FUNDAMENTALS OF
HUMAN NEUROPSYCHOLOGY

FUNDAMENTALS OF

HUMAN NEUROPSYCHOLOGY

Second Edition

BRYAN KOLB AND IAN Q. WHISHAW

UNIVERSITY OF LETHBRIDGE

W. H. FREEMAN AND COMPANY NEW YORK

LIBRARY OF CONGRESS CATALOGING IN PUBLICATION DATA

KOLB, BRYAN, 1947–
FUNDAMENTALS OF HUMAN NEUROPSYCHOLOGY.

(A SERIES OF BOOKS IN PSYCHOLOGY)
INCLUDES BIBLIOGRAPHIES AND INDEXES.
1. NEUROPSYCHOLOGY. 2. HUMAN BEHAVIOR. I. WHISHAW,
IAN Q., 1939–   . II. TITLE. III. SERIES. [DNLM:
1. NERVOUS SYSTEM—ANATOMY & HISTOLOGY. 2. NERVOUS
SYSTEM—PHYSIOLOGY. 3. NERVOUS SYSTEM DISEASES.
4. PSYCHOPHYSIOLOGY.   WL 102 K814f]
QP360.K64   1985   612'.8   84–24703
ISBN 0–7167–1672–0

PRINTED IN THE UNITED STATES OF AMERICA

3 4 5 6 7 8 HL 4 3 2 1 0 8 9 8 7 6

WE DEDICATE THIS BOOK TO KEVIN PITTMAN

Kevin Pittman represented to us what writing this book was all about. He was in the first class of our students to use the first edition as a text, became hooked on the subject matter, and was stimulated by the text to read on and to pursue a Ph.D. in neuroscience. His questions and criticisms frequently forced us to rethink our presentation and conclusions and provided one of the few real joys of teaching—evidence that we had forced others to think about issues that we believe are important. His sudden death in August, 1983, just a few months before he was to finish his Ph.D. at the University of British Columbia, was a blow to us all.

CONTENTS

PREFACE

The first edition of this book was written for undergraduate university students interested in an introduction to human neuropsychology. We have found that the book has been adopted more widely both within physiological and cognitive psychology, both for undergraduate and for graduate students, than we had anticipated. The first edition was also written in such a way that by the selection of relevant chapters it could be covered in one semester. We have attempted to retain these two objectives of the book. We have omitted the dates of many recent works from the text, instead presenting appropriate references at the end of each chapter. We still do not cite all the studies that might be relevant to particular issues, expecting that interested students will find more detailed accounts of the relevant literature in many of the reviews and texts that we do cite. We still simplify some of the more complex issues. Where facts are absent or unclear in their implications, we have still speculated and theorized. Nevertheless, the text is changed in some important ways. We have increased the biological content of the book in two ways: there are more detailed descriptions of cell structure, including descriptions of changes that cells might undergo if they are damaged, and there is a more detailed description of some of the evolutionary principles relevant to brain growth and development. We have also increased the clinical content of the book in two ways: there are descriptions of more motor and sensory disorders than was previously the case, and there is more information about the clinical application of neuropsychological tests. Finally, we have updated the information in most of the chapters, which has entailed changing the order of many of them, the division of three chapters in two, and the addition of five new chapters. Of course, we do not anticipate that every chapter in the book will be covered in a one-semester course. We do anticipate, however, that if a core group of chapters is covered in a course, the remaining chapters will provide useful supplementary reading for the interested student or useful reference material.

The following are the details of the changes that have been made. Chapter 2 has been expanded to include more information on the basic physiological properties of the nervous system and Chapter 4 has been enlarged to include a discussion of the evolutionary origins of the human brain. A new chapter (Chapter 8) provides a detailed account of the anatomical and functional organization of the neocortex in order to present new views about neocortical function and to provide a background for the chapters on motor and sensory functions. The sensory and motor chapters have been expanded to four chapters so that the organization of the motor and sensory systems receives, in part, a different discussion from the disorders of these systems. We have expanded our discussion of motor and sensory disorders to provide more background information about clinical disorders. We have found, for example, that cerebral palsy was a term that was common in clinical settings but received no mention in university courses, with the result that most students knew the term but did not know what it meant. We have enlarged the discussion of cerebral asymmetry so that one chapter (Chapter 14) discusses basic principles and the second (Chapter 15) discusses individual differences. These changes are made to respond to a growing body of information about asymmetry and to steadily increasing interest in cerebral asymmetry, as well as to the developing theoretical awareness that variations in asymmetry are commoner than was previously thought. There is now a chapter on spatial behavior (Chapter 23) that complements the psychologically oriented chapters on memory, language, and affect. Finally, we have added three new chapters discussing clinical applications of neuropsychology. This is to respond to the growing interest in the application of neuropsychology to neurological, psychiatric, and educational settings. To facilitate the interested student's pursuit of more detailed information, we have provided many new tables with basic references.

We still see the core of neuropsychology as the study of the neocortex, so that the more relevant behavioral chapters are grouped together (Chapters 13 to 23). Some chapters have been written with the view that the student can periodically review them alone (e.g., Chapters 3, 7, and 13). We feel that these chapters can be understood at a number of levels, depending on the reader's sophistication in the neurosciences. We find that our beginning students have little interest in history, for example, but as their interest in certain problems increases they find historical or other theoretical information more relevant.

Again, we must say that we are deeply indebted to our colleagues and students who have given us comments and advice about how to improve the book. Of course, the improvements are due to their help but the errors are attributable solely to us. We are grateful to Jill Becker, Brian Bland, Darryl Bruce, Robert Sutherland, and Case Vanderwolf for their helpful comments on given chapters. We are especially indebted to Terry Robinson for his extensive comments. We must also acknowledge the enthusiasm and faith of Buck Rogers of W. H. Freeman and Company in our ability to revise the book. Finally, we must again express our gratitude to Adria Allen for her heroic achievement in typing the many drafts of the chapters as we compiled them.

Bryan Kolb and Ian Q. Whishaw

PART ONE

BACKGROUND

In principle, it would seem simple to study human brain function: one need only study the behavior of people with known brain damage, note the behavioral changes, and from them infer the function of the region involved. Unfortunately, it is not quite so simple. There are significant technical and methodological problems that must be understood before any conclusions about brain-behavior relations can be made. Thus students of human neuropsychology must be familiar with the basic principles of brain function if they are to fully appreciate the nature of the neurological basis of complex cognitive processes.

Chapters 1 to 4 present background information about the anatomy and physiology of the brain, methodological problems in the study of the brain and behavior, and the evolutionary origins of the human brain. Although the beginning student may feel that this material is not relevant to the "real stuff" of neuropsychology, we emphasize that neuropsychological theories regarding human brain function are dependent on the basic data of neuroanatomy, neurophysiology, and neurochemistry. Chapters 1 to 4 are written for the beginning student who has not previously had a course in neuroscience, neuroanatomy, or physiological psychology. Students who have had such courses and feel comfortable in their knowledge of these areas can either review the material or proceed directly to Part Two. We recommend that students make use of the glossary found at the end of the text when they encounter words unfamiliar to them. Throughout the book, words listed in the glossary are printed in boldface type the first time they are used in the text.

1

ORGANIZATION
OF THE NERVOUS SYSTEM

As Oedipus approached the city of Thebes his way was blocked by the Sphinx, who posed a riddle to him: "What walks on four legs in the morning, two legs at noon, and three legs in the evening?" The answer given by Oedipus, "A man," was correct, for a person crawls as an infant, walks as an adult, and uses a cane when old. The riddle posed by the Sphinx is a riddle of the nature of human beings, and the reply by Oedipus indicates not only that he knew an answer but that he understood the underlying significance of the question. The riddle of human nature is still unanswered, and the object of this book is to pursue the answer in the place where it should most logically be found: the brain.

The simplest and most obvious questions to ask about the brain concern its size. Does size mean anything? Some information suggests that it does. The human brain weighs 400 grams at birth, 850 grams at 11 months, 1100 grams at three years, and 1450 grams at maturity. This suggests that the development of

adult behavior is related to brain size. Furthermore, at about 30 years of age the brain begins to grow smaller, until by 75 years it has lost on the average about 100 grams. This suggests the suspected decline in human abilities during aging may be related to decreased brain size. The brain has also grown bigger during evolution; for example, the brain of the great apes weighs about 400 grams, that of Java man weighed about 850 grams, and that of Peking man weighed about 1100 grams. This growth suggests that the evolution of modern man's abilities may have been dependent on the evolution of a greater brain size.

But despite these relations, there are facts about brain size suggesting that these conclusions are not unassailable. It is curious that modern man's direct hominoid ancestors, Neanderthal man and Cro-Magnon man, may have had slightly larger brains than modern man. It is also curious that the human brain may have gotten somewhat smaller in the last few thousand years. It is curious that although adult brain size is related to body size (larger people have larger brains than smaller people, and females, who are generally smaller than males, have proportionately smaller brains), the brain size of people of extraordinary ability is no different from the brain size of people of ordinary ability. It is curious that the brains of both gifted and ordinary people can vary in weight between 1100 and 2000 grams. Finally, it is curious that although human beings are apparently unique in their cultural achievements, dolphins may have larger brains, relative to body size, than humans have. Together, this information suggests that although brain size may be important, size alone does little toward answering the riddle of human nature.

The next most obvious questions to ask about the brain concern the relations between the brain's structure and behavior, and this is the focus of modern neuropsychology. Unfortunately, the complexity of the brain's structure makes it incredibly difficult to relate its components to individual capacities. The brain is composed of 180 billion cells, and of these, the 60 billion directly engaged in information processing each receive up to 15,000 physical connections from other cells. If there were no order in this complexity, it would be incomprehensible. Fortunately, some tentative answers about how this machinery works can be obtained because the cells of the brain are not organized haphazardly. They are arranged in assemblies, many of which are large and obvious enough to be identifiable on superficial examination. Although the brains of individuals vary in their features just as the faces of individuals vary, the different structures of the brain are common to all human beings. In fact, these structures seem to be common to all mammals. The anatomist Lorente de Nó, after examining the mouse brain through a microscope, remarked that its fine structure was little different from that of the human brain. Since many features of the brain are common to

most animals as well as to human beings, and since many of the behaviors of human beings and animals are similar, it is possible to learn about the function of the human brain by studying the brains of other animals, and to learn about the function of other animals' brains by studying the human brain. In the science of **neuropsychology** both kinds of study are pursued. Perhaps this procedure more than any other has influenced the organization of this book. Consequently, although we are specifically interested in discussing the functions of the human brain, throughout the book we shall frequently do so indirectly, through examination of the brains of other animals. It is our view that the answer to the riddle of the nature of human beings lies as much in the study of those other animals as it does in the study of human beings.

COMPOSITION OF THE NERVOUS SYSTEM

As we have stated, the nervous system is composed of cells, and these cells and their processes are grouped in an organized fashion. Since brain anatomy is the study of this organization, it is helpful to know how cells give the different parts of the brain their characteristic appearance.

Neurons and Glia

The germinal cells of a developing embryo give rise to two primitive types of nervous system cells: **neuroblasts** and **spongioblasts** (a blast is an immature cell). The neuroblasts develop into **neurons** (from the Greek for nerve), or *nerve cells,* which form the functional units of the nervous system. The spongioblasts develop into the **glial cells** (from *glia,* the Greek for glue), which provide various types of support functions to neurons. These two

TABLE 1–1

Glial cells and their function

Type	Function
Astroglia	Give structural support to and repair neurons
Oligodendroglia	Insulate and speed transmission of central nervous system neurons [a]
Schwann cells	Insulate and speed transmission of peripheral nervous system neurons
Microglia	Perform phagocytosis
Ependymal cells	Produce central nervous system fluid and insulate the brain's ventricles

[a]Central nervous system neurons are found within the brain and spinal cord; peripheral nervous system neurons are in the rest of the body.

types of cells, neurons and glia, make up the adult brain. Figure 1–1 shows the relative size, shape, and location of some neurons, and Table 1–1 summarizes some functions of glia.

Gray, White, and Reticular Matter. Different parts of the nervous system characteristically appear either gray, white, or mottled and are called gray, white, and reticular matter, respectively. Mixtures of capillary blood vessels and cell bodies of neurons have a gray-brown color and so areas composed predominantly of cell bodies constitute the **gray matter.** From the cell bodies of neurons, long processes, called axons, extend to form connections with other neurons in other brain areas. These processes are generally covered with an insulation of glial cells. The glial cells are composed of a fatty (lipid) substance with a high refractive index that gives them a white appearance, much as fat droplets in milk give it a white appearance. As a result, an area of the nervous system rich in axons covered with glial cells looks white and is called **white mat-**

ter. An area of nervous system where cell bodies and axons are mixed together is called a **reticular formation** (from the Latin *rete,* meaning net) because of its mottled gray and white, or netlike, appearance.

Nuclei and Tracts. A large number of cell bodies grouped together are collectively called a **nucleus** (from the Latin *nux,* meaning nut); a large collection of axons from neuron cell bodies is called a **tract** (from Old French, meaning path), or sometimes a fiber pathway. Since cell bodies are gray, nuclei are a distinctive gray; since glial cells make axons appear white, tracts are a distinctive white.

Staining

Because of their color, the larger nuclei and tracts of the brain can be seen in fresh brain tissue or brain tissue cut into thin sections, but the appearance of smaller nuclei and tracts must be enhanced to make them visible. The technique of enhancing differences in appearance is called staining and consists of placing brain tissue into different color dyes. Because there are variations in the chemical composition of cells, their various parts selectively take different dyes. Staining techniques aid immensely in differentiating brain tissue, and they are continually being refined. For example, if a nucleus of the brain is destroyed in some way, the axons leaving the cells die. Stains have been found that are selectively taken up by this dying tissue, making it easy to trace axons to their destinations.

A Wonderland of Nomenclature

To the beginning student, the terminology used to label nuclei and tracts of the nervous system might at first seem chaotic. Many structures have a number of names, often used interchangeably. For example, one structure, the **precentral gyrus,** is variously referred to

FIGURE 1–1. The nervous system is composed of neurons, of nerve cells, each of which is specialized for its function. The schematic drawings show the size, shape, location, and configuration of some neurons.

as the primary motor cortex, area 4, the motor strip, the motor homunculus, Jackson's strip, area pyramidalis, the somatomotor strip, and gyrus precentralis. Clearly such proliferation of terminology is an obstacle to learning, but it is some consolation to know that it reflects the culture and history of the neurosciences. There are many other examples of brain structures that have a number of names, some of which seem quite peculiar. Greek terminology is interchanged with English (e.g., mesencephalon for midbrain), Latin with English (fasciculus opticus for optic tract), and French for English (bouton termineau for synaptic knob). The neuroanatomist's imagination has sometimes strayed to body anatomy (e.g., mammillary bodies), to flora (amygdala, or almond), to fauna (hippocampus, or sea horse), and to mythology (Ammon's horn). Some terminology is a tribute to early pioneers: the fields of Forel, Rolando's fissure, and Deiters' nucleus. Other terms are colorful: substantia nigra (black substance), locus coeruleus (blue area), and red nucleus. Some names seem excessively long: nucleus reticularis tegmenti pontis Bechterewi. Other labels are based on the consistency of the tissue, for example, substantia gelatinosa (gelatinous substance); some seem somewhat mystifying: substantia innominata (nameless substance), zone incerta (uncertain area), nucleus ambiguus (ambiguous nucleus); and finally, some reflect a modern and more technical outlook, as with the nuclei A-1 to A-10.

In the present text, we have attempted to use consistent and simple terms, but in many cases alternate terms are widely used and so we have included them where necessary.

Approaches to the Study of Anatomy

Neuroanatomists study the structure of the brain with any of four main approaches: (1) comparative, (2) developmental, (3) cytoarchitectonic, and (4) biochemical.

The *comparative* approach consists of describing the brain's evolution from a primitive cord in simple wormlike animals to a large, complex "raveled knot" in the head of human beings. Since new types of behavior have developed as each new layer or protuberance has evolved, clues about the function of new areas can be gained by correlating structure and behavior. However, such analysis is not necessarily simple. The limbic system, a middle layer in the mammalian brain, evolved in amphibians and reptiles. Is its function to control new modes of locomotion, the orientation of the animals in a terrestrial world, new types of social behavior, or more advanced learning abilities? The answer is still uncertain. The comparative approach, however, has yielded a key piece of information in neuropsychology: mammals can be distinguished from other animals by their large neocortex (outer covering of brain tissue). Furthermore, this structure is particularly large in humans. It is understandable, then, that it is thought to have an important function in conferring abilities unique to mammals, and thus receives proportionately more attention in neuropsychology—particularly human neuropsychology—than other structures.

In the *developmental,* or ontogenetic, approach the changes in brain structure and size are described during the development of an individual. This approach allows for two useful perspectives. First, the development of new structures can be correlated with emerging behaviors, much as is done in comparative studies. Second, the immature brain can frequently provide the anatomist with a simplified model of the adult brain. The Spanish anatomist Ramón y Cajal pioneered this type of analysis to good effect. With the crude equipment and techniques available at the end of the 19th century he was unable to determine whether the adult brain is composed of a net of connected tissue or of individual units. But using embryonic tissue he was able to show that it is composed of units. Furthermore, by examining successively more mature animals he discovered how these units develop their adult form. Neuropsychologists widely assume that in newborn infants the neocortex is particularly immature in comparison to the rest of the nervous system. As a result, correlating the development of the neocortex with emerging behavior is viewed as a powerful method of uncovering its structural and functional relations.

Cytoarchitectonic analysis consists of describing the architecture of cells: their differences in structure, size, shape, and connections and their distribution in different parts of the brain. This type of analysis is possible because different parts of the nerve cell have affinity for different types of dyes, so that when the brain is cut into thin sections and stained, the cells can be examined under a microscope. The cytoarchitectonic approach has been used to particular advantage by neuroanatomists, such as Brodmann, who have described regional differences in cell structure and have constructed maps illustrating the topography of the regional differences. These maps have particular value, for they correlate rather well with maps that illustrate functional differences in brain areas. Cytoarchitectonic techniques are being continually refined as new and better microscopes, such as the electron microscope, are developed and new and more ingenious staining procedures are employed. Recently, for example, it was found that all of the processes of a single cell can be stained by injecting a protein, called horseradish peroxidase, into the cell through a very small glass pipette. With this technique not only can one cell's place in the brain be located but its connections with other cells can be traced.

The most recent analytical technique of studying brain structure is to describe its *biochemical* organization. It is now clear that discrete clusters of cells that send projections to other cell areas contain unique biochemical substances that play a special role in intercell communication. This finding illustrates a new dimension of brain organization, and it is of immense practical importance. First, the activity of these systems can be related to different aspects of behavior. Second, abnormalities in the functioning of these systems can be related to some types of abnormal behavior. For example, the chemical dopamine occurs in reduced levels in victims of Parkinson's disease and occurs in heightened levels in victims of certain types of schizophrenia. Third, as these biochemical systems become better understood, the means by which psychoactive drugs work will also be better understood. Various techniques for studying the biochemical organization of the nervous system include performing assays on different regions of the brain to determine their chemical composition, labeling a chemical of interest with a radioactive substance so that its course and destination in the brain can be found, and staining the tissue with dyes that produce distinctive colors in areas rich in particular biochemicals. The chemical organization of the brains of a number of animals has been mapped, and studies of the human brain show that its biochemical organization is similar to that of these animals' brains.

ORIGIN AND DEVELOPMENT OF THE BRAIN

The anatomical and functional organization of the adult human brain is difficult to grasp be-

A SPINAL CORD

Sensory

Motor

B BRAINSTEM

Prosencephalon

Mesencephalon

Rhombencephalon

Cerebellum

I

IV

III

II

C MAMMALIAN BRAIN

Cerebral hemisphere

Cerebellum

D HUMAN BRAIN

Telencephalon

Diencephalon

Mesencephalon

Metencephalon

Myelencephalon

FIGURE 1–2. Steps in the development of the brain. A. Spinal cord. B. Brainstem. C. Mammalian brain. D. Side view of the center of a human brain.

cause of the complicated clustering of nuclei and the intricate pathways of their axons. It is easier to understand the nervous system's organization by examining the way it developed phylogenetically. The nervous system developed in four somewhat general steps, as is shown diagrammatically in Figure 1–2.

1. The nervous system was first a simple tube, or *spinal cord,* receiving sensory fibers from the different segments of the body and sending motor fibers to them.

2. One end of the cord then became specialized to respond to special features of the sensory world and so made up the primitive brain, or *brainstem.*

3. The front and the hind ends of the brainstem then sprouted two new, large structures. In front, the cerebral hemispheres developed to become the initiators of movement; at the rear, the cerebellum developed to become the coordinator of movement. These final additions completed the *mammalian brain.*

4. With continued growth, the mammalian brain developed into the *human brain.*

The Spinal Cord

In primitive animals (and in the first weeks of mammalian embryonic development), some of the outer, or ectodermal, cells of the dorsal surface of the body formed a trough running the length of the body; the upper edges of the trough folded to form a tube (the precursor of the adult mammalian spinal cord). At this stage of development the body and the cord were arranged in segments, with sensory receptors on the body sending input to the dorsal part of the cord, while the cord sent axons from its ventral portion to control muscles in each of the segments. This primitive system, shown diagrammatically in Figure 1–2 A, provided the basis for the development of two important mammalian functions: the dorsal portion provided the neural basis of the somatosensory system (skin and muscle senses), whereas the ventral portion provided the neural basis for the execution of movement. In ancestral vertebrates, such as amphioxus, this was the extent of nervous system development.

The Brainstem

Further neural and functional specialization began at the front end of the spinal cord to form an *encephalon* (from the Greek, meaning in the head), or brain. This was probably because the first vertebrates were mobile and found it easier to travel predominantly in one direction; thus, it was adaptive to have special sensory analysis take place at "the-end-that-goes-first." At any rate, the front end formed three enlargements or vesicles (bladders). The cells surrounding each multiplied to form centers specialized for receiving and responding to particular features of the world. The front enlargement, the **prosencephalon** (forebrain), became specialized mainly for olfaction and possibly also taste. The second enlargement, the **mesencephalon** (midbrain), became specialized for vision and hearing. These parts of the brain made possible reception of the distant environment. The posterior enlargement, the **rhombencephalon** (hindbrain), became specialized for equilibrium and balance, and gave the animal better perception of its place in its immediate environment. The same organization found in the spinal cord continued to be maintained in the brain: the dorsal portion was sensory, the ventral portion motor. This relatively simple brain, similar to the brain of present fishes and amphibians, forms the basis of the brainstem of mammals. The general organization of the brainstem is shown in Figure 1–2 B.

The Mammalian Brain

The brain next developed primarily at its first and third segments. The prosencephalon developed to form two major new divisions: the **telencephalon** (endbrain) and **diencephalon** (between-brain). The most important addition in the telencephalon was the cerebral hemispheres, which functionally became the level of highest control for behavior. The rhombencephalon also divided to form two major new divisions: the *metencephalon* (across-brain) and the *myelencephalon* (spinal brain). The distinguishing feature was the growth of the cerebellum in the metencephalon, which became the coordinating center for all movement. The mammalian brain is diagrammed in Figure 1–2 C.

The Human Brain

The human brain evolved from the mammalian brain with no change to the basic design plan (see the sagittal, or side, view of the human brain in Figure 1–2 D). The only real difference between the two types of brains is that the cerebral hemispheres and the cerebellum of humans have become tremendously larger than those found in other mammals.

The Ventricles

The primitive spinal cord, remember, had the form of a tube with a hollow center. Further, Figure 1–2 shows that the central core of the brainstem and of the mammalian brain remains hollow. This cavity is not empty but is filled with fluid called **cerebrospinal fluid,** which is produced by **ependymal cells,** or glial cells, that line the inner surface of the cavity. The cavity is larger in some portions of its length than in others; these enlargements are called **ventricles** (from the Latin, meaning belly).

TABLE 1-2

The divisions of the nervous system

Primitive brainstem divisions	Mammalian brain divisions	Portion of fully developed brain	Behavioral division
Prosencephalon (forebrain)	Telencephalon (endbrain)	Neocortex Basal ganglia Limbic system Olfactory bulb Lateral ventricles	Forebrain
	Diencephalon (between-brain)	Thalamus Epithalamus Hypothalamus Pineal body Third ventricle	Brainstem
Mesencephalon (midbrain)	Mesencephalon (midbrain)	Tectum Tegmentum Cerebral aqueduct	
Rhombencephalon (hindbrain)	Metencephalon (across-brain)	Cerebellum Pons Fourth ventricle	
	Myelencephalon (spinal brain)	Medulla oblongata Fourth Ventricle	
			Spinal cord

There are four ventricles, numbered I to IV. It is conventional to call the lateral ventricles the first and second ventricles, the ventricle in the diencephalon the third ventricle, and the ventricle in the metencephalon and myelencephalon the fourth ventricle. The ventricle that was in the mesencephalon of the brainstem has become constricted and is called the cerebral aqueduct. The ventricles are distributed in the human brain exactly as in the mammalian brain.

ANATOMY OF THE HUMAN BRAIN

Table 1-2 summarizes the development of the brain from having three primary embryonic divisions to having five. In addition, the table shows some of the major brain structures found in each division of the fully developed brain. Whereas embryological neuroanato-mists have divided the nervous system into five major divisions, behaviorists are often content to divide it into three divisions to simplify discussion of its function. The lowest division is the **spinal cord,** which includes its connections with organs and muscles in the body. The middle division is the **brainstem,** which is equivalent to the embryologic or primitive premammalian brainstem and includes the diencephalon, the midbrain, and the hindbrain. The highest functional division is the **forebrain,** which includes all the structures in the telencephalon plus the thalamus of the diencephalon.

Many structures of the brain are labeled according to their location with respect to one another. Six conventional terms are used to indicate anatomical direction: *superior* (top), *lateral* (side), *medial* (middle), *ventral* (bottom), *anterior* (front), and *posterior* (back). Thus, one structure can be said to lie superior, lateral,

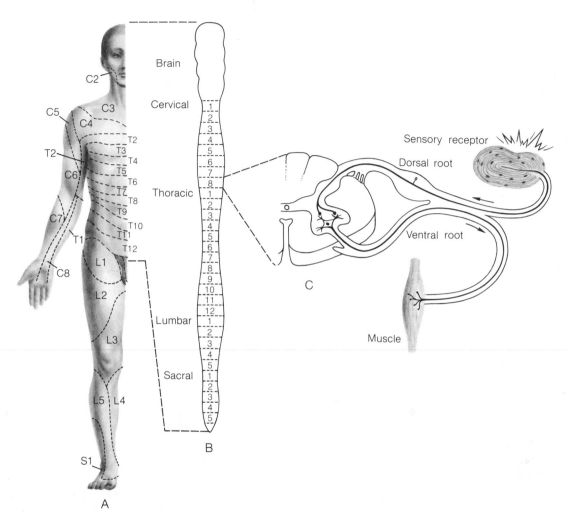

FIGURE 1–3. Relation between the dermatomes of the body and segments of the spinal cord. A. Body dermatomes. B. Spinal cord segments. C. Cross section through one segment of the spinal cord showing that sensory input from a dermatome arrives through the dorsal root, whereas motor output to the same dermatome goes through the ventral root. (After Truex and Carpenter, 1969.)

medial, ventral, anterior, or posterior to another. The nervous system is also symmetrically arranged and so consists of left and right sides. If two structures lie on the same side, they are said to be **ipsilateral;** if they lie on opposite sides, they are said to be **contralateral;** if they lie on both sides, they are said to be **bilateral.** Structures that are close to each other are said to be **proximal;** those far from each other are said to be **distal.** Finally, a process that is approaching the center is said to be **afferent;** one leaving it is said to be **efferent.**

THE SPINAL CORD

The spinal cord, the musculature, and the internal organs of the body have a segmentalorganization (see Figure 1–3). Each segment of the cord is linked with the organs and musculature of a given body segment. As Figure 1–3 B shows, there are 30 spinal cord segments: eight cervical (C), 12 thoracic (T), five lumbar (L), and five sacral (S). Figure 1–3 A shows the segments of the skin and musculature of the body, each labeled to match its corresponding cord segment. Each of the body segments, called a **dermatome** (meaning skin cut), encircles the body in a ring formation. Of course, because a human being has an upright posture the ring formation seen in a quadrupedal animal is distorted into the pattern shown in Figure 1–3 A. It is worth noting that because the cord and body have this segmental structure, rather good inferences can be made about the location of spinal cord damage or disease from changes in sensation or movement in body parts.

Figure 1–3 C shows a cross section of the spinal cord. Its outer portion consists of white matter or tracts, arranged so that with a few exceptions the superior tracts are sensory and the inferior tracts are motor in function. The inner portion of the cord, which has a butterfly shape, is gray matter, that is, composed largely of cell bodies. These are arranged so that the cells in the superior portion act as relays for sensory projections from the body, while the cells in the inferior portion send axons to connect with muscles or glands. As can be seen in Figure 1–3 C, two larger fiber tracts (or roots) of the **peripheral nerves** enter each section of the spinal cord, one on each side. The superior tracts contain projections from the receptors in the body, and the inferior tracts consist of axons from cells in the inferior gray matter that project to muscles or organs. Because of this arrangement, damage to the cord's superior regions will produce changes that are selectively sensory in nature, whereas damage to the inferior portion of the cord will produce changes that are selectively motor in nature.

THE BRAINSTEM

The Diencephalon

The diencephalon consists of the three thalamic structures (thalamus meaning inner room or chamber, though sometimes translated as couch on which the forebrain rests): the epithalamus (or upper room), the thalamus (described below with the forebrain), and the hypothalamus (or lower room) (see Figure 1–4). The diencephalon has often been called the interbrain and appropriately so, for in addition to having its own nuclei it is also a relay or thoroughfare for fibers connecting the forebrain and lower brainstem areas.

The **epithalamus** is of primitive origin, and its function in humans is not known. One of its structures is the **pineal body,** the only non-bilateral structure in the brain. This body has an interesting history, for Descartes, impressed by its solitary nature, suggested that it was the rendezvous between mind and matter and the source of the cerebral spinal fluid that powered movements. Although its function in humans is still not known, the pineal body of some animals plays a role in organizing biological rhythms.

The **hypothalamus** is composed of about 22 small nuclei, fiber systems that pass through it, and the pituitary gland. Although composing only about 0.3 percent of the brain's weight, its small size is deceiving because it is involved in nearly all aspects of behavior, including feeding, sexual behavior, sleeping,

FIGURE 1–4. Medial view through the center of the brain showing structures of the brainstem.

temperature regulation, emotional behavior, endocrine function, and movement. It has been a favorite area of study in animal neurobiology, but unfortunately less is known about the role of the hypothalamus in human behavior.

The Midbrain

The **midbrain,** shown in Figure 1–4, consists of two main subdivisions: the **tectum,** or roof, which is the area lying above the aqueduct, and the **tegmentum,** or floor, which lies below the aqueduct. The tectum consists primarily of two sets of bilaterally symmetrical nuclei: the **superior colliculi** (upper hills) are the anterior pair, and the **inferior colliculi** (lower hills) are the posterior pair. In birds and phylogenetically lower animals these sets of nuclei are their visual and auditory brains, respectively. In mammals, which have neocortical visual and auditory systems, these structures mediate

whole body movements to visual and auditory stimuli, respectively. The tegmentum contains four types of structures:

1. Next to the aqueduct are nuclei for some of the cranial nerves.

2. Beneath these are sensory fibers coming from the body senses.

3. Below these are motor fibers coming down from the forebrain.

4. Intermingled among these three structures are a number of motor nuclei such as the red nucleus and substantia nigra and some of the nuclei of the reticular system.

The Hindbrain

The **hindbrain** is organized in much the same way as the midbrain. Sensory nuclei of the vestibular system overlie the fourth ventricle; beneath the ventricle are more motor nuclei of the cranial nerves, ascending sensory tracts from the spinal cord, descending fiber tracts to the cord, and more nuclei composing the reticular activating system. Overlying the brainstem is the cerebellum.

The **cerebellum** (see Figure 1–4) is very old and was probably first specialized for sensory-motor coordination. The precise function of the cerebellum varies from one part of the structure to another, depending on the connections with the rest of the nervous system. Parts that receive most of their impulses from the vestibular system help to maintain the body's equilibrium, whereas parts receiving impulses mainly from the body senses are involved with postural reflexes and coordinating functionally related muscles. The major part of the cerebellum receives impulses from the neocortex and functions primarily to promote the efficiency of skilled movements.

The surface of the cerebellum is marked by narrow folds, or folia, beneath which lies a thick cortex of gray matter covering a larger central mass of white matter. Within the white matter are several nuclei. The cerebellum is attached to the brainstem by three major fiber pathways in which all afferent fibers pass to its cortex and all efferent fibers originate in the underlying cerebellar nuclei and then pass on to other brain structures.

Damage to the cerebellum results in impairments of equilibrium, postural defects, and impairments of skilled motor activity. Smooth movements may be broken down into sequential components, thus making movements jerky; ability to perform rapidly alternating movements may be impaired; and directed movements may overshoot their mark. In addition, muscle tone may be abnormal, so that movements are difficult to initiate.

The *reticular formation* consists of a complex mixture of nuclei and fiber tracts that stretch from the diencephalon through the hindbrain. These nuclei and fiber tracts have two distinguishing features: first, they do not have clearly defined sensory or motor functions; second, each sends fibers to a number of areas of the forebrain, brainstem, and spinal cord. The reticular formation is now well known as the *reticular activating system;* it obtained this distinction in the following way. Up to the 1940s it was thought that sleep could be attributed to a lack of sensory stimulation, whereas waking could be attributed to reception of an adequate amount of sensory stimulation. In 1949, Moruzzi and Magoun stimulated the brainstem of anesthetized cats while brain electrical activity was being recorded from them on an electroencephalogram, or EEG. The EEG of the cats consisted of large-amplitude slow waves, similar to those typically recorded from a sleeping animal, but when electrical brain stimulation was administered, a low-amplitude EEG pattern, similar to that commonly recorded from a waking cat, was recorded. As a result of their experiment, Moruzzi and Magoun proposed that the function of the reticular formation was to control sleeping and waking. Through the influence of these findings the reticular formation gradually came to be known as the reticular activating system, the function of which was to maintain "general arousal" or "consciousness." More recently, research has focused on the details of individual nuclear groups within the formation, and the results from these studies suggest a number of functions for different cell groups in this area.

There are 12 sets of **cranial nerves** (summarized in Table 5–1), which convey sensory information from the specialized sensory systems of the head and control the special movements of muscle systems in the head, e.g., movements of the eyes and tongue. A knowledge of their organization and function is important for neurological diagnosis; their functions and dysfunctions are discussed in Chapter 5.

FIGURE 1–5. Gyri and sulci. Lateral (A) and medial (B) views of the gyri. Lateral (C) and medial (D) views of the sulci.

THE FOREBRAIN

The forebrain is conventionally divided into five anatomical areas: (1) the neocortex, (2) the basal ganglia, (3) the limbic system, (4) the thalamus, and (5) the olfactory bulbs and tract. The following section will describe the first of these four structures. Since the content of this book is related substantially to the neocortex, it will be described in greatest detail.

The Neocortex

The **neocortex** comprises most of the forebrain by volume. It consists of four to six layers of cells (or gray matter) beneath which their axons form pathways (white matter). The term cortex (from the Latin, meaning bark) is used to refer to any outer layer of cells. Frequently the terms cortex and neocortex are used interchangeably, and so conventionally cortex refers to neocortex unless otherwise indicated. The neocortex has expanded the most during evolution; it comprises 80 percent of the human brain. Whereas the brainstems of a human being and a sheep are so similar in size that a novice may confuse them, their neocortexes can easily be distinguished. The human neocortex has an area of up to 2500 cm^2 but a thickness of only 1.5 to 3.0 mm. The cortex is wrinkled; this wrinkling is nature's solution to the problem of confining the huge neocortical surface area within a shell that is still small enough to pass through the birth canal. Just as a crumpled sheet of paper can fit into a smaller box than a flat sheet, folding of the neocortex permits the relatively fixed volume of the skull to contain more neocortex.

Fissures, Sulci, and Gyri. The wrinkled surface of the neocortex consists of clefts and ridges. A cleft is called a **fissure** if it extends deeply enough into the brain to indent the ventricles, and a **sulcus** if it is shallower. A ridge is called a **gyrus.** Figure 1–5 shows the location of some of the more important fissures, sulci, and gyri of the brain. There is *some* variation between the location of the features of the two sides of one individual's brain, and *substantial* variation in both the location and the features of the brains of different individuals. Two of the external features of the brain are relatively easy to locate: the lateral fissure, because it begins in a cleft on the anterior-inferior surface of the cortex, and the central sulcus, because it curves toward the posterior part of the brain as it moves medially across the superior surface of the cortex.

The Hemispheres and Lobes. As Figure 1–6 shows, the neocortex consists of two nearly symmetrical hemispheres, the left and the right, separated by the medial longitudinal fissure. Each hemisphere is subdivided into four lobes: frontal, parietal, temporal, and occipital.

The **frontal lobes** have fixed boundaries: they are bounded posteriorly by the central sulcus, inferiorly by the lateral fissure, and medially by the cingulate sulcus just above a large interhemispheric band of fibers called the corpus callosum. The anterior boundary of the **parietal lobes** is the central sulcus and their inferior boundary is the lateral fissure. The **temporal lobes** are bounded dorsally by the lateral fissure. The **occipital lobes** are separated from the parietal cortex medially by the parieto-occipital sulcus. On the lateral surface of the brain there are no definite boundaries between the occipital lobes and the parietal and temporal lobes. The areas between the lobes are sometimes referred to as the parietal-occipital area and the temporal-occipital area. It should be noted that the lobes are not functional regions but convenient anatomical regions. Nevertheless, because there are functional differences between them the terms are used in a rather loose and descriptive way to indicate different functional regions.

As shown in Figure 1–5, in a lateral view there are four major gyri in the frontal lobe: the superior, middle, and inferior and the precentral (which lies in front of the central sulcus). There are five in the parietal lobe: the superior and inferior, the postcentral (lying behind the central sulcus), and the supramarginal and angular (on either side of the lateral fissure). There are three in the temporal lobe: the superior, middle, and inferior gyri. Only the lateral gyrus is obvious in the occipital cortex.

Topography of the Neocortex. The several different kinds of maps that have been made of the neocortex are called **topographic maps.** These maps are constructed from information obtained by the application of specific research techniques:

1. **Projection maps** are constructed by tracing axons from the sensory systems into the brain, and tracing axons from the neo-

FIGURE 1–6. The location of the frontal, parietal, occipital, and temporal lobes of the human brain.

cortex to the motor systems of the brainstem and spinal cord.

2. **Functional maps** are constructed by stimulating areas of the brain electrically and noting the elicited behavior, or by recording the electrical activity of the cortex during certain behaviors. Functional maps can also be constructed by relating specific types of brain damage to changes in behavior.

3. **Cytoarchitectonic maps** are constructed from study of the distribution of different types of cells in the neocortex.

Projection Maps. Figure 1–7 shows an example of a projection map constructed by tracing the axons from the sensory systems to the neocortex, and by tracing the motor axons from the neocortex to subcortical motor systems. As the figure shows, the projections from the eye, the ear, and the body's somatosensory system can each be traced to a specific region of the neocortex: the visual system projects to the posterior occipital lobe, the auditory system projects to the superior temporal gyrus of the temporal lobe, and the somatosensory system projects to the area of the postcentral gyrus in the parietal lobe. The major motor projection appears to originate in the precentral gyrus of the frontal lobe. These areas are called **primary projection areas,** but it should be noted

FIGURE 1–7. A projection map. The dots indicate primary zones, which receive input from the sensory systems or project to spinal motor systems. The shaded areas are secondary zones. The unshaded areas are tertiary, or association, zones.

that the lateral view does not represent their entire extent, because they also project down into the gyri and fissures. The auditory zone, for example, is much larger within the lateral fissure.

Once the primary projection areas are described, the relation they have to the rest of the neocortex can be understood. The sensory systems send projections into areas that are adjacent to them, whereas the motor area receives fibers from an area adjacent to it. These areas, also indicated in Figure 1–7, are called **secondary projection areas.** The secondary areas receive fibers from (in the case of the motor projection) or send fibers to (in the case of sensory projections) **tertiary projection areas,** also frequently called association cortex.

It is clear from this topography that the neocortex is highly organized. It is also clear why the posterior neocortex is considered to be largely sensory, and why the anterior neocortex is considered to be largely motor. Finally, it is apparent why each of the lobes is thought to be associated with a particular general function: frontal with motor, parietal with somatosensory, occipital with visual, and temporal with auditory function. We wish toemphasize, however, that this is a simplified description of the neocortex. Motor fibers can be found coming from every part of the neocortex, and sensory fibers project to other areas. The map simply reflects the most concentrated projections of both kinds of fibers.

Functional Maps. Of the many functional maps of the somatosensory and motor areas, the best-known is by Penfield and his coworkers. During the course of brain surgery, they stimulated the brains of conscious people through thin wires, or electrodes, with low voltages of electric current. The protocol of such an experiment was to stimulate the cortical tissue briefly, observe whether the person made a movement or reported some sort of body sensation (itch, tickle, etc.), record the location and response, and then move the stimulating electrode to repeat the procedure. The results of several such experiments are shown diagrammatically in Figure 1–8. Areas that produced movement lie in the precentral gyrus in the primary motor projection area. Areas that produced sensations lie in the postcentral gyrus in the primary somatosensory area. For both the motor and sensory areas there is a point-to-point relation between parts of the body and parts of the neocortex. Note that in the figure these distributions of the body on the cortex are distorted, the face and hands being far larger proportionately than are other parts of the body. This topography is shown schematically by the cartoon men (or *homunculi*)drawn over the motor and sensory areas to indicate the parts of the body represented in different cortical areas.

The face and hands of the homunculi are larger because they are capable of finer perceptions and movements than are other body areas and so require proportionately more neocortex to represent them. The foot area lies in the longitudinal fissure (flexed up in Figure 1–8). The cortical representation of the eyes is actually not in the head region of the motor homunculus; they have their own area just anterior to the head area.

The visual and auditory systems have a neocortical distribution as precise as that for the motor and somatosensory systems. The visual field (the area of the world the eyes see) is represented across the visual projection area in the occipital lobe, whereas the sensory area for sound, the basilar membrane, is represented in the primary auditory area of the temporal lobe. The taste area of the brain lies across a tongue-shaped area in the postcentral gyrus in Figure 1–8. Whether or not the olfactory system has any representation in the neocortex is at present uncertain.

Cytoarchitectonic Maps. Cytoarchitectonic maps are constructed by examining the neurons of

B

FIGURE 1–8. A functional map. A. Electrical stimulation to precentral or postcentral gyrus through small electrodes. B. Movement or sensation is produced at the locations shown by the homunculi, or "little men." (After Penfield and Jasper, 1954.)

FIGURE 1–9. Brodmann's areas of the cortex. A few numbers are missing from the original sources, including areas 13–16 and 48–51. Some areas have histologically distinctive boundaries and are outlined with heavy solid lines; others, such as 6 and 18–19, have less distinct boundaries and are outlined with light solid lines; the remainder have no distinct boundaries but gradually merge into one another and are outlined with dotted lines. (From H. Elliott, *Textbook of Anatomy*. Philadelphia: Lippincott. Copyright © 1969. Reprinted with permission.)

number of layers distinguishes the neocortex from other brain areas, such as the limbic system, which has only three layers. The cell layers of the neocortex can be separated into two groups by function: the outer four layers receive axons from other brain areas; the inner two layers send axons to other brain areas. The cell layers are not distributed uniformly in the neocortex (in fact, it is debatable whether there are really six layers in all neocortical areas). For example, a primary sensory area such as the visual area has a large number of layer 4 cells receiving axons from the eyes but fewer layer 5 cells, whereas the primary motor area has a large number of layer 5 cells sending axons to subcortical motor systems but fewer layer 4 cells. Areas that are neither primary motor nor primary sensory have fewer cells in layers 4

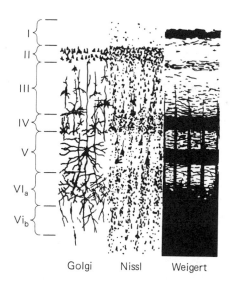

Golgi　　Nissl　　Weigert

FIGURE 1–10. Structure of the cortex revealed through the use of three different stains. The Golgi stain penetrates only a few neurons but reveals all of their processes, the Nissl stain highlights only cell bodies, and the Weigert myelin stain reveals the location of axons. Note that these staining procedures highlight the different cell types of the cortex and reveal that it is composed of a number of layers, each of which contains typical cell types. (After Brodmann, 1909.)

the neocortex and grouping areas with similar cell structure together. The many cytoarchitectonic maps of the neocortex differ chiefly in degree of complexity. The map presented in Figure 1–9 is by no means the simplest, but it is the most widely used, and it will be used throughout this book.

The neurons of the neocortex are arranged in about six layers, as is shown in Figure 1–10. The

TABLE 1–3

Functional areas and Brodmann cytoarchitectonic areas

Function	Brodmann area
Vision	
primary	17
secondary	18, 19, 20, 21, 37
Auditory	
primary	41
secondary	22, 42
Body senses	
primary	1, 2, 3
secondary	5, 7
Sensory, tertiary	7, 22, 37, 39, 40
Motor	
primary	4
secondary	6
eye movement	8
speech	44
Motor, tertiary	9, 10, 11, 45, 46, 47

and 5 and a greater density of cells in layers 2 and 3. It is on such differences in cell distribution, as well as differences in cell sizes and shapes, that cytoarchitectonic maps are based.

In **Brodmann's map,** a cytoarchitectonic map, shown in Figure 1–9, each of the areas is numbered, but the numbers themselves have no intrinsic meaning. To do his analysis Brodmann divided the brain at the central sulcus, and then worked through each half in random order, numbering new conformations of cells as he found them. Thus, he found areas 1 and 2 in the posterior section, then switched to the anterior section and found 3 and 4, and thereupon switched again, etc.

Table 1–3 summarizes some of the known relations between each of Brodmann's areas and its functions. As it turns out, the relation between structure and function is stunning. For example, area 17 corresponds to the primary visual projection area, and areas 18 and 19 to the secondary visual projection areas. Similar relations exist for other areas and functions. The boundaries of Brodmann's areas also appear to be related to function because the primary sensory and motor areas have fairly distinct boundaries and functions. The secondary areas have less distinct boundaries and the tertiary areas still less distinct ones. This has been taken to mean that they have less specified sensory or motor function and more associative or integrative function. At this point the best advice we can give a student with respect to Brodmann's system and its relation to function is to commit the numbers and the location of the primary and secondary areas to memory and then keep in mind that the remaining areas (composing the greater area of the neocortex) are tertiary cortex.

Cortical Connections

The various regions of the neocortex are interrelated by three types of axon projections: (1) relatively short connections between one gyrus and another, (2) longer connections between one lobe and another, and (3) interhemispheric connections, or **commissures,** between one hemisphere and another. Most of the interhemispheric connections link homotopic areas, or the same points, of the two hemispheres. Figure 1–11 shows the locations and names of some of these connections. The cortex also makes other types of connections with itself; cells in any area may, for example, send axons to cells in a subcortical area such as the thalamus, and the cells in the area of the thalamus may then send their axons to some other cortical area. These types of relations are more difficult to establish anatomically than those that are based on direct connections. Yet the connections are of considerable functional interest, for damage to a pathway is often reflected in behavioral deficits as severe as those suffered following damage to the functional areas they connect. A glance at Figure 1–11 will show that it would indeed be difficult to damage any area of the cortex without damaging one or more of its interconnecting pathways.

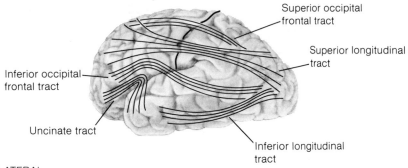

Superior occipital frontal tract

Superior longitudinal tract

Inferior occipital frontal tract

Uncinate tract

Inferior longitudinal tract

LATERAL

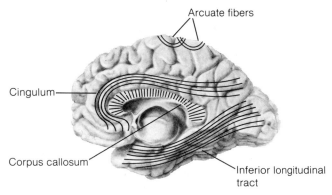

Arcuate fibers

Cingulum

Corpus callosum

Inferior longitudinal tract

MEDIAL

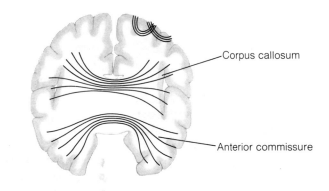

Corpus callosum

Anterior commissure

ANTERIOR

FIGURE 1–11. Connections between various regions of the cortex.

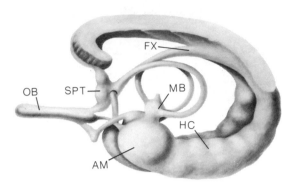

FIGURE 1–12. Model of the human limbic system. Major structures include the hippocampus (HC), amygdala (AM), septum (SPT), mammillary bodies (MB), olfactory bulbs (OB), and fornix (FX). (After Hamilton, 1976.)

Limbic Lobe

During the evolution of the amphibians and reptiles a number of three-layer cortical structures developed, sheathing the periphery of the brainstem. With the subsequent growth of the neocortex they became sandwiched between the new and the old brain. Because of the evolutionary origin of these structures some anatomists have referred to them as the reptilian brain, but the term limbic lobe (from the Latin *limbus,* meaning border or hem), coined by Broca in 1878, is more widely recognized today. The limbic lobe is commonly referred to as the **limbic system** (which may very well be a misnomer). The limbic lobe consists of a number of structures, including the **hippocampus** (sea horse), **septum** (partition), and **cingulate** (girdle) **gyrus,** which may all have different functions (see Figure 1–12). Nevertheless, the history of how the limbic "lobe" became the limbic "system" is one of the most interesting chapters of the neurosciences.

Initially, anatomists were impressed with the connections between the olfactory system and the limbic lobe. On this evidence it was suggested that the limbic structures were elaborated to deal with olfactory information, and so together they were called the **rhinencephalon,** or smell-brain. Because a number of experiments demonstrated that they had little olfactory function, for a time their putative olfactory function lay in a scientific limbo. Then in 1937, Papez, in what was thought at the time to be a scientific tour de force, asked, "Is emotion a magic product, or is it a physiologic process which depends on an anatomic mechanism?" He suggested that emotion, which had no known anatomic substrate, was a product of the limbic lobe, which had no recognized function. It is a historical irony that the structures he emphasized as primary, e.g., the hippocampus, have been subsequently found to have little emotional function, whereas those he ignored, such as the septum, may indeed have such a function. It would be inappropriate, however, to suggest that the function of the limbic structures is in any way settled. Recently a variety of different functions have been proposed for the different limbic structures. This hippocampus, for example, has been successively postulated to play a role in inhibition, learning, memory, organization of movement, and spatial orientation. Certainly to suggest that the limbic system is the emotional brain now seems as much an oversimplification as it is to say that the limbic system has only one function.

Basal Ganglia

The **basal ganglia** are a collection of nuclei lying mainly beneath the anterior regions of the neocortex (Figure 1–13). They include the **putamen** (shell), **globus pallidus** (pale globe), the **caudate nucleus** (tailed nucleus), and **amygdala** (almond). These nuclei have

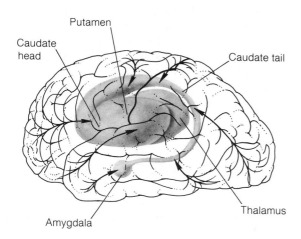

FIGURE 1-13. Relation between the basal ganglia and the cortex. Arrows indicate proposed projections of various cortical areas into basal ganglia structures.

intimate connections with the neocortex and thalamus, and they are connected by ascending and descending fibers to midbrain structures such as the red nucleus and substantia nigra. Figure 1-13 shows suggested relations to the neocortex.

The principal function of the basal ganglia has historically been described as motor. Damage to different portions of the basal ganglia can produce changes in posture, increases or decreases in muscle tone, and abnormal movements such as twitches, jerks, and tremors. The basal ganglia may have other functions, such as sequencing a number of complex movements into a smoothly executed response, as occurs during talking.

Thalamus

The **thalamus** can be divided into two areas, the ventral and dorsal thalami. The ventral thalamus provides a general, nonspecific input into the neocortex that may modulate the activity of the neocortex. The dorsal thalamus,

or thalamus proper, is composed of a number of nuclei, each of which projects to a specific area of the neocortex as shown in Figure 1-14. These nuclei receive input from the different body sensory systems or from other brain areas. The lateral geniculate body receives visual system projections, the medial geniculate body receives auditory system projections, and the ventral lateral posterior nuclei receive touch, pressure, pain, and temperature projec-

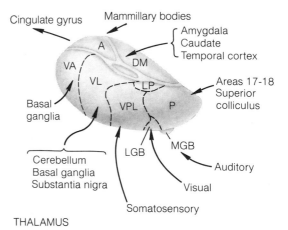

FIGURE 1-14. Relation between thalamic nuclei and various areas of the cortex to which they project. The arrows indicate the sources of input into the thalamus. DM, dorsal medial nucleus; VA, anterior ventral nucleus; VL, lateral ventral nucleus; LP, lateral posterior nucleus; VPL, lateral posterior ventral nucleus; P, pulvinar; LGB, lateral geniculate body; MGB, medial geniculate body.

tions from the body. In turn the lateral geniculate body projects to area 17, the medial geniculate body projects to area 41, and the ventral lateral posterior nuclei project to areas 1, 2, and 3. Note that the olfactory system does not project through the thalamus to the neocortex. A large area of the posterior secondary and tertiary cortex sends projections to and receives projections back from the pulvinar. Some of the subcortical motor nuclei, such as the globus pallidus, substantia nigra, and dentate nucleus, project to the anterior and lateral ventral nuclei, and these areas project to primary motor area 4 and secondary motor area 6. The dorsomedial nucleus receives projections from the amygdaloid complex, temporal neocortex, and caudate nucleus and projects to the remainder of the frontal lobe. The significance of some of these connections will be discussed in subsequent sections of the book.

THE CROSSED BRAIN

One of the most peculiar features of the organization of the brain is that each of its symmetrical halves responds to sensory stimulation from the contralateral side of the body or sensory world, and controls the musculature on the contralateral side of the body. (See Figure 1–15.) The visual system achieves this effect by crossing half the fibers of the optic tract as well as by reversing the image through the lens of the eye. Nearly all the fibers of the motor and somatosensory system cross. Projections from each ear go to each hemisphere, but there is substantial evidence that auditory excitation from one ear has a preferential route to the opposite hemisphere. As a result of this arrangement, along the center of the nervous system there are numerous crossings, or **decussations,** of sensory and motor fibers. Throughout the book details of this anatomy will be described where they are relevant to discussions of the function of each of these systems. It is sufficient to say here that because of this arrangement, damage to one side of the brain generally causes sensory and motor impairments not to the same side of the body but to the opposite side.

Anyone reflecting on this crossed arrangement must ask why it occurs and how. There have been a number of imaginative answers to each of these questions.

The Spanish anatomist Ramón y Cajal was obsessed, as he says, with the following

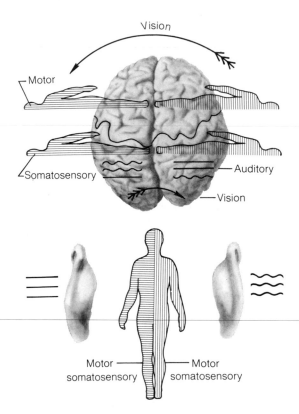

FIGURE 1–15. Schematic of the human brain from a dorsal view showing the projection of visual, auditory, and somatosensory input to contralateral areas of the cortex and the crossed projection of the motor cortex to the contralateral body.

thought: "Everything will have a simple explanation if it is admitted that the correct perception of an object implies the congruence of the cerebral surfaces of projection, that is,

those representing each point in space." He suggested that crossing in the visual system is necessary so that a continuous representation of an object is retained in the visual cortex. His explanation of what might happen in an uncrossed system is shown in Figure 1–16. He argued that since the lens reverses the image, and since each eye sees only part of the visual field, an uncrossed system would produce a representation in the cortex in which each half of the image was in one hemisphere but with the peripheries of the image juxtaposed in the center. He suggested that a prey taking the path of the external arrow shown in Figure 1–16 would be difficult to catch, since its path in the visual cortex would be discontinuous. Crossing the pathway introduces a continuous image. Cajal thought that reversal of the image's direction was not a problem, because it was compensated for by crossing the motor outflow from the brain.

A second theory advanced to explain crossing is the coil reflex theory shown in Figure 1–17. Coghill studied the development of movement in the primitive vertebrate *Amblystoma* and found that its first movement is a coil, which when repeated a number of times forms its basic swimming movement. In this animal, input from sensory receptors goes only to motor cells on the opposite side of the body through an interneuron at the rostral end. The sensory input is passed to successive motor cells in a rostral-to-caudal sequence, causing contraction of successive myotomes that by their action produce the coil. The coil allows the animal to flex away from a noxious stimulus, and as swimming develops, ensures that stimulation will elicit swimming at the animal's front end. Sarnat and Netsky suggest that this anatomical arrangement forms the basis for the crossed systems in all vertebrates. William Webster has suggested to us that this model explains why the olfactory system is the only sensory system that is uncrossed. The

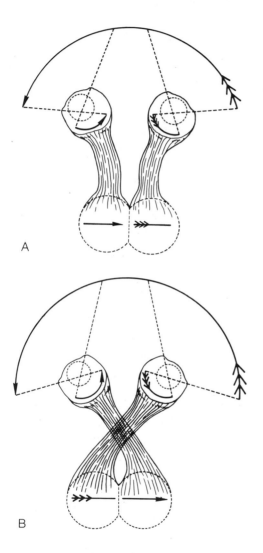

A

B

FIGURE 1–16. A. Illustration of the incongruous central projection of the images from the two eyes if there were no intercrossing of the optic nerves. B. Continuity of the visual image obtained by crossing the optic nerves. (From S. Ramón y Cajal. *Recollections of My Life*. Copyright © 1937. Reprinted with permission of the American Philosophical Society.)

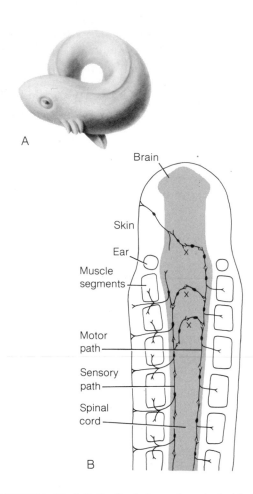

A

Brain

Skin

Ear

Muscle
segments

Motor
path

Sensory
path

Spinal
cord

B

FIGURE 1–17. A. Coil reflex in the embryonic *Amblystoma*. B. A diagram of the mechanism that accounts for the coil reaction. Sensory neurons are shown on one side of the body, motor neurons on the other. Excitation of a sensory neuron leads to excitation of an interneuron (X) and then to sequential contraction of the contralateral muscles in a head-to-tail direction. (After Coghill, 1929.)

assumption is that the primitive function of the olfactory bulb was to bring an animal to food, and so a primitive animal would coil toward an olfactory stimulus that signaled food. Therefore, it would have to contract muscles on the same side of the body and would use an uncrossed projection to the muscles. Further-

more, the Coghill model offers an explanation for why the brain's motor projections to the distal part of the body are also crossed. To be effective, an avoidance response of coiling would require a contralateral limb movement, once the limbs developed.

An imaginative explanation of how the nervous system became crossed has been proposed by Kinsbourne. He notes that invertebrates have an uncrossed and ventrally located nervous system, a dorsally located heart, and a posterior flow of blood in central blood vessels. Vertebrates have a crossed and dorsally located nervous system, a ventrally located heart, and an anterior flow of blood in ventral blood vessels. He proposes that in the transition from invertebrates to vertebrates the body rotated 180° with respect to the head. As a result, blood circulation reversed direction, the heart became located ventrally, the nervous system adopted a dorsal position, and decussations were formed by the rotation.

One weakness of Kinsbourne's theory is that it predicts that the sensory and motor pathways of the brainstem should be reversed in a dorso-ventral direction with respect to the spinal cord. This is not the case, for the dorsal portion of the midbrain is sensory, as is the dorsal portion of the spinal cord. A second weakness of the theory is that it does not explain why a 180° rotation would prove adaptive. It may have been a chance occurrence, or it may have occurred to effect the coil reflex. (Alternatively, we could suggest, tongue in cheek, that had the nervous system remained below the esophagus the brain could not have evolved lest it choke off respiration and the route of food to the stomach.)

PROTECTION

The brain and spinal cord are supported and protected from injury and infective invasion in three ways. (1) The brain is enclosed in a thick bone, the *skull,* and the spinal cord is encased in a series of interlocking bony *vertebrae.* (2) Within these bony cases are three membranes: the outer **dura mater** (from the Latin, meaning hard mother), a tough double layer of collagenous fiber enclosing the brain in a kind of loose sack; the middle **arachnoid** (from the Greek, meaning resembling a spider's web), a very thin sheet of delicate collagenous connective tissue that follows the contours of the brain; and the inner **pia mater** (from the Latin, meaning soft mother), which is a moderately tough membrane of connective-tissue fibers made from reticular, elastic, and collagenous fibers, that clings to the surface of the nervous tissue. (3) The brain is cushioned from shock and sudden changes of pressure by a fluid called the *cerebrospinal fluid* (CSF), which fills the ventricles inside the brain and circulates around the brain beneath the arachnoid layer, in the subarachnoid space. This fluid is a clear, colorless solution of sodium chloride and other salts and is made by a plexus of cells that evaginates into each ventricle. The CSF is made continually, and it flows from the ventricles, circulating around the brain, to be absorbed by the venous sinuses of the dura mater. Although it is unlikely that the CSF nourishes the brain, it may instead play a role in excreting metabolic wastes from the brain.

REFERENCES

Brodmann, K. *Vergleichende Lokalisationlehre der Grosshirnrinde in ihren Prinzipien dargestellt auf Grund des Zellenbaues.* Leipzig: J. A. Barth, 1909.

Coghill, G. E. *Anatomy and the Problem of Behavior.* Cambridge: Cambridge University Press, 1929. (Reprinted by Hafner, New York, 1963.)

Curtis, B. A., S. Jacobson, and E. M. Marcus. *An Introduction to the Neurosciences.* Philadelphia: Saunders, 1972.

Elliott, H. *Textbook of Neuroanatomy.* Philadelphia and Toronto: Lippincott, 1969.

Everett, N. B. *Functional Neuroanatomy.* Philadelphia: Lea and Febiger, 1965.

Hamilton, L. W. *Basic Limbic System Anatomy of the Rat.* New York and London: Plenum, 1976.

Kinsbourne, M., ed. *Asymmetrical Function of the Brain.* Cambridge: Cambridge University Press, 1978.

MacLean, P. D. Psychosomatic disease and the "visceral brain": Recent developments bearing on the Papez theory of emotion. *Psychosomatic Medicine* 11:338–353, 1949.

Papez, J. W. A proposed mechanism of emotion. *Archives of Neurology and Psychiatry* 38:724–744, 1937.

Passingham, R. E. Brain size and intelligence in man. *Brain Behavior and Evolution* 16:253–270, 1979.

Penfield, W., and E. Boldrey. Somatic motor and sensory representation in the cerebral cortex as studied by electrical stimulation. *Brain* 60:389–443, 1958.

Penfield, W., and H. H. Jasper. *Epilepsy and the Functional Anatomy of the Human Brain.* Boston: Little, Brown, 1954.

Ramón y Cajal, S. *Recollections of My Life,* Memoirs of the American Philosophical Society, vol. 8, 1937.

Ranson, S. W., and S. L. Clark. *The Anatomy of the Nervous System.* Philadelphia: Saunders, 1959.

Sarnat, H. B., and M. G. Netsky. *Evolution of the Nervous System.* New York: Oxford University Press, 1974.

Truex, R. C., and M. B. Carpenter. *Human Neuroanatomy.* Baltimore: Williams & Wilkins, 1969.

Van Valen, L. Brain size and intelligence in man. *American Journal of Physical Anthropology* 40:417–424, 1974.

2

PHYSIOLOGICAL ORGANIZATION
OF THE NERVOUS SYSTEM

When male Grayling butterflies are ready to copulate, they fly upward toward females passing overhead. The male's response to females is not unerringly accurate, because sometimes they fly toward other passing objects. This fact suggested to the ethologist Tinbergen that the most effective stimulus for releasing the male's approach response could be discovered with controlled experiments. Tinbergen made model butterflies, attached them to the line of a fishing rod, and "flew" them to determine which were the most effective in attracting males. Although the females are brightly colored, and the males can see color, it was not an important feature of the stimulus. The males were attracted by dark, large, and irregularly moving stimuli. Furthermore, these characteristics were mutually reinforcing, which suggested to Tinbergen that the nervous system of male butterflies has a "pooling station" that integrates the different features of the stimulating object.

Tinbergen's experiments are an example of excellent behavioral research that, although done with no knowlege or study of the physiology of the butterfly's nervous system, still gives clues about how that system must work. But knowledge of how the process of integration takes place, that is, of how the pooling station works, involves physiology. This is also true of neuropsychology. Much can be learned about people's behavior through careful observations and controlled experiments, but detailed knowledge of how the nervous system controls behavior requires study of its physiological organization. This requires knowing the structure of cells and how they work. Although an extensive knowledge of electrophysiology (the study of neuron activity) and neuropharmacology (the study of the biochemical activity of neurons) is not essential for understanding neuropsychology, a general understanding of them is helpful. The following sections give a brief description of (1) the physical features of neurons, (2) the electrical activity of neurons and the techniques used to record their activity, and (3) chemical communication between cells and the pharmacological techniques used to manipulate their communication.

NEURON STRUCTURE

Neurons are cells that are the integrating units of the nervous system, and although they share many of the characteristics of other cells in the body, they have special characteristics that make them particularly adapted to their function.

A broad analogy can be drawn between a neuron and a person. Neurons, once formed, do not regenerate, and unless they suffer lethal damage, most live as long as the person in which they are found. Each neuron is separated from physical contact with every other neuron, but it bridges this separation by communicating with a language that is part electrical and part chemical. Neurons vary enormously in size and shape, the differences making each neuron particularly adapted to its specialized function. Neurons are aggregated into communities, or nuclei, each of which makes a special contribution to behavior. Neurons are modifiable: they change their behavior with experience, they learn, they remember, and they forget. At times neurons can malfunction, causing disruptions in normal behavior. There are similarities in the behavior of neurons, but the full significance of their behavior can only be understood within the context of the community in which they function. In summary, this anthropomorphic analogy serves to caution us that the function of a neuron within the context of a working brain is not as simple as the neuron is small.

Figure 2–1 shows a neuron schematically. The neuron is enclosed in a specialized membrane and consists of a **cell body,** processes called **dendrites** (from the Greek, meaning

tree), a process called an **axon** (from the Greek, meaning axle), and little end feet, or *terminals,* at the ends of the axon. Associated with each of these parts are other specialized structures that are described where appropriate in the following sections. The dendrites collect information, which is then integrated at the **axon hillock** close to the cell body; a summary of the input received by the cell is then passed along the axon and through the end feet to other cells. ("Information" is used here loosely to mean any event or events that the cell actively codifies.)

Although neurons have these basic structures, their configurations differ from one another. For example, a *sensory* cell of the somatosensory system has one very long dendrite coursing from the skin to a point adjacent to its cell body, located near the spinal cord. Here the dendrite connects directly to its axon, which may then travel to the hindbrain. This sensory cell has developed a system of direct information transmission that requires no modification of the signal between receptor and brain. On the other hand, a *motor* cell in the inferior spinal cord has a number of dendrites collecting input and a long axon extending from the cord to muscles. This cell appears to be specialized to integrate a variety of inputs for a specific action.

Between these sensory and motor cells are many interneurons of various shapes. Some have a densely arborized dendritic system, suggesting that their primary function is to collect a great deal of diversified information for integration (for examples of different neuron types see Figure 1–1). Also, although many neurons communicate chemically—and we stress this feature of their function—some probably do communicate electrically.

The Cell Membrane

The cell membrane surrounds the entire cell and consists of a double layer of lipid (fat)

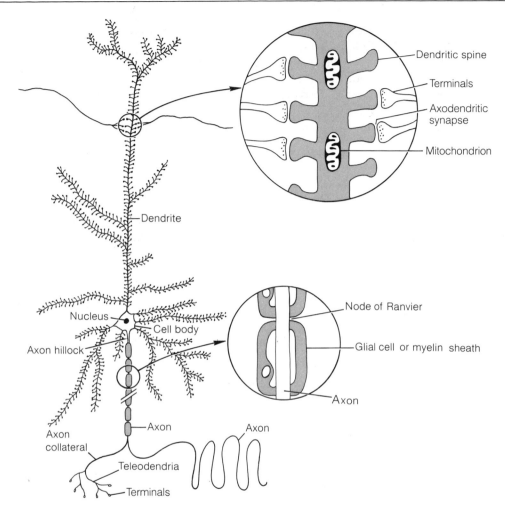

Dendritic spine

Terminals

Axodendritic synapse

Mitochondrion

Dendrite

Node of Ranvier

Nucleus

Cell body

Glial cell or myelin sheath

Axon hillock

Axon

Axon collateral

Axon

Axon

Teleodendria

Terminals

FIGURE 2–1. A typical neuron, showing some of its major physical features.

molecules. These molecules are polar in structure, each having a head and two tails; the heads face outward, the tails face inward. The inner portion made-up by the tails is believed to be largely impermeable to many substances, thus providing a barrier to the free movement of ions through the membrane. The membrane has four general functions. (1) It contains channels, specially designed spaces, that allow some ions to penetrate. It actively pumps other ions in and out of the cell. These processes allow the membrane to maintain a charge across its surface, with the inside of the cell negative with respect to the outside. (2) The membrane is the site of electrical changes that are involved in information transmission. (3) The membrane contains receptors to which peptides and hormones attach. These may be transported into the cell and carried to the cell nucleus. The hormones may act on chromosomes in the nucleus to initiate such processes as sexual differentiation of the cell and its functions. (4) The membrane contains sites for axon terminals as well as receptors. Transmitter substances from the terminals of one neuron attach to the receptors of another, where they induce changes in the electrical charge across the membrane.

The Cell Body (Soma)

The cell body, or **soma,** is defined as the area of cytoplasm (a semifluid substance filling the space outlined by the membrane) that surrounds the nucleus. The cell body contains a variety of substances that determine the structure and function of the cell. The major physical features of the cell body are illustrated in Figure 2–2. An important function of the cell body and its constituents is the manufacture and transportation of proteins and other substances. Some of the proteins may be destined to be secreted as transmitter sub-

stances, but most of them are required to maintain the many branching processes of the neuron. Other substances manufactured in the cell include enzymes for stimulating chemical reactions, receptors to which substances can attach to the cell's surface, and structural elements of the cell that maintain the shape or transport substances through its long axons and dendrites.

The Nucleus. Each cell contains a **nucleus.** Within the nucleus are **chromosomes** and a **nucleolus.** The chromosomes are composed of **deoxyribonucleic acid (DNA),** which combined with some proteins form almost all the genetic material of the cell. The DNA has two functions. First, it controls the growth and development of the cell into its mature form. Second, once the cell is mature, it continues to produce protein that is needed for maintaining the structure of the cell or for participating in the communication business of the cell. The nucleolus produces material called ribosomal

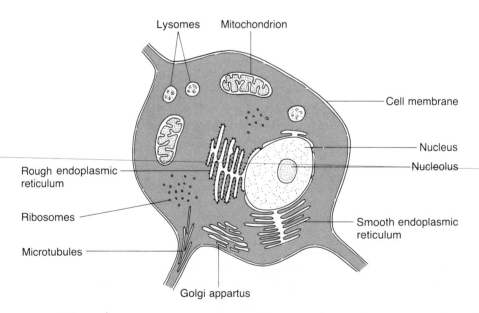

FIGURE 2–2. A typical cell body, showing some of its major physical features.

ribonucleic acid (rRNA), a form of **ribonucleic acid (RNA).**

It might be briefly mentioned here how the chromosomes and the nucleolus participate in protein production. Enzymes act on the DNA of the chromosomes to produce *messenger ribonucleic acid (mRNA)*, which contains the code for producing a protein such as an enzyme. The mRNA is transported into the cell cytoplasm. Here it joins with the ribosomal RNA, which has been transported from the nucleolus to the cytoplasm, to from a new structure called a *polyribosome*. The polyribosome is the template on which proteins are formed. Finally, once manufactured the proteins are used locally or are transported to other parts of the cell or are exported from the cell.

The Endoplasmic Reticulum. Extending throughout the cytoplasm is a nctwork of membranelike substance called the *endoplasmic reticulum* (ER). Some ribosomes become attached to the ER, giving it a rough appearance, and so this part is called the *rough* ER. This part of the ER is thought to make protein destined for export from the cell. The remaining part is called the *smooth* ER. When cells were first examined with a light microscope, a dense accumulation of material was seen around the nucleus. This was called Nissl substance. The substance had a great affinity for certain dyes, and so Nissl stains were, and still are, one of the most commonly used stains. When the electron microscope was developed, examination of the Nissl substance showed that it was in fact rough ER.

Light-microscopic examination of the cell shows clumps of material that are named the **Golgi apparatus.** Electron-microscopic examination of the Golgi apparatus shows that they are clusters of smooth ER. The Golgi apparatus is thought to collect proteins from the rough ER and cover them with a membrane so that they form granules. The granules are transported to other parts of the cell or are exported from it.

Lysomes. The cell body contains organelles of different sizes that are shaped like sacks, called **lysomes** (from the Greek *lyso-*, dissolution). Lysomes contain enzymes that degrade a wide variety of substances coming from within or outside the cell. Lysomes may leave a residue called **lipofuscin granules,** which appear in cells in increasing concentration with aging.

Mitochondria. Most of the processes of the cell require energy. This comes from the *mitochondria* (from the Greek *mito,* thread; *chondrion,* granule). They have a characteristic cigar shape, with a smooth outer membrane and an internal folded one. It is thought that they were originally primitive organisms that were incorporated into cells in a symbiotic relation. Brain cells derive all their energy from glucose, which is extracted from the blood as it is needed (there are no mechanisms for storage in the brain and so deprivation of glucose results in rapid cell death). The mitochondria take up glucose and break it down to form *adenosine triphosphate* **(ATP),** which is used by other components of the cell as an energy source. Another function of mitochondria is to store calcium, which is used in regulating the release of transmitter substances from the terminals.

Microtubules and Microfilaments. Cells contain different small fiberlike structures in both the cell body and the cell processes. **Microtubules** of various sizes are thought to be involved in the transport of substances from the cell body to the distal parts of the cell (orthograde transport) or from the distal cell elements to the cell body (retrograde transport). If an amino acid is injected near a cell, it is taken up by the cell, incorporated into protein, and then transported to the terminals. There seem to be two transport systems: some proteins can be seen to travel at 1 mm per day, others travel at 100 mm or faster per day. The existence of these transport systems has been used to trace connections between neurons. For example, if radioactively labeled materials are injected near cells, they are taken up and transported by the microtubules. If tissue that has been radioactively labeled is then placed on photographic film, it exposes the film, taking a picture of the route the labeled material has taken. The name of this procedure is *autoradiography*. Fluorescent dyes also may be injected near cells, incorporated into the cell, and then transported to the dendrites, cell body, or terminals depending on the dye, allowing them to be seen with a fluorescence microscope. This permits connections to be traced in a variety of directions. The function of **microfilaments** is uncertain, but they may be involved in controlling the shape, movement, or fluidity of the cytoplasm.

The Dendrites

The dendrites are actually extensions of the cell body that allow the neuron to increase the area of surface on which it receives information from other cells. The number of dendrites varies from neuron to neuron, some having a few, others over 20, and each dendrite may branch profusely. Dendrites vary from a few microns to millimeters in length and taper as they branch; some have rough projections called dendritic spines on which they receive terminals from other cells.

The Axon

The axon originates in the cell body at a transition point called the axon hillock. Its function is to transmit to other cells information that it receives from the axon hillock. Each cell has only one axon, which varies in length from a few microns to more than a meter in different cells. Most axons have branches called collaterals. At the end of the axon and its collaterals are fine terminations called teleodendria. The teleodendria are covered with little knobs, called terminals, which make junctions with other cells.

The Terminals

The terminals lie in close proximity to other cells. Sherrington coined the term *synapsis* (from the Greek, meaning union) for the "almost" connection between a terminal and another neuron; consequently the terminals became technically known as **synaptic knobs,** abbreviated to **synapses** when one is speaking in terms of function or more generally. They contain packages of chemical substances that when released influence the activity of other cells. Neurons may make actual contact with each other, but we will limit our description to the commonest "almost" connections.

The Synapse

There are three features of synapses that give some insight into their function. (1) The shape of the terminals, the appearance of their contents, and the way they connect with other structures show that there are different classes of synapses. For example, there are differences in the size of the granules in the terminals of different cells. Since the granules contain the transmitter, this shows that there are differences in the transmitter substances that different cells may contain. There are also differences in the density of the substances within the terminal, and there are differences in the density of the substances on the membrane with which they synapse. These features suggest that different synapses have different functions. Although no clear relations between the appearance of terminals and function are known, it is recognized that some synapses are able to inhibit the activity of post-

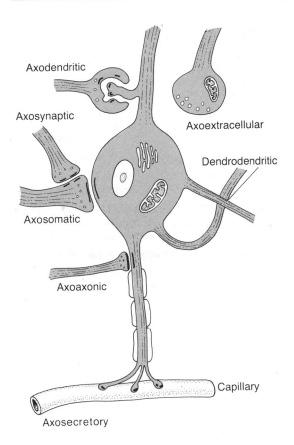

Axodendritic

Axosynaptic

Axoextracellular

Dendrodendritic

Axosomatic

Axoaxonic

Capillary

Axosecretory

FIGURE 2–3. Types of terminals in the central nervous system.

synaptic cells, whereas other synapses excite postsynaptic cells. (2) Synapses can make contacts with various portions of a cell; they are called axodendritic, axosomatic, axoaxonic, or axosynaptic, depending on whether they synapse with, respectively, dendrites, the cell body, axons, or synapses of other cells. Examples of these connections are given in Figure 2–3. Neurons may also make other contacts with each other: dendrites make dendrodendritic contacts, and the tubular portions of axons may overlie other axons and dendrites, making contact in passing. There are also terminals that do not synapse with other neur-

al elements, but rather secrete their transmitter into the extracellular space. These could be called axoextracellular synapses. If the nervous system is thought of as consisting of channels for information conduction, it can be appreciated that the variety of terminal locations provides many opportunities for unique or novel routes of communication. In addition to synapsing with other neural processes, terminals end on muscles, and they can terminate on capillaries, into which they may secrete hormones. (3) Inputs onto neurons are often highly segregated. This segregation can be illustrated by the seven inputs onto a pyramidal cell of the hippocampal formation, illustrated in Figure 2–4. Six of these inputs are segregated on segments of the cell; the seventh makes nonsegregated contacts. It is thought that synapses to the cell body have the potential to be more influential than those on the periphery, as we shall see in the next section. The nonsegregated inputs likely have a general modulatory action on the cell.

NEURON ELECTRICAL ACTIVITY

Much of the pioneering research done on the neuron's electrical activity, such as the work of Hodgkin and Huxley, used the giant axon of the squid, on the recommendation of the biologist Young. This axon measures up to a millimeter in diameter and is a hundred times larger than the axons of human nerve cells. The squid's axon is used to contract muscles that squirt water out the end of the squid's body to propel it through the water. Because effective propulsion requires all the muscles of the body to contract at the same time, the largest axons, which conduct the fastest, connect to the most distant muscles. Because of its size, the giant axon is easily removed from the squid by dissection and is easy to use for experiments on how electrical conduction takes place in axons.

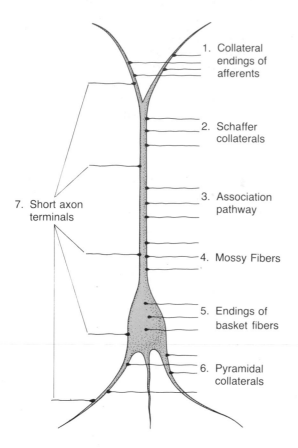

1. Collateral endings of afferents

2. Schaffer collaterals

3. Association pathway

7. Short axon terminals

4. Mossy Fibers

5. Endings of basket fibers

6. Pyramidal collaterals

FIGURE 2–4. Segregation of inputs onto a single hippo-campal pyramidal cell. (After Kandel and Schwartz, 1981.)

The Resting Potential

Neurons have a charge across their membrane. If a neuron is undisturbed, the charge remains relatively constant. This charge is called the **resting potential.** The following describes how it is maintained.

Probably everyone knows that if a salt is put into a liquid medium, it will dissolve into positive (+) and negative (−) ions, which will eventually become distributed equally through the solution. In distributing themselves the ions respond to two forces, concentration and charge, and the equilibrium they reach represents an equal distribution of both concentration and charge. The membrane of a nerve axon separates two fluid compartments, the intracellular and the extracellular fluid, each of which contains many ions. Of these, negatively charged organic ions (An^-) and chlorine ions (Cl^-), and positively charged potassium ions (K^+) and sodium ions (Na^+) are particularly important in electrical conduction. These ions would be equally distributed on both sides of the membrane if it did not act as a barrier to their easy passage. It does this in three ways. (1) It provides passive resistance to An^- ions because they are simply too large to pass through it; consequently they are retained in the intracellular fluid. (2) It is semipermeable to the other ions, allowing some of them to pass through more freely than others. Normally, K^+ passes more freely than Na^+ (Na^+, although smaller than K^+, is bound more strongly to water molecules, which add to its bulk). The permeability of the membrane also changes in certain situations, allowing these ions to pass more freely through the membrane at some times than they can at others. In particular, the membrane contains Na^+ channels and K^+ channels, which close or open to control the flow of these ions. (3) The membrane contains a pumping system, or Na^+-K^+ pump, which exchanges intracellular Na^+ for extracellular K^+. Since the membrane is less permeable to Na^+ than to K^+, Na^+ accumulates on the outside of the membrane. Some K^+ flows back out of the cell when pumped, to equalize the K^+ concentration across the membrane. The unlimited outward flow of K^+ is checked, however, by the accumulating extracellular charge carried by the Na^+ (like charges repel each other). As a result of the action of these three processes there are 350 times as many An^- ions and 20 times as many

K^+ ions on the inside of the cell membrane as on the outside, and nine times as many Cl^- ions and 20 times as many Na^+ ions on the outside of the cell membrane as on the inside, resulting in a negative charge on the inside of the cell in the range of −75 mV.

The Contribution of K^+ Ions to the Membrane Potential. The concentrations of various substances in the intracellular fluid and in the extracellular fluid are known. These values can be used to perform the following imaginary experiment. We erect a nerve membrane and place the stuff of the intracellular fluid on one side of it. This material contains a 385 mmol concentration of An^- ions and a 420 mmol concentration of K^+ ions. On the other side of the membrane we place a control fluid composed of large molecules that will not penetrate the membrane. Having placed the substance, we then measure the voltage across the membrane by placing electrodes connected to a voltmeter on each side of it. At first we find that there is no charge across the membrane, but gradually a charge develops until the inside of the membrane is negative by about −75 mV relative to the outside. After this, there is no further change. If the concentrations of the substances on each side of the membrane are then measured, it is found that all of the An^- ions are still on the same side of the membrane; none have escaped. When we measure the K^+ ion concentration, we find that 20 mmol of K^+ ions have crossed the membrane. How did they cross? How did such a small change in K^+ ion distribution produce such a large voltage shift? Why did the voltage across the membrane stop changing at precisely this level? We will answer each of these questions in turn.

The differential movement of ions across the membrane demonstrates that it is selectively permeable. Since there were no An^- ions placed on the outside portion of the membrane, An^- ions should have crossed to estab-lish equal concentration on each side. Since they did not cross, the membrane is obviously impermeable to them. Since some K^+ ions did pass through the barrier, it must contain holes large enough to let them pass, but small enough to block the larger An^- ions. These holes have been called K^+ channels. The existence of these channels has been confirmed in another way. If tetraethylammonium (TEA) is placed on the membrane, no K^+ ions escape: TEA blocks the K^+ ion channels.

In order to understand how a small change in K^+ ion concentration produces a large voltage, examine Figure 2–5. The cloud of "+" charges immediately outside the surface of the membrane represent the K^+ ions that have leaked across the membrane. The "−" charges immediately inside represent the An^- ions that could not cross the barrier. Note that the charge difference has accumulated only on the membrane: all other intracellular and extracellular fluid is in equilibrium. Thus, a small movement in K^+ ions creates a large

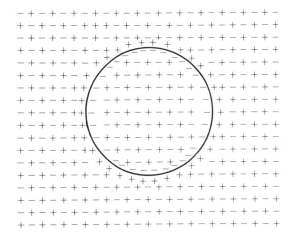

FIGURE 2–5. The net excess of positive charges outside the membrane of a nerve cell at rest represents a small fraction of the total number of ions inside and outside the cell. (After Kandel and Schwartz, 1981.)

transmembrane charge because the voltage difference is focused only on the surface of the membrane. It has been found that a difference of about 1200 charged ions across a square micrometer of membrane will produce a charge difference of 10 mV.

Figure 2–5 also shows why K^+ ions did not continue to leak across the membrane. A point was reached at which the concentration gradient pulling K^+ ions out of the cell was balanced by an electrostatic pressure that pulled them back in. When this equilibrium was reached, they stopped their migration. If you like, the "$-$" charges on the An^- ions held back any further escape of the "$+$" charges on the K^+ ions. Actually, in 1902, without performing this experiment, Julius Bernstein used an equation called the Nernst equation to predict the K^+ ion potential across the membrane. In the 1940s, when the experiment became feasible and was performed, it partly confirmed Bernstein's calculation.

The Contribution of Na^+ Ions to the Membrane Potential. As we have pointed out, experimental investigations did not quite confirm Bernstein's calculation of the K^+ ion potential. The calculated potential was accurate for glial cells, but apparently something else was leaking across the nerve membrane. The something else turned out to be Na^+ ions. Calculations of extracellular fluid concentrations show that there is a 440 mmol concentration of Na^+ ions in the extracellular fluid and only a 50 mmol concentration in the intracellular fluid. Na^+ ions leak into the cell to reduce this concentration difference. Experimental work has demonstrated that the Na^+ ions do not enter through the K^+ ion channels, because TEA does not block their inward flow. This result suggests that Na^+ ions have their own channels, a conclusion confirmed by the finding that *tetrodotoxin* (pufferfish poison) blocks the permeability of the membrane to Na^+ ions.

As we have noted above, K^+ ions stop flowing out of the cell because their movement is opposed by the electrostatic pressure that their outward flow creates across the membrane. Obviously, the inward flow of Na^+ ions redresses this situation. If there were no other checks, Na^+ ions would continue their inward flow, K^+ ions would continue to flow out, and the charge on the membrane would quickly run down. Something must intervene to prevent the unchecked inward flow of Na^+ ions.

The Na^+-K^+ Pump. If Na^+ ions continued to leak into the cell, they would balance the electrostatic disequilibrium produced by the outward flow of K^+ ions, and eventually K^+ ions would be depleted and the charge gradient would run down. Since this does not occur, it was suggested that the membrane contains pumps that pump Na^+ ions back out of the cell. Current theory holds that there is a Na^+-K^+ pump that extrudes Na^+, exchanging three Na^+ ions for every two K^+ ions. The K^+ ions, of course, quickly leak back out, but the Na^+ ions only slowly leak back in. The important result is that in the squid axon a charge of slightly less than -60 mV is maintained across the membrane. The operation of the Na^+-K^+ pump requires energy. It has been possible to demonstrate that its operation can be arrested with such metabolic poisons as *dinitrophenol* and *ouabain*.

To this point, we have not considered the contribution of Cl^-. Cl^- ions are free to cross the membrane passively. As a result, they respond to chemical and electrical gradients and do not affect the transmembrane potential established by the actively distributed Na^+ and K^+ ions.

Figure 2–6 shows a sketch of the charge across the membrane of an axon and a graph of the transmembrane voltage over a period of time. The voltage across the membrane is about -70 mV in mammalian nerves (the level

FIGURE 2–6. The nerve membrane, because of its permeability and through the action of the Na^+-K^+ pump, accumulates a charge, with the inside of the membrane negative with respect to the outside. This charge is about -70 mV and is called the resting potential.

actually varies between -55 and -90 mV in different animals). Provided that the membrane is undisturbed, the charge across the membrane will remain at that level indefinitely. This stable transmembrane potential is called the resting potential.

Stimulation

There are, of course, normal influences on the cell that change the voltage of the membrane in systematic ways. In addition, a wide variety of external agents such as electric currents and chemicals and irritation from manual displacement, foreign tissue, etc., can also produce changes in the membrane voltage. The normal processes provide the mechanisms for the normal functioning of the cell; the other processes more generally lead to various types of pathology. Despite these differences, both the nor-

mal and the abnormal influences act in very much the same way; thus, any influence or irritation that leads to a change in the voltage can be called a **stimulus,** and the process, whether normal or abnormal, can be called **stimulation.** In experimental situations stimulation is usually provided by giving brief pulses of electric shock to the axon through small wires called stimulating electrodes. The response of the axon is then recorded by measuring its voltage change with a voltmeter or oscilloscope attached to the axon by small wires called recording electrodes.

Passive Properties of a Neuron

When an axon or a neuron is electrically stimulated, the voltage across the membrane changes. Depending on the type of stimulation, the transmembrane potential could become larger or smaller. These changes are usually restricted to the area of tissue stimulated; that is, the effect decays over distance from the point of stimulation (in the same way that a wave decays in size as it moves away from the point where a stone is dropped into the water). The changes are also quite brief. Because the changes are produced by the action of an external agent, and not by the spontaneous actions of the membrane, they are called *passive changes*. The rate of decay and the duration of the changes are determined by properties of the axon that are referred to as its cable properties. These will not be discussed here. If stimulation produces a change that decreases the transmembrane voltage, the membrane is said to have become **depolarized.** If stimulation produces a change that increases the transmembrane voltage, the membrane is said to have become **hyperpolarized.** Depolarization is thought to be due to increased inward movement of Na^+ ions, whereas hyperpolarization is thought to be due to increased outward movement of K^+ ions. This suggests

FIGURE 2–7. Stimulation of the membrane causes it to become more permeable to Na^+ ions. As a result the transmembrane potential declines, or depolrizes. At about −50 mV, its threshold, the membrane becomes completely permeable and its charge momentarily reverses. At this point K^+ ions flow out of the cell, restoring the transmembrane potential. This sequence of changes is represented by the graphic display called an action potential.

that stimulation, whether chemical or electrical, regulates ion flow by changing the size of the channels in the membrane to decrease or increase ion movement.

The Action Potential

Although the neuron membrane responds to weak stimulation by decreasing its permeability to ions in a relatively orderly way, it undergoes a peculiar change of behavior if the stimulation is sufficiently intense to cause the transmembrane voltage to depolarize to about −50 mV. At about this voltage the membrane becomes completely permeable to Na^+; that is, Na^+ rushes into the cell until

the voltage across the membrane falls through 0 mV and even reverses to about +50 mV. The sudden permeability of the membrane occurs independently of any further stimulation once the membrane has depolarized to about −50 mV. The change in permeability is quite brief, about half a millisecond, after which the membrane becomes permeable to K^+, which flows out along both a chemical and an electrostatic gradient. The flow of K^+ ions restores and even overshoots the original resting potential. At this point the membrane again becomes resistant to the flow of Na^+ ions.

The Na^+-K^+ pump then resumes its action, and the resting potential of the membrane is restored. The voltage at which the membrane undergoes this autonomous change is called its **threshold.** The sudden reversal of polarity and the restoration of the resting potential are called an **action potential.** These are displayed graphically in Figure 2–7. One can say, therefore, that the threshold for eliciting an action potential is −50 mV.

What triggers the action potential? Hodgkin and Huxley have suggested that the ion conductance channels are controlled by "gates" embedded in the membrane. An example of what such a gate might look like is illustrated in Figure 2–8. In Figure 2–8 A, the charges across the membrane during a resting potential interact with the charges on the gating molecule to block the sodium channel. In Figure 2–8 B, stimulation reverses the membrane charge. This in turn interacts with the gating molecule, flipping open the Na^+ ion gate to permit the inward flow of sodium ions. According to this model the stimulus required to reverse the membrane voltage, opening a gate, would be an adequate stimulus for producing an action potential. The threshold for the action potential would be the actual voltage at which the gate flipped open. Current experimental work is being directed toward more precisely describing the gating mechanism.

Conduction of the Nerve Impulse

When an action potential occurs in a region of the nerve membrane, it acts as a stimulus, causing adjacent portions of the membrane to lose their permeability and undergo a similar voltage change. Consequently, an action potential triggered at one end of an axon will be conducted along its length. (Action potentials can travel in either direction, but they normally begin at the cell body and travel away from it.) This movement of the action potential along the length of the axon, shown in Figure 2–9, is called a **nerve impulse** (or, more colorfully and descriptively, firing or discharging). The rate at which the impulse travels along the axon, varying from one to 100 meters per second, is quite slow, but neurons can sustain a wide range of firing rates. Usually they fire fewer than 100 times a second, but they can fire as frequently as 1000 times per second.

The All-or-None Law

A peculiar property of a neuron's behavior is that its threshold is stable, and every action potential, and hence nerve impulse, once it is triggered has an identical threshold and height. Also, once the nerve impulses are initiated they require no further stimulus; the neuron provides all the energy required to maintain them. These properties of the neuron's behavior are formulated in the all-or-none law: action potentials either occur or they do not; there is no in-between condition.

Factors Determining Nerve Impulse Speed

The nerve impulse does not travel at exactly the same speed in all neurons. At least two factors affect speed. One factor is resistance to current along the axon. Impulse speed increases as resistance decreases, and resistance is most effectively decreased by increase of axon size. Therefore large axons conduct at a faster rate than small axons. Were the nervous system to rely only on this procedure, axons would have to be cumbersomely large. An alternative procedure has evolved that uses the glial cells to aid in speeding propagation. Schwann cells in the peripheral nervous system and oligodendroglia in the central nervous system wrap around some axons, forming a compact sheath of myelin (from the Greek, meaning marrow) against the cell membrane, as shown in Figure 2–10. Between each glial cell the membrane of the axon is exposed by a gap called a node of Ranvier. In these myeli-

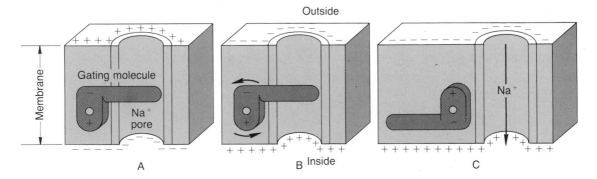

FIGURE 2–8. Hypothetical explanation for molecular events that underlie gating currents. A. Active membrane channel of a nerve cell at rest. B. Membrane changes during depolarization open the gate. C. Na$^+$ ions freely cross the membrane. (After Kandel and Schwartz, 1981.)

FIGURE 2–9. Because an action potential at one part of the axon stimulates adjacent areas of the axon to produce one, the action potential is propagated along the axon. (After Katz, 1967.)

FIGURE 2–10. The nerve impulse jumps from one inter-Schwann cell space, called a node of Ranvier, to the next. This process, saltatory conduction, greatly speeds impulse transmission.

nated axons the nerve impulse jumps along the axon from node to node, a type of conduction called saltatory conduction (from the Latin, meaning skip). Saltatory conduction is an extremely effective way of speeding the impulse because a small myelinated axon can conduct an impulse as rapidly as an unmyelinated axon 30 times as large.

The presence of myelin also conserves energy. Since the myelin prevents current flow along most of the length of the axon, the metabolic processes required for maintaining the resting potential need only be maintained at the nodes of Ranvier. Given the role of myelin, the devastating consequences of multiple sclerosis or Guillain-Barré disease, which cause demyelination, can be appreciated.

The Origin of the Nerve Impulse

Graded Potentials. So far we have described the events that occur on an axon when it is stimulated. What happens on dendrites, which are normally the origin of the cell's electrical activity? Dendrites have a membrane similar to the axons' and a similar resting potential, and they also undergo changes in potential when they are stimulated. But unlike the axon, the dendrites do not produce action potentials. If a dendrite is stimulated, the voltage changes from the resting potential in proportion to the intensity of the stimulation; the change then spreads along the dendrite away from the point of stimulation, getting smaller with distance (as the size of a wave in water decreases with distance from its source). These voltage changes undergone by dendrites are called **graded potentials,** which can occur as a decrease in transmembrane voltage (depolarization) or an increase (hyperpolarization), depending on the nature of the stimulation. How each of these occurs will be discussed after we have described how graded potentials trigger the nerve impulse on the axon.

Spatial and Temporal Summation. Because dendrites respond to stimulation with graded potentials they have some interesting properties. If a dendrite is stimulated at two points in close proximity, the graded potentials produced at each point will add. If the two stimuli are identical, the graded potential will be twice as large as would occur with only one stimulus. If the two stimuli are given at widely different points on the dendrite, the graded potentials will dissipate before they reach each other and will not add. Stimuli given at intermediate distances will produce additive graded potentials, but only at the points that receive the potentials from both sources. Also, the potentials will be smaller because they decay with distance. Similar rules apply when one stimulus hyperpolarizes the membrane and one depolarizes the membrane, with the difference that the graded potentials subtract. This property of adjacent graded potentials to add and subtract is called *spatial summation.*

Another type of change that can occur on dendrites is called *temporal summation.* The graded potential of a stimulated dendrite will decay with time after the stimulus has terminated. A second stimulus given some time later at the same site will produce a similar response. If the second stimulus is given soon after the first, the potentials will add, becoming larger than either is alone. The strength of the graded potential will be determined by the strength of the two stimuli and the interval between them. If one stimulus hyperpolarizes the membrane and the other depolarizes the membrane, then the two will subtract, and the graded potential will accordingly be decreased in size.

If the features of spatial and temporal summation of graded potentials are considered, it is possible to see how the nerve impulse is generated. It will be recalled that the threshold for an action potential is -50 mV. If the dendritic system is influenced so that it is depolarized to -50 mV, and if this graded potential spreads over the cell body to a point adjacent to the axon, then the necessary conditions for eliciting an action potential will be met. In fact, the point of transition between the cell body and the axon, called the axon hillock (Figure 2–1), is the site where the nerve impulse originates. As long as this area is depolarized below −50 mV by the spread of graded potentials, the cell will fire. However, if the graded potentials are not sufficiently strong to depolarize the axon hillock to the threshold, the cell will not fire. Thus, the origin of axonal firing can be traced to the influence of graded potentials from the dendrites of the cell. If the location of the axon hillocks is considered, it can be understood why synapses proximal to it will be the most influential in producing action potentials.

SYNAPTIC TRANSMISSION

The Origin of Graded Potentials: The Synapse, EPSPs, and IPSPs

The idea that chemicals play a role in the transmission of information from one neuron to another, from a neuron to a muscle, or from a neuron to a body organ originated with the experiments of Otto Loewi in 1921. He stimulated the nerves going to a frog heart, collected a fluid perfused through the ventricles of the heart, and transferred it to the heart of another frog. The activity of the second heart was changed by introduction of the fluid in the same way that the activity of the first heart was changed by electrical stimulation. The stimulated nerve had been releasing a chemical, and it was the chemical, not some direct action of the nerve, that was causing the heart's activity to change. It is now widely accepted that neurons communicate chiefly through the agency of the chemicals they release when they fire. These chemicals, known as **neurotrans**

mitters, are released by the terminals of the neuron.

Figure 2–11 shows a diagram of a terminal. The terminal is separated from other neurons by a very small space called the *synaptic space*. The membrane of the terminal is called the **presynaptic membrane,** and the membrane it synapses with is called the **postsynaptic membrane.** Penetrating the terminal from the axon are microtubules, which may transport precursor chemicals for the manufacture of neurotransmitters into the terminal. There are *mitochondria,* which provide energy for metabolic processes. There are also two types of vesicles in the terminal: **storage granules,** which are presumed to be long-term storage sites for neurotransmitters, and **synaptic vesicles,** which hold neurotransmitters for immediate use. On the postsynaptic membrane there are specialized proteins that act as *receptors* for the neurotransmitter. The synapse functions in the following way. When a neuron fires, some synaptic vesicles release their

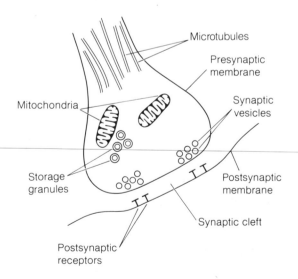

FIGURE 2–11. Diagram of the major features of a synapse.

neurotransmitter content into the synaptic space. The neurotransmitter binds weakly to the receptors on the postsynaptic membrane, after which it is quickly washed away by extracellular fluid and destroyed or is taken back into the presynaptic membrane for reuse.

At this point, we should pause briefly to note that there is quite a long delay, about 0.5 millisecond, in getting a message across a synapse. Only part of this time is taken up by the diffusion of the transmitter across the synaptic space. The remaining time is required to release the transmitter from the synapse. Terminals contain a large number of Ca^{2+} channels. The action potential opens these, so that Ca^{2+} ions enter the terminal. It is their entry that facilitates the release of transmitter by the synaptic vesicles into the synaptic space. There is a close relation between the amount of Ca^{2+} that enters the terminal and the amount of transmitter released.

How neurotransmitters, released by the firing of a presynaptic neuron, produce graded potentials in a postsynaptic neuron has been clarified in part by Eccles and his coworkers, who stimulated the axons of presynaptic neurons while recording from a postsynaptic cell body. Postsynaptic graded potentials followed each volley of presynaptic stimulation. These postsynaptic potentials, or PSPs, had a very small amplitude, 1 to 3 mV, but depending on which presynaptic axons were stimulated, they consisted either of depolarization or hyperpolarization of the postsynaptic membrane. Because depolarizing PSPs of course increase the probability of the neuron firing, they are called *excitatory postsynaptic potentials,* or *EPSPs,* and because hyperpolarizing potentials decrease the probability of the neuron firing, they are called *inhibitory postsynaptic potentials, or IPSPs.* It is now accepted that the EPSPs and IPSPs are produced by the action of neurotransmitters on the postsynaptic receptors of the cell. Neurotransmitters from certain synapses, called *excitatory neurotransmitters,* are responsible for EPSPs, whereas other neurotransmitters, called *inhibitory neurotransmitters,* are responsible for IPSPs. Eccles suggests that excitatory neurotransmitters produce EPSPs by making the membrane slightly more permeable to Na^+, which enters the cell, lowering the transmembrane voltage. Inhibitory neurotransmitters, on the other hand, make the membrane more permeable to K^+ and Cl^- ions; K^+ flows out and Cl^- flows into the cell, raising the transmembrane voltage.

It can now be seen that the origin of the graded potentials of dendrites can be traced to the release and action of neurotransmitters from the terminals of other neurons. It will be remembered that there are thousands of terminals synapsing with the dendrites and cell body of any one neuron; thus, the summed graded potential of the cell is produced by the action of all these inputs. The integration of these inputs by spatial and temporal summation determines whether the neuron will fire or not. If EPSPs predominate, and if there are enough of them to produce depolarization to threshold at the axon hillock, the neuron will fire. If IPSPs predominate, the neuron will not fire.

ANALYZING THE BRAIN THROUGH ITS ELECTRICAL ACTIVITY

The Integration of Neural Activity and Information Processing

It can be seen from the preceding sections that the dendritic system of the neuron sums the activity from many other neurons by producing graded potentials that will determine whether or not the neuron fires. The firing of the neuron is an all-or-none response, which will continue for as long as the firing threshold of the axon hillock is maintained.

Because the activity of nerve cells has an electrochemical basis the activity can be recorded with instruments sensitive to small changes in electrical activity. The several techniques for recording the brain's electrical activity include (1) intracellular unit and extracellular unit recording, (2) electroencephalographic (EEG) recording, and (3) evoked potential (EP) recording. Relating each of these types of activity to behavior can be used as a way of determining the function of particular brain areas, and as a way of determining the normality of function in a given brain area.

Unit Recording. If small wires or pipettes containing an ionized conducting solution are inserted into the brain so that their tips are placed in or near a nerve cell, the changes in a single cell's electrical potentials, i.e., **unit activity,** can be recorded in relation to some indifferent electrode or ground. *Intracellular* recordings are made from electrodes with very tiny tips, less than one-thousandth of a millimeter in diameter, which are placed in the cell, whereas *extracellular* recordings are made when an electrode tip is placed adjacent to one cell or a number of cells. Both techniques require amplification of the signal and some type of display. The cell's activity is either displayed on an oscilloscope for photographing or recorded on a tape recorder for computer analysis. In many experiments the signal is played through a loudspeaker so that cell firing is heard as a beep or pop. Both recording techniques require considerable skill to perform because it is difficult to place the electrode in or sufficiently close to the cell without killing it, and when a cell is "captured," it is often difficult to hold it for more than a few minutes or hours before the signal is lost.

Unit recording techniques provide a particularly interesting insight into the brain's function. For example, cell records obtained from the visual cortex of cats and monkeys reveal that each cell has a preferred stimulus and a preferred response pattern. Some cells fire to horizontal lines, others to diagonal lines, and still others fire only to lines that are oriented in a special way and that also move in a particular direction. Unit recording techniques have also been used to analyze such abnormal cell activity as occurs in epilepsy. In epilepsy, the activity of cells becomes synchronized in an abnormal pattern, and an understanding of epilepsy depends in part on analyzing and controlling this feature of the cell's behavior. Much of the information obtained with unit recordings has of necessity come from experiments performed on anesthetized animals. Future research is likely to repeat these tests in freely moving animals to confirm and elaborate on the findings.

EEG Recording. A simple technique for recording electrical activity of the brain was developed in the early 1930s by Hans Berger. He found that it was possible to record "brain waves" from the scalp. These waves, called **electroencephalograms,** or **EEGs,** have proved to be a valuable tool for studying problems such as sleep-waking, for monitoring depth of anesthesia, and for diagnosing epilepsy and brain damage.

To record a person's EEG a small metal disk is attached to the scalp, and the change in electrical activity in the area of this electrode is compared to some electrically neutral zone such as the earlobe. The electrical changes recorded on the scalp are rather small, usually much less than a millivolt, and so they must be amplified for display on an oscilloscope or on a paper chart recorder called an electroencephalograph, or EEG, machine.

The electrical activity recorded from the scalp is the sum of all neural activity, action potentials, graded potentials, etc., but it is mostly the measure of the graded potentials of dendrites. As a result, it represents the summed dendritic activity of thousands of nerve cells and can only be considered a rather general measure of the brain's activity. Although it can be used as a crude index of the brain's level of excitation, it tells very little about the activity of single cells as such. During a given EEG pattern any particular single cell may be active or inactive.

Bland and his colleagues have studied the relation of graded potentials and unit activity recorded from the same microelectrode in the dentate gyrus (part of the hippocampus) of freely moving rabbits (see Figure 2–12). In this example the rabbit is walking. The technique of recording both types of activity simultaneously from one electrode is made possible by the fact that they have different frequency ranges. The frequency of the rhythmic waves, or graded potentials, is slow, about four to seven cycles per second. The unit discharge is fast, each lasting about 2 milliseconds. When the line carrying the electric signal is split and the slow waves are filtered out of one of the lines, the unit activity is seen. The top trace of Figure 2–12 displays the rhythmic graded potentials that are characteristic of the cells in the hippocampus. The bottom trace shows

FIGURE 2–12. Dentate layer theta cells and simultaneous slow waves from the same electrode during freely moving behavior of the rabbit. Note the rhythmic slow wave *(theta)* activity and rhythmic cell discharges that occur during walking and that the cells discharge at the negative peak of the theta waves. (Courtesy of B. H. Bland.)

the action potentials or unit activity recorded from one of the cells. Even a casual glance at the figure shows that there is an important relation between the EEG activity and the unit activity. The unit activity occurs in bursts when the dendrites depolarize. If the graded potentials increase in amplitude, the cell may fire more frequently with each burst; if the frequency of the EEG rhythm speeds up, the bursts of unit activity will occur more frequently. In this way the graded potentials time or pace the unit activity. It is thought that the "information" transmitted by cells such as these is coded in terms of burst frequency, number of unit discharges per burst, the interunit discharge interval, etc. (Note: In this figure the electrical activity is recorded from an electrode placed just outside the cell, and so the wave amplitude and polarity are different from those described for squid axons, in which the electrodes were placed across the cell membrane.)

It is now thought that the nervous system works by a combination of analogue (how much) and digital, or binary (yes–no), principles. Analogue functions are a property of the dendritic system and its graded potentials and their unit activity; digital functions are a property of the axons. We can see how these principles determine behavior if we return to the opening description of the male Grayling butterfly's behavior. Recall Tinbergen's suggestion that in the male butterfly's nervous system there is a pooling station that integrates the different features (dark, large, and irregular) of a stimulus object to determine whether or not the male will approach the stimulus. Theoretically, all the male butterfly's behavior could be accounted for by the activity of one central neuron. The dendrites of that neuron would serve as the pooling station and the axon would be the system that initiates an approach response. If three channels of input coverged on the dendrites (one signaling darkness, one size, and one movement), simultaneous activity in the separate channels signaling dark, large, and irregular would produce EPSPs that when summed would trigger axonal firing and thus approach by the butterfly. Activity in only one channel might not be sufficient to fire the neuron; activity in two channels might be sufficient to produce a response, if input in each were particularly intense. At any rate, it can be seen that the analogue function of the dendrites will integrate the various sources of input, while the digital activity of the axon will determine whether or not approach is to occur. Of course, the analogue feature of dendritic integration can be put to many types of use, and the digital properties of the axon can be expressed in many codes (frequency, pattern of firing, etc.).

Many other factors contribute to information processing. Synapses proximal to the axon hillock may have special access to influence cell firing. Inhibition or excitation by more distal axosynaptic connections may allow for more subtle control of intercell communication. Some synapses may also change structurally with use or disuse, thus becoming increasingly or decreasingly effective in communicating. These factors are beyond the scope of the present discussion, but they are important to the brain's synthesizing and storage abilities.

Human EEG

It was originally thought that each cytoarchitectonic area of the brain had its own pattern of EEG activity, but it is now recognized that variations in patterns do not correlate closely with cytoarchitectonic areas. Figure 2–13 shows the characteristic resting rhythms obtained from different parts of the cortex. The patterns are obtained only under optimal conditions, when the person is awake, resting quietly, with eyes closed. The dominant rhythm of the posterior cortex is an eight to 12

cycles per second waveform called the alpha rhythm. The dominant rhythm of the precentral and postcentral sensorimotor area is 20 to 25 cycles per second beta rhythm. The secondary frontal areas have a 17 to 20 cycles per second beta rhythm. And the tertiary frontal area has eight to 12 cycles per second waves. The resting rhythms are replaced by low-voltage fast activity, or *desynchronization,* when the areas of brain are in an active mode. For example, in Figure 2–13 the alpha rhythm of the occipital (visual) cortex desynchronizes when the eyes are open. Penfield and Jasper have recorded from the motor cortex (area 4) while it was exposed during a surgical procedure. They found its EEG activity desynchronized during voluntary movement, e.g., arm movement. In some cases desynchronization was restricted to the cortical area representing the part of the body that was moved, e.g., moving the hand desynchronized only the EEG in the hand area.

Human EEG activity changes in a characteristic way during transitions from sleep to wakefulness (Figure 2–14). Generally, rhythms become slower in frequency and larger in amplitude as a person falls asleep. Large-amplitude slow waves are also present during coma and during anesthesia induced by some drugs, and they can appear in areas of the brain that have been subjected to trauma. A good rule of thumb in interpreting EEG activity is that when the brain is in an active mode, the desynchronized patterns occur, whereas when it is in an inactive mode, the slower, larger-amplitude patterns occur. Sometimes this rule is not easy to apply because it becomes difficult to define active (does one mean movement or sensory responsiveness?). Another factor making interpretation difficult is that it has been demonstrated that waveforms that appear to be the same on visual inspection can have quite a different pharmacological basis depend-

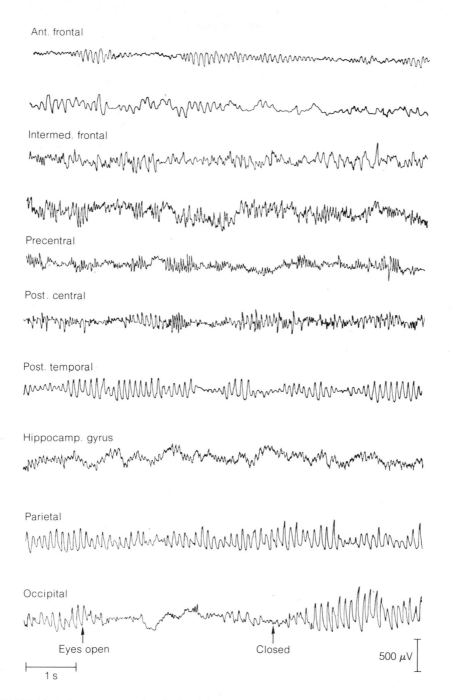

FIGURE 2–13. Spontaneous electrical activity, or resting rhythms, from different human cortical areas. Sample tracings were taken directly from the exposed cortex with bipolar silver chloride cotton-wick electrodes. (From W. Penfield and H. H. Jasper, *Epilepsy and the Functional Anatomy of the Human Brain.* Boston: Little, Brown. Copyright 1954. Reprinted with permission.)

ing on when they occur. For example, desynchronized EEG activity can be recorded from people in chronic states of coma. It may look exactly like the EEG activity recorded from an awake, alert, moving individual, yet be biochemically different. For people interested in pursuing the question of the relations between EEG activity and behavior, the classic view is illustrated succinctly by Figure 2–14. Vanderwolf and Robinson, in a very readable review, suggest that EEGs change with behavior and not with "behavioral state,"

as is illustrated in Figure 2–14. They would, for example, replace "excited" with "talking" or whatever, "relaxed" with "eyes closed," "drowsy" with "lying still," etc.

Electroencephalography is used clinically to detect malfunctioning brain areas, and so it is useful for diagnosing epilepsy, or for locating brain lesions or tumors. Large-amplitude spike-and-wave activity may indicate the presence of epilepsy, and slow waves in a behaviorally alert individual may indicate brain damage. Figure 6–5 shows some abnormal

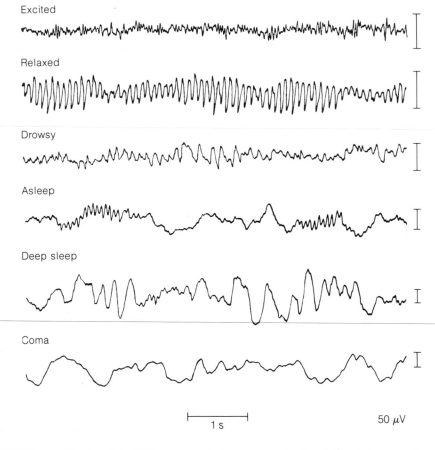

Excited

Relaxed

Drowsy

Asleep

Deep sleep

Coma

1 s

50 μV

FIGURE 2–14. Characteristic EEG recorded during various behavioral states in humans. (From W. Penfield and H. H. Jasper, *Epilepsy and the Functional Anatomy of the Human Brain*. Boston: Little, Brown. Copyright 1954. Reprinted with permission.)

EEG waves recorded from epileptics. Although the EEG is only a general measure of the brain's activity, rather sophisticated averaging procedures have been developed to localize areas that generate abnormal EEG activity.

Evoked Potentials

Evoked potentials, or **EPs,** consist of a short train of large slow waves and are like the EEG in that they are recorded from the scalp and largely reflect the activity of dendrites. But they occur only under special conditions. If a bright light or noise is presented very briefly, say for 250 milliseconds, electrodes placed on the cortex will record a large slow wave that is clearest and largest over the area of cortex processing the sensory event. For example, in the case of a bright light, the EP will be largest over the visual cortex. Since these potentials vary somewhat in their actual size and shape it is customary to average several together to obtain an accurate estimate of the "typical" EP. This average is often called an AEP, or **average evoked potential.** The evoked potential technique is very tricky because the size of the EP can be influenced by many variables. In animals, the most important variable seems to be movement, for the magnitude of the evoked potential may vary according to what the animal is doing. Movements that affect EP size may be as small and subtle as eye movements or changes in respiration. Nevertheless, the EP is considered by some people to be a useful indicator of the brain's activity in processing information.

Electrical Stimulation

Electrical stimulation of the brain requires some mention at this time because it is an efficient way of activating neurons. Usually a fine insulated wire with an uninsulated tip is placed in the brain so that the tip lies in a predeter-mined location. Low-voltage pulses of current, usually 60 to 100 pulses per second, are then passed through the electrode to stimulate neural tissue adjacent to its tip. Use of this technique on freely moving animals was pioneered by Hess, who developed the procedure of permanently attaching electrodes to the skulls of cats. The electrodes produced little discomfort to the animals and so they could receive brain stimulation while their reaction was observed. Hess found that virtually every behavior that a cat spontaneously performed could be induced by brain stimulation. The elicited behaviors were usually "stimulus bound"; that is, they lasted only as long as the stimulation was applied. Every part of the brain of many animals has since been mapped for the effects of electrical stimulation.

Electrical stimulation has also been used in surgery and as a treatment of some neurological disorders. In certain situations requiring brain surgery it is considered important not to damage areas of the brain involved in controlling speech. Under local anesthesia the patient's cortex is exposed and stimulated electrically to identify speech areas. During a stimulation test the patient is asked to speak, electrical stimulation is applied, and if it is found to disrupt speech in particular ways the stimulated area is defined as a speech area.

Therapeutic brain stimulation, although not widespread, has been used. A few seconds of electrical stimulation of the midbrain may arrest otherwise unmanageable pain for periods lasting many hours. Brief periods of stimulation given in the cerebellum have sometimes been found effective in arresting epileptic attacks.

Goddard has found that if certain portions of the limbic system are given from 1 to 2 seconds of stimulation each day, the stimulation, which initially has no observable effect on behavior, will begin to produce epileptic attacks. That is, the animals will show convulsions after stimulation. If the treatments are continued for a long enough period of time, the seizures may begin to occur spontaneously. This procedure has been given the name **kindling,** and it is providing a much needed model for studying human epilepsy.

ANALYZING THE BRAIN THROUGH ITS BIOCHEMICAL ACTIVITY

Neurotransmitters

As we have pointed out, neurons communicate with each other and with glands, muscles, and other body organs by releasing small quantities of substances, neurotransmitters, onto the receptors of the neurons or organs they synapse with. At the present time many different neurotransmitters are suspected to be active in the nervous system. Still, there are difficulties involved in identifying substances and their locations within the confined area of the brain, where many thousands of terminals connect with neurons that are only a few microns in size. In order to identify a chemical as a neurotransmitter a set of proofs should be met. These include the following:

1. The chemical is shown to be present in the terminals.

2. It is shown to be released when the neuron fires.

3. Placing the chemical on the innervated organ mimics the effect of nerve stimulation.

4. There is a chemical or an uptake mechanism present in the area of the synaptic space to inactivate the neurotransmitter.

5. Placing a substance in the synaptic space that will destroy or inactivate the neurotransmitter must block the effects of nerve stimulation.

At the present time, technology is simply unable to meet the rigor of all these demands, and so chemicals that are strongly suspected of having a neurotransmitter function are labeled putative (or supposed) transmitters.

Although all these criteria may not have been met for any transmitter in the brain, there is agreement that at least eight substances are neurotransmitters. These substances are listed in Table 2–1. In addition, at least 25 short peptides have been located in neurons and are thought to be involved in neurotransmission. These substances, listed in Table 2–2, include

TABLE 2–1

Neurotransmitters, receptor type with examples of receptor agonists and antagonists

Transmitter	Receptor type	Agonist	Antagonist
Acetylcholine	Nicotinic	Nicotine	Curare
	Muscarinic	Muscarine	Atropine
Biogenic amines			
Dopamine (DA)	D_1, D_2	Apomorphine	Haloperidol
Norepinephrine (NE)	$\alpha_1, \alpha_2, \beta_1, \beta_2,$	Clonidine	Phenoxybenzamine
Serotonin (5–HT)	$5-HT_1, 5-HT_2$	LSD	
Histamine	H_1, H_2		Promethazine
Amino acids			
α–Aminobutyric acid (GABA)		Muscimol	Picrotoxin
Glycine		Taurine	Strychnine
Glutamate		Kainic acid [a]	

[a]Kainic acid also acts as a neurotoxin, destroying many cells to which it binds.

TABLE 2–2

Neuroactive peptides

Gut-brain peptides
  Vasoactive intestinal polypeptide (VIP)
  Cholecystokinin octapeptide
  Substance P
  Neurotensin
  Methionine enkephlin
  Leucine enkephlin
  Insulin
  Glucagon

Hypothalamic-releasing hormones
  Thyrotropin-releasing hormone (TRH)
  Somatostatin (growth hormone release-inhibiting
    factor)

Pituitary peptides
  Adrenocorticotropin (ACTH)
  β–Endorphin
  α–Melanocyte-stimulating hormone (α–MSH)

Others
  Angiotensin II, bradykinin, vasopressin, oxytocin,
    carnosine, bombesin

After Kandel and Schwartz, 1981.

peptides that are also found in the gut, and may play a role in the central control of feeding and drinking, hormones that are released from the hypothalamus, peptides that are released from the pituitary, and others. At least two families of peptides act like opiates; that is, they have pain-suppressing properties in addition to producing other opiatelike effects. There are some general differences between the eight classical transmitters and the peptides. The former have low molecular weight, they are synthesized within the terminals, they act in high concentrations, and their effects are generally short-lasting. The "transmitters" are also synthesized from simpler substances, often obtained rather directly from food, in a few steps, each of which can be influenced by the action of various drugs. The peptides are formed in the cell body, they are fractions of larger peptide molecules, they are potent in small concentrations, and they appear to have long-lasting actions.

It was originally believed that any one neuron would only contain one transmitter in all its terminals. This rule has been referred to as *Dale's law*. The law was useful, for if a terminal at one location could be shown to contain a certain transmitter, then collaterals from the same neuron that ended in other locations could be supposed to contain the same transmitter. Now, the work of Hokfelt and his coworkers seems to show that the neuroactive peptides may coexist in terminals with the "classical" neurotransmitters. It is unclear in these situations whether the peptides are acting like transmitters in the full sense or whether they have modulatory actions on synaptic transmission.

Receptors

Transmitters have their action on receptors on the postsynaptic membrane. The receptors are proteins that bind the transmitter substance and to do so face outward to catch the transmitter. Receptors are thought to consist of two components, a *binding component,* which grasps the transmitter, and an *ionophore component,* which is a channel in the membrane that opens to let ions flow when binding occurs. Some receptors may also stimulate metabolic activity within the cell. This activity consists of a series of biochemical steps that take place within the postsynaptic cell and that in turn may regulate ion flow or may even change the number of receptors or change other structures within the cell. The latter postsynaptic chemicals are sometimes called second messengers. Such systems seem to contain the potential for modifying cells permanently, perhaps for such activities as learning.

The structure of receptors may determine the actions of a transmitter substance. It is apparent that many transmitter substances interact with more than one type of receptor (Table 2–1). This may allow the transmitter to have an excitatory function through one of its collaterals and an inhibitory function through other collaterals. Since pharmacological agents produce some of their actions by binding to receptors (Table 2–1), their choice of a particular receptor may allow them to modulate only part of a transmitter's actions. For example, acetylcholine receptors on nerve-muscle junctions are affected by a different group of drugs than acetylcholine receptors in many parts of the brain or in the autonomic system.

Distribution of Transmitters

The distribution of neurotransmitters in the brain can be determined in a number of ways. Samples of tissue can be taken from different brain areas and the concentrations of chemicals in the samples compared. This type of analysis gives only a relative measure of neurotransmitter distribution, and most neurotransmitters have been found in all regions of the brain, although in considerably varied concentrations. Generally it is not wise to conclude much about function from concentration differences; for example, a small quantity of neurotransmitter in one region may be just as important for a particular function as a large quantity in some other region. Another technique of determining distribution is to stain the brain tissue with stains that interact with neurotransmitters or with some chemical closely related to the neurotransmitter's function. For example, noradrenaline and dopamine can be stained by exposing sections of tissue to formaldehyde vapor and then illuminating the tissue with ultraviolet light. Both substances fluoresce with a green color, but to slightly different shades that can be distinguished. The presence of acetylcholine can be identified by staining tissue with a substance called butylthiocholine, which turns acetylcholinesterase, a chemical that breaks down acetylcholine, black. In most, but not all, brain sites acetylcholinesterase indicates the presence of acetylcholine.

Neurochemical mapping procedures have been revealing some extremely interesting insights into the organization of the brain. Some neurochemicals, although widely distributed in all regions of the brain, are located in neurons whose cell bodies are found in a number of restricted nuclei. The origin and distribution of some fibers of these systems in the rat are shown diagrammatically in Figure 2–15. These systems resemble hormone systems, except that hormones are carried from their origin throughout the body by the blood rather than by axons.

Brain Dysfunctions, Mental Illness, and Neurotransmitters

Since neurons containing specific neurotransmitters appear to be organized in systems, it seems pertinent to ask whether these different neurochemical systems can be associated with specific functions. Indeed, they seem to be. The problem, however, is not to find a function but to find the *appropriate* function.

Since before the turn of the century it has often been suggested that **psychosis**—e.g., an illness such as schizophrenia or manic-depressive behavior—was the result of brain malfunction. It was variously proposed that psychoses were due to actual brain damage, ingestion of toxins that poisoned the brain, or synthesis by the brain itself of a toxin that caused it to malfunction. These ideas were reinforced by the observation that various chemical agents, e.g., atropine, when ingested produced behavior resembling that of psychotics. Then, in 1952, French physicians observed that a preanesthetic agent, chlorpromazine, had a tranquilizing effect on surgical patients. When tried on psychotic patients, it was found to have striking therapeutic action. By 1955 it was in use in North America and was probably instrumental in drastically reducing the patient population of mental hospitals (Figure 2–16).

A DOPAMINE

B NORADRENALINE

C SEROTONIN

FIGURE 2–15. Location of cell bodies, shown as black dots, and the projections of dopamine, noradrenaline, and serotonin pathways in the rat. (From J. R. Cooper, F. E. Bloom, and R. H. Roth, *The Biochemical Basis of Neuropharmacology.* New York: Oxford University Press. Copyright 1978 by Oxford University Press, Inc. Reprinted with permission.)

Since then many other antipsychotic drugs have been introduced, and an intense search for the mechanisms of their action has been under way. Since many psychoactive drugs are now thought to produce their effects by modifying synaptic activity, the following sections will describe the synaptic organization and pharmacological influences of some of the better-known neurotransmitter systems.

Sites of Drug Action on Synapses

Figure 2–17 is a diagram of a generalized synapse showing many of the features typical of most synapses. The following is the sequence of biochemical events outlined in the diagram.

1. *Synthesis.* Precursor chemicals obtained from food or manufactured in the cell are transported down the axon into the synapse, where they are synthesized into the neurotransmitter.

2. *Storage.* The transmitter is stored in the synapse in one or more of several ways, at least one of which is in vesicles available for release.

3. *Release.* When the nerve discharges, some of the vesicles release their content into the subsynaptic space.

4. *Receptor interaction.* The released neurotransmitter crosses the synaptic space and binds weakly to specialized receptors on the postsynaptic membrane, where it initiates depolarization or hyperpolarization of the postsynaptic membrane. In many systems more than one type of postsynaptic receptor may be sensitive to the neurotransmitter.

5. *Inactivation* or

6. *Reuptake.* In some synapses the neurotransmitter is inactivated in the area of the synaptic space, in others it is taken back up into the synapse, and in some both mechanisms may be active.

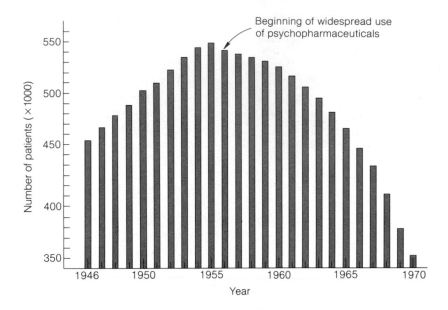

FIGURE 2–16. Numbers of resident patients in state and local government mental hospitals in the United States from 1946 through 1970. Note the dramatic change in the total population of patients in mental hospitals that began after 1955, when therapeutic use of psychoactive drugs began. (From V. C. Longo, *Neuropharmacology and Behavior*. San Francisco: W. H. Freeman and Company. Copyright 1972. Modified from D. H. Efron, ed., *Psychopharmacology: A Review of Progress*. Washington, D.C.: U.S. Department of Health, Education and Welfare, 1968.)

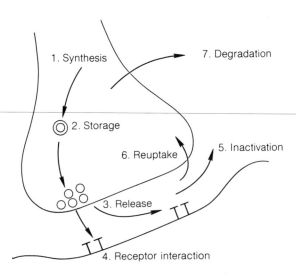

FIGURE 2–17. Steps in synaptic transmission in an idealized synapse.

7. *Degradation.* The free neurotransmitter within the synapse may be degraded to control interneuronal neurotransmitter concentrations.

Many of the chemicals that people ingest by accident, as recreational drugs, or as medicine may influence one or more of these steps in one or more neurochemical systems. This realization has revolutionized modern pharmacology and neuropharmacology, and it has led to an intense investigation directed toward disclosing the specific action of different drugs and toward synthesizing new drugs with specific actions. This investigation also involves a search for a neural substrate for such mental disorders as schizophrenia and depression, on the logic that if a particular drug can ameliorate one of these disorders, and if the transmitter substance on which the drug acts can be identified, then that might be taken as evidence that some excess or deficiency of that neurotransmitter may be causally related to the disorder. Although this line of reasoning has disclosed some intriguing possibilities, there are many pitfalls in the logic, and as yet there is no unequivocal evidence proving that any neurotransmitter is causally linked with a particular mental disease.

Classification of Psychoactive Drugs

Psychoactive drugs, drugs that affect cognitive functions, can be classified in a number of ways, among the most useful of which is by their behavioral effects. Table 2–3 summarizes such a classification. The table also shows the neurotransmitter systems on which various drugs in each category are thought to act and the effect the drug has on the respective neurotransmitter function. As pointed out above, drug may intervene in the process of intercell communication at any of a number of stages, but irrespective of its site of action it will have one of two effects: it will either increase or decrease the effectiveness of transmission at the synaptic junction. Thus, the arrows in Table 2–3 indicate by their direction whether the drugs listed have the effect of increasing (upward arrows) or decreasing (downward) activity at that synaptic junction.

Sedative-hypnotics are drugs that at low doses reduce anxiety, at medium doses produce sedation, and at high doses produce anesthesia or coma. They are a diverse group of drugs including barbiturates, benzodiazepines (known as minor tranquilizers, of which Valium is an example), and alcohol. They are widely used for their antianxiety actions. It is thought that these drugs depress the activity of the systems that produce arousal or initiation of behavior. At low doses the sedative-hypnotics may depress the activity of noradrenaline synapses, but their precise mechanism of action is unknown. At higher doses they may block neurotransmission in many systems and thereby produce anesthesia or even coma. The benzodiazepines are thought to act by facilitating γ-aminobutyric acid (GABA) function. Their

TABLE 2–3

Relation between psychoactive agents and neurotransmitter systems

Drug classification and drug	Neurotransmitter	Action
Sedative-hypnotics		
Barbiturates	Noradrenaline	↓
Benzodiazepines	γ–Aminobutyric acid (GABA)	↑
Alcohol	Noradrenaline	↓
Stimulants, antidepressants		
Amphetamine	Noradrenaline	↑
Cocaine	Noradrenaline	↑
Desipramine	Noradrenaline	↑
Imipramine	Serotonin	↑
Antipsychotic agents		
Chlorpromazine	Dopamine	↓
Reserpine	Dopamine, noradrenaline	↓
Opiates		
Heroin, morphine	Endorphins	↑
Psychedelics		
Atropine	Acetylcholine	↓
Muscarine	Acetylcholine	↑
Mescaline, cannabis	Noradrenaline	↑
LSD, psilocybin	Serotonin	↑ or ↓
	Noradrenaline	↑

action is not to stimulate the receptors directly but to make the receptor more responsive to GABA.

Stimulants are drugs that increase behavioral activity either by producing increases in motor activity or by counteracting fatigue. One group of stimulants, the amphetamines, is thought to potentiate release of noradrenaline from the presynaptic membrane and also to block the reuptake mechanism that reabsorbs noradrenaline back into the synapse after it has acted on the receptor. Both actions would increase the amount of noradrenaline available and the duration of its availability for action on the receptors. The amphetamines have antidepressant properties, but their major clinical use is to counteract narcolepsy, an uncontrollable tendency to fall asleep. Amphetamine is also given to hyperactive children, whom it may help by prolonging their attention span. Another group of stimulants includes cocaine and the tricyclic antidepressants, including desipramine and imipramine. There is good evidence that these drugs block the reuptake of noradrenaline and serotonin, thereby facilitating transmission by prolonging the time during which the neurotransmitter can act on the receptor. Some tricyclics, such as desipramine, have a more potent action on noradrenaline reuptake, whereas others, such as imipramine, more selectively block serotonin reuptake. The ability of cocaine to counteract depression was first documented by Sigmund Freud, but today the tricyclics, which are in some ways structurally similar to cocaine, are the treatment of choice for depression. Because different tricyclics are more effective than others in treating quite different depressive populations, van Praag has suggested that there may be at least two types of depression: one referable to reduced noradrenaline transmission, the other referable to reduced serotonin transmission.

The *antipsychotic agents* (often referred to as major tranquilizers) are drugs that have been effective in treating schizophrenia; the most widely used of them are chlorpromazine and reserpine. Although both drugs act on noradrenaline and dopamine systems, their antipsychotic action appears attributable to their action on dopamine. Chlorpromazine is thought to reduce dopaminergic transmission by blocking dopamine receptors, whereas reserpine reduces dopamine levels by destroying storage granules within the synapse. Although the effectiveness of these drugs in treating schizophrenia has led to the "dopamine hypothesis of schizophrenia," which states that schizophrenia may be related to excessive levels of dopamine, this hypothesis should be viewed with caution. Neurotransmitter systems have complex interactions with one another, and it is quite possible that schizophrenia is caused by imbalances in any of a number of known or unknown systems that normally check the level of dopamine transmission.

The *opiates,* such as heroin and morphine, although widely abused because of their addictive properties, are nevertheless among the most effective pain-relieving agents available. Their mechanism of action has been clarified recently by the discovery of endogenous, natural opiatelike substances in the brain. It has been suggested that these natural opiates, such as endorphins (a class name meaning that the chemicals act like opiates), are neurotransmitters in the brain, and that the opiates produce their effects by mimicking the postsynaptic stimulation from these neurotransmitters. The discovery that there are endogenous opiates has of course provoked tremendous excitement, particularly with respect to the possible new avenues they open up for controlling pain.

The *psychedelic drugs* are a mixed group of agents that alter sensory perception and cognitive processes. There are at least three major groups of psychedelics. (1) Acetylcholine psychedelics block or facilitate transmission in acetylcholine synapses. Drugs such as atropine block acetylcholine postsynaptic receptors, thus reducing acetylcholine action; those such as muscarine, on the other hand, stimulate these receptors much as acetylcholine does, thus mimicking acetylcholine activity. (2) Noradrenaline psychedelics include mescaline and possibly cannabis; they may act by stimulating noradrenaline postsynaptic receptors. (3) Serotonin psychedelics include LSD (lysergic acid diethylamide) and psilocybin, which may mimic serotonin by stimulating postsynaptic receptors of serotonin synapses or which may block the activity of serotonin neurons. In addition they may stimulate noradrenaline receptors.

In summary, it can be seen that many commonly used drugs interact with neurotransmitter systems in the brain. The object of this section was to point out the usefulness of considering drug action and behavior within the context of neurotransmitter function. Consequently, this should not be considered a comprehensive discussion of either neurotransmission or drugs. There are, of course, many more drugs that act on neurotransmission (curare, for example, blocks acetylcholine nerve-muscle junctions), and many other drugs have effects other than at neuron junctions (such as caffeine, which may stimulate metabolic activity in neurons). In addition, the seeming simplicity of neurotransmission is deceptive, because many neurotransmitter systems have a number of types of postsynaptic receptors that are sensitive to the effects of different drugs.

For example, the nerve-muscle acetylcholine receptors are blocked by curare, whereas the brain acetylcholine receptors are for the most part blocked by atropine. For a lucid and more detailed review of neuropharmacology we recommend the reader to Cooper, Bloom, and Roth; for a comprehensive source book on drugs and drug action we recommend Goodman and Gilman. Detailed information on cell structure and function may be found in Kandel and Schwartz and in Shepherd.

REFERENCES

Bland, B. H., P. Anderson, T. Ganes, and O. Sveen. Automated analysis of rhythmicity of physiologically identified hippocampal formation neurons. *Experimental Brain Research* 38:205–219, 1978.

Cooper, J. R., F. E. Bloom, and R. H. Roth. *The Biochemical Basis of Neuropharmacology.* New York: Oxford University Press, 1982.

Eccles, J. The synapse. *Scientific American* 212:56–66, Jan., 1965.

Goddard, G. V., and D. McIntyre. Some properties of a lasting epileptogenic trace kindled by repeated electrical stimulation of the amygdala in mammals. In L. V. Laitinen and K. E. Livingston, eds., *Surgical Approaches in Psychiatry.* Baltimore: University Park Press, 1973.

Goodman, L. S., and A. Gilman, eds. *The Pharmacological Basis of Therapeutics,* 4th ed. New York: Macmillan, 1970.

Hodgkin, A. L., and A. F. Huxley. Action potentials recorded from inside nerve fiber. *Nature* 144:710–711, 1939.

Hokfelt, T., O. Johansson, A. Ljungdahl, J. M. Lundberg, and M. Schultzberg. Peptidergic neurons. *Nature* (Lond.) 284:515–521, 1980.

Kandel, E. R., and J. H. Schwartz. *Principles of Neural Science.* New York: Elsevier North Holland, 1981.

Katz, B. How cells communicate. In J. L. McGaugh, N. M. Weinberger, and R. H. Whalen, eds., *Psychobiology.* Readings from Scientific American. San Francisco: Freeman, 1972.

Longo, V. C. *Neuropharmacology and Behavior.* San Francisco: Freeman, 1972.

Penfield, W., and H. H. Jasper. *Epilepsy and the Functional Anatomy of the Human Brain.* Boston: Little, Brown, 1954.

Shepherd, G. M. *Neurobiology.* New York: Oxford University Press, 1983.

Sinclair, B. R., M. G. Seto, and B. H. Bland. Theta cells in the CA1 and dentate layers of the hippocampal formation: Relations to slow wave activity and motor behavior in the freely moving rabbit. *Journal of Neurophysiology* 48:1214–1225, 1982.

Tinbergen, N. *The Animal in Its World.* London: Allen & Unwin, 1972.

Van Praag, H. M. Significance of biochemical parameters in the diagnosis, treatment, and prevention of depressive disorders. *Biological Psychiatry* 12:101–130, 1977.

3

TECHNIQUES, PROBLEMS, AND MODELS

A man was walking from Thistle to Down. The West Wind, resting on the mountains, said to the sun, "Let us amuse ourselves. See the jacket that the man has over his shoulders. Let us have a wager to see who can remove it." With that the wind blew down on the traveler, but the more fiercely he blew, the more tightly the traveler pulled in his jacket and buttoned it. After the wind was exhausted, the sun rose slowly into the center of the sky and shone on the traveler, who shortly unbuttoned the jacket and then removed it. The sun turned to the wind and said, "You see, the technique's the thing." The problem in using techniques in neuroscience involves not only knowing when to use the appropriate technique but knowing how to use it, and more importantly how to interpret the results obtained with it. A simple example will illustrate the problem.

Imagine four neuroscientists, α, β, δ, and γ, are studying an imaginary brain area called area 101. Area 101 consists of two local circuits, A and B, which generate, respectively, behaviors A and B. Circuit A, however, sends synapses onto circuit B so that behavior B occurs smoothly and not in jerks. Also in area 101 are fibers of passage that course through the neighborhood of circuits A and B but have nothing to do with either circuit. These fibers are responsible for the control of behavior C (see Figure 3–1).

Scientist α lesions area 101 and destroys circuits A and B and fibers of passage C. He concludes that area 101 produces a syndrome in which deficits in behaviors A, B, and C always go together; this becomes known as α's syndrome in neurology texts. When scientist β stimulates area 101 electrically, he obtains either behavior A, behavior B, or behavior C, depending on where his electrode is placed, but he concludes that they are independent and do not go together. In addition, he stimulates other areas of the brain and obtains behaviors A, B, and C (he is in fact stimulating fibers going to and coming from these areas), and he concludes that area 101 really is not all that important for controlling behaviors A, B, and C. Scientist δ chemically stimulates area 101

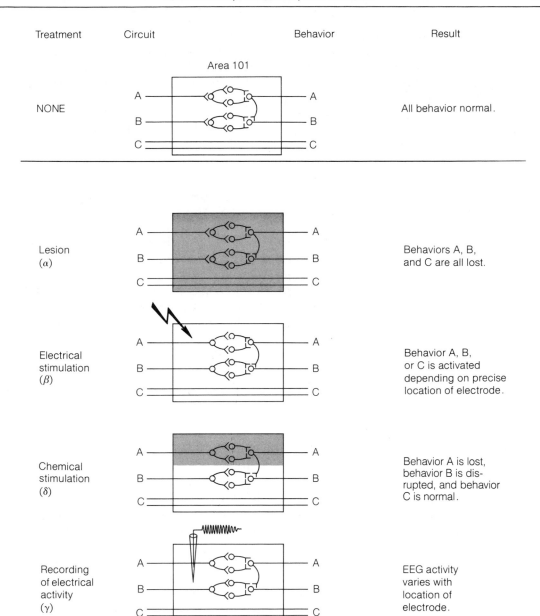

FIGURE 3–1. The different techniques of studying the brain used by scientists α, β, δ, and γ. Each uses a different procedure to study brain-behavior relations, and each arrives at a different conclusion regarding the function of area 101.

with a drug that blocks the synaptic activity in circuit A. She concludes that the area might control behavior A, that the drug also disrupts behavior B because it makes it so jerky, but that area 101 has nothing at all to do with behavior C. Finally, scientist γ records the electrical activity of circuits A and B and the fibers of passage. He finds two forms of electrical activity: one is related to the details of movement, and the other to the amount of sleep the animal had in the previous 24 hours. Scientist γ concludes that circuits A, B, and C all form some sort of functional system involved in sleep and movement.

Clearly, all four scientists are correct, but it is obvious that if they pooled their information they would not be able to construct the circuitry of area 101 without a unifying theory and considerably more experimentation to test the theory.

Something like the problem outlined for area 101 currently exists in the neurosciences, but on an absolutely massive scale. Many clinical disorders such as schizophrenia appear to occur because the brain is behaving abnormally, yet no lesions of the brain produce anything quite like schizophrenia. Many children with no apparent damage to the brain have incapacitating learning disorders, yet others with extensive brain damage are bright and intelligent and show little impairment in learning. These paradoxical effects have led one neuropsychologist we know to make the cryptic comment: "No brain is better than a bad brain." The beginning student will be mystified by these phenomena unless it is recognized that the brain is a large-scale, and considerably more complex, area 101, and that present neuropsychological theory is limited by the experimental techniques available.

There are six major techniques used in neuroscience: anatomy, biochemistry, lesions, stimulation, recording, and behavioral analysis. It is not possible to deal in depth with the problems posed in using the techniques because they are all multifaceted, but it might be useful to point out some of the more obvious difficulties that are encountered with each.

ANATOMY

The similarity in the anatomy of the brains of different animals is impressive, as is the similarity of the brains of individuals within any species. Still, there are problems in understanding function from an anatomical approach. First, there is individual variation in the size, topography, and structure of brains. Such differences can clearly be seen in the organization of the gyral patterns of two different individuals illustrated in Figure 3–2. Karl Lashley has noted that even inbred strains of laboratory animals have thalamic nuclei so different that individual animals can be distinguished. Second, some functions do not seem to be fixed to rigid anatomical boundaries. The best example of such flexibility in structure-function relations is the fact that in some people speech is localized in the right rather than the left hemisphere. As will be discussed in Chapter 15, it was once thought that deviations from standard (e.g., speech on the left in right-handed people) were anomalies, but it is now becoming recognized that the anomalies are the norm. When all the factors that influence localization are considered (e.g., sex, handedness, or age), it appears that the conventionally organized brain is in fact the brain of the minority. Third, the relation between brain mass and function has never been adequately explained. This applies both to the apparent diversity in brain size (consider the normal human brain has a range of 1000 to 2000 cm³) and to the fact that when parts of a brain area are removed, the remaining tissue has an amazing ability to keep getting the job done. We can illustrate the latter point with an amusing story. During the discussion of a surgical case, the question arose of how much temporal lobe could be removed without disrupting speech functions excessively. The professor of surgery, as well as the associate and the assistant professor, all expressed an opinion. It was clear from their estimates that a great deal more of the temporal lobe could be removed, while still sparing speech, if the surgery were done by a professor than if it were done by more junior surgeons! A final point to note with respect to anatomy is that although our anatomical knowledge continually improves, there are many brain areas whose function is poorly understood. To give two examples, the function of a large brainstem nucleus called the habenula is unknown, and the hippocampal formation is thought by different people to be involved in olfaction, emotion, long-term memory, short-term memory, and spatial navigation. The difficulty in making an appropriate correlation exists in part because people have maintained traditional, but unsupported, views, and in part because behavior theory is still too poorly developed to make adequate anatomical-functional correlations.

BIOCHEMISTRY

Remarkable progress has been made in understanding the biochemical organization of the brain. There are, however, some noticeable gaps in understanding how biochemical organization relates to behavior. These can be illustrated with four examples. First, one current theory of mental illness is that variations in the amount of turnover of neurotransmitters may be the basis of the symptoms of the various diseases. For example, increases in noradrenaline cause mania whereas decreases cause depression. Studies in rats have shown, however, that all brain noradrenaline can be removed without producing an unequivocal change in the animals' behavior. Second, another line of research has clearly demonstrated that decreases in the amount of dopamine are related to a motor disease called Parkinson's disease.

FIGURE 3–2. Reproduced from Wagner (1860), Table 3, showing the frontal lobe of the brain of Gauss (Figure I) compared with that of a worker, age 57 (Figure II). There is a difference, but part of it is explained by the "stenogyrencephalic" (numerous, narrow gyri) pattern in the former and an "eurygyrencephalic" (fewer, but broader, gyri) pattern in the latter. Both Retzius' types may occur in well-developed brains. (After Meyer, 1977.)

But here the surprising fact is that the symptoms of the disease do not appear until over 97 percent of central concentrations of dopamine are depleted. Clearly, the brain has mechanisms that compensate for dopamine insufficiency. The important point conveyed by these two examples is that relating fluctuating levels of neurotransmitters to behavior seems tenuous at best given some of the evidence currently available from experimental studies. Third, a great deal can be learned by direct manipulation of the biochemistry of the brains of animals, but these techniques cannot be used with humans. Studies with humans often involve such indirect measures as assays of the urine or cerebrospinal fluid for byproducts of chemical reactions. A high concentration of a byproduct in a schizophrenic patient may suggest that the precursor of the byproduct is the cause of the schizophrenia. It is equally likely, however, that the behavior of the schizophrenic patient is different from that of a normal person and the chemical changes are produced by the behavior and are not causal in the disease. If a schizophrenic patient were very active, for example, it might be expected that biochemical byproducts could be produced by the activity and not the schizophrenia. Such eventualities can be controlled for by having control subjects and experimental subjects engage in identical activities before tests are made, but such control procedures are very seldom used. A fourth problem in the biochemical research needs only brief mention but it is important. Nearly all patients are on some type of drug therapy. The drugs may modify both their brain function and their behavior, with the consequence that any test results obtained from the patient will be confounded by the drug treatments. There is very little that can be done about this problem except, whenever possible, to collect information from patients before they receive drug therapy.

BRAIN LESIONS

Effects of Brain Lesions on Behavior

The oldest and still most widely used approach to the problem of human brain function is to analyze the effects of lesion, or damage, of circumscribed regions of the central nervous system. In this approach the behavior of humans with restricted lesions resulting from head injury, vascular accidents, tumor, or brain surgery is compared with the behavior of normal control subjects on a variety of standardized behavioral tests. Similar research is done on nonhumans, with the difference that brain lesions can be more precisely located surgically in these species by gently sucking out small portions of tissue with a vacuum pump; by electrolytic lesion, passing strong electric current through a localized area of brain tissue; by heating or cooling tissue; or by placing toxic chemicals in restricted portions of tissue.

The rapid expansion of neuroscience in the past two decades has led to important advances in research methodology that antiquate the lesion technique. For example, with microtechniques a minute quantity of a chemical can be injected into a single neuron of a conscious animal, the effects of the chemical on the behavior of this neuron and others can be recorded, and, if special labeling materials are injected into these neurons, the cells and their connections can be located histologically after the death of the animal. Thus, because the macrotechniques of neuroscience research have become disused in favor of the microtechnology of the 1970s and 1980s, in recent years the study of the effects of brain lesions on behavior has come under widespread criticism.

There is a problem in neuropsychology, however: it is not feasible to use most of the modern microtechnology when studying human subjects. Furthermore, because the technology of human neuropsychology is limited, the most direct technique for studying the effects of brain lesions in humans is still to study the effects of analogous lesions in non-human animals. Hence, the lesion technique continues to be an important tool in all of neuropsychology. But its use is fraught with considerable problems. Although brain lesions are relatively simple to produce, the correct interpretation of their effects requires a thorough understanding of the problems involved. Below we shall consider the effects of brain lesions on brain function, the difficulties associated with the interpretation of lesion studies, and the difficulties in equating lesions in patients with varying neurological disturbances.

Interpreting Brain Lesion Effects

Brain lesions can have three quite different effects on behavior: (1) loss of function, (2) release of function, and (3) disorganization of function.

The most obvious and direct effect of brain lesions is a *loss of function*. For example, if the visual cortex is completely destroyed, pattern vision is permanently lost. Loss of function can also be partial, as when only a portion of the visual cortex is destroyed. It is a general rule that the larger the lesion, the greater the loss of function to be expected.

A *release of function* is said to occur if, after brain lesions, a new behavior appears or the frequency of a particular behavior is drastically increased. An example of new behavior occurs in victims of Parkinson's disease (the shaking palsy), who develop a tremor in the fingers and hands. Since the loss of some brain area or system could not produce the tremor directly, it is assumed that the lost area normally functioned to prevent tremor, and in its absence tremor is released. An example of increased frequency of a behavior occurs in victims of

frontal-lobe damage, who often perseverate on particular behaviors. For instance, say such a person were required to sort playing cards according to color, and after sorting several cards were then required to sort them by suit; it would be typical of persons with frontal-lobe damage to continue sorting by color. Perseverative behaviors imply that one function of the frontal lobe is to inhibit behavior, and in its absence behavior is released from inhibitory control.

Disorganization of function can also follow brain lesion such that bits or pieces of behavior still occur but not in the correct order, or at the wrong time and place. Thus, people with lesions in certain regions of the left hemisphere may be unable to make a cup of tea because they are unable to place the necessary behavioral components (heating water, pouring it over the tea bag into a teapot, pouring the tea into a cup, and adding sugar and/or milk) in the correct order. Instead, they might place the tea bag in the milk, add sugar to the teakettle, and pour the heated water onto the saucer. It is clear that these people are capable of all the pieces of the behavioral sequence; they are simply unable to organize them into the correct order.

It can be seen that the inferences drawn from the study of lesion effects depend on whether there is loss, release, or disorganization of function, or in some cases a combination of these effects. Behavior must be carefully described, and each of the three principal effects considered, before solid conclusions can be made from the study of brain lesions. A number of factors restrict the inferences one can make about brain function from the study of either humans or nonhumans with brain lesions. These include (1) locus of damage, (2) recovery from damage, (3) sparing of function, (4) side effects of damage, (5) disturbances in regions not directly damaged, (6) crowding, and (7) source of damage.

Locus of Damage. It has been recognized for hundreds of years that damage in the brainstem can have more devastating effects on behavior in general than a similar extent of damage in the neocortex. For example, in the winter of 1977 a young skier had a catastrophic spill in a downhill race and landed on his head at a speed in excess of 60 miles per hour. The resulting compression and twisting of the brainstem from the impact of the fall produced a lesion in the brainstem resulting in permanent coma. Autopsy studies of people with similar traumatic accidents indicate that the lesion in the brainstem responsible for the coma may be very small indeed. This observation stands in stark contrast to the famous case of Phineas Gage. Gage suffered an accidental removal of his frontal lobes when an iron bar was blown through his head, but, remarkably, he was merely stunned for a few seconds and managed to walk to medical assistance. The comparison of the skier and Gage is particularly surprising when one considers that Gage's lesion was 20 to 30 times larger than the skier's.

Recovery from Damage. Following brain injury there are often a number of behavioral changes that are transient and gradually disappear. A middle-aged man, Mr. B, suffered a small stroke in the left hemisphere and was subsequently unable to talk, read, or write. We followed his recovery over a period of six weeks, and he gradually began to regain his language skills, although even three months after the stroke he was still seriously impaired. When we next saw him, a year later, he was much improved and was capable of carrying on a conversation, although his speech was somewhat slower than normal because he had difficulty finding words. Mr. B. illustrates clearly the phenomenon of recovery of function. Although recovery processes such as those observed in Mr. B. are as yet poorly understood, their study is an important part of

lesion studies because they are a source of inferences regarding function. Had Mr. B. been examined two weeks after the stroke, the conclusions about the effect of his lesion would be rather different from those made a year later. This issue is further complicated by the variability of recovery in humans; the recovery period may take days, weeks, or, in some cases, even years, or recovery may not occur. Many people with lesions similar to Mr. B.'s never regain the ability to talk, read, and write, even with years of therapy.

Sparing of Function. It has long been known that brain injury sustained in infancy has far less severe effects on behavior than similar damage inflicted in adulthood; if the injury occurs early enough, it may have no effect at all on behaviors that have not yet developed at the time of injury. Thus, just as some functions recover with time, some functions are spared from disruption if the brain lesion occurs early in life. The best example of this phenomenon can be seen in the effects of left-hemisphere lesion on speech. Children who suffer cortical damage between about five and 10 years of age may initially experience a period in which they are unable to talk, but they usually recover this ability, and they are likely to do so more completely than Mr. B. did. On the other hand, children who suffer left-hemisphere damage before they begin to speak will not experience a period of language disturbance; they begin to speak at the usual time, or they may be retarded by only a few months. These children are said to have sparing of function, rather than recovery, since the function was never lost. Hence, the conclusions one may draw from brain–behavior relations obviously differ according to whether the brain damage was sustained early in life or in adulthood.

Side Effects of Damage. Brain damage may affect behavior not only directly but also indirectly. A common cause of epilepsy is brain damage in which cells in the region of the lesion are not destroyed but remain to act in an abnormal way, thereby producing the seizure disorder. The appearance of a seizure disorder complicates the study of brain lesions, since change in behavior may be secondary to the seizures. Furthermore, certain lesions may produce significant changes in personality that in turn obscure or distort the effects of the lesion on other behaviors. For example, Ms. P. was a 22-year-old undergraduate psychology major who suffered the rupture of a large aneurysm of the middle cerebral artery, resulting in extensive damage to the right temporal and parietal lobes. Prior to the accident she was an excellent student, but subsequent to it she was experiencing difficulties, especially in writing term papers—not because she was unable to read or write, but rather because she had become obsessed with writing the perfect paper, an obsession that resulted in no paper at all. Thus her lesion indirectly prevented her from writing by producing a change in personality.

Disturbances in Regions Not Directly Damaged. Changes in behavior following brain damage can sometimes be attributed to disturbances in regions not directly affected by the lesion. It is naive to assume that brain lesions affect only the region actually damaged, because any lesion initiates changes in those regions that are connected to the damaged area. For example, if lesions occur in the neocortex, cells die in the thalamus, because the axons of thalamic cells, which project to the neocortex, are damaged by the cortical lesion. Further, lesions in some regions of the brain have been shown to produce morphological, biochemical, and physiological changes in areas far removed from the damaged area. To illustrate, lesions of the hypothalamus destroy not only the cells in that region but also fibers of passage

coursing through it en route from lower centers of the brainstem to the forebrain. Thus, fibers projecting from the substantia nigra to the basal ganglia can be damaged by hypothalamic lesions, resulting in a reduction in the levels of dopamine in the caudate nucleus. It is therefore reasonable to assume that some effects of hypothalamic lesions are actually caused by imbalances in the basal ganglia, which creates difficulties in making inferences about hypothalamic function.

Crowding. There are circumstances when brain lesions can have unexpected effects. Such is the case with *crowding,* which seems to occur with brain lesions in very young children. There is recovery of function, but the recovery seems to be accomplished by the function being mediated by brain areas that would ordinarily not subserve it. In order for the area to take on this new responsibility it gives up control over some or all of the functions it might normally be responsible for. Hence, it is thought that the one function crowds out the other. That crowding can occur enormously complicates the interpretation of the effects of early lesions with respect to principles derived from studying the effects of lesions in adults.

Source of Damage. Although both naturally occurring and surgical lesions result in the death of neurons, not all brain lesions in a given zone of tissue produce exactly the same behavioral effects. Tumor patients frequently do not behave like patients with lesions from other causes, because tumors may produce pressure on widespread parts of the brain, resulting in symptoms unrelated to the region where the tumor actually resides. Furthermore, whereas the primary effects of tumors such as meningiomas result from pressure, the primary effects of infiltrating tumors such as glioblastomas may result from interference with the normal functioning of neurons in the affected area. An additional problem in equating lesions of different sources is that the extent of naturally occurring lesions is usually documented poorly, if at all. Various brain scans (see Chapter 5) can provide an estimate of the extent of the damaged region, but visual inspection provides the only certain measure. Since surgically induced lesions of the neocortex can be photographed at the time of surgery, these lesions provide a more precise relation between brain and behavior. However, even here there are other difficulties, since surgical lesions are not performed on normal brains. The patient would not be receiving surgery had there not been some prior neurological disorder; thus, there is a potential interaction between disease and surgery. For example, although epileptics are often nearly seizure-free after surgery, it is the usual practice to require continued medication, to ensure the absence of seizures. There is the added problem that years of poorly controlled seizures may have produced significant abnormalities in regions of the brain far removed from the lesion. Considering these problems, it is hardly surprising that there is controversy in the literature.

STIMULATION

Brain stimulation evokes three general types of effects: it produces relatively discrete actions, such as the twitching of a cat's paw when the appropriate portion of the motor cortex is stimulated; it produces an overall energizing effect on behavior, such as when the hypothalamus is stimulated and the animal displays approach or avoidance behavior, eating, sexual behavior, etc.; and it elicits abnormal electrographic effects on brain tissue, which themselves could lead to convulsions or other behaviors. The interpretation of just which type of effect is related to a particular behavior is not always easy, nor are results always wisely interpreted. Let us consider

some rather well-known results from the human brain stimulation studies of Wilder Penfield. The following is an account from an introductory textbook that summarizes one of Penfield's experiments.

We are in the operating room of the Montreal Neurological Institute observing brain surgery on Buddy, a young man with uncontrollable epileptic seizures. The surgeon wants to operate to remove a tumor, but first he must discover what the consequences will be of removing various portions of the brain tissue surrounding the tumor. . . . Suddenly, an unexpected response occurs. The patient is grinning; he is smiling; eyes opening when that area is stimulated. "Buddy, what happened, what did you just experience?" "Doc, I heard a song, or rather a part of a song, a melody." "Buddy, have you ever heard it before?" "Yes, I remember having heard it a long time ago, but I can't remember the name of the tune." When another brain site is stimulated, the patient recalls in vivid detail a thrilling childhood experience.

In a similar operation, a woman patient "relived" the experience she had during the delivery of her baby. As if by pushing an electronic memory button, the surgeon, Dr. Wilder Penfield, has touched memories stored silently for years in the recesses of his patients' brains. (Zimbardo and Ruch, 1975, pp. 48–49)

The interpretation placed on these results is that the brain stimulation was activating actual memory traces that had been placed in the brain many years before. Penfield himself also thought that something like this was occurring, for he remarked, "The astonishing aspect of the phenomenon is that suddenly he is aware of all that was in his mind during an earlier strip of time" (Penfield, 1969, p. 152). This interpretation of Penfield's results has contributed to the belief on the part of many people that information stored in long-term memory is permanent, although not always accessible. Elizabeth and Geoffrey Loftus have arrived at quite a different opinion on the basis of rereading the case reports. First, Penfield only rarely obtained the effect. Of 1132 cases only 40 showed the phenomena when given brain stimulation. Even considering the fact that only temporal-lobe stimulation evoked recall, these 40 cases comprised only 7.7 percent of the 520 cases that received temporal-lobe stimulation. Of the 40 cases many reported only hearing vague sounds or seeing vague things. When these are excluded, there remain only 22 responses obtained from 12 people seeming to indicate that actual memory traces were being rekindled. Even among these it is not clear that a memory was being activated, because one woman who reported being in a lumberyard stated afterward that in real life she had never been in one. Even if a few cases are examples of what could be memory rekindling, the possibility that something like a dream was being elicited cannot be ruled out.

In a review of these types of elicited response in his own patients and in the patients of others, Halgren makes the following points. First, the effects are uncommon, occurring in less than 8 percent of patients. Second, in nearly 50 percent of patients that show the effects, stimulation concomitantly activates an epileptiform activity called an afterdischarge. Three, there appears to be no relation between the location of stimulation and the category of the experience. Fourth, the same stimulation often evokes different effects. Fifth, after removal of the temporal lobe some patients may still experience the same phenomena. Sixth, only patients with certain types of personality appear to display the phenomena. Seventh, the phenomena appear to be related often to events of the moment and can be changed by altering the mood of the patient with suggestion. In sum, the evidence suggests that the phenomena may be an artifact of the abnormal electrical activity elicited by the stimulation, that they occur at some site distant from the stimulation electrode, and that they seem more related to auras that precede epileptic attacks or to hallucinations than to rekindled memory traces.

Of course, the lesson from the stimulation example given here is not that the phenomena are unreal or uninteresting. On the contrary, they are interesting, but they must be critically examined before generalizations about their significance are formed. The same type of critique must be made of other types of stimulation phenomena. It is well known that animals and humans will press a bar to obtain repeated trains of brain stimulation. Literally hundreds of studies have been carried out to explain this behavior. To date, explanations include: they like it, it produces an unpleasant aftereffect that can be erased with another stimulation, it produces movements that are reinforcing, it produces sensations that are reinforcing, it produces reinforcement followed by motivation, it produces abnormal brain activity that results in automaticlike behavior, etc. Of course, any or all of the interpretations may be correct, but the trick lies in interpreting the parameters within which any possible interpretation can be considered correct.

RECORDING

Interpreting the electrical activity recorded from the brain has its own special problems. Surprisingly, decisions about whether an electrical event is normal or abnormal are relatively easy to make. This is because a large number of cases can be collected to establish norms. It is interpreting the significance of normal electrical activity that can be difficult. Consider the patterns of EEGs recorded from the neocortex (Figure 2–14). The activated pattern (Figure 2–14, top) is obtained from a wide range of cortical areas, and in each it appears surprisingly similar, even though there is good evidence to indicate that each area has different functions. Apparently the activity has no localizing value with respect to determining what different areas do. To complicate things further, the activity looks very similar in different species of animals. The activated EEG obtained from a mammal even looks like recordings obtained from a housefly. Therefore, it is not possible, or at least not easy, to tell species apart by examining EEG activity.

The now-classic interpretation of cortical EEG–behavior relations is shown in Figure 2–14. Stated simply, a fast, desynchronized pattern is thought of as a sign of arousal or consciousness whereas successively larger and slower waveforms are thought to be correlates of relaxation, sleep, and coma. This interpretation is not without its problems. First, the activated pattern occurs during dream sleep. Although one may only hypothesize that the state of dream sleep is different from nondream sleep, a consensus that dream sleep is not like being awake and conscious is easy to reach. Because it was clear that the activated-EEG–conscious relation was negated by the presence of an activated EEG during dream sleep, dream sleep, was called paradoxical sleep. The introduction of this terminology, however, did nothing to change the anomalous EEG-behavior relation. Second, the EEG-consciousness relation is greatly complicated by the observation that an activated EEG occurs when people or animals are anesthetized with certain kinds of anesthetics. It even occurs when they are in a state of coma. Since such observations clearly negated the standard activated-EEG–consciousness relation, they were usually ignored. Third, there are times when conscious individuals display a slow-wave EEG. Even having the eyes go out of focus or closing them is sufficient to produce slow waves. It has been suggested, tongue in cheek, that these states should be called states of "paradoxical waking."

In a recent theoretical review, Case Vanderwolf and Terry Robinson have suggested that many of the difficulties with current EEG-behavior relations evaporate if the EEG is thought of as a correlate of behavior rather than as a correlate of consciousness, arousal, attention, etc. The first type of evidence that supports this view is that there are two types of activated-EEG activity, which are virtually indistinguishable to visual inspection but that can be identified by pharmacological manipulations. Whenever an activated pattern occurs in an immobile animal, irrespective of whether the animal is awake and alert, immobile in dream sleep, anesthetized, or in a coma, the activated EEG is the type that can be abolished by anticholinergic drugs such as atropine sulfate. Whenever the activated pattern occurs in a moving animal, irrespective of whether the movement occurs spontaneously or is a twitch or rapid eye movement during paradoxical sleep, the activated EEG is of a type that cannot be abolished by an anticholinergic agent. A second class of evidence for the new view is that whenever slow-wave activity appears, it occurs when animals are immobile, irrespective of whether they are awake and alert, asleep, anesthetized, or in coma. Slow-wave activity does not occur when animals move. This new synthesis not only questions the traditional view of EEG-behavior relations, it can be generalized to other kinds of brain events. In short, it suggests that such things as single-unit activity, evoked potentials, and slow direct-current shifts are more apt to be related to the behavior of subjects than to such states as consciousness, attention, arousal, motivation, etc. This view is, of course, not encouraging to those who believe that the object of neuroscience is to explain the latter kinds of states. It is encouraging to those who believe the object of neuroscience is to explain behavior.

BEHAVIOR

The rules of good science are usually explicitly taught in laboratory courses. Briefly, proper science involves: (1) Stating a theory composed of a set of postulates with all terms operationally defined. (2) Logical deductions or predictions about behavioral outcomes. (3) Comparison of prediction with the results of carefully controlled experiments, leading to a confirmation of the theory. This procedure is called the *hypothetico-deductive method.* There is also another way of doing science, but unfortunately it is seldom taught. It is the *empirico-inductive method.* It is empirical in the sense that reliance is made on experience and observation, without regard to systems and theories, and inductive in the same sense that meaningful generalizations or regularities are constructed from the results of the observations. Ideally, both approaches can be used together. The empirico-inductive method can be used to obtain new phenomena and new insights into behavior and then the hypothetico-deductive method can be used for its more formal strengths. Still, there are difficulties in proceeding in the study of behavior that neither approach can remedy. These include (1) methods of gathering information, (2) the question of the number of subjects that are required to make an observation real, (3) decisions about the proper behavior to be studied, and (4) problems of measurement. Examples of each are given below.

Information Gathering

The technique of gathering information in favor of a point has been in use for a long time. Early biological investigations, such as those done by Darwin, used just such a procedure. The most obvious mistake that can be made, and it is one that is often overlooked, is that of *exclusively* gathering information in favor of a position. This was the error made by the phrenologist Gall. He gathered thousands of bits of evidence that purported to support his theory that bumps on people's heads reveal something about their personality. What Gall failed to do was subject his observations to any test. The test that must be used is provided by statistical theory, called the null hypothesis. The null hypothesis states there is no difference between two things or groups. Evidence is then collected and the hypothesis is rejected or confirmed on the basis of the evidence. Gall's error was to state that a bump at point X indicated personality trait Y and then to collect examples. Had he stated his hypothesis: There is no difference between people with bumps at point X and people without bumps at point X, he would have been forced to examine all people with and without bumps and come to some sort of mathematical decision about whether the hypothesis could be rejected. The error in gathering information in favor of a point is made surprisingly often. For example, a scientist may state that recovery of function is common and proceed to gather examples of recovery until the point at which a reader is overwhelmed by the evidence. The evidence, however, may come from only a small portion of the population of people who incurred brain damage. Much of the early research on patients subject to psychosurgery contains errors of the same sort (see Valenstein); only confirmatory evidence was collected, and this evidence then perpetuated the popularity of the surgery.

Subject Number

There is an unwritten rule in behavioral science that the smaller the subject, the more subjects required to make valid decisions. Generally, a group should consist of 10 mice, six rats, two monkeys, or one elephant. We insist that we are unaware of any reasons why an observation on one elephant should be any more valid than an observation on one mouse. Another unwritten rule is that if differences are large, fewer subjects are required. Again, we do not believe that large differences are any more real than small ones. A third unwritten rule is that particularly interesting phenomena do not require the support of a lot of subjects. Here, one could argue that interest is often in the eye of the observer. Apart from these unwritten rules, it is often the case that neuropsychological and neurological journals publish articles based on the study of a single patient. Although these studies are often detailed and competent examinations of the behavior of a patient with a circumscribed lesion, they are of limited value in constructing a general theory of human neuropsychology because there are serious difficulties in generalizing from the behavior of one person to the behavior of all people. It is commonly recognized that the behavior of individuals varies enormously, but it is also necessary to recognize that brain structure also varies considerably from person to person. A mass of gray matter known as the massa intermedia, which connects the left and right thalami across the midline, is missing in nearly one-quarter of the population; at present there is no known relation between the presence or absence of this structure and behavior. Indeed, even though the convolutions of the human brain are drawn and photographed in every textbook of neurology and neuroanatomy, the pattern of convolutions is not precisely the same in any two brains (Figure 3–2).

To complicate matters, even when there is no gross variation in the structure of two brains, two normal people can vary on neuropsychological tests even to the point that one person appears brain damaged! It is because of such normal variation that most scientific studies of behavior require the use of at least simple statistics to clearly demonstrate the results. The nature of the statistics used generally determines the number of subjects that are used. Studies of individual cases run the risk of making serious errors in inference because of peculiarities in the subject's neuroanatomy or behavior, or an interaction of the two. Although in this book we emphasize studies of more than one patient, we still consider single-case studies, keeping in mind their weaknesses.

Choice of Behavior

There has been a longstanding debate about the behaviors that psychologists should select for examination. Many psychology textbooks reflect their bias in the choice of chapter headings, which include titles such as emotion, attention, arousal, and consciousness. Behaviorists, on the other hand, argue that only observable events can be adequately measured and studied. In part, the problem arose because psychology evolved from philosophy and problems of mind and mental states were questions that were important to philosophers. Many neuroscientists happened to agree with philosophers. Behaviorists rebelled against this approach. At some point every psychologist involved in research must come to a decision about what to study. We suggest that fewer mistakes are made when observable events are studied than when hypothetical or mental constructs are studied. The following example may serve to illustrate this point. The hippocampus produces a distinctive waveform called the hippocampal *theta* rhythm (see Figure 3–3). In their initial study, Green and Arduini suggested that it is a sign of arousal because whenever animals were excited, they displayed the activity. Routtenburg observed that the activity was present in rats before they habituated to a novel environment and suggested that it is related to motivation. Adey and his coworkers, however, observed that the frequency of the activity changed as cats mastered a T-maze and so suggested that the activity is related to learning. Finally, Graeff and his coworkers suggested that the activity is a correlate of fear because it appears when rats receive foot shock. Vanderwolf and his coworkers simply observed animals during spontaneous behavior. They found that the activity appeared in rats whenever they made a certain class of movements (including running, walking, and turning). As it turns out the movement hypothesis accounts for the data far

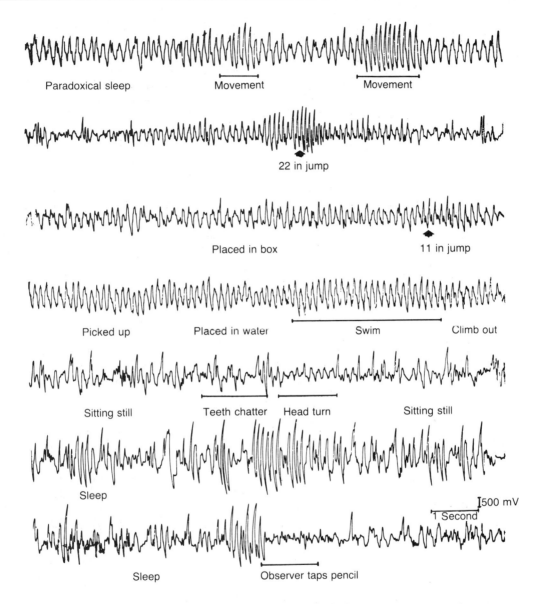

FIGURE 3–3. Electrical activity at a single hippocampal site during sleep and various behaviors in the rat. Note the following: rhythmical slow activity (RSA) during paradoxical sleep, struggling when held in the hand, swimming and head movement; large-amplitude irregular activity during sitting still while alert and while chattering the teeth; irregular slow activity and "spindling" during slow-wave sleep; and small-amplitude irregular activity when the rat was awakened but did not move about. Note also the following: increased RSA frequency and amplitude associated with twitching during paradoxical sleep and with jumping in avoidance tasks; different frequencies and amplitudes of RSA associated with head movements, swimming, jumping 11 in, and jumping 22 in. Calibration: 1 s, 500 μV; half-amplitude filters, 0.3 and 75 Hz. Electrode placement: CA1, hippocampus major. (After Whishaw and Vanderwolf, 1973.)

more simply and elegantly than the other hypotheses. Aroused, motivated, trained, or frightened rats may all have one behavior in common—they move. Just how dramatically an EEG waveform can change with changes in behavior is illustrated in Figure 3–3. Note that both the amplitude and the frequency of the rhythm change such that amplitude is large with large movements and frequency is fast with movements that are vigorous or involve rapid acceleration. Once one is adept at reading such records, it almost becomes possible to describe the behavior from the record. Vanderwolf has argued strongly against the study of mental events by stating that the brain is unlikely to be subdivided along the lines of a dictionary. He illustrates his point with the following story:

> Consider the case of Professor Omega, an imaginary researcher who suspected that the somatic muscles had a direct role in mental processes. Omega began his research by recording electromyographic activity (EMG) from m. pectoralis major during behavior in animals. His first finding was that on exposure of an animal to an unfamiliar Skinner box, EMG activity was high initially but declined progressively during continued exposure. Presentation of tones and flashing lights led to temporary increases in EMG activity. These findings suggested a role of the muscle in habituation and attention. When the animal was trained to press a lever in the box, EMG activity rose to a high level. Extinction procedures results in a decline to pretraining levels. These facts suggested a role for the muscle in conditioning and learning. Further research showed that EMG activity rose during food deprivation and fell after feeding, suggesting a role in motivational phenomena. Amphetamine increased EMG activity sharply, but anaesthetics abolished it. Tranquilizers had an intermediate effect. Omega concluded that the pectoralis muscle was probably the site of action of many drugs.
>
> To his surprise, Omega had great difficulty in publishing his results in scientific journals. In response to criticisms of his work, he pointed out that the methods and experimental design he had used were identical to those adopted by many researchers who had published papers purporting to show that the slow wave or unit activity of the neocortex, the hippocampus and many other parts of the brain is related to attention, learning, motivation, etc.
>
> The error made by Omega seems obvious to everyone because we know that EMG activity is strongly related to movement and posture. Any procedure whatsoever that alters behavior will alter EMG activity. Only recently has it become obvious that similar considerations apply in the brain since brain activity too is likely to be correlated with concurrent movement. (Vanderwolf, 1983, pp. 92–93)

In summary, the reader might consider that mental illnesses are not disorders of the mind but disorders of certain types of behaviors. Septal lesions do not produce emotional disorders, but they do increase the probability that rats will bite in certain unfamiliar situations. Children who write mirror-image letters may not do so because they have a reversed image of the world but because they perseverate in making the movements just used in writing a preceding letter. Hyperactive children do not have a disorder in paying attention but they are making movements incompatible with sitting still. Schizophrenic people do not have a split between cognitive and emotional functions, but they seldom make facial expressions. With practice it is possible to become quite adept at distinguishing between behavioral and nonbehavioral descriptions.

Measurement. It might be thought that of all the procedures used in neuropsychology, measurement of things or events might be the easiest to perform and replicate. This is not true. Many measures are made to obtain inferences about some other processes. For example, in the procedure of dichotic listening, different words are played through headphones to each ear and the subject is asked to recall as many words as possible. If more words are recalled from the right ear than from the left ear, the inference is made that speech is lateralized to the left hemisphere. The assumptions underlying this inference are relatively simple, yet there are so many variables that affect the result that Bryden has found it necessary to devote an entire book to the problem. Perhaps, one may ask, if a more objective measure of something like brain size were used the results would be more clear? This seems unlikely. There appear to be so many different ways to measure objects that almost any result can be obtained. Consider the following.

Probably everyone has had the feeling that their feet are not exactly the same size. Often the difference may manifest itself as greater discomfort of one foot while breaking in a new pair of shoes (we have never heard anyone suggest that the shoes might be different sizes). Differences in brain organization may be related to foot size. For example, people in medicine have known for a long time that damage to one hemisphere at an early age leads to smaller limbs in the contralateral body (Figure 3–4). Jere and Jerome Levy attempted to measure differences in foot size in normal people in order to make inferences about cerebral organization. They measured foot size in 150 individuals. They found that significantly more right-handed females had larger left than right feet, whereas significantly more right-handed males had larger right than left feet. Just the opposite result was obtained with left-handed females and males. The Levys' measures were made by converting foot size to shoe size and then converting differences to a seven-point rating scale. A number of studies attempted to repeat the Levys' work. Mascie-Taylor and his coworkers measured foot size using "standard anthropometric technique" (described elsewhere as heel to longest toe with the subject seated and with the toenails cut). They found

FIGURE 3–4. Growth asymmetry due to destruction of the left frontoparietal region at the time of birth. Such a case demonstrates the fact that growth has a cortical control quite aside from the effect of disuse, affecting limb size. (From W. Penfield and H. Jasper, *Epilepsy and the Functional Anatomy of the Human Brain.* Boston: Little, Brown. Copyright 1954. Reprinted with permission.)

that the left foot was longer than the right in both sexes, confirming seven previous studies. There were no handedness effects. Peters, Petrie, and Oddie measured the actual foot length from the heel to the longest toe in 365 seated subjects. They found no significant differences between the left and the right foot for any sex or handedness group, and they claimed partial support for their results from three other studies. Yanowitz, Satz, and Heilman traced the outline of 105 subjects' feet on a large sheet of paper. They found no differences in foot size with sex or handedness. The final score to date is: one study for sex and handedness effects, eight studies for a left-foot effect, and two studies for no differences, with three additional studies in partial support for no differences.

It might initially have been thought that measuring foot size is a relatively easy matter. This series of studies shows that it is not. Depending on the measuring device, the points across which length is measured, whether subjects are seated or standing, the time of day, and perhaps even shoe type worn before meas-urement, different measures can be obtained. In many of the studies the importance of these variables was not recognized, and in others the procedure was not described in sufficient detail to permit exact replication. It is interesting that the most objective measure, photography, was not used in any of the studies (see Figure 3–4). A photographic record of the feet would have permitted reevaluation of the results at any time by investigators interested in the question of appropriate measurement.

REFERENCES

Adey, W. R. Neurophysiological correlates of information transaction and storage in brain tissue. In E. Stellar and J. M. Sprague, eds., *Progress in Physiological Psychology,* vol. 1. New York: Academic, 1966.

Bryden, M. P. *Laterality: Functional Asymmetry in the Intact Brain.* New York: Academic, 1982.

Graeff, F. G., S. Quentero, and J. A. Grey. Median raphe stimulation, hippocampal theta rhythm and threat-induced behavioral inhibition. *Physiology and Behavior* 25:253–261, 1980.

Green, J. D., and A. Arduini. Hippocampal electrical activity in arousal. *Journal of Neurophysiology* 17:533–557, 1954.

Halgren, E. Mental phenomena induced by stimulation of the limbic system. *Human Neurobiology* 1:251–260, 1982.

Levy, J., and J. M. Levy. Foot-length asymmetry, sex, and handedness. *Science* 212:1418–1419, 1981.

Levy, J., and J. M. Levy. Human lateralization from head to foot: Sex-related factors. *Science* 200:1291–1292, 1978.

Loftus, E. F., and G. R. Loftus. On the permanence of stored information in the human brain. *American Psychologist* 35:409–420, 1980.

Mascie-Taylor, C. G. N., A. M. MacLarnon, P. M. Lanigan, and I. C. McManus. Foot-length asymmetry, sex, and handedness. *Science* 212:1416–1417, 1981.

Meyer, A. The search for a morphological substrate in the brains of eminent persons including musicians: A historical review. In M. Critchley and R. A. Hanson, eds., *Music and the Brain.* London: Heinemann Medical Books, 1977.

Penfield, W. Consciousness, memory, and man's conditioned reflexes. In K. Pribram, ed., *On the Biology of Learning.* Harcourt, Brace & World, 1969.

Penfield, W., and H. Jasper. *Epilepsy and the Functional Anatomy of the Human Brain.* Boston: Little, Brown, 1954.

Peters, M., B. Petrie, and D. Oddie. Foot-length asymmetry, sex, and handedness. *Science* 212:1417–1418, 1981.

Routtenburg, A. Hippocampal correlates of consumatory and observed behavior. *Physiology and Behavior* 3:533–535, 1968.

Vanderwolf, C. H. The role of the cerebral cortex and ascending activating systems in the control of behavior. In E. Satinoff and P. Teitelbaum, eds., *The Organization of Behavior*. New York: Academic, 1983.

Vanderwolf, C. H., and T. E. Robinson. Reticulo-cortical activity and behavior: A critique of the arousal theory and a new synthesis. *The Behavioral and Brain Sciences* 4:459–514, 1981.

Valenstein, E. *Brain Control*. New York: Wiley, 1973.

Whishaw, I. Q., and C. H. Vanderwolf. Hippocampal EEG and behavior: Changes in amplitude and frequency of RSA (theta rhythm) accompanying spontaneous and learned movement patterns in rats and cats. *Behavioral Biology* 8:461–484, 1973.

Yanowitz, J. S., P. Satz, and K. M. Heilman. Foot-length asymmetry, sex and handedness. *Science* 212:1418, 1981.

Zimbardo, P. G., and F. L. Ruch. *Psychology and life,* 9th ed. Glenview, Ill.: Scott, Foresman, 1975.

4

ORIGINS OF THE HUMAN BRAIN
AND BEHAVIOR

Although this book is primarily about the functions of the human brain as it now exists, one approach to understanding human brain function is to consider where our brain came from and to compare it with the brains of other animals. In this chapter we shall review the fossil record of the human brain and then examine the similarities and differences between the brains of living humans and nonhumans.

THE FOSSIL RECORD
OF THE HUMAN BRAIN

The recent and sudden proliferation of hominid fossil discoveries has sparked new interest in human evolution, especially in the evolution of the human brain. To fully appreciate the development of our brain, we must first consider who our ancestors were, where they arose, and how we appeared as their unlikely children.

Human Origins

Our story begins in 1859 with Darwin's publication of the *Origin of Species*. In it, Darwin carefully avoided the inflammatory subject of human ancestry, preferring to emphasize his studies of barnacles, extinct clams, and exotic animals from the far away Galapagos Islands. In fact, Darwin's only reference to human evolution appears at the end of the book, where he states: "Light will be thrown on the origin of man and his history." That was enough! There was an immediate public preoccupation with our alleged ancestral apes, reputedly leading one Victorian lady to have said, "Descended from apes! My dear, we hope it is not true. But if it is, let us pray that it may not become generally known." Our anatomical similarity to apes was difficult to ignore, and soon after the *Origin of Species* appeared, T. H. Huxley showed that anatomically we are more similar to apes than apes are to monkeys. (In fact, we now know that over 99 percent of our genes are identical with those of chimpanzees.) It was not until 1871 that Darwin concluded in his book *The Descent of Man* that humans descended from a "hairy, tailed quadruped, probably aboreal in its habits." In the following years the public belief emerged that being descended from apes need not be uncomfortable. It was presumed that humans were the pinnacle of a single lineage from extinct apelike animals, which were changed by the perfecting process of natural selection to become the very special product of evolution, *Homo sapiens sapiens*. The only flaws in this view are the facts that have emerged in the past two decades.

Although life may have been on earth for some 650 million years, the fossil record shows that true mammals made their appearance only about 150 million years ago, and that monkeylike mammals first appeared only about 25 million years ago. The fossil record of monkeys and apes is very poor, being largely composed of teeth, but it appears that *Ramapithecus,* the species often claimed to be ancestral to humans and other living apes, lived at least from eight to 14 million years ago. The fossil record has not yet revealed what occurred in primate evolution over the next four million years, but between three and four million years ago we see the first appearance of animals that appear humanlike; these creatures have been called australopithicines (meaning southern ape) and have to date been found only in Africa. It is the australopithicines and their descendants that are of particular interest to us, because these animals are the first to show a distinctly human characteristic: they walked upright. This observation is based both on the structure of the pelvis and on the discovery of fossilized footprints dated at 3.6 to 3.8 million years old, footprints that give some indication about how the foot was used. The impressions are hauntingly similar to ours, featuring a well-developed arch and big toe pointing straight ahead, rather than sideways as in apes; they almost could have been made by 20th-century humans. Still, some people argue that their feet were somewhat different, perhaps being specialized for tree climbing. It is thus clear that our common ancestor with modern apes is at least four million years removed, and probably much further. Who, then, are our direct ancestors?

We have noted that there is a tendency to perceive humans as the end product of a linear process of natural selection, but this view is in error. It is best to think of our recent evolution as being a bush, with our species the only surviving member, sitting alone on one branch. At the base of the bush lie the australopithicines (see Figure 4–1). Fossilized remains of what may be two distinct species (*Australopithicus africanus* and *A. afarensis*) have been discovered in East Africa and Ethiopia, along with their footprints, which we described above. (For a very enjoyable account of the discovery of the Ethiopian fossils we strongly recommend Johanson and Edey's book, *Lucy: The Beginnings of Humankind.*) The relationship between *A. africanus* and *A. afarensis* is controversial.

We are inclined to side with the view that they do indeed represent two distinct species, that *A. afarensis* may have been ancestral to *A. africanus,* and that the species coexisted for a long period of time, perhaps as long as a million years. Sometime about 2.3 million years ago a third type of australopithicine appears in the fossil records, only to disappear about 1.3 million years ago. These creatures, designated *A. robustus,* were apparently more heavily built than *A. africanus* and appear to have had a vegetarian diet. Thus, *A. robustus* had massive molars for grinding and developed large ridges around the eyes so that the jaw muscles could be firmly attached to the skull. The development of *A. robustus* is particularly interesting both because *robustus* lived side by side with its more slender cousin, *A. africanus,* and because they arose at about the same time and coexisted with a completely new genus, *Homo.*

The oldest fossils to be designated as *Homo* are those found in the Olduvai Gorge in 1964, dated at about 1.75 million years old. The specimens are of poor quality and bear a strong resemblance to *Australopithicus,* but Louis Leakey argued that the dental pattern is more similar to modern humans than to australopithicines and, more importantly, that the

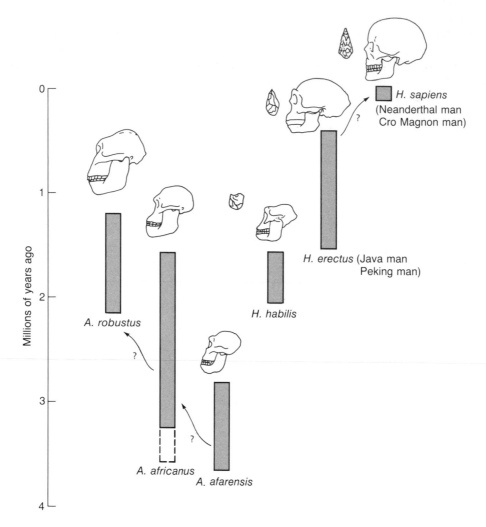

FIGURE 4–1. Summary of the recognized species of the human family. Question marks indicate that the proposed evolutionary relationships are uncertain. Notice the development of tools by *Homo*. (After Stanley, 1981, and Johanson and Edey, 1981.)

animal apparently made simple stone tools, which were also found in the Olduvai Gorge. Therefore Leakey named the species *H. habilus* (i.e., handyman). This designation has not been without controversy, and although it appears to have stuck, the importance of *H. habilus* in human evolution remains uncertain. Far more solid, however, is the importance of

another species of *Homo* (*H. erectus*, upright man, so named because of a mistaken notion that its predecessors were stooped), who first shows up in the fossil record about 1.6 million years ago, and lasts until at least 400,000 years ago. *Homo erectus* has a pivotal position in our history because it was a distinctive species very different from but coexistent with the australopithicines. The brain of this creature was strikingly larger than that of any previous animal, and unlike the australopithicines and *H. habilus,* he was a traveler; his remains have been found in East Africa as well as in Java (Java man) and China (Peking man). Finally, about 100,000 years ago Neanderthal man appeared throughout Europe. The designation of this species remains uncertain, some choosing to call it *H. neanderthalensis* and others calling it *H. sapiens neanderthalensis.* It really does not matter a great deal; Neanderthal man appeared very much like us, except that he was stockier, apparently being built more for strength than for swiftness. The oldest fossil remains of truly modern humans are about 40,000 years old and are widely known both as Cro-Magnon man and as *Homo sapiens sapiens.* The appearance of Cro-Magnon man was sudden, overlapping with Neanderthal man, although only for a few thousand years. Whether Neanderthal man is ancestral to Cro-Magnon man is unknown, but it does appear that Cro-Magnon man was rather different in behavior.

The creation of modern man, from the time at which a creature appeared humanlike to the time at which it was morphologically identical to modern man, took nearly four million years, but throughout much of this time span very little was happening. The final development of the human brain and its associated cognitive processes, however, was very rapid. *Homo erectus* had discovered the use of fire, but the anatomy of the throat is thought to be incompatible with complex speech as we now know it. Neanderthal man had a brain as large as ours, but he too may have had a poorly developed vocal apparatus, suggesting that language was still primitive. Nonetheless, Neanderthal man apparently buried his dead with flowers, arguably the first evidence of religious belief. By 25,000 years ago Cro-Magnon man was producing elaborate paintings on cave walls and carving ivory and stone

figurines, providing the first human culture. The tempo of change quickened in the last 10,000 years. Agriculture and animal husbandry were established in the Middle East by 7000 B.C., followed by ideographic writing in the same region by 3000 B.C. The modern age really began in about A.D. 1500; it is after this time that most of what we see around us today was invented or discovered. Hence although most of what we associate with modern humans is of very recent origin, the basic tools for use (i.e., the brain, free hands, and bipedal locomotion) have been with us a very long time. We can only wonder why it took us so long to use our brain as we now do. The tools of Cro-Magnon man were far more sophisticated than those of Neanderthal man, and unlike Neanderthal man, Cro-Magnon man began to paint cave walls about 25,000 years ago with artwork that is sophisticated even by modern standards. The bones of Cro-Magnon man are identical with those of modern humans; there is little reason to believe that our species has changed at all morphologically in the last 35,000 years.

In conclusion, as we have seen modern humans do not represent the final product of a gradual evolution from monkeys, as was envisioned in Victorian times. Several species of hominid creatures have arisen and disappeared, and throughout much of our recent evolutionary history there has been more than one species of hominid alive at once. None of our ancestors are alive today and, in spite of superficial resemblances to chimpanzees and gorillas, our ancestors diverged from the forerunners of modern apes at least four million years ago, when they developed an upright stance and bipedal locomotion. The importance of this difference cannot be underestimated. Bipedalism is not an easy accomplishment. As Gould has emphasized, bipedalism required a fundamental reconstruction of the anatomy, particularly of the foot and pelvis. By the time

Australopithicus appeared the change was large-ly over. We were already very different from those animals that became chimpanzees and gorillas, and all subsequent changes in our structure were probably only modifications of the existing structure, rather than a qualita-tive change such as was required to walk up-right.

Episodic Evolution of Humankind

Darwin believed that evolution was gradual, largely being shaped by processes of **natural selection** and **sexual selection.** The fossil record in Darwin's time was poorly docu-mented, but the absence of gradual change in the record was of little concern to Darwin; he simply rejected fossils as a source of evidence for evolution. A hundred years after Darwin the fossil record is well documented, but the data remain the same: there is no evidence for gradual change producing new species. Rath-er, speciation occurs very rapidly, probably in a few hundred or thousand years. Thus most species exhibit little significant change during their tenure on earth. They appear in the fossil record looking much the same as when they disappear from it. The view that evolution occurs very rapidly, adopted in the 1980s, marks a major shift in evolutionary biology, and it has important implications for how we view ourselves and our brain. First, the fact that our ancestors seem to appear suddenly in the fossil record is not an unusual characteristic of hominids; it is a characteristic of most spe-cies. Second, the fact that species appear sud-denly and then remain static for hundreds of thousands or even millions of years implies that transitional states are unlikely to be disco-vered. Fossilization of bone only occurs in optimal conditions, and so it is far more likely to find bones of animals that lived a static exist-ence for a million years than it is to find the bones of a transitional stage that may have existed for only a few hundred years. Hence

we may never discover the origins of each of the species depicted in Figure 4–1.

Brain Evolution

Unlike skulls and other bones, soft tissues such as brains do not leave fossil records. Therefore the size and organization of a fossil's brain must be inferred from the shape and size and other dimensions of the inside of the skull. Two measures are commonly considered: cra-nial capacity and sulcal pattern.

Cranial Capacity. The cranial capacity of a skull can provide a reasonable estimate of the size of an animal's brain, but we must be wary of assuming that brain size is an index of intelli-gence. Although it is true that large-brained animals such as chimpanzees appear more in-telligent than smaller-brained monkeys, we must consider three factors. First, intelligent animals are intelligent in different ways. Ani-mals living in such different ecologies as treetops and water may not require the same size brain to generate their movements. Sec-ond, there is a large variation in the size of brains within a given species. Although human brains average about 1300 cm^3, they range from about 1000 cm^3 to nearly 2000 cm^3, with an unreliable correlation with apparent intelli-gence. The organization of the neurons is probably far more important than the mere number. Finally, we must recognize that brain size is biased by body size. The larger one is, the more neurons are required to move the muscles. Nevertheless, in spite of these diffi-culties in interpreting brain size, one is still impressed with the dramatic change in cranial capacity between *A. afarensis* and *H. sapiens,* a difference that is roughly threefold (see Figure 4–2). The brain of the early australopithicines was about the same size as that of a modern chimpanzee, about 400 cm^3. None of the aus-tralopithicines developed particularly large

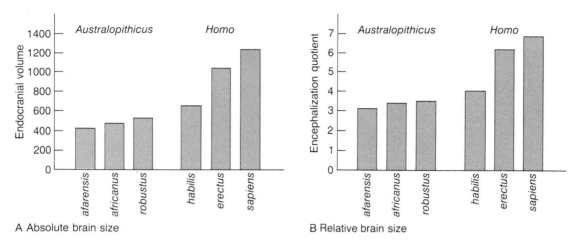

FIGURE 4-2. Endocranial volume (A) and encephalization quotients (B) for fossil hominids. Notice the sudden increase in brain size in *H. erectus.* (Data from McHenry, 1982.)

brains, in spite of the species' living about three million years. The first toolmakers *(H. habilus)* had slightly larger brains, but even theirs were modest, measuring only one-half the size of our brain. The great expansion in brain size obviously occurred in *H. erectus,* because the brain shows an increase in size equal to that of the entire australopithicine brain. The factors that caused the dramatic increase in brain size in *H. erectus* and *H. sapiens* must have done so rather quickly. The sudden appearance of large-brained *H. erectus* implies that there probably was not a gradual selection of individuals with larger brains, but rather having a larger brain must have conferred a large and immediate advantage. Many explanations have been proposed for this change in brain size (e.g., social development, the rigors of an ice age, changes in hunting practices, expansion into more temperature zones), but all of these must remain conjecture, especially since the australopithicines coexisted for thousands of years with *H. erectus* without showing any development of a larger brain.

Is it possible that the increase in cranial capacity in *Homo* is due to the fact that they are simply larger animals than the australopithicines? A number of authors, including Jerison and McHenry, have studied this possibility in detail, arriving at a uniform answer of "no." Arithmetical correction for differences in body weight can be performed in a number of ways, and in every case the *H. erectus* and *H. sapiens* brains are far larger than would be expected for an australopithicine of the same body size (see Figure 4-2). In sum, there is now little doubt that our brain has undergone a major expansion since we adopted a bipedal style of locomotion. Furthermore, whatever factors caused us to walk upright must have been very different from those that caused our brain to enlarge, since these two major changes are separated in time by nearly two million years.

Sulcal Pattern. The increase in cranial capacity is clearly a hallmark of hominid evolution but, as we have noted, mere size is not the major predictor of intelligence; cerebral organization is at least as important. Attempts to infer the organization of a brain from its size or shape are destined to be controversial, as Gall and his fellow phrenologists of the 18th century found out, but our curiosity about the origin of humankind encourages paleontologists and physical anthropologists to try anyway.

The simplest way to estimate organizational pattern is to examine the pattern of sulci and gyri on the surface of cerebral hemispheres. Although this is difficult to infer from the inside of the skull, it is possible to determine the position and relative size of the largest sulci, in part because of the indentations on the skull, which correspond to the location of the large cerebral arteries running along these sulci. A number of distinct sulcal patterns can be identified in this manner. Carnivores, ungulates, and primates, for example, have distinctive patterns that differentiate these mammalian orders. Distinctions among families of animals within orders is more difficult, however. Although the brains of chimpanzees and humans have distinctly different sulcal patterns (a pongid as opposed to a hominid pattern), the determination of one pattern or another from the fossilized skulls of australopithicines has proved to be a hazardous preoccupation. Whereas Holloway has argued that these skulls show a definite hominid pattern, Falk and others have been equally convinced that the pattern is either pongid or cannot be categorized at all. (Readers of the *American Journal of Physical Anthropology* can look forward to periodic new rounds in this debate!) In sum, although there is little doubt that consideration of cerebral organization is at least as important as studies of cranial capacity, the organization of the early hominid brain has not yet been demonstrated. Comparative neurology of living mammals, especially apes, is a more likely source of information about the reorganization of the human brain in hominid evolution, and so it is to these brains that we now direct our attention in the remainder of this chapter.

WHY STUDY NONHUMAN ANIMALS?

To many people, including many psychologists, human neuropsychology is seen as being wholly independent of the study of animals. It is the study of the *human* brain and *human* behavior. This view largely assumes that both human neuroanatomy and human cognitive processes (i.e., thinking) fundamentally differ from those of other animals. After all, humans talk, read, write, and do all sorts of things that no monkey or rat has ever done. It is our view that this line of reasoning is shortsighted and wrong. There is no compelling evidence of a qualitative difference in the structure of the human and chimpanzee brains (see below). One would surely expect there to be such a difference if neuropsychological processes in chimpanzees and humans were fundamentally different. Few psychologists who work with rats or chimps (or any other species) affect a strong interest in rats or chimps for the sake of these animals; their primary interest is in the human brain and in human brain–behavior relations.

Many psychologists agree that comparisons between humans and nonhuman primates such as monkeys and chimpanzees are reasonable, but many argue that comparisons with other species such as rats or cats are not. The evolutionary distance between humans and rats is viewed as too great to allow valid generalizations. Indeed, Lockhart and several other authors have argued that the laboratory rat in particular is an indefensible choice for behavioral research. They argue that it has been bred for laboratory work and so for many purposes is a freak, an unnatural animal, and a degenerate compared with its wild cousins. Although domesticated strains of Norway rats no doubt differ in some ways from their wild cousins, we are in complete agreement with Dewsbury's conclusion that there is little or no evidence that they are "inferior, freaks, unnatural animals or degenerates." Indeed, many aspects of neocortical function in laboratory rats are remarkably similar to those of other mammals, including primates. For example, the effects of frontal-cortex lesions in rats are strikingly similar to those of monkeys and, strangely enough, humans.

We are not proposing that rats are merely little men in white fur suits. They obviously are not. We are proposing that monkeys, rats, and other animals have an important role in the understanding of human brain–behavior relations, and that to dismiss research on them when discussing human neuropsychology is myopic, unreasonable, and enormously wasteful of valuable information. Furthermore, to insist that nonhuman research be done on primates is morally indefensible at this stage in our knowledge. Many species of nonhuman primates are becoming endangered, and many currently relevant questions can best be studied today through the use of animals that are in no danger of extinction.

What questions can best be addressed through study of nonhuman species? There are three such primary lines of neuropsychological research:

1. Studies directed toward an understanding of the basic mechanisms of brain function

2. Studies designed to produce models of human neurological disorders

3. Studies whose aim is to provide a description of the phylogenetic development of the brain

We shall consider each of these separately.

The chief purpose of cross-species comparisons in neuropsychology has been to arrive at an understanding of the basic mechanisms of brain function.

An early example of this method is Harvey's investigation of the function of the heart. In establishing that the blood is transferred by the heart from veins to arteries, Harvey used the fish as a model. In the absence of a secondary circulation to the lungs, the passageway from veins to arteries is apparent. Harvey argued that the pulmonary circulation in mammals had obscured our realization that the function of the heart is the same in all vertebrates. (Diamond and Chow, 1962, p. 174)

In this type of comparative work the species chosen for study depends on the nature of the question under study. For example, neurophysiologists may choose to study the neural activity of giant nerve fibers in the squid because the nerve is so large and accessible. It is assumed that fundamental properties of these nerves are generalizable to mammals and presumably to humans. In addition, sometimes species are merely chosen for convenience; Schneider chose to study hamsters in his work on subcortical visual mechanisms, not because of an intrinsic interest in hamsters, but because the superior colliculus is more accessible in them than in other mammals.

The second goal of comparative work is to produce models of human neurological disorders. The aim is to produce the disorder, then to manipulate numerous variables in order to try to understand the cause of the disorder and its course, and ultimately to formulate a treatment. For example, a model of Parkinson's disease has been developed in the rat—not out of interest in parkinsonian rats per se, but rather to find the causes of their abnormal behaviors and to find treatments to eliminate them. In this type of comparative work animals are really substitutes for humans, and it is assumed that similar principles underlie the cause and treatment of these disorders in humans and nonhumans alike. Indeed, there are strong grounds for supposing that this assumption is valid for the parkinsonian rat. We and our colleagues have found that these animals show most of the symptoms of parkinsonian humans and respond to various pharmacological manipulations in a manner analogous to that observed in humans.

The final rationale for using nonhuman species is to provide a neurology of mammalian behavior that emphasizes the phylogenetic development of the human brain. It is assumed that an understanding of the evolutionary development of the human brain is important both for human neuropsychology and, in a broader perspective, for anthropology and related fields. In addressing this question, the choice of species is critical. Experiments with rats, cats, dogs, and rhesus monkeys do not permit inferences regarding evolutionary development because these animals do not form an evolutionary sequence: rats were never ancestral to cats, nor cats to monkeys. All these species evolved independently from some primitive mammalian ancestor, as shown in Figure 4–3. To do comparative work from a phylogenetic perspective, it is necessary to choose closely related species that constitute what Hodos and Campbell have termed a quasi-evolutionary sequence. Thus, a series of animals should be used that includes the available living descendants of groups that are believed to be ancestors of more advanced forms (see Figure 4–4). For example, Masterton and his colleagues have studied the phylogenetic development of auditory processing by using opossums, hedgehogs, tree shrews, bushbabies, macaques, chimpanzees, and humans. Each succeeding species is believed to have evolved from a species something like the one listed before it.

NEUROANATOMICAL COMPARISONS

The most obvious question to ask is one of the easiest to answer: Is there a significant structural difference between the brains of humans and those of other animals—in particular, other primates? It is not necessary to review the evolution of the brain in detail (see Jerison; Sarnat and Netsky) to answer the question. The answer, quite simply, is that there are no qualitative differences, although there are clear quantitative differences. Consider the following points.

Brain Size

The most obvious characteristic of the human brain is that it is larger than the brains of most other animals. But what does that imply? After all, one might expect this difference simply because the human body is larger. Likewise, the elephant would be expected to have a larger brain than humans, and indeed it is roughly three times larger. Neuroanatomists long ago realized it was necessary to factor out body size, and Snell in 1891 and Dubois in 1897 compared the relative sizes of brains by taking body weight into account. From this earlier work of Snell, Dubois, and others, Jerison developed what he terms the **encephalization quotient,** or **EQ:** the ratio of actual brain size to expected brain size. The expected brain size is a kind of average for living mammals that takes body size into account. Thus, the average, or typical, mammal (which incidentally is the cat) has an EQ of 1.0. Animals that deviate from 1.0 have brains larger or smaller than would be expected for a mammal of that particular body size. Table 4–1 summarizes the EQs for common laboratory animals and for humans. Notice that the rat's EQ is only .4, whereas the human's is 6.30. The rat's brain, then, is only .4 times as large as expected for the typical mammal of that body size, and the brain of a human is 6.3 times as large as expected for the typical mammal of that body size. Notice that the chimpanzee brain is much larger than predicted for a typical mammal of that body size (EQ = 2.48), but the EQ is only about one-third as large as that of the human brain. The EQ makes it clear that the human

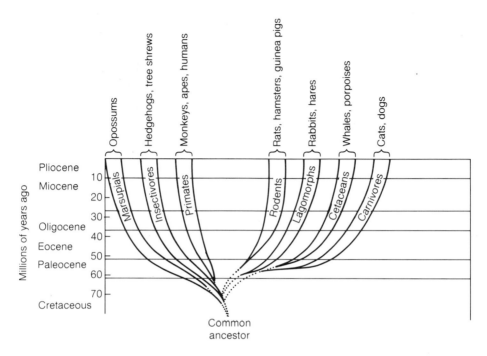

FIGURE 4–3. A phylogenetic tree showing the probable times of origin and affinities of the orders of mammals most commonly studied in comparative psychology and neuropsychology. (After Young, 1952.)

brain is really larger than those of other primates. (This high EQ is not unique to humans, however; the EQ of the dolphin is comparable, having a value of about 6.0.)

Brain Structure

What is the significance of the fact that the human brain is much larger than the brains of other primates? Is the human brain qualitatively different from those other brains, or is it just a larger version of the same basic brain? Stephan and Andy compared the brains of over 60 species of mammals and found that although nearly all structures of the brain increase in size as the EQ increases, it is the neocortex that shows the most dramatic increase. It would seem reasonable to suppose

that if the human brain is different in some way, the difference would most likely be found in the neocortex. This possibility can be considered by comparing the human brain with the brain of other primates using a variety of measures of neocortical structure, including (1) volume and distribution of neocortex and (2) cell density.

Total Neocortex. Stephan and Andy calculated what they called a progression index: the ratio of actual neocortex to the expected neocortex of a typical mammal. (This index is an analogue of the encephalization quotient, except that it measures only the neocortex.) The progression index shows that the volume of human neocortex is 3.2 times greater than the predicted volume for nonhuman primates

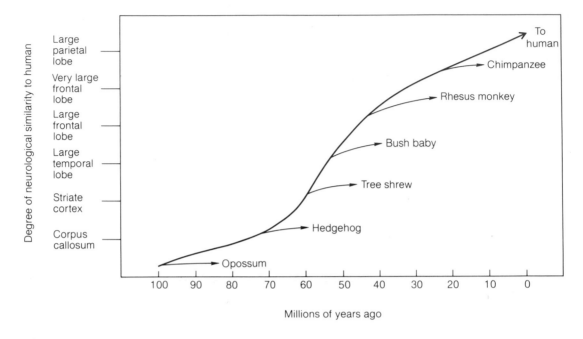

FIGURE 4–4. Phylogenetic relationships among the experimental subjects forming a quasi-evolutionary lineage. Notice that hedgehogs, tree shrews, bush babies, monkeys, and apes are living animals taken to be close approximations of the ancestors of humans. (After Masterton and Skeen, 1972.)

in general and nearly three times greater than that predicted for a chimpanzee of the same body weight. These figures mean that the increase in neocortex from the apes to humans is greater than would have been expected from the trends within the other primates. Where in the neocortex is this increase?

Passingham found that the increase in human neocortex does not appear to occur in the visual, somatosensory, or motor cortex. In fact, there is actually a decrease in the relative extent of area 17. But because there is a trend in primate phylogeny for visual (striate) cortex to decrease relative to total neocortex, this reduction in striate cortex is predictable.

Within primate phylogeny the association cortex increases progressively as a proportion of the total neocortex. Hence, although the association cortex makes up a greater propor-

tion of the human neocortex than would be expected from looking at the chimpanzee brain, Passingham concludes that, given the phylogenetic trend, humans do not have more association cortex than would be predicted for a primate with so much neocortex.

There has been some controversy over whether or not nonhuman primates have any association cortex analogous to the human speech zones. Passingham reviews the evidence and concludes that they do have a posterior speech zone, although the existence of a homologue of Broca's area is still in doubt. We shall return to this question in Chapter 21.

Cell Density. Although the human brain does not differ from other primate brains in gross anatomy, it is reasonable to suppose that

TABLE 4–1

Comparison of brain sizes of species most
commonly studied in neuropsychology [a]

Species	Brain volume (ml)	Encephalization quotient
Rat	2.3	0.40
Cat	25.3	1.01
Rhesus Monkey	106.4	2.09
Chimpanzee	440.0	2.48
Human	1350.0	6.30

[a]Values estimated by using Jerison's formula [EQ = $Ei/(12 \times Pi^{\frac{2}{3}})$ where Ei = actual brain size of species "i," Pi = body size of species "i"] and body and brain values. From Blinkov and Glesner, 1968.

it might differ in fine structure. And it does appear to do so in cell size and density: cell size increases and cell density decreases with increasing volume of neocortex. Thus, as the volume of neocortex increases, neurons increase in size but are spaced further apart, perhaps reflecting an increase in the number of synaptic connections. Although there is a marked change in cell size and density in humans as compared with other primates, Passingham calculates that these changes are predictable given the increase in volume of neocortex.

Conclusion

The overall conclusion that is forced on us for all the differences between human and other primate brains is the most parsimonious one: the main selection pressure was for a larger brain with more association neocortex. In other words, although the human brain is larger than would be expected for a primate of our body weight, this increase in brain size is attributable to a general increase in association cortex. There is no compelling evidence that there is a qualitative difference between the brains of humans and those of other mammals.

FUNCTIONAL COMPARISONS

Each mammalian species has a unique behavioral repertory. There has been a tendency to assume that the brain structures necessary to produce different behaviors must also be unique. This view ignores the fact that mammals share many similar behavioral traits and capacities, although the details of behavior may differ somewhat. For example, all mammalian mothers provide milk and maternal care for their young, although the details of care differ from species to species. Warren and Kolb have thus suggested that there are behaviors and behavioral capacities that could be designated **class-common behaviors:** behaviors common to all members of the phylogenetic class Mammalia. Hence, it is recognized that many behaviors are not species-specific; it is in these behaviors that generalizations in neuropsychology should be most meaningful.

If class-common behaviors are considered to be a basis for generalizing in neuropsychology, it is then possible to argue that there is no qualitative difference in the neural control of sensory, associative, and motor functions in mammals. This position is a direct contradiction of the widely held idea that function in mammals has undergone **encephalization**[1] and **encorticalization.** According to the former concept, during evolution there was a shift of function from lower centers, such as the brainstem, to higher centers, such as the

---

[1]There is some disagreement in the literature as to the use of the term encephalization. For example, Ruch, Patten, Woodbury, and Towe use the term to describe the idea that in the course of evolution the forebrain has increased its domination over the lower midbrain and spinal centers. Other authors use the term to describe the course of ontogenetic development of the brain. We are referring here, however, to the idea of a phylogenetic shift of function from lower to higher structures, especially within the neocortex, and we do not take issue with the other uses of the term.

neocortex and limbic system. According to the latter concept, as the neocortex developed, it assumed functions that were previously controlled by lower structures. If this view were correct, it would imply that the functions of the neocortex would be different in highly corticalized species, such as humans and chimpanzees, from the neocortical functions in species with less neocortex, such as rats or cats. As appealing and widespread as this idea is, it is based on inadequate evidence and can be discredited—as it previously has been by others such as Weiskrantz, Jerison, and Warren. The best evidence that lesions produce class-common behavioral effects actually comes from the very experiments that disconfirm the encephalization concept. So widely held is this concept of encephalization that it is incumbent on us to at least briefly review the evidence against it. This is most easily done by reviewing the evidence demonstrating functional similarities of the sensory, motor, and association cortex among all mammals.

The Visual System

Until recently there was believed to be a steady phyletic progression from rats to monkeys in the severity of the syndrome resulting from destruction of the visual cortex. Rats were considered to be less impaired than cats, cats less impaired than monkeys, and monkeys less affected than humans. Work done in the past five to 10 years has shown that this conclusion was in error, the error resulting from differences in experimental procedure with different species. For example, monkeys are not nearly as impaired as had been believed; earlier studies employed larger lesions that, going beyond the primary visual cortex, included surrounding cortex involved in the visual guidance of behavior. Also, the behavioral assessment techniques used in these studies were crude and misleading, and for one reason or another did

not accurately assess visual capacities after the removal of visual cortex. Recently, Humphrey studied a single monkey, with almost no striate cortex, over a period of years. He observed that the monkey could avoid obstacles and find even small objects such as currants with great efficiency. Humphrey was thus able to demonstrate that the effect of removing the visual cortex was really no more severe in the monkey than in the rat. There is no compelling evidence that the effects of visual cortex lesions differ in humans from those observed in monkeys or rats.

The Auditory System

In a recent review Ravizza and Belmore have shown that the effects of removing the auditory cortex are strikingly similar in many different species of mammals. Monkeys so treated are severely impaired in their ability to approach the site of a brief sound. They can, however, respond differentially to sounds presented at different spatial locations, if the required response is pressing a lever rather than walking through space. This result is apparently also true of other species such as opossums, hedgehogs, bush-babies, and cats. If the functions of the auditory cortex are similar in mammals, they should be affected in the same way by the same variations in experimental parameters, as is true in this illustration.

The Somatosensory System

The sense of touch is organized in a remarkably similar way in mammals, although the fine details vary somewhat. Figure 4–5 illustrates the organization of the somatosensory cortex of rats, cats, and monkeys, and it compares favorably with the similar organization of the human somatosensory cortex illustrated in Figure 1–8. Although the snout of the rat occu-

FIGURE 4–5. Functional divisions of the neocortex of three species of mammals as defined by electrical stimulation and recording. The regions not so defined are called association areas. (From C. N. Woolsey, Organization of somatic sensory and motor areas of the cerebral cortex. In H. F. Harlow and C. N. Woolsey, eds., *Biological and Biochemical Bases of Behavior.* Madison: University of Wisconsin Press, pp. 63–81. Copyright © 1958. Reprinted with permission.)

pies relatively more cortex than that of the monkey, the class-common basic organization is clearly similar.

The Motor System

As for the visual system, it was widely held a decade ago that the effects of motor cortex removal become progressively more serious as one goes from rats to cats to primates. For example, Lassek contrasted the effects of motor cortex removal in monkeys and carnivores, such as cats and dogs, by stating that removal of Brodmann's area 4 in primates causes "an enduring paralysis of isolated movements especially in the digits. A flaccid type of paralysis occurs in the proximal joints whereas the wrists and fingers pass through a period of moderate spasticity" (Lassek, 1954, pp. 65–66). On the other hand, "the motor cortex appears to be largely dispensable in mammals ranking below primates. Ablation of area 4 in the cat or dog is attended by only negligible and transitory deficits" (Lassek, 1954, p. 67).

Lassek's comparison between primates and carnivores is invalid, because it is based on different behaviors. The most profound deficits in monkeys were in manual activities, whereas only posture and locomotion were observed to be disturbed in cats and dogs. It is well known that in monkeys posture and locomotion are less severely disturbed by motor cortex lesions than are manual activities. Furthermore, more recent work on the effects of motor cortex removal in cats has shown a permanent impairment in the ability to manipulate objects and to make controlled extension responses with the forepaw. Rats are not capable of very refined movements of the digits of the forepaws, but even they have deficits in manipulation of food and objects following motor cortex removal. This deficit would easily be overlooked, however, if one simply observed rats making gross movements such as walking or swimming—activities that require little fine control of the digits.

To sum, careful observation shows no difference among mammals in the effects of motor cortex damage. The apparent differences described a decade ago do not reflect a functional difference within the motor cortex of various species, but rather a difference in their most obvious behaviors.

Association Areas

Since the association areas undergo such marked expansion in primates, and in humans in particular, it is reasonable to expect that there might be a qualitative difference in the functions of these regions. But the evidence to date does not support this proposition. Although the higher primates are doubtless capable of more complex associations (i.e., learning) than the lower mammals, lesions of the association cortex have remarkably similar general effects on mammals. This conclusion is in contradiction to much of the prevailing literature. For example, in 1969 Diamond and Hall made a convincing case that the cat had no association cortex in the temporal lobe that could be considered analogous to that found in the primate, suggesting a major difference between carnivores and primates. Recent anatomical and behavioral work indicates that this conclusion was unwarranted. The temporal region had simply not been properly identified in the cat. And Campbell has recently shown that lesions of the temporal association cortex produce deficits in visual learning by cats that are strikingly similar to those observed in primates.

PHYLOGENETIC TRENDS

We have concluded that the major difference between the brains of humans and other mammals is that there is an increase in the volume of neocortex but that the overall organization of the neocortex is similar in all mammals. We do not doubt that this conclusion is correct with respect to the gross functioning of the neocortex, but a careful examination of the details of cortical organization in mammals discloses two trends in mammalian brain development that must be considered when drawing conclusions from nonhuman species. First, there may be an increase in lateralization of function associated with an increase in EQ. Second, there may be an increase in the number of distinct anatomical and functional subregions within the neocortex as it expands in volume. We shall consider each trend in turn.

Lateralization of Function

One of the most striking characteristics of cerebral organization in humans is that many functions are relatively lateralized to one hemisphere or the other. It has been known for over a century that language functions are localized primarily in the left hemisphere of right-handed people and, although specific functions of the right hemisphere were not discovered until more recent times, it has been known for at least 30 years that visuospatial functions are localized primarily in the posterior regions of the right hemisphere. This asymmetry in cerebral organization is a significant feature of human brain organization (see Chapters 14 and 15), and its phylogenetic origins are of particular interest if we are to fully understand its significance in human brain function. Although once believed to be a uniquely human trait, cerebral asymmetry is now thought to represent the result of a trend toward asymmetrical organization of the cerebral hemispheres in the phylogenetic development of the mammalian brain. There is now evidence of anatomical asymmetries in the cerebral hemispheres of rodents, carnivores, and nonhuman primates as well as in the brain endocasts of australopithicines. Thus, just as the human brain is larger and has more cerebral cortex than expected for a mammal of its body size, it is probable that if a "lateralization quotient" analogous to the EQ could be calculated, the human brain would have greater lateralization of function than expected for a mammal of its body size. The presence of cerebral asymmetry in humans, however, does not represent a qualitative difference from other mammals.

Regional Specialization

Although functional and cytoarchitectonic subdivisions can be identified in the cortex of all mammalian species, there is a trend toward increasing numbers of *distinct* neocortical regions as the EQ increases. For example, whereas the auditory cortex of rats can be differentiated easily into only two or three subregions, the analogous cortex of monkeys can be differentiated into at least twice as many subregions. A similar trend is found in other sensory regions as well as in motor and association zones. If we assume that each cytoarchitectonically dissociable region has a distinct functional correlate, then an increase in the number of subregions provides a basis for potential differences between species as the total volume of neocortex increases. Many neuropsychologists believe that it is far-fetched to suppose that all of the cortical subregions in humans are hidden in some diminutive state in animals with modest EQs, as if awaiting some future expansion and development in the human brain, but new functional regions are unlikely to appear suddenly in the human brain. Rather, they presumably result from an elaboration of existing regions, although the processes involved in such an evolution remain a matter of speculation. (See Kaas for an interesting discussion of possible processes.)

Increasing neocortical differentiation into cytoarchitectonic and functional subregions probably provides a basis for increasing sophistication in the processing of sensory information and control of movement in animals with large brains. It does not imply qualitative differences between species, nor does it suggest that class-common behaviors are not mediated by class-common neural functions. It does imply, however, that although most principles of cerebral function can be inferred from studies using animals from throughout the class Mammalia, the fine details of neocortical processing in humans are best inferred from species with large EQs. Although neuroscience has made real progress in identifying general principles of cerebral organization in the past century, we have a very long way to travel before studies using nonhuman species will need to be concentrated on species with large brains such as monkeys and apes.

CONCLUSIONS

The divergence of the human brain from that of other living species has a history of at least four million years. The human brain has undergone a major expansion in the past two million years, but the evidence from the study of fossils as well as of contemporary mammals indicates that the human brain has not undergone a qualitative change. The brains of human and nonhuman primates today differ chiefly in overall size and in the volume of neocortex, rather than qualitatively in cerebral organization. Mammals have to deal with the same basic problems imposed by the environment, and the behavioral capacities to cope with these problems are class-common. The evidence indicates that class-common behaviors are mediated by class-common neural mechanisms sufficiently similar among mammals to permit valid generalizations across species. There is no strong evidence for unique brain-behavior re lations in any species within the class Mammalia. The possibility of considerable generalization across mammalian species does not imply that neuropsychologists should expend their major energies studying rats or monkeys. It does imply, however, that the results of studies on rats, monkeys, and animals of other species are valuable in understanding brain-behavior relations in humans and should not be ignored or dismissed simply because nonhumans do not talk.

REFERENCES

Blinkov, S. M., and J. I. Glesner. *The Human Brain in Figures and Tables*. New York: Basic Books, 1968.

Campbell, A. Deficits in visual learning produced by posterior temporal lesions in cats. *Journal of Comparative and Physiological Psychology* 92:45–57, 1978.

Campbell, C. B. G., and W. Hodos. The concept of homology and the evolution of the nervous system. *Brain, Behavior and Evolution* 3:353–367, 1970.

Dewsbury, D. A. Comparative psychologists and their quest for uniformity. *Annals of the New York Academy of Sciences* 223:147–167, 1973.

Diamond, I. T., and K. L. Chow. Biological psychology. In S. Koch, ed., *Psychology: A Study of a Science,* vol. 4. New York: McGraw-Hill, 1962.

Diamond, I. T., and W. C. Hall. Evolution of neocortex. *Science* 164:251–262, 1969.

Falk, D. A reanalysis of the South African australopithicine natural endocasts. *American Journal of Physical Anthropology* 53:525–539, 1980.

Gould, S. J. *The Panda's Thumb*. New York: Norton, 1980.

Hodos, W., and C. B. G. Campbell. Scale naturae: Why there is no theory in comparative psychology. *Psychological Review* 76:337–350, 1969.

Holloway, R. L. Revisiting the South African Tuang australopithicine endocast: The position of the lunate sulcus as determined by the stereoplotting technique. *American Journal of Physical Anthropology* 56:43–58, 1981.

Holloway, R. L., and M. C. de la Coste-Lareymondie. Brain endocast asymmetry in pongids and hominids: Some preliminary findings on the paleontology of cerebral dominance. *American Journal of Physical Anthropology* 58:101–110, 1982.

Humphrey, N. K. Vision in a monkey without striate cortex: A case study. *Perception* 3:241–255, 1974.

Jerison, H. J. *Evolution of the Brain and Intelligence*. New York: Academic, 1973.

Jerison, H. J. Fossil evidence of the evolution of the human brain. *Annual Review of Anthropology* 4:27–58, 1975.

Johanson, D., and M. Edey. *Lucy: The Beginnings of Humankind*. New York: Warner Books, 1982.

Kaas, J. H. The segregation of function in the nervous system: Why do sensory systems have so many subdivisions? *Contributions to Sensory Physiology* 7:201–240, 1982.

Kolb, B., and I. Q. Whishaw. Generalizing in neuropsychology: Problems and principles underlying inter-species comparisons. In T. E. Robinson, ed., *Behavioral Contributions to Brain Research*. New York: Oxford University Press, 1983.

Lassek, A. M. *The Pyramidal Tract*. Springfield, Ill.: Charles C Thomas, 1954.

Lockhart, R. B. The albino rat: A defensible choice or bad habit. *American Psychologist* 23:734–742, 1968.

Lumsden, C. J., and E. O. Wilson. *Promethean Fire: Reflections on the Origin of Mind*. Cambridge, Mass.: Harvard University Press, 1983.

Masterton, B., and L. C. Skeen. Origins of anthropoid intelligence: prefrontal system and delayed alternation in hedgehog, tree shrew and bushbaby. *Journal of Comparative and Physiological Psychology* 81:423–433, 1972.

McHenry, H. M. Fossils and the mosaic nature of human evolution. *Science* 190:425–431, 1975.

McHenry, H. M. The pattern of human evolution: Studies on bipedialism, mastication, and encephalization. *Annual Review of Anthropology* 11:151–173, 1982.

Passingham, R. E. Anatomical differences between the neocortex of man and other primates. *Brain, Behavior and Evolution* 7:337–359, 1973.

Passingham, R. E. Broca's area and the origins of human vocal skill. *Philosophical Transactions of the Royal Society of London* B 292:167–175, 1981.

Passingham, R. E. *The Human Primate*. San Francisco: Freeman, 1982.

Passingham, R. E. Primate specializations in brain and intelligence. *Symposium of the Zoological Society of London* 46:361–388, 1981.

Passingham, R. E., and G. Ettlinger. A comparison of cortical functions in man and the other primates. *International Review of Neurobiology* 16:233–299, 1974.

Ravizza, R. J., and S. Belmore. Auditory forebrain: evidence from anatomical and behavioral experiments involving human and animal subjects. In R. B. Masterson, ed., *Handbook of Behavioral Neurobiology*. New York: Plenum, 1978.

Ruch, T. C., H. D. Patten, J. W. Woodbury, and A. L. Towe. *Neurophysiology*. London: Saunders, 1965.

Sarnat, H. B., and M. G. Netsky. *Evolution of the Nervous System*. New York: Oxford University Press, 1974.

Schallert, T., I. Q. Whishaw, V. D. Ramirez, and P. Teitelbaum. Compulsive, abnormal walking caused by anticholinergics in akinetic, 6-hydroxydopamine–treated rats. *Science* 199:1461–1463, 1978.

Stanley, S. M. *The New Evolutionary Timetable*. New York: Basic Books, 1981.

Warren, J. M. Evolution, behavior and the prefrontal cortex. *Acta Neurobiologiae Experimentalis* 32:581–593, 1972.

Warren, J. M., and B. Kolb. Generalization in neuropsychology. In S. Finger, ed., *Recovery from Brain Damage*. New York: Plenum, 1978.

Weiskrantz, L. The interaction between occipital and temporal cortex in vision. In F. O. Schmitt and F. G. Worden, eds., *The Neurosciences: Third Study Program*. Cambridge, Mass.: MIT Press, 1974.

Woolsey, C. N. Organization of somatic sensory and motor areas of the cerebral cortex. In H. F. Harlow and C. N. Woolsey, eds., *Biological and Biochemical Bases of Behavior*. Madison: University of Wisconsin Press, 1958.

Young, J. Z. *The Life of Vertebrates*. New York: Oxford University Press, 1962.

PART TWO

BASIC NEUROLOGY

There are a number of reasons why it is very important to the student of neuro-psychology to have a basic grasp of clinical neurology. First, one method by which neuropsychologists study the normal function of the central nervous system is by studying it when it is behaving abnormally. It is therefore of fundamental importance to understand the ways in which the nervous system can become disordered, as well as the methods for identifying and studying these disorders. This need is particularly acute because different disorders affect the nervous system in distinctly different ways, and the inferences that can be drawn about normal function thus differ somewhat according to the exact disorder being studied.

Second, the principles of neuropsychology can be applied in a variety of ways to the treatment of people suffering from neurological disorders. This application, however, requires that the clinical neuropsychologist understand the nature of the disorders well enough to apply the theory most efficiently and appropriately. For example, it is pointless to consider occupational therapy in a person with certain disorders, since the disturbance of cognitive function is profound and irreversible. In other cases, people are able to function fairly normally, working around their sometimes considerable cognitive limitations. The neuropsychologist who fails to fully understand the nature of the disorders afflicting a given patient not only does the patient a disservice but also harms the credibility of the entire field of neuro-psychology itself.

Therefore, the two chapters of Part Two consider the clinical examination and specialized tests used to assess neurological disorders (Chapter 5) as well as providing a basic survey of such disorders (Chapter 6). These chapters introduce an array of specialized terms that are likely to overwhelm the beginning student, but with repeated exposure throughout the book they will become relatively simple and straightforward. One ought not be frightened of them.

5

THE NEUROLOGICAL EXAM
AND CLINICAL TESTS

People suspected of having some disorder of the nervous system are usually examined by a **neurologist,** a physician specializing in the treatment of such disorders. Although a comprehensive understanding of the neurological exam is not essential to an understanding of the basic principles of neuropsychology, a sense of what this exam entails is useful nevertheless, for a number of reasons. First, since a diagnosis is only as reliable as the procedure used to make it, the neuropsychologist should be aware of the limitations of diagnostic procedures. Second, since neuropsychologists often see clients who should be referred for a neurological exam, they should be aware of the procedures involved and the questions that are asked in this type of examination such that they can recognize when to make referrals and what information can be gained by the referral. Finally, since neuropsychological tests are extremely effective in spotting certain brain dysfunctions, the psychologist should be able to understand a neurological report in order to compare diagnoses and make recommendations.

The neurological examination is guided by the principle that every function is abnormal until it is examined and found to be normal. The neurologist first takes a history from the patient and makes a general assessment of the patient's appearance; i.e., what impression does the person's personality, facial appearance, and body structure make? The neurologist then examines every square centimeter of skin and mucous membrane, every orifice, every sensory system and motor function; listens to every sound over the chest, abdomen, head, and blood vessels; and examines every organ system. If what appears to be a deviation is found, it is evaluated with respect to the way and degree it is different from the body part on the opposite side, the body part of family members, and the theoretical norm for a person of like age and sex. In addition, the neurologist may recommend additional tests (EEG, brain scans, etc.) as indicated by the person's history or the initial neurological exam. At the end of an examination the neurologist writes a case summary. This usually consists of a summary of positive and negative historical and physical findings, a provisional diagnosis, a plan for further diagnostic tests to discriminate between diagnostic possibilities, and suggestions for therapy, therapeutic goals, etc. The following section summarizes the types of tests administered by the neurologist and some aspects of the rationale underlying their use.

THE NEUROLOGICAL EXAM

The History

The art of diagnosis has been described as coming to a correct answer with too little information. The neurologist's first step is to ask the patient about the problem, and it is a useful rule of thumb that the patient's first descriptive statement about his or her illness is the most important. Information is collected about the person's own background, with emphasis placed on previous disease, accidents, and the occurrence of symptoms such as headache, attacks of loss of consciousness, and sleep disturbances. Often, incidents that do not seem important to the person can be relevant to the diagnosis of the disorder. Family background is also significant because many diseases, such as epilepsy, have a high familial incidence. While the history is being taken, some aspects of the neurological exam are completed. For example, mental status is assessed (Is the person aware of where he or she is, the date, etc.?), facial features are examined for abnormalities or asymmetries, speech is assessed for abnormalities, and posture is observed. State of awareness is described by adjectives such as alert, drowsy, stuporous, confused, etc. Facial features and behavior reveal whether the person is agitated, anxious, depressed, apathetic, restless, etc. Some of the simpler aspects of memory may be tested by presenting digits and asking for their recall. Delusions and hallucinations are noted when present. The neurologist may also determine whether the person is left- or right-handed and the history of handedness in the family, since this may provide clues about which hemisphere controls speech. A number of simple tests for speech may be given: asking the meaning of words, having rhymes or words repeated (e.g., "la-la," "ta-ta"), having objects named, having the patient read and write.

Although the information obtained in a history gives clues about where emphasis should be placed in the subsequent neurological examination, the neuropsychologist should not accept uncritically the neurologist's evaluation of mental state. Many people who appear lucid on cursory examination are found to have severe impairments when thoroughly tested with appropriate neuropsychological tests.

The Physical Examination

To make a physical examination the neurologist puts out a number of instruments that then guide the course of the examination. These include (1) a measuring tape for measuring head and body size, the size of skin lesions, etc.; (2) a stethoscope for listening to the sounds of the heart, blood vessels, etc., and an otoscope for examining the auditory canal and drum; (3) a flashlight for eliciting pupillary reflexes; (4) tongue blades for depressing the tongue for eliciting the gag reflex, and for eliciting abdominal and plantar reflexes; (5) a vial of coffee for assessing smell, and vials of salt and sugar for taste; (6) a 256 cycle per second tuning fork for testing vibratory sensation and hearing; (7) a cotton wisp for eliciting the corneal reflex and for testing sensitivity to light touch, plastic tubes for testing temperature sensations, and pins for testing pain sensation; (8) a hammer for eliciting muscle stretch reflexes, such as knee jerk; (9) some coins and keys for testing **stereognosis,** the knowledge of objects through touch; and (10) a blood pressure cuff for taking blood pressure.

Examination of the Head

One of the most important parts of the neurological exam is the study of the head. Its general features such as size are assessed and a detailed examination is made of sensory and motor functions. The head is innervated by 12 sets of cranial nerves, many of which have both sensory and motor functions. These nerves have different origins within the brainstem, and their pathways occupy different portions of the brain. The study of their function may reveal malfunctions providing important clues about the location and nature of nervous system damage. Table 5–1 summarizes the cranial nerves, their function, and some of the commoner symptoms that occur after damage to them. Rather than discuss the function of each nerve in detail we shall give some examples from the visual system to illustrate the type of information the neurologist can obtain in the examination.

In examining the eye the neurologist first looks at its external covering, the eyelid. If it droops, a condition called **ptosis,** there is an indication of damage to some portion of the third nerve, which normally elevates it. The visual field can be examined for blind spots or reductions of sensitivity in the area that a person should normally be able to see. The occurrence of visual field defects can reveal quite precisely the existence of damage at nearly any location between the retina and the visual cortex (see Chapter 10). The pupil is controlled by two interocular smooth muscles: the pupilloconstrictor and the pupillodilator muscles of the iris, which act in opposition to each other. When the retina of one eye is illuminated with a light, the pupil constricts to block out most of the light, and at the same time the pupil of the unilluminated eye is constricted through a relay of the third nerve in the midbrain. Thus, the pupillary constriction and the lack of the consensual response of the opposite eye can be used as indicators of possible damage in the retina, optic tract, or midbrain. The pupils also constrict or accommodate when a person looks at a near object. Constriction to accommodation but not to light, the so-called **Argyll Robertson pupil,** has been used to diagnose syphilitic or other damage to midbrain relays of the third nerve. Examination of the optic fundus, or central area of the retina, is done with an ophthalmoscope, which is a light source with a viewing aperture. This allows the condition of blood vessels (which are visible on the retina) to be examined and determination of whether there is blurring or swelling in the central retina. The swelling, called **papilledema,** can indicate the presence of such abnormalities as brain tumors; because cerebrospinal fluid extends along the optic nerve, increased pressure in the brain will be reflected as retinal swelling. Finally, symmetrical movements of the eyes are controlled by the third, fourth, and sixth nerves, and asymmetries may indicate malfunctions of these nerves or of their central relays.

The Motor System

The motor system is examined to assess muscle bulk, tone, and power; to test for the occurrence of involuntary muscle movements such as shaking and tremors; and to assess the status of reflexes. In addition, coordination is examined by having a patient do such tasks as walking heel to toe in a straight line, touching the neurologist's finger and his or her own nose repeatedly, making rapid alternating movements of the fingers, tapping the foot as rapidly as possible, and so on. Generally, all the muscles of the body are tested in head-to-foot order, and the status of each can be recorded on a standard chart.

A knowledge both of reflex and muscle function and of the central motor pathways can

TABLE 5–1

The cranial nerves

Number	Name	Functions	Method of examination	Typical symptoms of dysfunction
I	Olfactory	(s)[a] Smell	Various odors applied to each nostril	Loss of sense of smell (anosmia)
II	Optic	(s) Vision	Visual acuity, map field of vision	Loss of vision (anopsia)
III	Oculomotor	(m)[a] Eye movement	Reaction to light, lateral movements of eyes, eyelid movement	Double vision (diplopia), large pupil, uneven dilation of pupils, drooping eyelid (ptosis), deviation of eye outward
IV	Trochlear	(m) Eye movement	Upward and downward eye movements	Double vision, defect of downward gaze
V	Trigeminal	(s,m) Masticatory movements	Light touch by cotton baton; pain by pinprick; thermal by hot and cold tubes; corneal reflex by touching cornea; jaw reflex by tapping chin, jaw movements	Decreased sensitivity or numbness of face, brief attacks of severe pain (trigeminal neuralgia); weakness and wasting of facial muscles, asymmetrical chewing
VI	Abducens	(m) Eye movement	Lateral movements	Double vision, inward deviation of the eye
VII	Facial	(m) Facial movement	Facial movements, facial expression	Facial paralysis
VIII	Auditory vestibular	(s) Hearing	Audiogram tests hearing; stimulate by rotating patient or by irrigating the ear with hot or cold water (caloric test)	Deafness, sensation of noise in ear (tinnitus); disequilibrium, feeling of disorientation in space
IX	Glossopharyngeal	(s,m) Tongue and pharynx	Test for sweet, salt, bitter, and sour tastes on tongue; pharyngeal or gag reflex by touching walls of pharynx	Partial dry mouth, loss of taste (ageusia) over posterior third of tongue, anesthesia and paralysis of upper pharynx
X	Vagus	(s,m) Heart, blood vessels, viscera, movement of larynx and pharynx	Observe palate in phonation, palatal reflex by touching palate	Hoarseness, lower pharyngeal anesthesia and paralysis, indefinite visceral disturbance
XI	Spinal accessory	(m) Neck muscles and viscera	Movement, strength, and bulk of neck and shoulder muscles	Wasting of neck with weakened rotation, inability to shrug
XII	Hypoglossal	(m) Tongue muscles	Tongue movements, tremor, wasting or wrinkling of tongue	Wasting of tongue with deviation to side of lesion on protrusion

[a] s and m refer to sensory or motor functions (or both) of the nerve.

make possible a fairly accurate estimate of the location and nature of possible central motor damage. Various types of motor dysfunction are also characteristic of certain motor diseases. For example, people with Parkinson's disease may show limb tremors when they are resting that are reduced or absent when they move. The analysis of reflexes can give important clues about the nature and function of nervous system damage, since some reflexes, such as the knee jerk, involve only spinal circuits, whereas others, such as abdominal reflexes, involve circuits that course through the brainstem, midbrain, or cortex. In addition, as we have indicated previously, different motor pathways cross from one side of the body to another at different levels of the nervous system. This arrangement allows the locations of lesions to be deduced, for when motor deficits occur in a person, a lesion must be located at a point where motor pathways lie adjacent.

The Sensory Systems

A complete sensory examination includes investigation of sensitivity to painful stimulation, touch, temperature, vibration sense, joint position sense, two-point discrimination, tactile localization, stereognosis (recognition of objects by touch alone), and **graphesthesia** (the ability to identify numbers or letters traced on the skin with a blunt object). These sensory tests allow the functions of individual sensory systems to be assessed and also give information about the location of possible dysfunctions. For example, if a person has no tactile sensation in a hand, there could be a problem with the spinal cord or with peripheral nerves. If the person can feel a stimulus but not recognize what it is, the problem is likely at a cortical level. Comparing functions of different sensory systems and comparing sensory functions with motor functions also give information about the location of possible dysfunctions.

For example, pain and pressure information from a given part of the body have separate routes through the spinal cord; pain fibers cross to the opposite side of the cord on entering, but the pathways are adjacent through the brainstem, where pressure fibers also cross. Thus, weakness in one modality and not the other may indicate a spinal problem, whereas weakness in both may indicate a problem in the brainstem or higher. Similarly, because sensory fibers lie adjacent to particular motor fibers at some levels of the nervous system but are separate at others, sensory and motor deficits that occur together provide diagnostic clues.

CLINICAL TESTS

A variety of clinical tests have been designed to quantify and augment the neurological exam and assist in diagnosis. It would be unusual for all the tests to be done on a single patient, but because all the tests are widely used we shall describe what they are intended to do.

Electroencephalography

Electroencephalography, more commonly called EEG analysis, consists of sampling the electrical activity of the cortex through electrodes posted on specific areas of the skull. The electrical fluctuations are usually amplified and displayed on an ink-writing polygraph. EEG analysis is only a very crude measure of the underlying brain activity, because it gives a measure of only the summed activity of millions of dendrites. Nevertheless, abnormalities in dendritic activity can be diagnostic of conditions of epilepsy, brain tumors, or other disorders. In cases of suspected epilepsy abnormal discharges may be present in the absence of overt epileptic signs such as convulsions, or the discharges may be elicited by various drugs or by such photic stimuli as a flashing strobe light. Differential recordings made with different combinations of electrodes can be used to quite accurately localize the source of abnormal brain activity.

Electromyography

Electromyography, or **EMG,** is the analysis of the electrical activity of muscles. The record is made by inserting a needle electrode into the muscle to be tested. When a normal muscle is completely relaxed, no electrical activity can be recorded, but as contraction occurs a characteristic recording, somewhat similar in appearance to an EEG recording, is produced. EMG recordings are useful for diagnosing the presence of damage or abnormalities in the nerves innervating the muscles from which recordings are being obtained. For example, in disease of the motor neurons of the spinal cord there is a marked reduction in the number of spikes present in the record, because there are fewer normal motor neurons to contract the muscles. By using the EMG the neurologist is able to diagnose the disorder and to evaluate its extent in the spinal cord.

Cerebrospinal Fluid Studies

Analysis of cerebrospinal fluid (CSF) provides the only method of looking at the subarachnoid space without opening the skull. CSF is most easily obtained by a puncture made in the lumbar, or lower, portion of the spinal column. CSF is removed for a variety of purposes: (1) to relieve intracranial pressure and to remove toxic, inflammatory, or other substances in the CSF, as would be found in disorders such as encephalitis or meningitis; (2) to allow an analysis of the CSF for the presence of blood (indicating a vascular accident) or a variety of other substances that might indicate the presence of a variety of central nervous system dysfunctions; (3) to introduce therapeutic sub-

stances into the subarachnoid space; and (4) to introduce air or opaque media for radiographic studies (see below).

Roentgenography

Roentgenography, or photography using x-rays, has been modified in a number of ways to serve in nervous system diagnosis. *Routine* x-rays are used to scrutinize the skull for evidence of fractures, calcification, or erosion of bone. **Contrast x-rays** can be obtained after special radio-opaque dye or air is injected into the ventricles or dye is injected into the arteries. Having a different density from surrounding areas, these introduced substances can be visualized, along with the outline of the arteries or ventricles, on the x-ray negatives. These procedures also make it possible to delineate the presence of occlusions or of swellings in the vessels, displacements of vessels or ventricles (indicative of the presence of a tumor), and sometimes actual visualization of a tumor.

The use of the x-ray technique after dye is injected into the vertebral or carotid artery is called **angiography;** Figure 5–1 shows an example of an angiogram. Angiography is particularly valuable in diagnosing and locating vascular abnormalities and some tumors, since they can be visualized in the x-ray. For example, if an artery appears displaced from its usual position, it can be inferred that something, such as a tumor, has developed, pushing the artery out of place. In **pneumoencephalography,** x-rays are taken after the cerebrospinal fluid is replaced by air introduced by a lumbar puncture. By manipulating the posture of the patient the radiologist is able to force the air to travel through the ventricular system. Since the air can be seen on an x-ray, it is possible to locate blockages in the ventricles, displacements in their position (as might occur with a tumor), or enlargements of them as occurs in hydrocephalus. Ventriculography is a similar technique, except that the air or an opaque me-

FIGURE 5–1. A normal carotid angiogram. The face is pointed down to the left. Number key: 2, callosomarginal artery; 4, internal carotid artery; 8, anterior cerebral artery; 9a, middle cerebral artery; 11, anterior choroidal artery; 13, posterior communicating artery; 16, ophthalmic artery; 18, approximate end of the Sylvian fissure. (From S. J. DeArmond, M. M. Fusco, and M. Dewey, *Structure of the Human Brain: A Photographic Atlas,* 2nd ed. New York: Oxford University Press. Copyright 1976, by Oxford University Press, Inc. Reprinted with permission.)

dium is introduced into the ventricle through a cannula inserted through the skull. It is chiefly used when there is an increase in intracranial pressure and when other procedures have not proved enlightening.

Radioisotope Scanning

In the radioisotope scan (or brain scan) an intravenous injection of a radioisotope is given, and the cranial surface is then scanned with a Geiger counter. Any alteration in blood supply can be detected, including the alterations associated with the growth of a tumor (see Figure 5–2).

Computer-Assisted Imaging

Several new techniques have been devised with which the brain can be imaged by the use of sophisticated computer technology. These include computerized transaxial tomography, positron emission tomography, and nuclear magnetic resonance.

FIGURE 5–2. Radioisotope scan (brain scan) showing a tumor as a darkened area. (From R. Bannister, *Brain's Clinical Neurology,* 5th ed. Oxford: Oxford University Press. Copyright 1978 by Oxford University Press, Inc. Reprinted with permission.)

Computerized Transaxial Tomography (CT Scan). With conventional x-rays the two-dimensional projections of a three-dimensional body appear on the x-ray films as overlapping structures that are difficult to distinguish from one another; the **CT scan,** on the other hand, provides a three-dimensional representation of the brain. The CT scan works on the mathematical principle that a three-dimensional object can be reconstructed from the infinite set of all its projections. In actuality, a finite set is used to produce a rough approximation. Briefly, the technique is as follows. A narrow beam of x-rays is passed through the brain from one side of the head and the amount of radiation not absorbed by the intervening tissue is absorbed by radiation detectors (Figure 5–3). The x-ray tube is moved laterally across the patient's head and the amount of radiation detected is recorded at 160 equally spaced positions. These data are stored in a computer. The x-ray beam is then rotated one degree and the procedure is repeated. In all, the beam is rotated through 180 degrees. When all the projections are completed, the resulting x-ray sums (160 × 180) are processed by the computer. A reconstruction of the patient's head in cross section is then printed out by the computer (see Figure 5–4). Ordinarily, eight or so cross sections are printed out, allowing a simple noninvasive examination of the patient's brain in about 25 minutes.

The CT scanner is an expensive apparatus, but it has become an indispensable tool in neurology because of its greater safety, speed, and accuracy compared with other x-ray techniques. Its greatest potential lies in locating tumors, assessing vascular accidents and head injuries, and in locating a variety of intracranial lesions or brain atrophy. In fact, neurologists have become so dependent on the CT scan that it is nearly impossible to attract neurologists to communities that do not have a CT scanner. As valuable as this machine is, however, it is not perfect and cannot identify many neurological abnormalities, such as epilepsy.

FIGURE 5–3. Schematic illustrations of imaging techniques. A. The CT scan makes use of a rapidly rotating x-ray source that takes hundreds of pictures, which are fed into a computer and compiled into one image. B. PET measures gamma rays resulting from the collision of a positron and an electron. Only those rays that strike opposite detectors are recorded, allowing the computer to determine the line along which the positron was emitted. C. Patients must lie down for the imaging procedures, with their heads placed within the machine.

FIGURE 5–4. Examples of CT scans. A. A blood clot from a hemorrhage caused by a blow to the skull; it is the white patch on the left side. Diagonally opposite the clot is a shallow pool of blood on the surface of the right hemisphere resulting from a "contracoup" injury. The ventricles (center) were compressed by the swelling on both sides of the brain. B. Scan of a meningioma in the right frontal lobe. The ventricles are quite distinct in this scan. (From S. S. Kety, Disorders of the Human Brain. *Scientific American,* 241:202–214, 1979. Copyright © 1979 by Scientific American, Inc. All rights reserved.)

Positron Emission Tomography (PET). **PET** is a visual technique in which the subject is given a radioactively labeled compound such as glucose, which is metabolized by the brain, and the radioactivity is later recorded by a special detector. Unlike the CT scan, PET measures the metabolic activity of different brain regions, the idea being that the most active areas at any given time will use more glucose and hence the radioactivity will be more concentrated there.

The detection of radiation in PET is not as straightforward as in traditional brain scans and requires some discussion. Briefly, elements become unstable when the number of electrons is not balanced by an equal number of oppositely charged protons. In the event that a compound has more protons than electrons, the excess protons can be released in the form

of neutrons and positrons. If the released positrons collide with electrons, both particles are annihilated, resulting in the formation of two gamma rays, each moving in opposite directions. Unlike electrons and positrons, which travel only short distances, gamma rays are very energetic and can travel a considerable distance. Thus in PET it is the gamma rays that are detected since they can escape the brain tissue and pass through the skull to strike detectors (Figure 5–3).

In most current applications of PET, the subject is given a compound such as fluorodeoxyglucose, containing fluorine 18, a very unstable form of fluorine with a half-life of only about 17 minutes. Since glucose is the only source of energy used by the brain, the fluorine is quickly transported to the brain, with the most active neural areas receiving the largest quantities. Positrons are emitted, gamma rays are formed when the positrons collide with electrons, the gamma rays leave the brain, and the detector monitors the number of them. The origin of the gamma rays can be mapped by a computer, thereby producing an image of the brain. Regions of higher metabolic activity will release more gamma rays, because they will take up more labeled glucose to support their neural activity. The computer color-codes the intensity of gamma radiation, producing a brain map in which different colors represent differences in brain activity.

This technique is not as accurate as the CT scan, and it is more expensive, but it offers the unique advantage that the image conveys information about metabolic processes taking place in the brain. At present, PET is being used largely as a research tool (see Chapter 14), but it is likely to become especially useful in the diagnosis and treatment of diseases that have a chemical origin.

Nuclear Magnetic Resonance (NMR). **NMR** is based on the principle that certain atoms, such as hydrogen, behave like tiny spinning magnets. Normally atoms are pointed randomly in different directions, but when they are placed in a magnetic field, they line up in parallel as they orient themselves with respect to the field's lines of force. Atoms spin, and because they are not perfectly symmetrical they wobble; the nuclei of different elements wobble at different frequencies since each element has a different weight. It turns out that if radio waves are beamed across the atoms at right angles to the magnetic field, they will cause the spinning nuclei to wobble synchronously. When the radio waves are turned off, the synchrony induces a voltage in the magnetic field (this is called magnetic resonance), which is picked up by a coil of wire around the tissue. As in the previous scanning techniques, the location of different wobbling

atoms is analyzed by computer and reconstructed as an image of the brain.

NMR images are most easily obtained from the resonance of hydrogen atoms, which is fortunate because the human body is rich in hydrogen and many hydrogen-rich molecules are known to be altered by many disease states. The images from NMR look very similar to those from CT scans, although the way they are generated is somewhat different. NMR shows the makeup and surroundings of cells whereas CT scans reveal only their density. Like PET, NMR is still largely experimental, but it is thought to be the scanner of the future. Some people believe that since NMR is more sensitive in detecting abnormalities than the CT scan, it will replace the CT scan in the next decade as the imaging technique of choice, although it is more expensive and demands higher overhead costs than the CT scan.

Neuromagnetic Measurement

Neurons maintain an electrical potential across their outer membrane, and when electrical potentials are summed, it is possible to record them, yielding the EEG, which reflects this activity. Under many conditions these same currents generate magnetic fields, which can also be recorded outside the skull, producing a magnetoencephalogram (MEG). It is only recently that the technology has become available for the measurement of these minute magnetic fields; but the technique has promise to offer a significant advance over conventional EEG. The principle advantages of MEG are that the potentials can be sensed at specific locations, which is very difficult with EEG, and that unlike electrical potentials, magnetic potentials are unaffected by the skull. MEG has been used successfully to localize epileptiform activity in the human brain, offering a better indication of the focus than standard EEG, although the cost is currently substantially higher than for EEG.

THE NEUROPSYCHOLOGICAL EXAM

Imaging systems are becoming indispensible in neurology, but they do not replace a careful neurological exam. Much can be learned about disease processes by a careful study of behavioral symptoms, especially in a careful investigation of the visual and somatosensory systems. As we shall see in subsequent chapters, the visual system courses directly through the brainstem, so that any abnormality in the brainstem can affect visual processing, including the control of eye movements, the precise symptoms depending on the locus of the pathology. Similarly, in the somatosensory system differences in effects on the senses of fine touch and pressure as opposed to effects on the senses of pain and temperature can be very useful in identifying disease processes in the spinal cord of the brainstem. Fancy machinery is an important addition to the neurologist's arsenal of tests, but it does not replace careful observation of behavior, either by the neurologist or, as we shall see throughout this book, the neuropsychologist.

The neurologist carefully examines primarily the sensory and motor functions but leaves other nervous system functions, especially those involved in cognition (i.e., thought) to the neuropsychologist. Indeed, it is not uncommon for patients to exhibit no neurological impairment at all in the neurological exam, only to be found to have clear neuropsychological deficits. This is because many neuropsychological deficits are not obvious without careful assessment of cognitive functions by tests of memory, intelligence, problem solving, and spatial relations, among others. These tests may take six to eight hours to administer, and so it is hardly surprising that a neurologist is unable to assess them in a cursory mental status exam. Neuropsychology is a relatively new field, but it has become a useful tool, and

in many cases a necessary one, in the diagnosis and treatment of neurological disorders. We shall discuss the procedures of neuropsychological assessment in detail at the end of the book because they are best discussed in the context of neuropsychological theory. However, in order to demonstrate the usefulness of neuropsychological assessment we shall provide an example here.

Mr. R., a 21-year-old left-handed man, had struck his head on the dashboard in a car accident two years prior to our seeing him. He was unconscious for a few minutes, but other than a cut on the right side of his forehead and amnesia for the period just before and after the accident, Mr. R. appeared none the worse for his mishap. Prior to his accident Mr. R. was an honor student at a university, with plans to attend professional or graduate school. However, a year after the accident he had become a mediocre student who had particular trouble completing his term papers on time, and although he claimed to be studying harder than he had before the accident, his marks had fallen drastically in courses requiring memorization. He was referred for a neurological exam by his family physician, but it proved negative and an EEG and a CT scan failed to demonstrate any abnormality. He was referred to us for neuropsychological assessment, which revealed several interesting facts. First, Mr. R. was one of about one-third of left-handers whose language functions are represented in the right rather than the left hemisphere. This discovery was significant not only in interpreting his difficulties but also in the event that Mr. R. should ever require neurosurgery, since the surgeon would want to respect the speech zones of the neocortex. In addition, although Mr. R. had a superior IQ, his verbal memory and reading speed were low-average, which is highly unusual for a person of his intelligence and education. These deficits indicated that his right temporal lobe may have been slightly damaged in the car accident, resulting in an impairment of his language skills. On the basis of our neuropsychological investigation we were able to recommend vocations to Mr. R. that did not require superior verbal memory skills, and he is currently studying architecture. This example illustrates that many effects of brain damage are subtle and difficult to detect without careful neuropsychological assessment. Even the most astute neurologist would have been unable to detect Mr. R.'s deficits without using extensive neuropsychological testing. Indeed, we anticipate that as neuropsychology continues to develop, neurology will place increasing demands on neuropsychological assessment as a tool in the diagnosis of cortical dysfunction.

REFERENCES

Barth, D. S., W. Sutherling, J. Engel, Jr., and J. Beatty. Neuromagnetic localization of epileptiform spike activity in the human brain. *Science* 218:891–894, 1982.

Bannister, R. *Brain's Clinical Neurology,* 5th ed. New York: Oxford University Press, 1978.

Curtis, B. A., S. Jacobson, and E. M. Marcus. *An Introduction to the Neurosciences.* Philadelphia: Saunders, 1972.

DeArmond, S. J., M. M. Fusco, and M. Dewey. *Structure of the Human Brain: A Photographic Atlas,* 2nd ed. New York: Oxford University Press, 1976.

Deecke, L., H. Weinberg, and P. Brickett. Magnetic fields of the human brain accompanying voluntary movement: Bereitschaftsmagnetfeld. *Experimental Brain Research* 48:144–148, 1982.

DeMyer, W. *Technique of the Neurologic Examination.* New York: McGraw-Hill, 1974.

Edelson, E. Scanning the body magnetic. *Science* 83(4):60–65, 1983.

Gordon, R., G. T. Herman, and S. A. Johnson. Image reconstruction from projections. *Scientific American* 233:56–68, Oct., 1975.

Jaffe, C. C. Medical imaging. *American Scientist* 70:576–585, 1982.

Kety, S. S. Disorders of the human brain. *Scientific American* 241:202–214, 1979.

Pykett, I. L. NMR imaging in medicine. *Scientific American* 246:78–88, 1982.

Raichle, M. E. Positron emission tomography. *Annual Review of Neuroscience* 6:249–267, 1983.

6

NEUROLOGICAL DISORDERS

The normal functioning of the central nervous system can be affected by a number of disorders, the commonest of which are headache, tumors, vascular disorders, infections, epilepsy, trauma from head injury, demyelinating diseases, and metabolic and nutritional diseases. The following is a brief overview of those disorders that a neuropsychologist is most likely to encounter either clinically or in the literature.

VASCULAR DISORDERS

A neuron or glial cell can be damaged by any process that interferes with its energy metabolism, whether it be a reduction in oxygen or glucose, an introduction of some poison or toxic substance, or, more important, an interruption in blood supply. Vascular disease can produce serious—even total—reduction of both oxygen and glucose, resulting in a critical interference of cellular energy metabolism. If such interference is longer than 10 minutes, all cells in the affected region die. Cerebral vascular diseases are among the most frequent causes

of death and chronic disability in the Western world. They are of particular concern to the neuropsychologist, because neuropsychology plays an important role in assessing the effects of vascular disorders on cognitive functioning, especially for the planning and assessment of rehabilitative efforts.

The brain receives its blood supply from two *internal carotid* and two *vertebral* arteries, one of each in either side of the body, as shown in Figure 6–1. The internal carotid arteries enter the skull at the base of the brain and give off a number of smaller arteries and two major arteries, the *anterior cerebral artery* and the *middle cerebral artery,* which irrigate the anterior and middle portions of the cortex. The vertebral arteries enter at the base of the brain and then join together to form the *basilar artery.* After giving off several smaller arteries that irrigate the cerebellum, the basilar artery then divides into the *posterior cerebral artery,* which irrigates the medial temporal lobe and the posterior occipital lobe (Figure 6–2).

The middle cerebral and posterior cerebral arteries are actually joined together on each

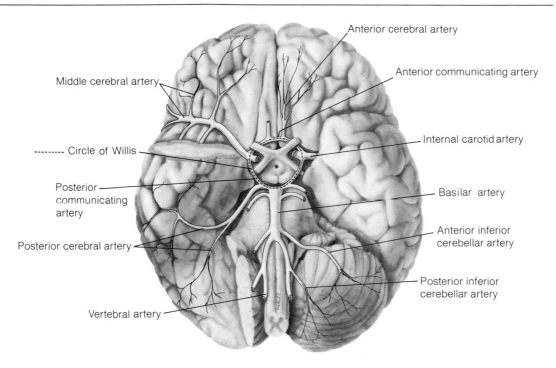

FIGURE 6–1. Major arteries of the brain viewed from below. The cerebellum and temporal lobe on the right hemisphere (left side of figure) have been cut away to reveal the pattern of irrigation, normally hidden from view. The connections formed by the anterior and posterior communicating arteries form the circle of Willis.

A Anterior cerebral artery   B Middle cerebral artery   C Posterior cerebral artery

FIGURE 6–2. Distribution of the major cerebral arteries in the hemispheres: top, lateral view; bottom, medial view.

side by the *posterior communicating artery,* and
the two cerebral arteries are joined by the
anterior communicating artery. These interconnections of arteries form the *circle of Willis,*
which may compensate a half of the brain that
has lost one of its carotid or vertebral arteries.
In swimming mammals the circle of Willis
may also rapidly equalize arterial pressure in
the two hemispheres during diving.

The distribution zones of the anterior, middle, and posterior cerebral arteries are shown in
Figure 6–2. Notice, however, that these arteries irrigate not only the cortex but also subcortical structures, as shown in Figure 6–3. Thus,
a disruption of blood flow to one of these
arteries has serious consequences for subcortical as well as cortical structures. As we shall see
in ensuing chapters, the occurrence of both
cortical and subcortical damage following
vascular accident is a major reason why studying the victims of vascular accidents is such a
difficult way to study brain function.

The veins of the brain are classified as external and internal cerebral veins and cerebellar
veins. The venous flow does not follow the
course of corresponding arteries but follows a
pattern of its own, eventually flowing into a
system of venous sinuses that drain the dura.
Because adequate illustration of the venous-
sinal drainage system requires more technical
detail than is appropriate for this book, the
interested reader is referred to more advanced
discussions for more detail.

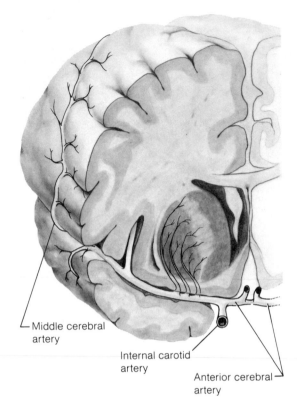

Middle cerebral
artery

Internal carotid
artery

Anterior cerebral
artery

FIGURE 6–3. Irrigation of the deep structures of the
brain by the same arteries as irrigate the surface structures. Interruption of the blood supply can thus produce
both cortical and subcortical damage. (After Raichle, de
Vivo, and Hanaway, 1978.)

Symptoms and Diagnosis
of Vascular Disorders

A common term used in discussion of cerebral
vascular disorder is stroke, or **cerebral vascular accident.** By **stroke** is meant a sudden
appearance of neurological symptoms as a result of severe interruption of blood flow.
Stroke can result from a wide variety of different vascular diseases, but not all vascular disorders produce stroke, for the onset of dys-

function can be insidious, spanning months or
even years. Stroke often produces an **infarct,**
an area of dead or dying tissue resulting from
an obstruction of the blood vessels normally
supplying the part.

Most disease of the cerebral vascular system
affects the arterial system, disease of venous
drainage being uncommon in the central nervous system. The type of damage, or **lesion,** its
extent, and its symptoms depend on a number
of factors, including especially the size of the
blood vessel involved, the health of the remaining vessels, the presence of preexisting
vascular lesions, the location of tissue in-

volved, the type of disorder, and the presence of anastomoses. These will now be discussed in turn.

Size of Blood Vessel. If small blood vessels, such as capillaries, are interrupted, the effects are more limited than the often devastating consequences of damage to large vessels, such as the major arteries diagrammed in Figure 6–2. Disturbance of these arteries can result in lesions that include large portions of the brain and produce serious deficits in behavior.

Health of Remaining Vessels. If a stroke or other cerebral vascular disorder occurs in one restricted portion of unusual weakness, the prognosis may be rather good, because vessels in surrounding zones are often able to supply blood to at least some of the deprived area. On the other hand, if a stroke affects a region that is surrounded by weak or diseased vessels, the effects may be much more serious, because there is no possibility of compensation; in addition, the surrounding weak zones may be at an increased risk of stroke themselves.

Presence of Preexisting Vascular Lesions. A small vascular lesion in a healthy brain will, in the long run, have a good prognosis for substantial recovery of function. However, in the event of preexisting vascular lesions, the effects of the second lesions may be extremely variable. The lesions can sum to obliterate a functional zone of brain tissue, producing serious consequences. Or, less commonly, the lesions can produce what is known as a serial lesion effect, in which case there is remarkably little chronic effect of the second lesion. Although the mechanism of the serial lesion effect is unknown (see Chapter 25), the phenomenon is assumed to result from the process of recovery from the first lesion.

Location of Tissue Involved. The behavioral symptoms following vascular lesions de-

pend, as with other lesions, on the exact location of damage. For example, a lesion in the primary visual cortex can produce an area of blindness, a lesion in the hippocampus can produce an impairment in memory, and a lesion in the medulla can produce arrest of breathing, resulting in death. Thus, the behavioral symptoms resulting from vascular disorder are important clues to the neurologist in locating the area of brain damage and assessing the extent.

Type of Disorder. Exact symptoms of vascular disorder depend on the precise nature of the disorder. Slowly developing disorders can be expected to produce symptoms that differ from those of disorders of sudden onset. Warning symptoms of many disorders may be similar, however; these include headache, if there is compression of the brain, as well as dizziness and vomiting.

Presence of Anastomoses. An **anastomosis** is a connection between parallel blood vessels that allows them to intercommunicate their blood flows. The presence of an anastomosis in the brain thus allows cerebral blood supply to take more than one route to a given region. If one vessel is blocked, a given region might therefore be spared an infarct because the blood has an alternate route to the affected zone. The presence of anastomoses is highly idiosyncratic among individuals, making it very difficult to predict the extent of damage resulting from a stroke to a given vessel. The difficulty is exacerbated by substantial variation in the exact route of even major blood vessels in the brain.

Types of Vascular Disorders

Of the numerous vascular disorders that affect the central nervous system, the commonest are encephalomalacias, cerebral hemorrhage, angiomas, and arteriovenous aneurysms, each of which will now be described.

Encephalomalacias. Encephalomalacias (encephalomalacia means literally "softening of the brain") are vascular disorders that produce a softening of the brain resulting from inadequate blood flow. Decreases in blood flow can have any of three causes: (1) a thrombosis: a plug or clot, in a blood vessel, of blood that has coagulated and remains at the point of its formation; (2) an **embolism:** a clot or other plug brought through the blood from another vessel and forced into a smaller one, where it obstructs circulation. An embolism can be a blood clot, a bubble of air, a deposit of oil or fat, or a small mass of cells detached from a tumor. Curiously, embolisms most frequently affect the middle cerebral artery of the left side of the brain; (3) reduction of blood flow such that not enough oxygen and glucose are supplied. This reduction in blood flow can result from a variety of factors that produce narrowing of the vessels. The commonest example of such narrowing is **cerebral arteriosclerosis,** a condition marked by thickening and hardening of the arteries. Other causes of narrowing include inflammation of vessels (vasculitis) or spasm of the vessels.

Aside from embolism, which produces sudden onset, encephalomalacias usually develop gradually, taking hours or sometimes days. The disease may also be episodic, in which case it may be termed cerebral vascular insufficiency or **transient ischemic** attacks to indicate the variable nature of the disorder. The onset of transient attacks is often abrupt, frequently occurring as fleeting sensations of giddiness or impaired consciousness.

Cerebral Hemorrhage. Cerebral hemorrhage is a massive bleeding into the substance of the brain. The most frequent cause is high blood pressure (hypertension). Other causes are congenital defects in cerebral arteries, blood disorders such as leukemia, or toxic chemicals. Onset of cerebral hemorrhage is abrupt and may quickly prove fatal. It usually occurs during waking hours, presumably because the person is more active and thus has higher blood pressure. Prognosis is poor in cerebral hemorrhage, especially if the patient is unconscious for more than 48 hours.

Angiomas and Aneurysms. Angiomas are congenital collections of abnormal vessels, including capillary, venous, or arteriovenous (A-V) malformations, that result in abnormal blood flow. Angiomas are composed of a mass of enlarged and tortuous cortical vessels that are supplied by one or more large arteries and are drained by one or more large veins, most frequently in the field of the middle cerebral artery. By causing abnormal blood flow, angiomas may lead to stroke, because they are inherently weak, or to inadequate distribution of blood in the regions surrounding the vessels. In some cases arterial blood may actually flow directly into veins after only briefly, or sometimes not at all, servicing the surrounding brain tissue.

Aneurysms are vascular dilations resulting from localized defects in the elasticity of the vessel. These can be visualized as balloonlike expansions of vessels, which are usually weak and prone to rupture. Although aneurysms are usually due to congenital defects, they may also develop from hypertension, arteriosclerosis, embolisms, or infections. Symptoms of aneurysm especially include severe headache, which may be present for years because of pressure on the dura from the aneurysm.

Treatment of Vascular Disorders

Most vascular disorders have no specific treatment, although the commonest remedies include support and surgery. Supportive measures include anticoagulants to dissolve clots or prevent clotting, agents to produce vasodilation, drugs to reduce blood pressure, and hypertonic solutions or steroids to reduce cerebral edema (swelling). Surgical techniques have been greatly improved in recent years but are practical only for some disorders. For example, the only certain cure for aneurysm is total removal, which is usually not feasible. Aneurysms are sometimes painted with various plastic substances, but the efficacy of this treatment is disputed. In the case of cerebral hemorrhage it may be necessary to operate to relieve the pressure of the blood from the ruptured vessel on the rest of the brain.

TRAUMATIC HEAD INJURIES

Brain injury is an all too common result of automobile and industrial accidents; *cerebral trauma* is the commonest form of brain damage in persons under the age of 40. Cerebral trauma may have significant effects on brain function in a number of ways. (1) The trauma may result in direct damage to the brain, such as in a gunshot wound, in which neurons and support cells are damaged directly. (2) Trauma may disrupt blood supply, resulting in ischemia and, if the interruption is prolonged, infarction. (3) Trauma may cause bleeding within the skull, leading to increased intracranial pressure and subsequent additional damage. (4) Like most tissues in the body, the brain swells when traumatized, leading to increased intracranial pressure and the possibility of brain damage. (5) Compound fracture of the skull opens the brain to infection. (6) Head trauma can produce scarring of brain tissue; the scarred tissue becomes a focus for later epileptic seizures. Indeed, the sudden appearance of epileptic seizures in adulthood can frequently be traced to head injury (particularly from automobile accidents) in preceding months or years.

Open Head Injuries

Open head injuries include traumatic brain injuries in which the skull is penetrated, as in gunshot or missile wounds, or in which fragments of bone penetrate the brain substance. Open head injuries show striking differences from closed head injuries; many people who have open head injuries do not lose consciousness and there is a tendency for localized, or focal, signs to undergo rapid and spontaneous recovery. Neurological signs are often highly specific, with the effects of the injuries often closely resembling those of surgical excision of a small area of cortex, as illustrated in the following case:

> . . . J. S. was injured in November 1944 by a bullet which penetrated the brain in the left parietal region. He did not lose consciousness and walked about two miles to meet the stretcher bearers. For about an hour after the injury he was unable to speak and thereafter his speech was slurred and hesitant. On examination, during which he was fully conscious and co-operative, he had slight right facial weakness and arm and leg reflexes were brisker on the right. The operation took place in a mobile Neurosurgical Unit 44 hours after wounding. . . . Five days after wounding, he was admitted to the Oxford Head Injuries Centre and was found to be in good general condition but had some numbness of the right hand, chiefly of the third and fourth digits although this had improved since injury. . . . Three months after injury, the hypalgesia of the right side of the face had persisted with slight loss to pin prick over the fingers and palm of the right hand as far as the wrist, and also slight decrease of vibration sense at the fingers and wrist of the right hand. His dysphasia was described as "not very marked" but he was hesitant in spontaneous speech. He read fairly well and retained the content of his reading "very well." (Newcombe, 1969, p. 6)

The specificity of neurological symptoms following open head injuries makes these patients especially good research subjects.

Three thorough investigations of World War II veterans with open head injuries have been published by Newcombe, Luria, and Teuber and his associates.

Closed Head Injuries

These injuries result from a blow to the head, which subjects the brain to a variety of mechanical forces. First, there is damage at the site of the blow or "coup." The brain is compacted by molding of the bone inward, even if the skull is not fractured. Second, this pressure on the brain at the time of the coup may force the brain against the opposite side of the skull, producing an additional bruise (contusion) known as a "countercoup" (see Figure 6–4 and the CT scan in Figure 5–4). Third, the movement of the brain may cause a twisting or shearing of nerve fibers in the brain, producing microscopic lesions. These may occur throughout the brain but are commonest in the frontal and temporal lobes. Fourth, the bruises and strains caused by the impact may produce bleeding (hemorrhage). Since the blood is trapped within the skull it acts as a growing mass (hemotoma), which exerts pressure on surrounding structures. Finally, as in blows to other parts of the body, blows to the brain produce swelling (edema), which is a collection of fluid in and around damaged tissue, producing another source of pressure on the brain tissue. Closed head injuries are commonly accompanied by a lack of consciousness that results from strain on fibers in the brainstem reticular formation, which often sustain permanent damage, even in cases of simple concussion. According

LATERAL VIEW

BASAL VIEW

FIGURE 6–4. A. Shading represents regions of the cerebral hemispheres most frequently damaged in cerebral contusion. B. Demonstration of how a blow to the forehead or occiput can produce a cerebral contusion on the frontal and temporal poles. Left, the blow (arrow) directly damages the brain; right, the blow causes the brain to be compressed forward, producing a countercoup injury. (Illustrations after Courville, 1945.)

to Lesak, the duration of loss of consciousness —or length of coma—can serve as a measure of the severity of damage because it correlates directly with mortality, and intellectual impairment, and deficits in social skills.

Closed head injuries resulting from motor vehicle accidents are particularly severe because the head is moving when the blow is struck, thereby increasing the velocity of the impact and hence multiplying the number and severity of small lesions throughout the brain. CT scans of motor vehicle accident victims suffering prolonged coma show diffuse brain injury and enlarged ventricles; these signs are associated with poor outcomes.

Two kinds of behavioral effects result from closed head injuries: discrete impairment of those functions mediated by the cortex at the site of the coup or the countercoup lesion; and more generalized damage widespread throughout the brain. The former effects are most commonly associated with damage to the frontal and temporal lobes, those areas most susceptible to closed head injury (see Figure 6–4). The latter effects, which result from minute lesions and lacerations scattered throughout the brain, are characterized by a general loss of complex cognitive functions including mental speed, ability to concentrate, and overall cognitive efficiency. These difficulties are usually reflected in patients' complaints of inability to concentrate or to do things as well as they could before the accident, even though the intelligence rating may still be well above average. Indeed, in our experience, bright people are the most affected by closed head injuries as they are acutely aware of a loss of cognitive skill that prevents them from returning to their previous competence level.

Closed head injuries that damage the frontal and temporal lobes also tend to have significant effects on people's personality and social adjustment. According to Lesak, relatively few victims of traffic accidents who have sustained severe head injuries ever resume their studies or return to gainful employment, or if they do reenter the work force, they do so at a lower level than before.

> Despite residual capacities that are often considerable, one combination or another of impaired initiative and apathy, lack of critical capacity, defective social judgement, childishness and egocentricity, inability to plan or sustain activity, impulsivity, irritability, and low frustration tolerance is likely to render these patients unemployable or only marginally employable. These same qualities also make a person who has sustained moderate to severe head injuries at best a nuisance at home, at worst a terror. By virtue of these qualities, and again despite their residual capacities, these patients are rarely able to form or maintain close relationships, so that those who have not been rendered silly and euphoric or apathetic by their injuries, are often lonely and depressed as well. (Lezak, 1983, p. 170)

The diffuse nature of chronic effects of closed head injuries is often not associated with any neurological signs, and patients are often referred for psychiatric evaluation. Psychological assessments are especially useful here, because seriously handicapping cognitive deficits may become immediately apparent in the course of a thorough assessment, even though they are not obvious in casual conversation. Many of these patients appear normal in a psychological examination with standard intelligence tests, or even commercial neuropsychological test batteries, but careful neuropsychological investigation may reveal severe cognitive deficits, a result that underscores the need for a careful and competent neuropsychological assessment (see Chapters 26 through 30).

EPILEPSIES

Epilepsy is a condition characterized by recurrent electrographic seizures of various types that are associated with a disturbance of consciousness. Although epileptic episodes have been termed convulsions, seizures, fits, and attacks, none of these terms is entirely satisfactory, since attacks vary greatly in nature. Epileptic seizures are very common; one person in 20 will experience at least one seizure during his or her lifetime. Most of these people are not truly epileptic, however, for the seizures do not recur. The prevalence of multiple seizures is much lower, about one in 200.

The cause of epileptic seizures was unknown until the development of the EEG by Berger in 1929. This technique made it possible to demonstrate that different varieties of epilepsy are associated with different abnormal electrical rhythms in the brain (see Figure 6–5). Sometimes epileptic seizures are classifiable as symptomatic seizures; that is, they can sometimes be identified with a specific cause, such as infection, trauma, tumor, vascular malformation, toxic chemicals, very high fever, and other neurological disorders. But other seizure disorders, called **idiopathic seizures,** appear to arise spontaneously and in the absence of other diseases of the central nervous system. The cause of the abnormal electric discharge within the cell is poorly understood, although it is likely that it causes some type of abnormality in the neuronal membranes.

Although it has long been known that epilepsy runs in families, it is unlikely that there is a single gene responsible for the seizures, because the incidence is lower than would be predicted from genetic models. It is more likely that certain genotypes have a predisposition to seizure problems given certain environmental circumstances.

Symptoms and Diagnosis

The most remarkable clinical feature of epileptic disorders is the discontinuity of symptoms, with widely varying intervals between attacks—minutes, hours, weeks, or even years. Thus it is almost impossible to describe a basic set of symptoms to be expected in all, or even most, people with the disease. Three symptoms, however, are found in many types of epilepsy. (1) An aura, or warning, of impending seizure. This may take the form of sensations such as odors, noises, and the like or may simply be a "feeling" that the seizure is going to occur. (2) Loss of consciousness. This may take the form of complete collapse or simply staring off into space. There is often amnesia, the victim forgetting the seizure itself and the period of lost consciousness. (3) Movements. It is common for seizures to have a motor component, although the characteristics vary considerably. In some cases there are shaking movements; in others, automatic movements such as rubbing the hands or chewing.

The diagnosis of epilepsy is usually confirmed by EEG. However, in some epileptics, seizures are difficult to demonstrate except under special circumstances (e.g., an EEG recorded during sleep), and not all persons with an abnormal EEG actually have seizures. In fact, some estimates suggest that four in 20 people actually have abnormal EEG patterns! Recently PET has provided a more reliable measure of functional abnormalities, although the cost remains prohibitive. Studies of cerebral blood flow (see Chapter 14) may provide a less expensive alternative (see Engle).

Types of Epilepsies

Several classification schemes have been published for epilepsy. Table 6–1 summarizes the one in common use.

Focal seizures are those that begin locally and then spread. For example, in Jacksonian seizures the attack begins with jerks of single parts of the body, such as a finger, a toe, or the

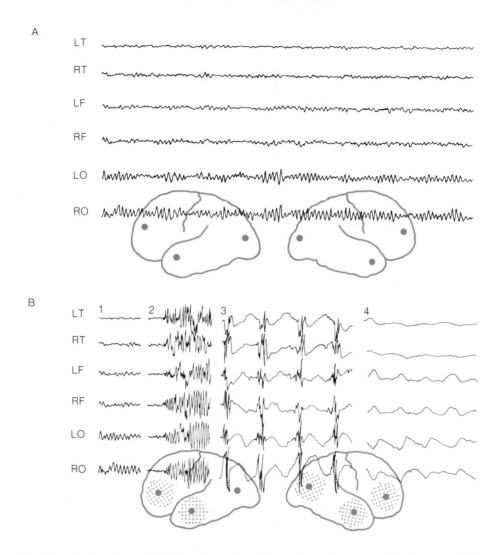

FIGURE 6–5. Examples of EEG recordings from different forms of epilepsy. LT: left temporal. RT: right temporal. LF: left frontal. RF: right frontal. LO: left occipital. RO: right occipital. Black dots on the hemispheres indicate the approximate recording sites. A. Normal adult EEG. B. Brief excerpts from an EEG during a grand mal seizure: (1) Normal recording preceding the attack. (2) Onset of attack. (3) Clonic phase of the attack. (4) Postictal period of coma. Shaded areas represent regions picked up by scalp electrodes. C. An episode of 3/sec spike-and-wave EEG characteristic of petit mal discharge. D. Hypsarrhythmia in the EEG of a child. Notice diffuse slow waves with occasional spikes. (From W. B. Hardin, Pathophysiology of clinical epilepsy. In I. S. G. Eliasson, A. L. Prensky, and W. B. Hardin, eds., *Neurological Pathophysiology,* 2nd ed. New York: Oxford University Press. Copyright 1978 by Oxford University Press, Inc. Reprinted with permission.)

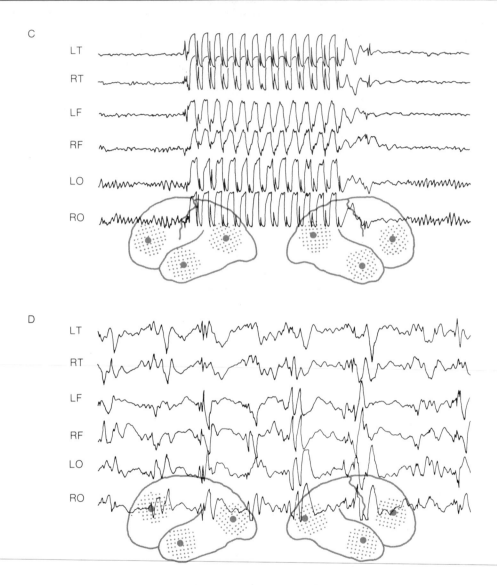

FIGURE 6–5 (continued)

mouth, and then spreads. If it were the finger, the jerks might spread to other fingers, then the hand, arm, and so on, producing a so-called Jacksonian march. Jackson made the prediction in 1870 that such seizures probably originated from the point (focus) in the neo-

cortex representing that region. He was later proved correct.

Complex partial seizures most commonly originate in the temporal lobe, and somewhat less frequently in the frontal lobe. Complex partial seizures are characterized by three common manifestations: (1) subjective feelings, such as forced, repetitive thoughts, alterations in mood, feelings of déjà vu, or hallucinations; (2) automatisms, repetitive stereotyped movements such as lip smacking or chewing, or the repetition of acts such as undoing buttons and the like; (3) postural changes, afflicted persons sometimes assuming catatonic, or frozen, postures.

Generalized seizures are bilaterally symmetrical without local onset. The **grand mal** attack is characterized by loss of consciousness and stereotyped motor activity. Typically, patients go through three stages: (1) a tonic stage, in which the body stiffens and breathing stops; (2) a clonic stage, in which there is rhythmic shaking; and (3) a post seizure (also known as postictal) depression, in which the patient is confused. About 50 percent of these seizures are preceded by an aura.

In the **petit mal,** or **absence attack,** there is loss of awareness during which there is no motor activity except blinking and/or turning the head, rolling the eyes, etc. These attacks are of brief duration, seldom exceeding about 10 seconds. The EEG record has a typical pattern known as 3/sec spike and wave.

Akinetic seizures are ordinarily only seen in children. Usually the child collapses suddenly and without warning. These seizures are often of very short duration, and the child may get up after only a few seconds with no postictal depression. The falls that these children have can be quite dangerous in themselves, and it is not uncommon for them to wear football helmets until the fits can be controlled by medication.

Myoclonic spasms are massive seizures that basically consist of a sudden flexion or extension of the body and often begin with a cry.

As mentioned earlier, seizures are not continual in any epileptic patients, even though the EEG may be chronically abnormal. Table

TABLE 6–1

Classification of the epilepsies

1. *Partial seizures (focal)*
   a. Simple partial seizures
      i. Motor (Jacksonian)
      ii. Sensory (Jacksonian)
      iii. Autonomic
   b. Complex partial seizures (temporal lobe, psychomotor)
      i. Absences
      ii. Complex hallucinations
      iii. Affective symptoms
      iv. Automatism
   c. Partial seizures secondarily generalized

2. *Generalized seizures*
   Bilaterally symmetrical without local onset
   a. Absence attacks (petit mal)
   b. Tonic-clonic (grand mal)
   c. Bilateral myoclonic
   d. Drop attacks (akinetic)

3. *Unclassified seizures*
   Because of incomplete data, includes many persons with apparently generalized seizures.

6–2 summarizes the great variety of circumstances that appear able to precipitate seizures. Although one is struck by the wide range of factors that may precipitate seizures, one consistent feature is that the brain is most epileptogenic when it is relatively inactive and the patient is sitting still.

Treatment of Epilepsy

The treatment of choice is use of an anticonvulsant drug, such as diphenylhydantoin (DPH, Dilantin), phenobarbital, and several others. Although the mechanism by which these drugs act is uncertain, they presumably inhibit the discharge of abnormal neurons by stabilizing the neuronal membrane. If medication fails to alleviate the seizure problem satisfactorily, surgery can be performed to remove the focus of abnormal functioning in patients with focalized seizures.

TABLE 6–2

Factors that may precipitate seizures
in susceptible individuals

Hyperventilation	
Sleep	
Sleep deprivation	
Sensory stimuli:	Flashing lights
	Reading-speaking, coughing
	Laughing
	Sounds: music, bells, etc.
	Reading
Trauma	
Hormonal changes:	Menses
	Puberty
	Adrenal steroids
	Adrenocorticotrophic
	hormone (ACTH)
Fever	
Emotional stress	
Drugs:	Phenothiazines
	Analeptics
	Tricyclic mood elevators
	Alcohol
	Excessive anticonvulsants

After Pincus and Tucker, 1974.

The surgical treatment of epilepsy dates back to the late 1800s, when Horsley and others removed the cortex in an attempt to alleviate seizures. The modern technique of surgery for epilepsy was pioneered by Otfrid Foerster in the 1920s in Germany. Wilder Penfield, stimulated by his studies with Foerster, began a prolonged scientific study of the surgical treatment of epilepsy in 1928, when he founded the Montreal Neurological Institute for that purpose. Penfield was soon joined by Herbert Jasper, who introduced EEG to the operating room, and by D. O. Hebb and Brenda Milner, who introduced the neuropsychological assessment of Penfield's surgical patients. Together these four and their colleagues developed a technique of cortical removal of the epileptogenic tissue from victims of focal epilepsy. The technique has been remarkably successful for this form of epilepsy. Their team approach to the treatment of a neurologi-

cal disease provides a model of the marriage of basic and applied disciplines in developing an effective treatment for a neurological disorder.

Today, epilepsy is a particularly important disease for the neuropsychologist, because patients treated surgically for the relief of epilepsy form one of the best patient populations for neuropsychological study. Because the extent of surgical removal can be carefully charted at surgery and correlated with both preoperative and postoperative behavior, neuropsychologists have an excellent source of information on brain-behavior relations in humans.

TUMORS

A **tumor** (or neoplasm) is a mass of new tissue that persists and grows independently of its surrounding structures and that has no physiologic use. Brain tumors do not grow from neurons but rather from glia or other support cells. The rate at which tumors grow varies widely, depending on the type of cell that gives rise to the tumor. Tumors account for a relatively high proportion of neurological disease, and next to the uterus, the brain is the commonest site for tumors. It is possible to distinguish between benign tumors, those not likely to recur after removal, and malignant tumors, those likely to recur after removal and that frequently progress, becoming a threat to life. Although the distinction between benign and malignant is well founded, the benign tumor may be as serious as the malignant one, since many benign tumors in the brain are inaccessible to the surgeon without risk to life. The brain is affected by many types of tumors, and no region of the brain is immune to tumor formation.

Tumors can significantly affect behavior in a number of ways. A tumor may develop as a distinct entity in the brain, a so-called encapsulated tumor, and produce effects by placing pressure on the rest of the brain (Figure 6–6). Encapsulated tumors are also sometimes cystic, which means they produce a fluid-filled cavity in the brain, usually lined with the tumor cells. Since the skull is of fixed size, any increase in its contents will functionally compress the brain, resulting in dysfunctions. Other tumors, so-called infiltrating tumors, are not clearly marked off from the surrounding tissue; they may either destroy normal cells and occupy their place or surround existing cells (both neurons and glia) and interfere with their normal functioning (Figure 6–7).

Symptoms and Diagnosis of Brain Tumors

The recognition of a brain tumor may be divided into three phases: (1) the suspicion that a tumor may be present, (2) the diagnostic confirmation of the tumor, and (3) the precise location of the tumor within the nervous system. The generalized symptoms of brain tumors, which result from increased intracranial pressure, include headache, vomiting, swelling of the optic disk (papilledema), slowing of the heart rate (bradycardia), mental dullness, double vision **(diplopia),** and, finally, convulsions. It would be rare indeed for a patient to exhibit all these symptoms, most of which result from a marked increase in intracranial pressure. Other signs and symptoms of tumors depend on the exact location of the tumor. Thus, a tumor in the speech zones would be more likely to disrupt speech than would a tumor in the visual cortex.

Types of Brain Tumors

There are three major types of brain tumors, distinguished on the basis of where they orig-inate: gliomas, meningiomas, and metastatic tumors. Each is discussed in turn.

Gliomas. Glioma is a general term for those brain tumors that arise from glial cells and infiltrate the brain substance. Roughly 45 percent of all brain tumors are gliomas. Gliomas, ranging from relatively benign to highly malignant, vary considerably in their response to treatment. Because the detailed description of types of gliomas is more important to the neurologist and neurosurgeon than to the neuropsychologist, we shall briefly describe only the most frequently occurring types of gliomas: astrocytomas, glioblastomas, and medulloblastomas.

Astrocytomas result from the growth of **astrocytes** and are usually slow growing. They account for about 40 percent of gliomas, being commonest in adults over 30 years of age. Because they are not very malignant, and because of their slow growth rate, they are relatively safe once treated. Thus, the prognosis is relatively good, with postoperative survivals occasionally being over 20 years.

The **glioblastoma** is a highly malignant, rapidly growing tumor commonest in adults, especially males, over 35 years of age. Glioblastomas account for roughly 30 percent of gliomas. This tumor may result from the sudden growth of spongioblasts, cells that are ordinarily formed only during development of the brain, although some texts suggest that astrocytes cannot be ruled out as the source of glioblastomas. The tumor may be made up of a variety of cell types (glioblastoma multiforme) or of a single cell type (glioblastoma unipolare). Because these tumors are so rapidly growing the life expectancy is usually short, seldom extending beyond one year after surgery.

Medulloblastomas are highly malignant tumors that are found almost exclusively in the cerebellum of children. Medulloblastomas

FIGURE 6–6. Frontal section showing a meningioma (arrow) arising in the dura and compressing the right cerebral hemisphere. Notice that the tumor has not infiltrated the brain. (From S. I. Zacks, *Atlas of Neuropathology*. New York: Harper & Row. Copyright 1971 by Harper & Row. Reprinted with permission.)

FIGURE 6–7. Frontal section showing a glioblastoma in the right cerebral hemisphere. Note the displacement of the ventricular system and the invasion of brain tissue. (From R. Bannister, *Brain's Clinical Neurology*, 5th ed. Oxford: Oxford University Press. Copyright 1978 by Oxford University Press, Inc. Reprinted with permission.)

account for about 11 percent of all gliomas. The tumor results from the growth of germinal cells that infiltrate the cerebellum or underlying brainstem. The prognosis for children with these tumors is poor; the postoperative survival period ranges from $1\frac{1}{2}$ to 2 years.

Meningiomas. Meningiomas are growths attached to the meninges and grow entirely outside the brain. These tumors are well encapsulated and are the most benign of all brain tumors. Although meningiomas do not invade the brain, they are often multiple and disturb brain function by producing pressure on the brain, often producing seizures as a symptom. Although most meningiomas lie over the hemispheres, some occur between the hemispheres. The latter location makes removal more complicated. It is not uncommon for these tumors to erode the overlying bone. If meningiomas are removed completely, they tend not to recur.

Metastatic Tumors. *Metastasis* is the transfer of disease from one organ or part to another not directly connected with it. Thus, a **metastatic tumor** in the brain is one that has become established by a transfer of tumor cells from some other region of the body, most commonly lung or breast. Indeed, it is not uncommon for the first indication of lung cancer to be evidence of brain tumor. In the event of metastasis to the brain, usually multiple metastatic tumors occur there, making treatment complicated and prognosis poor.

Other Tumors. We have considered only the major types of primary brain tumors, there being many more less common types. One of these, the pituitary adenoma, is a tumor of the pituitary region. Although the pituitary is not really part of the brain, tumors there produce pressure on the brain, and owing to the close relation between the hypothalamus and the pituitary, such tumors can produce significant functional abnormalities in the hypothalamus. For a detailed discussion of other brain tumors, we recommend Baker and Baker's extensive text.

Treatment of Brain Tumors

The most obvious treatment of brain tumors is surgery, which is the only way to make a certain histological diagnosis. If feasible, tumors are removed, but, as with tumors elsewhere in the body, success depends on early diagnosis. Radiotherapy is useful for treating certain types of tumors, such as glioblastomas and medulloblastomas, as well as for some metastatic tumors. Chemotherapy has not yet been very successful in the treatment of brain tumors owing in part to the difficulty in getting drugs to pass the blood-brain barrier and distribute in the tumor.

HEADACHES

Headache is so common among the general population that rare indeed is the person who has never suffered one. Headache may constitute a neurological disorder in itself, as in migraine; it may be secondary to neurological disease such as tumor or infection; or it may result from psychological factors, especially stress, as in tension headaches. The pain-sensitive structures within the skull that can be responsible for a headache include the dura, the large arteries of the brain, the venous sinuses, and the branches of the fifth, ninth, and 10th cranial nerves and the first to third cervical nerves. Pain can be elicited from these structures by pressure, traction, displacement, or inflammation.

Types of Headaches

Migraine. **Migraine** is perhaps the commonest neurological disorder, afflicting some 5 percent of the population at some time in their lives. It is experienced as an aching, throbbing pain, frequently unilateral and often coincident with the pulse beat. A migraine attack is often preceded by a visual disturbance (aura) that occurs within a restricted region of the visual field. This is experienced as a zone of flashing, whirling, or shimmering light that slowly increases in size, lasting 15 to 30 minutes. This aura is presumed to occur because vasoconstriction of one or more cerebral arteries has produced ischemia of the occipital cortex. The actual headache begins as the vasoconstriction reverses, thus ending the visual disturbance, and vasodilation occurs. The headache is manifested as an intense pain localized in one side of the head, although it frequently spreads on the affected side and sometimes to the opposite side as well. A severe headache can be accompanied by nausea and vomiting, and it may last for hours or even days. The frequency of migraine attacks varies from as often as one per week to as seldom as once in a lifetime. In cases where migraine is frequent the occurrence generally drops with aging and usually ceases in middle age. Migraine was generally believed to be rare prior to adolescence, but in recent years it has been recognized as afflicting children as well, although the actual incidence in this population is uncertain.

A large number of environmental factors appear to trigger migraine attacks, including anxiety, the termination of anxiety (relaxation), fatigue, bright light, and in many persons specific allergies, particularly to foods and wines.

Headache Associated with Neurological Disease. Headache, a common symptom of many nervous system disorders, usually results from distortion of the pain-sensitive structures. Common disorders producing headache include tumor, head trauma, infection, vascular malformations, and severe hypertension (high blood pressure). The characteristics and location of these headaches vary according to the actual disorder. For example, headache from brain tumor is almost always located on the same side of the head as the tumor, particularly in the early stages of the tumor. However, headaches related to brain tumor have no characteristic severity, for they vary from mild to excruciating. Likewise, hypertension headache, although it is nearly always located in the occipital region, is also highly variable in severity.

Muscle Contraction Headache. Muscle contraction headaches are the commonest form of headaches, also being known as tension, psychogenic, and nervous headache. These headaches result from sustained contraction of the muscles of the scalp and neck caused by constant stress or tension, especially if poor posture is maintained for any period of time. Patients describe their symptoms as steady, nonpulsing, tight, squeezing, pressing, or crawling sensations or as the feeling of having the head in a vise. The headaches may be accompanied by anxiety, dizziness, and bright spots in front of the eyes. In some people caffeine may exacerbate the headaches, presumably because anxiety is increased.

Nonmigrainous Vascular Headaches. A wide variety of diseases and conditions induce headache that is associated with dilation of the cranial arteries. The commonest causes are fever, anoxia, anemia, high altitude, physical effort, hypoglycemia, foods, and chemical agents. In addition, headache may result from congestion and edema of the nasal membranes, often termed "vasomotor rhinitis," which is assumed to represent a localized vascular reaction to stress.

Treatment of Headache

Migraine is treated by specific drugs at the time of attacks and by preventive measures between attacks. In an acute attack **ergotamine** compounds, often given in conjuction with caffeine, are useful in alleviating the headache, probably because they produce constriction of the cerebral arteries, thus reducing tension in this pain-sensitive structure. In addition, most migraine sufferers find the headache is reduced in a totally dark room. In view of the unpleasantness of migraine, the sufferer should try to avoid those circumstances that experience shows precipitate the attacks.

The most obvious treatment of headache arising from neurological disease is to treat the disease itself. Tension headache can be relieved by muscle-relaxant drugs, minor tranquilizers, application of heat to the affected muscles, and improvement of posture. They can also be prevented by avoiding the life situations that give rise to them.

INFECTIONS

Infection is the invasion of the body by disease-producing (pathogenic) microorganisms and the reaction of the tissues to their presence and to the toxins generated by them. The central nervous system can be invaded by a wide variety of infectious agents, including viruses, bacteria, fungi, and metazoan parasites. Thus, the diagnosis and treatment of infection are an important component of clinical neurology. Although infections of the nervous system usually spread from infection elsewhere in the body—especially the ears, nose, and throat—they also may be introduced directly into the brain as a result of head trauma, skull fractures,

or surgery. Infections of the nervous system are particularly serious because usually neurons and glia die, resulting in lesions.

There are a number of processes by which infections kill neural cells. First, infections may interfere with the blood supply to neurons, thus producing thrombosis, hemorrhage of capillaries, or even the complete choking off of blood vessels. Second, there may be a disturbance of glucose or oxygen metabolism in the brain cells that is serious enough to kill them. Third, the infection may alter the characteristics of the neural cell membranes, thus altering the electrical properties of the neurons, or alternatively, it may interfere with the basic enzymatic processes of the cell, producing any number of abnormal conditions. Fourth, a byproduct of the body's defense against infection is pus, a fluid composed basically of white blood cells, their byproducts and those of the infectious microorganisms, and a thin fluid called liquor puris. Pus impairs neuronal functioning in at least two ways: (1) it significantly alters the extracellular fluids surrounding a neuron, thus altering neuronal function, and (2) because pus occupies space, its production increases pressure on the brain, disturbing normal functioning. Fifth, and finally, infection often causes swelling (known as edema), which compresses the brain, again resulting in brain dysfunction.

Symptoms and Diagnosis of Infection

Many infections of the nervous system are secondary to infections elsewhere in the body and are accompanied by symptoms associated with those other infections, including lowered blood pressure and other changes in blood circulation, fever, general malaise, headache, and delirium. In addition, symptoms of cerebral infections include both generalized symptoms of increased intracranial pressure, such as headache, vertigo, nausea, convulsions, and mental confusion, as well as focalized symptoms of disturbance of specific brain functions.

Diagnostic studies of infection include CSF studies in addition to conventional methods of infection identification, such as smear and/or culture studies. CT scans and brain scans may also be used to diagnose and/or locate some infectious disorders.

Types of Infections

Unfortunately, there is a good deal of semantic disagreement about the terminology of infections. We shall use the term **encephalitis** for inflammation of the central nervous system caused by infection and the term **encephalopathy** for chemical, physical, allergic, or toxic inflammations. Note that, strictly speaking, encephalitis and encephalopathy do not refer to specific diseases, but rather to the effects of disease processes.

Four types of infections can affect the central nervous system: viral infections, bacterial infections, mycotic (fungi) infections, and parasitic infestations. We shall now discuss each of these types.

Viral Infections. A **virus** is an encapsulated aggregate of nucleic acid that may be made up of either DNA (deoxyribonucleic acid) or RNA (ribonucleic acid). Some viruses, such as those causing poliomyelitis and rabies, are called **neurotropic viruses,** because they have a special affinity for cells of the central nervous system. These are differentiated from **pantropic viruses** (such as those causing mumps and herpes simplex), which attack other body tissue in addition to the central nervous system. Most viral infections of the nervous system produce nonspecific lesions affecting widespread regions of the brain, as occur in diseases such as St. Louis encephalitis, rabies, and poliomyelitis.

Bacterial Infections. Bacterium is a loose generic name for any microorganism (typically one-celled) that has no chlorophyll and multiplies by simple division. Bacterial infections of the central nervous system result from an infestation of these organisms, usually via the blood stream. The commonest disorders resulting from bacterial infection are meningitis and brain abcess. In **meningitis,** the meninges are infected by any of a variety of bacteria. **Brain abcesses** are also produced by a variety of bacteria, secondary to infection elsewhere in the body. They begin as a small focus of purulent bacteria that cause necrosis (death) of cells in the affected region. As the organisms multiply and destroy more brain cells, the abcess behaves as an expanding mass, frequently hollow in the center; as it expands it produces increasing intracranial pressure.

Mycotic Infections. Invasion of the nervous system by a fungus is known as a **mycotic infection.** A fungus is any member of a large group of lower plants that lack chlorophyll and subsist on living or dead organic matter; the fungi include yeasts, molds, and mushrooms. Ordinarily the central nervous system is highly resistant to mycotic infections, but fungi may invade the brain whose resistance has been reduced by various diseases such as tuberculosis or malignant tumors.

Parasitic Infestations. A **parasite** is an organism that lives on or within another living organism (the host) at its expense. Several kinds of parasites invade the central nervous system and produce significant disease, the most important diseases being amebiasis and malaria. Amebiasis (also known as amebic dysentery), caused by an infestation of the protozoan ameba *(Entamoeba histolytica),* results in encephalitis and brain abcesses. Malaria is caused by protozoa of the genus *Plasmodium,* which are transmitted by the bites of infected mosquitoes. Cerebral malaria occurs when the plasmodia infect the capillaries of the brain, producing local hemorrhages and subsequent degeneration of neurons.

Treatment of Infections

Treatment varies with the type of infection. Viral infections are extremely difficult to treat, for there are no specific antidotes, the only treatment being to let the diseases run their course. Sedatives are sometimes administered to make the patient more comfortable. The important exception to this is the treatment of rabies. Once it is ascertained that a person has had contact with a rabid organism, antirabies vaccine is administered over a period of two to four weeks in order to produce an immunity before the disease actually develops. Once the disease does develop, rabies is fatal.

Bacterial cerebral infections have become less common with the introduction of antibiotic drugs, the usual treatment for these infections. In some cases it may be necessary to drain abcesses to relieve intracranial pressure, or to do spinal taps to remove CSF and reduce pressure where there is edema or a buildup of pus.

Neither mycotic nor parasitic infections can be satisfactorily treated, although antibiotics are often used to treat associated disorders.

DEGENERATIVE DISORDERS

Many diseases of the nervous system involve a progressive deterioration of brain tissue and behavior. In most cases there is a specific loss of some region or system in the brain, which produces a distinctive behavioral syndrome. The commonest degenerative disorders and their probable causes are summarized in Table

TABLE 6-3

Summary of common degenerative diseases

Disorder	Probable cause
Alzheimer's disease	Loss of cholinergic neurons in nucleus basalis of Meynert leading to development of senile plaques and neurofibrillary tangles
Pick's disease	Atrophy of frontal and temporal lobes from unknown causes
Cruetzfeldt- Jakob's disease	Generalized cortical atrophy from unknown causes
Korsakoff's syndrome	Atrophy of medial thalamus and mamillary bodies from chronic excessive alcohol consumption
Huntington's chorea	Degeneration of basal ganglia, frontal cortex, and corpus callosum due to a genetic abnormality
Parkinson's disease	Loss of striatal dopamine due to degeneration of the substantia nigra
Multiple sclerosis	Abnormal neural activity due to loss of myelin
Myasthenia gravis	Autoimmune disorder causing motor muscle receptors to decrease

6-3. We shall consider only the dementias (Alzheimer's, Pick's, and Creutzfeldt-Jakob's diseases) here, as the other disorders are described in detail elsewhere in the book. Parkinson's disease, Huntington's chorea, multiple sclerosis, and myasthenia gravis are discussed in Chapter 12 and Korsakoff's syndrome is considered in Chapter 20.

Alzheimer's disease accounts for about 50 percent of the patients diagnosed as demented and has generated a great deal of interest recently because it may provide a good model for the study of senility in general. Although a distinction was once made between the onset of senility prior to age 65 (presenile dementia of the Alzheimer type) and onset over 65 (senile dementia), there are no longer strong grounds for distinguishing between these disorders, since the pathology is similar. The term Alzheimer's disease is now commonly used to refer to both presenile and senile dementia. The disease begins insidiously, eventually afflicting about 5 percent of the population over 65. Postmortem study of the brains of Alzheimer's patients has recently led to a major breakthrough in our understanding of this and related diseases. It has been known for some time that the brains of these persons are characterized by abnormal neurofibrils (neurofibrillatory tangles), neuritic plaques, and the loss of nerve cells, but recent neurochemical studies have suggested that these changes may be due to a loss of acetylcholine cells in the base of the forebrain. Three small nuclei (the medial septal nucleus, the diagonal band of Broca, and the nucleus basalis of Meynert), which are in the basal forebrain lying just above the optic chiasm (see Figure 1–4), form cholinergic pathways that innervate the cortex. Careful study of the brains of Alzheimer's patients suggests that the plaque density in the cortex correlates with reductions in acetylcholine and a loss of cells in the nucleus basalis of Meynert, a result that has led to the hypothesis that Alzheimer's disease results from a degeneration of the nucleus basalis of Meynert.

Behaviorally, Alzheimer's disease is characterized by marked deficits in memory, language, and perception as well as by symptoms of depression. Indeed, it is not uncommon for Alzheimer's patients to be initially treated for depression. It is the loss of memory that has generated the most research interest; research on this is possible because memory can be easily studied in nonhuman species following the administration of drugs that are antagonistic to acetylcholine. The relation between Alzheimer's dementia and acetylcholine loss is important, for it suggests that the disorder could be treated with cholinergic agonists, although as yet there is no overwhelming evidence favoring this view.

Pick's and Creutzfeldt-Jakob's diseases are also dementias, although they are less common than Alzheimer's. The causes of these diseases are unknown but there is no compelling reason to believe that they result from cholinergic abnormalities. Pick's disease is characterized by symptoms that are virtually indistinguishable clinically from those of Alzheimer's disease, but at autopsy the diseases can be distinguished. In Pick's disease the cellular degeneration and atrophy are confined to the frontal and temporal cortex, and the plaques and tangles characteristic of Alzheimer's disease are not evident. Creutzfeldt-Jakob's disease differs from the other two in that its course is very rapid, leading in just a few months to stupor, coma, and death. Memory loss is prominent from the outset, but deterioration can be measured nearly day by day. At autopsy there is a generalized thinning of the cortex in addition to generalized abnormalities in subcortical structures.

MENTAL DISORDERS

The Diagnostic and Statistical Manual of Mental Disorders (DSM-III) of the American Psychiatric Association lists 16 different types of behavioral disorders (see Table 6–4); it can be safely assumed that some of these disorders result from abnormal brain function. However, current limitations in our knowledge about brain function make it impossible to ascertain whether a given behavioral disturbance results directly from abnormal brain functioning or from a response to environmental or social factors.

Two types of disorders likely to result from neurological abnormalities are the schizo-

TABLE 6–4

DSM-III categories of mental disorders

1. Disorders usually first evident in infancy, adulthood, or adolescence
2. Organic mental disorders
3. Substance-use disorders
4. Schizophrenic disorders
5. Paranoid disorders
6. Psychotic disorders not elsewhere classified
7. Affective disorders
8. Anxiety disorders
9. Somatoform disorders
10. Dissociative disorders
11. Psychosexual disorders
12. Factitious disorders
13. Disorders of impulse control not elsewhere classified
14. Adjustment disorder
15. Psychological factors affecting physical condition
16. Conditions not attributable to a mental disorder that are a focus of attention or treatment

phrenic and affective disorders, although even in these disorders an environmental influence cannot be ruled out. Both of these disorders have been alleged to result from abnormalities in the levels of neurotransmitters in the brain (dopamine for schizophrenia and noradrenaline and serotonin for depression); the principal treatment for both disorders is thus pharmacological in an attempt to correct the abnormality. Unlike Alzheimer's disease, however, it has not been possible to point to the loss of specific cells in the brain that might result in the neurochemical abnormalities. We shall consider current neurological theories of schizophrenia and affective disorders in detail in Chapter 22 in the broader context of the neurological control of affective behavior.

REFERENCES

Adams, H. E., M. Feuerstein, and J. L. Fowler. Migraine headache: Review of parameters, etiology, and intervention. *Psychological Bulletin* 87:217–237, 1980.

Alpers, B. J., and E. L. Mancall. *Clinical Neurology,* 6th ed. Philadelphia: Davis, 1971.

Bakal, D. A. Headache: A biopsychological perspective. *Psychological Bulletin* 82:369–382, 1975.

Baker, A. D., and L. H. Baker. *Clinical Neurology,* rev. ed. Philadelphia: Harper & Row, 1982.

Bannister, R. *Brain's Clinical Neurology,* 5th ed. New York: Oxford University Press, 1978.

Corkin, S. Acetylcholine, aging and Alzheimer's disease: Implications for treatment. *Trends in Neurosciences* 4:287–290, 1981.

Courville, C. B. *Pathology of the Nervous System,* 2nd ed. Mountain View, Calif.: Pacific Press, 1945.

Coyle, J. T., D. L. Price, and M. R. DeLong. Alzheimer's disease: A disorder of cortical cholinergic innervation. *Science* 219:1184–1190, 1983.

Eliasson, S. G., A. L. Prensky, and W. B. Hardin. *Neurological Pathophysiology,* 2nd ed. New York: Oxford University Press, 1978.

Engle, J. Functional localization of epileptogenic lesions. *Trends in Neurosciences* 6:60–65, 1983.

Forster, F. M. *Clinical Neurology,* 3rd ed. St. Louis, Mo.: Mosby, 1973.

Gloor, P. Contributions of electroencephalography and electrocorticography to the neuro-surgical treatment of the epilepsies. *Advances in Neurology* 8:59–105, 1975.

Hardin, W. B. Pathophysiology of clinical epilepsy. In S. G. Eliasson, A. L. Prensky, and W. B. Hardin, eds., *Neurological Pathophysiology,* 2nd ed. New York: Oxford University Press, 1978.

Lezak, M. D. *Neuropsychological Assessment,* 2nd ed. New York: Oxford University Press, 1983.

Lieberman, A., and J. Ransohoff. Treatment of primary brain tumors. *Medical Clinics of North America* 63:835–848, 1979.

McNeil, E. B. *The Psychoses.* Englewood Cliffs, N.J.: Prentice-Hall, 1970.

Newcombe, F. *Missile Wounds of the Brain.* London: Oxford University Press, 1969.

Pincus, J. H., and G. J. Tucker. *Behavioral Neurology.* New York: Oxford University Press, 1974.

Raichle, M. E., C. D. de Vivo, and J. Hanaway. Disorders of cerebral circulation. In S. G. Eliasson, A. L. Prensky, and W. B. Hardin, eds., *Neurological Pathophysiology,* 2nd ed. New York: Oxford University Press, 1978.

Rasmussen, T. Cortical resection in the treatment of focal epilepsy. *Advances in Neurology* 8:139–154, 1975.

Slager, U. T. *Basic Neuropathology.* Baltimore: Williams and Wilkins, 1970.

Terry, R. D., and P. Davies. Dementia of the Alzheimer type. *Annual Review of Neuroscience* 3:77–95, 1980.

Vinken, P. J., and G. W. Bruyn. *Handbook of Clinical Neurology.* New York: Wiley, 1969.

Zacks, S. I. *Atlas of Neuropathology.* New York: Harper & Row, 1971.

PART THREE

GENERAL PRINCIPLES OF BRAIN FUNCTION

At its simplest level of organization the nervous system consists of a sensory neuron that enters the spinal cord to synapse with a motor neuron. At more complex levels it consists of sensory neurons that interconnect with one or more interneurons that in turn connect to motor neurons. Chapter 7 presents some general theories about how sensory events are elaborated into motor events by the action of various groups of interneurons. Three important principles underly this discussion. (1) There is a *parallel* organization in the nervous system, in which the sensory systems and their subcomponents have preferential access to one or another motor system that is responsible for executing certain types of movements. (2) There is a *hierarchical* organization in the nervous system that emerges as successive levels of interneurons permit successively more complex or more adaptive behaviors. (3) There is development of *lateralization* of function such that the very highest levels of function serve somewhat different roles in the two hemispheres. Chapter 8 is devoted to the anatomical organization of the cortex, since it is the action of interneurons of this structure that are a central focus of the behavior of mammals in general and of humans in particular. Chapter 9 describes the organization and function of the sensory systems, and Chapter 10 describes disorders of sensory function. Chapter 11 describes the organization and function of the motor systems; Chapter 12 describes disorders of motor function.

The process of dividing the nervous system into sensory, integrative, and motor is rather traditional, but it can be argued that it is also artificial. This point should be kept in mind. On the one hand, it is a simple matter to argue that the entire nervous system is motor, and that movements begin at the sensory receptor. Indeed, changes in receptor activity can potentially—and usually do—lead to changes in motor activity, whether they are as simple as knee-jerk reflexes or as complex as orienting responses. On the other hand, it can be as convincingly argued that the entire nervous system is sensory, for any change in muscle activity brings about changes in the stimulation of sensory receptors. The anatomist Brodal has pointed out, commenting on the symptoms of a stroke that he had suffered, that when considering the functions of the damaged brain, practical divisions of function into sensory and motor are particularly difficult:

The *specificity of the morphological organization of the nervous system* is amazing. The more we know about the structure of the brain, the more we realize how this specificity can be traced to the minutest levels. It is the rule, rather than the exception, that even a small nucleus can be subdivided into parts or territories which differ with regard to cytoarchitecture, glial architecture, vasoarchitecture, fiber connections, synaptic arrangements and by its chemistry. . . . If one focuses attention on the fiber connections of the central nervous system one is struck by another feature of its organization: the *multiplicity of connections*. As a rule each small region receives fibers from a number of others and likewise emits fibers which pass to many other regions. . . . There may, of course, be great quantitative differences among the various contingents of afferent and efferent fibers of a nucleus. Nevertheless, a scrutiny of the fiber connections of the central nervous system as a whole leaves one with the conviction that there are morphological possibilities for an impulse from a certain part of the brain to be transmitted along circumvential routes of varying complexity to virtually every other part of the central nervous system! These multifarious interconnections between structures presumably provide possibilities for cooperation and integration of function between them and make it increasingly difficult and unjustified to describe a certain part of the brain as simply "motor," "visual," etc. (A. Brodal, Self-observations and neuro-anatomical considerations after a stroke. *Brain,* 96:687–688, 1973.)

7

A GENERAL THEORY OF
BRAIN ORGANIZATION AND FUNCTION

Once upon a time six blind people from Hindustan examined an elephant to satisfy their curiosity about what it was. Alpha, touching its body, thought it a wall; Beta, touching its tusk, thought it a spear; Delta, touching its trunk, thought it a snake; Gamma, touching its leg, thought it a tree; Terry, touching its ear, thought it a fan; and Tim, examining its tail, thought it a rope. This popular story illustrates a well-known problem in the neurosciences: How can a concept of brain functions be developed from the disparate descriptions given by the different branches of the neurosciences? This problem is compounded: How can anyone assimilate the staggering amount of data about the brain being collected each year by these different branches of neuroscience?

Fortunately, the answers to both of these questions, although not completely adequate, are at least practical and helpful. First, it is possible to sketch a silhouette of the elephant (i.e., a theoretical framework describing the brain's organization and function) that is agreed on by people in most neuroscience areas. Second, because much of the new in-

formation published each year is simply a more refined description of the composition of the "elephant's tusk," it adds little to knowledge about the elephant and so it can be temporarily ignored.

In this chapter, which gives a general overview of the brain's function, we emphasize the brain's hierarchical organization. That is, the brain is organized in a *functional* hierarchy, the higher levels providing the animal with more precision in its behavior. The concept of hierarchy is important because it prevents the attribution of behaviors to one anatomical area that are in fact controlled by another. Other important aspects of brain organization receive less emphasis in this chapter because they are discussed in some depth elsewhere. For example, the lateralization of the brain with respect to function, particularly in humans, is described in detail in Chapters 14 and 15. Also, within the hierarchically organized brain are a number of parallel systems. On the input side are the projections and relay stations of the five major senses, each with a similar yet partly independent organization; these are discussed in Chapters 9 and 10. On the output side are three relatively independent motor systems: one for whole body movements, one for relatively independent limb movements, and one for relatively independent finger movements; these are discussed in Chapters 11 and 12.

LEVELS OF FUNCTION FROM SPINAL CORD TO CORTEX

The idea that the brain is organized in functional levels is not new. It can be dated at least to the mid-19th century, to Herbert Spencer's speculations that each "step" in evolution added a new level of brain and accordingly a new level of behavioral complexity. Certainly it was the basic principle that underlay all of Hughlings-Jackson's writings on brain function. Because of the nature of the questions addressed, the evidence in this section comes primarily from animal studies. Nevertheless, the general principles are applicable to humans, as attested by evidence from clinical studies.

The typical question to which an experiment is addressed is something like: What can an animal do without a neocortex? The question is answered by surgically removing the animal's neocortex and studying changes in behavior. The question is then rephrased: What can an animal do if the neocortex and the basal ganglia in addition are removed? By removal of successively more brain tissue in different preparations, eventually the functions of the spinal cord can be studied in isolation from the rest of the brain. Thus, a brain area can be studied in isolation from some area to which it is normally connected, yielding information about what the removed structure did as well as what the remaining structures do.

Of course, the success of such research depends on the ability of a damaged nervous system to continue functioning after the surgical procedure is complete. As it turns out,

the brain has a remarkable ability to survive after parts are destroyed. This resiliency to insult was given popular exposure in 1700 by DuVerney; in a public demonstration he showed that when a nerve and muscle were dissected away from a frog, the nerve continued to function, for when touched it produced muscle contractions. In 1853 Pflüger demonstrated that a frog with only an intact spinal cord could survive and display quite complex responses. If acid was placed on the frog's right side, the right leg would reach up and remove the acid. If the right leg was restrained, then after a number of ineffective efforts, the left leg would be used to remove the acid. Other workers, among them Ridi in 1810, demonstrated that if parts of the brainstem were intact, amphibians could walk. In 1884 Fano studied the locomotor patterns of a tortoise with only a lower brainstem; attached to its tail was a brush dipped in aniline, which traced the animal's pathway as it walked. These early experiments were followed by more systematic research into the capacities of different portions of the nervous system as well as into the details of their structure.

The following section presents the case for levels of function by describing the capacities of spinal animals and animals with successively more intact nervous systems. Figure 7–1 lists each experimental preparation and the brain tissue that remains intact and summarizes the types of behavior the animal can perform. Parallel conditions that may occur in humans will be noted in the discussions following.

The Spinal Animal: Reflexes

The spinal animal has a comparatively simple nervous system. First, the cord is divided into segments (30 in humans), as is illustrated in Figure 1–3. Second, each segment consists of two symmetrical halves, each of which re-

ANATOMY	PREPARATION	BEHAVIORS
	Normal (cortex)	Performs sequences of voluntary movements in organized patterns; responds to patterns of sensory stimulation. Contains circuits for forming cognitive maps and for responding to distal things. Adds emotional value.
	Decorticate (basal ganglia)	Links voluntary movements and automatic movements sufficiently well for self-maintenance (eating, drinking) in a simple environment.
	Diencephalic (hypothalamus thalamus)	Voluntary movements occur spontaneously and excessively but are aimless; shows well-integrated but poorly directed affective behavior; thermoregulates effectively.
	High decerebrate (midbrain)	Responds to simple features of visual and auditory stimulation; performs automatic behaviors such as grooming; performs subsets of voluntary movements (standing, walking, turning, jumping, climbing, etc.) when stimulated.
	Low decerebrate (hindbrain)	Performs units of movement (hissing, biting, growling, chewing, lapping, licking, etc.) when stimulated; shows exaggerated standing, postural reflexes, and elements of sleep-waking behavior.
	Spinal (spinal cord)	Shows reflexes (stretching, withdrawal, support, scratching, paw shaking, etc.) to appropriate sensory stimulation.

FIGURE 7–1. Behavior that can be supported by different levels of the nervous system. Shading indicates the highest remaining functional area.

ceives sensory fibers from one unilateral body dermatome and sends motor fibers to the same body dermatome. Third, the dorsal (posterior in the upright-standing human) portion of the cord receives sensory input from fibers that enter the cord as a fiber bundle or **dorsal root.** The cell bodies of these neurons are just outside the cord, forming the **dorsal root ganglion.** The ventral portion (anterior in humans) contains the cell bodies of the motor neurons and is the origin of the collection of motor fibers that leave each segment in a nerve tract or **ventral root.** The division of the spinal cord into dorsal sensory and ventral motor segments is called the **Bell–Magendie law.** The story of the discovery of this law includes a long-lasting unpleasant controversy. François Magendie, a volatile and committed French experimental physiologist, reported in a three-page paper in 1822 that he had succeeded in cutting the dorsal and ventral roots of puppy dogs, animals in which the roots were sufficiently segregated to allow surgery. He found that sectioning of the dorsal roots was associated with loss of sensibility and that sectioning of the ventral roots was associated with loss of movement. As early as 1811, the Scot Charles Bell and English anatomists, using anatomical conclusions and the results from somewhat inconclusive experiments on rabbits, had suggested somewhat different functions for each of the roots. Following Magendie's paper, priority for the discovery was hotly disputed with at least some success on the part of Bell. Magendie's experiment has been called the most important ever conducted on the nervous system, for it enabled neurologists for the first time to localize nervous system damage from the symptoms displayed by patients.

In its overall function, the spinal cord is thought to be involved in simple behaviors called *reflexes*. In a sense this is true. The spinal animal cannot stand and move spontaneously. Nevertheless, there is a great deal of internal processing going on at the spinal level that

both elaborates and places constraints on behaviors that occur in response to sensory stimulation. An understanding of this function provides an appreciation of some of the general principles of how the nervous system works. The major thrust toward understanding spinal function came from the work of Sir Charles Sherrington and his coworkers. Sherrington, a British physiologist, published a monumental summary of his research in 1906. Sherrington's work brought forward the idea that complex behavior is formed by the chaining together of a number of simple reflexes. Some schools of psychology exhaustively studied this idea, but it has now been virtually abandoned. Although reflexes are thought of as simple in comparison to more complex aspects of behavior, when the nature of receptor, internal spinal cord, and muscle action are each considered in detail, the processes turn out to be more complex than can be completely dealt with in the present discussion.

To describe spinal reflexes, three aspects of spinal cord organization need to be considered: (1) the somatosensory or afferent nerves from the body, (2) the connections that the afferents make with interneurons and motor neurons in the spinal cord, and (3) the motor or efferent nerves that leave the cord for the muscles. Some aspects of the circuitry are illustrated in Figure 7–2.

Afferents. There are two general kinds of afferents from the body. Their distinguishing features are their size and their degree of myelination (actually, physiologists subdivide them into four or more groups). Large, well-myelinated fibers mediate the senses of fine touch, pressure, and position. Smaller, less well myelinated fibers mediate the senses of pain and temperature. Most of the fibers come from the skin, muscles, and tendons. Figure 7–2 shows an afferent, called the Ia afferent, that comes from the muscles. It comes from special receptors in the muscle and sends sig-

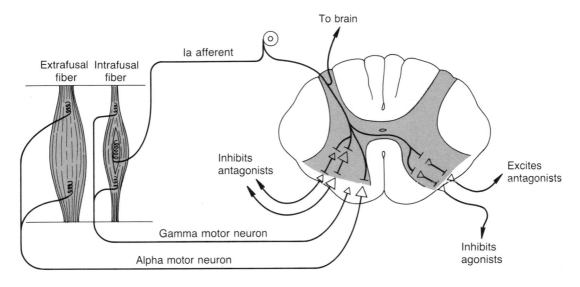

FIGURE 7–2. The stretch reflex. If a load is placed on a muscle, the muscle is stretched. Stretch activates the receptor in the intrafusal muscle fiber, sending a barrage of excitation to the motor neuron of the extrafusal fiber. It in turn contracts, resisting the stretch and relieving the tension of the intrafusal fiber. Note that input from the same afferent can inhibit antagonist muscles ipsilaterally and have the opposite actions on contralateral muscle groups.

nals to the brain about the position to which a limb has moved. As we shall see, it also signals its own muscle to contract to resist stretch.

Central Connections. In addition to projecting to the brain, somatosensory afferents make two kinds of connections in the spinal cord. They synapse in direct or monosynaptic connections with motor neurons, or they synapse with interneurons that in turn synapse with motor neurons. Most afferents have many collaterals, as is shown in Figure 7–2. Note that most synapses are with interneurons.

Efferents. There are two kinds of motor neurons: large motor neurons called *alpha motor neurons* and smaller ones called *gamma motor neurons*. The first type project to the working or *extrafusal* muscle fibers of the muscle, whereas the second type project to the sensory receptors, the *intrafusal* fibers (also

called muscle spindles) that are richly distributed throughout muscles.

An Example of a Spinal Reflex. How does the spinal cord produce reflexes? We have a tendency to think of reflexes as events that occur on special occasions, such as when a neurologist taps us on the knee. In fact, they are occurring from moment to moment to control the details of many aspects of movements that we make. We can appreciate this action by considering one reflex as an example. This is the *stretch reflex,* the one the neurologist elicits by tapping a patient on the knee.

Consider the reflex circuit illustrated in Figure 7–2. When the muscle is stretched by having a load placed on it, the muscle spindle is stretched and the receptor in its center is activated, sending a barrage of action potentials into the spinal cord. There is only one synapse between the afferent and the motor neuron that sends an axon to the same muscle, and so the discharge is transferred immediately to the muscle. The muscle contracts and its action counteracts the stretch, with the result that the muscle maintains its length, holding up the load. Contraction of the extrafusal fiber relieves the stretch on the intrafusal fiber and thus reduces the activity of the afferent.

The presence of the stretch reflex can be demonstrated in a clinical situation. If a subject, seated on a table with the lower part of the leg dangling from the edge of the table, is tapped on the tendon just below the knee (the tap is like a briefly applied load), the leg will swing upward briefly. This is because the tap on the tendon stretches the rectus femoris muscle of the upper leg, exciting its spindles and thereby activating a stretch reflex. Such stretch reflexes exist for all muscles, and many are routinely challenged by physicians during neurological examinations in order to test the integrity of different sections of the spinal cord. Obviously, if the stretch reflex is absent or exaggerated, the physician can suspect some abnormality in the appropriate section of the spinal cord. Stretch reflexes play an important role in controlling many aspects of behavior. If an object is dropped into one's outstretched hand, the hand will momentarily fall on impact with the object and then automatically return to its previous position. The stability of the hand's position is maintained through the stretch reflex of the biceps muscle. Stretch reflexes also help maintain posture. For example, standing still really consists of swaying slightly around a vertical position. When the eyes are closed, the amplitude of the oscillation is enhanced and contractions of the muscles, first on one side of the legs and then on the other, are readily perceptible, particularly in the large muscles of the upper forepart of the leg.

It seems worthwhile to describe two other aspects of the stretch reflex circuitry. When a group of muscles contract to produce a stretch,

what happens to the muscles around the same joint that normally oppose that movement? As is shown in Figure 7–2, collaterals from the afferent connect via interneurons to motor neurons of the antagonist muscles to inhibit their activity. The second point we can consider is how the brain produces movements through the circuit. Available evidence suggests that the brain simultaneously activates both the alpha and the gamma motor neurons, causing parallel contraction in both the extrafusal and intrafusal muscle fiber. During a voluntary movement the feedback from the muscle spindle, excited by the contraction, can both signal the brain that the limb has moved and signal the spinal cord about the resistance that the limb is meeting when it moves.

A number of other spinal reflexes require passing mention. The tendon receptor (also called the Golgi tendon organ) is situated in the tendon and is ideally placed to track the length of a muscle. The more a muscle contracts, the more likely the tendon organ is to be excited. It can monitor the length of the muscle and can also inhibit the muscle to slow the rate and extent to which it can be stretched. The latter action is called *the inverse stretch reflex*. There is a well-known reflex in people who have rigidity of central origin. If a limb is moved, it will stiffen and resist the movement but only up to a point. Quite suddenly it will relax and completely give way. This sudden release is called the *clasp-knife reflex* because it resembles the sudden last-minute loss of resistance in the blade of a pocket knife during closure. It was originally thought that this reflex is mediated by the tendon organ, but it is now thought that it is produced by afferents, called Ib afferents, that come from the muscle spindle.

A pinprick to the paw of a spinal cat or dog causes a flexion of the limb. This is a *withdrawal reflex* that removes the limb from danger. If the stimulus is mild, only the distal portion of the limb is withdrawn, but if the stimulus is made successively stronger, the size of the movement increases until the whole limb is withdrawn. The pain afferents produce withdrawal reflexes by exciting flexor muscles and inhibiting extensor muscles. Tactile stimulation, such as light pressure on the pads of the foot of a spinal dog, will cause the limb to extend. This *extensor reflex* is the basis of a supporting reaction prerequisite for standing. Afferents from the cutaneous receptors predominantly excite extensor motor neurons and inhibit flexor motor neurons. As such, the extensor reflex is exactly the opposite reaction to the withdrawal reflex.

So far we have described how a muscle responds to the stimulation of afferents within its own proximity. But muscles do not act in isolation. They are arranged in pairs around joints such that an *agonist* moves a joint in one direction and an *antagonist* moves it in the other direction. Muscles also work in groups that flex or extend limbs. These groups also act in concert with muscles on the opposite side of the body. For example, during walking flexors in one limb will be active in raising the limb while extensors are maintaining support with the other limb. The connections that we have described in the spinal cord (Figure 7–2) are not limited only to single muscles. Collateral from afferents will distribute themselves to interneurons and motor neurons in the same side of the cord and in the opposite side of the cord such that all muscle groups will act in concert in a coordinated fashion. The inhibition of one group of muscles that permits a second group to move is called **reciprocal inhibition.** Sensory afferents may also send collaterals to many other segments of the spinal cord in order to coordinate movements in other body parts. Again the appropriate connections are made directly or through interneurons. It can be seen that each motor neuron has many direct and indirect connections, and its activity will reflect the majority influence rather than just the influence of any single synaptic connection.

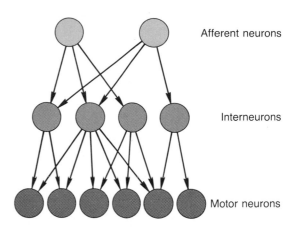

FIGURE 7–3. Lattice hierarchy. Top, afferent neurons; middle, interneurons; bottom, motor neurons. Note that different clusters of motor neurons are activated by different types of sensory stimulation. (After Gallistel, 1980.)

A model that explains how a limited number of motor neurons can participate in a large number of motor activities is shown in Figure 7–3. It is called a *lattice hierarchy.* The top units in the model represent different types of sensory stimulation, i.e., from the skin, tendons, or muscles. The middle group of units represent interneurons. The bottom group of units represents motor neurons. Note that through the connection of the interneurons each type of afferent stimulation can recruit a specific population of motor neurons and thus produce a specific movement. The same motor neurons can be used again and again but in different combinations. The lattice hierarchy explains how a fixed number of motor neurons can produce a wide variety of movements, and it also shows that there are certain constraints on how they are used. For example, a motor neuron could not be used at one and the same time to produce conflicting movements. The motor neurons have been described as analogous to the keys on a piano: there are a limited number of keys, yet when they are used in combination, a very large number of cords can be played singly, together, or in sequence to produce almost an infinite number of melodies.

Oscillators

Male spinal cats can make rhythmic movements of pelvic thrusting and female spinal cats can make rhythmic movements of treading. Spinal animals can also scratch with rhythmic movements to remove objects from the body. Grillner has demonstrated that a spinal cat suspended in a sling on a treadmill will display coordinated walking, and after some recovery from midspinal section it can use the isolated rear limbs for spontaneous walking. How are these movements produced? It is suggested that the spinal cord contains groups of neurons arranged in such a way that they reciprocally activate and inhibit each other in rhythmic fashion. Such reciprocally acting neuron pools are called *oscillators*. If the activity in an oscillator is self-sustaining, components of its activity could be used to power and time rhythmic movements of walking, scratching, pelvic thrusting, etc. It is thought that oscillators are located at many levels of the nervous system and are involved in timing movements such as chewing, licking, grooming, and long-lasting rhythmically occurring behaviors such as sleep, sexual cycles, and migration. Evidence that oscillators do in fact exist is persuasive. Early experimenters noted that fish with transected brains would make continuous movements of the fins in the absence of any sensory stimulation. In frogs and other animals it has been observed that the scratch reflex has an optimal frequency independent of the frequency eliciting it and that scratching may continue long after the stimulus has been removed. In invertebrates, which have relatively simple nervous systems, electrophysiological studies have identified and analyzed the general features of a number of different kinds of oscillators.

Feedback, Feedforward, and Gating

The analysis of spinal reflexes shows that they have a variety of properties that are not easily accounted for by "straight through" neural circuitry. Increasing intensities of stimulation do not lead to monotonically increasing response amplitudes. Sometimes, a response may also have a greater amplitude than that expected from the intensity of the stimulation. Presentation of two different kinds of stimulation can produce a response quite different from that found with the presentation of each stimulus alone. Each of these events can be explained by other properties of spinal cord organization.

Anatomists have observed that motor neurons give off collaterals before they leave the spinal cord. These collaterals synapse with an interneuron called the Renshaw cell (named after Renshaw, who first observed it). The Renshaw cell in turn synapses with the motor neuron (Figure 7–4 A). This circuit is an *inhibitory feedback loop*. Each time the motor neuron is excited, it dampens its own activity. This protects it from becoming excessively active. The utility of this action can be demonstrated by considering what happens when an animal is given an injection of the stimulant and poison strychnine. The strychnine-poisoned animal displays excessive muscle tone and can frequently be sent into convulsions by sensory stimulation. Strychnine blocks the Renshaw–motor neuron synapse (which is thought to contain glycine). Consequently, the motor neuron, no longer able to inhibit itself, can become excessively active and produce the violent muscular contractions that characterize a convulsion. Clearly, feedback has a protective influence to prevent excessive activation. Circuits that can be considered *feedforward* also exist. Stimulation of an afferent may send a

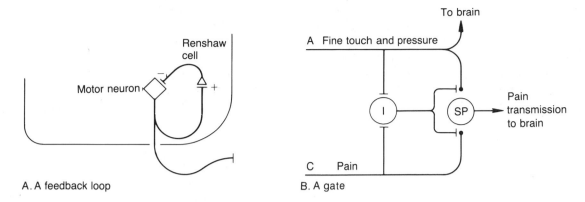

FIGURE 7–4. A. Renshaw arc. Note that the motor neuron can decrease its own ability to be reactivated. B. A model of the gate proposed by Melzack and Wall. Activation of the fine touch and pressure pathway excites the interneuron (I), but activation of the pain pathway inhibits it. The interneuron delivers presynaptic inhibition on transmission afferents to the secondary pain cell. Thus, fine touch and pressure activity decreases pain transmission.

message to the motor neuron and also send a message to the brain via a collateral. Should the brain act on the information that it receives, it would find the motor neuron already in a state of readiness for action. A startle response leading to postural adjustments that prepare a person to run can be considered an example of feedforward.

It is well known, and can be verified from personal experience, that a sensation of pain such as occurs with a burn, an itch, or a tickle can be reduced or stopped altogether by rubbing or scratching. How does rubbing, which activates fine touch and pressure receptors, reduce pain, which is mediated by a different receptor and different-size nerve fibers? Melzack and Wall, in a theory now considered to be classic, suggest that there are gates in the spinal cord that can be opened or closed to regulate the flow of certain kinds of sensory information. Figure 7–4 B gives an example of what such a gate might look like. Pathway A represents the fine touch and pressure system. It sends a collateral to an interneuron, I. Pathway C represents the pain-conducting system.

Note that there is a synapse in the pain pathway. When the events in the two pathways are varied, it can be seen that if the flow of information in the A pathway is increased relative to that in the C pathway, the A pathway will, through the interneuron, inhibit or gate activity in the C pathway. By the judicious placement of appropriately connected interneurons, many different kinds of gates serving different purposes can be constructed. There is experimental evidence that there are gates for pain in the spinal cord, and gates for pain suppression may also exist in various brain regions. For example, centrally placed gates may explain why, when one is paying attention to an interesting event, an uncomfortable or painful stimulus may go unnoticed.

Summary

A number of psychological theories that were popular in the first half of this century attempted to explain behavior in terms of simple stimulus-response (S-R) reflexes that are chained together in various ways. Unfortunately, students in psychology courses were abused by having to learn these theories. Studies by Sherrington and subsequently by other physiologists showed that even the simplest reflexes in the spinal cord provide little support for these theories. Sensory receptors that supply the spinal cord with input act as filters in that they are selective about the features of the stimuli to which they respond. The reflexes that a stimulus elicits are not related in a one-to-one fashion to either the duration or the intensity of the stimulation. In the frog, for example, a stimulus at any intensity or frequency might elicit only a 4 cycle/sec scratch reflex that continues well after the stimulus is removed. Different kinds of stimuli can also summate or negate. Even the same stimulus repeated can elicit quite different responses, as occurs when a toe pinch repeated a number of times elicits first a paw flexion response, then a lower limb flexion response, and finally a withdrawal response from the whole leg. Clearly, the spinal cord is not a passive channel for conducting information but is actively involved in transposing it through its own internal connections in a way that is consistent with their own moment-to-moment state. Many of the features of brain function are not understood as well as those of the spinal cord, but we may justifiably expect that they will not be less complex than those of the spinal cord. We may also expect that they will use many of the same principles of transposition that are found in the spinal cord, e.g., oscillators, feedforward, and feedback. It follows, therefore, that explanations of brain function will not be found in S-R–type theories but must be found by analyzing the programs that are formed by the multiple connections made by the brain's interneurons.

The Low-Decerebrate Animal: Support

In the low-decerebrate animal both the hindbrain and the spinal cord remain intact. The sensory input into the hindbrain comes predominantly from the head and is carried over cranial nerves IV to XII. Most of these nerves also have motor nuclei in the hindbrain whose efferent fibers control muscles in the head and neck. Whereas interneurons in the spinal cord are sometimes between sensory projections and motor projections, interneurons in the hindbrain have multiplied to form nuclei as well as more complex coordinating centers such as the cerebellum. Sensory input to the hindbrain is not limited to the cranial nerves, for, as we shall see, the spinal somatosensory system has access to hindbrain motor systems, just as the hindbrain has access to spinal motor systems. Before the function of the hindbrain is discussed, a description of the behavior of low-decerebrate animals might be helpful.

Low-decerebrate cats are described by Bazett and Penfield and by Bard and Macht in experiments in which the animals are kept alive for periods of weeks or months. The animals are generally inactive when undisturbed and show virtually no effective thermoregulatory ability, but otherwise they are relatively easy to maintain because they swallow food placed on their tongues and so can be fed. If the animals are stimulated lightly in any of a variety of sensory modalities—e.g., touch, pain, sounds—they right themselves from their normal lateral position into a crouched position. If the stimulation is stronger, they walk, somewhat unsteadily. These stimuli can also elicit some of the movements of the affective behavior of normal cats, because the cats are observed to bite, hiss, growl, and lash their tails.

One of the most characteristic additions to behavior accorded by an intact hindbrain is a peculiar kind of stiffness called **decerebrate rigidity:** excessive muscle tone, particularly in the antigravity muscles of the body, which are the strongest muscles. Because of this rigidity, when an animal is placed in an upright position, its limbs extend and its head flexes upward. Sherrington refers to this rigidity as exaggerated standing.

How is exaggerated standing produced? An experiment by Sherrington in 1898 showed that if the dorsal roots to the limb were cut, the limb immediately became flaccid. At the time, the observation that sectioning of afferents should abolish motor activity was quite surprising. Later, after muscle spindles had been described, it became clear that the rigidity was produced in part by brainstem excitation of gamma motor neurons. Note from Figure 7–2 that if they are excited, they cause the intrafusal muscle to contract. This excites the Ia afferents in the same way as if the entire muscle had been stretched. Activation of the Ia afferents then leads to contraction of the muscle. In the decerebrate animal all muscles that sustain posture against gravity are excited through the gamma motor system to produce exaggerated standing. Interestingly, the antigravity muscles in the sloth, which hangs upside down, are flexors and the decerebrate sloth displays flexor rather than extensor rigidity.

Against the background of decerebrate rigidity, a number of *postural reflexes* can be elicited by changes in head position. If the head of a standing animal is pushed down toward the floor, the front limbs flex and the hind limbs extend; if the head is pushed up, the hind legs flex and the front legs extend. The first type of posture would be used by a normal cat looking under a couch, the second by a normal cat looking up onto a shelf. Turning the head to the side elicits extension of the limbs on the same side and flexion of the limbs on the opposite side of the body; this type of response occurs in a normal cat that has turned its head to look at some object and is prepared to pursue it. When the animals are placed on their sides, they extend their lower limbs, which are in contact with the floor surface, and semiflex

their upper limbs, a static reaction that represents the first stage of the **righting reflex.**

There are two types of sleep in normal animals: *quiet sleep,* characterized by muscle tone, and *active sleep,* characterized by an absence of muscle tone. Low-decerebrate animals are described as showing characteristics of both types of sleep at different times. Animals left undisturbed gradually lose their rigidity and subside or droop into a prone posture. Any mild stimulus such as a noise or touch reinstates rigidity. This type of behavioral change seems analogous to quiet sleep. The animals also show a sudden collapse, accompanied by the loss of all body tone, which lasts from 15 seconds to 12 minutes. This type of behavioral change seems analogous to active sleep, particularly since some people with an illness called **narcolepsy** similarly collapse into active sleep.

The low-decerebrate animal's behavior, then, differs from the spinal animal's in a number of ways. First, responses such as tail lashing and biting are elicited by several modes of stimulation, which often summate. Such responses can be explained in the following way. In its simplest form tail lashing is a withdrawal reflex of the tail produced by noxious tail stimulation; it is a spinal reflex. Biting is a jaw reflex elicited by facial stimulation; it is mediated through the hindbrain by the sensory and motor components of the trigeminal (V) nerve. If the sensory component of the spinal reflexes taps into the motor components of hindbrain reflex circuits, and if the sensory components of the hindbrain reflexes tap into the motor component of spinal-cord reflex circuits, then pinching the cat's lip can produce tail withdrawal (tail lashing) as well as biting, and pinching the cat's tail can produce biting plus tail withdrawal. Spontaneous occurrence of these behaviors may either be elicited by spontaneous activity in the spinal–hindbrain circuits or be triggered by less obvious stimulation carried into the spinal–hindbrain circuits by other nerves such as the vagus (X) nerve. This principle of interlinking sensory and motor components of different levels is an organizational feature of all levels of brain function.

The **vestibular system,** by means of nerve VIII, makes an obvious contribution to the behavior of low-decerebrate animals. There are two vestibular receptors in the middle ear: the **saccule** signals when the head is oriented in the normal position; the utricle, which gives off steady signals even when the head is still, signals changes in orientation. It is probable that the upright posture of the head and body is maintained by the saccule or its motor nuclei in the hindbrain. The decerebrate rigidity of the low-decerebrate animal is no doubt the exaggerated product of unchecked activity in this system. When the head is moved, the posture of the animal changes in characteristic ways. These postural changes are probably mediated by the utricle and its motor nuclei.

Since part of the function of the vestibular system is to maintain and adjust posture it seems logical that a mechanism be built into the hindbrain to check its activity when an upright posture is not needed. Otherwise an animal might remain in a rigid position until its musculature were exhausted. Decerebrate animals do relax, which suggests that there is an inhibitory system in the hindbrain. The inhibition provided by this system is most likely the neurological basis of sleep. The observation that any type of stimulation can restore rigidity after relaxation occurs suggests that spinal and hindbrain sensory systems have input into the nuclei that maintain support and are capable of activating them. Stimulation from these systems probably provides part of the neurological basis for awakening.

The behavioral changes seen in low-decerebrate animals are paralleled in people who have brainstem damage of the type that essentially separates the lower brainstem from the rest of the brain. Barrett, Merritt, and Wolf have documented a number of such cases. These people may alternate between states of consciousness resembling sleeping and waking, make eye movements to follow moving stimuli, cough, smile, swallow food, display decerebrate rigidity, and display postural adjustments when moved. When cared for, people with such brain damage may live for months or years with little change in their condition.

The High-Decerebrate Animal: Voluntary and Automatic Behavior

The high-decerebrate animal has an intact midbrain containing, in the tectum, the coordinating centers for vision (superior colliculus) and hearing (inferior colliculus) and, in the tegmentum, a number of motor nuclei. Visual and auditory inputs are different from any sensory input received at lower levels because they allow the animal to perceive events at a distance. Correspondingly, it is not surprising to find that the high-decerebrate animal is able to respond to distant objects by locomoting toward them. However, the assessment of how active high-decerebrate animals are varies from study to study.

Bard and Macht report that high-decerebrate cats can walk, stand, resume upright posture when turned on their backs, and even run and climb when stimulated. Bignall and Schramm found that kittens decerebrated in infancy could orient to visual and auditory stimuli. The animals could even execute an attack response and pounce on objects at the source of a sound. In fact, Bignall and Schramm fed the cats by exploiting this behavior, for they placed food near the source of the sound; attacking the sound source the cats would then consume the food. Although the cats attacked moving objects, they gave no evidence of "seeing," for they bumped into things when they walked around. Woods has reported that high-decerebrate rats are active and make all the movements of normal rats; Grill and Norgren report that they are generally inactive and show normal locomotor abilities only when disturbed. Bignall and Schramm and Woods may have left some hypothalamic tissue intact, which would account for why their animals were more active than animals observed in other studies.

These experiments demonstrate that all the components (or subsets) of **voluntary movements**—movements that take an animal from one place to another, such as turning, walking, climbing, and swimming—are present at the level of the midbrain. Intact animals use voluntary movements in a variety of motivational conditions, e.g., to find food, water, or a new home territory or to escape a predator. These movements have also been variously called appetitive, instrumental, purposive, or operant. Voluntary movements, being executed through lower-level postural support and reflex systems, can also be elicited by lower-level sensory input; that is, a pinch or postural displacement can elicit turning, walking, or climbing. Thus, this new functional level is integrated with lower levels by both ascending and descending connections, exactly as the hindbrain and spinal levels are interconnected.

High-decerebrate animals are also able to effectively perform **automatic behaviors:** units of stereotyped behavior linked in a sequence. Grooming, chewing food, lapping water, and rejecting food are representative automatic behaviors of the rat. Generally, automatic behaviors (also variously called reflexive, consummatory, or respondent behaviors) are directed toward completing some sort of consummatory act and are not specifically directed toward moving an animal from one place to another. Grooming is an excellent example of an automatic behavior since it consists of a large number of movements

executed sequentially in an organized and quite stereotyped fashion. If a rat's fur is wet, it first shakes its back, then sits on its haunches and shakes its front paws, then licks water from them, wipes its snout rapidly with bilateral symmetrical movements, wipes its face with slight asymmetrical movements, and then turns to lick the fur on its body. Food rejection is similarly complex. If decerebrate rats are satiated and given food, they perform a series of movements consisting of tongue flicks, chin rubbing, and paw shaking to reject the food. These behaviors are similar to the rejection behaviors made by normal rats in response to food they find noxious. If the animals are not sated, they will lap water and chew food brought to their mouths.

There are a number of accounts of infants born with large portions of the forebrain missing. One child studied by Gamper (Figure 7–5) had no brain present above the diencephalon and only a few traces of the diencephalon intact, and it was thus anatomically equivalent to a high-decerebrate animal. This child showed many behaviors of newborn infants. It could sit up; it showed periodic sleep and wakefulness; it could suck, yawn, stretch, cry, and follow visual stimuli with its eyes. However, the child showed little spontaneous activity and if left alone remained mostly in a drowsy state. Brackbill studied a similar child and found that in responses to stimuli such as 60 to 90 decibel sounds it oriented in much the same way normal children did. Unlike normal children, however, the responses did not change in size and did not habituate to repeated presentation. She concluded that the forebrain is not important for eliciting responding but is important for attenuating and inhibiting responding. Generally, children born with such extensive brain abnormalities do not live long, and among those that live for a number of months there is no development of the complex behav-

FIGURE 7–5. Instinctive behavior and oral automatisms in Gamper's mesencephalic human. A. Yawning with spreading of arms. B. Oral adversive movements after the lips are touched, with deviation of the eyes. C. Coordinated gaze and snapping movements after finger was removed. D. Spontaneous sucking of own hand. E. Oral adversion to the left side with deviation of head and eyes and tonic neck reflexes in the arms. (From E. Gamper, *Ztschr. ges. Neurol. Psychiat.* 104:49, 1926.)

iors seen in normal children. They appear to have the same behavioral capacities of high-decerebrate animals.

In summary, the midbrain adds at least three new components to behavior. First, the presence of the auditory and optic systems allows the animals to receive sensory input that originates at some distance. Most evidence suggests that these sensory systems respond to only the simpler features of stimuli such as intensity and place. Second, these sensory systems appear to be linked with voluntary motor systems that allow the animal to respond to distant stimuli by moving toward or away from them. Third, the midbrain appears to contain programs that allow the animals to chain together a number of movements to form complex behaviors of the consummatory type, called automatic behaviors.

The Diencephalon: Affect and Motivation

Probably the diencephalon has been studied more than any other brain structure, yet its contribution to the organization of behavior is not well understood. The diencephalic animal has an intact olfactory system, enabling it to smell odorous objects at a distance. The hypothalamus and pituitary are also intact, and their control over body hormonal systems no doubt integrates the body's physiology with the brain's activity. In physiological literature the hypothalamus is thought to be involved in homeostasis, that is, maintaining body temperature, water balance, energy reserves, etc. Diencephalic animals do maintain normal body temperature, but they do not eat or drink well enough to maintain themselves. In the traditional literature of physiological psychology, diencephalic functions are often discussed under the headings of affect and motivation. Although these terms have never been defined to everyone's satisfaction, the diencephalon does seem to add a dimension of affect and motivation to behavior if the terms are used in the sense that behavior becomes "energized." Some examples of the diencephalic animal's behavior will illustrate this point.

As we have mentioned, high-decerebrate

animals show many of the component behaviors of rage, but the behaviors are not
energetic, well integrated, or sustained. Cannon and Britton studied forebrain-lesioned
cats and described what they called "quasi-
emotional phenomena" (or sham rage, described below) such as are usually seen in an
infuriated animal; the behavior consists of
lashing the tail, arching the trunk, making limb
movements, displaying claws, snarling, and
biting. Sympathetic signs of rage are present,
including erection of the tail hair, sweating of
the toe pads, dilation of the pupils, mictura-
tion, high blood pressure, high heart rate, and
increases in adrenalin and blood sugar. These
emotional attacks sometimes last for hours.
Bard removed various amounts of forebrain
and brainstem and found that for this effect to
occur it was necessary to leave at least the
posterior portion of the hypothalamus intact.
Clinical reports indicate that similar sham
emotional attacks can occur in people who
have suffered hypothalamic lesions; thus, there
are reports of people who show unchecked
rage behavior, or who literally laugh until they
die.

One of the most pronounced features of the
diencephalic animal's behavior is its constant
activity; this has been observed by Sorenson
and Ellison and by Grill and Norgren in rats
and by Goltz in dogs. We have watched
diencephalic rats and found that although they
attempt to eat, they are unable to remain still
long enough to ingest more than a few grams
of food over periods lasting for hours. Since
normal animals deprived of food and water
become active, it is possible to argue that the
diencephalic animal's hyperactivity is driven
by a deficiency condition; that is, the animal is
searching for food or water. Grill and Norgren, however, have found that feeding the
animals as much as control rats does not arrest
hyperactivity.

These two examples of diencephalic behavior suggest to us that the diencephalon adds
an "energizing" dimension to behavior that
may justify labeling the behavior affective or
motivated. Britton and Cannon, however,
were aware of the inappropriateness of the rage
behavior of the diencephalic cat (it is overdone
and not directed) and so they called it sham
rage, to distinguish it from the directed rage of
the normal cat. Perhaps the hyperactivity of
the diencephalic animal should be called sham
motivation to distinguish it from the goal-
oriented behavior of the normal animal. In this
sense the sham affect and sham motivation of
the diencephalic animal are something like the
exaggerated standing observed in low-
decerebrate animals. Under appropriate forebrain control it can be manipulated for functional purposes, but in the absence of that control the behavior of the animal is excessive and
seems inappropriate. (These are classic examples of Jacksonian release phenomena.) At present it is unknown whether the energizing
aspect of the diencephalic animal's behavior
can be attributed to the hormonal or to the
neural connections of the diencephalon.

The Basal Ganglia: Self-Maintenance

Decortication is removal of the neocortex
(either alone or with the limbic system as well),
leaving the basal ganglia and brainstem intact.
Decorticate animals have been studied more
closely than any others because they are able to
maintain themselves without special care in
laboratory conditions.

The first careful experiments were done by
Goltz with decorticate dogs (Chapter 13), but
the most thorough studies have used rats as
subjects. Experiments by ourselves and our
colleagues show that within a day after surgery
they eat and maintain body weight on a wet
mash diet, and eat dry food and drink water

brought in contact with the mouth. With a little training at drinking (holding the water spout to the mouth) they find water and become able to maintain themselves on water and laboratory chow within 10 days. They have normal sleep-waking cycles, run, climb, and swim, and even negotiate simple mazes (which admittedly they learn with great difficulty). The hyperactivity characteristic of diencephalic animals is greatly reduced.

What is observed in the decorticate rat, and what is presumably conferred by the basal ganglia, is the ability to link automatic movements to voluntary movements so that the behaviors are biologically adaptive. A major portion of this linking probably involves inhibition or facilitation of voluntary movements. For example, the animal walks until it finds food or water and then the basal ganglia inhibit walking to allow the consummatory act to occur. As well as inhibiting voluntary movements at specific times, the basal ganglia probably also help them to occur.

The most thorough study of animals without a basal ganglia has been done by Jaime Villablanca and Charles Olmstead in cats. In this species the basal ganglia can be removed without damaging the motor fibers projecting from the cortex to the brainstem. Villablanca and Olmstead suggest that the basal ganglia are involved in the fine-tuning of motor and sensory responses. Their cats displayed a compulsive approach syndrome. They followed people, attempting to make contact with them and stick to them. They would return again and again after being repeatedly pushed away. They attempted to grasp any nearby moving object and would approach any sensory stimulus. They were docile, purred continually, and made treading responses in the presence of people. Their movements were abnormal. They lost placing responses for months after surgery, their reaching movements were poorly controlled,

they had difficulty in pressing a bar, and they were hyperactive. Thus, the cats seemed to display all cat-type behaviors, but the acts were often inappropriate and were poorly executed, suggesting that the problem was "tuning" rather than performance per se. Some of the features of the behavior of cats with damaged basal ganglia are reminiscent of those of monkeys and cats that have the amygdala (another portion of the basal ganglia) removed. These animals display a constellation of abnormalities referred to as the Klüver-Bucy syndrome. They display "psychic blindness" in that they do not seem to recognize familiar objects. They examine every object by placing it in their mouth. They orient to every visual stimulus. They seem to show an absence of the emotional behaviors of anger and fear. They also show increased sexual activity. The constellation of syndromes displayed by animals with both kinds of brain damage suggests not only a deficit in fine-tuning but also an inability to recognize the significance of various objects.

The Cortex: Sequencing Voluntary Movement, Pattern Perception, and Cognitive Mapping

What the cortex *does* can also be ascertained by studying what the decorticate animal (with the neocortex alone removed or with the limbic system also removed) *cannot* do. The cortex has diverse functions, and these may not have a single organizing principle. Nevertheless, generalizing from the following deficits, it appears that the cortex constructs sequences or patterns of voluntary movements in response to external and internal cues, discriminates pattern in sensory input, and executes a number of complex behaviors that seem to involve cognitive mapping.

Sequencing Voluntary Movements. Studies on decorticate animals seem to suggest more about what they can do than what they cannot do. All the elementary movements that an animal might require seem to be part of their behavioral repertory. They can walk, eat, drink, mate, etc., in a seemingly adequate fashion. Yet they do not build nests, although they engage in some nest-building behaviors. They do not hoard food, although they might carry food around. They do not keep themselves as clean as normal animals, although they seem to perform most of the movements of grooming. Because of the nature of these deficits, Vanderwolf and his coworkers have suggested that the cortex is involved in sequencing voluntary movements. Their general argument has been made a number of times in different forms. One version of the argument suggests that the cortex contains motor scores that direct the sequence in which subcortically coded elementary movements are executed. A second version of the idea is that the cortex has a general inhibitory action in deleting certain subcortically coded movements so that other appropriate movements can occur.

Pattern Perception. It is well known that the function of the cortical sensory areas is to discriminate patterns. Klüver, using monkeys, found that animals with visual cortex lesions were unable to discriminate between two objects that differed in their pattern (i.e., horizontal as opposed to vertical stripes), but that they were able to respond to lights in different locations or of different brightness. Bauer and Cooper, and Goodale, have made a similar point with respect to visual cortex function in rats. Their research suggests that whereas the superior colliculus and other midbrain visual centers are adequate for discriminating place and intensity, the neocortex is required for pattern discrimination. Other studies on other sensory systems agree that the function of the cortical sensory areas is to discriminate patterns. For example, a decorticate animal may discriminate "beep, beep, beep" from "bop, bop, bop" but be quite unable to discriminate "beep, bop, beep" from "bop, beep, bop."

Cognitive Mapping. There are a number of paradigms used to study learning in animals. A series of experiments by David Oakley and Ian Steele Russell have looked at classical conditioning, operant conditioning, approach learning, cue learning, etc., in decorticate rats and rabbits and have found that the decorticate animals perform tasks as well or almost as well as normal animals. These experiments confirm that the cortex is not necessary for learning per se. In the first part of this century Edward Tolman suggested that animals have the ability to make maps of their environment and then navigate through that environment using information from the maps. For example, if a rat is trained to travel from the south corner of the room to the north corner and then at some later time is placed in the west corner, it is able to travel to the correct north corner even if it has never experienced taking that route. Classical and operant conditioning theory cannot explain this result. It therefore seems likely that the animal has an ability to form maps of its environment that it can use in novel ways at a later date. Very little is known about the neural circuitry that makes cognitive mapping possible, but available evidence suggests that such maps are formed extremely rapidly, sometimes in one or two trials. This suggests that the maps are formed by specific cognitive processes that are a property of inbuilt neural connections. In other words, they are not formed by some sort of rote trial-by-trial learning procedure. We have recently tested the ability of decorticate rats to navigate using either a cognitive mapping strategy or a cue-learning strategy. The animals were tested in a task called the Morris water task, designed in Scotland by Richard Morris. The apparatus consisted of a large circular pool filled with tinted water in which a platform was hidden just below the surface at a fixed location. The animals, placed in the pool at different locations, were required to locate the hidden platform. The only cues that they could use for guidance were surrounding room cues. Normal rats mastered this task in a few trials, but the decorticates never learned to navigate to the platform and seemed to find it occasionally only by chance. If the platform was raised above the water so that it was visible, the decorticate rats quickly learned to swim to it.

The results of this experiment suggest to us that the cortex contains processing capacities that are different from those used by subcortical structures. John O'Keefe and Lynn Nadel have suggested that the hippocampus plays a special role in such mapping and also argue that other abilities such as language use similar cognitive abilities. What is particularly interesting about cognitive mapping abilities is that they seem designed to deal with distal as opposed to proximal events or cues. A proximal cue can be detected and increases in size or intensity as it is approached. Animals such as salmon can navigate for thousands of miles by following an odor cue, which presumably increases in intensity as its source is approached. A distal cue, however, need not be approached or avoided and is used only because of its relative position. It guides navigation to some other fixed place. We suggest that if the cortex has some special organizational principle, it is the ability to deal with distal things or events. Decorticate rats, for example, cannot make placing responses with their limbs. In part, such responses require that they move a limb from one location to another on the assumption that there will be an object there to contact. They are able to use their tongue to lick, but they seem unable to pro-

trude it to retrieve an object at a distance. They are impaired in their ability to reach for and retrieve objects with their paws. Again these are movements that seem specifically designed to deal with distal things. Decorticate rats are also extremely impaired in go-no-go tasks. Such a task requires that an animal sit and wait for a specific period of time before engaging in some act. Their impairment here seems to be an inability to deal with an event distant in time. The idea that the cortex has evolved to deal with distal events seems particularly supported by the use of language in humans, for language is designed not only to communicate at a distance but also to communicate about things that are distant in place, order, or time.

The Generality of Levels of Function

After summarizing some of the available information on levels of function, it seems appropriate to ask: Are the results from these lesion studies consistent with those obtained from research using other approaches? The answer is that there is a good relation. For example, Flynn and his coworkers have studied the organization of predatory behavior in the cat by stimulating the brainstem electrically. Stimulation in the midbrain gives responses that are not associated with the autonomic signs of arousal that typically accompany attack behavior elicited by hypothalamic stimulation. Similarly, many other stimulation studies on rats and other animals confirm that the simpler components of motor behavior are organized in the lower brainstem (e.g., Bernston and Micco, Buchholz, and Robinson).

Another source of confirmatory evidence for levels of function is studies on the electrical activity (EEG) of the forebrain. Vanderwolf and his colleagues find that the electrical activity of the neocortex and hippocampus changes with behavior in such a way that "activated" patterns of EEG always occur during voluntary movements but not always with automatic behaviors. The hippocampal EEG of the rat shows this relation most clearly (see Figure 7–6): a rhythmical wave pattern called **theta activity** (having a frequency of 4 to 7 Hz) is found to be correlated with voluntary movements (type 1) but is generally absent during automatic movements (type 2). According to the argument that the forebrain's function is to produce patterns of movements by putting together subsets of voluntary movement, it is understandable that the forebrain is in an "active mode" during these behaviors. It is controlling voluntary movements to ensure that they are appropriate in sequence, time, and place. The forebrain need not be active in the same way during automatic movements, since, once the animal is in a posi-tion to perform them, they are executed whol-ly at lower functional levels. It is instructive that Bland and Vanderwolf have reported that interference with the theta activity of the hip-pocampus will disrupt voluntary but not more automatic behaviors, whereas facilitating the theta activity facilitates voluntary but not more automatic behaviors.

Why Levels?

Why is the brain organized into functional levels integrated in such a way that each level controls a large number of behaviors? Evelyn Satinoff suggests that the answer has three parts. First, the selective pressure for the de-velopment of new brain was to refine the animal's ability to respond to specific features of the world. A good example is thermo-

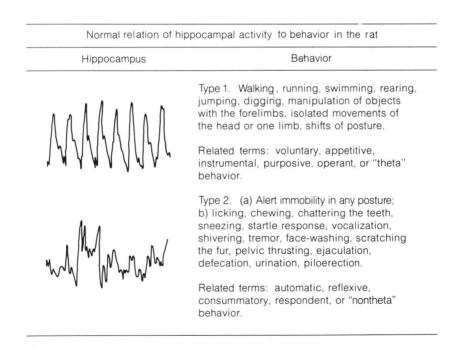

Normal relation of hippocampal activity to behavior in the rat	
Hippocampus	Behavior
	Type 1. Walking, running, swimming, rearing, jumping, digging, manipulation of objects with the forelimbs, isolated movements of the head or one limb, shifts of posture.
	Related terms: voluntary, appetitive, instrumental, purposive, operant, or "theta" behavior.
	Type 2. (a) Alert immobility in any posture; b) licking, chewing, chattering the teeth, sneezing, startle response, vocalization, shivering, tremor, face-washing, scratching the fur, pelvic thrusting, ejaculation, defecation, urination, piloerection.
	Related terms: automatic, reflexive, consummatory, respondent, or "nontheta" behavior.

FIGURE 7–6. Hippocampal activity in relation to spontaneous behavior in the rat. (After Vanderwolf et al., 1975.)

regulation: any physiological or behavioral response intended to maintain normal body temperature. Response to temperature change in spinal animals begins at temperature extremes of 36 to 41°C; in decerebrates the range narrows to 37 to 39°C; in diencephalics it is around 38°C; whereas in normal animals thermoregulatory responses are ongoing to maintain a precise body temperature that seldom deviates more than a fraction of a degree. The second part of the answer is that the brain took a great deal of time to evolve, and the development of any new structure conferring a new behavior had to integrate its activity through the systems already present. The third part is that once a new ability was developed it was frequently co-opted to be used for other purposes in addition to those for which it was initially evolved. For example, upright walking on four legs was evolved to move an animal rapidly from one place to another, but the upright posture, once developed, could then be used as the support for shivering. As Schallert et al. point out, it is therefore not surprising to find some aspects of walking and thermoregulation related. In fact, Satinoff has used this logic to explain why many components of thermoregulation are found at different levels. Another example might be that once an animal was able to balance on its hind legs to rear or jump, its front paws were free for manipulating objects. As a consequence of these three developments, we find behaviors integrated at each level in such a way that the entire organization of the brain can be viewed as a hierarchy of functional levels.

There is one additional reason the brain is organized in levels. The process of brain evolution was determined in a very real way by the sequence in which animals evolved into new habitats. In an aquatic environment they first had to develop locomotion. In a terrestrial environment the form of locomotion had to be modified; the animal required supporting reactions to lift it from the ground and legs to enable it to traverse various terrestrial obstacles. Once animals could travel on land, the development of new types of feeding abilities and thermoregulatory abilities became advantageous. For those animals that were highly mobile, new types of guidance systems became useful. Finally, once animals were dispersed, the ability to communicate over great distances became advantageous. It can be postulated that had animals evolved in some other way and encountered various environmental obstacles in another sequence the functional organization of the brain might be quite different from what we now find it to be.

FUNCTIONAL LEVELS AND LATERALIZATION OF THE CORTEX

Since the mid-19th century the anterior cortex has been recognized as being more involved than the posterior cortex in motor functions and the posterior cortex as being more involved than the anterior cortex in sensory functions. It has also been recognized that the cortex can be divided into three types of areas:

1. Primary sensory and motor areas
2. Secondary sensory and motor areas
3. Tertiary, or association, areas

From this knowledge Luria and others have proposed a general theory of cortical function. In presenting Luria's general theory of cortical function we do not intend to argue that the cortex is not made up of a number of separate channels that are involved in separate and independent sensory and motor processes. This may very well be the case. Nevertheless, on the basis of the available evidence it seems obvious that the cortex is involved in integration in an important way. We feel that at a beginning level it is easier to understand the processes of integration from Luria's holistic perspective.

Organization of the Cortex

Luria divides the cortex into two functional units (Figure 7–7). The first, the posterior portion of the neocortex (parietal, temporal, and occipital lobes), is the *sensory* unit. It receives sensory impressions, processes them, and stores them as information. The second, the anterior cortex (frontal lobe), is the *motor* unit. It formulates intentions, organizes them into programs of action, and executes the programs. In both cortical units there is a hierarchical structure with three cortical zones arranged functionally one above the other. These zones are distinguished by the cytoarchitecture and can therefore be described with Brodmann's numbering system.

The Sensory Unit. In the sensory unit the *primary zones* consist of the projection areas of vision (area 17), audition (area 41), and body senses (areas 1 to 3). In these zones the general features of sensory stimulation are organized in an array representing the topography, intensity, and pattern of stimulation. The *secondary zones* comprise the projection areas of these primary zones; in the case of vision, for example, areas 18 and 19. The secondary zones retain the modality (e.g., visual) of sensation but have a less fixed topographic organization (e.g., for vision its re-representation of the retina). The *tertiary zones* lie on the boundary of the occipital, temporal, and parietal cortex and include Brodmann's areas 5, 7, 21, 22, 37, 39, and 40—an area of about one-quarter of the posterior unit's total mass. The function of the tertiary zones is to integrate the excitation arriving from the different sensory systems. It is in these tertiary zones, Luria believes, that sensory input is translated into symbolic pro-

The sensory unit

The motor unit

FIGURE 7–7. A. The first functional unit of the cortex: the sensory unit. (Dark-shaded areas are primary zones; medium shaded, secondary zones; light shaded, tertiary zones.) Sensory input travels from primary to secondary to tertiary and is concomitantly elaborated from sensation into symbolic processes. B. The second functional unit of the cortex: the motor unit. Symbolic processes from the first functional unit are translated into intentions in the tertiary zones and then into patterns of action in the secondary and primary zones. (After A. R. Luria, *The Working Brain*. The Copyright Agency of the USSR. Reprinted with permission.)

cesses, and that concrete perception is translated into abstract thinking.

The Motor Unit. The motor unit, or frontal lobes, also consists of three hierarchically organized zones. The *primary zone* is the motor strip, area 4, which is the final cortical motor command area. The *secondary zone* is the premotor area, area 6, where motor programs are prepared for execution by the primary area. The most important part of this functional unit is the *tertiary zone,* comprising the prefrontal, or granular frontal, cortex: areas 9, 10, 45, 46, 47. It is here that intentions are formed. Luria describes the tertiary zone of the frontal unit as the most highly integrated area of function: "the superstructure above all other parts of the cerebral cortex."

An Example of Cortical Function

Luria conceives of the cortex as working in the following way: sensory input enters the primary sensory zones, is elaborated in the secondary zones, and is integrated in the tertiary zones of the posterior unit. For an action to be executed, activity from the posterior tertiary sensory zones is sent to the tertiary zone of the frontal unit, then to its secondary zone, and then to the primary zone, where execution is initiated.

To give a very simplified example of how Luria's model of the cortex might function, say one were walking along and came upon a soccer game. In the primary visual area the actual perception of the movements of people and the ball would occur. In the secondary zone, recognition that those activities constituted a soccer game would occur. In the tertiary zone the sounds and movements of the game would be synthesized into the realization that one team had scored and was ahead and that the game had a certain significance for league standings, etc. These cortical events could lead, in the tertiary zone of the frontal cortex, to formation of the intent to play soccer. The programs to execute this intent would be formulated in the secondary frontal zones. The actual movements to execute the programs would be initiated in the primary zone of the frontal cortex and the lower structures it controls.

Using the same example of a soccer game we can describe the effects of brain lesions. A lesion in the primary visual area would produce a blind spot in some part of the visual field, requiring the person to move his or her head backward and forward to see the entire game. A lesion in the secondary area might produce a perceptual deficit making the person unable to recognize the activity as a soccer game. A lesion in the tertiary area might make it impossible for an individual to recognize the significance of a soccer game in its abstract form; e.g., that one team wins, that league standings change, etc. A lesion in the prefrontal area might prevent the formation of the intention to become a soccer player and join a club, buy a uniform, get to practice on time, etc. A lesion in the secondary frontal zone might make it difficult for the individual to execute the sequences of movements required in plays. Finally, a lesion in the primary zone might make it difficult for the individual to execute the discrete movements, e.g., kicking the ball, required in the game. Again, this example is a grossly oversimplified version of Luria's model and the possible effects of brain lesions according to the model.

Properties of the Cortical Zones

Diminishing Specificity. A cortical area is said to show *specificity* if it analyzes only one mode of sensory input, e.g., visual or auditory. According to Luria, the lowest cortical zones are very specific in function (e.g., the primary visual zone analyzes only visual input), whereas the highest zones are very nonspecific (e.g., the tertiary zone analyzes all sensory information—visual, auditory, tactile, etc.). In other words, the primary zones process a specific sensory modality, recording chiefly its primary features of intensity and spatial distribution, whereas the higher zones process the more abstract features, with the highest zone synthesizing the abstract features of a number of modalities.

Progressive Lateralization. A cortical area is said to show *lateralization* if it has a function that is not shared by the homotopic area of the contralateral hemisphere. Speech, for example, is lateralized in the left hemisphere of most right-handed people. Luria postulates that there is progressive lateralization at higher levels of the cortical hierarchy. In other words, lateralization should be expected to be absent in primary visual area 17 but should be expected to be most pronounced in the tertiary areas. These expectations appear to be correct, because the most lateralized functions (speech in the left, spatial perception in the right) are functions of the tertiary zones. Lateralization does not appear to be as pronounced in the tertiary zone of the frontal cortex, if available evidence is accepted, but Luria predicts that this area, which he describes as the superstructure above all other cortical structures, should show the most pronounced lateralization.

Assessment of Luria's Model

Although Luria's model is a useful way to begin thinking about how the cortex works, it contains some pitfalls, at least three of them worthy of mention. First, whereas it is extremely difficult to make distinctions between sensory and motor functions at any level of nervous system function, it is more so at the level of the cortex. Consider the following points. (1) Any movement we make produces changes in sensation, just as changes in sensation provoke movement. It could be argued, then, that movement is partly a sensory function, since it produces changes in sensation, and that sensation is partly a motor function, since it provokes movement. (2) The perception of the same object in different instances can produce different responses. For example, a dog perceiving a man begins to bark and run away; then, "recognizing" the man as its master, it runs forward wagging its tail. (We can all

recall similar experiences of our own in which changes in perception have produced changes in behavior.) Since in Luria's model perception occurs in the posterior unit, changes in perception could arguably produce changes in movement; thus, posterior cortex is partly motor and not entirely sensory. In fact, many neuropsychologists argue just that point. (3) It might be thought that the corticospinal tract from area 4 of the motor cortex is "very motor"; Sherrington in fact called cells of this tract upper motor neurons. The sensory tracts in the dorsal cord carrying fine touch and pressure directly from body sensory receptors might be thought to be "very sensory." Yet Adkins, Morse, and Towe have shown that the two are intertwined functionally: the corticospinal fibers give off collaterals to the ascending sensory fibers presumably to amplify the input on the sensory channel. When a motor tract is found to perform such functions, it is difficult to argue that it is purely motor in its function. We could give many other similar examples of sensory-motor integration, but suffice it to say that the terms sensory and motor are used relatively: the former means more sensory than motor; the latter, more motor than sensory.

A second difficulty with Luria's model is that it is not clear just how much behavior is elaborated through a circuit that involves sequential processing from primary to tertiary sensory cortex and then from tertiary to primary motor cortex. As we shall see in subsequent chapters, there are ways in which information can bypass frontal cortex completely, and other ways in which it can bypass primary motor cortex.

A third problem with Luria's model is that although it seems to account for our perception of how we process information and behave, it is quite possible that our perceptions are in error. In our description of the organization of the cortex (Chapter 8) we point out that there is anatomical evidence that the cortex may be made up of many parallel sensory-motor systems any of which could be selectively removed by appropriate anatomical manipulation. One could, for example, selectively delete pain or color perception abilities or one could selectively delete short-term memory for auditory-verbal, for auditory-nonverbal, or for visual events. A good example of parallel processing comes from studies on the visual system. The visual systems that mediate circadian rhythms, pupillary constriction to light, and pattern vision are quite separate anatomically and they function in a largely independent fashion. It is quite possible that all cortical systems are organized as independent parallel systems in much the same way. The only difficulty in adopting this view is that it does not lend itself easily to an explanation of how perception is integrated. We must therefore accept that Luria's model is simply that: a model, from which it should be expected that there will be deviations. Should it be found in the future that the deviations are excessive, the model will no doubt be dropped in favor of one more closely corresponding to the true situation.

APPLICATIONS FOR HIERARCHICAL PRINCIPLES

As we stated earlier, it was John Hughlings-Jackson who adopted (from the psychology of Herbert Spencer) the idea of a hierarchically organized nervous system and applied its principles to the analysis of the brain's function. Some 50 years later the usefulness of Hughlings-Jackson's approach was reaffirmed by Henry Head, and again by Luria still another 50 years later. The following sections describe some of the ways in which hierarchical principles have been used in the analysis of behavior. It should be noted that when levels of function, or centers, are used in

these theoretical approaches to problems, the structures are *theoretical constructs;* that is, a known structure is not necessarily being described.

Brain Damage

Using the concept of functional levels for clinical diagnosis, Hughlings-Jackson reasoned that two types of symptoms should follow brain damage: loss of function, or negative symptoms, and release of function, or positive symptoms. The *negative symptoms* were those behaviors that, being absent after brain damage, were presumably generated by the damaged area. The *positive symptoms* were those that emerged or became commoner after brain damage and were thus presumed to reveal the function of remaining structures. We can illustrate these types with a hypothetical example. Say a person stops eating, becomes excessively active, is unable to sleep, and is given to outbursts of rage at the slightest provocation. The negative symptoms are the absence of normal quiet behavior, sleep, and eating; the positive symptoms are hyperactivity and excessive emotional response. These symptoms, reminiscent of the behavior of diencephalic animals, suggest that the diencephalon is released from normal forebrain control—which could occur because of a tumor or an infection in the forebrain. (Symptoms not unlike these have been associated with encephalitis or infections of the forebrain.) Quite often positive symptoms take bizarre forms, yet if they are thought of as reflecting lower levels of function, situations in which they are, or once were, appropriate can be found. For example, Denny-Brown has described the reappearance of rooting and sucking reflexes in adults who have suffered some forms of frontal-lobe damage. With such damage and loss of normal frontal-lobe function, the normal smooth flow of behavior disappears, and the disappearance is labeled the negative symptom. The frontal lobe also inhibits lower levels that produce reflexive behavior, so that in its absence reflexive behaviors reemerge, and they are labeled as positive symptoms. Although the positive symptoms appear peculiar in the adult, by the logic of this example they were once appropriate, for they supported feeding in infancy. The disappearance of both the positive and the negative symptoms can be used as a diagnostic indicator to gauge the rate and extent of recovery from brain damage.

Insanity

Hughlings-Jackson's concept of insanity was entirely hypothetical. When he discussed brain damage, he generally had particular anatomical structures in mind—e.g., frontal cortex, basal ganglia, spinal cord—but with reference to insanity he reasoned that at the highest level, the cortex, there must be sublevels that are also arranged hierarchically. Disorders of these levels, he reasoned, would produce insanity with positive symptoms manifest as aberrant behaviors. In fact, he reasoned that the highest levels of the hierarchy would be the most complex in structure and therefore the most susceptible to dysfunction. In his own words:

> Cases of insanity should, I think, be classified and investigated on the basis supplied by the doctrine of evolution of nervous centers. We shall have enormous help in the work Spencer has done in his *Psychology*. We have already explained that we use the term dissolution as the opposite of evolution. Insanity is dissolution, beginning in the highest nervous system processes. Moreover, of course, what we call the scientific investigation of insanity is really an experimental investigation of mind; and in this regard the slightest departures from a person's standard of mental health are to be studied, and not only the cases of patients who require to be kept in asylums. (Hughlings-Jackson, 1932, p. 4)

Although Hughlings-Jackson's reasoning has been little applied to the study of mental disorders, it may become increasingly relevant since those disorders are increasingly studied as neuropsychological problems. His conceptualizations suggest that at the very least the problem in some types of mental disorders lies in the highest zones of the cortex. For example, the inappropriate chatter of hebephrenic schizophrenia resembles in some respects fluent aphasia; thus, it could be taken as a positive symptom of a dysfunction of the highest language zones.

Dreams and Illusions

Hughlings-Jackson considered both dreams and illusions to be positive symptoms revealing the activity of particular brain structures released from inhibition. Dreams, he thought, were released by the inhibition through sleep of higher levels of the brain that were normally inhibitory. Illusions, hallucinations, and similar phenomena had an analogous cause, with the difference that higher centers were inactivated by mental disease, drugs, or brain damage. His intriguing suggestion has never been put to the test. It is interesting to contrast Hughlings-Jackson's theory with Freud's wish-fulfillment theory of dreams, which was predicated on the absence of the ego (or rational part of the personality) during sleep. There are similarities in the two theories.

Development

Perhaps no area of psychology makes more use of hierarchical concepts than developmental psychology (for example, see Bronson): many aspects of the development of behavior are believed to reflect the maturation of successively higher levels of the nervous system. From a developmental perspective negative symptoms (the absence of certain behaviors) can be attributed to the immaturity of higher centers, whereas positive symptoms (e.g., play behavior, hyperactivity) can be considered as reflecting the activity of lower centers. Developmental approaches to brain function analysis have an advantage over brain transection studies insofar as they can reveal brain organization in intact individuals.

SPECIAL PROBLEMS OF CORTICAL FUNCTION

Two problems of cortical function have been repeatedly debated: mass action and equipotentiality. According to the **mass action hypothesis,** the entire brain participates in every behavior, and therefore the removal of any cortical tissue produces, with respect to any task, a deficit that is proportional to the amount of tissue removed. According to the **equipotentiality hypothesis,** each portion of a given area is able to encode or produce the behavior normally controlled by the entire area. Since these two ideas are either explicit or implicit focal points in many discussions of cortical function their status warrants brief review. As can be seen from their definition they are more sophisticated reformulations of the old problem of localization of function.

Mass Action

The idea of mass action was most recently and most clearly formulated by Karl Lashley, between 1920 and 1950. Lashley developed his work largely in reaction to strict localizationists, who adopted the view that each restricted portion of the cortex has a function, and that damage to that area produces a loss of only that function. He envisioned that mass action applies largely to complex behaviors, for he argued in 1939:

It has been assumed that properties of experience are represented at the level of some simple nervous activity or in a single locus: sensations in the sensory areas, volitional patterns in the motor regions or particular forms of intelligent behavior in restricted coordinating centers. Such conceptions of localization are oversimplified and must be abandoned. Nothing is known of the physiological basis of conscious states, but there is some reason to believe that these states can be correlated only with the summated activity of all centers simultaneously excited. (Lashley, 1939, p. 341)

Of numerous experiments undertaken to examine the problem of mass action, none can be called conclusive. It is generally agreed, however, that Lashley's arguments are not a refutation of the idea that function is localized. It is clear that functions are localized to some extent, although to what extent and how are under debate. It is also clear that damage to many brain areas can produce deficits in a given task. The more relevant question asked today is: How is performance disrupted by a specific lesion? Language, for example, can be disrupted by damage to Wernicke's area, to Broca's area, and to the arcuate fasciculus connecting the two. But language can also be disrupted by deafness at an early age, by damage to areas of the thalamus, and by damage to the nerves controlling the face muscles. In each case careful experimentation can delineate the contribution of each of these factors.

Equipotentiality

If it is accepted that function is localized, at least in a general sense, within an area of the brain, how is that organization achieved? Many people have been impressed by the demonstration that destruction of a portion of a particular "functional" area produces a general behavioral deficit followed by either substantial recovery or only a slight general impairment of function. Usually only complete destruction of an area produces sustained impairment. From such findings it has been concluded that each portion of the tissue within a given area must have the capacity to encode or produce the behavior normally controlled by the entire area. According to Lashley's formulation, equipotentiality means that every point within an area is able to encode a particular habit. To demonstrate this point it is worthwhile considering two of the most convincing types of supporting evidence.

If a portion of area 17 of the visual cortex is destroyed, the cells in the lateral geniculate nucleus that project to that area die. The extent of remaining visual cortex can be estimated by counting the remaining lateral geniculate cells. Lashley trained rats on a visual discrimination task and then removed various portions of area 17. The rats were able to retain the habit with as few as one-fiftieth of the total number of cells in their visual system (682 of about 34,100). Humphrey also reported that a monkey with a small remnant of visual cortex restricted to the left hemisphere was able to localize objects in space, reach out and touch objects in a precise fashion, and avoid bumping into obstacles placed in natural and artificial settings. Similarly, we have examined a person with extensive bilateral damage to the visual cortex who was still able to process visual information with a visual field a couple of centimeters in diameter. This is not to argue that large visual area lesions do not produce visual distortions: they do. But the point is that a small portion of visual cortex can process a substantial amount of visual information. This suggests that there is some degree of equipotentiality within the primary visual area.

In experiments designed to examine recovery in the motor cortex, Glees and Cole defined the thumb area of the motor cortex in monkeys by electrical stimulation. They then removed this area and followed the course of recovery of thumb movements from the flaccid paralysis caused by the lesion. After complete recovery the brain was reexposed, and they found that the borders of the lesion now produced thumb movements although they had not during the first stimulation session. This area was then removed and flaccid paralysis occurred, followed again by recovery. These findings are consistent with an enormous amount of clinical evidence that the cortex does have the capacity to reorganize and compensate for damage.

What accounts for this capacity? Lashley suggested that a pattern of excitation is reduplicated throughout an entire functional area, enabling any portion of the area to sustain the response. Recently, Pribram has reformulated Lashley's idea with an imaginative hypothesis. He suggests that the brain might operate on holographic principles, producing interference patterns similar to those formed in holographic photography. A hologram, which is formed by the interference patterns of light reflected from an object, has two properties that make it a relevant equipotentiality model. First, the image is distributed across the negative in such a way that the negative can be divided into two or many pieces, each of which contains the entire image. Second, each negative can contain many different superimposed pictures that can be recalled when illuminated with varying wavelengths of light. Holograms can be stored in solids, and each bit of information can be stored throughout the solid and still be individually retrievable. In experimental work, some 10 billion bits of information have been stored holographically in a cubic centimeter, and it has been estimated that it is feasible for holographic processes to handle the phenomenal amount of information stored by a human brain in a lifetime.

Another explanation of equipotentiality is that there are large overlapping fields of neurons engaged in each function. Under normal conditions those with the most direct control of a behavior are functional and hold the others under inhibition. If the more prepotent areas are damaged, neurons with lower thresholds are released from inhibition and become functional, thus restoring the behavior. One of several other ideas is that neurons sprout when their terminals are damaged and innervate surrounding intact areas to produce a

measure of recovery. At the present time a combination of these two processes is viewed as being adequate to explain both recovery and the latency required for recovery. Thus, it would be appropriate to say that a more restricted concept of overlapping field of control is considered more adequate today than the general equipotentiality theory of Lashley.

REFERENCES

Adkins, R. J., R. W. Morse, and A. L. Towe. Control of somatosensory input by cerebral cortex. *Science* 153:1020–1022, 1966.

Bandler, R. J., C. C. Chi, and J. P. Flynn. Biting attack elicited by stimulation of the ventral midbrain tegmentum of cats. *Science* 177:361–366, 1972.

Bard, P. A diencephalic mechanism for the expression of rage, with special reference to the sympathetic nervous system. *American Journal of Physiology* 84:490–515, 1928.

Bard, P., and M. B. Macht. The behavior of chronically decerebrate cats. In G. E. W. Wolstenholm and C. M. O'Connor, eds., *Ciba Foundation Symposium on Neurological Basis of Behavior*. London: J. and A. Churchill, 1958.

Barrett, R., H. H. Merritt, and A. Wolf. Depression of consciousness as a result of cerebral lesions. *Research Publications of the Association for Research in Nervous and Mental Disease* 45:241–276, 1967.

Bauer, J. H., and R. M. Cooper. Effects of posterior cortical lesions on performance on a brightness discrimination task. *Journal of Comparative and Physiological Psychology* 58:84–92, 1964.

Bazett, H. C., and W. G. Penfield. A study of the Sherrington decerebrate animal in the chronic as well as the acute condition. *Brain* 45:185–265, 1922.

Beach, F. A. Effects of cortical lesions upon the copulatory behavior of male rats. *Journal of Comparative Psychology* 29:193–245, 1940.

Bernston, G. G., and D. J. Micco. Organization of brainstem behavioral systems. *Brain Research Bulletin* 1:471–483, 1976.

Bignall, K. E., and L. Schramm. Behavior of chronically decerebrate kittens. *Experimental Neurology* 42:519–531, 1974.

Bland, B. H., and C. H. Vanderwolf. Diencephalic and hippocampal mechanisms of motor activity in the rat: effects of posterior hypothalamic stimulation on behavior and hippocampal slow wave activity. *Brain Research* 43:67–88, 1972.

Bland, B. H., and C. H. Vanderwolf. Electrical stimulation of the hippocampal formation: behavioral and bioelectrical effects. *Brain Research* 43:89–106, 1972.

Brackbill, Y. The role of the cortex in orienting: orienting reflex in an encephalic human infant. *Developmental Psychology* 5:195–201, 1971.

Brazier, M. B. A. The historical development of neurophysiology. In J. Field, H. W. Magoun, and V. E. Hall, eds., *Handbook of Physiology*, vol. 1. Washington, D.C.: American Physiological Society, 1959.

Bronson, G. The hierarchical organization of the central nervous system: implications for learning processes and critical periods in early development. *Behavioral Science* 10:7–25, 1965.

Brooks, D. M. The role of the cerebral cortex and of various sense organs in the excitation and execution of mating activity in the rabbit. *American Journal of Physiology* 120:544–553, 1973.

Buchholz, D. Spontaneous and centrally induced behaviors in normal and thalamic opossums. *Journal of Comparative and Physiological Psychology* 90:898–908, 1976.

Cannon, W. B., and S. W. Britton. Pseudoaffective medulliadrenal secretion. *American Journal of Physiology* 72:283–294, 1924.

Denny-Brown, D. The nature of apraxia. *Journal of Nervous and Mental Diseases* 126:9–32, 1958.

Flynn, J., H. Venegas, W. Foote, and S. Edwards. Neural mechanisms involved in a cat's attack on a rat. In R. E. Whalen, R. F. Thompson, M. Verzeano, and N. M. Weinberger, eds., *The Neural Control of Behavior*. New York: Academic, 1970.

Freud, S. *The Standard Edition of the Complete Psychological Works of Sigmund Freud.* J. Stachey and A. Freud, eds. London: Hogarth, 1950.

Gallistel, C. R. *The Organization of Action.* Hillsdale, N.J.: Lawrence Erlbaum Associates, 1980.

Gamper, E. In J. Field, H. W. Magoun, and V. E. Hall, eds., *Handbook of Physiology*, vol. 2. Washington, D.C.: American Physiological Society, 1959.

Glees, P., and J. Cole. Recovery of skilled motor functions after small repeated lesions of motor cortex in macaque. *Journal of Neurophysiology* 13:137–148, 1950.

Goltz, F. On the functions of the hemispheres. In G. von Bonin, ed., *The Cerebral Cortex.* Springfield, Ill.: Charles C Thomas, 1960.

Goodale, M., and R. M. Cooper. Cues utilized by normal and posterior neodecorticate rats in the Yerkes brightness discrimination task. *Psychonomic Science* 3:513–514, 1965.

Granit, R. *Receptors and Sensory Perception.* New Haven: Yale University Press, 1955.

Grill, H. J., and R. Norgren. Chronically decerebrate rats demonstrate satiation but not baitshyness. *Science* 201:267–269, 1978.

Grill, H. J., and R. Norgren. Neurological tests and behavioral deficits in chronic thalamic and chronic decerebrate rats. *Brain Research* 143:299–312, 1978.

Grillner, S. Locomotion in the spinal cat. In R. B. Stein, ed., *Control of Posture and Locomotion.* New York: Plenum, 1973.

Hughlings-Jackson, J. Remarks on dissolution of the nervous system as exemplified by certain post-epileptic conditions. In J. Taylor, ed., *Selected Writings of John Hughlings-Jackson,* vol. 2. London: Hodder and Stoughton, 1932.

Humphrey, N. K. Vision in a monkey without striate cortex: a case study. *Perception* 3:241–255, 1974.

Jung, R., and R. Hassler. The extrapyramidal motor system. In J. Field, H. W. Magoun, and V. E. Hall, eds., *Handbook of Physiology*, vol. 2. Washington, D.C.: American Physiological Society, 1959.

Klüver, H. Functional significance of the geniculo-striate system. In H. Klüver, ed., *Visual Mechanisms*. Lancaster, Pa.: Cattrell, 1942.

Klüver, H., and P. C. Bucy. Preliminary analysis of the functions of the temporal lobes in monkeys. *Archives of Neurology and Psychiatry* 42:979–1000, 1939.

Kolb, B., and I. Q. Whishaw. Decortication of rats in infancy or adulthood produced comparable functional losses on learned and species-typical behaviors. *Journal of Comparative and Physiological Psychology* 95:468–483, 1981.

Kuhn, R. A. Functional capacity of the isolated human spinal cord. *Brain* 73:1–51, 1950.

Lashley, K. S. The mechanisms of vision. XVI. The functioning of small remnants of the visual cortex. *Journal of Comparative Neurology* 70:45–67, 1939.

Lashley, K. S. Functional determinants of cerebral localization. In F. A. Beach, D. O. Hebb, C. T. Morgan, and H. W. Nissen, eds., *The Neuropsychology of Lashley*. New York: McGraw-Hill, 1960.

Liddell, E. G. T., and C. S. Sherrington. Reflexes in response to stress (mystatic reflexes). *Proceedings of the Royal Society of London* 96:212–249, 1924.

Luciani, L. *Human Physiology*. London: Macmillan, 1915.

Luria, A. R. *The Working Brain*. Harmondsworth: Penguin, 1973.

Melzack, R., and P. D. Wall. Pain mechanisms: A new theory. *Science* 150:971–979, 1965.

Morris, R. G. M. Spatial localization does not require the presence of local cues. *Learning and Motivation* 12:239–260, 1980.

Oakley, D. A. Cerebral cortex and adaptive behavior. In D. A. Oakley and H. C. Plotkin, eds., *Brain, Evolution and Behavior*. London: Methuen, 1979.

O'Keefe, J., and L. Nadel. *The Hippocampus as a Spatial Map*. Oxford: Oxford University Press, 1978.

Pinel, J. P. J., and D. Treit. Burying as a defensive response in rats. *Journal of Comparative and Physiological Psychology* 92:708–712, 1978.

Pribram, K. H. *Languages of the Brain*. Englewood Cliffs, N.J.: Prentice-Hall, 1971.

Robinson, T. E. Electrical stimulation of the brain stem in freely moving rats: I. Effects on behavior. *Physiology and Behavior* 21:223–231, 1978.

Satinoff, E. Neural organization and evolution of thermal regulation in mammals. *Science* 201:16–22, 1978.

Schallert, T., I. Q. Whishaw, M. DeRyck, and P. Teitelbaum. The postures of catecholamine-depletion catalepsy: their possible adaptive value in thermoregulation. *Physiology and Behavior* 21:817–820, 1978.

Sherrington, C. S. *The Integrative Action of the Nervous System*. New Haven: Yale University Press, 1906.

Sorenson, C. A., and G. D. Ellison. Striatal organization of feeding behavior in the decorticate rat. *Experimental Neurology* 29:162–174, 1970.

Tolman, E. C. *Behavior and Psychological Man*. Berkeley: University of California Press, 1961.

Vanderwolf, C. H. Hippocampal electrical activity and voluntary movement in the rat. *Electroencephalography and Clinical Neurophysiology* 26:407–418, 1969.

Vanderwolf, C. H., B. Kolb, and R. K. Cooley. Behavior of the rat after removal of the neocortex and hippocampal formation. *Journal of Comparative and Physiological Psychology* 92:156–175, 1978.

Vanderwolf, C. H., R. Kramis, L. A. Gillespie, and B. H. Bland. Hippocampal rhythmical slow activity and neocortical low voltage fast activity: relations to behavior. In K. H. Pribram and R. L. Isaacson, eds., *The Hippocampus: A Comprehensive Treatise.* New York: Plenum, 1975.

Villablanca, J. R., and C. E. Olmstead. The striatum: a fine tuner of the brain. *Acta Neurobiologica Experimentalis* 42:227–229, 1982.

Villablanca, J. R., C. E. Olmstead, and I. de Andres. Effects of caudate nuclei or frontal cortical ablations in kittens: responsiveness to auditory stimuli and comparisons with adult-operated littermates. *Experimental Neurology* 61:635–649, 1978.

Whishaw, I. Q., T. Schallert, and B. Kolb. An analysis of feeding and sensorimotor abilities of rats after decortication. *Journal of Comparative and Physiological Psychology* 95:85–103, 1981.

Woods, J. W. Behavior of chronic decerebrate rats. *Journal of Neurophysiology* 27:634–644, 1964.

8

PRINCIPLES
OF NEOCORTICAL ORGANIZATION

Mr. Higgins decided that he should learn French so that he could enjoy French literature. After a year's intensive study Higgins was almost fluent in French but it became clear to him that in order to really understand French, he was going to have to study Latin. Higgins had always been interested in Latin and so he plunged into it, only to find after a year's intense study that in order to master Latin, he really must study old Greek. Higgins was determined to learn French, and so he began a serious study of Greek. Alas, after a year's intense study of Greek, Higgins determined that he must now learn Sanskrit if he were to really appreciate Greek. This posed a problem, for there were few scholars of Sanskrit, but with a few months' effort, he managed to locate an old man in India who was a true scholar of Sanskrit. Excited at the possibility of soon learning French, Higgins moved to India to begin his study of Sanskrit. After six months the old man died. Demoralized because he did not yet have a good knowledge of Sanskrit, Higgins returned home and concluded that it was not possible to really learn French.

This story illustrates the difficulty for the psychologist who wishes to study the neurological bases of human behavior. The psychologist obviously must study the basic structure and organization of the brain, especially the neocortex, and must keep abreast of the latest developments in neuroanatomy, neurochemistry, and neurophysiology. The problem for the psychologist, however, is in knowing where to stop. The microstructure of mitochondria in the presynaptic ending may be fascinating and necessary to know in order to understand how a neuron functions, but will this knowledge make it any easier to study the neurological control of language? There is, of course, no easy answer to this question; the psychologist must avoid being trapped by Sanskrit but must be aware of where French came from. In this chapter, which is an elaboration of our discussion of the organization of the neocortex in the last chapter, we outline some of the details of cortical organization that we feel are necessary for the psychologist to know before beginning the study of the functional organization of the cortex. We have simplified much of the material, hoping to avoid a regression to Sanskrit, but the student should be aware that our discussion has been simplified and that a good deal more is known about the details (Greek and Sanskrit) of cortical organization than we have presented.

We shall make six points in this chapter, each of which will be considered separately: (1) the cortex is composed of many types of neurons, which are organized into six layers, (2) the cortex is organized into functional columns, (3) there are multiple representations of sensory and motor functions in the cortex, (4) these representations exhibit plasticity, (5) cortical activity is influenced by feedback loops from several forebrain regions, and (6) the cortex functions using both hierarchical and parallel processing.

CELLS AND LAYERS OF THE CORTEX

We described the layered structure of the cerebral cortex in Chapter 1. Here we shall consider the types of cells that make up the layers, the nature of the connections of the layers, and the functions of the layers.

Two main categories of nerve cells can be easily distinguished in the cortex by their general shape. **Pyramidal cells,** which have cell bodies in the general shape of a pyramid, represent the major efferents of the cerebral cortex and are found in layers II, III, and V (Figure 8–1). The pyramidal cells of layer V are the largest, projecting to the brainstem and spinal cord. Those in layers II and III are smaller and project to other cortical regions (Figure 8–2). **Stellate cells** (star-shaped cells) are interneurons and represent a collection of different types of cells, which are named largely on the basis of the configuration of their axons and dendrites. For example, one type of stellate cell is the basket cell, whose axon projects horizon-

tally, forming synapses that envelop the postsynaptic cell (hence the name basket). Stellate cells also include granule cells, double-bouquet cells, chandelier cells, and fusiform cells, among others. Stellate cells are found in all the layers of the cortex, but the heaviest concentration of them is in layer IV, especially in the sensory cortex. Stellate cells receive afferents from subcortical structures, as well as providing interconnections between the cortical afferents and efferents, as summarized in Figure 8–2.

The cells of the middle layers of the cortex (especially in and around layer IV) can be conceived as composing a zone of *sensory analysis,* whereas the cells of layers V and VI can be conceived as composing a zone of *output* from the cortex. It is therefore hardly surprising that the sensory cortex has a relatively large layer IV and a small layer V whereas the motor cortex has a relatively small layer IV, but a correspondingly larger layer V. Figure 8–2 illustrates this difference and shows that although the different cortical layers can be distinguished throughout the cortex, the thickness of the layers is far from uniform: the fourth layer may be virtually absent in the motor cortex, and the sensory cortex is far thinner overall than is the motor cortex.

Figure 8–2 also illustrates another feature of cortical organization. Afferents to the cortex are of two general types: specific and nonspecific. *Specific afferents* are those afferents that terminate in relatively discrete regions of the cortex, usually in only one or two layers. These include projections from the thalamus as well as those from the amygdala. Most of these projections terminate in layer IV although projections from the amygdala and certain thalamic nuclei may terminate in the more superficial layers. Nonspecific afferents are those afferents that terminate diffusely over large regions of the cortex, in some cases over all of the cortex. The noradrenergic projections from the brainstem, the choli-

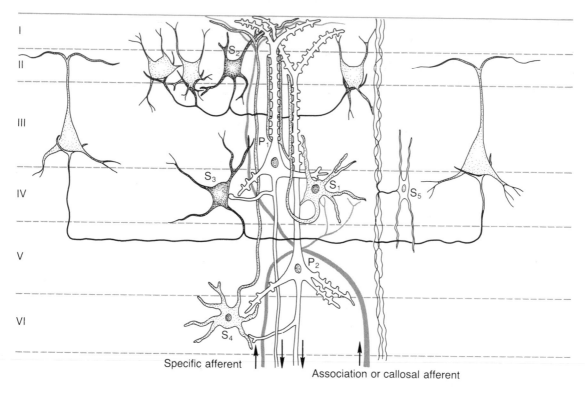

Specific afferent

Association or callosal afferent

FIGURE 8–1. Illustration of the most important neocortical cell types. Pyramidal cells (P_1 and P_2) are found in layers 3 and 5. These cells are found throughout the cortex and include several types of cells (S_1–S_5). Thalamic afferents arrive in layer 4 and synapse on stellate interneuron S_1. Associative or callosal afferents feed into the more superficial layers to synapse on interneurons or on the long apical dendrites of pyramidal neurons. Basket-type stellate interneurons (S_2) establish connections within the superficial layers, likely functioning to inhibit the cells to which they project. Larger basket interneurons (S_3) located in the deeper layers may also spread inhibition laterally in the deeper layers. Fusiform-type stellate cells (S_4) are primarily located in layer 6, sending excitatory axons vertically. Double-bouquet-type stellate cells (S_5) may secure the spread of excitation over the entire depth of the cortex when layer 4 is stimulated by incoming afferents. (Adapted from Szentágothai, 1969.)

nergic projections from the basal forebrain, and the projections from certain thalamic nuclei are examples of nonspecific afferents. Nonspecific afferents often terminate in many or all the layers of the cortex and presumably serve some general function such as the enhancement of ongoing cortical activity.

Finally, it should be realized that most of the interactions between the layers of the cortex are with cells directly above or below, with relatively less interaction with cells more than a couple of millimeters laterally on either side (see Figure 8–1). This vertical bias in cortical organization forms the basis for a second type of neocortical organization: the column.

CORTICAL COLUMNS

If a microelectrode is moved vertically through the sensory cortex from layer I to layer VI, all the neurons encountered appear functionally

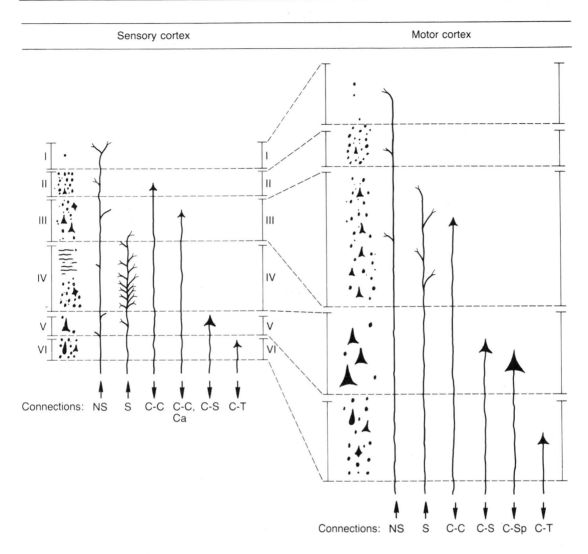

Sensory cortex   Motor cortex

Connections: NS   S   C-C   C-C, C-S   C-T
                               Ca

Connections: NS   S   C-C   C-S C-Sp C-T

FIGURE 8–2. Schematic illustration of the neuronal elements of sensory and motor cortex. The sensory cortex is much thinner than the motor cortex, and the size of each layer is markedly different in the sensory and the motor cortex. The specific (S) and nonspecific (NS) inputs to the cortex illustrate the different distribution of these afferents to the different laminae. The outputs from the cortex arise from different layers, depending on the destination. Cortical-cortical (C-C) efferents arise from layers 2 and 3, callosal (Ca) efferents arise from layer 3, cortical-subcortical (C-S) and cortical-spinal (C-Sp) efferents arise from layer 5, and cortical-thalamic (C-T) efferents arise from layer 6, as illustrated. (After Shepherd, 1979.)

very similar. For example, if an electrode is placed in the somatosensory cortex and lowered vertically from layer I to VI, neurons in each layer are excited by a particular tactile stimulus (e.g., a light touch) in a particular part of the body (e.g., the left thumb). The cells of layer IV are activated earliest by an afferent input, as would be expected by the direct afferent connections to layer IV. Cells of the other layers must necessarily have longer latencies, since they would have at least one more synapse on an interneuron in layer IV before receiving the sensory input. The pyramidal neurons of layer V are the last to be activated, again as would be expected since these are the efferents. The functional similarity of cells across all six layers at any point in the cortex suggests that the simplest functional unit of the cortex is a vertically oriented column of cells that composes a minicircuit. Thus, the cortex is organized into narrow vertical columns 0.5 to 1.0 mm wide, running from the cortical surface to the white matter, in which each neuron in such a column is functionally similar to the others. (Figure 8–3). Afferents terminate on interneurons in layer IV and these interneurons transmit information vertically to synapse on other interneurons or pyramidal cell dendrites. Little information transfer occurs laterally, the principle direction of information travel being vertical. Physiological studies have shown that adjacent columns are maximally excited by different afferents, providing further evidence that each column functions as a minicircuit. For example, in the somatosensory system each cell in one column might be responsive to the movement of hairs, whereas cells in an adjacent column might respond to the movement of a joint (Figure 8–3). Each of the columns has a somatosensory function, but for each column the particular feature of somatosensation coded is different. It is apparent that a single vertical column 1 mm in diameter is hardly sufficient to analyze all the

sensations of a particular aspect of touch from the whole body. Thus, there must be multiple columns for this, and indeed there are. Columns for skin touch intermingle in a mosaic pattern within the somatosensory cortex with columns for joint position, hair movement, stretch, etc. Although the various columns appear to mingle at random at any point on the cortex, there is a rather highly organized structure inherent in the mosaic. Columns responsive to different sensations in the thumb are grouped together, as are those for the hand, leg, trunk, face, etc., so that if one were to look at the cortex from above, there would be regions devoted to the hand, face, leg, etc., as illustrated in Figure 8–4 B.

Although we have used the somatosensory system as an example of columnar organization, such organization is a feature of the entire neocortex, although little is known about the details of columnar organization outside the somatosensory and visual cortex. Furthermore, outside the somatosensory and motor cortexes, the mosaic of the columns would not form a neat homunculus but would appear more like strips or patches of functionally related columns.

MULTIPLE REPRESENTATIONS

When Penfield and his colleagues stimulated the motor and somatosensory strips of their patients at the Montreal Neurological Hospital, they found that it was possible to identify regions of the pre- and postcentral gyri, respectively, that appeared to represent localized body parts such as the leg, hand, and face (see Figure 1–8). In order to summarize their observations, they constructed a homunculus in which different body parts are represented in discrete regions of the cortex. We must remember, however, that the homunculus that they

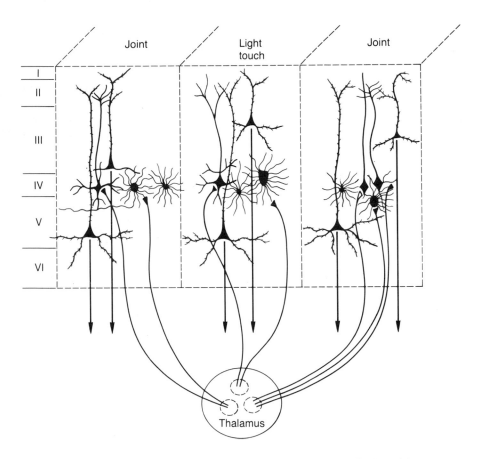

FIGURE 8–3. Highly schematic diagram illustrating the columnar organization of the neocortex. Thalamic input synapses on stellate cells, with interneurons and pyramidal cells tranferring information vertically. In this example each column is specific for a submodality of somatosensation. Interneurons between the columns are not drawn.

drew is imaginary and was not actually observed in each patient. By stimulating dozens of points in different patients they were able to determine the boundaries of the motor and sensory fields, but the detailed organization was really just an educated guess. Subsequent studies by Woolsey and his colleagues using nonhuman subjects confirmed Penfield's findings, as there appeared to be analogous representations in other species (see Figure 4–5). Like Penfield, however, Woolsey did not

actually observe a detailed map on the cortical surface but rather observed something like illustration Figure 8–4 B. That is, the stimulation allowed the investigators to identify a series of functional bands corresponding to different parts of the body. The fact that the cortical representation is not one-to-one with the body surface is not unreasonable, since it is in accord with the common experience that some body parts are indeed less sensitive to touch than are others (e.g., the back as opposed

Traditional Homunculus	Schematic Bands	Multiple Representations

FIGURE 8–4. Three conceptions of the organization of the somatosensory cortex in the postcentral gyrus of the monkey. A. Representation of a traditional homunculus. B. Major body parts represented as functional bands. C. Multiple representations of the body in which each architectonic field contains one representation. The traditional homunculus was mapped using large electrodes, whereas the multiple representations were discovered using microelectrodes. (After Kaas, Nelson, Sur, Lin, and Merzenich, 1979.)

to the face). Similar representations of the visual and auditory fields, as well as of the motor cortex, were constructed, leading to the general consensus that the sensory world is represented directly in a number of regions in the cortex. It is this view that is described in most current introductory psychology, neurology, and biology textbooks, but the actual story appears to be somewhat more complex.

We have seen that the cortex is functionally organized into columns, with adjacent col-

umns devoted to different aspects of sensory input. For example, we saw in Figure 8–3 that within the somatosensory cortex one column might code touch and an adjacent column might code pressure. How are these distinct sensations accounted for within the single representation of the body? Recent experiments using microelectrodes to study somatosensory representation in the monkey brain have shown that they are not. The somatosensory area is actually composed of three, and perhaps four, smaller representations of the body, as illustrated in Figure 8–4 C. It can be seen that within the leg area, for example, there are at least three separate representations, each one coding some different aspect of somatosensation. Each of the subareas has its own pattern of sensory activation and its own distinctive pattern of connections. It is now clear that although Penfield's maps are useful summaries of his observations, owing to his relatively crude procedures they led to the erroneous belief that there is a single representation of the body surface in the postcentral gyrus. In fact, there are multiple representations of the body surface, each of which appears to function independently of the others.

Evidence of multiple representations of somatosensation leads to the question of whether the visual world and the auditory world are also represented repeatedly in the cortex. Indeed they are, as we shall see in the next chapter. Furthermore, there is good evidence that there are also multiple representations of the body in the motor system. Both Penfield and Woolsey identified a complete motor representation on the medial surface of the cortex, which Woolsey termed the **supplementary motor cortex** (Figure 4–5), and according to Evarts, there is little doubt that significant functional divisions exist within the motor cortex of the precentral gyrus. Similarly, the cortex lying just in front of the primary motor cortex (the *premotor cortex* on Brodmann's areas 6 and 8) may contain one or more additional representations.

STABILITY OF SENSORY REPRESENTATIONS IN THE CORTEX

One of the striking things about the stimulation studies of Penfield and his colleagues is the remarkable variation among patients in the exact organization of the sensory and motor representations. Part of this variation is almost certainly due to slight differences in the testing procedure from patient to patient, but there is reason to believe that much of the variation can be accounted for by genetic and experiential factors. It is generally assumed that sensory representations in the cortex occupy fixed, presumably genetically programmed, locations throughout life. Although it has been recognized that people with pre- or postnatal disorders frequently have unusual sensory or motor representations, such as the remarkable dexterity of toe use in people with no hands, these peculiar phenomena have generally been attributed to the apparent plasticity of the infant nervous system. Recent evidence questions this assumption, leading us to consider an important change in our conceptions of sensory and motor organization.

In their studies of somatosensory organization in monkeys, Merzenich and Kaas severed the median nerve of the right hand. This nerve normally innervates the palmer side (also referred to as the glabrous side) of the thumb and first two fingers and the right side of the palm. Immediately following nerve section, the cortex in areas 3b and 2 that was previously responsive to stimulation of the skin serviced by the median nerve became unresponsive. However, in most monkeys, small fragments of cortex that were formerly devoted to the glabrous digits became immediately responsive to the dorsal surface of these digits, which is innervated by other nerves. Over several weeks these small fragments of newly responsive cortex enlarged to represent more of the skin surface of the dorsal digits. Furthermore, representations of skin surfaces bordering the skin field of the median nerve began to expand to occupy the denervated zone. Some of these expansions were truly remarkable, as some skin sites, which were formerly entirely outside the denervated zone, moved to fall completely within it, allowing more distal skin sites to expand into the evacuated "territory." These results, which have also been found in other mammalian species, have important implications for principles of cortical organization.

First, they imply that cortical, and presumably subcortical, representations of sensory surfaces are plastic, even in mature individuals. Second, map changes may involve significant changes in anatomical organization, either in terms of the effectiveness of synapses or in the development of new synaptic contacts or both. Third, the dramatic reorganization observed in the cortex may not be a curious effect of peripheral nerve injury but may actually reflect a normal process of dynamic organization in the cortex. In other words, it may be that there is a normal competition of inputs for neocortical space, a competition that is influenced by peripheral effects, including environmental stimulation. It is well known that environmental stimulation can influence a variety of neocortical characteristics, including cortical weight and thickness, and so it may not be surprising that cortical organization might also be influenced by environmental stimulation. Indeed, the common observation that movements and sensations are changed after prolonged experience in a cast may have its foundation in significant changes in the organization of cortical sensory and motor representation, changes that can be reversed by therapy.

In sum, maps apparently change, the apparent stability in them being a consequence of balanced competition. Changing the balance results in an orderly sequence of change that produces a new balance and a new organization. Merzenich and Kaas speculate that it should be possible to change this balance not only by removing an input but also by increasing or decreasing the levels of activity produced by given skin surfaces or by a given set of receptors. Thus, somatosensory cortical fields may be subject to alterations related to sensory use. In fact, there is preliminary evidence that learning a sensory-motor skill could actually modify a cortical map, and the modifications could be responsible, at least in part, for the increased skill. The fact that these changes occur in mature individuals also implies that it may be possible to teach old dogs new tricks after all. On the other hand, the apparent difficulty may imply that there is a relative loss in the plasticity of neocortical fields with age, although this is purely speculation.

FEEDBACK LOOPS

Governments, universities, corporations, and other large institutions are normally run by a relatively small group of people that form a cabinet, council, board, etc. This group may make the final decisions on behalf of a very large number of people (millions in the case of governments), but it does not normally reach its decisions without significant input from other bodies. The commonest source of such input is the committee, which may include people from the inner group as well as a larger sample of people from outside. The committee is given a mandate from the upper group, and then later reports back to it with recommendations. An analogous organization is found in the brain in the form of cortical-subcortical feedback loops. If the cortex is conceived as the cabinet or board, various subcortical regions such as the thalamus, striatum, and amygdala can be considered to be committees. These regions receive inputs from the cortex and in turn send outputs back to the cortex. These structures also have other outputs to the brainstem, just as information from committees may go directly to civil servants or employees, but it is the input to the cortex that is especially important in the current context, for it must have a significant effect on cortical functioning. The principal cortical-subcortical feed-

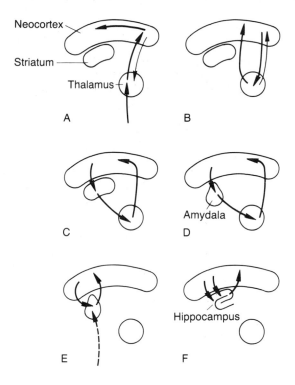

Neocortex

Striatum

Thalamus

A   B

Amydala

C   D

Hippocampus

E   F

FIGURE 8–5. Schematic diagrams illustrating the cortical-subcortical feedback loops. A and B show two different thalamic loops, C shows the cortical-striatal-thalamic loop, D the cortical-amygdala-thalamic loop, E the cortical-amygdala loop, and F the cortical-hippocampal loop. Each of these feedback loops presumably functions to modify ongoing cortical activity.

back loops are illustrated in Figure 8–5, and we shall consider each separately.

Cortical-Thalamic Loops

The thalamus plays a central role in the functioning of the neocortex since it provides the major sensory afferents to the cortex (Figure 1–14). In addition, however, the thalamus receives projections back from the cortex, projections that likely function to inhibit or to excite thalamic-cortical connections (Figure 8–5 A and B). For example, if one is startled while walking through a park at night, the cortical-thalamic projection could function

to amplify the sensory afferents to the cortex. Since the thalamus plays a key role in providing the cortex with specific afferents, we should not be surprised to discover that disruptions of thalamic functioning have significant consequences on neocortical functioning. In Korsakoff's syndrome the medial thalamus is destroyed by chronic alcohol ingestion, leading to severe memory loss and various signs suggestive of frontal-lobe damage. Since the medial thalamus provides the principal subcortical afferents to the frontal cortex, the frontal-lobe symptoms presumably result from a disturbance of cortical function secondary to the thalamic damage.

Cortical-Striatal Loops

The striatum is one of the major efferent targets of the cortex. Unlike the cortical projections to the brainstem, however, the striatum does not send heavy projections in turn to the spinal cord but rather sends its major projections back to the cortex by way of the thalamus (see Figure 8–5 C). The principal function of the striatum therefore must be to modify cortical activity rather than to control behavior directly, since the only way the striatum can effectively change behavior is by influencing cortical function. The striatum must have an especially important role in the control of movement since striatal damage can produce a wide range of movement disorders. The best-known of these disorders is Parkinson's disease, in which an absence of dopamine in the striatum produces a bewildering array of motor (as well as cognitive) symptoms, which we shall discuss in detail in Chapter 12.

Cortical-Amygdala Loops

The amygdala has two different feedback loops to the cortex. The first is indirect, via the medial thalamus, and the second is direct, as illustrated in Figures 8–5 D and E. The function of the cortical-amygdala loop is not well understood, but the role of the amygdala in the control of affective behavior suggests that it may play some role in adding affective tone to cortical activity. For example, a ferocious dog may generate a strong affective response in us as it charges up, in part because the amygdala adds affective tone to the visual input of the dog. Indeed, in the absence of the amygdala laboratory animals appear to have absolutely no fear of threatening objects. We have seen amygdalectomized cats take leisurely strolls through rooms housing large monkeys, whereas no normal cat would even contemplate doing such a thing.

Cortical-Hippocampal Loops

The hippocampus does not provide the large source of cortical afferents that the thalamus, striatum, or amygdala do, but it does receive cortical input and does influence neocortical activity. The hippocampus is probably one of the most intensely studied and poorly understood structures in the forebrain, as is attested by the numerous theories regarding its function. As we shall see in later chapters, the hippocampus has a crucial role in memory and may have a role in many other functions including movement, affect, language, and spatial behavior. This role is most likely due largely to the major cortical-hippocampal projections, but it is likely that the hippocampus has some influence on cortical function as well, via feedback loops through the thalamus or limbic cortex.

HIERARCHICAL AND
PARALLEL PROCESSING

In the previous chapter we emphasized the hierarchical nature of brain organization. Within the cortex, we suggested that Luria's

concept of primary, secondary, and tertiary cortex provides a useful conceptual model of cortical function. Having considered the cortex in more detail in this chapter, we are now ready to elaborate on Luria's simple model in order to incorporate features such as multiple representations and feedback loops and to consider a second type of cortical processing, namely parallel processing. We shall begin by reconsidering the types of cortex.

Cortical Types

We have seen that the sensory and motor regions are very different in their laminar structure. The motor cortex is thicker overall and the relative sizes of the layers in the two types of cortex are rather different. We have also seen in Chapter 7 that in addition to primary sensory and motor cortex there is secondary cortex, which is closely associated with specific primary regions, and tertiary cortex, which is multimodal and not specifically associated with any primary sensory or motor region. Careful anatomical and behavioral studies have shown, however, that the division of cortex into three types is an oversimplification. First, secondary cortex can be distinguished as two separate types of cortex on the basis of its cortical-cortical connections (Figure 8–6). One secondary region, which we shall refer to as secondary I, receives projections from primary cortex and projects to the premotor cortex (area 6) as well as to the other secondary region, which we shall refer to as secondary II. This latter region sends its projections to the prefrontal cortex, to the limbic system, and to tertiary cortex. Second, it must be recognized that there may be more than one functional route from primary cortex through the secondary regions to tertiary cortex. For example, Mishkin and his colleagues have shown that there is one distinct route beginning in area 17 that is concerned with determining the *what* of

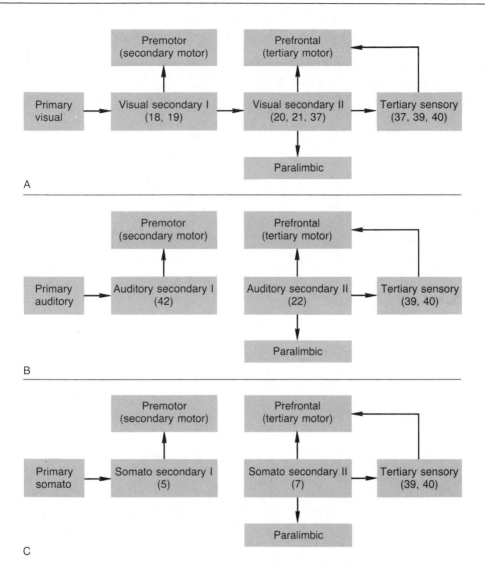

FIGURE 8–6. Schematic diagrams illustrating the principal serial connections between the primary, secondary (I and II), and tertiary zones and the motor zones.

visual information, and a complementary second route, which also begins in area 17, that is concerned with determining the *where* of visual information (see Chapter 23 for a detailed discussion of this research). Both routes are hierarchical and both are within the "visual system," but they are nearly completely independent of each other. Third, there is an additional type of cortex that Pandya has labeled **paralimbic cortex.** This cortex is not primary, secondary, or tertiary neocortex but rather is older cortex, being composed of roughly three layers. It is in two places: (1) on the medial surface of the temporal lobe, where it is known as pyriform, entorhinal, and parahippocampal cortex (Figure 17–1), and (2) just above the corpus callosum in each hemisphere, where it is referred to as cingulate cortex (Brodmann's areas 23, 24, 25, and 32). The paralimbic cortex receives projections from secondary II regions and thus offers an alternate route for sensory information to follow, rather than just from secondary to tertiary cortex. Hence, we can see that although the cortex is clearly hierarchical, there are several hierarchical pathways that may be followed, not just one, as is implied by Luria's simple model.

Parallel Processing

In the traditional view of the thalamic-cortical pathways of the sensory systems, each of the primary sensory areas receives input from a single thalamic nucleus, as illustrated in Figure 8–7 A. The identification of multiple sensory areas has coincided, however, with the discovery that the thalamic-cortical connections are actually made up of parallel pathways with overlapping projections, as illustrated in Figure 8–7 B. The organization of these parallel pathways can best be understood by considering several features of thalamic-cortical anatomy, which appear to be common to each of the sensory systems.

First, Diamond suggests that the neocortex of a sensory system should be conceptualized as forming a *field*. A field is defined as a constellation of small cortical areas constituting one continuous larger cortical area, functionally unified by the reception of sensory projections in a given modality. Thus, there would be fields for vision, audition, and somatosensation and possibly for visceral sensation (taste and olfaction). Second, there is a *core* area within each field that is characterized by the maximum development of

A Traditional hierarchical model

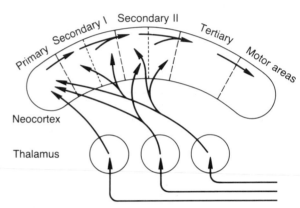

B Hierarchical/parallel model

FIGURE 8–7. Highly schematic diagrams illustrating the traditional hierarchical model and the hierarchical/parallel model of cortical processing. A. In the hierarchical model sensory inputs progress serially from the thalamus to the primary, secondary, and tertiary regions respectively before going to the motor cortex. B. The hierarchical/parallel model recognizes additional cortical regions and multiple thalamic inputs. Sensory input may be processed as in the straight hierarchical model or it may proceed directly to secondary areas via direct thalamic projections that miss the primary zone altogether. For additional explanation, see text.

the fourth layer. This is Luria's primary zone. There is one thalamic nucleus that projects principally, if not exclusively, to the core area. In the visual system, the core area would be area 17, and the projections would arise in the lateral geniculate nucleus. For the auditory system, the core area would roughly correspond with area 41, and the pathway would originate in the ventral division of the medial geniculate nucleus. In the somatosensory system the core area is probably area 3b, and the thalamic projections originate in the ventral posterior nucleus. Third, at least one thalamic nucleus projects to all subdivisions in the field (e.g., the pulvinar in the visual system) and at least one thalamic nucleus projects to more than one subdivision but fewer than all the subdivisions of the field (e.g., the lateral nucleus in the visual system). The fourth principle is that the laminar distribution for these thalamic projections differs, with the core projection terminating in layer IV and the other projections terminating in layer I, rather than in layer IV, in regions where the terminations overlap with the core projections. Therefore, although there are indeed parallel pathways to the sensory cortex, the function of the parallel projections is almost certainly different from that of the primary projections to the core area.

OVERVIEW OF CORTICAL ORGANIZATION

Our discussion of cortical organization has emphasized that the neocortex can be considered in terms of its laminar and columnar organization; in a broader view in terms of its relation with subcortical structures, especially the thalamus; and in terms of its cortical-cortical interactions. What is left now is for us to consider the functional implications of this organization. Two general principles can be established. The first is that functions are localized in parallel in the cortex both at a microlevel at any point in the cortex and at a broader level within distinct cortical regions. The second is that imposed on this

parallel organization is an overall hierarchical organization. We shall consider each in turn.

Parallel Processing

The fact that the anatomical and electrophysiological evidence clearly indicates a parallel organization of the sensory, and probably the motor, systems in the cortex implies that these parallel areas may have distinct, independent functions. Thus, cortical columns have functions that can be distinguished from one another and so do each of the larger individual representations of the sensory surface. It follows therefore that damage or disorganization of individual columns or of individual sensory representations could produce a specific behavioral effect. In view of the size and mosaic pattern of the columns it is improbable that direct cortical damage could selectively destroy one class of columns (although some selective neurotoxin could at least in principle perform this feat), but direct cortical damage certainly could interfere with the functioning of a single sensory representation within a larger sensory field. The neurological literature confirms this expectation, as it provides numerous examples of highly specific functional deficits arising from restricted cortical lesions. For example, there are numerous case reports of human patients suffering limited combinations of losses of vibratory, pain, tactile pattern, or joint position sense following different parietal lobe lesions, and analogous specific symptoms have been reported frequently for visual and auditory modes as well. (We must add a cautionary note that one should be wary of claims of specific deficits consequent to cerebral injury since, in our experience, deficits that appear remarkably specific in the clinic become far less so under careful, systematic examinations in the laboratory!)

Hierarchical Processing

The pattern of cortical-cortical projections both within the sensory fields and beyond implies that a dominant feature of cortical processing must be hierarchical, or serial. Although it is recognized that each of the sensory representations provides a unique contribution to the overall perception, it is certainly the case that the core area of each sensory field is more critical to sensory experience than any of the others. Hence, even though damage to individual sensory representations within the secondary regions might produce specific symptoms, damage within the core area produces a more severe and generalized effect on perception. Furthermore, interruption of pathways from one zone to another (primary to secondary I, secondary I to secondary II, secondary II to tertiary, etc.) produces behavioral symptoms, known as a **disconnection syndrome,** that persist in spite of the continuing activity of the individual sensory areas. For example, disconnection of the sensory field from tertiary cortex will produce what appears to be a loss of "memory" or "perception," as the individual may be unable to name an object even though the visual system has accurately represented the object in the neocortex. If this sensory representation is not passed on to the appropriate effectors, it will appear as though the sensory representation itself was absent. (We shall proceed with a detailed discussion of this phenomenon in Chapter 19.)

The existence of both serial and parallel systems in the cortex has several implications for cortical processing. First, perception appears to be a product of the nearly simultaneous activation of a number of topographic sensory representations, unified by serial cortical connections. For example, depression of the skin activates neurons in each of the four somatosensory representations at about the same time, but since a spatially unified perception of the sensory event is generated, it is likely that the serial organization within the sensory field has a major role in providing a single experience from the multiple cortical representations of a single sensory event. Second, differences in the perception of a given stimulus from one person to the next may result from variations in the relative size of each of the parallel sensory representations within a sensory field. Thus, our six blind men from Hindustan could each have examined the same region of the elephant but owing to individual differences in somatosensory representations, they might still have arrived at different impressions of the animal. Or, put another way, beauty really is in the eye (or sensory field!) of the beholder. Similarly, individual differences in motor skills may be at least partly due to individual differences in the cortical organization of motor circuitry. Third, Merzenich and Kaas propose that differences in the perception of a given stimulus by the same person at different times may be the result of variations in the contributions of individual topographic representations to perception under different conditions of expectancy, set, or other factors, a possibility that could probably be extended to include the motor system as well. These variations likely result from some plasticity in the nature of the serial processing as the sensory representation in the cortex proceeds to the paralimbic regions. Recall, for example, that the size of cortical representations can be affected by environmental stimulation, so that changes in perceptions over time may result from real changes in the size and nature of cortical representations.

REFERENCES

Diamond, I. T. The functional significance of architectonic subdivisions of the cortex: Lashley's criticism of the traditional view. In J. Orback, ed., *Neuropsychology after Lashley*. Hillsdale, N.J.: Lawrence Erlbaum Associates, 1982.

Diamond, I. T. The subdivisions of neocortex: A proposal to revise the traditional view of sensory, motor, and association areas. *Progress in Psychobiology and Physiological Psychology* 8:1–43, 1979.

Graybiel, A. M., and D. M. Berson. On the relation between transthalamic and transcortical pathways in the visual system. In F. O. Schmitt, F. G. Worden, G. Adelman, and S. G. Dennis, eds., *The Organization of the Cerebral Cortex*. Cambridge, Mass.: MIT Press, 1981.

Jones, E. G. Anatomy of cerebral cortex: Columnar input-output organization. In F. O. Schmitt, F. G. Worden, G. Adelman, and S. G. Dennis, eds., *The Organization of the Cerebral Cortex*. Cambridge, Mass.: MIT Press, 1981.

Kaas, J. H., R. J. Nelson, M. Sur, C.-L. Lin, and M. M. Merzenich. Multiple representations of the body within the primary somatosensory cortex of primates. *Science* 204: 521–523, 1979.

Merzenich, M. M., and J. H. Kaas. Principles of organization of sensory-perceptual systems in mammals. *Progress in Psychobiology and Physiological Psychology* 9:1–42, 1980.

Merzenich, M. M., and J. H. Kaas. Reorganization of mammalian somatosensory cortex following peripheral nerve injury. *Trends in Neurosciences* 5:434–436, 1982.

Pandya, D. N., and B. Seltzer. Association areas of the cerebral cortex. *Trends in Neurosciences* 5:386–390, 1982.

Shepherd, G. M. *The Synaptic Organization of the Brain,* 2nd ed. New York: Oxford University Press, 1979.

Szentágothai, J. Architecture of the cerebral cortex. In H. H. Jasper, A. A. Ward, and A. Pope, eds., *Basic Mechanisms of the Epilepsies*. Boston: Little, Brown, 1969.

Wise, S. P., and E. V. Evarts. The role of the cerebral cortex in movement. *Trends in Neurosciences* 4:297–300, 1981.

9

ORGANIZATION OF THE SENSORY SYSTEMS

The human sensory systems present some of the most obvious evidence of brain function to the average person. We are aware of sensations (e.g., sight, hearing, and touch) all our waking hours, and most people accept that the brain is responsible for these sensations. To recognize the role of the brain is one matter, to understand how nervous tissue can turn energy (such as light waves) into meaningful sensations, which in turn lead to thoughts, is another. The operation of the sensory systems is complex, and in spite of intense research effort over the past three decades, represents a large area of ignorance in neuropsychology. In this chapter we shall present the general workings of the three major sensory systems (vision, audition, and touch), identifying principles that allow us to understand the basic operation of these and the other sensory systems. We do not propose to present a detailed description of the physiological mechanisms of sensory processing, as this is beyond the scope of our concern. (The interested reader is directed to Uttal, Masteron, or other standard texts for detailed accounts of each of the sensory systems.) Since naturally occurring lesions seldom respect the boundaries of individual components of the sensory systems, we are forced to rely principally on anatomical, physiological, and functional evidence from nonhuman species, especially cats and monkeys, although data from humans are considered whenever available.

GENERAL PRINCIPLES OF THE SENSORY SYSTEMS

Each of the sensory systems can be understood in terms of a number of principles, some of which will be described here before we discuss specific sensory systems.

Receptors

In each sensory system there are specialized cells called *receptors*. The function of these receptors is to transduce sensory energy (e.g., light waves) into neural activity in the form of either graded potentials or action potentials.

The receptors in each sensory system are different, and so the sensory energy that they can detect is different. For vision, light energy is converted into chemical energy in the receptors of the retina, and this chemical energy is in turn converted into neural activity. In the auditory system, sound waves are converted into mechanical energy in the form of the movement of the little bones in the ear and the movement of the basilar membrane, which contains the actual hair receptors. It is only after the receptor hair cells are activated that a neural discharge occurs. In the somatosensory system, mechanical energy in the form of touch, pressure, vibration, etc., activates mechanoreceptors, which in turn generate neural activity. For taste and olfaction, various molecules carried by the air or contained in food fit themselves into receptors of various shapes to activate relevant neural activity. For pain sensation, a very curious transduction step is thought to occur between tissue damage, the adequate stimulus, and neural activation. It is thought that tissue damage releases a chemical from tissue that is called neurokinin. This in turn is thought to act like a neurotransmitter to activate pain fibers. The neurokinin explanation does have the virtue of accounting for why tissue damage can result in pain sensations that last for hours or days.

Receptive Fields

Not only do receptors act as filters in letting only certain forms of energy activate them, they also have what are called **receptive fields.** For some sensory systems the receptive field is fairly straightforward. For example, for vision, if the eyes are fixated, all the visual world that can be seen forms the receptive field for vision. If one eye is closed, the remaining world that can be seen by the other eye forms the receptive field for that eye. Within that eye is a cup-shaped retina, which contains thousands of receptor cells. Because of the

shape of the retina, each cell points in a particular direction, like a telescope pointing at a particular part of the world, and the little part of the world that each receptor receives light from forms its receptive field. For skin receptors, the part of the skin on which they are located forms their receptive field; this will generally consist of a few square millimeters of tissue, but the receptive field for all tactile reception will consist of the body surface. The function of receptive fields is of course to allow stimuli to be located in space or on the body surface. Some systems such as olfaction are not very good at this: we do have two nostrils but there is some question about how sensitive they are to the directionality of odors. On the other hand, in the auditory system both ears hear most sounds, so that location is done not so much by differences in detection but by differences in loudness; that is, the ear closest to the sound hears it as loudest. For sensations of taste, there are interesting topographic organizations for the receptors sensitive to different stimuli. Receptors for sweet substances are mainly on the tip of the tongue, whereas receptors for bitter substances are mainly on the back of the tongue, with the receptors for saltiness and sourness along the tongue margins. Hence, there are different receptive fields for tastes, but the location of the fields may have more to do with deciding questions of ingestion than with localizing the substance per se. The tip of the tongue is a good place for sweet receptors, because sweet foods are good to eat and can be swept into the mouth. Bitter foods, however, are usually poisonous and so when detected on the back of the tongue they can be coughed out.

Localization and Detection

An important question each sensory system must answer is: Where is it? The receptive fields of individual receptors overlap, which has heuristic value for localizing a stimulus and for identifying it. If one receptor is more activated by a stimulus than another, then the object in question must be located more precisely in the receptive field of that receptor. In vision, a light source will produce a gradient of illumination across the retina that differentially activates different receptors, thus permitting the light source to be localized. Movement of the light could be tracked by the change in illuminance on the receptors. We must note, however, that in many sensory systems there are cells specialized for detecting moving objects; for example, many hair receptors on the body are only activated if the stimulus is moving in a particular direction.

Sensory systems must also answer questions such as: Is it there? and, What is it? Detection of a stimulus is often determined by receptor density and overlap. Tactile receptors on the fingers are numerous as compared with the back, and the fingers have remarkably good discrimination abilities as compared with the back. In the visual system the organization of receptors has two quite different arrangements to facilitate detection. In the fovea the receptors (called cones) are small and densely packed to make fine discriminations in bright light. In the periphery of the retina the receptors (called rods) are larger and more scattered, but large numbers of rods give their input to only a few neurons. Their discrimination ability is not good, but their ability to detect light (e.g., a lighted match at the distance of two miles on a dark night) is quite remarkable.

Neural Relays

Each sensory system requires three to four neurons, connected in sequence, to get information from the receptor cells to the cortex (e.g., the visual and somatosensory systems

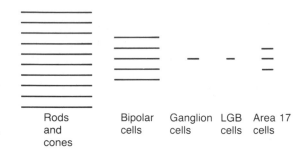

Rods and cones   Bipolar cells   Ganglion cells   LGB cells   Area 17 cells

FIGURE 9–1. Diagrammatic representation of the numbers of cells at each level of the visual system. Both the length and the numbers of lines represent cell numbers.

have three, and the auditory system has four). Two important events can occur at the synapses between the neurons in the relays. First, some kind of motor response can be produced. For example, axons from pain receptors first synapse in the spinal cord, where they can produce a withdrawal reflex. They next synapse in the brainstem, where they can produce whole limb or body movements, presumably withdrawal from the noxious stimulus. Finally, they synapse in the thalamus, where, in conjunction with their connections in the cortex, they can produce anticipation of and hence avoidance of the noxious stimulus. The second thing that can happen at a synapse is that the code carrying the message can be modified in a variety of ways; for example, descending impulses from the cortex can block or amplify it, or the code can simply be made more elaborate or more precise. When one considers the convergence of the sensory systems with each relay and their subsequent divergence when they reach the cortex, it becomes apparent that there must be a change in the code from level to level. This is illustrated in Figure 9–1 for the visual system. Lashley calculated that there are about nine million rods and cones, 3.5 million bipolar cells, 0.2 million ganglion cells, 0.03 million lateral geniculate cells, and 0.6 million area 17 cells at the different levels in the rat visual system. It seems quite obvious that there is not a straight-through point-to-point correspondence from one relay to the next, but rather a recoding in successive relays.

Information Transmission

In some of the sensory systems it takes one or more cells to transduce the stimulus energy into neural energy (e.g., for taste, one taste receptor; for vision, a light-sensitive cell and then a bipolar cell), but once transduced all sensory information from all sensory systems is coded by action potentials. The sensory information is conducted into the brain by bundles of axons, called *nerves* until they enter the brain or spinal cord and *tracts* thereafter, and every nerve carries the same kind of signal. This raises some interesting questions. How do action potentials code the differences in sensations? How do action potentials code the features of sensations themselves? The answers to parts of these questions seem easy and the answers to other parts are very difficult. The presence of a stimulus can be coded by an increase or decrease in the discharge rate of a neuron, and the amount of change can code the intensity. Qualitative changes such as red as opposed to green can be coded by activity in different neurons or even by different levels of discharge in the same neuron. What is less clear, however, is how we perceive such sensations as touch, sound, and smell as different. One explanation is that the neural areas that process these sensations in the cortex are distinct. Another explanation is that we learn through experience to distinguish them. A third explanation is that each sensory system has a preferred link with certain kinds of movements, which ensures that they remain distinct at all levels of neural organization. Of course, this question requires a great deal more study,

but it should be noted that such distinctions are not always clear. There are people who can hear in color or identify smells by the sounds that they make. This ability is called *synesthesia,* or mixed senses. Of course, everyone who has shivered during certain notes of a piece of music (or at the noise that chalk or fingernails can make on a blackboard) has felt sound.

Sensory Subsystems

There are multiple pathways in each sensory system, from the sensory receptor to the brain, that form subsystems with specialized functions. We are used to thinking of the visual system as a single system, but if we refer to the schematic illustration Figure 9–2, it can be seen that the visual system is really made up of a number of subsystems. There is a pathway to the superoptic nucleus of the hypothalamus that controls daily rhythms of feeding and sleeping, etc.; a pathway to the pretectum in the midbrain that controls pupillary responses to light; a pathway to the superior colliculus in the midbrain that controls head orienting to objects; a pathway to the pineal body that controls long-term circadian rhythms; a pathway to the visual cortex that controls pattern perception, depth perception, color vision, and tracking of moving objects; and a pathway to the frontal cortex that controls voluntary eye movements. The pathways to many of these "visual centers" are often more indirect than is illustrated in the figure and involve other brain centers as well. Further, just as there are many visual systems projecting into different brain regions, there are multiple subsystems projecting to the visual cortex. Thus, there are a number of parallel visual systems going through the visual cortex, each of which may have a rather specialized output. For example, the systems for pattern perception, color vision, depth perception, and visual tracking may be as inde-

Visual System	Postulated Function
1. Superoptic nucleus	Controls daily rhythms (sleep, feeding, etc.) in response to day-night cycles.
2. Pretectum	Produces changes in pupil size in response to light-intensity changes.
3. Superior colliculus	Head orienting, particularly to objects in peripheral visual fields.
4. Pineal body	Long-term circadian rhythms.
5. Accessory optic nucleus	Moves eyes to compensate for head movements.
6. Visual cortex	Pattern perception, depth perception, color vision, tracking moving objects.
7. Frontal eye fields	Voluntary eye movements.

FIGURE 9–2. Schematic representation of visual subsystems. Each pathway and each number represents a subsystem as indicated in the text.

pendent from one another as are the systems that code hearing and the systems that code taste. The fact that they are in close anatomical proximity may not mean that they are functionally identical or interchangeable.

Multiple Representation

The neocortex re-represents the sensory field, not once but a number of times. Therefore the entire retina (or visual field) is represented several times in the visual cortex. Each sensory system has a primary area, which has one representation, and two secondary areas, each of which has several representations. The same principle of multiple representation applies to each sensory system, but as yet the functional differences in each of the representations are not fully understood. Nevertheless, it is likely that each representation is devoted to coding one specific aspect of a sensory modality.

THE VISUAL SYSTEM

Visual Receptors

A schematic illustration of the eye and the visual receptor surface, the retina, is presented in Figure 9–3. When light enters the eye, it is bent slightly by the cornea and then more profoundly by the lens so that images are focused on the receptors at the back of the eye. An unusual feature of the eye is that light must travel through the outer layers of the retina in order to strike the photoreceptive cells that lie on its inner surface. The chemical reactions that light induces in the receptors actually occur at the distal end of the receptor. The barrier provided by the retinal cells has little effect on our visual acuity for two reasons. First, the cells are relatively transparent and the photoreceptors are extremely sensitive; they can be excited by the absorption of a single quantum of light. Second, many of the fibers skirt the central portion, or fovea, of the retina to facilitate light access to the receptors. This

accounts for why the fovea is seen as a depression on the retinal surface.

The human retina contains two types of photoreceptive cells, rods and cones, both of which function to transduce light energy into action potentials. Rods, sensitive to dim light, are utilized mainly for night vision. Cones are better able to transduce bright light and are used for daytime vision and color vision. There are three types of cones, each type being maximally responsive to wavelengths producing hues of red, blue, or yellow, respectively. Rods and cones differ in their distribution across the retina; cones are packed together densely in the foveal region and rods are more sparsely distributed in the periphery of the retina. The significance of this distribution can be appreciated at night when, to see something, it is best to look slightly away from it.

The photoreceptive cells are connected to very simple cells called bipolar cells. The receptor cells induce graded potentials in the bipolar cells. The bipolar cells in turn induce action potentials in ganglion cells. As is illus-

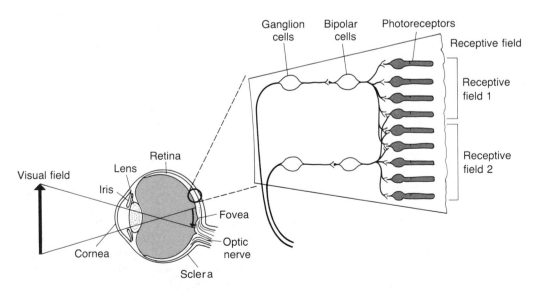

FIGURE 9–3. A. Anatomy of the eye. B. Anatomy of the retina. (After Bailey, 1981.)

trated in Figure 9–3, it is the ganglion cells that actually send axons into the brain.

Visual Pathways

The axons of ganglion cells leave the retina to form the optic nerve. Just before entering the brain the optic nerves partly cross, forming the *optic chiasm* (from the Greek, meaning a cross-shaped crossing). At this point about half of the fibers from each eye cross, as is illustrated in Figure 9–4 A, in such a way that each visual half-field will be represented in the opposite hemisphere of the brain. Having entered the brain, the ganglion cells divide, forming a number of separate pathways. The largest of these is the geniculostriate system: the projection that goes to the lateral geniculate nucleus or body (LGB) of the thalamus and then to the visual cortex. The ganglion cells of the geniculostriate system synapse in the LGB. Each LGB has six well-defined layers: layers 2, 3, and 5 receive fibers from the ipsilateral eye and layers 1, 4, and 6 receive fibers from the contralateral eye. The topographic relation of the visual field is also maintained in the LGB, with the central portion representing the central visual field and the peripheral portions representing the peripheral visual field. The LGB cells project to the visual cortex, where they are distributed in such a way that the visual field is again topographically represented. This representation is illustrated in Figure 9–4 B. The representation is quite easy to remember if it is noted that everything is upside down and backward. The central part of the visual field is represented at the back of the brain and the peripheral part is represented toward the middle of the brain. The upper part of the visual field is represented below the calcarine fissure and the lower part of the visual world is represented above the calcarine fissure. Of course, we have already noted that the left visual field is represented in the right hemisphere and the right visual

field is represented in the left hemisphere. Other visual pathways go to the superior colliculus, accessory optic nucleus, pretectum, and superoptic chiasmatic nucleus, as is illustrated in Figure 9–5. It should also be noted in Figure 9–5 that the projections to the superior colliculus can reach the cortex through relays in the lateral posterior-pulvinar complex of the thalamus.

Visual Cortex

In addition to their main projections to area 17 of the cortex the thalamocortical pathways terminate in the cortex to produce several independent representations of the retina. The precise number of these retinal representations is not known for humans, but in monkeys there may be as many as 10 independently organized fields, as illustrated in Figure 9–6. The entire visual field is systematically represented in each field, although the details of this representation are still uncertain in the inferotemporal cortex. These visual representations are not mere copies of one another, as the size of each field is different, the core area being the largest, and there are significant differences in organization. The visual areas of the owl monkey in Figure 9–6 illustrate this. For example, whereas the upper and lower visual fields are independently represented in most of the fields, they are not so represented in area DI. Careful examination of the regional representation of the retina also shows marked differences between the regions. In area DM, for example, it is the central retina that is principally represented, with few cells responding to visual stimuli at the periphery. In contrast, there are many cells in both area 17 and in area V II that respond to stimuli in the periphery and relatively fewer cells responsive to stimuli in the center of the visual field. Similarly, cells in area 17 are unresponsive to color, whereas

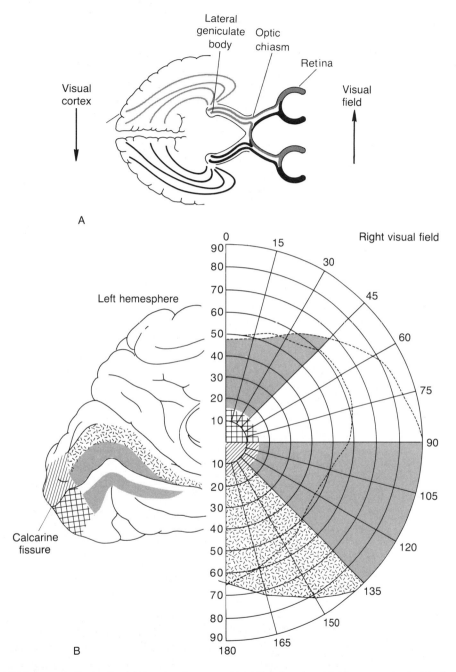

FIGURE 9–4. A. Projection of the visual system. Note that the visual fields are projected to the contralateral visual cortex. B. Projection of the right visual field on the left hemisphere (medial view). Note the relation between the topography of the visual field and the topography of the cortex. (After Poggio, 1968.)

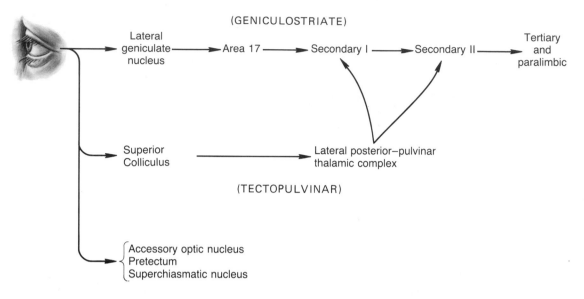

FIGURE 9–5. The connections of the visual system. One subsystem, the geniculostriate system, is specialized for pattern analysis; the other, the tectopulvinar system, is specialized for the detection of and orientation to visual stimuli. Note that the systems converge in the tertiary visual cortex.

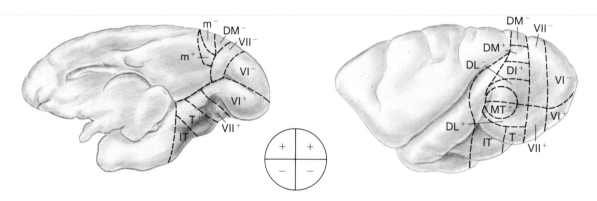

FIGURE 9–6. The representation of the visual field in the cortex of the owl monkey as seen medially (top) and dorsolaterally (bottom). The symbols from the visual field chart are superimposed on the cortex. (Redrawn from Allman, 1977.)

cells in some temporal areas are maximally excited by certain hues.

Properties of Cells in Visual Areas

By the use of microelectrodes neurophysiologists have recorded the activity of cells in anesthetized cats and monkeys while visual stimuli are presented on a screen placed in the animals' visual field. As we have noted, cells at each level of the visual system are responsive to a specific region of the visual field, known as the receptive field. Cells at each level of the visual system differ in two ways, however. First, the

receptive fields tend to be larger at each succeeding level toward the secondary cortex.
Second, cells in different levels of the visual
system respond to different properties of visual
stimulation. The nature of the visual input that
maximally excites cells at each level has been
extensively investigated, but there is still disagreement over exactly what the cells are responding to. (For a discussion of this controversy see Held, Leibowitz, and Teuber,
1978.) Nevertheless, some characteristics of
the cells have been agreed on.

As an overall generalization, the farther
along a cell is in the visual system, the more
complex the visual stimulus must be to excite
it. For example, cells in the retina are most
responsive to spots of light falling in the center
of their receptive fields. In some retinal cells
this light produces a rapid increase in the firing
rate of the cell, and in others it produces an
inhibition of all firing of the cell. In contrast,
cells in area 17 are most responsive to bars of
light of particular orientation. Some cells are
most responsive to bars of light oriented at 90°
from the horizontal, whereas others are most
responsive to bars oriented at other angles.
Cells in areas 18 and 19 require more complex
stimuli, being most responsive to bars of light
oriented at a particular angle and moving in a
particular direction. Still more complex cells
are maximally responsive to more complicated
patterns of light, such as corners; in inferotemporal cortex cells may require a very specific
shape for maximum response (e.g., a hand or
face), yet they can tolerate substantial changes
in the size of the stimulus, a characteristic that
may be a physiological basis for object con-
stancy.

THE AUDITORY SYSTEM

Auditory Receptors

To understand how the ear transduces sound
waves into action potentials we must take a
look at the anatomy of the ear, as illustrated in

Figure 9–7. When sound waves strike the ear-
drum it vibrates. The vibrations are transmitted via three small bones (ossicles) to the fluid
of the inner ear. One of the ossicles (the stirrup)
acts on the fluid like a tiny piston, driving the
fluid back and forth in the rhythm of the sound
waves. These movements of the fluid cause a
thin membrane, called the basilar membrane,
to resonate. Finally, the movement of the basilar membrane causes movements of the auditory receptors, hair cells, in the organ of Corti,
whose membrane potentials are altered, resulting in neural activity. The basilar membrane
and the organ of Corti are within a spiral-
shaped structure known as the cochlea, and it is
the structure of the cochlea and the basilar
membrane that allows the hair cells to code
different frequencies of sound. The basilar
membrane is not a uniform structure; it is narrow (100 μm) and taut near the ossicles and
wider (500 μm) and floppier near the apex of
the cochlea. It was Helmholtz in the late 1800s
who proposed that owing to this structure,
different portions of the basilar membrane
resonate with different frequencies of sound.
Although he was not precisely correct, it was
not until 1960 that von Bekesy was able to
directly observe the basilar membrane to show
that a traveling wave moves along it, starting
at the oval window. The peak of the wave
on the basilar membrane varies with the frequency of the sound, higher sounds causing
maximum peaks near the base of the basilar membrane and lower sounds causing
maximum peaks near the apex. As a rough
analogy, consider what happens when a
garden hose is shaken at one end. If it is shak-
en very quickly, the waves are very small
and the first wave on the hose reaches its peak
size very quickly. In contrast, if the hose is
shaken very slowly, the first wave reaches its
peak farther down the hose. The difference
between the basilar membrane and the hose
is that the basilar membrane is very short (33
mm) and there is only one peak, whereas

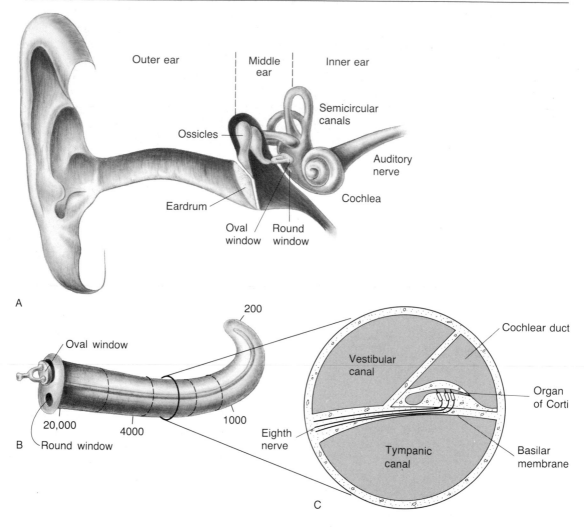

FIGURE 9–7. A. Anatomy of the ear. B. Anatomy of the cochlea and basilar membrane.

on the longer hose the wave travels along the hose, repeating itself. The hair cells in the organ of Corti are maximally disturbed at the point of the peak of the wave, resulting in the maximal neural response of hair cells at that point. A signal composed of many frequencies will cause several different points along the basilar membrane to vibrate and will excite hair cells at all of these points.

As in the visual system, each of the receptor cells in the auditory system has its own receptive field, as do each of the cells in the higher auditory centers. The receptive field of the hair cells is not a point in space, as in the visual system, but rather a particular frequency of sound. Thus, in contrast to the retinotopic maps in the visual system, the auditory system is composed of tonotopic maps.

Auditory Pathways

The axons of the hair cells leave the cochlea to form the major part of the auditory nerve, the eighth cranial nerve. The nerve first projects to the level of the medulla in the lower brainstem, synapsing either in the dorsal or the ventral cochlear nuclei, or in the superior olivary nucleus. The axons of cells in these areas form the lateral lemniscus, which terminates in discrete zones of the inferior colliculus. Two distinct pathways emerge from the colliculus, coursing to the ventral and the dorsal medial geniculate bodies, respectively (Figure 9–8). The ventral region projects to the core auditory cortex, AI, and the dorsal region projects to the secondary regions, thus corresponding to the general pattern of multiple independent ascending pathways to the cortex. In contrast to the visual system, the projections of the auditory system provide both ipsilateral and contralateral inputs to the cortex, so that there is bilateral representation of each cochlear nucleus in the cortex. The majority of the input is contralateral, however, a fact of importance in understanding the studies of cerebral asymmetry in Chapter 14.

Auditory Cortex

In contrast to studies of the visual and the somatosensory cortex, there has been relatively little research on the auditory cortex of primates, most of the research having been done with cats, in which direct homologies in the auditory cortex are uncertain (see Figure 9–9). Nevertheless, there are sufficient data to provide a basis for general principles of auditory cortical organization in primates. We include the cat in our discussions, however, to aid the interested reader in understanding the animal literature on the auditory cortex, most of which is based on work with cats.

There are several auditory areas in the cortex, because different regions of the medial geniculate nucleus project to independent tonotopically organized cortical zones in both cats and monkeys. These zones include the core auditory cortex (AI) and at least four other zones surrounding it.

Direct homologies are uncertain in cats and monkeys for the secondary zones; they may correspond to areas R, AL, CM, and PL in the owl monkey and to areas T, PAF and VPAF, AII, and AAF in the cat. In the human, the core area is within Heschl's gyrus (see Figure 9–9) and is surrounded by seven secondary areas. Although the auditory cortex is normally thought of as being in the temporal lobe, it can be seen in Figure 9–9 that it actually extends into the parietal lobe, both into the parietal operculum (the tissue on the parietal side of the Sylvian fissure) and into the inferior parietal cortex, at the caudal end of the Sylvian fissure. The tonotopic organization of each of the auditory areas remains to be completely mapped, although in general it appears that low tones are represented caudally and high tones more rostrally, in each subfield that has been mapped.

There may be a species difference in the organization of the secondary cortex, as there is a marked anatomical asymmetry in humans that has not been described in cats or monkeys (see Figure 14–1). In right-handed people the planum temporale is larger on the left whereas Heschl's gyrus is larger on the right. There is uncertainty over the posterior boundary of auditory cortex in the monkey since it may include more parietal cortex than previously suspected, so that it is difficult to be certain that there is no asymmetry, although there are no compelling grounds at present for believing there to be one.

Properties of Cells in the Auditory Cortex. Microelectrode studies have shown that single neurons in the auditory system code the frequency (or pitch) of sounds, different

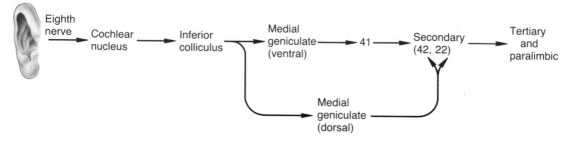

FIGURE 9–8. The major connections of the auditory system.

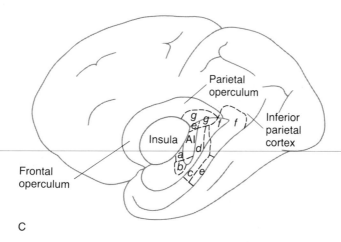

FIGURE 9–9. Representations of the auditory regions of the brains of the cat (A), owl monkey (B), and human (C).

neurons being maximally sensitive to different sound frequencies. In general, cells in subcortical nuclei are responsive to a broader band of frequencies than are cells higher in the system. Thus, a neuron in the cochlear nucleus may have a tuning curve with maximum sensitivity at 7000 Hz and reduced sensitivity to frequencies between 1000 and 12,000 Hz, as compared with a neuron in AI, whose tuning curve is also maximally sensitive to 7000 Hz but is partially responsive to frequencies between only 5000 and 9000 Hz. In some of the secondary areas the specificity of frequency is reduced slightly, because the cells are also responsive both to very small differences in arrival time in the two ears (as little as 30 μs, or 300 millionths of a second) and to other special characteristics of sound such as harmonics. It is likely that there are cells in the secondary, and possibly tertiary, auditory areas that are maximally sensitive to phonemes (e.g., da, la, ma), although this has not yet been demonstrated.

THE SOMATOSENSORY SYSTEM

The visual and auditory systems are known as *exteroceptive systems* because they are sensitive to stimuli from the external environment. The somatosensory system also has an exteroceptive function, but in addition it is a *proprioceptive* system, which provides information about the relative position of body segments to one another and the position of the body in space, and an *interoceptive* system, which records internal bodily events such as blood pressure. The somatosensory system is therefore not a single sensory system but a multiple one composed of several submodalities: (1) touch-pressure, which is sensation elicited by mechanical stimulation of the body surface; (2) position sense or kinesthesia, which results from mechanical disturbances in the muscles and joints; this system has two subcomponents,

the sense of static limb position and the sensation of limb movement; (3) heat and cold; and (4) pain, which is elicited by noxious stimulation.

Somatosensory Receptors

The somatosensory system does not have a single type of receptor cell; it has at least 20 different types of receptor cells, each transducing a different form of energy. Furthermore, the receptor surface of the somatosensory system is much larger than that of any other senses, because there are receptors in all body tissues except the brain itself. The basic organization of the receptors is the same as in the other two systems, however, as the membrane potential of each is altered by a particular form of energy, and each has its own receptive field, which is an area of body tissue.

1. *Hair receptors.* Hair receptors are located in hair follicles and are exquisitely sensitive to the bending of a hair. There are a number of types of hair receptors, each with distinctive morphological and physiological properties.

2. *Touch receptors.* Touch receptors are quite varied in the spectrum of stimuli that excite them and the morphology of their receptor specializations. They respond to stimulus characteristics such as vibration, skin indentation, and certain types of hair movements, with some receptors responding to the velocity of onset of stimulation and others to the duration of stimulation, or to moving stimuli. Touch receptors include Pacinian corpuscles, field receptors, Meissner's corpuscles, Merkel cell-neurite complexes, Ruffini endings, and C mechanoreceptors.

3. *Temperature receptors.* Temperature receptors (cold receptors and warm receptors) are sensitive to temperature change, showing a discharge that is related to skin temperature. Cold receptors are excited by decreases in skin temperature when the initial skin temperature

ranges from approximately 15 to 40°C. Warm receptors respond maximally to increases in temperature in the approximate range of 30 to 48°C. Other types of receptors (some touch receptors and nociceptors) also respond to rapid temperature changes, but they are not specialized *just* for temperature changes as are the temperature receptors.

4. *Nociceptors.* Nociceptors are receptors that are sensitive to mechanical or thermal stimuli that begin near levels that damage the tissue. In addition, some of these fibers respond to chemical stimuli. There are four types of nociceptors: mechanical nociceptors, mechanical and thermal nociceptors, deep pressure-pain receptors, and visceral afferents. The discharge of each of these receptor types is associated with the experience of pain.

5. *Joint receptors.* These receptors are responsive to the movements and positions of limbs. There are at least three types, including Ruffini endings, Paciniform endings, and Golgi receptors.

6. *Muscle and tendon receptors.* These receptors are located in the muscles and tendons, responding primarily to stretch and contraction of these organs. They include muscle spindle receptors and Golgi tendon organs.

It should be apparent from our brief overview of the somatosensory receptors that the central representation of the information from all these receptors must be very complex indeed if there is to be a representation of all this information in the cortex, and if it is all to be integrated to allow us a perception of touch.

Somatosensory Pathways

The somatosensory system can be seen as two subsystems, one for fine touch, pressure, and kinesthesis, and one for pain and temperature. Fibers that form the first system leave the receptors and ascend via the dorsal columns of the spinal cord to synapse in the cuneate and gracile nuclei of the lower brainstem. The fibers then cross to the opposite side of the brain to form the medial lemniscus, which terminates in the ventroposterior region of the ventrobasal thalamus (see Figure 9–10). This thalamic nucleus then projects primarily to area 3b, as well as 1, to form independent somatotopic maps, as illustrated in Figure 8–4. In contrast to this pattern, the fibers of the pain and temperature system leave the receptors to synapse in the dorsal horn (the substantia gelatinosa) of the spinal cord. The cells in this area then cross over to the other side of the cord and form the lateral spinothalamic tract, which primarily terminates in the dorsal portions of the ventrobasal thalamus (ventroposterior oral and ventroposterior superior) as well as the posterior thalamus. These nuclei project in turn to areas 3a (ventroposterior oral), 2 (ventroposterior superior), 5 (lateral posterior), and SII (posterior). Thus, we see that as in the other sensory systems there are multiple pathways to independent representations of the receptor surface.

Somatosensory Cortex

We previously discussed somatosensory cortical organization as an example of sensory neocortical organization in Chapter 8 (see Figure 8–4), and so we shall not repeat the details here. Like the other sensory systems, the somatosensory system is composed of a primary core area, a secondary cortex, and a tertiary projection area. The core area is not so anatomically distinct in this system, presumably because the somatosensory system is composed of so many subsystems, but Kaas has suggested that there are grounds for considering it to be area 3b. In this case, areas 3a, 2, and 1 are likely secondary I cortex, and areas 5 and SII (area 43) are secondary II cor-

FIGURE 9–10. Major connections of the somatosensory system. It has two major subsystems, one for fine touch, pressure, and kinesthesis, and the other for pain and temperature, which converge on the somatosensory cortex.

tex. The tertiary projections fall in parts of areas 7 and 40.

Properties of Cells in Somatosensory Areas

Microelectrode studies have suggested that at least five basic sensations are independently coded throughout the somatosensory system: light touch to the skin, deep pressure to the fascia below the skin, joint movement, pain, and temperature. Within the thalamus, cells are highly specific, any given cell being maximally responsive to only one mode of stimulation. Within the next higher level, in the cortex, the cells are just as specific to particular stimuli, but a given cell is responsive to a smaller region of skin. Thus, in the cortex there is increased discrimination of spatial location on the receptor surface. In addition some cells, especially in the hand region, have very complex properties, responding to movement of stimuli in one direction or another or to the precise orientation of tactile stimuli on the skin surface. These neurons likely play some special role during movements of the hand designed to

explore the shape of an object, and they play a role in stereognosis, the ability to perceive a three-dimensional structure tactually. There may be other properties of these cells in areas 7 and 40 that integrate visual and tactile information in coding the position of the body in extrapersonal space, a problem we shall return to in Chapter 23.

PERCEPTION

We have reviewed the basic organization of the sensory systems, illustrating the neural pathways from the receptors to the tertiary cortex, and identifying principles that govern the operation of the sensory systems. We have described a very sterile picture, however, since our experiences of sensory stimuli are far richer than the description of the anatomy and physiology would lead us to believe. Our sensory impressions are obviously affected by our past experience, the contexts in which they occur, the affective state that we are in, and so on. There is certainly far more to the sensory systems than the transduction of physical energy into nervous activity. Our subjective experience of the physical energy is perception, and it is perception, rather than sensory transduction, that is of most interest to the psychologist.

Sensation and perception can be distinguished quite simply: **sensation** is the result of activity of receptors and their associated afferent pathways to the corresponding neocortical sensory areas; **perception** is the result of activity of cells in the cortex beyond the first synapse in the sensory cortex. Thus, in the neocortex sensory information is transformed into a percept by such factors as experience and context; the percept may differ in a number of ways from the sensory information sent to the neocortex. For example, if a motorist comes on a road sign partially covered with mud and reading "ST," she would most likely stop her vehicle because her perception is of the word "STOP" although her sensation was only of "ST." From her previous experience with road signs the motorist's sensation is transformed by mediation processes to a perception with considerable meaning.

The clearest proof that perception is more than sensation is the transformation of the same sensory stimulation into totally different perceptions, and the fact that perceptions are affected by the context of the sensory input. The classic demonstration of the former effect is such ambiguous figures as Rubin's vases (see Figure 9–11). The figure may be seen either as a vase or as two faces, and if one fixates on the dot in the center the perceptions alternate even though the sensory stimulation remains constant. Similarly, the Müller-Lyer illusion in Figure 9–11 demonstrates the influence of context. The top line is perceived as longer than the bottom although both are the same length. The contextual cues (the arrowheads) alter the perception of line length. Ambiguous figures and illusions involve complex perceptual phenomena that are mediated by the neocortex at a

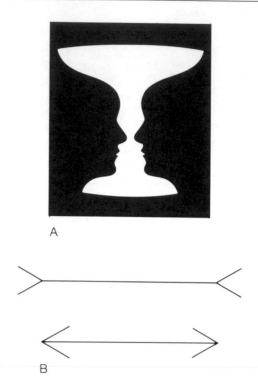

A

B

FIGURE 9–11. Demonstration of the distinction between sensation and perception. A. An ambiguous or reversible figure first described by Rubin. The figure can be seen as a vase or as two faces. B. The Müller-Lyer illusion: the top line appears longer than the bottom line because of contextual cues (the arrowheads).

functional level beyond the primary sensory cortex. They also illustrate the complexity of perceptual phenomena produced by the secondary and tertiary sensory regions, and allow us some insight into the bases of cognitive processes.

The distinction between sensation and perception is particularly useful to neuropsychology because it allows different predictions to be made of the effects of lesions to lower (sensory) and upper (perceptual) components of the sensory systems. Specifically, damage to the sensory system up to and including the core sensory cortex should produce distortions of the details of the world around us, whereas damage to the higher sensory regions of the neocortex, and the areas receiving projections from these parasensory regions, should result in deficits in understanding or comprehending the meaning of the incoming sensory information. These predictions are indeed confirmed by the evidence, which we review in the next chapter.

REFERENCES

Allman, J. M. Evolution of the visual system in the early primates. *Progress in Psychobiology and Physiological Psychology* 7:1–53, 1977.

Andersen, R. A., P. L. Knight, and M. M. Merzenich. The thalamocortical and corticothalamic connections of AI, AII, and the anterior auditory field (AAF) in the cat: Evidence for two largely segregated systems of connections. *Journal of Comparative Neurology* 194:663–701, 1980.

Bailey, C. H. Visual system I: The retina. In E. R. Kandel and J. H. Schwartz, eds., *Principles of Neural Science*. New York: Elsevier, 1981.

Burton, H., and E. G. Jones. The posterior thalamic region and its cortical projection in New World and Old World monkeys. *Journal of Comparative Neurology* 168:249–302, 1976.

Cowey, A. Why are there so many visual areas? In F. O. Schmitt, F. G. Worden, G. Adelman, and S. G. Dennis, eds., *The Organization of the Cerebral Cortex*. Cambridge, Mass.: MIT Press, 1981.

Galaburda, A., and F. Sanides. Cytoarchitectonic organization of the human auditory cortex. *Journal of Comparative Neurology* 190:597–610, 1980.

Held, R., H. W. Leibowitz, and H.-L. Teuber. *Perception. Handbook of Sensory Physiology*, vol. VIII. New York: Springer-Verlag, 1978.

Imig, T. J., and A. Morel. Organization of the thalamocortical auditory system in the cat. *Annual Review of Neuroscience* 6:95–120, 1983.

Imig, T. J., M. A. Ruggero, L. M. Kitzes, E. Javel, and J. F. Brugge. Organization of auditory cortex in the own monkey *(Aotus trivirgatus)*. *Journal of Comparative Neurology* 171:111–128, 1977.

Jones, E. G., S. P. Wise, and J. D. Coulter. Differential thalamic relationships of sensory-motor and parietal cortical fields in monkeys. *Journal of Comparative Neurology* 183:833–882, 1979.

Kaas, J. H. What, if anything, is SI? Organization of first somatosensory area of cortex. *Physiological Reviews* 63:206–231, 1983.

Kandel, E. R., and J. H. Schwartz. *Principles of Neural Science*. New York: Elsevier, 1981.

Lashley, K. S. The mechanisms of vision. XVI. The functioning of small remnants of the visual cortex. *Journal of Comparative Neurology* 70:45–67, 1939.

Ludel, J. *Introduction to Sensory Processes*. San Francisco: Freeman, 1978.

Masterton, R. B., *Sensory Integration. Handbook of Behavioral Neurobiology*, vol. 1. New York: Plenum, 1978.

Merzenich, M. M., and J. F. Brugge. Representation of the cochlear partition on the superior temporal plane of the macaque monkey. *Brain Research* 50:275–296, 1973.

Poggio, G. F. Central neural mechanisms in vision. In V. B. Mountcastle, ed., *Medical Physiology*. St. Louis: Mosby, 1968.

Uttal, W. R. *The Psychobiology of Sensory Coding*. New York: Harper & Row, 1973.

Van Essen, D. C. Visual areas of the mammalian cerebral cortex. *Annual Review of Neuroscience* 2:227–263, 1979.

10

DISORDERS OF SENSATION AND PERCEPTION

The following account by Saletsky, who suffered a bullet wound to the brain in the battle of Smolensk in 1943, gives a vivid illustration of the difference between sensation and perception.

> The instructor gave me a needle, spool of thread, some material with a pattern on it, and asked me to try to stitch the pattern. Then he went off to attend to other patients—people who'd had their arms or legs amputated after being wounded, or half their bodies paralyzed. Meanwhile, I just sat there with the needle, thread and material in my hands wondering why I'd been given these; I sat for a long time and did nothing. Suddenly the instructor came over and asked: "Why are you just sitting there: Go ahead and thread the needle!" I took the thread in one hand, the needle in the other, but couldn't understand what to do with them. How was I to thread the needle? I twisted it back and forth but hadn't the slightest idea what to do with any of these things. When I first looked at those objects, but hadn't yet picked them up, they seemed perfectly familiar—there was no reason to think about them. But as soon as I had them in my hands, I was at a loss to figure out what they were for. I'd lapsed into a kind of stupor and wouldn't be able to associate these two objects in my

mind—it was as though I'd forgotten why they existed. (Luria, 1976, pp. 47–48)

Clearly the patient's problem was not simply one of visual sensation or of movement; he was able to pick up the needle and thread without difficulty. The problem was not restricted to the recognition of objects, as demonstrated by two other exerpts:

> I tried to figure out what directions north, south, east, and west were by the sun, but just couldn't. I even had trouble understanding where the sun should have been—whether to the right or the left. I confused east with west and couldn't remember what those words meant. When someone passed by, I asked him how to get to Kazanovka. But he just smirked and walked on, since the settlement was right there—you could see it through the hedges. I still couldn't believe it and asked another person. "Look for yourself," he said, "it's right here!" And sure enough, when I looked around, I recognized the houses in Kazanovka. Its so weird—I simply can't orient myself to a place, just have no sense of space. (Luria, 1976, p. 58)

> I went into the hall to look for a bathroom I'd been told was next door. I went up to the room and looked at the sign on the door. But no matter

how long I stared at it and examined the letters, I couldn't read a thing. Some peculiar, foreign letters were printed there—what bothered me most was that they weren't Russian. When a patient passed by, I pointed to the sign and asked him what it was. "It's the men's room," he replied. "What's the matter with you, can't you read?" I stood there as though rooted to the spot, simply unable to understand why I couldn't read that sign. After all, I could see, I wasn't blind. But why was it written in a foreign alphabet? Wasn't someone playing a joke on me—a sick man? (Luria, 1976, p. 62)

These disorders vividly demonstrate the complexity of deficits in sensation and perception. In this case there is little doubt that the patient could "see" in the sense that the term is normally used, but there is equally little doubt that he had a severe visual impairment. Alterations of this sort pose a peculiar problem for the neuropsychologist. To the patient these alterations are often quite obvious, whether they are the outright and persistent loss of some sensory ability, or more subtle disabilities, which are only noticed on certain occasions. To the neuropsychologist, these alterations present a challenge, as they must be demonstrated and quantified, a difficult task when the patient is unable, or unwilling, to describe how the sensory world has changed. The psychologist's task is made more complicated by the fact that patients easily misinterpret their condition, making accurate description a real challenge in some cases. Studies of sensory processing in human patients are therefore among the most tedious of all neuropsychological investigations, and many sensory dysfunctions continue to represent large areas of ignorance in neuropsychology. The nature of many sensory disorders has still not been adequately investigated and conceptions of many disorders are based on clinical description. Clinical description cannot take the place of careful quantification, however, and many clinical descriptions in the literature

(or in patients' files) are based on cursory observation and do not accurately describe the condition. Furthermore, clinical shorthand expressions such as "agnosia" conceal the diversity of mechanisms that can be disturbed, providing an illusion of understanding because a condition has been named. We must be wary of being trapped into thinking that because a patient is described as having "object agnosia" that this patient's symptoms and neurological condition are similar to those of other patients with the same label. It is only by careful description of the patient's perceptual abilities that the source of particular symptomatology can be identified. The question to keep asking in studies of disorders of sensation and perception is, "Why does a particular symptom appear?"

In this chapter we shall briefly survey the types of functional sensory abnormalities most commonly encountered in the visual, auditory, and somatosensory domains. We shall not be overly concerned with trying to localize the disorders to specific cortical regions, in part because so little is known about this, and in part because we shall return to many of these disorders in our more detailed discussions of clinical syndromes in later chapters.

TYPES OF DISORDERS

At the risk of oversimplifying, we can identify two broad categories of sensory disorders: (1) complete or partial loss of some sensory process, and (2) distortion or loss of some aspect of perception, in spite of apparent awareness of the existence of the sensory stimulus. We shall consider each of these separately.

Complete Loss

Evidence of complete loss of sensory ability would seem rather simple to demonstrate, but we shall see that the absence of response to sensory input does not necessarily provide evidence of the absence of sensory processing. Consider the following. If the optic nerve is severed before it enters the brain, there can be little doubt that a person will be blind in the visual field served by the nerve. Let us suppose, however, that the nerve enters the brain, making its first synapse in the thalamus or brainstem. If the primary sensory cortex is damaged, sensory input can still get to the secondary cortex, and so we might ask: Are such people completely blind? They claim to be blind, and they act as though they are blind, but testing can show that they do have certain visual capacities, which they are apparently unaware of, and with which they make no, or only poor, motor responses. The difficulty is obvious: At what point do we conclude that there is a complete loss of sensory ability? As a rule of thumb, we can conclude that complete loss of sensory function is only certain after the sensory nerve or nucleus of the first synapse is damaged. Damage in the primary sensory areas has the severest effect on sensation, but even in cases of complete removal, it is normally possible to demonstrate some type of response to sensory input, although in the visual system it is far less than might be expected, given that several other intact representations of the retina are still functional.

Partial Loss or Distortion

It follows from our discussion of cortical organization of the sensory systems that damage beyond the primary area in one of the multiple representations of a given sensory system would be expected to produce some type of relatively specific sensory or perceptual impairment. This is easier to predict than to prove. Damage to restricted regions of the cortex, or to connections between cortical areas, is often claimed to produce relatively specific perceptual abnormalities, but careful neuro-psychological examination normally finds a more general impairment in perception than initially believed. Nevertheless, even though the perceptual eficits are less specific than we might have predicted, there is little doubt that people can have disturbances in sensory processing that are quite different from an apparent loss in sensory function. Saletsky did not claim to be blind and did not act blind; he had some disorder in visual processing that occurred even though he was able to perceive that something was in the visual world. This condition is clearly different from our first complaint of complete loss and certainly must have a different anatomical basis. It is likely that partial loss is most commonly a result of damage to secondary regions or to connections between secondary regions, although it is still an unproved hypothesis that damage to individual sensory representations will produce specific loss of some sensory or perceptual function.

EFFECTS OF LESIONS OF THE VISUAL SYSTEM

The nature of a visual disturbance will depend on the location of the damage (see Figure 10–1). Destruction of the retina or optic nerve of one eye produces **monocular blindness,** the loss of sight in that eye. A lesion of the medial region of the **optic chiasm** severs the crossing fibers, producing **bitemporal hemianopsia,** loss of vision of both temporal fields. A lesion of the lateral chiasma results in a loss of vision of one nasal field, or **nasal hemianopsia.** Complete cuts of the optic tract, lateral geniculate body, or area 17 will result in **homonymous hemianopsia,** blindness of one entire visual field. Should this lesion be partial, as is often the case, **quadrantic hemianopsia** occurs: destruction of only a portion of the visual field. Lesions of the occipital lobe frequently spare the central, or macular, region

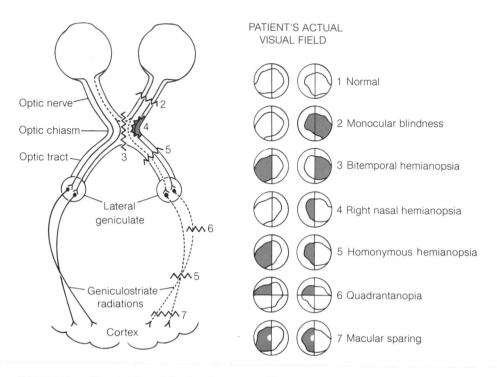

PATIENT'S ACTUAL
VISUAL FIELD

Optic nerve

Optic chiasm

Optic tract

Lateral
geniculate

Geniculostriate
radiations

Cortex

1 Normal

2 Monocular blindness

3 Bitemporal hemianopsia

4 Right nasal hemianopsia

5 Homonymous hemianopsia

6 Quadrantanopia

7 Macular sparing

FIGURE 10–1. Visual defects following damage at different levels of the visual system as denoted by numbers. A darkened region in the visual field denotes a blind area. (After Curtis, 1972.)

of the visual field, although the reason is uncertain. The most reasonable explanations of this **macular sparing** are: (1) The macular region receives a double vascular supply, from both the middle and the posterior cerebral arteries, making it more resilient to large hemispheric lesions. Or (2) the foveal region of the retina projects to both hemispheres, so that even if one occipital lobe is destroyed, the other receives projections from the fovea. Macular sparing helps to differentiate lesions of the tract or thalamus from cortical lesions, since macular sparing occurs only after lesions (usually large) of the visual cortex.

Small lesions of the occipital lobe often produce **scotomas,** small blind spots in the visual field. A curious aspect of these defects is that people are often totally unaware of them, be-

cause of **nystagmus,** constant tiny eye movements, and "spontaneous filling in." Because the eyes are in constant motion the scotoma moves about the visual field, allowing the brain to perceive all the information in the field. If the eyes are held still, the visual system actually completes objects, faces, etc., resulting in a normal percept of the stimulus, just as we are unaware of our own blind spot. The visual system may cover up the scotoma so successfully that its presence can only be demonstrated to the patient by "tricking" the visual system. This can be achieved by placing objects entirely within the scotoma and, without allowing the patient to shift his or her gaze, asking what the object is. If no object is reported, the examiner moves the object out of the scotoma and it will suddenly appear in the intact region of the patient's visual field, thus demonstrating the existence of a blind region.

More complex effects on visual perception result from lesions in the visual system beyond the primary visual cortex. It is in these higher levels, especially in areas 20 and 21, that cerebral asymmetry becomes apparent, for lesions on the right produce larger deficits in perception of complex visual forms, such as faces and geometric patterns, whereas lesions on the left produce larger deficits in perception of verbally related material. For example, lesions in the region of Brodmann's area 39, particularly in the angular gyrus, produce **dyslexia,** deficits in reading, because letters no longer form meaningful words. We shall return to these perceptual deficits soon, in our discussion of partial loss of visual functions.

Evidence for Two Visual Systems

Curiously, in neuropsychology, many ideas about brain function that were introduced around the turn of the century were extremely insightful although usually based on inference from only a few patients; most such ideas were ignored until the 1960s and 1970s. The idea that there are two parallel visual systems is a good case in point.

In 1918 Holmes reported a series of patients with unique visual deficits. These patients all had intact vision in the center of the visual field—that is, they could identify objects when asked to—but they often failed to notice objects that were within their range of vision. They had difficulty as well in following moving objects with their eyes, judging depth, and orienting themselves visually in the space around them. These deficits implied to Holmes that there might be two components to the visual system: one to discriminate visual stimuli, and a second to locate and attend to stimuli in the visual field. This theory was sup-

ported by a phenomenon reported the previous year: Riddoch described patients who were apparently blind but were able to grasp objects in motion and could indicate the direction of motion, even if they reported not having seen the object! Weiskrantz recently dubbed this phenomenon blindsight, implying functional vision in cortically blind people. Weiskrantz and others have extended Riddoch's observations. For example, we recently observed a man who suffered from nearly total cortical blindness, exhibiting only macular sparing. At one meter, this man could see a region about the size of a quarter. He was, however, capable of detecting objects outside this region. If an examiner moved his finger slowly into the area of vision and asked the patient to indicate when he first saw it, he failed to note its presence until it moved into the macular region. If the examiner moved his fingers rapidly in an oscillating motion and slowly moved toward the center of the visual field, no object was reported until it reached the macular region, but this report was accompanied by the statement, "Oh, I saw that way out to the side!" Curiously, even with repeated practice the subject failed to acknowledge the oscillating fingers until they reached the macula, at which point he reported observing them earlier. Weiskrantz has labeled this phenomenon "hindsight in blindsight."

Riddoch and Holmes, and later others, have supplied evidence supporting the notion of two functional visual systems corresponding to the two anatomical pathways illustrated in Figure 9–5. The detection, location, and following of objects by the eyes are thought to be primarily functions of the tectopulvinar system, whereas form and color analysis are primarily functions of the geniculostriate system. Animal studies support this conclusion; several groups have developed convincing animal models of two anatomical and functional visual systems in species as diverse as hamsters and monkeys. Schneider, for example, demonstrated that ablation of the superior colliculus has little effect on pattern discrimination but produces deficits in orientation to visual stimuli. Conversely, lesion of the striate cortex severely disrupts pattern vision but does not impair orientation to visual stimuli.

Partial Loss of Visual Functions

Partial loss of sensory function can be described in terms of clearly defined perceptual deficits or clinical syndromes called **agnosias** (from the Greek *a,* not, and *gnosis,* perception). We shall consider psychological studies of visual perceptual deficits in this section and agnosias in the next.

We have summarized the major types of visual disorders in Table 10–1, identifying three types of partial loss of visual functions: visuoperceptual disturbances, visuospatial disturbances, and visuomotor disturbances.

TABLE 10–1

Summary of visual disorders

Anopia: complete or partial loss of visual field (anopia, hemianopia, scotoma)

Visuoperceptual disturbances
Impaired discrimination of complex stimuli
Impaired visual recognition
Impaired color recognition
Impaired figure-ground differentiation
Impaired visual integration

Visuospatial disturbances
Defective localization of points in space
Defective judgment of direction and distance
Defective topographic orientation
Unilateral visual neglect

Visuomotor disturbances
Defective eye movements
Defective assembling performance
Defective graphomotor performance

Modified from Benton, 1979.

Visuoperceptual Disturbances. Individuals with complete, or nearly complete, visual fields may have disturbances in at least six types of visuoperceptual skills. First, they may be impaired at the discrimination of complex stimuli. Although it is uncommon for individuals to have difficulty in discriminating single attributes of stimuli such as size, brightness, or length, patients with temporal lobe excisions are impaired at discriminating between complex visual configurations that differ in some subtle characteristic. For example, Meier and French found that temporal lobe patients had great difficulty in picking out one of four patterns of concentric circular patterns, differentiated on the basis of only one cue, as different from the others (see Figure 10–2). Second, individuals may be unable to recognize stimuli. Thus, when presented with an object or other visual stimulus, the individual is unable to identify it. In its simplest form, this could be attributed to an inability to name things rather than an inability to actually recognize them. Although many cases of apparent inability to recognize are undoubtedly due to difficulties in naming, most workers in the field conclude that this cannot account for all recognition deficits. For example, there are people whose primary complaint is an inability to recognize familiar faces. Recognition deficits may present a form of complex visual discrimination deficit, for objects (or faces) that normal people perceive as being very different may only be differentiated on the basis of relatively subtle cues, which only become distinctive with visual experience. Third, individuals may be unable to name or to use colors correctly, even though they can pass tests of color blindness and can name objects appropriately. There are many different disabilities in color perception that are observed clinically, and we shall consider them in more detail in our discussion of color agnosia. Fourth, impairment in the ability to

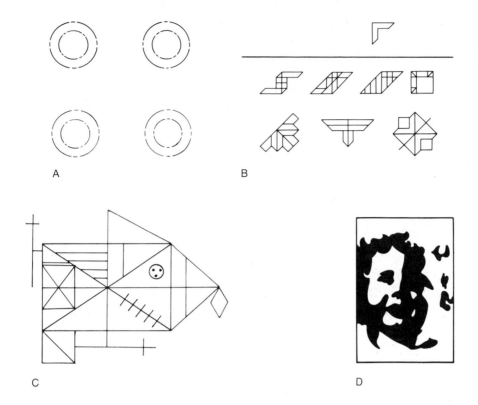

FIGURE 10–2. Examples of tests for visual disorders. A. Meier and French's test, in which the subject must identify the drawing that is different. B. Sample of the Gottschaldt hidden-figure test. The task is to detect and trace the sample (upper drawing) in each of the figures below. C. Rey-Osterith figure. The subject is asked to copy it as exactly as they can. D. Sample of the Mooney closure test. The task is to identify the face in the ambiguous shadows.

separate figure from ground is a common feature of visuoperceptual deficits. This difficulty is easily shown by tasks such as the Gottschaldt figures, illustrated in Figure 10–2, or by Luria's test of visual recognition, illustrated in Figure 10–3. Although the cause of this disorder is not known, it is common, being observed in a significant proportion of persons with focal brain disease, independently of the locus of the lesion. Fifth, individuals with posterior lesions, especially right posterior temporal, are impaired at synthesizing the content of a picture. This can be demonstrated in any test in which the

visual material is ambiguous and must be interpreted in some manner. In a simple example, the Mooney visual closure test requires that a person examine a complex pattern of shadows, integrating the information to identify an object, often a face (see Figure 10–2). In a more difficult test, the McGill picture anomalies, a person is to identify what is wrong or unusual in a drawing, such as the Mona Lisa hanging in a monkey cage.

It is evident that the disorders of visuoperceptual abilities are often subtle, and that they are very different from **anopias** (i.e., blindness). The anatomical bases of the lat-

FIGURE 10–3. Luria's test of visual recognition of crossed-out figures is found to be difficult for sufferers of visual agnosias. One response to the crossed-out watch was "chick hatching from an egg and some funny circles."

ter disabilities are less certain, although they presumably arise from damage in secondary or tertiary zones, especially of the right hemisphere.

Visuospatial Disturbances. Faulty appreciation of spatial aspects of visual experience may lead to a number of disorders grouped under the rubric of visuospatial. Although we consider these disorders in detail in Chapter 23, we shall briefly review them in the context of visual disorders.

Benton has grouped these disorders into four basic categories, as summarized in Table 10–1. Defective localization of points in space can be demonstrated easily by asking a person to touch points in space, defined by the investigator's finger, while maintaining a fixed forward gaze. A second class of visuospatial disorders can be observed in persons with difficulties in judging the directional orientation

and distance or length of stimuli. Hence they are impaired at estimating the angle of orientation of lines or the length of the lines. Further, they may be impaired at perception of depth, although this has not been as thoroughly studied. A third type of visuospatial disturbance is a deficit in topographical orientation. In this case people have great difficulty in describing how to travel from one place to another, or even in describing the floor plan of their own home. People with these difficulties are frequently lost, apparently being unable to appreciate their spatial location using prominent landmarks as cues. Finally, individuals may exhibit a symptom known as **unilateral visual neglect.** In this disorder they completely fail to respond to stimuli in one or the other lateral visual fields, almost as though they were anopic. It can be shown, however, that they are not anopic but rather fail to respond to stimuli in the visual field. We return to this disorder in our discussion of symptoms of parietal lobe damage in Chapter 16.

Visuomotor Disturbances. We use the term visuomotor disturbance to refer to any deficit in making movements directed by visual stimuli, of which there are at least three distinct types. The first disorder is one in moving the eyes to scan visual stimuli. Normal subjects have a very complex but consistent manner of looking at objects, pictures, etc. This organized pattern is completely disrupted in many subjects with perceptual disorders, who may produce largely random eye movements as illustrated in Figure 10–4. Inability to scan visual material normally may be an important factor in many of the visuoperceptual disorders described above, although it has not been systematically studied. The two other forms of visuomotor disturbances are quite different; both require the subject to reconstruct something pre-

A

B

a

b

c

d

FIGURE 10–4. Eye movements during the examination of a visual stimulus. A. The concentration of normal eye movements (by a normal subject) to distinctive features of the face (eyes, nose, mouth); these movements are directed more at the left side of the photograph. B. The eye movements of a normal subject examining a sphere *(a)* and a bust *(b); c* and *d* represent the eye movements of an agnosic subject examining the same shapes. Note the random movements of the agnosic subject. (From A. R. Luria, *The Working Brain*. The Copyright Agency of the USSR. Reprinted with permission.)

sented visually. In the first case, a deficit sometimes described as **acopia** (from the Greek, meaning not copy) or a *graphomotor* dysfunction, the person is to draw a geometric figure that is placed in front of him or her. Difficulties in copying the Rey-Osterith figure (Figure 10–2) provide a good example of this difficulty. The drawings are frequently badly distorted or have material missing. The final type of visuomotor disturbance is a deficit in visuomotor construction. That is, the subject is to construct, often with blocks, some design or structure that is placed in front of them. Like the copy of the Rey-Osterith, the construction is often drastically altered, frequently with only superficial resemblance to the original. This type of disturbance is often referred to as **constructional apraxia,** a disorder we shall return to in later chapters.

Visual Agnosias

Visual agnosia is the term coined by Sigmund Freud for the inability to combine individual visual impressions into complete patterns—thus, the inability to recognize objects or their pictorial representations, or to draw or to copy them. This definition includes many of the visual deficits that we described above, but we present them here as clinical syndromes, since they are often encountered in this form in the neurological literature. There are several types of commonly observed visual agnosias, summarized in Table 10–2 and described below. (For a particularly interesting case history of visual agnosia in an artist, see Wapner, Judd, and Gardner.)

Visual Object Agnosia. A person with visual object agnosia when shown an object can see it but is unable to name it, demonstrate its use, or remember having seen it before. Hécaen and Albert describe one patient who identified a bicycle as "a pole with two wheels,

TABLE 10–2

Summary of the major agnosias

Type	Deficit	Most probable lesion site
Visual agnosias		
Object agnosia	Naming, using, or recognizing objects	Areas 18, 19, 20, 21 on left + corpus callosum
Agnosia for drawings	Recognition of drawn stimuli	Areas 18, 19, 20, 21 on right
Prosopagnosia	Recognition of faces	Areas 20, 21 on right
Color agnosia	Association of colors with objects	Areas 18, 19 on right
Color anomia	Naming colors	Speech zones or connections from areas 18, 19, 37
Achromatopsia	Distinguishing hues	Areas 18, 19, 37
Visual spatial agnosia	Stereoscopic vision, topographical concepts	Areas 18, 19, 37 on right
Auditory agnosias		
Amusia	Tone deafness; melody deafness; disorders of rhythm, measure, or tempo	Areas 42, 22 on right
Agnosia for sounds	Identifying meaning of nonverbal sounds	Areas 42, 22 bilaterally?
Somatosensory agnosias		
Asterognosia	Recognition of objects by touch	Areas 5, 7
Anosognosia	Awareness of illness	Areas 7, 40 on right
Anosodiaphoria	Response to illness	Areas 7, 40 on right
Autotopagnosia	Localization and naming of body parts	Areas 7, 40? on left
Asymbolia for pain	Reaction to pain	Area 43?

one in front, one in back." Visual object agnosias are rare, leading to controversy over their existence and the precise location of the lesion leading to this condition. Hécaen and Angelergues found only four instances of object agnosia among 415 patients with cortical lesions. The general consensus is that a lesion of the left occipital lobe extending into subcortical white matter is necessary for the condition to occur. It is common for the damage to be bilateral, often including the corpus callosum and the inferior longitudinal fasciculus in the right hemisphere.

Visual Agnosia for Drawings. Visual agnosias affect recognition of a variety of drawn stimuli, including realistic representations of simple objects, complex scenes, schematic reproductions of objects, geometric figures, meaningless forms, incomplete figures, and abstract drawings. The lesion producing this condition is most likely located in secondary and tertiary visual cortex areas 18 through 21 in either hemisphere, although lesions in the right hemisphere seem to be implicated more frequently.

Prosopagnosia: Agnosia for Faces. In 1947, Bodamer described the inability of three patients to recognize faces although they were able to recognize objects, forms, and colors. This deficit, although rare, has since been confirmed by many others and is known as prosopagnosia (from the Greek *proso*, face; *a*, not; and *gnosis,* perception). According to Hécaen and Albert, sufferers from the disorder, although able to differentiate one face from another, cannot recognize previously known faces by relying only on the visual perception of them. Some individuals may even be unable to recognize their own faces in a mirror! There is little agreement on the best explanation of prosopagnosia. Many studies have demonstrated that lesions of the right hemisphere alter the perception or memory of faces, implying that prosopagnosia results from damage to some critical area in the right hemisphere, but the damage necessary is uncertain (see Meadows; and Benson et al.). Less severe disturbances in the recognition and memory of faces are much commoner than prosopagnosia. It appears that memory of faces is impaired by lesions of the right temporal lobe, and perception of faces by lesions of the right parietal lobe.

Color Agnosia. Impaired color recognition can take any of three different forms: achromatopsia, color anomia, and color agnosia. **Achromatopsia** is an inability to distinguish different hues although normally pigmented cells are present in the retina. It can be described as cortical color blindness, which differs from congenital color blindness in that achromatopsia affects all parts of the color spectrum. All colors appear less bright, and the environment is "drained of color" or, in severe cases, totally lacking color. Meadows concluded that achromatopsia results from *bilateral* lesions of areas 18, 19, and probably 37. **Color anomia** (from the Greek for no meaning), or color aphasia, is an inability to name colors and is generally associated with other aphasic symptoms. **Color agnosia** is an inability to associate particular colors with objects or particular objects with colors. Hécaen and Albert characterize color agnosia as (1) preservation of color perception as determined by tests of

color discrimination, and (2) inability to select all colors of the same hue from a group of colored objects, to pick out or point to colors on command, to name colors in the absence of aphasia, and to evoke the specific colors of color-specific objects such as a tomato, grass, etc.

Anatomical studies have not conclusively indicated which lesions result in the various types of disturbances in color perception and recognition. Meadows presented a theoretical anatomical model, which we have altered somewhat in Figure 10–5. It is assumed that lesions of areas 18, 19, and 37 produce achromatopsia because the cells responsible for color coding have been destroyed. Color aphasia or anomia results from a lesion of the speech zones or a disconnection of the speech zones from areas 18, 19, and 37, thus isolating the regions from one another. Color agnosia could result from a variety of lesions that disconnect the color cells from the memory functions. In this case, color could be seen but not recognized. Correlated defects in linguistic ability could result from damage to the connections with the language zones or to the language zones themselves.

Visual Spatial Agnosias. A variety of disorders of spatial perception and orientation have been described. These deficits, caused mainly by right posterior hemispheric lesions (particularly in the right parietal and occipital cortex), include defective stereoscopic vision, loss of topographical concepts, and neglect of one side of the world. We shall return to spatial agnosias in our discussion of the parietal lobes.

Are Faces Special?

Faces convey a wealth of social and affective information to humans. This importance of faces as visual stimuli led Teuber to postulate a special mode for the analysis of faces that is

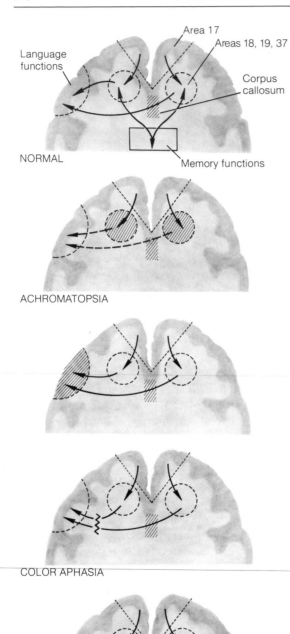

analogous to the left hemisphere's apparent innate predisposition for the analysis of words. When the visual system encounters words, a special processing mechanism in the tertiary visual region of the left hemisphere is invoked to allow their comprehension. Teuber suggested that when faces are encountered, they are analyzed by a special processing mechanism in the right hemisphere so that they are recognized in a manner analogous to words. An intriguing study by Yin supports Teuber's hypothesis. Yin found that the memory of photographs of faces was impaired in patients with right posterior lesions but that this handicap was reduced when the photographs were presented upside down or when other complex visual stimuli, such as houses, were used instead. Yin concluded that photographs of faces presented upright are processed by a special mechanism that is disrupted by right posterior lesions. Because faces presented upside down do not stimulate the special mechanism, right posterior lesions do not affect the recognition of these stimuli.

The Teuber-Yin theory raises several questions. First, if there is a special processing mechanism for faces, where is it located? The tertiary cortex of the right parietal lobe is a likely candidate but, as we noted earlier, prosopagnosia is not very common, even in the presence of large right parietal lesions that produce many other deficits (see Chapter 16). Second, there is some doubt as to the nature of the special perceptual mechanism. Teuber appears to have assumed it to be a mechanism devoted to combining features of facial stimuli into a

FIGURE 10–5. Cerebral function demonstrating possible mechanisms of various abnormalities of color vision. Each diagram represents a schematic section through the brain illustrating visual association cortex (areas 18, 19, and 37), language functions, and a theoretical memory function. Memory functions are drawn as a single box, but it is understood that this is theoretical and may not actually represent a brain structure. (After Meadows, 1974.)

whole, or gestalt, but it is uncertain how this mechanism would be specific for faces. Finally, Yin's experiment confounds both perceptual and memory functions. If the Teuber-Yin view is correct, orientation would be expected to have an effect on a purely perceptual test as well. Kolb and his colleagues failed to confirm this prediction. They presented subjects with photographs of faces as illustrated in Figure 10–6. Each of the two lower photographs is a composite of the left or the right side of the original face shown in the upper photograph. Asked to identify which of the composite photographs most resembled the original, normal subjects consistently matched the left side of the original photograph to its composite, whether or not the photographs were presented upright or inverted. This finding is not

FIGURE 10–6. An example of the split-faces test. Subjects were asked which of the two bottom pictures, B or C, most closely resembles the top picture, A. Picture C was chosen by controls significantly more often than B. Picture C corresponds to that part of A falling in the subjects' left visual field. (After Kolb, Milner, and Taylor, 1983.)

predicted by the Yin–Teuber theory. Furthermore, patients with either right temporal or right parietal removals failed to match consistently to either side of the face in either the upright or the inverted presentation.

As intriguing an idea as the Teuber–Yin theory is, we believe that the data on facial perception and memory warrant a more parsimonious interpretation: the posterior part of the right hemisphere is specialized for the processing of complex visual patterns, whether they be faces, geometric patterns, or the like. Perception of faces is particularly sensitive to the effects of right posterior damage because faces are especially complex and because there are so many different faces, many of which superficially appear highly similar. Indeed, the uniqueness of individual human faces is based on very small differences, and mastery of the differentiation of faces requires considerable practice, and possibly includes a genetic predisposition. In this regard, deficits in facial perception might result, in part, from deficits in the identification of the distinctive features used in differentiation, rather than in the flawed formation of an actual gestalt of a particular face. As we noted, if the normal pattern of visual scanning of faces is disrupted, recognition of faces might be impaired, in spite of a relatively intact percept of a given face. Indeed, the difficulty that normal adults initially have in differentiating individuals of an unfamiliar race may imply that one must learn to scan the faces of different racial groups in particular ways to identify the cues necessary for accurate identification.

Finally, we consider the perception of our own face. This provides a unique example of visual perception since our own image of our face largely comes from looking in a mirror, thus providing a reversed image, whereas others' image of our face comes from direct view. Inspection of Figure 10–6 illustrates the implications of this difference. The top photograph is the image that other people see of this woman and, since there is a left visual field bias in our perception, most right-handers choose the bottom right as the picture most resembling the original. Consider the choice of the woman herself, however. Her common view of her face is the reverse of ours and hence she is more likely to choose (and in fact did) the other composite photograph as that most resembling her own face. One intriguing consequence of our biased self-facial image is our opinion of personal photographs. Many people complain about not being photogenic, that their photographs are never taken at the correct angle, that their hair wasn't just right, etc. The problem may be rather different: we are accustomed to seeing ourselves in a reversed mirror image and hence when we view a photograph, we are biased to look at the side of our face that we do not normally selectively perceive. Indeed, we appear not to see ourselves as others see us!

EFFECTS OF LESIONS OF THE AUDITORY SYSTEM

The classic identification of the neocortex with the capacity for visual sensation led to the prediction by Munk in the 1880s that bilateral damage to the auditory cortex would result in "psychic deafness," a term later replaced in the 1930s with "cortical deafness." Although people with bilateral damage to the auditory cortex are relatively rare, both the available clinical evidence and evidence from animal studies do not support this prediction. There is in fact little disruption of sensitivity to changes in frequency or intensity after either bilateral or unilateral auditory cortex lesions in any mammal studied. Nonetheless, the auditory cortex is involved in certain types of complex auditory analysis, which can be documented both in terms of audioperceptual and audiospatial deficits as well as by auditory agnosias.

Audioperceptual Deficits

There are at least five relatively independent impairments in audioperception following temporal lobe lesions, which include core, secondary, and tertiary auditory regions (see Table 10–3). First, although the processing of simple acoustic information is accomplished normally after cortical damage, the detection of brief sounds is markedly impaired. For example, Tallal and Piercy found that patients with lesions including auditory cortex were impaired at discriminating 43-ms sounds of changing frequency but performed normally when the duration of the sounds was increased to 95 ms. A second, related impairment is observed in the judgment of the simultaneity of brief sounds. Cortical lesions appear to increase the time needed *between* sounds in order to discriminate the sounds. This impairment is presumably related to the common complaint among left temporal and parietal lobe patients that people are talking quickly. It is not so much the quickness of the speech but the inability of these people to discriminate between sounds quickly presented, a difficulty commonly encountered by normal people during

the acquisition of a new language. A third audioperceptual impairment is also related to timing of auditory stimuli, namely the judgment of temporal order in sounds heard. If a normal subject is presented with two sounds, a temporal separation of only 50 to 60 ms is sufficient to identify correctly which of the two sounds was presented first. Subjects with temporal lobe lesions may require as much as 500 ms (a tenfold increase) in order to perform at the same level. Each of these first three audioperceptual impairments appears to be more severe following left than right temporal lobe lesions, a result suggesting that these auditory skills are especially important in the discrimination of speech sounds. It is therefore not surprising that left but not right temporal lobe lesions produce a marked deficit in the discrimination of speech sounds, the fourth audioperceptive impairment. For example, persons with such lesions asked to repeat pairs of oppositional phonemes, such as da-ta, ba-pa, or sa-za, have difficulty doing so correctly. Instead, they repeat da-da, ba-ba, and so on. In a more difficult test, known as dichotic listening, subjects are presented two words or digits simultaneously, one to each ear. Persons with left temporal lobe lesions have a marked deficit in the recall of dichotically presented digits or words, although they have no difficulty if the words are presented monaurally. Rather than being specific to the right ear the deficit appears in both ears, suggesting some sort of deficit in selectively attending to and differentiating simultaneous speech sounds. One might predict that people so afflicted would have a very difficult time listening to a conversation in the midst of much background talking, such as at a party. Finally, there is an audioperceptual symptom that is specific to the right temporal lobe, namely the perception of certain characteristics of music. Milner gave patients the six subtests of the Seashore Measures of Musical

TABLE 10–3

Summary of auditory disorders

Audioperceptual
  Defective detection of brief sounds
  Defective discrimination of simultaneously
    presented sounds
  Defective judgment of temporal order of sounds
  Defective discrimination of speech sounds
  Defective discrimination of time, loudness,
    timbre, and tonal memory in music

Audiospatial
  Impaired binaural localization of sounds

Talents test: pitch discrimination, loudness, rhythm, time, timbre, and tonal memory. Patients with right temporal lobe lesions were impaired at all of the tests, although they were significantly worse than left temporal lobe patients only on the tests of time, loudness, timbre, and tonal memory, the difference being largest on the last two subtests. The timbre test measures the ability to distinguish between complex sounds that differ only in harmonic structure. It consists of 50 pairs of tones; for each pair the subject must judge whether the tone quality of the two is the same or different. On the tonal memory test a sequence of notes is played twice in rapid succession; the sequences are identical except that one note in the sequence is changed in the second playing. The subject must compare the two tonal patterns and identify, by its number in the sequence, the note that was changed at the second playing. Thus, the deficit in the analysis of music observed after right temporal lobe damage is enhanced as the subtests become more difficult, including an element of timing or temporal ordering, a result that is parallel to the deficit in processing speech sounds after left temporal lobe damage.

Audiospatial Impairment

Like the visual system, the auditory system functions to identify the spatial location of sensory information, but unlike the visual system, deficits in spatial localization are difficult to demonstrate reliably. Studies of cats with complete removal of the auditory cortex show a complete inability to localize sound but smaller, subtotal lesions leave localization unaffected. If this result can be generalized to humans, it would be expected that subtotal removal of the temporal lobe would have a limited effect on audiospatial localization whereas complete removal would be more

likely to impair this ability. To date, the data are conflicting, but there is some evidence that large temporal-parietal lesions, especially of the right hemisphere, do impair the ability to localize sounds in space. (See de Renzi for a review of the controversial data.)

Auditory Agnosias

An auditory agnosia is the impaired capacity to recognize the nature of nonverbal acoustic stimuli. Like visual agnosias, auditory agnosias presumably result from a variety of perceptual disturbances, although these are not as well understood as those in visual agnosias. The commonest auditory agnosias are *amusia* (agnosia for music) and agnosia for other sounds (see Table 10–2).

Amusia. Amusias can be subdivided into various forms, including tone deafness (the inability to discriminate various tones in a scale) and melody deafness (impaired recall or recognition of a melody) as well as disorders of rhythm, measure, or tempo. To date there are only scattered case reports of these various amusias, and there are no compelling quantitative studies demonstrating double dissociation to show they are independent. Lesions resulting in amusias usually have been located in the right middle temporal regions.

Agnosia for Sounds. Agnosia for sounds is characterized by an inability to identify the meaning of nonverbal sounds, such as a bell ringing. Sounds either may sound all alike to the patient or, if they are distinguished, may be confused for one another. Thus, in the former case all sounds may be labeled as bird song, whereas in the latter case bird song and bell tinkling may be confused. Some individuals remain able to recognize speech and music, but more usually amusia and word deafness are associated.

To date, the location of the lesions resulting in agnosia for sounds is uncertain, although the evidence favors bilateral temporal damage. We suspect that the syndrome of perceiving all sounds as similar may result from damage, perhaps bilateral, to secondary auditory areas. On the other hand, different sounds may be confused because the auditory percept is disconnected from the verbal or memory components necessary to label the sound, much as is proposed as the cause of color agnosia (Figure 10–5).

Is Music Special?

In 1926, Henschen reported 16 patients who had musical agnosia but had no language deficit. Since preservation of musical abilities in aphasic musicians had been documented many times since the 1930s, Henschen concluded that the two functions are in opposite sides of the brain. This argument was not unanimously accepted, and today it is difficult to find a convincing case of amusia in the absence of a language or perceptive disorder. Nevertheless, there is some evidence that Henschen's idea may be partly correct. For example, left hemisphere lesions can produce aphasia while leaving singing ability relatively intact. Thus, we are inclined to agree with Henschen: we think it reasonable to propose that some aspects of music and language are juxtaposed in the brain and to expect right hemisphere lesions to produce a condition of amusia analogous to the aphasia that results from left hemisphere lesions. Further support for this idea comes from the common clinical observation that many severely aphasic patients can carry a tune and can even sing the words to previously learned songs. We saw a middle-aged woman with severe left hemisphere damage and dense

aphasia who was able to sing with some coaxing and even managed a recognizable version of the national anthem—much to the surprise of herself, us, and the attending nurses.

Proof of Henschen's proposal requires more than case histories, however, and this proof has been very elusive. In the past two decades there have been many experiments on normal subjects as well as numerous case reports of amusias in musicians, but there is still no clear consensus on the nature of hemispheric processing of music. A major difficulty appears to be that people listen to or perform music differently. In particular, there is good reason to suppose that musical training or practice may change the way in which music is processed. Werner observed in 1948 that "musically experienced listeners have learned to perceive a melody as an articulated set of relations among components rather than as a whole." If Werner is correct, we might predict that musical training causes a shift in processing from the right hemisphere to include processing by both hemispheres, or even predominantly by the left, a prediction that finds some support in studies of normal subjects (e.g., those of Bever and Chiarello). There is little supporting evidence for this view in the neurological literature, and so this intriguing idea is still best considered as a hypothesis.

Overall, we are impressed with the conclusions of a particularly thoughtful review by Brust, who concludes that current conceptions of the cerebral organization of music, including the view that increasing musical sophistication causes a shift in locus of musical processing, are oversimplifications. The door would seem wide open for imaginative studies of cerebral processing of musical perception and production in both brain-damaged and normal people, especially if we are to demonstrate the specialness of music.

EFFECTS OF LESIONS OF THE SOMATOSENSORY SYSTEM

Alterations in somatic sensation and its various submodalities, including touch-pressure, appreciation of limb position and limb motion, and sensitivity to temperature and pain, are powerful indices of posterior cortical damage, although the tedious nature of the assessment discourages most neuropsychologists from doing thorough assessments. Nevertheless, it is now possible to identify a number of sensory and perceptual deficits associated with damage to the postcentral gyrus (areas 3a, 3b, 1, and 2) and the adjacent cortex (areas 5, 7, and SII).

Verger in 1902 and Dejerine in 1907 published the first descriptions of somatosensory loss resulting from cortical lesions. Symptoms of the Verger-Dejerine syndrome include loss of tactile localization, loss of sense of a limb's position in space, loss of tactile form discrimination, and impaired recognition of objects by touch (astereognosis). On the basis of thorough clinical studies Head elaborated the Verger-Dejerine syndrome, and he concluded in 1920 that lesions of the somatosensory cortex produce three largely independent effects: (1) the threshold for appreciation of the intensity of tactile, thermal, or painful stimuli is raised; (2) stereognosis is impaired; and (3) spatial recognition is impaired, because information about the spatial position of a limb is lost. This distinction of three types of disorders holds today, and we shall consider them using Head's categorization (see Table 10–4).

Somatosensory Thresholds

Damage to the postcentral gyrus is normally associated with marked changes in somato-

TABLE 10–4

Summary of somatosensory disorders

Somatosensory thresholds
  Raised threshold for the detection of touch, temperature, and painful stimuli
  Impaired sense of limb motion and position
Somatoperceptual
  Impaired tactile appreciation of object qualities (astereognosis)
  Simultaneous extinction
Somatospatial
  Impaired arm or limb placement in the absence of visual guidance

sensory thresholds. The most thorough studies of these changes were made by Semmes and her colleagues on war veterans with missile wounds to the brain and by Corkin, Milner, and Rasmussen, who assessed patients with cortical resections for relief of epilepsy. Both groups found that lesions of the postcentral gyrus produced abnormally high sensory thresholds, impaired position sense, and deficits in stereognosis. For example, in the Corkin et al. study, patients performed poorly at detecting light touch to the skin (i.e., pressure sensitivity), at determining if they were touched by one or two sharp points (two-point threshold), and at the localization of points of touch on the skin contralateral to the lesion. If blindfolded, the patients also had difficulty in reporting whether the fingers of the contralateral hand were passively moved or not. Whereas the Semmes and Corkin groups are agreed on the effects of damage to the postcentral gyrus, they fail to agree on the effects of damage beyond the postcentral gyrus. In their study of war veterans Semmes and her colleagues found an apparent asymmetry in the somatosensory system: missile wounds in the right hemisphere produced a sensory defect indicating that somatosensory function was diffuse throughout the right hemisphere. In the left hemisphere, by contrast, only lesions that invaded the region of the postcentral gyrus produced deficits. The apparent asymmetry in somatosensory function is remarkable, and surprising, for two reasons: first, lesions to primary areas in the visual and auditory systems do not produce asymmetrical effects, and second, many of the lesions studied must have been outside the primary sensory zone. Corkin and her colleagues failed to find any evidence of asymmetrical organization in their surgical patients, however; a result that leads us to question the nature of cerebral injuries in the two patient populations. Because the cerebral injuries in the war veterans occurred naturally, these lesions would be less restricted than those of the surgical patients, whose injuries would normally be limited to cortical tissue. For this reason, the data from the latter patients must be given more weight, but the issue is not yet resolved.

Lesions of the postcentral gyrus may produce a variety of other deficits not reported by the Semmes and Corkin studies. For example, Luria reported a symptom that he calls **afferent paresis:** movements of the fingers are clumsy because the person has lost the necessary feedback about their exact position. If lesions of the postcentral gyrus cause loss of representation of the face area in the left hemisphere, another defect is often observed: *motor aphasia,* a transient aphasia in which the person appears unable to figure out how to position the lips and tongue to pronounce the desired sounds. Although motor aphasia is possibly analogous to Luria's afferent paresis, motor aphasia is not observed following lesions to the homologous region in the right hemisphere.

Somatoperceptual Disorders

The presence of normal somatosensory thresholds does not preclude the possibility of other types of somatosensory abnormalities. First, both the Semmes and the Corkin group noted a deficit in stereognosis, a disturbance that can be demonstrated in tests of tactile appreciation of object qualities, illustrated in Figure 10–7. In these tests subjects are told to palpate shapes or have objects placed on the palm of their hand, and the task is to match the original to one of several alternatives, which are also out of view. According to Teuber, subjects with impaired somatosensory thresholds almost always exhibit astereognosis, although the association is not mandatory. Subjects who only demonstrate astereognosis are less common, normally having more posterior lesions that also result in "spatial deficiencies," which we consider below.

A second somatoperceptual disorder, simultaneous extinction, can only be demonstrated by special testing procedures. The logic in this test is that a person is ordinarily confronted by an environment in which many sensory stimuli impinge on him or her simultaneously, yet the person is able to distinguish and perceive each of these individual sensory impressions. Thus, single stimuli presented to a subject represent an unnatural situation that may underestimate, or miss altogether, sensory disturbances. Hence in order to present more complicated sensory stimulation, two tactual stimuli are presented simultaneously to homologous or heterologous body parts. The objective of such double simultaneous stimulation is to uncover situations in which each of the two stimuli would be reported if each were applied alone but in which only one of the two stimuli would be reported if both were applied together. Bender has described a failure to report one stimulus as **extinction.** Damage to the somatic secondary cortex, especially in the right parietal lobe, is most commonly associated with extinction, although it can occur from damage to other regions as well.

FIGURE 10–7. Examples of tests for tactile appreciation of objects. A. A pattern is placed for five seconds on the subject's palm, and then placed within the array. The task is to identify the original by palpating all six patterns. B. A duplicate of one of the patterns is palpated by the subject. The task is to identify, again by palpation, the matching pattern in the array. (After Teuber, 1968.)

As Teuber has noted, much remains to be done in exploring the role of intensity, place, and timing of the stimuli that tend to produce extinction, not only in the tactual but also in the visual and auditory modes. One intriguing finding is that stimulation of nonhomologous body points (e.g., one side of the face and the contralateral hand) may reveal "rostral dominance." That is, the subject is more likely to report the contact impinging on the face than that on the hand. Similar results are often found in studies of recovery of sensory orientation in animals, and rostral dominance should probably be studied more extensively in human patients.

Somatospatial Disorders

People with posterior parietal damage, including the secondary somatosensory regions in areas 5 and 7, frequently have difficulty in accurate placement of the limbs to points in space, especially in the absence of visual guidance. One basis for this disorder could be the loss of sensory feedback about limb position (i.e., kinesthesis), thus making limb placement difficult. However, as we shall see in later chapters, this disorder could also result from a loss of the normal marriage of tactile and visual information, presumably due to damage to tertiary cortex.

Somatosensory Agnosias

There are two major types of somatosensory agnosias: *astereognosia* (from the Greek *stereos,* meaning solid), the inability to recognize the nature of an object by touch, and *asomatognosia* (from Greek *somatos,* meaning body), the loss of knowledge or sense of one's own body and bodily condition. Although astereognosia is essentially a disorder of tactile appreciation, discussed earlier, we include it here since this behavior is often described clinically as an agnosia.

Astereognosia. Astereognosias have been recognized since 1844. In 1885, Wernicke divided tactile agnosias into two categories: primary agnosia and secondary agnosia, or asymbolia. Primary agnosia is an inability to recognize tactile qualities of an object, allegedly because of an inability to evoke tactile images. In *asymbolia,* the tactile images are preserved but are disconnected or isolated from other sensory representations; thus, the full significance of the object cannot be appreciated. According to classic neurological doctrine, the principal locus for astereognosia is the posterior parietal cortex, roughly areas 5 and 7. The Corkin study reviewed earlier failed to observe this effect, for tactile agnosias were consistently correlated with defects in sensation, implying that the lesion included primary sensory regions. Clinical cases of tactile agnosia in the absence of primary sensory defect have been reported, but they are admittedly rare.

Asomatognosia. Asomatognosia, the loss of knowledge about one's own body and bodily condition, is one of the most curious of all agnosias. It is an almost unbelievable syndrome—until one has actually observed a person neglecting part of his or her body or denying an obvious illness. There are a variety of different asomatognosias, including **anosognosia,** the unawareness or denial of illness; **anosodiaphoria,** indifference to illness; **autotopagnosia,** an inability to localize and name body parts; and asymbolia for pain, the absence of normal reactions to pain. A case study of a patient with asomatognosia is described in Chapter 16.

Asomatognosias may be for one or both sides of the body. Unilateral anosognosias and anosodiaphorias, resulting from lesions of the posterior parietal region in the right hemisphere, are most commonly of the left side of the body. Autotopagnosias result from lesions of the left parietal cortex. The lesion location responsible for asymbolia for pain has not yet been established, although it most frequently results from left hemisphere lesions, possibly because SII either has suffered a lesion or has been disconnected from affective regions of the brain.

HIGHER-LEVEL SENSORY SYSTEM INFLUENCES

As we have seen, the secondary and tertiary sensory zones produce a selective picture of the external world by a process known as perception. Normal perception may be disrupted either directly or indirectly. *Direct* disruption occurs either by an absence of sensory input, in which case there may be no perception at all, as in blindness or deafness, or by a lesion of the secondary and tertiary sensory zones, in which cases there is an agnosia. *Indirect* disruption also can occur if higher-level control of the perceptual process is altered. As Figure 10–8 shows, sensory information is relayed to the frontal and anterior temporal lobes in the form of a perception; these higher levels in turn project back on the sensory systems. Thus, a feedback loop is formed whereby perceptions can be influenced by previous experience, cognitive set, ongoing behavior, and so on—influences beyond the scope of the sensory representation of the external world. Consider the following possibilities.

If the sensory input is ambiguous, the perception may be influenced either by cognitive set or by a change in behavior. For example, imagine that you are walking through a park at dusk. Shapes become indistinct in the darkness because the sensory input is inadequate to provide a clear percept of your surroundings. If you are worried that a mugger might be hiding in the bushes (i.e., your set is for muggers), every noise and shape is perceived in that context. On the other hand, if you have no such set, the higher levels may produce behavior necessary to gather more information. Noises and vague shapes are explored to provide a clearer sensory representation and hence modify the perception.

The influence of the higher levels may also sometimes be inhibitory on the sensory sys-

A NORMAL

Higher levels ⇄ Perception
(frontal, temporal   (secondary, tertiary
lobes)   sensory cortex)

↑

Sensation
(primary sensory
cortex)

B ABNORMAL
SCHIZOPHRENIA, DRUGS

Higher levels ⟶ Perception

↑

Sensation

DREAMS

Higher levels ⟶ Perception

↑

Sensation

HALLUCINATIONS

Higher levels ⇄ Perception

Sensation

ILLUSIONS

Higher levels ⇄ Perception

↑

Sensation

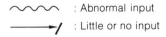

∿∿∿ : Abnormal input

⟶/ : Little or no input

FIGURE 10–8. A. The role of higher levels in the activity of the sensory systems. Sensory input travels to the frontal and temporal (anterior and medial) lobes, which can in turn influence the perception via a feedback loop. B. Hypothetical disturbances in the higher-level control of sensory systems resulting in various perceptual phenomena.

tems, preventing perceptions from dominating behavior. For example, one is unlikely to flee suddenly from the park because of one's perceptions concerning muggers. Fleeing is inhibited and frequently so-called displacement activities, behaviors such as whistling or humming, are produced instead.

The higher levels also allow sensory input to be interpreted in the context of behavior. If you move your eyes, you do not perceive the world to move because there is **corollary discharge:** input from the frontal lobe informing the perceptual systems of the eye movement. If you gently push down on your eyelid with your finger, the eye moves but there is no corollary discharge, and so the world is perceived as moving when it did not. In the absence of higher-level input, the sensory stimulation is perceived literally and possibly erroneously. (The effects of frontal-lobe lesions on corollary discharge are discussed in Chapter 18).

Finally, the higher levels add the influence of experience to sensory input (recall our motorist who perceived "ST" as "STOP"). In the absence of higher-level input, sensory input is difficult to interpret, and perhaps can even be meaningless. Nakamura and Mishkin beautifully demonstrated this phenomenon in a recent experiment. They surgically removed the frontal cortex, parietal cortex, and portions of the temporal cortex of monkeys, leaving the visual and limbic systems intact. The remarkable result was that although the visual and limbic systems were intact, the monkeys were behaviorally blind. Food could only be found by tactile and auditory cues, fearful objects were ignored, and unfamiliar environments were explored using only tactile cues. Two monkeys were kept alive for 200 days and they remained behaviorally blind. Although the visual system was intact, it was unable to influence behavior because the sensory input was disconnected either from the motor output or from the descending influence of higher cortical areas.

Higher-Level Control Disorders and Perceptual Disorders

Seeing the sensory systems as hierarchical and as being influenced by higher-level input makes it possible to understand a number of complex perceptual phenomena such as illusions, hallucinations, and dreaming, in addition to the complex perceptual disturbances found in drug intoxication or schizophrenia. We consider these phenomena below.

During the surgical treatment of epilepsy, Penfield, working with Jasper and with Perrot, discovered that stimulating the neocortex produces several remarkable phenomena: **illusions** (perceptual distortions), hallucinations (apparent perception of sights, sounds, etc., not actually present), and dreamlike states similar to what Hughlings-Jackson had described as dreamy states or psychical seizures in epileptic attacks. These phenomena reported by Penfield are of great interest, because they provide a key to understanding illusions, hallucinations, and dreams under more normal circumstances.

Penfield reported illusions of four basic forms. (1) Auditory illusions (sounds seem louder, fainter, more distant, or nearer) occurred when the superior temporal gyrus (area 22) of either hemisphere was stimulated. (2) Visual illusions (objects seem nearer, farther, larger, or smaller) occurred predominantly when the right temporal lobe was stimulated. (3) Illusions of recognition in which present experience seems either familiar (déjà vu) or strange, unreal, and dreamlike occurred predominantly when the right temporal lobe was stimulated. (4) Emotional illusions such as feelings of fear, loneliness, or sorrow occurred when either temporal lobe was stimulated.

Hallucinations took the form of dreamlike states in which familiar voices, music, scenes, etc., were experienced as being there, even when the patient knew that they could not be. Like illusions, the auditory hallucinations occurred when area 22 of either hemisphere was stimulated, whereas the visual hallucinations occurred primarily when the right temporal lobe was stimulated. An example of the responses of one of Penfield and Jasper's patients follows.

This French Canadian veteran, age 24, had had seizures for 6 years. His attacks were ushered in by a dizziness in which there was a sense of rotation. Then he might hear a voice calling "Sylvère, Sylvère, Sylvère." Sylvère was his own first name. As the years passed the warning changed to a feeling of nausea which he located behind his sternum. The warning gave him time to lie down so that he would not fall. There was a lapse of consciousness which might only last for 30 seconds. At times there was a major convulsive seizure.

Psychical precipitation. He volunteered the information that an attack was sometimes precipitated when he sought to recall the name of a person or to reflect whether or not he had seen a thing before. He illustrated this in a conversation with Dr. Robert Sears as follows, "Now, for example, if I thought I had seen you somewhere, perhaps in a crowd, and if I tried to make certain in my mind whether I had seen you or not, I might have an attack."

The precipitating factor seemed to be the intellectual process involved in comparing the present experience with the memory of past similar experiences. This is the same mechanism which must be interfered with during perceptual illusions. In an *illusion of familiarity* ("déjà vu") there is false activation of the mechanism. When this patient tried to make normal use of that mechanism he evidently precipitated an epileptogenic discharge in the temporal cortex.

The focus of the seizures was shown by preoperative electroencephalograms to be right temporal. Ventricular pneumography showed some enlargement of the right temporal horn of the ventricle.

Right osteoplastic craniotomy was carried out.

There was evidently an *arteriovenous anastomosis* within the temporal lobe. The substance of the temporal cortex was of normal consistency on its lateral aspect but the superior surface of the temporal lobe became quite abnormal where it lay in contact with the insula. Here it was yellow and tough. This toughness extended into the uncus and amygdaloid nucleus where it was grayish-yellow in color.

The Rahm stimulator was set at 50 cycles and 1 volt for points 1 to 5. After that it was changed to 2 volts for succeeding stimulations. The following were some of the responses to stimulation.

Numbers 1 to 13 mark the sites of origin of somatic sensory and motor responses. Curiously enough, at point 11 the patient opened his mouth. This was followed by a *sneeze* and chewing movements.

14. "Just like someone whispering, or something, in my left ear. It sounded something like a crowd." Warning was then given but no stimulation. He reported, "Nothing."

15. "Again someone trying to speak to me, a single person." When asked, he added, "Oh a man's voice, I could not understand what he said."

16. (While the electrode was held in place.) The patient said, "Something brings back a memory, I could see Seven-Up Bottling Company—Harrison Bakery."

Warning given again, but no stimulus applied. Again he was not fooled and replied, "Nothing."

17. (While the electrode was held in place.) "Again something I have heard of but I cannot remember it." On questioning he added that it was a word but he could not remember what word.

18. (Stimulus applied without warning the patient.) He said he was a little drowsy, then, "Someone was there in front of me right where the nurse is sitting."

19. (During stimulation.) "I am trying to find the name of a song. There was a piano there and someone was playing. I could hear the song, you know. It is a song I have sung before but I cannot

find out quite what the title of the song is." The electrode was removed. After listening to the above dictation the patient added, "That was what I was trying to do when you finished stimulating!"

19. (Repeated without warning.) After withdrawal of the electrode, he said, "Someone speaking to another and he mentioned a name, but I could not understand it." When asked whether he saw the person, he replied, "It was just like a dream." When asked if the person was there he said, "Yes, sir, about where the nurse with the eyeglasses is sitting over there."

19. (Repeated again without warning the patient and without questioning him.) "Yes, 'Oh Marie, Oh Marie'—someone is singing it." He was then asked who it was and replied, "I don't know, Doctor, I cannot recognize the voice."

19. (Repeated again without warning.) He observed, while the electrode was being held in place, "Again, 'Oh Marie, Oh Marie.' " He explained that he had heard this before. "It is a theme song," he said, "on a radio program. The program is called the 'Life of Luigi.' " The patient then discussed the identity of the song with Dr. Sears and he ended by singing the well known refrain, "Oh Marie, Oh Marie." All in the operating room recognized the song.

21. "Someone telling me in my left [contralateral] ear 'Sylvère, Sylvère!' It could have been the voice of my brother."

23. "It is a woman calling something but I cannot make out the name."

24. (Deep stimulation with coated needle, the point being directed toward the buried transverse gyrus of Heschl.) "Buzzing sound."

25. (Stimulation without warning.) "There is someone near my left eye."

25. (Repeated without warning.) "Oh my left eye! I see someone." Then he explained that there were men and women. "They seemed to be sitting down and listening to someone. But I do not see who that someone might be."

22. Nausea.

19 was restimulated several times toward the close of exploration. Instead of causing him to hear the song, it produced nothing. The voltage was increased from 2 to 3 and the stimulation was

repeated. This made him feel nauseated and he vomited, but it resulted in nothing else. (Penfield and Jasper, 1954, pp. 452–455)

The illusions and hallucinations described by Penfield and Jasper are remarkably similar to those observed in dreams or during epilepsy, sensory deprivation, drug intoxication, and other disorders. It is imperative to emphasize, however, that brain stimulation produces these states only in epileptic patients and not in patients with other neurological disorders, implying that epileptic brains are significantly different from other brains. Nonetheless, the similarity of spontaneous illusions and hallucinations to those observed by Penfield and Jasper is of great interest because it implies that these phenomena can be understood as disturbances in the normal functioning of the sensory systems.

Illusions. A variety of theoretical explanations have been proposed for illusions, but they are difficult to test empirically. Many such theories assume that illusions result from a failure of sensory and higher-level input to become synthesized, since normal perception is assumed to rely on the integration of input from these sources. The result is a distorted perception of the world.

Hallucinations. Hallucinations can be thought to result from stimulation of the sensory cortex without stimulation of the receptors. Normally the higher levels (presumably the frontal lobe) exert an influence to resolve this discrepancy. If this frontal influence is absent, a pathological state occurs. An example will illustrate. It is a common occurrence to "see" nonexistent things out of the corner of one's eye, to "hear" nonexistent noises, or to "feel" nonexistent irritations on the skin. Ordinarily this sensory input is confirmed or discarded by the higher levels, which direct

orienting behavior to investigate the perceived stimulation. But what if this behavioral response were not produced? Consider what happens if you intentionally inhibit your response to reach for a possible insect on your skin: the stimulation becomes intolerable, both becoming more intense and increasing your uncertainty about the significance of the stimulation—even though there may be absolutely nothing here. Normally behavior is produced to resolve the ambiguity, but schizophrenics or people under the influence of psychogenic drugs may fail to produce this behavior normally, if at all. The result may be perception of stimuli not actually present. Support for this admittedly speculative proposal comes from indirect evidence of frontal-lobe dysfunction in both schizophrenia and drug intoxication. The neurochemistry of the tertiary zones of the frontal lobes is known to differ from that of other neocortical regions, because there are catecholaminergic synapses in the frontal lobe and apparently few, if any, elsewhere in the neocortex. Since schizophrenia and the effects of psychogenic drugs are generally thought to produce major changes in dopaminergic synapses in the neocortex and elsewhere, it is reasonable to suggest that the frontal lobe's higher-level infuences on perception may be impaired. Although this interpretation is speculative, it is heuristic, providing a reasonable neuropsychological explanation of disordered perception in schizophrenia and drug intoxication.

Dreams. Remember that Penfield and Jasper produced "dreamy states" by electrically stimulating the higher-level sensory zones of the temporal lobes, especially of the right temporal lobe—suggesting that dreams may normally result from activation of the temporal lobes, possibly more so of the right than of the left. As electrophysiological work in cats has shown, sensory input from the receptors is blocked during dreaming, correlating with the common observation that people are difficult to arouse during dreaming. As Hughlings-Jackson originally proposed, it seems probable that during dreaming input from the frontal lobe and sensory systems is at least partially blocked from reaching the sensory zones. As a result the sensory zones are released from the influence of this source of higher control. These zones can still be influenced, however, by the medial temporal regions. Thus, the temporal lobe memory system activates the sensory zones—which may account, in part, for the realism of many dreams. This admittedly speculative proposal obviously fails to explain *why* the temporal lobe (and hence dreaming) should be activated during certain periods of sleep, but it does explain the perceptual component of dream activity. Probably the sensory zones are activated by an ascending input from the brainstem, although the genesis of this input remains uncertain. One testable prediction of this model can be made: patients from whom a temporal lobe, especially the right lobe, has been surgically removed should have significantly different dream activity, both in the content and nature of the sensory experience and, possibly, even in the frequency of dreaming. This remains to be studied.

SUMMARY AND QUESTIONS

Two fundamental principles describe the functional organization of the sensory systems:

1. The sensory systems are arranged hierarchically from the receptors at the bottom to the neocortex at the top, with complexity increasing at each higher level.

2. Function is lateralized at the highest levels.

Lesions in the primary visual, somatosensory, and auditory systems produce serious deficits in sensory discrimination by significantly reducing acuity. Often after lesions in the secondary zones acuity is preserved but, although intellectual functioning is not disturbed, there is an inability to recognize objects or patterns. Further, there is tentative evidence of specific neurological substrates of illusions, hallucinations, and dreaming.

A nagging question remains: How much of a sensory system must be spared to allow modality-specific processing? Why, for example, does unilateral removal of area 41, the primary auditory area, have negligible effects on resolution? A second question is: Do specific agnosias in fact consistently occur in the absence of other deficits? This issue has raised heated debate since the concept of agnosia was first proposed, and it is far from settled. The disagreement has its historical roots in the debate over localization of function. If functions are truly localized, it is logical to presume that somewhere there are people who have specific agnosias (e.g., for faces) and exhibit no other deficits. In principle, this would seem simple to determine. Skepticism develops, however, when there is consistent question about how thoroughly patients have been examined for other disorders. Given the considerable controversy over whether Broca's area is really necessary for language, the problem of convincingly demonstrating specific agnosias comes into perspective.

REFERENCES

Benson, D. F., J. Segarra, and M. L. Albert. Visual agnosia-prosopagnosia, a clinicopathological correlation. *Archives of Neurology* 30:307–310, 1974.

Benton, A. Visuoperceptive, visuospatial, and visuoconstructive disorders. In K. M. Heilman and E. Valenstein, eds., *Clinical Neuropsychology*. New York: Oxford University Press, 1979.

Bever, T. G., and R. J. Chiarello. Cerebral dominance in musicians and nonmusicians. *Science* 185:537–539, 1974.

Bodamer, J. (1947). Cited by H. Hécaen and M. L. Albert. *Human Neuropsychology*. New York: Wiley, 1978.

Brust, J. C. M. Music and language: Musical alexia and agraphia. *Brain* 103:367–392, 1980.

Corkin, S., B. Milner, and T. Rasmussen. Somatosensory thresholds. *Archives of Neurology* 23:41–58, 1970.

Critchley, M., and R. A. Henson, eds. *Music and the Brain*. London: Heinemann Medical Books, 1977.

Curtis, B. Visual system. In B. A. Curtis, S. Jacobson, and E. M. Marcus, *An Introduction to the Neurosciences*. Philadelphia and Toronto: Saunders, 1972.

Dejerine, J. A propos de l'agnosie tactile. *Revue de Neurologie* 15:781–784, 1907.

Hebb, D. O. *The Organization of Behavior*. New York: Wiley, 1949.

Hécaen, H., and M. L. Albert. *Human Neuropsychology*. New York: Wiley, 1978.

Henschen, S. E. On the function of the right hemisphere of the brain in relation to the left hemisphere in speech, music and calculation. *Brain* 49:110–123, 1926.

Holmes, G. Disturbances of vision by cerebral lesions. *British Journal of Ophthalmology* 2:353–384, 1918.

Holms, G. Disturbances in visual orientation. *British Journal of Ophthalmology* 2:385–407, 1918.

Kolb, B., B. Milner, and L. Taylor. Perception of faces by patients with localized cortical excisions. *Canadian Journal of Psychology* 37:8–18, 1983.

Konorski, J. *Integrative Activity of the Brain*. Chicago: The University of Chicago Press, 1967.

Ludel, J. *Introduction to Sensory Processes*. San Francisco: Freeman, 1978.

Luria, A. R. *The Working Brain*. New York: Penguin, 1973.

Luria, A. R. *The Man With a Shattered World*. Chicago: Regnery, 1976.

Meadows, J. C. Disturbed perception of colours associated with localized cerebral lesions. *Brain* 97:615–632, 1974.

Meadows, J. C. The anatomical basis of prosopagnosia. *Journal of Neurology, Neurosurgery and Psychiatry* 37:489–501, 1974.

Meier, M. S., and L. A. French. Lateralized deficits in complex visual discrimination and bilateral transfer of reminiscence following unilateral temporal lobectomy. *Neuropsychologia* 3:261–272, 1968.

Milner, B. Laterality effects in audition. In V. B. Mountcastle, ed., *Interhemispheric Relations and Cerebral Dominance*. Baltimore: Johns Hopkins University Press, 1962.

Milner, B., and H.-L. Teuber. Alteration of perception and memory in man: Reflections on methods. In L. Weiskrantz, ed., *Analysis of Behavioral Change.* New York: Harper & Row, 1968.

Nakamura, K., and M. Mishkin. Blindness in monkeys after lesions of nonvisual cortex. *Society Neuroscience Abstracts* 3:571, 1977.

Oscar-Berman, M., S. Blumstein, and D. DeLuca. Iconic recognition of musical symbols in lateral visual fields. Cited by Wyke, 1977.

Petras, J. M. Connections of the parietal lobe. *Journal of Psychiatric Research* 8:189–201, 1971.

Petrides, M., and S. D. Iverson. Restricted posterior parietal lesions in the rhesus monkey and performance on visuospatial tasks. *Brain Research* 161:63–77, 1979.

Piercy, M., H. Hécaen, and J. de Ajuriaguerra. Constructional apraxia associated with unilateral cerebral lesions—left and right cases compared. *Brain* 83:225–242, 1960.

Pohl, W. Dissociation of spatial discrimination deficits following frontal and parietal lesions in monkeys. *Journal of Comparative and Physiological Psychology* 82:227–239, 1973.

Ravizza, R. J., and S. M. Belmore. Auditory forebrain: Evidence from anatomical and behavioral experiments involving human and animal subjects. In R. B. Masterton, ed., *Sensory Integration. Handbook of Behavioral Neurobiology,* vol. 1. New York: Plenum, 1978.

Renzi, E. de, *Disorders of Space Exploration and Cognition.* New York: Wiley, 1982.

Renzi, E. de, and P. Faglioni. Normative data and screening power of a shortened version of the token test. *Cortex* 14:41–49, 1978.

Semmes, J., S. Weinstein, L. Ghent, and H.-L. Teuber. Correlates of impaired orientation in personal and extra-personal space. *Brain* 86:747–772, 1963.

Semmes, J., S. Weinstein, L. Ghent, and H.-L. Teuber. *Somatosensory Changes after Penetrating Brain Wounds in Man.* Cambridge, Mass.: Harvard University Press, 1960.

Sweet, W. H. Cerebral localization of pain. In R. A. Thompson and J. R. Green, eds., *New Perspectives in Cerebral Localization.* New York: Raven Press, 1982.

Tallal, P., and M. Piercy. Developmental aphasia: Rate of auditory processing and selective impairment of consonant perception. *Neuropsychologia* 12:83–93, 1974.

Teuber, H.-L. The brain and human behavior. In R. Held, H. W. Leibowitz, and H.-L. Teuber, eds., *Perception. Handbook of Sensory Physiology,* vol. VII. Berlin: Springer-Verlag, 1978.

Teuber, H.-L., and S. Weinstein. Performance on a formboard task after penetrating brain injury. *Journal of Psychology* 38:177–190, 1954.

Thomas, R. K., and V. K. Weir. The effects of lesions in the frontal or posterior association cortex of rats on maze III. *Physiological Psychology* 3:210–214, 1975.

Wapner, W., T. Judd, and H. Gardner. Visual agnosia in an artist. *Cortex* 14:343–364, 1978.

Warrington, E. K., M. James, and M. Kinsbourne. Drawing disability in relation to laterality of cerebral lesions. *Brain* 89:53–82, 1966.

Warrington, E. K., and P. Rabin. Perceptual matching in patients with cerebral lesions. *Neuropsychologia* 8:475–487, 1970.

Warrington, E. K., and A. M. Taylor. The contribution of the right parietal lobe to object recognition. *Cortex* 9:152–164, 1973.

Warrington, E. K., and L. Weiskrantz. An analysis of short-term and long-term memory defects in man. In J. A. Deutsch, ed., *The Physiological Basis of Memory*. New York: Academic, 1973.

Werner, H. *Comparative Psychology of Mental Development*. New York: International Universities Press, 1948.

Wyke, M. A. Musical ability: A neuropsychological interpretation. In M. Critchley and R. A. Henson, eds., *Music and the Brain*. London: Heinemann Medical Books, 1977.

11

ORGANIZATION OF THE MOTOR SYSTEMS

Animals are able to execute a remarkable number of movements. They can swim, crawl, walk, jump, and fly as well as use parts of their body, such as the limbs and mouth, for more discrete manipulations. Essentially, the entire brain can be described as having evolved for producing movements, and so it is partly for the sake of simplicity that a part of the brain is designated and discussed here as the motor system. The findings we present in this chapter suggest that the motor system can be subdivided into a number of subsystems so organized that they can differentially control whole body movements, independent movements of limbs, and independent finger movements. This organization can be seen in the development of movement and in the anatomical organization of the motor system. We review some of the supporting evidence in the following sections.

THE DEVELOPMENT OF MOVEMENT

The development of movement can be described from two general perspectives: phy-
logenetic and ontogenetic. From a phylogenetic perspective it is readily apparent that the movements we refer to as whole body movements evolved rather early. Primitive vertebrates and fish are restricted largely to whole body movements, which they use in swimming. Amphibians make whole body movements similar to those of fish but have developed limbs as well, with which they can make patterned movements for locomotion. The ability to make relatively independent movements of the limbs developed only later, when mammals evolved; many mammals use one or two limbs independently of the others to engage in such behaviors as eating, nest-building and fighting. Relatively independent movements of the fingers, however, are seen only in primates and are most highly developed in humans. Thus, the phylogenetic story suggests the independent sequential evolution of whole body movements, relatively independent limb movements, and relatively independent finger movements. This sequential evolution suggests that there should have been a parallel evolution of brain structures to produce them. Subcortical motor systems are

clearly involved in the production of whole body movements, such as those used in swimming and walking, whereas the motor systems of the neocortex evolved to produce relatively independent movements of the limbs. Of the cortical motor systems, the cells projecting directly to the spinal motor cells appear to have been the most recent evolutionary development, and they are responsible for producing relatively independent finger movements.

Two developmental studies might be mentioned in this section for the purpose of illustrating the sequences of movement evolution: those by Coghill and by Twitchell. Coghill described the ontogeny of movement in the newt *Amblystoma*. The animal is interesting because it develops locomotion in a series of stages that permitted Coghill to correlate the anatomical changes in its nervous system with the development of new patterns of locomotion. The first movements made by *Amblystoma* are coiling movements of the whole body. The coiling is gradually modified until repeated alternating coils propel the animal through the water. Since the development of swimming in *Amblystoma* recapitulated that of swimming in vertebrates, Coghill was moved to observe, "With the attainment of locomotion *Amblystoma* has passed one of the most significant landmarks in the evolution of animal behavior." The development of *Amblystoma* does not stop with swimming, for the newt grows first front limbs and then hind ones. At first its walking movements are secondary to swimming movements, its limbs being used only in conjunction with whole body coiling. As the animal matures the coiling diminishes in amplitude until the body is carried as a fixed trunk by the coordinated movements of the legs. This stage of motor development reached by *Amblystoma* is fairly representative of the locomotion of most amphibians and reptiles on land.

Everyone is aware of the development of locomotion in human infants. Infants are at first unable to walk, but with development they learn first to crawl and then to walk. The way in which infants learn to reach and grasp is less obvious. The ontogeny of relatively independent arm movements and relatively independent finger movements is seen most clearly in the second of the two developmental studies mentioned above: Twitchell's 1965 description of the development of the grasping reaction in human infants. Before birth the infant's movements are essentially whole body movements, but after birth the infant gradually develops the grasping reaction, the ability to reach out with one limb and bring objects toward itself. The grasping reaction develops in a number of stages. Shortly after birth the infant can flex all the joints of an arm in such a way that it could scoop something toward its body, but it is not at all clear that this movement is executed independent of other body movements. Between one and four months of age the infant can grasp objects that come in contact with its hands but can do so only by closing all the fingers of a hand simultaneously. Between three and 11 months it orients its hand toward, and gropes for, objects that have contacted it. Between eight and 11 months it develops the "pincer grasp," using the index finger and thumb in opposition to each other. The development of the pincer grasp is extremely significant, because it allows the infant to make a very precise grasping movement as well as to manipulate small objects or objects located in hard-to-reach places. In fact, in his baby book Dr. Benjamin Spock advises parents of babies of this age to observe them using the pincer grasp to pick up objects as small as pieces of dust. In summary, then, we see the sequential development of an independent limb movement quite clearly in the development of the infant's grasping reaction: first scooping, then reaching and grasping with all fingers, then independent movements of the fingers, as seen in the pincer grasp. Maturation of the motor cortex, as measured by its degree of **myelinization,** parallels the development of the grasping reaction: small motor fibers from the precentral gyrus become myelinated at about the time that reaching and grasping develop; the giant Betz cells of the precentral gyrus become myelinated at about the time the pincer grasp develops. As we shall discuss in more detail later, these different motor fibers are thought to control arm movements and finger movements respectively.

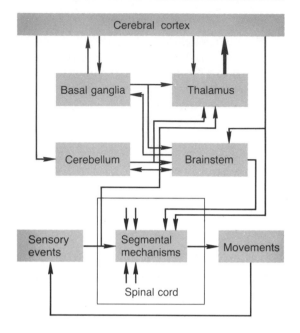

FIGURE 11–1. Diagrammatic representation of the organization of the motor system showing its major structures and connections.

THE ANATOMY
OF THE MOTOR SYSTEM

The motor system can be divided into a number of subsystems. These have a hierarchical organization and a parallel organization, which are illustrated in Figure 11–1.

All projections from the brain must go to the motor neurons of the spinal cord. For this reason the projection from the motor neurons of the spinal cord to muscles is referred to as the *final common path*. Note also that the spinal cord receives projections from the sensory receptors, from the brain, and also from other segments of the spinal cord. The projections from the cortex, which is at the top of the functional hierarchy, take two routes to the spinal cord. One is direct and the other is indirect, through other systems. It has been suggested by some researchers that this feature of cortical organization shows the cortex to be a good executive: it is able to give direct commands to all subordinate levels as well as give indirect commands subordinate through administrative channels. Between the cerebral cortex and the spinal cord are four major systems: the basal ganglia, the thalamus, the cerebellum, and the brainstem. Of these four systems only the brain-

stem projects directly to the spinal cord. Thus there are two parallel projections to the spinal cord, one from the cerebral cortex and one from the brainstem. The remaining structures all have a modulatory role in the control of movement. The cerebellum is known to be involved in ensuring that movements are executed precisely. The thalamus is a major relay for most sensory input to the cortex, and some of its nuclei are also involved in communication that takes place between different areas of the cortex and the basal ganglia and cortex. It is difficult to describe the function of the basal ganglia in only a few words, but it might be noted that its connections are optimal for modulating activity in the cortex, thalamus, and brainstem. In the following sections we shall describe the contributions of different parts of the nervous system to movement beginning with the spinal cord and ending with the cortex.

The Spinal Cord

The spinal cord is composed of a core of cells surrounded by fiber tracts; the cells comprise the gray matter of the cord and the fiber tracts make up its white matter (Figure 11–2 A). The dorsal and ventral extensions of the gray matter, the "butterfly" pattern, subdivide the white matter into three funiculi (from the Latin for cord): the dorsal, the lateral and the ventral funiculi. The funiculi are partly subdivided with respect to sensory and motor functions. The *dorsal funiculi* contain proprioceptive pathways; that is, fibers from skin and muscle receptors that carry information about the position and movements of the body. The *lateral* and *ventral funiculi* consist mainly of descending motor pathways, although the ascending sensory pathways for pain and temperature

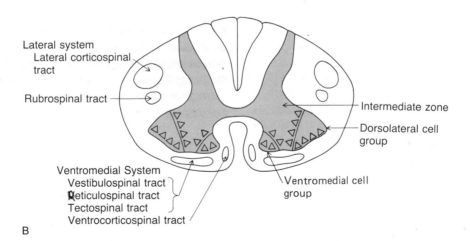

FIGURE 11–2. A. Major structures of the spinal cord. B. Location of the lateral and ventromedial systems and the interneurons and motor neurons of ventral columns.

lie in the junctional area between these two funiculi. The gray matter can also be subdivided; the upper portion is called the *dorsal column* and the lower the *ventral column*. The cells in the dorsal column mainly receive and relay sensory information, whereas those in the ventral column are interneurons and motor neurons involved in controlling movement.

The Motor Tracts. The motor tracts from the brain to the spinal cord are segregated into two groups as they descend through the spinal cord. This spatial separation has important implications for the differences in function between them. Figure 11–2 B shows the location of these tracts. One group of tracts, located in the lateral funiculi of the spinal cord, makes up the *lateral system*. There are two major tracts in the lateral system: the *lateral corticospinal tract* and the *rubrospinal tract*. They originate in the cortex and the *red nucleus*, respectively. The second group of tracts, located in the ventromedial portion of the spinal cord, makes up the *ventromedial system*. These tracts include the *vestibulospinal tracts*, the *reticulospinal tracts*, and the *tectospinal tracts* from the brainstem and the ventral corticospinal tract, which originates in the neocortex. As we shall later describe, the division of the motor tracts into two systems has functional implications. The tracts in the lateral system are largely concerned with producing distal movements (limb movements), whereas those of the ventral system are largely concerned with producing proximal movements (body movements).

Motor Neurons and Interneurons. Few cells of the central motor system project to muscles. The special cells that do, called **motor neurons,** are located in only a few places: in the nuclei of the cranial nerves and in the ventral portions of the spinal gray matter. As it turns out, no cells of the motor system of most nonprimates, and only a few cells in primates, connect directly with motor neurons. Rather, most connections are made via **interneurons** that lie in close proximity to the motor neurons. The motor neurons are located in two zones of the ventral columns of the spinal cord. There is a lateral cell group called the *dorsolateral cell group,* and there is a medial group called the *ventromedial cell group* (Figure 11–2 B). The interneurons are located more dorsally and medially in the *intermediate zone* of the spinal gray matter. Motor neurons and interneurons for the cranial nerves are similarly arranged, but for simplicity we shall describe only the spinal cord projections.

The motor neurons have a topographical organization in the ventral zone of the spinal cord: motor neurons located dorsally and laterally innervate the distal musculature, including the fingers, hand, and arm; motor neurons located more medially innervate the proximal musculature of the trunk and shoulders; and motor neurons in the ventromedial cell group innervate the axial musculature, that is, the musculature of the body midline (Figure 11–3 A).

The interneurons are similarly organized: the interneurons located in the dorsolateral portion of the intermediate zone connect to dorsolateral motor neurons; interneurons located in the ventromedial portion of the intermediate zone connect to ventromedial motor neurons. As a result, the dorsolateral interneurons eventually control distal musculature, and the ventromedial motor neurons eventually control proximal musculature. Figure 11–3 A shows this relation among body musculature, motor neurons, and interneurons.

In addition to the relation between these neurons and body muscles, there is a lateral-medial organization of the spinal cells. More laterally placed cells tend to produce extensor

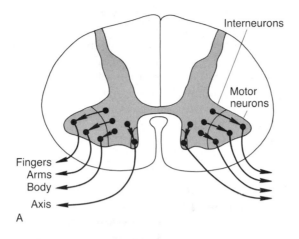

Interneurons

Motor
neurons

Fingers
Arms
Body
Axis

A

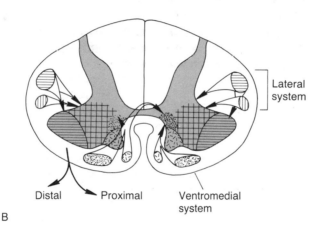

Lateral
system

Distal   Proximal   Ventromedial
system

B

FIGURE 11–3. A. Topographic relation between interneurons, motor neurons, and the body locations to which motor neurons project. B. Projection of fibers in the motor pathways onto interneurons and motor neurons.

movements when active and more medially located cells tend to produce flexor movements. Since extensor and flexor movements are produced by different muscle groups both the organization with respect to body muscles and the organization with respect to movements suggest that the interneurons and motor neurons are arranged in pools that control specific muscle groups.

Relation Between Motor Tracts and Spinal Neurons. Lawrence and Kuypers and others have described the relation between the descending motor tracts of the spinal cord and the interneurons and motor neurons of the spinal gray matter. If the axons of the descending tracts are lesioned and the spinal cord stained for degenerating terminals, each system develops a different pattern of degeneration (see Figure 11–3 B). The lateral corticospinal tract connects primarily with motor neurons in the dorsolateral portion of the ventral zone, and with inter-neurons in the dorsolateral portion of the intermediate zone. The rubrospinal tract connects with interneurons in the dorsolateral portion of the intermediate zone; thus, the lateral system connects primarily with the distal musculature. The tracts of the ventromedial system synapse with interneurons in the ventromedial portion of the intermediate zone; thus, the ventromedial system connects primarily with the proximal and axial musculature. The ventromedial fibers are also distributed bilaterally in the ventromedial zone. In summary, then, the lateral system controls movements of the fingers, hands, arms, and shoulders unilaterally; the ventromedial system controls movements of the body axis and the proximal portion of the limbs bilaterally.

Projections to Motor Neurons. Each motor neuron receives thousands of terminals from other neurons, and so to contract a muscle, it must ultimately reflect the majority opinion from these various sources. Some of the major sources of input are diagrammati-

cally illustrated in Figure 11–4. Note that comparatively very little of the input onto a motor neuron is direct; rather, most comes indirectly through interneurons. There are two major sources of sensory input: one from sensory receptors in muscles and the other from cutaneous (skin) receptors. Only one class of muscle afferent, the primary spindle receptor that mediates the stretch reflex (Chapter 7), makes a monosynaptic connection with motor neurons. There are two major projections from the brain: one is from the cortex and the other is from the brainstem. Most of the direct connections from the brain are made by projections from the cortex; brainstem fibers mainly make connections with interneurons. As we shall later describe, the direct connections are special because they permit more fractionated movements such as individual finger movements. There are two major spinal projections to the motor neurons. *Intersegmental* fibers come from other segments of the spinal cord, and many of these are collaterals from sensory afferents. *Propriospinal* fibers are from cells that have their origin wholly within the spinal cord; their cell bodies may be in the same segment or in other segments of the spinal cord. Propriospinal neurons are located in boththe dorso-

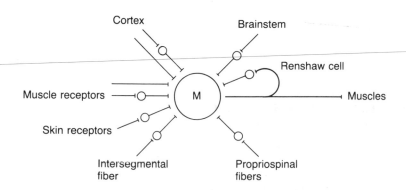

FIGURE 11–4. Summary of fibers that project directly or indirectly onto motor neurons.

lateral and the ventromedial motor neuron pools. Propriospinal neurons likely help to integrate movements that involve many spinal cord segments. Finally, the motor neurons also communicate with themselves and interneurons through a collateral given off to the Renshaw interneuron. Through this feedback loop the motor neuron is thought to be able to modulate its own activity.

The variety of connections to a motor neuron, illustrated in Figure 11–4, represents only a small portion of the afferents that it receives. The afferents from the body include at least seven different fiber types, each of which may have its own preferred type of input. There are at least nine fiber projections from the brain, which also make their own preferred input. The intersegmental and propriospinal inputs come from many different spinal cord segments. In considering this array of inputs, it must be noted that the connections are not haphazard. It is thought that the connections and the interneurons are highly organized. The afferents from the body and from the brain are segregated with respect to the movements that they are likely to elicit. It is also thought that the interneurons and motor neurons are arranged in assemblies, each of which is involved in producing certain classes of movements, such as flexion or extensor movements or stepping movements.

Motor Programs

Animals perform many movements, which when seen in isolation from other movements seem so stereotyped that they appear to be produced by some fixed internal circuitry. A hypothetical network of neurons interconnected in such a way that they produce such specific movements is called a **motor program.** The motor programs may be for movements as simple as a reflex or as complex as

walking. What evidence is there that motor programs exist? It turns out there is a great deal of evidence, from many different sources. Motor programs also seem to have a rather specific relation to certain kinds of sensory stimulation, so that some people call them *sensory-motor programs;* that is, programs that are dependent on activity in certain sensory channels with which they are linked preferentially. In Chapter 7 we pointed out that stimulation of certain sensory afferents in spinal animals produces certain reflex responses. These responses can be thought of as the product of rather simple sensory-motor programs. Through introspection we know that the sensory receptors on our body lead us to have certain sensations, including those of movement, fine touch and pressure, and pain and temperature. Physiologists who have examined the afferent nerves from sensory receptors have noted that they are divisible into four classes of neurons differing in size and degree of myelination. The two largest fiber groups, which are well myelinated, convey information about movement, position, and fine touch and pressure. The next smaller group of fibers are also myelinated and convey information about pain and temperature, particularly the aspects of these sensations that we describe as bright or sharp. The smallest fibers are unmyelinated and convey information about the aspects of temperature and the pain that we describe as dull and aching. Stimulation of these different afferents has been found to give rise to certain types of movements. Generally, stimulation of the larger fibers produces monosynaptic reflexes, such as the stretch reflex, or multisynaptic reflexes, such as those involving extensor movements to maintain contact with an object. For example, pressure on the pads of the feet produces limb extension to maintain contact with the ground. Stimulation of smaller fibers usually produces flexion movement of a general type that will withdraw the limb from stimulation. What seems both interesting and important in this organization is that sensory stimulation does at least two things: it produces movement and it produces sensation. Generally, withdrawal movements are associated with sensations of unpleasantness whereas extension movements are associated with sensations of pleasantness. More detailed physiological studies have attempted to correlate activity in certain fiber types more specifically with certain movements. To date these studies provide ample evidence that something like a specific relation between fiber type and movement type exists; however, these relations are not perfect, and combined activation in two or more fiber types might be the necessary stimulus for some movements.

Movements produced by the brain are probably also the product of motor programs. A large part of the analysis of the motor system is directed toward understanding these motor programs. The existence of some motor programs has been demonstrated by brain transection studies such as those described in Chapter 7. The exaggerated standing displayed by the decerebrate animal or the stereotyped forward progression displayed by the thalamic animal are examples of activity in motor programs that come to dominate the animal. The existence of motor programs is also revealed in motor diseases in which stereotyped movements occur repeatedly and interfere with the normal flow of behavior. Ingestion of certain drugs and some types of prolonged drug therapy can also produce stereotyped movements that seem to be due to repeated activation of one or another motor program. In fact, it is thought by many that normal behavior will be shown eventually to be the result of the sequential activation of many individual motor programs in sequence. What makes analysis of the programs difficult

is that they are modified by sensory events, by central events, by motor programs that have just been activated, and by experience. Nevertheless, their existence simplifies to some extent our understanding of how movements are produced.

The Brainstem

The brainstem has a more complex architecture than the spinal cord. Nevertheless, the basic plan of the spinal cord can be recognized in the arrangement of structures within the brainstem. The sensory and motor fibers of the spinal cord have their continuation in the sensory and motor fibers of the 12 cranial nerves that enter the brainstem. The proprioceptive fibers of the dorsal funiculus synapse in the dorsal column nuclei at the base of the brainstem and then continue through the brainstem as the medial lemniscus to terminate in the thalamus. Fibers conducting information about pain and temperature also continue through the brainstem as the lateral spinothalamic tract to terminate in the thalamus. The interneurons of the spinal intermediate zone continue rostrally to form the reticular formation. The spinal motor neuron cell groups have their counterparts in the motor nuclei of the cranial nerves. The spinal ventromedial cell group differentiates into the hypoglossal (XII) nucleus and then more rostrally into nuclei that control eye movements [the abducens (VI), trochlear (IV), and oculomotor (III) nuclei]. The lateral motor neuron cell group, which innervates distal musculature of the body, has its counterpart in the nuclei that control facial movements [the facial (VII), hypoglossal (XII), and trigeminal (V) nuclei]. In particular, the medial facial nucleus, which innervates the ear muscles, may be the counterpart of the more medially located dorsolateral motor neurons, whereas the lateral facial nucleus, which innervates muscles of the mouth and muscles around the eyes, may be the counterpart of the more laterally located motor neurons.

Brainstem Origins of the Ventromedial System The brainstem contains a number of nuclear groups that send fiber tracts to the spinal cord. Tracts that form the ventromedial system originate in the vestibular nuclei, the reticular formation, and the tectum. The vestibulospinal tract is the origin of information from the vestibular system of the middle ear, and it functions to maintain posture and balance. The tectospinal tract contains fibers that originate in the superior colliculus, the midbrain, and the visual center. Its function is to produce orienting movements to visual stimuli. The reticulospinal tracts come from many cell groups in the reticular formation. In turn, it receives projections from most of the sensory systems of the brainstem and spinal cord. Its descending pathways are probably involved in producing various organized movements including walking, swimming, and running. The pathways of the ventromedial brain system are illustrated in Figure 11–5. Note that with the exception of the tectospinal pathway they do not cross in the brainstem, but they do project bilaterally to medially located interneurons in the intermediate zone of the spinal cord. The axons of fibers in the lateral system give a large number of collaterals to many interneurons in many spinal cord segments. This feature of their distribution as well as their termination within the medially located interneurons of the spinal cord suggests that they produce whole body movements involving many muscle groups of the axial and proximal body musculature. The fibers of the ventromedial system also project to the extraocular motor neurons in cranial nerves III, IV, and VI as well as to the vagus (X) glosopharyngeal (IX) and spinal accessory (XI) nuclei. Through these nuclei they control eye and head movements as well as some movements of the oral cavity.

The reticulospinal projection also includes fibers from noradrenaline, serotonin, and perhaps dopaminergic neurons. These projections are thought to be involved in the modulation of movement rather than in the production of movement per se. At least, the absence of dopamine results in general slowing of movement as in Parkinson's disease (Chapter 12).

Brainstem Origins of the Lateral System The red nucleus of the midbrain sends its crossed projection, the rubrospinal tract, through the lateral system of the spinal cord (Figure 11–5 B). It also sends projections to the cranial nuclei that control facial movements [the facial (seventh) and hypoglossal (12th) nuclei]. The rubrospinal fibers terminate on interneurons of the lateral portion of the intermediate zone of the spinal cord. They have fewer collaterals and make connections with fewer spinal cord segments than fibers of the ventromedial system. Their organization and termination suggests that their function is to control independent movements of the distal musculature such as movements of the hands, feet, arms, and legs. The rubrospinal tract also gives off collaterals to the sensory trigeminal nucleus (the fifth nerve, which receives fibers from the face) and it gives off collaterals to the dorsal column nuclei (nuclei that receive and relay proprioceptive input from the body). These connections suggest that it has a modulatory action on sensory input from the body.

The Cortex

The cortex can produce and control movement in two ways. (1) It sends fibers, called cortico-

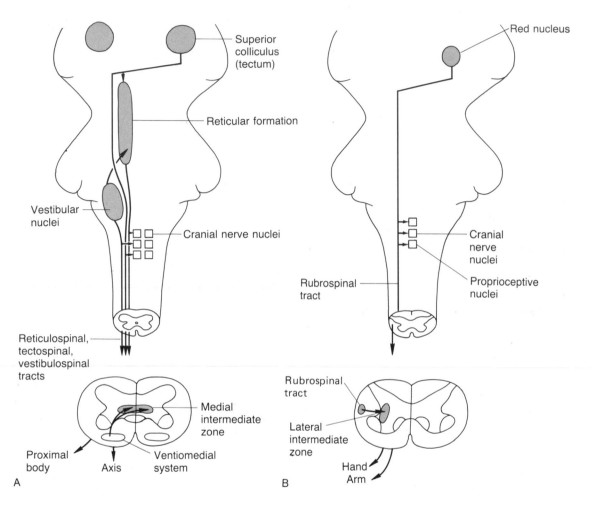

FIGURE 11–5. A. Brainstem structures that contribute fibers to the ventromedial system. B. Brainstem structures that contribute fibers to the lateral system. (After Ghez, 1981.)

fugal fibers ("cortico" meaning cortex and "fugal" meaning flight), to brainstem motor nuclei and to ventral horn interneurons and motor neurons of the spinal cord. The fibers that go to the motor nuclei are called *cortico-bulbar* fibers, and those that go to the spinal cord are called *corticospinal* fibers. The cortico-bulbar and corticospinal motor fibers allow the cortex to control movement relatively directly. (2) There are corticofugal fibers that go to the brainstem nuclei that give rise to the tracts forming the lateral and ventromedial systems, described above. These projections allow the cortex to modulate movement through existing subcortical movement systems. An important feature of the cortical motor projections is the way in which they parallel the subcortical motor systems. Remember that the subcortical motor system has two components: the lateral system, which controls more distal movements, and the ventromedial system, which controls more proximal movements. The projections from the cortex divide in the same way. Part of the corticofugal fibers join the lateral system and terminate on brainstem nuclei, cranial nuclei, and spinal cord interneurons and motor neurons that control distal movements. The other part of the corticofugal fibers join the ventromedial system to terminate on brainstem nuclei, cranial nuclei, and spinal cord interneurons and motor neurons that control axial and proximal body musculature.

A diagram showing the projections of the corticofugal pathways is given in Figure 11–6. Figure 11–6 A shows the route of the corticofugal fibers that form the lateral system. Some of these fibers connect to the red nucleus, some connect to the motor nuclei of the cranial nerves, and still others descend into the pyramids (large pyramidal-shaped protuberances at the base of the brain), where they cross in the pyramidal decussation to form the lateral corticospinal tract. The fibers of the lateral system end mainly on interneurons in the lateral part of the intermediate zone and on more laterally located motor neurons. Through these connections the projections control distal movements. (In humans some connections are made with the more medially located interneurons and motor neurons.)

The corticofugal fibers of the lateral system come mainly from areas 4 and 6, motor areas of the frontal cortex, but accompanying this projection are corticofugal fibers from areas 3, 1, and 2, parietal somatosensory cortex. These fibers terminate on the dorsal-column nuclei and on cells in the dorsal columns of the spinal cord. The degree of relationship between sensory and motor cortex is not fully understood, but they are traditionally included together as part of the corticofugal motor projection. The projections to the sensory nuclei are thought to be involved in modulating sensory input. For

example, Adkins, Morse, and Towe have shown that if the pyramidal tract, which contains this projection, is electrically stimulated, the somatosensory field in the cortex expands, presumably to increase the area of skin from which each cortical cell gathers information. This would, presumably, be useful in such situations as when an insect is detected on the skin and the cortex needs to amplify signals from the skin to precisely localize the insect.

Figure 11–6 B shows the route of corticofugal fibers in the ventromedial system. Some of the fibers terminate on brainstem nuclei, particularly those involved in controlling eye movements and head movements, whereas others continue on the same side of the brainstem into the pyramids and spinal cord to form the ventral corticospinal tract. These fibers terminate bilaterally on the most medially located interneurons and motor neurons. Through these connections they control whole body movements.

The Relation Between Motor Cortex and Subcortical Motor Systems

We have described the organization of the motor cortex previously. It is topographically organized such that its different parts control different body movements. This topographical organization is often represented by a homunculus in humans or by a corresponding cartoon in other animals. What relation does the motor cortex have to the lateral and ventromedial systems that we have just described? Kuypers and Brinkman and others have described the corticofugal projections in a number of species of animals, but the projections in the monkey will serve for the purposes of illustration (Figure 11–7). First, the motor cortex sends projections to the subcortical nuclei of the lateral and ventromedial systems. The part of motor cortex representing the limb and dis-

FIGURE 11–6. A. Corticospinal projections that contribute to the lateral system. B. Corticospinal projections that contribute to the ventromedial system. (After Ghez, 1981.)

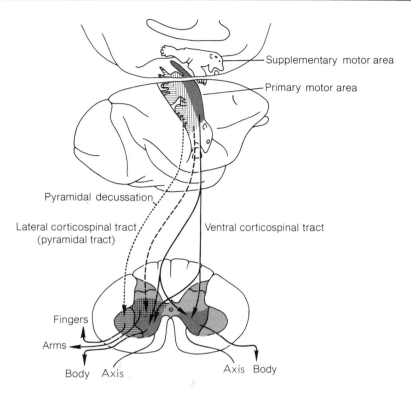

Supplementary motor area

Primary motor area

Pyramidal decussation

Lateral corticospinal tract
(pyramidal tract)

Ventral corticospinal tract

Fingers

Arms

Body   Axis

Axis   Body

FIGURE 11–7. The relation among primary motor cortex, descending tracts, spinal cord inter-neurons, motor neurons, and body musculature. (After Lawrence and Kuypers, 1968.)

tal part of the body sends projections to the red nucleus whereas the part representing the medial part of the body sends projections to nuclei of the ventromedial system. These projections are not illustrated in Figure 11–7. The projections that are illustrated are those that make up the corticospinal tracts. The different parts of the homunculus have the following relations with these tracts and their terminations in the spinal cord.

1. Projections from the digit area of the motor cortex mainly connect directly to motor neurons in the dorsolateral cell group of the spinal gray matter. This pathway decussates at the junction of the medulla and spinal cord, forming protuberances on the ventral aspect of

the brainstem that are called the pyramids. Hence these fibers form a portion of what is known as the pyramidal tract. This direct corticomotor neuron projection is found only in animals capable of independent movements of the digits: primates, including humans, and also hamsters and raccoons, which have good control of the digits. Animals such as cats have no direct connections and no independent digit control.

2. Cells in the digit, hand, and limb area of the motor cortex project to the interneurons in the dorsolateral portion of the intermediate zone in the contralateral half of the spinal cord. They also form part of the pyramidal tract. Because of their origin and termination, these

fibers are thought to be responsible for producing relatively independent hand and arm movements.

3. Cells in the body area of the motor cortex project to the interneurons of the ventromedial portion of the intermediate zone both ipsilaterally and contralaterally. Part of this projection follows the crossed pyramidal tract and part remains uncrossed to form the ventral corticospinal tract; thus this projection, unlike the former two, is bilateral. Because of its origin and termination, this system is thought to control movements of the body and proximal limbs for such activities as walking or turning.

Cortical Access to Motor Systems

So that finger, arm, and body movements can be used under sensory and cognitive control, all regions of the cortex must have access to the different motor pathways. Kuypers and Lawrence and others have described a number of alternate routes through which movements can be controlled.

Figure 11–8 shows some of these alternatives. Figure 11–8 A shows the three corticospinal projections (already described) from area 4 that control finger, arm, and body movements respectively. Figure 11–8 B shows indirect projections from area 4 into the lateral system through the red nucleus, and into the ventromedial system through the other brainstem nuclei. Additional projections may occur indirectly through the basal ganglia. The existence of these projections has been shown both anatomically and electrophysiologically. In the electrophysiological experiments the spinal tracts were sectioned and the motor cortex was then stimulated electrically. Such stimulation no longer produced movements of the figers, but it still produced movements of the limbs and body, thus demonstrating that the motor

cortex makes connections with the subcortical motor systems.

Figure 11–8 C shows how other areas of the cortex obtain access to the motor pathways in area 4. Because only the postcentral gyrus projects into area 4, other posterior cortical regions must project into frontal cortex and from there into area 4. Brinkman and Kuypers and Haaxma and Kuypers have demonstrated such connections both anatomically and through behavioral studies.

Figure 11–8 D shows that there are alternate connections from frontal cortex and parietal cortex that bypass primary motor cortex and project into the brainstem motor systems either directly or indirectly via the basal ganglia. Note that although these projections give these areas of the cortex access to control of arm movement via the lateral system and of body movements via the ventromedial system, they have no access to the control of finger movements. Finger movements must be controlled through area 4 of the cortex. In general, these projections most probably control orientation of the head, body, and eyes, since stimulation of this cortex produces these types of movements. In addition to interhemispheric and corticofugal projections, the motor cortex has intrahemispheric connections through the corpus callosum for all body parts except the hand area.

Species and Individual Differences in Corticospinal Projections

It is immediately obvious to anyone who observes the behavior of animals that there are striking differences in the movements that they make. Some of these differences seem to be due to differences in connections made by the descending motor pathways to the brainstem cranial nuclei and spinal cord. The corticospinal pathway can be selectively sectioned in the pyramids of the ventral brainstem (the

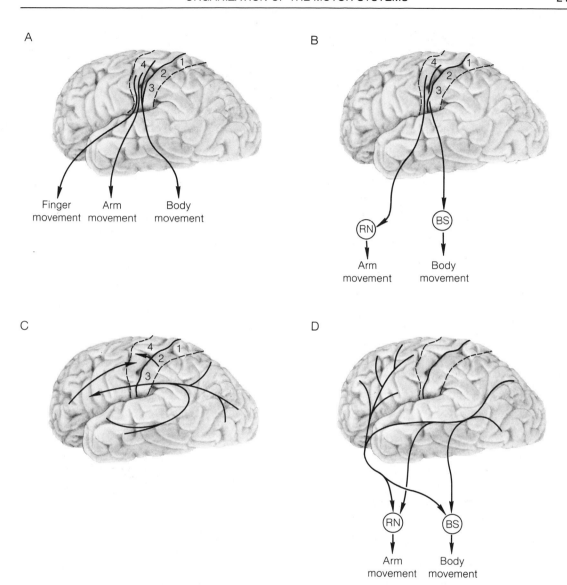

FIGURE 11–8. Motor pathways from the cortex. A. The corticospinal tracts. B. Indirect projections from area 4 to the lateral system via the red nucleus (RN), and to the ventromedial system via other brainstem (BS) nuclei. Additional connections may be made through the basal ganglia. C. Connections of different areas of the cortex to area 4. D. Connections of frontal and parietal cortex to the subcortical nuclei of the lateral and ventromedial systems.

pyramids are composed of the corticospinal fibers and are easy to reach surgically because of their superficial location). When this projection is cut, the terminations of the fibers can be determined by locating the degenerating terminals with the reduced silver staining technique and the Nauta stain and its modifications. Kuypers and others have studied terminal distribution in different species; an example of some of their results is illustrated in Figure 11–9. Some animals, sometimes described as being primitive, such as the opossum, have no terminals in the ventral column. Terminals are restricted to the dorsal column. Other species, such as the cat, which is unable to make independent digit movements, have no terminals on motor neurons but do have terminals on interneurons. Animals such as the rhesus monkey, which can make independent digit movements, have terminals only on the most laterally located motor neurons. Finally, animals such as the chimpanzee (and humans) have terminals on all motor neurons and interneurons. These results suggest that the direct connections permit fractionated movements whereas the indirect connections permit relatively independent limb movements. The opossum should be capable of few independent limb movements, the cat should be able to make such movements, and the rhesus monkey should be able to make independent digit movements, whereas humans and the chimpanzee should be capable not only of fractionated movements of the digits but of other parts of the body as well, which is indeed the case.

Studies that have been done on animals of different ages show that the corticospinal terminations on interneurons and motor neurons are not established at birth. The connections are made gradually, with development, and as they are made there is a concomitant development of more fractionated movements. In

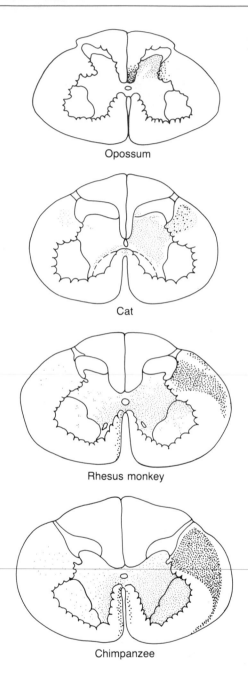

FIGURE 11–9. Distribution of corticospinal fibers from the left hemisphere to low cervical spinal gray matter in the opossum, cat, rhesus monkey, and chimpanzee. (After Kuypers, 1981.)

addition, studies on fiber diameter show that the thickest fibers, which are capable of the most rapid information conduction, make up only a small fraction of all the corticofugal fibers, but it is they that make the most direction connections with motor neurons. These fibers also tend to mature and become functional last in development. Thus, the largest and fastest fibers are those that have the latest maturation and are also those that are responsible for late-maturing fractionated movements.

Examination of corticofugal pathways in humans shows that there is considerable variation among individuals. Nyberg-Hansen and Rinvik have described some of these variations; they include no uncrossed corticospinal tract, no crossed corticospinal tract, and two crossed or two uncrossed corticospinal tracts. The functional significance of such variations is simply not known. Yakovlev and Rakic have examined the size of the corticospinal pathways, and they note that 80 percent of individuals have larger tracts on the right side of the spinal cord. In the remaining 20 percent the pattern is reversed. It might be thought that this asymmetry is related to handedness; that is, most people are right-handed and receive larger corticospinal projections on the right. This study found that there is not a perfect relation between handedness and the size of the corticospinal pathways. Thus at present this anatomical bias has not conclusively received a functional correlate.

BRAIN LESIONS

As can be seen from its anatomical organization, the motor system can be divided into cortical and subcortical systems. The cortical system controls all body movements, including arm and finger movements. The subcortical system controls distal movements through its lateral spinal cord projection, and proximal movements through its ventromedial spinal cord projection. To analyze the contributions made by these different systems Lawrence and Kuypers studied rhesus monkeys, which have a motor anatomy quite similar to that of humans. They made three types of lesions in the monkeys. They cut the corticospinal tracts at the level of the pyramidal decussation in the medulla. They then subdivided the animals in this group into two groups, each of which received a second lesion. In one group they lesioned the rubrospinal tracts, either in the brain or in the cord, by cutting their lateral columns. In the other group they lesioned the tracts of the ventromedial column in the brain, or cut the ventromedial columns in the cord. The logic of this protocol was that first the functions of the corticospinal projections could be assessed, and then, since this system overlaps to some extent with the remaining lateral and ventromedial pathways, their function could be assessed independently in the absence of the cortical projections.

The Function of the Corticospinal System

Within six to eight hours after surgery animals with corticospinal lesions were able to right themselves from a lateral posture, but their limbs tended to hang loosely or were poorly placed on the floor. Within 24 hours they could stand, grip the cage, and take a few climbing steps. They attempted to bite food, but for the first 10 to 15 days they could not swallow and so needed to be specially fed. Once they began to eat they would reach through their cage bars for food. However, they were hesitant to fully extend their arms and frequently caught their fingers on the opening. Once they reached the food their fingers closed in concert, but weakly, and grasping was associated with a hooking circumduction of the whole arm. Gradually, speed and strength of movements increased, yet the animals continued to display two striking deficits. First, they were not able to grasp food with the pincer grasp of the thumb and index finger opposed. Second, once they had grasped food with a whole-hand grip, they had difficulty in releasing it; to do so they rooted for it with their snouts. During locomotion, however, they had no difficulty in releasing the bars of the cage.

In summary, following corticospinal lesions, locomotion was minimally disturbed, whereas independent movements of the limbs in the absence of body movement were initially impaired but recovered to near-normal levels. In contrast, the animals never recovered the ability to fully use movements of the hand, as in releasing food, or to use relatively independent movements of the fingers to grasp food or manipulate objects. Beck and Chambers measured the functions of monkey limbs after lesions of the corticospinal tract. Their results comport with those given above. The monkeys showed slowed reaction times on two-choice tasks using the affected limb, showed greater loss of strength in flexion than in extension, and showed weaker flexion at the wrist than at the elbow or shoulder. From these and other observations it can be concluded that the corticospinal pathways provide speed, strength, and agility to limb movements and the capacity to make discrete movements of the extremities—in particular the relatively independent movements of the fingers. The recovery from the initial difficulties in moving the limbs presumably can be attributed to actions of the rubrospinal projection of the lateral system.

The Function of the Rubrospinal System

Once the corticospinal system had been removed, lesions were made in some animals in the rubrospinal system, either in the brain or by lateral cord section. After the lesions the animals were able to sit unsupported, stand, walk, run, and climb. The most striking changes in movement occurred in the limbs, particularly the forelimbs. When the animals were sitting, the limbs hung loosely from the shoulder with the hand and fingers extended. The arm was not used discretely for reaching for food, but if food was within reach, the arm was carried by a shoulder movement to rake food in toward the mouth with the hand extended. If the hand fell on the food, it was unable to grasp and hold it. In contrast to these deficits in using the limb for independent movements of reaching and grasping for food, it was used well, although somewhat weakly, in locomotor activities such as walking and climbing. Thus, interruption of the rubrospinal system severely disrupts the relatively independent use of the limbs in reaching and grasping but spares their ability to participate in whole body movements.

The Function of the Ventromedial System

Animals that had the corticospinal system removed received a second lesion in the brainstem nuclei of the ventromedial system or by section of the ventromedial columns of the cord. Animals with such lesions showed striking abnormalities in posture but were considerably less impaired in the use of their extremities. They showed a prolonged inability to achieve upright posture and severe difficulty in moving the body or in moving the limbs at the proximal joints. They also showed pronounced flexion of the head, limbs, and trunk, which lessened with recovery but did not disappear. They were not able to sit up for 10 to 40 days and required frequent repositioning and had to be fed by stomach tube. When they were able to sit, they were unsteady and tended to slump forward with the shoulders elevated. Slight movements or sudden sounds made them fall, and when starting to fall, they failed to make corrective movements to support themselves. The animals had great difficulty in walking; they walked with a narrow-based gait, frequently veered off target, and bumped into things. In contrast to the severe impairments of body movement, the distal parts of the limbs and hands were less impaired. The animals could cling to cage bars, reach and grasp food, and bring it to their mouths. When reaching for food, they executed movements mainly at the elbows and hands while the rest of the body remained relatively immobile. Thus, interruption of the ventromedial system disrupted body movements relatively selectively, leaving limbs, controlled by the rubrospinal system, relatively unimpaired.

SENSORY-MOTOR INTEGRATION

There are close anatomical relations between the sensory and motor systems. In the spinal cord sensory afferents form monosynaptic or disynaptic connections with motor neurons. At the level of the cortex, somatosensory cortex (areas 3, 1, 2) has direct projections to motor cortex (area 4). Furthermore, there is a direct projection from somatosensory receptors to motor cortex: this projection is well developed from the distal portion of the limbs. Given the close anatomical relations between sensory and motor systems, it might be asked: How interdependent are they functionally? Is movement possible in the absence of sensory input?

There is a large amount of literature on the effect of deafferentation (particularly on removing somatosensory input by cutting the dorsal roots of the spinal cord) on animal locomotion. The major result of these studies shows that there is a surprisingly wide range of movements that are possible in the absence of sensory information from one or more limbs. Taub has examined the effects of deafferentation on movements of the rhesus monkey. If only one forelimb is deafferented, the animal tends to neglect the limb and use its other limbs. If this is prevented by binding the contralateral forelimb, the animal will learn to make very good use of the deafferented limb. If both forelimbs are deafferented, then after a period of recovery lasting a few weeks, very effective use is possible. The animal can climb, walk, cling to the bars of its cage, and even reach for objects using the pincer grip. The capacity involved in making these movements does not need to be exercised before deafferentation. Taub has deafferented preterm monkeys (removed from the uterus and replaced after surgery) and found that they displayed good postnatal development of movement. Of course, the monkeys do have vision, so that it is possible that their movements are performed under visual guidance. To examine this possibility, Taub sutured the infants' eyes closed and found that they still displayed effective locomotion. They could even reach and use the pincer grasp, provided that they were trained so that they knew there were objects they could reach for. These experiments demonstrate that there are central programs for movement that can operate in the absence of sensory stimulation or sensory feedback. Of course, movements are not completely normal and many spinal reflexes are absent, but the unambiguous development of ambulation, climbing, and reaching satisfactorily demonstrates the existence of the central motor programs.

It would be misleading to leave the topic of deafferentation without describing some features of the disabilities that do follow deafferentation in humans. Walking is disturbed and knowledge about the location of limbs is severely impaired. The importance of sensory information for normal walking in humans is demonstrated by the ataxia shown by people who suffer from a genetic disorder called Friedreich's ataxia. These people have degeneration of the dorsal funiculi, which contain the afferents conducting fine touch and pressure information from the body. They have little or no position sense, and they have a poor sense of passive movement and vibration. When they walk, they support their body on a broad base, legs apart, and they tend to shuffle, reel, and stagger. Similar difficulties have been observed in a patient who had had accidental section of the dorsal columns (Chapter 12). For humans, walking involves a bit of a balancing act; weight must be shifted from one leg to the other, and balancing is required as weight is carried forward on one limb. This balancing obviously requires afferent input, for ataxia does not lessen with time or practice. Thus, locomotion is more severly impaired in people than in monkeys, but the difference is due to the more complex mode of locomotion used by humans (monkeys walk with four feet on the ground) and not to the inability to produce movement.

It is well known that people who have lost a limb still have a central image of the limb. This phenomenon is referred to as a phantom limb. Melzack and Bromage have shown that in normal people who have a limb anesthetized a phantom limb develops very quickly even when they are prevented from seeing the limb. When they were asked to report on the location of the limb, however, they were usually in error with respect to its location. When they saw their limb in a location in which they had not expected to see it, they were surprised by it and often thought that it might belong to someone else. These observations demonstrate rather dramatically that afferent input is necessary for knowing about the location and movement of body parts even though images of them may exist in its absence.

THE BASAL GANGLIA

The basal ganglia comprise a collection of nuclei in the forebrain that make connections with the midbrain, diencephalon, thalamus, and cortex. The basal ganglia make no direct connections to the spinal cord, but they have been traditionally considered as part of the motor system. This tradition is in large part based on clinical observations that damage to various parts of the basal ganglia produces such change in movements as akinesia (an absence of spontaneous movements) and hyperkinesia (excessive slow or rapid involuntary movements).

The anatomical relations between structures that make up the basal ganglia, including their afferent and efferent connections, are shown in Figure 11–10. The architecture of these structures and their relations to the cortex suggests that they form a loop for modulating motor functions. Projections from all parts of the cortex enter the neostriatum in a topographical fashion. The neostriatum then projects through the external and internal pallidum (also called the globus pallidus) and from there goes to the ventral and lateral thalamus and then terminates in the premotor and motor cortex. Thus, superficially at least, it appears that all parts of the cortex are able to exert a modulating influence of some sort on the motor cortex. The neostriatum is composed of the caudate nucleus and the putamen, and it is phylogenetically the most recent structure in the basal ganglia. The pallidum, in turn, is related to the diencephalon in terms of development. The amygdala is often included anatomically as a basal ganglia structure, but it is also often discussed functionally as being

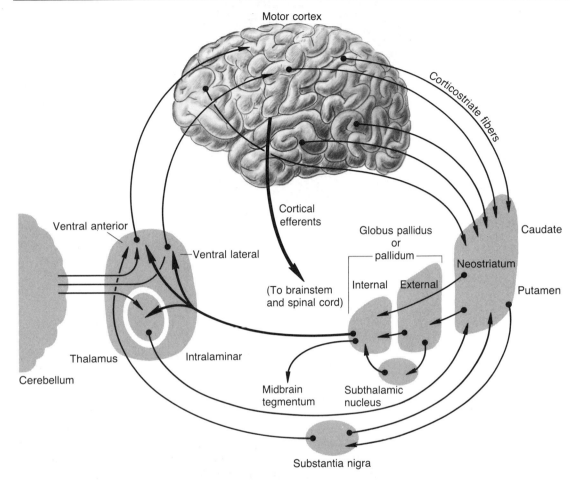

FIGURE 11–10. Circuitry showing the relation between the basal ganglia and cortex. Note that projections from all parts of the cortex enter the basal ganglia but that only motor cortex receives projections from the basal ganglia. (After DeLong, 1974.)

part of the limbic system. The basal ganglia receive input from the subthalamic nucleus of the diencephalon and from the substantia nigra of the midbrain, and they receive connections from the cerebellum via a relay in the thalamus.

Understanding basal ganglia function is complicated not only by the nature of its circuitry but also by the difficulties involved in interpreting the effects of damage to their components. Motor fibers from the cortex pass

through or close to the basal ganglia, making it difficult to determine whether behavioral changes are due to damage to the basal ganglia themselves or to these fibers of passage. The symptoms of basal ganglia disorders are also different depending on how they are damaged. If the dopamine-containing projection from the substantia nigra is severed, a condition of rigidity and akinesia, called Parkinson's disease, ensues (Chapter 12). It is likely that cells

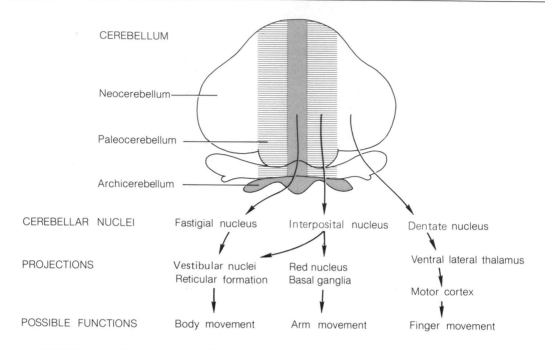

FIGURE 11–11. Projections from different cerebellar areas to spinal cord motor pathways controlling different portions of body musculature.

that normally function to inhibit movement are released from substantia nigra inhibition and thus excessively impede voluntary movements. If cells within the basal ganglia are damaged, quite different symptoms occur. Involuntary movements become common. Thus, it seems that cells within the basal ganglia are involved in checking these types of movements. If, however, the entire structure is removed, as reported by Villablanca and Olmstead (Chapter 7), a syndrome consisting of a "release of following" or "approach" behavior occurs. Neither the akinetic or hyperkinetic symptoms are displayed.

Early theories of basal ganglia function suggested that they were involved in making the postural adjustments against which the cortex produced more skilled or precise movements. More recently it has been suggested that they are involved in making slow movements, whereas the corticospinal systems are involved in rapid ballistic movements. Evidence cited in favor of this idea is that parkinsonian patients display a poverty of movement, yet preserve normal reaction times. Also, Kornhuber and DeLong, on the basis of clinical and single-cell recording evidence, suggest that rapid movements released by basal ganglia diseases may be due to the loss of the restraining influence of the slow movements. These ideas are of course difficult to reconcile with the type of basal ganglia symptoms that follow complete basal ganglia removal. In fact, the studies of Villablanca and Olmstead suggest that the persistent following behaviors and exaggerated "positive" behavior of their cats is due less to a disorder of motor behavior per se than to an inability to modify their behavior in response to the negative consequences of their actions. A still more recent theory of neostriatum function, which is based on cell structure and connections, has been proposed by Groves. He suggests simply that there is an inhibitory circuit and an excitatory circuit in the neostriatum that together are involved in preparing the motor system for the production of voluntary movements.

CEREBELLAR ACCESS TO MOTOR SYSTEMS

The cerebellum is generally thought of as an important part of the motor system, but rather than sending projections directly to motor neurons or their interneurons, it projects to a number of nuclei that then join, either directly or indirectly, the lateral or ventromedial systems of the spinal cord. Figure 11–11 gives a simplified representation.

The archicerebellum composes the entire cerebellum in fishes and is the first cerebellar structure to differentiate in the human fetus. In mammals it makes up the more medial and ventral portion of the cerebellum. Projections from the archicerebellum pass from its medial cerebellar nuclei to the reticular formation and the vestibular nuclei. Tracts from these areas form part of the ventromedial projection of the spinal cord, which, as we have seen, is instrumental in controlling more proximal movements of the body, such as posture and locomotion. Tumors or damage to this area disrupt upright posture and walking but do not substantially disrupt other movements such as reaching, grasping, and finger movements. For example, a person with medial cerebellar damage may, when lying down, show few symptoms of such damage.

The paleocerebellum is the dominant cerebellar structure in quadrupeds from amphibians to mammals and seems closely related to the development and use of the limbs in locomotion. Projections from the nuclei of this area go to the red nucleus, and possibly to the other brainstem nuclei as well. Thus, this system is probably involved in the control of limb movements through the lateral system and body movements through the ventromedial system. The predominant effect of damage to this area, although such damage is rare, is an increase in rigidity of the limbs, which disrupts distal movement more than proximal movement.

The neocerebellum makes up the outermost lateral portion of the cerebellum. Although well developed in animals capable of nonsymmetrical limb movements, it shows its greatest development in primates. Projections from the lateral nuclei that serve this area go to the ventral thalamus and from there to the precentral motor cortex. Thus, this area has access to the corticospinal tract that controls more distal movements of the arms and fingers as well as proximal movements of the body. Damage to the neocerebellum produces weakness and a tendency to fatigue, difficulty in localizing or pointing to body parts correctly, and a variety of deficits in the control of the extremities such as overshooting the mark when pointing, flailing at the joints, staggering, and an inability to carry out repeated rhythmic movements.

In summary, therefore, the development and anatomy of these three cerebellar areas and their relations to other portions of the motor system suggest that they form an integral part of these systems and participate in differentially controlling whole body movements and relatively independent movements of the limbs and of the fingers.

REFERENCES

Adkins, R. J., R. W. Morse, and A. L. Towe. Control of somatosensory input by cerebral cortex. *Science* 153:1020–1022, 1966.

Beck, C. H., and W. W. Chambers. Speed, accuracy, and strength of forelimb movement after unilateral pyramidotomy in rhesus monkeys. *Journal of Comparative and Physiological Psychology* 70:1–22, 1970.

Bowen, F. P. Behavioral alterations in patients with basal ganglia lesions. In M. D. Yahr, ed., *The Basal Ganglia*. New York: Raven Press, 1976.

Bucy, P. C., J. E. Keplinger, and E. B. Siqueira. Destruction of the "pyramidal tract in man." *Journal of Neurosurgery* 21:385–398, 1964.

Coghill, G. E. *Anatomy and the Problem of Behavior*. New York and London: Hafner, 1964.

DeLong, M. R. Motor functions of the basal ganglia: Single-unit activity during movement. In F. O. Schmitt, and F. G. Worden, eds., *The Neurosciences: Third Study Program*. Cambridge, Mass.: MIT Press, 1974.

Denny-Brown, D. The nature of apraxia. *Journal of Nervous and Mental Diseases* 126:9–33, 1958.

Elliott, H. C. *Textbook of Neuroanatomy*. Philadelphia and Toronto: Lippincott, 1969.

Ghez, C. Introduction to the motor systems. In E. R. Kandel and J. H. Schwartz, eds., *Principles of Neural Science*. New York: Elsevier, 1981.

Groves, P. M. A theory of the functional organization of the neostriatum and the neostriatal control of voluntary movement. *Brain Research Reviews* 5:109–132, 1983.

Kuypers, H. G. J. M. Anatomy of descending pathways. In V. B. Brooks, ed., *The Nervous System. Handbook of Physiology,* vol. VII. Bethesda, Md.: American Physiological Society, 1981.

Kuypers, H. G. J. M. The descending pathways to the spinal cord, their anatomy and function. In J. C. Eccles and J. P. Schade, eds., *Organization of the Spinal Cord,* vol. 11. Amsterdam: Elsevier, 1964.

Kuypers, H. G. J. M., and J. Brinkman. Precentral projections to different parts of the spinal intermediate zone in the rhesus monkey. *Brain Research* 24:29–48, 1970.

Kuypers, H. G. J. M., and D. G. Lawrence. Cortical projections to the red nucleus and the brain stem in the rhesus monkey. *Brain Research* 4:151–188, 1967.

Lawrence, D. G., and H. G. J. M. Kuypers. The functional organization of the motor system in the monkey. I. The effects of bilateral pyramidal lesions. *Brain* 91:1–14, 1968.

Lawrence, D. G., and H. G. J. M. Kuypers. The functional organization of the motor system in the monkey. II. The effects of lesions of the descending brain-stem pathways. *Brain* 91:15–36, 1968.

Melzack, R., and P. R. Bromage. Experimental phantom limbs. *Experimental Neurology* 39:261–269, 1973.

Nyberg-Hansen, R., and E. Rinvik. Some comments on the pyramidal tract, with special reference to its individual variations in man. *Acta Neurologica Scandinavia* 39:1–30, 1963.

Sherrington, C. *The Integrative Action of the Nervous System,* 2nd ed. New Haven: Yale University Press, 1961.

Tank, E. Motor behavior following deafferentation in the developing and motorically mature monkey. In R. M. Herman, ed., *Neural Control of Locomotion*. New York: Plenum, 1976.

Twitchell, T. E. The automatic grasping response of infants. *Neuropsychologia* 3:247–259, 1965.

Yakovlev, P. I., and P. Rakic. Patterns of decussation of bulbar pyramids and distribution of pyramidal tracts to two sides of the spinal cord. *Transactions of the American Neurological Association* 91:366–367, 1966.

12

DISORDERS OF THE MOTOR SYSTEMS

Many more disorders of movement are attributable to malfunctions of various portions of the brain than can be discussed in this chapter. More comprehensive descriptions can be found in texts of clinical neurology such as those by Baker and Baker and Walton. In addition, many disorders have been dealt with in discussions of special issues in other chapters, and these will be referred to in the appropriate places. This chapter is limited to a description of those disorders that are relatively common or are of particular interest because of the insights they give into the organization and function of various parts of the nervous system. Brain lesions of an experimental nature will not be dealt with in detail since a more idealized discussion of experimental lesions has been given in Chapter 11. This chapter is so organized that disorders of the motor neurons and spinal cord will be described first, followed by general disorders of movement, and then disorders of the basal ganglia and neocortex. A final section will deal with "higher-order"

motor disorders, which are disorders of the control of movement rather than of movement per se. Table 12–1 gives some commonly used terms for movement disorders.

DISORDERS OF MOTOR NEURONS AND THE SPINAL CORD

This section provides descriptions of a select number of spinal cord disorders. These include myasthenia gravis, a disorder of the muscle receptor; poliomyelitis, a disorder of the motor neuron cell body; multiple sclerosis, a disorder of myelinated motor fibers; and paraplegia and Brown-Séquard's syndrome, which are due to complete or hemitransections of the spinal cord, respectively.

Myasthenia Gravis

Myasthenia gravis (severe muscle weakness) is a disorder characterized by muscular fatigue after muscles have been exercised a few times.

TABLE 12–1

Some commonly used terms for movement disorders

Apraxia: Inability to carry out purposeful movements or movements on command in the absence of paralysis or other motor or sensory impairments. Usually follows damage to cortex tertiary areas.

Ataxia: Failure of muscular coordination or an irregularity of muscular action. Commonly follows cerebellar damage.

Athetosis: A condition in which ceaseless slow, sinuous writhing movements occur, especially in the hands. Due to abnormal function of the extrapyramidal system.

Catalepsy: A condition marked by muscular rigidity in which voluntary movements are reduced or absent but posture is maintained. It is a feature of Parkinson's disease due to dopamine loss.

Cataplexy: Complete loss of movement and posture during which muscle tone is absent but consciousness is spared.

Chorea: Literally means "dance" but refers to the ceaseless occurrence of a wide variety of jerky movements that appear to be well coordinated but are performed involuntarily.

Hemiplegia: Complete or partial paralysis to one half of the body. Usually follows damage to the contralateral motor cortex.

Palsy: Means a paralysis of movement and usually refers to persisting movement disorders due to brain damage acquired perinatally.

Paralysis: Complete loss of movement or sensation (but more commonly movement) in a part of the body. Usually permanent after damage to motor neurons; temporary after damage to motor cortex (area 4).

Paraplegia: Paralysis or paresis of the lower torso and legs, as can occur following spinal cord damage.

Paresis: Slight or incomplete paralysis or often a general loss of movement, such as follows syphilitic infection.

Spasticity: An increase in the tone of certain muscle groups involved in maintaining posture against the force of gravity. If the limb is moved against the rigidity, resistance will initially increase but then tone will suddenly melt (clasp-knife reflex). Spasticity is thought to be produced by damage to the extrapyramidal motor fibers from the neocortex.

Tardive dyskinesia: The occurrence of slow, persistent movements, particularly of the mouth and tongue. Usually follows long-term treatment with antipsychotic drugs.

It may be apparent after a short period of exercise or work, toward the end of a long conversation, or sometimes even after a few repetitions of a movement. Recovery follows a period of rest. Its rapid onset after exercise distinguishes it from other disorders such as depression or general fatigue. Examination of muscles shows that there is no obvious muscle pathology. Myasthenia can occur in people of any age, but it is commonest in the third decade of life, and women are more often affected. All the muscles of the body may be affected, but those supplied by the cranial nerves are usually involved first. Here the initial symptoms are diplopia (double vision), ptosis (drooping of the eyelid), weakness of voice, and difficulty in chewing and swallowing or holding up the head. In some people only the limbs are involved. Usually the symptoms are the most apparent at the end of the day and are relieved after sleep. The severity of the disease varies from a mild unilateral ptosis in some people to an incapacitating generalized weakness with a threat of loss of life coming from respiratory paralysis in others.

Muscular weakness is due to a failure of normal neuromuscular transmission. It has long been known that drug treatment that prevents the destruction of acetylcholine (ACh), allowing it to remain in the area of the neuromuscular junction for a longer period of time, will partially reverse symptoms.

The breakdown of acetylcholine in the synaptic space requires the enzyme acetylcholinesterase (AChe). The action of AChe can be blocked by drugs such as physiostigmine (eserine), which permits the accumulation of ACh. If, on the other hand, the neuromuscular junction is partially blocked with drugs such as curare, neuromuscular weakness is enhanced. There are at least three possible explanations of myasthenia in terms of transmitter function. The terminal may release an insufficient supply of ACh, the postsynaptic receptors may be reduced in number or function ineffectively, or there may be an excessive supply of AChe in the vicinity of the terminal. Research in the past 15 or so years suggests that the problem is with the receptor.

In 1967, Changeux, Kasai, and Lee, a group of chemists studying snake venomen, isolated the toxin *α-bungaratoxin,* a venom that acts by binding irreversibly with the motor end plate, thereby causing paralysis. Their discovery led to the chemistry that made possible isolation of the nicotinic receptor for acetylcholine (AChR). When the receptors were bound with α-bungaratoxin, they could be separated from the muscle. In 1973 Patrick and Lindstrom in the United States injected the receptor, isolated from the electric eel *Torpedo* (the electric organ of the animal is a rich source of receptors), into rabbits in order to induce the formation of antibodies to the receptor. It was intended that these in turn could be labeled and used to locate the receptors. When the antibodies formed, however, the rabbits became "myasthenic," with symptoms similar to those shown by humans. Their weakness was reversed by physiostigmine and enhanced by curare. The explanation for their myasthenia was that antibodies formed to attack the foreign receptors also attacked the rabbits' own receptors, which appeared identical. This finding suggests that the disease in humans might be an autoimmune disease; that is, humans form antibodies to their own AChR. Subsequently, antibodies to human AChR have been found in a majority of myasthenic patients' serum. Furthermore, drainage of the lymph fluid, which contains antibodies, improved symptoms, whereas replacing it returned symptoms. Finally, Albuquerque and coworkers in 1976 demonstrated that the receptor responsiveness in myasthenic muscle is reduced, and Fambrough, Drachman, and Satyamurti showed that there is a reduction in the number of receptors of the myasthenic muscle.

Although the receptor model of myasthenia provides a palatable explanation, it does leave some unresolved problems. It is not known how the production of antibodies starts, and it is not completely clear how the antibodies inactivate the receptors. It is also unclear why circulating antibodies are absent in some patients and why all the muscles of the body are not equally affected.

Treatment now has two objectives. First, AChe therapy is used to relieve symptoms. Second, for prolonged relief, attempts are made to arrest the disease with thymectomy (thymus removal) and with immunosuppressive drug treatment. As a result of treatment mortality is currently very low.

Poliomyelitis

Poliomyelitis is an acute infective disease caused by a virus that has a special affinity for the motor neurons of the spinal cord and sometimes also for the motor neurons of the cranial nerves. In extreme infections it causes paralysis and wasting of the muscles. If it attacks the motor neurons of the respiratory centers, death can result from asphyxia. Not all people who are infected by the virus show symptoms of the disease, but they nevertheless can pass on the disease to others. Infections in individuals can be accelerated by exercise, exertion, or minor surgical operations. Even exercise of a limb may hasten the viral attack on the motor neurons that innervate that limb. The disease usually occurred sporadically until the Salk and Sabin vaccines were developed in the 1960s. Many of those infected by the virus after vaccination against it showed no symptoms, others showed signs of a mild infection, and others developed fever, headache, malaise, etc., but only a minority developed paralysis. Paralysis usually reached its maximum within the first 24 hours and improvement occurs after about a week. Of the muscles that were paralyzed, only a portion remained permanently paralyzed, so that after an attack considerable recovery of movement was possible. The process of recovery often lasted for over a year. It is not known why the virus has a special affinity for motor neurons, but this type of predilection of some viruses for certain classes of brain cells is thought to be a possible cause of other brain disorders such as Parkinson's disease and schizophrenia.

Multiple Sclerosis (MS)

Multiple sclerosis ("sclerosis" is from the Greek meaning hardness) is a disease characterized by the loss of myelination largely in motor, but also in sensory, tracts. The loss of myelin is not uniform but occurs in patches. In many cases the early manifestations of the disease are followed by improvement, so that remissions and relapses are a striking feature of the disease. The course of the disease may run from a few years to as long as 50 years. The eventual condition may be one in which the affected person is confined to bed with the classic feature of ataxic paraplegia.

The first pathological accounts of the disease were given in the early part of the 19th century. The "units" of the disease consist of small circumscribed lesions in which the myelin sheath and sometimes the axons are destroyed. Eventually a "sclerotic plaque" may form in these

areas. The cause of MS is still not known. It has been thought that it is due to an infection, a virus, environmental factors, or an immune response of the central nervous system. It often occurs a number of times in the same families, but there is not clear evidence that it is inherited or that it is transmitted from one individual to another. MS is most prevalent in Northern Europe and somewhat less common in North America. It is rare in Japan and more southerly or tropical countries. In regions in which it occurs its incidence of 50 per 100,000 still makes it one of the commonest structural diseases of the nervous system. Only Parkinson's disease is equally as common. It occurs in females as compared with males in a ratio of about 6 to 4, and progress of the disease is often more rapid in females than in males.

The onset of MS is usually rapid; symptoms are fully apparent within a day or two. In onehalf of affected persons the first symptoms are weakness or loss of control over the limbs, in 30 percent the symptoms are blindness or other disorders of vision in one or both eyes, and in 20 percent the symptoms are sensory sensations, tremors, epilepsy, or vertigo. The motor symptoms usually consist of a loss of power in the lower limbs or arms. Muscular wasting is rare because of the patchy nature of the disease and because muscles receive multiple innervation from many motor neurons. The first symptoms usually appear in adulthood, and after remission symptoms may not occur again for years. In cases in which the disease is fatal, the average age of death is between 65 and 84 years. There are no specific treatments for the disease other than to treat the symptoms and encourage the affected persons to continue working and leading an active life as long as possible. Some people with MS are described as displaying an optimistic euphoria, possibly because the disease has attacked diencephalic structures, which is thought to be helpful in their management.

Affected persons, however, may also occasionally show symptoms of apathy and depression.

Paraplegia

Paraplegia (from the Greek *para,* beyond, and *plegia,* stroke) is a condition in which both lower limbs are paralyzed (quadraplegia is the paralysis of all four extremities). It is a direct consequence of a complete transection of the spinal cord. Immediately after a complete section, the cord distal to the section is devoid of all activity, and all movement, sensation, and reflexes are absent. Due to loss of reflex activity, thermoregulatory control is absent (leaving the skin cool and dry without sweating) as is bladder control (requiring drainage of the bladder to prevent urinary retention). This condition, called spinal shock, lasts from four days to about six weeks. Gradually, there is a return of some spinal reflexes until a stabilized condition is reached after a year or so. No sensations, voluntary movements, or thermoregulatory control ever reappears below the lesion. Even though no sensation is felt, certain reflexes can be elicited. A pinprick, for example, may elicit a withdrawal reflex such as the *triple response,* which consists of flexion of the hip, knee, and ankle. Later, extensor activity may become sufficiently strong that weight may be briefly supported, but spinal circuits are too dependent on brain facilitation to permit prolonged standing in its absence. After a year or two a paraplegic person may be in one of a number of conditions. (1) *Paraplegia in extension,* in which tone predominates in extensor muscles, resulting in a predominantly extensor posture. In this condition (about two-thirds of all paraplegics) the withdrawal reflex has a high threshold. (2) *Paraplegia in flexion,* in which flexor spasms predominate and major flexor activities can occur, including the flexor withdrawal reflexes and excretory and sexual

reflexes. (3) *Flaccid paralysis,* in which no tone is present, occurs in less than 20 percent of paraplegics.

Brown-Séquard Syndrome

Brown-Séquard syndrome refers to the consequences of a unilateral section through the spinal cord. Since some of the ascending and descending pathways are uncrossed and some are crossed, symptoms will occur on both sides of the body below the cut. Contralateral to the side of section there will be a loss of pain and temperature sensation, since these pathways cross at the point that they enter the cord. Sensations of fine touch and pressure will be preserved, since their pathways do not cross until they reach the caudal medulla. Ipsilateral to the section there will be a loss of fine touch and pressure, but not pain and temperature; sensation and voluntary movements of distal musculature will be lost. According to Nathan and Smith, walking recovers well within two to three days because control of this movement is bilateral.

GENERAL DISORDERS OF MOTOR FUNCTION

This section describes three disorders that are due primarily, but not exclusively, to dysfunctions in subcortical areas. In each case the effects of the disorders are widespread and involve most brain or behavioral functions in general. These disorders include cerebral palsy, hydrocephalus, and disorders of sleep.

Cerebral Palsy

Cerebral palsy is usually defined as a disorder primarily of motor function caused by perinatal brain trauma. Any simple definition is difficult, however, because (1) the motor symptoms take many forms, (2) there can be many different accompanying cognitive impairments, and (3) the disorder has diverse causes. As such cerebral palsy cannot be called a disease, a syndrome, or even a condition since, depending on the nature of the brain damage, it will take different forms in every individual. Because brain damage is involved, it is not curable, but it often is amenable to therapy and training. "Cerebral palsy" has its most useful meaning in an administrative sense, for it covers individuals who are handicapped in many different ways by motor disorders due to nonprogressive brain abnormalities. A more detailed discussion of the problems of definition, form, incidence, treatment, etc., has been presented by Cruickshank.

Cerebral palsy was first described in the medical literature in 1853 by the London physician William Little. He recognized that the motor abnormalities of some babies are related to abnormal parturition, difficult labor, premature birth, and asphyxia. He also recognized the permanent nature of the disabilities and their associated intellectual impairments; changes in personality, such as irritability and temper tantrums; and epilepsy. More importantly, he pointed out that the problems could be severely aggravated by subsequent improper training and education.

The incidence of cerebral palsy is not precisely known because many cases are not reported, but it is estimated at about six per 1000 births. The number of males and females afflicted is about equal. Estimates on degree of impairment suggest that about 10 percent of afflicted persons require no special services, 65 percent need services on an ambulatory basis, and about 25 percent need special schooling or custodial care. With respect to type of cerebral palsy by motor symptoms, about 50 percent of persons with the disorder are spastic, about 25 percent are athetoid, about 10 percent are

afflicted with rigidity, and about 10 percent are ataxic. As might be expected, cerebral palsy has many causes, the most frequent of which are listed in Table 12–2. Nearly 50 percent of all cases are due to birth injury or injury suffered during development, 9 percent are secondary to convulsions, and 8 percent are due to prematurity. Smaller numbers result from other diverse causes. Incidence is also importantly related to the mother's ability to carry a baby to term, and to factors such as her body size, health habits, and weight gain during pregnancy.

Donhoff has described the medical features of the movement disorders and the part of the body involved, that is, spastic, ataxic, choreiform, etc. In addition to these characteristics, the degree of the impairment (mild, moderate, or severe), with a description of muscle tone (hypertonic, hypotonic) and other associated dysfunctions may also be specified. Lesions involving the corticospinal tracts, basal ganglia, brainstem, and cerebellum are presumed to be responsible for the disorders. Yet in cerebral palsy clear-cut relations between lesion and clinical findings are difficult to make. A conservative classic interpretation would associate corticospinal damage with spasticity, basal ganglia damage with dyskinesia, and cerebellar damage with ataxia. Simply because many of these brain systems traverse the entire brain and make many connections throughout it, localization is difficult.

Hydrocephalus

Hydrocephalus is characterized by an increase in the volume of the cerebrospinal fluid (CSF). This can occur in two ways. In the first enlarged ventricles are a secondary result of shrinkage or atrophy of surrounding brain tissue. This is more likely to occur in adults. The second, more typical cause of hydrocephalus is due to obstruction of the flow of CSF that

TABLE 12–2

Potential causes of cerebral palsy

I. *Hereditary*
   1. Static—familial athetosis, familial paraplegia, familial tremor
   2. Progressive—demyelinating diseases of viral or undetermined origin (chromosomal breakages are rare in cerebral palsy, as are disorders of metabolism)

II. *Congenital (acquired in utero)*
   1. Infection rubella, toxoplasmosis, cytomegalic inclusions, herpes simplex, and other viral or infectious agents
   2. Maternal anoxia, carbon monoxide poisoning, strangulation, anemia, hypotension associated with spinal anesthesia, placental infarcts, placenta abruptio
   3. Prenatal cerebral hemorrhage, maternal toxemia, direct trauma, maternal bleeding diathesis
   4. Prenatal anoxia, twisting or kinking of the cord
   5. Miscellaneous toxins, drugs

III. *Perinatal* (obstetrical)
   1. Mechanical anoxia—respiratory obstruction, narcotism due to oversedation with drugs, placenta previa or abruptio, hypotension associated with spinal anesthesia, breech delivery with delay of the after-coming head
   2. Trauma—hemorrhage associated with dystocia, disproportions and malpositions, injudicious forceps applications, holding back of head, pituitary extract induction of labor, sudden pressure changes, precipitate delivery, caesarean delivery
   3. Complications of birth—"small for date" babies, prematurity, immaturity, dysmaturity, postmaturity, hyperbilirubinemia and isoimmunization factors (kernicterus due to Rh factor, ABO incompatability), hemolytic disorders, "respiratory distress" disorders, syphilis, meningitis, and other infections, drug addiction reactions, hypoglycemia reactions, hypocalcemic reactions

IV. *Postnatal-Infancy*
   1. Trauma (subdural hematoma, skull fracture, cerebral contusion)
   2. Infections (meningitis, encephalitis, brain abscess)
   3. Vascular accidents (congenital cerebral aneurism, thrombosis, embolic, hypertensive encephalopathy, sudden pressure changes)
   4. Toxins (lead, arsenic, coal tar, derivatives)
   5. Anoxia (carbon monoxide poisoning, strangulation, high altitude and deep pressure anoxia, hypoglycemia)
   6. Neoplastic and late neurodevelopmental defects (tumor, cyst, progressive hydrocephalus).

From E. Denhoff, Medical aspects. In W. M. Cruickshank, Ed., *Cerebral Palsy*. Syracuse, N.Y.: Syracuse University Press, 1976, p. 33. Reprinted with permission.

results in a buildup of pressure in one or more ventricles, eventually causing their expansion. This type is more typical in infants. It is not certain that a simple overproduction of CSF is ever a cause of hydrocephalus.

Figure 12–1 is a drawing made from a cast of the lateral ventricles. Normally the ventricles are filled with CSF. In all, there is only about 130 cm^3 of CSF in an adult and about one-third of this is in the spinal cord's great lumbar cistern. The clear, colorless fluid is made by the choroid plexus in the ventricles. Most of the CSF is made in the lateral ventricles. From there it flows through the interventricu-

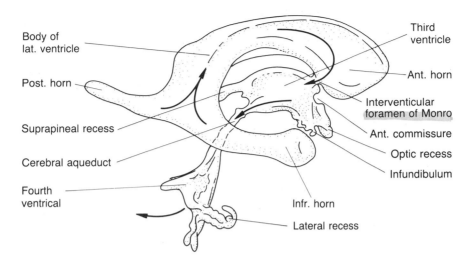

Body of
lat. ventricle

Post. horn

Suprapineal recess

Cerebral aqueduct

Fourth
ventrical

Third
ventricle

Ant. horn

Interventicular
foramen of Monro

Ant. commissure

Optic recess

Infundibulum

Infr. horn

Lateral recess

FIGURE 12–1. Drawing of a cast of the ventricular system of the brain as seen from the side. The arrows show the direction of flow of cerebral spinal fluid. (After Everett, 1965.)

lar foramina (windows) of Monro into the third ventricle, through the cerebral aqueduct, and then into the fourth ventricle. It finally escapes through three little holes in the roof of the fourth ventricle. These are the two laterally located foramina of Luschka and the medial foramina of Magendie. (The mnemonic is: lateral, Luschka; medial, Magendie). The fluid then enters the subarachnoid space, beneath the arachnoid covering of the brain and spinal cord. It finally is absorbed into the veins and is carried away by the bloodstream.

The circulation in the ventricles can be blocked at either of the interventricular foramina, causing an increase in pressure followed by expansion of either lateral ventricle. It can also be blocked at the level of the cerebral aqueduct, causing hydrocephalus of the first three ventricles, or be blocked by closure of the foramina in the roof of the fourth ventricle, producing hydrocephalus of the entire ventricular system. If CSF flow is suddenly obstructed, there is a rapid rise in intracranial pressure, ventricular dilation, and finally coma. If CSF pathways are

gradually obstructed, as might be produced by a tumor, increase in pressure and dilation is less rapid and symptoms may include the gradual appearance of visual disturbances, palsies, dementia, etc.

Infant hydrocephalus is characterized by a conspicuous enlargement of the head. It usually occurs during the first few months of life. As many as 27 of 100,000 newborn babies may suffer from hydrocephalus. In about 14 percent of cases there is a malformation that impedes CSF circulation; inflammation or trauma produce most other cases. About 4 percent of cases are due to tumors. As the ventricles distend they push the cerebral hemispheres into a balloon shape. Because the skull bones are not yet fused, continued pressure causes the expansion of the head in all directions. If expansion damages the cortex, intelligence may be impaired and dementia may result. If the cortex is undamaged, intelligence may be unimpaired even after the cortex is stretched into a sheet of tissue less than a centimeter thick. If untreated, hydrocephalus often causes death or severe mental or motor disabilities. It can now be treated with some success by inserting a valve and tube into one lateral ventricle that passes into a jugular vein to drain into the cardiac atrium.

Disorders of Sleep

Sleep is a behavior characterized by the absence of obvious responses to most surrounding events and the absence of most kinds of voluntary movements. Originally, sleep was thought to be a passive act that resulted when sensory stimulation was low. This view was seemingly supported by Bremer, who in 1935 transected the brain between colliculi of cats (called the *cerveau isolé* preparation) and observed that large-amplitude slow waves characteristic of sleep were a permanent feature of the cat's EEG as long as it survived. If the transection was made lower down (the *encéphale isolé* preparation), the cat showed normal sleep and waking EEG cycles. Bremer believed that the difference between these two preparations was that the cranial nerves provided stimulation in the latter preparation, whereas in the former they were separated from the forebrain and could not do so. Bremer's idea, also referred to as the passive hypothesis of sleep, has not received much support. Experiments that deprived humans of sensory stimulation showed that deprivation did not induce or prolong sleep. Perhaps the single most influential experiment performed to oppose the passive view was that by Moruzzi and Magoun in 1949. They implanted stimulating electrodes into the reticular formation of cats and recording electrodes into the neocortex. When the reticular formation was stimulated, the slow waves of the cortex were replaced by a pattern of low-voltage fast activity characteristic of a waking cat. The fast activity outlasted the period of stimulation by a considerable duration. A mapping study suggested that a pathway from the reticular system to the forebrain was responsible for producing the "waking-like" EEG pattern. The consequence of Moruzzi and Magoun's experiment was that the dominant hypothesis of sleep became what is known as the active hypothesis. Stated simply, the hypothesis is that sleep is produced by the activity of certain brain structures. The hypothesis has led to the search for the brain structure that produces sleep, and in the course of this search, it has been found that sleep as a behavior is very complex. There seem to be at least two different kinds of sleep, which are produced by the interaction of a number of different brain structures. Ironically, "the structure" that produces sleep has not yet been satisfactorily identified. Nevertheless, enough is now known about sleep mechanisms for a beginning explanation to be available for a number of classic disorders of sleep. In addition, sleep laboratories have been set up in a number of places to specialize in the study and treatment of the disorders of sleep.

Before we give a description of the disorders of sleep, it is important to point out that sleep is a very variable phenomena as displayed by different individuals and by the same individual at different stages of life. We have all been subjected to the idea that eight hours of sleep each night is necessary for good health. In fact, there are both long and short sleepers. Some people have been found to stay healthy on as little as an hour of sleep each day, whereas other people may sleep as much as 10 to 12 hours a day. Webb and his associates have studied long sleepers (longer than 9.5 hours per day) and short sleepers (less than 4.4 hours per day) and found little difference in their overall health. It does seem reasonable to state, then, that the proper amount of sleep is an individual affair. Short sleepers may not be able to sleep any longer and long sleepers may not function efficiently after only a short period of sleep. The definition of what constitutes adequate sleep must therefore be made within the context of an individual's past sleep history.

Initially, sleep was thought to be one behavioral state. Subsequent studies have shown that it is comprised of at least two states that periodically alternate with each other during a complete sleep session. Based on their respective EEG activity patterns, one state is called *D-sleep,* for its characteristic desynchronized EEG pattern, and the other is called S-sleep, for its characteristic slow-wave EEG pattern. D-sleep is characterized by a desynchronized or waking-like EEG, during which rapid eye movements (REMs) and twitches of the fingers, toes, and other body parts occur in short bursts. S-sleep is characterized by a slow-wave EEG of various degrees. Large movements such as tossing and turning occur. S-sleep is generally divided into four stages: stage 1 has the least amount of slow-wave activity and stage 4 has the most slow-wave activity. The two types of sleep occur in an alternating pattern in the "average" individual. This alternation is illustrated in Figure 12–2. When sleep begins, stages 1 to 4 of S-sleep appear in

succession and then give way to D-sleep. After a period of D-sleep, S-sleep again occurs, and so on throughout the night. As a night's sleep progresses, however, stage 4 sleep becomes less frequent and the periods of D-sleep tend to last longer.

What accounts for the two types of sleep and their alternation? The answer to this question is intimately linked to the question of the function of sleep. A biological explanation of sleep is that it is an adaptive process to conserve energy at night (a time during which food-gathering would be difficult). A problem to be overcome, however, is that the process of evolution has placed a premium on developing rhythms of locomotor activity (thought to occur every two or so hours, during which food gathering, etc., would occur). The activity cycles would obviously be incompatible with a full night's sleep. In order to cope with the dual demands of conserving energy and of maintaining activity cycles, an innovative adaptation occurred. Periodically, when a waking cycle should occur, immobility was maintained by inhibiting the musculature selec-

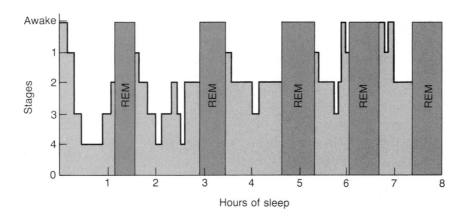

FIGURE 12–2. Course of events during a typical night's sleep from one individual. Stages represent those defined by EEG recordings. The stippled areas represent S-sleep; the dark areas represent D-sleep. Note: Stage 4 S-sleep typically occurs early in the evening; D-sleep increases in duration as the night's sleep progresses. (After Hartmann, 1967.)

tively, while only the brain entered the active cycle.

Experimental evidence supports this hypothesis rather well. Pompiano has recorded from the brainstem, spinal cord, motor neurons, and musculature during S- and D-sleep. During D-sleep there is an increase in the activity of certain brainstem and spinal cord pathways while at the same time motor neuron and muscle activity are almost completely suppressed. Presumably, some central structure is actively suppressing movement. Morrison has located this structure, just below the cerebellum. When this area is damaged in cats, they display gross body movements rather than paralysis during D-sleep. The inhibition does not completely extend to the cortex, however, for physiological measures of brain activity show that during paralysis oxygen use, temperature, and metabolic activity increase, supporting the EEG data that the brain is in an active state. (The activity may be so intense that excitement occasionally breaks through the inhibition to produce movements of the eyes, fingers, toes, etc.) Peripherally, however, in the absence of muscle activity, all thermoregulation stops and body temperature falls toward room temperature. In addition, any gross body movements such as rolling around are effectively blocked. It is still not entirely understood why central activity does not manifest itself in consciousness. Part of the explanation may be that sensory input is blocked, for Pompiano has shown in cats that the thresholds for activating central changes to sensory stimulation are greatly increased. Part of the explanation may also be that the inhibition blocks some critical part of brain activity that is necessary for consciousness. Nevertheless, although consciousness seems blocked and recall is incomplete, studies by Dement, Kleitman, and others have shown by waking up sleeping people that D-sleep is a time during which vivid dreaming invariably occurs.

Disorders of sleep are generally classified into two major groups: (1) narcolepsy, which is characterized by excessive sleep or brief inappropriate episodes of sleep, often associated with other symptoms; and (2) insomnia, which is characterized by an inadequate amount of sleep, an inability to fall asleep, or frequent inconvenient arousals from sleep. Both types of disorders can have a variety of causes, including brain damage, viral infections, drug abuse, etc. They may, however, also occur in the absence of obvious precipitating factors. In addition to these two types of disorders there are many other behaviors that occur during sleep that are disturbing to the afflicted individual. These include night terrors, sleepwalking, teeth grinding, and myoclonic jerks (sudden vigorous movements), but they are usually transitory, infrequent, or not sufficiently disruptive to be called sleep disorders per se.

Narcolepsy. Narcolepsy is defined as an inappropriate attack of sleep. The afflicted individual has an overwhelming impulse to fall asleep or simply collapses into sleep at inconvenient times. The attacks may be infrequent or occur many times a day. The disorder is surprisingly common: estimates suggest that as many as 0.02 percent of the population may suffer from these attacks. Men and women seem equally affected. Although there is a high incidence of narcolepsy in the families of afflicted individuals, no genetic causality has been demonstrated. Symptoms usually appear in people when they are between the ages of 10 and 20 years, and once sleep attacks are developed they continue throughout life. Amphetamine-like stimulants and tricyclic antidepressants have been found useful in treatment.

Narcolepsy has four characteristic features: (1) sleep attacks, (2) cataplexy, (3) sleep paralysis, and (4) hypnagogic or hypnopompic hallucinations. All the symptoms do not necessarily occur at once or in the same individual, but they do occur together sufficiently often to be considered interrelated. We shall describe each of the symptoms in turn.

1. *Sleep attacks.* Sleep attacks are brief, often irresible episodes of sleep that last about 15 minutes and can occur at any time. Their onset is sometimes recognizable but they can also occur without warning. The episodes are most apt to occur during times of boredom or after meals, but they can also occur during sexual intercourse, scuba diving, baseball games, etc. After a brief sleep attack the individual may awaken completely alert and be refractory to a second attack for a number of hours.

2. *Cataplexy.* Cataplexy (from the Greek *cata,* down, and *plexy,* strike) is a complete loss of muscle tone or a sudden paralysis that results in "buckling" of the knees or complete collapse. The attack may be so sudden that the fall results in injury, particularly because the collapse involves a loss of muscle tone and loss of reflexes necessary to break the fall. During the attack the patient remains conscious, and if the eyelids are open, or are opened, the patient can recall visual events that occur during the attack. In contrast to sleep attacks, cataplectic attacks usually appear at times of emotional excitement, such as when a person is laughing or angry. If emotions are held under tight control, the attacks can be prevented.

3. *Sleep paralysis.* Sleep paralysis is an episode of paralysis that occurs at the transition periods between wakefulness and sleep. The period of paralysis is usually brief but can last as long as 20 minutes. Sleep paralysis has been experienced by half of all people, if classroom surveys are an indication of its frequency. In contrast to cataplexy, the paralyzed individual can easily be aroused by touching or name-calling, and if the individual is experienced with the attacks, he or she can terminate them by using a strategy such as grunting.

4. *Hypnagogic and hypnopompic hallucinations.* Hypnagogic (from the Greek *hypno,* sleep, and *gogic,* enter into) hallucinations are episodes of hallucination in the auditory, visual, or tactile modalities that occur during sleep paralysis as the individual is falling asleep. Hypnopompic (*pompic,* leading away) hallucinations are similar experiences that occur during paralysis as the individual is awakening. The hallucinations are generally frightening: the individual may feel a monster or something equally terrifying is lurking nearby. The same kinds of hallucinations can occur during episodes of cataplexy. A curious feature of the hallucinations is that the individual is conscious and often aware of things that are actually happening, so that the hallucinations are even more bizarre because they can become intermixed with real events.

The symptoms of narcolepsy fit together to form what Rechtschaffen and Dement feel may be a syndrome involving the unwanted sudden onset of D-sleep. Recall from the description of sleep types that D-sleep is characterized by muscular paralysis and vivid dreams. The parallel in narcolepsy is the cataplex and sleep paralysis and the hypnagogic hallucinations that are common in both conditions. Two types of evidence support Rechtschaffen and Dement's view. First, during an attack of cataplexy or sleep paralysis, and even though individuals are conscious, they experience hallucinations that have a dreamlike character. Second, EEG recordings taken from narcoleptics have shown that rather than going through an hour or so of S-sleep, they enter D-sleep almost immediately. Individuals who suffer from narcolepsy display the symptoms described above at different times and in different combinations, but the usual pattern is that the sleep attacks appear first (usually without other symptoms). Cataplexy, which may be a sudden onset of D-sleep, will develop in about 70 percent of patients. Sleep paralysis with hallucinations occurs in about 30 percent of patients. It may involve entering a D-sleep stage before losing consciousness with sleep, or regaining consciousness during a D-stage of sleep.

There may be other forms of narcolepsy, but they have received less experimental description than the form just described. It is thought that individuals may suffer from a type of narcolepsy in which they are prone to enter S-sleep. Obviously one of the problems with describing this type of narcolepsy is that it is difficult to distinguish it from genuine fatigue. At least one distinguishing feature of S-sleep narcolepsy is that individuals still feel fatigued when they wake up, unlike D-sleep narcoleptics, who feel refreshed.

Insomnia. Studies on people who claim that they do not sleep, do not sleep well, or wake up frequently from sleep show that their insomnia can have many causes. Rechtschaffen and Monroe recorded EEGs before and during sleep from poor sleepers and found that they exaggerated the length of time that it took them to get to sleep. But the individuals did have decreased D-sleep, they made more body movements, and they went through more changes in sleep stages than did normal individuals. When awakened from S-sleep, they also claimed that they were not sleeping. The investigators concluded that even though these poor sleepers did sleep by EEG criteria, they did not seem to benefit completely from the restorative properties of sleep. Surveys suggest that as many as 14 percent of people claim to suffer from insomnia, but the causes are divergent and include general factors such as anxiety, depression, fear of sleeping, environmental disturbances, and travel into new time zones. Some factors in insomnia seem directly related to the sleep situation. These include (1) nightmares, (2) sleep apnea,

(3) restless legs syndrome, (4) myoclonus, (5) drug-induced insomnia, and (6) insomnia due to brain damage.

1. *Nightmares.* Nightmares are intense frightening dreams that lead to arousal. They are commoner than night terrors *(parvor nocturnus)*. Night terrors are attempts to fight or flee accompanied by panic and such utterances as bloodcurdling screams. Nightmares occur during D-sleep, but night terrors occur during stage 4 S-sleep. Night terrors are usually brief (one to two minutes), and the individual is usually amnesiac for the episode. Both kinds of events are commoner in children than adults, perhaps because adults are more experienced with disturbing dreams and so are not easily awakened. Both types of events can be sufficiently disturbing to disrupt sleep and lead to insomnia.

2. *Sleep apnea.* Sleep apnea (from the Greek for not breathing) is a cessation of respiration that occurs periodically, lasting about 10 or more seconds, and occurs only during sleep. There are two types of sleep apnea. *Obstructive sleep apnea* occurs mainly during D-sleep and seems to be due to a collapse of the oropharynx during the paralysis of D-sleep. Patients with this problem invariably have a history of loud snoring: sounds produced as a consequence of the difficult breathing through the constricted air passage. The obstruction can be reduced through surgical intervention. *Central sleep apnea* stems from a central nervous system disorder. It occurs primarily in males and is characterized by a failure of the diaphragm and accessory muscles to move. Apnea periods may last for up to three minutes. Both types of sleep apnea require all-night recording sessions to detect. Both types interrupt sleep, for the individual is awakened partly or fully by oxygen debt. Although individuals may be unaware of their apnea, they complain of chronic daytime fatigue. Similar apnea in newborn

babies may be a causal factor in the unexplained sudden deaths attributed to sudden infant death syndrome.

3. *Restless legs syndrome.* This is characterized by a severe, difficult to describe, generalized painlike sensation felt in the legs, which is relieved by leg movements. The movements produce insomnia in the individual and any partner by delaying sleep onset.

4. *Myoclonus.* Nocturnal myoclonus is sudden body jerks that occur when an individual is falling asleep. It is sometimes accompanied by dreamlike sensations or images. The movements usually wake up everyone in the bed.

5. *Drug-induced insomnia.* Many drugs, whether stimulants or sedatives, eventually lead to insomnia. Hypnotics and sedatives may at first promote sleep, but habituation occurs. They also deprive the user of D-sleep. Stimulants directly reduce sleep, but they may have their greatest effect on S-sleep. Drug withdrawal is usually an effective treatment.

6. *Insomnia due to brain damage.* Brain-damage-induced insomnia is relatively rare, but Guilleminault and coworkers and Fischer-Perroudon, Mouret, and Jouvet have described patients who showed reduced sleep or no sleep following brain damage. It has been suggested that the neurotransmitter serotonin is required for sleep induction and that serotonin function was impaired by the brain damage in these patients. The insomnia was relieved by treatment with the precursor to serotonin, 6-hydroxytryptophan. The same treatments given to insomniacs of other types has not typically proved to be effective. Certain viral infections, such as the *encephalitis lethargica* of the 1920s, described by von Economo, can lead to insomnia that is so longlasting it can prove fatal. One treatment given for this type of insomnia was to anesthetize the patients for eight to 10 days, with brief timeouts for feeding, until recovery occurred. It is likely that the virus of encephalitis attacks brain centers responsible for sleep induction. Nauta has described a rat analogue of this condition: he observed that rats with large anterior hypothalamic lesions became excessively active and insomniac until they died.

DISORDERS OF THE EXTRAPYRAMIDAL SYSTEM

Classically, the extrapyramidal system consists of motor structures that do not send motor fibers to the spinal cord through the pyramidal tract. Often the term is used in a more restricted sense, to refer to the basal ganglia and their major pathways. The lack of clarity of the term "extrapyramidal" is widely recognized and so will not be discussed here. Nevertheless, there is a group of diseases having clinical symptoms marked by abnormalities in movement and posture that are referable to dysfunctions of the basal ganglia and so are traditionally called extrapyramidal disorders. The major symptoms of these disorders are an excess of spontaneous, aimless movements, and a persistent increase in motor tone with no essential change in spinal reflexes. Clinically, two groups of symptoms are distinguished: *hyperkinetic-dystonic* syndromes, characterized by an excess of motor activity (including chorea, ballism, athetosis, Wilson's disease, and perhaps Tourette's syndrome), and the *hypokinetic-rigid* syndrome (Parkinson's disease). These disorders are described in the following sections.

Huntington's Chorea

Huntington's chorea (chorea is from the Greek for dance) is a genetic disorder that results in intellectual deterioration and abnormal movements as the afflicted reach certain ages in life. George Huntington was eight years old when he first saw people with "that disorder," as it was then called. He was driving with his father in his native New York when they came upon two women who were tall, thin, and twisting and grimacing. No doubt the disorder was familiar to his father and grandfather, who were both physicians. Nevertheless, the sight of these women left such a profound impression on him that he studied the disease when he later became a physician. In 1872, when he was 22, he wrote the first complete description of the disease. The history of the disease and its origin in the United States have been told by Vessie, who traced it to the village of Bures in England in 1630. At that time whole families in Bures and its vicinity were branded and tried as witches. Some family members, who had or carried the disease, sailed to America among the 700 passengers of the John Winthrop fleet in 1630. In 1653, Ellin Wilkie (name fictitious), who had arrived with Winthrop, apparently had the disorder, for she was tried and hanged for witchcraft. Her granddaughter was later tried and pardoned in 1692. Part of the early history of establishing the genetic basis for the disease involved tracing the family background of afflicted individuals whose ancestors had arrived among the Winthrop passengers and who had moved to other areas of the country. In other countries that were colonized by Europeans, there have been similar family histories constructed that trace the disease back to one or a few immigrants. In actuality, Huntington's chorea is relatively rare, with death rates of 1.6 per million population per year. It is commonest among white Europeans and their descendants; it is very rare in other racial groups such as Japanese and blacks. The number of people who will develop the disease is now thought to be on the decline because of advances in genetic counseling.

Huntington's chorea, or hereditary chorea, is a progressive degenerative disease. The first symptom is usually a reduction of activity and restriction of interest. The first restless and involuntary movements may be attributed to hysteria or some other disorder. The first movements usually appear within a year of the onset of the psychiatric symptoms. The involuntary movements are initially slight and consist of little more than continuous fidgeting, but they slowly increase until they are almost incessant. The movements never involve single muscles but include whole limbs or parts of a limb. They are also irregular and follow no set pattern. A reliable sign of the disease is that a sustained muscular contraction is not possible: when an object is held, grip fluctuates, and the tongue cannot be held protruded. Eventually, the movements become uncontrollable and affect the head, face, trunk, and limbs, impeding speech, swallowing, walking, writing, or other voluntary movements. Sometimes individuals may attempt to mask the abnormal movements with purposeful ones. The main feature of the dementia is that it is what is called the subcortical type. There are emotional and personality changes, impairments of recent memory, defective ability to manipulate acquired knowledge, and slowing of information processing. Apraxia, aphasia, and agnosias, which result from certain cortical diseases such as Alzheimer's disease, do not develop. The emotional changes that result include anxiety, depression, mania, and schizophrenia-like psychoses. Suicide is not uncommon in younger patients.

The first symptoms of the disorder usually occur in people 30 to 50 years of age. About 5 percent of cases, sometimes called "juvenile chorea," begin before age 20. In contrast with adult cases, juvenile cases may exhibit muscle rigidity and slow movements, somewhat similar to those in Parkinson's disease, and they may also have muscle spasms, tremor, disturbances of eye movement, and epilepsy. Adult patients live an average of 12 years after disease onset, but the progress of the disease is far more rapid in the juvenile cases.

Huntington's chorea is transmitted as an autosomal dominant with complete penetrance. Thus, half of all offspring of an affected individual will develop the disease. The location of the gene is not yet known, and genetic analysis is further complicated by the suggestion that there may be three distinct chorea types: a juvenile form characterized by rigidity, a midlife form characterized by emotional impairments, and a form in older people that occurs without the emotional impairment. At present there is no known way of determining whether a family member will develop the disease before symptoms appear. This is unfortunate, because the disease may be passed on to children before it is known whether an individual is a carrier.

At autopsy the brains of Huntington's chorea individuals show shrinkage and thinning of the cerebral cortex. The basal ganglia is also grossly atrophied and shows a marked loss of its intrinsic neurons. One dominant explanation of the disease is that there is an imbalance among the various neurotransmitter systems of the basal ganglia. A simplified model of the transmitter systems involved is illustrated in Figure 12–3. They include: (1) a glutamate projection from the cortex to the basal ganglia, (2) a γ-aminobutyric acid (GABA) projection from the basal ganglia to the substantia nigra, (3) a dopamine (DA) projection from the substantia nigra to the basal ganglia, (4) and acetylcholine (ACh) neurons in the basal ganglia. It is postulated that the intrinsic neurons of the basal ganglia (GABA and ACh neurons) die during the course of the disease, leaving a largely intact nigrostriatal DA pathway. As a result of the decrease in inhibition of the DA cells by the GABA pathway, there is an increase in DA

release in the basal ganglia. The hyperactivity of the dopamine system is thought to produce the characteristic abnormal movements. Exactly how the movements are produced is not clear, but if the basal ganglia have a modulatory function on the corticobulbar and corticospinal systems, then their release from modulation could certainly produce the typical abnormal movements. Support for the idea that there is an increase in dopamine activity comes from two sources. First, biochemical analysis of the brain tissue at autopsy shows a significant increase in dopamine levels. Second, drugs that tend to ameliorate chorea are those that block dopamine, such as major tranquilizers, whereas those that aggravate chorea are dopamine agonists, such as amphetamine.

Over the past 10 years there has been a surge of interest in the mechanisms that produce Huntington's chorea. A volume edited by Chase, Wexler, and Barbeau has been devoted to the disease. An animal model has also been

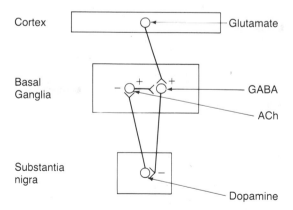

FIGURE 12–3. Model of transmitter systems involved in Huntington's chorea. It is thought that ACh and GABA neurons in the basal ganglia die, and as a result dopamine cells are released from GABA inhibition and become hyperactive, thus producing abnormal movements. The death of GABA cells may be produced by excessive activity of the glutamate pathway.

developed that offers at least a partial explanation of how the disease progresses. In the animal model it has been found that an analogue of glutamate called kainic acid will attach to glutamate receptors and kill cells by overstimulating them. When kainic acid is injected into the basal ganglia of rats, many neurons containing GABA and ACh as well as other transmitters are destroyed. Accordingly, an explanation of the cell loss in humans is that the glutamate pathway from the cortex to the basal ganglia becomes hyperactive and destroys cells in the basal ganglia with which it connects. There is some independent support for this suggestion, but there are also some unanswered questions. For example, the rat models of Huntington's chorea do display some learning impairments, but they do not display abnormal movements. In addition, there is still no explanation of how the disease takes different forms or why it has an age-related onset. These unanswered questions provide fruitful areas for future investigation.

Sydenham's Chorea

Sydenham's chorea is named after the English physician Thomas Sydenham (1624–1689). It also goes by its German name, St. Vitus' dance, although it is likely that the group dances of the Middle Ages that received this name were not performed by people with the disorder that Sydenham described. (St. Vitus was martyred under Diocletian and was the patron saint of those afflicted with compulsive dancing: it was to St. Vitus' shrine near Strassburg that the afflicted went for treatment.) Sydenham's chorea is relatively rare, and so few cases have come to autopsy or have received biochemical examination. Where autopsy has been performed, diffuse changes in the basal ganglia and cortex have been observed.

Sydenham's chorea occurs in children and young people five to 20 years of age and is thought to be due to acute childhood rheumatism or other infections. Heredity may play some part in the etiology, since some families appear susceptible to acute rheumatism. People of European ancestry are more susceptible than other races, and the disorder is three times more likely to occur in females than in males.

The onset of the chorea is insidious, and the child may at first be thought to be clumsy. As movements become more obvious the child is described as fidgety, restless, or unable to keep still. The involuntary movements are usually described as quasi-purposive and follow one another in a disordered fashion. They include bilateral facial movements: frowning, raising the eyebrows, smiling, and other movements of the mouth and tongue, and the eyes and head may be rolled from side to side. When severe, the facial movements may interfere with chewing and swallowing, so that special feeding may be required. Movements of the upper limbs involve all joints. For example, the limb may be flexed with the fingers closed and will then be flung out in full extension. Lower limb movements usually are less pronounced and are most frequently distal. Voluntary movements are generally not impaired, but muscle tone is increased such that voluntary movements become exaggerated. Usually the child is emotionally excitable and suffers from insomnia. The chorea disappears during sleep.

Most affected persons recover in two to three weeks, but they may have a number of attacks at intervals of about a year. No obvious disabilities have been described after recovery. Treatment consists of confining the individual to bed until the movements cease. Drug therapy with sedatives and major tranquilizers appears to be helpful in reducing the chorea.

Hemiballism

Hemiballism is a term applied to involuntary movements that occur on one side of the body. It consists of violent movements of the limbs, which resemble a forceful throwing movement. These movements exhaust and incapacitate the person and can lead to death unless arrested. The first summary of persons with this disorder was made by Martin in 1927. He reviewed 21 patients in all and called the disorder "syndrome of the Body of Luys" because of the frequent association of damage to this structure and the contralateral movements in the patients. Descriptions of the disorder are infrequent. The body of Luys is now called the subthalamic nucleus, and as noted in Chapter 11, it forms part of the basal ganglia. Symptoms can be the result of vascular disease, tumor, or infection involving this structure. Stereotaxic surgery of the thalamus has been found successful in treating the disorder, presumably because the lesion cuts the flow of information between the basal ganglia and the motor cortex.

Athetosis

The term athetosis (from the Greek, meaning without fixed position) was coined by the American physician William Alexander Hammond in 1871. The German anatomists Cecil and Oscar Vogt described a number of cases between 1911 and 1924 in which there was bilateral atrophy of the basal ganglia. The symptoms of the disease resemble chorea but the movements are slower, coarser, and more writhing than choreic movements. Athetosis, particularly if it is bilateral, may be congenital or result from damage to the basal ganglia. It may also develop during adolescence as a progressive disorder terminating in rigidity. Sometimes *torsion dystonia* is used as a description of athetosis in which movements involve more proximal parts of the body.

Congenital athetosis is first noticed when a child is several months to two years old. The child makes peculiar movements and is often hypotonic, being referred to as a "floppy infant." Facial movements include frequent grimaces of all kinds associated with involuntary laughing and crying. If athetosis is unilateral, the facial movements may be exaggerations of normal ones. In the limbs distal movements are commoner than proximal movements. The hand is usually flexed at the wrist, and this position is frequently interrupted by slow writhing movements of flexion and extension. The movements usually completely interfere with the voluntary movements of the limbs, and the person may attempt to restrain the hand by holding it or leaning on it. The movements always become exaggerated when voluntary movements are attempted. Athetosis has proved difficult to treat. A variety of drugs including major and minor tranquilizers have not been consistently effective and the results of attempts to arrest the movements with thalamic surgery have been inconsistent.

Wilson's Disease

Wilson's disease, also known as hepatolenticular degeneration, is a progressive disease of early life that is due to an autosomal recessive gene. It was first described by Wilson in 1912, and although one of the rarest disorders of movement, it is one of the first for which a rational treatment became available. It is characterized by a disorder of copper metabolism in which copper concentrations of the brain and liver increase, leading to a degeneration in certain brain regions, particularly the basal ganglia, and to cirrhosis of the liver. A particularly good diagnostic sign of the disease is corneal pigmentation (the Kayser-Fleischer ring), which consists of a 2-mm-diameter zone of golden-brown pigmentation on the cornea. It is due to deposit of copper and may be present before nervous system symptoms develop. The disorder leads to increasing muscular rigidity, tremor, and progressive dementia. The incidence of the gene is about one per 1000 population and it is found in all races. Symptoms of the disease usually become apparent between 10 and 25 years of age. Choreiform movements of the face and hands are the first symptoms and occur when the person is at rest, but they are reduced by relaxation. The rigidity is general and resembles that of Parkinson's disease. Loss of emotional control occurs, with involuntary laughing and crying, and there is always mental deterioration, ending in mild dementia. Individuals may survive from one to six years or longer when untreated. When treated with D-penicillamine, the disease is arrested, and if treatment occurs early, subjects remain symptomfree. D-penicillamine acts by binding, or chelating, copper, aiding in its excretion.

Gilles de la Tourette Syndrome

The Gilles de la Tourette syndrome (TS) was described by Gilles de la Tourette in a two-part paper published in 1885. In most important ways this paper is still a remarkably good description of the disorder. Until Tourette's review this syndrome was seen either as an undifferentiated chorea or a symptom of hysteria, and it went by a variety of different names depending on where it had been observed. The symptoms of the syndrome have a tendency to evolve and become more elaborate with age. Tourette described three stages to the syndrome. In the first stage only multiple tics (twitches of the face, limbs, or of the whole body) occur. In the second stage inarticulate cries are added to the multiple tics. In the third stage the emission of articulate words with echolalia (repeating what others have said, but also repeating actions) and coprolalia (corpro from the Greek for dung, but now meaning obscene or lewd, and lalia meaning speech) are added to the multiple tics and inarticulate cries. The following is a case history reported by Tourette that illustrates most of the major features of the syndrome.

Case VIII: Miss X. by Professor Pitres of Bordeaux. Miss X., fifteen years old, spent several months at the Longchamps hydrotherapy institution at Bordeaux during the winter of 1883, where she was treated for convulsive attacks of chorea and ejaculations of loud vulgar and obscene words. Miss X. was very intelligent, she learned the lessons given her by her teacher with the greatest ease, and she played the piano well. She was tall and largely built. She was not well disciplined.

Her mother had never had a neurological disease. Her father had a convulsive, though not painful, facial tic. She had a strange, almost crazy, aunt, who lived alone. She had fits of hysteria, morbid hunger, and sometimes long periods of melancholy in which she refused to talk to anyone.

When nine, Miss X. began having violent and irregular choreiform tics of the face, arms, and legs. At the same time she occasionally uttered a few vulgar words. After a few months the attacks disappeared. A year later they came back again. The tics first reappeared in the shoulders, then in the arms, and then in the face, where they were accompanied by loud guttural sounds. These indistinct sounds became very clearly articulated when she was thirteen. At that time her most frequent words were "get away, go away, imbecile." A little later her words became more frequent and much clearer, and were rough and lewd. She remained that way until the present.

Miss X. belonged to an upper-class family. Her education was excellent. She never left her mother, who surrounded her in continuous, tender loving care. One had to wonder how and where she picked up the words she continually uttered: e.g., "In God's name, fuck, shit, etc." When she is in her calm normal state such words never pass her lips.

Whenever Miss X. was in the presence of someone she was afraid of, or who intimidated her, she was able to suffocate the sounds by a sheer effort of will. By clenching her teeth convulsively she could prevent the words from being understood. All one heard then was a kind of vague growling. As soon as she was alone the usual words poured out in added abundance.

The words were always pronounced with a series of convulsive tics of the face, the shoulders, the trunk. Often, convulsive attacks happened without any word being spoken. At other times the words could be smothered and rendered incomprehensible by an intense effort of will. During sleep, spasmodic movements and involuntary words ceased altogether.

Professor Pitres sent us some additional observations on October 27: It would seem that "Miss de M.," has not clearly presented the echolalia phenomena. To be sure we have not sought them out by pronouncing the coarse words that are so familiar to her. On the contrary, the patient's mother has tried to substitute the vulgar words with indifferent words and banale exclamations. To this end she ordered the governess to shout out several times a day in front of her daughter, "Oh my God!" or "Mother!" The governess fulfilled her duty faithfully, but the patient did not repeat the exclamations that she had heard.

One single fact observed by the governess seemed to have some bearing on echolalia. One evening in 1883, while Miss X. was undressing to go to bed, a dog came and barked under the window of her room. She immediately began involuntarily to echo the dog's barking. She was unable to sleep till one in the morning because her body was continually wracked by muscular spasms that accompanied the noisy barking, exactly like the dog's. Here is another bit of curious information: Miss X. had quite a pronounced tendency to imitate actions and to take up queer postures that she had seen and that had struck her. One day she was walking with her governess in a fairground, and she spied a cardboard model of Gargantua whose mouth opened and shut with a regular motion, gobbling up everything that was presented. The child looked at the astonishing sight for a moment, and the for rest of the walk she never stopped opening and shutting her mouth, involuntarily, just as she had seen it done by Gargantua. (*Gilles de la Tourette, 1885,* pp. 41–42; translated by Lorna Whishaw)

Tourette recognized that individuals with the syndrome could be intelligent and productive and that they were not neurotic or psychotic. He also noted that the syndrome, or parts of it, ran in families and thus seemed hereditary. Tourette pointed out that there was no treatment (although the symptoms lessened or disappeared during fevers), so that the symptoms were likely to be with the person for life. Recently there has been renewed interest in TS largely through the work of the Tourette Society in North America. Many TS patients have been misdiagnosed as troublemakers, hysterics, schizophrenics, etc., no doubt because they seemed intelligent yet displayed bizarre behavior. This is now changing, and there is great interest in trying to understand the cause of the disorder in terms of brain function. Much of the research that has been done to date has been summarized in an edited work by Friedhoff and Chase.

The incidence of TS is less than one in 100,000, but the incidence can vary with the degree of professional knowledge about the disorder. In our area, which has a population base of about 100,000, a child psychiatrist interested in the disorder has diagnosed over 10 cases. Thus, the incidence may actually be somewhat higher. From work by Shapiro and Shapiro the following features of TS are known. TS occurs in all racial groups, and the male to female ratio is about 3 to 1. TS seems to be hereditary because between 30 to 40 percent of TS individuals have a family member with the disorder or who displays various types of tics. It also seems commoner for female members to transmit the disorder. Neverthe-less, the genetic basis of the disorder is not known, and it has been suggested that there are hereditary and nonhereditary groups of TS individuals. The average age of onset ranges between two and 15 years, with a median of seven years, and by 11 years symptoms have appeared in 97 percent of cases. The most frequent symptoms are tics involving the eye, head, or face (97 percent), followed by the neck and shoulders (97 percent), upper limbs (81 percent), and lower limbs and body (55 percent). Complex movements including touching, hitting, and jumping occur in between 30 to 40 percent of cases. Coprolalia may develop in up to 60 percent of cases and then disappear in a third of these. As noted above, TS is not associated with neuroses, psychoses, or other disorders. EEG activity is frequently normal although some patients may display some abnormalities. Evoked potential studies show that the premovement potentials that are associated with willed, voluntary movements do not occur with the tics in TS patients, which testifies to the involuntary nature of the movements.

It is thought that TS has a subcortical origin, possibly in the basal ganglia. This idea is supported in part by studies that have found Tourette-like symptoms in patients with other basal ganglia disorders that have been induced by other diseases or by long-continued use of major tranquilizers. There have been very few autopsy examinations of the brains of TS patients, and of those that have been done there is one report of an excessive number of small cells in the basal ganglia and other reports that the cells there are normal. A major piece of evidence that implicates the basal ganglia comes from effective drug therapy. To date, the most consistent improvements are obtained with antidopaminergic agents such as haloperidol; thus it is thought that there may

be some abnormality in the dopamine system in the basal ganglia. Clonidine, a noradrenaline receptor agonist, also is reported to be effective in some cases. A number of neuropsychological studies have been done, and there is a suggestion from these that there are abnormalities in some cognitive functions usually supported by the right hemisphere. The results of the neuropsychological studies will be considered in Chapter 29.

Tardive Dyskinesia

Tardive dyskinesia (from the French and Greek, meaning later-appearing abnormal movements) is a disorder caused mainly by long-term use of antipsychotic agents (phenothiazines and butyrophenones) that act primarily as dopamine blocking agents. People with tardive dyskinesia display an excess of motor activity, especially of the face and tongue. The movements disfigure the face and become so severe that they interfere with eating. They usually do not appear until individuals have been taking antipsychotic agents for months or years. Once developed, tardive dyskinesia is extremely difficult to treat. Lowering the dosage of drug treatment tends to worsen the symptoms. Stopping drug use may not always lead to lessening of the symptoms. If symptoms do stop with a "drug holiday," they may begin again almost immediately with renewed drug treatment. Not all patients treated with antipsychotics develop tardive dyskinesia, but it is more likely to occur in older patients, those who may have some form of brain damage, and in females. Because tardive dyskinesia is a serious side effect of antipsychotic therapy, the drugs are only administered where this type of treatment is mandatory. Even then it has been suggested that patients or their family be apprised of the possibility of developing tardive dyskinesia and required to sign a consent form before medication is begun.

Parkinson's Disease

The individual symptoms of Parkinson's disease have been described by physicians from the time of Galen, but their occurrence as a syndrome was not recognized. In 1817, James Parkinson, a London physician, published an essay in which he argued that several different motor symptoms could be considered together as a group forming a distinctive condition. His observations are interesting not only because his conclusion was correct but also because he made his observations in part at a distance by watching the movements of parkinsonian victims in the streets of London. Parkinson's disease has been called at different times the shaking palsy or its Latin equivalent, *paralysis agitans,* but received its commoner designation from Charcot, who suggested that the disease be renamed to honor James Parkinson's recognition of its essential nature.

Parkinson's disease is fairly common, estimates of its incidence varying from 0.1 to 1.0 percent of the population. It is also of considerable interest for a number of other reasons. First, the disease seems related to the degeneration of a brain nucleus called the **substantia nigra,** and to the loss of the neurotransmitter substance dopamine, which is produced by cells of this nucleus. The disease therefore provides an important insight into the role of this brainstem nucleus and its neurotransmitter in the control of movement. Second, because a variety of pharmacological treatments for Parkinson's disease relieve to some extent different features of its symptoms, the disease provides a model for understanding pharmacological treatments of motor disorders in their more general aspects. Third, although Parkinson's disease is described

as a disease entity, the symptoms vary enormously among people, thus making manifest the complexity with which the components of movement are organized to produce fluid motion. Fourth, because many of the symptoms of Parkinson's disease strikingly resemble changes in motor activity that occur as a consequence of aging, the disease provides indirect insight into the more general problems of neural changes in aging.

There are four major symptoms of Parkinson's disease: tremor, plastic (cogwheel) rigidity, akinesia, and disturbances of posture, each of which may be manifest in different body parts in different combinations. Since some of the symptoms involve the appearance of abnormal behaviors and others the loss of normal behaviors we shall discuss the symptoms in these two major categories: positive and negative. Positive symptoms are behaviors not seen in normal people or seen only so rarely and then in such special circumstances that they can be considered abnormal. Negative symptoms are marked not by any particular behavior but rather by an absence of a behavior or by an inability to engage in an activity.

Positive Parkinsonian Symptoms. Since positive symptoms are common in Parkinson's disease they are thought to be held in check, or inhibited, in normal people but released from inhibition in the process of the disease. The commonest positive symptoms are the following. (1) *Tremor at rest.* This consists of alternating movements of one or both of the distal limbs when they are at rest, but which stop during voluntary movements or during sleep. The tremors of the hands often have a "pill-rolling" quality, as if a pill were being rolled between the thumb and forefinger. (2) *Muscular rigidity.* Muscular rigidity consists of increased muscle tone simultaneously in both extensor and flexor muscles. It is particularly evident when the limbs are moved passively at a joint; movement is resisted but with sufficient force the muscles yield, for a short distance, then resist movement again. Thus, complete passive flexion or extension of a joint occurs in a series of steps, giving rise to the term "cogwheel rigidity." This should be contrasted with the "clasp-knife rigidity" of hemiplegia, in which initial resistance to flexion or extension gives way suddenly, permitting free movement of the joint. The rigidity may be sufficiently severe to make all movements difficult. One man less severely afflicted by rigidity was moved to comment, "The slowness of movement is conscious but not willed. That is, I form a plan in my mind; for instance, I wish to uncork that bottle. Then I deliberately invoke the effort that sets the muscles in motion. I'm aware of the slowness of the process; I'm unable to increase [its speed], but I always get the bottle open." (3) *Involuntary movements.* These may consist of continual changes in posture, sometimes to relieve tremor and sometimes to relieve stiffness, but often for no apparent reason. These small movements or changes in posture, sometimes referred to as *akathisia* or "cruel restlessness," may be concurrent with general inactivity. Other involuntary movements are distortions of posture, such as occur during oculogyric crisis (turns of the head and eyes to one side), which last for periods of minutes to hours. Since the positive symptoms are "actions," they are caused by the activity of some brain area. Before drug therapy became commoner, one of the treatments used to stop them was to localize the source of the symptom and make a lesion there. For example, tremor was treated by lesions made in the ventral thalamus.

Negative Parkinsonian Symptoms. After detailed analysis of negative symptoms in severely parkinsonian patients Martin divided them into five groups. (1) *Disorders of posture.* These are disorders of fixation and equilibrium. A disorder of fixation consists of an inability to maintain, or difficulty in maintaining, a part of the body (head, limbs, etc.) in its normal position in relation to other parts. Thus, a person's head may droop forward, or a standing person may gradually bend further forward until he or she ends up on the knees. Disorders of equilibrium consist of difficulties in standing or even sitting when unsupported. In less severe cases individuals may have difficulty standing on one leg, or, if pushed lightly on the shoulders, they may fall passively without taking corrective steps or attempting to catch themselves. (2) *Disorders of righting.* These consist of difficulty in achieving a standing position from a supine position. (3) *Disorders of locomotion.* Normal locomotion requires support of the body against gravity, stepping, balancing while the weight of the body is transferred from one limb to another, and pushing forward. Parkinsonian individuals have difficulty initiating stepping, and when they do, they shuffle with short footsteps on a fairly wide base of support because they have trouble maintaining equilibrium when shifting weight from one limb to the other. Often parkinsonian individuals who have begun to walk demonstrate **festination:** they take faster and faster steps and end up running forward. (4) *Disturbances of speech.* These consist mainly of difficulties in the physical production of sound; rigidity may play a prominent role in these disturbances. (5) *Akinesia.* **Akinesia** refers to a poverty or slowness of movement, which may also manifest itself in a blankness of facial expression, lack of blinking, swinging of the arms when walking, spontaneous speech, or normal movements of fidgeting. It is also reflected in difficulty in making repetitive movements, such as tapping, even in the absence of rigidity. People who sit motionless for hours show akinesia in its most striking manifestation. Other negative symptoms include difficulty in chewing and swallowing, but these symptoms do not fit easily or clearly into any of the above five categories.

The symptoms of Parkinson's disease begin insidiously, often with a tremor in one hand and with slight stiffness in the distal portions of the limbs. Movements may next become slower, the face becoming masklike with loss of eye blinking and poverty of emotional expression. Thereafter the body may become stooped, while the gait becomes a shuffle with the arms hanging motionless at the sides. Speech may become slow and monotonous, and difficulty in swallowing saliva may make drooling a problem. Although the disease is progressive, the rate at which the symptoms worsen is variable, and only rarely is progression so rapid that a person becomes disabled within five years; usually 10 to 20 years elapse before symptoms cause incapacity. One of the most curious aspects of Parkinson's disease is its on-again/off-again quality: symptoms may suddenly appear and as suddenly disappear. Partial remission of Parkinson's disease may also occur in response to interesting and activating situations. Sacks recounts an incident in which a parkinsonian patient leaped from his wheelchair at the seaside and rushed into the breakers to save a drowning man, only to fall back into his chair immediately afterward and become inactive again. Although remission of some symptoms in activating situations is common, remission is not usually as dramatic as is recounted in this case.

Causes of Parkinsonism. There are three major types of Parkinson's disease: idiopathic, postencephalitic, and drug-induced. Parkinson's disease may also result from arteriosclerosis, may follow poisoning by carbon monoxide or manganese intoxication, or may result from syphilis or the development of tumors. As is suggested by its name, the *idiopathic* cause of Parkinson's disease is not known. Its origin may be familial, or it may be part of the aging process, but it is also widely thought that it might have a viral origin. It most often occurs in people who are over 50 years of age. The *postencephalitic* form originated in the sleeping sickness *(encephalitis lethargica)* that appeared in the winter of 1916–1917 and vanished by 1927. Although the array of symptoms was bewilderingly varied, such that hardly any two patients seemed alike, Constantin von Economo demonstrated a unique pattern of brain damage associated with a virus infection in the brains of patients who had died from the disease. A third of those affected died in the acute stages of the sleeping sickness, in states either of coma or of sleeplessness. Although many people seemed to completely recover from the sickness, most subsequently developed neurological or psychiatric disorders and parkinsonism. The latency between the initial and subsequent occurrences of the disease has never been adequately explained. The third major cause of Parkinson's disease is more recent, and is associated with ingestion of various drugs, particularly major tranquilizers that include reserpine and several phenothiazine and butyrophenone derivatives. The symptoms are usually reversible, but they are difficult to distinguish from those of the genuine disorder.

Although parkinsonian patients can be separated into clinical groups on the basis of cause of the disease, it is nevertheless likely that the mechanisms producing the symptoms have a common origin. Either the substantia nigra is damaged, as occurs in idiopathic and postencephalitic cases, or the activity of its cells is blocked, as occurs in drug-induced parkinsonism. The cells of the substantia nigra contain a dark pigment (hence its name); in Parkinson's disease this area is depigmented by degeneration of the melatonin-containing neurons of the area. Why the relatively selective degeneration occurs is not known, but it is possible that in viral causes the virus disturbs the metabolic pathways related to the formation of the pigment. The cells of the substantia nigra are the point of origin of fibers that go to the basal ganglia in particular, but also, in the rat (and probably also in humans), project to the frontal cortex and to the spinal cord. The neurotransmitter at the synapses of these projections is dopamine. It has been demonstrated by bioassay of the brains of deceased parkinsonian patients, and by analysis of the major metabolite of dopamine, homovanallic acid, which is excreted in the urine, that the amount of brain dopamine is reduced by over 90 percent and is often reduced to undetectable amounts. Thus, the cause of Parkinson's disease has been identified with some certainty as a lack of dopamine or, in drug-induced cases, with a lack of dopamine action. However, dopamine depletion may not account for the whole problem in some people, since decreases of noradrenaline have been recorded, and there have been a number of reports that cells in some of the nuclei in the basal ganglia may degenerate as well.

The Nature of the Motor Defect. It is not known precisely how a reduction in brain dopamine produces Parkinson's disease, but Martin has performed the best analysis of the disease's negative symptoms. He compared the function of mechanisms controlling posture and locomotion in normal people with those controlling locomotion in parkinsonian patients.

In normal people postural reflexes are under the control of vision; the labyrinths, or balance receptors, of the middle ear; and proprioception, or sensation, from muscles and joints. Of

these three senses proprioception appears to be the most important, because whereas adequate locomotion can still occur in the absence of vision and labyrinthine function, locomotion is severely impaired if proprioception is absent. Martin described the difficulties of a man whose proprioceptive pathways of the spinal cord had been cut accidentally. His locomotor difficulties appear in some ways surprisingly like those of people with Parkinson's disease.

> This patient, in spite of years of physiotherapy and training, has never regained the ability to walk in any normal manner. His greatest difficulty is in starting to walk and in propelling himself forward. When he first began to walk—about a year after his injury—he held his hands out in front of him, which, of course, had the effect of bringing his center of gravity forward. Now, after several years of practice, he advances his hands less and he bends his head and body forward. He walks on a wide base and rocks his body but he does not bend his legs and so shows no proper stepping. If he loses his balance, he shows no reaction to protect his equilibrium and he has learned to fall with his body relaxed. When he falls he cannot rise without help. He is also unable to rise from a chair. He cannot crawl or place himself in the all-fours posture. When standing or walking he is entirely dependent on vision and falls down if he closes his eyes. At first he was unable to maintain his position on an ordinary chair when he closed his eyes but he had gradually acquired the ability to do this. (Martin, 1967, p. 32)

When Martin tested labyrinthine and proprioceptive function in Parkinson's disease patients, he found the receptors and their afferent pathways intact, but still neither seemed to function to aid locomotion. Perhaps the important feature in locomotion for humans is its bipedal nature, which requires balancing as weight is shifted from one limb to the other. Proprioception may be particularly important for this aspect of walking, and it is balance that the person with Parkinson's disease seems intent on preserving with the wide-based, shuffling walking style. The mechanisms for normal locomotion seem intact, for if walking is brought more directly under visual control, it appears quite normal. Martin accomplished increased visual control by having the patients walk over a series of wood blocks: as the patients walked over the blocks, walking suddenly and dramatically become normal, but it ceased to be so when the last of the blocks was reached. Actually, visual stimuli are not essential; parkinsonian individuals may walk briefly with normal stepping motions if asked to do so. The initiation of normal walking in people is usually accomplished by leaning forward and rocking from side to side. These movements, which will unbalance parkinsonian individuals, are resisted, making initiation of walking difficult. But leaning them forward (or having them carry something before them, which accomplishes the same effect) and rocking them from side to side, both of which are automatic reflexes of walking, can reinstate more normal walking. Thus, in Parkinson's disease, when the proprioceptive system in intact and the stepping mechanisms of the motor system are functional, normal walking nevertheless fails to occur. Thus, it can only be concluded that the connection between sensory input and motor output is not being made. Since dopamine is implicated in Parkinson's disease, and since a primary projection of the dopamine system is from the substantia nigra to the basal ganglia, it can be concluded that dopamine is required in the basal ganglia to maintain the connection between the proprioceptive sensory system and the movement system.

How is Parkinson's disease related to the anatomical projections of the motor system we outlined in the Chapter 12? There is, of course, no certain answer to this question, but the defects in such movements as righting, leaning forward, and rocking from side to side,

and the absence of arm swinging when walking, etc., all suggest disturbed control of the ventromedial system that controls body movements and walking. The basal ganglia are known to make major connections with this system. The corticospinal system may function more normally, since affected individuals can write, although their writing tends to become small, possibly because of reduced arm movements. In opposition to this viewpoint, however, Weaver and Brooks and others report that in patients with Parkinson's disease fine motor skills involving the digits are severely impaired.

Treatment of Parkinson's Disease. There is no known cure for Parkinson's disease, and none will be in sight until the factors that produce the progressive deterioration of the substantia nigra are known. As a result, treatment is symptomatic and directed toward support and comfort. The major symptoms of parkinsonism are influenced by psychological factors, a person's outcome being affected by how well he or she can cope with the disability. As a result, individuals should be counseled early regarding the meaning of symptoms, the nature of the disease, and the potential for most of them to lead long and productive lives. Physical therapy should consist of simple measures such as heat and massage to alleviate painful muscle cramps, and training and exercise to cope with the debilitating changes in movement.

The drug treatments for Parkinson's disease are of considerable theoretical as well as practical interest. In recent years understanding of the structure and function of synapses has been greatly advanced. Parkinson's disease provides an excellent model for understanding brain function with respect to synaptic action, because a specific constellation of symptoms has been linked with changes in a known neurotransmitter. Pharmacological treatment has two main objectives: first, increase the activity in whatever dopamine synapses remain; second, suppress the activity in structures that show heightened activity in the absence of adequate dopamine action. Drugs such as L-dopa, which is converted into dopamine in the brain; amantadine; amphetamine; monoamine oxydase inhibitors; and tricyclic mood elevators are used to potentiate effective dopamine transmission. Naturally occurring anticholinergic drugs, such as atropine and scopolamine, and synthetic anticholinergics, such as benztropine (Cogentin) and trihexyphenidyl (Artane), are used to block the cholinergic systems of the brain that seem to show heightened activity in the absence of adequate dopamine activity.

The Effectiveness of Drug Therapy. The effectiveness of drug therapy depends on the progression of the disease, as has been described by Hornykiewicz. Unless dopamine is depleted by more than 80 percent, the disease is clinically silent. Manifestation of symptoms seems prevented in two major ways: the remaining dopamine fibers become overactive, and there is a proliferation of D-2 receptors, allowing the remaining excitatory pool of DA to have a greater effect, a phenomenon called **denervation supersensitivity.** Other compensatory actions may also be occurring, including decreases in serotonin and GABA activity, which are thought to inhibit dopamine function, decreases in the number of D-1 receptors (which have inhibitory functions in comparison to D-2 receptors), and increases in the activity of that portion of the noradrenaline system that normally facilitates dopamine action. Once dopamine depletion reaches the point that these compensatory actions are no longer effective, the symptoms of the disease start appearing. L-dopa, the most effective treatment, does not become effective until denervation supersensitivity appears; that is, until the disease is well developed. As denervation supersensitivity becomes more pronounced, L-Dopa becomes difficult to administer in a dose that does not produce side effects. In the early stages of the disease, L-dopa therapy may reverse denervation supersensitivity, making treatment ineffective. A "drug holiday" is thought to be useful for restoring the receptor proliferation that is the prerequisite of effective L-dopa therapy. The best description of the effects of drug therapy on the condition of Parkinson's disease is given in a series of case histories described by Sacks. Although drugs such as L-dopa have been called miracle drugs, they are not a cure for the disease. Generally it is necessary to treat each patient as an individual, experimenting with different available drugs and with different dosages. In some cases symptoms are dramatically relieved and patients are immensely helped; in other cases the drug treatments may prove to have side effects as unpleasant and as debilitating to the patient as the disease symptoms. An additional complexity in treatment is the progressive nature of the disease. Drug therapy must be continually reevaluated, and it may become ineffectual in the latter stages of the disease. The following is an example of the "side effects" on a patient, Miss N., described by Sacks.

> In September for the third time I gave her L-dopa and her responses were not quite different from either of the first two times. She complained of rapid breathing and difficulty in catching her breath, and she had the beginnings of respiratory crises. She developed very rapid "saluting" tics in both of her arms, her hand flying from her lap to her face three or four times every minute. She also developed palilalia, repeating her words innumerable times. Her reaction at this time was remarkably similar to that of her room-mate Miss D., so much so that I wondered if either was automatically "imitating" the other. By the mid-

dle of September, Miss N. was . . . [producing tics] 60 times to the minute, 60 minutes to the hour, and saying an incessant palilalic repetition of the following verse she had learned years before:

I thought it said in every tic,
I am so sick, so sick, so sick.
Oh death, come quick, come quick,
    come quick!
Come quick, come quick, come quick,
    come quick!

Since she was exhausting herself and maddening her fellow patients, I again found it necessary to stop L-dopa.

Following this excited state Miss N. showed a severe "rebound" when L-dopa was stopped, becoming so rigid, tremulous, akinetic and voiceless, and having so much difficulty in swallowing, that we had to tube-feed her. This "withdrawal reaction" continued for the remainder of September without any lessening in severity whatever. (From *Awakenings,* by Oliver Sacks. Copyright © 1973 by Oliver Sacks. Reprinted by permission of Doubleday & Company, Inc., and Gerald Duckworth & Co., Ltd.)

It is unlikely that L-dopa would produce such side effects if given to normal people. It does so in parkinsonian patients because postsynaptic receptors proliferate as dopamine end feet degenerate; there being fewer and fewer synapses, there are concomitantly more and more receptors. Thus, as parkinsonian symptoms develop and as L-dopa becomes more necessary it also unfortunately produces more side effects.

Psychological Aspects of Parkinson's Disease. Although Parkinson's disease patients are often described as manifesting many features of depression, they are also widely thought to show no psychological changes that parallel their motor disabilities. This latter view may be incorrect. On the basis of clinical observations, Sacks suggests that there are cognitive changes parallel to those reflected in motor activity. Sacks emphasizes festination and resistance as positive symptoms of cognitive activity. As mentioned earlier, festination is manifest as an acceleration of walking, but it is also seen as a rushing of speech and even thought. Resistance, however, has the opposite effect: as soon as speech or thought is attempted, it may be blocked by resistance. Thus, the two positive effects are in a sense opposites, and parkinsonian individuals might find themselves embattled, festination counteracted by resistance. Sacks has also emphasized that there are negative components of the disease in cognitive function. There is an impoverishment of feeling, libido, motive, and attention; individuals may sit for hours apparently lacking the will to enter or continue on any course of activity.

Bowen has reported on the performance of parkinsonian patients on a number of more formal neurological and psychological tests. Although verbal IQ was normal, patients performed significantly less well on memory tests than their spouses, who were used as the control group. Parkinsonian patients also showed significant deficits on tests of extrapersonal orientation, personal orientation, the Wisconsin card-sorting test, and Aubert's test of setting an illuminated rod to the vertical. (These tests, which are sensitive to frontal-lobe damage are described in some detail in Chapter 18.) Thus, Parkinson's disease would seem to be associated with cognitive changes, particularly those changes normally found in patients with frontal-lobe or basal ganglia lesions. In a sense this association is not so surprising, because there are intimate relations between the functions of the basal ganglia and of the frontal cortex, and because there are dopamine projections into the frontal cortex that might be expected to degenerate in the same way that those of the basal ganglia degenerate. Having also tested patients before and after L-dopa treatment Bowen reports that test performance is not noticeably improved by drug therapy.

Animal Models of Parkinson's Disease. In recent years considerable attention has been given to developing animal models of Parkinson's disease. Although no animal models reliably produce all the symptoms of the human condition, many symptoms resembling those of parkinsonism appear in animals with experimentally reduced dopamine concentrations. Specifically, the injection of the **neurotoxin** 6-hydroxydopamine into the ventricles or into specific brain areas can greatly deplete dopamine by destroying the terminals of DA neurons. Animals so treated show many symptoms resembling those of Parkinson's disease, including akinesia, rigidity, abnormal postures, and compulsive fidgeting. Some of these symptoms can be relieved by administration of anticholinergic drugs or L-dopa, but the threshold for eliciting side effects is nearly the same as the threshold for relief of symptoms. The animal models provide insights into the neurological basics of the disease and will be useful in the development of new pharmacological treatments and assessment of their therapeutic value. Also, in some relatively new developments, a number of people have reported that embryonic brain cells transplanted into adult rats will grow and seemingly make normal connections. This has been demonstrated for dopamine and noradrenaline cells: if the animals are previously depleted of these neurotransmitters, the brain grafts will begin to restore brain concentrations of the neurotransmitters, and to restore as well some features of more normal behavior. Theoretically, these results offer an unexpected new approach to the treatment of Parkinson's disease.

DISORDERS OF CORTICAL FUNCTION

The account that we give here of disorders of cortical function is limited to two dysfunctions: hemiplegia and apraxia. In the first, there is clear impairment of movement, which can also be accompanied by various psychological and intellectual deficits such as aphasia and agraphia. Only the movement dysfunctions will be described here; those such as aphasia, agraphia, and alexia are described in detail in Chapter 21 and elsewhere. Unlike all the preceding disorders of movement, apraxia is a disorder in which posture and movement are "normal" but skill is lost. Rather than a disorder of movement per se, it is a disorder of the systems that command movement.

Hemiplegia

The characteristics of hemiplegia are a loss of voluntary movements on one side of the body, changes in postural tone, and changes in the status of various reflexes. Hemiplegia results from cortex damage that occurs contralateral to the motor symptoms. Once referred to as a pyramidal, as opposed to an extrapyramidal, disorder, it is now recognized that the complete range of symptoms is not produced by pyramidal tract damage only, and thus they must result from damage to extrapyramidal cortical fibers as well. In infancy damage may result from birth injury, epilepsy, or fever. Infant hemiplegia is usually discussed under the umbrella of cerebral palsy. In young adults hemiplegia is usually caused by rupture of a congenital aneurysm, an embolism, a tumor, or a head injury. The largest group are the middle-aged to elderly, and their hemiplegia is usually due to hemorrhage occurring as a consequence of high blood pressure and a degenerative condition of the blood vessels.

The commonest site of a vascular disease producing a hemiplegia is in the middle cerebral artery, which supplies the greater part of the main motor area (Figures 6–1 and 6–2). The motor pathways from the cortex run through the internal capsule, and so a small lesion in this area can also cause similar impairments to those that follow cortical damage.

Damage to the motor cortex first produces a loss of all voluntary movement on the contralateral side of the body and a paralysis of movement in which muscles are in an almost flaccid state and reflexes are absent. The course and rate of recovery in individuals is quite variable, as has been described by Twitchell (see also Chapter 25). Within a period of days to weeks the muscles become *spastic;* that is, there is an increase in muscle tone until the tone is greater than normal *(hypertonus)*. At the same time there is an increase in tendon (stretch) reflexes until they are more responsive than normal *(hyperreflexia)*. The spasticity is most pronounced in the antigravity muscles (the antigravity muscles are also called *physiological extensors* even though the action of some of them is to produce flexion; for example, flexors hold the arm up against gravity, and flexion, or curling down, of the toes helps maintain standing against gravity). Once spasticity is developed it affects posture in a definite, recognizable pattern. The arm is abducted and flexed at the elbow, with the fingers tightly curled into the palm (an exaggeration of the posture of the adducted arm typical of a person running or sitting). The extension of the leg is exaggerated, giving it a pillarlike character that also permits it to be used for walking. Inability to move the joints independently, however, requires that the leg be moved as a whole: steps with the affected leg are initiated by raising the pelvis on that side and bringing the leg through

with circumduction from the hip, keeping the knee extended. Spasticity is dependent on posture. When a person takes a quadrupedal position, the arms become spastic in an extended position. It is important to note here that the spasticity is still serving the function of antigravity support: spasticity is not a property of independent muscles, but occurs in groups of muscles in a purposeful way.

The spasticity of hemiplegia has a number of characteristics that distinguish it from the rigidity of extrapyramidal disorders such as Parkinson's disease. It is unidirectional as a result of being greater in antigravity muscles. The resistance of the spastic muscle to passive movement is greater with rapid compared with slow movements. Tendon reflexes are hyperactive. Finally, the limbs show a clasp response after initially resisting forced movement. For example, when an attempt is made to extend the forearm, resistance to the forced movement gradually increases and then quite suddenly melts away (as noted in Chapter 11, the name comes from the sudden snap of the blade of a jackknife, which when closed is stiff during the first half of the closure and then suddenly snaps shut). By contrast the rigidity of Parkinson's disease is bidirectional, is independent of the velocity of movement, is not accompanied by hyperactive reflexes, and clasp-knife responses do not occur. On the other hand, decerebrate rigidity is very much like spasticity and as such is a good animal analogue of spasticity, except that the clasp-knife response is absent.

The damage that produces hemiplegia also results in changes in a number of reflexes that are diagnostically important. Scratching the sole of the foot of a normal person with a dull object produces a downward flexion of all toes. In hemiplegia there is an upward flexion, especially of the big toe, and outward fanning of the toes (Figure 12–4). This response is caused by activation of physiological flexors and is often accompanied by flexion of the leg at the knee and hip. The response is called the *Babinski sign* or *extensor plantar response*. It has been referred to as the single most important sign in clinical neurology because it reliably indicates damage to cortical motor neurons (or as they are sometimes called, upper motor neurons). This sign is in fact only one of a family of flexion responses that occur after motor cortex or pyramidal tract damage. Two other reflexes are absent in hemiplegia. In normal people, stroking the abdominal muscles causes their retraction (the abdominal reflex) and stroking the inner thigh causes retraction of the testicles (cremasteric reflex): these reflexes are absent after cortical lesions.

Since the neocortex is the source of the pyramidal tract, which projects to the spinal cord through the pyramids, as well as being the sourse of motor fibers that project to other brain areas involved in movement, it can be asked: What contribution do each of the different motor projections make to the motor

disturbances of hemiplegia? Damage to the pyramidal tract produces loss of fine move ments of the distal limbs, loss of strength, and loss of movement speed. It also produces loss of reflexes: the Babinski sign is present and abdominal and cremasteric re lexes are absent (see Chapter 11 for a description of the contribution of the pyramidal tract to reaching movements made by monkeys). Damage to the nonpyramidal motor efferents is thus responsible for the spasticity and the exaggerated stretch reflexes. The distinction between the contributions of the two efferent systems is important because they are partly separate as they traverse the brain and so central damage can be localized to some extent by the degree to which one or other group of symptoms is present.

Hemiplegia also involves abnormalities in muscles other than the limbs. There is difficulty in deviating the eyes and rotating the head opposite to the side of the lesion, weakness of voluntary movements of the lower face (such as in retracting the lips and pursing them), and weakness in the jaw and tongue

FIGURE 12–4. The Babinski sign. Top: The normal adult response to stimulation of the lateral planar surface of the foot. Bottom: The normal infant and abnormal adult response. (After Gardner, 1968.)

on the opposite side. Emotional expressions (smiling, crying) are usually not affected. Because muscles of the head are under greater bilateral control than those of the limbs, most of these affected movements show relatively rapid recovery.

There is a great deal of variation in the recovery that occurs after hemiplegia, but treatment may have one or a combination of objectives. The person may be trained to use the unaffected side, to use the affected side as much as spasticity and residual abilities allow, or to make movements that lessen spasticity so that voluntary movements can in turn be performed as much as is possible. The last procedure is described in detail by Bobath. Briefly, it is based on the fact that the strength of spasticity is related to posture. For example, rotation of the body between the shoulder and pelvis lessens both flexor and extensor spasticity, whereas if the arm is extended and the head turned toward the arm, flexion spasticity is lessened. Treatment of hemiplegia of course is constrained by accompanying intellectual impairments, which differ depending on the size of the lesion or the hemisphere in which it is located.

Apraxia

Steinthal coined the term apraxia in 1871, but the symptoms had first been described some five years earlier by Hughlings-Jackson. He noted that some aphasic patients were totally unable to perform voluntary movements, such as protruding the tongue, even though there was no evidence of weakness in the muscles involved and the tongue could be protruded as part of licking the lips after drinking. Although this symptom was subsequently noted by several authors, it was Leipmann who began the first detailed analysis of apraxic symptoms. In 1900 he reported the case of an aphasic man who was unable to carry out hand movements when asked to do so. Curiously, he could follow directions if the required movement was a whole body movement, such as sitting down, and could make *spontaneous* hand movements. In the ensuing years Leipmann studied many patients with this unusual movement problem, and in 1920 he proposed his now classic theory of apraxia of which two important points are: (1) apraxia results from lesions of the left hemisphere or of the corpus callosum; (2) there are several different types of apraxia, each most likely resulting from damage to a specific locus in the left hemisphere.

Strictly defined, *apraxia* means no action (the Greek *praxis* means action). The term apraxia, however, is hardly ever used in this strict sense; today it is used to describe all sorts of missing or inappropriate actions that cannot be clearly attributed to paralysis, paresis, or other more primary motor deficits on the one hand, or to lack of comprehension, motivation, etc., on the other.

Defining Apraxia. Until recently discussion of apraxia was invariably of specific case histories rather than of carefully designed scientific studies. The result was conflicting interpretations of the behaviors described. Consider the following case as an example.

A woman with a biparietal lesion had worked for years as a fish-filleter. With the development of her symptoms, she began to experience difficulty in carrying on with her job. She did not seem to know what to do with her knife. She would stick the point in the head of a fish, start the first stroke and then come to a stop. In her own mind she knew how to fillet fish, but yet she could not execute the maneuver. The foreman accused her of being drunk and sent her home for mutilating fish.

This same patient also showed another unusual phenomenon which might possibly be apraxic in nature. She could never finish an undertaking. She would begin a job, drop it, start another, abandon that one, and within a short while would have four or five uncompleted tasks on her hands. This would cause her to do such inappropriate actions as putting the sugar bowl in the refrigerator, and the coffee pot inside the oven. (Critchley, 1966, pp. 158–159)

Although we can agree with Critchley that the filleter had a motor problem that cannot be readily attributed to paralysis or paresis, we could argue that she had forgotten how to fillet fish, that she had an agnosia for fish, knives, etc., that she had attention problems, that she was absentminded, and so on. A more systematic analysis of her behavior is obviously required if we are to understand her deficit.

The several standard clinical tests often used to assess apraxia have similar weaknesses. For example, a patient may be asked to demonstrate the use of a particular object in its absence, e.g., to comb the hair or to hammer a nail. An apraxic person's response may be to do nothing or else to use a part of the body as if it were the implement—to stroke a finger through the hair as if it were a comb, or to hit the table with a fist as though it were a hammer. A normal person would pretend to be holding the comb or hammer. Another test of apraxia might be to ask a person to perform such symbolic movements as saluting or waving good-bye; the person might remain still or respond by making an unrecognizable movement. Although these tests are useful for "on the spot" assessments of apraxia, they do not permit objective quantification or more penetrating analysis.

Clinical description presents a further difficulty, namely that classifications of apraxia tend to be somewhat arbitrary. Also, new types of apraxias tend to proliferate not because actual new symptoms are discovered but because either new questions are put to the patients or new ways of assessing the responses are developed. As a result there are such terms as ideational apraxia, ideomotor apraxia, limb kinetic apraxia, etc., the definitions of which are often disputed. Finally, slight variations in lesion location might often be used as justification that one apraxia differs from another. Rather than pursue this type of analysis, let us turn to a different approach.

Recently a number of laboratories have begun to analyze apraxias under fairly rigorous experimental conditions. The objectives of these experiments are to (1) use a standard test, (2) quantify the response, (3) define the range of motor responses that are impaired, and (4) categorize those responses that are unimpaired. The goal of this research is to eventually specify what function each area of the cortex has in generating particular movements.

In any study of apraxia it is necessary to distinguish between deficits that result from direct damage to the motor system and those that result from damage to other areas that "command" it. With respect to finger, hand, and arm movements it can be noted whether the deficit is unilateral. (Remember, one hemisphere controls the contralateral limb; thus, a deficit in only the contralateral limb can be most parsimoniously attributed to motor system damage.) Because other movements (face, head, body) are controlled bilaterally, a deficit in their control is most likely to be apraxic. Most studies of apraxia also include tests for paralysis and paresis; clearly, it is pointless to try to determine whether a paralyzed limb is under voluntary control.

Table 12–3 summarizes two groups of tests of motor behaviors. The tests listed in part A of the table—hand strength, finger-tapping speed, etc.—are ones on which people with cortical damage usually show no impairment or only unilateral impairment. Therefore, these tests are not particularly useful for diagnosing apraxia, although they are good for

TABLE 12–3

Effects of right- or left-hemisphere lesions on various motor behaviors

A. Tests in which there is no bilateral impairment[a]	Basic reference
1. Hand strength	Kimura, 1977
2. Finger-tapping speed	Carmon, 1971
3. Steadiness in static position	Haaland et al., 1977
4. Unidirectional moving steadiness	Haaland et al., 1977
5. Repetitive screw rotation	Kimura, 1980
6. Imitation of single hand posture	Kimura and Archibald, 1974
7. Imitation of single oral movements	Mateer and Kimura, 1977
8. Imitation of single facial movements	Kolb and Milner, 1981

B. Tests in which there is bilateral impairment	Basic reference
1. Demonstration of object use	de Renzi et al., 1968
2. Rapid directed arm movements	Wyke, 1967, 1968
3. Finger tapping—two keys	Wyke, 1967
4. Finger tapping—rhythms	Luria, 1973
5. Stylus maze	Haaland et al., 1977
6. Pegboard	Haaland et al., 1977
7. Pursuit rotor	Heilman et al., 1975
8. Manual sequence box	Kimura, 1977
9. Imitation of multiple oral movements	Mateer and Kimura, 1977
10. Imitation of multiple facial movements	Kolb and Milner, 1981
11. Oral movements on request	Poeck and Kerschensteiner, 1975
12. Imitation of meaningful single oral movements (e.g., kiss, whistle)	de Renzi et al., 1966

[a]Note that in the absence of damage to the motor cortex there may be no impairment at all on these tests.

assessing paralysis or paresis; that is, they are good control tests for assessing the ability to make movements.

Listed in part B of Table 12–3 are tests on which either no impairment or bilateral impairment has been demonstrated. These, then, are tests of apraxia; they are assumed to require higher-level control for their execution. Figures 12–5 and 12–6 show examples of two of these tests. In the Kimura box test (Figure 12–5) the person is asked to either push the button, pull the lever, or depress the bar as a test of paresis, and then is asked to make the responses in sequence. The manipulanda are connected to timers and counters that record accuracy and speed. In the test in Figure 12–6, a test for paresis, the person is asked to make any one of the individual movements. If the person is able to make the individual movements, he or she is then asked to watch and repeat each of the sequences of movement. The person's response is scored for the accuracy of each movement, for the number of correct movements, and for the sequence of response.

It is clear that these tests are very objective; the responses can be quantified, and different laboratories can use the tests with little difficulty. Furthermore, the tests can be designed to analyze different contributions to motor con-

FIGURE 12–5. Kimura box test. Subjects are required to learn the movement series of (1) pushing the top button with the index finger, (2) pulling the handle as shown, and (3) pressing down on the bar with the thumb. Apraxic subjects are impaired at this task, and they may be unable to learn it at all, even with extended practice.

trol, as a comparison of the tasks shown in Figures 12–5 and 12–6 illustrates. The box test primarily requires movement of the distal musculature of the hand and fingers in a fairly discrete spatial locus. The arm movement test, on the other hand, requires movements of both the distal and proximal musculature over a large spatial area. In view of what is known about the differential input of the frontal and parietal cortex in the control of proximal and distal musculature, it is likely that tests of these kinds will be differentially affected by lesions to different regions of the cortex. This likelihood, however, remains to be studied.

Asymmetry of Movement Control. One of the most important proposals in Leipmann's theory of apraxia was that the left hemisphere

plays a special role not shared by the right hemisphere in the control of movement. This feature of apraxia is reflected in all the studies cited in part B of Table 12–3. In each study a bilateral impairment was produced by a left hemisphere lesion.

Another line of evidence supporting Leipmann's left hemisphere proposal comes from a study by Milner and her colleagues. They taught patients a complex series of arm movements prior to intracarotid sodium Amytal injections. After the injections the patients were required to perform the movements. Only injections into the speaking hemisphere disrupted the movements, even though the movements were to be performed with the ipsilateral limb (controlled by the contralateral motor cortex that had not received an injection). Thus, the results of sodium Amytal injections support the results of lesion studies in confirming a special role for the left hemisphere in the control of movement.

Confronted with the left hemisphere's special control of many types of movement the reader will immediately be moved to ask whether the right hemisphere might not also control certain types of movements. In fact, there is a group of movements that can be selectively disrupted by right hemisphere lesions. These are used in tests in which a variety of components are to be assembled to form an object. Such tasks include (1) assembling pieces of a jigsaw puzzle together to form a picture; (2) drawing a clock face, map, etc.; (3) copying a design with sticks of various lengths; (4) building bridges, towers, etc., with blocks; and (5) copying designs with different colored blocks. Deficits on such tests are sometimes called constructional apraxias.

What is special about these constructional tasks? All of them require that objects be ordered in extrapersonal space. Dealing with the spatial relations of objects is believed to be a function of the right hemisphere, especially of

FIGURE 12–6. Serial arm movements and copying test. Subjects are asked to copy each of the series (1–6) as accurately as they can. Subjects with left posterior lesions including of tertiary parietal cortex are especially impaired.

the right parietal cortex. Although left parietal lesions can also produce some similar deficits, their occurrence may have a different cause: left hemisphere deficits may result from the person's inability to adjust the parts of his or her own body, rather than the inability to adjust the position of an external object. This theoretically interesting proposition has yet to be clearly tested experimentally.

Are Aphasia and Apraxia Correlated? Since many apraxias stem from left hemisphere lesions, are they secondary to deficits in comprehension? Although aphasia frequently accompanies apraxia, three lines of evidence indicate that the symptoms can be dissociated. First, de Renzi gave patients tests of aphasia and apraxia; the test scores were poorly correlated. Second, patients with surgical excisions outside the speech zones may have no detectable dysphasias but may be dyspraxic, especially when tested on objective tests of movement-copying skills. Third, whereas surgical removal of speech areas may produce severe aphasia, the accompanying apraxia is surprisingly mild; cortical damage does not appear to be sufficient to produce dense apraxia, although it can be enough to produce dense aphasia.

Neuroanatomical Basis of Apraxia. Classical neurological theory concerning the basis of apraxia is derived from a model originally proposed by Leipmann and subsequently popularized by Geschwind. Briefly, Leipmann proposed that the left parietal cortex (specifically around area 40) is the critical region for control of complex movement. This control would be mediated via the left frontal lobe and area 4 in control of the right side of the body. Disruption anywhere along this route in the left hemisphere would produce apraxia of the right limbs. Control over the limbs of the left

side was proposed to be mediated through a series of corticocortical connections running from the left parietal cortex to the left frontal cortex and finally to the right frontal cortex via the corpus callosum. This model is often cited in psychology and neurology texts, but it has several serious shortcomings, each of which we shall consider in some detail.

First, since there are clearly separable "motor systems," each with unique anatomical input, models and studies of apraxia should consider separately different types of movements. Thus, assessment of apraxic syndromes should carefully consider the control of distal (finger, toe, and face) movements, hand and limb movements, and whole body movements. The Leipmann-Geschwind model does not consider different movement types separately, nor have most studies of apraxic behaviors. It is possible that subtypes of apraxia can be determined on the basis of the system(s) disrupted. For example, Kolb and Milner compared the performance of patients with unilateral cortical excisions at copying of both arm and facial movement sequences and did indeed find evidence of differential input of the frontal and the parietal cortex to the control of movement. Whereas left parietal lobe lesions significantly disrupted the copying of arm movement sequences, these lesions had no significant effect on the copying of facial movement sequences. In contrast, left frontal-lobe lesions had relatively little effect on the copying of arm movement sequences but produced larger impairment in the copying of facial movement sequences. Unfortunately, Kolb and Milner did not try to separate the control of limb, hand, and finger movements in their study. Nonetheless, their results show that it is possible to dissociate the relative contribution of different cortical areas to the control of different types of movements. A similar dissociation has also been made by Kimura in her study of stroke patients. An important additional finding by Kimura, however, was that the complexity of the movement is important. She found that patients with either left anterior or left posterior lesions were inferior to those with equivalent right hemisphere damage at tasks requiring the reproduction of a series of multiple oral or manual sequences. However, on a test requiring the reproduction of single movements the only group significantly impaired was the left anterior group, whereas on single hand postures the only group impaired was the left posterior group.

Second, since the posterior parietal and prefrontal cortex have no direct projections onto the spinal motor neurons, theories emphasizing their importance in apraxia must attempt to specify just how it is that these regions might influence movement. Indeed, although it is widely assumed that the posterior parietal and prefrontal cortexes are the primary cortical regions for the production of apraxia, patients with circumscribed cortical excisions do not typically demonstrate chronic abnormalities on standard clinical tests of apraxia and, compared with stroke patients, have relatively minor impairments on tests of movement copying; even massive removals of the left hemisphere produce rather small movement-copying deficits when compared with the performance of persons with naturally occurring lesions. The implications of this cannot be underestimated: the direct contribution of the prefrontal and the parietal cortex (and the connections between them) to praxis must be less than is generally implied from clinico-anatomical studies. The failure to demonstrate unequivocal apraxia-like disorders in nonhuman species with cortical ablations may therefore not reflect a species difference as is commonly presumed, but rather the severity of movement impairment may actually be equivalent in humans and nonhumans with surgical removals of the cortex.

Third, the Leipmann-Geschwind model does not recognize the likely role of the basal ganglia and thalamus in apractic syndromes. These regions provide major access routes for the cortex to influence motor output. The fact that cortical excisions have far lesser effects on praxis than do strokes, which presumably affect both the cortex and the basal ganglia and/or the thalamus, implies that damage to subcortical structures may be essential in order to produce severe clinical apraxia.

Fourth, since the limbs and face, but not the hands, are connected via the corpus callosum, it should be determined whether or not the extent of bilateral apraxia is similar in tests of hand, finger, face, and limb movements. Although the importance of transcallosal connections has been emphasized in accounts of apractic syndromes, emphasis usually has been placed on the inability of the hand ipsilateral to the speaking hemisphere to perform movements to verbal command. Few attempts have been made to carefully describe the abilities of the limbs, fingers, and face to perform particular movements. In one attempt to consider this problem Milner and Kolb studied the ability of four patients, in whom the corpus callosum had been severed as a treatment for epilepsy, to copy meaningless sequences of arm or facial movements with either the left or the right hand. The data showed that the subjects were very badly impaired at copying these movements, even when compared with patients with left parietal lesions. Perhaps most surprisingly, in the arm movements the patients were equally impaired with either hand, a result that would not be predicted from previous clinicoanatomical studies, and certainly not by the Leipmann-Geschwind model. Unfortunately, the movement sequences in the Kolb and Milner study confounded both limb and finger movements, although most of the errors of movement appeared to be in the positioning of the arms, rather than the fingers. Since the transcallosal connections of the fingers and arms are different, this impression should be followed up with additional studies.

In sum, although the Leipmann model of the neuroanatomical basis of apraxia has been a useful one, it does not account for the data and must be reevaluated in the light of what is now known about the organization of the intact and dysfunctioning motor systems.

REFERENCES

Albuquerque, E. X., J. E. Rash, R. F. Mayer, and J. R. Satterfield. An electrophysiological and morphological study of the neuromuscular junction in patients with myasthenia gravis. *Experimental Neurology* 51:536–563, 1976.

Baker, A. B., and L. H. Baker. *Clinical Neurology.* Cambridge: Harper & Row, 1982.

Bobath, B. *Adult Hemiplegia: Evaluation and Treatment.* London: Heinemann Medical Books, 1970.

Bremer, F. Cerveau isolé et physiologie du sommeil. *Comptes Rendus de la Société de Biologie* 118:1235–1242, 1935.

Brinkman, J., and H. G. J. M. Kuypers. Cerebral control of contralateral and ipsilateral arm, hand and finger movements in the split-brain rhesus monkey. *Brain* 96:653–674, 1973.

Carmon, A. Sequenced motor performance in patients with unilateral cerebral lesions. *Neuropsychologia* 9:445–449, 1971.

Changeux, J.-P., M. Kasai, and C.-Y. Lee. The use of a snake venom toxin to characterize the cholinergic receptor protein. *Proceedings of the National Academy of Sciences* 67:1241–1247, 1970.

Chase, T. N., N. S. Wexler, and A. Barbeau, eds. *Huntington's Disease. Advances in Neurology,* vol. 23. New York: Raven Press, 1979.

Crithley, M. *The Parietal Lobes.* New York: Hafner, 1965.

Cruickshank, W. M. *Cerebral Palsy.* Syracuse, N.Y.: Syracuse University Press, 1976.

Dement, W., and N. Kleitman. Cyclic variations in EEG during sleep and their relation to eye movements, body motility and dreaming. *Electroencephalography and Clinical Neurophysiology* 9:673–690, 1957.

Denhoff, E. Medical aspects. In W. M. Cruickshank, ed., *Cerebral Palsy.* Syracuse, New York: Syracuse University Press, 1976.

Economo, C. von. *Encephalitis Lethargica: Its Sequence and Treatment.* Oxford: Oxford University Press, 1931.

Everett, N. B. *Functional Neuroanatomy.* Philadelphia: Lea and Febiger, 1965.

Fambrough, D. M., D. B. Drachman, and S. Satyamurti. Neuromuscular junction in myasthenia gravis: Decreased acetylcholine receptors. *Science* 182:293–295, 1973.

Friedhoff, A. J., and T. N. Chase, eds. *Gilles de la Tourette Syndrome. Advances in Neurology,* vol. 35. New York: Raven Press, 1982.

Gardner, H. *Fundamentals of Neurology.* Philadelphia: Saunders, 1968.

Geschwind, N. The apraxias: Neural mechanisms of disorders of learned movement. *American Scientist* 63:188–195, 1975.

Gilles de la Tourette, G. Étude sur un affection, nerveuse charactérisée pale l'ineoordination motrice accompanagnée de'écholalie et de copralalie (Jumping, Latah, Myriachit). *Archives of Neurology* 9:19–42, 158–200, 1885.

Haaland, K. Y., C. S. Cleeland, and D. Carr. Motor performance after unilateral damage in patients with tumor. *Archives of Neurology* 34:556–559, 1977.

Haaxma, R., and H. G. J. M. Kuypers. Intrahemispheric cortical connections and visual guidance of hand and finger movements in the rhesus monkey. *Brain* 98:239–260, 1975.

Hammond, W. A. *A Treatise of the Diseases of the Nervous System.* New York: Apple-Century-Crofts, 1871.

Hartmann, E. *The Biology of Dreaming.* Springfield, Ill.: Charles C Thomas, 1967.

Heilman, D. M., H. D. Schwartz, and N. Geschwind. Defective motor learning in ideomotor apraxia. *Neurology* 25:1018–1020, 1975.

Hornykiewicz, O. Parkinson's disease. In T. J. Crow, ed., *Disorders of Neurohumoural Transmission.* New York: Academic, 1982.

Huntington, G. On chorea. *Medical Surgical Reporter* 26:317–321, 1872.

Kimura, D. Acquisition of a motor skill after left-hemisphere damage. *Brain* 100:527–542, 1977.

Kimura, D. Left-hemisphere control of oral and brachial movements and their relation to communication. *Philosophical Transactions of the Royal Society of London* B298:135–149, 1982.

Kimura, D. The neural basis of language and gesture. In H. Avakina-Whitaker and H. A. Whitaker, eds., *Studies in Neurolinguistics.* New York: Academic, 1976.

Kimura, D. Neuromotor mechanisms in the evolution of human communication. In H. D. Steklis and M. J. Raleigh, eds., *Neurobiology of Social Communication in Primates: An Evolutionary Perspective.* New York: Academic, 1980.

Kimura, D., and Y. Archibald. Motor functions of the left hemisphere. *Brain* 97:337–350, 1974.

Kolb, B., and B. Milner. Performance of complex arm and facial movements after focal brain lesions. *Neuropsychologia* 19:491–503, 1981.

Leipmann, H. Die linke Hemisphäre und das Handeln. In *Drei Aufsätze aus dem Apraxiegebiet.* Berlin: Springer, 1908.

Little, W. J. *Deformities of the Human Frame.* London: Longmans, 1853.

Luria, A. R. *The Working Brain.* New York: Penguin, 1973.

Martin, J. P. *The Basal Ganglia and Posture.* London: Ritman Medical Publishing, 1967.

Martin, M. P. Hemichorea resulting from a local lesion of the brain (Syndrome of the Body of Luys). *Brain* 50:637, 1927.

Mateer, C., and D. Kimura. Impairment of nonverbal oral movements in apraxia. *Brain and Language* 4:262–276, 1977.

McLennan, J. E., K. Nakano, H. R. Tyler, and R. S. Schwab. Micrographia in Parkinson's disease. *Journal of Neurological Science* 15:141–152, 1972.

Milner, B. Hemispheric asymmetry in the control of gesture sequences. *Proceedings of XXI International Congress of Psychology* Paris, 1976, 149.

Moruzzi, G., and H. W. Magoun. Brain stem reticular formation and activation of the EEG. *ELectroencephalography and Clinical Neurophysiology* 1:455–473, 1949.

Nathan, P., and M. Smith. Effects of two unilateral cordotomies on the mobility of the lower limbs. *Brain* 96:471–494, 1973.

Nauta, W. J. H. Hypothalamic regulation of sleep in rats: An experimental study. *Journal of Neurophysiology* 9:285–316, 1946.

Parkinson, J. Essay on the shaking palsy. Reprinted in M. Critchley, ed., *James Parkinson.* London: Macmillan, 1955.

Patrick, J., and J. Lindstrom. Autoimmune response to acetylcholine receptor. *Science* 180:871–872, 1973.

Poeck, K., and M. Kerschensteiner. Analysis of the sequential motor events in oral apraxia. In K. J. Zülch, O. Creutzfeldt, and B. C. Galbraith, eds., *Cerebral Localization.* Berlin: Springer-Verlag, 1975.

Pompeiano, O. Mechanisms of sensorimotor integration during sleep. In E. Stellar and L. Sprague, eds., *Progress in Physiological Psychology,* vol. 3. New York: Academic, 1970.

Rechtschaffen, A., and W. Dement. Studies on the relation of narcolepsy, cataplexy, and sleep with low voltage random EEG activity. *Research Publications: Association for Research in Nervous and Mental Disease,* XLV: 488–498, 1967.

Rechtschaffen, A., and L. J. Monroe. Laboratory studies of insomnia. In A. Kales, ed., *Sleep: Physiology and Pathology.* Philadelphia and Toronto: Lippincott, 1969.

Renzi, E. de, A. Pieczuro, and L. A. Vignolo. Ideational apraxia: A quantitative study. *Neuropsychologia* 6:41–52, 1968.

Renzi, E. de, A. Pieczuro, and L. A. Vignolo. Oral apraxia and aphasia. *Cortex* 2:50–73, 1966.

Sacks, O. *Awakenings.* New York: Doubleday, 1973.

Twitchell, T. E. The restoration of motor function following hemiplegia in man. *Brain* 74:443–480, 1951.

Vessie, P. R. On the transmission of Huntington's chorea for 300 years—the Bures family group. *Journal of Nervous and Mental Disorders* 76:533–565, 1932.

Vogt, C. Sur l'état marlové du striatum. *Journal of Psychiatry and Neurology* 31:256, 1924–25.

Walton, J. N. *Brain's Diseases of the Nervous System.* New York and Toronto: Oxford University Press, 1977.

Weaver, L. A., and G. W. Brooks. The effects of drug-induced Parkinsonism on the psychomotor performance of chronic schizophrenics. *Journal of Nervous and Mental Diseases* 133:148–154, 1961.

Webb, W. B. *Sleep the Gentle Tyrant.* Englewood Cliffs, N.J.: Prentice-Hall, 1975.

Wilson, S. A. K. Progressive lenticular degeneration: A familial nervous disease associated with cirrhosis of the liver. *Brain* 34:295, 1912.

Wyke, M. The effect of brain lesions in the performance of an arm-hand precision task. *Neuropsychologia* 6:125–134, 1968.

Wyke, M. Effect of brain lesions on the rapidity of arm movement. *Neurology* 17:1113–1120, 1967.

PART FOUR

GENERAL PRINCIPLES OF HUMAN NEUROPSYCHOLOGY

This section delivers the core of neuropsychology. Chapter 13 gives the history of neuropsychology, describing how the major hypotheses of brain function were developed to shape current thinking and research on its function. Chapters 14 and 15 describe the fascinating division of function, almost unique to humans and certainly most elaborated in them, between the two cerebral hemispheres. This division has been not only an object of study in its own right but has also provided a key that opens new insights into cortical function. Chapters 16, 17, and 18 describe the functions of the lobes. Of course, they do not work in isolation and so Chapter 19 describes their functional interrelations.

13

THE DEVELOPMENT OF NEUROPSYCHOLOGY

The term neuropsychology was apparently first alluded to by D. O. Hebb, in a subtitle to his 1949 book *The Organization of Behavior: A Neuropsychological Theory*. Although neither defined nor used in the text itself, the term was probably intended to represent a study that combined the neurologist's and physiological psychologist's common interests in brain function. By 1957 the term had become a recognized designation for a subfield of the neurosciences, since Heinrich Klüver, in the preface to *Behavior Mechanisms in Monkeys,* suggested that the book would be of interest to neuropsychologists and others. (Klüver had not used the term in the 1933 preface to the same book.) The term was given wide publicity when it appeared in 1960 in the title of a collection of K. S. Lashley's writings—*The Neuropsychology of Lashley*—most of which were rat and monkey studies. But again neuropsychology was not used or defined in the text.

The term, then, is of relatively recent origin. We define neuropsychology as the study of the relation between brain function and behavior. Although the study draws information from many disciplines—e.g., anatomy, biology, biophysics, ethology, pharmacology, physiology, physiological psychology, and philosophy—its central focus is the development of a science of human behavior based on the function of the human brain.

Although neuropsychology was developed only recently (as was much of science itself), its contemporary definition is strongly influenced by two traditional foci for experimental and theoretical investigations in brain research: the *brain hypothesis,* the idea that the brain is the source of behavior; and the *neuron hypothesis,* the idea that the unit of brain structure and function is the neuron. In this chapter the development of these two ideas is traced, after which the more recent advances leading to the modern science of neuropsychology are described. It will be seen that although the science is new, its major ideas are not. A consensus that these were important ideas was not easily arrived at, however. For much of our past we humans were groping in the dark for concepts that would help to describe the brain's function. From time to time an idea was serendipitously formulated, was sometimes grasped, sometimes examined, and then was discarded only to be later rediscovered. Today we are still finding, examining, and reexamining ideas. Through this history we hope to encourage the reader to become a participant and to see the science not as a dogma but as a dialogue about some of the ideas that have emerged.

THE BRAIN HYPOTHESIS

The Brain Versus the Heart

Since earliest times humans have believed that their behavior is controlled by a soul, spirit, or rational system. We have also held a variety of views about its nature and location; among the earliest that survive in record were those of Alcmaeon of Croton (ca. 500 B.C.) and Empedocles (ca. 490–430 B.C.). Alcmaeon located mental processes in the brain, and so subscribed to what is now called the brain hypothesis; Empedocles located mental processes in the heart, and so subscribed to what could be called the cardiac hypothesis.

The relative merits of those two hypotheses were debated for the next 2000 years, evidence and logic being presented in support of each. For example, Plato (420–347 B.C.) developed the concept of a tripartite soul and placed its rational part in the brain because that was the part of the body closest to the heavens. Aristotle (384–322 B.C.) had a good knowledge of brain structure and realized that, of all animals, humans have the largest brain relative to body size. Nevertheless, he decided that because the heart was warm and active it was the source of mental processes; the brain, because it was cool and inert, served as a radiator to cool the blood. He explained away the large size of the brain as evidence of a relation to intelligence by stating that humans' blood is richer and hotter than other animals' and so requires a larger cooling

system. Physicians such as Hippocrates (430–379 B.C.) and Galen (A.D. 129–199) described some aspects of brain anatomy and argued strongly for the brain hypothesis. They were no doubt influenced by their clinical experience. For example, before becoming the leading physician in Rome, Galen had spent five years as a surgeon to gladiators and was well aware of the behavioral consequences of brain damage. He went to great pains to refute Aristotle on logical grounds, for example, by pointing out that the nerves from the sense organs go to the brain, not to the heart. He also did experiments to compare the effects of pressure on the heart and brain. He noted that light pressure on the brain caused cessation of movement and even death, whereas pressure on the heart caused pain but did not arrest voluntary behavior.

Although the cardiac hypothesis is no longer a serious scientific position, it left its mark on our language. In literature as in everyday speech, matters of emotion are frequently referred to the heart: love is symbolized by an arrow piercing the heart; a person distressed by unrequited love is said to be heartbroken; an unenthusiastic person is said to be not putting his or her heart into it; an angry person is said to have boiling blood. Thus, it was not initially obvious what organ controlled behavior, and elegant arguments for the brain hypothesis developed only gradually and then only as a result of logical argument, careful observation, and experimentation.

Localization of Function: Early Developments

Of course, simply knowing that the brain controls behavior is not enough: formulation of a complete hypothesis required knowledge of *how* it controls behavior. Much of the research directed to this end has addressed the issue of **localization of function:** the notion that given behaviors are controlled by given areas of the brain. Theories of localization of function are as old as theories about nervous system involvement in mental processes. Today, localization of function is generally used to mean that functions are distributed among different segments of the neocortex: visual perception in the occipital lobe, auditory perception in the temporal lobe, etc. This idea took some time to develop: the first problem to be solved was whether mental processes were the product of the brain or mind; the second problem was locating the control of different aspects of behavior within the brain.

Modern thinking about the mind began with René Descartes (1596–1650). Descartes replaced the Platonic concept of the tripartite soul with that of a unitary mind that is the reasoning or rational soul. Being nonmaterial and having no spatial extent, the mind is fundamentally different from the body. The body is a machine that is material and thus clearly has spatial extent; it responds reflexively to sensory changes by action of the brain. Nonhuman animals have only bodies and no rational minds; thus, their behavior can be explained, according to Descartes, as purely mechanical action. However, any account of human behavior requires that the functions of both mind and body be considered. In proposing that the mind and body are separate but can interact, Descartes originated the *mind-body problem,* namely: What is the relation between the mind and the body, or, more simply, how do they interact? Some *dualists* (as those holding mind and body to be separate are called) have argued that the two causally interact, but they have never convincingly explained how. Other dualists have avoided this problem by reasoning either that the two function in parallel without interacting or that the body can affect the mind but the mind cannot affect the body. Thus, both dualist positions allow for theorizing about behavior without considering mind. Those philosophers called *monists* avoid the mind-body problem by postulating that the mind and body are both the same and either are both material or both nonmaterial. Clearly, the latter monist position might be an embarrassing one for a neuroscientist.

The belief, widely held through Descartes' influence, that the mind was an indivisible substance forced two conclusions, also widely held. First, since the mind was indivisible, theories that subdivided brain function could not be correct. (Some of the history of this debate will be traced in subsequent pages.) Second, since mind existed apart from the body, the functions of mind would require separate consideration; complete understanding of the body and how it worked would not bring complete understanding of human behavior. During the 19th century physiologists would often describe the physiology of some newly discovered reflex system and then speculate as to how mind worked through it. (Even today some physiologists devote a portion of their writing to the problem of mind—for example, Eccles, *The Neurophysiology Basis of Mind: The Principles of Neurophysiology,* 1956.) Many modern neuroscientists assert that the body portion of the mind-body polarity is their proper domain of study and ignore the mind or dismiss it by saying that, although it may very well exist, it cannot be studied by using recording or stimulating electrodes. Others, more skeptical, refer to the mind as the bogey in the brain, the ghost in the machine, or, as some psychologists have referred to it, the little green man in the head. They argue, as does the philosopher Gilbert Ryle, that mind is simply a term for the brain and its activities and not a separate entity, just as city is a term for a collection of buildings and people and not a separate thing. Still others, equating mind with the soul, keep their views on the mind private and make no pretense that once everything about neural systems is known the mind-body problem will be solved.

Prior to Descartes there had been a persistent belief, held by Galen and many subsequent writers, that mind was located in the fluid of the ventricles rather than in the matter of the brain. This belief was reinforced in the 10th century when it came to be thought that the muscles were moved by being filled with a fluid that traversed the nerve centers. Ventricular fluid was the prime candidate for being that fluid. In fact, some of the theories of how fluid in different ventricular cavities controlled different aspects of behavior are quite elegant. The cogent arguments of Andreas Vesalius (1514–1564) finally discredited the ventricular theories. Vesalius dissected brains and noted that the relative size of the ventricles in animals and humans is the same. He concluded that since rational man distinguished himself by having the largest brain, it is the brain and not the ventricles that mediate mental processes. Descartes, however, was the first to locate mental processes precisely within brain tissue. He located the mind in the pineal body, on the logic, first, that this body is the only structure in the nervous system not composed of two bilaterally symmetrical halves, and, second, that it is located in proximity to the ventricles. (The rest of the brain was seen not as functioning neural tissue but as the cortex, or bark, that protected the important internal mechanisms.) Thus, by thinking of the mind as unified and located precisely in a single structure, Descartes simultaneously initiated the debate on localization of function and enunciated the negative position.

Localization of Function: The Phrenologists

The argument *for* localization of function began with the phrenological theory of Franz Josef Gall (1758–1828) and Johann Casper Spurzheim (1776–1832). Their theory, in the broad lines of its arguments, is of such scope and brilliance that it could not be ignored, but its details are so improbable that it was immediately rejected by most of their contemporaries. Their theory of localization of function stunningly resembles modern theories; had their methodology been a little different they could have anticipated much of modern neuropsychology.

Gall and Spurzheim, both anatomists, made a number of important discoveries in neuroanatomy that alone would have given them a place in history. They realized that the cortex is composed of functioning cells that are connected with the subcortical structures. They described the crossing of the pyramids and recognized that the spinal cord is divided into white and gray matter. They also recognized that the two symmetrical halves of the brain are connected by commissures. But as soon as they went beyond anatomy and attempted to ascribe functions to different parts of the brain, everything they did was conceptually brilliant but hopelessly in error.

From observations made in early youth Gall believed that students with good memories had large, protruding eyes. He thought it possible that a well-developed memory area of the brain located behind the eyes could cause them to protrude. From this beginning, Gall and Spurzheim undertook to examine the external features of the skull and to correlate its bumps and depressions with what they thought to be important aspects of behavior. A bump on the skull indicated a well-developed underlying cortical gyrus and therefore a greater faculty for a particular behavior; a depression in the same area indicated an underdeveloped gyrus and a concomitantly reduced capacity. Thus, a person who had a high degree of what they called **amativeness** had a large bump in the area shown in Figure 13–1, whereas a person who had a low score on this trait had a depression in this same area. Their behavioral traits consisted of a long list of faculties such as wit, inquiry, and faith. Each of these faculties, which they had devised or had borrowed from English or Scottish psychology, they assigned to a particular portion of the skull or by inference to the underlying portion of the brain. Figure 13–2 shows the resulting map. Spurzheim called the study of the rela-

A

B

FIGURE 13–1. According to phrenologists, depressions (A) and bumps (B) on the skull indicate the size of the underlying area of brain, and when correlated with personality traits, indicate the part of the brain controlling the trait. Gall, examining a patient (who because of her behavior became known as "Gall's Passionate Widow"), found a bump at the back of her neck that he thought located the center for amativeness in the cerebellum. Flourens refuted this hypothesis by removing the cerebellum from a dog to show that the cerebellum was involved in coordinating movement. As phrenology was popularized, bumps and depressions were indicated on the head in places that were no longer adjacent to the brain—as occurred with amativeness, as shown in this figure. (From C. H. Olin, *Phrenology*. Philadelphia: Penn Publishing Co., 1910.)

tion between the skull's surface features and the person's faculties **phrenology.**

Gall and Spurzheim went to considerable effort to gather evidence for their theory, and Gall states that he devoted himself to observation and waited patiently for nature to bring her results to him. In developing his idea of the carnivorous instinct, Gall examined the skull of meat- and plant-eating animals and detailed evidence from over 50 species, including anecdotal evidence from his own lapdog. He studied the behavior of men, including an account of a parricide and a murderer and the details on 25 other skulls. He included descriptions about people who delighted in witnessing death or in torturing animals, or who historically were noted for cruelty and sadism, and he even considered evidence from numerous paintings and busts. One might ask why it was that he "made thousands of observations on this subject, and never found an exception." Young makes the telling point that Gall's entire method was geared toward seeking confirmations. He never considered the possibility that his observations should meet certain standards or that they should be tested in any objective way. Even when he made good observations that may have been subjected to more rigorous examination, he gave them little more weight than any anecdote. Gall also placed no emphasis on evidence from cases of brain damage. He has been credited with giving the first complete account of a relation between left frontal brain damage and aphasia (Figure 13–2), yet he felt this type of finding was not evidence per se but rather confirmation of a finding that was already established by phrenological evidence.

Despite the ingenuity behind Gall and Spurzheim's research it failed, for four reasons. First, the psychology of faculties bore little relation to real behavior: faculties such as faith, self-love, and veneration were hope-

FIGURE 13–2. Originally Gall's system had 27 faculties. As phrenology (Spurzheim's name for the theory) expanded, the number of faculties increased. The figure shows the location of faculties according to Spurzheim. Language, indicated in the front of the brain, actually derived from a case study of Gall's: a soldier had received a knife wound that penetrated the frontal lobe of his left hemisphere through the eye. The soldier became aphasic; he was thus the first comprehensive report of aphasia following left frontal damage.

lessly impossible to define and to quantify objectively. The first breakthroughs in localization came only when people chose an objective behavior, such as speech, to correlate with an area of the brain. The second cause of failure was their belief that the superficial features of the skull, the analysis of which they called cranioscopy, could be used to estimate brain size and shape. Incredibly, they failed to realize that the outer skull did not mirror the inner skull or the surface features of the neocortex. Had they instead investigated gyral size, history might have been kinder to them. But they thought of gyral patterns as random wrinkles, such as those that might be found in a crumpled shirt, and so gave them to attention. They might have discovered the asymmetries, such as the larger planum temporale of the left posterior cortex, which is now thought to reflect lateralization of language to the left hemisphere. The third cause of failure was that phrenology invited quackery and thus, indirectly, ridicule by association. Because its followers devoted themselves to extremely superficial personality analysis, the entire endeavor was quickly brought into disrepute. In the eyes of their contemporaries, however, there was a more damning criticism—the fourth cause of their failure. Gall and Spurzheim had postulated that the brain is the organ of the mind, that personality characteristics are innate, and that the brain (or mind) is composed of independent functioning units. The prevailing opinion still reflected Descartes: the mind is nonmaterial and functions as a whole. Since these views are still held by many people today, it is possible to understand the hostility their criticism evoked nearly 200 years ago.

In reflecting on the contributions made by phrenological thought, it should not be believed that phrenology has been entirely abandoned. Hebb has remarked that it takes about 50 to 100 years for scientific ideas to become common sense, and if they are wrong, another 100 years to get rid of them. Perhaps the second figure should be revised upward: phrenological ideas are still widely held. Despite the periodic failure of scientific attempts to correlate appearance and various aspects of behavior, it is not uncommon to hear people accord virtues to others solely on the basis of their physical appearance. Readers may ask themselves how accurate they would be if asked to judge intelligence on the basis of photographs of others. Social psychologists have found that university students are not unwilling to make such judgments; they do so using the rule: beauty equals intelligence. In fairness to Gall, we may note that at least some of his science, inaccurate as it appears to have been, attempted an actual physical measurement.

Localization of Function: The First Experiments

Because of its weaknesses and the hostility it provoked, Gall and Spurzheim's phrenology had little chance of success. Nevertheless, Pierre Flourens (1794–1867) is generally credited with the definitive demolition of their science. Flourens, who accepted the concept of a unified mind, buttressed philosophical arguments against Gall and Spurzheim with experimentation. Nor was he above using ridicule to discount them, as the following story from Flourens' book *Comparative Psychology,* excerpted by Krech, shows:

> The famous physiologist, Magendie, preserved with veneration the brain of Laplace. Spurzheim had the very natural wish to see the brain of a great man.
>
> To test the science of the phrenologist, Mr. Magendie showed him, instead of the brain of Laplace, that of an imbecile.
>
> Spurzheim, who had already worked up his enthusiasm, admired the brain of the imbecile as he would have admired that of Laplace. (Krech, 1962)

In his experimental work, Flourens developed the technique of lesioning the brains of animals to study the changes produced in their behavior. He concluded that the cerebrum is the seat of intelligence, that the cerebellum coordinates locomotion, and that the medulla oblongata, since damage to it arrested respiration and resulted in death, is the seat of the principle of life. He concluded that there is no localization of function in the cerebrum, that all intellectual faculties resided there coextensively. He argued that loss of function is correlated with the extent of ablation of cortical tissue; that if all tissue was gone all intellectual functions were gone, and that if sufficient tissue remained intact there was recovery of all function.

Not only did Flourens make a number of important contributions to experimental psychology, he encumbered it with a number of millstones, some of which it has still not completely removed. He was a strict Cartesian, even to the point of dedicating his book to Descartes. He argued that the cortex had no motor or sensory functions. It would be years before brain stimulation studies showed him to be wrong on this point. Still, the idea that there is uncommitted cortex (now called association cortex) available for all sorts of hypothetical higher functions is still widely believed, although it is no more than a Flourensian notion applied to a more circumscribed portion of the cortex. Currently, a number of lines of investigation are committed to demonstrating that the idea of uncommitted cortex is a fallacy. Flourens invested the cortex with the properties that Descartes had ascribed to the mind, including the functions of will, reason, and intelligence, and advocated that the only proper approach to their function is through introspection. Even today, Hebb finds it necessary to advocate that neuroscientists should be behaviorists and study observable events rather than directing their studies toward mentalistic constructs. Finally, the idea that the mind is indivisible has had its advocates in this century, including people such as Lashley, who came to doubt that psychological functions could be localized successfully, and Finger and Stein, who imply that the nonspecific potential of the cortex permits extensive possibilities for recovery of function. Perhaps the most commonly applied erroneous Flourensian notion is in pedagogy, where it is expressed as, "Most people never use more than 10 percent of their brain."

The conclusion that Flourens' experiments devastated Gall and Spurzheim was persuasive at the time, but is difficult to support in retrospect. Most of Flourens' experiments were performed with pigeons and chickens —animals with virtually no neocortex. His behavioral tests were assessments of activities such as eating and wing flapping and bore no relation to the faculties proposed for the cortex by Gall and Spurzheim. Finally, many of the deficits from which his animals appeared to suffer may have been the result of postsurgical shock, brain swelling, or removal of far more tissue than the forebrain. Certainly subsequent workers who removed only the cerebrum did not find that pigeons lost all intellectual faculties as Flourens had defined them.

Localization of Language

Gall and Spurzheim's theory of localization of function was in disrepute for about 50 years while Flourens' concept of holistic function was dominant. Jean Baptiste Bouillaud (1796–1881), however, by supporting Gall's idea that language function is localized in the frontal lobe, provided the impetus for localization theory to take a new direction. On 21 February 1825 he read before the Royal Academy of Medicine, in France, a paper in which he argued from clinical studies that function is localized in the neocortex, and specifically that speech is localized in the frontal lobes just as Gall had suggested. (Gall had correlated that frontal cortex with language after studying a penetrating brain injury.) Observing that acts such as writing, drawing, painting, and fencing were carried out with the right hand, Bouillaud also suggested that the part of the brain that controlled them might possibly be the left hemisphere. Why, he asked, should people not be left-brained for the movements of speech as well? A few years later, in 1836, Marc Dax read a paper in Montpellier about a series of clinical cases demonstrating that disorders of speech were constantly associated with lesions of the left hemisphere. Dax's manuscript was published by his son in 1865.

Though neither Bouillaud's nor Dax's work had much impact when it was first presented, Ernest Auburtin, Bouillaud's son-in-law, took up Bouillaud's cause. At a meeting of the Anthropological Society of Paris in 1861 he reported the case of a patient who ceased to speak when pressure was applied to his exposed anterior lobes. He also gave the following description of another patient, with a challenge:

> For a long time during my service with M. Bouillaud I studied a patient, named Bache, who had lost his speech but understood everything said to him and replied with signs in a very intelligent manner to all questions put to him. This man, who spent several years at the Bicetre, is now at the Hospital for Incurables. I saw him again recently and his disease has progressed; slight paralysis has appeared but his intelligence is still unimpaired, and speech is wholly abolished. Without a doubt this man will soon die. Based on the symptoms that he presents, we have diagnosed softening of the anterior lobes. If, at autopsy, these lobes are found to be intact, I shall renounce the ideas that I have just expounded to you. (Stookey, 1954)

Paul Broca (1824–1880), founder of the society, attended the meeting and heard Auburtin's challenge. Five days later he received a patient, Leborgne, who had lost his speech and was able to say only "tan" and utter an oath. He had paralysis on the right side of his body but in other respects he seemed intelligent and normal. Broca invited Auburtin to examine Tan, as he came to be called, and together they agreed that if Auburtin was right, Tan should have a frontal lesion. Tan died on 17 April 1861, and the next day Broca submitted his findings to the Anthropological Society. The left anterior lobe was the focus of Tan's lesion. By 1863, Broca had collected eight more cases similar to Tan's and stated:

> Here are eight instances in which the lesion was in the posterior third of the third frontal convolution. This number seems to me to be sufficient to give strong presumptions. And the most remarkable thing is that in all the patients the lesion was on the left side. I do not dare draw conclusions from this. I await new facts. (Joynt, 1964)

It is usual to credit Broca with four contributions to the study of cortical function: describing a behavioral syndrome that consists of an inability to speak despite the presence of intact vocal mechanisms and normal comprehension, coining the word aphemia to describe this syndrome, correlating aphemia with an anatomical site now known as Broca's area, and elaborating the concept of *cerebral dominance* of language in the left hemisphere, or, as he phrased it, "nous parlons avec l'hemisphere gauche."

Largely because these contributions marked a change in the approach to analysis of brain function they have been carefully scrutinized by historians, some of whom have judged them as either not original, not enduring, or not accurate. First, the clinical symptoms that he described were already known, as is demonstrated by Auburtin's account of the aphasic Bache—and this Broca acknowledged. Second, the term aphemia was criticized by Trousseau, who argued that it meant infamy and was thus inappropriate as a clinical designation. Trousseau suggested the word aphasia, which Broca criticized as also inappropriate, since it meant "the state of a man who has run out of arguments"; but it nevertheless became universally accepted whereas aphemia was discarded. Third, language and the frontal lobes had previously been correlated by Gall, Bouillaud, and Auburtin, whose priority Broca recognized. Fourth, Broca's anatomical analysis was criticized by Pierre Marie, who reexamined the brains of Broca's first two patients, Tan and Lelong, 25 years after Broca's death. Marie pointed out in his article, "The Third Left Frontal Convolution Plays No Particular Role in the Function of Language," that Lelong was probably a victim of a senile dementia, with general nonspecific atrophy of the brain common in senility, and was not aphasic, and that Tan had additional extensive damage in his posterior cortex that may have accounted for his aphasia. In fairness, Broca had been aware of Tan's posterior damage but had concluded that, whereas the posterior damage contributed to his death, the anterior damage had occurred earlier, producing his aphasia. A fifth criticism is that Dax was the first to suggest the doctrine of cerebral dominance. This Broca also acknowledged, although, according to Joynt, he was never able to establish to his own satisfaction that Dax had read a paper in Montpellier in 1836 in which he stated that speech was lateralized on the left.

There is substance to the details of all these criticisms, but in a way they miss the mark, for Broca's more enduring contribution was to synthesize the theory of localization of function, the clinical descriptions of brain-damage effects, and neuroanatomy with such clarity that it excited neuroscientists and the lay public alike and so altered the direction neurobehavioral analysis was to take.

Wernicke-Sequential Programing and Disconnection

From Broca's description of aphasia resulting from left frontal lesions (as confirmed by findings from a number of other sources), Broca could be interpreted as having made two rather simple, but fundamental, points for localization:

1. A behavior is controlled by a specific brain area.

2. Destroying the area selectively destroys the behavior.

People who interpreted Broca in this way have been called strict localizationists. There were, however, those who disagreed with these points of both logical and clinical grounds. Among the most notable to dissent were Hughlings-Jackson, Bastian, and Wernicke.

The position of Carl Wernicke (1848–1904) initially gained widest recognition (and it was he who, like Broca, had an area of the brain named after him). He also made two findings devastating to strict localization: first, there is more than one language area; second, damage that spared an area could produce deficits indistinguishable from those that followed damage to the area per se. The first finding suggested that behaviors such as language are *sequentially programed;* the second advanced the concept of disconnection.

Theodore Meynert (1833–1892) first suggested that the cortex behind the central fissure is sensory in function and in addition described the projection of the auditory nerve to the cortex of the Sylvian fissure of the temporal cortex. He suspected a relation between hearing and speech and even described two cases of aphasic patients with lesions in this auditory projection area. It was his associate Wernicke, however, who subsequently described the details of this temporal lobe aphasia—or, as it has come to be called, **Wernicke's aphasia** or **fluent aphasia**—and placed it within a theoretical framework.

Wernicke described four major features of the aphasia that made it different from what Broca described:

1. There was damage in the first temporal gyrus, in what is now known as Wernicke's area.

2. There was no contralateral hemiplegia or paralysis.

3. The patients could speak fluently, but what they said was confused and made little sense—hence the term paraphasia.

4. Although the patients were able to hear, they could not understand or repeat what was said to them.

In addition to describing a new kind of aphasia, Wernicke provided a model for how language is organized in the left hemisphere: it involves sequential programming of activity in two language areas (see Figure 13–3). Wernicke theorized that the sound images of objects are stored in the first temporal gyrus (**Wernicke's area**), whence they are sent over a pathway (later identified as the arcuate fasciculus) to **Broca's area,** where the representations of speech movements are retained. If the temporal lobe were damaged, speech movements could occur but the speech would make no sense, because the person would be unable to monitor what he said. Because damage to Broca's area produces loss of speech movements without the loss of sound images, aphasia is not accompanied by a loss of comprehension.

Wernicke suggested that if the fibers connecting the two speech areas were damaged (disconnected), then, without damage to Bro-

ca's or Wernicke's area, a speech deficit would occur. Wernicke called such a disconnection **conduction aphasia:** both speech sounds and movements would be retained, as would comprehension, but speech would still be paraphasic because the person would not be able to judge the congruity of what he or she said.

The analysis of brain lesion effects by subsequent neurologists was much influenced by Wernicke's concept of disconnection, because it provided a methodology linking anatomy and behavior in such a way that it permitted prediction of new brain syndromes and the testing of hypotheses. Using this methodology, Déjérine in 1892 was able to describe a case in which dyslexia—loss of the ability to read—resulted from disconnecting the visual area from Wernicke's area. And Wernicke's student Liepmann (1863–1925) was able to show that **apraxia,** an inability to make movements in response to commands, followed disconnection of motor areas from sensory areas. The importance of the idea of disconnection cannot be overemphasized, for the behavioral deficit that follows a disconnection without a lesion in a given locus can be identical to a deficit that follows damage to that locus. As a result, any concept of strict localization of function becomes unworkable.

Electrophysiological Confirmation of Localization

The work of clinical neurologists such as Broca, Wernicke, and others seemed to indicate that behavior was somehow localized in the neocortex. Although many were excited by the idea, others maintained strong objections; what was needed was a different research approach that would support one or the other position. Almost on cue, this was provided by the development of the technique for electrically stimulating the brain.

FIGURE 13–3. Wernicke's (1874) model showing how language is organized in the brain. Sounds enter the brain on the auditor pathway *(a)*; sound images are stored in Wernicke's area (*a'*) and are sent to Broca's word area (*b*) for articulation over the motor pathway (*b'*). Lesions on the pathway *a-a'-b-b'* could produce different types of aphasia, depending on lesion location. It is curious that Wernicke drew all his language models on the right hemisphere and not the left, which is the dominant hemisphere for language, as Wernicke believed. It is amazing that his model was that of an ape, which could not speak, as Wernicke knew. (After C. Wernicke, *Der Aphasische Symptomencomplex.* Breslau, Poland: M. Cohn and Weigert, 1874.)

In 1870, Gustav Theodor Fritsch (1838–1929) and Eduard Hitzig (1838–1907) published their extraordinary paper "On the Electrical Excitability of the Cerebrum." Hitzig had previously elicited eye movements by stimulating the temporal cortex of a man, and he may have derived the idea of stimulating the cortex from an observation made while dressing a wound, that mechanical irritation of the brain caused twitching in the contralateral limbs. Working in Hitzig's bedroom they performed a successful preliminary experiment with a rabbit and then examined the effects of stimulating the exposed neocortex of a dog. At the time nearly everyone was of the opinion that the neocortex was inexcitable by electrical stimulation. They demonstrated that not only is the neocortex excitable, it is selectively excitable. Direct application of galvanic current to portions of the anterior neocortex caused movements on the opposite side of the body, whereas stimulation of the posterior neocortex produced no movement. They also found that stimulation of restricted portions of the anterior neocortex elicited movement of particular body parts, which suggested that on the neocortex there are *centers* or topographic representations of the different parts of the motor system. In sum, their findings contributed toward overthrowing three dictums that had been defended by Flourens. They showed that (1) the cortex is excitable, (2) the cortex plays a role in producing movement, and (3) function is localized. Over the next few years David Ferrier (1843–1928) refined the stimulation technique and confirmed Fritsch and Hitzig's results in monkeys, dogs, cats, rabbits, guinea pigs, pigeons, fish, and frogs. Fritsch and Hitzig summarized the interpretation of their findings in the conclusion to their 1870 paper:

Furthermore, it may be concluded from the sum of all our experiments that, contrary to the opinions of Flourens and most investigators who followed him, the soul in no case represents a sort of total function of the whole cerebrum, the expression of which might be destroyed by mechanical means in toto, but not in its individual parts. Individual psychological functions, and probably all of them, depend for their entrance into matter or for their formation from it, upon circumscribed centers of the cerebral cortex. (Fritsch and Hitzig, 1960)

Although Fritsch and Hitzig may have stimulated the cortex of wounded soldiers, the first experiment in which electrical stimulation on the cortex of a human was formally reported was performed by R. Bartholow (1831–1904) in Cincinnati, in 1874. Mary Rafferty, a patient in his care, had a cranial defect that exposed the posterior part of each cerebral hemisphere. The following is an extract from his report of that experiment:

Observation 3. *To test faradic reaction of the posterior lobes.* Passed an insulated needle into the left posterior lobe so that the non-insulated portion rested entirely in the substance of the brain. The other insulated needle was placed in contact with the dura mater, within one-fourth of an inch of the first. When the circuit was closed, muscular contraction in the right upper and lower extremities ensued, as in the preceding observations. Faint but visible contraction of the left orbicularis palpebrarum, and dilation of the pupils, also ensued. Mary complained of a very strong and unpleasant feeling of tingling in both right extremities, especially in the right arm, which she seized with the opposite hand and rubbed vigorously. Notwithstanding the very evident pain from which she suffered, she smiled as if much amused. (Bartholow, 1874)

Bartholow's work was not met with acclaim. In fact its publication caused such an outcry that he was forced to leave Cincinnati. Also, it is unlikely that he had stimulated the cortex, because in his account his electrodes were inserted about an inch into the brain tissue. Nevertheless, he had demonstrated that the electrical stimulation technique could be used on people; that is, the technique could be used with a conscious person, who could report the subjective sensations produced by stimulation. (The pain that Mary was reported to have suffered was not caused by stimulation of pain receptors in the brain—since there are none—but was probably a genuinely evoked sensation from brain stimulation.) It was not long before electrical stimulation was being used on humans in other experimental situations. And, of course, from there it has evolved into a standard part of many brain surgery procedures.

The Antilocalization Position of Goltz

In his extremely vigorous history (1926) of this period, Henry Head labeled Wernicke and others of his school the "diagram makers." This somewhat derogatory term was a reference to their oversimplification of the deficits that followed brain damage, as well as to their selection ("lop and twist," as he phrased it) of symptoms to fit their models. In fact, Head's criticisms were not unreasonable, because in the period preceding and following 1900 there was a proliferation of maps and diagrams showing the supposed location of all types of functions. Furthermore, Head argued, they persisted in concluding that because we have words for behaviors such as speech, eating, walking, etc., there must be one place in the brain that controlled each behavior. Head preferred to argue that there were many forms of speech, eating, walking, etc., each of which was probably controlled by many different parts of the brain. Rather than review the complexities of the work through this period, it is perhaps more instructive to look at the type of evidence brought forward in opposition to localization of function. The most instructive

opposition came from Goltz's experiments with dogs.

When Fritsch and Hitzig made their historical discovery that stimulation of a restricted portion of the neocortex resulted in specific movements, they concluded that the cortex was "the place of entry of psychic functions into matter." The electrophysiological localization of Fritsch and Hitzig, Ferrier, and others led quite logically to the view that the cortex produced and controlled specific movements as well as other behaviors. The experiments performed by Friedrich L. Goltz (1834–1902) in 1892 were intended specifically to question this position. Goltz's methodology resembled Flourens' in that he was addressing the question of what would happen if the entire neocortex were removed from an animal. But unlike Flourens he chose dogs with a well-developed neocortex and a repertory of easily observable mammalian behaviors. He took his animals throughout Europe and displayed them everywhere, and he even made sure that when they were sacrificed to confirm brain lesion extent, many of the important neurologists and physiologists of the day had a chance to examine the brains to ensure that the lesions were complete.

Goltz reasoned that if a portion of the neocortex had a function, then removal of the cortex should lead to a loss of that function. Goltz removed the neocortex, most of the basal ganglia, and parts of the midbrain from three dogs, which he then studied for 57 days, 92 days, and 18 months, respectively. The dog that survived for 18 months was studied in the greatest detail. It was more active than a normal dog, alternated sleep-waking periods (though these were shorter than normal), and panted when warm and shivered when cold. It walked well on uneven ground and was able to catch its balance when it slipped. If placed in an abnormal posture, it corrected its position. After hurting a hind limb on one occasion it trotted on three legs, holding up the injured limb. It was able to orient to touches or pinches on its body and snap at the object that touched it, although its orientations were not very accurate. If offered two portions of food—the first a piece of meat soaked in milk, the second a piece of meat soaked in bitter quinine—it accepted the first and rejected the second. It responded to light and sounds, although its response thresholds were elevated.

Goltz interpreted his findings as indicating a general lowering of the will and intellect that was proportional to the size of the lesion. He argued that his findings did not support the localization-of-function hypothesis. With reference to experiments of his time, he stated that if stimulation of a particular portion of the brain were found to produce movement, and if the stimulated area were concluded to be a motor center, it followed that removal of this area should abolish movement. Goltz's experiments had elegantly demonstrated that cortical removal did not abolish movement. In fact, decortication did not appear to completely abolish any function, though it seemed to reduce all functions to some extent. This demonstration appeared to be a strong argument against localization of function.

Hughlings-Jackson and Hierarchical Organization

Goltz's experiments should not be ignored, because they reiterated what had been said previously by Flourens and because arguments very much like them were to be made again through the first half of the 20th century, particularly by Lashley. The fundamental difference between Goltz and those whom his experiments were intended to criticize was to be resolved by the hierarchical concept of brain function proposed by the English neurologist John Hughlings-Jackson (1835–1911), who has been described as the founder of modern neurology. Hughlings-Jackson was extremely prolific, writing over 300 papers, but his work was often not given the attention it deserved, perhaps because he was more reflective and philosophical than is usually popular.

Hughlings-Jackson thought of the nervous system as being organized in a number of layers arranged in a functional hierarchy. Each successively higher level would control more complex aspects of behavior but do so through the lower levels. Often Hughlings-Jackson described the nervous system as having three levels: the spinal cord, the basal ganglia and motor cortex, and the frontal cortex. But equally often he designated no particular anatomical area for a nervous system level. He had adopted the theory of hierarchy from Herbert Spencer's argument that the brain evolved in a series of steps, each of which brought animals the capacity to engage in a constellation of new behaviors. But what Hughlings-Jackson did with the theory was particularly novel. He suggested that diseases or damage that affected the highest levels would produce *dissolution,* the reverse of evolution: the animals would still have a repertory of behaviors, but they would be simpler, more typical of an animal that had not yet evolved the missing brain structure.

If the logic of this argument is followed, it becomes apparent how the results from Goltz's experiments can be reconciled with those of his opponents. Goltz's dogs were "low-level" dogs: they were able to walk and to eat, but if food had not been presented to them—had they been required to walk in order to find food—they would have failed and starved. For them walking would not have served a useful biological function. Similarly, all the other behaviors of the dogs were low-level behaviors. For example, they could thermoregulate by shivering and panting, but had they been placed in a situation requiring them to perform a complex series of acts to leave a cold or warm area for a neutral thermal zone, they would have failed and so would not have been able to behaviorally thermoregulate as do normal dogs. It can be seen, therefore, that Hughlings-Jackson's concepts allowed the special role of the cortex in organizing purposeful behavior to be distinguished from the role of subcortical areas in supporting the more elementary components of behavior.

Hughlings-Jackson applied his concepts of hierarchical organization to many other areas of behavior, including language and aphasia. It was his view that every part of the brain is involved in language, with each part making some special contribution. The relevant question was not where language is localized but what unique contribution is made by each part of the cortex. Thus if, for example, the nondominant hemisphere is not involved in language but in spatial organization, then damage to that hemisphere would be revealed not just in spatial disabilities but also in language impoverishment because spatial concepts cannot be employed. With respect to this logic Hughlings-Jackson was particularly modern —so much so, in fact, that his ideas are receiving more serious consideration today than they did in his own time.

THE NEURON HYPOTHESIS

The second major influence on modern neuropsychology was the development of what has become known as the *neuron hypothesis:* the hypothesis that the nervous system is composed of discrete, autonomous cells, or units, that can interact but are not physically connected. The opposite position, known as the *nerve net hypothesis,* that the nervous system is composed of a continuous network of interconnected fibers, was held at one time. At the cellular level, support for the neuron theory depended on the solutions to three problems:

1. How the nervous system conducts information
2. How it is constructed
3. How it is itself interconnected and how it is interconnected with muscles

The first problem was solved by advances in physiology and physiological recording techniques, the second by advances in anatomy, and the third by advances in biochemistry and pharmacology.

Information Conduction

Early views of how the nervous system moves muscles involved some type of hydraulic theory requiring gas or liquid to flow through nerves into muscles. Such theories have been called balloonist theories, since movement was thought to be caused by the filling and emptying of muscles. Certainly Descartes espoused the balloonist hypthesis, for he argued that a fluid from the ventricles flowed through nerves into muscles to make them move (Figure 13–4). Francis Glisson in 1677 made a direct test of the balloon theory by immersing a man's arm in water and measuring the change in the water level when the muscles of the arm were contracted. Since the water level did not rise, Glisson concluded that no fluid entered the muscle. Swammerdam in Holland had reached the same conclusion from similar experiments on frogs, but his manuscript had lain unpublished for 100 years.

Isaac Newton may have been the first person to advance a theory of nerve function that approximates a modern view. In 1717 he suggested that nerves were not hollow tubes but were solid. He then postulated that they worked by the vibration of an "elastic aether" that was propagated along their length. Albrech von Haller (1708–1777) seems to have developed the concept of nerve irritability; that is, when irritated by touch or chemicals, the

FIGURE 13–4. The concept of reflex originated with Descartes. In this example heat from the flame causes a thread in the nerve to be pulled, releasing ventricular fluid through an opened pore. The fluid flows through the nerve, causing not only the foot to withdraw but also the eyes and head to turn to look at it, the hands to advance, and the whole body to bend to protect it. His concept was stimulated by the mechanical principles of displays used in water gardens fashionable in France in his day. A visitor in the gardens would step on a plate that mechanically caused statues to hide, appear, or squirt water. In actual fact, his use of the reflex concept was for behaviors that would today be considered more than reflexive, whereas what is held as reflexive today was not so conceived by Descartes. (From R. Descartes, *Traité de l'Homme*. Paris: Angot, 1664.)

nerves would make muscles move. Haller was aware that electricity was a candidate for the medium of nerve conduction, but he and others of his time, thinking of electrical conduction in a wire, believed that nerves lacked the insulation prerequisite for conduction.

The impetus to adopt a theory of electrical conduction came from Stephen Gray, who in 1731 attracted considerable attention by demonstrating that the human body could be electrified. In an ingenious demonstration he showed that static electricity from a rod could pass through the body: when a charged glass tube was brought close to the feet of a boy suspended by a rope, a grass-leaf electroscope was attracted to the boy's nose. It was only much later, however, that Luigi Galvani (1737–1798) demonstrated that electrical stimulation of a frog's nerve could cause muscle contraction, and Friedrich Humboldt (1769–1859) confirmed that nerves contain intrinsic "animal" electricity. In 1859, F. Pflüger suggested that electricity does not flow along the nerve but sets up a wave motion within it. Finally, in 1886 J. Bernstein developed the theory that the membrane of a nerve is polarized, and that the action potential is a propagated depolarization of this membrane. Many of the details of ionic conduction were worked out during the past 30 years, and A. L. Hodgkin and A. F. Huxley received the Nobel Prize in physiology in 1963 for their pioneering efforts in this field.

As successive findings brought hydraulic models of conduction into disfavor and more dynamic electrical models into favor, hydraulic theories of *behavior* were also critically reassessed. For example, Freud's theory of behavior, involving the different levels id, ego, and superego, is very much a hydraulic model. Although conceptually useful for a time, it had no impact on concepts of brain function, because almost as soon as the theory was proposed it became clear that the brain does not function as a hydraulic system.

Nervous System Structure

Early views of the nervous system showed little concern for its structure, probably because to superficial examination it resembled little more than jelly. There was a general awareness that nerves led to muscles, and it was widely believed that the nerves were hollow, fluid-containing tubes. One of the first cellular anatomists, Anton van Leeuwenhoek (1632–1723), examined nerves with a primitive microscope but was unable to find hollow tubes. By 1717 he had described what may have been a nerve fiber surrounded by myelin. Van Leeuwenhoek also described what he called globules, but it is doubtful that these were cell bodies. They may have been either blobs of fat or optical aberrations produced by the crude microscopes of the day. From van Leeuwenhoek's time until the 1830s, when the achromatic microscope was developed, the frequency of artifacts aroused a general distrust of microscope results. However, in 1781, Felice Fontana did succeed in describing the nerve fiber. Then, in 1833, using the achromatic microscope, Christian G. Ehrenberg described nerve cells in the brain; in 1836, Gabriel G. Valentin described the cell body, nucleus, and nucleolus; and in 1838, Robert Remak distinguished myelinated and nonmyelinated fibers and suggested that fibers connect to cell bodies. From these findings and others Theodor Schwann in 1839 enunciated the cell theory; that is, that cells are the basic structural unit of the nervous system. It was not until 1849, however, that Rudolf A. van Koelliker had definitely established that nerve fibers are linked to the cell body.

Understanding of cell structure was advanced chiefly by improvements in technology. The earliest anatomists who tried to examine the substructure of the nervous system were faced with a gelatinous white substance. In 1809, Johann C. Reil developed the technique of fixing and hardening tissue by placing it in alcohol to remove fluid from the plasma. A more effective fixer, chromic acid, was found by Adolph Hannover in 1840. The formaldehyde technique, the preferred modern fixative procedure, was discovered in 1893 by Ferdinand Blum. In the 1830s Luigi Rolando devised techniques for cutting thin sections of tissue, and in 1842 Benedikt Stilling discovered that the tissue could be cut into extremely thin sections if it was first frozen. The technique of freezing permitted serial reconstruction of fibers and of cellular tissue components and also permitted a more effective use of stains.

The most exciting development in neuroanatomy was the technique of staining, which allows different portions of the nervous system to be visualized. In 1858, Joseph von Gerlach devised the carmine stain, which turns cells and their processes red; in 1882, Carl Weigert developed a technique for staining myelin; and, in 1894, Franz Nissl developed the methylene blue technique (Nissl stain), which stains cell bodies but not fibers, revealing many of their internal structures. The most amazing cell stain was developed by Camillo Golgi in 1875. Impregnating tissue with silver nitrate, Golgi found that a few cells would take up the stain, and that each of these cells in its entirety—cell body, dendrites, and axons—became encrusted with reduced silver. Thus, finally the entire neuron and all its processes could be visualized at one time.

As cells were visualized with microscopes it became clear that, far from resembling a bowl of jelly, the brain has an enormously intricate substructure with components arranged in complex clusters, each of which is interconnected with many others. Psychologists who were fractionating behavior into parts and faculties could only have been encouraged by the details of the brain revealed by the anatomists. There was a genuine theoreticians' banquet on hand, and for every conceivable behavioral trait there was a newly discovered nucleus or pathway begging to be attached. The feast may have been too rich, for the clear message from anatomists to psychologists was that things were probably more complex than they appeared to be. This may have been why for the first half of this century many psychologists turned away from the brain and not toward it for enlightenment.

Nervous System Connections

Was the brain a net of physically interconnected fibers, or a collection of discrete units? If it were an interconnected net, then it would follow that changes in one part would, by diffusion, produce changes in every other part. Since it would be difficult for a structure thus organized to localize function, a netlike structure would favor a holistic or gestalt type of brain function and psychology. Alternatively, a structure of discrete units would favor psychology based on localization of function, since—at least theoretically—each unit could function autonomously.

The concept of a nerve net originated in 1855 with Franz von Leydig, who observed and described numerous interlacing fibrils in the nervous system of a spider. Later, J. von Gerlach (1820–1896), while studying dendrites in vertebrates, found what he considered a similar network. In 1883, Golgi dismissed Gerlach's hypothesis of an interlinking network of dendrites, suggesting instead that axons were interconnected, forming an axonic net. A number of anatomists opposed Golgi's idea; the most definitive work in opposition was done by Santiago Ramón y Cajal (1852–1934), using Golgi's own silver staining technique. In 1891, summarizing Cajal's work on nerve cells, Wilhelm Waldeyer coined the term neuron (from the Greek for nerve) and popularized the *neuron hypothesis,* which states that neurons are not physically connected through their axons. Golgi and Cajal jointly received the Nobel Prize in 1906; each in his acceptance speech argued his position on the neuron hypothesis, Golgi supporting the nerve net and Cajal supporting the position now considered to be correct, the neuron hypothesis.

Largely because of the development of the electron microscope, more recent work in the early part of the 20th century fully supports the neuron hypothesis. It is accepted that axons have terminal knobs on their ends, and that cells are separated by gaps, which are bridged by chemical messengers. (It is a nice historical irony that something like the idea that a fluid passes from the end of a nerve to activate a muscle turns out to be true.) It has been repeatedly demonstrated that neurons have a certain autonomy of function; thus, localization of function could be argued at the level of the cell. On this principle Hebb, in 1949, brilliantly advanced association learning theory by proposing that individual cells could, by being activated at the same time, come to form cell assemblies (a semi-mini-nerve net, if one likes) that form the structure in which memory is housed.

In conclusion, many of the constituent concepts of the neuron hypothesis were formulated at roughly the same time as the developments in behavior we reviewed earlier, and they did so almost in parallel, seemingly without influencing how people thought behavior was produced. But the influence was there: knowing that the nervous system is composed of a uniform substance allowed it to be viewed as a single organ, knowing that it is electrically active led to experiments in which it was stimulated, knowing that some parts of the nervous system are composed of cell bodies and other parts of fibers permitted speculation about the relative effects of cell damage versus fiber damage, and being able to see subtle differences in cell structure in a microscope permitted the development of cytoarchitectonic maps that are strikingly similar and that gave support to functional maps constructed from lesion studies. Thus, although it may seem that behavior was effectively studied in ignorance of the brain's fine structure, actually it was not—and it is unlikely that it will be in the future. In fact, the discovery that cells are organized in neurochemical systems may now be the predominant influence on how we think about behavior. In our view, although the influence of cell study on psychological theory has perhaps lagged somewhat, it is likely that the neuron hypothesis is catching up and may soon begin to shape psychological theory.

THE DEVELOPMENT OF MODERN NEUROPSYCHOLOGY

Given the 19th-century developments in knowledge about brain structure and function—the brain and neuron hypotheses, the concept of the special nature of cortical function, the concepts of localization of function and of disconnection—it seems surprising that psychologists did not become more interested in the brain earlier. Why was a science of neuropsychology not developed by 1900 rather than by 1949, when we first dated the use of the term? There are several possible reasons for the latency. One factor was that in the 1920s neurologists, such as Henry Head, rejected the classical approach of Broca, Wernicke, and others, arguing that their attempt to correlate behavior and anatomical site was little advanced over the approach of the phrenologists. This criticism was partly reasonable at the time, since some people, such as K. Kleist, had attempted to correlate every aspect of behavior and language with a particular anatomical location. A second reason was the intervention of two world wars, which disrupted the development of science in many countries. A third reason may have been that psychologists, who traced their origins to philosophy rather than to biology, were not interested, directing their atten-

tion instead to behaviorism, psychophysics, and the psychoanalytical movement.

A number of modern developments have made a contribution to the growth of neuropsychology as an identifiable discipline in the neurosciences. These deserve some mention and include (1) neurosurgery; (2) psychometrics, the method of measuring human abilities, and statistical analysis; and (3) technological advances.

1. Neurosurgery. Penfield and Jasper have provided a brief but informative history of neurosurgery. Brain surgery was clearly performed by prehistoric peoples because skulls that had been subject to surgery (the skulls show postsurgical healing) have been obtained from the Neolithic period of man in Europe and from the early Incas in Peru. It is likely that these early peoples had found surgery to have a beneficial effect for some types of brain problems. Later Hippocrates gave written directions for trephining the side of the head opposite to the site of a local convulsion as a means of therapeutic intervention. During the period between the 13th and 19th centuries there were a number of attempts, some quite successful, to relieve various symptoms with surgery. The modern era began once antisepsis, anesthesia, and the principle of localization of function were developed. In the 1880s a number of surgeons reported the success of operations for the treatment of abscesses, tumors, and epilepsy-producing scars. Subsequently, the Horsley-Clarke stereotaxic device was developed for holding the head, local anesthetic procedures were developed so that the patient could contribute to the success of surgery by responding to the effects of localized brain stimulation, and devices such as the EEG and pneumoencephalographs were developed to locate the area of brain malfunction more precisely before surgery began. The value of the idea of localization of function cannot be underestimated in this account. The first surgeons used signs of trauma on the skull as a means of localizing brain damage, but once it was realized that a variety of behavioral symptoms could be used to localize damage the surgeon had a far better idea where to make the surgical penetration.

The development of neurosurgery as a practical solution to some types of brain abnormality has had a profoundly positive influence on neuropsychology. In animal research the ablation technique was developed to the point that it became one of the most important sources of information about brain–behavior relations. Yet in human research, most information came from patients with relatively poorly defined lesions; strokes produced damage that included subcortical structures as well as the cortex and brain trauma produced lesions that were diffuse, irregular, or incomplete. Furthermore, patients lived for years after injury and histological localization was thus impossible. Neurosurgery provided a serendipitous solution to all these problems. Surgical removal of cortical tissue was often so localized that it equaled that produced in animals. Since the surgeon drew a map of the lesion and sometimes even electrically stimulated the surrounding tissue the location of the lesion was known in advance. The variation in surgical technique in producing such things as focal lesions, hemispherectomies, and commissurectomies also allowed for refined analysis of the contributions of different brain areas to behavior. As information about behavior was obtained from patients with circumscribed lesions it became in turn useful for diagnostic purposes in new patient populations.

2. Psychometrics and Statistical Evaluation. The first experiments on individual differences in psychological function were made

by an astronomer, Friedrich Wilhelm Bessel, in 1796. Bessel had become curious about the dismissal of an assistant at the Greenwich observatory near London for being one or so seconds slower than his superior in observing stars and setting clocks. Bessel began a study of reaction time and found quite large differences among people. Individual differences were very much a part of Gall and Spurzheim's phrenology, but unlike their idea of localization of function, this feature of their science attracted little interest among neuroscientists. Charles Darwin's English cousin, Francis Galton, maintained a laboratory in London in the 1880s where for three pennies he measured physical features, perceptions, and reaction time with an eye to finding individual differences that could explain why some people were superior to others. Galton's elegant innovation was to apply the statistical methods of Quetlet, a Belgian statistician, to his results and so rank his subjects relativistically on a frequency distribution. This innovation was essential for the development of modern psychological tests. It was fitting that Galton's work was directed to describing individual differences, since Darwin's evolutionary theory of natural selection required individual differences with which to work. Yet the measures that Galton selected were not those that permitted him to distinguish the characteristics of people who were eminent from those who were ordinary.

Modern test procedures for intelligence were developed by the French physician, biologist, and psychologist Alfred Binet for the purposes of solving a quite practical problem. Binet experimented with a wide variety of measurements, including those of head size, facial features, and handwriting style, and found them to be inadequate for distinguishing mental differences. Then in 1904 the Minister of Public Instruction commissioned Binet to develop tests that could identify retarded children and so single them out for special instruction. In 1905, in collaboration with Simon, he produced what is now known as the 1905 Binet-Simon scale. The tests were derived empirically by administering questions to 50 normal three- to 11-year-old children and some mentally retarded children and adults. The tests were designed to evaluate judgment, comprehension, and reason, which Binet thought were essential features of intelligence. The scale was revised in 1908, unsatisfactory tests were deleted, others were added, and the student population was increased to 300 children aged three to 13 years. From the tests a *mental level* was calculated, which was a score that 80 to 90 percent of normal children of a particular age attained on the test. In 1916 Terman in the United States produced the Stanford-Binet test, in which IQ, mental age divided by chronological age times 100, was first used. In 1940, D. O. Hebb gave IQ tests to brain-damaged people in Montreal, with the resultant surprising discovery that lesions in the frontal lobes—until then considered the center of highest intelligence —did not decrease IQ scores. This counterintuitive finding identified the utility of using such tests for brain-damage assessment and effectively created a bond of common interest between neurology and psychology. Many of the clever innovations used for assessing brain function in various patient populations are strongly influenced by intelligence testing methodology. Particularly notable is the fact that the tests are brief, easily and objectively scored, and are standardized using statistical procedures. Many neuropsychologists use features of IQ scores to assess regional brain contributions to IQ, whereas others only use IQ as a measure of general psychological function for the purposes of evaluating other test results. Although the concept of "mental testing" as it is used in many applications has been criticized a number of times, even harsh critics, such as Gould, feel that it has an appropriate use in neuropsychology. In fact, it is likely that mental tests will themselves be modified by advances in neuropsychology.

3. Advances in Technology. Because the advances that have been made in technology are so numerous, and are also discussed elsewhere, they will not be detailed here. What should be remembered is the frequently echoed statement, "Methods give the results." This was Flourens' exclamation when he advocated the experimental method rather than Gall's anecdotal and confirmatory approach. It was also Fritsch and Hitzig's statement when they overthrew Flourens' dogma on the electrical excitability of the cortex. Improved approaches not only include theory and methodology but also technology. It has been only through technological advance that the internal structure of neurons could be visualized, their electrical activity recorded, and their biochemical activity analyzed and modified. It is only through technology that the processes of disease, degeneration, and regeneration in the nervous system can be understood. In fact, it is often the case that the methodology and the results are so intimately linked that they cannot be dissociated. For this reason, technological advances provide new opportunities to review old and well-mellowed ideas, and it is why old and well-mellowed ideas should be thrown into the mill of technological innovation for confirmation.

SUMMARY

This chapter traces the advance of our understanding that the brain is the organ of the mind and that the cell is the material from which it is constructed. It was not enough to speculate that it is so, as some of the ancients were correctly able to do, it was necessary to support the hypothesis with fact. The thrust and parry of this endeavor not only provide the history, they give definition to the present science of neuropsychology. To have met Flourens is to have been introduced to issues of recovery of function, to have met Wernicke and Déjérine is to have been introduced to disconnection theory, to have met Leipmann is to have been introduced to an origin of hypotheses on the neural organization of movement, to have met Gall and Dax and Broca is to have been introduced to the puzzle of asymmetry of function, and to have met van Leeuwenhoek is to have received an introduction to advances that will come from the technology of double labeling of cells. Still, the hypotheses that have flowered in this history are sufficiently broad and vague that they will require generations of careful examination before they can be sketched in colors that reflect their truth. We leave the reader with the advice that to know history is to be able to replicate, to advance it, and perhaps to confound sphinxes with it.

REFERENCES

Bartholow, R. Experimental investigation into the functions of the human brain. *American Journal of Medical Sciences* 67:305–313, 1874.

Beach, F. A., D. O. Hebb, C. T. Morgan, and H. W. Nissen. *The Neuropsychology of Lashley*. New York, Toronto, and London: McGraw-Hill, 1960.

Benton, A. L. Contributions to aphasia before Broca. *Cortex* 1:314–327, 1964.

Brazier, M. A. B. The historical development of neurophysiology. In J. Field, H. W. Magoun, and V. E. Hall, eds., *Handbook of Physiology*, vol. 1. Washington, D.C.: American Physiological Society, 1959.

Broca, P. Remarks on the seat of the faculty of articulate language, followed by an observation of aphemia. In G. von Bonin, ed., *The Cerebral Cortex*. Springfield, Ill.: Charles C Thomas, 1960.

Broca, P. Sur le siège de la faculté du langage articulé. *Bulletin of the Society of Anthropology* 6:377–396, 1865.

Clark, E., and C. D. O'Malley. *The Human Brain and Spinal Cord*. Berkeley and Los Angeles: University of California Press, 1968.

Descartes, R. *Traité de l'Homme*. Paris: Angot, 1664.

Eccles, J. C. *The Neurophysiological Basis of Mind: The Principles of Neurophysiology*. Oxford: Clarendon Press, 1956.

Flourens, P. Investigations of the properties and the functions of the various parts which compose the cerebral mass. In G. von Bonin, ed., *The Cerebral Cortex*. Springfield, Ill.: Charles C Thomas, 1960.

Fritsch, G., and E. Hitzig. On the electrical excitability of the cerebrum. In G. von Bonin, ed., *The Cerebral Cortex*. Springfield, Ill.: Charles C Thomas, 1960.

Geschwind, N. *Selected Papers on Language and Brain*. Dordrecht, Holland; and Boston: D. Reidel Publishing Co., 1974.

Goltz, F. On the functions of the hemispheres. In G. von Bonin, ed., *The Cerebral Cortex*. Springfield, Ill.: Charles C Thomas, 1960.

Gould, S. J. *The Mismeasurement of Man*. New York: Norton, 1981.

Head, H. *Aphasia and Kindred Disorders of Speech*. London: Cambridge University Press, 1926.

Hebb, D. O. *The Organization of Behavior: A Neuropsychological Theory*. New York: Wiley, 1949.

Hebb, D. O., and W. Penfield. Human behavior after extensive bilateral removals from the frontal lobes. *Archives of Neurology and Psychiatry* 44:421–438, 1940.

Joynt, R. Paul Pierre Broca: His contribution to the knowledge of aphasia. *Cortex* 1:206–213, 1964.

Klüver, H. *Behavior Mechanisms in Monkeys*. Chicago: The University of Chicago Press, 1933, 1957.

Krech, D. Cortical localization of function. In L. Postman, ed., *Psychology in the Making*. New York: Knopf, 1962.

Lenneberg, E. H. *Biological Foundations of Language*. New York: Wiley, 1967.

Luciani, L. *Human Physiology*. London: Macmillan, 1915.

Luria, A. R. *The Working Brain*. New York: Penguin, 1973.

Olin, C. H. *Phrenology*. Philadelphia: Penn, 1910.

Penfield, W., and H. Jasper. *Epilepsy and the Functional Anatomy of the Human Brain*. Boston: Little, Brown, 1954.

Pribram, K. H. *Languages of the Brain*. Englewood Cliffs, N.J.: Prentice-Hall, 1971.

Rothschuk, K. E. *History of Physiology*. Huntington, N.Y.: Robert E. Krieger, 1973.

Stookey, B. A note on the early history of cerebral localization. *Bulletin of the New York Academy of Medicine* 30:559–578, 1954.

Taylor, J., ed. *Selected Writings of John Hughlings-Jackson*, vols. 1 and 2. London: Hodder, 1931.

Wernicke, C. *Der Aphasische Symptomenkomplex*. Breslau, Poland: M. Cohn and Weigert, 1874.

Young, R. M. *Mind, Brain and Adaption in the Nineteenth Century*. Oxford: Clarendon Press, 1970.

14

PRINCIPLES OF CEREBRAL ASYMMETRY

It is over 100 years since Dax and Broca discovered that damage to the left hemisphere produced an inability to talk whereas damage to the right hemisphere did not affect speech production. Since then it has been generally accepted that the left hemisphere plays a special role in language that is not shared by the right hemisphere. But language is not the only special function of the left hemisphere; at the beginning of this century Leipmann compared the movements of patients with lesions of either the left or the right hemisphere and demonstrated that the left hemisphere has a role in controlling movement that is not shared by the right. The special functions of the right hemisphere remained a mystery until comparatively recently, when the work of Zangwill, Hécaen, Milner, and others showed that it is more involved than the left in the analysis of the visuospatial dimensions of the world.

Although these findings superficially appear to simplify the problem of understanding lateralization, the problem is complicated by the following three variables:

1. Laterality of function can be affected by environmental factors as well as genetically determined factors such as gender and handedness; the cerebral organization of some left-handers and females appears to have less functional asymmetry than right-handers and males.

2. Laterality is relative and not absolute, for both hemispheres play a role in nearly every behavior; thus, although the left hemisphere is especially important for the production of language, the right hemisphere also has some language capabilities.

3. Whereas a functionally asymmetrical brain was once believed to be a uniquely human characteristic—one that suggested a straightforward relation between asymmetry and language—this idea has proved to be naive and incorrect. There is evidence that certain songbirds, rats, cats, monkeys, and apes have a functionally and anatomically asymmetrical brain.

This chapter addresses the basic principles of cerebral asymmetry; the next chapter examines the factors that produce variations in the "basic pattern" of cerebral asymmetry. The answers to most questions about the nature of cerebral asymmetry are as yet incomplete, but our tentative answers take into account information about the brain's anatomical and functional asymmetry, the relation of hand preference and gender to asymmetry, the influence of culture and education on asymmetry, the nature of lateralized functions, and finally the incidence of asymmetry in nonhumans.

ANATOMICAL ASYMMETRY IN THE HUMAN BRAIN

According to Hughlings-Jackson, Gratiolet first observed in the 1860s that the convolu-

tions on the left hemisphere mature more rapidly than those on the right. Anatomical asymmetry was described again in the late 1800s by a number of authors, but these observations were largely ignored until the 1960s, when von Bonin reviewed the earlier literature and Geschwind and Levitsky described significant anatomical asymmetry in a large series of human brains. The latter authors reported that the **planum temporale,** which is the cortical area just posterior to the auditory cortex (Heschl's gyrus) within the **Sylvian fissure,** was larger on the left in 65 percent of the brains studied. On the average, the planum temporale on the left was nearly 1 cm longer than on the right (see Figure 14–1 and Table 14–1). This report generated renewed interest in anatomical asymmetries in humans and

FIGURE 14–1. Anatomical differences between the two hemispheres are visible in the temporal lobes. A. The Sylvian fissure on the left (top) has a gentler slope than the fissure on the right. B. A knife has been moved along the Sylvian fissure of each hemisphere and through the brain, cutting away the top portion. The planum temporale (darkened area) is larger on the left than on the right. (B after Geschwind, 1972.)

TABLE 14–1

Summary of studies demonstrating anatomical asymmetry

Measure	Basic reference
A. Asymmetries favoring the left hemisphere	
1. Greater specific gravity	Von Bonin, 1962
2. Longer Sylvian fissure	Ebberstaller, 1884; LeMay and Culebras, 1972; Heschl, 1878
3. Larger insula	Kodama, 1934
4. Doubling of cingulate gyrus	Ebberstaller, 1884
5. Relatively more gray matter	Von Bonin, 1962; Gur et al., 1980
6. Larger planum temporale	Geschwind and Levitsky, 1968; Galaburda et al., 1978; Teszner et al., 1972; Witelson and Pallie, 1973; Wada et al., 1975; Rubens et al., 1976; Kopp et al., 1977
7. Larger lateral posterior nucleus	Eidelberg and Galaburda, 1982
8. Larger inferior parietal lobule	LeMay and Culebras, 1972
9. Larger area Tpt of temporoparietal cortex	Galaburda and Sanides, 1980
10. Wider occipital lobe	LeMay, 1976
11. Longer occipital horn of lateral ventricles	McRae et al., 1968; Strauss and Fitz, 1980
12. Larger total area of frontal operculum	Falzi et al., 1982
B. Asymmetries favoring the right hemisphere	
1. Heavier	Broca, 1875; Crichton-Browne, 1880
2. Longer internal skull size	Hoadley and Pearson, 1929
3. Doubling of Heschl's gyrus	Economo and Horn, 1930; Chi et al., 1977
4. Larger medial geniculate nucleus	Eidelberg and Galaburda, 1982
5. Larger area of convexity of frontal operculum	Wada et al., 1975
6. Wider frontal lobe	LeMay, 1976

other animals, and it put to rest the notion that the two hemispheres are structurally identical.

Many anatomical differences between the two hemispheres of the brain have now been reported. The major differences can be summarized as follows:

1. The right hemisphere is slightly larger and heavier than the left hemisphere, but the specific gravity of the left hemisphere exceeds that of the right hemisphere. Von Bonin suggested that these differences may indicate that there is actually more gray matter in the left than in the right hemisphere, a proposal that has been confirmed by Gur and his colleagues.

2. There is a marked asymmetry in the structure of the temporal lobes. Geschwind and Levitsky's finding that the planum temporale is larger on the left has now been replicated by numerous other investigators, although the percentage of cases having a larger planum temporale on the left varies from 65 to 90 percent in different samples. In contrast, the primary auditory cortex of Heschl's gyrus is larger on the right, as there are usually

two Heschl's gyri on the right and only one on the left (see Figure 14–1). Thus, there is a complementary asymmetry in the temporal lobes, an asymmetry that may provide an anatomical basis for the functional dissociation of the temporal lobes in language and in musical functions, respectively. This complementary specialization of the hemispheres may be present very early in cerebral development, as the anatomical asymmetries are present as soon as the temporal gyri are recognizable, normally during the last trimester of fetal life.

3. The asymmetry in the cortex of the temporal lobes is correlated with a corresponding asymmetry in the thalamus. Thus, Eidelberg and Galaburda found that the lateral posterior nucleus, which projects to the parietal cortex just caudal to the planum temporale, is larger on the left whereas the medial geniculate nucleus, which projects to the primary auditory cortex, is larger on the right. This anatomical asymmetry complements an apparent functional asymmetry in the thalamus, the left thalamus being dominant for language functions.

4. The slope of the Sylvian fissure is different in the two sides of the brain, being gentler on the left than on the right (see Figure 14–1). This difference can be seen by gross inspection of the brain as well as from angiograms, since the middle cerebral artery follows the course of the Sylvian fissure. The region of the temporal-parietal cortex lying ventral to the Sylvian fissure therefore appears larger on the right. We shall see that this enlarged region has a specialized role in integrating the spatial characteristics of sensory stimuli.

5. The frontal operculum (Broca's area) is organized differently on the left and right. The area visible on the surface of the brain is about one-third larger on the right than on the left, whereas the area of cortex buried in the sulci of the region is greater on the left than the right. This asymmetry probably reflects the functional dissociation of the regions, the left side being involved in producing language and the right one possibly influencing tone of voice (see Chapter 22).

6. The distribution of various neurotransmitters is asymmetrical, in both cortical and subcortical regions. Thus, there are asymmetries in the distribution of acetylcholine, GABA, noradrenaline, and dopamine, the particular asymmetry being dependent on the structure under consideration. (See Falzi et al., Glick et al., and Oke et al.)

7. The right hemisphere extends farther anteriorly than the left, the left hemisphere extends farther posteriorly than the right, and the occipital horns of the lateral ventricles are five times more likely to be longer on the right than on the left. These asymmetries presumably reflect some as yet unspecified gross difference in cerebral organization.

8. The details of anatomical asymmetry are affected both by sex and handedness, as we shall see in the next chapter.

Because these anatomical asymmetries of the left hemisphere center primarily on the language areas, it is tempting to speculate that they evolved to subserve the production of language. Moreover, the presence of these asymmetries in preterm infants might be taken as support for the proposition that humans have an innate predisposition for language. It should be noted, however, that the brains of australopithicines share many of these asymmetries, but they did not have a vocal apparatus that would allow language as we conceive of it. Furthermore, some asymmetries, such as a heavier and larger right hemisphere, as well as a longer Sylvian fissure, can also be seen in many nonhuman species. Finally, we caution that undue emphasis has been placed on finding anatomical asymmetries that can be associated with language. Enlarged areas in the left hemisphere must be balanced by smaller areas elsewhere on the same side or larger areas in other lobes on the contralateral hemisphere.

Perhaps a more concerted study of asymmetries favoring the right hemisphere will cast light on the still poorly understood special functions of the right hemisphere.

ASYMMETRY IN NEUROLOGICAL PATIENTS

Cerebral asymmetry was first established by the study of patients with neurological disease that was lateralized to one hemisphere. The improvement in neurosurgical treatment for neurological disorders, especially epilepsy, has provided a large source of subsequently healthy subjects that are normally very willing to participate in neuropsychological studies. Thus, a good deal is now known from these patients about both the lateralization and the localization of functions in the cerebral cortex, and it is information from these patients that forms the basis for a large part of the remainder of this book. In this section we consider the evidence demonstrating lateralization of function in these patients, emphasizing the study of patients with lateralized lesions and those undergoing commissurotomy as well as of those who received unilateral hemisphere anesthetization with intracarotid injections of sodium Amytal.

Patients with Lateralized Lesions

The oldest method of studying hemispheric specialization has been to study the effects of circumscribed unilateral lesions that occur as a result of strokes, surgery, etc., and to infer the function of the area from behavioral deficits. However, for it to be concluded that the area has a special or lateralized function it is also necessary to show that lesions in other areas of the brain do not produce a similar deficit. The method that has proved strongest for demonstrating lateralization of function is one that Teuber calls double dissociation, an inferential technique premised on the following observations. It has been consistently demonstrated that lesions in the left hemisphere of right-handed patients can produce deficits in language functions (speech, writing, and reading) that do not follow lesions of the right hemisphere. Thus, the functions of the two hemispheres can be said to be dissociated. On the other hand, anecdotal and experimental evidence suggests that performance of spatial tasks, singing, playing musical instruments, and discriminating tonal patterns is more disrupted by right hemisphere than by left hemisphere lesions. Since right hemisphere lesions disturb tasks not disrupted by left hemisphere lesions and vice versa, the two hemispheres can be said to be doubly dissociated. A similar logic is used for localizing functions within a hemisphere. That is, behavioral tests that are especially sensitive to damage to a specific locus and not to others can be used to localize functions within a hemisphere, as illustrated in Table 14–2. Two hypothetical neocortical regions, 102 and 107, are doubly dissociated on tests of reading and writing: damage to area 102 disturbs reading, whereas damage to area 107 impairs writing. In principle, this logic can be extended to functionally dissociate additional areas concurrently by triple dissociation, quadruple dissociation, and so on.

In order to illustrate the nature of lateralized functions as observed in neurological patients, we contrast two cases from the Montreal

TABLE 14–2

Hypothetical example of double dissociation behavioral test

		Reading	Writing
Neocortical lesion site	102	Impaired	Normal
	107	Normal	Impaired

Neurological Hospital, neither of which was aphasic at the time of assessment (see Figure 14–2). The first patient, case P. G., was a 31-year-old man who had developed seizures over six years before his surgery. At the time of his admission to the hospital his seizures were poorly controlled by medication, and subsequent neurological investigations revealed a large lesion, which turned out to be a glioma, in the anterior part of the left temporal lobe. Preoperative psychological tests showed this man to be of superior intelligence, with the only significant deficits being on tests of verbal memory. Two weeks following surgery, psychological testing showed a general decrease in intelligence ratings and a further decrease in the verbal memory scores. Performance on other tests, including tests of the recall of the Rey-Osterith figure (see Figure 10–2) were normal. The second patient, case S. K., had an astrocytoma removed from the right temporal lobe. In contrast to the results from P. G., preoperative testing of this patient showed a low score on the recall of the Rey-Osterith figure (see Figure 14–2). Two weeks after surgery, repeat testing showed a marked decrease of the performance IQ rating and a decline of the nonverbal memory score, both on simple designs and on an alternate form of the Rey-Osterith figure. Comparison of these two patients provides a clear example of double dissociation: the patient with removal of the left temporal lobe was impaired only on verbal tests, whereas the patient with removal of the right temporal lobe was impaired only on nonverbal tests. Furthermore, both patients performed normally on many tests, providing evidence for localization, as well as lateralization, of function.

Patients with Commissurotomy

Epileptic seizures may begin in a restricted region of one hemisphere and then spread via the fibers of the corpus callosum to the homologous location in the opposite hemisphere. To prevent the spread of the seizure when medication has failed to impose control, the procedure of cutting the 200 million nerve fibers of the corpus callosum was performed in the early 1940s by William Van Wagnen, an American neurosurgeon. The procedure initially appeared to be too variable in its therapeutic outcome and was subsequently abandoned until the 1960s, when research by Myers and Sperry with nonhuman species led to a reconsideration of the procedure. Two Californian surgeons, Bogen and Vogel, thus performed complete sections of the corpus callosum and a smaller commissure known as the **anterior commissure** in a new series of about two dozen patients suffering from intractable epilepsy. The procedure was medically beneficial, leaving some patients virtually scizure-free afterward, and the procedure appeared to have rather minimal effects on the everyday behavior of the patients. More extensive psychological testing by Roger Sperry and his colleagues soon demonstrated, however, that these patients have a unique behavioral syndrome: a syndrome that has provided new insights into the nature of cerebral asymmetry.

Figure 14–3 illustrates the effect of commissurotomy on the normal function of the brain. After sectioning, the two hemispheres are independent; each receives sensory input from all sensory systems, and each can control the muscles of body, but the two hemispheres can no longer communicate with one another. Because the functions in these separate cortexes or "split brains" are thus isolated, sensory information can be presented to one hemisphere and the hemisphere's function studied without the other hemisphere having access to the information.

From the numerous studies performed on split-brain patients it is now widely recognized

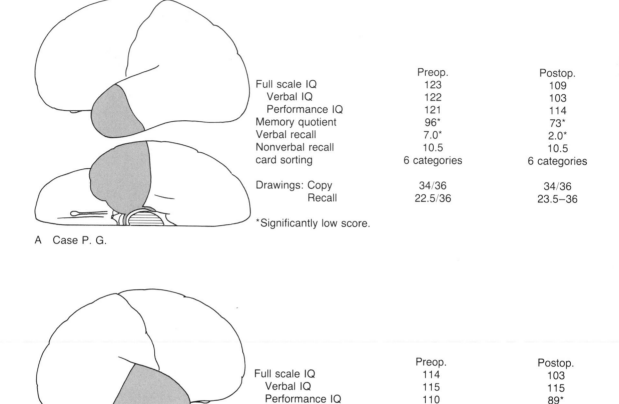

	Preop.	Postop.
Full scale IQ	123	109
Verbal IQ	122	103
Performance IQ	121	114
Memory quotient	96*	73*
Verbal recall	7.0*	2.0*
Nonverbal recall	10.5	10.5
card sorting	6 categories	6 categories
Drawings: Copy	34/36	34/36
Recall	22.5/36	23.5–36

*Significantly low score.

A   Case P. G.

	Preop.	Postop.
Full scale IQ	114	103
Verbal IQ	115	115
Performance IQ	110	89*
Memory quotient	121	101
Verbal recall	16.0	12.0
Nonverbal recall	7.5	5.5*
Card sorting	3 categories	5 categories
Drawings: Copy	31/36	28/36*
Recall	11/36*	13/36*

*Significantly low score.

B   Case S. K.

FIGURE 14–2. A comparison of psychological test results for a patient with a left temporal lobec-tomy (A) and a patient with a right temporal lobectomy at the Montreal Neurological Hospital. The region removed is represented by the darkened zone, estimated by the surgeon at the time of operation. (Modified from Taylor, 1969.)

that when the left hemisphere has access to information, it can initiate speech and hence communicate about the information. The right hemisphere apparently has reasonably good recognition abilities but is unable to initiate speech because it lacks access to the speech mechanisms of the left hemisphere. An exam-ple will serve to illustrate.

FIGURE 14–3. The effect of commissurotomy on connections between the hemispheres and to the sensory and motor systems. Note that although the connections between the visual (V), auditory (A), somatosensory (S), and motor (M) cortical regions and the receptors and effectors are unaffected, the connections between homotopic points in the two hemispheres are severed. Each hemisphere therefore functions independently of the other and without access to the other's sensations, thoughts, or actions.

Patient N. G., a California housewife, sits in front of a screen with a small black dot in the center. She is asked to look directly at the dot. When the experimenter is sure she is doing so, a picture of a cup is flashed briefly to the right of the dot. N. G. reports that she has seen a cup. Again she is asked to fix her gaze on the dot. This time, a picture of a spoon is flashed to the left of the dot. She is asked what she saw. She replies,

"No, nothing." She is then asked to reach under the screen with her left hand and to select, by touch only, from among several items the one object that is the same as she has just seen. Her left hand palpates each object and then holds up the spoon. When asked what she is holding, she says "pencil." (Springer and Deutsch, 1981, pp. 29–30)

The behavior of patient N. G. provides a clear demonstration of the behavior of the two hemispheres when they are not interacting. The picture of the cup was presented to the speaking left hemisphere, which could, of course, respond. The picture of the spoon was presented to the right hemisphere and, since the right hemisphere does not speak and the speaking left hemisphere was not presented a picture, N. G. failed to correctly identify the picture (see Figures 14–4 and 14–5). The abilities of the right hemisphere are demonstrated when the left hand, which is controlled by the right hemisphere, is used to identify the object. Finally, when asked what the still-out-of-sight left hand is holding, the left hemisphere does not know and incorrectly guesses "pencil."

The special capacities of the right hemisphere in facial recognition (see Chapter 10) can also be demonstrated in the split-brain patient. Levy devised the chimeric figures test, which consists of faces and other patterns that have been split down the center and recombined (see Figure 14–6). When the recombined faces were presented selectively to each hemisphere, the patients appeared unaware of the gross discordance between the two sides of the pictures. When asked to pick out the picture they had seen, they chose the face seen in the left visual field and thus by their right hemisphere, demonstrating that the right hemisphere has a special role in the recognition of faces.

In sum, careful and sometimes ingenious studies of patients with commissurotomies have provided clear evidence of the complementary specialization of the two cerebral hemispheres. It must be recognized, however, that as interesting as these patients are, they represent only a very small population and their two hemispheres are by no means normal. Most of these patients had focal lesions, which caused the initial seizure disorder, and some may have had brain damage early in

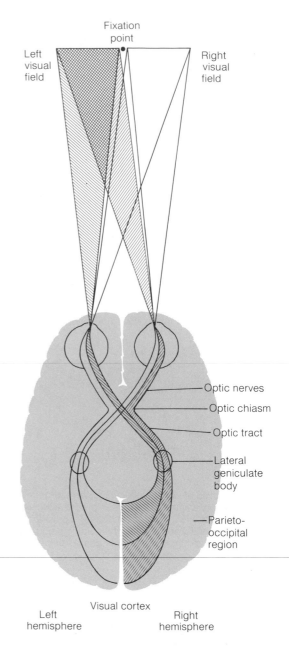

FIGURE 14–4. Visual pathways are crossed; thus, visual fields (and not eyes) are represented in each hemisphere. All the field left of the fixation point (shaded region) is represented in the right visual cortex, and all the field right of the fixation point is represented in the left visual cortex.

Left
visual
field

Key

Right
visual
field

Key   Key

FIGURE 14–5. Visual input is transferred from the left visual field to the left visual cortex via the corpus callosum. Cutting the callosum would prevent such a transfer.

life, leading to significant reorganization of cerebral function. Thus, generalizations and inferences must be made cautiously with these fascinating patients. We shall return to them in Chapter 19.

Brain Stimulation

In the early 1930s Wilder Penfield and his associates at the Montreal Neurological Institute pioneered the use of surgical treatment for epilepsy in patients whose seizures were poorly controlled by drug therapy. The logic of this procedure is to remove the region of cortex where the abnormal discharge originates. Since this is an elective therapeutic surgery it can be planned for, and considerable care can be taken to ensure that areas of the cortex that are critical for the control of speech and movement are not damaged. To identify speech and movement areas, as well as to localize the extent of the epileptogenic tissue, the surgeon stimulates the exposed cortex and records the responses of the conscious patient. Careful study of hundreds of patients in Montreal by Penfield and his students, especially Theodore Rasmussen, and more recently by George Ojemann and his colleagues at the University of Washington, has provided clear evidence of cerebral asymmetry: stimulation of the left hemisphere can block the ability to speak whereas stimulation of the right hemisphere seldom does so. The importance of this technique for neuropsychology cannot be underestimated. Following surgery, in which the surgeon has localized speech and language functions and removed the damaged brain, psychologists often have the opportunity to study patients and to correlate the results of cortical stimulation and psychological assessment, the work of Rasmussen and Brenda Milner at the Montreal Neurological Institute providing an excellent example of such collaboration.

Application of an electric current to the cortex of a conscious patient has four general effects, three excitatory and one inhibitory. First, stimulation can produce localized movements, localized dysthesias (numbness or tingling in the skin), light flashes, or buzzing

Chimeric stimuli

FIGURE 14–6. Composite faces used by Levy et al. to demonstrate the special role of the right hemisphere in facial recognition. Commissurotomy patients were shown the chimeric stimuli (composite pictures) A through D. When asked to choose the face they had seen from among the array of original pictures, 1 through 8, the patients chose the face that was in the left visual field, as the right-hand side of the figure illustrates. (From J. Levy, C. Trevarthen, and R. W. Sperry, Perception of bilateral chimeric figures following hemispheric deconnection. *Brain,* 95:61–78, 1972. Reprinted with permission of Oxford University Press, Oxford.)

sensations. These are normally evoked respectively from primary motor, somatosensory, visual, and auditory areas and pathways and are produced by stimulation of either hemisphere with about the same frequency, a result that illustrates the often overlooked fact that the brain has symmetrical as well as asymmetrical functions. Second, stimulation can produce what Penfield called "interpretive" and "experiential" responses, an example of which was provided in Chapter 10. These uncommon but often highly reliable phenomena include alterations in the interpretation of the patient's surroundings, such as déjà vu, fear and dreaming states, and the reproduction of visual and/or auditory aspects of specific previous experiences. These phenomena usually occur from tissue showing epileptogenic discharge, but there is an asymmetry in their occurrence: stimulation of the right temporal lobe produces these phenomena more frequently than stimulation of the left temporal lobe, which suggests that the right hemisphere has perceptual functions not shared by the left hemisphere. Third, stimulation of the left frontal or temporal regions may accelerate the production of speech. Ojemann suggests that this acceleration may result from a type of "alerting response" and may occur in other cognitive processes, especially memory, although this is difficult to demonstrate unequivocally. Finally, stimulation blocks function. This effect is most evident in complex functions such as language and memory and is *only* apparent when current is applied while the patient is actively engaged in these behaviors. Stimulation to the same site in a quiet patient is without discernible effect. Disruption of speech is a well-documented effect of stimulation of the left hemisphere (see Chapter 21 for a detailed account of this), but it is only recently that stimulation of the right hemisphere has been shown to disrupt behavior. Ojemann and his colleagues have reported that stimulation of the right hemisphere disrupts judgments of line orientation, labeling of facial expressions, and short-term memory for faces, the effects coming almost exclusively from the temporoparietal cortex: a result consistent with the presumed role of this cortex in visuospatial behavior. Unfortunately the authors fail to report data on the effects of stimulation of the left hemisphere on visuospatial behaviors, although they presumably expect that, like the effect of stimulation of the right hemisphere on language, stimulation of the left hemisphere would have negligible effects on visuospatial functions. Perhaps they will test this assumption in future studies.

In sum, stimulation of the cortex has proved a useful tool in demonstrating both localization and lateralization of function. The effect of disrupting stimulation is frequently quite localized, often changing as the site of stimulation is moved as little as a few millimeters, and it is often very reliable within individual patients. Indeed, this technique probably provides the best degree of localization of function that is presently available in the study of brain-behavior relations in humans. One additional intriguing aspect of data from cortical stimulation is that there is a great deal of variation from patient to patient in the exact location and extent of sites with particular effects on behavior. One can speculate that this variation forms a basis for individual differences in skills, as people presumably have different amounts of cortex devoted to particular functions. A correlational study between stimulation results and different cognitive skills would seem to be a very worthwhile endeavor for a surgeon-psychologist team.

Carotid Sodium Amytal

Although language is usually located in the left hemisphere, a small percentage of people, most of them left-handed, have language represented in the right hemisphere. In the event of elective surgery for the treatment of disorders such as epilepsy, avoiding inadvertent damage to the speech zones requires that the surgeon be certain of their location. To achieve certainty in doubtful cases Wada pioneered the technique of injecting sodium Amytal into the carotid artery to produce a brief period of anesthesia of the ipsilateral hemisphere. This procedure results in an unequivocal localization of speech, for injection into the speech hemisphere results in an arrest of speech lasting up to several minutes, and as speech returns it is characterized by aphasic errors. Injection into the nonspeaking hemisphere may produce no, or only brief, speech arrest. The carotid Amytal procedure has the advantage that each hemisphere can be studied separately in the functional absence of the other, anesthetized one. Since the period of anesthesia lasts several minutes it is possible to study a variety of functions, including memory and movement, to determine the capabilities of one hemisphere in the absence of the anesthetized one.

The test is always performed bilaterally, with the two cerebral hemispheres being injected on separate days in order to be sure that there is no residual drug effect from the injection of the first hemisphere at the time of injection of the opposite side. At the Montreal Neurological Hospital, where Wada initially developed the procedure, a small catheter is inserted under x-ray control by a neuroradiologist well up into the internal carotid artery and an angiogram is carried out. The patient is then moved to the testing room and a dry run is carried out to familiarize the patient with the tests that will be done during and after the drug injection, and to establish a baseline performance level against which to compare the postinjection performance. He or she is then given a series of simple tasks, involving immediate and delayed memory for both verbal (sentences or words) and nonverbal (photographs of faces or objects) material, for the same purpose. Moments before the drug is injected, the patient lies flat on his or her back with both knees drawn up, both hands raised, and the fingers and toes moving. The patient is asked to count backward from 20, and without warning the neurosurgeon injects the drug through the catheter over a two to three second period. Within seconds, there are dramatic changes in behavior.

The contralateral arm and leg fall to the bed with a flaccid paralysis and there is no response whatsoever to a firm pinch of the skin of the affected limbs. If the injected hemisphere is nondominant for speech, the patient may continue to count and carry out the verbal tasks while the temporary hemiparalysis is present, although there is often a period of up to 20 to 30 seconds during which the patient appears confused and is

silent, but typically can resume speech with urging. When the injected hemisphere is dominant for speech, the patient typically stops talking and remains completely aphasic until recovery from the hemiparesis is well along, usually in four to 10 minutes. Speech is tested by asking the patient to name a number of common objects presented in quick succession, to count and recite the days of the week forward and backward, and by simple naming and spelling. In addition to aphasia and paresis, patients with injections of either hemisphere are totally nonresponsive to visual stimulation in the contralateral visual field. For example, there is no reflexive blinking or orientation toward suddenly looming objects. Finally, injection of the speaking hemisphere not only produces contralateral hemiparesis but also renders the ipsilateral side dyspraxic, as we described in our discussion of apraxia in Chapter 12.

The sodium Amytal test, like direct brain stimulation, has been very useful in determining which hemisphere controls speech. Table 14–3 shows the relation between hand preference and the lateralization of cerebral speech processes for a large sample of patients, who were studied by Rasmussen and Milner. As would be expected from the data from brain stimulation, there is a strong preponderance for left hemisphere speech representation: 96 percent of the right-handers and 70 percent of the left-handers show speech disturbance after Amytal-injection into the left hemisphere and

TABLE 14–3

Speech lateralization as related to handedness

Handedness	No. of cases	Speech representation (%)		
		Left	Bilateral	Right
Right	140	96	0	4
Left	122	70	15	15

After Rasmussen and Milner, 1977.

not after injection into the right. Curiously, 4 percent of their right-handed sample had their speech functions lateralized to the right cerebral hemisphere. This figure certainly overestimates the proportion of right hemisphere speech in the normal population (remember that all of these patients had epileptogenic lesions), but it does remind us that speech is sometimes found in the right hemisphere of right-handed people. The results for left-handed patients support the view that the pattern of speech representation is less predictable in left-handed and ambidextrous subjects than in right-handers, but that the majority of left-handers do have speech represented in the left hemisphere. It is interesting, however, that whereas none of the right-handers showed evidence of bilateral speech organization, in 15 percent of the non-right-handers there was some significant speech disturbance following injection of either side. These patients probably did not have a symmetrical duplication of language functions in the two hemispheres, as injection of one hemisphere tended to disrupt naming (e.g., names of the days of the week) whereas injection of the other hemisphere disrupted serial ordering (e.g., ordering the days of the week). Hence, although people may have bilateral representation of speech, this representation is probably asymmetrical and need not imply that the person has "two left hemispheres." Further study of these patients would likely have revealed that visuospatial functions were bilaterally, and asymmetrically represented as well, although this is mere conjecture on our part.

ASYMMETRY IN THE INTACT BRAIN

The study of neurological patients demonstrates a clear functional difference between the hemispheres, particularly in the control of language. We have noted earlier, however, that there are many problems in trying to make inferences about the functioning of the normal brain from clinical studies of the dysfunctioning brain. Thus, just because a specific behavioral symptom is associated with damage to a particular brain area does not necessarily mean that the region once controlled the disrupted function. Confirmation is needed from the study of normal brains, especially since the two hemispheres are unlikely to function independently in the intact brain but must play some type of complementary role with each other in nearly all behaviors. The challenge is to devise ways of studying the contribution made by each hemisphere to behavior in the intact brain.

One approach to the study of the normal brain forms the subfield of neuropsychology called **laterality.** The logic of laterality studies is to take advantage of the anatomical organization of the sensory and motor systems in order to "trick" the brain into revealing its mode of operation. Laterality research now forms a very large and growing subfield within human neuropsychology, a field that itself now forms the basis for entire textbooks. We shall review the major findings and problems in laterality research and refer the reader interested in details to the recent account by Bryden.

Asymmetry in the Visual System

The organization of the visual system provides an opportunity to selectively present each hemisphere with specific visual information. Figure 14–4 shows the relation between each visual field and its field of projection in the visual cortex: visual stimuli in the left visual field are projected to the right visual cortex, whereas stimuli in the right visual field travel to the left visual cortex. By using a special instrument called a **tachistoscope** visual information can be presented to each visual field independently. Subjects are asked to fixate on a center point marked by a dot or cross (see Figure 14–4). An image is then flashed in one visual field for about 50 milliseconds—a time short enough to allow the image to be processed before the eyes can shift from the fixation point. By comparing the accuracy with which information from the two visual fields is processed it is possible to infer which hemisphere is best suited to process different types of information.

In the early 1950s Mishkin and Forgays first used the tachistoscopic procedure to demonstrate that normal right-handed subjects could identify English words presented to the right visual field more accurately than when they were presented to the left visual field. Mishkin and Forgays believed that acquired directional reading habits (i.e., left to right in English) were responsible for this bias, but the studies with the Californian commissurotomy patients a decade later suggested another interpretation: information presented to only one visual field is processed most efficiently by the hemisphere that is specialized to receive it. Words presented to the left hemisphere are therefore processed more efficiently than words presented to the nonverbal right hemisphere. This conclusion was very important not only because it was consistent with the clinical inferences about cerebral specialization but also because it suggested that differences between the processing carried out by the right and left hemispheres could be studied in normal subjects.

The strongest evidence that visual field differences in tachistoscopic studies are measuring functional asymmetries in the brain is that the visual field asymmetries in tachistoscopic tasks are the same as the asymmetries demonstrated with neurological patients. Thus, a right visual field advantage is found with normal subjects in a variety of tasks using verbal material such as words

and letters, and a left visual field advantage is found for stimuli thought to be processed by the right hemisphere, including faces and other visuospatial stimuli (see Table 14–4).

Asymmetry in the Auditory System

The auditory system is not as completely crossed as is the visual system: both hemispheres receive projections from each ear. However, the crossed connections do appear better developed and may have preferred access to the cortex. Thus, sounds projected to the right ear are processed primarily by the left hemisphere, and those to the left ear are processed primarily by the right hemisphere, as shown in Figure 14–7.

In the early 1960s Doreen Kimura, working at the Montreal Neurological Institute, was presenting patients with pairs of spoken digits (e.g., "two" and "six"), one of which was heard in each ear through headphones connected to a stereo tape recorder. Each patient was presented with three pairs of digits and then asked to recall as many of the six digits as possible, in any order. Kimura was interested in the auditory processing capacities of patients with temporal lobe lesions, but she noticed that all subjects, regardless of lesion locus, recalled more digits that had been presented to the right ear than had been presented to the left ear. The right-ear advantage was also found in normal control subjects. This led Kimura to propose that when two different stimuli are presented simultaneously to each ear, the pathway from the right ear to the speaking hemisphere has preferred access, whereas the ipsilateral pathway from the left ear is relatively suppressed. Thus, during a dichotic task, the stimulus to the left ear must travel to the right hemisphere and then across the cerebral commissures to the left hemisphere. The more difficult route via the left ear puts stimuli into this ear at a disadvantage, and words played to the right ear

TABLE 14–4

Summary of relative asymmetry of function in studies of normal subjects

	Task	Left hemisphere dominance [a]	Right hemisphere dominance
Visual (tachistoscope)	Letters	1.2	1.0
	Words	1.5	1.0
	Two-dimensional point localization	1.0	1.2
	Dot and form enumeration	1.0	1.2
	Matching of slanted lines	1.0	1.1
	Stereoscopic depth perception	1.0	1.3
	Faces	1.0	1.2
Auditory (dichotic listening)	Words	1.9	1.0
	Nonsense syllables	1.7	1.0
	Backward speech	1.7	1.0
	Melodic pattern	1.0	1.2
	Nonspeech sounds (cough, laugh, etc.)	1.0	1.1
Manual	Skilled movements	1.0	1.0
	Free movements during speech	3.1	1.0
	Tactual dot (Braille)		Significantly higher

[a] Numbers indicate the ratio of hemisphere dominance for each task.
Adapted from Kimura, 1973.

are recalled more accurately. Having found a right-ear advantage for the perception of dichotically presented speech stimuli, it was an obvious next step to search for tasks that gave a left-ear superiority. In 1964, Kimura reported just such an effect in the perception of melodies. Two excerpts of instrumental chamber music were played simultaneously through headphones, one to each ear. After each pair, four excerpts, including the two that had been played dichotically, were presented binaurally and the subject's task was to identify the two that had been heard previously. The amazing result was that Kimura found a left-ear advantage for normal subjects on this task.

It should be noted that not all subjects show the expected ear advantages in dichotic studies, the effects are not large when they occur (seldom exceeding a twofold difference in accuracy in the two ears), and dichotic results are apparently affected by various contextual and practice effects. Nonetheless, the Kimura studies have played a seminal role in laterality studies, since they complemented the results from the neurological literature. As a result, they opened up an entire field of research to anyone with imagination and a stereo tape recorder. More importantly, her experiments provided a noninvasive technique for identifying the hemisphere dominant for language, a question of special clinical importance, particularly in left-handed patients. Furthermore, the test has other clinical uses since patients with left temporal lobe damage are very poor at this task and patients with damage to the corpus callosum exhibit an almost complete inhibition of words presented to the left ear, even though they can recall words presented to this ear if there is no competing stimulus to the right ear. In sum, the dichotic listening proce-

FIGURE 14–7. Auditory pathways from the ears to the cerebral auditory receiving areas in the right and left hemispheres are partially crossed. Although each hemisphere can receive input from both ears, the neural connections from one ear to the hemisphere on the opposite side are stronger than those to the hemisphere on the same side. When ipsilateral (same side) and contralateral (opposite side) inputs compete in the auditory neural system, it is thought that the stronger contralateral input inhibits or occludes the ipsilateral signals. (After Kimura, 1973.)

dure has proved to be an invaluable tool both clinically and in the field of laterality.

Asymmetry in the Somatosensory System

Experiments of laterality in somatosensation have not been as popular as those on vision and audition. Nevertheless, the somatosensory system is almost completely crossed, a feature that allows an easy comparison of the two sides, just as in vision or audition (see Figure 14–8). By blindfolding subjects and requiring them to perform various tasks, such as reading Braille or palpating objects with each hand

separately, it is possible to identify differences in efficiency of performing by the two hands, differences that can be taken to imply functional asymmetry in cerebral organization.

One type of research has compared the performance of the left and right hands in the recognition of various shapes, angles, and patterns by testing each hand separately. The left hand of right-handed subjects is superior at nearly all tasks of this type. For example, Rudel et al. found that both blind and sighted

FIGURE 14–8. Somatosensory and motor pathways are almost wholly crossed; each hand is served primarily by the cerebral hemisphere on the opposite side.

subjects read Braille more rapidly with the left hand. Some children are actually fluent readers with the left hand but totally unable to read with the right. Since Braille patterns are spatial configurations of dots, this observation is congruent with the proposal that the right hemisphere has a role in processing spatial information not shared by the left hemisphere.

A second type of somatosensory test utilizes an analogue of the dichotic procedure, the **dichaptic** test, which was used first by Witelson. She simultaneously presented a different, unfamiliar complex shape that could not be seen to each hand. The subjects felt the objects and then were allowed to look at an array of objects and select those they had previously touched. The results showed a left-hand—hence right hemisphere—superiority in the recognition of objects. More recently, Gibson and Bryden have been able to dissociate the performance of the left and right hands. In their experiment, subjects were dichaptically presented with cutouts of irregular shapes or letters made of sandpaper, which were moved slowly across the fingertips. Their subjects showed a right-hand advantage for identifying letters and a left-hand advantage for identifying nonsense shapes.

Perhaps the most elegant somatosensory study was carried out by Nachson and Carmon in 1975. They presented subjects with two different tasks, one that they described as "spatial" and another described as "sequential." In these tasks the index, middle, and ring fingers were stimulated by tapered metal rods. Depending on the task, the subjects had to respond by pressing microswitches next to the rods. Thus in the spatial task one finger was stimulated once, another twice, and a third not at all. The subject's task was to indicate the pattern of stimulation by pressing the appropriate microswitches. In the sequential task, the three fingers were stimu-

lated in random order and the subjects had to press the switches in the same sequence as they had been stimulated. With bimanual presentation, subjects made more errors with the left hand on the sequential task and more errors with the right hand on the spatial task. This result is important, for it implies that the left hemisphere has a special role in sequential analysis, a capacity that would presumably be very important in the control of complex movement, a control that we have already seen may be a special function of the left hemisphere.

Asymmetry in the Motor System

Although the motor system has a significant uncrossed component, clinical studies, first by Wyke and more recently by Kimura and others, have suggested that there is a functional asymmetry in the control of the movement. Following the logic of the study of asymmetry in the intact sensory systems, it would seem reasonable to look for asymmetries in motor control. One difficulty that immediately confronts us, however, is that since there is an asymmetry in the accuracy of response to sensory input, the study of motor asymmetries is potentially confounded by the fact that the two sides do not start off equally. For example, if we found that the right hand reacted to verbal stimuli faster than the left hand, we would be unable to conclude that this was due to a motor asymmetry per se; it could be due entirely to the perceptual asymmetry. Two different types of experiments have therefore been devised to assess motor asymmetries: (1) direct observation of motor asymmetry, and (2) interference tasks. We shall consider each separately.

Direct Observation. If there is an inherent asymmetry in the control of movement, it is possible that this asymmetry might be observ-

able when people are engaged in other behaviors. For example, perhaps the right hand is
more active during the performance of verbal
tasks, which do not require a manual response,
and the left hand is more active during the
performance of nonverbal tasks, which also do
not require a manual response. To examine this
possibility Kimura and her students have done
a number of intriguing experiments. It is a
common observation that people often gesture
when talking. By videotaping subjects talking
or humming, Kimura was able to show that
right-handed people tend to gesture with their
right hands when talking but are equally likely
to scratch, rub their nose, or touch their body
with either hand. Kimura interpreted the
observed gesturing with the limb contralateral
to the speaking hemisphere to indicate a relation between speech and certain manual activities. Since differences in gesturing, which
favor the right hand in right-handed subjects,
could simply reflect a difference in preferred
hand rather than imply a functional asymmetry
in motor control, another series of studies
compared hand movement asymmetries during analogous verbal and nonverbal tasks. The
procedure involved videotaping right-handed
subjects while they assembled blocks in three
different types of tests. The first type, a "neutral task," required subjects to combine
white blocks to form a 5-by-5 matrix. The
second type, a "verbal task," required subjects
to combine blocks with letters on them in a
series of crossword-puzzle tasks. In the third
type, a "nonverbal task," subjects did jigsaw
puzzles with the same size blocks as in the
preceding types of tasks. Analysis of the
movements showed that in the neutral task,
subjects manipulated blocks with the right
hand while supporting them with the left.
Other movements seldom occurred. On the
verbal tasks, most task-directed movements
showed a right-hand preference. In contrast,
on nonverbal tasks, task-directed movements

showed a leftward shift from the neutral condition, subjects now making far more movements with the left hand. These results suggest that the two hemispheres may have
complementary roles in the control of movement, an asymmetry that is moderated by a
native hand preference.

Another fascinating observation of lateralization of movement control is that concentration on a difficult problem frequently causes
the eyes, and often the head, to turn laterally to
the left or right. Careful study indicates that
right-handed people usually turn head and eyes
to the right when solving verbal problems, but
look up and to the left when solving numerical
and spatial problems. This phenomenon,
labeled *lateral eye gaze,* has been interpreted as
resulting from predominant activation of the
hemisphere most vigorously involved in processing the material of the task. In other words,
people gaze right while doing a verbal problem
because the activation of the left hemisphere
"spills over," affecting motor activation toward the right side. The converse is true of
spatial or numerical tasks. This phenomenon,
although slow in gaining credibility among
many neuropsychologists, is interesting and
provocative.

Interference Tasks. A variety of laboratories
have recently examined a well-known phenomenon that most people manifest: the difficulty in doing two complex tasks at the same
time. If subjects are asked to balance a dowel
on their left or right index fingers while talking, they are able to maintain the balance much
longer with the left hand than with the right.
Similar results are also reported for other
complex tasks such as tapping a sequence of
movements with the fingers; speaking interferes only with performance of the left
hand. Perhaps the most interesting interference study we know of is an unpublished

experiment by Hicks and Kinsbourne. They persuaded several unemployed musicians to come to their laboratory daily to play the piano. The task was to learn a different piece of music with each hand so that the two pieces could be played simultaneously. Once the musicians had mastered this very difficult task, the experimenters then asked them to speak or to hum while playing. Evidently speaking disrupted playing with the right hand and humming playing with the left hand.

As interesting as interference studies may be, interference effects are poorly understood and appear to be capricious. It is a common observation that as we become proficient at motor tasks we are less prone to interference effects. Consider the difficulty in talking while learning to play tennis; an interference paradigm of little challenge to a tennis professional. Interference studies provide a useful way to study the roles of the two hemispheres in the control of movement, but much more work will be needed before we can identify the complementary roles of the two hemispheres in movement. It will be necessary to identify which types of movements each hemisphere is especially good at controlling since these movements will likely be resilient to interference effects. Further, there should be studies of the capacities of the hemispheres to produce simultaneous finger versus limb movements. Perhaps finger movements are more sensitive to interference effects when performed by the right than the left hemisphere. Studies of interference effects are important, however, as they may provide fresh insights into the nature of apraxia in clinical populations.

What do Laterality Studies Tell Us about Brain Function?

Laterality studies provide an important complement to the study of neurological patients and have served as the basis for much of the current theorizing about the nature of cerebral asymmetry. It should be recognized that they are a very indirect measure of brain function and that they are far from being the ideal tools they are often assumed to be. Consider the following problems.

Measures of laterality do not correlate perfectly with invasive measures of cerebral asymmetry. For example, dichotic-listening studies show a right-ear bias for words in about 80 percent of right-handed subjects, but sodium Amytal testing and brain stimulation show language to be represented in the left hemisphere in over 95 percent of right-handers. What causes this discrepancy?

Measures of laterality do not correlate very highly with one another. We might expect that tachistoscopic and dichotic measures of laterality in the same subjects would be highly concordant, but they are not. Perhaps these tests are not really measuring the same things after all?

There is no simple way to correlate individual differences in the neural pathways to the cortex, or the functional representations in the cortex, with individual performance on laterality tests. Individual differences in the brains of normal subjects almost certainly add a great deal of variance to the results, but there is currently no way of identifying a systematic relation between anatomy and performance.

The strategies that subjects adopt in laterality tasks can significantly alter performance. If subjects are instructed to pay particular attention to words entering the left ear in dichotic tasks, they can do so, abolishing the right-ear effect. Subjects can also enter tests with preconceived biases, which may affect test performance. Finally, laterality effects may simply be a result of experiential, rather than biological, factors. Suspicion is reinforced by the observation that repeated testing of the same subjects does not always produce the same results.

Laterality studies are very easy to do and can be done by most undergraduate psychology majors if they have access to a tachistoscope or a stereo tape recorder. Although this is good pedagogically, it has encouraged a proliferation of experiments on small samples of subjects in which the experimenters are not always fully aware of the tenuous nature of the inferences about brain function. We cannot emphasize strongly enough that laterality studies are just one technique of drawing inferences about cerebral functioning. Theories about hemispheric organization must consider data from many sources, only one of which is the study of the intact brain.

MEASURES OF CEREBRAL BLOOD FLOW AND METABOLIC RATE

In 1890 Roy and Sherrington first postulated that when regions of the brain are functionally activated, the blood supply will correspondingly increase in these areas. The measurement of moment-to-moment variations of cerebral blood flow is difficult but is thought to be accurate, and measurements have been made since 1890 using some ingenious techniques. The modern development of computerized systems for collecting and synthesizing large amounts of data has made possible the parallel development of highly reliable techniques for measuring both local cerebral blood flow and local cerebral glucose metabolism. In the former procedure, a solution containing a substance such as xenon 133, which accumulates in areas of increased blood flow, is injected into an artery while special detectors on the skull monitor its concentration. (In a new, less accurate variant of this procedure the xenon 133 is inhaled.) If a subject is asked to palpate an object with one hand, an increase in xenon 133 concentration is found over the somatosensory zones of the contralateral hemisphere, suggesting their involvement in tactile processing. The measurement of glucose metabolism takes advantage of the PET scanner (see Chapter 5). Since there is a close link between functional activity and local metabolism in the brain, it is possible to infer the relative functional activity of local regions of the brain by measuring the rate of glucose metabolism. In this method a short-lived radioactive tracer ($[^{18}F]$-2-deoxy-2-fluoro-D-glucose, abbreviated $[^{18}F]$-FDG), is intravenously injected while a subject is engaged in a task. When this glucose is metabolized, a labeled product of the metabolism ($[^{18}F]$-FDG phosphate) is essentially trapped in the tissue for a few minutes and can be measured by a PET scanner.

The use of both of these techniques is still in its infancy and a significant increase in resolution is required before effective mapping of active cortex can be carried out. With improved instrument resolution the situation will be different, and both procedures will become major techniques in the study of cerebral functioning, in both the study of localization and of lateralization of functions (see the review by Reivich).

Localization of Function

Owing to the low resolution and slow speed of these procedures cortical activation lasting only a few seconds will be missed, and so most studies to date have utilized simple tasks, which are repeated over a period of several minutes. Nevertheless, the results are exciting. Regional blood flow measurements have been used to determine the normal resting pattern of activity of the brain when subjects are sitting still with their eyes closed and ears plugged. A highly reliable resting pattern emerges in which the frontal lobe receives relatively more blood, roughly 15 percent more than the mean for the entire hemisphere. This pattern of cerebral activation changes markedly during basic auditory, visual, and tactile stimulation or during rhythmic movements. For example, auditory input bilaterally activates both superior temporal gyri, visual input activates the contralateral occipital cortex, and simple tactile object discrimination with the hand, mouth, or foot activates the corresponding part of the contralateral sensorimotor areas. Similarly, rhythmic movements of the hand, fingers, lips, and toes activate the respective contralateral sensorimotor regions as well. Activation is not restricted just to the primary sensory and motor regions, however, as it is usually accompanied by activation in at least part of the frontal lobe. For example, rhythmic movements often activate the supplementary motor cortex and tactile discrimination is associated with an increase in activity in the superior frontal sulcus, observations that are consistent with the proposed role of the frontal cortex in sensory processing and movement (see Chapter 18).

Lateralization of Function

Both regional blood flow and FDG systems have been used to identify asymmetries in cerebral functioning. As might be expected, there is an asymmetrical uptake of the tracers when subjects either listen to or engage in conversation (see Figure 14–9). For example, when a subject is listening to speech, both hemispheres show regional changes in cerebral activation especially within the auditory cortex, but the left hemisphere also shows increased activation in Broca's and Wernicke's areas. When speaking, subjects also show activation of the motor representation of the face, mouth, and the supplementary motor cortex. Somewhat curiously, repetition of what has been called "automatic" speech,

such as naming the days of the week over and over again, fails to produce an increase in activity in Broca's area, a result that would not have been predicted from the idea that this area is involved in producing movement or from the sodium Amytal or stimulation results discussed earlier. In contrast to the left side increase during speech perception, there is an increase in right side uptake of tracer in the temporal lobe when subjects are played the tonal memory and timbre tests of the Seashore Musical Aptitude Test, a result consistent with Milner's demonstration that right temporal lobe lesions impair performance of these tests. Finally, Dabbs and others have found evidence that there may be an overall difference in blood flow to the two hemispheres: the right hemisphere receives slightly more blood flow than the left. This may be because the right hemisphere is larger or it may also occur for other reasons.

In sum, measures of regional blood flow and glucose uptake hold great promise for the future, once the instrumentation can be improved to make possible faster and finer resolution. The cost of these procedures will remain prohibitive, however, and so it is likely that only a small number of laboratories will be able to perform this type of research. Further, it should be recognized that with the available technology quickly occurring cognitive events (e.g., less than 45 s duration) cannot be measured.

ELECTRICAL RECORDING

The electrical activity of the brain of normal subjects can be recorded (as noted in previous chapters) by both the EEG and the average evoked potential (AEP). Since the two hemispheres function differently, and since the EEG and AEP reflect the function of neurons, it follows logically that there ought to

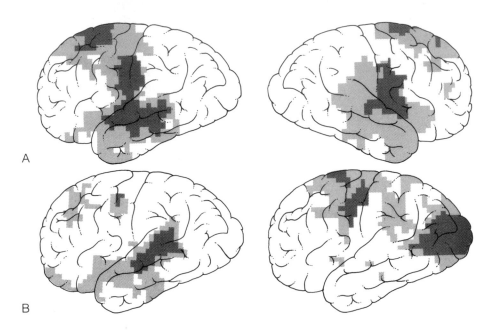

A

B

FIGURE 14–9. Relating brain function to regional blood flow. Because the pattern of blood flow varies with the behavioral task the relative importance of different areas in different functions can be inferred: light shading indicates the average level of blood flow; dark shading indicates higher-than-average blood flow; the absence of shading indicates lower-than-average blood flow. A. Speaking activates the mouth-tongue-larynx of the motor and somatosensory cortex, the supplementary motor area, and the auditory cortex. These images, averaged from nine different subjects, show differences in the activity of the left and right hemispheres: in the left hemisphere the mouth area is more active and the auditory cortex, including part of area 22, is considerably more active. B. Sensory perception changes the pattern of blood flow in the cortex, revealing the localization of areas that mediate the processing of sensory information. During the study at the right the subject followed a moving object with his eyes, resulting in high activity in the visual cortex and frontal eye fields. During the study at the left the same subject listened to spoken words, resulting in increased activity localized to the auditory cortex. Note that the position of the Sylvian and central fissures is approximate; the actual position could be determined only by opening the skull. The squared shapes are an artifact of the recording and averaging procedure and thus do not accurately indicate the shapes of areas in the brain. (Simplified from Lassen, Ingvar, and Skinhøj, 1978.)

be asymmetry in the EEGs and AEPs recorded from the two hemispheres. Indeed, over the past 10 years numerous experiments have attempted to demonstrate this asymmetry, and there have been promising results, for on some behavioral tasks EEGs and AEPs do appear to be asymmetrical over the two hemispheres. The results are far from conclusive, however. In a recent review, Donchin et al. conclude that the literature is fraught with serious methodological inadequacies related to recording techniques, behavioral tasks, data analysis, and the like. These problems are not unsurmountable, however, and the development of new techniques, such as the one described by Gevins and his colleagues, is intriguing and may prove to be more reliable than the more traditional approaches. In sum, although interhemispheric differences in EEG and AEP recordings are apt to be minute, the

TABLE 14–5

Summary of data on cerebral lateralization[a]

Function	Left hemisphere	Right hemisphere
Visual system	Letters, words	Complex geometric patterns Faces
Auditory system	Language-related sounds	Nonlanguage environmental sounds Music
Somatosensory system	?	Tactual recognition of complex patterns Braille
Movement	Complex voluntary movement	?
Memory	Verbal memory	Visual memory
Language	Speech Reading Writing Arithmetic	
Spatial processes		Geometry Sense of direction Mental rotation of shapes

[a] Functions of the respective hemispheres that are predominantly mediated by one hemisphere in right-handed people.

techniques are promising as a means of investigating hemispheric lateralization.

WHAT IS LATERALIZED?

It is tempting to conclude that the functional asymmetries described so far represent a larger fundamental difference in the basic cognitive processes of the left and right hemispheres. However, before considering this issue we will summarize the data, since any theoretical statements are best considered in light of the available information.

Table 14–5 summarizes the major data and illustrates the range of functions lateralized principally in the left and right hemispheres respectively. In right-handed people the left hemisphere has a role in language and in controlling complex voluntary movement that is not shared by the right hemisphere, whereas the right hemisphere has a role in the control of

visuospatial abilities not shared by the left hemisphere.

Theoretical Arguments

There have been three principal arguments regarding the fundamental difference between the hemispheres. The first clear proposal was made by Semmes in 1968. On the basis of her previous studies of World War II veterans suffering from penetrating brain injuries she concluded that the left hemisphere functions as a collection of focalized regions, whereas the right hemisphere functions more diffusely, in a manner consistent with Lashley's notions of mass action and equipotentiality. Her logic was as follows. She had noticed that small lesions of the left hemisphere produced a wide variety of specific deficits (e.g., impaired spelling and reading), the precise deficit depending on the locus of the lesion; similar-sized lesions within the right hemisphere were frequently without obvious effect. In contrast, large lesions of *either* hemisphere produced a large number of deficits. To account for this differential effect Semmes argued that a person with a small lesion of the right hemisphere exhibits no deficits because specific functions are not localized in discrete regions in the right hemisphere, the functions being diffusely represented. A large lesion of the right hemisphere produces many more deficits than would be predicted from the total of smaller lesions because an entire functional field is removed—a proposition that is consistent with Lashley's idea of mass action. Large lesions of the left hemisphere produce many deficits simply because many small focal regions have been destroyed; the total is equal to the sum of the parts.

Semmes proposed that this differential organization of the two hemispheres is advantageous for efficient control of their respective functions. The diffuse organization of the right hemisphere is seen as advantageous for spatial abilities, since spatial analysis requires that different kinds of information (visual, auditory, tactual) be integrated into a single percept. Language functions are not integrated in the same manner, but remain as individual units.

From Semmes's basic idea subsequent writers such as Levy, Sperry, Bogen, Ornstein, and Jaynes have proposed a second argument: namely that the hemispheres represent two distinct modes of cognitive processing.

> The left hemisphere operates in a more logical, analytical, computer-like fashion, analyzing stimulus information input sequentially, abstracting out the relevant details to which it attaches verbal labels; the right hemisphere is primarily a synthesizer, more concerned with the overall stimulus configuration, and organizes and processes information in terms of gestalts or wholes. (Harris, 1978, p. 463)

Although this second theory has recently stimulated interest among philosophers and the general public, it is important to remember that it is entirely an inference, one that has jumped a long way from the data summarized in Table 14–5. There is no direct support of the model, and there are good reasons to approach Semmes's results with caution. Her critical result—the absence of deficits from small right hemisphere lesions—may reflect our ignorance about the functions of the right hemisphere rather than an absence of deficits. Recall that until the 1950s and 1960s right hemisphere lesions had few known effects, and even today we understand the left, verbal, hemisphere far better than we do the right.

The third theoretical position, proposed by Kimura, is that although the left hemisphere mediates verbal function, it is specialized not for verbal function per se, but rather for certain kinds of motor function, both verbal and nonverbal. Kimura's argument is based on two premises. First, lesions of the left hemisphere disturb the production of voluntary movement, an impairment correlated with disturbance in speech. Second, Kimura proposes that verbal communication evolved from a stage that was primarily gestural, though with vocal concomitants, to one that is primarily vocal but that retains the capacity for manual communication. Since the neurological control of speech and language thus evolved out of a system of motor control of gesture, the left hemisphere is not specialized for language per se, but rather for motor control.

Kimura's theory is radically different from the previous ideas of Semmes and others, and it unfortunately does not consider in the same detail the question of the right hemisphere. Nevertheless, we prefer Kimura's theory because it is closely tied to the available data, the role of the left hemisphere in movement is testable, and it is possible to extend the theory to include the right hemisphere. For example, it could be argued that the two hemispheres became specialized for different aspects of motor control. The left hemisphere is specialized for fine motor control and the right hemisphere for gross motor movement in space.

Kimura discusses one aspect of cerebral asymmetry that other writers do not: the question of laterality in nonhuman species. Presumably any theory of what is lateralized in the human brain must eventually consider whether the nonhuman brain is asymmetrically organized, and if so, what is lateralized in those species. We consider this question in the next chapter.

Preferred Cognitive Mode

From the previous theoretical arguments it is possible to speculate that individual differences in the behavior of normal subjects result, at least in part, from individual differences in how the cerebral hemispheres are organized and how functions are lateralized. Thus, subjects who are very logical, analytical, and verbal could be assumed to be more efficient in using their left hemispheres to solve problems in everyday life, whereas subjects who are predominantly concerned with wholes or general concepts could be assumed to be more efficient in using their right hemispheres. For example (a tongue-in-cheek one), two professors, Alpha and Beta, are both excellent scholars, but they are totally different in how they work and think.

Alpha is meticulous and leaves no detail to chance; when learning new material he masters every detail and has total command of the topic. Alpha is verbal and can easily win debates with his quick thinking and elegant arguments. His writing is clear and concise with flawless grammar and spelling. Alpha is athletic, being a nationally ranked tennis player. Curiously, he is only mediocre at other sports, but with prolonged practice he is able to master their details as well. Finally, Alpha's office is neat and tidy, with every item carefully placed in its correct location. On his desk is the project he is currently working on and nothing else.

Beta, on the other hand, only appears to learn the generalities of new material, and seldom recalls the minute details. He grasps ideas quickly, however, and is often able to tie very diverse concepts into a meaningful picture. His thinking often appears muddled to those around him, for he has difficulty expressing his ideas, but given enough time he often impresses his colleagues with his insight into problems. His writing is poor in comparison to Alpha's, for he expresses himself with tortuous constructions and is plagued by grammatical and spelling errors about which he appears totally unconcerned. Nevertheless, Beta has a remarkable knack for asking the correct questions and tying together seemingly diverse literature. Like Alpha, Beta is athletic, but unlike Alpha, Beta acquires the general motor skills of new sports rapidly, although he has never been able to become a top participant in any event. Beta's office is messy and his desk is a pile of papers and books, because he works on several projects concurrently.

Alpha and Beta represent extremes of what could be described as left hemisphere and right hemisphere individuals, respectively. The fundamental difference between them is that each attacks problems by using what has been described as a different **preferred cognitive mode.** Alpha is analytical, logical, verbal, and meticulous, whereas Beta is a synthesizer, more concerned with organizing concepts into meaningful wholes. Thus, in both the cognitive and the motor skills of Alpha and Beta there is a basic difference that is assumed to reflect a fundamental difference in either brain organization or the "dominance" of one hemisphere over the other.

As intriguing as this analysis of Alpha and

Beta appears to be, we caution that it is pure speculation, without empirical basis. It is probable that factors other than brain organization may contribute to preferred cognitive mode. For example, a recent study by Webster and Thurber demonstrates that cognitive set can affect some tests of lateralization. They repeated Witelson's dichaptic test (described earlier), but added an additional variable. One group (the gestalt group) was encouraged to learn the shapes by imagining the overall appearance, or gestalt, whereas a second group (the analytic group) was encouraged to identify distinctive features and list them to themselves. This manipulation demonstrably influenced the degree of left-hand superiority, for the gestalt group had a significantly larger performance difference between the hands than did the analytic group. Although the basis for this effect is uncertain, it implies that strategies used by subjects can significantly influence tests of lateralization. It thus seems reasonable to assume that differences in preferred cognitive mode may reflect socialization or environmental factors in addition to neuronal, biological, or constitutional factors. Nevertheless, that individual differences in behavior result in part from individual differences in brain organization seems a provocative assumption worthy of serious study.

CONCLUDING REMARKS

We have shown how the two hemispheres of the human brain are both anatomically and functionally asymmetrical. Two important points must be emphasized before we consider variations in the "textbook pattern" of cerebral asymmetry in the next chapter, lest we leave the reader with two common misunderstandings.

First, many functions of the cerebral hemispheres are not asymmetrical. Rather, they are symmetrical. In a recent examination in our undergraduate course in human neuropsychology we asked the question: In what ways is the human brain symmetrical? Thinking it to be a trick question, a majority of the students answered: "It isn't symmetrical, it's asymmetrical." This is wrong, of course, since many functions, especially of the primary sensory and motor areas, appear identical on the two sides of the brain. Furthermore, we must realize that the functional differences between the two hemispheres are not absolute, but rather are relative. Just because sodium Amytal renders one hemisphere aphasic does not mean that language functions are only carried out in the aphasic hemisphere.

Second, cerebral site is at least as important in understanding brain function as cerebral side, a fact that is often overlooked when people theorize about cerebral organization. Thus, although the frontal lobes are asymmetrical, the functions of the two frontal lobes are more similar to one another than they are to those of the posterior cortex on the same side. In fact, it is often very difficult to localize lesions in neurological patients to one hemisphere in the absence of neurological data, even though the site (frontal as opposed to temporal or parietal) may be immediately obvious. Perhaps it is best to think of the functions of the cerebral cortex as being localized, and hemispheric side as being only one way in which it is localized.

REFERENCES

Amaducci, L., S. Sorbi., A. Albanese, and G. Gainotti. Choline acetyltransferase (ChAT) activity differs in right and left human temporal lobes. *Neurology* 31:799–805, 1981.

Bonin, G. von. Anatomical asymmetries of the cerebral hemispheres. In V. B. Mountcastle, ed., *Interhemispheric relations and cerebral dominance.* Baltimore: Johns Hopkins Press, 1962.

Broca, P. Sur la faculté du langage articulé. *Bulletins et Mémoires de la Société D'Anthropologie de Paris* 6:377–393, 1865.

Bryden, M. P. *Laterality: Functional Asymmetry in the Intact Brain.* New York: Academic, 1982.

Cain, D. P., and J. A. Wada. An anatomical asymmetry in the baboon brain. *Brain, Behavior and Evolution* 16:222–226, 1979.

Carmon, A., Y. Harishanu, E. Lowinger, and S. Lavy. Asymmetries in hemispheric blood volume and cerebral dominance. *Behavioral Biology* 7:853–859, 1972.

Chi, J. G., E. C. Dooling, and F. H. Gilles. Left-right asymmetries of the temporal speech areas of the human fetus. *Archives of Neurology* 34:346–348, 1977.

Crichton-Browne, J. On the weight of the brain: Its component parts in the insane. *Brain* 2:42–67, 1880.

Cunningham, D. F. *Contribution to the Surface Anatomy of the Cerebral Hemispheres.* Dublin: Royal Irish Academy, 1892.

Deuel, R. K., and C. C. Moran. Cerebral dominance and cerebral asymmetries on computed tomogram in childhood. *Neurology* 30:934–938, 1980.

Donchin, E., M. Kutas, and G. McCarthy. Electrocortical indices of hemispheric utilization. In S. Harnad, R. W. Doty, L. Goldstein, J. Jaynes, and G. Krauthamer, eds., *Lateralization in the Nervous System.* New York: Academic, 1977.

Eberstaller, O. Zur Oberflächenanatomie der Grosshirnhemisphären. *Wien. Med. Blätter* 7:479–482, 542–582, 644–646, 1884.

Economo, C. V., and L. Horn. Über Windungsrelief, Masse und Rindenarchitektonik der Supratemporalfläche, ihre individuellen und ihre Seitenunterschiede. *Zeitschrift für Neurologie und Psychiatrie* 130:678–757, 1930.

Eidelberg, D., and A. M. Galaburda. Symmetry and asymmetry in the human posterior thalamus. *Archives of Neurology* 39:325–332, 1982.

Falzi, G., P. Perrone, and L. A. Vignolo. Right-left asymmetry in anterior speech region. *Archives of Neurology* 39:239–240, 1982.

Fried, I., C. Mateer, G. Ojemann, R. Wohns, and P. Fedio. Organization of visuospatial functions in human cortex: Evidence from electrical stimulation. *Brain* 105:349–371, 1982.

Galaburda, A. M., M. LeMay, T. L. Kemper, and N. Geschwind. Right-left asymmetries in the brain. *Science* 199:852–856, 1978.

Geschwind, N. Language and the brain. *Scientific American,* 226:340–348, 1972.

Geschwind, N., and W. Levitsky. Left-right asymmetries in temporal speech region. *Science* 161:186–187, 1968.

Gevins, A. S., J. C. Doyle, B. A. Cutillo, R. E. Schaffer, R. S. Tannehill, J. H. Ghannam, V. A. Gilcrease, and C. L. Yeager. Electrical potentials in human brain during cognition: New method reveals dynamic patterns of correlation. *Science* 213:918–921, 1981.

Gevins, A. S., G. M. Zeitlin, J. C. Doyle, C. D. Yingling, R. E. Schaffer, E. Callaway, and C. L. Yeager. Electroencephalogram correlates of higher cortical functions. *Science* 203:665–668, 1979.

Gibson, C., and Bryden, M. P. Dichaptic recognition of shapes and letters in children. *Canadian Journal of Psychology* 37:132–143, 1983.

Glick, S. D., D. A. Ross, and L. B. Hough. Lateral asymmetry of neurotransmitters in human brain. *Brain Research* 234:53–63, 1982.

Gordon, H. W., and J. E. Bogen. Hemispheric lateralization of singing after intracarotid sodium amylobarbitone. *Journal of Neurology, Neurosurgery, and Psychiatry* 37:727–738, 1974.

Gur, R. C., I. K. Packer, J. P. Hungerbuhler, M. Reivich, W. D. Obrist, W. S. Amarnek, and H. Sackheim. Differences in distribution of gray and white matter in human cerebral hemispheres. *Science* 207: 1226–1228, 1980.

Hampson, E., and D. Kimura. Hand movement asymmetries during verbal and nonverbal tasks. *Canadian Journal of Psychology,* in press.

Harris, L. J. Sex differences in spatial ability: Possible environmental, genetic, and neurological factors. In M. Kinsbourne, ed. *Asymmetrical Function of the Brain*, Cambridge, Mass.: Cambridge University Press, 1978.

Heschl, R. L. Über die vordere quere Schlafentwindung des menschlichen Grosshirns. Vienna: Braumüller, 1878.

Hicks, R. E. Intrahemispheric response competition between vocal and unimanual performance in normal adult human males. *Journal of Comparative and Physiological Psychology* 89:50–61, 1975.

Hoadley, M. D., and K. Pearson. Measurement of internal diameter of skull in relation to "pre-eminence" of left hemisphere. *Biometrika* 21:94–123, 1929.

Hughlings-Jackson, J. *Selected Writings of John Hughlings-Jackson.* J. Taylor, ed. New York: Basic Books, 1958.

Kimura, D. The asymmetry of the human brain. *Scientific American* 228:70–78, 1973.

Kinsbourne, M. Eye and head turning indicates cerebral lateralization. *Science* 176:539–541, 1972.

Kinsbourne, M., and J. Cook. Generalized and lateralized effects of concurrent verbalization on a unimanual skill. *Quarterly Journal of Experimental Psychology* 23:341–345, 1971.

Kinsbourne, M., and R. E. Hicks. Functional cerebral space: A model for overflow, transfer and interference effects in human performance. In J. Requin, ed., *Attention and Performance,* vol. VII. New York: Academic, 1978.

Kodama, K. Beitrage zur Anatomie des Zentralnervensystems der Japaner. VIII. Insula Reil ii. *Folia Anatomica Japan* 12:423–444, 1934.

Kopp, N., F. Michel, H. Carrier, A. Biron, and P. Duvillard. Étude de certaines asymmetries hemispheriques du cerveau human. *Journal of the Neurological Sciences* 34:349–363, 1977.

Lassen, N. A., D. H. Ingevar, and E. Skinhøj. Brain function and blood flow. *Scientific American* 239:62–71, 1978.

LeMay, M. Asymmetries of the skull and handedness. *Journal of the Neurological Sciences* 32:243–253, 1977.

LeMay, M. Morphological aspects of human brain asymmetry. *Trends in Neurosciences* 5:273–275, 1982.

LeMay, M., and A. Culebras. Human brain-morphologic differences in the hemispheres demonstrable by carotid arteriography. *New England Journal of Medicine* 287:168–170, 1972.

Levy, J. The origins of lateral asymmetry. In S. Harnad, R. W. Doty, L. Goldstein, J. Jaynes, and G. Krauthamer, eds., *Lateralization in the Nervous System*. New York: Academic, 1977.

Levy, J., C. Trevarthen, and R. W. Sperry. Perception of bilateral chimeric figures following hemispheric deconnection. *Brain* 95:61–78, 1972.

Mazziotta, J. C., M. E. Phelps, R. E. Carson, and D. E. Kuhl. Tomographic mapping of human cerebral metabolism: Auditory stimulation. *Neurology* 32:921–937, 1982.

McRae, D. L., C. L. Branch, and B. Milner. The occipital horns and cerebral dominance. *Neurology* 18:95–98, 1968.

Milner, B. Hemispheric specialization: Scope and limits. In F. O. Schmitt and F. G. Worden, eds., *The Neurosciences: Third Study Program*. Cambridge, Mass.: MIT Press, 1974.

Mishkin, M., and D. G. Forgays. Word recognition as a function of retinal locus. *Journal of Experimental Psychology* 43:43–48, 1952.

Morrell, L. K., and J. G. Salamy. Hemispheric asymmetry of electrocortical responses to speech stimuli. *Science* 174:165–166, 1971.

Nachson, I., and A. Carmon. Hand preference in sequential and spatial discrimination tasks. *Cortex* 11:123–131, 1975.

Nishizawa, Y., T. K. Olsen, B. Larsen, and N. A. Lassen. Left-right cortical asymmetries of regional cerebral blood flow during listening to words. *Journal of Neurophysiology* 48:458–466, 1982.

Oke, A., R. Keller, I. Mefford, and R. N. Adams. Lateralization of norepinephrine in human thalamus. *Science* 200:1411–1413, 1978.

Rasmussen, T., and B. Milner. The role of early left brain injury in determining lateralization of cerebral speech functions. *Annals of the New York Academy of Sciences* 299:355–369, 1977.

Reivich, M. The use of cerebral blood flow and metabolic studies in cerebral localization. In R. A. Thompson, and J. R. Green, eds., *New Perspectives in Cerebral Localization*. New York: Raven Press, 1982.

Rodney, M. L. Motor sequencing and hemispheric specialization. Unpublished doctoral dissertation. University of Waterloo, Canada, 1980.

Roland, P. E., E. Skinhøj, N. A. Lassen, and B. Larsen. The role of different cortical areas in man in the organization of voluntary movements in extrapersonal space. *Journal of Neurophysiology* 43:137–150, 1980.

Roy, C. S., and M. B. Sherrington. On the regulation of the blood supply of the brain. *Journal of Physiology* 11:85, 1890.

Rubens, A. B. Anatomical asymmetries of human cerebral cortex. In S. Harnad, R. W. Doty, L. Goldstcin, J. Jaynes, and G. Krauthamer, eds., *Lateralization in the Nervous System*. New York: Academic Press, 1977.

Rubens, A. B., M. W. Mahowald, and J. T. Hutton. Asymmetry of the lateral (Sylvian) fissures in man. *Neurology* 26:620–624, 1976.

Rudel, R. G., M. B. Denckla, and E. Spalten. The functional asymmetry of Braille letter learning in normal sighted children. *Neurology* 24:733–738, 1974.

Seitz, M. R., B. A. Weber, J. T. Jacobson, and R. Morehouse. The use of averaged electroencephalic response techniques in the study of auditory processing related to speech and language. *Brain and Language* 11:261–284, 1980.

Semmes, J. Hemispheric specialization: A possible clue to mechanism. *Neuropsychologia* 6:11–26, 1968.

Sergent, J. Role of the input in visual hemispheric asymmetries. *Psychological Bulletin* 93:481–512, 1983.

Sperry, R. W. Lateral specialization in the surgically separated hemispheres. In F. O. Schmitt and F. G. Worden, eds., *The Neurosciences: Third Study Program*. Cambridge, Mass.: MIT Press, 1974.

Springer, S. P., and G. Deutsch. *Left Brain, Right Brain*. San Francisco: Freeman, 1981.

Strauss, E., and C. Fitz. Occipital horn asymmetry in children. *Annals of Neurology* 18:437–439, 1980.

Taylor, L. B. Localisation of cerebral lesions by psychological testing. *Clinical Neurology* 16:269–287, 1969.

Teszner, D., A. Tzavaras, and H. Hécaen. L'asymetries droite-gauche du planum temporale: À-propos de l'étude de 100 cerveaux. *Revue Neurologique* 126:444–449, 1972.

Teuber, H.-L. Physiological psychology. *Annual Review of Psychology* 6:267–296, 1955.

Wada, J. A., R. Clarke, and A. Hamm. Cerebral hemispheric asymmetry in humans: Cortical speech zones in 100 adult and 100 infant brains. *Archives of Neurology* 32:239–246, 1975.

Wada, J., and T. Rasmussen. Intracarotid injection of sodium Amytal for the lateralization of cerebral speech dominance. *Journal of Neurosurgery* 17:266–282, 1960.

Webster, W. G., and A. D. Thurber. Problem solving strategies and manifest brain asymmetry. *Cortex* 14:474–484, 1978.

Witelson, S. F., and W. Pallie. Left hemisphere specialization for language in the newborn: Neuroanatomical evidence of asymmetry. *Brain* 96:641–646, 1973.

Zangwill, O. L. *Cerebral Dominance and Its Relation to Psychological Function*. Springfield, Ill.: Charles C Thomas, 1960.

15

VARIATIONS IN CEREBRAL ASYMMETRY

Cerebral asymmetry is one of the most remarkable features of cerebral organization and continues to be a source of much theorizing in both the popular and the scientific literature. An important feature of cerebral asymmetry is that there is considerable individual variation in the pattern of left-right differences in both anatomical and functional asymmetry. By studying the nature of this variation we may be able to fractionate the processes that are lateralized and gain insights into the nature of cerebral asymmetry.

INDIVIDUAL VARIATION IN ANATOMICAL ASYMMETRY

No two brains are alike. Brains differ in their size, gyral patterns, distribution of gray and white matter, cytoarchitectonics, vascular patterns, neurochemistry, etc. The question is whether variations in anatomical organization are related in any meaningful way to factors such as handedness or gender, and whether variations are correlated with functional differences.

Handedness

Witelson thoroughly reviewed the evidence for anatomical asymmetries in relation to handedness, finding evidence that hand preference is correlated with right-left asymmetry in the parietal operculum, frontal cortex, occipital region, vascular patterns, and cerebral blood flow (see Table 15–1). The overall conclusion is that in comparison to right-handers, a higher proportion of left-handers show no asymmetry or a reversal of the direction of anatomical asymmetry. Is this difference of functional significance? To examine this, Radcliffe and his colleagues correlated the asymmetry in the course of the Sylvian fissure, as revealed by carotid angiogram, with the results of carotid sodium Amytal speech testing. They found that left- and right-handers with speech in the left hemisphere had a mean right-left difference of 27° in the angle formed by the vessels leaving the posterior end of the Sylvian fissure. Left- and right-handers with speech in the right hemisphere or with bilaterally represented speech had a mean difference of 0°. Thus the anatomical asymmetry in their population was

TABLE 15–1

Variations in anatomical asymmetry related to handedness

Measure	Handedness	Anatomical Differences		
		Left larger (%)	Right larger (%)	No difference (%)
Blood volume	Right	25	62	13
	Left	64	28	8
Parietal operulum	Right	67	8	25
	Left	22	7	71
Frontal width	Right	19	61	20
	Left	27	40	33
Occipital width	Right	66	9	25
	Left	38	27	35
Occipital horns	Right	60	10	30
	Left	38	31	31

Data from Hochberg and LeMay (1975), LeMay (1977), Carman et al. (1972), and McRae et al. (1968).

related to speech representation and not necessarily to handedness. In other words, the location of speech was a better predictor of individual variation in anatomical organization than was handedness. Handedness may appear more closely related to anatomical anomalies because there is more variance in lateralization of speech in left-handers. A series of studies by Yakovlev and his colleagues is germane. In a careful study of over 300 cases they found that in 80 percent of the cases the pyramidal tract descending to the right hand contains more fibers than does the same tract going to the left hand. Apparently, there are more fibers descending to the right hand both from the contralateral left hemisphere and from the ipsilateral right hemisphere than there are to the left hand. In addition, the contralateral tract from the left hemisphere crosses at a higher level in the medulla than does the contralateral tract from the right hemisphere. To date, data are only available for 11 left-handers, but the pattern is remarkably similar to that observed in the population at large: nine of 11 (82 per-

cent) of these cases had the typical right-side bias. Since two-thirds of these left-handers could have been expected to have speech on the left, there appears to be a closer relation between locus of language and pyramidal tract organization than between handedness and the organization of the pyramidal tract.

A difficulty in accounting for variations in anatomical asymmetries is that there are both left- and right-handers in whom there is a marked dissociation between morphological and functional asymmetry. Thus, carotid Amytal testing may show speech to be in the left hemisphere, but the enlarged temporoparietal speech zone is inferred from neurological studies to be in the right hemisphere. Consider also that a large percentage of the right-handed cases summarized in Table 15–1 do not show the "expected asymmetries" but have reversed asymmetries or no differences at all. These cases do pose a significant interpretation problem, and they suggest that other as yet unknown variables may also account for individual differences in both left- and right-handers.

Gender

Less of the variance in anatomical asymmetry of the cerebral hemispheres can be associated with differences between males and females than with differences related to handedness. Although it is frequently stated that the cerebral hemispheres of females are less symmetrical than those of males, this conclusion is based largely on nonsignificant trends or impressions. We are aware of only three statistically reliable differences related to gender in humans. First, according to Wada there are more females than males exhibiting a reversed asymmetry pattern in the planum temporale, although the predominant pattern is still like that observed in males. Second, de Lacoste-Utamsing and Holloway reported that the posterior part of the corpus callosum (the **splenium**) is significantly larger in females than in males. These authors also noted a qualitative difference: the female splenium is bulbous and widens markedly with respect to the body of the callosum; the male counterpart is approximately cylindrical and is relatively continuous with the body of the corpus callosum. Third, Landsdell and Davie studied pneumoencephalograms of neurological patients for the presence of the massa intermedia (a band of tissue joining the thalami but absent in about one-third of males and one-quarter of females) and correlated performance on the verbal and nonverbal sections of the Wechsler-Bellevue intelligence test. Whereas males with a massa intermedia had lower nonverbal scores than those without this structure, there was no comparable result in females. One interpretation of this result is that the presence of the massa intermedia in males produces competition and interference between the lateralized functions of the two hemispheres. This hypothesis remains to be proved, however.

The absence of more evidence of sex differences in anatomical organization in humans does not mean that there is not a major difference related to gender. There are now numerous reports of large sex differences in both the neocortex and the hypothalamus of rats, which appear related to hormonal variables. There is no reason to believe that similar differences are not present in humans, although they have not been demonstrated yet.

HANDEDNESS AND FUNCTIONAL ASYMMETRY

As the term sinister—usually used to mean wicked or evil, but originally meaning left-handside in Latin—implies, left-handedness has historically been viewed as somewhat strange or unusual. The most commonly cited figure for left-handedness is 10 percent, representing the number of people who write with the left hand, but when other criteria are used, estimates range from 1 to 30 percent. The problem is that handedness is not absolute; some people are nearly totally left-handed, whereas others are ambidextrous (that is, they use either hand with equal facility). A rather useful distribution of handedness has been described by Annett (Table 15–2), who asked over 2000 adults to indicate the hand they used to perform each of 12 different tasks. It can be seen that the incidence of left-handedness on Annett's tasks varied from a low of about 6 percent when cutting with scissors to a high of about 17 percent when dealing cards.

Theories of Hand Preference

The many theories put forward to account for hand preference can be categorized according to their environmental, anatomical, or genetic emphases.

Environmental Theories. The three variations of environmental theories of handedness

TABLE 15–2

Percentages of "left," "right," or "either"
responses to each question[a]

	Left (%)	Either (%)	Right (%)
Dealing cards	17.02	3.32	79.66
Unscrewing jar	16.50	17.49	66.01
Shoveling	13.53	11.89	74.58
Sweeping	13.49	16.89	69.62
Threading needle	13.10	9.74	77.16
Writing	10.60	0.34	89.06
Striking match	9.95	8.74	81.31
Throwing ball	9.44	1.29	89.47
Hammering	9.22	2.54	88.24
Using toothbrush	9.18	8.49	82.33
Using racket	8.10	2.59	89.31
Using scissors	6.20	6.81	86.99

[a] Percentages based on 2321 respondents. Adapted from Annett, 1970.

stress the utility of behavior, reinforcement, or accident as the major determining variable. The first variation, the behavioral, sometimes called the theory of the Pelopennesian Wars or the sword and shield hypothesis, is that a soldier who held his shield in his left hand better protected his heart and improved his chance of survival. Since the left hand was holding the shield, the right hand became more skilled in various movements and eventually was used for most tasks. According to a female variant of this theory, it is adaptive for a mother to hold an infant in her left hand so that it will be soothed by the rhythm of the mother's heart; the mother, like the soldier, then has the right hand free and so uses it for executing skilled movements. Such theories have difficulties, the most obvious being failure to consider the possibility that right-handedness preceded, and thus is responsible for, the behavior.

The second variant of environmental theories, that of reinforcement, has been elabo-

rated by Collins. It is based on some ingenious experiments on "handedness" in mice: Collins raised mice in a world biased in such a way that the mice were forced to use either their left or right paws to obtain food located in a tube adjacent to the wall of their home cage. He found that the proportion of adult right- or left-pawed mice was directly related to the type of world in which they were raised. Thus, he suggested, their preference was established by the contingencies of reinforcement received in the environment in which they spent the first few weeks of life. This view can be adapted to humans. The child's world is also right-handed in many ways, which reinforces the use of that hand. In addition, children in the United States were once forced to write with their right hands. Although emphasizing the potential importance of environmental factors, Collins' theory does not account for the difference between familial and nonfamilial handedness or the relation of handedness to cerebral dominance. It also seems to be negated by what happened when children were given their choice of which hand to learn to write with in United States schools: the incidence of left-handed writing rose only to 10 percent, which is the norm in most societies that have been studied.

According to the third variant of environmental theories, there is a genetically determined bias toward being right-handed, but left-handedness occurs through some cerebral deficit caused by accident. To account for the familial aspect of left-handedness Bakan has argued that there is a high probability of stressful births among left-handers, which increases the risk of brain damage and so maintains the incidence of left-handedness. This theory would predict that some consistent deficit in cognitive functioning in adult left-handers should result from their brain damage, but no such deficit has been shown. It could be argued that since the alleged damage occurs in infancy, the brain compensates in such a way that the only symptom that appears in adulthood is left-handedness, but this argument is hardly compelling support for the theory.

Anatomical Theories. Of the several anatomical theories of handedness, two, which are well documented, explain handedness by alluding to anatomical asymmetry. In the first theory right-handedness is attributed to enhanced maturation and ultimately greater development of the left hemisphere. Generalizing from this assumption, it is predicted that nonfamilial left-handers should show an asymmetry mirroring that of right-handers, whereas familial left-handers should show no anatomical asymmetry. These predictions are difficult to assess because no studies have specifically considered anatomical asymmetry with respect to handedness or with respect to familial history and handedness. A major problem with this theory is that it simply pushes the question one step backward, asking not "why handedness?" but instead "why anatomical asymmetry?"

The second theory addresses this problem in part. As Morgan has pointed out, many animals have a left-sided developmental advantage that is not genetically coded. For example, there is a left-sided bias for the location of the heart, the size of the ovaries in birds, the control of birdsong, the size of left temporal cortex in humans, the size of the left side of the skull in the great apes, and so on. This predominance of left-favoring asymmetries puts the more celebrated left-hemisphere speech dominance in the more general perspective of all anatomical asymmetries. Since neither genetic evidence nor genetic theory accurately predicts these human asymmetries, Morgan assumes that they all result from some fundamental asymmetries in human body chemistry. The problem with Morgan's theory applied to handedness is that it fails to explain left-handedness in the presence of other "normal" asymmetries such as the location of the heart.

Genetic Theories. Of the many genetic models for handedness, most postulate a dominant gene or genes for right-handedness and a recessive gene or genes for left-handedness, but none of these models can accurately predict the probability of left-handedness.

The two best attempts to develop genetic models of handedness are those of Annett and of Levy and Nagylaki. Annett has proposed that there may be a gene for right-handedness but not for left-handedness. In the absence of the right-handed gene the displayed handedness will be random. The incidence of right-handedness would be slightly higher in this group because of environmental factors predisposing the choice of the right hand. The theory proposed by levy and Nagylaki is somewhat more complex. This theory is a two-gene, four-allele model. That is, there is a gene for handedness and a gene for hemispheric representation of speech. The gene for left-handedness is recessive as is the gene for having speech in the right hemisphere. Genetic theories have been criticized on a number of grounds (see Hardyck and Petrinovich), and none is totally satisfactory. For example, there is no attempt to differentiate between familial and nonfamilial left-handers.

From this brief review of theories of handedness it is clear that we do not know why there is handedness, and we may never know. (To the multiplicity of theories of handedness we add our own: a man named Noah was disliked by his fellow townspeople because he was right-handed and they were southpaws, and because he insisted on building an ark in the desert. A great flood came and everyone was drowned except Noah and his right-handed family. The rest is history.)

Cerebral Organization in Left-Handers

There appears to be a widespread belief in the neurological literature that cognitive functions are more bilaterally organized in left-handers than in right-handers. This conclusion likely arose from the aphasia literature, in which there are reports that aphasia occurs more often in left-handers than in right-handers with comparable damage but that recovery from aphasia is more rapid and complete in left-handers. Careful examination of the literature suggests, however, that these conclusions are based largely on compilations of scattered individual cases rather than on systematic studies of unselected cases. Two recent large-scale studies suggest that the well-known difference between cerebral organization in left- and right-handers may be wrong. First, in the last chapter we discussed the sodium Amytal procedure and reported the data of Rasmussen and Milner. They found that 70 percent of left-handers appeared to have language represented in the left hemisphere, 15 percent in the right hemisphere, and 15 percent bilaterally. Second, Kimura reported the incidence of aphasia and apraxia in a consecutive series of 520 patients selected only for unilateral brain damage. The frequency of left-handedness in her population was within the expected range, and these patients did not have a higher incidence of either aphasia or apraxia than right-handers. In fact, the incidence of aphasia was approximately 70 percent of the incidence in right-handers, exactly what would be predicted from the Amytal studies. Thus, although a small proportion of left-handers may have bilateral speech or right hemisphere speech, the majority of left-handers do not.

It has been suggested that on the basis of family background left-handers can be subdivided into two populations differing in cerebral organization: familial left-handers, who have a family history of left-handedness, and nonfamilial left-handers, who have no family history of left-handedness. According to Hécaen and Sauguet, nonfamilial left-handed patients with unilateral lesions perform like right-handed patients on neuropsychological tests. In contrast, familial left-handers perform much differently, suggesting to Hécaen and Sauguet that they have a different pattern of cerebral organization. Although this conclusion is interesting, it must be considered cautiously. First, the distinction between familial and nonfamilial left-handers can be criticized on the grounds that the designation to one group or the other is based on loose criteria. Normally, subjects are merely asked if they have any left-handed relatives. In our experience, people are very unreliable at accurately reporting this information. Future studies should actually measure the handedness of the relatives. Second, it is possible that familial left-handers have a different pattern of cerebral organization because they represent the left-handers that do not have speech exclusively located in the left hemisphere. This is an empirical question and could easily be tested.

In sum, we can find little evidence that the cerebral organization of speech or nonspeech functions differs from right-handers in the 70 percent of left-handers with speech represented in the left hemisphere. One caveat must be attached to the conclusion that there is no difference in cerebral organization between left- and right-handers: There is a larger incidence of left-handedness among mentally defective children and children with various neurological disorders than is found in the general population. This is not surprising, however, because if the dominant hemisphere is injured at an early age, handedness and dominance can move under the control of what would normally not be the dominant hemisphere. Since there are so many more right-handed children, by probability alone it would be expected that more right-handed children with left-hemisphere damage would switch to right-hemisphere dominance than would switch in the reverse direction. That this can occur, however, cannot be used as grounds for predicting cognitive deficits or differences in cerebral organization in the general population of left-handers.

SEX DIFFERENCES IN CEREBRAL ASYMMETRY

One of the most obvious sources of individual variation in the behavior of humans is gender: males and females behave differently. The question is whether any differences in cognitive behavior between males and females can be attributed to biological differences between the brains of the two sexes. There is substantial anecdotal and experimental evidence of cognitive differences between males and females, and there have been several attempts to relate these to differences in brain organization. If any one principle can be abstracted to distinguish the sexes, it is that females tend to be more fluent than males in the use of language, whereas males tend to be better than females at spatial analysis. These differences have been attributed to the possibility of a difference in the pattern of cerebral organization between the sexes, but before considering the theories we shall review the data.

Evidence of Sex Differences

Evidence supporting the argument that there are significant sex differences in cerebral organization derive primarily from studies of normal subjects, laterality studies, cerebral

blood flow measurements, and neurological patients.

Normal Subjects. The place to start in the study of cognitive differences between males and females is with *The Psychology of Sex Differences,* a book published by MacCoby and Jacklin in 1974. In their thorough review of the literature to 1974 they found four reliable sex differences. First, girls have greater verbal ability than boys. At about age 11, the sexes begin to diverge, with female superiority increasing through high school and possibly beyond. Girls score higher on tasks involving both receptive and productive language, and on "high-level" verbal tasks (analogies, comprehension of difficult written material, creative writing) as well as on lower-level measures (fluency). A simple demonstration of this sex difference can be seen when males and females are asked to fill in the blanks as illustrated in Figure 15–1. In this test the first letter of each of four words is provided. The task is to fill in missing letters to make a meaningful sentence. Females are much better at this task than males. Overall the magnitude of female superiority at verbal skills is small, in the range of one-quarter of a standard deviation. Second, males excel in visual-spatial ability. Thus, on tests of recall and detection of shapes, mental rotation of two- or three-dimension figures, geometry, maze learning, map reading, aiming at and tracking objects, and geographical knowledge, males perform better on average than do females. Simple tests, that can be used to demonstrate this sex difference are illustrated in Figure 15–1. For example, in the water level task used by Thomas, subjects are shown a tipped flask and asked to indicate the water level. Thomas reports that among 62 randomly chosen college men the error in estimating the angle of the water was about 2° off the horizontal. Of 91 women, 28 (31 percent) showed the same performance as men,

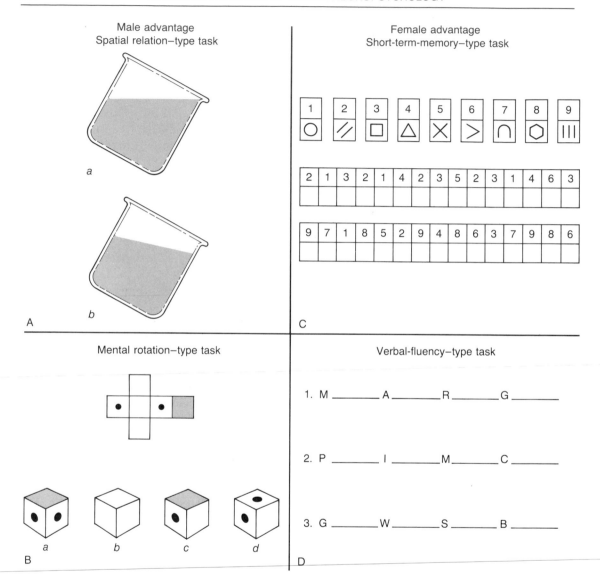

FIGURE 15–1. Examples of four types of tasks that reliably show sex-related differences. A. The top drawing shows a line drawn to indicate waterline in which the response indicates comprehension of the concept of horizontality of fluid level. The bottom illustration shows the line drawn incorrectly, indicating no comprehension of the concept. This response is typical of about two-thirds of females. B. This task, which is similar to those in the spatial relations test of the Differential Aptitude test, requires the subject to choose the one box from the bottom four that could be made from the plan above. Males typically find this task much easier than females. C. In this test the subject must fill in the empty boxes in the bottom rows with the appropriate symbols from the examples at the top. This is similar to the digit symbol test on the Wechsler Intelligence tests. When given a larger number of boxes to fill and a time limit of 90 seconds, females complete 10 to 20 percent more items than males. D. This test of verbal fluency requires the subject to fill in each blank in order to form words that make a sentence. Females are faster at this type of test than males.

whereas the remainder showed an error of 15 to 20°. In other words, although the men in his sample appreciated that the water level remained horizontal, 69 percent of the women did not. In developmental studies Thomas reports that by 12 years of age most males indicate that the water level is horizontal, but that females who perform in this way do so at a somewhat later age. Like the verbal advantage of females, the spatial advantage of males is not absolute, the difference being only about .4 of a standard deviation. Third, boys excel in mathematical ability. Although the two sexes are similar in their early acquisition of quantitative concepts and their mastery of arithmetic, beginning at about age 12 to 13 boys' mathematical skills increase faster than girls'. The better mathematical skills of boys is partly a function of the number of mathematics courses taken, since boys do take more courses, but this accounts for only part of the difference. Recently, a controversy has arisen over the basis of this sex difference (see Benbow and Stanley), but there is little argument over the fact that males perform better at math. Fourth, males are physically more aggressive than females. A sex difference is present as early as social play begins, at age two to three years, and remains through the college years. Studies with nonhuman primates, largely rhesus monkeys, show that the increased aggression in males is probably a result of androgen both pre- and postnatally. How this influences the brain is unknown.

The appearance of sex differences in the performance of what appears to be simple tests has important implications for neuropsychological assessment, since gender may be important in predicting what normal performance level should be. Consider the following example. Whishaw and Kolb gave school-age children three tests that are widely used in neuropsychological assessment and found sex differ-

ences on two of the tests (Figure 15–2). On the Draw-A-Bicycle test (see Chapter 30 for the scoring procedure) males performed better than females; on the Chicago Word Fluency test (the test requires the subject to write as many words beginning with "s" as possible in five minutes and and as many four-letter words beginning with "c" as possible in four minutes) females performed better—at some ages by as much as 10 words—than males. On the copy and recall of the Rey figure (See Figure 10–2), there was no sex difference. The appearance of reliable sex differences on these clinical tests implies that separate norms are necessary for the clinical assessment of males and females, although to date separate norms are not available for very many clinical tests.

The sex differences described by MacCoby and Jacklin have often been described as a "spatial" advantage for males and a "verbal" advantage for females, but more recent research has indicated that this dichotomy is too simple; there is a broader pattern of differences that cannot be labeled easily as verbal and spatial. According to Harshman's recent review, females excel at both perceptual speed (see Figure 15–1) and visual memory, whereas males are better at perceptual closure (see Figure 10–2) and the disembedding of visual patterns from complex arays (see Figure 10–2). The fact that females are superior at perceptual speed and visual memory is not predicted from a simple "verbal" description of their superior abilities, although males still appear to perform best at "spatial-type" tests. Finally, some researchers have been impressed by anecdotal evidence that men appear to excel at chess and musical composition. In the Soviet Union, where chess is a national pastime, no women have achieved grand-master status, and women compete in separate tournaments. In music women appear to be as competent in performing as men, but fewer excel in com-

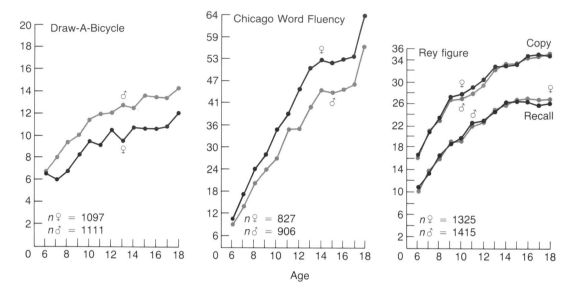

FIGURE 15–2. Performance of males and females of different ages on three neuropsychological tests. A. On the Draw-A-Bicycle test males obtain higher scores than females. B. On the Chicago Word Fluency test females perform better than males. C. On the Rey Copy and Recall tests there is no difference in the performance between males and females. (Whishaw and Kolb, unpublished.)

position. It has been suggested that men have an advantage in these fields because both involve heavy spatial loading. Harris described the spatial structure of music as follows:

For instance, there is the sense in which certain kinds of sounds naturally seem to belong in certain parts of space relative to other sounds. Why are high notes and low notes *called* high notes and low notes? Why does the flute seem to float above the bassoon, and the violin above the cello? Pitch and resonance seem to impart "spatial" qualities to sound in more than a merely metaphorical sense. . . .

There are many other examples of spatial structure in music, including cross-relations (appearance in different voices of two tones of mutually contradictory character that normally are played as a melodic progression in one voice); cross-rhythms (simultaneous use of conflicting rhythmic patterns); bitonality; and polytonality.

Perhaps the ability to recognize and to execute and, above all, to create, a melodic pattern is a spatial ability not unlike the visual detection of an

embedded figure or the mental rotation of a geometrical form so as to anticipate how it will look from a different spatial prespective. The recognition of counterpoint or of variations on a theme may depend on similar abilities to [disassemble] a figure from a complex background, to remember it, and to follow it through a variety of transformations. (Harris, 1978, pp. 424–525)

There may be substance to the argument that sex differences in chess and musical composition can be attributed to spatial factors, but it is also easy to suggest cultural and environmental reasons why women have not excelled in these areas. Similar arguments about the spatial aspects of literature could also be advanced, but it would be somewhat more difficult to demonstrate sex differences in creative writing ability.

Laterality Studies. If the differences described above are real, one might expect to find a difference between the sexes in the distribution of verbal and spatial functions between the hemispheres in laterality studies. The literature on sex-related differences in lateralization is characterized by inconsistencies, however. As Bryden emphasizes, procedural differences, small samples, and great variability plague this research, and it is difficult to be certain that observed differences truly reflect differences in laterality in the population. Nonetheless, he concludes that the majority of the verbal dichotic and verbal tachistoscopic studies that show any sex-related effects indicate a greater degree of lateralization in males. Furthermore, although sex-related differences are not as consistent on tests of spatial processing, there is some evidence that males are more lateralized on tests in both the visual and the tactual modalities. We must emphasize, however, that sex differences in the degree of perceptual asymmetries can be profoundly influenced by the way in which the subjects approach the task. For example, women may tend to use verbal strategies to solve spatial problems and to encode spatial displays, and this may generate a laterality effect, not because of a difference in cerebral lateralization of function between the sexes, but because of a difference in strategy or preferred cognitive mode used to solve the task. On the basis of the evidence to date, we must concur with Bryden that this alternative seems at least reasonably plausible.

Cerebral Blood Flow. Some of the variance in studies of changes in cerebral blood flow during cognitive activity is apparently related to gender as well as to handedness. Gur and his colleagues found that females and left-handers have a higher rate of cerebral blood flow and a greater percentage of fast-perfusing tissue than do right-handed males. All groups showed an increase in blood flow to the left hemisphere during verbal tasks and a complementary increase in blood flow to the right hemisphere during spatial tasks, but females and male left-

handers showed reliably greater increases than right-handed males. The authors took these data to suggest possible differences in the distribution of gray and white matter in the two hemispheres of males and females, although confirmation of this hypothesis awaits necropsies. The authors failed to find support for a simple difference between verbal and spatial processing in the two sexes, however, as both sexes exhibited an increase in left hemisphere blood flow during the verbal task and in the right hemisphere during the spatial task.

Neurological Patients. Although Lansdell first reported a sex-related difference in the effects of left- and right-temporal lobectomies in 1962, it was a series of papers by McGlone in the late 1970s and early 1980s that proved to be seminal for the study of sex differences in neurological patients. On the basis of her studies of stroke patients with lateralized lesions she made three clear and testable proposals: (1) There is a sex-related difference in the effects of left- and right-hemisphere strokes on the performance of the Wechsler Adult Intelligence Scale (WAIS), (2) Aphasia is commoner in males than in females, and (3) there is a greater degree of functional asymmetry in right-handed men than in right-handed women. McGlone's conclusions are important both because they have led many researchers to consider the possibility of sex-related differences in their studies of neurological patients, and because the ideas that have come from her work, as well as from subsequent work by others, provide new insights into the nature and complexity of cerebral asymmetry. We shall thus consider the data from neurological patients in some detail.

McGlone's initial studies showed a double dissociation of the effects of left- and right-hemisphere lesions in males on the performance of the verbal and performance subscales of the WAIS (see Chapter 26 for details of the

WAIS). Left hemisphere lesions were associated with a decline in verbal IQ whereas right hemisphere lesions were correlated with a depression of the performance IQ. In contrast, she failed to find a selective verbal or performance deficit after unilateral brain injury in females; females with either left or right hemisphere lesions exhibited a severe depression of verbal intelligence and memory. Furthermore, in McGlone's population aphasia was three times more likely in males than in females. McGlone interpreted these results as indicating greater functional asymmetry in males than in females. Although there has been some support for her conclusions, there appear to be five reasons to suggest that some revision may be in order.

First, Inglis and Lawson reviewed the literature and found 16 studies that reported the effects of lateralized lesions on the performance of the verbal and performance subscales of the WAIS. By performing various statistical procedures with these data they showed that whereas left and right hemisphere lesions differentially affected verbal and performance subscales in males, as McGlone had found in her smaller sample, left hemisphere lesions in females depressed both IQs equivalently and right hemisphere lesions failed to depress either IQ (see Figure 15–3). Thus, in contrast to McGlone, Inglis and Lawson found an equivalent effect of left hemisphere lesions on verbal IQ in the two sexes, a result suggesting that left hemisphere lesions are

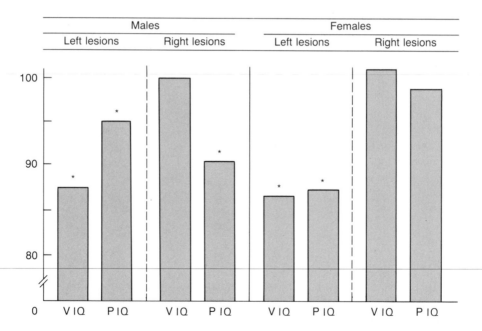

FIGURE 15–3. Summary of Inglis and Lawson's tabulation of studies reporting verbal and performance IQ scores in neurological patients. A clear sex difference emerged in which males with left hemisphere lesions exhibited a depression in verbal IQ whereas males with right hemisphere lesions exhibit a complementary deficit in performance IQ. In contrast, females with left hemisphere lesions show reductions in both verbal and performance IQs whereas females with right hemisphere lesions show no significant depression in either IQ scale.

equally disruptive to verbal behaviors in males and females. Second, several groups have failed to find any evidence of a difference between the sexes in the incidence of aphasia. For example, Hier and Kaplan tabulated the frequency of aphasia in three large samples ($n = 767$) and found the ratio of men to women aphasics to be about 1.2:1. Similarly, De Renzi and his colleagues found the same ratio, in a sample of 1244 patients, to be 1:1.1. Third, aside from performance IQ data, there is little compelling evidence that right hemisphere lesions in females are less disruptive to nonverbal behaviors. For example, Hier, Mondlock, and Caplan found no evidence of a sex difference in the incidence of a variety of symptoms commonly associated with right hemisphere damage, including anosognosia, simultaneous extinction, contralateral neglect, drawing, prosopagnosia, constructional apraxia, or dressing apraxia. One might have expected a difference on these symptoms if the female brain were less lateralized. Fourth, our reanalysis of the effects of small left or right hemisphere excisions on the verbal and performance IQs of patients studied by Kolb and Milner revealed only a quantitative difference in performance: males tend to show greater effects than females of small cerebral excisions on verbal and performance IQs after left and right hemisphere lesions, respectively. Finally, a recent study by Kimura showed that the pattern of cerebral organization *within* each hemisphere may differ between the sexes. Although males and females were nearly as likely to be aphasic following left hemisphere lesions, males were likely to be aphasic and apraxic after damage to either the anterior or the posterior cortex, whereas females were far more likely to experience speech disorders and apraxia after anterior than posterior lesions. Kimura also reported data from a small sample of patients that suggest an analogous sex-related difference following right hemisphere lesions. Anterior, but not posterior, lesions in females impaired performance of the block design and object assembly subtests of the WAIS, whereas males were equally affected on these tests by either anterior or posterior lesions.

Taken together, the data from neurological patients support the idea that unilateral lesions have different effects in males than in females. How the sexes differ in cerebral organization is simply not known at present. McGlone's conclusion that the female brain is more symmetrical than the male brain appears to be too simple to account for the data. Kimura's results suggest that there may be intrahemispheric differences in cerebral organization, but her study needs to be replicated by others. Further, there should be an examination of cortical stimulation data to see if speech is differentially affected by posterior stimulation in males and females. Finally, we must be aware that apparent differences between the sexes, especially left-right ones, may reflect different strategies of problem solving in the two sexes rather than real neurological differences. For example, if women tend to solve relatively nonverbal problems with verbal strategies, unilateral brain damage would appear to have less specific effects in women than men; left hemisphere lesions in females would depress performance of both verbal and "nonverbal" tests whereas right hemisphere lesions might appear to have little effect on either type of task.

In sum, gender appears to account for some of the observed variability in cerebral asymmetry, although more research is needed to determine how much of the variance is accounted for by gender and how gender interacts with handedness. Gender may be important in accounting for the observed behavioral differences between males and females and should be studied systematically, particularly in neurological patients.

Explanations of Sex Differences

We can identify six different explanations commonly advanced to account for sex differences: (1) differential brain organization, (2) hormonal effects on cerebral function, (3) genetic sex-linkage, (4) maturation rate, (5) environment, and (6) preferred cognitive mode. We shall consider each briefly.

Differential Brain Organization. We have considered sex differences in cerebral organization as inferred from studies of neurological patients, anatomy, and laterality studies. There is now good evidence that lesions differentially affect males and females, but it has not been proved that this is due to differences in brain organization.

Hormonal Effects. The neocortex of rodents, and probably mammals in general, has receptors for gonadal hormones, and so it is not unreasonable to presume that hormones could affect cerebral functioning. Preliminary evidence from studies of rats suggests that neonatal castration or ovariectomy may alter cortical growth, but there is no similar evidence for primates.

Genetic Sex-Linkage. A variety of authors have proposed that the major factor in differential spatial ability is genetic. It is postulated that a recessive gene on the X (female) chromosome is responsible. Every normal person has 46 chromosomes arranged in 23 pairs, one set from the male and one from the female. The twenty-third pair is composed of the sex chromosomes; if both are X, the child is female (XX), whereas if one is X and the other Y, the child is male (XY). If a gene is re-cessive, the trait will not be expressed unless the gene is present on both chromosomes—provided they are the same, as in females (XX). However, the gene need be present only on one chromosome if the other chromosome is different, as in the sex chromosomes of males (XY). Thus, if a mother carried the gene on both sex chromosomes, all of her sons will present the trait, but whether her daughters will present it depends on whether the father also carries the recessive gene. Notice that for boys it is irrelevant whether or not the father carries the trait; males, then, have a greater chance of expressing the trait than girls, who require that both parents give them the gene. Figure 15–4 illustrates the principle. If this model were accurate, there would be a near-zero correlation between the spatial ability if a father provided the Y chromosome, but there would be a significant correlation between mother and son as well as between father and daughter. These correlations have indeed been claimed.

For the model in Figure 15–4 the number of males and females who would possess the trait can be predicted: 50 percent of males and 25 percent of females. From this we can predict that 25 percent of females will exceed the average male's score; this percentage is consistently observed.

Maturation Rate. Developmental studies indicate that a fundamental difference in male and female cerebral maturation may help to account for the sex differences observed in adulthood. It has long been known that girls begin to speak sooner than boys, develop larger vocabularies during childhood, and as children use more complex linguistic constructions than do boys. Further, the speech of young girls may be better enunciated than boys' speech, and girls are generally better readers than boys. Although developmental studies of laterality in chil-

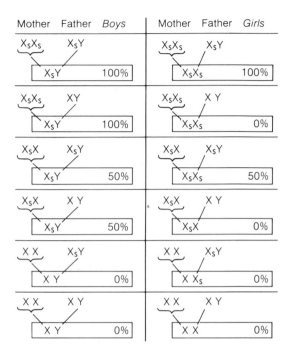

Mother	Father	*Boys*		Mother	Father	*Girls*
X_sX_s	X_sY			X_sX_s	X_sY	
	X_sY	100%			X_sX_s	100%
X_sX_s	XY			X_sX_s	$X\ Y$	
	X_sY	100%			X_sX_s	0%
X_sX	X_sY			X_sX	X_sY	
	X_sY	50%			X_sX_s	50%
X_sX	$X\ Y$			X_sX	$X\ Y$	
	X_sY	50%			X_sX	0%
$X\ X$	X_sY			$X\ X$	X_sY	
	$X\ Y$	0%			$X\ X_s$	0%
$X\ X$	$X\ Y$			$X\ X$	$X\ Y$	
	$X\ Y$	0%			$X\ X$	0%

FIGURE 15–4. Model demonstrating sex-linked recessive trait for spatial ability. The percentages represent the number of offspring having the genotype for spatial ability. That genotype in males (S_sY) is more likely than in females (S_xX_s), since males have only a single X chromosome. Since the gene for spatial ability (s) is recessive, females require both X chromosomes to carry the gene before the trait is expressed. (After Harris, 1978.)

dren have yielded conflicting results, dichotic and tachistoscopic studies frequently indicate an earlier evolution of asymmetry in girls than in boys. Since it is well known that females attain physical maturity at an earlier age than do males, it is reasonable to propose that the male brain matures more slowly than the female brain, and that maturation rate is a critical determinant of brain asymmetry. That is, the more slowly a child matures, the greater the observed cerebral asymmetry. A study by Waber demonstrates just this finding. She reported that, regardless of sex, early maturing adolescents performed better on tests of ver-

bal than of spatial abilities, whereas the late-maturing ones did the opposite. This study, then, implies that maturation rate may affect the organization of higher cortical function. Since, on average, females mature faster than males, superior spatial abilities in males may be directly related to their relatively slow development.

The relation between maturation rate and cerebral asymmetry has an intriguing implication for the genetic model of spatial ability. It may be that what is transferred by the recessive gene is maturation rate, not spatial ability per se. Thus, superior spatial skills are an indirect effect of maturation rate, which is determined by the presence of the recessive gene. To test this prediction it would be necessary to show that females who develop slowly are the same ones who perform as well as the average male on spatial tests and whose spatial ability correlates with their parents as predicted in Figure 15–4. This study has not been done.

Environment. Probably the most influential psychological view of sex-related differences is that different environmental factors shape the behavior of males and females. For example, in the case of spatial ability, it is presumed that male children are expected to exhibit greater independence than females, and thus engage in activities such as exploring and manipulating the environment—activities that improve spatial skills. In a recent review, Harris considered all the research support for this argument and concluded that although a few studies can be found to support the view, the bulk of the evidence fails to support it. For example, in the Thomas et al. study on the horizontality of a liquid (15–1), women who had failed the task were repeatedly shown a bottle half-filled with red water that was tilted at various angles. They were asked to adjust the "pretend waterline" by moving a disk, half red, half white, in a second bottle. Even when the subjects simply had to adjust the pretend water-line to match the visible real waterline, the women failed to show much improvement and were likely to state that "water is level when the bottle is upright but is inclined when the bottle is tilted." Males or females who perform correctly state that "water is always level." A priori, one would have expected females to have had as much experience as males with tilting vessels, and that even if they had not, special instruction would be helpful. This, however, does not seem to be the case. In sum, although environmental theories may be appealing, there is no evidence that the observed sex differences in verbal and spatial behaviors can be accounted for solely on the basis of environmental or social factors.

Preferred Cognitive Mode. We have mentioned several times that the strategies that males and females use to solve different tasks may be at least partly responsible for the observed sex differences. It may be that genetic, maturational, and environmental factors predispose males and females to prefer different modes of cognitive analysis. In other words, females develop in such a way that they prefer to solve problems primarily by using a verbal mode. Since this mode is less efficient at solving spatial problems, the female exhibits an apparent deficit. By the same logic, females should do better than males at primarily verbal tasks. This proposition has yet to be thoroughly investigated.

Summary

There is evidence of at least four significant cognitive sex-related differences: verbal differences, visuospatial differences, differences in mathematical ability, and differences in aggression. Although the causes of cognitive sex-related differences are unknown, they are most likely biological. Consider the following data. Harshman and his associates recently completed a very ambitious study of the interaction of sex and handedness on cognitive abilities, finding a significant sex × handedness interaction. That is, sex-related differences in verbal and visuospatial behavior varied as a function of handedness. It is difficult to imagine how social or environmental factors alone could account for this type of result. It is thus most plausible to account for sex-related differences as at least partly due to neurological factors that may be modulated by the environment.

ENVIRONMENTAL EFFECTS ON ASYMMETRY

Environment is known to produce significant effects on brain growth in laboratory animals and so it is reasonable to presume that different environments might differentially affect the human brain and produce variance in the pattern of cerebral asymmetry. Two environmental variables would seem to be especially good candidates to consider: culture and literacy. We shall consider each separately.

Cultural Effects on Asymmetry

Most studies of cultural differences have centered on the study of language. It has been proposed that non-European languages such as Japanese or Chinese might have more right hemisphere involvement since there seems to be more **prosody** (or song) to them. It has also been suggested that bilinguals may have a different pattern of language organization than unilinguals. Laterality studies have lent some support to the idea that Asian and native American languages may be more bilaterally represented but, as we have seen, laterality studies can be influenced by many factors such as strategy or task requirements, and so one would want to be very cautious about making inferences regarding cultural differences in brain organization from these studies. (See Uyehara and Cooper and Obler et al. for good discussions of the difficulties.)

Studies of neurological patients have provided no evidence for culturally or linguistically based differences in cerebral organization. A good example is a study by Rapport, Tan, and Whitaker. They evaluated the language functions of seven Chinese-English polyglots, whose mother tongue was Malay, Cantonese, or Hokkien, using carotid sodium Amytal, cortical stimulation, and clinical examination. They found that all of these patients were left hemisphere dominant for both the Chinese and the English languages; there was no consistent evidence for increased participation by the right hemisphere for language functions. Although bilinguals probably have all languages located in the left hemisphere, this does not rule out the possibility that the language zones may be enlarged in the left hemisphere or that they might be slightly different in microorganization. Recall that experience is known to alter somatosensory organization (see Chapter 8), so that an analogous effect on the language zones would seem to be a reasonable expectation. It is likely, however, that the major effects of language and environment on the brain are on the development of particular styles of problem solving (i.e., cognitive mode), which are heavily culture-dependent, rather than on changes in cerebral asymmetry per se.

Literacy, Hearing, and Asymmetry

Both education and congenital deafness have been alleged to alter hemispheric specialization. The evidence that schooling changes cerebral organization is scanty and inconclusive. Laterality studies do not generally support the idea, nor do studies on the frequency and quality of aphasias in illiterate populations, as illiterate aphasics do not appear to differ from educated aphasics. There is some evidence that congenital deafness may alter cerebral processing, however. Although left hemisphere damage produces aphasia in American Sign Language, possibly because of the praxic requirements, several laterality studies have failed to find the expected right visual field effects for words in deaf subjects. For example, Kelly and Tomlinson-Keasey found that in contrast to hearing children, deaf children have a left-visual field advantage for most visually presented material. The data suggest that in the absence of verbal auditory input, young deaf children rely heavily on the right hemisphere to process visual stimuli. There is no evidence that the brain itself has been changed by the lack of auditory input, it may simply be the strategy or mode of processing that has changed. Studies of aphasic and apraxic deaf people with left, but not usually right, hemisphere lesions are consistent with this view.

In summary, although environmental experience may affect the way in which stimuli are processed, there is no evidence that environment actually changes the organization of the cerebral hemispheres. The bulk of the evidence implying environmental influence on cerebral organization derives from laterality studies, but the susceptibility of performance on dichotic or tachistoscopic tasks to task variables in the same subjects leaves us with a healthy skepticism. Convincing evidence must come from neurological patient's, and to date this evidence has favored a view that the "basic left-for-language and right-for-space" organization of the cerebral hemispheres is unaffected by experience.

ASYMMETRY IN NONHUMANS

Cerebral asymmetry in the human brain is a crucial element in neuropsychology. Those pressures that led to the development of an asymmetrical brain are unknown, but language and handedness are often considered to be strong candidates. Various factors such as gender, culture, and education are often claimed to influence asymmetry, especially insofar as they relate to language. It is implicitly assumed in many discussions of the nature of asymmetry and its role in behavioral diversity in humans that cerebral asymmetry is linked with specially human intellectual characteristics, but asymmetry may not be a uniquely human characteristic. If this is the case, then theories regarding the nature of asymmetry and the reasons for variations in it must be reevaluated in light of the evidence from nonhuman species. Our intent is not to review all the studies seeking to find asymmetry in the nonhuman brain, but rather to highlight the most stimulating and robust data gathered thus far in birds and mammals, beginning with anatomical asymmetry, then going on to handedness, and finally to cognitive behaviors.

Anatomical Asymmetry in Nonhumans

Anatomical asymmetry in the brains of nonhuman primates was first noticed by Cunningham in 1892. As in human brains, there is a greater upward slope in the Sylvian fissure on the right in the chimpanzee, orangutan, and gorilla brains, and the right frontal pole is longer than the left in baboons. Similarly, the gyral patterns in the two hemispheres of cats are asymmetrical in about 45 percent of cases, although the asymmetries are not constant from cat to cat. Although most rodents do not have gyrencephalic brains, making the analysis of gyral patterns difficult, the existence in the rat brain of both morphological and neurochemical asymmetries has been established. Like the right hemisphere of the human, that of the rat is larger and heavier than the left, and the right frontal pole extends farther anterior than does the left. The neocortex of the right hemisphere is thicker in the posterior parietal and visual cortex, a difference that Diamond and her colleagues find to be modulated both by age and by sex. In addition to those morphological asymmetries, neurochemical asymmetries have been found in noradrenaline concentrations, GABA turnover, and the uptake of serotonin, noradrenaline, and choline. Finally, the right hemisphere of cats, mice, and rabbits is also heavier than the left. The presence of morphological and neurochemical asymmetries in nonhumans is especially intriguing because at least some of them parallel those reported for humans.

Thus, the right hemisphere of both humans and other mammals is apparently heavier and extends farther anterior than the left. Further, the Sylvian fissure of at least the great apes is asymmetrical in a pattern resembling that observed both in humans and in australopithicine endocasts.

Handedness

Consistent preference for the use of one hand in a variety of manipulations is a defining characteristic of handedness in humans. Although some cats, rats, and monkeys have strong hand preferences that are consistent on several different tasks, most do not. Mike Warren began a beautiful series of experiments in the 1960s by looking at the hand preferences in cats and monkeys in a wide range of manipulations including different types of unilateral cortical damage. In a recent review, he was unequivocal in his conclusions. (1) The distribution of hand preferences in nonhuman species is symmetrical, with no disproportionate number of right- and left-handed individuals. (2) The hand preferences of nonhuman mammals are frequently inconsistent in different testing situations and are strongly affected by learning. (3) Hand preferences are not a heritable trait in rats, cats, and mice.

Cognitive Behavior

Fernando Nottebohm reported a startling discovery in 1971. In severing the canary left hypoglossal nerve, but not the right, he found severe disruption of birdsong in the canary. Subsequently, he has found similar results from lesions all along the pathway from the hypoglossal nerve to the higher cerebral nuclei on the left but not on the right. If the left nerve is severed in young canaries, the right hypoglossal nerve assumes the control of birdsong —a finding remarkably similar to that of human children with left hemisphere damage in infancy who subsequently develop language centers in the right hemisphere. Although Nottebohm's results are provocative, he has also found that some highly vocal species such as parrots do not have lateralized control of song, whereas some relatively inarticulate birds (e.g., domestic fowl) do. Furthermore, although he has carefully examined the structure of forebrain vocal control nuclei, he has failed to find any consistent right-left asymmetry.

Nottebohm's studies lead one to wonder if similar asymmetries might be present in mammals, but few mammals have the rich vocalizations of birds. Most studies of functional asymmetries in mammals have focused therefore on other behaviors, especially postural/motor behaviors and cognitive behaviors.

Postural/Motor Behaviors. Studies of postural/motor asymmetries have been conducted largely with rats. For example, Denenberg and his colleagues have reported that under certain conditions of environmental enrichment in infancy, there are asymmetrical effects of left and right cortical ablations on measures such as open field activity and turning preference. Similarly, R. G. Robinson has found that damage to the right frontal cortex produces a postoperative period of hyperactivity not seen after left neocortical damage, a result that we have been able to replicate. Further, there are now dozens of studies of postural asymmetries and rotational (circling) behavior in a variety of species. For example, Glick and his colleagues have found that rats given amphetamine tend to circle consistently to one side or the other. Since amphetamine increases dopamine levels in the brain, particularly in the caudate nucleus, they hypothesized that such circling could be induced by differential amounts of dopamine levels in the two caudate nuclei. Bioassays of rats confirmed this hypothesis, for normal rats have a 10 to 15 percent asymmetry in dopamine content in the two caudate nuclei, a difference that is potentiated by amphetamine to 25 to 30 percent. Furthermore, the biochemistry and behavior are associated, because rats rotate toward the side with the lower level of dopamine. In recent years there has been great interest in the neural correlates of circling behavior because of the ease of using this behavior an assay of asymmetrical behavior, which can be correlated with neuroanatomy and neurochemistry (see the review by T. E. Robinson). Studies of postural/motor asymmetries in nonhuman species have an uncertain relation to cognitive asymmetries in humans, but they do suggest that one should study postural/motor asymmetries in humans. For example, T. E. Robinson has suggested that the basis of asymmetrical hand preference in humans may be related to neurochemical asymmetries. This is an intriguing idea, since to date there is no obvious neuroanatomical correlate of handedness in humans.

Cognitive Behaviors. If anything akin to cerebral asymmetry in humans is to be demonstrated in other mammals, it seems reasonable to expect that tests of perception, orientation in space, sequencing of movement, and affective behavior would reveal it. To date, the results have been disappointing, as unequivocal evidence of functional asymmetry in monkeys has been elusive. Studies of the visual system have consistently yielded negative results, which is surprising considering the anatomical similarity of the visual system in humans and other primates. For example, one might have predicted an asymmetry in the perception of faces in monkeys, in which facial expression is a significant social cue, but work by both Hamilton and Overman has yielded no evidence at all for asymmetrical processing of faces or facial expressions.

Studies of functional asymmetry in the auditory system are somewhat more encouraging. Dewson removed the superior temporal gyrus in rhesus monkeys (roughly area 22), producing a lasting deficit on an auditory-visual task if the lesion was in the left hemisphere but not if it was in the right. The monkeys were required to press a panel that activated one of two acoustic stimuli, either a 1 kHz tone or white noise. They were then presented with two panels, one green, one red. If the tone was heard, the monkeys pressed the red panel; if the white noise was heard, they pressed the green panel to receive the reward. Superior temporal gyrus lesions on the left impaired performance of this task, whereas lesions to the analogous area on the right did not.

Prudence dictates a measure of caution in interpreting this exciting result. The number of cases is small and the results of histological examination are not yet available. The possibility of asymmetry in the auditory system is confirmed, however, by the work of Petersen and Beecher. They compared the ability of Japanese macaques to discriminate among communicatively relevant sounds and irrelevant sounds. The animals were able to discriminate communicatively relevant sounds presented to the right ear better than those presented to the left ear. The researchers suggest that the Japanese macaques engage in left hemisphere processing in a way that is analogous to that of humans. The results of the experiments on the auditory system are exciting and may be an important step in demonstrating laterality in the nonhuman primate brain.

Studies of rats have proved as equivocal as those with monkeys. Denneberg and his coworkers have reported that under certain conditions ablations of the right hemisphere of rats have different effects on affective behavior, and others have found subtle asymmetrical effects of unilateral forebrain lesions in certain types of learning tasks. In contrast, in an extensive study of praxic, spatial, and social behavior of rats with left or right hemidecortications, we were completely unable to demonstrate any functional asymmetry whatsoever, even though we have consistently observed anatomical asymmetries between the two hemispheres of rats. These results are puzzling and disappointing since it is a general principle of human cerebral organization that the highest cognitive functions are the *most* lateralized behaviors. Nevertheless, the data show that asymmetries in rats are the most obvious in relatively simple behaviors such as turning or general activity.

Summary

The brains of nonhuman mammals exhibit clear anatomical asymmetry, which may be analogous to that observed in humans. Evidence of functional asymmetry has been more elusive, however. There is little doubt that nonhumans do not show asymmetrical hand preference, although there is preliminary evidence of other behavioral asymmetries that may have analogues in humans. The demonstration of anatomical asymmetry in non-human brains implies that asymmetry in the human brain is not directly related either to handedness or to language. We are inclined to believe that the hemispheres of mammals are more likely to be specialized for praxic, perceptual, spatial, and/or affective behavior, but the behavioral evidence from studies of nonhumans does not yet lend a great deal of credence to this suggestion. It would seem safe to conclude, therefore, that even if evidence of functional asymmetry is eventually forthcoming in nonhuman mammals, lateralization of function is a far less salient feature of the cerebral cortex of rodents than of humans.

CONCLUDING REMARKS

The discovery of systematic relations between normal variations in cerebral organization and individual differences in cognitive abilities represents one of the most challenging goals of neuropsychology. The complexity of the human brain makes the task difficult, but the problems are not intractable. Each of us has unique behavioral capacities, as well as short-comings (i.e., "Achilles lobes"), which must surely be related to cerebral organization in some manner. Demonstrations of variations related to handedness imply that some variance is innate, although environmental variables must almost certainly modify cerebral organization. Finally, we must point out that although we have emphasized variations in the asymmetrical organization of the cerebrum, the individual variance within each hemisphere may be as large as between the hemispheres.

REFERENCES

Annett, M. A classification of hand preference by association analysis. *British Journal of Psychology* 61:303–321, 1970.

Bakan, P., G. Dibb, and P. Reed. Handedness and birth stress. *Neuropsychologia* 11:363–366, 1973.

Benbow, C. P., and J. C. Stanley. Sex differences in mathematical ability: fact or artifact? *Science* 210:1262–1264, 1980.

Bryden, M. P. *Laterality: Functional Asymmetry in the Intact Brain.* New York: Academic, 1982.

Collins, R. L. Toward an admissible genetic model for the inheritance of the degree and direction of asymmetry. In S. Harnad, R. W. Doty, L. Goldstein, J. Jaynes, and G. Krauthamer, eds., *Lateralization in the Nervous System.* New York: Academic, 1977.

Dennenberg, V. H. Hemispheric laterality in animals and the effects of early experience. *The Behavioral and Brain Sciences* 4:1–50, 1981.

Dennenberg, V. H., J. Garbanati, G. Sherman, D. A. Yutzey, and R. Kaplan. Infantile stimulation induces brain lateralization in rats. *Science* 201:1150, 1978.

De Renzi, E. The influence of sex and age on the incidence and type of aphasia. *Cortex* 16:627–630, 1980.

Dewson, J. H. Preliminary evidence of hemispheric asymmetry of auditory function in monkeys. In S. Harnad, R. W. Doty, L. Goldstein, J. Jaynes, and G. Krauthamer, eds., *Lateralization in the Nervous System*. New York: Academic, 1977.

Diamond, M. C., R. E. Johnson, and C. A. Ingham. Morphological changes in the young, adult, and aging cerebral cortex, hippocampus, and diencephalon. *Behavioral Biology* 14:163–174, 1975.

Diamond, M. C., G. M. Murphy, Jr., K. Akiyama, and R. E. Hohnson. Morphologic hippocampal asymmetry in male and female rats. *Experimental Neurology* 76:553–565, 1982.

Glick, S. D., T. P. Jerussi, and B. Zimmerberg. Behavioral and neuropharmacological correlates of nigrostriatal asymmetry in rats. In S. Harnad, R. W. Doty, L. Goldstein, J. Jaynes, and G. Krauthamer, eds., *Lateralization in the Nervous System*. New York: Academic, 1977.

Goy, R. W., and B. S. McEwen. *Sexual Differentiation of the Brain*. Cambridge, Mass.: MIT Press, 1980.

Gur, R. C., R. E. Gur, W. D. Obrist, J. P. Hungerbuhler, D. Younkin, A. D. Rosen, B. E. Skolnick, and M. Reivich. Sex and handedness differences in cerebral blood flow during rest and cognitive activity. *Science* 217:659–660, 1982.

Gur, R. C., I. K. Packer, J. P. Hungerbuhler, M. Reivich, W. D. Obrist, W. S. Amarnek, and H. A. Sackheim. Differences in the distribution of gray and white matter in human cerebral hemispheres. *Science* 207:1226–1228, 1980.

Hamilton, C. R. An assessment of hemispheric specialization in monkeys. *Annals of the New York Academy of Sciences* 299:222–232, 1977.

Hardyck, C., and L. F. Petrinovich. Left-handedness. *Psychological Bulletin* 84:384–404, 1977.

Harris, L. J. Sex differences in spatial ability: Possible environmental, genetic, and neurological factors. In M. Kinsbourne, ed., *Asymmetrical Function of the Brain*. Cambridge: Cambridge University Press, 1978.

Harshman, R. A., E. Hampson, and S. A. Berenbaum. Individual differences in cognitive abilities and brain organization, part I: Sex and Handedness. differences in ability. *Canadian Journal of Psychology* 37:144–192, 1983.

Hécaen, H., M. DeAgostini, and A. Monzon-Montes. Cerebral organization in left-handers. *Brain and Language* 12:261–284, 1981.

Hécaen, H., and J. Sauguet. Cerebral dominance in left-handed subjects. *Cortex* 7:19–48, 1971.

Herron, J. *Neuropsychology of Left-Handedness*. New York: Academic, 1980.

Hier, D. B., and J. Kaplan. Are sex differences in cerebral organization clinically significant? *Behavioral and Brain Sciences* 3:238–239, 1980.

Hier, D. G., J. Mondlock, and L. R. Caplan. Behavioral abnormalities after right hemisphere stroke. *Neurology* 33:337–344, 1983.

Hochberg, F. H., and M. LeMay. Arteriographic correlates of handedness. *Neurology* 25:218–222, 1975.

Holloway, R. L., and M. C. de la Coste-Lareymondie. Brain endocast asymmetry in pongids and hominids: Some preliminary findings on the paleontology of cerebral dominance. *American Journal of Physical Anthropology* 58:101–110, 1982.

Inglis, J., and J. S. Lawson. A meta-analysis of sex differences in the effects of unilateral brain damage on intelligence test results. *Canadian Journal of Psychology* 36:670–683, 1982.

Inglis, J., and J. S. Lawson. Sex differences in the effects of unilateral brain damage on intelligence. *Science* 212:693–695, 1981.

Inglis, R., M. Rickman, J. S. Lawson, A. W. MacLean, and T. N. Monga. Sex differences in the cognitive effects of unilateral brain damage. *Cortex* 18:257–276, 1982.

Kelly, R. R., and C. Tomlinson-Keasey. The effect of auditory input on cerebral laterality. *Brain and Language* 13:67–77, 1981.

Kertesz, A., and N. Geschwind. Patterns of pyramidal decussation and their relationship to handedness. *Archives of Neurology* 24:326–332, 1971.

Kimura, D. Sex differences in cerebral organization for speech and praxic functions. *Canadian Journal of Psychology* 37:19–35, 1983.

Kimura, D. Speech representation in an unbiased sample of left-handers. *Human Neurobiology,* in press.

Kolb, B., A. MacKintosh, I. Q. Whishaw, and R. J. Sutherland. Evidence for anatomical but not functional asymmetry in the hemidecorticate rat. *Behavioral Neuroscience* 98:44–58, 1984.

Kolb, B., and B. Milner. Performance of complex arm and facial movements after focal brain lesions. *Neuropsychologia* 19:491–503, 1981.

Kolb, B., R. J. Sutherland, A. J. Nonneman, and I. Q. Whishaw. Asymmetry in the cerebral hemispheres of the rat, mouse, rabbit, and cat: The right hemisphere is larger. *Experimental Neurology* 78:348–359, 1982.

Lacoste-Utamsing, C. de., and R. L. Holloway. Sexual dimorphism in the human corpus callosum. *Science* 216:1431–1432, 1982.

Lake, D. A., and M. P. Bryden. Handedness and sex differences in hemispheric asymmetry. *Brain and Language* 3:266–282, 1976.

Lansdell, H. A sex difference in effect of temporal-lobe neurosurgery on design preference. *Nature* 194:852–854, 1962.

Lansdell, H., and J. Davie. Massa intermedia: Possible relation to intelligence. *Neuropsychologia* 10:207–210, 1972.

Levy, J. Possible basis for the evolution of lateral specialization of the human brain. *Nature* 224:614–615, 1969.

Levy, J., and T. Nagylaki. A model for the genetics of handedness. *Genetics* 72:117–128, 1972.

MacCoby, E., and C. Jacklin. *The Psychology of Sex Differences.* Stanford, Calif.: Stanford University Press, 1974.

Manning, A. A., W. Gobel, R. Markman, and T. LaBrech. Lateral cerebral differences in the deaf in response to linguistic and nonlinguistic stimuli. *Brain and Language* 4:309–321, 1977.

McGlone, J. Sex differences in the cerebral organization of verbal function in patients with unilateral brain lesions. *Brain* 100:775–793, 1977.

McGlone, J. Sex differences in human brain asymmetry: A critical survey. *Behavioral and Brain Sciences* 3:215–263, 1980.

McGlone, J., and W. Davidson. The relation between cerebral speech laterality and spatial ability with special reference to sex and hand preference. *Neuropsychologia* 11:105–113, 1973.

McGlone, J., and A. Kertesz. Sex differences in cerebral processing of visuospatial tasks. *Cortex* 9:313–320, 1973.

McKeever, W. F., H. W. Hoemann, V. A. Florina, and A. D. Van Deventer. Evidence of minimal cerebral asymmetries in the congenitally deaf. *Neuropsychologia* 14:413–423, 1976.

Miceli, G., C. Caltagirone, G. Gainotti, C. Masullo, M. C. Silveri, and G. Villa. Influence of age, sex, literacy and pathologic lesion on incidence, severity and type of aphasia. *Acta Neurological Scandinavia* 64:370–382, 1981.

Morgan, M. Embryology and inheritance of asymmetry. In S. Harnad, R. W. Doty, L. Goldstein, J. Jaynes, and G. Krauthamer, eds., *Lateralization in the Nervous System*. New York: Academic, 1977.

Nottebohm, F. Asymmetries in neural control of vocalization in the canary. In S. Harnad, R. W. Doty, L. Goldstein, J. Jaynes, and G. Krauthamer, eds., *Lateralization in the Nervous System*. New York: Academic, 1977.

Nottebohm, F. Brain pathways for vocal learning in birds: A review of the first 10 years. *Progress in Psychobiology and Physiological Psychology* 9:85–124, 1980.

Obler, L. K., R. J. Zatoree, L. Galloway, Jr., and J. Vaid. Cerebral lateralization in bilinguals: Methodological issues. *Brain and Language,* 15:40–54, 1982.

Overman, W. H., Jr., and R. W. Doty. Hemispheric specialization of facial recognition in man but not in macaque. *Society for Neuroscience Abstracts* 4:78, 1978.

Petersen, M. R., M. D. Beecher, S. R. Zoloth, D. B. Moody, and W. C. Stebbins. Neural lateralization: Evidence from studies of the perception of species-specific vocalizations by Japanese macaques *(Macada puscata)*. *Science* 202:324–326, 1978.

Porac, C., and S. Coren. *Lateral Preferences and Human Behavior*. New York: Springer-Verlag, 1981.

Rapport, R. L., C. T. Tan, and H. A. Whitaker. Language function and dysfunction among Chinese- and English-speaking polyglots: Cortical stimulation, Wada testing, and clinical studies. *Brain and Language* 18:342–366, 1983.

Ratcliffe, G., C. Dila, L. Taylor, and B. Milner. The morphological asymmetry of the hemispheres and cerebral dominance for speech: A possible relationship. *Brain and Language* 11:87–98, 1980.

Robinson, R. G. Differential behavior and biochemical effects of right and left cerebral infarction in the rat. *Science* 205:707–710, 1979.

Robinson, T. E., J. B. Becker, and D. M. Camp. Sex differences in behavioral and brain asymmetries. In M. Myslobodsy, ed., *Hemisyndromes: Psychobiology, Neurology, and Psychiatry*. New York: Academic, 1984.

Sherman, G. F., A. M. Galaburda, and N. Geschwind. Neuroanatomical asymmetries in non-human species. *Trends in Neurosciences* 5:429–431, 1982.

Thomas, H., W. Jamison, and D. D. Hummel. Observation is insufficient for discovering that the surface of still water is invariantly horizontal. *Science* 191:173–174, 1973.

Tzavaras, A., G. Kaprinis, and A. Gatzoyas. Literacy and hemispheric specialization for language: Dichotic listening in illiterates. *Neuropsychologia* 19:565–570, 1981.

Uyehara, J. M., and W. A. Cooper, Jr. Hemispheric differences for verbal and nonverbal stimuli in Japanese- and English-speaking subjects assessed by Tsunoda's method. *Brain and Language* 10:405–417, 1980.

Waber, D. P. Sex differences in cognition: A function of maturation rate? *Science* 192:572–573, 1976.

Walker, S. F. Lateralization of functions in the vertebrate brain: A review. *British Journal of Psychology* 71:329–367, 1980.

Warren, J. M. Functional lateralization in the brain. *Annals of the New York Academy of Sciences* 299:273–280, 1977.

Warren, J. M. Handedness and cerebral dominance in monkeys. In S. Harnad, R. W. Doty, L. Goldstein, J. Jaynes, and G. Krauthamer, eds., *Lateralization in the Nervous System.* New York: Academic, 1977.

Webster, W. G. Functional asymmetry between the cerebral hemispheres of the cat. *Neuropsychologia* 10:75–87, 1972.

Webster, W. G., and I. H. Webster. Anatomical asymmetry of the cerebral hemispheres of the cat brain. *Physiology and Behavior* 14:867–868, 1975.

Witelson, S. F. Early hemisphere specialization and interhemispheric plasticiy: An empirical and theoretical review. In S. J. Segalowitz and F. A. Gruber, eds., *Language Development and Neurological Theory.* New York: Academic, 1977.

Witelson, S. F. Sex and the single hemisphere: Right hemisphere processing for spatial processing. *Science* 193:425–427, 1976.

Witelson, S. F. Neuroanatomical asymmetry in left-handers: A review and implications for functional asymmetry. In J. Herron, ed., *Neuropsychology of Left-Handedness.* New York: Academic, 1980.

Wittig, M. A., and A. C. Petersen. *Sex-Related Differences in Cognitive Functioning.* New York: Academic, 1979.

Yakovlev, P. E. A proposed definition of the limbic system. In C. H. Hockman, ed., *Limbic System Mechanisms and Autonomic Function.* Springfield, Ill.: Charles C Thomas, 1972.

Yakovlev, P. I., and P. Rakic. Patterns of decussation of bulbar pyramids and distribution of pyramidal tracts on two sides of the spinal cord. *Transactions of the American Neurological Association* 91:366–367, 1966.

Yeni-Komshian, G., and D. Benson. Anatomical study of cerebral asymmetry in the temporal lobe of humans, chimpanzees and rhesus monkeys. *Science* 192:387–389, 1976.

16

THE PARIETAL LOBES

The patient with a gross lesion of the parietal lobe presents obvious and profound abnormalities of behavior. The interpretation of these abnormalities presents one of the most challenging puzzles in neuropsychology. A major source of the challenge is the absence of satisfactory nonhuman animal models of parietal lobe function. Parietal lobe function and organization are exceedingly complex. As a consequence of this complexity Luria has hypothesized that some portions of the parietal lobe constitute the specifically human portions of the brain. However, to date there is no clear evidence that such portions are exclusive to the human animal. In this chapter, we do not attempt to catalogue the myriad of behavioral abnormalities associated with parietal lobe disease. We instead present a simple theoretical model of parietal lobe function. The model is based on a similar one by Luria and is supported with appropriate descriptions of the major symptoms of parietal lobe disorder.

ANATOMY OF THE PARIETAL LOBES

The parietal lobe is the region of cerebral cortex underlying the parietal skull bone; this area is roughly demarcated anteriorly by the central fissure, ventrally by the Sylvian fissure, dorsally by the cingulate gyrus, and posteriorly by the parietal-occipital sulcus (see Figure 16–1). The principal regions of the parietal lobe include the postcentral gyrus (Brodmann's areas 1, 2, and 3), the superior parietal lobule (areas 5 and 7), the inferior parietal lobule (areas 40 and 43), and the angular gyrus (area 39). These areas can be divided into two functional zones: an anterior zone including areas 1, 2, 3, and 43 as well as portions of areas 5 and 7, and a more posterior zone including the posterior portions of areas 5 and 7 as well as areas 39 and 40. The anterior zone is principally primary and secondary somatosensory cortex; the more posterior zone is true association cortex.

The principal afferents to the parietal cortex project from the lateral and posterior thalamus, hypothalamus, and primary and secondary sensory areas. The parietal lobe in turn sends its major projections to the frontal and temporal association cortex (Figure 16–2) as well as to subcortical structures including the lateral and posterior thalamus and the posterior region of the striatum, midbrain, and spinal cord. The corticocortical projections to the frontal lobe

Postcentral gyrus

Superior parietal lobule

Angular gyrus

Supramarginal gyrus

A

B

FIGURE 16–1. Gross anatomy of the parietal lobe. A. The major gyri. B. Brodmann's cytoarchitectonic regions.

reflection of cytoarchitectural or physiological unity. It is therefore not surprising that the parietal lobe does not have a unitary function. However, if the anterior (somatosensory) and posterior (association) zones are considered as functionally distinct regions, two independent functions of the parietal lobes can be identified. One is primarily concerned with somatic sensations and perceptions; the other is specialized for integrating sensory input from the somatic, visual, and auditory regions. This latter area extends beyond the formal boundary of the parietal lobe to include posterior portions of the temporal lobe, specifically area 37.

provide sensory input to the frontal lobe, because there are no direct sensory projections to this region. The descending projections to the striatum and spinal cord in particular likely function as a guidance system in the control of movements in space (as described later in the chapter).

A THEORY OF PARIETAL LOBE FUNCTION

No unitary theory of parietal lobe function is possible because the parietal lobe is an artifact of gross anatomical definition rather than a

A

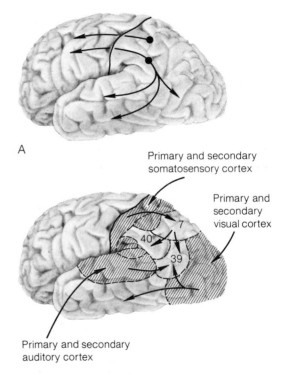

Primary and secondary somatosensory cortex

Primary and secondary visual cortex

Primary and secondary auditory cortex

B

FIGURE 16–2. A. Schematic of the long corticocortical projections of the parietal lobe to the frontal and temporal lobes. B. Schematic of the short corticocortical projections from the primary and secondary somatosensory, visual, and auditory cortex to the tertiary zone of the parietal lobe.

To discuss these two basic functions, we must first briefly review the hierarchical organization of the sensory systems (discussed in Chapter 7). Recall that the lowest cortical zone (Luria's primary zone), which receives projections from the thalamus, consists of highly specific neurons responsive to a single sensory modality. Lesions in the primary zones produce fundamental sensory losses, such as the scotoma that follows damage to area 17 in the visual system. The next cortical zone (Luria's secondary zone; Pandya's parasensory zone) comprises the projection areas of the primary zones, which synthesize the sensory input into more complex forms. Again, the neurons, although more complex, are highly modality-specific, i.e., most are responsive to stimulation in just one modality. Lesions in this zone produce agnosias. Finally, in the highest zone (Luria's tertiary zone) sensory modalities overlap, enabling the sensory systems to integrate their input and to work in concert with one another and with information already stored in the nervous system.

The anterior portion of the parietal lobe forms the primary and secondary zones of the somatic senses (see Figure 16–2), whereas the posterior region of the parietal lobe, in conjunction with the posterior temporal cortex, forms the tertiary zone. We are primarily concerned here with the function of the tertiary zone, the somatosensory functions having previously been discussed in Chapter 9.

Lesions of the tertiary zone do not produce deficits in vision, hearing, or somatic sensation or perception, but they do produce severe disturbances in the integration and analysis of sensory information. An example of this type of sensory integrating process is known as *cross-modal matching*. Say an object is placed in a person's hand and palpated but kept out of sight, and the person is then asked to choose the object visually from among a group of objects. The person must integrate the tactile and visual input to arrive at the solution— that is, to form a single percept of the object. Cross-modal matching can occur among any combination of visual, auditory, and somatic stimuli; in each case the matching is assumed to occur in the tertiary cortex where the inputs overlap. Lesions of this zone would be predicted to impair cross-modal matching, and indeed there is evidence that this is the case.

Another aspect of this integrative function of the tertiary cortex was seen in a patient of ours with a left posterior parietal astrocytoma. She was able to identify a clock as a clock, but she was totally incapable of telling the time from the position of its hands. Thus, she did not have a visual agnosia, but rather a more complex deficit: she was unable to integrate the visual information necessary to decipher the meaning of the position of the hands.

We have greatly simplified the integrative function of the tertiary cortex of the parietal-temporal junction (we expand on it in the next section). Nevertheless, this integrative function demonstrably represents the highest form of sensory analysis. This function is frequently also called cognition, a term in psychology essentially encompassing the mental abilities described by such English-language terms as reasoning, thought, and perception.

Asymmetry of Tertiary Sensory Function

One of the principles of hierarchical organization is that cerebral asymmetry is far more likely to be found at the highest functional levels. Thus, as would be expected, the greatest asymmetry is found in the cognitive functions of the tertiary zone. From our discussion of cerebral asymmetry in Chapter 14 we would expect the left parietal-temporal cortex to have a special role in language processes and the right parietal-temporal cortex to have a special role in spatial processes, and this is indeed the case. We shall describe each of these functions separately.

The left parietal-temporal region is specialized for processing symbolic-analytic information such as is found in language and arithmetic, in which the incoming sensory stimulation stands for, or abstractly symbolizes, something else. For example, the word "cat" describes a four-legged furry feline and assumes the characteristics of the animal (a form of cross-modal matching) even though the word itself in no way resembles a cat. Auditory, visual, and somatic input of a real object is therefore integrated and represented by an abstract stimulus that itself has auditory, visual, and somatic properties. One hears or reads the word "cat"—or, if the word is written in raised lettering, one can somatically "read" by touch the word "cat"—and in each case the object is understood. Geschwind, Luria, and others have proposed that this ability of cross-modally matching the various attributes of a real stimulus into an abstract, symbolic representation is the necessary foundation for the evolution of language. They hypothesize that the function is performed by the angular and supramarginal gyri, roughly areas 39 and 40. And, as previously mentioned, they question the existence of these regions in nonhuman primates on anatomical grounds, although their absence remains to be proved.

The right tertiary sensory zone is specialized for processing a different aspect of sensory input from that of the left. Analysis of visual, auditory, and somatic input requires that the information not only of *what* is incoming be integrated but also of *where* it is coming from. In other words, only when the spatial characteristics of sensory inputs are integrated can a complete perception of the world around us be developed. The complexity of this integration can be demonstrated in a number of ways. For instance, a student in a classroom is able to describe the room from the professor's point of view, even if the student has never stood where the professor stands. To do this, the student must construct an integrated spatial representation of the room, primarily visual and auditory, and then rotate the representation so that the professor's position is assumed. The complexity of this cognitive process is underscored by the observation, made by Piaget and others, that this ability does not develop in children until about 10 years of age.

Parietal Lobe Motor Functions

Mountcastle and his colleagues have proposed that the tertiary parietal cortex receives afferent signals not only of the sensory representation of the world but also of the position and movement of the body in space; the region uses this information to function as "a command apparatus for operation of the limbs, hands, and eyes within immediate extrapersonal space." Thus the parietal lobe not only integrates sensory and spatial information to allow accurate movements in space but also functions to direct or guide movements in the immediate vicinity of the body. Note, however, that the parietal lobe is not thought to control the details of muscular contraction during execution of movements—a function of the frontal lobe (principally area 4) and subcortical structures. Rather, it directs or aims movements toward behavioral goals. Note also that the parietal lobe is not considered to be the *only* motor command system, but rather one of several, each providing a different control function, as yet unspecified.

This view of parietal lobe function accords with much anatomical and behavioral data. It is known that the parietal lobe has substantial efferents to subcortical motor structures, including the basal ganglia and spinal cord. These motor projections contribute to the control of proximal movements (e.g., gross limb movements), but not to distal movements (e.g., fine digit control), which are primarily controlled by area 4 of the frontal lobe. Thus, parietal lobe lesions would be expected to disturb gross movements of the arms (in space) but to have little effect on distal movements of the fingers or face. Consistent with this prediction is the observation that parietal lobe lesions produce severe bilateral apraxia when limb movements are required, but only mild apraxia when facial movements are required (see Chapter 12).

Like other functions of the parietal lobe, motor control of the left and right parietal cortex is asymmetrical. Because (as noted earlier) the left hemisphere has a special role in controlling movement, the theory would be expected to be more applicable to the left parietal lobe than to the right. Kimura has proposed that the left parietal control function provides a system for accurate internal representation of moving body parts and thus is important for controlling changes in their spatial positions. She argues that apraxia results from a disturbance in this function of controlling accurate positioning of limb and oral musculature. To move a limb from one position to another a person must have an accurate representation of where the limb is currently positioned. Without this information, changes of position are awkward and frequently in error. The right parietal lobe also has a motor function, as observed in constructional apraxia, discussed in Chapter 12. We propose, however, that the two motor functions are totally dissimilar, for the right directs motor movements for reproducing the spatial properties of objects in the world. Right parietal lesions disturb the motor control of drawing or constructional abilities, because the inadequate sensory-spatial representation deprives the frontal motor system of sufficient information to carry out the appropriate movements.

Thus, drawings are distorted, blocks are assembled in bizarre designs, maps lack spatial organization, etc.

Further Implications of the Theory

This relatively simple model of parietal lobe function allows us to make inferences about the organization of other cognitive functions such as memory and personality.

Memory. For sensory input to be effectively integrated it must be held long enough to be used. It could therefore be predicted that parietal lobe dysfunction would disturb short-term, or working, memory—that is, the memory for things that have just happened. For example, a person asked to repeat the digits 3292401 must hold them briefly in order to process and to repeat them, and indeed left parietal temporal lesions seriously impair the ability to recall strings of digits. On the other hand, if there is no primary sensory defect, or agnosia, then a person with this lesion should be able to remember the digits with repeated practice, provided the mechanisms involved in long-term storage (located primarily in the medial temporal lobes) are intact. This prediction appears to be confirmed by observation. Furthermore, there is an asymmetry in this short-term memory function: the left parietal-temporal region is involved primarily in holding verbal material and the right parietal-temporal region primarily in holding nonverbal material, such as the spatial location of particular sensory inputs.

Personality. We have seen that a person's behavior is influenced by the integration of sensory stimuli to produce a unified perception of the world. If a lesion in the left parietal lobe occurs, producing a disturbance of abstract symbolic integration, then behaviors such as talking, reading, and writing are disturbed. Similarly, a disturbance of spatial integration resulting from lesion of the right parietal lobe produces a disturbance in behaviors requiring spatial orientation. Thus, since changes in sensory integration alter our behavior, it follows that how the affected person appears to others (that is, the person's personality) will be altered. And indeed, right parietal-temporal lesions commonly produce profound changes in personality. Luria describes a group of such patients with lesions (tumors and aneurysms) of the right parietal-temporal region who showed a severe loss of direct orientation in space and time.

> They firmly believed that at one and the same time they were in Moscow and also in another town. They suggested that they had left Moscow and gone to the other town, but having done so, they were still in Moscow where an operation had been performed on their brain. Yet they found nothing contradictory about these conclusions. Integrity of the verbal-logical processes in these patients, despite the profound disturbance of their direct self-perception and self-evaluation, led to a characteristic overdevelopment of speech, to verbosity, which bore the character of empty reasoning and which masked their true defects. (Luria, 1973, p. 168)

EFFECTS OF PARIETAL LOBE LESIONS

Although we have described a simple theory of how parietal lobe function is organized, we have not discussed in any detail the bewildering array of symptoms characteristic of patients with parietal lobe lesions. In this section we take a brief historical look at the interpretations of the symptoms of left and right parietal lobe disease. We then describe some of the typical symptoms observed in patients with parietal lobe lesions.

Symptoms of Left Parietal Lobe Lesions

In 1924, Josef Gerstmann described a patient with an unusual symptom following a left parietal stroke—finger agnosia: the patient was unable to name or indicate recognition of the fingers on either hand. This discovery aroused considerable interest, and over the ensuing years other symptoms were reported to accompany finger agnosia, including right-left confusion, **agraphia** (inability to write), and **acalculia** (inability to perform mathematical operations). These four symptoms collectively became known as the **Gerstmann syndrome.** Gerstmann and others argued that these symptoms accompanied a circumscribed lesion in the left parietal lobe, roughly corresponding to the **angular gyrus** (area 39). If these four symptoms occurred as a group, the patient was said to demonstrate the Gerstmann syndrome, and the lesions could be localized in the angular gyrus. The storm of controversy that followed such claims continues to this day. The major issue is whether all these symptoms occur together, and whether these are the only symptoms.

The important question from our point of view is whether these symptoms occur: they do. Do they ever occur as a pure syndrome? They probably do, but not often enough that the syndrome would be a useful diagnostic tetrad in routine investigations. Today various other symptoms of left parietal lesions are known; many of these are illustrated in the following case history.

On 24 August 1975, Mr. S., an 11-year-old boy, suddenly had a seizure, which was characterized by twitching on the right side of the body, particularly the upper limb and face. He was given anticonvulsant medication and was symptom-free until 16 September 1975, when he began to write upside down and backward, at which time he was immediately referred to a neurologist, who diagnosed a left parietal malignant astrocytoma. Careful neuropsychological assessment revealed a number of symptoms characteristic of left parietal lesions. (1) Mr. S. had several symptoms of disturbed language function: he was unable to write even his name (agraphia), had serious difficulties in reading (dyslexia), and spoke slowly and deliberately, making many errors in grammar **(dysphasia).** (2) He was unable to combine blocks to form designs and had difficulties learning a sequence of novel movements of the limbs, suggestive of apraxia. (3) He was very poor at mental arithmetic **(dyscalculia)** and could not correctly solve even simple additions and subtractions. (4) He had an especially low digit span, being able to master the immediate recall of only three digits, whether they were presented orally or visually. (5) He was totally unable to distinguish left from right, responding at chance on all tests of this. (6) He had right hemianopia, probably because his tumor had damaged the geniculostriate connections. As Mr. S.'s tumor progressed, movement of the right side of his body became disturbed, because the tumor placed pressure on the frontal lobe. By the end of October 1975 Mr. S. died, neither surgery nor drug therapy being able to stop the growth of the tumor.

The symptoms that Mr. S. exhibited resemble those of other patients we have seen with left parietal lesions. Curiously, he did not have finger agnosia, one of the Gerstmann symptoms, illustrating the point that even very large lesions do not produce the same effects in every patient. Thus, a parietal syndrome cannot be identified as Gerstmann tried to do.

Symptoms of Right Parietal Lobe Lesions

A perceptual disorder following right parietal lesions was described by Hughlings-Jackson in 1874. However, not until the 1940s was the effect of right parietal lesions clearly defined by Paterson and Zangwill. A classic paper by McFie and Zangwill, published in 1960, reviewed much of the previous work and described several symptoms of right parietal lesions, which are illustrated in the following patient.

Mr. P., a 67-year-old man, had suffered a right parietal stroke. At the time of our first seeing him (24 hours after admission) he had no visual field defect or paresis. He did, however, have a variety of other symptoms. (1) Mr. P. neglected the left side of his body and of the world. When asked to lift up his arms, he failed to lift his left arm but could do so if one took his arm and asked him to lift it. When asked to draw a clock face, he crowded all the numbers onto the right side of the clock. When asked to read compound words such as ice cream or football, he read "cream" and "ball." When he dressed, he did not attempt to put on the left side of his clothing (a form of dressing apraxia), and when he shaved, he shaved only the right side of his face. He ignored tactile sensation on the left side of his body. Finally, he appeared unaware that anything was wrong with him and was uncertain as to what all the fuss was about (anosagnosia). Collectively, these symptoms are referred to as **contralateral neglect;** we shall return to them shortly. (2) He was impaired at combining blocks together to form designs (constructional apraxia) and was generally impaired at drawing freehand with either hand, copying drawings, or cutting out paper figures. When drawing, he often added extra strokes in an effort to make the pictures correct, but the drawings generally lacked accurate spatial relations. Notice, in Figure 16–3 that the attempted drawing of a cube is spatially distorted and contains many superfluous lines. (3) He had a topographical disability, being unable to draw maps of well-known regions from memory. He attempted to draw a map of his neighborhood, but it was badly distorted with respect to directions, the spatial arrangement of landmarks, and distances. In spite of all these disturbances Mr. P. knew where he was and what day it was, and he could recognize his family's faces. He also had good language functions: he could talk, read, and write normally.

The contralateral neglect observed in Mr. P. is one of the most fascinating symptoms of brain dysfunction. Typically there is neglect of visual, auditory, and somesthetic stimulation on the side of the body and/or space opposite to the lesion, which may be accompanied by denial of the deficit. Recovery passes through two stages. The first, **allesthesia,** is charac-

A

B

FIGURE 16–4. A. Composite drawing of the region damaged (as inferred from brain scans) in 13 patients with contralateral neglect as described by Heilman and Watson. The area of greatest overlap is the right inferior parietal lobule. B. Composite drawing of the region of overlap among lesions producing deficits in Warrington and Taylor's test of recognition of objects seen in unfamiliar views. The shaded region is the one of maximal overlap. Note the similarity between A and B.

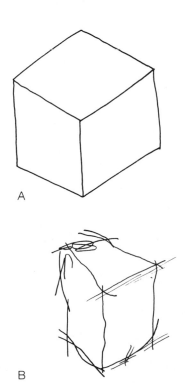

A

B

FIGURE 16–3. A. The model. B. The copy done by a patient with a right parietal stroke. Note the addition of lines to try to make the drawing correct.

terized by the person's beginning to respond to stimuli on the neglected side, but doing so as if the stimuli were on the good side. The person responds to and orients to visual, tactile, or auditory stimuli on the left side of the body as if they were on the right. The second stage is called **simultaneous extinction:** the person responds to stimuli on the hitherto neglected side unless both sides are stimulated simultaneously, in which case he or she notices only the stimulation on the side ipsilateral to the lesion.

Neglect presents several obstacles to understanding. For example, where is the lesion that can produce this effect? Figure 16–4 is a composite drawing of the region damaged (as inferred from brain scans) in 13 patients with neglect as described by Heilman and Watson. The area of most overlap among the lesions was the inferior parietal lobule. It should be noted, however, that neglect is occasionally observed following lesions to the frontal lobe and **cingulate cortex,** as well as to subcortical structures including the superior colliculus and lateral hypothalamus. It is not clear, however, whether the same phenomenon results from these various lesions.

A second problem is why neglect occurs at all. There are two main theories: (1) that neglect is caused by defective sensation or perception, (2) that it is caused by defective "attention" or orientation. The strongest argument favoring the theory of defective sensation is that a lesion to the parietal lobes, which receive input from all the sensory regions, could disturb the integration of sensation. Denny-Brown termed this function *morphosynthesis* and its disruption *amorphosynthesis*. In a current elaboration of this view it is hypothesized that neglect follows right parietal lesion because the integration of the spatial properties of stimuli becomes disturbed; as a result, although stimuli are perceived, their location is uncertain to the nervous system and subsequently they are ignored. The neglect is hypothesized to be unilateral because it is assumed that in the absence of right hemisphere function, the left hemisphere is capable of some rudimentary spatial synthesis that prevents neglect of the right side of the world. This rudimentary spatial ability cannot compensate, however, for the many other behavioral deficits resulting from right parietal lesion.

Critchley and later others, proponents of the second theory, have suggested that neglect results from an inability to attend to input that has in fact been registered. This view has most recently been elaborated by Heilman and Watson. They propose that neglect is manifested by a defect in orienting to stimuli; the defect results from disruption of a system whose function is to "arouse" the individual when new sensory stimulation is present.

We are inclined to favor the first theory, of defective perception, for two reasons. First, it is consistent with the general theory of parietal lobe function; second, it does not require that an additional function be postulated for the parietal lobe.

Another common symptom of right parietal lobe lesion (which we did not look for in Mr. P.) has been described by Warrington and her colleagues: patients with right parietal lesions, although capable of recognizing objects shown in familiar views, are badly impaired at recognizing objects shown in unfamiliar views. For example, a side-view photograph of a bucket is recognized easily; a top-view photograph of the same bucket is recognized with great difficulty (see Figure 16–5). Warrington concludes that the deficit is not in forming a gestalt, but rather in perceptual classification, the mechanism whereby two or more stimulus inputs are allocated to the same class. Such allocation can be seen as a type of spatial matching in which the common view of an object must be spatially rotated to match the novel view. Warrington and Taylor suggest that the focus for this deficit is roughly the inferior parietal lobule, the same region proposed as the locus of contralateral neglect (Figure 16–4).

Balint's Syndrome

In 1909 Balint described a patient with a rather peculiar visual symptomatology. The patient showed no obvious signs of mental impairment, as he displayed no aphasia or apraxia, had full visual fields, and could recognize, use, and name objects, pictures, and colors normally. In spite of this, the patient did have three

FIGURE 16–5. Drawing of a bucket in familiar (A) and unfamiliar (B) views. Patients with right parietal lesions have difficulty in recognizing objects in unfamiliar views such as this one.

unusual symptoms. First, although he spontaneously looked straight forward, when an array of stimuli was placed in front of him, he directed his gaze 35 to 40° to the right and perceived only what was lying in that direction. This symptom includes a component of neglect of the left visual field, but in addition there is neglect of part of the right visual field. Second, once the patient's attention was directed toward an object, no other stimulus was noticed. With urging, he could identify other stimuli placed before him, but he would quickly relapse into his previous neglect. Balint concluded that the patient's field of attention was limited to one object at a time, a disorder that made reading very difficult since each letter was perceived separately. Third, the patient had a severe deficit in reaching under visual guidance. Balint described this symptom as **optic ataxia,** a term that is not strictly appropriate, but it has stuck anyway. A disorder of reaching is commonly observed in parietal lobe patients, as illustrated in a case described by Damasio and Benton.

> She consistently misreached for targets located in the nearby space, such as pencils, cigarettes, matches, ashtrays and cutlery. Usually she under-reached by 2 to 5 inches, and then explored, by tact, the surface path leading to the target. This exploration, performed in one or two groping attempts, was often successful and led straight to the object. Occasionally, however, the hand would again misreach, this time on the side of the target and beyond it. Another quick tactually guided correction would then place the hand in contact with the object. . . . In striking contrast to the above difficulties was the performance of movements which did not require visual guidance, such as buttoning and unbuttoning of garments, bringing a cigarette to the mouth, or pointing to some part of her body. These movements were smooth, quick and on target. (Damasio and Benton, 1979, p. 171)

Balint's patient turned out to have bilateral softening of the region of areas 39 and 40. The syndrome does not seem to occur with unilateral lesions, although it has been reported by others in patients with bilateral lesions. It thus can be considered quite rare. Nevertheless, the deficits in directing gaze and reaching are important in understanding parietal lobe function since, as we shall see, there are cells in areas 5 and 7 of the monkey that fire during reaching movements to objects in space.

Summary of the Major Symptoms

Our survey of the literature indicates 15 major reliable symptoms of parietal lobe damage. Table 16–1 summarizes these symptoms, indicates the most probable lesion locus, and provides basic references in which these disorders have been quantified. Details of all these symptoms can be found in Chapters 10, 12, 16, and 22.

Left and Right Parietal Lobes Compared

Although we have discussed the left and right parietal lobes separately and have described

TABLE 16–1

Summary of major symptoms of parietal lobe damage

	Symptoms	Most probable lesion site	Basic reference
1.	Disorders of tactile function	Areas 1, 2, 3	Semmes et al., 1960 Corkin et al., 1970
2.	Visual or tactile agnosia	Areas 5, 7, 37?	Hécaen and Albert, 1978 Brown, 1972
3.	Apraxia	Areas 7, 40 left	Brown, 1972 Geschwind, 1975 Kimura, 1980
4.	Constructional apraxia	Areas 7, 40	Piercy et al., 1960
5.	Disorders of language (alexia, aphasia)	Areas 39, 40 left	Hécaen and Albert, 1978
6.	Acalculia	Areas 39, 40 left	Hécaen, 1969
7.	Impaired cross-modal matching	Areas 37, 40	Butters and Brody, 1968
8.	Contralateral neglect	Areas 7, 40 right	Heilman and Watson, 1977
9.	Poor short-term memory	Areas 37, 40	Warrington and Weiskrantz, 1973
10.	Disorders of body image	Area 7?	Hécaen and Albert, 1978
11.	Right-left confusion	Areas 7, 40 left	Semmes et al., 1960 Benton, 1959
12.	Disorders of spatial ability	Areas 7, 40 right	Semmes et al., 1963 Benton, 1969
13.	Disorders of drawing	Area 40	Warrington et al., 1966
14.	Defects in eye movement	Area 7, 40?	Tyler, 1968
15.	Misreaching	Areas 5, 7	Damasio and Benton, 1979

functional asymmetry, there is little doubt that lesions to the two hemispheres produce some overlapping. See Table 16–2, taken from the classic paper by McFie and Zangwill. Notice that lesions of either hemisphere are associated with behavioral deficits on four of their seven tests, although particular deficits were more likely to follow damage to one hemisphere. This partial overlap of symptoms is a common feature of lesions of association cortex and implies functional overlap between the highest functions of the hemispheres. The partial overlap may be related to the concept of preferred mode of cognitive processing, introduced in Chapter 14. There we noted that many problems can be solved by using either a verbal cognitive mode or a spatial nonverbal cognitive mode, and that genetic, maturational, and environmental factors may predispose different people to use different modes. For example, a complex spatial problem, such as reading an upside-down map, can be solved either directly, by "spatial cognition" (the directions to travel are intuited spatially), or by "verbal cognition" (the spatial information is encoded into words and the problem is solved by being "talked" through step by step). There are people who are highly verbal and prefer the verbal mode even when it is less efficient; lesions of the left parietal lobe of these people would be expected to disturb functions that ordinarily are preferentially disrupted by right parietal lesions, as can be seen in Table 16–2. Little direct evidence favors this explanation of functional overlap, but we believe it is a provocative idea that accounts in part for individual differences as well as for the apparent functional overlap revealed by lesion studies.

Clinical Neuropsychological Assessment

As we have seen, restricted lesions of the parietal cortex produce a wide variety of behavioral changes. It is logical to assume that behavioral tests used to evaluate brain damage in neurologically verified cases could be used to predict the locus and extent of brain damage or dysfunction in new cases. (See Chapter 26 for more detail on the rationale of neuropsychological assessment.) In this section we briefly summarize a number of tests that have proved to be sensitive and valid predictors of brain injury (see Table 16–3). Although these tests do not assess all the symptoms summarized in Table 16–1, they assess a broad

TABLE 16–2

Effects of left and right parietal lobe lesions compared

	Percent of subjects with deficit [a]	
	Left (%)	Right (%)
Unilateral neglect	13	67
Dressing disability	13	67
Cube counting	0	86
Paper cutting	0	90
Topographical loss	13	50
Right-left discrimination	63	0
Weigl's sorting test	83	6

[a]Note the small but significant overlap in symptoms of left and right lesions respectively.
Based on data presented by McFie and Zangwill, 1960.

range of parietal lobe functions. It would be highly unusual for a person to perform normally on all these tests but show other symptoms of parietal lobe damage.

The two-point discrimination test assesses somatosensory thresholds. Recall that following lesions of the postcentral gyrus the somatosensory threshold increases in the contralateral side of the body. The test requires the blindfolded subject to report whether he or she felt one or two points touch the skin (usually on the palm of the hand or the face). The distance between the points is at first very large (e.g., 3 cm) and is gradually reduced until the subject can no longer perceive two points. In extreme cases the process is reversed: the distance must be increased to find that at which the subject first perceives two points.

The Seguin-Goddard form board is a test of tactile form recognition. The blindfolded subject palpates 10 blocks of different shapes (e.g., a star or triangle) and attempts to place them in similarly shaped holes on a form board. When the test is completed, the form board and blocks are removed and the subject is asked to draw the board from memory. The precise locus of the lesion producing deficits on this test is controversial, and no claims have been proved. Nevertheless, research on tactile performance in monkeys with parietal lesions (see below) indicates that blindfolded tactual recognition is probably sensitive to lesions of areas 5 and 7, whereas in humans the drawing part—a test of both memory and cross-modal matching—is probably sensitive to lesions in the tertiary zone (areas 37 and 40).

Visual perceptual capacity is easily assessed by either the Mooney closure test or the Gollin incomplete figure test. In both tasks a series of incomplete representations of faces or objects is presented, and the subject must combine the elements to form a gestalt to identify the picture. These tests are especially sensitive to right parietal-cortex damage.

TABLE 16–3

Standardized clinical neuropsychological tests for parietal lobe damage

Function	Test [a]	Basic reference
1. Somatosensory	Two-point discrimination	Corkin et al., 1970
2. Tactile form recognition	Seguin-Goddard form board Tactile patterns	Teuber and Weinstein, 1954 Benton et al., 1983
3. Visual perception	Gollin incomplete figures Mooney closure test	Warrington and Rabin, 1970 Milner, 1980
4. Spatial relations	Semmes locomotor map Right-left differentiation	Semmes et al., 1963 Benton et al., 1983
5. Language: speech comprehension 　　　　　reading comprehension	Token test Token test	de Renzi and Faglioni, 1978
6. Apraxia	Kimura box test	Kimura, 1977

[a] These are standardized tests validated on large samples of patients with known localized brain damage.

The Semmes body placing and locomotor map tests are described in detail in Chapter 18 and so will not be discussed here. In the right-left differentiation test a series of drawings of hands, feet, ears, and so on is presented in different orientations (upside down, rear view, etc.), and the subject's task is to indicate whether the drawing is of the left or right body part. In a verbal variant of this test subjects are read a series of commands (e.g., "Touch your right ear with your left hand"), which are to be carried out, rather than pointing to pictures. Both of these tests are very sensitive to left parietal lobe damage, but caution is advised, because subjects with left frontal lobe damage are also frequently impaired at these tasks.

The token test is an easily administered test of language comprehension. Twenty tokens—four shapes (large and small circles, large and small squares) in each of five colors (white, black, yellow, green, red)—are placed in front of the subject. The test begins with simple tasks (e.g., touching the white circle) and becomes progressively more difficult (e.g., touching the large yellow circle and the large green square). A reading comprehension test can also be given by having the subject read the instructions out loud and then perform according to them.

It is unfortunate that there are no standardized tests of apraxia analogous to the token test for aphasia. However, the Kimura box test (see Figure 12–5) is probably the best test currently available, and it may provide the desperately needed analogue. The subject is required to make three consecutive movements of pushing a button with the index finger, pulling a handle with four fingers, and pressing a bar with the thumb. This test is done very poorly by apraxics, and many of them appear unable to perform this very simple series of movements even with extensive practice.

Together, these nine tests provide a simple, standardized, and thorough collection of tests of parietal lobe damage. We shall discuss the uses of these tests in Chapters 26 through 30.

NONHUMAN PARIETAL LOBE FUNCTIONS

Certain claims have made studies of the organization of the parietal lobe of nonhumans especially important to our discussion of parietal lobe function in humans. Luria, Geschwind, and others claim that the tertiary zone of the human parietal lobe either is not found in the nonhuman or functions differently there. This difference is taken to be significant in understanding the differences between humans and other primates. Unfortunately, the parietal cortex of nonhumans has drawn far less interest than the frontal and temporal cortex; current knowledge about nonhuman parietal lobe function lags far behind knowledge about other association areas, although recent reviews by Hyvarinen and by Lynch are an important step forward. To date, four types of experiments on the parietal lobes of nonhuman primates are relevant to this discussion: (1) those comparing neuroanatomical structure of the subregions of the parietal lobes; (2) those examining the behavioral capacities of different primates, especially on tests of cross-modal matching; (3) those examining the effects of parietal lobe lesions on behavior; and (4) those examining the properties of cells in the parietal cortex.

Neuroanatomical Structure of Parietal Lobes

Luria, Geschwind, and Konorski have all argued that there are fundamental differences between the parietal lobes of humans and nonhuman primates. Luria and Geschwind have claimed that there is no homologue of the angular gyrus in nonhumans, and Konorski has questioned the existence of the **arcuate fasciculus,** which connects the posterior part of the parietal-temporal junction with the frontal cortex. In a thorough review of this issue Passingham and Ettlinger conclude that Konorski was in error, because there is clear evidence that the arcuate fasciculus exists in nonhuman primates, and to date there is no unequivocal evidence of major differences between the angular gyrus in

FIGURE 16–6. Gross anatomy of the parietal lobes of the monkey, cat, and rat. Tertiary zones are tentative pending further behavioral and anatomical work. The brains are not drawn to the same scale. Note that no evolutionary progression from one species to another is implied (see Chapter 4).

humans and in other primates. Indeed, they point out that the only clear neuroanatomical difference between humans and other primates is the larger size of the human brain. Figure 16–6 provides a tentative summary of the extent and location of parietal cortex in the monkey, cat, and rat. The location and existence of areas 39 and 40 in all three species is uncertain and somewhat controversial. Brodmann, for example, pointed out that his monkey area 7 should be thought of as an undifferentiated area comparable to areas 7, 39, and 40 in humans. We have drawn these regions on the basis of available cytoarchitectonic, behavioral, and neuroanatomical degeneration studies.

Nonhuman Primate Cross-Modal-Matching and Language Skills

Cross-modal-matching ability has been widely implicated as a necessary correlate of language skills in humans, and it has been suggested that nonhuman primates do not naturally have language because they lack this cognitive function. Because it is assumed that cross-modal matching is performed by the angular and supramarginal gyri, and because there are suggestions that nonhumans may not possess a homologue of this region, it is of particular interest to know whether nonhuman primates are capable of performing this behavior.

A variety of experimental situations have been devised to test this question. In the simplest of these tests an animal is presented three objects: one (the sample) it can see but not touch, and two others it can touch but not see. One of the hidden objects is identical to the sample. The subject's task is to select this one after palpating each of the hidden ones. If the chosen object matches the sample, the animal is given a food reward. By using this procedure Davenport and his colleagues have unequivocally demonstrated cross-modal-matching abilities in chimpanzees, for they not only can match a visually presented object with the tactile equivalent but also can match photographs of an object with its tactile equivalent.

Until recently monkeys were reported to fail or give equivocal results in a matching task, but Jarvis and Ettlinger have shown that various species of monkeys are clearly capable of cross-modal matching and that early failures were an artifact of testing procedures. Furthermore, when they compared the performance of chimpanzees and rhesus monkeys on the same test problems, they found no clear superiority in the performance of the chimps. This result is surprising, for the chimpanzee has the larger parietal association cortex of the two.

The results of these studies imply one of two conditions: either cross-modal matching is not a correlate of language (although perhaps it is a prerequisite for language), or nonhuman primates are capable of some language abilities. Research on several species of apes has indicated that they are indeed capable of acquiring certain language abilities, such as the American Sign Language; thus, the neocortical organization of humans and other great apes may not differ qualitatively. We shall return to this issue in our discussion of language (Chapter 21); we conclude here that there is no compelling behavioral evidence for a significant difference between the parietal lobe function in humans and their nearest primate relatives.

Behavior Following Parietal Lobe Lesions in Nonhumans

The behavioral effects of parietal lobe lesions in monkeys are summarized in Table 16–4. Each of the symptoms listed is also observed in humans, although the symptoms are less obvious than they are in humans. Unfortunately, there are few studies in which the lesions have been limited to a single cytoarchitectonic area, the lesions usually being placed in the anterior parietal (areas 1, 2, and 3) or posterior parietal (areas 5 and 7) regions.

TABLE 16–4

Summary of major symptoms of parietal lobe lesions in monkeys

Symptom	Lesion site	Representative reference
1. Disorders of tactile function	Areas 1, 2, 3, 5, 7	Semmes and Turner, 1977 LaMotte and Mountcastle, 1979 Moffet et al., 1967
2. Disorders of spatial ability	Areas 5, 7	Sugishita et al., 1978 Pohl, 1973
3. Unilateral neglect	Areas 5, 7	Denny-Brown and Chambers, 1958 Heilman and Watson, 1977
4. Defects in eye movements	Areas 5, 7	Latto, 1978 Lynch, 1980
5. Misreaching	Areas 5, 7	Peele, 1944 Milner et al., 1977

Tactile Function. Lesions of areas 1, 2, and 3 produce deficits in various tactile-related behaviors. Simple tactile discriminations (e.g., roughness) are disturbed by lesions of primary parietal cortex, whereas most posterior lesions produce a wide variety of symptoms, including deficits in tactile form discrimination, impairment of limb position sense, and deficits in tactile placing and the grasping response.

Spatial Ability. Monkeys with posterior parietal lesions have an impaired perception of the relations among objects in space, although apparently not of the relation between the monkey's own body and objects in space. Such monkeys are also deficient in finding their home cages when released in the center of an animal room, and they direct manual searches in the dark in the wrong direction. All these symptoms suggest a general spatial disturbance, which we shall return to in Chapter 23. In addition, the monkeys are impaired at visual guidance of movements in space. Petrides and Iverson studied the performance of monkeys on a behavioral analogue of the route-finding tests (e.g., mazes and maps) used to study special ability in humans. They chose a "bent

wire" problem, using metal rods bent to form various routes.

A ring-shaped sweet was threaded on the wire, and the monkey's task was to remove the sweet so that it could be eaten. Monkeys with parietal lesions took significantly longer to remove the sweets; indeed, they completely failed to solve about half of the problems. These data demonstrate a visuospatial deficit analogous to those seen in humans with similar lesions.

Unilateral Neglect. Although unilateral neglect is less conspicuous in monkeys than in humans with parietal lobe lesions, several authors have reported that unilateral parietal-cortex lesions in monkeys produce a phenomenon similar to the contralateral neglect. For example, Watson and Heilman and their associates have observed that monkeys display extinction to simultaneous visual and somethesthetic stimulation and decreased response to threat contralateral to the lesions, occasionally even ignoring food on the side contralateral to the lesion.

Defective Eye Movements. Workers at a number of laboratories have noticed abnormal visual search patterns following posterior parietal lesions in monkeys, and careful study by Lynch and his colleagues has shown several abnormalities in optokinetic nystagmus, which is involuntary, rapid movements of the eyeball elicited by stimuli moving through the visual field.

Misreaching. Monkeys with parietal lesions reach with poor accuracy and may appear ataxic as they try to grasp objects with either the fore or hind feet. The reaching deficit is characterized by slowness of movement, abnormal shaping of the hand and fingers during reaching, and an error in the angle of reach of the limb with respect to a target.

We are unaware of any studies of lesions in the posterior parietal cortex of cats, although lesions in primary somatosensory cortex do disrupt tactile discrimination. More research has been done with rats, and we have found deficits in spatial navigation and limb placement from the presumed analogue of posterior parietal cortex lesions in humans.

Microelectrode Studies

In the 1960s the parietal cortex of the monkey was considered to be a somatosensory area, the anterior zone to be involved in basic somatosensation, and the posterior zone to have some sort of "associate somatic" function. Over the past decade research using microelectrodes to study single units has painted a somewhat different picture, in which the functions of areas 1, 2, and 3, area 5, and several subareas of area 7 can be dissociated. We have described the characteristics of units in areas 1, 2, and 3 in Chapters 8 and 10, and so we shall focus our discussion on areas 5 and 7.

Area 5. The majority of neurons in area 5 are activated by passive joint rotation or the stimulation of muscles and other deep tissues. More important, however, is the fact that area 5 neurons are most responsive during active movement. Mountcastle and his colleagues found that many cells were only responsive to projections of the arm or manipulations by the hand within the immediate space around the animal *to obtain an object such as food.* This observation was unexpected and fascinating since these same cells were not active during other movements in which the same muscles were used differently, implying that the function of the cells was not simply "somatic." Hyvarinen suggests that area 5 seems to have an important role in somatosensory exploration, reaching for and manipulation of objects. For successful reaching in space, the positions of several joints have to be coordinated; damage to these neurons would impair reaching, and we have seen that this is the case. The neural circuits connecting the posterior parietal cortex with the frontal and limbic cortex (see Chapter 8) may be responsible for the selective activation of area 5 neurons in the presence of goal objects, but this remains to be proved.

Area 7. Far from being a "somatic association zone," the units in area 7 reveal it to be a truly multimodal region, as we suggested in our theoretical view of the parietal lobe at the beginning of the chapter. Cells in area 7 respond to somatic stimulation, as might be expected in a somatic secondary region, but there are also cells responsive to visual and to auditory stimulation. Further, there are cells in this area that are active during eye movements, cells that may be analogous to those active during visually guided reaching movements.

The details of the characteristics of the cells of area 7 are complex and beyond us here, but some simple generalizations can be made. First, the cells in area 7 have a role in directing movements toward somatosensory, visual, and auditory targets. When the head or a limb moves toward a position in space, cells in area 7 are very active, suggesting that they have a major role in coordinating the changes in joint position to direct the movement to the position in space. It may not be surprising, therefore, that removal of the posterior parietal cortex produces apparent neglect; in the absence of area 7 the brain may detect the stimuli normally but be unable to direct the appropriate movements, resulting in part of the neglect syndrome.

Second, area 7 appears to be functionally differentiated into smaller regions, each of which may have a special role in a particular type of movement. Thus, one zone has cells responsive to both somatic and visual stimuli, another to somatic and auditory stimuli, and another to chemical and somatic stimuli. The first zone may be involved in visual and somatic guidance of limb and hand movements, the second in auditory and somatic guidance of the head, and the third in chemical and somatic guidance of the tongue, although this is purely speculative.

The identification of units in the parietal cortex that appear to have a role in the control of movement in space with respect to specific targets is important, for these properties are consistent with two effects of parietal lobe lesions in humans. First, parietal lobe individuals appear to have a deficit in coordinating segmental movements involving changes in joint position, an effect one might expect if area 7 units were damaged. Second, parietal lobe individuals have difficulty in manipulating objects in space (constructional apraxia), another effect that might be expected if area 7 units were damaged.

REFERENCES

Balint. R. Seelenlahmung des "Schauens," optische Ataxie, raumliche Störung der Aufmerksamkeit. *Monatsschr. Psychiatr. Neurol.* 25:51–81, 1909.

Benton, A. L. *Right-Left Discrimination and Finger Localization.* New York: Hoeber-Harper, 1959.

Benton, A. L., K. deS. Hamsher, N. R. Varney, and O. Spreen. *Contributions to Neuropsychological Assessment.* New York: Oxford University Press, 1983.

Benton, A. L. Disorders of spatial orientation. In P. Vincken and G. Bruyn, eds., *Handbook of Clinical Neurology,* vol. 3. Amsterdam: North-Holland Publishing Co., 1969.

Bolster, R. B. Cross-modal matching in the monkey *(Macaca fasicularis). Neuropsychologia* 16:407–416, 1978.

Brown, J. *Aphasia, Apraxia and Agnosia.* Springfield, Ill.: Charles C Thomas, 1972.

Butters, N., and B. A. Brody. The role of the left parietal lobe in the mediation of intra- and cross-modal associations. *Cortex* 4:328–343, 1968.

Corkin, S., B. Milner, and T. Rasmussen. Somatosensory thresholds. *Archives of Neurology* 23:41–58, 1970.

Critchley, M. *The Parietal Lobes.* London: Arnold, 1953.

Damasio, A. R., and A. L. Benton. Impairment of hand movements under visual guidance. *Neurology* 29:170–178, 1979.

Davenport, R. K., C. M. Rogers, and I. S. Russell. Cross-modal perception in apes. *Neuropsychologia* 11:21–28, 1973.

Denny-Brown, D., and R. A. Chambers. The parietal lobes and behavior. *Research Publications of the Association for Research in Mental Disease* 36:35–117, 1958.

Gerstmann, J. Some notes on the Gerstmann syndrome. *Neurology* 7:866–869, 1957.

Geschwind, N. The apraxias: Neural mechanisms of disorders of learned movement. *American Scientist* 63:188–195, 1975.

Geschwind, N. Disconnexion syndromes in animals and man. *Brain* 88:237–294, 1965.

Gravbiel, A. M. Studies on the anatomical organization of posterior association cortex. In F. O. Schmitt and F. G. Worden, eds., *The Neurosciences: Third Study Program*. Cambridge, Mass.: MIT Press, 1974.

Hall, R. D., and E. P. Lindholm. Organization of motor and somatosensory neocortex in the albino rat. *Brain Research* 66:23–38, 1974.

Hécaen, H. Aphasic, apraxic and agnosic syndromes in right and left hemisphere lesions. In P. Vincken and G. Bruyn, eds., *Handbook of Clinical Neurology,* vol. 4. Amsterdam: North-Holland Publishing Co., 1969.

Hécaen, H., and M. L. Albert. *Human Neuropsychology*. New York: Wiley, 1978.

Heilman, K. M., and R. T. Watson. The neglect syndrome—A unilateral defect of the orienting response. In S. Harnad, R. W. Doty, L. Goldstein, J. Jaynes, and G. Krauthamer, eds., *Lateralization in the Nervous System*. New York: Academic, 1977.

Hyvarinen, J. *The Parietal Cortex of Monkey and Man*. Berlin: Springer-Verlag, 1982.

Jarvis, M. J., and G. Ettlinger. Cross-modal recognition in chimpanzees and monkeys. *Neuropsychologia* 15:499–506, 1977.

Kimura, D. Acquisition of a motor skill after left hemisphere damage. *Brain* 100:527–542, 1977.

Kimura, D. Neuromotor mechanisms in the evolution of human communication. In H. D. Steklis and M. J. Raleigh, eds., *Neurobiology of Social Communication in Primates: An Evolutionary Perspective*. New York: Academic, 1980.

Kolb, B., R. J. Sutherland, and I. Q. Whishaw. A comparison of the contributions of the frontal and parietal association cortex to spatial localization in rats. *Behavioral Neuroscience* 97:13–27, 1983.

Kolb, B., and I. Q. Whishaw. Dissociation of the contributions of the prefrontal, motor, and parietal cortex to the control of movement in the rat: An experimental review. *Canadian Journal of Psychology* 37:211–232, 1983.

Konorski, J. *Integrative Activity of the Brain*. Chicago: The University of Chicago Press, 1967.

LaMotte, R. H., and V. B. Mountcastle. Disorders of somesthesis following lesions of the parietal lobe. *Journal of Neurophysiology* 42:400–419, 1979.

Latto, R. The effects of bilateral frontal eye-field, posterior parietal or superior collicular lesions on visual search in the rhesus monkey. *Brain Research* 146:39–53, 1978.

Luria, A. R. *The Working Brain*. New York: Penguin, 1973.

Lynch, J. C. The functional organization of the posterior parietal association cortex. *Behavioral and Brain Sciences* 3:485–499, 1980.

Lynch, J. C. The role of parieto-occipital association cortex in oculomotor control. *Experimental Brain Research,* 41:A32, 1980.

Lynch, J. C., V. B. Mountcastle, W. H. Talbot, and T. C. T. Yin. Parietal lobe mechanisms for directed visual attention. *Journal of Neurophysiology* 40:362–389, 1977.

McFie, J., M. F. Piercy, and O. L. Zangwill. Visual spatial agnosia associated with lesions of the left cerebral hemisphere. *Brain* 73:167–190, 1950.

McFie, J., and O. L. Zangwill. Visual-constructive disabilities associated with lesions of the left cerebral hemisphere. *Brain* 83:243–260, 1960.

Milner, A. D., E. M. Ockleford, and W. Dewar. Visuo-spatial performance following posterior parietal and lateral frontal lesions in stumptail macaques. *Cortex* 13:350–360, 1977.

Milner, B. Complementary functional specializations of the human cerebral hemispheres. In R. Levy-Montalcini, ed., *Neurons, Transmitters, and Behavior.* Vatican City: Pontificiae Academiae Scientiarum Scripta Varia, 1980.

Moffet, A., G. Ettlinger, H. B. Morton, and M. F. Piercy. Tactile discrimination performance in the monkey: The effect of ablation of various subdivisions of posterior parietal cortex. *Cortex* 3:59–96, 1967.

Mountcastle, V. B., J. C. Lynch, A. Georgopoulos, H. Sakata, and C. Acuna. Posterior parietal association cortex of the monkey: Command functions for operation within extra-personal space. *Journal of Neurophysiology* 38:871–908, 1975.

Passingham, R. F., and G. Ettlinger. A comparison of cortical functions in man and other primates. *International Review of Neurobiology* 16:233–299, 1974.

Paterson, A., and O. L. Zangwill. Disorders of space perception associated with lesions of the right cerebral hemisphere. *Brain* 67:331–358, 1944.

Peele, T. L. Acute and chronic parietal lobe ablations in monkeys. *Journal of Neurophysiology* 7:269–286, 1944.

Petras, J. M. Connections of the parietal lobe. *Journal of Psychiatric Research* 8:189–201, 1971.

Petrides, M., and S. D. Iverson. Restricted posterior parietal lesions in the rhesus monkey and performance on visuospatial tasks. *Brain Research* 161:63–77, 1979.

Piercy, M., H. Hécaen, and J. de Ajuriaguerra. Constructional apraxia associated with unilateral cerebral lesions—Left and right cases compared. *Brain* 83:225–242, 1960.

Pohl, W. Dissociation of spatial discrimination deficits following frontal and parietal lesions in monkeys. *Journal of Comparative and Physiological Psychology* 82:227–239, 1973.

Renzi, E. de, and P. Faglioni. Normative data and screening power of a shortened version of the token test. *Cortex* 14:41–49, 1978.

Semmes, J., and B. Turner. Effects of cortical lesions on somatosensory tasks. *Journal of Investigations in Dermatology* 69:181–189, 1977.

Semmes, J., S. Weinstein, L. Ghent, and H.-L. Teuber. Correlates of impaired orientation in personal and extra-personal space. *Brain* 86:747–772, 1963.

Semmes, J., S. Weinstein, L. Ghent, and H.-L. Teuber. *Somatosensory Changes after Penetrating Brain Wounds in Man.* Cambridge, Mass.: Harvard University Press, 1960.

Sugishita, M., G. Ettlinger, and R. M. Ridley. Disturbance of cage-finding in the monkey. *Cortex* 14:431–438, 1978.

Teuber, H.-L. and S. Weinstein. Performance on a formboard task after penetrating brain injury. *Journal of Psychology* 38:177–190, 1954.

Tyler, H. R. Abnormalities of perception with defective eye movements (Balint's syndrome). *Cortex* 4:154–171, 1968.

Warrington, E. K., M. James, and M. Kinsbourne. Drawing disability in relation to laterality of cerebral lesion. *Brain* 89:53–82, 1966.

Warrington, E. K., and P. Rabin. Perceptual matching in patients with cerebral lesions. *Neuropsychologia* 8:475–487, 1970.

Warrington, E. K., and A. M. Taylor. The contribution of the right parietal lobe to object recognition. *Cortex* 9:152–164, 1973.

Warrington, E. K., and L. Weiskrantz. An analysis of short-term and long-term memory defects in man. In J. A. Deutsch, ed., *The Physiological Basis of Memory*. New York: Academic, 1973.

17

THE TEMPORAL LOBES

In the late 19th century three major effects of temporal lobe lesions on behavior were documented: in 1874 Wernicke described a language deficit, in 1899 Bekhterev reported memory impairment, and in 1888 Brown and Schaefer noted a disorder of affect and personality. Only in the past 30 years, however, have the functions of the temporal lobes—especially of the right—been elaborated. In this chapter (following the format of the previous chapter, on the parietal lobes) we review temporal lobe anatomy, present a simple theoretical model of temporal lobe function, describe the basic symptoms of temporal lobe damage in humans, and briefly describe the effects of temporal lobe lesions in nonhumans.

ANATOMY OF THE TEMPORAL LOBES

The temporal lobe comprises all the tissue below the Sylvian fissure anterior to an imaginary line running roughly from the end of that fissure to the boundary of area 37 with area 19, and the boundary of areas 22 and 37 with the parietal association areas 39 and 40 (see Figure 17–1). The region enclosed by these boundaries includes not only neocortex (six layers) on the lateral surface but also phylogenetically older cortex known as **archicortex** and **paleocortex** (three layers) on the medial surface. The neocortical regions include Brodmann's areas 20, 21, 22, 37, 38, 41, and 42. These areas are also sometimes described by the gyri that form them (illustrated in Figure 17–1): Heschl's gyrus (areas 41 and 42), the superior temporal gyrus (roughly area 22), the middle temporal gyrus (roughly areas 21, 37, and 38), and the inferior temporal gyrus (roughly areas 20 and 37). The older cortex includes both the cortex on the medial surface of the temporal lobe, which forms the fusiform gyrus, parahippocampal gyrus, and uncus, and the hippocampus and amygdala (see Figures 17–1 and 17–2), which are subcortical. Thus, the temporal lobe includes auditory cortex, association cortex, and limbic cortex.

The temporal lobe is rich in internal connections, afferent projections from the sensory systems, and efferent projections to the parietal and frontal association regions, limbic sys-

FIGURE 17–1. Gross anatomy of the temporal lobe. A. The three major gyri visible on the lateral surface of the temporal lobe. B. Brodmann's cytoarchitectonic zones on the lateral surface. C. The gyri visible on a medial view of the temporal lobe.

tem, and basal ganglia. The left and right temporal lobes are connected via the corpus callosum and anterior commissure, the neocortex through the former and the archicortex through the latter.

A THEORY OF TEMPORAL LOBE FUNCTION

Being an arbitrarily defined anatomical region, the temporal lobe does not have a unitary function, since it houses primary and secondary auditory cortex, tertiary sensory cortex, and limbic cortex. However, if the primary and secondary auditory cortex are considered separately from the association and limbic cortex, three basic functions of the temporal lobes can be identified: one primarily concerned with auditory sensations and auditory and visual perception, one specialized for long-term storage of sensory input, and one functioning to add affective tone to sensory input.

The latter two functions are best understood by considering the analysis of sensory stimuli as they enter the nervous system. When a sensory stimulus is received, several processes must occur to allow the motor system to act on the information. First, a percept must be formed, which requires that information about a given stimulus be integrated from different sense modalities, especially vision, audition, and somesthesis. This integration is the primary function of the tertiary area of the parietal lobe. Second, information may either be stored for future use or compared with material stored previously. Higher animals characteristically are able to store large amounts of information, which allows flexibility and adaptability to motor output. Storage requires two components. First, there must be a mechanism that functions to store and to retrieve information; this mechanism appears to be in the temporal lobes, especially the hippocampus. Second, there must be a mechanism for the actual storage of information; there are few clues about the location of this mechanism because brain lesions do not selectively destroy memories. We return to the problem of where memory is stored in Chapter 20.

The third function of sensory-input analysis

FIGURE 17–2. Top: Lateral view of the left hemisphere illustrating the relative positions of the amygdala and hippocampus buried deep in the temporal lobe. The dashed lines A and B indicate the approximate location of each section illustrated below. Bottom: Frontal sections through the left hemisphere illustrating the cortical and subcortical regions of the temporal lobe. A, amygdala; C, caudate nucleus; DM, dorsomedial nucleus of the thalamus; FG, fusiform gyrus; GP, globus pallidus; H, hippocampus; ITG, inferior temporal gyrus; LT, lateral thalamus; MTG, middle temporal gyrus; P, putamen; STG, superior temporal gyrus; TS, temporal stem; U, uncus. Shaded region is the lateral ventricle.

is assigning connotative or affective properties to stimuli—that is, associating them with motivational or emotional significance. This function is crucial for learning because stimuli

become associated with their positive, negative, or neutral consequences, and behavior is modified accordingly. In the absence of this system all stimuli would be treated as equivalent, and there would be a loss of affective response to them. Associating affective properties with particular stimuli is also a function of the temporal lobe, especially the medial temporal cortex and amygdala. Indeed, because of this function the medial temporal cortex has been called the association cortex of the limbic system. To date, most research on temporal lobe function has been done on memory processes and very little on affective processes, partly because studying memory mechanisms is easier than studying affective mechanisms objectively. Indeed, both cognitive psychologists and neuropsychologists barely pay lip service to this latter function, although most would agree it plays an important role in the way we think and behave.

Although possible in principle at least, the anatomical separation of memory and affective functions in the temporal lobe has proved difficult to demonstrate. Visual or auditory input leaving the secondary sensory regions (see Figure 17–3) proceeds to the tertiary region of the temporal lobe, which includes areas 20, 21, 37, and 38. There are no strong empirical grounds for functionally differentiating these regions in humans, although work on nonhuman primates suggests that the anterior and posterior regions are likely to have different functions. The posterior region (area 37?) is primarily a sensory integrative region functionally associated with areas 39 and 40. The anterior region is primarily concerned with directing nervous system "attention" to particular aspects of the sensory input, such as trying to remember a particular face from a large number (area 20?), the storage of visual and auditory memories (area 21?), and the association of affective properties with particular stimuli (area 38?). The sensory analysis

FIGURE 17–3. The flow of activity from the visual and auditory regions forward through the temporal lobes to the medial regions including the amygdala and hippocampus is illustrated. Note that sensory input analyzed in either the temporal or the parietal lobe eventually arrives at the frontal lobe.

performed in the tertiary zone then proceeds primarily to the medial regions of the temporal lobe, where, probably, the memory and affective systems are first clearly distinguished—although this has not been proved. The medial temporal cortex then projects primarily to the amygdala and hippocampus, which are relatively specialized for affective and memory functions respectively. Note, however, that the amygdala and hippocampus are probably not absolutely dissociated, because there is evidence in nonhuman primates that memory defects are more severe when the amygdala is also damaged, and affective changes have been associated with hippocampal lesions in cats (comparable data are not available from studies of primates).

Asymmetry of Temporal Lobe Function

The sensitivity of the temporal lobes to epileptiform abnormalities, combined with the favorable outcome of treatment of epilepsy by surgical removal of the abnormal temporal lobe, has allowed neuropsychologists to carefully study the complementary specialization of the temporal lobes. Comparison of the effects of left and right temporal lobectomy by Milner and her associates has revealed that specific memory defects vary according to which side the lesion is on: damage to the left temporal lobe is associated with deficits in verbal memory; damage to the right temporal lobe, with deficits in nonverbal memory. Little is known, however, about the relative role of the left and right temporal lobes in affective behavior; we are unaware of any studies specifically addressing the asymmetry of this function in the temporal lobes. The only hint of asymmetry comes from unquantified clinical observations that left and right temporal lobe lesions appear to have different effects on personality.

In reviewing the literature on the effects of unilateral temporal lobectomy one is often struck by the relatively minor effects of removal of such a large zone of the cerebral hemispheres. However, it is incorrect to assume from these studies that removing both temporal lobes would have the effect merely of adding the symptoms of damage to each alone. Bilateral temporal lobe removal produces dramatic effects on both memory and affect that are orders of magnitude greater than those observed following unilateral lesions. (See Chapters 20 and 22 for detailed discussion of the effects of bilateral lesions on memory and affect respectively.) Thus, although the temporal lobes are relatively specialized in their functions, there is substantial functional overlap: do not be overly impressed by the apparent functional asymmetry.

SYMPTOMS OF TEMPORAL LOBE LESIONS

Eight principal symptoms are associated with disease of the temporal lobes: (1) disturbance of auditory sensation and perception, (2) disturbance of selective attention of auditory and visual input, (3) disorders of visual perception, (4) impaired organization and categorization of verbal material, (5) disturbance of language comprehension, (6) impaired long-term memory, (7) altered personality and affective behavior, and (8) altered sexual behavior. Disorders of auditory sensation and perception were discussed in Chapter 10 and will not be repeated here. We discuss each of the remaining symptoms separately. Table 17–1 summarizes the major symptoms of temporal lobe damage, lists the most probable lesion sites, and cites basic references.

Disturbance of Selection of Visual and Auditory Input

Lesions of the temporal lobes outside the primary and secondary auditory and visual zones produce neither deficits of sensation nor agnosias, producing instead disturbance in focusing attention on specific aspects of sensory input. This is best understood by first considering sensory selection in normal subjects.

People have a limited capacity to process the wealth of information in their environment and hence must select which inputs to process. This selectivity is generally not conscious, for the nervous system automatically scans input and selectively perceives the environment. (Conscious control can be exerted, of course, as when one searches for a mailbox to post a letter.) Selectivity in auditory perception is

TABLE 17–1

	Summary of major symptoms of temporal lobe damage		
	Symptoms	Most probable lesion site	Basic reference
1.	Disturbance of auditory sensation	Areas 41, 42, 22	Vignolo, 1969 Hécaen and Albert 1978
2.	Disturbance of selection of visual and auditory input	Areas 20, 21, 22, 37, 38	Sparks et al., 1970 Dorff et al., 1965 Milner, 1958
3.	Disorders of visual perception	Areas 20, 21	Milner, 1968 Meier and French, 1968
4.	Impaired organization and categorization of material	Areas 21, 38 left	Wilkins and Moscovitch, 1978 Read, 1981
5.	Disturbance of language comprehension	Area 22 left	Hécaen and Albert, 1978
6.	Poor long-term memory	Areas 21, hippocampus (and possibly amygdala)	Milner, 1970
7.	Changes in personality and affect	Areas 21, 38 plus amygdala	Blumer and Benson, 1975 Pincus and Tucker, 1974
8.	Changes in sexual activity	?	Blumer and Walker, 1975

best illustrated by the problem of listening to two conversations simultaneously. Because it is impossible to process the two competing inputs concurrently, the auditory system adopts one of two strategies: either one conversation is ignored, or attention shifts back and forth from one conversation to the other. In either case there is a selection of input. Selective perception in the visual system operates similarly. For example, because it is not possible to watch all events of a gymnastics meet simultaneously, attention either is focused entirely on one event or is shifted from one event to another.

Let us now consider the person with temporal lobe damage. We shall see that there is an impairment of both auditory and visual selection of input, which is ordinarily demonstrated only by special testing procedures. Selective attention of auditory input can be tested by using a dichotic-listening technique. As we noted in Chapter 14, if a series of pairs of words is presented dichotically, more of the words presented to the right ear will be reported; if tonal sequences are presented dichotically, there will be a left-ear advantage. Exploiting this technique in patients with temporal lobe lesions, Schulhoff and Goodglass have demonstrated that left temporal lobe lesions result in an overall drop in the number of words reported, whereas right temporal lesions result in an overall drop in the number of tonal sequences recognized, although the expected ear advantages are still present in both cases. One explanation for this effect is that the nervous system has difficulty focusing selectively on the input into one ear and attempts to process all the input concurrently; as a result performance drops severely. Analogous findings are reported for visual input as well. Dorff et al. presented two different visual stimuli simultaneously, one to each visual field. Lesions of the left temporal lobe impaired

recall of content of the right visual field, whereas lesion of the right temporal lobe impaired recall of content of both visual fields. Again, it may be that the nervous system is now unable to focus on distinctive features of the stimuli to allow efficient perception and storage of the input. In the case of visual input, however, it is noteworthy that right temporal lesions produce bilateral deficits, whereas left temporal lesions produce unilateral deficits. This difference implies that the right temporal lobe may have a greater role than the left temporal lobe in selective attention to visual input.

Disorders of Visual Perception

Although individuals with temporal lobectomies do not normally have large defects in their visual fields, they do have deficits in visual perception. This was first demonstrated by Milner, who found that her patients with right temporal lobe removals were impaired at the interpretation of cartoon drawings in the McGill picture anomaly test. For example, in one item illustrating a monkey in a cage there is an oil painting on the wall of the cage—an obvious oddity or anomaly. But patients with right temporal lesions, although able to accurately describe the contents of the picture, were impaired at recognizing the anomalous character of this and other pictures. Similarly, on a test of visual closure such as the Mooney series or tests requiring the discrimination of complex patterns (see Figure 10–2), temporal lobe patients perform very poorly. Perhaps one of the most interesting visual perceptual deficits, however, is in facial perception and recognition. When Kolb et al. presented patients with the split-faces test described in Chapter 10 (see Figure 10–6), they found that those with right temporal lobe resections failed to show a bias for that portion of the face falling in the left visual field, suggesting that these patients were perceiving faces abnormally. This conclusion is consistent with reports that right temporal lobe patients are impaired at the recognition and recall of faces or photographs of faces. Furthermore, right temporal lobe patients do not appear able to perceive subtle social signals such as discreet but obvious glances at one's watch, a gesture often intended as a cue to break off a conversation. Presumably the patients fail to perceive the significance of the visual signal.

Categorization of Material

If one is asked to learn a list of words such as "dog, car, bus, apple, rat, lemon, cat, truck, orange," it is a common experience that the words will be categorized into three different classes, namely animals, vehicles, and fruit. If the list is later recalled, the items are likely to be recalled by category, and recall of the categories is likely to be used as an aid in recall. The ability to organize material is especially important for language and memory. For example, it makes possible comprehension of extended sentences, including both the meaning of individual sentences and the information that is inferred from the sentences. Organization of sensory input appears to be a function of the temporal lobes. Studies by Jaccarino-Hiatt and by Wilkins and Moscovitch have shown that patients with left temporal lobectomies are impaired at their ability to do this type of organization, even with single words or pictures of familiar objects. Thus, patients have difficulty in placing words or pictures into discrete categories, even when they are requested to, and they also have difficulty in using categories that most of us use automatically. For example, Milner has found that when such patients are given a category name (e.g., animal) and asked

to recall exemplars of the category (e.g., dog, cat, rat), they have difficulty, even though they are fluent in other types of tests. Given that temporal lobe patients have difficulty in relatively simple types of categorization tasks studied in the laboratory, one can imagine that their difficulty in spontaneous organization may represent a significant deficit in cognition, especially in memory for complex material.

Language

Since the time of Wernicke, lesions of the left temporal association cortex (primarily area 22) have been associated with disturbed recognition of words, the extreme form being "word deafness": an inability to recognize words as such despite intact hearing of pure tones (a deficit given detailed discussion in Chapter 21).

In addition to producing deficits in language comprehension, lesions of temporal cortex beyond area 22 alter language processes in subtle ways. For example, Jaccarino-Hiatt has shown that nonaphasic patients with left temporal lobectomies have protracted latencies in producing word associations such as in "table-chair," "night-day," etc. Furthermore, people with right temporal lobectomies are excessively talkative, suggesting a loss of inhibition of talking. (Excessive talkativeness is, however, a clinical impression not quantitatively documented.) In view of the temporal lobe's role in affect it would be interesting to know if the affective connotation of language is diminished by temporal lobectomy (we are unaware of any studies of this sort).

Memory

To many neuropsychologists the study of the temporal lobes is synonymous with the study of memory. In fact, in most physiological psychology and neuropsychology texts index references to the temporal lobes lead one to a discussion of amnesia. The interest in temporal lobes is synonymous with the study of memory, which was stimulated in the early 1950s by the discovery that bilateral removal of the medial temporal lobes, including the hippocampus and amygdala, resulted in amnesia for all events after the surgery (anterograde amnesia). It is now clear that both the hippocampus and the temporal neocortex are important for memory functions. Milner and her associates have demonstrated that disturbances of memory result from damage to area 21; the disturbance increases in direct proportion to the amount of hippocampus damaged. Studies by the same investigators have further indicated a strong asymmetry of temporal lobe memory function (both cortical and hippocampal): lesions of the left temporal lobe result in impaired recall of verbal material, such as short stories, word lists, and so on, whether presented visually or aurally; lesions of the right temporal lobe result in impaired recall of nonverbal material, such as geometric drawings, faces, tunes, and similar material. However, unlike parietal lobe lesions, temporal lobe lesions do not disturb the immediate recall of material such as strings of digits; thus, the temporal and parietal lobes have complementary rather than redundant roles in memory.

The following two patients demonstrate the role of the left and right temporal lobes in memory. Mr. B., a 38-year-old man, was suffering from an astrocytoma in the left temporal lobe. Prior to the onset he had been a successful executive in an oil company and was noted for efficiency. As his tumor developed he became forgetful, and at the time of hospital admission his efficiency had dropped drastically; he had begun to forget appointments and other important events. Forgetfulness had become such a problem that he had begun to write notes to himself to cover his memory problem, but he often mislaid the notes, leading to even greater embarrassment. On formal tests of memory he had special difficulty in recalling short stories read to him a few minutes earlier. For example, in one test he was read the following story from the Wechsler memory scale and asked to repeat it as exactly as possible. "Anna Thompson of South Boston, employed as a scrub woman in an office building, was held up on State Street the night before and robbed of fifteen dollars. She had four little children, the rent was due and they had not eaten for two days. The officers, touched by the woman's story, made up a purse for her." Mr. B. recalled: "A woman was robbed and went to the police station where they made her a new purse. She had some children too." This is very poor performance for a person of Mr. B.'s intelligence and education. On the other hand, his immediate recall of digits was good; he could repeat strings of seven digits accurately, illustrating the integrity of his left parietal lobe functions. Similarly, his recall of geometric designs was within normal limits, illustrating the asymmetry of memory functions, for his right temporal lobe was still intact.

Ms. C. illustrates the complement of Mr. B.'s syndrome. She was a bright 22-year-old college student who had an indolent tumor of the right temporal lobe. When we first saw her, following surgery, she complained of memory loss. She was within normal limits on formal tests of verbal memory, such as the story of Anna Thompson, but was seriously impaired on formal tests of visual memory, especially geometric drawings. For example, in one test she was shown geometric designs for 10 seconds and then asked to draw them from memory. Ten minutes later she was asked to draw them again. She had difficulty with immediate recall (see Figure 17–4), and after 10 minutes was unable to recall any of the drawings at all.

FIGURE 17–4. Illustration of impaired recall of geometric figures in the case of Ms. C. In each set shown (A, B, C) the top drawing is the original stimulus and the bottom drawing is Ms. C's sketch made immediately after viewing each figure for 10 seconds. Note that Ms. C's impairment is worse with the more complex figures. Ms. C. was unable to recall even the simplest figure 10 minutes after viewing it.

Affect and Personality

Although the temporal lobe has been known to be associated with disturbance of affect in humans for nearly 100 years, knowledge about the details of this role is still surprisingly frag-mentary. Penfield and others reported that stimulation of the anterior and medial temporal cortex produces feelings of fear, an effect also occasionally obtained from the amygdala as well. Temporal lobe epilepsy traditionally has been associated with personality characteristics in which there is an overemphasis on trivia and the petty details of daily life. Pincus and Tucker describe several symptoms of this personality, including pedantic speech, egocentricity, perseveration on discussion of personal problems (sometimes referred to as "sticky," because one is stuck talking to the person), paranoia, preoccupation with religion, and proneness to aggressive outbursts. This constellation of behavior produces what is described as a *temporal lobe personality*, although very few people combine all these traits. Similar personality traits occur following temporal lobectomy. There appears to be a relative asymmetry in the symptoms, as right temporal lobectomy appears more likely than left temporal lobectomy to be associated with paranoia, pedantic behavior, egocentricity, talkativeness, and stickiness. This observation has not been quantified, however, and warrants further study. Finally, although temporal lobe epilepsy has long been linked anecdotally to psychosislike episodes, Slater and associates in 1963 first demonstrated a statistical relation between the occurrence of temporal lobe epilepsy and psychosis. Since no such relation has been described between temporal lobectomy and epilepsy, it has been suggested that a chronic abnormally discharging temporal lobe may produce abnormalities in either the biochemistry or the electrophysiology of the brain, leading to psychotic behavior. We return to this issue in Chapter 22.

Sexual Behavior

The role of the temporal lobe in sexual behavior is poorly understood, but it has long been known that bilateral destruction of the entire temporal lobe results in a dramatic increase in sexual behavior that is indiscriminantly directed heterosexually and homosexually and toward inanimate objects. This condition is neither common nor well studied in humans, and it does not occur following unilateral temporal lobe removal. Indeed, although we are unaware that the sexual behavior of people with unilateral temporal lobectomies has been the subject of any formal studies, we have never heard any complaints of either increased or decreased sexual activity in our experience with these people. Temporal lobe epilepsy is associated with altered sexual behavior, however: Blumer and Walker found 70 percent of their patient sample to have experienced a change in sexual activity, most commonly a decrease in sexual interest (see Table 17–2). Among these patients it was not unusual for sexual arousal to occur as rarely as once a year. This result must be interpreted cautiously, however, for the data may not reflect the function of the temporal lobes so much as the effect of chronic abnormal electrical activity on temporal and limbic structures.

Clinical Neuropsychological Assessment of Temporal Lobe Damage

A number of standardized assessment tools have proved to be sensitive and valid predictors of temporal lobe injury (see Table 17–3). Like

TABLE 17–2

Summary of the changes in sexual behavior of 50 temporal lobe epileptics

Symptom	Number of patients showing symptom
Chronic global hyposexuality	29
Postoperative hypersexuality	2[a]
Hypersexuality induced by medication	1
Postictal sexual arousal	4[b]
Ictal sexual arousal	1
Homosexual behavior	2
	35 (70%)

[a]Both patients were preoperatively hyposexual.
[b]One patient also with homosexual behavior, another patient also with hypersexuality induced by medication (Mysoline).
From Blumer and Walker, 1975, p. 207.

TABLE 17–3

Standardized clinical neuropsychological tests for temporal lobe damage		
Function	Test	Basic reference
1. Auditory processing capacity	Dichotic words and melodies	Sparks et al., 1970
2. Visual processing capacity	McGill picture anomalies	Milner, 1958
3. Verbal memory	Wechsler memory scale; logical stories and paired associates	Milner, 1975
4. Nonverbal memory	Rey complex figure	Taylor, 1969
5. Language	Token test	de Renzi and Faglioni, 1978

clinical neuropsychological tests of parietal lobe function, these tests do not assess all the symptoms summarized in Table 17–1, but it would be highly unusual for a person to perform normally on all these tests if there were damage to either temporal lobe.

Auditory and visual processing capacity can be assessed using dichotic listening and the McGill picture anomalies, as described earlier in the chapter. The picture-anomalies task is not as sensitive an indicator today as it was when first used in the 1950s, perhaps because television viewing has made the average person more sophisticated in visual perceptual abilities. Nevertheless, a poor score on this test almost invariably denotes right temporal abnormality.

The best test of general verbal memory ability is the Wechsler memory scale. However, because the Wechsler memory quotient is affected by nonspecific disorders of attention, two subtests—paired associates and logical stories—are often used as a purer measure of verbal memory capacity. Paired associates require a subject to learn a series of word pairs (e.g., north-south, cabbage-pen) such that when one word is read (e.g., north, cabbage) the paired associate word (south, pen) can be recalled. An example of the logical memory test was presented earlier in the chapter, in reference to Mr. B.'s verbal memory defect.

The Rey complex figure test has proved to be one of the best tests of the nonverbal memory function of the right temporal lobe (see Figure 10–2). A printed copy of a complex geometric pattern is placed before the subject with the instructions, "Copy the drawing as accurately as you can." Forty-five minutes later the subject is asked to reproduce as much of the figure as he or she can remember. Although the scoring criteria provide an objective measure of nonverbal memory, the test has the drawback that depressed or poorly motivated subjects may perform poorly, not because there is right temporal lobe damage, but because they refuse to seriously try to recall the figure. There is no easy solution to this problem, since all tests of nonverbal memory are subject to this complication.

Finally, a deficit in language comprehension could be the result of a lesion in any of the language zones of the left hemisphere (that is, in the parietal, temporal, or frontal lobe); there is currently no neuropsychological assessment tool that can localize the area of damage within the left hemisphere. For this reason we once again recommend the token test as the test of choice for language comprehension. Additional tests (described in Chapter 21) may prove useful after the initial screening with the token test.

TEMPORAL LOBE FUNCTIONS
IN NONHUMANS

In the 1950s studies of memory defects in humans with temporal lobe lesions led to the suggestion that the temporal lobes of humans might have functions unlike those of nonhumans, since severe memory defects could not be unequivocally demonstrated in nonhumans. An influential paper by Diamond and Hall in 1969 kindled interest in evolutionary questions regarding the temporal lobe. They proposed that the primate temporal lobe is special, and they questioned whether or not carnivores even have a temporal lobe homologous to that of primates. Since Diamond and Hall's paper, research has indicated that this view is incorrect: both primates and carnivores appear to be good models of temporal lobe function in humans. Without exhaustively surveying research on nonhuman temporal lobe function, we shall demonstrate that the symptoms of temporal lobe lesions in nonhumans qualitatively resemble those observed in humans.

Anatomy of Nonhuman
Temporal Lobes

The cortical extent of the temporal lobes of nonhumans is defined by cytoarchitecture, thalamic projections, and the electrophysiological properties of temporal lobe cells. Figure 17–5 illustrates the general evolutionary increase in temporal lobe neocortex in primates, especially in comparison to the rat. Indeed, it has been proposed that a major difference between primates and other mammals is the increase in size of both the temporal and the frontal lobes relative to the remaining cerebral cortex. Note the similarity, however, in the regions of the temporal lobes in cats and monkeys: both demonstratethe same cortical sub-

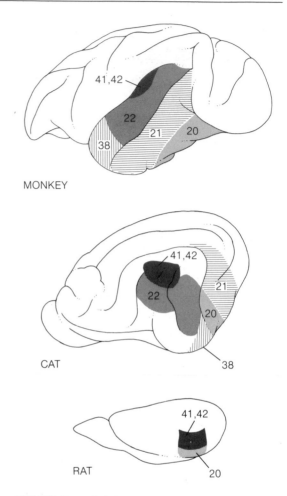

FIGURE 17–5. Relative sizes and locations of the temporal cortex of the monkey, cat, and rat. Depiction of area 22 in the cat may be an overestimate, because the zone's posterior region (the posterior ectosylvian gyrus) has both auditory and visual functions and may actually be analogous to area 37 as well. The brains are not drawn to the same scale. No evolutionary progression from one species to another is implied.

tical subareas, although the temporal neocortex may make up a larger percentage of the monkey brain. All mammalian species have the equivalent of medial temporal cortex, hippocampus, and amygdala.

Effects of Temporal Lobe Lesions in Nonhumans

All the major deficits associated with temporal lobe lesions in humans (with the exception of language deficits) are observed in nonhumans (see Table 17–4). Moreover, many of the effects of temporal lesions are much easier to study in cats and monkeys than in humans. As a result, research on nonhuman animals has greatly clarified understanding of the human temporal lobe.

Auditory Processing

Dewson and his colleagues have demonstrated that unilateral lesion of the superior temporal gyrus (area 22) of the monkey produces deficits in the performance of tasks requiring complex analysis of auditory input. For example, in one experiment monkeys with unilateral lesions confined to area 22 were trained to discriminate between paired sequences of auditory elements, combinations of pure tone (T) and white noise (N). Four sequences were presented: T-T, T-N, N-N, and N-T. The animals' task was to learn to press two bars in a unique sequence for each auditory pair. For example, for T-T the animals were trained to press the left bar twice; for T-N, to press the left bar, then the right. Monkeys with le-

sions of area 22 were severely impaired at this task. The auditory sensitivity of these animals proved to be normal, but there was a deficit in auditory memory. Lesions of the visual association cortex (areas 20 and 21) had no effect on performance of this task.

Dewson has also demonstrated cerebral asymmetry in auditory processing in monkeys; lesions in area 22 on the left result in larger effects on auditory discrimination and association than similar lesions on the right. However, a crucial experiment remains to be done. Wollberg and Newman have shown that area 22 has cells differentially responsive to species-typical vocalizations such as hoots, howls, etc. The question is whether lesions of area 22 (especially on the left) would disturb perception of species-typical vocalizations. If so, a symptom analogous to "word deafness" in people might be demonstrated (although this may be pushing the analogy somewhat).

Visual Processing

Converging evidence from studies using monkeys has revealed a sequential pathway for processing visual information that begins in the core visual cortex (area 17) and proceeds through the secondary regions of the temporal

TABLE 17–4

	Summary of symptoms of temporal lobe lesions in monkeys		
	Symptom	Lesion site	Representative reference
1.	Disorders of auditory processing	Areas 41, 42, 22	Cowey and Dewson, 1972
2.	Disorders of visual processing	Areas 20, 21, 38	Ungerleider and Mishkin, 1982
3.	Visual categorization	Area 21	Wilson and DeBauche, 1981
4.	Memory	Hippocampus, amygdala	Mishkin, 1978 Horel and Pytko, 1982
5.	Sexual behavior	Amygdala, limbic cortex	Klüver and Bucy, 1939

cortex, which includes the temporal cortex right to the tip of the temporal pole (areas 20, 21, and 38). Researchers at the National Institute of Mental Health (see Macko et al.) have mapped the visual pathway through the temporal lobe using a type of 2-deoxyglucose tracing procedure, which is a far more accurate analogue of the technique described in Chapter 14 for tracing the visual pathway in humans. The results revealed two distinct visual pathways, one traveling from area 17 through the temporal lobe and eventually to the frontal cortex, and another traveling from area 17 via the parietal cortex to the frontal lobe. It has been suggested that the former route has a special role in object recognition whereas the latter route has a special role in spatial vision, conjectures that are in basic accord with the observed symptoms.

A number of investigators have been able to functionally distinguish among the posterior temporal cortex (roughly area 20), an area anterior to it (roughly area 2l), and the anterior and medial limbic cortex (roughly area 38 plus medial cortex) in monkeys and cats. Lesions of the posterior cortex produce an inability to discriminate and select the essential cues from a visual stimulus and to maintain attention to them. Thus, the animal has difficulty in distinguishing complex visual stimuli from one another, just as the human does with deficits in discriminating complex visual stimuli such as faces from one another. Lesions of area 21 produce a different type of deficit, in which the animal has difficulty in forming visual memories. The monkeys are able to discriminate among complex visual stimuli but are unable to remember the visual image for more than a few moments, and they are thus impaired at problems requiring such visual memory. Finally, lesions of the anterior zone, including the amygdala, produce deficits in the process of associating visual stimuli with their reinforcement properties. To demonstrate this, a monkey is presented with two visual stimuli, such as a square and a cross. A food reward is associated with one of the stimuli; if the monkey chooses the correct stimulus, it is reinforced with a peanut or raisin. Once this problem is mastered, the reward properties of the stimuli are reversed, the previously rewarded stimulus now being unrewarded and vice versa. This task therefore requires the animal to associate changing reward properties with the visual stimuli, a requirement that is difficult to meet in the absence of the anterior temporal cortex and/or amygdala.

Finally, neurons of the temporal lobe have been found that are specifically responsive to faces, a result that complements the demonstrations of impaired facial perception and recognition in humans with right temporal lobe removals. Perret and his associates have found many cells in monkeys that respond selectively to human faces and photographs of monkey faces, despite inversion, rotation, or changes in size or color of the face! It remains to be seen if removal of these cells impairs facial recognition in monkeys, however.

Categorization

Like human temporal lobe patients, who have difficulty in organizing and categorizing material, monkeys with lesions of inferotemporal cortex (roughly area 21) are impaired at categorical perception of visual stimuli. Wilson and DeBauche trained monkeys to discriminate between pairs of stimuli that differed in length, orientation, or texture. For example, food reward was obtained for choosing a line 10 mm as opposed to 55 mm in length. After successful solution of this problem the monkeys were given pairs of stimuli in which the correct one was the one closest to the originally correct stimulus. For stimuli differing in length the animals were given lines that were 10, 15, 20, 25, 30, 35, 40, 45, 50, or 55 mm long.

Normal animals easily discriminated between lines clearly in a different category (i.e., long and short) but did poorly with lines of similar length within each category. Monkeys with inferotemporal lesions did not show categorical perception. That is, when given a pair such as 15 and 40 mm, they responded at chance. These results cannot be accounted for by a simple deficit in visual acuity, because monkeys with damage in area 17 did exhibit categorical perception. The authors conclude that the temporal lobe normally functions to process visual stimuli in such a way as to treat visual inputs as members of classes, a conclusion consistent with the demonstrations of impaired categorization in humans as well as monkeys with temporal lobe lesions.

Memory

A clear demonstration of a severe memory defect in nonhuman animals analogous to that resulting from bilateral temporal lobe removal in humans has been elusive. As a result, many propose that the functions of the medial temporal lobe in humans reflect an evolutionary shift. Until recently, studies meant to demonstrate analogous memory defects in nonhumans assumed that the critical structure for memory storage is the hippocampus, and it was repeatedly found that bilateral hippocampal lesions in rats, cats, and monkeys failed to produce the human syndrome of anterograde amnesia. A recent study by Mishkin sheds light on this apparent discrepancy: memory loss after removal of both the hippocampus and the amygdala in monkeys was much more severe than after removal of either structure alone. Mishkin suggested that both structures have an important role in memory. This hypothesis remains to be studied further, especially in humans, where the amygdala is virtually always removed along with the hippocampus. It may

be that the role of the amygdala has been underestimated in studies of humans. With respect to memory functions of area 21, we have already noted that these lesions in monkeys produce visual memory deficits, again consistent with the results of Milner's human studies.

Affect

Bilateral lesions of the amygdala, hippocampus, and lateral temporal cortex are known to produce alterations in affect in both monkeys and cats, but the precise role of each of these structures in affective control is not well understood. The amygdala and anterior temporal neocortex may have similar roles in affective control; Horel et al. reported that lesions of both regions reduced both attack and escape behavior and made the animals less reluctant to approach novel stimuli. In addition, it is known that monkeys with lesions of either the anterior temporal cortex of the amygdala do not survive in the wild, because they no longer associate with other members of their species. By contrast, animals with more posterior lesions in the temporal lobe are still social creatures, behaving normally in the social group.

Sexual Behavior

Bilateral destruction of the temporal lobes is known to produce profound changes in sexual behavior—chiefly increasing sexual activity —in a variety of mammals. The crucial structure for this effect is the amygdala and its related archicortex and paleocortex. The hippocampus appears to play a minor role, and there is no clear indication of the role of the temporal neocortex in sexual behavior. It would be expected that damage to area 20 produces impaired discrimination of visual sexual objects, but this possibility has not been studied.

Summary

The detailed studies of temporal lobe processes, especially those related to visual processing, beautifully illustrate how studies of nonhuman brain function can provide crucial clues to understanding human brain function. It is impossible to do many needed studies in humans because neither surgical nor naturally occurring lesions conform to the anatomical subdivisions of the temporal lobe. A difficulty, however, is that results from studies of the temporal lobe in monkeys appear to be most similar to results from studies of the right temporal lobe function in humans, there not yet being any compelling evidence of asymmetrical processing of visual information in monkeys. Perhaps generalizations to left temporal function can be made in the future when we have a better appreciation for the basis of cerebral asymmetry.

REFERENCES

Blumer, D., and D. F. Benson. Personality changes with frontal and temporal lesions. In D. F. Benson and F. Blumer, eds., *Psychiatric Aspects of Neurologic Disease*. New York: Grune & Stratton, 1975.

Blumer, D., and E. A. Walker. The neural basis of sexual behavior. In D. F. Benson and D. Blumer, eds., *Psychiatric Aspects of Neurologic Disease*. New York: Grune & Stratton, 1975.

Campbell, A. Deficits in visual learning produced by posterior temporal lesions in cats. *Journal of Comparative and Physiological Psychology* 92:45–57, 1978.

Cowey, A., and J. H. Dewson. Effects of unilateral ablation of superior temporal cortex on auditory sequence discrimination in *Macaca mulatta*. *Neuropsychologia* 10:279–289, 1972.

Dewson, J. H. Preliminary evidence of hemispheric asymmetry of auditory function in monkeys. In S. Harnad, R. W. Doty, L. Goldstein, J. Jaynes, and G. Krauthamer, eds., *Lateralization in the Nervous System*. New York: Academic, 1977.

Diamond, I. T., and W. C. Hall. Evolution of neocortex. *Science* 164:251–262, 1969.

Dorff, J. E., A. F. Mirsky, and M. Mishkin. Effects of unilateral temporal lobe removals on tachistoscopic recognition in the left and right visual fields. *Neuropsychologia* 3:39–51, 1965.

Geschwind, N. Disconnexion syndromes in animals and man. *Brain* 88:237–294, 585–644, 1965.

Hécaen, H., and M. L. Albert. *Human Neuropsychology*. New York: Wiley, 1978.

Horel, J. A. The neuroanatomy of amnesia: A critique of the hippocampal memory hypothesis. *Brain* 101:403–445, 1978.

Horel, J. A., E. G. Keating, and L. J. Misantone. Partial Klüver-Bucy syndrome produced by destroying temporal neocortex or amygdala. *Brain Research* 94:349–359, 1975.

Horel, J. A., and D. E. Pytko. Behavioral effect of local cooling in temporal lobe of monkeys. *Journal of Neurophysiology* 47:11–22, 1982.

Iwai, E., and M. Mishkin. Two visual foci in the temporal lobe of monkeys. In N. Yoshii and N. A. Buchwald, eds., *Neurophysiological Basis of Learning and Behavior*. Osaka, Japan: Osaka University Press, 1968.

Jaccarino-Hiatt, G. Impairment of cognitive organization in patients with temporal-lobe lesions. Unpublished Ph.D. thesis, McGill University, 1978.

Jones, B., and M. Mishkin. Limbic lesions and the problem of stimulus-reinforcement associations. *Experimental Neurology* 36:362–377, 1972.

Jones, E. G. The anatomy of extrageniculostriate visual mechanisms. In F. O. Schmitt and F. G. Worden, eds., *The Neurosciences: Third Study Program*. Cambridge, Mass.: MIT Press, 1974.

Klüver, H., and P. C. Bucy. Preliminary analysis of the temporal lobes in monkeys. *Archives of Neurology and Psychiatry* 42:979–1000, 1939.

Kolb, B., B. Milner, and L. Taylor. Perception of faces by patients with localized cortical excisions. *Canadian Journal of Psychology* 37:8–18, 1983.

Macko, K. A., C. D. Jarvis, C. Kennedy, M. Miyaoka, M. Shinohara, L. Sokoloff, and M. Mishkin. Mapping the primate visual system with [2-^{14}C]deoxyglucose. *Science* 218:394–397, 1982.

Meier, M. S., and L. A. French. Lateralized deficits in complex visual discrimination and bilateral transfer of reminiscence following unilateral temporal lobectomy. *Neuropsychologia* 3:261–272, 1968.

Milner, B. Memory and the medial temporal regions of the brain. In K. H. Pribram and D. E. Broadbent, eds., *Biological Bases of Memory*. New York: Academic, 1970.

Milner, B. Psychological aspects of focal epilepsy and its neurosurgical management. *Advances in Neurology* 8:299–321, 1975.

Milner, B. Psychological defects produced by temporal lobe excision. *Research Publications of the Association for Research in Nervous and Mental Disease* 38:244–257, 1958.

Milner, B. Visual recognition and recall after right temporal lobe excision in man. *Neuropsychologia* 6:191–209, 1968.

Mishkin, M. Memory in monkeys severely impaired by combined but not by separate removal of amygdala and hippocampus. *Nature* 273:297–298, 1978.

Nonneman, A. J., and B. Kolb. Lesions of hippocampus or prefrontal cortex alter species typical behavior in the cat. *Behavioral Biology* 12:41–54, 1974.

Penfield, W., and H. H. Jasper. *Epilepsy and the Functional Anatomy of the Human Brain*. Boston: Little, Brown, 1959.

Perret, D. E., E. T. Rolls, and W. Cann. Visual neurons responsive to faces in the monkey temporal cortex. *Experimental Brain Research* 47:329–342, 1982.

Pincus, J. H., and G. J. Tucker. *Behavioral Neurology*. New York: Oxford University Press, 1974.

Read, D. E. Solving deductive-reasoning problems after unilateral temporal lobectomy. *Brain and Language* 12:116–127, 1981.

Renzi, E. de, and P. Faglioni. Normative data and screening power of a shortened version of the token test. *Cortex* 14:41–49, 1978.

Schulhoff, C., and H. Goodglass. Dichotic listening: Side of brain injury and cerebral dominance. *Neuropsychologia* 7:149–160, 1969.

Slater, E., A. W. Beard, and E. Glithero. The schizophrenia-like psychosis of epilepsy. *British Journal of Psychiatry,* 109:95–150, 1963.

Sparks, R., H. Goodglass, and B. Nickel. Ipsilateral versus contralateral extinction in dichotic listening from hemispheric lesions. *Cortex* 6:249–260, 1970.

Taylor, L. B. Localization of cerebral lesions by psychological testing. *Clinical Neurosurgery* 16:269–287, 1969.

Ungerleider, L. G., and M. Mishkin. Two cortical visual systems. In D. J. Ingle, M. H. Goodale, and R. J. W. Mansfield, eds. *The Analysis of Visual Behavior*. Cambridge, Mass.: MIT Press, 1982.

Vignolo, L. A. Auditory agnosia: A review and report of recent evidence. In A. L. Benton, ed., *Contributions to Clinical Neuropsychology*. Chicago: Aldine, 1969.

Weiskrantz, L. The interaction between occipital and temporal cortex in vision: An overview. In F. O. Schmitt and F. G. Worden, eds., *The Neurosciences: Third Study Program*. Cambridge, Mass.: MIT Press, 1974.

Wilkins, A., and M. Moscovitch. Selective impairment of semantic memory after temporal lobectomy. *Neuropsychologia* 16:73–79, 1978.

Wilson, M., and B. A. DeBauche. Inferotemporal cortex and categorical perception of visual stimuli by monkeys. *Neuropsychologia* 19:29–41, 1981.

Wolberg, Z., and J. D. Newman. Auditory cortex of squirrel monkey: Response patterns of single cells to species-specific vocalizations. *Science* 175:212–214, 1972.

18

THE FRONTAL LOBES

There is no cerebral structure in which lesions can produce such a wide variety of symptoms, and thus a more bewildering range of interpretations, than the frontal lobes. Some authors have assigned the human frontal lobes the "highest" conceivable functions such as intellectual synthesis and the control of ethical behavior, whereas other authors demote them, failing to see any special importance in them. In this chapter we first describe the anatomy of the frontal lobes, then present a basic model of frontal lobe function. The effects of frontal lobe damage on human behavior are well documented. We attempt to summarize these effects in an effort to make sense of the extravagant claims as to the function of this vast area. We consider the question of whether the frontal lobes are really special in humans, and discuss the idea that the frontal lobes are part of a functional system that includes a number of subcortical structures. First, however, it is necessary to review the anatomy of the frontal lobes.

ANATOMY OF THE FRONTAL LOBES

The frontal lobes of the human brain comprise all the tissue in front of the central sulcus. It is certainly not anatomically homogeneous, however; several areas are functionally and anatomically distinct. These include area 4, or primary motor cortex; area 6, or premotor cortex; Broca's area; medial cortex; and prefrontal cortex (see Figure 18–1). The functions of area 4 were described in Chapter 11.

In 1948, Rose and Woolsey noticed that the frontal lobes of all the mammalian species they examined had a region that received projections from the dorsomedial nucleus of the thalamus. They termed this region **prefrontal cortex.** The dorsomedial nucleus has three divisions, each of which projects to a distinct region of the prefrontal cortex, and each of which is functionally and anatomically distinct. In primates these regions are known as the dorsolateral cortex (roughly

LATERAL VIEW

MEDIAL VIEW

FUNCTIONAL MAP

FIGURE 18–1. A. Lateral and medial views of Brodmann's cytoarchitectonic map of the frontal lobe. B. Approximate boundaries of functional zones of the frontal lobe. Note that area 6 includes two functional zones: the premotor cortex on the lateral surface and the supplementary motor cortex on the medial surface.

areas 9, 10, 44, 45, and 46), **orbital frontal cortex** (so called because of its relation to the orbit of the eye, and roughly including areas 11, 12, and 47), and the frontal eye fields (including portions of areas 8 and 9). At one time the prefrontal cortex was called the frontal granular cortex, since the fourth layer of this region has large granular cells that clearly distinguish it from areas 4 and 6, which have no granular fourth layer but have instead a large fifth layer of giant pyramidal cells. This terminology is seldom used today because although all mammalian species have a prefrontal cortex, not all have granular cells and hence a frontal granular cortex.

The transcortical and extracortical connections of the frontal lobe, and in particular of the prefrontal cortex, are exceedingly complex. Briefly, the prefrontal cortex receives afferents from the visual, auditory, and somatosensory areas by way of the parietal cortex. It also receives fibers from many subcortical structures, the most important being the caudate nucleus, the dorsomedial thalamus, the amygdala, and the hypothalamus. The prefrontal cortex sends heavy projections to the parietal and temporal association cortex and cingulate cortex, as well as to subcortical structures including the basal ganglia, dorsomedial thalamus, amygdala, hippocampus, hypothalamus, and other lower brainstem structures. As might be expected, each of the three subregions of the prefrontal cortex has its own separate connections, which are frequently connected to discrete regions of the structures mentioned above.

The complexity and breadth of the frontal lobe connections no doubt contribute to the puzzling array of behavioral changes observed in people with lesions in this region. With respect to understanding the functions of the frontal lobes, the most important connections may well be those with the "motor" structures such as the basal ganglia, those with the limbic system, and those with the parietal and temporal association cortex.

A THEORY OF FRONTAL LOBE FUNCTION

Background

Historically, claims about the functions of the frontal lobes have been extravagant and extreme. From the time of Gall until the 1930s the frontal lobes were thought by most to be the seat of highest intellect. Functions as varied as "abstract behavior," foresight, intellectual synthesis, ethical behavior, affect, and self-awareness were proposed by a variety of writers. Hebb's discovery in 1939 brought these prevailing views into question. Administering standard intelligence tests to patients with frontal lobe removals for treatment of epilepsy, Hebb discovered that IQ was not reduced—an astonishing observation in light of the prevailing belief. This test has been repeated by many others with the same results: IQ is not lowered by frontal lobe lesions, and sometimes may actually be raised!

A major reason for the extremes of views regarding frontal lobe functions was that neurologists and neuropsychologists often based their conclusions on single cases. Many of these patients had tumors, and it is now well known that tumor patients frequently do not behave like patients with lesions resulting from other causes. Tumors may produce pressure on widespread parts of the brain, resulting in symptoms unrelated to the region where the tumor actually resides. Furthermore, tumors may include subcortical structures or may result in the production of abnormal electric discharges that themselves may alter the function of widespread areas of brain tissue. An additional problem is that often frontal lobe tumors are larger than tumors elsewhere in the brain. It may be that the large size of the frontal lobes allows a tumor to grow for longer periods without specific motor, sensory, or language problems arising as symptoms.

The advent of frontal lobotomies in psychosurgery provided large numbers of patients with frontal lobe lesions, but studies on these patients did little to reduce extravagant claims of frontal lobe function. Although IQs after frontal lobotomy were lower than those obtained much earlier, they were not, according to a study by Rosvold and Mishkin in 1950, lower than IQs obtained just prior to surgery. In other words, the lower IQ was caused not by the lobotomy per se, but by the psychiatric disease process necessitating the lobotomy. Hence the serious flaw in using psychosurgical patients in neuropsychological research. Because no groups of patients with similar psychiatric disease have lesions elsewhere in the brain, the effects of the disease cannot be separated from the effects of the lesion. Furthermore, we now know that severe psychotic disease of the type that might lead to psychosurgery produces serious deficits in neuropsychological test results without surgery.

In 1923 Feuchtwanger did one of the first systematic studies of large numbers of patients with lesions other than tumors or lobotomies. His monograph should not have been ignored, as it was, by North American neuropsychology. Teuber has summarized the results of Feuchtwanger's study of 400 cases of gunshot wounds: 200 frontal and 200 nonfrontal. All the wounds resulted from injuries during World War I.

A careful reading of Feuchtwanger's monograph would have prepared us for the surprises of the forties and fifties of this century: The increasing evidence is that frontal lesions, on the whole, have less effect on test intelligence, on categorizing, and on a variety of complex reaction-time tasks than lesions in other areas of the human brain. He concluded that specific changes were not to be sought, either in the intellectual sphere, or in that of "attention" or "memory," including recent memory. Instead, the more pervasive changes were those of mood and attitude, ranging from euphoria, or, less frequently, depression to a curious form of "other-directedness" on the patient's part—an incapacity for making plans. These changes were independent, in Feuchtwanger's view, from the occasional alterations in motor control: restlessness, hyperkinetic behavior, or, more rarely, slowing and torpor. (Teuber, 1964, p. 415)

During the 1950s, 1960s, and 1970s research on the frontal lobes has clarified many of the contradictions and inconsistencies of the earlier work. A theoretical model of frontal lobe function is now possible that provides a unified explanation of the various symptoms of frontal lobe damage.

Hierarchical Organization

Before the hierarchical organization of the frontal lobe is discussed, the organization of the cortical input to the motor system must be reviewed briefly. The cortical motor system is thought to comprise three levels of function. The first level is composed of neurons whose cell bodies reside in area 4 and whose axons largely synapse directly on spinal motor neurons or cranial nerve motor nuclei. This level is specialized for controlling fine hand, finger, and facial movements. Lesions in this level produce severe chronic deficits in fine motor control and also reduce speed and strength of limb movements.

The second level of cortical motor function is composed of neurons whose cell bodies lie primarily in areas 4, 6, and 8 of the frontal cortex and 5 and 7 of the parietal cortex. These neurons contribute to two descending systems: one controlling limb movements; the other,

body movements. All neurons of the limb-control system synapse in the red nucleus, although many synapse earlier as well, primarily in the basal ganglia. Similarly, all neurons of the axial system synapse in the brainstem reticular formation, but, again, many of these neurons synapse en route to the brainstem in the basal ganglia. Cortical lesions in this level of control do not abolish limb or axial movements, since subcortical structures (i.e., red nucleus, basal ganglia, thalamus, etc.) can still operate to produce basic limb and axial movements. Rather, the lesions alter more complex aspects of limb and axial movements, producing more subtle deficits. Lesions in areas 5 and 7 contribute to apraxias, probably because of damage in the visual and tactile guidance of limb and axial movements. The effects of lesions in areas 6 and 8, although still poorly understood, appear to impair the smooth transition of separate axial, limb, and hand movements into a fluid series of movements.

The third level of motor control is composed of the neurons forming the prefrontal cortex. These neurons receive input from the tertiary zones of the parietal and temporal cortex; they send efferents to cortical neurons in both the first and second levels as well as to the basal ganglia and brainstem nuclei of the motor system. The prefrontal cortex has a nonspecific role in movement control, and it probably plays little role in actually controlling the components of movement. Rather, the prefrontal cortex controls the overall motor programs and adds flexibility to motor output by modifying behavior with respect to specific internal and external factors. Because of this flexibility, ongoing behavior requires continual monitoring, as do its consequences, such that behaviors are appropriate to particular circumstances. In the absence of this function, behavior becomes stereotyped, inflexible, and maladaptive. The prefrontal cortex also provides the highest control of affective behavior and is able to effect control of basic emotional behavior by virtue of its intimate connections with the limbic system. Lesions of the prefrontal cortex therefore usually produce alterations in basic aspects of personality and social behavior and interfere as well with the planning and execution of complex behavioral programs. People with prefrontal lesions are therefore seldom able to hold jobs and have difficulty looking after many daily activities. They are typically late for appointments and are often unable to maintain close relations even with their immediate families.

The three levels of cortical motor control are hierarchical with respect to final motor output, the first level being the closest to it and the third level being the most removed. Whereas the first level synapses directly on spinal motor neurons, the second level and, to a greater extent, the third level have multiple synapses en route to the spinal motor neurons. Thus, the effects of lesions in the first level are easily specified, since no other levels in the nervous system can assume the functions affected. But at the higher levels the effects of cortical lesions become progressively more difficult to define, because there are subcortical levels of control before the final motor output, in the spinal cord and cranial nerve nuclei.

Asymmetry of Frontal Lobe Function

In view of the asymmetry in parietal and temporal association cortex function it could be expected that the frontal lobes are organized asymmetrically. This is indeed the case. Furthermore, as expected from the principles of hierarchical organization of the neocortex, this asymmetry is found principally in the prefrontal cortex, the highest level of the motor hierarchy. In keeping with the general asymmetrical organization of the cerebrum, the special role of the left frontal lobe is in control of movement primarily related to language, and that of the right frontal lobe is in control of movement primarily related to nonverbal abilities. Like that of the parietal and temporal lobes, the asymmetry of frontal lobe function is relative rather than absolute; studies of patients with frontal lesions indicate that both frontal lobes play a role in nearly all behavior. Milner has emphasized this point, noting that the laterality of frontal lobe lesions is far less striking than that observed from more posterior lesions.

SYMPTOMS OF FRONTAL LOBE LESIONS

The effects of lesions in the lower levels of the motor system were discussed in Chapter 12. Our primary concern here is with the effects of lesions to the prefrontal cortex. However, in our discussion two factors may produce discrepancies between our conclusions and others'. First, we deal primarily with the effects of *unilateral* frontal lesions. As with the temporal lobe there is reason to believe that some effects of bifrontal lesions cannot be duplicated by lesions of either hemisphere alone. Table 18–1 summarizes a study comparing the behavioral effects of unilateral and bilateral lesions. People with bifrontal lesions are severely impaired at reporting the time of day and in decoding proverbs, effects seldom seen following unilateral frontal lesions. Although its cause is uncertain, this effect is consistent with the results of much animal work—that is, unilateral frontal lesions have little or no effect on certain tasks whereas bifrontal lesions have severe effects.

The second factor in any discrepancy is that we have mainly drawn our conclusions from studies using patients with surgical removals for the relief of epilepsy or the excision of benign tumors and patients with missile wounds of the brain. This choice of patients presents the difficulty that some phenomena may not be observed in them. For example, Denny-Brown and others described the release of hand and foot grasp reflexes, which appear to result only from very large frontal lesions, possibly bifrontal, such as result from slow-growing tumors or abcesses.

There appear to be about 14 reliable symptoms of prefrontal damage (Table 18–2); we discuss each of them separately and in some detail. We cannot describe patients with all of these symptoms, because few patients would have lesions so large as to include all the functional subregions. Whenever possible, however, we illustrate the symptoms with examples.

Fine Movements

Damage to the primary motor cortex is normally associated with a chronic loss of the ability to make fine independent finger movements, presumably due to a loss of direct corticospinal projections onto motor neurons. In addition, there is a loss of speed and power in both hand and limb movements. Details of these impairments are found in Chapter 12.

TABLE 18–1

Relative frequency of defective performance on neuropsychological tests

| Test | Percentage of group showing a deficit | | |
	Left (%)	Right (%)	Bilateral (%)
Verbal fluency	70	38	71
Verbal learning	30	13	86
Block construction	10	50	43
Design copying	10	38	43
Time orientation	0	0	57
Proverbs	20	25	71

Adapted from Benton, 1968.

Movement Programming

In a classic paper in 1950, Lashley asked how movements are put together in a particular order. How is it, he asked, that a violinist can play an arpeggio so quickly and flawlessly? Clearly, each note is not "thought of" separately. Furthermore, how is it that during a tennis game a player can make very rapid movements, seemingly much too fast to have considered each movement itself? Lashley presumed that this function—serially ordering complex chains of behavior in relation to varying stimuli—must somehow be a function of the neocortex. Although he believed this to be a function of the entire neocortex, it appears more likely to involve only the frontal lobes.

To date, the major support for this role of the frontal lobes comes from two lines of work: studies of the supplementary motor cortex and a single study of movement-copying of patients with frontal excisions. Although removal of the supplementary motor cortex results in a transient disruption of nearly all voluntary movements, including speech if the removal is on the left, there is rapid recovery and the only permanent disability appears to be in the performance of rapid alternating movements with the hands, and reduction in typing speed. It has been suggested that the cause of this sparse symptomatology from rather large lesions is that both the left and the right supplementary motor cortexes participate in the control of movement, much as both the left and the right face areas do. This suggestion receives support from observations that both supplementary areas show an increase in blood flow during *unimanual* tasks in humans; in monkeys, cells in both the left and the right areas show increased activity regardless of which is moving.

The lack of information about the effects of lesions of the supplementary motor cortex in

TABLE 18–2

Summary of major symptoms of frontal lobe damage

Symptom	Most probable lesion site	Basic reference
1. Loss of distal movements	Area 4	Kuypers, 1981
2. Poor movement programming	Supplementary motor Dorsolateral?	Roland et al., 1980 Kolb and Milner, 1981
3. Poor voluntary eye gaze	Areas 8, 9	Teuber, 1964 Guitton et al., 1982
4. Poor response inhibition	Areas 9, 10	Milner, 1964; Perret, 1974
5. Reduced corollary discharge	Dorsolateral	Teuber, 1964
6. Disorders of temporal ordering	Dorsolateral	Milner, 1974 Petrides and Milner, 1982
7. Impaired spatial orientation	Dorsolateral	Semmes et al., 1963
8. Reduced behavioral spontaneity	Orbital	Milner, 1964 Jones-Gotman and Milner, 1977
9. Impaired associative learning	Dorsolateral	Drewe, 1975 Petrides, 1982
10. Impaired olfactory discrimination	Orbital	Potter and Butters, 1980
11. Impaired social behavior	Orbital, dorsolateral	Blumer and Benson, 1975
12. Altered sexual behavior	Orbital	Walker and Blumer, 1975
13. Aphasia	Area 44	Brown, 1972
14. Disorder associated with damage to the face area	Face	Taylor, 1979

humans makes it difficult to infer its functions. Nonetheless, on the basis of lesion, stimulation, and blood flow studies, Roland et al. have proposed that the supplementary motor areas are "programming areas for motor subroutines." Movements that are composed of changes of sequences of fast, isolated muscular contractions are hypothesized to be programmed here to allow them to be run off quickly. Evidence for this idea comes from their observation that human speech, a form of voluntary movement composed of sequences of fast, isolated muscle contractions, is correlated with a bilateral increase in blood flow to the supplementary motor cortex. Similarly, movements of both the fingers and the limbs are associated with increased blood flow here, implying a general role of the supplementary motor cortex in the programming of movements, possibly both in the initiation of movement and in the execution of established subroutines of especially fast movements.

Further evidence favoring a role of the frontal cortex in movement programming comes from a study by Kolb and Milner. They asked patients with localized unilateral frontal removals, most of which did not include the supplementary motor cortex, to copy a series of arm or facial movements, as illustrated in Figures 12–6 and 18–2. Although the patients had mild impairment in copying the arm movements, it was a small effect compared with the performance of patients with left parietal lobe lesions. In contrast, both left and right frontal lobe patients were very poor at copying a series of facial movements. On analysis of the facial movement task, the frontal lobe groups made more errors of sequence than normal controls or other groups of patients. In other words, one deficit observed in the frontal lobe groups was difficulty in ordering the various components of the sequence into a chain of movements. The components were recalled correctly, but in the wrong order. To be sure, the frontal lobe patients made other sorts of errors as well, including intrusions (making movements not belonging in the sequence) and omissions (leaving movements out).

The results of the Kolb and Milner study complement the work of Roland and his associates, implicating the frontal lobe in movement programming. Both lines of work imply that this function is bilaterally represented in the frontal cortex, and it may be that the supplementary motor area has an especially important role in movement programming, although the larger region of the frontal lobe would seem to be involved in the programming of some types of movement.

The observation that the copying of facial but not arm movements was severely disrupted in the frontal lobe patients of Kolb and Milner implies that the frontal lobe may play a special role in the control of the face, perhaps even including the tongue. We shall see below that frontal lobe patients exhibit relatively little spontaneous facial expression, a result in accord with the possible special role of the frontal lobe in the control of the face.

Deficits in Voluntary Gaze

A number of studies using quite different procedures have been reported in which frontal lobe lesions produce alterations in voluntary eye gaze. For example, Teuber presented patients with an array of 48 patterns on a screen. The patterns could be distinguished by either shape or color or both (see Figure 18–3). At a warning signal a duplicate of one of the 48 patterns appeared in the center of the array, and the subject's task was to find the matching pattern and to identify it by pointing to it. Patients with frontal lobe lesions were impaired at finding the duplicate pattern.

Luria recorded patients' eye movements as they visually examined a picture of a complex scene. The eye movement patterns of the patients with large frontal lobe lesions were quite different from those of normal control subjects or of patients with more posterior lesions. For example, if a normal control was asked about the age of the people in a picture, his or her eyes fixed on the heads; if asked how they are dressed, the eyes fixed on the clothing, etc. Patients with large frontal lobe lesions tended to glance over the picture more or less at random, and a change in the question about the picture failed to alter the direction or the pattern of eye movements.

In a recent study Guitton and his colleagues examined a different type of oculomotor defect in frontal lobe patients. They examined the ability of patients to make voluntary eye movements toward or away from briefly appearing targets presented at randon to the right or the left of fixation. Normally if a stimulus cue is briefly presented in either visual field, a person will make a quick eye movement, called a saccade, toward the stimulus. Frontal lobe patients had no difficulty at this, and so Guitton et al. added a second feature to the task.

FIGURE 18–2. Patients with frontal lesions were impaired at copying the series of facial movements *abc, def, ghi, jkl,* and *mno.* Individual movements were performed correctly, but the series were not combined properly. (After Kolb and Milner, 1981.)

Rather than make eye movements toward a target, the patients had to make eye movements to the same place in the opposite visual field. The task therefore requires an inhibition of the normal saccade and a voluntary saccade to the homotopic point opposite. Frontal lobe patients had two deficits on this variation of the task. First, whereas normal subjects failed to inhibit a short-latency response toward the cue in about 20 percent of trials, frontal lobe patients had much more difficulty in inhibiting the initial saccade. Second, following the initial saccade in the incorrect direction, normal subjects had no difficulty in making a large corrective saccade toward the opposite field. In contrast, patients with frontal lesions, which included the frontal eye fields, had difficulty in executing the corrective responses *when the response had to be generated by the damaged hemisphere*. In other words, they had difficulty in moving the eyes to the field contralateral to the frontal lesion. Corrective movements could be made normally in the field opposite the undamaged hemisphere.

The difficulty of patients with frontal lesions in the visual search and the saccade tasks points to the importance of the frontal cortex for certain aspects of oculomotor control. Only the Guitton study has localized the effect in the frontal eye fields, but it is likely that the most severe deficits in search tasks are associated with damage to the frontal eye fields as well.

Impaired Response Inhibition and Inflexible Behavior

Perhaps the most commonly observed traits of frontal lobe patients tested by clinical neuropsychologists are impaired response inhibition and inflexible behavior. Patients with frontal lobe lesions consistently perseverate on responses in a variety of test situations, particularly those in which there are changing demands.

The best example of this phenomenon is observed in the Wisconsin card-sorting test, which has been extensively studied by Milner. Figure 18–4 shows the test material as it appears to the subject. The subject is presented with four stimulus cards, bearing designs that differ in color, form, and number of elements. The subject's task is to sort the cards into piles in front of one or another of the stimulus cards. The only help the subject is given is being told whether the choice is correct or incorrect. The test works on this principle: the correct solution is first color; once the subject has figured out this solution, the correct solution then becomes, without warning, form. Thus, the subject must now inhibit classifying the cards on the basis of color and shift to form. Once the subject has succeeded at selecting by form, the correct solution again changes unexpectedly, this time to number of elements. It will later become color again and so on. Shifting response strategies is particularly difficult for persons with frontal lesions, who may continue responding to the original stimulus (color) for as many as 100 cards until testing is terminated. Throughout this period they may comment that they know that color is no longer correct. They nevertheless continue to sort on the basis of color. For example, one person stated (correctly): "Form is probably the correct solution now so this [sorting to color] will be wrong, and this will be wrong, and wrong again." Such perseveration is common on any task in which a frontal lobe patient is required to shift response strategies, demonstrating that the frontal lobe is necessary for flexibility in behavior. It is important to note that on card-sorting tasks the subjects must not be given any hint that they are to expect a change in the correct solution, because many frontal lobe patients improve dramatically when given this warning. The cue apparently allows enough flexibility in behavior to solve the problem.

FIGURE 18–3. Visual search test adapted from Pop-pelreuter (1917). The subject must locate a duplicate of the stimulus object placed inside the central base.

It appears from Milner's work that the principal locus of this effect (on card sorting, at least) is roughly around Brodmann's area 9 in the left hemisphere. Lesions elsewhere in the left, and often the right, frontal lobe will also produce a deficit on this task, although a somewhat attenuated deficit.

Performance of the Stroop test further demonstrates loss of behavioral flexibility and response inhibition following frontal lobe damage. Subjects are presented with a list of color words (blue, green, red, etc.), each word being printed in colored ink but never in the color denoted by the word (e.g., the word "yellow" is printed in blue, green, or red ink). The subject's task is to name the color in which each word is printed as quickly as possible. Correct response requires an inhibition of reading the color name, an inhibition that is difficult for many control subjects. Perret found that patients with left frontal lesions were unable to inhibit reading the words and thus were impaired at this task.

Corollary Discharge

If one pushes on the eyeball, the world appears to move. If one moves one's eyes, the world remains stable. Why? Teuber proposed that for a movement to take place there must be a signal to produce the movement and also a signal that the movement is going to occur. Thus, when one moves the eyes, there is a signal that it will happen and the world stays still. If the eyes are moved mechanically, there is no such signal and the world moves. This signal has been termed corollary discharge, or **reafference.**

In 1954 Teuber and Mishkin began to study this process, using a task first designed by Aubert in 1861. If you tilt your head sideways in a lighted room, vertical lines between the ceiling and floor do not tilt; they remain upright. If you tilt your head or body in the dark while looking at a luminous line, the mechanism still works, but not as well. If the task is made more difficult so that you must try to orient a tilted luminous line to the vertical in the dark while your head is also tilted sideways, there will be errors of a few degrees. The task is very difficult. Teuber and Mishkin discovered that if patients with frontal lesions were strapped into a chair that was then tilted, and the task was to set a luminous line to vertical, they were much more severely impaired than patients with more posterior lesions or than controls. This impairment disappeared if the chair was upright, indicating that the problem was not one of orienting the line but of doing so in an abnormal attitude.

On the basis of this study as well as others on cats, rats, and monkeys (see below), Teuber argued that the deficit in the tilted-chair experiment is one of corollary discharge. Stated simply, voluntary movements involve two

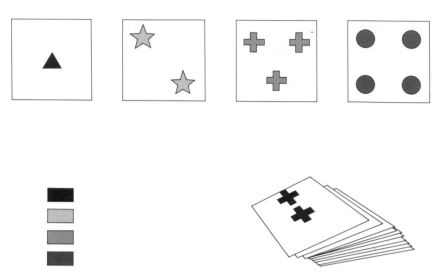

FIGURE 18–4. The Wisconsin card-sorting test, showing test material as presented to the subject. (From B. Milner, Some effects of frontal lobectomy in man. In J. M. Warren and K. Akert, eds., *The Frontal Granula Cortex and Behavior,* p. 315. Copyright © by McGraw-Hill, Inc. Used with the permission of McGraw-Hill Book Co.)

sets of signals rather than one. There are simultaneously the movement command, through the motor system, to effect the movements, and a signal (corollary discharge) from the frontal lobe to the parietal and temporal association cortex that presets the sensory system to anticipate the motor act. Thus, a person's sensory system is able to interpret changes in the external world in light of information about the person's movement. For example, when one is running, the external world remains stable, even though the sense organs are in motion, because there is corollary discharge from the frontal lobe to the parietal-temporal cortex signaling that the movements are occurring. A frontal lesion can therefore not only disturb the production of a movement but also interfere with the message to the rest of the brain that a movement is taking place. By this indirect means, perception of the world by the posterior association cortex is altered.

Temporal Organization of Behavior

One of the most characteristic manifestations of frontal lobe disease is a profound disturbance in organizing everyday activities. This normally manifests itself as an inability to select and execute plans, sometimes disturbing behaviors as simple as planning and preparing a simple meal, the end result being that frontal lobe patients achieve rather little in life. In order to study the nature of this deficit in frontal lobe patients, Milner and her associates have focused on two requirements of temporal ordering: memory for the order of events and self-ordering of tasks. We shall consider each separately.

Memory. Many reports from the 1930s and 1940s suggested that the frontal lobes play a role in some types of memory. Although consistent with research on nonhuman primates, this conclusion is, in a broad sense, not correct, because frontal lobe lesions do not generally interfere with the long-term storage of material. However, one special function is mediated by the frontal lobes: memory for recency. That is, individuals with frontal lobe lesions are impaired at remembering the order of events, although the memory of the events themselves does appear intact. Further, there is relative asymmetry in the frontal lobes in this regard: the right frontal lobe appears more important for memory for nonverbal or pictorial recency; the left frontal lobe appears more important for verbal recency. For example, if a subject is read a series of words and then asked which of two words was read most recently, the frontal lobe patient will have difficulty recalling, although he or she may clearly recall that both words were read. This latter storage function is performed by the temporal lobe. Nonverbal function can be tested by showing photographs instead of reading words; again, the order of presentation of the photographs is forgotten.

At first glance, the impaired memory for recency appears to be an exception to the theoretical role of the frontal lobe in motor control. However, it is essential to motor control that behaviors be distinguished from one another in time. In other words, the order in which behaviors are performed must be remembered, especially in the learning of complex skilled movements. Thus, it could be predicted that frontal lobe patients with impaired recency memory for words or photographs would also be impaired at remembering the order of individual movements. This prediction remains to be tested.

Self-Ordering. Many tasks in everyday life require that we generate our own plans to solve them. In a task designed to explore this ability Petrides and Milner presented subjects with stacks of cards on which was displayed an array of 12 stimuli, including words or drawings in parallel versions of the task. The stimuli in the arrray remained constant, but the position of each stimulus varied randomly from card to card. The subject's task appeared rather simple: Go through the stack and point to only one item on each card, taking care not to point to the same item twice. Thus the subjects themselves initiated the plan to follow and determined the order of responding. Although the task appears easy to us, frontal lobe patients did not find it so: left frontal lobe lesions were associated with impaired performance of both verbal and nonverbal versions of the task, whereas right frontal lobe lesions were associated only with poor performance on the nonverbal test.

Petrides and Milner suggest that in contrast to the recency tests, the self-ordered tasks require subjects to organize and carry out a sequence of responses. From the moment the subjects begin responding, they must constantly compare the responses they have made to those that still remain to be carried out. Hence, this type of task demands an accurate memory as well as an organized strategy. When questioned about their approach to the task at the end of testing, patients with frontal lesions were less likely than other subjects to report that they had used a particular strategy, and when they had, the strategy often appeared to be ill-defined and to have been used inconsistently. The deficit is unlikely to have been one of simple memory, since temporal lobe patients, who would have been expected to have defects of memory, performed normally at this task.

The greater defect following left frontal than right frontal lesions may be consistent with the suggestion that the left hemisphere plays a special role in the programming of responses, whether the production of simple sequences of movements such as on the Kimura manual sequence box or on more complex tests such as these.

Spatial Orientation

Semmes and her colleagues were the first to demonstrate clearly that patients with frontal lobe lesions have a deficit in spatial orientation. To do this, they devised parallel tests of personal orientation (egocentric spatial relations) and of extrapersonal orientation (allocentric spatial relations), both diagrammed in Figure 18–5. In the egocentric test the subject's task was to point to the location on his or her body represented by the various numbers shown on the figure. In the allocentric task the subjects carried a series of maps, one map at a time, in a room where nine dots were painted on the floor in an evenly spaced pattern. The subject's task was to pace out on the floor the route laid out on a given map.

Because the parietal cortex is known to be involved in spatial relations, Semmes expected

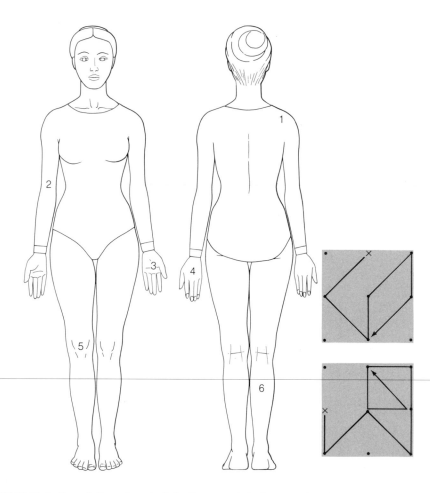

FIGURE 18–5. Sample items from tests by Semmes et al. of personal and extrapersonal orientation. A. In the personal-orientation task the subject is required to touch parts of his or her own body as indicated by the numbers on the diagram. B. In the extrapersonal-orientation task the subject follows a map painted on the floor to progress from point to point.

the maximal deficits on both of these tasks to result from parietal lesions. But this was not the case. The results showed a double dissociation of egocentric and allocentric spatial relations: the frontal lobe patients were impaired at the egocentric test and not the allocentric, whereas the parietal lobe patients were badly impaired at the latter test and only slightly at the former. Furthermore, performances on both tests were more severely affected by lesions of the left than of the right hemisphere. Semmes et al. interpreted the impairment following frontal-cortical damage as a difficulty with behaviors that depend on the accurate assessment of one's body orientation in space. In contrast, the impairment following parietal-cortex damage was interpreted as a difficulty with behaviors involving the spatial relations among external stimuli.

Why personal orientation should be disrupted by frontal lobe lesions and, in view of the right hemisphere's importance in spatial processing, why these deficits should result primarily from lesions in the left hemisphere cannot be easily explained. Teuber has proposed that maximum flexibility of behavior requires that the nervous system keep an ongoing record of where the individual is at any given instant—a kind of corollary discharge of all ongoing behavior. Thus, according to Teuber, deficits in personal orientation result from an absence of corollary discharge. Further, it could be argued that since the left hemisphere is specialized for control of complex movement it may be the most efficient location for this behavioral recording system. Both of these conjectures remain to be proved.

Although patients with right frontal lobe lesions are not severely impaired at the Semmes tests, they are impaired at other tests of spatial orientation. In particular, patients with right frontal lobe lesions have difficulty in successfully solving finger and stylus maze tests. For example, in Corkin's study of stylus maze

performance, subjects had to learn to trace a route in a maze, which was out of sight, using a stylus. Each time an incorrect alley was entered a bell rang, providing subjects with feedback about their performance. Whereas control subjects made an average of about 100 errors in solving this admittedly difficult task, patients with right, but not left, frontal lobe lesions failed to learn the task and were discontinued after about 350 errors. Furthermore, patients with right frontal lobe lesions performed more poorly at this task than did patients with right temporal or parietal lobe lesions, who also were impaired at it. It is unclear why the patients with right frontal lobe lesions were so poor at the task, but it does suggest that the frontal cortex has an important role in spatial orientation. We shall return to this issue in our more extended discussion of spatial behavior in Chapter 23.

Spontaneous Behavior

According to Zangwill, in a detailed study of the early literature, such authors as Feuchtwanger and Kliest observed that although patients with left frontal lesions anterior to Broca's area were not aphasic, they did have a type of verbal deficit. Zangwill described it as "a certain loss of spontaneity of speech" and a "difficulty in evoking appropriate words or phrases." Subsequent studies by a variety of authors—Milner and, later, Ramier and Hécaen among others—have been able to quantify this deficit. These researchers gave patients tests similar to Thurstone's word fluency test; patients were asked to write or to say, first, as many words starting with a given letter as they could think of in five minutes, then as many four-letter words starting with a given letter. Patients with frontal lobe lesions have a low output of words in this test, producing an average of 35 words in total in Milner's sample. Although the principal locus of this defect appears to be in the left orbital frontal region, lesions in the right orbital frontal region may also produce a large reduction in verbal fluency. Again we see less asymmetry in the frontal lobes than one might expect. The following case is an example of low spontaneous verbal fluency from a lesion of the right frontal lobe.

Mrs. P., a 63-year-old woman with a B.A. degree, was suffering from a large astrocytoma of the right frontal lobe. Her word fluency is reproduced in Figure 18–6, where four features of frontal lobe damage in this test performance are illustrated. First, her total output of words is remarkably low: only eight words beginning with "s" and six words beginning with "c." (Control subjects of similar age and education produce a total of about 60 words in the same time period.) Second, we see rule-breaking, which is a common characteristic of frontal lobe patients on this test. We told her several times that the words starting with "c" could have only four letters. She replied: "Yes, yes, I know, I keep using more each time." Even though she understood the instructions she could not organize her behavior to follow them successfully. Third, her writing is not fluid but rather jerky, much like that seen in a child learning to write, implying that her tumor had invaded area 4 or 6. Finally, Mrs. P. insisted on

FIGURE 18–6. Word fluency. Left: Mrs. P.'s lists. Right: A normal control subject's lists. Both subjects were given five minutes to write as many English-language words as possible starting with the letter "s" and four minutes to write as many four-letter words as possible starting with the letter "c." Note Mrs. P.'s low output and her rule-breaking in the four-letter "c" words. (Mrs. P. was multilingual, although English was her first language.)

talking throughout the test—complaining that she simply could not think of any more words—and kept looking around the room for objects starting with the required letter.

Although one locus of low verbal fluency anterior to Broca's area appears to be in the orbital cortex, patients with lesions in the central face area actually have even lower verbal fluency scores, according to Milner. Although a peculiar result, it appears solid and reliable, and suggests that the face area has some special role in certain aspects of verbal abilities.

A study by Jones-Gotman and Milner raises the question of whether this verbal fluency deficit might have a nonverbal analogue. The researchers devised an ingenious experiment in which they asked patients to draw as many different drawings, which were not supposed to be representational, as they could in five minutes. The patients were then asked to draw as many different drawings as they could, but this time using only four lines (a circle was counted as a single line). The results showed a beautiful analogue to the verbal fluency results. As can be seen in Figure 18–7, lesions in the right frontal lobe produced a very large drop in the production of *different* drawings. Normal controls drew about 35 drawings, left frontal lobe patients about 24 drawings, and right frontal lobe patients about 15 drawings. This deficit appears to be related to an impoverished output, high perseveration, and, in some cases, the drawing of nameable things. As with verbal fluency, lesions in the central face

FIGURE 18–7. Design fluency. Left: A normal control subject's drawings, showing perseveration. Right: A frontal lobe patient's drawings, showing lack of spontaneity. (Adapted from Jones-Gotman and Milner, 1977.)

area actually appeared to produce a larger deficit than the more anterior lesions. There is not yet a clear indication whether orbital frontal lesions affect design fluency more than dorsolateral lesions do. More patients must be studied.

The question arises of whether patients with frontal lobe lesions might actually show a reduced spontaneity of behavior in general. Since frontal lobe patients have been described as "pseudodepressed" (see below), this might indeed be the case, but we are aware of only two studies that have actually recorded the spontaneous behavior of patients. Kolb and his colleagues found the following. (1) Patients with frontal lobe removals displayed fewer spontaneous facial movements and expressions than did normal controls or patients with more posterior lesions. (2) There were dramatic differences in the number of words spoken by frontal lobe patients during a neuropsychological interview: patients with left frontal removals rarely spoke, whereas patients with right frontal lesions were excessively talkative. Hence it would seem worthwhile to study in detail the spontaneous behavior of patients with frontal lesions to determine whether altered spontaneity is a general feature of their behavior. The following quotation from Hécaen and Albert suggests that it might be.

> Lack of initiative or spontaneity is a characteristic feature of frontal lobe pathology. These are linked to a general diminution of motor activity. The patient no longer voluntarily carries out the necessary daily activities of life, such as getting out of bed in the morning, washing or dressing himself, feeding himself, or even urinating or defecating in the toilet. These latter activities may be carried out at any time or place, without regard for the social consequences. The actual ability to carry out the various activities of daily living is not impaired —the patient is neither paralyzed, apraxic, nor confused. When he is vigorously urged to do something, he can do it. What is impaired is the ability to initiate spontaneously a desired or an automatic motor task.
>
> It is this rupture between the patient and the external world, this diminution of activity in manipulating real objects, this reduction of interpersonal exchange that appear to be a loss of interest on the part of the patient. Whether there is a true loss of interest or an apparent loss of interest due to an impairment of spontaneous initiation of activity, the effect on the examiner remains the same. (Hécaen and Albert, 1975, p. 139)

Associative Learning

It has often been claimed that patients with large frontal lobe lesions are unable to regulate their behavior by external stimuli. Thus, for example, Luria and Homskaya described patients with massive frontal lobe tumors who could not be trained to respond consistently with the right hand to a red light and with the left hand to a green light, even though the patients could indicate which hand was which and could repeat the instructions. As with many other frontal lobe symptoms, however, there are very few experimental studies of this phenomenon in patients with more restricted cortical injuries, although a recent study by Petrides is intriguing. He asked frontal lobe patients to learn arbitrary associations between colors and spatial locations or between colors and hand postures. For example, in the former test, patients were presented with six blue lights and six white index cards placed in a row on a table in front of them. Each light was associated with one and only one of the index cards, and the subjects' task was to learn which card was associated with which light. Damage to either the left or the right hemisphere resulted in poor performance on this task, as well as on an analogous task in which different-colored lights and six hand postures had to be associated in a similar way. Again, the behavioral impairments in the frontal lobe patients could not be attributed to a deficit in memory since temporal lobe patients with poor performance on other tests of memory performed normally at these tasks.

The deficits observed in associative learning tasks imply that frontal lobe lesions impair the ability to utilize external cues to guide responses, although the details of this deficit await further study. Nonetheless, it seems likely tht a disorder of this sort would render behavior inflexible and disorganized, symptoms we have already seen to be characteristic of frontal lobe patients.

Olfaction

Although olfaction is seldom studied in human subjects, behavioral evidence from studies of nonhuman subjects led Potter and Butters to investigate olfactory detection and discrimination in frontal lobe patients. Their results showed that although olfactory detection was still normal, olfactory discriminatory ability was severely impaired in their patients. The orbital frontal cortex of other species is known to have significant olfactory input and cells there are known to respond to specific odors, so that it is likely that the same is true in humans. Thus, the orbital frontal cortex may be the core olfactory cortex, a surprising possibility in view of the more strictly motor functions that we have described to this point. The importance of olfaction in social and sexual behavior, even in humans, may be significant in understanding the olfactory functions of the frontal cortex, although this is pure speculation at this point, the subject requiring a good deal more study.

Social Behavior and Personality

One of the most obvious and striking effects of frontal lobe damage in humans is a marked change in social behavior and personality. Perhaps the most publicized example of personality change following frontal lobe lesion is that of Phineas Gage, first reported by Harlow in 1868. Gage was a dynamite worker and survived an explosion that blasted an iron tamping bar (3 ft 7 in long, 1.25 in wide at its widest point) through the front of his head (see Figure 18–8). After the accident his behavior changed completely. He had been of average intelligence and was "energetic and persistent in executing all his plans of operation." His posttrauma personality is described as follows:

> The equilibrium or balance, so to speak, between his intellectual faculties and animal propensities seems to have been destroyed. He is fitful, irreverent, indulging at times in the grossest profanity, manifesting but little deference for his fellows, impatient of restraint or advice when it conflicts with his desires, at times pertinaciously obstinate, yet capricious and vacillating, devising many plans of operation, which are no sooner arranged than they are abandoned in turn for others appearing more feasible. A child in his intellectual capacity and manifestations, he has the animal passions of a strong man. (Blumer and Benson, 1975, p. 153)

Gage's injury affected primarily the left frontal lobe from the medial orbital region upward to the precentral region.

Although Gage's skull has been examined carefully, the first person with extensive frontal damage to actually undergo close scrutiny at autopsy was a furrier who fell 100 feet from a window. He suffered a compound fracture of the frontal bones and severe injury to the right frontal lobe but, remarkably, was never unconscious and was confused only briefly. Before the fall the man had been good-natured and sociable, but afterward he became nasty and cantankerous. Autopsy, about a year after the accident, revealed deep scarring of the orbital part of

FIGURE 18–8. Bust and skull of Phineas Gage, showing the hole in the frontal bone made by the iron rod blown through his head. (From C. Blakemore, *Mechanics of the Mind.* Cambridge: Cambridge University Press, p. 3. Copyright © 1977. Reprinted with permission of Cambridge University Press.)

both frontal lobes, although more extensively on the right.

From soon after the turn of the century until about 1950 there were many excellent psychiatric studies of the effect of brain lesions on personality. A consistent finding of this work (especially Kliest's) was that damage to the orbital regions of the frontal lobe was associated with more dramatic changes in personality than dorsolateral lesions, although the latter also had significant effects. Although there are abundant clinical descriptions of the effects of frontal lobe lesions on personality, there are few systematic studies. At least two types of personality change have been clinically

observed in such patients: Blumer and Benson have termed them as showing **pseudodepression** and as being **pseudopsychopathic.** Patients classified as showing pseudodepression exhibit such symptoms as outward apathy and indifference, loss of initiative, reduced sexual interest, little overt emotion, and little or no verbal output. Patients classified as pseudopsychopathic exhibit immature behavior, lack of tact and restraint, coarse language, promiscuous sexual behavior, increased motor activity, and a general lack of social graces. Incontinence is not uncommon with large traumatic lesions or tumors in the frontal lobes. The following two case histories illustrate the pseudodepressed and pseudopsychopathic frontal personalities, respectively.

At the age of 46, a successful salesman sustained a compound depressed fracture of the left frontal bone in a traffic accident. Treatment included debridement and amputation of the left frontal pole. Recovery was slow, and 9 months after the injury he was referred for long-term custodial management. By this time, he had recovered motor function with only a minimal limp and slight hyperreflexia on the right side, had normal sensation, no evidence of aphasia, and normal memory and cognitive ability (IQ 118). Nonetheless, he remained under hospital care because of marked changes in personal habits.

Prior to the accident, the patient had been garrulous, enjoyed people, had many friends and talked freely. He was active in community affairs, including Little League, church activities, men's clubs, and so forth. It was stated by one acquaintance that the patient had a true charisma, "whenever he entered a room there was a change in the atmosphere, everything became more animated, happy and friendly."

Following the head injury, he was quiet and remote. He would speak when spoken to and made sensible replies but would then lapse into silence. He made no friends on the ward, spent most of his time sitting alone smoking. He was frequently incontinent of urine, occasionally of stool. He remained unconcerned about either and was frequently found soaking wet, calmly sitting and smoking. If asked, he would matter-of-factly state that he had not been able to get to the bathroom in time but that this didn't bother him. Because of objectionable eating habits he always ate alone on the ward. His sleep pattern was reversed; he stayed up much of the night and slept during the day. He did not resent being awakened or questioned. He could discuss many subjects intelligently, but was never known to initiate either a conversation or a request. He could give detailed accounts of his life prior to the accident, of the hospitals he had been in, the doctors and treatment he had had but there was an unreality to his conversation. When asked, he would deny illness, state emphatically that he

could return to work at any time, and that the only reason he was not working was that he was being held in the hospital by the doctors. At no time did he request a discharge or weekend pass. He was totally unconcerned about his wife and children. Formerly a warm and loving father, he did not seem to care about his family. Eventually, the family ceased visiting because of his indifference and unconcern. (Blumer and Benson, 1975, pp. 156–157)

A 32-year-old white male was admitted for behavioral evaluation. History revealed that he had sustained a gunshot wound in Vietnam 5 years previously. A high-velocity missile had entered the left temple and emerged through the right orbit. Infection necessitated surgical removal of most of the orbital surface of the right frontal lobe. On recovery, he was neither paralyzed nor aphasic but suffered a remarkable change in personality.

Prior to injury he had been quiet, intelligent, proper, and compulsive. He was a West Point graduate and spent the ensuing years as a military officer attaining the rank of captain. Both as a cadet and later as an officer, he was known to be quiet, strict, and rigid. He was considered a good commander, trusted by his men, but never shared camaraderie with his troops or with his peers.

Subsequent to injury, he was outspoken, facetious, brash, and disrespectful. There was no evidence of self-pity, although he frequently made rather morbid jokes about his condition (for example, "dummy's head"). On admission to the hospital, he had just failed at an extremely simple job.

He was not aphasic but misused words in a manner that suggested inability to maintain specific meanings. For instance, when asked whether the injury had affected his thinking his response was, "Yeah—it's affected the way I think—it's affected my senses—the only things I can taste are sugar and salt—I can't detect a pungent odor—ha ha—to tell you the truth it's a blessing this way." When the examiner persisted, "How had it affected the way you think?" his response was "Yes—I'm not as spry on my feet as

I was before." He was never incontinent, but did show a messiness in attire. His remarks to the nurses and other female personnel were open and frank but were never blatantly sexual. His premorbid IQ was reported at about 130. Present examination showed a full-scale IQ of 113. (Blumer and Benson, 1975, pp. 155–156)

Blumer and Benson are probably correct in their assertion that all the elements of these syndromes are observable only after bilateral frontal lobe damage. Nevertheless, some elements of these two rather different syndromes can be observed in most, if not all, persons with frontal lobe lesions. Pseudodepression appears most likely to follow lesions of the left frontal lobe; pseudopsychopathic behavior, lesions of the right frontal lobe.

Sexual Behavior

Changes in sexual behavior are among the most difficult symptoms of frontal lobe damage to properly document, largely because of social taboos against investigating people's sex lives. To date, there are no such empirical studies, but there is anecdotal evidence that frontal lesions do alter libido and related behavior. Orbital frontal lesions may introduce abnormal sexual behavior (such as public masturbation) by reducing inhibitions, although the actual frequency of sexual behavior per se is not affected. On the other hand, dorsolateral lesions appear to reduce interest in sexual behavior, although the patients are still capable of the necessary motor acts and can perform sexually if led through the activity "step by step."

Broca's Aphasia

The first symptom of prefrontal cortex damage to be described was the disturbance of language following lesion of the left frontal lobe, by Broca in 1861. After studying additional patients Broca and others proposed that the third frontal convolution of the left hemisphere, area 44, is specialized for producing motor programs for speech, a function Broca described as the "motor image of the word." In this type of aphasia the person has difficulty speaking, doing so only slowly and deliberately. Curiously, although this symptom of frontal lobe damage was the first to be described, it remains the most controversial even to this day. Some question its existence; others, granting that it might really occur, question its nature. We shall return to this problem in our discussion of language in Chapter 21. To date there are no clear indications what area 44 in the right frontal lobe does. It is certain, however, that loss of this zone does not produce aphasia.

Symptoms Associated with Damage to the Face Area

Over the years Taylor and his colleagues have accumulated some remarkable data from a small group of patients with localized surgical removals of the precentral and postcentral gyri containing, respectively, the motor and sensory representations of the face (see Figure 18–1 B). Unlike removal of the hand area (see Chapter 10), removal of the face area is seldom associated with long-lasting somatosensory deficits on the face, even if both the sensory and motor representations are removed completely. This finding is in keeping with the evidence that the face area is represented bilaterally in the cortex. There has been no systematic study of the facial motor abilities of patients with removal of both precentral and postcentral gyri, but Kolb and Milner found them able to perform normally the facial sequences illustrated in Figure 18–2. Furthermore, although they had difficulty in making individual facial movements in the initial postoperative period, especially on the side of the face contralateral to the lesion, they appeared to have regained normal voluntary facial control a month after surgery, although closer examination might have revealed subtle defects. In addition, their faces were expressive, and they displayed normal spontaneous facial expressions at frequencies well within normal limits.

In the immediate postoperative period patients with left hemisphere facial area lesions are aphasic, being impaired at both language comprehension and production as well as being alexic. However, these symptoms subside rapidly, probably having resulted from swelling and trauma associated with the surgical procedure. Within about six months to a year of surgery only a slight residual expressive dysphasia remains. Yet these same patients are severely impaired at certain other language tests.

> They achieve an even lower score on the word fluency test than do our frontal lobe patients. They are also unable to make effective use of phonetic elements of language. When asked . . . to discriminate phonemes embedded in nonsense words, face area patients correctly identify less than one half of the 108 sounds they have heard, whereas other patient groups score significantly higher on the task. (Taylor, 1979, p. 171)

In addition, these same patients are very poor spellers, occasionally writing words that are unrecognizable. Their low verbal fluency is complemented by a very low design fluency; patients with right facial area lesions are worse at design fluency than frontal lobe patients, even with very large anterior lesions. This lack of spontaneity in verbal and design fluency is remarkable, considering the normal spontaneity of facial expressions noted above.

In summary, unilateral removal of the face area results in no significant chronic loss in sensory or motor control of the face (presumably because of its bilateral representation in the cortex) but results surprisingly in chronic

deficits in phonetic discrimination, spelling, verbal fluency, and design fluency. Taylor has preliminary data suggesting that these deficits may result primarily from damage to the precentral motor representation of the face, rather than to the postcentral sensory representation. The origin of these deficits is, however, unexplained to date.

Clinical Neuropsychological Assessment of Frontal Lobe Damage

Considering the number and variety of symptoms associated with frontal lobe damage, surprisingly few standardized neuropsychological tests are useful for assessing frontal lobe function. The available tests (see Table 18–3) are very good, however. As with the parietal and temporal lobe tests discussed in the previous two chapters, it would be highly unusual for a person to perform normally on all these tests if there were damage to either frontal lobe.

The Wisconsin card-sorting test (Figure 18–4), described earlier, is the best available test of dorsolateral frontal cortex function. Briefly, the subject is told to sort the cards into piles in front of one or another of the stimulus cards bearing designs that differ in color, form, and number of elements. The correct solution shifts unbeknownst to the subject once he or she has figured out each solution.

The Semmes body-placing test (Figure 18–5), also described earlier, is a simple, easily administered test of personal spatial orientation. Left frontal lobe patients do more poorly on this test than other patient groups, although left parietal lobe patients often are impaired as well. For this reason the Semmes test should be given in conjunction with a left-right differentiation test (see Chapter 16), which often helps to differentiate between left frontal and left parietal patients. Although both groups are likely to be impaired at left-right discrimin-

TABLE 18–3

Standardized clinical neuropsychological tests for frontal lobe damage

	Function	Test	Basic reference
1.	Response inhibition	Wisconsin card-sorting test	Milner, 1964
2.	Personal spatial orientation	Semmes body placing	Semmes et al., 1963
3.	Verbal fluency	Thurstone word fluency	Milner, 1964
			Ramier and Hécaen, 1970
4.	Motor	Hand dynamometer	Taylor, 1979
		Finger tapping	Reitan and Davison, 1974
		Sequencing	Kolb and Milner, 1981
5.	Aphasia: language	Token test	de Renzi and Faglioni, 1978
	comprehension		
	spelling		Taylor, 1979
	phonetic discrimination		Taylor, 1979

ation and perform below control levels, the parietal lobe patients are likely to be reduced to chance performance, whereas the frontal lobe patients are more likely to perform above chance levels.

The Thurstone word fluency test, recall, requires subjects to say or write as many words as possible beginning with a given letter in five minutes, and then as many four-letter words beginning with a given letter in four minutes. Although subjects with lesions anywhere in the prefrontal cortex are apt to do poorly on this test, subjects with facial area lesions perform the worst, those with orbital lesions performing only slightly better. Performance is of course poorest when the lesion is in the left hemisphere.

Tests of motor function include tests of strength (hand dynamometer), finger-tapping speed, and movement sequencing. Strength and finger-tapping speed are significantly reduced contralateral to a lesion that is in the vicinity of the precentral or postcentral gyri. Motor sequencing can be assessed by using the facial sequence test (Figure 18–2), although this test requires considerable practice in both administering and scoring. Simpler tests of movement programming such as the Kimura

box test (Chapter 12) are not suitable because frontal lobe patients are unlikely to perform very poorly unless the lesion extends into the basal ganglia.

As in previous chapters we recommend the token test as a quick aphasia screening test, to be followed if necessary by more extensive aphasia testing (Chapter 21). Although it is widely believed that damage to Broca's area results in deficits in language production only and not in comprehension, we shall see in Chapter 21 that this is not strictly true. Left frontal lesions in the vicinity of Broca's area produce deficits in comprehension as well as in production. Spelling is seriously impaired by facial area lesions and can be assessed by any standardized spelling test. Phonetic differentiation, a test described by Stitt and Huntington and used for neurological patients by Taylor, is another means of assessing facial area function. A series of nonsense words, such as "agma," is presented and the subject's task is to identify the first consonant sound. This test proves difficult even for controls, but it is most poorly performed by subjects with facial area damage, especially on the left. However, frontal lobe lesions outside the facial area also may impair performance significantly on this test.

In the absence of language deficits it may prove difficult to localize frontal lobe damage in either the left or the right hemisphere with neuropsychological tests, presumably because the two frontal lobes significantly overlap in function. Clinical evaluation of personality as pseudodepressed or pseudopsychopathic (as discussed earlier) may prove useful in localizing the dysfunction to the left or the right hemisphere, respectively, but caution is advised; unfortunately no standardized quantitative measures of these symptoms are available.

FRONTAL LOBE FUNCTION IN NONHUMANS

From the assumption, prevalent in the 1930s and 1940s, that the frontal lobes house the highest human intellectual capacities, it was logical to conclude that they must be unique to humans. The fact that the frontal lobes markedly increase in size phylogenetically supported this view. The frontal lobes of humans are not, however, special. The frontal lobes have changed remarkably little functionally through phylogeny; thus, nonhuman frontal lobes provide an excellent model for the study of human frontal lobes.

An exhaustive survey of the effects of frontal lobe damage in nonhumans being beyond the scope of this book, we shall discuss only the major findings. We shall consider mainly nonhuman primates and rats, largely because the most is known about these species, and because they represent extremes in the anatomical size of the frontal cortex and in diversity of behavior. Surely if the effects of lesions to the frontal lobes of rats, monkeys, and humans are similar, the functions of the frontal lobes are likely to be similar across mammalian phylogeny.

Anatomy of the Frontal Lobes of Nonhumans

In 1948 Rose and Woolsey point out that all mammals appear to have a frontal lobe composed of regions receiving projections from the dorsomedial nucleus of the thalamus (which they termed prefrontal cortex) as well as from the motor thalamus that projects to areas 4 and 6.

Figure 18–9 shows how the frontal cortex has generally increased as a proportion of the neocortex during mammalian evolution. In all mammals there is a region of prefrontal cortex, and in all but marsupials and monotremes this region appears to be anatomically dissociable into three regions, as is the human frontal lobe. In the rat, dog, and monkey there is clear evidence that these regions are functionally dissociable as well.

Effects of Frontal Lobe Lesions in Nonhumans

As with parietal and temporal lesions, all the major symptoms of frontal lobe lesions in humans (with the exception of language deficits) can be observed in nonhumans. Unilateral lesions in the frontal cortex of nonhumans seldom produce behavioral effects as large as those observed in humans, however, so that most studies have investigated the effect of bilateral lesions; we shall restrict our discussion to such studies (Table 18–4). We shall further limit our review to studies of premotor and prefrontal damage, the effects of damage to area 4 having been discussed in Chapters 11 and 12.

Movement Programming

Serially ordering complex chains of behavior in relation to varying stimuli is as necessary a component of higher-level motor control in

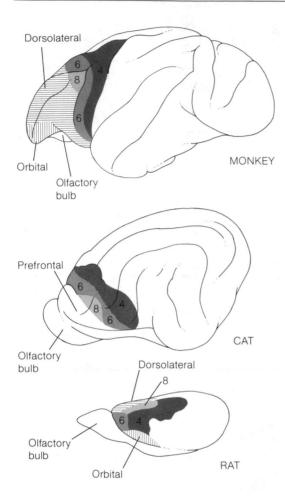

FIGURE 18–9. The frontal lobes of the monkey, cat, and rat. Notice the marked expansion of the frontal neocortex in primates. It is not currently possible to dissociate the prefrontal cortex of the cat into subzones analogous to those in the human, monkey, and rat. The brains are not drawn to the same scale. No evolutionary progression from one species to another is implied.

nonhumans as it is in humans. Many authors, most notably Pribram, have emphasized the role of the frontal cortex of the monkey in the highest levels of motor control (or, in Pribram's term, "executive" control) of behavior.

However, few studies have directly addressed the issue of the frontal lobe's role in apraxia in nonhumans. In a recent study, Deuel trained monkeys to open a complex latch box in which correct performance required a series of movements, including sliding a bolt along a track, lifting the bolt out, turning a crank 180°, and depressing a knob on the front of a box. To obtain a food reward, the monkeys had to perform these movements correctly and, more important, in the correct sequence. Deuel found that small dorsolateral lesions profoundly impaired performance, whereas parietal lobe lesions did not. Gentile et al. found an analogous disruption of a latch-opening task in rats with frontal cortex but not parietal cortex lesions. These motor tasks, similar to the Kimura box test used for studying human subjects, suggest that the frontal lobe of nonhuman primates is important in praxic functions.

We have studied this function in a different way, by observing the chaining together of movement components of species-typical behavior. Both rats and hamsters with frontal lobe removals are impaired at such chaining to perform complex behaviors, such as nest building, grooming, and food hoarding. Thus, when hamsters with frontal lobe lesions attempt to build a nest, the component behaviors of picking up nest material in the mouth, carrying it to the desired location, putting it down, and manipulating it into the proper position are performed correctly but not in the proper order—a deficit strikingly reminiscent of apraxia in primates.

When discussing humans, we considered the possibility that the supplementary motor cortex might have an important role in programming movements. To date, there have been few studies of monkeys or rats with lesions including the supplementary motor cortex, although this would seem to be a worthwhile endeavor.

TABLE 18–4

Summary of major symptoms of frontal lobe damage in nonhuman primates

	Symptom	Lesion site	Representative reference
1.	Loss of distal movements	Area 4	Lawrence and Kuypers, 1968
2.	Poor movement programming	Dorosolateral	Deuel, 1977
3.	Poor voluntary eye gaze	Area 8	Latto, 1978
4.	Impaired response inhibition	Orbital	Mishkin, 1964
5.	Reduced corollary discharge	Dorsolateral?	Bossom, 1965
6.	Disorders of temporal ordering	Dorsolateral	Pribram and Tubbs, 1967
7.	Impaired spatial orientation	Dorsolateral	Mishkin, 1964
8.	Reduced behavioral spontaneity	Orbital?	Myers, 1972
9.	Impaired associative learning	Dorsolateral	Petrides, 1982
10.	Impaired olfactory discrimination	Orbital	Tanabe et al., 1975
11.	Impaired social and affective behavior	Orbital, dorsolateral	Butter and Snyder, 1972 Miller, 1976
12.	Alterations in mobility	Orbital, dorsolateral	Gross and Weiskrantz, 1964 Ruch and Shenkin, 1943
13.	Impaired habituation	Dorsolateral?	Butter, 1964

Deficits in Voluntary Gaze

Lesions of the frontal eye fields (area 8) of monkeys impair performance on search tasks analogous to Poppelreuter's search task for humans. Eye movements are not a prominent feature of the behavior of cats, dogs, and rats, and we are unaware of any studies examining eye movements following area 8 lesions in these species. Nevertheless, there is evidence that all these species have frontal eye fields, because stimulation there produces eye movements. We would be surprised if lesions to this region did not have some effect on eye movements.

Impaired Response Inhibition and Inflexible Behavior

Impaired response inhibition and inflexible behavior are behavioral deficits analogous to perseveration in card-sorting tasks by humans with frontal lobe damage. Such behavior is a commonly observed effect of frontal lobe le-

sions in rats, cats, dogs, and monkeys; it can be demonstrated on a wide variety of standard laboratory learning tasks. For example, if an animal is trained to find food under a food well located to its left, and the food reward is then shifted to a location under another food well to the animal's right, the animal with the frontal lobe lesion persists in looking under the original food well. This perseverative responding may persist even with extended training, as we have observed rats to perseverate for up to a hundred incorrect choices in a row before adapting to the correct response. Normal control animals typically make fewer than five or 10 incorrect choices before altering response strategy. The primary focus for this perseverative response is the orbital frontal cortex, although this behavior also follows dorsolateral lesions.

Corollary Discharge

There are two sources of evidence that the nonhuman primate frontal lobe plays a role in corollary discharge: studies of frontal eye field cells and experimental use of prisms on the eyes. Bizzi and others have found that cells in the frontal eye fields fire simultaneously with movements of the eyes. These cells cannot be causing the eyes to move, for to do so they would have to fire prior to the eye movements (just as to accelerate an automobile you must first depress the gas pedal). Rather, these cells must be monitoring the ongoing movement— a process suspiciously similar to what would be expected from a region involved in corollary discharge.

Further evidence comes from a beautiful experiment by Bossom. In the early 1960s Held, Hein, and others performed experiments by fitting prisms to the eyes of animals and humans. As a result, whatever the subject saw was systematically displaced from its true location, all lines appearing subjectively curved and tilted, in keeping with the distortions imposed by the optics of the prism. After the prisms were worn for a few hours the distortions and displacements diminished, and acts such as reaching for objects were performed normally. On abrupt removal of the prisms the distortions were reinstated, requiring readaptation before perception was again normal. An important feature of these experiments was that passively sitting for a few hours did not produce the perceptual change; to induce the adaptation, the individual had to move about in the environment. This requirement implied that adaptation to the prism occurred in the motor system rather than in the sensory systems. With these experiments in mind, Bossom selectively removed frontal, temporal, parietal, or occipital cortex in monkeys to see which lesion, if any, would disrupt prism adaptation. As one would predict from the work of Held, only frontal lesions impaired adaptation to the distorting prisms; parietal, temporal, and occipital lesions did not. Teuber interprets this experiment as showing that cor-

ollary discharge is necessary for the adaptation to occur. In other words, the effects of movement must be monitored with respect to sensory input such that the brain can adjust the movements to make them accurate. To date, these studies have not been performed on other species (including humans), but they are suggestive and worthy of further study.

Temporal Organization

In the 1930s Jacobsen gave impetus to a revolution in research on the frontal lobes when he observed that chimpanzees with frontal lobe lesions are impaired at a task called delayed response. In the delayed-response task, the animal is shown where food is located (e.g., under one of two cups) but is prevented from responding for some period of time, usually a few seconds. After this delay, the animal is allowed to respond, and its accuracy in choosing the correct hiding place for the food is measured. Monkeys, dogs, cats, and rats with frontal lesions are severely impaired at this task. The task was originally assumed to be a measure of short-term memory, but it later became clear that the spatial component of the task was essential to the deficit, since the animals are quite capable of forming object-discrimination learning sets that have no spatial component. Nevertheless, there is reason to believe that, like humans with frontal lobe lesions, these species suffer a deficit in recent memory. From experiments by Harlow and later by Pribram and Tubbs it was observed that such monkeys could not keep trials separate in memory; that is, what had happened on the last trial as opposed to the previous one. Pribram and Tubbs found that if repeated trials on problems such as delayed response were separated by longer and longer periods of time, the performance of the monkeys improved. This could not be due simply to the spatial aspects of the task, because they remained constant; nor could it be a simple memory problem, because the period between hiding the food and the response was kept constant. The important variable was the time between trials. As the interval between trials lengthened, the trials became more distinct to the animals and therefore easier to tell apart, suggesting a defect in recency memory analogous to that observed in humans with frontal lobe lesions. This phenomenon has not, to our knowledge, been studied in rodents or carnivores.

Spatial Orientation

Monkeys, cats, dogs, rats, and hamsters with frontal lesions have all displayed deficits in learning problems and behaviors that require the use of spatial cues. In a classic study, Pohl was able to double dissociate the parietal and frontal lobes on two spatial tasks in a manner analogous to that done by Semmes and Teuber in humans. Pohl selected the two tasks of spatial reversal and landmark reversal. In the former task, after monkeys learned that food was placed under a cup to one side of them, the reward was shifted, without any cues or warning, to the cup on the opposite side. Once the animals had solved this reversal, the food was reversed again. Basically, the task requires the animal to learn egocentric orientation: the relation of objects in space to the animal itself. Warren has suggested that this task is probably the best test of frontal lobe damage in animals; the data support this view.

In the landmark-reversal task, a test of allocentric orientation, the animal must learn the spatial relation between two objects: in this case, the food cup and some object located elsewhere. For example, the food will be found under the cup closest to a pop bottle located a few inches behind the cups. Once this relation has been learned, the task is reversed—i.e.,

the reward is now to be found under the cup farthest from the pop bottle. The results of the landmark-reversal task have shown that frontal lobe lesions (especially dorsolateral lesions) impair acquisition of the spatial-reversal task, whereas parietal lobe lesions impair acquisition of the landmark-reversal task. This nice example of double dissociation is analogous to that observed in humans who have frontal and parietal lobe lesions.

Spontaneous Behavior

Behavioral spontaneity in humans was assessed by measuring verbal fluency, design fluency, and spontaneous facial expressions. It is difficult to find analogies of these behaviors in nonhuman species, although two studies are suggestive. In the first, Myers examined the frequency of spontaneous facial expressions and vocalizations in rhesus monkeys. These monkeys have a rich repertory of vocalizations (hoots, howls, etc.) and facial expressions that are as important in social communication as facial expression and certain basic vocalizations (characteristic utterances such as "hmm," crying, laughing, etc.) are among humans. Myers reported that frontal lobe removal resulted in drastically reduced frequencies of facial expressions and vocalizations. Indeed, it was this observation that led Kolb and Milner to study facial expressions in humans with frontal lobe lesions. Unfortunately, because Myers failed to quantify this observation, it is difficult to assess the magnitude of the change in the number of expressions. In the second study, Kolb found that guinea pigs, who are normally very vocal, showed dramatic reductions (over 80 percent) in vocalizations following orbital frontal lesions. Although these observations do not conclusively establish reduced spontaneity of behavior as a frontal symptom in nonhumans, they suggest that further study may be fruitful. On the other hand, a large body of literature appears to contradict this conclusion. It has long been known that rats and monkeys with orbital frontal lesions increase locomotor activity. However, this paradoxical result may not be as inconsistent with the literature on humans as it appears. Although to date general locomotor activity levels of human frontal lobe patients have not been systematically studied, numerous case studies (for example, see Ackerly) report increased locomotor activity in these people, especially if the lesion is on the right. It thus appears that frontal lesions may have differential effects on spontaneous levels of locomotor and other behaviors in both humans and nonhumans. This problem deserves additional study.

Associative Learning

Like humans with frontal lobe lesions, monkeys with such lesions are impaired at learning arbitrary associations between a set of stimuli and a set of responses. In a monkey analogue of his associative learning task, which we described earlier, Petrides trained monkeys to make different movements of a manipulandum when presented with different objects. In contrast to his control monkeys, who rapidly acquired the task, monkeys with prefrontal lesions including area 8 and part of area 6 were unable to learn it, although they were able to master unrelated tasks.

Olfaction

There are relatively few studies of olfactory-guided behavior in animals with frontal lesions, but it is known that both rats and monkeys are severely impaired at odor discriminations following orbital frontal lesions. In ad-

dition, cells have been identified in the orbital gyrus of the monkey that are specific to certain odors. These data add credence to the suggestion that there may be a region in the frontal cortex of mammals that can be considered to be the primary olfactory cortex.

Social Behavior

Several studies show that the frontal lobe lesions in rats, cats, and monkeys significantly alter social behavior. In one interesting study, Butter and Snyder removed the dominant (so-called alpha) male from each of several groups of monkeys. They removed the frontal lobes from half of the monkeys. When the animals were later returned to their groups, they all resumed the position of dominant male, but within a couple of days all the frontal monkeys were deposed and fell to the bottom of the group hierarchy.

Analogous studies of wild monkeys have shown similar results: frontal monkeys fall to the bottom of the group hierarchy and eventually die, because they are helpless alone. It is not known exactly how the social behavior of these animals has changed, but there is little doubt that it is as dramatic as the changes in the social behavior of humans.

Mobility

Perhaps the oldest established effect of frontal cortex removal in both rats and monkeys is an increase in activity, the first report dating back to Ferrier in 1886. Although there are actually few modern studies, the available data appear reliable, showing both rats and monkeys with orbital damage to be excessively active, an effect that is potentiated by food deprivation. Animals with dorsolateral lesions are not normally hyperactive, but they frequently appear hyperreactive to environmental stimuli, a behavioral response that often distracts them while performing neuropsychological tests.

Activity has not been studied systematically in human frontal lobe patients, but in our experience many such patients are hyperactive indeed, and it may present a real challenge to keep them settled in a testing situation. Further studies of general activity in both humans and other animals are needed before the nature of the disorder is understood.

Habituation

Habituation is a gradual quantitative response decrement that results from repeated exposure to a stimulus. For example, when one first enters a bakery, the odor are distinctive, but if one works in the same bakery, there is rapid habituation to the odors and they are no longer noticed. A number of studies using monkeys, rats, and cats have suggested that frontal cortex, possibly the dorsolateral region, is involved in normal habituation. Animals with frontal cortex lesions fail to habituate normally, if at all, to novel stimuli or environments, whereas stimulation of the frontal cortex accelerates habituation to similar stimuli. Thus, in the absence of frontal cortex the animals' behavior appears stereotyped and repetitive, behavior that may contribute to their increased locomotor activity. We are unaware of any studies of habituation in humans with frontal lobe lesions, but the reliability of this observation in a variety of nonhuman species suggests the worthiness of such studies.

Summary

There is no evidence that the frontal lobes of humans are qualitatively special, for frontal lobe lesions in species as diverse as rats and humans affect behavior in remarkably similar ways. It is probable that, in phylogeny, a significant specialization and elaboration of a basic movement control function has occurred, and that the complexity of movement control is highly correlated with the relative volume of the frontal lobe in mammals.

FRONTAL LOBE SYSTEMS

We have noted several times that the prefrontal cortex is part of a system that has an important role in the control of movement. Rosvold and his colleagues have postulated that there are actually two frontal lobe systems. One, a *dorsolateral system,* may involve the dorsolateral cortex, the anterodorsal sector of the caudate nucleus, the lateral portion of the dorsomedial thalamus, and the hippocampus. The other, an *orbital system,* may include the orbital cortex, the ventrolateral sector of thc caudate nucleus, the medial portion of the globus pallidus, the medial region of the dorsomedial thalamus, the septal nuclei, and the possibly the amygdala. Lesions of structures in either system would be expected to produce behavioral effects qualitatively similar to those observed from lesions of the dorsolateral or orbital regions respectively. Although there is anatomical and behavioral support for this type of frontal lobe system in nonhumans, it remains mostly theoretical for humans. Nevertheless, two lines of evidence tend to support the idea for humans. First, movement disorders, especially Parkinson's disease, produce symptoms that are similar to those of frontal lobe lesions—in particular reduced spontaneity of behavior, changed social behavior, and impaired corollary discharge. Second, Korsakoff's disease, which results from prolonged alcoholism (see Chapter 20), also produces several symptoms similar to frontal lobe damage. For example, Korsakoff's patients are as impaired at the Wisconsin card-sorting test as are frontal lobe patients.

Although the idea that there are two frontal lobe systems is intriguing, it is unlikely to derive much empirical support from human neuropsychology in the near future. The model must rely on research with nonhuman species.

REFERENCES

Ackerly, S. S. A case of bilateral frontal lobe defect observed for thirty years. In J. M. Warren and K. Akert, eds., *The Frontal Granular Cortex and Behavior*. New York: McGraw-Hill, 1964.

Benton, A. L. Differential effects of frontal lobe disease. *Neuropsychologia* 6:53–60, 1968.

Bizzi, E., and P. H. Schiller. Single unit activity in the frontal eye fields of unanesthetized monkeys during head and eye movement. *Experimental Brain Research* 10:151–158, 1970.

Blakemore, C. *Mechanics of the Mind*. Cambridge: Cambridge University Press, 1977.

Blumer, D., and D. F. Benson. Personality changes with frontal and temporal lobe lesions. In D. F. Benson and D. Blumer, eds., *Psychiatric Aspects of Neurologic Disease*. New York: Grune & Stratton, 1975.

Bossom, J. The effect of brain lesions on adaptation in monkeys. *Psychonomic Science* 2:45–46, 1965.

Brown, J. *Aphasia, Apraxia and Agnosia*. Springfield, Ill.: Charles C Thomas, 1972.

Butter, C. M. Habituation of responses to novel stimuli in monkeys with selective frontal lesions. *Science* 144:313–315, 1964.

Butter, C. M., and D. R. Snyder. Alterations in aversive and aggressive behaviors following orbital frontal lesions in rhesus monkeys. *Acta Neurobiologiae Experimentalis* 32:525–565, 1972.

Corkin, S. Tactually guided maze-learning in man: Effects of unilateral cortical excisions and bilateral hippocampal lesions. *Neuropsychologia*, 3:339–351, 1965.

Denny-Brown, D. The frontal lobes and their functions. In A. Feilnig, ed., *Modern Trends in Neurology*. New York: Hoeber-Harper, 1961.

Deuel, K. K. Loss of motor habits after cortical lesions. *Neuropsychologia* 15:205–215, 1977.

Divac, I. Neostriatum and functions of prefrontal cortex. *Acta Neurobiologiae Experimentalis* 32:461–478, 1972.

Drewe, E. A. Go-no-go learning after frontal lobe lesions in humans. *Cortex* 11:8–16, 1975.

Eichenbaum, H., R. A. Clegg, and A. Feeley. Reexamination of functional subdivisions of the rodent prefrontal cortex. *Experimental Neurology* 79:434–451, 1983.

Ferrier, D. *Functions of the Brain*, 2nd ed. London: Smith and Elder, 1886.

Feuchtwanger, E. As cited in Teuber, 1964.

Fuster, J. M. *The Prefrontal Cortex*. New York: Raven Press, 1980.

Fuster, J. M., and R. H. Bauer. Visual short-term memory deficit from hypothermia of frontal cortex. *Brain Research* 81:393–400, 1974.

Gentile, A. M., S. Green, A. Nieburgs, W. Schmelzer, and D. G. Stein. Disruption and recovery of locomotor and manipulatory behavior following cortical lesions in rats. *Behavioral Biology* 22:417–455, 1978.

Goldman, P. S., and H. E. Rosvold. Localization of function within the dorsolateral prefrontal cortex of the rhesus monkey. *Experimental Neurology* 27:291–304, 1970.

Goldstein, K. Mental changes due to frontal lobe damage. *Journal of Psychology* 17:187–208, 1944.

Griffin, J. O. Neurophysiological studies into habituation. In G. S. Horn and R. A. Hinde, eds., *Short Term Changes in Neural Activity and Behavior*. New York: Cambridge University Press, 1970.

Gross, C. G., and L. Weiskrantz. Some changes in behavior produced by lateral frontal lesions in the macaque. In J. M. Warren and K. Akert, eds., *The Frontal Granular Cortex and Behavior*. New York: McGraw-Hill, 1964.

Guitton, D., H. A. Buchtel, and R. M. Douglas. Disturbances of voluntary saccadic eye-movement mechanisms following discrete unilateral frontal-lobe removals. In G. Lennerstrand, D. S. Lee, and E. L. Keller, eds., *Functional Basis of Ocular Motility Disorders*. Oxford: Pergamon, 1982.

Harlow, H. F., R. T. Davis, P. H. Seftlage, and D. R. Meyer. Analysis of frontal and posterior association syndromes in brain damaged monkeys. *Journal of Comparative and Physiological Psychology* 45:419–429, 1952.

Hebb, D. O. Intelligence in man after large removals of cerebral tissue: Report of four left frontal lobe cases. *Journal of General Psychology* 21:73–87, 1939.

Hécaen, H., and M. L. Albert. Disorders of mental functioning related to frontal lobe pathology. In D. F. Benson and D. Blumer, eds., *Psychiatric Aspects of Neurologic Disease*. New York: Grune & Stratton, 1975.

Held, R. Dissociation of visual function by deprivation and rearrangement. *Psychology Forschung* 31:338–348, 1968.

Jacobsen, C. F. Studies of cerebral function in primates. *Comparative Psychology Monographs* 13:1–68, 1936.

Jones-Gotman, M., and B. Milner. Design fluency: The invention of nonsense drawings after focal cortical lesions. *Neuropsychologia* 15:653–674, 1977.

Kliest, K. As cited in Zangwill, 1966.

Kolb, B. Brain-behavior relationshps in the frontal cortex of the rat: A comparative review. *Brain Research Reviews,* in press.

Kolb, B., and B. Milner. Observations on spontaneous facial expression after focal cerebral excisions and after intracarotid injection of sodium Amytal. *Neuropsychologia* 19:514–515, 1981.

Kolb, B., and B. Milner. Performance of complex arm and facial movements after focal brain lesions. *Neuropsychologia* 19:505–514, 1981.

Kolb, B., R. J. Sutherland, and I. Q. Whishaw. A comparison of the contributions of the frontal and parietal association cortex to spatial localization in rats. *Behavioral Neuroscience* 97:13–27, 1983.

Kolb, B., and L. Taylor. Affective behavior in patients with localized cortical excisions: An analysis of lesion site and side. *Science* 214:89–91, 1981.

Kolb, B., and I. Q. Whishaw. Dissociation of the contributions of the prefrontal, motor, and parietal cortex to the control of movement in the rat: An experimental review. *Canadian Journal of Psychology* 37:211–232, 1983.

Konorski, J., H.-L. Teuber, and B. Zernicki. The frontal granular cortex and behavior. *Acta Neurobiologiae Experimentalis* 32:119–656, 1972.

Kuypers, H. G. J. M. Anatomy of the descending pathways. In V. B. Brooks, ed., *The Nervous System, Handbook of Physiology,* vol. 2. Baltimore: Williams & Wilkins, 1981.

Lashley, K. S. The problem of serial order in behavior. In F. A. Beach, D. O. Hebb, C. T. Morgan, and H. W. Nissen, eds., *The Neuropsychology of Lashley.* New York: McGraw-Hill, 1960.

Latto, R. The effects of bilateral frontal eye-field, posterior parietal or superior collicular lesions on visual search in the rhesus monkey. *Brain Research* 146:35–50, 1978.

Lawrence, D. G., and H. G. J. M. Kuypers. The functional organization of the motor system in the monkey: I. The effects of bilateral pyramidal lesions. *Brain* 91:1–14, 1968.

Luria, A. R. *The Working Brain.* New York: Penguin, 1973.

Markowitsch, H. J., and M. Pritzel. Comparative analysis of prefrontal learning functions in rats, cats and monkeys. *Psychological Bulletin* 84:817–837, 1977.

Miller, M. H. Dorsolateral frontal lobe lesions and behavior in the macaque: Dissociation of threat and aggression. *Physiology and Behavior* 17:209–213, 1976.

Milner, B. Some cognitive effects of frontal-lobe lesions in man. *Philosophical Transactions of the Royal Society of London* B298:211–226, 1982.

Milner, B. Some effects of frontal lobectomy in man. In J. M. Warren and K. Akert, eds., *The Frontal Granular Cortex and Behavior.* New York: McGraw-Hill, 1964.

Milner, B. Hemispheric specialization: Scope and limits. In F. O. Schmitt and F. G. Worden, eds., *The Neurosciences: Third Study Program.* Cambridge, Mass.: MIT Press, 1974.

Mishkin, M., Perseveration of central sets after frontal lesions in monkeys. In J. M. Warren and K. Akert, eds., *The Frontal Granular Cortex and Behavior.* New York: McGraw-Hill, 1964.

Mishkin, M., and F. J. Manning. Non-spatial memory after selective prefrontal lesions in monkeys. *Brain Research* 143:313–323, 1978.

Myers, R. E. Role of the prefrontal and anterior temporal cortex in social behavior and affect in monkeys. *Acta Neurobiologiae Experimentalis* 32:567–579, 1972.

Nauta, W. J. H. Neural associations of the frontal cortex. *Acta Neurobiologiae Experimentalis* 32:125–140, 1972.

Orgogozo, J. M., and B. Larsen. Activation of the supplementary motor area during voluntary movement in man suggests it works as a supramotor area. *Science* 206:847–850, 1979.

Pandya, D. N., and H. G. J. M. Kuypers. Cortico-cortical connections in the rhesus monkey. *Brain Research* 13:13–36, 1969.

Passingham, R. Information about movements in monkeys *(Macaca mulatta). Brain Research* 152:313–328, 1978.

Penfield, W., and J. Evans. The frontal lobe in man: A clinical study of maximum removals. *Brain* 58:115–133, 1935.

Perret, E. The left frontal lobe of man and the suppression of habitual responses in verbal categorical behavior. *Neuropsychologia* 12:323–330, 1974.

Petrides, M. Motor conditional associative learning after selective prefrontal lesions in the monkey. *Behavioural Brain Research* 5:407–413, 1982.

Petrides, M., and B. Milner. Deficits on subject ordered tasks after frontal- and temporal-lobe lesions in man. *Neuropsychologia* 20:249–262, 1982.

Pohl, W. Dissociation of spatial discrimination deficits following frontal and parietal lesions in monkeys. *Journal of Comparative and Physiological Psychology* 82:227–239, 1973.

Poppelreuter, W. *Die psychischen Schädigungen durch Kopfschuss im Kriege 1914/16,* vol. 1. Leipzig: Leopold Voss Verlag, 1917.

Potter, H., and N. Butters. An assessment of olfactory deficits in patients with damage to prefrontal cortex. *Neuropsychologia* 18:621–628, 1980.

Pribram, K. H. The primate frontal cortex—executive of the brain. In K. H. Pribram and A. R. Luria, eds., *Psychophysiology of the Frontal Lobes.* New York: Academic, 1974.

Pribram, K. H., and W. E. Tubbs. Short-term memory, parsing and the primate frontal cortex. *Science,* 156:1765–1767, 1967.

Ramier, A.-M., and H. Hécaen. Role respectif des atteintes frontales et de la lateralisation lésionnelle dans les deficits de la "fluence verbale." *Revue de Neurologie* 123:17–22, 1970.

Reitan, R. M., and L. A. Davison. *Clinical Neuropsychology.* New York: Wiley, 1974.

Renzi, E. de, and P. Faglioni. Normative data and screening power of a shortened version of the token test. *Cortex* 14:41–49, 1978.

Roland, P. E., B. Larsen, N. A. Lassen, and E. Skinhøj. Supplementary motor area and other cortical areas in organization of voluntary movements in man. *Journal of Neurophysiology* 43:118–136, 1980.

Rose, J. E., and C. N. Woolsey. The orbitofrontal cortex and its connections with the mediodorsal nucleus in rabbit, sheep and cat. *Research Publications of the Association of Nervous and Mental Disease* 27:210–232, 1948.

Rosenkilde, C. E. Functional heterogeneity of the prefrontal cortex in the monkey: A review. *Behavioral and Neural Biology* 25:301–345, 1979.

Rosvold, H. E. The frontal-lobe system: Cortical-subcortical interrelationships. *Acta Neurobiologiae Experimentalis* 32:439–460, 1972.

Rosvold, H. E., and M. Mishkin. Evaluation of the effects of prefrontal lobotomy on intelligence. *Canadian Journal of Psychology* 4:122–126, 1950.

Ruch, T. C., and H. A. Shenkin. The relation of area 13 on the surface of the frontal lobes to hyperactivity and hyperphagia in monkeys. *Journal of Neurophysiology* 6:349–360, 1943.

Semmes, J., S. Weinstein, L. Ghent, and H.-L. Teuber. Impaired orientation in personal and extrapersonal space. *Brain* 86:747–772, 1963.

Shipley, J. E., and B. Kolb. Neural correlates of species-typical behavior in the Syrian Golden Hamster. *Journal of Comparative and Physiological Psychology* 19:93–103, 1977.

Stitt, C., and D. Huntington. Some relationships among articulation, auditory abilities and certain other variables. *Journal of Speech and Hearing Research* 12:576–593, 1969.

Tanabe, T., H. Yarita, M. Iino, Y. Ooshima, and S. F. Takagi. An olfactory projection area in orbitofrontal cortex of the monkey. *Journal of Neurophysiology* 38:1269–1283, 1975.

Taylor, L. Psychological assessment of neurosurgical patients. In T. Rasmussen and R. Marino, eds., *Functional Neurosurgery.* New York: Raven Press, 1979.

Teuber, H.-L. The riddle of frontal lobe function in man. In J. M. Warren and K. Akert, eds., *The Frontal Granular Cortex and Behavior*. New York: McGraw-Hill, 1964.

Teuber, H.-L. Unity and diversity of frontal lobe function. *Acta Neurobiologiae Experimentalis* 32:615–656, 1972.

Teuber, H.-L., and M. Mishkin. Judgment of visual and postural vertical after brain injury. *Journal of Psychology* 38:161–175, 1954.

Tyler, H. R. Disorders of visual scanning with frontal lobe lesions. In S. Locke, ed., *Modern Neurology*. London: J. and A. Churchill, 1969.

Walker, E. A., and D. Blumer. The localization of sex in the brain. In K. J. Zulch, O. Creutzfeldt, and G. C. Galbraith, eds., *Cerebral Localization*. Berlin and New York: Springer-Verlag, 1975.

Warren, J. M., H. B. Warren, and K. Akert. The behavior of chronic cats with lesions in the frontal association cortex. *Acta Neurobiologiae Experimentalis* 32:345–392, 1972.

Warren, J. M., and K. Akert, eds. *The Frontal Granular Cortex and Behavior*. New York: McGraw-Hill, 1964.

Zangwill, O. L. Psychological deficits associated with frontal lobe lesions. *International Journal of Neurology* 5:395–402, 1966.

19

DISCONNECTION SYNDROMES

So far we have emphasized the importance of neocortical and subcortical regions in controlling various aspects of behavioral. We have associated particular behavioral deficits with different brain lesions and from these deficits have tried to infer the function of the missing region. In looking at brain function in this way we have postponed discussion of the function of the connections between various regions. In this chapter we consider the function of various cerebral connections and the effects of cutting them. The process of cutting connections is called *disconnection,* and the ensuing behavioral effects are therefore called *disconnection syndromes*. We begin by reviewing the major connections of the cerebral hemispheres.

ANATOMY OF CEREBRAL CONNECTIONS

There are three major types of connections of the neocortex: projection fibers, commissural fibers, and association fibers.

Projection Fibers

Projection fibers include ascending fibers from lower centers to the neocortex, such as projections from the thalamus, as well as descending fibers from the neocortex to the brainstem and spinal cord.

Commissural Fibers

Commissural fibers primarily function to join the two hemispheres and include principally the corpus callosum, anterior commissure, and hippocampal commissure. The **corpus callosum** provides the major connection of neocortical areas. Most homologous regions of the hemispheres are interconnected by this route, although there are exceptions. For example, area 6 has heavy connections not only with the contralateral area 6 but also with areas 4, 5, 7, and 39. Area 4, on the other hand, directly connects only with the contralateral area 4.

Furthermore, the prefrontal cortex and inferior parietal lobule are only partially interconnected, because portions of these regions are not connected with the contralateral hemisphere.

The *anterior commissure* is much smaller than the corpus callosum and functions to interconnect portions of the anterior temporal lobe, the amygdala, and the paleocortex of the temporal lobe surrounding the amygdala. In humans reported to have been born with no corpus callosum (a condition called agenesis of the corpus callosum), the anterior commissure is greatly enlarged to connect far greater regions of the neocortex.

The hippocampal commissure interconnects the hippocampal formations of the two hemispheres. Little is known about the significance of these connections.

Association Fibers

Two types of association fibers can be distinguished: (1) long fiber bundles that interconnect distant neocortical areas, and (2) short subcortical U-fibers that interconnect adjacent neocortical areas. The long fiber bundles include the uncinate fasciculus, the superior longitudinal fasciculus, the cingulum, the inferior longitudinal fasciculus, and the inferior frontal occipital fasciculus. These pathways were illustrated in Figure 1–11.

THE BEHAVIORAL EFFECTS OF DISCONNECTION

The clinical effects of disconnection were first seriously considered by Wernicke in 1874. He predicted the existence of an aphasic syndrome (conduction aphasia) that would result from severing fiber connections of the anterior and posterior speech zones. Later, in 1892, Déjérine was the first to demonstrate a distinctive behavioral deficit resulting from pathology of the corpus callosum. However, in a series of papers published around 1900 Leipmann most clearly demonstrated the importance of severing connections as an underlying causal factor in the effects of cerebral damage. Having carefully analyzed the behavior of a particular patient, Leipmann predicted a series of disconnections of the neocortex that could account for the behaviors. In 1906, after the patient died, Leipmann published the postmortem findings, which supported his hypothesis. He wrote extensively on the principle of disconnection, particularly with respect to the idea that some apraxias might result from disconnection. He reasoned that if a patient were given a verbal command to use the left hand in a particular way, only the verbal left hemisphere would understand the command. To move the left hand a signal would then have to travel from the left hemisphere through the corpus callosum to the right hemispheric region that controls movements of the left hand, as illustrated in Figure 19–1. Interrupting the portion of the corpus callosum that carried the command from the left hemisphere to the right would disconnect the right hemisphere's motor region from the command. Thus, although the subject comprehended the command, the left hand would be unable to follow it (see Figure 19–1). This apraxia would occur in the absence of weakness or incoordination of the left hand, as would occur if there were a lesion in the motor cortex of the right hemisphere, which controls the actual movement of the left hand.

Leipmann's deduction, although brilliant, was ignored for a number of reasons. First, it was published in German and so was not widely read by English-speaking neurologists; Leipmann's papers have only recently been translated into English by Doreen

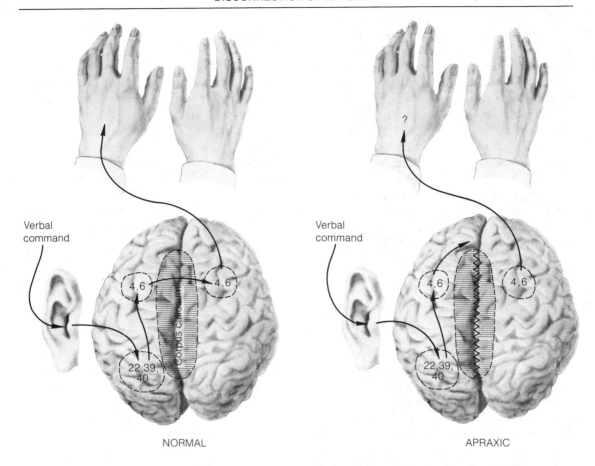

NORMAL   APRAXIC

FIGURE 19–1. Leipmann's theory of apraxia resulting from lesion of the corpus callosum. (The jagged line indicates section of the callosum.) The verbal command has no way of reaching the motor cortex (area 4) of the right hemisphere to move the left hand. Geschwind proposed that bilateral apraxia could result from a lesion disconnecting the posterior speech zone (areas 22, 39, and 40) from the motor cortex of the left hemisphere. In this case the verbal command cannot gain access to either the left or the right motor cortex.

Kimura. Second, except in the extremely unusual case of a patient with a natural lesion of only the corpus callosum, any observed behavioral deficits could be attributed to damage of gray matter itself without reference to connections. Third, a large number of animal studies consistently purported to demonstrate that no significant behavioral effects followed the cutting of the corpus callosum. Not until the late 1950s and 1960s

did it become clear that the results from the animal studies could be largely attributed to crude behavioral testing.

An important series of papers by Myers and by Sperry in the early 1950s revived interest in the effects of disconnecting neocortical regions. They examined the behavioral effects of severing the corpus callosum of cats. Their work confirmed others' earlier observations that the animals were virtually indistinguishable from their unoperated coun- terparts, and indeed appeared normal under most tests and training conditions. Unlike the previous studies, however, their studies re- vealed that under special training procedures the animals could be shown to have severe deficits. Thus, if the sensory information were allowed separate access to each hemisphere, each could be shown to have its own indepen- dent perceptual, learning, and memory proces- ses. Myers' and Sperry's remarkable results were quickly duplicated by dozens of labor- atories around the world. The corpus callosum did indeed have an important function. This conclusion has been clearly demonstrated in the subsequent studies by Sperry and his col- leagues on the effects of surgical disconnection of the cerebral hemispheres of humans for the treatment of intractable epilepsy (see Chapter 14).

The success of the Myers and Sperry experi- ments stimulated interest in other connections of the brain. Geschwind and his colleagues began to reassess the clinical effects of naturally occurring neocortical lesions as possibly in- dicating disconnection of various regions of the cerebral hemispheres. In parallel work, Mishkin and his colleagues began to construct animal models of human disconnection syn- dromes; by disconnecting related neocortical regions from one another, they have demon- strated their critical interdependence. In the remainder of this chapter we first discuss the work of Sperry on the "split-brain" pa- tient, this patient providing an excellent model of disconnection syndromes. Next we reconsider Geschwind's reinterpretation of three classic symptoms of cortical damage (aphasia, apraxia, and agnosia) as discon- nection syndromes. Finally, we briefly study Mishkin's animal models of disconnection in the visual and somesthetic systems, the only systems that have been studied in this way to date.

A HUMAN MODEL OF DISCONNECTION

Epileptic seizures may begin in a restricted region of one hemisphere (most frequently the temporal lobes) and then spread via the fibers of the corpus callosum or anterior com- missure to the homologous location in the opposite hemisphere. These seizures can us- ually be controlled by anticonvulsant medi- cation, but in some cases the medication is of little value, and the seizures may actually become life-threatening because they recur of- ten, sometimes several times in an hour. To relieve this seizure condition, the corpus callo- sum and anterior commissure can be surgically sectioned to prevent the spread of abnormal electrical activity from one hemisphere to the other.

From Leipmann's early theorizing it should be possible to demonstrate conditions such as apraxias in patients with this sort of surgery. Sperry and his colleagues have extensively studied the effects of hemispheric discon- nection on behaviors related to both sensory and motor systems.

Olfaction

Unlike all the other senses, the olfactory sys- tem is not crossed. The input from the left nostril goes straight back to the left hemi- sphere, and the input from the right nostril goes to the right hemisphere. Fibers travel- ing through the anterior commissure join the olfactory regions in each hemisphere, just as fibers traveling through the corpus callosum join the motor cortex of each hemi- sphere.

If the anterior commissure is severed, odors presented to the right nostril cannot be named, because the left hemisphere, where speech is centered, is disconnected from the informa- tion. Similarly, the right hemisphere has the information but has no control of speech. The olfactory function is still intact, however, because the patient can use the *left* hand to pick out an object, such as an orange, that corresponds to the odor smelled. In this case, no connection with speech is necessary, the right hemisphere both containing the olfactory information and controlling the left hand. If requested to use the right hand, the patient would be unable to pick out the object because the left hemisphere, which controls the right hand, is disconnected from the sensory information. Thus, the patient appears normal with one hand and anosmic with the other (see Figure 19–2).

Vision

As described previously (see Figure 14–4), the visual system is crossed. Information flashed tachistoscopically to one visual field travels selectively to the corresponding region of the visual cortex. Recall that by using this procedure researchers have demonstrated left and right visual field superiorities for different types of input. For example, verbal material (such as words) is more accurately perceived when presented to the right visual field, presumably because the input travels to the left, speech, hemisphere. On the other hand, various types of visuospatial input produce a left visual field superiority, since the right hemisphere appears to have a more important role in analyzing this information. Note, however, that the visual field superiority observed in normal subjects is *relative*. That is, words presented to the left visual field, and hence right hemisphere, are sometimes perceived, although not as accurately or consistently as when they are presented

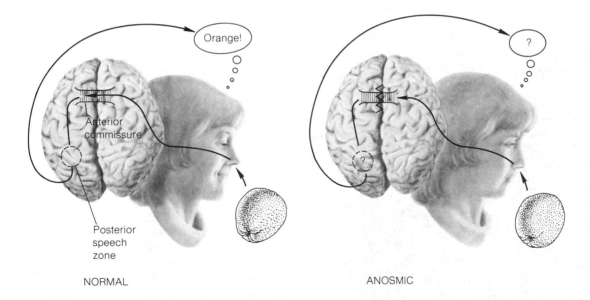

NORMAL   ANOSMIC

FIGURE 19–2. Anosmia resulting from section of the anterior commissure. (The jagged line indicates the lesion of the anterior commissure.) Olfactory input to the right nostril travels directly back into the right hemisphere and crosses the anterior commissure, thus gaining access to the left (speech) hemisphere. When the pathway is severed, the left hemisphere has no way of knowing what odor the right hemisphere perceived.

to the right visual field. The relative effects of course occur because either hemisphere potentially has access to input to the opposite hemisphere via the corpus callosum, which joins the visual areas (see Figure 14–5). In the commissurotomy patient there is no longer such access because the connection is severed. Since speech is housed in the left hemisphere of right-handed patients, visual information presented to the left visual field will be disconnected from verbal associations because the input goes to the right, nonlinguistic, hemisphere. Similarly, complex visual material presented to the right visual field will be inadequately processed, because it will not have access to the visuospatial abilities of the right hemisphere. It follows that if material is appropriately presented, it should be possible to demonstrate aphasia, agnosia, alexia, and acopia in a patient who ordinarily exhibits none of these symptoms. This is indeed the case, as we now demonstrate.

Consider the language-related deficits aphasia, alexia, and agnosia. If verbal material were presented to the left visual field, the commissurotomy patient would be unable to read it or to verbally answer questions about it, since the input is disconnected from the speech zones of the left hemisphere. Presentation of the same verbal material to the right visual field presents no difficulties, since the visual input projects to the verbal left hemisphere. Similarly, if an object is presented to the left visual field, the patient would be unable to name it and thus would appear to be either agnosic or aphasic. If presented to the right visual field, this same object would be correctly named, because the left visual cortex "perceives" the object and has access to the speech zones. Thus, we can see that the split-brain patient is aphasic, alexic, and agnosic if verbal material or an object requiring a verbal response is visually presented

to the right hemisphere but appears normal if material is presented to the left hemisphere.

A further deficit can be seen if the patient is asked to copy a complex visual figure. As discussed earlier, the right hemisphere is specialized for the perception of complex visual material. Since the right hemisphere controls the left hand we might predict that the left hand would be able to copy the figure but that the right hand, deprived of the expertise of the right hemisphere, would be severely impaired. The left hand draws the figure well, whereas the right hand cannot and is thus acopic.

Somesthesis

Like the visual system, the somatosensory system is completely crossed. Sensations of touch in the left hand travel to the right hemisphere, whereas those in the right hand travel to the left hemisphere. An object placed in the left hand can be named because the tactile information projects to the right hemisphere, crosses to the left, and subsequently has access to the speech zones. Similar, if a subject is blindfolded and the right hand molded to form a particular shape, the left hand is able to copy it because the tactile information goes from the right hand to the left hemisphere, then across the corpus callosum to the right hemisphere, and the left hand forms the same shape.

If the two hemispheres are disconnected from each other, the somatosenory functions of the left and right parts of the body become independent. For example, if some object is placed in the left hand of a blindfolded patient, who is then asked to choose the presented object from an array of objects, the left hand can pick out the object whereas the right hand cannot. If an object is placed in a blindfolded patient's right hand, the patient can name it, but not if it is placed in the left hand, because the sensory input is disconnected from the left, speech, hemisphere.

The disconnection effects can also be demonstrated without the use of objects. For example, if the patient is blindfolded and one hand is shaped in a particular way, the opposite hand is unable to mimic the posture. One hand has no way of "knowing" what the other hand is doing in the absence of input coming from the opposite hemisphere via the corpus callosum. If the patient is not blindfolded, however, he or she can find out what the opposite hand is doing simply by looking at it.

Audition

The auditory system is somewhat more complex than the other systems because it has both crossed and uncrossed connections (see Figure 14–8). Although the left hemisphere appears to receive most of its input from the right ear, it also receives input from the left ear. Words played into the left ear can therefore travel directly to the left hemisphere or can go to the right hemisphere and then to the left via the corpus callosum. In normal subjects dichotic listening tasks clearly show that the contralateral input is preferred because words presented to the right ear are selectively perceived over words presented to the left ear. Remember, however, that this difference is relative, some words presented to the left ear also being reported.

The bilateral anatomical arrangement just described appears to reduce the effects of disconnection, but nevertheless one effect has been demonstrated. In the dichotic listening task input from the left ear is totally suppressed; the patient reports only those words played to the right ear. That is, digits or words played to the right ear are reported, but no input to the left ear is reported. This is a little surprising, since words played to the left ear, even under these conditions, would have been

expected to attain some direct access to the left hemisphere. This direct access does not appear to occur.

Movement

Because the motor system is largely crossed, disconnection of the hemispheres could be predicted to induce several kinds of motor difficulties. First, on any task involving either a verbal command for the left hand to follow or verbal material for the left hand to write, a form of apraxia and agraphia could be expected, because the left hand does not receive instruction from the left hemisphere. That is, the left hand would be unable to follow the command (apraxia) or write (agraphia). These disabilities would not be seen in the right hand, which has access to the speech hemisphere. Similarly, if the right hand were asked to copy a geometric design it might be impaired (acopia) because it is disconnected from the right hemisphere, which ordinarily has a preferred role in the drawing of this type of material. These symptoms of disconnection are in fact observed in commissurotomy patients, although the severity of the deficit declines significantly over time after surgery, possibly because the left hemisphere's ipsilateral control is being used.

A second situation that might be expected to produce severe motor deficits in commissurotomy patients is one in which the two arms must be used in cooperation. Ordinarily, one hand is informed of what the other is doing via the connection of the corpus callosum. Preilowski and later Zaidel and Sperry carefully examined the effect of disconnection on this type of bimanual cooperative movement. Patients required to make alternating tapping movements of the index fingers were severely impaired at the task. Similarly, in a task similar to an Etch-a-Sketch, one requiring that a line inclined at an angle be traced, callosal patients did very poorly. This task requires the use of two cranks, one operated by each hand; one makes the tracing pen move vertically, whereas the other makes the tracing pen move horizontally. A high degree of manual cooperation is required to trace the line smoothly. If the hemispheres have undergone disconnection, this cooperation is severely retarded since the left and right motor systems are unable to gain information as to what the opposite side is doing, except indirectly, by the patient's watching them.

Dramatic illustrations of conflict between hands can be seen in the following descriptions.

> In one case the patient (W. J.) would repeatedly pick up a newspaper with his right hand and lay it down with his left hand. This would be performed several times until finally the left hand threw the newspaper on the floor. Another patient (R. Y.) was described by a physiotherapist: "He was buttoning his shirt with his right hand and the left hand was coming along just behind it undoing the buttons just as quickly as he could fasten them." However, as in the praxic impairments described earlier, instances of intermanual conflict were generally confined to the first postoperative months and again seemed related to the age of the patient and extent of extra-callosal damage. It is of interest to note that the same patients while inhibiting these episodes of intermanual conflict were able to use their left hand in a purposeful and cooperative manner when "not thinking of what they were doing." For example, they could pour coffee out of a pot held in the right hand into a cup held by its handle with the left hand. The above-mentioned peculiarities in motor functions were observed only in the complete split-brain patients. (Preilowski, 1975, p. 119)

The Problem of Partial Disconnection

Results from tests of callosal patients raise the question of whether a partial section of the corpus callosum would have as severe effects as a complete disconnection. Recently, surgeons have experimented with partial surgical disconnection of the hemispheres, hoping to attain the same clinical relief from seizures but with fewer neuropsychological side effects. Although the results are still preliminary, partial disconnection, in which the posterior part of the corpus callosum is left intact, appears to combine markedly milder effects than complete commissurotomy with the same therapeutic benefits for epilepsy. For example, Sperry and colleagues have found that patients with partial disconnection are significantly better at motor tasks such as the Etch-a-Sketch. Research on monkeys with partial commissurotomies suggests that the posterior portion of the corpus callosum (splenium) subserves visual transfer (as does the anterior commissure), whereas the region just in front of the splenium affects somatosensory transfer. The functions of the more anterior portions of the corpus callosum are largely unknown, but presumably transfer of motor information may be one function.

Conclusions

The results of studies on surgical disconnection of the hemispheres indicate that many symptoms, including aphasia, alexia, agnosia, agraphia, acopia, and apraxia, can be demonstrated *in the absence of any direct damage to particular cytoarchitectural or functional neocortical regions.* They can also occur for one side of the body and not the other. Symptoms such as aphasia, agnosia, etc., can be thought of as resulting from disconnection of cortical regions rather than as necessarily resulting from damage to cortical regions. We shall return to this idea below.

LESION EFFECTS REINTERPRETED AS DISCONNECTION SYNDROMES

In 1965, Geschwind published a theoretically significant monograph, "Disconnexion Syndromes in Animals and Man," that tied together a vast amount of literature and anticipated many of the effects of callosal surgery. Although Geschwind's arguments are complex, his thesis is that certain types of behavioral deficits can be seen as resulting from disconnections between the hemispheres, within a hemisphere, or a combination of both. The value of this monograph is not the review of data, but rather its forceful reintroduction of the concept first proposed by Déjérine and Leipmann nearly 70 years earlier, that disconnecting neocortical regions can cause a variety of neurological symptoms. To demonstrate the utility of the model we discuss only the three classic symptoms of left hemisphere damage: apraxia, agnosia, and alexia.

Apraxia

Earlier in this chapter we noted that if a lesion of the corpus callosum disconnected the left hand from the left hemisphere, that hand would be unable to respond to verbal commands and would be considered apraxic (see Figure 19–1). Suppose, however, that the right hand is unable to respond to verbal commands. Geschwind speculated that this deficit results from a lesion in the left hemisphere that disconnects its motor cortex, which controls the right hand from the speech zone; thus, the right hand could not respond to verbal commands and would be considered apraxic.

Although Geschwind's model can explain bilateral apraxia in some patients, it must be emphasized that disconnection is not the only cause of apraxia. Because the posterior cortex has direct access to the subcortical neural

mechanisms of arm and body movements (as described in Chapter 11), parietal input need not go through the motor cortex except for control of finger movements. Furthermore, as we noted earlier, patients with sections of the corpus callosum are initially apraxic but show substantial recovery despite a disconnection of the motor cortex of the left and right hemispheres.

Agnosia and Alexia

Geschwind theorized that agnosia and alexia can be produced by disconnections of the posterior speech area from the visual association cortex. They can be produced by a lesion that disconnects the visual association region on the left from the speech zone in addition to a lesion which disconnects the right visual association cortex from the speech zone by damaging the corpus callosum, as illustrated in Figure 19–3. Thus the patient, although able to talk, is unable to identify words or objects because the visual information is disconnected from the posterior speech zone in the left hemisphere.

Conclusions

In this section lesions that disconnect regions within or between hemispheres were demonstrated to at least theoretically be able to produce many neuropsychological symptoms is likely that the effects of naturally occurring lesions result from a combination of direct damage to a region and disconnection of different regions. If so, localization of brain damage on the basis of behavior becomes more complicated.

EXPERIMENTAL VERIFICATION OF DISCONNECTION EFFECTS

Disconnection of different neocortical regions to produce a variety of behavioral symptoms

Posterior speech zone

17, 18, 19

NORMAL

AGNOSIC, ALEXIC

FIGURE 19–3. Geschwind's model of agnosia and alexia resulting from disconnection of the visual cortex from the posterior speech zone. (The jagged lines indicate the lesion of the pathways.) Normally, the visual input of both hemispheres travels to the posterior speech zone and tertiary sensory cortex, where it is processed to allow speech describing the written word or object. In the absence of the connection this is no longer possible, and agnosia and alexia result.

can be used experimentally to demonstrate the function of various brain regions. Downer, for example, devised an ingenious experiment to demonstrate the effects of temporal lobectomy. He removed one temporal lobe in a monkey that had previously undergone a split-brain operation. He then showed that if only the hemisphere with the temporal lobectomy receives visual information, the monkey acts like Klüver and Bucy's monkeys, being completely tame and placid. On the other hand, when the visual input is restricted to the intact hemisphere, the monkey is normal and far from tame. So astounding was this phenomenon that it was a first widely doubted, but since it has been replicated by other investigators it is now generally accepted. The experiment clearly demonstrates that the two hemispheres can act independently of each other.

Mishkin and others have exploited the disconnections of different brain areas in animals to demonstrate the functional connections in the hierarchical organization of the visual system and, more recently, the somatosensory system. This research clearly demonstrates the usefulness of the disconnection approach and has led to significant progress in our understanding of the sensory systems.

The Visual System

Previous discussion of the visual system's hierarchical nature did not consider the connections between the system's various regions. These are summarized in Figure 19–4 A. In each hemisphere connections run from area 17 to area 18 and 19 in the same hemisphere. Connections from 18 and 19 cross the corpus callosum to the analogous area on the opposite

A

B

C

side, as well as connecting with area 20 on the same side. Area 20 connects to area 21 and the amygdala on the same side, and on the opposite side via the anterior commissure. What would happen to vision if the connections were cut? This question has been addressed in experiments using monkeys as subjects.

Consideration of this question requires that monkeys first be tested to determine their visual capabilities. The easiest method is to teach the animal a visual discrimination such as between a "+" and a "0." Food reinforcement is associated with one stimulus and not with the other. The monkey's task is to identify the correct stimulus and respond to it. Control monkeys learn this problem in 100 to 150 trials or fewer, and so if a monkey that has been operated on fails to learn this problem in 1000 trials, it is assumed that it will not learn it at all; the lesion can thus be inferred to have some important effect on the monkey's ability to discriminate visual stimuli.

By using tasks of this sort, Mishkin and others have demonstrated that bilateral lesions in areas 17, 18, and 19, or in 20 and 21, result in impaired, or abolished, solution of visual-discrimination problems. Because unilateral lesions do not have such an effect, what seems to be necessary is one intact area each of 17, 18, and 19, and one intact area 20 and 21. There is, however, one constraint: the remaining regions must be connected. Thus, in Figure 19–4 B a lesion in area 17 on the right and in 20 and 21 on the left does not disturb performance, since there is still an intact system that can be used. If the connection between the hemispheres is now severed, the neocortical areas

FIGURE 19–4. Disconnection effects in the visual system of monkeys. A. The visual system is intact. B. The left visual cortex still has access to the visual association cortex of the right hemisphere, and so vision is still possible. C. The intact components of the visual system are disconnected, producing major visual deficits. (After Mishkin, 1979.)

are still intact but not connected, and the result is failure on the visual–discrimination problem (Figure 19–4 C). Clearly the neocortical regions do not function properly if they are not connected to each other.

Mishkin first studied the region of areas 20 and 21, thinking them to be the final step in the neocortical visual system. More recently he has studied the problem of how visual stimuli might gain what he calls "motivational" or "emotional" significance. Recall that the Klüver–Bucy monkeys with bilateral temporal lobectomies attached no significance to visual stimuli. Thus, they would repeatedly taste nasty-tasting objects, or place inedible objects in their mouths. In his 1965 paper Geschwind proposed that this symptom represented a disconnection of the amygdala from the visual system. That is, theoretically at least, although an animal's visual sensory system might be intact, the animal would behave as if it were not because it is disconnected from another system that attaches meaning to visual information. Figure 19–5 A illustrates the additional connections when the amygdala is included in an extended visual system. Areas 20 and 21 connect with the amygdala on the same side and on the opposite side via the anterior commissure.

To test Geschwind's proposal, Mishkin devised the experiment illustrated in Figure 19–5 parts B and C. The amygdala was lesioned on the left and the inferior temporal cortex on the right. This arrangement left one complete system of areas 17, 18, 19, 20, 21 and amygdala, and using it the monkey's performance on visual problems was normal, as would be expected. The anterior commissure was then cut, leaving all the necessary pieces of the system intact but disconnecting the intact amygdala from the neocortical portion of the system. Performance on visual problems instantly deteriorated, indicating that there was some in-terruption of the normal processing of visual material, as would be predicted from Geschwind's model. Other experiments by Mishkin and his colleagues have demonstrated that the orbital frontal cortex may also play an important role in the system, possibly to guide behavioral responses to biologically relevant visual information.

In another application of the disconnection model to studying the visual system, Nakamura and Mishkin have shown blindness in monkeys after disconnection of the intact visual system from nonvisual regions. Monkeys received unilateral decortications in which only those regions removed as shown in Figure 19–4, in addition to the limbic cortex, were spared. Then the cerebral commissures and contralateral optic tract were severed. Unexpectedly, the animals were blind! None of the animals showed any detectable reaction to visually presented stimuli, whether these were food, fearful objects, threats, or sudden movements. When placed in an unfamiliar environment, they bumped into obstacles and found food objects only by touching them accidentally or exploring for them tactually. Although some of the monkeys showed some recovery over time, others did not, remaining functionally blind even two years after surgery. Further experiments revealed that electrophysiologically the visual cortex was still functioning, yet the animals behaved as though it no longer functioned at all. The results point to an important role of the nonvisual cortex in visual perception and demonstrate the importance of studying connections as well as areas of a functional system.

The Somatosensory System

The logic used in studying the connection of the visual system can be applied to the study of the somatosensory system. Consider the following type of experiment. A monkey is trained to discriminate between two objects by touch alone, using just one hand. Once this problem is learned, the opposite hand, when tested, performs well on the task, either because the information stored in the trained hemisphere is accessible to that hand (see Figure 19–6) or because the information is stored in both hemispheres. The next step is to cut the corpus callosum. Failure of the left hand to solve the problem would indicate that memory of the task is stored in the trained hemisphere. The hand indeed fails, indicating that the memory of the task is stored in the trained hemisphere. Notice, however, that the trained hand will still be able to solve the problem. The next question to ask is: Which connections within the trained hemisphere are necessary to continue to perform normally on this task? Mishkin proposes that the connections are something like those diagrammed in Figure 19–6. That is, the primary somatosensory cortex is connected to the secondary somatosensory cortex of both hemispheres. This region in turn is connected to the medial temporal region and/or the orbital frontal region. If this is true, then the following predictions can be made. First, a lesion at point *a* in Figure 19–6 B would render the left hand unable to do a task learned by the right hand because the memory is in the trained hemisphere, as noted above. Second, a lesion of *b* or *c* would render the right, trained hand unable to do the problem because the primary area is disconnected from the remainder of the system. These predictions remain to be tested directly. Notice that if there were

FIGURE 19–5. Disconnection of affect from visual input. A. The connections of the normal visual system, including both the callosal and anterior commissural connections. B. Even if parts of the system are damaged, it can still function. C. If the anterior commissure is severed, visual input is separated from affect, resulting in visual deficits. (After Mishkin, 1979.)

FIGURE 19–6. Mishkin's somatosensory model. A. The major intracortical connections of the somatosensory system involved in performing a tactile discrimination. Input travels from the hand to areas 1, 2, and 3, to area 43, and then to the medial temporal and orbital frontal areas. This input then travels to the motor cortex to produce a response. B. A lesion at *a* would render the left hand unable to perform a task learned by the right because the memory is in the left hemisphere. Also, *b* and *c* show that lesions at these points would render the trained right hand unable to perform the task because the primary area is disconnected from the remainder of the system. (After Mishkin, 1979.)

lesions to *b* or *c*, the callosum would not have to be cut, because the memory is not stored in the opposite hemisphere.

CONCLUSIONS

We have demonstrated that the connections of various cortical and subcortical regions are as important as the regions themselves in understanding the effects of brain damage. Conditions such as apraxia, agnosia, and alexia may be produced by disconnections of neocortical regions that normally function as part of an interconnected system. In humans it is extremely difficult to know whether behavioral symptoms are a result of disconnection or of regional damage, but in experimental work with nonhumans the data are much clearer. Mishkin and his colleagues have clearly shown that the visual and possibly the somatosensory systems are composed of a series of sequential steps beginning with the primary sensory cortex and terminating in the medial temporal lobe and/or orbital frontal cortex.

REFERENCES

Akelaitis, A. J. A study of gnosis, praxis and language following section of the corpus callosum and anterior commissure. *Journal of Neurosurgery* 1:94–102, 1944.

Downer, J. L. de C. Changes in visual gnostic functions and emotional behavior following unilateral temporal pole damage in the "split-brain" monkey. *Nature* 191:50–51, 1961.

Gazzaniga, M. S. *The Bisected Brain*. New York: Appleton-Century-Crofts, 1970.

Geschwind, N. Disconnexion syndromes in animals and man. *Brain* 88:237–294, 585–644, 1965.

Klüver, H., and P. C. Bucy. Preliminary analysis of functions of the temporal lobes in monkeys. *Archives of Neurology and Psychiatry* 42:979–1000, 1939.

Mishkin, M. Analogous neural models for tactile and visual learning. *Neuropsychologia* 17:139–152, 1979.

Myers, R. E. Functions of the corpus callosum in interocular transfer. *Brain* 57:358–363, 1956.

Nakamura, R. K., and M. Mishkin. Blindness in monkeys following non-visual cortical lesions. *Brain Research* 188:572–577, 1980.

Nebes, R. D. Hemispheric specialization in commissurotomized man. *Psychological Bulletin* 81:1–14, 1974.

Preilowski, B. Bilateral motor interaction: Perceptual-motor performance of partial and complete "split-brain" patients. In K. J. Zulch, O. Creutzfeldt, and G. C. Galbraith, eds., *Cerebral Localization*. Berlin and New York: Springer-Verlag, 1975.

Sperry, R. W. Lateral specialization in the surgically separated hemispheres. In F. O. Schmitt and F. G. Worden, eds., *Neurosciences: Third Study Program*. Cambridge, Mass.: MIT Press, 1974.

Spiegler, B. J., and M. Mishkin. Evidence for the sequential participation of inferior temporal cortex and amygdala in the acquisition of stimulus-reward associations. *Behavioural Brain Research* 3:303–317, 1981.

Zaidel, D., and R. W. Sperry. Some long term motor effects of cerebral commissurotomy in man. *Neuropsychologia* 15:193–204, 1977.

PART FIVE

HIGHER FUNCTIONS

Just as there has been a long tradition in neurology of studying the lobes of the brain, so has there been a long tradition in psychology of studying memory, language, emotional behavior, and spatial behavior. Chapters 20 through 23 examine brain function from the perspective of the psychologist by focusing on the problems in which psychologists have traditionally had an interest. Of course, some of the things discussed in Part Four will come up again, but the perspective should be sufficiently different and fresh to make the retelling of the tale worthwhile.

20

MEMORY

Psychologists began studying memory in the mid-19th century, the first monograph, Ebbinghaus's, being published in 1885. Memory, however, has not been the sole province of psychologists. It has been a topic of interest to philosophers from the time of Plato and Aristotle, and more recently it formed an important part of Freud's psychoanalytic theory. The neuropsychological study of memory dates back to about 1915, when Karl Lashley embarked on a lifetime project to identify the neural locations of learned habits. In most of his experiments he either removed portions of the neocortex or made cuts of fiber pathways in hopes of preventing transcortical communication between sensory and motor regions of the cortex. After hundreds of experiments Lashley was still unable to interfere with specific memories. In 1950 he concluded that "it is not possible to demonstrate the isolated localization of a memory trace anywhere in the nervous system. Limited regions may be essential for learning or retention of a particular activity, but . . . the engram is represented throughout the region."

Ironically, only three years later, in 1953, a neurosurgeon, William Scoville, inadvertently made one of the most influential findings in neuropsychology, when he operated on the now famous patient H.M. Bilateral removal of the hippocampus in H.M. made him amnesic for virtually all events following the operation. From Lashley's extensive work no one could have predicted that removal of any structure, let alone a structure that was once believed to be primarily olfactory in function, would result in a person remembering things from the distant past but not from the recent past! The surgery had interfered with the process of storing or retrieving new memories but had not touched stored memories themselves. The case of H.M. revolutionized the study of the memory process and shifted the emphasis from a search for the location of memory to an analysis of the process of storing memories. Indeed, Scoville and Milner's description of H.M. is probably the second most influential observation ever made in neuropsychology, with only Broca's surpassing it. Today, few areas in experimental psychology are as active as those relating to the processes involved in human memory.

In this chapter we describe the role of the temporal, frontal, and parietal lobes in memory. Specific attention is paid to the complementary specialization of the left and right hemispheres for the storage of verbal and nonverbal material, respectively. We review the various disorders of memory, neuropsychological theories of memory, and studies of memory processes in nonhumans. But before we consider the facts regarding the pathology of memory let us examine several theoretical issues.

THE NATURE OF MEMORY

What Is Memory?

Memory is a process that results in a relatively permanent change in behavior. It is never observed and is always inferred. In other words, we cannot identify memories in the brain, but since behavior changes with experience, we logically infer that some process must occur to account for the behavioral change. The lesson to be learned from Lashley is that no region in the nervous system can be pointed to as the place where we remember. Lesions to a number of brain regions disturb memory, but these regions do not house memory or memories. They can be said only to be more involved in the process of remembering than other regions. It is likely that groups of neurons in different parts of the brain, especially in the cerebral hemispheres, are more or less important for the remembering of different types of information (e.g., verbal, pictorial), but even this specialization is relative rather than absolute. It does not happen, for example, that a person is totally amnesic for verbal material but remembers nonverbal material.

If memories are not stored as discrete things

in the brain, how might they be stored? This complex question has no clear answer as yet, but an analogy may help illustrate the kind of process that could be involved. Imagine a hill; water poured onto the soil at its top runs down the hill, eroding small channels in the earth. If more water is poured on the hill, most of it follows the same route of the first water, further deepening the channels. Still more water continues the process. Since the water will always take the same route down the hill, we could say that there is a "memory" for that route. In neurological terms we could conceive of the brain as the hill and the process of memory as the route. Sensory experience enters the brain (top of the hill), flows through the brain (the channels in the hill), and produces behavior (leaves the hill) at the bottom. We can see, therefore, that the memory was not stored in a place but, rather, was a function of the activity of the entire brain. We do not wish to belabor this analogy, nor for it to be taken literally, but it does demonstrate a simple way in which to conceive of memory as a process of neuronal connectivity rather than as a thing to be found in the brain.

What Do We Remember from an Experience?

To consider the pathology of memory we must first examine what is normally remembered. In his classic book *Remembering* (1932), Bartlett made the point that remembering cannot be regarded as the mere revival of previous experience; rather, it is a process of active reconstruction. In his words:

> Remembering is not the re-excitation of innumerable fixed, lifeless and fragmentary traces. It is an imaginative reconstruction, or construction, built out of the relation of our attitude towards a whole active mass of organized past reactions or experience . . . and to a little outstanding detail which commonly appears in image or in language form. It is thus hardly ever really exact, even in the most rudimentary

cases of rote recapitulation. . . . (Bartlett, 1932, pp. 213–214)

It looks as if what is said to be reproduced is, far more generally than is commonly admitted, really a construction serving to justify whatever impression may have been left by the original. It is this "impression," rarely defined with much exactitude, which most readily persists. So long as the details which can be built up around are such that they would give a "reasonable" setting, most of us are fairly content, and are apt to think that what we build we have literally retained. (Bartlett, 1932, p. 176)

In other words, events are not stored in toto; only certain critical elements are stored from which the event can be reconstructed. The more cues or elements that are provided contextually, the more exactly the event can be reconstructed and "remembered."

Consider our hill analogy again. If only a trickle of water (minimal sensory input) is poured on the hill, the water will trace only part of the route to the bottom, bypassing many of the small side channels. As more water (i.e., more contextual information) is added, it travels faster down the hill, tracing more and more of the various channels originally followed (i.e., "remembers" the route more precisely).

After a long delay, remembering may identify correctly the essential elements of sensory experience yet incorporate additional elements that, although compatible with the essential sensory experience, are erroneous. It is widely believed that this incorrect embellishment of the critical experience may account for the fallibility of eyewitness evidence in which plausible but erroneous details are "remembered." To return to our hill analogy, if water has not been poured on the hill recently, the channels become less distinct because of environmental processes such as wind erosion and so on. The major channels remain passable, but many of the smaller channels may be lost. When water is

again poured on the hill, it retraces the major route but the details of the smaller side channels are lost and new ones, which may or may not coincide with the original, are formed.

Bartlett's proposition that remembering is reconstruction is particularly important in understanding the pathology of memory. An apparent defect in memory could result from a disorder not only in the storage of sensory experience but also in the later reconstruction of sensory experience from the critical features. Indeed, in some disorders, such as the amnesia associated with Korsakoff's disease (see below), a deficit in reconstruction may well prove to be a significant component.

Two Types of Memory

In 1890 William James distinguished between what he called *primary* memory, one that endured for a very brief period of time, and *secondary* memory, "the knowledge of a former state of mind after it has already once dropped from consciousness" (James, 1890, p. 648). Not until 1958, however, were separate short-term and long-term memories specifically postulated by Broadbent, although a number of authors (e.g., Miller) had hinted at this possibility. Since Scoville and Milner's description of H. M. the concept of two memory systems, short-term and long-term, has become central to neuropsychological theory. Neuropsychological evidence now supports the concept, since patients may suffer one kind of memory loss and not the other.

An experiment by Hebb nicely demonstrates the two kinds of memory behaviorally. College students were asked to repeat strings of digits, such as 83759247. The number of digits that can be recalled is termed the memory span. The maximum memory span is about eight. There is little hope of repeating eight digits unless we listen very carefully and then repeat them at once. The memory is brief, and it is striking that even with sustained concentration items in short-term memory fade very quickly and are lost. In Hebb's experiment, nine digits were read aloud to the subjects. Since nine digits are beyond the memory span of most subjects, few correctly recalled the nine. The subjects were then read another set of digits, then a third, and so on, for a total of 24 sets of nine digits. However, unknown to the subjects, every third set repeated the first set. The results showed (see Figure 20–1) that although the short-term memory for nine digits is very brief, the subjects gradually learned the repeating series, as it was evidently stored in long-term memory. Hebb proposed that listening to a set of digits does more than set up a short-term memory. He suggested that some other long-term change must also be beginning and is left behind in the nervous system. Although hearing another string of digits appears to completely wipe out the first set, only the short-term memory is wiped out completely, since long-term memory gradually develops as the repeating set is learned.

Hebb went a step further from the behavioral data and developed a theory of the neurological basis of short-term and long-term memory in his 1949 book. His genius

lay in using the associational learning theory of Hull and his contemporaries in the 1930s and 1940s and in using what was known of nervous system activity to describe the basis of learning and memory. Hebb argued that short-term memory is an active process of limited duration, and that long-term memory involves an actual structural change in the nervous system.

Hebb realized from the earlier anatomical work of Lorente de Nó that neurons in the brain are interconnected with many other neurons, and, in turn, each neuron receives input from many synapses on its dendrites and cell body. The resulting neuronal loops (see Figure 20–2) contain neurons whose output signal may be either excitatory or inhibitory. Although the neuronal loops are usually drawn as though they were in the cortex, many of the loops probably run from the cortex to the thalamus or other subcortical structures, such as the hippocampus, and back to the cortex. Because each neuron is believed to both send and receive thousands of outputs and inputs, the number of possible neuronal loops is truly immense.

In Hebb's theory each psychologically important event, whether a sensation, percept,

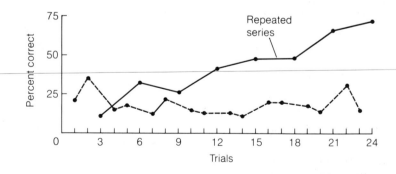

FIGURE 20–1. Performances on the Hebb recurring-digits test. Subjects were read sets of nine digits to recall immediately. Unbeknownst to the subjects every third set repeated the first set. The subjects gradually learned the repeating series, but they continued to do poorly on the novel series. (After Hebb, 1961.)

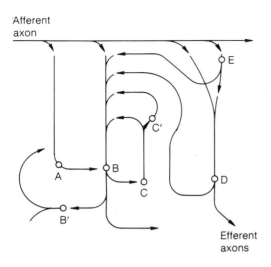

Afferent
axon

Efferent
axons

FIGURE 20-2. Simplified diagram of the interconnections of neurons to form neuronal loops. The entering
axon excites four neurons, A, B, D, and E. Of these, B and
D send impulses out of the system (efferent axons) to
excite other systems. A-B-B', B-C, and B-C-C' form
closed loops. (After Hebb, 1972.)

memory, thought, emotion, etc., is conceived
to be the flow of activity in a given neuronal
loop. Hebb proposed that the synapses in a
particular path become functionally connected
to form a **cell assembly.** At this point Hebb
made the assumption that if two neurons,
A and B, are excited together, they become
linked functionally. In Hebb's words:
"When an axon of cell A is near enough to
excite a cell B and repeatedly or persistently
takes part in firing it, some growth process or metabolic change takes place in one
or both cells such that A's efficiency, as one
of the cells firing B, is increased" (Hebb,
1949, p. 62). In Hebb's view the most probable
way in which one cell could become more
capable of firing another is that synaptic
knobs grew or became more functional,
increasing the area of contact between the
afferent axon and efferent cell body and
dendrites.

In Hebb's view the cell assembly is a system
that is initially organized by a particular sensory event but is capable of continuing its
activity after the stimulation has ceased. Hebb
proposed that to produce functional changes in
synaptic transmission the cell assembly must
be repeatedly activated. After the initial sensory input the assembly would therefore re-
verberate. Repeated reverberation could then
produce the structural changes. Clearly this
conception of information storage could explain the phenomena of short-term and long-
term memory: short-term memory is reverberation of the closed loops of the cell assembly; long-term memory is more structural, a
lasting change in synaptic connections.

In Hebb's theory there is yet another factor
in long-term memory. For the structural
synaptic changes to occur there must be a
period in which the cell assembly is left relatively undisturbed. Hebb referred to this process of structural change as consolidation, a
period believed to require 15 minutes to an
hour. Its existence was supported by observations that retention failed when brain function
was disrupted soon after learning, as, for example, in the amnesia for events just prior to a
concussion. The description of H.M.'s case
invited a logical extrapolation of Hebb's
theory: the hippocampus was assumed to be
especially important to the process of consolidation, although just how it is involved
could not be specified. New material is not
remembered because it is not consolidated; old
material is remembered because it was consolidated before the hippocampal damage.

Finally, Hebb assumed that any cell assembly could be excited by others. This idea
provided the basis for thought or ideation.
The essence of an "idea" is that it occurs
in the absence of the original environmental
event that it corresponds to.

The beauty of Hebb's theory is that it
attempted to explain psychological events by

the physiological properties of the nervous system. Now, over 30 years since Hebb's landmark volume, his theory remains the best attempt to combine the principles of psychological reality and the facts of neuroscience. In a recent, thoughtful review Goddard revisited the cell assembly and found that, with a few modifications, it is still a sound metaphor for psychological activity. Goddard bases his argument largely on recent work providing physiological confirmation for Hebb's argument that there are separate neurological substrates for short-term and long-term memory. On the basis of earlier work by Eccles and others, Bliss and Gardner-Medwin demonstrated unequivocally in 1973 that electrical stimulation of a neuron can produce either brief or long-lasting changes in synaptic transmission, according to the characteristics of the brain stimulation. Brief pulses of current are delivered to an axon over a few seconds and the magnitude of the response is recorded from areas known to receive projections from the stimulated axon. After a stable baseline of response to the stimulation has been established the stimulation is changed to one of high frequency, driving the system very hard. This high-frequency stimulation is then discontinued and the brief test pulses are resumed. The magnitude of the postsynaptic response can thus be compared with the original baseline and the time course of the decay of changes in response magnitude can be measured as well. Two significant findings emerge from this study. First, response magnitude markedly increases immediately after the high-frequency stimulation (see Figure 20–3). This increase declines over time and returns to baseline, the rate of decline depending on the details of the stimulation. This short-term increase is called *posttetanic potentiation*. Second, the change in response magnitude may not decline to baseline but instead remain elevated, possibly for days or as long as is technically practical to

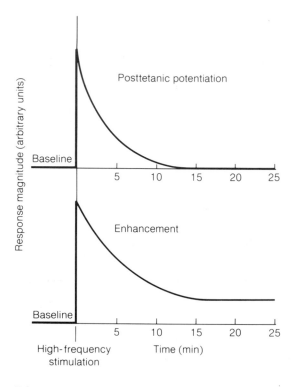

FIGURE 20–3. Time course of change in response magnitude following high-frequency stimulation. In the upper curve the response magnitude returns to baseline, a phenomenon described as post tetanic potentiation. In the lower curve the response strength does not return to baseline, indicating enhancement. (After Goddard, 1979.)

measure it. McNaughton has labeled this phenomenon *enhancement*. In some cases enhancement may be present after two months, and Barnes has shown that enhancement is prolonged by occasional repetition of the high-frequency stimulation. The original studies of posttetanic potentiation and enhancement were done on the hippocampus, but these phenomena can be demonstrated elsewhere in the brain.

Goddard emphasized the similarity between the phenomena of short-term memory and posttetanic potentiation and between long-term memory and enhancement. He proposed that these physiological events provide a strong basis for Hebb's neuropsychological theory. As attractive as the physiological work is as a model of short-term and long-term memory, it is still a substantial theoretical leap to understanding the effects of lesions on memory, such as the differential effects of temporal lobe and parietal lobe lesions on short-term and long-term memory respectively. This apparent complication may be resolved in the future as more is learned about the mechanisms of enhancement and posttetanic potentiation. The important point for us now is that there is tentative evidence to support Hebb's theory. As Goddard states:

> It is a tribute to Hebb that, even though some of his postulates concerning synaptic mechanisms were wrong, it is only by adopting his theoretical perspective that [we] have been able to see how the newly discovered details of synaptic plasticity have any importance at all. (Goddard, 1979, p. 22)

Terminology

The terminology in studies of disorders of memory can be confusing. **Amnesia** refers to the partial or total loss of memory. A difficulty in recalling events prior to the onset of the amnesia is known as **retrograde amnesia.** An inability to remember events subsequent to the onset of the amnesia is known as **anterograde amnesia.** These amnesias are usually not complete but patchy, some events being remembered and others not.

THE TEMPORAL LOBES AND MEMORY

The first suggestion that the temporal lobes might play a critical role in human memory was provided by Bekhterev in 1899. He reported a patient who had shown a severe memory impairment, and he demonstrated on autopsy a bilateral softening in the region of the uncus, hippocampus, and adjoining medial temporal cortex (see Figure 17–2).

In the 1950s the importance of the hippocampus in human memory was clearly demonstrated in reports describing several patients with bilateral hippocampal damage. Scoville and Milner's patient H.M. is the most thoroughly studied, having been followed for more than 30 years. He was a motor winder by trade and had experienced generalized epileptic seizures that had grown progressively worse in frequency and severity despite very high doses of medication. On 23 August 1953 William Scoville performed a bilateral medial temporal lobe resection in an attempt to stop the seizures. Afterward H.M. experienced a severe anterograde memory impairment that has persisted with little improvement to this day.

The Case of H.M.

H.M.'s IQ is above average (118 on the Wechsler Adult Intelligence Scale), and he performed normally on several different types of perceptual tests such as the Mooney closure test (see Chapter 10). H.M.'s memory for events prior to the surgery is good, as is his capacity to recall remote events such as incidents from his school days or jobs he held in his late teens or early twenties, prior to his surgery. Socially, H.M. is quiet and well mannered. He dresses neatly but has to be reminded when to shave. He speaks in a monotone but articulates his words well and has a vocabulary in keeping with his above-average intelligence. His language comprehension is normal and he understands complex verbal material, including jokes.

H.M.'s recall of personal events is interesting and enlightening, as witnessed by the following description. Notice his severe handicap in everyday life and his ability to remember some events but only after prolonged repetition.

H.M. has been cared for all this time by his mother, who usually accompanies him wherever he goes. It so happened, however, that in 1966 the mother was in Hartford Hospital, recovering from a minor operation, just when H.M. was about to leave for Boston. It was his father, therefore, who packed H.M.'s clothes for him and brought him to meet us at Dr. Scoville's office prior to the journey. The father had also taken the patient to visit his mother in hospital that very morning, the third such visit within a week. Yet when he questioned H.M., he seemed not to remember any of these visits, although he expressed a vague idea that something might have happened to his mother. On the journey to Boston, he kept saying that he felt a little uneasy and wondered if something might be wrong with one of his parents, though he could not be sure which one. On being asked who had packed his bag for the trip, he said "Seems like it was my mother. But then that's what I'm not sure about. If there is something wrong with my mother, then it could have been my father." Despite our explaining the situation to him repeatedly during the journey, H.M. was never able to give a clear account of what had happened, and was still feeling "uneasy" when he reached Boston, wondering if something was "wrong" with one of his parents. Gradually, this uneasiness wore off, and although he was told repeatedly that he could telephone home any time he wished, he no longer seemed to know why he should do so. Next day he appeared completely unaware that there had been any question of illness in his family. When asked again who had packed his suitcase, he said "It must have been my mother. She always does these things." It seemed to us instructive how the emotional tone (one of concern and uneasiness), which was associated with the vague knowledge of his mother's illness, appeared to fade away nearly as rapidly as his knowledge of the events provoking it.

During three of the nights at the Clinical Research Center, the patient rang for the night nurse, asking her, with many apologies, if she would tell him where he was and how he came to be there. He clearly realized that he was in a hospital but seemed unable to reconstruct any of the events of the previous day. On another occasion he remarked "Every day is alone in itself, whatever enjoyment I've had, and whatever sorrow I've had." Our own impression is that many events fade for him long before the day is over. He often volunteers stereotype descriptions of his own state, by saying that it is "like waking from a dream." His experience seems to be that of a person who is just becoming aware of his surroundings without fully comprehending the situation, because he does not remember what went before.

In December, 1967 (eighteen months after the visit to Boston), H.M.'s father died suddenly, and H.M. is said to have become temporarily quite irritable and intractable, rushing out of the house in anger one evening. The cause of the anger was finding that some of his guns were missing. These had been prize possessions of which he often spoke and which he had kept in his room for many years, but an uncle had claimed them as his legacy after the father's death. The patient was upset by what to him was an inexplicable loss, but became calm when they were replaced in his room. Since then, he has been his usual even-tempered self. When questioned about his parents two months later, he seemed to be dimly aware of his father's death. In these and similar respects, he demonstrates some capacity to set up traces of constant features of his immediate environment. In this instance, the continued absence of one of his parents may have served as an unusually effective clue. Until then, H.M.'s entire life had been spent at home with his father and mother.

After his father's death, H.M. was given protected employment in a state rehabilitation centre, where he spends week-days participating in rather monotonous work, programmed for severely retarded patients. A typical task is the mounting of cigarette lighters on the cardboard frames for display. It is characteristic that he cannot give us any description of his place of work, the nature of his job, or the route along which he is driven each day, to and from the centre.

In contrast to the inability to describe a job after six months of daily exposure (except for week-ends), H.M. is able to draw an accurate floor plan of the bungalow in which he has lived for the past eight years. He also seems to be familiar with the topography of the immediate neighbourhood, at least within two or three blocks of his home, but is lost beyond that. His limitations in this respect are illustrated by the manner in which he attempted to guide us to his house, in June, 1966, when we were driving him back from Boston. After leaving the main highway, we asked him for help in locating his house. He promptly and courteously indicated to us several turns, until we arrived at a street which he said was quite familiar to him. At the same time, he admitted that we were not at the right address. A phone call to his mother revealed that we were on the street where he used to live before his operation. With her directions we made our way to the residential area where H.M. now lives. He did not get his bearings until we were within two short blocks of the house, which he could just glimpse through the trees." (Milner, Corkin, and Teuber, 1968, pp. 216–217)

Formal Tests of H.M.'s Memory

H.M.'s memory has been the subject of literally dozens of papers. The following summarizes some of the major findings on the extent of his amnesia, the central feature of which is a failure in long-term retention for most events, in the absence of any general intellectual impairment or perceptual disorder.

1. *Learning and Memory*. H.M. is impaired at virtually any kind of learning task in which there is a delay between presentation and recall, particularly if interfering material is presented between trials. For example, when shown

photographs of people, he fails to recognize them two minutes later if asked to repeat digits in the interim. He is severely deficient on tests of verbal learning and recall and cannot master sequences of digits beyond his immediate span. H.M. is also impaired at nonverbal tasks such as the delayed recall of a complex geometric design and the recognition of recurrent nonsense patterns.

2. *Maze-Learning Tests*. H.M. has been tested on both stylus and tactile maze tests. In the former test a wood board has metal bolt heads sticking out as shown in Figure 20–4. The subject must discover and remember the correct route and is told only when he makes errors. H.M. failed to acquire the route even after extensive testing. He did, however, solve a radically shortened version of the maze, although it took him 155 trials. In the tactile maze test, the subject must learn a similar sort of problem, although in this case he is blindfolded and runs his fingers through alleys, again having to discover the correct route himself. Once again, H.M. failed to learn the complete maze but eventually solved a shortened version of it.

FIGURE 20–4. A visually guided stylus maze. The black circles represent metal bolt heads on a wood base. The task is to discover and remember the correct route, indicated here by the line. Deficits on this task are correlated with the amount of right hippocampus damaged. (After Milner, 1970.)

3. *Classical Conditioning*. The question of whether H.M. can be classically conditioned has not been resolved. In 1962 Kimura attempted to condition galvanic skin responses, which were to be elicited by electric shock, to previously neutral stimuli. The experiment had to be abandoned, as it turned out that H.M. showed no GSR response to the shock, even at levels of shock intensity that normal control subjects found disagreeably painful. H.M. apparently noticed the shocks but did not complain. The cause of this unexpected result has not been determined. Although classical conditioning has not been demonstrated in H.M., work by Warrington and Weiskrantz implies that H.M. probably can be classically conditioned. They classically conditioned an eyeblink response in two severe amnesics and demonstrated retention over an interval of 24 hours. This significant retention occurred in spite of the subjects' denial that they had ever seen the conditioning apparatus.

4. *Response to Internal States*. H.M.'s deficit in GSR implies that he may show a more general deficit in autonomic or other internal signals. For example, it has been noted that he rarely comments on such internal states as hunger, thirst, pain, and fatigue. In order to document these clinical observations, Hebben et al. examined his thermal pain perception and his reports of hunger before and after meals. Although H.M.'s somatosensory thresholds appeared normal, he was very poor at discriminating different levels of stimuli found painful by normal subjects and never gave reports of pain after stimuli that others found quite painful. A similar neglect of internal state was seen in his report of hunger. On a scale of 0 to 100 where 0 is "famished" and 100 is "too full to eat another bite," H.M. consistently reported 50, whether he was about to eat or had just eaten. In an attempt to influence his subjective report of satiety, the authors supplied him with as

much food as he could eat in one sitting. After he had consumed a complete dinner, his empty tray was removed, and without explanation another full dinner was provided. He apparently did not behave as if anything unusual had happened, and after having eaten the second dinner, except for the salad, he reported simply that he was finished. At that time, however, he rated his satiation at 75! H.M. is clearly impaired at monitoring pain and hunger, although the structural damage responsible for this is uncertain. Hippocampal damage alone is unlikely to produce all the observed effects. Presumably the amygdalectomy plays a significant role, although Anderson's study of the effects of amygdalectomy in humans makes no mention of effects such as those reported for H.M.

5. *Motor Learning*. Although H.M. has a severe memory defect on tests of kinesthetic memory, memory for words, and visual location, he is surprisingly competent at motor learning. In one experiment Milner trained H.M. on a mirror-drawing task that required tracing a line between the double outline of a star while seeing the star and his pencil only in a mirror (Figure 20–5). This task is initially difficult even for normal subjects, but they improve with practice. H.M. had a normal learning curve and although he did not remember having performed the task previously, he retained the skill on following days. Subsequently, Corkin trained H.M. on a variety of manual-tracking and coordination tasks. Although his initial performances tended to be inferior to those of control subjects, he showed nearly normal improvement from session to session.

More recently, Cohen and Corkin showed an analogous result on the "Tower of Hanoi puzzle," a well-studied problem involving a number of pegs and a number of blocks of different sizes. To begin the problem, all the blocks are arranged on the "source" peg in size

FIGURE 20–5. H.M. shows clear improvement in motor tasks. In this test the subject's task is to trace between the two outlines of the star while viewing his or her hand in a mirror. The reversing effect of the mirror makes this a difficult task initially. Crossing a line constitutes an error. (After Blakemore, 1977.)

order, with the smallest on the top and the largest on the bottom. The task is to move these blocks one at a time onto a "goal peg," with the largest block again at the bottom and the smallest at the top, while never placing a block onto one smaller than itself. Thus, successful solution requires the use of additional pegs in a specific order. Normal subjects require a decreasing number of moves for solution over successive trials. Despite his inability to remember particular moves and whether they advance or retard solution, H.M.'s performance improved systematically over days, even though his commentary during each trial sounded as though he were solving the puzzle for the first time. In short, H.M. was able to learn the procedures or operations necessary for successful performance of this cognitive skill, despite markedly impaired declarative memory for the task. We shall return to this dissociation in our discussion of amnesia.

The dissociation between the impairment in motor learning and other types of tasks implies that motor skills are acquired independently of the hippocampal system. The question of where this might be has not been examined to date, although there is a substantial literature on the acquisition of motor skills by normal subjects. Perhaps psychologists studying motor skills will consider this question in neurological patients.

Additional Evidence for a Hippocampal Role in Memory

Much has been written and theorized about H.M., but, as we have emphasized throughout the book, studies of single cases are not a legitimate basis for neuropsychological theory. If, for example, H.M. were in some way unusual, as he might very well be, conclusions about the hippocampus and memory drawn from this one subject might be grossly overstated. H.M.

is not unusual, however, as we shall see in the evidence described in this section.

Other Examples of Bilateral Hippocampectomy

Milner has studied two other patients with severe memory defects who also are believed to have bilateral hippocampal damage. They showed many of the same phenomena seen in H.M. Once case, P.B., was a civil engineer whose left temporal lobe had been resectioned for relief of seizures. After surgery he had severe anterograde amnesia, which persisted and worsened until he died from unrelated causes 15 years later. At autopsy P.B. was found to have an atrophic right hippocampus opposite the surgically excised left hippocampus. Penfield and Milner proposed that P.B.'s right hippocampus was dead at the time of the operation, resulting in severe amnesia like H.M.'s.

Effect of Unilateral Hippocampal Lesions on Memory

Patients with unilateral lesions of the hippocampus do not suffer from H.M.'s severe amnesia, but they do have significant memory deficits. The role of the hippocampus in memory can be assessed by correlating the amount of hippocampus removed in the temporal lobectomy with the performance on memory tests. That is, since the surgeon removed only as much of the hippocampus as necessary to stop the abnormal epileptiform activity, different patients lose different amounts of hippocampus. Table 20–1 summarizes the results of such an analysis on the right hippocampus. Performance on maze-learning tasks is correlated with damage to the right hippocampus: the larger the removal, the larger the deficit. The same is true of a face-recognition task. On a test of spatial position (Figure 20–6) the subject marks the circle indicated on an exposed eight-inch line,

TABLE 20–1

Summary of tests that correlate degree of memory defect with amount of unilateral hippocampal removal [a]

| | Site of lesion | | |
	Left hippocampus	Right hippocampus	Basic reference
Tactile maze learning	−	×	Milner, 1965
Visual maze learning	−	×	Corkin, 1965
Facial recognition	−	×	Milner, 1968
Spatial block span + 1	−	×	Corsi, 1972
Spatial position	−	×	Corsi, 1972
Spatial association	−	×	Petrides, 1983
Spatial memory	−	×	Smith and Milner, 1981
Self-ordered design recall	−	×	Petrides and Milner, 1982
Recall of nonsense syllables	×	−	Corsi, 1972; Samuels et al., 1972
Recall of word lists	×		Jaccarino-Hiatt, 1978
Digit span + 1	×	−	Corsi, 1972
Nonspatial association	×	−	Petrides, 1983
Self-ordered word recall	×	−	Petrides and Milner, 1982

[a] × = significant impairment; − = normal performance.

A

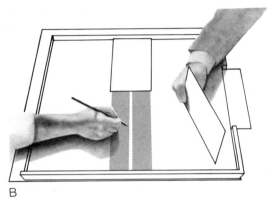

B

FIGURE 20–6. A procedure to test memory for spatial position. A. The subject marks the circle indicated on the exposed line to the left. B. After a short delay the subject attempts to reproduce this position as accurately as possible on the line on the right. (After Milner, 1972.)

then, after a short delay, attempts to repro-duce this position on another eight-inch line. Again, performance is related to the extent of right hippocampus removed. In an ingen-ious experiment Corsi devised a spatial analogue to Hebb's recurring-digits test. A series of blocks is presented, and the sub-ject learns to tap out a sequence on a block board, illustrated in Figure 20–7. Just as there is a memory span for digits, normal subjects show a memory span for blocks: the maximum number that can be remembered. The subjects,

Examiner's view

FIGURE 20–7. Sketch of Corsi's block-tapping task. The subject must copy a sequence tapped out by the examiner on the blocks. The blocks' numbers are visible on the examiner's side but not on the subject's. (After Milner, 1971.)

patients, and normal control, are then tested on a series of block sequences that are one more than span. As on the Hebb repeating-digits experiment, one sequence repeats itself every third trial. Normal subjects learn the repeating sequence over several trials, although they are still poor at the novel sequences. Subjects with damage to the right hippocampus do not learn the repeating sequence or do so very slowly (Figure 20–8), whereas subjects with other cor-tical lesions perform as controls do. This test appears to be the best available noninvasive test of right hippocampal function. More recently, the size of right hippocampal removal has been associated with a deficit in two additional tests of spatial learning and memory, a finding adding credence to the notion that the right hippocampus may play a role in spatial orienta-tion.

The left-hand column of Table 20–1 summa-rizes a similar analysis of left hippocampal function. Recall of nonsense syllables (e.g., "PTB") is impaired in direct relation to the amount of hippocampus removed, as is per-formance on Hebb's repeating-digits test (see Figure 20–8), a nonspatial association test (see

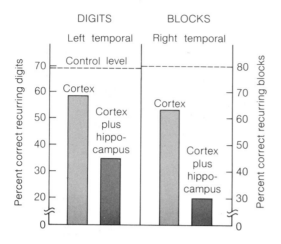

FIGURE 20–8. Summary of double dissociation of left and right hippocampal function. Left temporal lesions, including radical removal of the hippocampus, produced severe deficits on acquisition of the recurring digits, whereas right temporal lesions, including radical removal of the hippocampus, produced serious deficits on acquisition of recurring-block sequences. (Redrawn after Milner, 1970, 1971.)

Chapter 17), and a test of recall of self-ordered word learning (see Chapter 18).

These results illustrate that both hippocampi are essential for normal memory, and that the left and right hippocampi can be functionally dissociated. The left is more important in the memory of verbal material, the right in the memory of visual and spatial material.

Stimulation of the Hippocampus During Surgery

If it is assumed that stimulation of the hippocampus disrupts its functioning, then stimulation would be expected to impair memory functions. Chapman et al. stimulated the hippocampus bilaterally in two epileptic patients and unilaterally in 13 others and found that bilateral stimulations produced retrograde amnesia that persisted for a few hours and

reached back about two weeks. Immediate memory (digit span) and more remote memories were intact. Unilateral stimulation produced similar but lesser effects on memory.

Although these results appear to support the hypothesized role of the hippocampus in memory, there are problems with this interpretation. In their series at the Montreal Neurological Institute Rasmussen and his colleagues stimulated the hippocampus in well over 300 patients undergoing surgery for temporal lobe epilepsy. Whenever the hippocampal stimulation produced hallucinatory or interpretational responses, there were significant alterations of electrical activity on the temporal cortex. This implies that disturbances of memory from hippocampal stimulation may result from disruption of normal activity elsewhere in the brain. Furthermore, Doty and Overman found that electrical stimulation of the anterior commissure of monkeys prevented acquisition of a visual learning task, but that stimulation elsewhere in the temporal lobe had no effect.

In conclusion, the results of stimulation of the hippocampus are somewhat ambiguous. Stimulation of the temporal lobe does disrupt memory, but the cause and principal locus of this effect have yet to be clearly demonstrated.

Carotid Sodium Amytal Memory Testing

Memory tests during sodium Amytal testing (see Chapter 14) have shown that if one hippocampus is damaged and the drug is injected into the contralateral hemisphere, there is amnesia for material presented during the action of the drug.

In memory testing during sodium Amytal, only very simple tests can be used, because the drug wears off within a few minutes. Before the drug injection the patient is presented with both verbal and nonverbal items and is told to remember them. For example, the patient is shown two pictures (e.g., hand and cup) and asked to name them and to remember them. He or she is then distracted with mental arithmetic before being asked to recall the names of the pictures. A similar procedure is used for recall of a sentence (e.g., Peter is in the garden). After this baseline testing, injection is made into one hemisphere and testing is repeated, with the difference that the patient is shown two new pictures and given a new sentence to remember. After the drug has worn off, the patient is tested for recall and, failing this, recognition of all the items.

Table 20–2, summarizing the incidence of amnesia following injections ipsilateral to a lesion, shows that although free recall is generally poor, recognition is very good. The table also shows that either hemisphere is capable of storing both verbal and nonverbal memories. In other words, the right hemisphere appears capable of storing the sentences, although not as efficiently as the left hemisphere.

Table 20–3 compares the effects of injection into the hemisphere ipsilateral and contralateral to a lesion. Injection into the contralateral (normal) hemisphere allows the efficiency of the impaired hemisphere's memory to be tested. Table 20–3 shows that if a patient suffers from temporal lobe epilepsy with a unilateral focus, then, in the absence of the intact hemisphere during the period of anesthetization, the epileptic hemisphere is badly impaired at recognizing the pictures or sentences (47 percent failure). This is to be compared with only 5 percent failure of recognition when the injection is made into the epileptic hemisphere. Comparison of the two failure rates indicates that normal memory function requires at least one temporal lobe to be functioning normally. Injection into the side contralateral to the lesion produces an unaccept-

TABLE 20–2

Percent failure of recall and recognition after injection of sodium Amytal ipsilateral to lesion

	Free recall %	Recognition %
Pictures	60	0
Sentences	72	6

After Milner, 1975.

TABLE 20–3

Percent failure of recognition after injection of sodium Amytal ipsilaterally and contralaterally to lesion

| | Side of injection | |
	Ipsilateral to lesion %	Contralateral to lesion %
Unilateral epileptic focus	5	47
Bilateral epileptic focus	26	35

After Milner, 1975.

able memory loss because neither hippocampus is operative. Table 20–3 also illustrates that patients with bilateral epileptic foci have significant memory defects when either hemisphere is injected, again implying that one normally functioning temporal lobe is necessary for normal memory. Patients with bilateral epileptic foci are clearly poor risks for surgery, since injection of either hemisphere leaves the patient with unacceptable memory defects.

To summarize, there are three principal findings from the sodium Amytal studies. First, if the drug is injected ipsilaterally to the damaged hemisphere, the patient retains 90 to 95 percent of both the verbal and the nonverbal material. Thus, both temporal lobes are capable of storing both types of memories. This result does not impugn the previously described studies indicating an asymmetry in memory function, since the memory tests are very simple and do not nearly tax a person's mnemonic abilities. Second, injection of the drug contralateral to the damaged temporal lobe results in substantial memory impairment, retention dropping to about 50 percent. In other words, if the injection is made into the intact hemisphere, the damaged hemisphere is impaired at storing the new material. Third, if injection ipsilateral to a known lesion results in impaired memory, there are strong grounds for predicting that the patient suffers from a bilateral lesion, as in the case of P.B. described above.

Role of the Temporal Neocortex in Memory

Although we have emphasized the role of the medial temporal lobes (hippocampus) in memory, the neocortex of the lateral temporal lobes is also important. Lesions of the anterior temporal lobe sparing the hippocampus result in a variety of memory impairments, although the global amnesia of H.M. is not observed. Milner and her colleagues have double dissociated the effects of damage to the neocortex of the temporal lobe of each hemisphere on several memory tasks. They conclude that lesions of the right temporal lobe result in impaired memory of nonverbal material, whereas lesions of the left temporal lobe result in impaired memory of verbal material. These findings are summarized in Table 20–4, where it can be seen that removal of the right temporal lobe produces deficits on nonverbal tests, including recall of complex geometric figures, paired-associate learning of nonsense figures, and recognition of nonsense figures (see Figure 20–9), of tunes, and of previously seen photographs of faces. No deficits are seen, however,

on tests of verbal memory. Removal of the left temporal lobe, on the other hand, produces deficits on verbal tests, such as recall of previously presented stories and of pairs of words, and recognition of words or numbers and of recurring nonsense syllables; such removal has little effect on the nonverbal tests. These studies indicate that although damage to the medial temporal lobe is associated with severe deficits of memory, so too is damage restricted to just the temporal neocortex associated with memory disturbance.

In a clever experiment, Jones found that patients with left hemisphere lesions could improve their verbal memory by encoding verbal information with the assistance of visual imagery. Thus, memory for a list of paired-associate words improved significantly if the person was told to remember pairs; for example, elephant-bouquet would be remembered by visualizing an elephant holding a bouquet with its trunk. Similarly, patients with right temporal lesions could benefit from the use of verbal encoding. Thus, for example, in the case of "elephant-bouquet" the patient was instructed to verbally encode the pair in a sentence such as "the elephant ate the bouquet." H.M. did not benefit from instructions to use these strategies, indicating that one intact hippocampus is necessary for this type of encoding scheme to be of value.

Summary. Lesions to the temporal lobes produce significant and often tragically severe deficits in long-term memory. These deficits are not modality-specific, as they occur to both visual and auditory material no matter how the material is initially presented or memory is assessed. The deficits are material-specific, however, as left temporal lesions specifically impair memory for verbal material and right temporal lesions impair memory of nonverbal material. Although

TABLE 20–4

Summary of the effects of left or right temporal lobectomy on various tests of memory [a]

	Site of lesion		
	Left temporal lobe	Right temporal lobe	Basic reference
Geometric recall (Rey)	–	×	Taylor, 1969
Paired-associate nonsense figures	–	×	Prisko, 1963
Recognition of nonsense figures	–	×	Kimura, 1963
Recurring nonsense figures	–	×	Kimura, 1963
Recognition of faces	–	×	Warrington and James 1967; Milner, 1968
Recognition of tunes	–	×	Shankweiler, 1966
Recall of stories	×	–	Milner, 1967
Paired-associate words	×	–	Milner, 1967
Recognition of words, numbers	×	–	Milner, 1967
Recurring nonsense syllables	×	–	Corsi, 1972

[a] × = significant impairment; – = normal performance.

there is no question of memory defects following temporal lobe lesions, there is substantial controversy over what the critical focus for the lesion is to produce the maximal deficit and why there are deficits at all. We address the first question in the next section and save discussion of the last question for our discussion of theories of amnesia.

PROBLEM: ROLE OF THE HIPPOCAMPUS IN MEMORY

Having emphasized the role of the temporal lobes, and especially of the hippocampus, in long-term memory a note of caution is desirable. Not even 30 years of study on amnesia and the temporal lobes have established with certainty that the hippocampus is the critical structure in the temporal lobe amnesic syndrome. Certainly the extent of hippocampal involvement and the severity of memory impairment are correlated, but unresolved issues remain that must be confronted.

Functions of the Hippocampus in Nonhumans

The profound amnesia found in patients with bilateral medial temporal damage has not been observed in nonhumans with hippocampal damage, despite dozens of attempts to find it. In 1954 Mishkin established that bilateral removal of the temporal neocortex in nonhumans produces a severe and enduring impairment in learning visual material but does not affect auditory and tactile modes—a pattern of effects unlike the modality independent global amnesia observed in humans. Furthermore, in these same studies little or no impairment was found to follow bilateral hippocampectomy. The initial attempts at demonstrating hippocampal involvement in the memory processes of nonhuman species thus proved disappointing. But since 1954 at least five clear effects of bilateral hippocampal lesions in nonhumans, principally monkeys and rats, have emerged in the literature.

First, there is a tendency to perseverate on responses. That is, once an animal with

FIGURE 20–9. Example from Kimura's recurring non-sense figures test. Subjects are shown a series of cards, on each of which is an unfamiliar design. Some designs recur, and it is the subject's task to say whether he or she has seen each design before. Right temporal lesions impair recognition on this task.

a bilateral hippocampal lesion begins a response it will perseverate on that response. This deficit could be interpreted as a kind of memory deficit, since the animal may not "remember" what it has just done or what the consequences of that act were. But this behavior is more frequently interpreted as evidence of some type of response disinhibition. This interpretation is compatible with Warrington and Weiskrantz's idea that human amnesics have difficulty in controlling and restraining the influence of prior learning on present performance.

The second effect is a deficit in the ability of animals with hippocampal lesions to order serially long chains of behavior. Thus, Sainsbury, Kolb, and others have shown that rats and hamsters with hippocampal lesions cannot build nests, hoard food, exhibit maternal behavior, and so on, largely because they appear to be unable to chain together the various motor acts necessary for the complex outcome. This deficit could explain some learning defects as well, since Winocur and Breckenridge have made a similar proposal to account

for impaired maze performance. The idea that hippocampal animals cannot sequence motor acts is supported by the bulk of the recent hippocampal EEG literature, which has shown that rhythmic waves in the hippocampus are related to the moment-to-moment details of movement (see Chapter 7).

The third effect, demonstrated in experiments by a number of groups, is a memory defect in animals with hippocampal lesions, a defect that may be analogous to some aspects of the memory defect in amnesics. For example, several experiments have shown that learning and memory in hippocampal animals are disrupted by interfering stimuli. Correll and Scoville found that when monkeys with bilateral medial temporal lesions were required to learn six pattern discriminations concurrently, they were severely impaired. The animals received only a single trial at a time on the individual problems, but trials on each of the six problems were interspersed with trials on the other five problems. Thus the presentation of one set of patterns interfered with the learning of other patterns. Interference need not come from concurrent learning, however: Jarrard found that if rats with hippocampal lesions were forced to run in a wheel after learning a spatial task, their performance was impaired relative to that of controls or hippocampal rats that did not experience the interpolated activity.

Fourth, Olton and his colleagues have now done dozens of experiments designed to show that hippocampal lesions in rats impair the acquisition of certain mazes because the animals have a type of short-term memory ("working memory") defect. For example, when rats were tested in a multi-arm maze in which some arms were always baited with food and others were never baited, Olton et al. found that the rats with damage to the hippocampal system were not impaired at learning which arms were baited but rather were impaired at recalling which arms had been successfully entered to find food on any given day. This effect in intriguing, and it has generated considerable controversy. No doubt it will be explored further in the coming years.

Finally, the most recent analysis of the hippocampus has been based on an ingenious set of experiments initiated by O'Keefe, Nadel, and Black. They have argued that the hippocampus functions to "construct spatial maps" by which animals locate themselves in space. This argument is supported by their own neurophysiological evidence that there are cells in the hippocampus that fire either when the animal finds itself in a particular spot in the environment, or when it encounters a strange object or the absence of an expected one. Hippocampal lesions are proposed to disturb maze learning, nest building, food hoarding, etc., because of the spatial requirement of the tasks.

In summary, lesions of the hippocampus of nonhuman species are known to produce perseverative responses, deficits in response sequencing, sensitivity to interfering stimuli, and spatial deficits. There is, however, no compelling evidence of a multimodal global amnesia. The failure to find the profound amnesia clinically observed in humans has been a serious obstacle to the understanding both of hippocampal function and of the amnesic syndrome.

Solutions

Failure to find global amnesia in nonhuman species has prompted a number of explanations. One argument is that there is an evolutionary break between humans and other species. Because humans and other animals are undeniably different, this absence of global amnesia could be another example of the differences in hippocampal anatomy, physiology, and apparent functions across all other mam-malian species studied, as well as of the general conservatism of development in nervous system evolution (see Chapter 4).

A second possibility is that behavioral studies of hippocampectomized rats and monkeys have not used tests comparable to the ones used on people. Although more attractive than the first alternative, this also appears unlikely, since the memory deficits in nonhuman species generally appear to be minor compared with the global amnesia of H.M. and similar patients. Nevertheless, this possibility cannot be discounted yet in view of an intriguing series of experiments done by Gaffan, who attempted to devise behavioral tests more similar to those used to study human amnesics. In one experiment two monkeys were trained on a picture-recognition task somewhat similar to one used previously for amnesics by Warrington. The monkeys were shown a series of 25 pictures, each of which appeared twice per training session. The task was to make a response to a picture on its second appearance in a session, but to make no response on its first appearance. The difficulty of the test was varied by changing the average separation between the first and second presentation of pictures within a session. After the monkeys had learned the task with up to 18 intervening items, the fornix (a major output of the hippocampus) was surgically transected. After surgery neither monkey could reliably perform the task with more than three intervening items. The impairment was severe and was most plausibly ascribed to a memory defect similar to that observed in human amnesics. Gaffan's results are suggestive, but two problems must be considered experimentally before the memory impairments can be considered analogous to those in human amnesics. First, global amnesia is multimodal, and Gaffan has studied only visual problems to date. Second, Gaffan sectioned the fornix rather than directly damaging the hippocampus, thus making his

experiment a somewhat indirect study of hippocampal function.

A final possibility is that the neuropathology
responsible for the amnesia in humans has been
inaccurately localized. The hippocampal damage is generally assumed to produce the amnesic syndrome, but a series of studies by Horel
and Misantone and more recent studies by
Mishkin bring this notion into serious question. Horel notes that major efferents of the
temporal cortex pass through a narrow channel
known as the temporal stem (Figure 20–10), en
route to the dorsomedial thalamus, frontal
lobe, basal ganglia, and contralateral temporal
lobe. After a careful examination of the literature Horel concludes that it is virtually impossible to surgically remove the hippocampus
without damaging the temporal stem, and that
the more hippocampus removed, the greater
the damage to the temporal stem. Horel therefore concludes that damage to the temporal
stem, and not to the hippocampus, may be
critical in the amnesic syndrome. Some of the
most convincing evidence favoring Horel's
hypothesis comes from the autopsy data of
Penfield and Milner's patient P.B., discussed
earlier. Although autopsy confirmed Penfield
and Milner's predictions that the hippocampus
was damaged bilaterally, the posterior portion
of one hippocampus was intact and appeared to
be nearly normal, whereas the temporal stem
appeared to be completely degenerated. Horel
proposed that the bilateral damage to the temporal stem was responsible for P.B.'s amnesia,
not the partial hippocampal damage. Horel
supports his claim with studies showing that
temporal stem lesions in monkeys have severe
consequences for visual discrimination learning. Although he has yet to examine auditory
or tactile learning, Horel's proposal must be
considered seriously, especially in light of
more recent work by Mishkin, who has
emphasized a slightly different anatomical
argument. Hippocampal lesions in humans

usually are accompanied by damage to the
amygdala as well. When Mishkin varied the
extent of amygdala and hippocampal damage
in monkeys, he found that although bilateral
hippocampal or amygdala lesions alone had
little effect on a simple visual learning problem, simultaneous bilateral removal of the two
areas produced a severe memory disorder.
Furthermore, in another study, Zola-Morgan,
Squire, and Mishkin found that whereas
monkeys with combined amygdala and hippocampal lesions exhibited a severe memory
impairment, monkeys with temporal stem
lesions did not, although the latter lesions
did disturb visual discrimination learning.
These results suggest that although temporal stem lesions may impair memory on certain
tasks, it is hippocampal and amygdala damage that may mimic the human amnesic
syndrome. If so, a rapprochement between
the findings for the effects of hippocampal
lesions in humans and nonhumans may be
close at hand.

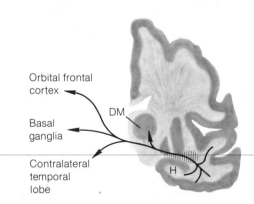

Orbital frontal cortex

DM

Basal ganglia

Contralateral temporal lobe

H

FIGURE 20–10. Major efferents of the temporal cortex
pass through the temporal stem (shaded area) en route
to the dorsomedial thalamus (DM), orbital frontal cortex,
basal ganglia, and contralateral temporal lobe. Noting
that removal of the hippocampus (H) invariably damages
the temporal stem, Horel posits that global amnesia may
result from damage to the temporal stem rather than to
the hippocampus.

THE PARIETAL LOBES
AND MEMORY

Warrington and her colleagues have presented evidence that the parietal lobes may be involved in short-term memory. They studied three patients with fairly restricted left parietal lesions who had severely impaired digit span but surprisingly intact memory of paired-associate words and short stories. Warrington has therefore argued that the left parietal lobe has an important role in the storage of short-term memory. Two objections can be raised to this conclusion. First, Warrington does not convincingly demonstrate that the memory defect is not a secondary effect of aphasia, since all three of her patients were in fact dysphasic. Second, she does not demonstrate the effect to be specific to the left parietal lobe, for the lesions extend beyond this region. Despite these objections, there are indications that she is correct. For example, Table 20–5 summarizes the digit span and IQs of a series of nonaphasic patients with parietal removals (see Kolb and Milner for brain maps of the cortical excisions). Notice that the digit spans are significantly lower for the patients with left parietal lesions than for those with right parietal lesions. (Digit spans are also significantly reduced for groups with left frontal or left temporal lesions, although not as severely as the left parietal group.)

The left parietal lobe may be divisible into functional subregions, for Warrington and Weiskrantz report that patients with left parieal lesions have deficits on one type of short-term memory and not on another. They found that some patients apparently have defects in short-term recall of visually presented digits or letters but not for the same stimuli presented aurally. These patients have alexia but not aphasia. On the other hand, Luria reports patients with just the opposite difficulty: specific deficits for aurally presented but not visually presented

TABLE 20–5

Summary of mean IQs and scaled digit-span scores on Wechsler Adult Intelligence Scale for patients reported by Kolb and Milner

		Full-scale IQ	Digit span [a]
Parietal	Left n = 6	98.2	6.8 [b]
	Right n = 5	102.8	11.0
Frontal	Left n = 9	104.2	8.2 [c]
	Right n = 9	107.2	9.7
Temporal	Left n = 10	105.1	9.1 [c]
	Right n = 10	108.6	10.8
Normal controls	n = 10	114.3	10.1

[a] Refers to scaled score on Wechsler Adult Intelligence Scale.
[b] Differs significantly (p < .05) from homologous contralateral lesion.
[c] Differs significantly (p < .05) from all other groups.

verbal items. Luria's patients were aphasic but not alexic. Figure 20–11 shows Warrington and Weiskrantz's provisional anatomical location for these doubly dissociable deficits.

Note that the short-term memory deficits reported both by Luria and by Warrington and Weiskrantz occur in the absence of long-term memory defects. In other words, patients may exhibit surprisingly intact recall of verbal material over long delays in spite of markedly reduced short-term recall. This phenomenon implies that short-term and long-term memory are parallel processes and that material is stored separately in both. Neurologically, the parietal lobe appears to be involved in short-term memory and the temporal lobe in long-term memory.

If the left parietal lobe is participating in the short-term storage of verbal material, is it possible that the right parietal lobe is participat-

FIGURE 20–11. Provisional anatomical loci for most severe auditory and visual short-term memory defects. (After Warrington and Weiskrantz, 1973.)

pating in the short-term storage of nonverbal information? Although we are not aware of any published data on this point, the idea seems reasonable. One might expect, for example, that the span on the Corsi block-tapping test would be reduced in patients with right parietal lesions, and preliminary data from Milner show that this may be the case.

THE FRONTAL LOBES AND MEMORY

Historically there have been extravagant claims that the frontal lobes are responsible for the highest intellectual functions, but until quite recently there was no evidence that the frontal lobes are involved in memory. In 1963, Prisko devised an experiment based on previous work with experimental animals. It was essentially a "compound-stimulus" task in which two stimuli in the same sensory modality were presented in succession, separated by a short interval. The subject's task was to report whether the second stimulus of the pair was identical with the first. On half the trials the stimuli were the same and on the other half they were different. Thus, the task required the

subject to remember the first stimulus of a pair in order to compare it with the second, while suppressing the stimulus that occurred on previous trials. Prisko used pairs of clicks, light flashes, tones, colors, and irregular nonsense patterns as the stimuli. The same stimuli were used repeatedly in different combinations. Patients with unilateral frontal lobe removals showed a marked impairment at matching the clicks, flashes, and colors.

The poor performance of the frontal lobe patients is unlikely to have resulted from a defect of short-term or long-term memory, because the subjects performed normally on tests of these functions. Milner noted that in the Prisko test the subject is required to suppress the memory of previous trials and concentrate only on the predelay stimulus. If this behavior is no longer possible after the frontal lesion, then, when a few stimuli constantly recur, the interfering effects of previous trials may seriously impair test performance. That is, because there is difficulty in discriminating the most recent stimulus from others that appeared earlier, the frontal lobe patient's temporal discriminations become rather blurred. This possibility was tested more directly in an experiment by Corsi.

In Corsi's experiment there were two tasks, one verbal and one nonverbal, and the subjects were required to decide which of two stimuli had been seen more recently. In the verbal task the subjects were asked to read pairs of words presented on a series of cards (e.g., cowboy-railroad). From time to time a card appeared bearing two words with a question mark between them. The subject had to indicate which of the words he or she had read most recently. Sometimes both words had been seen before, but at other times only one had been. In the latter case the task became a simple test of recognition, whereas in the former case it was a test of recency memory. Patients with left temporal removals showed a mild deficit in recognition, as befits their difficulty with verbal memory; the frontal lobe patients performed normally. However, on the recency test both frontal lobe groups (left and right) were impaired, although the left-side group was significantly worse.

The nonverbal task was identical with the verbal, except that the stimuli were photographs of paintings rather than words. Patients with right temporal lobe removals showed mild deficits on recognition, consistent with their visual memory deficit, whereas those with right frontal lobe lesions performed normally. On the recency test the frontal lobe groups were impaired, but now the right-side group was significantly worse. Thus, Corsi's experiments confirm Prisko's results indicating a deficit in the memory of the temporal ordering of events, a conclusion corroborated by Petrides' more recent experiments showing deficits in self-ordered tasks in patients with frontal lobe lesions (see Chapter 18). The data from these studies are consistent with the hypothesis that the frontal lobes play some role in the memory processes needed to separate events in time, but Prisko's data also suggest that frontal lobe patients may have another type of memory deficit related to their sensitivity to interference from exposure to new material.

This possibility was tested directly by Moscovitch and Milner. In their experiment patients were read five different lists of 12 words each and were instructed to recall each list immediately after presentation. In the first four lists the words were all drawn from the same taxonomic category, such as sports, followed by a fifth list from a different category, such as professions. Normal subjects show a decline in the number of words correctly recalled from list 1 to 4 (that is, they exhibit proactive interference), but they also exhibit an additional

phenomenon on list 5: they recall as many words as they did for list 1, thus demonstrating what is referred to as "release from proactive interference." Frontal lobe patients also showed strong proactive interference, as would be expected from the Prisko experiments, but surprisingly they failed to show release from proactive interference on list 5. These data imply that frontal lobe lesions produce yet another memory defect that is not observed in patients with large temporal lobe lesions, although a similar memory abnormality is observed in certain other types of amnesic syndromes such as Korsakoff's syndrome (see below).

Finally, yet another deficit in memory in frontal lobe patients has been demonstrated in a test of movement copying. In their study of the copying of complex arm and facial movements in patients with cortical lesions, Kolb and Milner found that in addition to errors of sequence, frontal lobe patients made many errors of intrusion and omission. Hence, when asked to copy a series of three discrete facial movements (see Figure 18–2), frontal lobe patients left one movement out (error of omission) or added a movement seen in a previous sequence (error of intrusion). The errors of intrusion may represent another example of interference effects, but the errors of omission imply a type of short-term memory defect. Specific short-term memory deficits have been suggested previously by Moscovitch to account for the performance of frontal lobe patients on certain memory tests, and the data from Kolb and Milner's patients tend to support this view.

In summary, although frontal lobe lesions are not associated with deficits in standard tests of memory function, frontal lobe lesions do produce disturbances in certain memory functions. In particular, frontal lobe patients show an increased susceptibility to interference, have a poor memory for temporal order, show poor release from proactive interference, and may have difficulty with short-term memory for certain types of material. It is important to note, however, that the disturbances of memory observed in frontal lobe patients are not observed in patients with medial temporal lobe damage or parietal lobe damage but they are seen in patients with certain amnesic syndromes. This dissociation suggests that some amnesic syndromes may result in part from frontal lobe damage rather than from temporal lobe damage, as is often assumed. We shall return to this point shortly.

AMNESIA FROM DIENCEPHALIC LESIONS

Global amnesia results not only from bilateral removal of the temporal lobes but also from damage to the diencencephalon. Evidence of diencephalic amnesia comes from two sources: patient N.A. and patients with Korsakoff's syndrome.

Patient N.A.

N.A. (born 9 July, 1938) was injured on 15 December 1960 when a miniature fencing foil entered his right nostril and punctured the base of the brain after taking an obliquely upward course, slightly to the left. According to the medical records, he was confused and disoriented for several days but was never unconscious. The major neurological symptom was a paralysis of upward eye gaze and an unresponsiveness of the pupils to light. The most interesting behavioral effect, however, was a profound loss of recent memory. Although N.A. has a retrograde amnesia extending perhaps one year back before his injury, he has a severe anterograde amnesia for events after his accident in 1960. N.A.'s memory disturbance is similar to that of

H.M.: both patients have a persistent anterograde amnesia, but it is more pronounced for verbal material than for nonverbal material in N.A., a result consistent with the predominantly left-side lesion of N.A. N.A. is impaired at many tests of nonverbal memory, however, including tests of facial memory, maze learning, recall of the Rey figure, and the Kimura recurring figures; he is just not as impaired at these tests as H.M. Recent CT scans have identified a lesion in the region of the left dorsomedial thalamic nucleus. This nucleus provides the major afferent pathway to the frontal lobe, and although this thalamic region receives input from the amygdala, it has no anatomical relationship to the hippocampus.

Korsakoff's Syndrome

Long-term alcoholism, especially when accompanied by malnutrition, has long been known to produce defects of memory. In the late 1800s a Russian physician, S. S. Korsakoff, called attention to a syndrome that he found to accompany chronic alcoholism, the most obvious symptom being a severe loss of memory. He wrote:

> The disorder of memory manifests itself in an extraordinarily peculiar amnesia, in which the memory of recent events, those which just happened, is chiefly disturbed, whereas the remote past is remembered fairly well. . . . This reveals itself primarily in that the patient constantly asks the same questions and repeats the same stories. At first, during conversation with such a patient, it is difficult to note the presence of psychic disorder; the patient gives the impression of a person in complete possession of his faculties; he reasons about everything perfectly well, draws correct deductions from given premises, makes witty remarks, plays chess or a game of cards, in a word, comports himself as a mentally sound person. Only after a long conversation with the patient, one may note that at times he utterly

confuses events and that he remembers absolutely nothing of what goes on around him: he does not remember whether he had his dinner, whether he was out of bed. On occasion the patient forgets what happened to him just an instant ago: you came in, conversed with him, and stepped out for one minute; then you come in again and the patient has absolutely no recollection that you had already been with him. Patients of this type may read the same page over and over again, sometimes for hours, because they are absolutely unable to remember what they have read. . . . With all this, the remarkable fact is that, forgetting all events which have just occurred, the patients usually remember quite accurately the past events which occurred long before the illness. What is forgotten usually proves to be everything that happened during the illness and a short time before the beginning of the illness. (Oscar-Berman, 1980, p. 410)

Korsakoff's syndrome has been studied intensely in the past decade since the seminal paper of Sanders and Warrington in 1971, as Korsakoff's patients are far more readily available than individuals with other forms of global amnesia such as H.M. and N.A. Talland has described six major symptoms of Korsakoff's disease:

1. *Anterograde amnesia*. The patients are unable to form new memories. On formal memory tests they are especially bad at learning paired-associate lists.

2. *Retrograde amnesia*. The patients have an extensive impairment of remote memory that covers most of their adult life. This is easily demonstrated by their very poor recognition of famous faces from years past, faces that most normal people as well as N.A. and H.M. recognize accurately.

3. *Confabulation*. Patients make up stories about past events rather than admit memory loss. These stories are often based on past experiences and are therefore often plausible. For example, when asked where he was last night,

a man told us that he had been at the Legion with his pals. He had not, but this had been a common practice in the past and so was a plausible story.

4. *Meager content in conversation*. Korsakoff patients have little to say in spontaneous conversation, presumably in part because of their amnesia.

5. *Lack of insight*. Many patients are virtually completely unaware of their memory defect.

6. *Apathy*. Indifference and incapacity persevere in ongoing activities. The patients lose interest in things quickly and generally appear indifferent to change.

These symptoms are all observed in patients who otherwise appear quite normal. They have normal IQs, are alert and attentive, appear motivated, and generally lack other neurological signs of cerebral deficit such as abnormal EEG.

The symptoms of Korsakoff's syndrome may appear suddenly within the space of a few days. The cause is a thiamine (vitamin B_1) deficiency resulting from prolonged intake of large quantities of alcohol. The syndrome, which is usually progressive, can be arrested by massive doses of vitamin B_1 but cannot be reversed. Prognosis is poor, with only about 20 percent of patients showing much recovery over a year on a B_1-enriched diet. Many patients demonstrate no recovery even after 10 to 20 years.

Although there has been some controversy over the exact effect that the vitamin deficiency has on the brain, it is currently believed that there is damage in the medial thalamus, and possibly in the mammillary bodies of the hypothalamus, as well as generalized cerebral atrophy. It was widely believed that the severe memory defect results from hypothalamic damage because the mammillary bodies are a major recipient of hippocampal efferents through the fornix. There are four reasons to doubt this. First, in many cases only the medial thalamus is degenerated and not the mammillary bodies; the reverse is not observed. Second, the hippocampus appears not to project through the fornix to the mammillary bodies, but rather to the subiculum, which is the cortex lying near the hippocampus, and the subiculum appears in turn to project to the mammillary bodies. Third, there is considerable controversy over whether lesions to the fornix itself even produce amnesia. For example, Woolsey and Nelson report a case in which there was no apparent neuropsychological disturbance (that is, no obvious memory defect) from a malignant tumor that had destroyed the fornix bilaterally. Garcia-Bengochea et al. sectioned the fornix bilaterally as a treatment for epilepsy in 14 patients and reported that amnesia did not ensue. There have been two reports of memory loss after fornical section, but because these patients have not come to autopsy it is uncertain just where the lesion is. In sum, the bulk of the evidence suggests that damage to the dorsomedial thalamus, not damage to the hippocampal system, produces the memory loss. Finally, two cases, which were thoroughly studied by Mair et al.; have come to autopsy. Both of these patients had bilateral lesions in the medial nuclei of the mammillary bodies as well as cell loss in the dorsomedial thalamic nucleus. In sum, it is likely that damage to both diencephalic structures is necessary for severe amnesia; perhaps lesions to either area can produce a milder form of amnesia.

Diencephalic Contributions to Memory

It is clear that the role of the hippocampus in memory has been overrated, as global amnesia can result from damage to structures other than the hippocampus. There are clear differences, however, between the memory loss experienced by diencephalic and temporal lobe patients. For example, whereas temporal lobe patients show normal release from proactive interference, diencephalic patients do not. Further, individuals with Korsakoff's syndrome have an extensive loss of past memories; temporal lobe patients do not. Note, however, that N.A. does not share this symptom with Korsakoff individuals, suggesting that diencephalic amnesia is not a unitary phenomena. Moscovitch has suggested that Korsakoff individuals may have two problems: a diencephalic lesion and frontal lobe deterioration, the latter conclusion based on evidence from CT scans that show frontal atrophy in over 80 percent of Korsakoff amnesics.

In sum, we have seen that damage to the frontal, temporal, and parietal cortex, damage to the hippocampus and amygdala, and damage to the medial diencephalon can all produce disturbances of memory, each of which is dissociable from the others. Memory is obviously not a unitary phenomenon, and theories regarding the nature of memory and amnesias must now consider both the types of memory disturbance and the presumed neuroanatomical loci.

OTHER SOURCES OF MEMORY LOSS

Convulsive therapy with metrazol-induced seizures was introduced by von Meduna in 1933 after the correlation between schizophrenia and epilepsy was observed to be extremely low; von Meduna proposed that they were mutually exclusive. In 1937, Cerletti and Bini replaced the previous agents with electricity: *electroconvulsive shock therapy* (*ECT or ECS*).

The method of ECT is to apply a 70 to 120 volt alternating current (AC) for about half a second through temporal electrodes. Treatments are usually given one to three times a week, lasting for two to four weeks. To protect the body from the physical consequences of the convulsions, tranquilizers, muscle relaxants, and sometimes atropine are given just prior to the shock.

The clearest effect of ECT on psychological functioning is an adverse effect on memory, a consequence that has been studied thoroughly, especially by Squire and his colleagues. In a recent review, Taylor et al. reached several conclusions regarding the nature of the memory loss: (1) Bilateral ECT frequently induces memory changes, even with the standard number of treatments, e.g., eight or nine; (2) the effects of ECT on memory appear to be cumulative, with greater effects seen with successive treatments; (3) the majority of cognitive and memory defects appear to be entirely reversible with a return to pretreatment levels of function or better within six to seven months; (4) some subtle but persistent defects may be found some months after ECT, especially in personal or autobiographical material; and (5) the persistent defects tend to be of an irritating rather than a seriously incapacitating nature.

The predominantly anterograde amnesia in ECT patients suggests a similarity between them and temporal lobe patients. Since the hippocampus and amygdala are probably the most epileptogenic structures in the brain, it would not be surprising if the observed amnesia following ECT was a result of disruption of medial temporal structures. The fact that hippocampal seizure activity is known to produce cell death in the hippocampus leads to the question of whether there are permanent structural changes in the hippocampus of ECT patients, but this remains to studied.

There have been claims that unilateral ECT has significantly less effect on memory than bilateral ECT. The evidence for this is contradictory and not altogether convincing. In a review on ECT Robertson and Inglis conclude that manipulation of electrode placements is the most promising line of research to prevent or reduce memory impairments, but that much basic research remains to be done. It seems reasonable to expect that unilateral ECT on the left might preferentially disturb verbally mediated memory, whereas unilateral ECT on the right might preferentially disturb nonverbal memory. Indeed, there is preliminary evidence these expectations may be correct. Most of the claims made about the therapeutic powers of ECT remain unproved. In view of unpublished studies by Corkin showing that prolonged repetition of ECT has a very detrimental effect on general neuropsychological functioning, one wonders whether the risk is worth it.

Transient Global Amnesia

In 1958 Fisher and Adams described a previously unrecognized amnesic syndrome: transient global amnesia. The onset is sudden and includes both retrograde and anterograde amnesia, without apparent precipitating cause. Although this syndrome has been subsequently confirmed by many others, little is known of the etiology. It has been linked to concussion, migraine, hypoglycemia, and epilepsy, but the most likely explanation appears to be vascular interruption in the territory of the posterior cerebral artery, from either a transient ischemic attack or an embolism.

Transient global amnesia has usually been assumed to be a one-time event from which there is complete recovery. A recent review by Markowitsch questions these assumptions: the attacks are frequently repeated and there is evidence of permanent memory loss. Indeed, a thorough study by Mazzucchi et al. shows that there is significant chronic memory loss; this is normally overlooked because of the dramatic recovery from global amnesia and because-careful memory testing is seldom done on these people.

Traumatic Amnesia

Head injuries commonly produce a form of amnesia, the severity of the injury determining the characteristics of the amnesia. There is typically a transient loss of consciousness followed by a short period of confusion. The period of retrograde amnesia generally shrinks over time, frequently leaving a residual retrograde amnesia of only a few seconds to a minute for events immediately preceding the injury. Further, there is usually an additional period of posttraumatic amnesia (i.e., antero-grade amnesia).

Duration of the posttraumatic amnesia varies. In one series of patients with severe head injuries Whitty and Zangwill found that 10 percent had durations of less than one week, 30 percent had durations of two to three weeks, and the remaining 60 percent had durations of over three weeks. Unfortunately, the authors fail to specify how long the amnesia lasted in the third group. Sometimes certain events, such as the visit of a relative or some unusual occurrence, may be retained as "islands of memory" during this amnesic period. According to Whitty and Zangwill the posttraumatic amnesia commonly ends quite sharply, often after a period of natural sleep.

Infantile Amnesia

One form of amnesia is experienced by every-one and is therefore particularly intriguing: events or things experienced or learned in infancy are forgotten. (We refer readers to the excellent review by Campbell and Spear for more detail.)

The most paradoxical aspect of infantile amnesia is that the early years are generally regarded as being a time of critical importance in a child's development, yet these years are not remembered in adulthood. The evidence suggests that memory of early childhood begins in late preschool or early school years. Although there are some snatches of memory here and there from early childhood, it is difficult to know whether they are true memories or have resulted from repetition of favorite stories by parents.

Infantile amnesia appears to have three plausible explanations. First, the information may still be there but be no longer retrievable. A fascinating experiment done by Yerkes in 1912 is germane to this theory. Yerkes trained worms in a Y-maze, one end of which had a shock grid and the other, moist earth. Once the worms had learned this problem Yerkes decapitated the creatures and retested the body on the maze over the ensuing days. The body appeared to retain the habit for a while, but appeared to lose the skill as a new head grew. To our knowledge this experiment has not been replicated, but the message of the data is intriguing: as the forebrain develops it either disrupts the memory or blocks its retrieval. Because in human ontogeny the brain clearly develops functionally in a caudorostral sequence, a similar explanation of infantile amnesia is plausible. In other words, as the new areas in the forebrain (i.e., cerebral hemispheres) mature and become functional, they preclude access to the memories laid down earlier.

A second, similar explanation of infantile amnesia suggests that one memory system is used by infants and another develops for adults. Memories are lost because they are not stored in the new, adult system.

A third explanation is that the problem is cellular. As neurons mature, more and more dendritic processes grow. They interfere with the established memories, which are thus lost.

Commissurotomy

Commissurotomy patients, although not amnesic, show a disturbance of memory for both visual and verbal material, and like frontal lobe patients, they make many intrusion and omission errors on tests of movement copying. The cause of the memory deficit is unknown.

THEORIES OF AMNESIA

On the whole, models of amnesia have been unsatisfactory for two reasons: either they have been restricted to very simple aspects of memory, or they have been based on communications theory or complex human cognitive theory and are consequently difficult to reconcile with both neuropsychology and neurophysiology. Despite these shortcomings there is no shortage of theories. (Weiskrantz noted, tongue in cheek, that there are now more theories of the human amnesic syndrome than there are amnesic subjects.) For present purposes, however, theories of amnesia can be grouped into two broad categories: sequential processing theories, in which it is assumed that there is a defect in the sequential processing of information, and structural theories, in which a blockage in a particular form of memory is assumed.

Sequential-Processing Theory

In most of the sequential-processing theories of memory it is assumed that there is a deficit in the processing of memory storage or retrieval. It is also assumed that memory traces are sequentially transferred from short-term to long-term memory. The oldest and most widely known sequential-processing model is the consolidation model, dating back to Müller and Pilzecker in 1900. In the modern version of this theory it is assumed that for memory to become permanent, some structural change takes place, e.g., perhaps a synapse becomes larger or more effective. Thus, like gelatin, which takes time to set, memory takes time to be "consolidated." Amnesia is presumed to result when the process of consolidation is disrupted and the memory trace fails to produce a structural change and is lost. Applied to the patient H.M., this theory suggests that his short-term memory is intact and his long-term memory storage system is intact, but that hippocampal damage has resulted in the loss of the process of consolidation. Another version of the processing model is the hypothesis that memory really is stored after all, but the system that is responsible for retrieving memory traces is lost. This aspect of the theory is useful for explaining the behavior of Korsakoff individuals, who are apparently able to remember some things but can retrieve them only with prompting. For example, if told that someone's name is John, they are unable to remember John's name a few minutes later, but if asked if his name is Mark or John, they may promptly answer, "John." What is important to note about sequential theories is that storage systems are thought to be intact but the systems of storage and/or retrieval are thought to be absent or ineffective.

Structural Theory

If we consider all the evidence in the amnesic literature, we must immediately be struck with the fact that there seems to be at least two kinds of long-term memory. We must also be struck with the fact that some kind of distinction can be made between "knowing" something and "knowing that you know it." Amnesics commonly appear unaware of their memories. For example, on tests on which amnesics display long-term retention the subjects claim to have no recollection of ever having performed the test before, although they have obviously retained the task. Similarly, amnesics do not suffer from the "tip of the tongue phenomenon" of normal subjects, who "know they know" but are unable to demonstrate the retention. Squire has suggested that these two types of memory be called procedural and declarative. **Procedural** memory is the modification of behavior that takes place when a skill or an operation is mastered. **Declarative** memory is the ability to recount when and how the procedure was acquired. In the case of H.M., an example of procedural memory capacity would be his ability to acquire mirror drawing, whereas an example of declarative memory impairment would be his inability to recall that he had been trained at the task. Weiskrantz has insightfully noted that this dissociation may be analogous to the "blindsight" of occipital patients (see Chapter 10). There are at least two ways to account for how declarative and procedural memory can be anatomically distinguished. One way is to postulate that there is a disconnection between the language systems that are necessary for declarative memory and the motor systems that seem modified during procedural memory acquisition. Another sort of explanation is to postulate that memory traces are laid down at least twice. One location in which they are stored would be in the system that executes the behavior. A second location would be in some sort of language-related memory store. The first memory trace would permit appropriate task execution, whereas the second would monitor the execution and would record relevant details of time, place, success, etc. The idea that there is such a dichotomy in the nervous system has a certain appeal because there is overwhelming evidence that almost every level of the nervous system is capable of learning of some sort and thus of what we are calling procedural memory, whereas only certain "higher-level" structures appear capable of declarative memory. On the

basis of this logic it seems clear that hippocampal-amygdala systems are necessary for declarative memory but not for procedural memory. Theoretically, something like the model illustrated in Figure 20–12 might apply. In response to a command, a task may be executed through a series of neural structures involving the efferent systems of the frontal cortex. For simplicity, this is referred to as the "procedural route." Simultaneously, performance, and the context in which it occurs, is monitored through a system that must both be partly separate from the procedural route and include hippocampal-amygdala circuitry. For simplicity, we call this the declarative route. Both systems will involve a variety of subcortical relays and feedback loops, etc., which are not illustrated. Damage to subcortical circuitry (e.g., the diencephalon) and to feedback loops

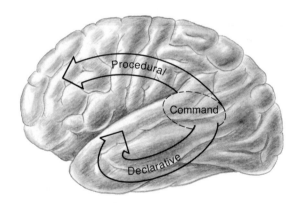

FIGURE 20–12. A model of memory systems that accounts for the retention of procedural memory and the loss of declarative memory in amnesic patients. The declarative system must be partly independent from the procedural system and it must involve hippocampal-amygdala circuitry. The model proposes that in response to a command, procedural memory is encoded in afferent systems of the frontal cortex involved in task execution, whereas the declarative system involves monitoring task execution and noting the details about time, place, circumstance, etc. Subcortical circuitry and feedback loops are not shown.

(e.g., the thalamus) may account for why amnesia can be produced by a variety of different lesions. Finally, since procedural memory is intimately dependent on the efferent systems within which it is encoded, it should be rather robust to neural insult that spares those efferent systems.

S.: A CASE OF TOTAL RECALL

We would be remiss if having presented H.M., the man who cannot form new memories, we were to close this chapter without mentioning S., the man who could not forget. So remarkable are the contrasts between the two that the neural capacity lost to H.M. through surgery seems to have been present in S. to excess. Of course, the notion is unlikely to ever be confirmed. Nevertheless, if H.M. has in any way shaped our notion of memory, so, too, should S.

S. was a newspaper reporter who never took notes at briefings as did other reporters, and so came to the attention of his employer. When questioned on the matter, S. repeated verbatim the transcript of the briefing. S. had not considered himself unusual, although he had wondered why other people relied so much on written notes. Nonetheless, at his employer's urging he went to see a psychologist. In this way S. met Luria, with whom he began a 30-year study of his memory. Luria published an account of this investigation, and to this day *The Mind of the Mnemonist* is one of the most readable accounts of unusual memory.

We can document S.'s memory abilities by referring to Table 20–6. S. could look at this table for two or three minutes and then repeat it from memory: by columns, by rows, by diagonals, in reverse, in sums, or as a single number. Tested unexpectedly as many as 16 or

TABLE 20–6

Example of tables memorized by S.

6	6	8	0
5	4	3	2
1	6	8	4
7	9	3	5
4	2	3	7
3	8	9	1
1	0	0	2
3	4	5	1
2	7	6	8
1	9	2	6
2	9	6	7
5	5	2	0
×	0	1	×

With only two to three minutes study of such a table, S. was able to reproduce it in reverse order, horizontally, or vertically, or to reproduce the diagonals.

more years later, S. could repeat the performance without error.

For a good part of his life S. supported himself as a mnemonist, that is, a person who exhibits his memory in performances to audiences. During the course of his work he consigned hundreds of such lists, or lists of names, letters, nonsense syllables, etc., to memory and was able to recall any of these at some later date.

S.'s ability to commit things to memory hinged on three processes. He could visualize the stimuli mentally, recalling them simply by reading them from his internal image. He also made multisensory impressions of things. This ability, called synesthesia, involves processing any sensory event in all sensory modalities simultaneously. Thus, a word was recorded as a sound, a splash of color, an odor, and a taste as well as an object with texture and temperature. Finally, S. used the pegboard technique used by many other mnemonists; that is, he used a number of standard images with which he associated new material. In actuality, whereas most mnemonists used this technique as their primary memory device, S. seemed to use it somewhat less, relying more on his internal visual images and his multisensory impressions. Here are some examples of how he saw numbers:

> "Even numbers remind me of images. Take the number 1. This is a proud, well-built man; 2 is a high-spirited woman; 3 a gloomy person (why, I don't know); 6 a man with a swollen foot; 7 a man with a mustache; 8 a very stout woman—a sack within a sack. As for the number 87, what I see is a fat woman and a man twirling his mustache." (Luria, 1968, p. 31)
>
> "For me, 2, 4, 6, 5 are not just numbers. They have forms. 1 is a pointed number—which has nothing to do with the way it's written. It's because it's somehow firm and complete. 2 is flatter, rectangular, whitish in color, sometimes almost a gray. 3 is a pointed segment which rotates. 4 is also square and dull; it looks like 2 but has more substance to it, it's thicker. 5 is absolutely complete and takes the form of a cone or a tower—something substantial. 6, the first number after 5, has a whitish hue; 8 somehow has a naive quality, it's milky blue like lime." (Luria, 1968, p. 25)

From Luria's description of S. it seems safe to conclude that there was absolutely no limit to his ability to remember. At least Luria, in the many tests that he gave S., was never able to reach such a limit. What was his ability with respect to short-term memory, long-term memory, and forgetting?

Luria never really tested S. to determine whether he had a short-term memory of the sort that most of us have. That is, once given an item of information did S. forget it a short while later? Luria's report seems to suggest that S. had no short-term memory—everything was put into long-term storage. In fact, S. worried about his inability to forget and attempted to devise strategies for forgetting. He tried to write things down just as most of us do when we do not wish to carry them about as a memory, but the technique did not work.

> "Writing something down means I'll know I won't have to remember it . . . so I started doing this with small matters like phone numbers, last names, errands of one sort or another. But I got nowhere, for in my mind I continued to see what I'd written. . . . Then I tried writing all the notes on identical kinds of paper, using the same pencil each time. But it still doesn't work." (Luria, 1968, p. 70)

S. tried other strategies: burning the paper in his mind, or putting things on the blackboard and covering them up or erasing them in his mind. But none of these techniques worked either.

Did S. forget? We have already said that his long-term memory was amazing, but from Luria's account he did not seem to forget in the same way as the rest of us. When he missed an item, it was not because it was forgotten but because it was hidden from view or hard to see. He was always able to find it. Here is how he accounted for some of the items he had missed in a list:

> "I put the image of the *pencil* near a fence . . . the one down the street, you know. But what happened was that the image fused with that of the fence and I walked right on past without noticing it. The same thing happened with the word *egg*. I had put it up against a white wall and it blended in with the background. How could I possibly spot a white egg up against a white wall?" (Luria, 1968, p. 36)

S.'s ability to use his imagination was not limited to memorizing things. He could raise his heart rate from 70–72 to 100 beats per minute by imagining that he was exercising and could lower it to 64–66 by imagining that he was relaxing. He could also raise and lower the temperature of his hand by imagining that it was in warm or cold water. He could deal with pain by imagining that he was no longer in his body, and he could stop his sense of time passing by imagining that the hands of a clock no longer moved. He was even able to dark-adapt himself in a lighted room by imagining that he was in a darkened room. This incredible control he had over his autonomic system contrasts with H.M., who was reported to show no changes of galvanic skin response even when receiving mild skin shock.

Did S. pay a price for his memory abilities? Luria clearly takes the position that he did. Luria characterizes S. as a person with little aim in life and seemingly dull and superficial. Luria suggests that S. was not able to reason, to categorize, and to see order in things seen by ordinary people. He also had little ability to deal with metaphors; he visualized and interpreted them literally (e.g., to weigh one's words) and so was puzzled by what was meant by them. He had difficulty in understanding what was meant by simple statements and had greater difficulty understanding the sense of poetry.

In summary we can agree with Luria that S. did have an apparently limitless memory. But whether he payed a penalty for it is another matter. Because Luria's assessments of this question were clinical, not experimental, it is impossible to assess in any objective way the nature and degree of S.'s supposed impairment. (In fact, we also had some difficulty with the meaning of the poetry given to S. to interpret, and in many other situations we saw ourselves responding as S. did.) We conclude from the case of S., then, not that he paid a price, but that he was a person who had no short-term memory but a limitless long-term memory, and so was just the opposite of H.M., who has a short-term memory but no long-term memory. Whatever explanation of memory eventually evolves from the study of the nervous system, it will have to account for each of these extremes.

REFERENCES

Anderson, R. Cognitive changes after amygdalectomy. *Neuropsychologia* 16:439–451, 1978.

Barnes, C. A. Memory deficits associated with senescence: A neurophysiological and behavioral study in the rat. *Journal of Comparative and Physiological Psychology* 93:74–104, 1979.

Bartlett, F. C. *Remembering*. Cambridge: Cambridge University Press, 1932.

Bekhterev, V. M. Demonstration eines Gehirns mit Zerstörung der vorderen und inneren Theile der Hirnrinde beider Schlafenlappen. *Neurol. Zbl.* 19:990–991, 1900.

Blakemore, C. *Mechanics of the Mind*. Cambridge: Cambridge University Press, 1977.

Bliss, T., and A. Gardner-Medwin. Long-lasting potentiation of synaptic transmission in the dentate area of unanesthetized rabbit following stimulation of the perforant path. *Journal of Physiology* 232:357–374, 1973.

Broadbent, D. E. *Perception and Communication*. London: Pergamon, 1958.

Campbell, B. A., and N. E. Spear. Ontogeny of memory. *Psychological Review* 79:215–236, 1972.

Cermak, L. S., ed. *Human Memory and Amnesia*. Hillsdale, N.J.: Lawrence Erlbaum Associates, 1982.

Chapman, L. F., R. D. Walter, C. H. Markham, R. W. Rand, and P. H. Crandall. Memory changes induced by stimulation of hippocampus or amygdala in epilepsy patients with implanted electrodes. *Transactions of the American Neurological Association* 92:50–56, 1967.

Cofer, C. N. An historical perspective. In C. N. Cofer, ed., *The Structure of Human Memory*. San Francisco: Freeman, 1975.

Cohen, N. J., and S. Corkin. The amnesic patient H.M.: Learning and retention of a cognitive skill. *Neuroscience Abstracts* 7:235, 1981.

Corkin, S. Acquisition of motor skill after bilateral medial temporal-lobe excision. *Neuropsychologia* 6:255–265, 1968.

Corkin, S. Tactually-guided maze-learning in man: Effects on unilateral cortical excisions and bilateral hippocampal lesions. *Neuropsychologia* 3:339–351, 1965.

Correll, R. E., and W. B. Scoville. Effects of medial temporal lesions on visual discrimination performance. *Journal of Comparative and Physiological Psychology* 60:175–181, 1965.

Corsi, P. M. Human memory and the medial temporal region of the brain. Unpublished Ph.D. thesis, McGill University, 1972.

Doty, R. W., and W. H. Overman. Mnemonic role of forebrain commissures in macaques. In S. Harnad, R. W. Doty, L. Goldstein, J. Jaynes, and G. Krauthamer, eds., *Lateralization in the Nervous System*. New York: Academic, 1977.

Ebbinghaus, H. *Memory*. New York: Teachers College, 1913. (Originally published in 1885.) Reprinted by Dover, New York, 1964.

Fisher, C. M., and R. O. Adams. Transient global amnesia. *Transactions of the American Neurological Association* 83:143, 1958.

Gaffan, D. Monkeys' recognition memory for complex pictures and the effect of fornix transection. *Quarterly Journal of Experimental Psychology* 29:505–514, 1977.

Garcia-Bengochea, F., O. de La Torre, and O. Esquivel. The section of the fornix in the surgical treatment of certain epilepsies. *Transactions of the American Neurological Association* 79:176–179, 1954.

Goddard, G. V. Component properties of the memory machine: Hebb revisited. In P. W. Jusczyk and R. M. Klein, eds., *The Nature of Thought: Essays in Honour of D. O. Hebb*. Hillsdale, N.J.: Lawrence Erlbaum Associates, 1980.

Hebb, D. O. *Organization of Behavior*. New York: Wiley, 1949.

Hebb, D. O. *Textbook of Psychology*. Toronto: Saunders, 1972.

Hebb, D. O. Distinctive features of learning in the higher animal. In J. F. Delafresnaye, ed., *Brain Mechanisms and Learning*. London: Blackwell, 1961.

Hebben, N., K. J. Shedlack, H. B. Eichenbaum, and S. Corkin. The amnesic patient H.M.: Diminished ability to interpret and report internal states. *Neuroscience Abstracts* 7:235, 1981.

Hirst, W. The amnesic syndrome: Descriptions and explanations. *Psychological Bulletin* 91:435–460, 1982.

Horel, J. A. The neuroanatomy of amnesia: A critique of the hippocampal memory hypothesis. *Brain* 101:403–445, 1978.

Horel, J. A., and L. G. Misantone. Visual discrimination impaired by cutting temporal lobe connections. *Science* 193:336–338, 1976.

Iversen, S. Do hippocampal lesions produce amnesia in animals? *International Review of Neurobiology* 19:1–49, 1976.

James, W. *The Principles of Psychology*. New York: Henry Holt, 1890.

Jaccarino-Hiatt, G. Impairment of cognitive organization in patients with temporal-lobe lesions. Unpublished Ph.D. thesis, McGill University, 1978.

Jarrard, L. E. Role of interference in retention by rats with hippocampal lesions. *Journal of Comparative and Physiological Psychology* 89:400–408, 1975.

Jones, M. K. Imagery as a mnemonic aid after left temporal lobectomy: Contrast between material-specific and generalized memory disorders. *Neuropsychologia* 12:21–30, 1974.

Kimura, D. Right temporal-lobe damage: Perception of unfamiliar stimuli after damage. *Archives of Neurology* 8:264–271, 1963.

Kolb, B., and B. Milner. Performance of complex arm and facial movements after focal brain lesions. *Neuropsychologia* 19:491–503, 1981.

Lashley, K. D. In search of the engram. *Symposia of the Society for Experimental Biology* 4:454–482, 1950.

Luria, A. R. *The Mind of a Mnemonist*. New York: Basic Books, 1968.

Mair, W. G. P., E. K. Warrington, and L. Weiskrantz. Memory disorder in Korsakoff's psychosis. *Brain* 102:749–783, 1979.

Markowitsch, H. J. Transient global amnesia. *Neuroscience and Biobehavioral Reviews* 7:35–43, 1983.

Mazzucchi, A., G. Moretti, P. Caffarra, and M. Parma. Neuropsychological functions in the follow-up of transient global amnesia. *Brain* 103:161–178, 1980.

McNaughton, B. L. Dissociation of short- and long-lasting modification of synaptic efficacy at the terminals of the perforant path. *Society for Neuroscience Abstracts* 3:517, 1977.

Milner, B. Some cognitive effects of frontal-lobe lesions in man. *Philosophical Transactions of the Royal Society of London* B298:211–226, 1982.

Milner, B. Disorders of learning and memory after temporal lobe lesions in man. *Clinical Neurosurgery* 19:421–446, 1972.

Milner, B. Interhemispheric differences in the localization of psychological processes in man. *British Medical Bulletin* 27:272–277, 1971.

Milner, B. Psychological aspects of focal epilepsy and its neurosurgical management. *Advances in Neurology* 8:299–321, 1975.

Milner, B. Visually-guided maze learning in man: Effects of bilateral hippocampal, bilateral frontal, and unilateral cerebral lesions. *Neuropsychologia* 3:317–338, 1965.

Milner, B. Visual recognition and recall after right temporal-lobe excision in man. *Neuropsychologia* 6:191–209, 1968.

Milner, B. Memory. Unpublished neuroscience seminar. Montreal Neurological Institute, 1975.

Milner, B., and B. Kolb. Performance of complex arm and facial movements after cerebral commissurotomy. *Neuropsychologia,* in press.

Milner, B. Brain mechanisms suggested by studies of temporal lobes. In F. L. Darley, ed., *Brain Mechanisms Underlying Speech and Language*. New York: Grune & Stratton, 1967.

Milner, B. Memory and the medial temporal regions of the brain. In K. H. Pribram and D. E. Broadbent, eds., *Biology of Memory*. New York: Academic, 1970.

Milner, B., S. Corkin, and H.-L. Teuber. Further analysis of the hippocampal amnesic syndrome: 14-year follow-up study of H.M. *Neuropsychologia* 6:215–234,
1968.

Mishkin, M. Memory in monkeys severely impaired by combined but not by separate
removal of amygdala and hippocampus. *Nature* 273:297–298, 1978.

Mishkin, M. Visual discrimination performance following partial ablations of the temporal
lobe: II. Ventral surface vs. hippocampus. *Journal of Comparative and Physiological Psychology* 147:187–193, 1954.

Moscovitch, M. Multiple dissociations of function in amnesia. In L. S. Cermak, ed., *Human
Memory and Amnesia.* Hillsdale, N.J.: Lawrence Erlbaum Associates, 1982.

Müller, G. E., and A. Pilzecker. Experimentelle Beiträge zur Lehre vom Gedächtnis.
Zeitschrift für Psychologie 1:1–288, 1900.

O'Keefe, J., and L. Nadel. *The Hippocampus as a Cognitive Map.* Oxford: Oxford University
Press, 1978.

Olton, D. S., J. T. Becker, and G. E. Handelmann. Hippocampus, space and memory.
Behavioral and Brain Sciences 2:313–366, 1979.

Olton, D. S., and B. C. Papas. Spatial memory and hippocampal function. *Neuropsychologia*
17:669–682, 1979.

Oscar-Berman, M. Neuropsychological consequences of long-term chronic alcoholism.
American Scientist 68:410–419, 1980.

Penfield, W., and G. Mathieson. An autopsy and a discussion of the role of the hippocampus
in experiential recall. *Archives of Neurology* 31:145–154, 1974.

Penfield, W., and B. Milner. Memory deficit produced by bilateral lesions in the hippocampal zone. *Archives of Neurology and Psychiatry* 79:475–497, 1958.

Petrides, M. Effects of frontal- and temporal-lobe excisions in man on the performance of
associative-learning tasks. *Neuropsychologia,* in press.

Petrides, M., and B. Milner. Deficits on subject-ordered tasks after frontal- and temporal-
lobe lesions in man. *Neuropsychologia* 20:249–262, 1982.

Posner, M. I. *Cognition: An Introduction.* Glenview, Ill.: Scott, Foresman, 1973.

Prisko, L. Short-term memory in focal cerebral damage. Unpublished Ph.D. thesis, McGill
University, 1963.

Rasmussen, T., and B. Milner. Clinical and surgical studies of cerebral speech areas in man.
In K. J. Zulch, O. Creutzfeldt, and G. C. Galbraith, eds., *Cerebral Localization.* Berlin
and New York: Springer-Verlag, 1975.

Robertson, A. D., and J. Inglis. The effects of electroconvulsive therapy on human learning
and memory. *Canadian Psychological Review* 18:285–307, 1977.

Sainsbury, R. S., and G. W. Jason. Fimbria-fornix lesions and sexual-social behavior in the
guinea pig. *Physiology and Behavior* 17:963–967, 1976.

Samuels, I., N. Butters, and P. Fedio. Short-term memory disorders following temporal-
lobe removals in humans. *Cortex* 8:283–298, 1972.

Sanders, H. I., and E. K. Warrington. Memory for remote events in amnesic patients. *Brain*
94:661–668, 1971.

Schacter, D. L., and H. F. Crovitz. Memory function after closed head injury: A review of
the quantitative research. *Cortex* 13:150–176, 1977.

Scoville, W. B., and B. Milner. Loss of recent memory after bilateral hippocampal lesions. *Journal of Neurology, Neurosurgery and Psychiatry* 20:11–21, 1957.

Serafetinides, E. A., R. D. Walter, and D. G. Cherlow. Amnestic confusional phenomena, hippocampal stimulation, and laterality factors. In K. H. Pribram and R. Isaacson, eds., *The Hippocampus,* vol. II. New York: Plenum, 1975.

Shankweiler, D. Defects in recognition and reproduction of familiar tunes after unilateral temporal lobectomy. Paper presented at the 37th Annual Meeting of the Eastern Psychological Association, New York, 1966.

Shipley, J. E., and B. Kolb. Neuronal correlates of species-typical behavior in the Syrian Golden Hamster. *Journal of Comparative and Physiological Psychology* 91:1056–1073, 1977.

Smith, M. L., and B. Milner. The role of the right hippocampus in the recall of spatial location. *Neuropsychologia* 19:781–793, 1981.

Squire, L. R. The neuropsychology of human memory. *Annual Review of Neuroscience* 5:241–273, 1982.

Squire, L. R. A stable impairment in remote memory following electroconvulsive therapy. *Neuropsychologia* 13:51–58, 1975.

Squire, L. R., and N. J. Cohen. Remote memory, retrograde amnesia, and the neuropsychology of memory. In L. S. Cermak, ed., *Human Memory and Amnesia*. Hillsdale, N.J.: Lawrence Erlbaum Associates, 1982.

Squire, L. R., and R. Y. Moore. Dorsal thalamic lesion in a noted case of human memory dysfunction. *Annals of Neurology* 6:503–506, 1979.

Talland, G. A. *The Pathology of Memory*. New York: Academic, 1969.

Taylor, J. R., R. Tomphins, R. Demers, and D. Anderson. Electroconvulsive therapy and memory dysfunction? Is there evidence for prolonged defects? *Biological Psychiatry* 17:1169–1193, 1982.

Taylor, L. Localization of cerebral lesions by psychological testing. *Clinical Neurosurgery* 16:269–287, 1969.

Teuber, H.-L., B. Milner, and H. G. Vaughan. Persistent anterograde amnesia after stab wound of the basal brain. *Neuropsychologia* 6:267–282, 1968.

Warrington, E., and M. James. An experimental investigation of facial recognition in patients with unilateral cerebral lesions. *Cortex* 3:317–326, 1967.

Warrington, E. K., and L. Weiskrantz. Further analysis of the prior learning effect in amnesic patients. *Neuropsychologia* 16:169–177, 1978.

Warrington, E. K., and L. Weiskrantz. An analysis of short-term and long-term memory defects in man. In J. A. Deutsch, ed., *The Physiological Basis of Memory*. New York: Academic, 1973.

Weiskrantz, L. A comparison of hippocampal pathology in man and other animals. *Functions of the Septo-Hippocampal System,* Ciba Foundation Symposium. Amsterdam: Elsevier, 1978.

Weiskrantz, L., and E. K. Warrington. The problem of the amnesic syndrome in man and animals. In K. H. Pribram and R. Isaacson, eds., *The Hippocampus,* vol. II. New York: Plenum, 1975.

Whitty, C. W. M., and O. L. Zangwill. Traumatic amnesia. In C. W. M. Whitty and O. L. Zangwill, eds., *Amnesia*. London: Butterworth, 1966.

Winocur, G., and C. B. Breckenridge. Cue-dependent behavior of hippocampally damaged rats in a complex maze. *Journal of Comparative and Physiological Psychology* 82:512–522, 1973.

Woolsey, R. M., and J. S. Nelson. A symptomatic destruction of the fornix in man. *Archives of Neurology* 32:566–568, 1975.

Yerkes, R. M. The intelligence of earthworms. *Journal of Animal Behavior* 2:332–352, 1912.

Zaidel, D., and R. W. Sperry. Memory impairment after commissurotomy in man. *Brain* 97:263–272, 1974.

Zangwill, O. L. Remembering revisited. *Quarterly Journal of Experimental Psychology* 24:123–138, 1972.

Zola-Morgan, S., L. Squire, and M. Mishkin. The neuroanatomy of amnesia: Amygdala-hippocampus versus temporal stem. *Science* 218:1337–1339, 1982.

21

LANGUAGE

It is tempting to analyze the neurological correlates of language functions by considering the theoretical sensory-integrative, memory, and motor functions of the respective regions of association cortex. The activity of the association cortex of the left hemisphere integrates, however, to form a functional language system that is far more complex than an isolated analysis of the parietal, temporal, and frontal lobes would suggest. Thus, details of the neural mechanisms of language have been among the most difficult of the brain's functions to study. This difficulty has been compounded by the absence of language in other species, making models of the neural correlates of language difficult to test experimentally. In this chapter we briefly review the history of thought regarding the neurological basis of language, examine the cortical and subcortical speech zones as mapped by stimulation and lesion studies, consider disorders of language and theoretical models of language, and, finally, examine the phylogenetic origins of language.

HISTORICAL VIEWS

A brief review of the historical development of ideas about language function is the most effective approach to studying the organization of the neurological basis of language function. In the early 1800s, Gall, in his phrenology, was the first to propose a relation between localized regions of the brain and specific behaviors. Bouillard agreed with Gall and attempted to provide clinical proof that the organ of language resided in the anterior lobes of the brain. Indeed, in 1825 Bouillard even proposed asymmetry of brain function, suggesting that the left hemisphere had a special role in complex movement such as fencing, writing, and speech. This proposal was supported a little later by Dax, in 1836, when he described a series of cases demonstrating that disorders of language were consistently associated with lesions of the left hemisphere. Although the hypothesis that speech is localized in the frontal lobe of the left hemisphere was revived in 1861 by Auburtin, it was Broca who provided the anatomical proof of the theory, and it is an irony of science that the anterior speech zone became known as Broca's area. The primary disturbance resulting from damage to Broca's area appeared to be a defect in the motor component of speech production. In 1875 Wernicke demonstrated that a lesion in the temporal-parietal cortex produced a form of language disturbance that differed from that described by Broca. This region became known as Wernicke's area. Wernicke proposed that Broca's area was the center of language production, whereas Wernicke's area was the center of language understanding. Wernicke's proposals led to a flurry of "brain diagrams" in the late 1800s, each purporting to describe how lesions to Broca's and Wernicke's areas, as well as to associated regions and their interconnections, could produce specific disturbances in language functions.

Although the localizationists held the dominant view at the turn of the century, there were dissenting voices, most notably those of Hughlings-Jackson, Freud, Marie, and Head. Hughlings-Jackson contended that language is a dynamic process that derives from the integrated function of the whole brain, and although he conceded a special role for the left hemisphere in language, he believed that the right hemisphere and subcortical structures must also play a significant role in language function. He argued that the more complex a task is, the greater the number of regions and structures in the brain that must be involved. For example, the ability to write one's name involves a much smaller, more localized brain region than the ability to write a book. Thus, a person might be unable to write a book after damage to virtually any region of the association cortex, but the ability to write one's name would be impaired only by a restricted lesion in the temporal-parietal cortex. By the 1920s

the pendulum had swung in favor of a holistic view of language function, especially after the publication of Head's elegant and influential attack on localizationists in 1926. Not until the 1950s and 1960s did the localizationist view of language function regain credibility, primarily through Geschwind's theoretical writings.

Today it is reasonable to say that the primary language functions of the brain are housed in broadly defined language zones in the left hemisphere, including Broca's and Wernicke's areas, as well as in other zones of association cortex within the left hemisphere, especially the tertiary zone of the left temporal cortex. Lesser, and poorly understood, roles are played by the association cortex of the right hemisphere and by subcortical structures, including especially the basal ganglia and posterior thalamus. This view of the neurology of language thus represents a compromise between the extremes of inflexible wiring diagrams of the late 1800s and the holistic views of the 1920s.

SPEECH ZONES AS MAPPED BY STIMULATION AND ABLATION

The zones of the neocortex involved in language, and particularly in speech, have been identified by careful investigations of the effects both of cortical stimulation during surgery and of the effects of surgery on behavior. Accumulating results from hundreds of patients has made it possible to construct statistically defined regions of the neocortex specifically concerned with language processes.

Electrical Stimulation

The investigations undertaken by Penfield and his associates on patients undergoing surgical

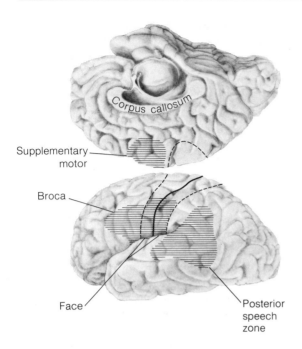

Supplementary motor

Broca

Face

Corpus callosum

Posterior speech zone

FIGURE 21–1. Shaded areas indicate the zones in which electrical stimulation may interfere with speech. Note that the posterior area is much larger than the classical Wernicke's area. Speech is also disrupted by stimulation in the face or supplementary motor area of the right hemisphere. A. Medial view of the left hemisphere. B. Lateral view of the left hemisphere.

treatment of epilepsy were the first to clearly identify the extent of the neocortical speech zones. Subsequent work by others has confirmed Penfield's findings and has clarified and extended them by the use of more quantitative behavioral recording techniques. The major findings are as follows:

1. Stimulation of a number of cortical areas (Figure 21–1) with a low-voltage electric current interferes with speech. These areas include the classical areas of Broca and Wernicke in the left hemisphere, as well as the sensory and motor representations of the face in both hemispheres and in a region known as the supplementary motor area, or MII, of both hemispheres. (See Figure 4–5 for an illustration of the organization of MII.)

2. Penfield and Roberts conclude that stimulation produces two effects on speech:

a. Positive effects, meaning vocalization, which is not speech but rather a sustained or interrupted vowel cry, such as "Oh. . . ." Vocalization can be elicited by stimulation of either the face area or the supplementary motor region of either hemisphere.

b. Negative effects, meaning the inability to vocalize or to use words properly. These include a variety of aphasia-like errors:

i. Total arrest of speech or an inability to vocalize spontaneously; this occurs from stimulation throughout the shaded zones in Figure 21–1.

ii. Hesitation and slurring of speech: hesitation occurs from stimulation throughout the zones of Figure 21–1; slurring occurs primarily from stimulation of the face area in either hemisphere.

iii. Distortion and repetition of words and syllables; distortion differs from slurring in that the distorted sound is an unintelligible noise rather than a word. These effects occur primarily from stimulation of the classical speech zones, although occasionally from the face area as well.

iv. Confusion of numbers while counting; for example, a patient may jump from "six" to "nineteen" to "four" and so on. Confusion in counting results from stimulation of Broca's or Wernicke's area.

v. Inability to name despite retained ability to speak. "An example is 'That is a . . . I know. That is a. . . .' When the current was removed, the patient named the picture correctly. Another example is, 'Oh, I know what it is. That is what you put in your shoes.' After withdrawal of the stimulating electrodes, the patient immediately said 'foot' "(Penfield and Roberts, 1959, p. 123). Naming difficulties arise from stimulation throughout the anterior (Broca's) and posterior (Wernicke's) speech zones.

vi. Misnaming; may occur when the subject uses words related in sound such as "camel" for "comb," uses synonyms such as "cutters" for "scissors," or perseverates by using the same name twice. For example, a picture of a bird may be named correctly but the next picture, a table, is also called a bird. Misnaming, like naming difficulties, occurs during stimulation of both the anterior and the posterior speech zones.

3. Ojemann and Mateer report that during stimulation in the region of Broca's area, patients are unable to make voluntary facial movements similar to those illustrated in Figure 18–2. Curiously, stimulation of these same points may also disrupt phonemic discrimination as measured by the phonetic differentiation test described in Chapter 18. These authors also describe defects in short-term memory resulting from stimulation in roughly the zone identified from lesion studies and described in Figure 20–11.

4. Most reports agree that the extent of the cortical language zones as marked by stimulation varies considerably among subjects, although there is little indication of what this variation may reflect. In this regard, it would seem worthwhile to correlate the size of the speech zones with performance on a variety of verbal tests. Perhaps verbal ability is positively correlated with the size of the speech zones, a suggestion that has intuitive appeal but that is obviously speculative and remains to be proved.

Several important conclusions can be drawn from these results. First, the data do not support strict localizationist models of language, since stimulation of the anterior and posterior speech zones has remarkably similar effects on speech functions. Second, stimulation of the neocortex much beyond the classical areas of Broca and Wernicke disturbs speech functions. The area involved is remarkably similar to the speech zones defined more recently by regional blood flow studies (see Chapter 14). Compare, for example, Figures 14–9 and 21–1. Third, stimulation of the speech zone affects more than just talking, for there are deficits in voluntary motor control of facial musculature as well as of short-term memory. Fourth, removal of the cortex surrounding the posterior speech zone, mapped in Figure 21–1, does not produce lasting aphasia, even though fibers connecting the visual areas to the speech regions may be disrupted. Thus, it seems clear that these connections are not essential in the coordination of these two areas. Fifth, it has proved difficult to classify the transient aphasia following surgery, because each patient appears to be unique. There is also little evidence for a distinctive type of aphasia associated specifically with damage to either the anterior or posterior speech zones. In other words, there is no evidence for pure motor or sensory aphasias as postulated by Wernicke. Sixth, chronic speech and language deficits occur only if lesions are made within the classical speech zones (see Figure 21–2). Although stimulation of the face areas and supplementary motor zones produces speech arrest, removal of these zones has no chronic effect on speech. Recall, however, that face-area lesions do chronically impair other language functions (see Chapter 18).

One issue arising from the study of lesion patients is the relative importance of the anterior and posterior speech zones. Recall (Chapter 13) that in 1906 Marie published his celebrated paper claiming that Broca's area plays no special role in language. His conclu-

FIGURE 21–2. Summary of the effects of lesions on speech. Damage to the darker two areas produces chronic aphasia, damage to the lighter areas produces transient aphasia, and damage beyond these areas does not produce aphasia.

sion was based on the study of cases in which there appeared to be destruction of Broca's area without aphasia and of cases in which there was Broca's aphasia without damage to Broca's area. Marie undoubtedly overstated his case, but his point was well taken and led to a controversy that persists to this day. We are inclined to agree with Zangwill's suggestion that although Broca's area undoubtedly plays a significant role in the normal control of articulate speech, damage to the area does not have the severe consequences on language that lesions in the posterior speech zone have. Furthermore, the severity of aphasia is far more variable following lesions to Broca's area than to Wernicke's area. Some Broca's area patients

may have only mild articulatory disorders, whereas others have severe disturbances of both expression and comprehension. Jefferson was probably correct in his suggestion that this variability reflects the extent of subcortical damage in addition to the damage to Broca's area itself.

Subcortical Components in Language

At the same time that Broca was describing a cortical center for speech control, Hughlings-Jackson proposed that subcortical structures are critical to language. In 1866 he wrote: "I think it will be found that the nearer the disease is to the corpus striatum, the more likely is the defect of articulation to be the striking thing, and the farther off, the more likely it is to be one of mistakes of words." Although he was the first to propose that aphasias result from subcortical damage, this proposition was not seriously considered until 1959, when Penfield and Roberts proposed that the thalamus, especially the **pulvinar,** functions to coordinate the activity of the cortical speech zones. In recent years evidence from stimulation and lesion studies has supported Hughlings-Jackson's proposal, although the importance and the precise role of the thalamus is still under debate.

In the course of surgical treatment of **dyskinesia,** electrodes are placed in the thalamus and an electric current applied in order to precisely define the electrode's position. For example, movements evoked by stimulation would indicate placement in motor thalamus, whereas somatosensory changes such as tingling sensations in the skin would indicate placement in the somatosensory thalamus. When the electrode is properly placed, a stronger current is passed, producing a lesion intended to relieve the dyskinesia. Careful study of language functions during these procedures, especially by

Ojemann and by Cooper and their respective colleagues, has indicated that the pulvinar and the lateral posterior-lateral central complex of the left thalamus have a role in language not shared by other subcortical structures (see Figure 1–14). Stimulation of the left ventrolateral and pulvinar nuclei of the thalamus produces speech arrest, difficulties in naming, **perseveration,** and reduced speed of talking. Stimulation has also been reported to produce positive effects on memory, because it improves later retrieval of words heard during stimulation. As a result it has been proposed that the thalamus has some role in activating or arousing the cortex.

Lesions of the ventrolateral thalamus and/or pulvinar on the left have been associated with a variety of disturbances of speech and language processes. Symptoms include postoperative dysphasia, which is usually transitory; increased verbal response latency; decreases in voice volume; alterations in speaking rate and slurring or hesitation in speech; and impaired performance on tests of verbal IQ and memory.

To summarize, there is evidence that the left posterior thalamus, including the pulvinar, lateral posterior, and lateral ventral regions, has a significant role in language. The nature of this role is still uncertain.

DISORDERS OF LANGUAGE

Before the neurology of language is given a theoretical description, the disorders of language must first be considered, since theoretical formulations of language function must be able to account for the disorders observed. We first describe the types of deficits observed in language and then consider the classification of aphasias.

Language Deficits and Neurological Damage

Normal language depends on a complex interaction among sensory integration and symbolic association, motor skills, learned syntactic patterns, and verbal memory. **Aphasia** refers to a disorder of language apparent in speech, writing (agraphia), or reading (alexia) produced by injury to brain areas specialized for these functions. Thus, disturbances of language due to severe intellectual impairment, loss of sensory input (especially vision and hearing), or paralysis or incoordination of the musculature of the mouth (**anarthria**) or hand (for writing) are not considered to be aphasic disturbances. These disorders may accompany aphasia, and they complicate the study of it.

Goodglass and Kaplan have broken language disturbances down into nine basic types, which we have subgrouped into disorders of comprehension and of production of language.

Disorders of Comprehension. Disorders of comprehension can be either auditory or visual, each related to the sensory modality of presentation of verbal material.

1. *Auditory comprehension.* Comprehension of auditory input may be disturbed even though the primary auditory cortex per se is not damaged. For example, a person may act as though a word was not heard at all (so-called word deafness) or as though only fragments of the word were heard. The commoner defect is not in failing to recognize that a word was spoken but rather in failing to attach meaning to the word (much as if it were spoken in a foreign language unknown to the hearer). In some cases auditory comprehension is particularly impaired when words are presented in isolation rather than in the context of a sentence. In some aphasics comprehension of in-

dividual words is intact, but certain grammatical constructions are not discriminated properly. For example, the phrases "the lost man's wallet" and "the man's lost wallet" involve the same words but have totally different meanings.

2. *Visual comprehension.* Because comprehension of written material (i.e., reading) is based on prior mastery of auditory language, it is not surprising that deficits in reading (*alexia*) accompany deficits in auditory comprehension. A disturbance of reading is commonly associated with impaired comprehension of auditory material, but these two symptoms may occur independently of each other. As with auditory defects, defects in visual comprehension may involve a deficit in recognizing individual letters or words as being letters or words, or a deficit in attaching meaning to the symbols written on a page.

Disorders of Production. There are at least eight disorders of production, which range from an inability to form words to an inability to place words together to form a spoken or written sentence.

1. *Articulation.* Speaking requires the ability to make the sounds of vowels and consonants, which will then be placed in different combinations to form words and sentences. People with severe deficits in articulation are unable to produce simple sounds, even by imitation. Noises may actually be produced, but frequently each attempt to form a word produces the same nonsense syllable. In milder forms the person may be able to articulate many sounds, especially vowel sounds, but usually will have extreme difficulty in making difficult sounds such as consonant blends. For example, one man that we saw would say "huah" for "ch" and "buh" for "bl." Deficits in articulation may result from any of three different causes.

First, there may be a defect in the peripheral speech mechanisms of the larynx, pharynx, and tongue. This disorder is not an aphasia but is termed **dysarthria.** Second, there may be a defect in choosing the desired sound from all those available in a person's repertory. Third, there may be a deficit in the motor system that prevents the desired sound from being properly pronounced.

2. *Word finding.* Words are formed by combining sounds; to do this correctly it is necessary to choose the appropriate words from the large available repertory. Virtually all aphasics suffer from some restriction in the repertory of words available, and even when words are produced, it takes longer than normal to do so. If this difficulty in finding words occurs in the absence of other aphasic symptoms, the disorder is called **anomia.** Difficulty in word finding often results in the person's deliberately choosing a word that approximates the intended idea when the intended word cannot be found. For example, one woman we saw substituted words such as "cow" for "milk" and "cigar" for "pipe."

3. *Paraphasia.* Goodglass and Kaplan define **paraphasia** as the production of unintended syllables, words, or phrases during the effort to speak. Paraphasia differs from difficulties in articulation in that sounds are correctly articulated, but they are the wrong sounds, and either distort the intended word (e.g., "pike" instead of "pipe") or produce a completely unintended word (e.g., "my mother" instead of "my wife").

4. *Loss of grammar and syntax.* Words must be placed together to produce proper grammar and syntax. Some individuals are totally unable to place words together into grammatically

correct sequences and so restrict their sentences to short utterances of two or three words.

Choosing correct verb tenses may be especially difficult, in which case nearly all verbs are in the present tense, usually of a simple form such as "He go." It is curious that many of these aphasics are able to produce long strings of memorized sequences such as in counting numbers or reciting days of the week and months of the year; some individuals can even recite previously learned poetry or prayers or repeat sentences they have just heard. The preservation of these abilities, however, in the face of an inability to produce spontaneous sentences, demonstrates that some associative ability is missing or seriously impaired.

5. *Repetition*. Although many aphasics can repeat aurally presented material, others cannot, even though other language functions may appear fairly intact. Disorders of repetition may result either from deficits in comprehension or articulation—in which case there are associated aphasic symptoms—or from a selective dissociation between auditory-input and speech-output systems. In the latter case, of selective dissociation, the disorder of repetition may be the only significant language disturbance and may go unnoticed except through special testing.

6. *Verbal fluency*. Verbal fluency is the ability to produce words in uninterrupted strings. Low verbal fluency may be associated with word-finding difficulty or may occur in the absence of any other language disturbances. Recall that frontal lesions, even on the right, may reduce word output even though no other deficits in language use or production are known.

7. *Writing*. Writing, one of the most complex of language abilities, may be disturbed in a wide variety of ways. First, it may result from

disturbance in movement of the limb to produce letters and words—although this disorder would not be a disturbance of language per se. At a more complex level, writing may be impossible *(agraphia)* because of inability to recall the form of letters or the correct movements necessary to produce them. Many of the deficits observed in oral language may also occur in written language, as in **paragraphia,** which is the writing of the incorrect word, or in perseveration, which would involve writing the same word repeatedly.

8. *Prosody*. Prosody (from the Greek for song) refers to the tone or accent of language. Normally the term is used to refer to the loudness of voice, the relative duration of different phonemes, and the vocal pitch. The closest physical correlates are intensity, time pattern, and vocal frequency respectively. Monrad-Krohn described three classes of prosodic abnormality: *hyperprosody*, an excessive or exaggerated prosody, sometimes characterizing mania and only occasionally observed in aphasics; *dysprosody*, a distorted prosody in which listeners perceive a foreign accent (usually Welsh or German in native English speakers); and *aprosody*, an attenuation or lack of normal prosody, such as is often observed in people with Parkinson's disease. We shall return to prosody in our discussion of affect in the next chapter.

Classification of Aphasias

Since the time of Wernicke people have attempted to describe different types of aphasias by identifying clusters of symptoms associated with particular brain lesions. This has proved to be a difficult task, partly because so few cases are thoroughly studied, and partly because so few well-studied cases ever come to autopsy. Thus, there is constant debate over which lesions produce which cluster of aphasic symptoms. Although many researchers have considered different types of aphasias to be totally independent of one another, there is no convincing empirical proof of this claim. As Brown puts it:

All disorders of speech understanding, even those with the most limited pathology, are likely to have an expressive element, while some defect in speech comprehension should be a constant feature of the motor aphasias. The importance of this finding has certainly not received proper attention in the literature. One need only point to the fact that there is not one careful study ofspeech comprehension in restricted cases of Broca's aphasia, nor a comparable study, of the much rarer word-deafness, of the true state of expressive speech. (Brown, 1972, p. 14)

In spite of considerable disagreement over the number of types of aphasias, there are several that most workers in the field agree on. These are summarized in Table 21–1. Broadly

TABLE 21–1

Definition of aphasic syndromes [a]		
Syndrome	Type of speech production	Type of language errors
A. *Fluent*		
Wernicke	Fluent speech, without articulatory disorders	Neologism and/or anomias, or paraphasias; poor comprehension; poor repetition
Transcortical, sensory	Fluent speech, without articulatory disorders	Verbal paraphasias and anomias; poor comprehension
Conduction	Fluent, sometimes halting speech, but without articulatory disorders	Phonemic paraphasias and neologisms; phonemic groping; poor repetition
Amnesic	Fluent speech, without articulatory disorders	Anomia and occasional paraphasias
B. *Nonfluent*		
Broca, severe	Laborious articulation	Speechlessness with recurring utterances or syndrome of phonetic disintegration; poor repetition
Broca, mild	Slight but obvious articulatory disorders	Phonemic paraphasias with anomia; agrammatism; dysprosody
Transcortical motor	Marked tendency to reduction and inertia, without articulatory disorders	Uncompleted sentences and anomias; naming better than spontaneous speech
Global	Laborious articulation	Speechlessness with recurring utterances; poor comprehension; poor repetition
C. *"Pure"*		
Alexia without agraphia	Normal	Poor reading
Agraphia	Normal	Poor writing
Word deafness	Normal	Poor comprehension; poor repetition

[a] After Mazzocchi and Vignolo, 1979.

defined, aphasias can be classified into three general categories: **fluent aphasias,** in which there is fluent speech but difficulties either in auditory verbal comprehension and/or the repetition of words, phrases, or sentences spoken by others; **nonfluent aphasias,** in which there are difficulties in articulating but relatively good auditory verbal comprehension; and "pure aphasias," in which there are selective impairments of reading, writing, or recognition of words. Within each of these broad categories of aphasia, numerous subtypes are often distinguished, including Wernicke's aphasia, isolation syndrome, conduction aphasia, anomic aphasia, and Broca's aphasia.

1. *Wernicke's aphasia.* Classically Wernicke's, or sensory, aphasia is the inability to comprehend words or to arrange sounds into coherent speech. Luria has proposed that this type of aphasia has three characteristics. First, to hear and make out the sounds of speech, one must be able to qualify sounds—that is, to include sounds in the system of phonemes that are the basic units of speech in a given language. An example will illustrate. In the Japanese language the sounds "l" and "r" are not distinguished; a Japanese hearing English cannot distinguish these sounds because the necessary template is not in the brain. Thus, although this distinction is perfectly clear to English-speaking persons, it is not to native Japanese. This is precisely the problem that a person with Wernicke's aphasia has in his or her own language: the inability to isolate the significant phonemic characteristics and to classify sounds into known phonemic systems. The second characteristic of Wernicke's aphasia is that there is a defect in speech. The affected person can speak, and may speak a great deal, but he or she confuses phonetic characteristics, producing what is often called word salad. The third characteristic is an impairment in writing. A person who cannot discern pho-

nemic characteristics cannot be expected to write, because he or she does not know the graphemes that combine to form a word.

2. *Isolation syndrome,* or transcortical aphasia. Isolation syndrome, or transcortical aphasia, is a curious type of aphasia in which individuals can repeat and understand words and name objects but cannot speak spontaneously, or they are also unable to comprehend words although they can still repeat them. This type of aphasia is presumed to be caused by loss of the secondary sensory cortex (association cortex). Comprehension could be poor because words fail to arouse associations. Production of meaningful speech could be poor because even though the production of words is normal, words are not associated with other cognitive activity in the brain.

3. *Conduction aphasia.* Conduction aphasia is a paradoxical deficit: people with the disorder can speak easily, name objects, and understand speech but cannot repeat words. The simplest explanation for this problem is that there is a disconnection of the "perceptual word image" in the parietal-temporal cortex and the "motor image of the word" in the frontal cortex. This explanation is not very convincing. There has never been any clear proof that cutting the connections actually causes this syndrome, and there is considerable debate over whether this symptom really occurs in the absence of other symptoms, especially impaired short-term memory.

4. *Anomic aphasia,* or amnestic aphasia. People with anomic aphasia comprehend speech, produce meaningful speech, and can repeat speech but have great difficulty in finding the names of objects. For example, we saw a patient who when shown a picture of a ship anchor simply could not think of the name and finally said, "I know what it does. . . . You use it to anchor a ship." Although he had actually used the word as a verb he was unable to use it as a noun. This symptom is most likely to

result from a lesion in the angular gyrus, but nearly all aphasics have some naming difficulties. Luria and Hutton emphasize that this type of aphasia cannot be explained simply; it appears likely that the same symptom may result from any one of three causes. First, to name an object one must identify its distinguishing characteristics. A person having difficulties in isolating these characteristics will not name it properly. Second, to name an object, having isolated its characteristics, one must also develop the auditory form of the word. Thus, a person who does not retain the word's auditory structure will be unable to produce it. Finally, to produce the word, one must select the appropriate word from those expressing ideas closely associated with it. For example, when asked to name a butterfly, a person may have difficulty in choosing the correct word from associated words such as moth, fly, insect, etc. In failing to do so the person may utter the word "moth" or even "bird." Clearly this problem is quite different from the inability to identify distinguishing characteristics. It is possible that each of these three naming problems represents a separate neurological deficit, but this possibility is rather difficult to prove.

5. *Broca's aphasia.* In Broca's aphasia a person has difficulty in speaking, although he or she continues to understand speech. Broca's aphasia is also known as motor, expressive, or nonfluent aphasia. This aphasia features a pattern of speech in which a person speaks in a very slow, deliberate manner with very simple grammatical structure. Thus, all the forms of a verb are likely to be reduced to the infinitive or the participle. Nouns are most apt to be expressed only in the singular, and conjunctions, adjectives, adverbs, and articles are very uncommon. Only the key words necessary for communication are used.

There is still no adequate explanation for Broca's aphasia. Broca assumed that the prob-

lem was an impairment of the "motor image of the word," but it is uncertain what this supposition implies about brain function. Certainly, however, the deficit is not one of making sounds, but rather one of switching from one sound to another.

Localization of Lesions in Aphasia

Distinct variation in the language disorders of different aphasics is readily apparent clinically and has been recorded for over a century. It is logical to presume that the individual symptomatology is related to the precise pathology, but this is difficult to prove. The possibility of defining the site and extent of lesions in vivo has been greatly increased by the introduction of new scanning procedures, especially the CT scan.

The first systematic attempt to correlate pathology with brain scan data was published by Benson in 1967. He correlated the locus of pathology as inferred from radioisotope brain scans (see Chapter 5) and found that patients classified as nonfluent aphasics, whom he characterized as having low verbal output, dysprosody, dysarthria, and obvious articulatory disorders, had lesions located anterior to the central fissure; fluent aphasics, whom he classified as having paraphasia, with "press of speech and a distinct lack of substantive words," had a posterior lesion. Benson thus felt that an anterior or a posterior localization could be reliably diagnosed in a majority of aphasics based solely on their verbal output. Although Benson's study was an important step in localizing lesions in aphasia, radioisotope scans are rather gross measures. The advent of the CT scan provided not only a means of producing an anterioposterior distinction but also of measuring the dorsoventral extent of a lesion. Two groups have been particularly successful in using CT scans in the study of aphasia. The first, Naeser and her colleagues, have described the relation between CT scans and aphasia using the procedure illustrated in Figure 21–3. Basically, the locus of pathology is determined from the scan and the relation between the pathology and the cortical language areas inferred from the known relations between the ventricles and the cortical areas. The second, Mazzocchi and Vignolo, have attempted to control for intersubject differences in the orientation of the CT scan by using a slightly different method. In essence, this consists of determining the angle of the CT sections, tracing the contours of the lesion on each CT section, and transferring them onto a standard lateral diagram of the hemisphere, as illustrated in Figure 21–4. The results of these two procedures are in general agreement with Benson's conclusions: Wernicke's aphasia (a fluent aphasia) is correlated with damage in the posterior speech zone and Broca's aphasia (a nonfluent aphasia) is correlated with damage to the anterior speech zone. In addition, both groups have shown that global aphasia results from larger lesions in the left hemisphere, usually including both the anterior and the posterior speech zones, and that other types of aphasia (e.g., conduction aphasia) may have similar anatomical correlates.

NEUROLOGICAL MODELS OF LANGUAGE

We noted earlier that there have been two major theoretical positions on the neurology of language: localizationism and nonlocalizationism. Although neither position is completely tenable today, in recent years Geschwind's reformulation and clarification of Wernicke's localization model has proved conceptually useful, forming a basis for more moderate positions on the neurology of language function.

The Wernicke-Geschwind Model

The Wernicke-Geschwind model is built on the assumption that the neural basis of speech and language involves the following structures: Broca's area, Wernicke's area, the arcuate fasciculus (which connects Broca's area with Wernicke's area), the precentral and postcentral face area, the angular gyrus, and the auditory and visual cortex (see Figure 21–5). Broca's area is assumed to house programs for the complex coordination of muscles for speech; Wernicke's area, the mechanism for transforming auditory input into meaningful units, or words; the arcuate fasciculus joins the anterior and posterior speech zones; the face area directs the movements of the face, tongue, etc.; and the angular gyrus combines sensory input to house "visual patterns" of letters, words, etc., and acts in some way to convert a visual stimulus into the appropriate auditory form. Geschwind has neatly summarized how these parts of the cortex function in the production of language.

> When a word is heard, the output from the primary auditory area of the cortex is received by Wernicke's area. If the word is to be spoken, the pattern is transmitted from Wernicke's area to Broca's area, where the articulatory form is aroused and passed on to the motor area that controls the movement of the muscles of speech. If the spoken word is to be spelled, the auditory pattern is passed to the angular gyrus, where it elicits the visual pattern. When a word is read, the output from the primary visual areas passes to the angular gyrus, which in turn arouses the corresponding auditory form of the word in Wernicke's area. It should be noted that in most people comprehension of a written word involves arousal of the auditory form in Wernicke's area. Wernicke argued that this was the result of the

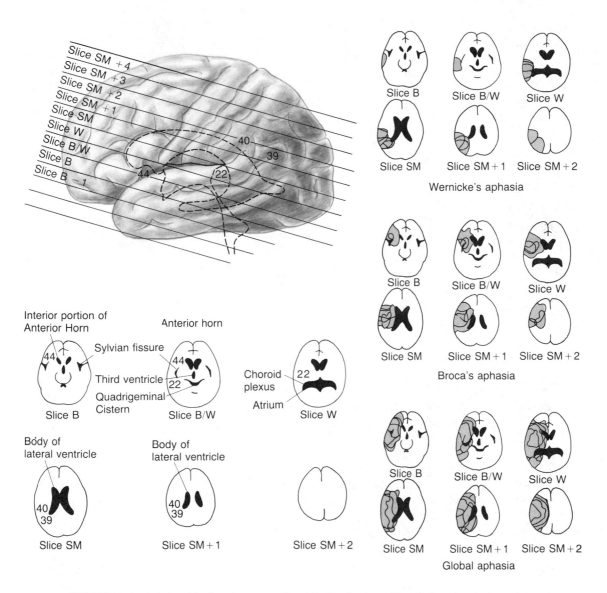

FIGURE 21–3. A. Lateral (ton) and cross-sectional (bottom) veiws of the relation of major language areas to the shape of the ventricles on CT-scan slices. B. Cross-sectional composite CT-scan lesion sites for four Wernicke's, three Broca's, and five global aphasics. (After Naeser et al., 1981.)

way most people learn written language. He thought, however, that in people who were born deaf, but had learned to read, Wernicke's area would not be in the circuit.

According to this model, if Wernicke's area is damaged, the person would have difficulty comprehending both spoken and written language. He should be unable to speak, repeat, and write

Wernicke's aphasia

Broca's aphasia

Global aphasia

FIGURE 21–4. Maps of lesions in individual cases of Wernicke's, Broca's, and global aphasia. The lower row of global aphsics shows examples that spare Wernicke's area. (After Mazzocchi and Vignolo, 1979.)

correctly. The fact that in such cases speech is fluent and well articulated suggests that Broca's area is intact but receiving inadequate information. If the damage were in Broca's area, the effect of the lesion would be to disrupt articulation. Speech would be slow and labored but comprehension should remain intact. (Geschwind, 1972, p. 344)

Further, damage to the arcuate fasciculus would not be expected to disturb either the comprehension or the production of speech, but rather should make it difficult to repeat speech, because the auditory recognition and speech production regions would be disconnected.

Two other abilities can be considered in this model: reading and writing. In theory, these abilities require the integrity of the angular gyrus to act as a way station between the visual and auditory regions (see Figure 21–5). To be meaningful, visual input must be translated into auditory form in this region. Similarly, before a word can be written, the auditory input must be translated into visual form. Thus, people with lesions of the angular gyrus would be expected to be unable to read or write. Although these people can speak and can comprehend speech, they cannot recognize a word spelled aloud, nor can they spell a word aloud.

Problems with the Wernicke-Geschwind Model

However popular and useful the Wernicke-Geschwind model of language function has been, its rigid localizationist bias leaves it open to a number of criticisms. (1) As we described earlier, stimulation of speech zones does not always interrupt speech, and when speech is interrupted, the interruption is of the same type in both the anterior and posterior speech zones. Indeed, Ojemann has recently found that stimulation-induced naming errors are

1 Spoken word ⟶ Areas 41, 42 ⟶ Wernicke (area 22) ⟶ Hear and comprehend word

2 Cognition ⟶ Wernicke ⟶ Broca ⟶ Face ⟶ Cranial nerves ⟶ Speak

3 Written word ⟶ Area 17 ⟶ Areas 18, 19 ⟶ Area 39 (angular G) ⟶ Wernicke ⟶ Read

FIGURE 21–5. Geschwind's model of the neurology of language, showing the regions of the cortex involved. Items 1 to 3 illustrate how the model explains different language functions.

more likely to occur from stimulation of the anterior speech zone than of the posterior zone! Furthermore, Ojemann and Mateer report that stimulation of the same sites disrupted both the production of sequential oral-facial movements and the ability to discriminate phonemes such as "la" and "ba." The apparent functional homogeneity within widespread regions of the speech zones is difficult to reconcile with a strict localizationist view of language function. Different effects would be expected from different portions of the speech circuitry. (2) Studies of lesion patients do not support a distinction between disorders of language production and understanding, since both expressive and receptive speech disorders are present in all aphasic patients with naturally occurring lesions, and surgical destruction of portions of the language zones seldom results in permanent aphasia. (3) The model does not include subcortical components

of language, regions that play a significant, even if poorly understood, role in language. (4) The studies of Penfield and of Rasmussen and their colleagues indicate that the corticocortical connections from the visual and auditory regions to the speech zones, and the arcuate fasciculus joining the speech zones themselves, can apparently be surgically removed without aphasia being incurred. This observation contradicts Geschwind's case studies, which show that accidental lesions of the cortex surrounding Wernicke's area produce aphasia. The discrepancy is explained by the considerable difference between the lesions in the patients studied by Geschwind and those done surgically. For example, the surgical lesions are shallower, bleed less, and are precise and restricted to the cortex; natural lesions almost certainly include subcortical damage, and remaining cortex may function abnormally.

In summary, although the Wernicke-Geschwind model of localization of language function is conceptually useful, it presents several serious difficulties. Other models have been proposed in recent years (e.g., those of Brown, of Caplan and Marshall, and of Whitaker), but none is totally acceptable. A comprehensive model of language function must incorporate stimulation and lesion data and include subcortical structures as well as mechanisms of affective control. Such a model remains to be proposed.

ASSESSMENT OF APHASIA

Since the World War II there has been widespread interest in establishing a standard systematic procedure of aphasia assessment, for use both in providing standardized clinical descriptions of patients and in facilitating comparison of patient populations in neuropsychological research. In the past 25 years a number of manuals on aphasia testing have appeared. Table 21–2 summarizes the most widely used. The first group of tests are considered to be test batteries, for they provide a large number of subtests designed to systematically explore the language capabilities of the subject. They typically include tests of (1) auditory and visual comprehension; (2) oral and written expression including tests of repetition, reading, naming, and fluency; and (3) conversational speech. Because these test batteries have the disadvantages of being lengthy and requiring special training to administer, some brief aphasia screening tests have been devised. The two most popular, the Halstead-Wepman and the token test, are frequently used as part of standard neuropsychological test batteries (see Chapter 26), being short and easy to administer and to score. These tests do not replace the de-

TABLE 21–2

Summary of the major tests of aphasia

Test	Basic reference
Aphasia test batteries	
Boston diagnostic aphasia test	Goodglass and Kaplan, 1972
Functional communicative profile	Sarno, 1969
Neurosensory center comprehensive examination for aphasia	Spreen and Benton, 1969
Porch index of communicative ability	Porch, 1967
Minnesota test for differential diagnosis of aphasia	Schuell, 1965
Wepman-Jones language modalities test for aphasia	Wepman and Jones, 1961
Aphasia screening tests	
Halstead-Wepman aphasia screening test	Halstead and Wepman, 1959
Token test	de Renzi and Vignolo, 1962

tailed examination of the aphasia test batteries, but they can be used to identify language disorders. If a fine description of the linguistic deficits is desired, the more comprehensive aphasia batteries must be given.

ASSESSMENT OF DYSLEXIA

The assessment of reading disorders is becoming a special branch of the study of language. This is because it is possible to be more objective in the analysis of reading than is possible for writing and speaking, because there is a large pedagogical science of reading, and because in addition to the **acquired dyslexias** (impairments in reading that follow brain damage), **developmental dyslexias** (failure to learn to read during development) are common and require diagnosis and remediation.

Coltheart has argued that the most objective approach to the study of reading is the model-building approach. In model building (the models are much like algorithms) the model is constructed and then reading-disabled individuals are tested in order both to define the impairment and to test the utility of the model. The model-building approach differs from classical neurological approaches in which dyslexia is defined in terms of whether it occurs in conjunction with other disorders, such as dysgraphia or dysphasia, and the primary intent is to correlate the impairment with the locus of brain damage. The model-building approach can be traced to Hinshelwood's analysis, first published in 1900. Hinshelwood recognized that there are different types of reading disorders, including (1) the inability to name letters (letter blindness), (2) the inability to read words (word blindness), and the inability to read sentences (sentence blindness). The Hinshelwood taxonomy and its subsequent elaboration has led to the current hypothesis that reading is composed of a number of independent abilities, which may have an independent anatomical basis. Figure 21–6 gives in flowchart form some different types of impairments in reading that have been encountered. In addition to the impairment, the question to be asked in order to identify it is also given. The following are brief descriptions of these impairments.

1. *Attentional dyslexia.* When one letter is present, naming is normal. When other letters are present, naming is difficult. Even if the letter is specially colored, underlined, has an arrow pointing to it, and is pointed to by the tester, it may be named incorrectly. The same phenomenon may occur when one as opposed to more than one word is present.

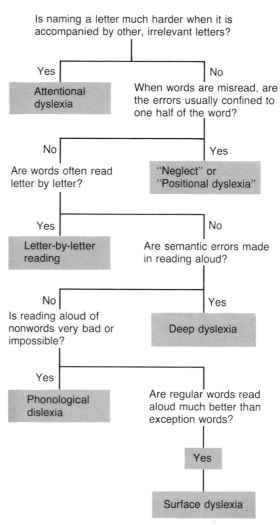

FIGURE 21–6. Flow chart for the analysis of dyslexia. (After Coltheart, 1981.)

2. *Neglect.* Persons may misread the first half of a word (e.g., "whether" as "smother"), or they may misread the last part of a word (e.g., "strong" as "stroke"). This syndrome has received little investigation.

3. *Letter-by-letter reading.* Affected individuals read words only by spelling them out

to themselves (aloud or silently). When the spelling is done silently, it can be detected by the increase in time taken to read long words. Frequently, the person can write but then has difficulty in reading what was written.

4. *Deep dyslexia.* The key symptoms in this disorder are semantic errors: persons with deep dyslexia read semantically related words in place of the word they are trying to read (e.g., "tulip" as "crocus" and "merry" as "Christmas"). Nouns are the easiest for them to read, followed by adjectives and then verbs. Function words present the greatest difficulty. Deep-dyslexic people also find it easier to read concrete than abstract words and are completely unable to read nonsense words. They are also generally impaired at writing and in short-term verbal memory (digit span).

5. *Phonological dyslexia.* The one symptom is an inability to read nonwords aloud; otherwise reading may be nearly flawless.

6. *Surface dyslexia.* The surface dyslexic is unable to recognize words directly but can understand them by using letter-to-sound relations; that is, the word can be understood if it is sounded out. This reading procedure works well as long as the words are regular ones (home, dome), but not if the words are irregular ("come" will be read as "comb"). Spelling is also impaired but is phonetically correct. Surface dyslexia will not occur in languages that are totally phonetic (such as Italian). Surface dyslexia is a common symptom of children who have difficulty in learning to read.

The explanation of reading that comes from the model-building approach is that reading is composed of a number of independent skills or subsystems, one or another of which may not be functioning in an impaired reader. Marshall cleverly demonstrates this idea with the following example of two lines of poetry that can be read either for sense or for sound:

Kuh! Sie Kuh! Sie kann der . . .
Wer Du ja Wanduhr?

The sound reader will read this as "Goosey, Goosey Gander, / Where do you wander?" The sense reader will read it as "Cow! You Cow! / Who do you think you are, you and your clock on the wall?" (We could not read these at all!) The central idea to be obtained from this example is that in normal readers sense and sound are computed in parallel, whereas in the dyslexic, one or the other process may be absent. The deep-dyslexic patient is unable to process for sound and so attempts to read for sense. The surface dyslexic is able to

FIGURE 21–7. Examples of subsystems used in reading. Note that speech from print can follow a number of different routes and can be independent of comprehension or pronunciation. (After Coltheart, 1981.)

process for sound but not for sense. A model of how parallel systems may be organized and interact is illustrated in Figure 21–7. Note that there are two quite separate ways of obtaining-speech from print, and a still different way of producing letter-names.

The important features of the model-building approach are that it does not demand that anatomical-functional relations be used, it can be equally applied to other disorders of speech, and it may eventually give an alternative perspective of how the anatomical organization of language must be arranged.

ORIGINS OF SPEECH AND LANGUAGE

Origins of Language

Speculations about human language origins are centuries old, but recently there has been some progress in providing evidence for some of the more plausible theories.[1] An obvious explanation of speech is that it slowly evolved from various kinds of vocalizations. Hewes has reviewed many of the variants of this theory, including the "pooh-pooh" theory (speech evolved from noises associated with strong emotion), the "bow-wow" theory (speech evolved from noises first made to imitate natural sounds), the "yo-he-ho" theory (speech evolved from sounds made to resonate with natural sounds), and the "sing-song" theory (speech evolved from noises made while playing or dancing). These examples by no means exhaust the list of imaginative theories of speech origin. A major difficulty with these kinds of theories is that it is very hard to col-

lect evidence to support them. Nevertheless, Steklis and Raleigh argue strongly for this type of theory. The evidence they put forth includes the following: the theory is parsimonious, involving as it does a direct, rather than an indirect, explanation; many nonhuman primates use nonemotional types of vocalizations in a rudimentary communicative style; and the evolution of new types of skilled movements would have provided a neural basis for the refined movements of the vocal system prerequisite for speech.

In addition to this theory, there are two other major theories that deserve consideration, if not for their explanatory power, then at least because they are supported by a substantial amount of research. One theory postulates that language in its present form is of recent origin. The second theory postulates that language is very old and only gradually evolved into its present form from its original gestural base. In a sense, these two theories are compatible, in that language may have evolved in a gestural form and then been rapidly transformed into a vocal form.

Speech as a Recently Evolved Ability

Let us consider the evidence that language has a relatively recent origin. Swadish developed a list of 100 basic lexical concepts that he expected to be found in every language. These included such words as I, two, woman, sun, green, etc. He then calculated the rate at which these words would have changed as new dialects of language were formed. His estimates suggest that the rate of change was 14 percent every 1000 years. When he compared the lists of words spoken in different parts of the world, his estimates suggested that between 10,000 and 100,000 years ago everyone spoke the same language. According to Swadish's logic it would be expected that language would

---

[1] A beautiful little paper by Hewes summarizes the history of theories of the phylogenesis of speech. It is recommended for anyone interested in the problem.

have had its origins at about this time because diversification would have begun almost as soon as language developed. Of course, hominids have been around for four million years, so how can one rule out the possibility that they were speaking at a much earlier date? Lieberman has studied the properties of the vocal tract that enable modern humans to make the sounds that are used for language. Modern humans have a low larynx and a large throat. Modern apes and newborn humans have neither of these characteristics and cannot produce all the sounds used in human speech. On the basis of skull reconstructions, Lieberman suggests that Neanderthal man was also unable to make the sounds necessary for modern speech. Specifically, he would not have been able to produce the vowels "a," "i," and "u." If Lieberman's hypothesis about the structure of Neanderthal man is correct and if modern humans evolved from Neanderthal man (and we must point out that both assumptions have been seriously questioned), then it can be concluded that modern speech did not exist before about 60,000 years ago, before the appearance of Cro-Magnon man. Another line of evidence for recent speech goes like this. The ability to write and the ability to speak seem to have a lot in common. Most notably, they both require very fine movements and many movement transitions. Therefore, it is possible that speech and writing appeared at about the same time. Alexander Marshack has found that the first symbols that humans made date back to about 30,000 years ago. Accordingly, this would be evidence that speech appeared at about this time. What seems to link these three separate lines of evidence together to make the recency hypothesis plausible is that the first appearance of modern humans, *Homo sapiens sapiens,* can be dated to about 40,000 years ago. Possibly the evolution of modern humans was quite sudden and one of their adaptive strategies was

language. In opposition to the notion of recently acquired speech, Holloway argues from paleontological evidence, e.g., the size of Broca's area as revealed by endocasts, that rudimentary language was probably displayed by Australopithecine roughly 2.5 to 3.5 million years ago.

Speech as a Gestural Language

The origins of the gestural theory of language can be dated to the 15th century. This theory suggests that primitive gestures and other body movements gradually evolved into modern language. It is assumed that effective hunting and farming and the maintenance of social groups required some kind of communication system, and that this need was the impetus for the evolution of language. Until recently there was no evidence that supported the gestural theory, but now at least two lines of research can cite evidence in its favor. The evidence from the first line of research is that gestural language and vocal language depend on the same neural systems. The evidence from the second line is that nonhuman primates are able to use gestures or symbols for at least rudimentary communication. The first evidence is important because if the neural systems were different, it would weaken the argument that one type of language evolved into the other. The second is important, for it shows that a similar, although much smaller brain is capable of language, thus making it unnecessary to evolve an entirely new neural system for speech.

It has long been thought that the evidence required to demonstrate support for the idea that gestural language evolved into vocal language would be an experiment showing that gestural languages and vocal language depend on the same brain structure. As early as 1878

Hughlings-Jackson suggested that a natural experiment, the loss of language in people using sign language, would provide the appropriate evidence, and he even observed a case that seemed to indicate sign language was disrupted by a left hemisphere lesion, as is vocal language. A definitive review of similar cases by Kimura confirms that lesions disrupting vocal speech also disrupt signing. Of a total of 11 patients with signing disorders following brain lesions, nine right-handers had disorders following a left hemisphere lesion. One left-handed patient had a signing disorder following a left hemisphere lesion, and one had a signing disorder following a right hemisphere lesion. These proportions are identical with those found for vocal patients who become aphasic. These results strongly favor the idea that the language systems that control vocal speech also control signing. They offer little support for any alternate view (e.g., that signing, being more spatial in nature than vocal speech, is controlled by the right hemisphere).

On the basis of other evidence, Kimura favors the idea that gesture and speech depend on the same neural systems. She examined the ability of stroke patients to perform sequences of face or arm movements that required transitions of posture from one movement to the next (i.e., the type of movements required for sign language). Lesions in the language zone that produced aphasia, particularly in the left parietal cortex, also disrupted the ability to make postural transitions. Tasks that required repetitive movements such as tapping or turning a screw were not disrupted.

In summary, it seems that there is a similarity between lesions that produce vocal language disturbances and those that disrupt the movements required for gestural language. But at this point one must ask if emotional sounds and facial expressions were also precursors of language or whether there may have been something special about certain kinds of gestures. The evidence seems not to support the idea that emotional sounds or expressions evolved into language. First, emotional expressions in apes cannot be conditioned for use as signs with the ease with which gestures can be conditioned. Second, the neural mechanisms controlling emotional expressions in both apes and man are different from those controlling language. Myers has shown that frontal lesions disrupt emotional expression in monkeys, and Kolb and Milner have found that frontal, but not parietal, lesions disrupt emotional expressions in humans.

If it is true that gestures had evolved into vocal language by the time *Homo sapiens sapiens* appeared, it is possible to make at least one testable prediction. It is very likely that the first gestures were genetically rather than culturally transmitted. These gestures should still be genetically transmitted and so should still be found in all groups of humans. A subset of this group of gestures should also be used by man's close relatives, the apes. The begging gesture, hand outstretched, of chimpanzee and human is likely an example of these gestures.

A question that can be raised with respect to gestural theories is why there is a shift to vocalizing. Hewes proposes that this derives from facial expressions, which themselves derive from gesturing. Two reasons are given for the increased use of the face: (1) as the individual increases the use of tools the hands are full and cannot be used for gesturing; (2) as language becomes more complicated there are clearly upper limits to the number of possible facial and manual expressions. A relevant observation that supports the gestural proposal is that hand gestures still accompany language. Indeed, in the absence of a common language people elaborate hand and facial gestures to communicate.

Myers has proposed a slightly different version of the gestural theory. He argues that the development of language is a logical consequence of the increasing development of the control of facial musculature. Prosimians are unable to produce facial expressions, rhesus monkeys and other monkeys are able to produce a limited range of facial expressions, and chimpanzees have a complex repertory of facial movements, but only humans have developed the movements for speech and the necessary changes in the vocal tract. Myers proposes that Broca's area creates a qualitatively different type of vocal output. This idea is not entirely inconsistent with the Kimura's notion described above. In fact, Kimura notes that the same movement transitions required for arm gestures are necessary for vocal speech, for example, in the transition from "be-ba-be" or "de-da-de." She argues, however, that these transitions are produced by the left parietal cortex rather than by Broca's area.

Evidence for Language-like Processes in Apes

Although no nonhuman primates have a verbal language analogous to the human's, one approach to the study of human language is to attempt to trace the phylogenetic origins of speech. Some recent demonstrations of languagelike processes in apes have generated interest in this approach, and the results have important implications for understanding human brain function—and may also have practical applications. For example, are there alternate forms of communication that can be substituted for the lost speech of the aphasic? In this section we shall consider the evidence for language-like processes in apes, the theories of the phylogenetic development of language, and the applications to humans of research on the phylogenetic origins of language in nonhumans.

Several people have tried to teach chimpanzees to talk. The most persistent attempts were undertaken by Hayes and by the Kelloggs, who raised chimps in their homes with the idea that they might learn to talk if raised with humans from birth. They did not. Viki, Hayes's chimp, with extensive training learned to make noises for about four words, none of them properly formed. For example, the word "cup" sounded like "krup" when Viki "said" it. These early studies were dismal failures in view of the obvious neurological similarity between apes and humans. Then in the 1960s two totally new approaches appeared virtually simultaneously. Both were based on the premise that auditory communication must be bypassed and something visual used. The Gardners pioneered the use of American Sign Language (Ameslan); Premack used plastic symbols. It is interesting that Yerkes, in 1925, first proposed the idea of teaching sign language to chimps. The notion was apparently not considered a worthwhile endeavor!

The Gardners began by bringing Washoe, a year-old chimp, into their home. The aim was to teach Washoe the hand movements, or signs, that refer to various objects or actions (known as exemplars) that are found in Ameslan. These signing gestures, analogous to words in spoken language, have specific movements that begin and end in a prescribed manner in relation to the signer's body (see Figure 21–8). The Gardners molded Washoe's hands to form the desired shapes in the presence of the exemplar of the sign, reinforcing her for correct movements. In addition, rather than using verbal language, the Gardners used Ameslan to communicate with each other in Washoe's presence. Thus, Washoe was raised in an environment filled with signs. Washoe learned, and learned well. She was able to correctly sign for objects and to ask for objects with high accuracy. Most

CAT

Draw out 2 whiskers with thumb and index finger

CATERPILLAR

Pull hand along arm

FRUIT

Fingertip and thumbtip on cheek; twist

ORANGE

Squeeze in front of chin

ME

Index finger points to and touches chest

FOND

Cross over heart

FIGURE 21–8. Examples from American Sign Language (Amesian). The Gardners and others taught such symbols to the chimpanzees in their studies. (After Gustason et al., 1975.)

of her errors were in the same class. For example, she might use the sign for cat when identifying a dog.

Washoe also picked up signs by observing the signing of others. One example was the sign for "smoke." Apparently several of the workers on the project smoked, and, using Ameslan, they would request, in front of Washoe, smokes (cigarettes) from fellow workers. Washoe was fascinated by smoking, and soon added the sign to her vocabulary. Another example was the sign for toothbrush. This sign is made by moving an extended forefinger back and forth in front of the teeth. Washoe learned this sign on her own as well. Washoe's signing did not include nouns only but also pronouns and action verbs. For example, she could sign statements such as "You go me," meaning "Come with me."

Two questions are whether chimpanzees generalize the use of specific signs, and whether they can make up their own signs. In one experiment to test this question, a chimp had been taught five food-related signs: food, fruit, drink, candy, and banana. The test was to show her new fruits and vegetables and to ask her what they were. The result was fascinating, as a couple of examples will illustrate. When a radish was shown, the chimp (who had previously eaten radishes) signed "cry-hurt-food"; for a watermelon she signed "candy-drink" or "drink-fruit." The sign "fruit" was used 85 percent of the time to label fruit, but only 15 percent of the time for vegetables, whereas "smell" was used 65 percent of the time to label citrus fruits, presumably because chimps eat the outer skin, which is rather aromatic when bitten into.

Another experiment addressed the question of abstraction. Could the chimps learn verbal commands, and could they generalize back and forth from signs to words? To test this idea, a chimp was trained on English words such as "spoon." Having learned that the verbal word spoon referred to an object, he was then taught the Ameslan sign for spoon, but not in the presence of the object, rather in relation to the auditory representation, the word "spoon." Would the chimp, if asked what the object was, be able to make the "jump" and sign for the object? The answer was yes.

A large number of chimps have now been studied, and although there are clear differences among the individual animals, all have mastered a large number of signs. Attempts to teach Ameslan to other species of great apes have proved very successful; Patterson has found gorillas to have an even better predisposition to acquire sign language than chimpanzees.

Premack approached the study of language abilities of chimpanzees in a different way. He taught his chimpanzee, Sarah, to read and write with variously shaped and colored pieces of plastic, each representing a word (see Figure 21–9). Premack first taught Sarah that different symbols represented different nouns, just as Washoe had been taught in sign language. Thus, for example, Sarah learned that a pink square was the symbol for banana. Sarah was then taught verbs so that she could write and read such combinations as "give apple" or "wash apple." Her comprehension could easily be tested by writing messages to her (hanging up symbols) and then observing her response. This was followed by much more complicated tutoring in which Sarah successfully mastered the interrogative (Where is my banana?), the negative, and finally the conditional (if, then). It is readily apparent that Sarah had mastered a fairly complicated communication system analogous to simple human language.

A more recent project has demonstrated even more complex language learning in the chimpanzee. After carefully studying the results of the Gardners' and Premacks' projects, Rumbaugh and his colleagues at the Yerkes Regional Primate Center launched Project

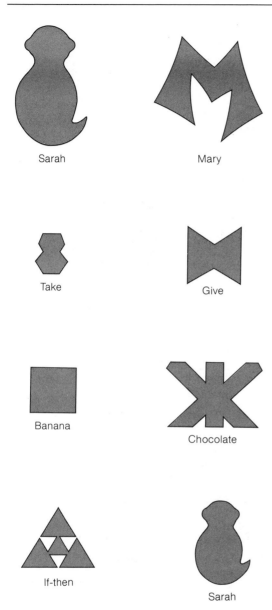

Sarah

Mary

Take

Give

Banana

Chocolate

If-then

Sarah

FIGURE 21–9. An example of a "conversation," using plastic symbols, with Premack's chimpanzee, Sarah. Note that the message is written from top to bottom. (After Ann James Premack and David Premack, Teaching language to an ape. Copyright © 1972 by Scientific American, Inc. All rights reserved.)

Lana. This project involved teaching their chimp, Lana, to communicate by means of a keyboard programmed by a computer. The keyboard was composed of nine stimulus elements and nine primary colors, which could be combined together in nearly 1800 combinations (lexigrams), as illustrated in Figure 21–10, to form a language now known as Yerkish. This project differs from the previous ones in being a collaborative effort of a psychologist, linguists, and computer specialists.

Lana had to learn simply to type out her messages on the keyboard. She was first trained to press keys for various single incentives; the requirements then became increasingly complex as she mastered the various types of statements, such as the indicative (Tim move into room), the interrogative (Tim move into room?), the imperative (Please Tim move into room), and the negative (Don't Tim move into room). Lana is now capable of strings of six lexigrams and makes few errors, most being "typing errors" or errors caused by distraction.

One of the initial goals of Project Lana was to engage in conversation with a chimpanzee. This has been accomplished by having the experimenter type messages on the board and then allowing Lana to respond. She actually learned to initiate conversation on her own, and engaged in conversations such as that illustrated in Table 21–3.

Further studies by Rumbaugh's group have demonstrated that chimpanzees are capable of symbolic communication with one another: two chimpanzees in adjoining rooms were able to use Yerkish to ask each other for specific foods. Further study showed they could even communicate reliably with regard to sharing tools for obtaining foods. When forced to rely on nonsymbolic means of communication, such as facial expression or body posture, their joint accuracy declined from 95 percent to 10

DESIGN ELEMENTS

EXAMPLES OF LEXIGRAMS

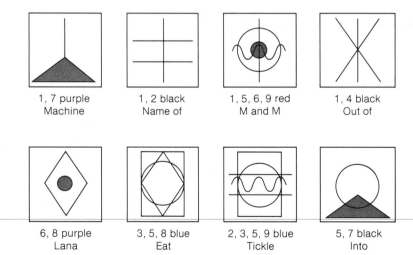

FIGURE 21–10. A. The nine basic design elements in Yerkish that are combined together to form lexigrams. B. Examples of lexigrams. (From E. von Glaserfeld, The Yerkish language and its automatic parser. In D. M. Rumbaugh, ed., *Language Learning by a Chimpanzee*. New York: Academic Press. Copyright © 1977. Reprinted with permission.)

TABLE 21–3

A conversation with Lana

Lana:	Milk name-of this.
Tim:	Yes.
Lana:	Milk this. ? Time give Lana coffee.
Tim:	No. (Although at times he has honored this request, this time he elected not to, for milk, not coffee, was the incentive appropriate to her state of heightened food motivation.)
Lana:	? Tim move milk coffee. (This was the first suggestion that she was going to ask Tim to move something from one point to another in space. She had not received specific training to ask that this be done.)
Tim:	(No response.)
Lana:	? Tim move behind room.
Tim:	Yes. (Thereupon Tim set down the pitcher of milk and moved behind the room to the general area of the vending devices where the milk would ordinarily be loaded into the machine. Lana's response was to hoot with apparent agitation; she also displayed piloerection and a furrowed brow. In a few seconds, Tim returned to the anteroom, picked up the milk, and stood once again in Lana's full view.)
Lana:	Milk of this coffee. ? Tim give milk name-of. ? Tim move milk behind. . . . (The sentence was not completed; however, Tim interpreted it to mean that Lana did not know how to finish what promised to be a novel question and one that was quite appropriate to the context.)
Tim:	? Behind what.
Lana:	? Tim move milk behind room. (With this statement Lana had asked for the first time that a person move something other than his own body from one point to another in space.)
Tim:	Yes. (He then loaded the vending device with milk, and Lana began to work for it by requesting it repeatedly.)

From Rumbaugh and Gill, 1977, p. 175.

percent. This latter result implies that the chimpanzees comprehend the symbolic and communicative functions of the symbols that they use and are not using subtle nonsymbolic cues to communicate.

Lenneberg and others have argued that human mathematical abilities are derived from the same foundation as language. Thus, whether chimpanzees possess the ability to acquire and use mathematical skills is an important question. Rumbaugh and his colleagues on Project Lana have begun to consider this problem. Lana has learned the concept of "more" and "less" and can accurately determine whether a group of four washers is more or less

than a group of five washers, when surface area, mass, and spatial arrangement of the washers are varied randomly. The question now under study is whether Lana can learn names of precise numbers and the ordinal relations involved among the numbers 1 through 10.

A Word of Caution

As provocative as the language studies in apes have proved to be, there have been criticisms. Terrace and his colleagues have raised an important issue that must be addressed before we know how relevant the ape language studies are to the study of human language. As Terrace notes, although apes can learn vocabularies of visual symbols, the important question is not whether the apes have a good memory for symbols but whether the apes can spontaneously combine such symbols by using a systematic grammar to create new meanings. After all, Terrace notes that whereas pigeons and other animals can learn complex chains of responses to obtain a food reward, these responses are not related one to another as words in a sentence are. For example, a pigeon can be trained to peck on four keys of different colors in a particular sequence regardless of the physical position of the colors; nevertheless, colors do not combine to form a grammatical sentence. Likewise, whereas an ape may produce sequences of symbols that a human observer sees as grammatically related, it does not follow that the ape was aware of the inferred relations. If, for example, in response to the question "What that?" Washoe signed "Water bird" in the presence of a swan, Washoe's response clearly appears creative and meaningful.

> Nevertheless, there is no basis for concluding that Washoe was characterizing the swan as a "bird that inhabits water." Washoe had a long history of being asked "what that?" in the presence of objects such as birds and bodies of water. In this instance, Washoe may have simply been answering the question, "what that?" by identifying correctly a body of water and a bird, in that order. Before concluding that Washoe was relating the sign "water" to the sign "bird," one must know whether she regularly placed an adjective (water) before, or after, a noun (bird). That cannot be decided on the basis of a single anecdote, no matter how compelling that anecdote may seem to an English-speaking observer. (Terrace et al., 1979, pp. 895–896)

To support their argument Terrace and his colleagues carefully analyzed more than 19,000 multisign utterances of an infant chimpanzee (Nim) as well as reanalyzing film of Washoe and other chimps. Although they found evidence for what appeared to be grammatical construction, that conclusion was invalidated by analyses of videotapes and films showing that most of the apes' utterances were prompted by their teachers' prior utterances and could thus be adequately explained by simple nonlinguistic processes. Indeed, the authors were struck both by the absence of creativity in the apes' utterances and by the dependence of their utterances on the prior utterances of their teachers. This is quite unlike the advanced multiword sequences produced by young children.

We do not wish to belittle the remarkable achievements of the ape language projects, but for the moment it is best to proceed with caution and to resist overly rich interpretations of the language capabilities of apes. In view of the utility of Ameslan as a human language, it might initially appear that the machine language (e.g., Yerkish) studies were unnecessary and perhaps redundant. In view of Terrace's criticisms, however, it can easily be seen that the machine languages are more objective and easier to quantify and to analyze than Ameslan. Thus, the machine language approach is more likely to satisfy the criticisms of Terrace and his colleagues.

Applications of the Chimpanzee Studies

A major implication of the work with chimpanzees is that communication does not require talking or even the ability to talk. Thus, a person with severe aphasia could potentially be taught some other form of language. In view of the reports that strokes produce impairment in Ameslan signing in deaf patients, either the Premack symbols or the Project Lana Yerkish would seem more appropriate for this purpose. Glass, Gazzaniga, and Premack have used

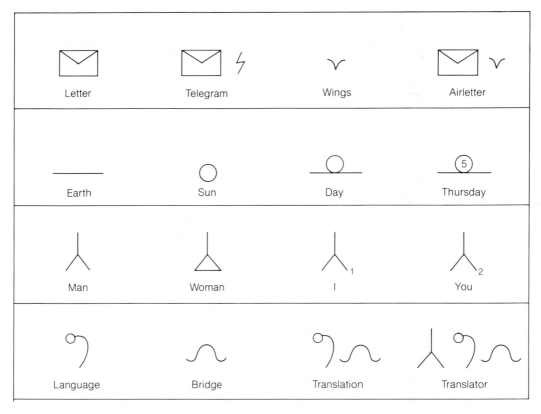

FIGURE 21–11. Examples of the Bliss language system. The symbols are pictorial and build on one another logically. This system has proved useful for teaching nonvocal children, and it holds promise for use with aphasic adults.

Premack symbols with encouraging results. Interestingly, noun symbols were learned readily, whereas verbs sometimes took weeks to learn. This difference is reminiscent of the observation that the right hemisphere of the split-brain patient is unable to process natural-language verbs.

It is relevant in this context to note that a symbol language was devised and published by Bliss in 1942. This language, known as Bliss Symbols or semantographics, is essentially similar to a simplified Chinese, being the clear, pictorial representation of real things as we see them. Each symbol looks like the object it represents; abstractions and intangibles are represented by geometric objects associated with them. The language is composed of 100 symbol elements that are recombined to form different words, as illustrated in Figure 21–11.

The simplicity of this system is apparent. The language has now been tried with non-vocal children with very favorable results. For example, Harris-Vanderbeiden and her colleagues implemented a modified Bliss system for children with cerebral palsy. With about 20 hours of training these children had all mastered at least some symbols that could be used for communication. One child who had an IQ of about 56 learned about 75 symbols, which she could use for both respondent and expressive communication.

To our knowledge this system has not yet been applied to aphasic patients, but it appears very promising. It is considerably more complex than the chimpanzee symbol systems used to date, and its pictorial component might make it a better choice for aphasic persons than Yerkish.

REFERENCES

Benson, D. F. Fluency in aphasia. *Cortex* 3:373–394, 1967.

Bliss, C. W. *Semantography*. Sydney, Australia: Semantography Publications, 1942.

Brown, J. *Aphasia, Apraxia and Agnosia*. Springfield, Ill,: Charles C Thomas, 1972.

Brown, J. The neural organization of language: Aphasia and lateralization. *Brain and Language* 3:482–494, 1976.

Caplan, D., and J. C. Marshall. Generative grammar and aphasic disorders: A theory of language representation in the human brain. *Foundations of Language* 12:583–596, 1972.

Chomsky, N. On the biological basis of language capabilities. In R. W. Rieber, ed., *Neuropsychology of Language*. New York: Plenum, 1976.

Coltheart, M. Acquired dyslexias and normal reading. In R. N. Malatesha and H. A. Whitaker, eds., *Dyslexia: A Global Issue*. The Hague: Martinus Nijhoff, 1984.

Coltheart, M. Disorders of reading and their implications for models of normal reading. *Visible Language* XV:245–286, 1981.

Cooper, I. S., I. Amin, R. Chandra, and J. M. Waltz. A surgical investigation of the clinical physiology of the LP-pulvinar complex in man. *Journal of Neurological Science* 18:89–110, 1973.

Gardner, B. T., and R. A. Gardner. Two-way communication with an infant chimpanzee. In A. M. Schrier and F. Stolinitz, eds., *Behavior of Nonhuman Primates,* vol. 4. New York: Academic, 1971.

Geschwind, N. Language and the brain. *Scientific American* 226:76–83, 1972.

Glaserfeld, E. von. The Yerkish language and its automatic parser. In D. M. Rumbaugh, ed., *Language Learning by a Chimpanzee*. New York: Academic, 1977.

Glass, A. U., M. S. Gazzaniga, and D. Premack. Artificial language training in global aphasics. *Neuropsychologia* 11:95–103, 1973.

Goodglass, H., and E. Kaplan. *The Assessment of Aphasia and Related Disorders*. Philadelphia: Lea and Febiger, 1972.

Green, E. Psycholinguistic approaches to aphasia. *Linguistics* 53:30–50, 1969.

Gustason, G., D. Pfetzing, and E. Zawoklow. *Signing Exact English*. Silver Spring, Md.: Modern Signs Press, 1975.

Halstead, W. C., and J. M. Wepman. The Halstead-Wepman aphasia screening test. *Journal of Speech and Hearing Disorders* 14:9–15, 1959.

Harris-Vanderbeiden, D., W. R. Brown, P. MacKenzie, S. Reinen, and C. Scheibel. Symbol communication for the mentally handicapped. *Mental Retardation* 34–37, 1975.

Hayes, K. J., and C. H. Nissen. Higher mental functions of a home reared chimpanzee. In A. M. Schrier and F. Stolinitz, eds., *Behavior of Nonhuman Primates,* vol. 4. New York: Academic, 1971.

Hewes, G. W. Language origin theories. In D. M. Rumbaugh, ed., *Language Learning by a Chimpanzee.* New York: Academic, 1977.

Holloway, R. L. Human paleontological evidence relevant to language behavior. *Human Neurobiology* 2:105–114, 1983.

Hughlings-Jackson, J. Notes on the physiology and pathology of learning. In J. Taylor, ed., *Selected Writings of John Hughlings-Jackson.* London: Hodder, 1932.

Jefferson, G. Localization of function in the cerebral cortex. *British Medical Bulletin* 6:333–340, 1949.

Kellogg, W., and L. Kellogg. *The Ape and the Child.* New York: McGraw-Hill, 1933.

Kimura, D. Neuromotor mechanisms in the evolution of human communication. In H. D. Steklis and M. J. Raleigh, eds., *Neurobiology of Social Communication in Primates: An Evolutionary Perspective.* New York: Academic, 1979.

Kimura, D. Neural mechanisms in manual signing. *Sign Language Studies* 33:291–312, 1981.

Larsen, B., E. Skinhøj, and N. A. Lassen. Variations in regional cortical blood flow in the right and left hemispheres during automatic speech. *Brain* 101:193–209, 1978.

Lenneberg, E. H. *Biological Foundations of Language.* New York: Wiley, 1967.

Lieberman, P. *On the Origins of Language: An Introduction to the Evolution of Human Speech.* New York: Macmillan, 1975.

Luria, A. R., and J. T. Hutton. A modern assessment of basic forms of aphasia. *Brain and Language* 4:129–151, 1977.

Marshall, J. C. Biological constraints on orthographic representation. *Philosophical Transactions of the Royal Society of London,* B298:165–172, 1982.

Mateer, C. Asymmetric effects of thalamic stimulation on rate of speech. *Neuropsychologia* 16:497–499, 1978.

Mazzocchi, F., and L. A. Vignolo. Localisation of lesions in aphasia: Clinical–CT scan correlations in stroke patients. *Cortex* 15:627–654, 1979.

Menzel, E. W. Communication about the environment in a group of young chimpanzees. *Folia Primatologia* 15:220–232, 1971.

Miller, G. A. *Language and Speech.* San Francisco: Freeman, 1981.

Monrad-Krohn, H. The third element of speech; prosody and its disorders. In L. Halpern, ed., *Problems of Dynamic Neurology.* Jerusalem: Hebrew University Press, 1963.

Myers, R. E. Comparative neurology of vocalization and speech: Proof of a dichotomy. *Annals of the New York Academy of Sciences* 280:745–760, 1976.

Naeser, M. A., R. W. Hayward, S. A. Laughlin, and L. M. Zatz. Quantitative CT scan studies in aphasia. I. Infarct size and CT numbers. *Brain and Language* 12:140–164, 1981.

Newcombe, F., and Marshall, J. C. On psycholinguistic classifications of the acquired dyslexias. *Bulletin of the Orton Society* 31:29–46, 1981.

Ojemann, G. A. Models of the brain organization for higher integrative functions derived with electrical stimulation techniques. *Human Neurobiology* 1:243–250, 1982.

Ojemann, G. A., ed. The thalamus and language. *Brain and Language* 2:1–120, 1975.

Ojemann, G. A., and C. Mateer. Human language cortex: Localization of memory, syntax, and sequential motor-phoneme identification systems. *Science* 205:1401–1403, 1979.

Ojemann, G. A., and C. Mateer. Cortical and subcortical organization of human communication: Evidence from stimulation studies. In H. D. Steklis and M. J. Raleigh, eds., *Neurobiology of Social Communication in Primates: An Evolutionary Perspective*. New York: Academic, 1979.

Patterson, F. G. The gestures of a gorilla: Language acquisition in another pongid. *Brain and Language* 5:72–97, 1978.

Penfield, W., and L. Roberts. *Speech and Brain Mechanisms*. Princeton, N.J.: Princeton University Press, 1959.

Porch, B. E. *Porch Index of Communicative Ability*. Palo Alto, Calif.: Consulting Psychologists Press, 1967.

Premack, A. J., and D. Premack. Teaching language to an ape. *Scientific American* 227:92–99, 1972.

Premack, D. *Intelligence in Ape and Man*. Toronto: Wiley, 1976.

Rasmussen, T., and B. Milner. Clinical and surgical studies of the cerebral speech areas in man. In K. J. Zulch, O. Creutzfeldt, and G. C. Galbraith, eds., *Cerebral Localization*. Berlin and New York: Springer-Verlag, 1975.

Renzi, E. de, and L. A. Vignolo. The token test: A sensitive test to detect disturbances in aphasics. *Brain* 85:665–678, 1962.

Ricklan, M., and I. S. Cooper. Psychometric studies of verbal functions following thalamic lesions in humans. *Brain and Language,* 2:45–64, 1975.

Rumbaugh, D. M., and T. V. Gill. Lana's acquisition of language skills. In D. M. Rumbaugh, ed., *Language Learning by a Chimpanzee*. New York: Academic, 1977.

Sarno, M. T. *The Functional Communication Profile: Manual of Directions*. New York: Institute of Rehabilitation Medicine, New York University Medical Center, 1969.

Savage-Rumbaugh, E. S., D. M. Rumbaugh, and S. Boysen. Symbolic communication between two chimpanzees. *Science* 201:641–644, 1978.

Schuell, H. *Differential Diagnosis of Aphasia with the Minnesota Test*. Minneapolis: University of Minnesota Press, 1965.

Searleman, A. A review of right hemisphere linguistic capabilities. *Psychological Bulletin* 84:503–528, 1977.

Spreen, O., and A. L. Benton. *Neurosensory Center Comprehensive Examination for Aphasia*. Victoria, Canada: University of Victoria, 1969.

Steklis, H. D., and M. J. Raleigh. Requisites for language: Interspecific and evolutionary aspects. In H. D. Steklis and M. J. Raleigh, eds., *Neurobiology of Social Communication in Primates: An Evolutionary Perspective*. New York: Academic, 1979.

Swadesh, M. *The Origin and Diversification of Language*. J. Sherzer, ed. Chicago: Aldine-Atherton, 1971.

Terrace, H. S., L. A. Petitto, R. J. Sanders, and T. G. Beyer. Can an ape create a sentence? *Science* 206:891–902, 1979.

Wepman, J. M., and L. V. Jones. *Studies in Aphasia: An Approach to Testing*. Chicago: University of Chicago Education-Industry Service, 1961.

Whitaker, H. A. *On the Representation of Language in the Human Brain*. Edmonton, Canada: Linguistic Research, Inc., 1971.

Zangwill, O. L. Excision of Broca's area without persistent aphasia. In K. J. Zulch, O. Creutzfeldt, and G. C. Galbraith, eds., *Cerebral Localization*. Berlin and New York: Springer-Verlag, 1975.

22

EMOTIONAL PROCESSES

Virtually any alteration of central nervous system activity can change an individual's personality; impairments of movement, perception, language, or perception affect how an individual behaves and is perceived by others. Nevertheless, the scientific study of changes in personality, emotion, and social behavior following brain injury lags far behind the study of cognitive functions, in large part due to the difficulties in defining, recording, and evaluating these behaviors. Over the past decade a view has emerged that there is both a lateralization of control of certain emotional processes, the right hemisphere being dominant, and a localization of control to the frontal and medial temporal regions. Further, it has been proposed that certain major psychiatric disturbances such as schizophrenia and depression may result from abnormalities in the normal cerebral control of emotional behavior.

In this chapter we shall summarize current thinking and research on the neurological control of emotional processes in the normal and abnormal brain. We begin by reviewing the development of thought regarding the neurology of emotional behavior before considering

more recent experimental investigations of this question. Finally, we shall consider biological bases of schizophrenia and depression and conclude with a brief consideration of psychosurgery.

HISTORICAL VIEWS

In 1937, Papez proposed that the structures of the limbic lobe form the anatomical basis of emotions. Papez reasoned that the limbic structures acting on the hypothalamus produce emotional states. Although the neocortex plays no part in producing emotional behavior, Papez believed it to be necessary to transform events produced by limbic structures into what we experience as "emotions." Papez based his theory on observations of patients with rabies, since this disease affects the hippocampus and causes such emotional and behavioral changes as anxiety, rage, terror, and so on. The Papez theory had the appeal at the time of combining behavioral phenomena having no known neurological substrates with anatomical structures having no known function.

The idea of an emotional brain gained instant approval because of the predominance of Freudian thinking then. That an ancient, deep part of the central nervous system controls emotions and instincts unconsciously, with the neocortex producing consciousness, was a concept with natural appeal for a Freudian-based psychology. In 1939, Klüver and Bucy rediscovered an extraordinary behavioral syndrome that had first been noted by Brown and Schaefer in 1888. The observed behavior, resulting from bilateral anterior temporal lobectomy in monkeys, included (1) tameness and a loss of fear; (2) indiscriminate dietary behavior, the monkeys being willing to eat many types of previously rejected foods; (3) greatly increased autoerotic, homosexual, and heterosexual activity, with inappropriate object choice; (4) **hypermetamorphosis,** or a tendency to attend to and react to every visual stimulus; (5) a tendency to examine all objects by mouth; and (6) visual agnosia.

The **Klüver-Bucy syndrome** has subsequently been observed in people with a variety of neurological diseases. For example, Marlowe et al. reported a patient with Klüver-Bucy symptoms resulting from meningoencephalitis.

As regards his visual functions, the patient seemed unable to recognize a wide variety of common objects. He examined each object placed before him as though seeing it for the first time, explored it repetitively and seemed unaware of its significance. As a result, he exhibited difficulty in the spontaneous employment of tools and other mechanical devices, but could initiate utilization of such objects by imitating the gestures of others, and could care for at least some daily needs in this way. Thus, when handed his razor, he would regard it in a bewildered fashion, but would accompany another patient to the bathroom and imitate all movements of his escort, even the most idiosyncratic, with precision; he could in this way succeed in shaving. Other ordinary tasks could be performed on the same imitative basis. Difficulties in recognition, it should be added, extended to people as well as to objects; he failed, for example, to recognize his parents during innumerable hospital visits. However, his ability to match simple pictures, geometric designs, letters of the alphabet and objects was demonstrably preserved when the tasks were taught non-verbally. Visual orientation was defective, the patient losing his way around the hospital when unattended, and visual distractibility was prominent; he seemed unable to distinguish between relevant and irrelevant objects and actions.

Behavioral patterns were distinctly abnormal. He exhibited a flat affect, and, although originally restless, ultimately became remarkably placid. He appeared indifferent to people or situations. He spent much time gazing at the television, but never learned to turn it on; when the set was off, he tended to watch reflections of others in the room on the glass screen. On occasion he became facetious, smiling inappropriately and mimicking the gestures and actions of others. Once initiating an imitative series, he would perseverate copying all movements made by another for extended periods of time. In addition, he commonly generated a series of idiosyncratic, stereotyped gestures employing primarily his two little fingers which he would raise and touch end-to-end in repetitive fashion.

He engaged in oral exploration of all objects within his grasp, appearing unable to gain information via tactile or visual means alone. All objects that he could lift were placed in his mouth and sucked or chewed. He was commonly observed to place his fingers in his mouth and suck them. He did not attempt to pick up objects directly with his mouth, using his hands for that purpose, but was observed to engage in much olfactory behavior. When dining he would eat with his fingers until reprimanded and a fork placed in his hand; he was thereafter able to imitate use of a fork, but failed to remaster the task of eating with utensils spontaneously. He would eat one food item on his plate completely before turning to the next. Hyperbulimia was prominent; he ingested virtually everything within reach, including the plastic wrapper from bread, cleaning pastes, ink, dog food, and feces. Although his tastes were clearly indiscriminate, he seemed to prefer liquids or soft solids.

The patient's sexual behavior was a particular source of concern while in hospital. Although vigorously heterosexual prior to his illness, he was observed in hospital to make advances toward other male patients by stroking their legs and inviting fellatio by gesture; at times he attempted to kiss them. Although on a sexually mixed floor during a portion of his recovery, he never made advances toward women, and, in fact, his apparent reversal of sexual polarity prompted his fiancée to sever their relationship. (Marlow, Mancall, and Thomas, 1975, pp. 55–56)

The appearance of the Klüver-Bucy syndrome apparently requires that the amygdala and inferior temporal cortex be removed bilaterally. H.M., the amnesic patient described in Chapter 20, does not exhibit the syndrome in spite of bilateral removal of the medial temporal structures.

At about the time of Klüver and Bucy's discovery a less dramatic but in many ways more important discovery was made. Jacobson studied the behavior of chimpanzees on a variety of learning tasks following frontal lobe removals. In 1935, he reported his findings on the effects of the lesions at the Second International Neurology Congress in London. He casually noted that one particularly neurotic chimp appeared more relaxed following the surgery, leading a Portuguese neurologist, Egas Moniz, to propose that similar lesions in people might relieve various behavioral problems. Thus was born psychosurgery and the frontal lobotomy! Unbelievably, not until the late 1960s was any systematic research done on the effects of frontal lobe lesions on the affective behavior of nonhuman animals. Hence frontal lobotomies in humans were performed without an empirical basis. Experiments by several laboratories have now clearly shown that frontal lobe lesions in rats, cats, and monkeys all have severe effects on social and affective behavior. For example, frontal lesions in monkeys virtually eliminate social interaction, even when the surgical candidate is the dominant alpha monkey of the group. Social responses that remain following surgery are inappropriate and frequently lead to severe fights in which the frontal monkey is inevitably the loser. Removals of the neocortex other than the frontal lobes in monkeys has reduced or negligible effects on social behavior, implying that the frontal lobe is the primary neocortical zone involved in social behavior. Indeed, we noted earlier that one of the most characteristic results of frontal lobe injury in humans is a marked, often dramatic alteration of personality.

Few would seriously argue today that the neocortex does not play a significant role in social behavior. In the nearly five decades since Papez's model was first proposed the pendulum of thought regarding the neurological control of affective behavior has gradually swung from the extreme view placing this function in the limbic system to a view emphasizing the importance of the neocortex. Indeed, limbic structures such as the hippocampus appear to have a minor role in the control of what Papez described as emotional behavior. Rather, the major forebrain structures involved in affective behavior now appear to be the orbital frontal cortex, the amygdala, and portions of the anterior temporal cortex. These structures are intimately related anatomically, forming a system with important input to the hypothalamus.

LOCALIZATION OF EMOTIONAL PROCESSES

The place to start in trying to identify the source of changes in emotional behavior is in the clinic. In the 1930s clinicians were reporting detailed observations of patients with large unilateral lesions, noting an apparent asymmetry in the effects of left and right hemisphere lesions. The best-known descriptions are those of Goldstein, who suggested that left hemisphere lesions produce "catastrophic" reactions characterized by fearfulness and depression, whereas right hemisphere lesions produce "indifference." The first systematic study of these contrasting behavioral effects was done by Gainotti, who showed that catastrophic reactions occurred in 62 percent of his left hemisphere sample, compared with only 10 percent for his right hemisphere cases. In contrast, indifference was commoner in the right hemisphere patients, occurring in 38 percent, as compared with only 11 percent of the left hemisphere cases. Significantly, however, Gainotti reported that catastrophic reactions were associated with aphasia, and indifference reactions with neglect.

Although it is tempting to assume that the emotional reactions observed in stroke patients reflect complementary functioning of the two hemispheres in emotional processes, our experience with patients undergoing cortical resections suggests that the situation is more complex. In general, right hemisphere excisions appear to release talking, left hemisphere lesions to reduce it. (Remember that none of these patients are aphasic, nor do they exhibit persistent neglect.) These effects are especially obvious following frontal lobe lesions. The content of talking released by right hemisphere lesions has not been carefully studied, but it is our impression that it is significantly affected by the lesion site. Patients with right frontal lesions characteristically make poor jokes and puns and tell pointless stories, often liberally embellished with profanity. Further, the right frontal lobe patient is usually intensely amused by the stories he or she is telling and will persist even if others are ambivalent to them. On the other hand, lesions of the right temporal and/or parietal lobe produce a totally different type of talking in individuals that is characterized by excessive concern for their personal lives. They often go to great lengths to rationalize their personal shortcomings, and they are generally unaware that others may be bored with their talking. Many of these patients also exhibit symptoms of paranoia, often being convinced that friends or family either are not supportive or are against them. They are excessively suspicious of neuropsychological assessments, insisting either that the assessments are unnecessary or that they would rather do them when they are "feeling better."

It is obvious that a simple left/right distinction of catastrophic/indifference is far too simple; both the site and the side of the lesion are important in understanding the changes in emotional behavior. This ought not to surprise us, however, since the same is true of cognitive behaviors. In order to understand the organization of emotional processes we must therefore attempt to fractionate the components of the behaviors as we have done for the study of cognitive processes. As a first step, we can separate the production of emotion, which is often called mood, from the perception and discrimination of emotion in others, which we shall call interpretation.

Production of Emotional Behavior

Mood is inferred largely by facial expression, tone of voice, and frequency of talking, and so these are sensible behaviors to study first in an analysis of emotional behavior in brain-damaged people. Another way to study emotional behavior is to assess mood and related behaviors with various rating scales, both with self-administered scales and by ratings of others. Finally, behavior can be studied using sodium Amytal, with which one hemisphere is briefly anesthetized. We shall consider each of these approaches separately.

Facial Expression and Spontaneous Talking. Kolb and Milner used an ethological recording technique to measure the frequency of spontaneous facial expressions in patients with cortical excisions. Excisions of either the left or the right frontal lobe significantly reduced the occurrence of spontaneous facial expressions, whereas face area, temporal, or posterior lesions had no differential effect (see Figure 22–1). On the other hand, during routine neuropsychological testing, left

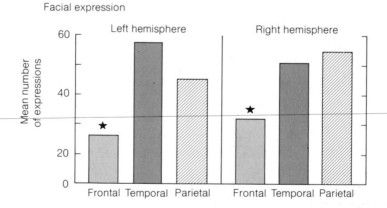

FIGURE 22–1. Relative frequencies of spontaneous talking (A) and facial expressions (B) during routine neuropsychological testing. Note that frontal lobe lesions significantly reduce the number of facial expressions. The level of spontaneous talking is significantly reduced for left frontal lesions and increased for right frontal lesions. Stars indicate significant difference from other groups with same-side lesions. (After Kolb and Milner, 1981; Kolb and Taylor, 1981.)

frontal lesions significantly reduced the incidence of spontaneous talking in patients, whereas right frontal lesions significantly increased it. Lesions elsewhere in the cortex had no effect on this behavior. The release of spontaneous talking in right frontal lobe patients is particularly interesting because these same patients could produce very few words in a test of verbal fluency.

Kolb and Milner's study suggests that the frontal lobe may have some special role in the control of facial expressions and movements, but the study provides no evidence of an asymmetry of this control. Two studies of patients with larger, more diffuse unilateral lesions have shown an asymmetry, however, as large right hemisphere lesions are reported both to reduce facial expression and to abolish the normal asymmetry in facial expression (laterality studies are discussed below). Left hemisphere lesions were without significant effect on either measure. Taken together, studies of facial expression in patients with unilateral lesions suggest that although there is some evidence of an asymmetry in the control of facial expression, there is also evidence of participation of both frontal lobes in its control. Perhaps separate frontal and right hemisphere roles will be differentiated in future studies.

Tone or Prosody. Spoken language carries two types of information: information derived directly from the content, and information inferred from the tone of voice used. There is little doubt that the former is a function of the left hemisphere, and there is now good reason to suspect that the latter is a function of the right hemisphere. For example, when Tucker et al. asked patients to express particular affective states such as anger, happiness, and sadness when they read emotionally neutral sentences, patients with right hemisphere lesions produced the sentences with relatively flat affect in comparison to those with left hemisphere lesions. This absence of tone in speech has been termed *aprosodia* and can be measured on a wide-band spectogram, as was done by Kent and Rosenbek.

Abnormalities in the tone of voice in right hemisphere patients has led Ross to propose that there may be a set of aprosodias analogous to aphasias in left hemisphere speech (see Table 22–1). Motor aprosodia, which is suggested to be an inability to produce affective components of language, is proposed to result from damage in the region of Broca's area in the right hemisphere, whereas sensory aprosodia, a deficit in the interpretation of the emotional components of language, is presumed to result

TABLE 22–1

	Aprosodias			
Ross's proposed classification of aprosodias	Spontaneous prosody and gesturing	Prosodic repetition	Prosodic comprehension	Comprehension of emotional gesturing
Motor	Poor	Poor	Good	Good
Sensory	Good	Poor	Poor	Poor
Global	Poor	Poor	Poor	Poor
Conduction	Good	Poor	Good	Good
Transcortical motor	Poor	Good	Good	Good
Transcortical sensory	Good	Good	Poor	Poor
Mixed transcortical	Poor	Good	Poor	Poor
Anomic (alexia with agraphia)	Good	Good	Good	Poor

from damage to the region in the right hemisphere analogous to Wernicke's area. Ross's proposal may have merit and deserves serious consideration, but at present it is without much scientific support. Furthermore, like aphasias, which are virtually never purely of one type, aprosodias are certainly not as pure as Ross has suggested.

Temporal Lobe Personality. One way in which to quantify social or affective behavior is to have patients and their friends complete rating scales of various behavioral traits such as "anger," "sadness," and "religiosity." In their study of the behavior of temporal lobe patients Bear and Fedio asked them and their friends to do just this, with the scales related to the traits summarized in Table 22–2. Each of these traits had previously been attributed to temporal lobe epileptics, who presumably have temporal lobe lesions producing their epileptic condition. The epileptic patients self-reported a distinctive profile of humorless sobriety, dependence, and obsessionalism; raters discriminated the temporal lobe patients on the basis of nearly every trait listed in Table 22–2 but rated them most strongly on the traits described as "circumstantiality," "philo-

TABLE 22-2

Summary of characteristics attributed to temporal lobe epileptics [a]	
Emotionality	Deepening of all emotions, sustained intense manic-depressive disease
Elation, euphoria	Grandiosity, exhilarated mood; diagnosis of manic-depressive disease
Sadness	Discouragement, fearfulness, self-depreciation; diagnosis of depression, suicide attempt
Anger	Increased temper, irritability
Aggression	Overt hostility, rape attacks, violent crimes, murder
Altered sexual interest	Loss of libido, hyposexualism; fetishism, transvestism, exhibitionism, hypersexual episodes
Guilt	Tendency to self-scrutiny and self-recrimination
Hypermoralism	Attention to rules with inability to distinguish significant from minor infraction; desire to punish offenders
Obsessionalism	Ritualism; orderliness; compulsive attention to detail
Circumstantiality	Loquacious, pedantic; overly detailed, peripheral
Viscosity	Stickiness; tendency to repetition
Sense of personal destiny	Events given highly charged, personalized significance; divine guidance ascribed to many features of patient's life
Hypergraphia	Keeping extensive diaries, detailed notes; writing autobiography or novel
Religiosity	Holding deep religious beliefs, often idiosyncratic multiple conversions, mystical states
Philosophical interest	Nascent metaphysical or moral speculations, cosmological theories
Dependence, passivity	Cosmic helplessness, "at hands of fate"; protestations of helplessness
Humorlessness, sobriety	Overgeneralized ponderous concern; humor lacking or idiosyncratic
Paranoia	Suspicious, overinterpretative of motives and events; diagnosis of paranoid schizophrenia

[a] After Bear and Fedio, 1977.

sophical interests," and "anger" (see descriptions in Table 22–2). Furthermore, right and left temporal lobe patients could be distinguished: the right temporal patients were described as more obsessional and the left temporal ones as more concerned with "personal destiny" (see Table 22–2). These ratings are in general accord with our clinical experience and quantify the clinical impressions of a temporal lobe personality observed by many others. Unfortunately, similar studies have not yet been carried out with patients having larger lesions or lesions of the frontal lobes.

Affect under Sodium Amytal

From the above studies it is reasonable to expect that patients under the effects of carotid sodium Amytal would exhibit changes in personality related to the side of drug injection. For example, from Gainotti's results a depressive-catastrophic reaction could be predicted to follow injection of the speaking hemisphere, and an indifference reaction to follow injection of the nonspeaking hemisphere. Study results are, however, contradictory. The most widely cited results are those collected by Terzian and by Rossi and their respective colleagues. They report that injections of the left hemisphere indeed provoke a catastrophic reaction as the drug wears off. The patient "despairs and expresses a sense of guilt, of nothingness, of indignity, and worries about his own future or that of his relatives, without referring to the language disturbances overcome and to the hemiplegia just resolved and ignored." As the drug wore off after injection of the right hemisphere a "euphorical" reaction was reported, as the patient "appears without apprehension, smiles and laughs and both with mimicry and words expresses considerable liveliness and sense of well-being." These results are provocative, but unfortunately a number of groups have been unable to confirm them. For example, in one report on 104 patients Milner noted only rare depression, and there was no systematic asymmetry in the euphoria. Furthermore, Kolb and Milner found no asymmetry in either the frequency or the quality (e.g., happy or sad) of facial expressions following injection of the left and right hemispheres respectively (see Figure 22–2).

The difference between the results of the Italian investigators and Milner's group is unlikely to be resolved in the near future. There is one relevant methodological difference: in the two Milner series each patient could be used as his or her own control, because both hemispheres were injected, although on different days. In the Terzian and Rossi studies most patients were injected in only one hemisphere. In any event, until such results are replicated by others they should be interpreted with caution.

Summary

As summarized in Table 22–3, emotional or social behavior is markedly altered by cerebral lesions. Taken together, the studies lead to several conclusions. First, lesions of the left and right hemispheres have differential effects on emotional behavior. Second, occurrences of aphasia and unilateral neglect are significant factors in predicting occurrences of depressive-catastrophic and indifference reactions, respectively; these reactions are uncommon in the absence of aphasia and neglect. Third, the frontal lobes appear to have a special role in producing facial expression; there is no evidence for asymmetry in this function. Fourth, the frontal lobes are asymmetrical in their role in spontaneous talking: left frontal lesions appear to inhibit spontaneous talking, whereas right frontal lobe lesions appear to release it. Fifth, temporal lobe damage is associated with a constellation of behavioral symptoms, many of

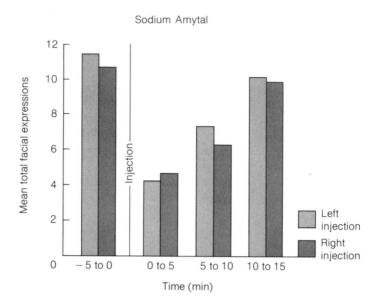

FIGURE 22–2. Changes in facial expression following injection of sodium Amytal into the left or right hemisphere. Note that injection into each hemisphere abolished expression briefly; gradual recovery followed. There was no evidence of asymmetry. (After Kolb and Milner, 1981.)

TABLE 22–3

Summary of experiments on production of emotional behavior in neurological patients

	Behavior	Characteristics	Basic reference
1.	Clinical behavior of patients with natural lesions	Catastrophic reactions from left hemisphere lesions; indifference from right hemisphere lesions	Gainotti, 1969; 1972; Goldstein, 1939
2.	Facial expression	Reduced by frontal lesions Reduced by right hemisphere lesions Asymmetry altered	Kolb and Milner, 1981 Buck and Duffy, 1980 Bruyer, 1981
3.	Spontaneous speech	Decreased by left frontal lesions; increased by right frontal lesions	Kolb and Taylor, 1981
4.	Tone or prosody of speech	Right hemisphere lesions impair mimicry of emotional states	Tucker et al., 1977
5.	Temporal lobe traits	Temporal lobe personality	Bear and Fedio, 1977; Waxman and Geschwind, 1974; Sachdev and Waxman, 1981
6.	Sodium Amytal	A. Catastrophic reactions to left injection; indifference reactions to right injection	Terzian, 1964; Rossi and Rosandini, 1967
		B. No evidence of asymmetrical effects	Rovetta, 1960; Milner, 1967; Kolb and Milner, 1981

which are associated with damage to just the left or the right hemisphere. Finally, the occurrence of many traits of personality or emotional behavior that are characteristic of brain-damaged groups in persons without known brain damage leads us to speculate that differences in cerebral organization, whether genetically or environmentally derived, form the basis of different human personalities. For example, one could speculate that people who are hypercritical may have relatively smaller temporal lobes or that people without much facial expression have smaller frontal lobes. Since we have noted previously that people vary widely in their performance on neuro-psychological tests of cognitive behavior as well, it would be interesting to explore the relation between the performance on measures of cognitive and emotional behavior *in the same normal subjects*. Concordance of measures on the two types of tests would be provocative indeed.

INTERPRETATION OF AFFECTIVE STIMULI BY NEUROLOGICAL PATIENTS

Emotional behavior might appear to be abnormal not only because a person is unable to produce the appropriate behavior but also because a person misinterprets the social or emotional signals coming from others. The interpretation of affective stimuli by neurological patients has been studied in a number of ways, each of which is considered separately (see Table 22–4).

Judgment of Mood

Heilman and his colleagues asked patients to judge the mood of a speaker after listening to him read a sentence in which he successively feigned anger, joy, etc. Patients with right hemisphere lesions, largely temporal-parietal, were more impaired at the task than patients with analogous left hemisphere lesions. This impairment at perceiving emotional tone in language is referred to by Ross as a sensory aprosodia, and he predicts it to result from temporal-parietal lesions on the right, just as Heilman et al. report. It is likely, however, that patients with right temporal lobectomies, who, it should be recalled, are impaired at musical perception, will be quite impaired at the judgment of emotional tone whether or not the analogue of Wernicke's area is removed. A preliminary study by Tompkins and Mateer suggests this may be true, but more study is required.

Comprehension of Humor

The ability to make and appreciate humor is one of our most intriguing behaviors and certainly contributes to our personality. Little is known about the neurological basis of humor competence, except for two nice studies by Gardner and his associates. In their first study they examined the comprehension and appreciation of humorous material following left or right hemisphere lesions. They asked patients to choose the funniest of four cartoons, which were either with or without captions (Figure 22–3). The results showed that all of the patients were impaired at the task, but there was an asymmetry in the pattern of errors. Patients with left hemisphere lesions did well on the cartoons *without* captions, whereas patients with right hemisphere lesions did well on the cartoons *with* captions. Further, the behavior of the two patient groups differed. Those with left hemisphere lesions behaved "normally"; those with right hemisphere lesions tended to exhibit one of two extreme reactions: either they laughed at nearly every item, even when their understanding was doubtful, or, more commonly, they displayed little reaction to

TABLE 22-4

Summary of experiments on interpretation of emotionally relevant stimuli in neurological patients

1.	Judgment of mood in others	Right hemisphere lesions impair comprehension	Heilman et al., 1975
		Right temporal lesions impair perception of intonation	Tompkins and Mateer, 1983
2.	Judgment of propositional affect	Left hemisphere lesions impair comprehension	Kolb and Taylor, 1981
3.	Comprehension of verbal humor	Left hemisphere lesions impair comprehension of captioned cartoons; right hemisphere lesions alter understanding of jokes	Gardner et al., 1975 Brownell et al., 1983
4.	Comprehension of nonverbal humor	Right hemisphere lesions impair comprehension	Gardner et al., 1975
5.	Matching pictures of emotional facial expressions	Right hemisphere lesions impair performance	DeKosky et al., 1980; Kolb and Taylor, 1981; Cicone et al., 1980

any item, even when their understanding seemed adequate. Thus, although both left and right hemisphere damage impaired the appreciation of humor, the right hemisphere lesions appear to have had a more fundamental effect on the patients' behavior.

In a second study, Brownwell et al. assessed the appreciation of jokes by patients with right hemisphere damage. They hypothesized that the appreciation of jokes presupposes two elements: sensitivity to the surprise element entailed in the punch line of the joke, and appreciation of the coherence that results when the punch line has been integrated with the body of the joke. In other words, the surprise element must be appreciated as being related to the content of the prelude; if it is not, the humor is lost. In order to study the verbal humor of their patients, they presented subjects with a short story leading up to a punch line, followed by four alternate endings. One ending was a surprise that followed the story, one was a surprise that was a nonsequitur with the story, and the other two contained no surprise but were statements that followed the coherence of the story. Consider the following example. "The neighborhood borrower approached Mr. Smith on Sunday afternoon and inquired: 'Say Smith, are you using your lawnmower this afternoon?' 'Yes, I am,' Smith replied warily. The neighborhood borrower then answered: 'Fine, then you won't be needing your golf clubs, I'll just borrow them.' "

In the Brownwell study the subjects did not receive the last sentence but were given four choices. (1) Correct ending: "Fine, then you won't be needing your golf clubs, I'll borrow them." (2) Nonsequitur ending: "You know, the grass is greener on the other side." (3) Neutral ending: "Do you think I could use it when you're done?" (4) Sad ending: "Gee, if only I had enough money, I could buy my own."

Patients with right hemisphere damage did poorly at this test because although they reliably chose surprise endings, they were as likely to choose a nonsequitur as the correct ending. The patients recognized that a joke must end in a surprise, and they recognized which endings were surprising, but they could not establish an interpretation of the story that tied the ending coherently to the body of the joke.

Taken together, the Gardner studies imply that right hemisphere patients in particular have an atypical sense of humor, a result concordant with clinical descriptions of these patients as having inappropriate responses to jokes, stories, or conversations. There is no hint concerning where this deficit is most likely to arise, although on the basis of clinical reports, the frontal lobe would seem the obvious place to look.

Judgment of Facial Expression

There has been considerable interest in the perception of facial expression in normal subjects over the past decade, in large part due to the seminal work of Ekman and his colleagues. It is now recognized that people are capable of discriminating about six different classes of facial expression (happy, sad, angry, surprised, afraid, and disgusted), and that this ability transcends cultural or linguistic barriers. Thus, people from New Guinea recognize the same categories of facial expressions as do people from France. In order to study the ability of patients with cerebral lesions to appreciate different facial expressions, Kolb and Taylor did a series of experiments in which subjects were to match different photographs of faces on the basis of emotion inferred from the facial expression, or from verbal captions given to the photographs. Patients with right hemisphere lesions were especially poor at matching facial expressions, a result consistent with the inferred role of the right hemisphere in the processing of faces (see Chapter 10). A surprising finding, however, was that lesions in the right hemisphere had no focal effect—surprising since facial-recognition deficits are

localized to the posterior cortex. It thus appears that the frontal cortex has some role in the appreciation of facial expression, although not in facial perception per se. In an unpublished study Kolb and Taylor asked the same patients to match facial expressions with different verbal descriptions and found a nonspecific impairment: patients with lesions in the prefrontal, temporal, or posterior parietal cortex of either hemisphere were impaired at the test. That this was not merely a test sensitive to cerebral damage is shown by the fact that the patients with central lesions, largely in the face area, performed flawlessly at the task. Thus, as in the tests of humor described earlier, both right and left hemisphere lesions may produce an impairment, but the impairments observed from right hemisphere lesions appear to be larger, even in some tests in which there is a verbal component. A similar conclusion has been reached by DeKosky et al., who did analogous experiments with patients having larger left or right hemisphere lesions.

Judgments of Emotional Situations

Like the appreciation of facial expression, the comprehension of emotional situations is central to understanding emotion in others. Cicone et al. asked patients to match a target scene, such as a man being held up, with one of four other scenes that displayed the same emotion, although in a different situation. Thus, given a choice of a man winning a lottery, a woman shopping, a man in quicksand, and a child eating ice cream, the match to a man being held up would be the man in quicksand, for both pictures represent frightening situations. Right hemisphere patients were more impaired than left hemisphere patients on a purely visual form (drawings of scenes) and were as impaired on a verbal version (spoken or written

FIGURE 22–3. Examples from the study by Gardner et al. of sense of humor in neurological patients. Patients with right hemisphere lesions had difficulty in choosing the funny captionless cartoon (this page), whereas patients with left hemisphere lesions had difficulty in choosing the funny captioned cartoon (opposite page). The appreciation of humor is of course idiosyncratic and difficult. These cartoons may not strike everyone as being especially humorous, but most people will be able to identify which cartoon has an element of humor when compared with the other choices. (After H. Gardner, P. K. Ling, L. Flamm, and J. Silverman, Comprehension and appreciation of humorous material following brain damage. *Brain*, 98:399–412. Copyright © 1976. Reprinted with permission.)

form). These authors conclude that the difficulty in understanding emotional situations is general among right hemisphere patients, whereas it is secondary to language impairment in left hemisphere patients. This may be true, but the degree of impairment in verbal tasks is almost certainly related to the size of the lesion in the right hemisphere patients. Kolb and Taylor found that their patients with small right hemisphere excisions were not im-

paired at judging emotion from verbal descriptions of emotional situations, whereas patients with equivalent left-side lesions were. For example, the patients were asked to pair the correct emotion with a propositional statement such as "This man is at a funeral"; left but not right hemisphere lesions reduced accuracy relative to that of controls.

Much more study of the judgment of emotional situations is needed, but as a general conclusion it appears that right hemisphere lesions have a greater effect on this ability than left hemisphere lesions, a result consistent with the inappropriateness of much behavior in patients with right hemisphere lesions, especially those including the frontal lobe.

Summary

The interpretation of emotionally significant stimuli is impaired by cerebral lesions, just as the production of emotional behavior is impaired by the same lesions. Damage to either hemisphere appears to influence the interpretation of stimuli, although damage to the right hemisphere appears to have greater effects, even on the interpretation of certain types of verbal stimuli. A major challenge for future studies is the demonstration of focal effects of right hemisphere lesions on the interpretation of emotional stimuli. It is likely that frontal and posterior regions have a different interpretive role but there is no evidence as yet to indicate what this difference might be.

LATERALITY STUDIES

In recent years, attention has turned in laterality studies to the lateralization of affective processes. The basic logic applied in these studies has been to present material to one hemisphere, using dichotic or tachistoscopic techniques (see Chapter 14), in order to demonstrate a difference in the performance of the two hemispheres. If one hemisphere were superior to the other at recognizing tone of voice or facial expression, for example, it could be inferred that the superior hemisphere had some dominant role in this function. We shall review briefly these studies, dividing them into studies of the production of affective behavior and studies of the perception of emotional stimuli.

Production of Affective Behavior

Few studies have examined the neuropsychology by which affective behaviors are produced in normal subjects. All these studies have centered on the study of eye movements and facial expression. One study, by Schwartz et al., involved observing the direction of horizontal eye movements made during emotional and nonemotional tasks. Emotionally loaded statements, such as "Picture and describe the last situation in which you cried," produced significantly more gaze shifts to the left than to the right, whereas nonemotional questions such as "What is the primary difference between the meanings of the words 'recognize' and 'remember'?" produced more gaze shifts to the right than to the left. By use of the hypothesized relation between gaze shift and lateralization, these results were interpreted as demonstrating a special role of the right hemisphere in regulating emotional processes. These data are provocative, but they are not a very direct measure of affective behavior.

A series of studies by Campbell has demonstrated that facial expressions are not always symmetrical, but rather strongly tend to occur predominantly on the left side of the face. The asymmetries may range from the hardly noticeable, such as the flicker of a smile on the left side of Mona Lisa's face (on the right of the painting, of course), to the pronounced, such as a raised eyebrow, wink, or lopsided smile, on the left side of the face. In one study Moscovitch and Olds surreptitiously recorded the laterality of facial expressions of people in restaurants, finding a left-side preponderance of facial expression. They confirmed this observation by carefully analyzing video recordings of people recounting sad and humorous stories, again finding a left-side bias in facial expressions. Asymmetrical production of facial expression can be interpreted as showing that the right hemisphere is specialized in that function, a conclusion consistent with its presumed specialization in the perception of facial expressions. It is tempting to speculate that right hemisphere specialization in expressing and interpreting facial expression is analogous to the left hemisphere specialization in expressing and interpreting language, but this has yet to be proved. In our discussion of the Teuber-Yin theory of facial perception (Chapter 10) we noted that the apparent specialization of the right hemisphere in the perception of faces could easily be interpreted as a specialization for the perception of complex visual stimuli, of which faces are an example.

Perception of Relevant Stimuli

Normal Subjects. To date, in studies of perception of emotionally loaded stimuli, only the visual and auditory modalities have been examined. For both modalities the stimulus usually is presented to one hemisphere selectively, either alone or in competition with information simultaneously presented to the opposite hemisphere. Two procedures have been used for the visual presentation. In one procedure, faces with different expressions (e.g., sad and happy) are presented tachistoscopically to the left or right visual field, and the subject is asked to identify the facial expression. The results show the left visual field to be superior at correct identification. This superiority can be interpreted as demonstrating a right hemisphere specialization for the perception of facial expression, an important aspect of nonverbal communication. The second procedure involves an ingenious technique devised by Dimond. By the use of special contact lenses Dimond and his colleagues were able to selectively project several types of films to the left or right hemisphere. Subjects rated each film on a scale of 1 to 9 on the four emotional dimensions of humorous, pleasant, horrific, or unpleasant. Films presented to the right hemisphere were judged more unpleasant and horrific and produced greater autonomic nervous system activation (as measured by heart rate) than when presented to the left hemisphere of other subjects. Dimond and his colleagues concluded that the two hemispheres hold an essentially different emotional view of the world. Curiously, if the films were shown to both hemispheres simultaneously, the ratings closely resembled those of the right visual field (the left hemisphere), suggesting that left hemisphere perception is dominant. It could be predicted that a left hemisphere lesion might result in a more negative view of the films, although this has not been studied.

Studies of asymmetries in the auditory perception of emotions have generally employed a dichotic-listening technique, which generally shows a left-ear superiority for emotional material such as laughing, crying, etc.

One of the most compelling experiments was conducted by Ley and Bryden. They employed a number of short sentences spoken in happy, sad, angry, and neutral voices. These sentences were dichotically paired with neutral sentences of similar semantic content. Subjects were instructed to attend to one ear and to report the emotional tone of the target sentence and indicate its content by checking off items on a multiple-choice recognition sheet. Virtually every subject showed a left-ear advantage for identifying the emotional tone of the voice and at the same time a right-ear advantage for identifying the content. This result is analogous to that of Dimond et al., who found that the two hemispheres deal with visual material in a different way.

Summary

Laterality studies generally confirm the conclusions from studies of neurological patients: the right hemisphere has a predominant role in emotional behavior. Nevertheless, this conclusion is not universally accepted, although the data appear to favor it. For example, in a thoughtful review Tucker concluded that the right hemisphere has a special role in mediating negative emotions, whereas the left hemisphere is more implicated in positive emotions. There is little reason to believe that the brain is arranged in this manner, however, and it seems more parsimonious to us to view the right hemisphere as being more involved than the left in all aspects of emotional behavior. The nature of this role is a matter for debate and will become an increasingly important focus for research over the coming decade.

NEUROBIOLOGY OF SCHIZOPHRENIA AND DEPRESSION

We have considered the effects of cerebral damage on emotional processes, emphasizing the role of both the right hemisphere and the frontal and medial temporal structures in emotional behavior. Accumulating evidence from the fields of neuropsychology, neurochemistry, psychiatry, and neurology indicates that the loss of specific neurotransmitter systems may also produce abnormalities in emotional behavior, abnormalities that are quite different from those resulting from cortical injury. Recall, for example, that a loss of the cholinergic projections from the nucleus basalis of Meynert is thought to produce Alzheimer's disease, whereas a loss of dopamine projections to the striatum is responsible for the symptoms of Parkinson's disease. Could analogous losses of other specific transmitter pathways be the cause of two of the most debilitating diseases of emotional behavior, schizophrenia and depression? Although there is little doubt that environmental factors play a significant role in the etiology of both of these disorders, there is now good reason to believe that environmental factors may interact with abnormalities of transmitter systems in the brain and with other as yet unknown variables to produce both depression and schizophrenia. We first review the transmitter pathways, before considering their role in emotional behavior.

Amine Pathways

Three biogenic amines, which are putative transmitters in the brain, are believed to be important in emotional behavior: dopamine, noradrenaline, and serotonin. Each of these substances is manufactured in a restricted region of the brainstem and sent via long axons to various places, specially in the forebrain (see Figure 22–4).

Dopaminergic Projections. There are two principal dopaminergic projection systems to the forebrain. The nigrostriatal system arises from cell bodies in the substantia nigra, whose

axons project primarily to the caudate nucleus and putamen. It is the loss of these projections that is responsible for Parkinson's disease. The mesocortical system begins with cell bodies in the tegmentum, in a region just above the substantia nigra known as the ventral tegmental area of Tsai. Axons of these neurons project to the limbic system, including certain regions of

FIGURE 22–4. Schematic drawings of central biogenic aminergic tracts. A. Dopaminergic tracts. B. Noradrenergic and serotoninergic tracts. (After Sachar, 1981.)

the frontal lobe. It is an abnormality of these cells that is believed to occur in schizophrenia.

Noradrenaline. Noradrenergic innervation of the brain arises from cell bodies at the level of the pons in and around a nucleus known as the locus ceruleus. Fibers from this region form six major noradrenergic tracts projecting to the hypothalamus, thalamus, limbic system, neocortex, cerebellum, and spinal cord (see Figure 22–4). An abnormality in noradrenaline may be responsible for some symptoms of depression.

Serotonin. Serotonin-containing neurons are found in nine clusters of cells lying in the midline region of the pons and upper brainstem known as the raphe regions. These neurons project widely throughout the brain, as illustrated in Figure 22–4, innervating all those structures also receiving projections from dopamine or noradrenaline neurons. Like noradrenaline, serotonin has a putative role in depression.

The Dopamine Theory of Schizophrenia

From research on drug action, on autopsied brains, on the metabolites of psychotic patients, and on the observed side effects of movement-disorder treatments one conclusion is supported: There is evidence favoring the presence of an abnormality in the mesocortical dopamine system of schizophrenics. Perhaps the strongest evidence favoring a dopaminergic role in schizophrenia comes from studies of the action of antipsychotic drugs. Antipsychotic drugs, or **neuroleptic drugs,** are known to act on the dopamine synapse, and dopamne agonists, which enhance the action of dopamine (cocaine, amphetamine, and 1-DOPA), can induce psychotic symptoms that are almost indistinguishable from classic paranoid schizophrenia.

Further, if a schizophrenic takes heavy doses of amphetamine, the schizophrenic symptoms are heightened.

Since there is no evidence of cell loss as in Parkinson's or Alzheimer's disease, we must ask what type of abnormality in the dopamine system is responsible for schizophrenic symptoms. There are five possibilities: (1) too much dopamine is released by the dopaminergic neurons; (2) too little dopamine is released and the receptors are hypersensitive, a condition known as *denervation supersensitivity;* (3) dopaminergic receptors are hypersensitive to the normal amount of dopamine released; (4) some other system, which is antagonistic to dopamine, is underactive; or (5) there is a malfunction of a feedback pathway that controls some component of the dopamine system. Studies of postmortem schizophrenic brains have demonstrated that schizophrenics have up to twice as many dopamine receptors as normal controls, lending credence to the second or third suggestion, but we must be cautious since most of the evidence favoring any dopaminergic abnormality in schizophrenia is still circumstantial.

If the mesocortical dopamine system is involved in schizophrenia, then we might expect that those regions of the cortex receiving dopaminergic projections (medial temporal and prefrontal) would show other abnormalities. This is indeed the case. Studies of regional blood flow and glucose uptake have both shown evidence that the frontotemporal regions are functionally abnormal. Further, Risberg has studied regional blood flow in a subject before and after amphetamine intoxication and found the major change to be a large increase in frontal blood flow. Finally, in our studies of the neuropsychological test performance of patients with schizophrenia we have found evidence of bilateral frontal and temporal lobe dysfunction in the presence of normal parietal lobe function.

We return to neuropsychological studies of schizophrenic patients in Chapter 29.

The dopamine theory of schizophrenia is far from proved and has important weaknesses. One is that although neuroleptic drugs block dopamine receptors rapidly, the core symptoms of schizophrenia disappear gradually over several weeks. Could this be due to actions of the drugs on other systems, actions that take weeks to become effective? Further, CT scans of schizophrenic patients reveal an enlarged ventricle, implying that schizophrenics may suffer from brain atrophy. Sachar wonders if this implies that in some forms of schizophrenia the psychotic episodes are secondary to a primary lesion of the brain that has not yet been recognized. Thus, the dopamine hypothesis, even if correct for the psychotic phase, may be inadequate to account for the entire illness, and the search continues for the primary brain disturbance. In view of the evidence of frontal-temporal dysfunction in schizophrenia, the place to look would seem to be in these regions.

Neurobiological Hypotheses of Depression

The existence of genetic elements in a large proportion of depressive disorders implies an associated biological abnormality, but no such abnormality has ever been conclusively identified in the brain or body fluids of any depressed person. Evidence favoring a biological abnormality derives largely from studies of the influence of antidepressant drugs on depressive symptoms and neurotransmitters, and from studies of neuroendocrine function in depressed individuals.

Neurotransmitters. The most prevalent idea is that depression involves a functional deficiency in monoamines; depression is hy-

pothesized to result from a deficiency of serotonin or noradrenaline or both, and antidepressants work by increasing the availability of these amines. Like the dopamine theory of schizophrenia, the data in support of a monoamine theory of depression are largely circumstantial, and there is the difficulty that antidepressant drugs are very slow to work, even though their action on the monoamine synapse is believed to be rapid. Nevertheless, most authors believe that brain noradrenergic and serotoninergic pathways are strongly implicated in the chemical pathology of depressive disorders. The role is not a simple one, however, and cannot be viewed as merely a "too little or too much" hypothesis.

Neuroendocrine Function. Both noradrenaline and serotonin modulate the secretion of hormones by the hypothalamus. There are many clinical signs of hypothalamic disturbance in depression, the best established abnormality being an oversecretion of the hormone cortisol. Normally, the secretion of cortisol fluctuates, peaking at about 8:00 a.m. and virtually ceasing in the evening. In contrast, about 50 percent of depressed patients secrete excessive amounts of cortisol (about two times the normal level), especially in the evening. Carroll and his colleagues have shown that whereas normal people or patients with other psychiatric diagnoses show a suppression of cortisol secretion when given dexamethasone, about 40 percent of depressed people show no suppression at all. The dexamethasone suppression test (DST) is becoming a standard clinical test for depression and is proving particularly useful because the absence of suppression is a good predictor of positive outcome from antidepressant therapy.

Cortical Function in Depression. We have seen that there are abnormalities both in monoamine levels and in neuroendocrine function in depressed persons, but we still must consider what effects these abnormalities might have on neocortical function. First, since serotonin is a vasodilator, its absence would be predicted to reduce blood flow because of relative vasoconstriction. It does: both blood-flow and PET studies have shown a bilateral reduction of cerebral activity in depressed persons. Second, diffuse depression of cerebral activity might be expected to produce nonspecific neuropsychological symptoms in which the extent of the deficit would be revealed by the difficulty of the test, rather than by the specific function assessed. This appears to be the case. Third, since serotonin is hypothesized to play a key role in sleep-waking cycles, it might be expected that EEG studies would reveal cortical abnormalities in the sleep-waking cycle. They do: Kupfer and his colleagues have found that slow-wave sleep is abnormal and that the onset of paradoxical sleep (rapid eye movement sleep or dreaming) is more rapid in depressed people, and they believe this measure to be as sensitive as the DST as a clinical test for depression. Finally, it might be predicted that some depressed people would exhibit only regional cortical depression because of some local disruption of neurotransmitter levels and thus that there might be different types of depressions characterized by different patterns of cerebral dysfunction. This hypothesis is difficult to test, but both Flor-Henry and Ross have proposed unique and testable models of this sort, although neither enjoys much empirical support to date.

Summary

Although our understanding of the biological bases of schizophrenia and depression is only at a very elementary level, the available data imply that both disorders have biological correlates that are of particular interest to neuropsychologists. In particular, evidence of frontal-temporal dysfunction in schizophrenia is consistent with neuropsychological theories that these regions are especially important in the control of emotional processes. Although symptoms of schizophrenia can be expected to differ from those resulting from the effects of cortical lesions, it seems reasonable to study schizophrenic patients using the same methods found to be useful with lesion patients. With this in mind, Pittman and Kolb have found reductions in facial expression and changes in spontaneous talking in schizophrenic patients, and Kolb and Whishaw have found abnormalities in the interpretation of facial expression in schizophrenic subjects as well. By studying the effects of both removal (brain lesions) and disruption (schizophrenia) of frontal and temporal zones it may thus be possible to better understand the neurological bases of emotional behavior, an understanding that would be of enormous practical benefit in treating people with biologically based disorders of emotional processing.

PSYCHOSURGERY

The debate over the use of surgery to treat emotional disorders has become a contentious issue, especially in the United States, over the past decade. We do not wish to enter the debate but rather will describe psychosurgery and its uses. For an excellent discussion of the psychosurgery issue, we recommend the recent text by Valenstein.

What Is Psychosurgery?

Psychosurgery is defined by Valenstein as destruction of some region in the brain in order-to alleviate severe and otherwise intractable psychiatric disorders. In order to distinguish current psychosurgical techniques from earlier and cruder "lobotomy" operations, the term *psychiatric surgery* has been suggested as a substitute by some, although the term refers to the same procedures. Brain surgery intended to repair damage in order to alleviate symptoms resulting from known neurological disease is not considered psychosurgery, even if the patient has severe behavioral and emotional symptoms. Brain surgery to alleviate intractable pain is normally considered to be psychosurgery since the brain operations are performed on normal brain tissue and because serious emotional disturbances often accompany chronic pain.

The belief that mental aberrations are related to disturbances of brain function goes back to primitive peoples. The practice of opening the skull (trepanning) for magical-medical purposes was apparently performed extensively over the world dating back at least to about 2000 B.C. Modern psychosurgery is normally traced to the Portuguese neurologist Egas Moniz, who started the prefrontal procedures in 1935. On the basis of studies of a small sample of monkeys and chimpanzees by Jacobsen, Moniz reasoned that destruction of the frontal lobe of psychiatrically ill people might be beneficial. Although he initially used alcohol injected into the frontal lobes to induce a frontal lesion, he soon switched to a technique in which nerve fibers were cut with a special knife called a leucotome (from the Greek *leuco,* white nerve fibers; *tome,* a cutting instrument). The procedure involved drilling holes over the frontal lobes and inserting a leucotome into the white matter to sever the frontal connections. Later modifications in the procedure were made in the United States by Freeman and Watts, including the Freeman-Watts procedure of drilling the holes in the temples and the lateral transorbital procedure of Free-

man in which the leucotome was inserted through the bony orbit above the eyeball. It is impossible to estimate accurately how many psychosurgical procedures were performed worldwide, although Valenstein feels that the best estimate for the United States is about 35,000 between 1936 and 1978.

The introduction of antipsychotic drugs in the mid-1950s led to a sharp reduction in the number of psychosurgical operations, but there still were a significant number of psychiatric patients who were not helped by the drugs. There has thus been a continuing interest in surgical intervention to change behavior, but since the 1960s there has been a change in the nature of the psychosurgical procedures employed, in part because of advances in the neurosciences. There are currently about 12 different targets of psychosurgical operations, which are summarized in Figure 22–5. These procedures generally produce smaller lesions than the original lobotomy-type procedures.

Who Receives Psychosurgery?

According to Valenstein, there is general agreement among psychiatrists and neurosurgeons who recommend or practice psychosurgery about who are the most appropriate patients for these operations. The major group of patients are described as "suffering from very intense and persistent emotional responses." This is taken to include patients suffering from depression, obsessive-compulsive disorders, anxiety, and phobias. Further, there is a group of patients in which psychosurgery is performed for pain symptoms, the pain usually being described as "intense, persistent, crippling, and intractable." Normally, all these disturbances are claimed to be of long duration and resistant to other treatments such as drugs, ECT, and psychotherapy.

FIGURE 22–5. Approximate brain targets of psychosurgical operations currently in use. *Frontal lobe procedures:* (1) bimedial leucotomy; (2) yttrium lesions in subcortical white matter; (3) orbital undercutting; (4) bifrontal stereotaxic subcaudate tractotomy; (5) anterior capsulotomy (destruction of fibers of internal capsule); (6) mesoloviotomy (similar to rostral cingulotomy, but lesion invades genu—"knee"—of corpus callosum). *Cingulotomies:* (7) anterior cingulotomy; (8) mid-cingulotomy; (9) posterior cingulotomy. *Amygdalectomy:* (10) amygdalectomy or amygdalotomy. *Thalamotomies:* (11) dorsomedial, centromedian, and parafascicular nuclei; (12) anterior thalamotomy. *Hypothalamotomy:* (13) posterior, ventromedial, and lateral hypothalamic targets. (After Valenstein, 1980.)

It is difficult to estimate the amount of psychosurgery currently performed. Valenstein estimates that 141 neurosurgeons in the United States performed approximately 400 operations per year during 1971–73, a figure that has declined steadily since then. In England, approximately 200 to 250 psychosurgical procedures have been performed per year through 1970–77, a figure that represents a rate by population about twice as high as in the United States. Less psychosurgery seems to be performed in Canada, however, the rate being about one-half that of the United States.

Comment

The effectiveness of psychosurgery as a treatment for psychiatric disorders is not easily assessed. The United States has formed a commission (National Commission for the Protection of Human Subjects of Biomedical and Behavioral Research) with the mandate of studying psychosurgery and making recommendations to the government regarding the further practice of psychosurgery in the country. The differences of opinion are large and the necessary scientific data are few, making any decision regarding psychosurgery very difficult indeed. For the neuropsychologist, an important question must be the issue of the cognitive price to be paid for surgical destruction of normally functioning brain tissue. We have seen throughout this text that virtually any cortical damage is associated with cognitive loss, often of an unexpected nature. There are now two extensive neuropsychological studies (see Corkin, and Mirsky and Orzack) that have shown there are surprisingly few deficits in cognitive functioning after cingulotomy, but we are unaware of any similar studies of patients undergoing other types of psychosurgical procedures. Thus, although there may be claims that psychosurgery is effective as a treatment of various disturbances, the cognitive price paid by the patients remains unstudied. As we have noted before, absence of evidence does not constitute evidence of absence. At present, we believe that with the possible exception of psychosurgery for the relief of chronic pain, there is little justification for the use of psychosurgical procedures un-

til more is known about them. As we shall discuss in relation to recovery of function from brain lesions (Chapter 25), the processes following brain lesions are extremely complex and are poorly understood. Changes may continue for years after brain damage (e.g., calcification), and so follow-up studies must do careful analyses of patients over the course of years. We are inclined to believe that for many patients psychosurgical procedures may be equivalent to using a sledgehammer for a hangnail. It may be a "cure," but the cost may not be worth it.

REFERENCES

Bear, D. M., and P. Fedio. Quantitative analysis of interictal behavior in temporal lobe epilepsy. *Archives of Neurology* 34:454–467, 1977.

Benson, D. F., and D. Blumer, eds. *Psychiatric Aspects of Neurological Disease.* New York: Grune & Stratton, 1975.

Blumer, D. Temporal lobe epilepsy and its psychiatric significance. In D. F. Blumer and D. Benson, eds., *Psychiatric Aspects of Neurological Disease.* New York: Grune & Stratton, 1975.

Brown, S., and E. A. Schaefer. An investigation into the functions of the occipital and temporal lobe of the monkey's brain. *Philosophical Transactions of the Royal Society,* part B, 179:303–327, 1888.

Brown, W. A., R. Johnston, and D. Mayfield. The 24-hour dexamethasone suppression test in a clinical setting: Relationship to diagnosis, symptoms, and response to treatment. *American Journal of Psychiatry* 136:543–547, 1979.

Brownwell, H. H., D. Michel, J. Powelson, and H. Gardner. Surprise but not coherence: Sensitivity to verbal humor in right-hemisphere patients. *Brain and Language* 18:20–27, 1983.

Bruyer, R. Asymmetry of facial expression in brain damaged subjects. *Neuropsychologia* 19:615–623, 1981.

Bryden, M. P. *Laterality: Functional Asymmetry in the Intact Brain.* New York: Academic, 1982.

Buchtel, H., F. Campari, C. de Risio, and R. Rota. Hemispheric differences in discriminative reaction time to facial expressions. *Italian Journal of Psychology* 5:159–169, 1978.

Buck, R., and R. J. Duffy. Nonverbal communication of affect in brain-damaged patients. *Cortex* 16:351–362, 1980.

Campbell, R. Asymmetries in interpreting and expressing a posed facial expression. *Cortex* 14:327–342, 1978.

Campbell, R. The lateralisation of emotion: A critical review. *International Journal of Psychology* 17:211–229, 1982.

Carlsson, A. Does dopamine have a role in schizophrenia? *Biological Psychiatry* 13:3–21, 1978.

Carmon, A., and I. Nachshon. Ear asymmetry in perception of emotional nonverbal stimuli. *Acta Psychologia* 37:351–357, 1973.

Carroll, B. J., G. C. Curtis, and J. Mendels. Neuroendocrine regulation in depression. II. Discrimination of depressed from non-depressed patients. *Archives of General Psychiatry* 33:1051–1058, 1976.

Chaurasia, B. D., and H. K. Goswami. Functional asymmetry in the face. *Acta Anatomica* 91:154–160, 1975.

Chorover, S. L. The psychosurgery evaluation studies and their inpact on the commission's report. In E. Valenstein, ed., *The Psychosurgery Debate*. San Francisco: Freeman, 1980.

Cicone, M., W. Wapner, and H. Gardner. Sensitivity to emotional expressions and situations in organic patients. *Cortex* 16:145–158, 1980.

Corkin, S. A prospective study of cingulotomy. In E. Valenstein, ed., *The Psychosurgery Debate*. San Francisco: Freeman, 1980.

Danly, M., and B. Shapiro. Speech prosody in Broca's aphasia. *Brain and Language* 16:171–190, 1982.

Davis, K. L., and P. Berger. Pharmacological investigations of the cholinergic imbalance hypotheses of movement disorders and psychosis. *Biological Psychiatry* 13:23–49, 1978.

DeKosky, S. T., K. M. Heilman, D. Bowers, and E. Valenstein. Recognition and discrimination of emotional faces and pictures. *Brain and Language* 9:206–214, 1980.

Dimond, S. J., and L. Farrington. Emotional response to films shown to the right or left hemisphere of the brain measured by heart rate. *Acta Psychologia* 41:255–260, 1977.

Dimond, S. J., L. Farrington, and P. Johnson. Differing emotional response from right and left hemispheres. *Nature* 261:690–692, 1976.

Ekman, P., W. V. Friesen, and P. Ellsworth. *Emotion in the Human Face*. New York: Pergamon, 1972.

Farley, I. J., K. S. Price, E. McCullough, W. Deck, W. Hordynsku, and O. Hornykiewicz. Norepinephrine levels in chronic paranoid schizophrenia: Above-normal levels in limbic forebrain. *Science* 200:456–458, 1978.

Flor-Henry, P. On certain aspects of the localization of the cerebral systems in regulating and determining emotion. *Biological Psychiatry* 14:677–698, 1979.

Flor-Henry, P., and Z. J. Koles. EEG studies in depression, mania and normals: Evidence for partial shifts of laterality in the affective psychoses. *Advances in Biological Psychiatry* 4:21–43, 1980.

Gainotti, G. Emotional behavior and hemispheric side of the lesion. *Cortex* 8:41–55, 1972.

Gainotti, G. Reactions "catastrophiques" et manifestations d'indifférence au cours des atteintes cerebrales. *Neuropsychologia* 7:195–204, 1969.

Gardner, H., P. K. Ling, L. Flamm, and J. Silverman. Comprehension and appreciation of humorous material following brain damage. *Brain* 98:399–412, 1975.

Goldstein, K. *The Organism: A Holistic Approach to Biology, Derived from Pathological Data in Man.* New York: American Book, 1939.

Haggard, M. P., and A. M. Parkinson. Stimulus and task factors as determinants of ear advantages. *Quarterly Journal of Experimental Psychology* 23:168–177, 1971.

Haug, J. O. Pneumoencephalographic studies in mental disease. *Acta Psychiatrica Neurologia Scandinavia,* suppl. 165, 38:1–104, 1962.

Hécaen, H., J. de Ajuriaguerra, and J. Massonet. Les troubles visuo-constructifs par lesion parieto-occipitale droite. *Encephalé* 40:122–179, 1951.

Heilman, K., M. R. Scholes, and R. T. Watson. Auditory affective agnosia. *Journal of Neurology, Neurosurgery and Psychiatry* 38:69–72, 1975.

Kent, R. D., and J. C. Rosenbek. Prosodic disturbance and neurological lesion. *Brain and Language* 15:259–291, 1982.

King, F. L., and D. Kimura. Left-ear superiority in dichotic perception of vocal nonverbal sounds. *Canadian Journal of Psychology* 26:111–116, 1972.

Klüver, H., and P. C. Bucy. Preliminary analysis of the temporal lobes in monkeys. *Archives of Neurology and Psychiatry* 42:979–1000, 1939.

Kolb, B., and B. Milner. Observations on spontaneous facial expression after focal cerebral excisions and after intracarotid injection of sodium Amytal. *Neuropsychologia* 19:505–514, 1981.

Kolb, B., and L. Taylor. Affective behavior in patients with localized cortical excisions: Role of lesion site and side. *Science* 214:89–91, 1981.

Kolb, B., and I. Q. Whishaw. Performance of schizophrenic patients on tests sensitive to left or right frontal, temporal, or parietal function in neurological patients. *Journal of Nervous and Mental Disease* 171:435–443, 1983.

Kupfer, D. J. Toward a unified view of affective disorders. In M. Zales, ed., *Affective and Schizophrenic Disorders.* New York: Brunner/Mazel, 1983.

Kupfer, D. J., and M. E. Thase. The use of the sleep laboratory in the diagnosis of affective disorders. *Psychiatric Clinics of North America* 6:3–25, 1983.

Ley, R. G., and M. P. Bryden. A dissociation of right and left hemispheric effects for recognizing emotional tone and verbal content. *Brain and Cognition* 1:3–9, 1982.

Ley, R. G., and M. P. Bryden. Hemispheric differences in processing emotions and faces. *Brain and Language* 7:127–138, 1979.

McHugh, P. R., and M. F. Folstein. Psychiatric syndromes of Huntington's chorea. In D. F. Benson and D. Blumer, eds., *Psychiatric Aspects of Neurological Disease.* New York: Grune & Stratton, 1975.

Malamud, N. Organic brain disease mistaken for psychiatric disorder. In D. R. Benson and D. Blumer, eds., *Psychiatric Aspects of Neurological Disease.* New York: Grune & Stratton, 1975.

Marlowe, W. B., E. L. Mancall, and J. J. Thomas. Complete Klüver-Bucy syndrome in man. *Cortex* 11:53–59, 1975.

Mathew, R. J., J. S. Meyer, D. J. Francis, K. M. Semchuk, K. Mortel, and J. L. Claghorn. Cerebral blood flow in depression. *American Journal of Psychiatry* 137:1449–1450, 1980.

Milner, B. Brain mechanisms suggested by studies of the temporal lobes. In C. H. Millikan and F. L. Darley, eds., *Brain Mechanisms Underlying Speech and Language*. New York: Grune & Stratton, 1967.

Mirsky, A. F., and M. H. Orzack. Two retrospective studies of psychosurgery. In E. Valenstein, ed., *The Psychosurgery Debate*. San Francisco: Freeman, 1980.

Moscovitch, M., and J. Olds. Asymmetries in spontaneous facial expressions and their possible relation to hemispheric specialization. *Neuropsychologia* 20:71–82, 1982.

Papez, J. W. A proposed mechanism of emotion. *Archives of Neurology and Psychiatry* 38:725–744, 1937.

Robinson, R. G., and B. Szetela. Mood change following left hemispheric brain injury. *Annals of Neurology* 9:447–453, 1981.

Ross, E. D. The aprosodias: Functional-anatomical organization of the affective components of language in the right hemisphere. *Archives of Neurology* 38:561–569, 1981.

Ross, E. D., and A. J. Rush. Diagnosis and neuroanatomical correlates of depression in brain-damaged patients. *Archives of General Psychiatry* 38:1344–1354, 1981.

Rossi, G. F., and G. Rosandini. Experimental analysis of cerebral dominance in man. In C. H. Millikan and F. L. Darley, eds., *Brain Mechanisms Underlying Speech and Language*. New York: Grune & Stratton, 1967.

Rovetta, P. Discussion of paper "Amytal intracarotides per lo studio della dominanza emisferica." *Rivista di Neurologia* 30:460–470, 1960.

Sachar, E. J. Psychobiology of schizophrenia. In E. R. Kandel and J. H. Schwartz, eds., *Principles of Neural Science*. New York: Elsevier North-Holland, 1981.

Sachdev, H. S., and S. G. Waxman. Frequency of hypergraphia in temporal lobe epilepsy: An index of interictal behaviour syndrome. *Journal of Neurology, Neurosurgery, and Psychiatry* 44:358–360, 1981.

Sackeim, H. A., M. S. Greenberg, A. L. Weiman, R. C. Gur, J. P. Hungerbuhler, and N. Geschwind. Hemispheric asymmetry in the expression of positive and negative emotions. *Archives of Neurology* 39:210–218, 1982.

Sackheim, H., R. S. Gur, and M. Saucy. Emotions are expressed more intensely on the left side of the face. *Science* 202:434–436, 1978.

Safer, M., and H. Leventhal. Ear differences in evaluating emotional tones of voice and verbal content. *Journal of Experimental Psychology: Human Perception and Performance* 3:75–82, 1977.

Schwartz, G. E., R. J. Davidson, and F. Maer. Right hemisphere lateralization for emotion in the human brain: Interactions with cognition. *Science* 190:286–288, 1975.

Snyder, S. H. *Biological Aspects of Mental Disorder*. New York: Academic, 1980.

Terzian, H. Behavioral and EEG effects of intracarotid sodium Amytal injection. *Acta Neurochirurgica* 12:230–239, 1964.

Tompkins, C. A., and C. A. Mateer. Right hemisphere appreciation of intonational and linguistic indications of affect. Unpublished manuscript, 1983.

Tucker, D. M. Lateral brain function, emotion, and conceptualization. *Psychological Bulletin* 89:19–46, 1981.

Tucker, D. M., R. T. Watson, and K. M. Heilman. Discrimination and evocation of affectively intoned speech in patients with right parietal disease. *Neurology* 27:947–950, 1977.

Valenstein, E. S., ed. *The Psychosurgery Debate*. San Francisco: Freeman, 1980.

Van Praag, H. M. Significance of biochemical parameters in the diagnosis, treatment and prevention of depressive disorders. *Biological Psychiatry* 12:101–131, 1977.

Watson, S. J., P. A. Berger, H. Akil, M. J. Mills, and J. D. Barchas. Effects of naloxone on schizophrenia: Reduction in hallucinations in a subpopulation of subjects. *Science* 201:73–76, 1978.

Waxman, S. G., and N. Geschwind. Hypergraphia in temporal lobe epilepsy. *Neurology* 24:629–636, 1974.

23

SPATIAL BEHAVIOR

In modern accounts of cerebral organization it is assumed that spatial processing is a special function of the right hemisphere, but it is only since about 1960 that this view has gained widespread acceptance. Hughlings-Jackson was the first to propose that the right hemisphere might have some special perceptual function to complement the language functions of the left hemisphere. In his famous paper of 1874, "On the Nature of the Duality of the Brain," he predicted that a person with damage restricted to the posterior part of the right hemisphere would have a distinctive syndrome. "The patient would have difficulty in recognizing things; he would have difficulty in relating what had occurred, not from lack of words, but from a prior inability to revive images of persons, objects and places, of which the words are symbols. . . . He could not put before himself ideal images of places one after another; could not re-see where he had been, and could not therefore tell of it in words" (Taylor, 1932, p. 144). Hughlings-Jackson was proposing a spatial-perceptual function for the right hemisphere, although he admitted that the evidence for his position was not strong, remarking that, "as will be seen, my facts are very few" (ibid, p. 145). A series of papers by a number of investigators between 1876 and 1905 described various cases with spatial-perceptual difficulties, confirming Jackson's view that such disorders ought to exist. Although most of these cases appeared to have bilateral damage, rather than right posterior damage, a view nonetheless persisted at the turn of the century that the right hemisphere might have a special role in the mediation of spatial thinking.

World War I led to further advances in the understanding of spatial disturbances accompanying brain injury, but the possibility that there was an association between spatial deficits and right hemisphere damage was largely ignored. By 1950 a large number of "spatial deficits" had been described (see Table 23–1), but the main point that had escaped notice was the asymmetrical representation of spatial function in the two hemispheres, perhaps

TABLE 23–1

Summary of types of "spatial" deficits
described in the clinical literature

Behavior	Basic reference
1. Impaired eye movements to points in space	Balint, 1909; Tyler, 1968
2. Poor localization of visual, auditory, or tactile stimuli in space	Head, 1920; Shankweiler, 1951; Holmes, 1919
3. Misreaching for objects	Brain, 1941
4. Neglect for left hemispace	Brain, 1941; Oxbury et al., 1974
5. Right/left confusion	Benton, 1959
6. Constructional apraxia	Benton, 1979
7. Amnesia for routes and locations	Paterson and Zangwill, 1944
8. Impaired performance on mazes	Corkin, 1965; Milner, 1965
9. Defective locomotion in space	Semmes et al., 1963
10. Poor drawing	McFie and Zangwill, 1960
11. Impaired performance at tests of mental spatial transformations (geometry, mazes, mental rotation, etc.)	DeRenzi, 1982
12. Inability to determine visual or tactile line orientation	Benton et al., 1978; DeRenzi, et al., 1971
13. Defective shape discrimination	DeRenzi and Scotti, 1969

because most of the published reports were single-case studies, which could be easily discounted. It was the systematic studies of Zangwill, Hécaen, and their coworkers in the 1950s that forced a reexamination of the role of the right hemisphere in spatial performance. There now is little doubt that the right hemisphere has a dominant role in most spatial

behavior, but that certain disorders of spatial processing are observed only in people with damage to the left hemisphere or with bilateral damage, and so the control of spatial behavior is not the exclusive domain of the right hemisphere. In this chapter we shall consider the nature of spatial behavior, the abnormalities of spatial processing observed after different types of brain damage, and the anatomical correlates of spatial behavior, especially as inferred from recent studies of spatial processing in rats and monkeys with cerebral lesions.

THE NATURE OF SPACE

The concept of "space" has many interpretations that are by no means equivalent. Our body occupies space, it moves through space, it interacts with things in space, and it can mentally rotate and manipulate representations of space. Other objects also occupy space and maintain relations in space with one another and with us. Yet, as O'Keefe and Nadel illustrate in their important book, it is extraordinarily difficult to come to grips with the nature of space. Philosophers have asked whether objects exist without space, or conversely, whether space exists without objects. Is space a feature of the universe or merely a creation of our brain? How are the concepts of space developed as humans grow from a baby? Anyone who has banged his or her head on a cupboard door can quickly realize the difference in spatial perspective between crawling babies and standing adults. Small animals' (e.g., dogs, cats, and children) representation of space must be very different if only because they are always looking up and are in constant danger of having their personal space violated by our feet. Pilots and birds must have a very different concept of space than do those with more restricted vistas. It should be obvious that to say a person has a "spatial deficit" or the right hemisphere is "spatial" is not very informative, even as a shorthand description. Table 23–1 summarizes such deficits, including disorders as diverse as confusion in naming left and right, the inability to localize sounds in space, amnesia for the position of things in space, and the inability to move the eyes or to use a map. Given this range of disorders, which are loosely grouped together as spatial deficits, it is obvious that we must try to fractionate "spatial behavior" into its constituent parts if we are to understand the brain-behavior relations involved.

One way to fractionate spatial behavior is to consider the space around an individual as being composed of three functionally different subspaces (Figure 23–1), each of which may have a distinct neural representation. First, there is the body surface, on which stimuli can be localized to a place. An inability to localize points on the body or neglect of the body would represent a disorder of body space. Second, there is the space immediately around the individual, which Grüsser has termed the grasping space. Abnormalities of reaching would be an example of a disorder of this subspace. Finally, beyond the grasping space is a region that can be called action space. Several different strategies may be necessary for operations in this space. For example, within action space sedentary objects maintain an absolute

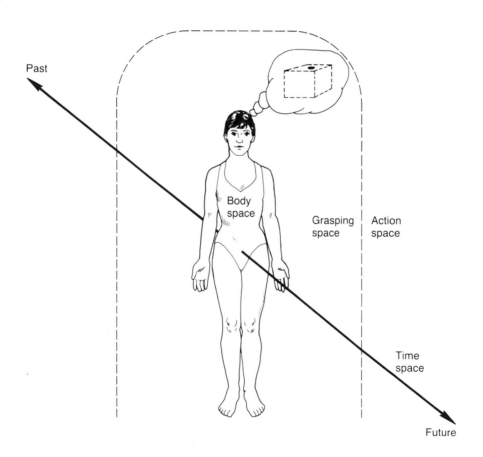

FIGURE 23–1. A conceptual model of the compartments of space.

relation to one another but the relation of objects to moving humans is relative to our position. A flower may be to the right of a tree if we are facing north, but although the flower and tree are in the same absolute positions, their relative position of left and right is reversed should we face south. We shall see that there are grounds for believing that neural representations of the absolute and the relative position of objects are dissociable.

Our fractionation of space into three subspaces provides a useful vehicle for understanding how the brain represents space. In particular, it forces us to think of space not as a homogenous thing, but rather as something that can be broken down into constituent parts, just as language and memory are not things, but are shorthand descriptions for large classes of behavior. Furthermore, these subspaces are the areas in which people and other animals operate, and so we can be reasonably assured that each subspace has some type of neural representation. What we do not know is how separable each representation is.

Two other aspects of space deserve mention before we consider the disorders of space. The first is imaginary space, that is, our cognitive representation of the external world; the second is the distinction between places and routes. We shall consider each in turn.

Cognitive Space

It seems obvious that the subspaces of the physical world must have cognitive representations in the brain. For example, we can mentally draw a map of a route from one point to another, or imagine looking at an object from the side opposite our actual vantage point without actually moving. Cognitive representations of space are dependent on experience and change with experience. Children are unable to form complex cognitive representations, especially of action space. As they ma-

ture, they are able to produce more accurate representations, but these are notoriously fragile, even in normal people. Virtually everyone has lost their way in a new place, often because of one wrong turn, and our cognitive representations of geography are continually being changed by travel. Kolb's representation of the eastern part of North America was of a series of cities from Chicago to Montreal, separated by short distances. The territory west of Chicago was, however, vast, and cities were far apart. This cartography was a product of his western upbringing and was only changed when he attempted to drive from Ontario to Nova Scotia in an afternoon.

The important point about cognitive representations of space is that each of our subspaces can be represented cognitively. Thus we can have a mental image of body parts, even when they are absent as in phantom limbs, and of things and places in space, whether they are visible or not. We shall therefore consider disorders of cognitive representations of different subspaces as we discuss the disorders of each subspace.

Within the realm of cognitive space, we can include the dimension of time. Time is obviously cognitive—we do not actually observe it—but the concept of time is conceptually different from a mental map of places, although places can exist within different dimensions of time. Little is known about the neurological representation of time, but we do know that people with frontal lobe damage often have a blithe disregard for time and have difficulty in temporally organizing their behavior. We do not know, however, how people make neural representations of long-range plans that extend their commitment for years into the future or how they create neural constructs of their pasts that enable them to place themselves within a culture constrained by ancient traditions and histories. These issues will remain beyond the scope of this chapter!

Places and Routes

As we go about our business in space we learn not only *where* things are but also how to get from one place to another. This is the distinction between places and routes. As we consider disorders of each subspace it will be useful to keep this distinction in mind, for we shall see that the neural representation of places and routes may be separable. Indeed, it could be argued that knowledge about where things are is primarily a function of the right hemisphere in humans, but that knowledge about routes to places is a function of both hemispheres, the precise role depending on the way in which the route is coded. For example, if a route is coded verbally (e.g., turn left, go straight, turn right), we would anticipate that the left hemisphere is dominant. In contrast, if a route is coded in relation to the position of things or places, such as when we have a vague feeling about where we left our shoes last night, the right hemisphere would likely be dominant. Given this distinction, we should not be surprised to find that both left and right hemisphere lesions produce certain specific deficits in "spatial behavior."

DISORDERS OF BODY SPACE

Let us first consider the nature of body space. Perhaps the most obvious component of body space is the skin surface. If our skin receptors are stimulated by something, we can immediately identify the spatial location on the body. In addition, we can synthesize the tactile information to identify the shape (a spatial configuration) of many things that touch us. As you sit reading this page you can identify both the spatial position of objects touching you as well as the shape of those objects without moving. Perhaps one leg is against the table; you can identify the table and feel the straight edge.

Perhaps your feet are crossed; you can identify this experience and feel the shape of one shoe against the other, and so on. Further, if an unidentified object were presented to you while you were blindfolded, it would be possible to scan and identify the object, even if only one finger were allowed to contact it. Body space includes more than just tactile experience, however. It also includes knowledge about the body. In particular, you are aware of the existence and position of different body parts and can identify similar body parts in others.

We have seen in earlier chapters that disorders of body space can be localized to the parietal lobes. Damage to the primary somatosensory cortex may raise the threshold for the detection of tactile stimuli, thus making spatial localization impossible. Similarly, damage to the primary or secondary cortex may render a person unable to recognize objects by touch (astereognosia); a spatial configuration of the object can no longer be constructed. Finally, parietal lobe damage can produce various agnosias related to body parts or conditions (e.g., finger agnosia, contralateral neglect, and autotopagnosia). It seems clear that information from the body can be considered "spatial" information, and that disorders related to this information can be conceptualized as a spatial disorder, insofar as the disorder is one of determining *where* something is, rather than *what* something is. We shall return to this distinction later.

DISORDERS OF GRASPING SPACE

Grasping space is that space immediately around the individual in which objects can be touched directly, or indirectly using tools. Unlike body space, grasping space is external to the body, and behaviors related to grasping space are movements directed toward points immediately around the individual. The most obvious movements within grasping space would be with the arms and hands, but they could also be of the head, tongue, or legs. In addition, movements of the eyes can be considered movements in grasping space since eye movements are necessary to detect where things are as well as to direct movements with respect to things. Movements in grasping space could be directed by nearly any type of sensory input, but we shall restrict our consideration to visual and auditory input since the most is known about the role of these stimuli in spatial behavior.

Disorders of Visual-Spatial Function

The visual system is organized to perceive at any given moment only a small part of the visual world and to be able to analyze in detail only an even smaller part of it, and so it is obvious that a prerequisite of visual processing is the detection and localization of visual stimuli that are to be processed. One way to explore the visual world is to make eye movements, which are often directed toward stimuli that are first perceived in the periphery and function to move the stimuli into the visual field of the fovea. A second way to explore the visual world is to move the body with respect to visual stimuli. Perhaps the commonest way to do this is by reaching for objects and bringing them closer for more detailed inspection, although moving to a stimulus serves the same purpose. In either case, however, the stimulus must first be detected and "noticed" or "attended to" before visually guided movements can occur. Disorders of visual-spatial exploration could thus result from defects in attending to visual stimuli or in making the necessary eye or body movements toward them.

Disorders of visual-spatial exploration were described first by Badal in 1889, but it was Balint and later Holmes who first analyzed defective visual exploration in detail. (For a discussion of Balint's syndrome and Holmes's patients see Chapter 10.) There now appear to be about eight different defects of visual exploration, which usually result from bilateral lesions of the posterior cortex and do not occur all at once (see Table 23–2). Perhaps the most dramatic symptoms are those first described by Balint. Figure 23–2 shows a patient studied by Allison and his colleagues who had bilateral posterior cortical lesions resulting in small lower temporal quadrant field defects accompanied by dramatic deficits in the visual control of reaching and other movements (so-called optic ataxia) as well as by deficits in eye movements.

A manifestation of visual disorientation noted by the nursing staff five months after operation was when he attempted to light a cigarette. He took it out of the packet and put it in his mouth, then clumsily took a match out of the matchbox and lit it, afterwards directing the flame towards his lower lip, missing the cigarette. . . . He could not pour fluid from a bottle into a glass but spilled it on the table cloth [Figure 23–2]. He was unable to shake hands without first groping for the proferred hand. It could be demonstrated that visual memory was intact and did not contribute to his errors. When an object (e.g., a match-

TABLE 23–2

Deficits in visual-spatial exploration
1. Displaced visual attention
2. Inability to perceive more than one stimulus
3. Defective visual control of movement (optic ataxia)
4. Inability to follow a moving target
5. Defective accommodation and convergence
6. Inability in maintaining fixation
7. Inability to voluntarily direct gaze to targets (gaze apraxia)
8. Abnormal visual search

FIGURE 23–2. A patient with Balint's syndrome demonstrates a visual-spatial deficit in his attempt to pour fluid into a glass. (After Allison et al., 1969.)

box) was held up either above his head, to the right or to the left and he was asked to note its position, close his eyes for a moment and then point in the general direction in which he had seen the object, he did this correctly. Therefore, it appeared that his ability to remember the position of an object in space was not impaired. (Allison et al., 1969, 324–326)

This patient shows a clear disorder in grasping space. His visual acuity was good and his verbal abilities (apart from reading, which requires eye movements) were seemingly normal, but his visual-spatial abilities were grossly defective. His control of movements by visual guidance was especially bad, as was his ability to localize the position of objects in space.

In order to dissociate the many deficits that people like this one suffer from, various investigations have centered on two aspects of visual function within grasping space, namely visual localization and depth perception.

Consider the following representative studies. To demonstrate a disorder of spatial localization independent from a disorder of reaching or pointing, Hannay et al. projected one or two dots on a screen for 300 ms. Two seconds later an array of numbers, each of which identified a point where a dot may have been, was projected, and the task was to indicate the position of the dot. Patients with right-hemisphere lesions were impaired at this task in comparison to those with left hemisphere lesions and normal controls. This deficit is not simply a manifestation of neglect, since errors were equally distributed in the left and right visual fields. It is apparent that an inability to localize points in space would make it difficult indeed to direct movements within grasping space, resulting in an apparent "spatial" deficit.

An important cue to spatial location of objects is depth. To discover its importance, try catching a ball with one eye closed. The discovery of a profound impairment in depth perception has been claimed dating back to Balint, but a significant problem of interpretation arises when the inference of impaired depth is based on misreaching, since an impairment might result from many different deficits. Nonetheless, there is now good evidence that depth perception can be markedly abnormal in the presence of good acuity. A study by Carmon and Bechtoldt provides a compelling example. Their patients were presented with random dot stereograms developed previously by Julesz to study cues necessary to perceive depth. Subjects look into eyepieces and are shown an apparently random array of dots. When viewed with one eye alone, the array has no contour or depth, the pattern looking rather like a complex crossword puzzle with black and white boxes. However, when each eye independently views a stereogram, a striking figure-ground contour suddenly appears because of slight disparities between the stereograms shown to the two eyes. Most normal subjects and patients with left hemisphere damage easily perceive the contours, but patients with right hemisphere damage are very poor at this test, illustrating a defect in depth perception. This result has been replicated by others, supporting the idea that the mechanism involved in at least some aspects of the perception of depth are more strongly represented in the right hemisphere.

Disorders of Auditory-Spatial Analysis

The localization of sounds in space is an important feature of auditory processing. Normally, identification of the spatial location of sounds rests on the detection of the difference in time, intensity, and phase with which two ears are stimulated by sound, although scanning head movements may also be necessary if the difference between the ears is small. Studies with cats by Neff and others have established that bilateral removal of the temporal cortex abolishes the ability to localize sounds, but evidence from unilateral ablations of temporal cortex in humans is not entirely consistent. Overall, it appears that temporal lobe damage is likely to impair sound localization and that right temporal lobe damage has greater effects than similar damage to the left. These deficits are probably relatively small and may not be noticed at all by people in their daily life—a situation in sharp contrast to the effects of right hemisphere lesions on visual-spatial analysis.

Anatomical Correlates of Grasping Space

Deficits in behaviors related to grasping space appear most likely to follow parietal cortex damage, most likely within the secondary and tertiary areas. It will be recalled from our discussion of the parietal cortex that various

investigators have identified neurons in the posterior parietal cortex of monkeys that respond to stimuli within grasping space. It is likely that these are cells that can be used to guide the limbs during voluntary movements toward targets in various spatial locations. Furthermore, there are neurons that appear to have a role in head or eye movements toward stimuli in grasping space, again providing evidence that the parietal cortex has a special role in the control of behavior within grasping space. Evidence for an asymmetry in the neural representation of grasping space in humans is not overwhelming, although some investigators have found a small asymmetry favoring the right hemisphere.

DISORDERS OF ACTION SPACE

Action space refers to the space beyond our immediate grasp in which we move in our daily activities. It thus includes places that we may be in or go to, things that we may interact with, routes that we might follow, and the cognitive representations of all these things. The cognitive representation of action space is especially important, for a disturbance in it can produce profound disruption of a person's overt behavior. Much of our behavior in action space requires that we first mentally manipulate objects or places in order to determine the best course of action, or that we draw or otherwise represent things and places in action space. For example, if we wish to go from point A to point B, we must first take stock of where we are, next mentally determine the shortest or most efficient path, and then set out. As we progress on our route we must monitor our progress relative to landmarks and our mental route. Cognitive manipulations of representations of objects or places need not produce movement to be considered aspects of action space, however. If we are asked what in direction Paris is from Cairo, we must manipulate a mental representation to answer the question, even though we will not actually be moving. Further, if we are asked to imagine that a cube is hanging directly above us and is suspended from one corner, we can easily imagine looking up at the cube and count the number of corners that are visible. Action space thus includes the space in which we move and the representation of this space. It would therefore seem to be that portion of space many people are referring to when they say that the right hemisphere is "spatial." We shall see, however, that many aspects of action space may be carried out by the left hemisphere rather than by the right.

The discussion of action space is complicated by the variety of behaviors that can occur within it. To facilitate our discussion we have divided action space into five separate parts, each of which will be considered separately: (1) left/right confusion, (2) egocentric and allocentric orientation, (3) topographical disorientation, (4) spatial thought, and (5) spatial memory.

Left/Right Confusion

The confusion of left and right is not strictly a disorder of action space, as it can occur within body or grasping space as well. The important point is not exactly where in space it occurs, but that the neural representation of left and right may be in the left or the right hemisphere, depending on the exact demands of the behavior examined.

The distinction between left and right is complex, for it requires an appreciation of a person's point of view and of that of others. Moreover, the distinction between left and right requires not only the comprehension of position but also the use of a word to label the position. The classical view of left/right confusion is that it is a symptom of left parietal damage. Recall, for example, that Gerstmann was sufficiently convinced about the reliability of this symptom to include it in his "syndrome" of left parietal lobe damage. Left/right confusion is known to be associated with language disorders, and so it is reasonable to wonder if this deficit is only a result of disturbed language processing, rather than a real "spatial" deficit. This is unlikely. First, no simple relation holds between aphasia and left/right confusion, although the symptoms can certainly occur together. Second, left/right confusion is a common symptom of reading disabilities in children, but apart from an obvious difficulty with reading, these children do not have a language disturbance. Third, the presence of left/right confusion is often dependent on the way in which subjects are tested. For example, people with left posterior lesions show a severe left/right confusion when tested with the body-placing test of Semmes or if they are asked to decide whether drawings of body parts are of the left or the right. In contrast, Ratcliff found that similar left posterior patients, but not right posterior patients, could perform normally when a slight twist was added to the task. In his version, schematic drawings of a man were shown to subjects in either an upright or an inverted orientation. One of the hands was marked with a black dot, and the subject's task was to say "right" or "left" depending on the hand marked. The right posterior group made significantly fewer errors than the left posterior group for the upright orientation, but the reverse was obtained with the inverted orientation. In fact, the left hemisphere patients actually performed slightly better than the control group with the inverted orientation! This result is remarkable, and it makes the important point that left/right confusion can occur from lesions in either hemisphere, depending on the nature of the test. Since left/right confusion has essentially been viewed as a left parietal lobe symptom it seems worthwhile to reevaluate it in light of Ratcliff's study. Further, we must now be alert to the fact that relatively minor modifications of a "spatial" task may make rather larger differences in how the brain handles the problem.

Egocentric and Allocentric Orientation

Action space is often conceptualized as consisting of two components. The first, which is known as egocentric or personal space, is space in which the body is the referent for the location of things. Left and right or front and back are terms referring to egocentric space since they are relative to the position of our body. An object or position moves relative to the body if we turn and face in the opposite direction. The second space, which is known as allocentric or extrapersonal space, is space that is fixed with respect to the position of the body. The absolute position of New York is fixed regardless of where we stand. A number of investigators have argued that this distinction is neurologically significant, with the frontal lobe playing a special role in egocentric orientation and the parietal lobe playing a role in allocentric orientation. This dichotomy is easier to propose than to prove.

In their study of the effects of penetrating head wounds in World War II veterans, Semmes and her colleagues showed that frontal lesions were more disruptive to a test of body placing than parietal lesions, but that parietal lesions disrupted the following of various routes (see Figure 18–5). Semmes et al. concluded that these data supported their theory, since they believed the body-placing task to be an egocentric task and the route-walking task to be an allocentric one. There is now considerable literature from the study of both humans and monkeys to support the belief that personal and extrapersonal orientation may be dissociable, but the neurological basis is not so

straightforward as Semmes and her colleagues suggested. This is best illustrated by the problem of left and right discussed earlier. Left and right are obviously egocentric, and so we would anticipate left/right confusion from frontal lesions. This does not occur. Further, although frontal lesions do produce deficits on egocentric spatial tasks, they also produce deficits that are not simply tests of personal orientation. For example, the deficit in maze learning described by Milner and by Corkin for frontal lobe patients is not really one of egocentric disorientation. It is the relative position of the lines or routes in the mazes that is the key to the solution.

Overall, the data suggest that the right parietal cortex is primarily concerned with allocentric orientation and that the frontal cortex is concerned with egocentric orientation as well as having some more global, and as yet unspecified, role in the control of action space.

Topographical Disorientation

There are many clinical reports of patients with a gross disability in finding their way about surroundings, even those with which they were familiar before the onset of their disease. Many of these reports are difficult to interpret because the patients also experienced other spatial deficits such as left/right confusion, contralateral neglect, deficits of sensory-spatial analysis, and visual field defects. Nevertheless, topographical disorientation has been observed in patients in whom it has been claimed that other spatial deficits were minimal. DeRenzi summarizes a case thoroughly studied by Meyer at the turn of the century that nicely illustrates the nature of topographical disorientation:

(1) Whenever he left his room in the hospital, he had trouble in finding the way back, because at any chosen point of the route he did not know whether to go right, left, downstairs or upstairs

(on one occasion, he walked from the main floor down to the basement, instead of going up to the first floor, where his bed was located). When he eventually arrived in front of his own room, he did not recognize it unless he chanced to see some distinguishing feature, such as the black beard of his roommate, or a particular object on the bedside table. . . .

(2) When taken to sections of the city he knew before his illness and required to lead the way, he tried hard to find familiar landmarks, such as a signboard, the name of a street, the tramcar numbers, etc., but this information, though effectively indicating to him he was near his home, failed to provide clues for choosing the right direction. . . .

(3) Required to provide verbal information concerning routes or places well known before the disease, he performed fairly well as long as he could rely on purely verbal knowledge. Thus he was able to give the names of the intermediate stations on the railway line he used daily, or the location of the main building of the city. Yet, he met with considerable difficulty when the way had to be retraced from spatial memory; for instance, when required to tell how he would walk between two sites chosen at random in the city, he could only say the initial street and then he became confused. . . .

(4) He grossly mislocated cities and states on a map of his country as well as of Europe, a task with which he was familiar, since he had been a post-office clerk. (DeRenzi, 1982, p. 213)

Although topographical disorientation has been reported from both left and right hemisphere lesions, it is commoner in people with right hemisphere damage. Efforts to quantify the behavioral deficits have largely concentrated on having patients draw maps or follow routes, often from maps. In general, people with right hemisphere lesions and topographical disorientation are very poor at drawing geographical maps or floor plans, although this may be a symptom of a more general disability in drawing (see Figure 23–3). Perhaps the most commonly used test of topo-

graphical orientation is the route-following test of Semmes described earlier (see Figure 18–5). The results have been inconsistent, however, in different laboratories with different patient populations. In general the results show that posterior lesions of either hemisphere can disrupt route walking and that neither left/right confusion nor aphasia significantly affects performance. It seems safest to conclude that topo-

FIGURE 23–3. Top: A copy of the Rey figure by a patient with a right parietofrontal missile wound. (After Ratcliff, 1982.) Bottom: Drawing of the floor plan of a right fronto-parietal tumor patient's house by a psychologist (left) and by the patient (right). (Redrawn from McFie et al., 1950.)

graphical orientation requires the integrity of the parietal cortex and that both left and right parietal cortex play complementary roles. Perhaps the left functions to verbally code topographical locations and the right to code topographical location in some other, nonverbal, manner.

Spatial Thought

The terms "spatial thought" and "conceptual spatial performance" have been used to describe the processes needed to solve problems that require mental rotation or manipulation of stimuli in order to reach some solution to a problem. We have argued, however, that it is simpler to consider these processes as those of action space. For example, when asked to describe what would be seen from a pilot's perspective in an airplane, an observer on the ground must mentally assume the perspective of the pilot looking down, rather than the real perspective of actually looking up. Similarly, when asked to solve tests such as the folding or unfolding of patterns (see Figure 15–1), one must mentally manipulate the patterns to arrive at the correct solution. It would seem likely that the right parietal and perhaps right temporal lobes would be necessary for these types of manipulations, although the contribution of the analogous left hemisphere regions cannot be ruled out if verbal mediation can be used to solve the task. There are surprisingly few studies showing a clear dissociation between the effects of left and right hemisphere lesions on tasks of spatial thinking, a fact that is all the more remarkable when one realizes that many popularized versions of the nature of hemispheric asymmetry are based on a distinction between verbal and spatial modes of thinking! There is evidence that the posterior region of the right hemisphere is more critical for certain maze tests that are

solved mentally, but much more research is necessary on this topic.

Perhaps one of the most interesting examples of a disorder in spatial thought is found in two clever studies by Bisiach and his associates. Patients were asked to give a verbal description of a place that was previously ascertained to be familiar to them: the cathedral square in Milan. The subjects were first requested to imagine themselves facing the front of the cathedral from the opposite side of the square and to describe the scene. Then they were requested to imagine the vantage point to be the central entrance of the cathedral, facing the opposite direction as before. Patients with contralateral neglect failed to describe details of the left side of the square regardless of their vantage point. In other words, when they switched from the first to the second vantage point, they then described the side of the square that they had previously neglected. Their neglect is clearly not one of memory, nor is it attributable to field defects or other primary sensory loss. Neglect in this test is likely due to a loss of a cerebral representation or "image" of part of the external world, the lost part varying with the frame of reference of the representation.

Spatial Memory

It is a common experience to be able to remember where we have seen something, even though we may have only incidentally noticed it and did not deliberately pay attention to its location. Consider the common experience of knowing exactly *where* on a page you read something, but being unable to recall much else about the context in which the material was read. This phenomenon may be a unique form of memory since other visual attributes of stimuli are seldom encoded incidentally with such consistency. The loss of memory for the location of things thus may be quite debilitating, especially since spatial location may be an important cue for recalling the observed thing at all. As is the case with lesion-induced deficits in other forms of memory, those lesions that most disrupt performance of short-term spatial memory can be doubly dissociated from those producing deficits on long-term spatial memory. We consider each separately.

Short-Term Spatial Memory. DeRenzi and his colleagues have extensively studied short-term spatial memory using a variety of tasks, including some similar to Corsi's spatial span task (Figure 20–7). In general, the results confirm the conclusion that the posterior temporal cortex and parietal cortex play a prominent role in short-term spatial memory. As might be expected, the right posterior cortex plays the more critical role in spatial memory, especially if the tasks are difficult, although aphasic patients with left hemisphere lesions may perform poorly on tests in which verbal mediation might easily be used.

Long-Term Spatial Memory. The right frontal lobe and right hippocampus appear to play a dominant role in long-term recall of spatial position. In their studies of maze learning by patients with cortical excisions both Milner and Corkin found patients with right frontal or right hippocampal ablations to perform very poorly, although the basis for the impaired performance may be different in the two groups. Similarly, Milner and her colleagues have shown that right hippocampal ablation is especially detrimental to the acquisition of Corsi's span + 1 task, and that right temporal lobe patients are very poor at learning the spatial location of objects. What is not known, however, is whether frontal or hippocampal lesions interfere with previously acquired spatial memories. It is likely that they do not.

In sum, the bulk of the evidence implicates the right hemisphere in spatial memory. The right parietal cortex appears to be the most critical for short-term spatial recall, whereas the right hippocampus and temporal cortex play major roles in the long-term recall of spatial material. The frontal cortex also appears to play a role in long-term spatial memory, although the nature of this role is unknown.

ANATOMICAL CORRELATES OF SPATIAL BEHAVIOR

Although spatial processing is now generally believed to be a major function of the right hemisphere, the relative contributions of parietal, temporal, and frontal regions to different aspects of spatial behaviors have not yet been demonstrated. Put another way, there are no known Broca's or Wernicke's areas or H.M.'s for spatial behavior. There has, however, been a good deal of interest in studying this question in nonhuman species, particularly in rats and monkeys, and it is to these studies that we shall direct our discussion for the remainder of the chapter.

Studies of spatial behavior in nonhuman species have been conducted largely along three general lines of work. First, Mishkin and his colleagues have been investigating posterior neocortical subareas for visual-spatial ability in monkeys. Second, the roles of the frontal and parietal cortexes of rats and monkeys have been contrasted in order to try to identify differences in their contributions to spatial orientation. Third, largely stimulated by the book by O'Keefe and Nadel, there has been a good deal of interest in the role of the hippocampus in spatial orientation and spatial memory in rats. We shall consider each of these lines of work separately.

Temporal and Parietal Mechanisms in Spatial and Object Vision

Over the past 20 years Mishkin and his associates have carried out a series of important experiments that have been guided by the hypothesis that the appreciation of an object's qualities and its spatial location depends on the processing of different kinds of visual information in the inferior temporal and the posterior parietal cortex, respectively. Given that damage to the temporal cortex of humans produces an impairment in visual recognition and that damage to the parietal cortex produces a constellation of visual-spatial impairments, Mishkin assumed an occipital-temporal system would be specialized in object perception (locating *what* an object is) whereas an occipital-parietal system would be specialized in spatial perception (locating *where* an object is). By using the techniques of double dissociation and disconnection he has been able to show just this. Lesions of the para-sensory cortex of the temporal lobe of monkeys impair the ability of the animals to discriminate objects (see Chapter 19 for details), whereas lesions of parietal parasensory cortex impair the ability of the animals to learn spatial relations. The most commonly used test of the latter function is a "landmark" test. In this test an animal is presented with two identical stimuli; the problem is to correctly identify which of the stimuli has a reward hidden under it. The only cue to the solution is the presence of another stimulus, a visual "landmark," that is closer to one of the two stimuli than to the other; it is the spatial relation between the landmark and the stimulus objects that tells the animal the location of the reward. Monkeys with temporal lobe lesions, who may have difficulty with object discrimination, usually perform normally at this

task, whereas monkeys with posterior parietal lesions, who are unimpaired at object discrimination, perform poorly at this task as well as at variants of it. Mishkin concludes that the inferior temporal cortex participates mainly in the acts of noticing and remembering an object's qualities, not its position in space, and conversely, the posterior parietal cortex seems to be concerned with the perception of spatial relations among objects, not their intrinsic qualities.

Parietal and Frontal Contributions to Spatial Orientation

Evidence that the frontal cortex might play a significant role in visually guided behavior in monkeys first came from studies of delayed-response-type tasks by Mishkin and Pribram in the early 1950s. In their studies monkeys observed food being placed under one of two stimuli, which differed only in their position on a test board. After a delay of some seconds or minutes, the animals were allowed to choose one of the stimuli and obtain the hidden reward. Although the initial studies confounded the delay and the spatial component, subsequent studies by Mishkin and Goldman and their colleagues demonstrated that the spatial component of the task was critical for demonstrating a deficit. Since the correct position of the food well was always relative to the body of the monkey (left, right) it was suggested that the frontal cortex might play a role in egocentric spatial orientation. As a direct test of this possibility, Pohl compared the performance of monkeys with frontal or parietal lesions on both delayed-response and landmark tasks, obtaining a beautiful double dissociation: frontal lesions impaired performance on only the delayed response task, whereas parietal lesions impaired performance on only the landmark task. Pohl's experiment appeared to provide strong support for the personal-extra-personal distinction between the frontal and the parietal cortex advanced by Semmes from her study of war veterans. Unfortunately, as we have seen for Semmes's studies with humans, Pohl's distinction is not as clear as first appeared. It now appears that frontal monkeys and rats are impaired at many tests of spatial orientation that cannot be described as tests of personal orientation (see Table 23–3). For example, in collaboration with Robert Sutherland, we have found that rats with frontal lesions are very poor at learning the location of a hidden object when the only cues available are the relations of objects to one another. In our studies, which utilize an ingenious task devised by Richard Morris, rats are placed in a large, circular, water-filled tank in which there is a hidden platform (clear Plexiglas) just below the surface of the water in a constant location. The only cue to the location of the platform is the relation between the platform and the cues in the room (see Figure 23–4). Whereas rats with parietal lesions learn the location of the platform in fewer than 10 trials, rats with frontal lesions are very slow to acquire this knowledge. Curiously, Sutherland has found that rats with frontal lesions are only impaired at the acquisition of this task; rats taught the task prior to frontal surgery remember the location of the platform as well as control animals postoperatively.

TABLE 23–3

Visual-spatial deficits in monkeys and rats
with neocortical lesions

Lesion	Task	Basic reference
Parietal		
A. Monkeys	Landmark	Pohl, 1973; A. D. Milner et al., 1977; Ungerlieder and Brody, 1977; Brody and Pribram, 1978; Ungerleider and Mishkin, 1982
	Stylus maze	A. D. Milner et al., 1977
	Patterned string	Ungerleider and Brody, 1977
	Home-cage finding	Sugishita et al., 1978
	Route following	Petrides and Iverson, 1979
B. Rats	Lashely and Hebb-Williams mazes	Boyd and Thomas, 1977; Thompson, 1979; McDaniel and Thomas, 1978
	Radial arm maze	Kolb et al., 1983
Frontal		
A. Monkeys	Delayed-response type	Mishkin and Pribram, 1955, 1956; Goldman and Rosvold, 1970; Goldman et al., 1971
	Personal orientation	Brody and Pribram, 1978
	Extrapersonal orientation	Brody and Pribram, 1978
B. Rats	Delayed-response type	Kolb et al., 1974; Wikmark et al., 1973
	Radial arm maze	Kolb et al., 1983
	Spatial-reversal type	Divac, 1971; Nonneman et al., 1974
	Morris water task	Kolb et al., 1983; Sutherland et al., 1982

Radial arm maze

Grice box

Morris water maze

FIGURE 23–4. Three mazes used to study spatial behavior in animals. The radial arm maze was designed as a test of foraging behavior in animals by Olton. The rat must learn which alleys contain food and which alleys have been visited on any given day. The Grice box is a test of left/right differentiation in animals. The food is placed in one alley until the animal has learned its location, then the position of the food is reversed to the other alley, and so on. The animal must thus learn that the location of the food shifts and adjust its behavior accordingly. The Morris water maze requires the animal to learn the location of a submerged, invisible platform. The only cue to the position of the platform is its spatial relation with cues about the room.

This result implies that the frontal cortex may have some role in the learning of the spatial relations among objects in complex environments, but not in the actual orientation of behavior relative to the environment. This may be a function of a posterior cortical structure, although this remains to be proved.

There is little doubt that both the frontal and the parietal cortex play a significant role in spatially guided behavior in both rats and monkeys, but the precise role of each region is still uncertain. Nevertheless, at least three generalizations are possible. First, in studies with both rats and monkeys, relatively small lesions of the anterior frontal or posterior parietal cortex produce deficits in spatial behavior. Second, in both rats and monkeys lesions of the frontal cortex produce more global effects on spatial behavior than do lesions of the parietal cortex. Third, contrary to the predictions of Semmes and her colleagues, the impairments following frontal cortex lesions are found in tasks that require learning the relations between stimuli in space, that is, extrapersonal relations. Brody and Pribram believe the frontal cortex is essential to the ability to perform tasks in which spatial context varies, regardless of whether the tasks are personal or extrapersonal. For example, in the water task used for rats, the precise relation between the cues and the hidden platform varies as the rat moves around the tank. The cues, which might identify the location of the platform, thus vary depending on whether the rat approaches the platform from the east or the west. This interpretation of the frontal deficit is consistent with the idea that humans and nonhumans with frontal lobe lesions have a general deficit in generating flexible response patterns in the face of novel changing environmental demands. The ambiguity in many spatial tasks therefore provides an ideal situation in which to demonstrate this behavioral inflexibility and does not represent a spatial deficit in the same way that damage to Mishkin's visual-spatial parietal system does. We note that this interpretation is speculative and requires additional study, but we feel it is a reasonable explanation for why frontal lesions produce a relatively global deficit in spatial behavior. A further speculation is that frontal lobe individuals might be expected to have deficits in tests of "spatial thinking" since many of these tests are ambiguous at best. This remains to be studied.

Hippocampal Contributions to Spatial Orientation

The possibility that the hippocampus plays a central role in spatial processing arose from a comprehensive and provocative book by O'Keefe and Nadel, who proposed that the hippocampus functions to create "cognitive maps" of environments. There are now four lines of evidence supporting this proposal, each of which we shall consider separately.

Electrophysiological Evidence. In the course of studying the properties of cells in the hippocampal formation of rats, O'Keefe discovered that some cells were excited by the position of the animal, regardless of how it got there. Thus, a cell might fire when a rat walked past a spot on the wall, but it might in addition fire just as strongly if the rat were carried past the spot. Furthermore, if the spot were removed from the wall, the cell would no longer be excited when the rat passed the previously significant location. Similar cells have now been found in a number of laboratories using both rats and rabbits, and although these cells represent a minority of the cells in the hippocampus, there can be little doubt of their existence or of the nature of the stimuli that activate them, namely spatial position.

Foraging Behavior. One of the most amazing abilities of animals is their capacity to keep track of all the places they have found or stored food. For example, in their studies of the foraging behavior of birds, Cowie et al. found that marsh tits could keep track of hundreds of locations where they had stored food. Recognizing this capacity of animals, David Olton devised an ingenious task in which to study the neurological correlates of foraging behavior in rats. His task, known as the Olton maze or the radial arm maze, features a series of arms, which may or may not contain food (see Figure 23–4). The animal's task is to visit each arm once to obtain food, and so it must keep track of where it has been on any given day. A further wrinkle can be added to the task by placing food only in certain alleys so that the animals must keep track not only of which alley they have visited but also of which alleys contain food. Dozens of laboratories now have mazes of this type, and it is clear that hippocampal lesions disrupt performance on it. One difficulty with the Olton maze is that its successful solution requires knowledge about *where* things are in space as well as *memory* for where the animal has been. Olton and his colleagues have emphasized a deficit of memory in the hippocampal animal, but this has not been universally accepted and will no doubt remain a matter of intense study for some time to come.

Navigation. The Morris water task described earlier provides an ideal test of the role of the hippocampus in spatial behavior. The target must be located using distal visual cues because it is hidden from view (see Figure 23–4). Both Morris and his colleagues and Sutherland and Whishaw have shown that hippocampal lesions of various types produce severe multimodal deficits in the learning of a number of variations of the Morris task. That the hippocampus plays a different role than the frontal cortex in the performance of this task is shown by the fact that hippocampal lesions impair both acquisition and retention of the task. (It will be recalled that frontal lesions resulted only in poor acquisition of the task.)

Humans. Further evidence for the role of the hippocampus in spatial behavior comes from Milner's work with human temporal lobe patients. Those patients with removals of the temporal lobe that include significant portions of the hippocampal formation are impaired at many tasks of both spatial learning and memory, and H.M. is seriously impaired in his attempt to find his way about the world.

The relative contribution of the hippocampus to spatial orientation and memory remains to be determined, but any theory of spatial behavior must clearly find some role for it. The role of the hippocampus is likely to be a controversial and popular topic for some time to come. This is because it is unlikely that the sole function of the hippocampus is in either spatial mapping or memory, and because many people think spatial mapping must be the function of the cortex rather than of the architecturally more simple hippocampus.

Summary

On the basis of human clinical studies it has been inferred that the posterior-parietal and posterior-temporal regions of the right hemisphere (roughly areas 7, 39, and 40) are especially important for the control of many types of spatial behavior. Studies using nonhuman species confirm the important role of this region in spatial analysis, emphasizing in particular the contributions of a visual-parietal pathway in spatial behavior. The frontal cortex and hippocampus also play a role in spatial behavior, but the nature of their contributions remains uncertain. Behaviorally, we have seen that it is naive to talk of spatial behavior as a general ability, as there are many types of very different behavioral capacities that are frequently described as "spatial."

REFERENCES

Allison, R. S., L. J. Hurwitz, J. G. White, and T. J. Wilmot. A follow-up study of a patient with Balint's syndrome. *Neuropsychologia* 7:319–333, 1969.

Archibald, Y. M. Time as a variable in the performance of hemisphere-damaged patients on the Elithorn Perceptual Maze Test. *Cortex* 14:22–31, 1978.

Becker, J. T., J. A. Walker, and D. S. Olton. Neuroanatomical bases of spatial memory. *Brain Research* 200:307–321, 1980.

Benton, A. L. *Right-Left Discrimination and Finger Localization.* New York: Hoeber-Harper, 1959.

Benton, A. L. Disorders of spatial orientation. In P. J. Vinkey, and G. W. Bruyn, eds., *Handbook of Clinical Neurology,* vol. 3. Amsterdam: Elsevier North-Holland, 1969.

Benton, A. L. Spatial thinking in neurological patients: Historical aspects. In M. Potegal, ed., *Spatial Abilities: Development and Physiological Foundations.* New York: Academic, 1982.

Benton, A. L. Visuoperceptive, visuospatial, and visuoconstructive disorders. In K. M. Heilman and E. Valenstein, eds., *Clinical Neuropsychology.* New York: Oxford University Press, 1979.

Benton, A. L., A. Elithorn, M. L. Fogel, and M. Kerr. A perceptual maze test sensitive to brain damage. *Journal of Neurology, Neurosurgery, and Psychiatry* 26:540–544, 1963.

Benton, A. L., K. deS. Hamsher, N. R. Varney, and O. Spreen. *Contributions to Neuropsychological Assessment.* New York: Oxford University Press, 1983.

Benton, A. L., and H. Hécaen. Stereoscopic vision in patients with unilateral cerebral damage. *Neurology* 20:1084–1088, 1970.

Benton, A. L., N. R. Varney, and K. deS. Hamsher. Visuospatial judgement: A clinical test. *Archives of Neurology* 35:364–367, 1978.

Bisiach, E., E. Capitani, C. Luzzatti, and D. Perani. Brain and conscious representation of outside reality. *Neuropsychologia* 19:543–552, 1981.

Bisiach, E., and C. Luzzatti. Unilateral neglect of representational space. *Cortex* 14:129–133, 1978.

Boyd, M. G., and R. K. Thomas. Posterior association cortex lesions in rats: Mazes, pattern discrimination, and reversal learning. *Physiological Psychology* 5:455–461, 1977.

Brain, W. R. Visual disorientation with special reference to lesions of the right cerebral hemisphere. *Brain* 64:244–272, 1941.

Brody, B. A., and K. H. Pribram. The role of frontal and parietal cortex in cognitive processing. *Brain* 101:607–633, 1978.

Butters, N., M. Barton, and B. A. Brody. Role of the parietal lobe in the mediation of cross modal associations and reversible operations in space. *Cortex* 6:174–190, 1970.

Butters, N., C. Soeldner, and P. Fedio. Comparison of parietal and frontal lobe spatial deficits in man: Extrapersonal vs. personal (egocentric) space. *Perceptual and Motor Skills* 34:27–34, 1972.

Carmon, A., and H. P. Bechtoldt. Dominance of the right cerebral hemisphere for stereopsis. *Neuropsychologia* 7:29–39, 1969.

Coltheart, M., K. Patterson, and J. C. Marshall, eds. *Deep Dyslexia.* London: Routledge, 1980.

Corkin, S. Tactually-guided maze-learning in man: Effects of unilateral cortical excisions and bilateral hippocampal lesions. *Neuropsychologia* 3:339–351, 1965.

Corkin, S. The role of different cerebral structures in somaesthetic perception. In E. C. Carterette and M. P. Friedman, eds., *Handbook of Perception,* vol. 6. New York: Academic, 1978.

Cowie, R. J., J. R. Krebs, and D. F. Sherry. Food storing by marsh tits. *Animal Behavior* 29:1252–1259, 1981.

DeRenzi, E. *Disorders of Space Exploration and Cognition.* New York: Wiley, 1982.

DeRenzi, E., P. Faglioni, and P. Previdi. Spatial memory and hemispheric locus of lesion. *Cortex* 13:424–433, 1977.

DeRenzi, E., P. Faglioni, and G. Scotti. Judgement of spatial orientation in patients with focal brain damage. *Journal of Neurology, Neurosurgery, and Psychiatry* 34:489–495, 1971.

DeRenzi, E., P. Faglioni, and G. Scotti. Tactiles, spatial impairment and unilateral cerebral damage. *Journal of Nervous and Mental Disorders* 146:468–475, 1968.

DeRenzi, E., and G. Scotti. The influence of spatial disorders in impairing tactual discrimination of shapes. *Cortex* 5:53–62, 1969.

Divac, I. Frontal lobe system and spatial reversal in the rat. *Neuropsychologia* 9:209–217, 1971.

Goldman, P. S., and H. E. Rosvold. Localization of function within the dorsolateral prefrontal cortex of the rhesus monkey. *Experimental Neurology* 27:291–304, 1970.

Goldman, P. S., H. E. Rosvold, B. Vest, and T. W. Galkin. Analysis of delayed-alternation deficit produced by dorsolateral prefrontal lesions in the rhesus monkey. *Journal of Comparative and Physiological Psychology* 77:212–220, 1971.

Grüsser, O. J. The multimodal structure of the extrapersonal space. In A. Hein and M. Jeannerod, eds., *Spatially Oriented Behavior.* New York: Springer, in press.

Hannay, H. J., N. R. Varney, and A. L. Benton. Visual localization in patients with unilateral brain disease. *Journal of Neurology, Neurosurgery and Psychiatry* 39:307–313, 1976.

Head, H. *Studies in Neurology.* London: Oxford University Press, 1920.

Hécaen, H., J. de Ajuriaguerra, and J. Massonet. Les troubles visuoconstructifs par lésions parieto-occipitales droites. Rôle des perturbations vestibulaires. *Encephale* 1:122–179, 1951.

Hécaen, H., C. Tzortzis, and M. C. Masure. Troubles de l'orientation spatiale dans une pereuve de recherce d'itineraire lors des lésions corticales unilaterales. *Perception* 1:325–330, 1972.

Hécaen, H., C. Tzortzis, and P. Rondot. Loss of topographical memory with learning deficits. *Cortex* 16:525–542, 1980.

Holmes, G. Disturbances of visual space perception. *British Medical Journal* 2:230–233, 1919.

Holmes, G., and G. Horax. Disturbances of spatial orientation and visual attention, with loss of stereoscopic vision. *Archives of Neurology and Psychiatry* 1:385–407, 1919.

Jackson, J. H. On the Nature of Duality of the Brain. *Brain* 38:80–103, 1915.

Klingon, G. H., and D. C. Bontecou. Localization in auditory space. *Neurology* 16:879–886, 1966.

Kolb, B., A. J. Nonneman, and R. K. Singh. Double dissociation of spatial impairments and perseveration following selective prefrontal lesions in rats. *Journal of Comparative and Physiological Psychology* 87:772–780, 1974.

Kolb, B., R. J. Sutherland, and I. Q. Whishaw. A comparison of the contributions of the frontal and parietal association cortex to spatial localization in rats. *Behavioral Neuroscience* 97:13–27, 1983.

McDaniel, W. F., and R. K. Thomas. Temporal and parietal association cortex lesions and spatial and black-white reversal learning in the rat. *Physiological Psychology* 6:300–305, 1978.

McFie, J., M. F. Piercy, and O. L. Zangwill. Visual-spatial agnosia associated with lesions of the right cerebral hemisphere. *Brain* 73:167–190, 1950.

McFie, J., and O. L. Zangwill. Visual-constructive disabilities associated with lesions of the left hemisphere. *Brain* 83:243–260, 1960.

Milner, A. D., E. M. Ockleford, and W. Dewar. Visuo-spatial performance following posterior parietal and lateral frontal lesions in stumptail macaques. *Cortex* 13:350–360, 1977.

Milner, B. Interhemispheric differences in the localization of psychological processes in man. *British Medical Bulletin* 27:272–277, 1971.

Milner, B. Visually-guided maze learning in man: Effects of bilateral hippocampal, bilateral frontal, and unilateral cerebral lesions. *Neuropsychologia* 3:317–338, 1965.

Mishkin, M., M. E. Lewis, and L. G. Ungerleider. Equivalence of parieto-preoccipital subareas for visuospatial ability in monkeys. *Behavioural Brain Research* 6:41–55, 1982.

Mishkin, M., and K. H. Pribram. Analysis of the effects of frontal lesions in monkeys: I. Variations of delayed alternation. *Journal of Comparative and Physiological Psychology* 48:492–495, 1955.

Mishkin, M., and K. H. Pribram. Analysis of the effects of frontal lesions in monkeys: II. Variations of delayed response. *Journal of Comparative and Physiological Psychology* 49:36–40, 1956.

Mishkin, M., and L. G. Ungerleider. Contribution of striate inputs to the visuospatial functions of parieto-preoccipital cortex in monkeys. *Behavioural Brain Research* 6:57–77, 1982.

Morris, R. G. M. Spatial localization does not require the presence of local cues. *Learning and Motivation* 12:239–260, 1981.

Morris, R. G. M., P. Garrud, J. Rawlings, and J. O'Keefe. Place navigation impaired in rats with hippocampal lesions. *Nature* 297:681–683, 1982.

Neff, W. D. Localization and lateralization of sound in space. In A. V. S. De Reuck and J. Knights, eds., *Hearing Mechanisms in Vertebrates*. Ciba Foundation Symposium. London: Churchill, 1969.

Nonneman, A. J., J. Voigt, and B. E. Kolb. Comparisons of behavioral effects of hippocampal and prefrontal cortex lesions in the rat. *Journal of Comparative and Physiological Psychology* 87:249–260, 1974.

O'Keefe, J., and L. Nadel. *The Hippocampus as a Cognitive Map*. New York: Clarendon Press, 1978.

Olton, D. S. The function of septo-hippocampal connections in spatially organized behaviour. In *Functions of the Septo-Hippocampal System,* Ciba Foundation Symposium 58. New York: Elsevier North-Holland, 1978.

Olton, D. S., J. T. Becker, and G. E. Handelmann. Hippocampus, space and memory. *Behavioral and Brain Sciences* 2:313–366, 1979.

Oxbury, J. M., D. C. Campbell, and S. M. Oxbury. Unilateral spatial neglect and impairments of spatial analysis and visual perception. *Brain* 97:551–564, 1974.

Patterson, A., and O. L. Zangwill. Disorders of visual space perception associated with lesions of the right cerebral hemisphere. *Brain* 67:331–358, 1944.

Petrides, M., and S. K. Iversen. Restricted posterior parietal lesions in the rhesus monkey and performance on visuospatial tasks. *Brain Research* 161:63–77, 1979.

Pohl, W. Dissociation of spatial discrimination deficits following frontal and parietal lesions in monkeys. *Journal of Comparative and Physiological Psychology* 82:227–239, 1973.

Ratcliff, G. Disturbances of spatial orientation associated with cerebral lesions. In M. Potegal, ed., *Spatial Abilities: Development and Physiological Foundations.* New York: Academic, 1982.

Ratcliff, G. Spatial thought, mental rotation and the right cerebral hemisphere. *Neuropsychologia* 17:49–54, 1979.

Ratcliff, G., and G. A. B. Davies-Jones. Defective visual localization in focal brain wounds. *Brain* 95:49–60, 1972.

Ratcliff, G., and F. Newcombe. Spatial orientation in man: Effects of left, right, and bilateral posterior cerebral lesions. *Journal of Neurology, Neurosurgery, and Psychiatry* 36:448–454, 1973.

Ratcliff, G., R. M. Ridley, and G. Ettlinger. Spatial disorientation in the monkey. *Cortex* 13:62–65, 1977.

Semmes, J. A non-tactual factor in astereognosis. *Neuropsychologia* 3:295–315, 1965.

Semmes, J., S. Weinstein, L. Ghent, and H.-L. Teuber. Correlates of impaired orientation in personal ånd extra-personal space. *Brain* 86:742–772, 1963.

Shankweiler, D. Performance of brain damaged patients on two tests of sound localization. *Journal of Comparative and Physiological Psychology* 54:375–381, 1951.

Smith, M. L., and B. Milner. The role of the right hippocampus in the recall of spatial location. *Neuropsychologia* 19:781–793, 1981.

Sugishita, M., G. Ettlinger, and R. M. Ridley. Disturbance of cage finding in the monkey. *Cortex* 14:431–438, 1978.

Sutherland, R. J., B. Kolb, and I. Q. Whishaw. Spatial mapping: Definitive disruption by hippocampal or medial frontal cortex damage in the rat. *Neuroscience Letters* 31:271–276, 1982.

Sutherland, R. J., I. Q. Whishaw, and B. Kolb. A behavioural analysis of spatial localization following electrolytic, kainate- or colchicine-induced damage to the hippocampal formation in the rat. *Behavioural Brain Research* 7:133–153, 1983.

Taylor, J. *The Selected Writings of John Hughlings-Jackson.* London: Hodder, 1932.

Teuber, H.-L, and S. Diamond. Effects of brain injury in man on binaural localization of sounds. Paper read at Eastern Psychological Association Meetings, Atlantic City, March, 1956. As cited by DeRenzi, 1982.

Thomas, R. K., and V. K. Weir. The effects of lesions in the frontal or posterior association cortex of rats on maze III. *Physiological Psychology* 3:210–214, 1975.

Thompson, R. Hippocampal and cortical function in a maze devoid of left and right turns. *Physiology and Behavior* 23:601–603, 1979.

Tyler, H. R. Abnormalities of perception with defective eye movements (Balint's syndrome). *Cortex* 4:154–171, 1968.

Ungerleider, L. G., and B. A. Brody. Extrapersonal spatial orientation: The role of posterior parietal, anterior frontal, and inferotemporal cortex. *Experimental Neurology* 56:265–280, 1977.

Ungerleider, L. G., and M. Mishkin. Two cortical visual systems. In D. Ingle, M. A. Goodale, and R. J. W. Mansfield, eds., *Analysis of Visual Behavior.* Cambridge, Mass.: MIT Press, 1982.

Wikmark, R. G. E., I. Divac, and R. Weiss. Retention of spatial delayed alternation in rats with lesions in the frontal lobes. *Brain, Behavior and Evolution* 8:329–339, 1973.

PART SIX

DEVELOPMENT
AND RECOVERY

There are two tremendously powerful ways of studying how the brain works. Its growth and the behavior that flows from that growth can be correlated, or its recovery from damage and the reconstitution of behavior that follows can be correlated. This section deals with these processes. Chapter 24 examines the emergence of behavior from the developing brain, and Chapter 25 examines the emergence of behavior after brain damage. The two processes have much in common. It is noteworthy that in development there is a hierarchical emergence of behavior that has as some of its other characteristics a rostral–caudal organization (maturation occurs in the head first and the back last) and a proximal–distal organization (maturation proceeds from the body to the limbs). Many of the same principles seem to apply for recovery, in that lower functions recover more rapidly than higher functions and recovery often has a rostral–caudal and proximal–distal progression.

24

DEVELOPMENT OF FUNCTION

Developmental neuropsychology is becoming an area of increasing interest for many reasons. Some people are attracted to the area because they believe that children are neurologically simpler than adults and therefore easier to study. Others believe that analysis of the behavior and development of children will give important clues about the relative contributions of heredity and environment to the development of particular behaviors. Still others are compelled by practical necessity: they must develop programs for children with special problems in school. The growth of developmental neuropsychology as a field of inquiry has raised further questions. Why does the brain in early life appear to be so flexible in compensating for injury and for variations in the environment? Is there an optimal environment in which development should occur? Is there an optimal method of instruction that should be used in education? How can one brain be so much more efficient than another that appears so similar under superficial examination? Thus, the object of developmental neuropsychology is to better understand ner-

vous system function in early life, and to see whether such an understanding can contribute answers to questions such as the above.

METHODOLOGY

Behavioral changes related to neural function can be examined in three ways. The first is to look at nervous system maturation and correlate it with the development of specific behaviors. The second, the converse, is to look at behavior and then make inferences about neural maturation. The third is to relate brain malfunction or damage to behavioral disorders or cognitive deficits. Although each of these procedures is widely used, each is associated with methodological difficulties that deserve comment.

Initially, the first-named method, relating neural development to the emergence of specific behaviors, might seem ideal. The development of both the nervous system and behavior is orderly and similar in sequence from person to person, suggesting that correlations may be made easily. This approach has not been as useful as was expected, for a number of reasons. (1) The nervous system develops in a relatively unremitting way, whereas behavioral changes depend on education and learning. Thus, a behavior may emerge in one environment but not in another. (2) Because age-related changes in the human nervous system are directly observable only in extraordinary circumstances, it is impossible to observe relevant neural substrate may be difficult to identify. For example, hundreds of studies on animals have attempted, with little success, to determine some anatomical or biochemical substrate of memory. This general failure bodes ill for such correlations in humans, because in theory it is easier to correlate a neural-behavioral change in animals. (3) Behaviors deemed important may also be irrelevant. For example, there is a tendency to emphasize school behaviors as the most important for study; although these are certainly important, it must be remembered that the human brain did not evolve in a school-like environment. The basic functions and abilities of the brain may be revealed by the study of much more fundamental processes. Reading requires spatial skills and sequencing ability. How reading skills develop may be better understood by analyzing these more basic abilities than by studying reading per se. Because developmental research focused on nervous system changes is difficult to conduct, most of it is done with animal models. Nevertheless, the principles obtained from this research should be applicable to humans.

The second approach, the analysis of nervous system function by inference from sequential changes in behavior, is not widely used. This is partly because the psychologists most interested in human development have not been primarily interested in brain function. Also, hypotheses about brain function are hard to verify, because the human nervous system cannot be manipulated during development. Nevertheless, this approach is important be-cause it is the only way models of the function of the normal human nervous system can be obtained.

The third approach, relating brain malfunction to behavioral disorders, is widely used in adult neuropsychology, but it has drawbacks when applied to developmental problems. First, much evidence suggests that the function of an immature brain may not be comparable to that of an adult brain. Freud's work, and subsequently Piaget's, suggests, first, that the immature brain might be incapable of certain adult functions, and, second, that there is no *one* immature brain. That is, the brain may be changing such that principles applicable at one age are inappropriate for another age. This discontinuity may be one reason why estimates of intelligence obtained from very young children correlate poorly with their adult intelligence. Another obstacle to directly applying adult neuropsychology to developing brains is the plasticity or adaptability of the immature brain. Brain damage occurring in infancy may often go unnoticed because an undamaged portion of the brain adopts the function of the damaged zone. For example, if the speech zones of an infant's left hemisphere are damaged, speech may develop on the right. Such does not occur in an adult. Nevertheless, this approach remains important and provides major clues about the organization of the developing brain.

We point out these pitfalls in developmental neuropsychology not to deter study of developmental problems, but to caution that the neuropsychology of children may not be identical to that of adults. True, when adult standards are used, infants may look surprisingly like adults in a number of ways. But this similarity could be an artifact of researcher expectation: if the infant's brain is expected to be like the adult's, and if it is therefore studied only with tests initially designed for the study of adults, then phenomena peculiar to infants and children may be ignored.

The remainder of this chapter is divided into four sections. The first section looks at developmental problems from a neurological perspective; that is, what can be learned about behavior from studying the development of the nervous system. By its nature this area is largely experimental, leans heavily on animal research, and provides some good basic insights into developmental issues. The second section consists largely of work done on the development of cognitive functions from which inferences are made about nervous system organization and development. As might be expected, it is informative, but its interpretation is speculative. The third section describes the effects of brain damage suffered in infancy and compares these with the effects suffered by adults. The fourth section combines the different lines of research discussed in the chapter and presents a view of cognitive development that we believe may prove useful for understanding development.

A NEURAL PERSPECTIVE
ON DEVELOPMENT

Cellular Basis of Brain Development

The process of brain growth and differentiation consists of a series of biological changes occurring at a particular age and in a relatively fixed sequence. These include (1) the migration of cells, (2) the formation and growth of axons, (3) the formation of dendrites, (4) the formation of synaptic connections, and (5) myelinization. Because of either deficits in the genetic program, intrauterine trauma, the influence of toxic agents, or other factors, peculiarities or errors in development can occur that may contribute to obvious and severe deformities such as those listed in Table 24–1. Less pronounced deficits may become manifest in such things as learning disabilities

or may contribute only to subtle differences in individuality. In the following sections each of the above-named biological processes is briefly described, as are abnormalities that occur when the process is not properly completed.

Cell Migration. Nerve cells form by division in the inner, or ventricular, lining of the brain and migrate from there to the surface of the brain. Once a group of cells has arrived at the surface, differentiation (formation of axons, dendrites, etc.) begins. Subsequently a new group of cells migrates from the inner lining through the layers already present to form a new outer layer. Thus, a structure such as the cortex matures from its inner to its outer surface. The mechanisms that guide migration are not known.

Migration can stop prematurely, leaving a group of cells that should normally appear as an outer layer instead scattered among inner layers of cells. Caviness and Sidman have made a major study of disturbed cell migration in the cortex of a genetic mutant mouse called the reeler mouse. In this animal the first-generated cells lie near the surface whereas the last-generated lie deepest, creating a cortex that is inverted from that of a normal mouse. Despite their aberrant position the cells receive and give off appropriate connections, but the mice have an abnormal, reeling movement. Cases of failure or incomplete cell migration in humans have also been described.

Axonal Growth. Sprouting axons grow in a given direction either because the cell body is oriented in a particular way or because of other, unknown factors. The growing end of the axon, called the growth cone, was first recognized and described by Ramón y Cajal in the 1890s. He wrote:

I had the good fortune to behold for the first time that fantastic ending of the growing axon. In my

TABLE 24–1

Types of abnormal development

Type	Symptom
Anencephaly	Absence of cerebral hemispheres, diencephalon, and midbrain
Holoprosencephaly	Cortex forms as a single undifferentiated hemisphere
Lissencephaly	The brain fails to form sulci and gyri and corresponds to a 12-week embryo
Micropolygyria	Gyri are more numerous, smaller, and more poorly developed than normal
Macrogyria	Gyri are broader and less numerous than normal
Microencephaly	Development of the brain is rudimentary and the person has low-grade intelligence
Porencephaly	Symmetrical cavities in the cortex, where cortex and white matter should be
Heterotopia	Displaced islands of gray matter appear in the ventricular walls or white matter, caused by aborted cell migration
Agenesis of the corpus callosum	Complete or partial absence of the corpus callosum
Cerebellar agenesis	Portions of the cerebellum, basal ganglia, or spinal cord are absent or malformed

sections of the three-day chick embryo, this ending appeared as a concentration of protoplasm of conical form, endowed with ameboid movements. It could be compared with a living battering ram, soft and flexible, which advances, pushing aside mechanically the obstacles which it finds in its way, until it reaches the area of its peripheral distribution. This curious terminal club, I christened the growth cone. (Ramón y Cajal, 1937)

In general, the axon grows at a rate of seven to 170 micrometers (μm) per hour. Axon branching occurs at the growth cone. It is possible that the growth cone forms synapses and retains the capacity to renew growth, which may thus underlie the formation of new synapses during the course of learning.

A major unanswered question in developmental neurobiology concerns the forces that initiate and guide axonal growth. Axons have specific targets that they must reach if the neuron is to survive and become functional. Some axons grow because they are towed from their cell bodies by a structure that is growing away from the region, such as when the muscles grow away from the spinal cord early in development. Other axons traverse enormous distances and are able to overcome obstacles such as being moved to another location, having their cell bodies rotated, or having their targets moved. Although the forces that guide this homing are not understood, there are several possibilities: axons may follow an electrical or chemical gradient or a particular physical substrate, or they may send out many branches, or shoots, and when one reaches an appropriate target the others follow. It is also possible that several such mechanisms may be operative simultaneously or sequentially.

The formation of appropriate neural pathways may be disrupted in any of a number of ways. Axons may be unable to reach their target if their way is blocked, as may happen following scarring from head trauma during the early months of life. Their development may be disrupted by anoxia, ingestion of toxic materials, malnutrition, etc. Several reports of anomalous fiber systems in mutant strains of mice also suggest that abnormalities could have a genetic basis. There have been cases in which the corpus callosum is of abnormal size or is absent, and cases in which the fiber pathways in the hippocampal system are abnormal. In a number of albino animal species, and possibly also in human albinos, the ipsilateral optic pathway is reduced in size and area of distribution. Since the brain processes information sequentially, similar disruption of transcortical or interhemispheric connections during development could be related to the cognitive difficulties that some humans have. In fact, it has been suggested that some learning disorders might originate in delayed, incomplete, or inappropriate formation of the cortical fiber system.

Axonal development might also be disrupted if the axons' target is damaged, in which case the axonal system may degenerate or may occupy an inappropriate target. Should the latter event occur the behavior supported by the invaded area may also be disrupted. In a well-documented study of abnormal fiber growth Schneider has shown that if the optic tectum in the hamster is removed on one side at birth, the fibers that should normally project to it project instead to the opposite side. This aberrant pathway is functional, but in a curious way. If a visual stimulus is presented to the eye contralateral to the damaged tectum, the hamster turns in the direction opposite to that of the stimulus. The message has traveled from the eye to the wrong tectum, a tectum that would ordinarily receive input from the opposite side of the world. The abnormalities of posture and movement seen in some sorts of athetosis and dystonia in children may occur because fiber systems supporting posture and movement invade the wrong target, causing an intended movement to be disrupted by an inappropriate movement. Should this be the case, it is not surprising that lesions in the thalamus, which might sever such an abnormal connection, can result in improved posture and movement.

Dendritic Growth. The growth of dendrites parallels that of axons, growth and division also occurring at a growth cone. Generally, the growth of dendrites is timed to intercept the axons that are to innervate them. During development all dendrites go through a phase in which they have dendritic spines; later the dendrites of some cells lose their spines, whereas others reduce the number of their spines. The significance of dendritic spines is not well understood, but it is possible that they receive a particular class of synapse.

In studies of abnormalities of dendrites it is difficult to determine whether a disorder is specifically dendritic or is secondary to inappropriate cell location, abnormal innervation, ingestion of a neurotoxin, etc. Reduced afferent innervation is known to lead to a reduction in the number of dendritic spines. Studies of the cerebral cortex in various mental retardation conditions indicate a number of dendritic abnormalities. Dendrites may be thinner, with fewer than normal numbers of spines; the dendrites may be short stalks with small spines; or there may be simply a reduction in spine number. What causes these changes is not known, but the histology gives the general impression that the embryonic condition is retained.

Synaptic Formation. It is clear from many studies that a given brain region sends axons to only a limited number of other regions, and that synapses are made only in a specific part of certain cells in that region. The locations of synapses are determined in part by genetic instruction, in part by the orientation of the cell when the axons arrive, in part by the timing of axon arrival (axons apparently compete for available space), and in part by the use that they are given once a connection is made. In addition, the pharmacology of the synapse is flexible. For example, it has been found that individual neurons can become either noradrenergic or cholinergic depending on their environment. Malfunctions in any of these features of synaptic formation may cause abnormal brain development.

Myelination. Myelination is the process by which the support cells of the nervous system begin to surround axons and provide them with insulation. Although nerves can become functional before myelinization, it is assumed that they reach adult functional levels as myelination is completed. Thus, myelination provides an index of the maturity of structures from which axons project and to which they project.

If myelination is used as an index of maturation, then the anatomical developmental work of Flechsig indicates that the neocortex begins a sequential development at a relatively early age. The primary sensory areas and motor areas show some myelinization just before term. The secondary cortical areas become myelinated within the next four postnatal months, and by the fourth month the tertiary areas of the cortex are becoming myelinated. Although myelination begins during the early postnatal period, it continues to increase beyond 15 years of age and may increase in density as late as 60 years of age. Any disruption in this ongoing process can potentially cause neural and hence behavioral abnormalities.

ENVIRONMENTAL INFLUENCES ON DEVELOPMENT

The environment in which development occurs can profoundly influence behavior, as has been suggested by anecdotal reports about how deprivation has produced impoverished behavior in children. For example, Singh and Zingg report that children raised by wolves behave like wolves and are difficult to socialize; on the other hand, Skeels reports that children removed from substandard orphanages develop normal intelligence by adulthood whereas those that are not removed remain retarded. These reports have been fully confirmed by Harlow in formal studies on the effects of early deprivation on the maturation of monkeys. How do the conditions of early environment affect nervous system development? There are several possibilities, each of which has received some support in recent experimental work. (1) The nervous system develops independently, but requires stimulation for maintained function. (2) The nervous system develops independently in part, but requires stimulation for continued maturation beyond some point. Inappropriate stimulation may change the system's properties. (3) The properties of the nervous system are not innate, but develop only with appropriate stimulation. Experimental work has been advanced most by studies using the visual system as a model and such work has provided support for each of these possibilities. In all cases the importance of stimulation is emphasized. The term **functional** validation is sometimes used to express the idea that to become fully functional a neural system requires stimulation at some point.

Environmental Influences on Brain Size

The simplest measure of the effects of environment on the nervous system is brain size. Environmental influences on animal brain size have been investigated; domestic animals have brains up to 10 to 20 percent smaller than those of animals of the same species and strain raised in the wild. These differences are apparently related to factors that occur early in life, since animals born in the wild and later domesticated have brains the same size as animals raised in the wild. The part of the brain that seems to be most affected by a domestic upbringing is the cortex, which is reduced in size by as much as 35 percent in some animals. This reduction may be related to smaller eye and retina size.

An extensive laboratory experimental literature now exists on the effects of environmental manipulation on brain size and anatomy. Exposure to an enriched environment increases brain size, most noticeably in the neocortex, with the greatest increase occurring in the occipital neocortex. Related to increased size are increases in the density of glial cells, in the number of higher-order dendritic spines on neurons, in the number of synaptic spines, and in the size of synapses. These changes are most pronounced if enriched experience is given in early life; similar less pronounced effects can be obtained with more prolonged exposure given in later life. In addition to these anatomical changes, enriched animals can perform better than their impoverished counterparts on a number of tests of learning and memory. However, given that the enriched environment of the laboratory experiment may be less than or only equivalent to that of a wild habitat, these findings mean that exposure to an impoverished laboratory retards the development of the nervous system and reduces performance on a number of tests.

Environmental Influences on Function— Examples from the Visual System

Clinical studies have shown that disturbances of the optics of the eye, e.g., cataracts and astigmatism, during early life cause long lasting impairments of vision even after the optical defects are corrected. These impairments, called **amblyopia**—dimness of vision without obvious impairment of the eye—are

presumed to be caused by changes in the central nervous system. Behavioral studies have shown that amblyopia can be produced in animals; its cause has been extensively analyzed in studies using cats and monkeys. This area of research now provides one of the most penetrating insights into factors affecting development and deserves careful study.

Hubel and Wiesel and others have described the response patterns of normal cells in area 17 of the visual cortex. They recorded the activity of cells in anesthetized animals while visual stimuli were presented on a screen placed in the animal's visual field. The cells respond to a number of properties of a visual stimulus, including its orientation and direction; they also respond according to which eye it is presented to and are affected by binocular disparity (the different view each eye has of the stimulus). Using a profile of the activity of cells in a normal cat's area 17, Hubel and Wiesel addressed the question of the function of area 17 in kittens whose eyes had not yet opened. In eight-day-old kittens they found that although the cells are sluggish and become fatigued quickly, they show the properties of the adult cat's cells to the first presentation of visual stimulation. The results of this and similar studies suggest that the visual system has normal response capacity before being stimulated by light. What, then, of the environment's contribution?

To assess the contributions of the environment two conditions of visual deprivation have been used: **binocular deprivation** and **monocular deprivation**. In the first, animals are deprived by being reared in the dark or by their eyelids being sutured before they open. This deprivation produces no change in the retina, and only mild changes in the lateral geniculate nucleus, the major relay of the visual cortex. By contrast, cells in the visual cortex undergo disturbances of protein synthesis and have fewer and shorter dendrites, fewer spines, and 70 percent fewer synapses than normal. Analysis of the properties of these cells shows that after a number of months of early deprivation there are severe abnormalities, which disappear to some extent with normal visual experience. Deprivation in later life does not produce the same initial period of abnormality. Thus, visual stimulation in early life is important for continued development of visual cells, but the visual system retains some ability to compensate.

The second deprivation condition, monocular deprivation, surprisingly has a severer effect than binocular deprivation. If one eyelid is sutured during early life, the eye appears to be essentially blind for a period of weeks after opening, although its function does improve somewhat with time. Cell-recording studies show either that stimulation in the deprived eye cannot activate cells in the cortex or that in those few cases in which it can the cells are highly abnormal. The experiments also show that the earlier deprivation occurs, the shorter the deprivation period required and the severer the effects. These results confirm that deprivation can retard development, and that early deprivation is the most influential. The experiments also suggest that factors other than deprivation alone must be operative to produce the severe effects found.

Apparently competition also contributes to the severity of deficits in the deprived eye. Kratz et al. found that if the normal eye of an animal was removed after the other eye had been deprived for five months, the deprived eye gave comparatively normal responses in 31 percent of the cells, compared with only 6 percent when the normal eye was present. This finding is confirmed by a number of more indirect experiments. These results imply that the deprived portion of the visual system has the capacity to function but is inhibited from doing so by the good portion of the visual system. If inhibition of function is removed, the deprived portion of the visual system begins to function.

Can the visual system be changed by manipulation less drastic than complete sensory deprivation? Hirsch and Spinelli fitted kittens with lenses that brought a set of horizontal stripes into focus on one retina and a set of vertical stripes into focus on the other retina. After later removal of the lenses, they found that cells responded only if the stimulus was oriented close to the horizontal when viewed with the eye that had seen horizontal during the exposure period, and only to a stimulus oriented close to the vertical when viewed with the eye that had seen vertical stripes during the exposure period. These findings have been confirmed for kittens raised in an environment of stripes or of spots or in an environment organized to be devoid of movement. In fact, work by Blakemore and Mitchell indicates that one hour of exposure on day 28 after birth is sufficient to bias a cortical unit to respond to a particular pattern.

In summary, this work suggests that the visual system is genetically programmed to make normal connections and normal responses but can lose much of this capacity if it is not exercised during the early months of life. When part of the system is deprived, in addition to loss of capacity caused by the deprivation, the system is inhibited by the remaining functional areas, and the defect is potentiated. Removal of inhibition can permit some degree of recovery. Finally, if the environment is so arranged that the system is exposed to stimuli of one type, the cells in the system are biased to respond to stimuli of that type.

Although these conclusions come from experiments performed on a relatively low level of the visual system, the results can be generalized to other sensory systems and cortical areas. For example, our inability to perceive certain sounds in languages unfamiliar to us may result partly from disuse, inhibition, or the development of an incompatibility set within the auditory cortex. These experiments suggest speculative questions about the function of the brain. Under normal circumstances, how much do used portions of the brain tend to place inhibition on unused portions of the brain? Does the development of language in one hemisphere inhibit its development in the other hemisphere? These questions will be asked in future experiments undertaken to analyze the secondary and tertiary areas of the cortex.

A BEHAVIORAL PERSPECTIVE ON DEVELOPMENT

Asymmetry

Just as asymmetrical function of the adult's brain has been a focal point for neurological study, so has the development of asymmetry been a focal point for development studies. Most of the research with children has been designed to demonstrate lateralization of function, emphasizing the question of the age at which asymmetry first appears. The central theoretical issue in this research revolves around the hypotheses of maturation of asymmetry as opposed to invariance of asymmetry. According to the *maturation hypothesis* asymmetry develops with aging, is not necessarily hemisphere-specific, and may be influenced in important ways by environmental events. According to the *invariance hypothesis* functions are asymmetrically located in the hemispheres because they depend on certain anatomical circuitry of the brain, and this in turn is presumably genetically determined. If and when a particular behavior becomes lateralized may still depend on both the age the behavior de-

velops and the form in which it is acquired. Because of the complexities of the questions that are asked, the results of many studies on asymmetry are equivocal. Some of the difficulties in interpretation have been reviewed by Bryden. Let handedness serve as an example. Handedness for writing cannot, obviously, be determined in infants. Therefore, an assumption has to be made that hand strength or some other measure will serve as an indication of handedness. Even if a good correlation is obtained between a measure such as hand strength and the hand subsequently used for writing, by chance such a relation would be expected, since most people are right-handed. Even if perfect correlations were subsequently obtained, environmental influences must still be accounted for; after all, children copy their parents. Then, a neural substrate has to be found. This is likely to be difficult. For speech it is thought that the large left temporal planum is the substrate, yet it is larger on the left in only about 60 to 70 percent of people, whereas speech is lateralized to the left in a much higher proportion of people. At the present time the invariance hypothesis is strongly favored. It is thought that each hemisphere has a special potential for acquiring various functions, and that this relation between hemisphere and function would only be changed if brain damage were incurred. Even then, however, the way in which a hemisphere acquires a functional capacity may be hemisphere-specific. As will be pointed out in the following sections, under certain circumstances both hemispheres may learn to speak, but each will be constrained in its use of language in specific ways. Table 24–2 gives examples of the earliest ages and side of lateralization of a number of representative functions. Undeniably, lateralization is found even in the very immature brain, and it is this that provides compelling support for the invariance hypothesis.

TABLE 24–2

Studies showing age of asymmetry for different behaviors

System	Age	Dominance	Reference
Auditory			
Speech syllables	Preterm	Right ear	Molfese and Molfese, 1980
Music	22–140 days	Left ear	Entus, 1977
Phonemes	22–140 days	Right ear	Entus, 1977
Words	4 years	Right ear	Kimura, 1963
Environmental sounds	5–8 years	Left ear	Knox and Kimura, 1970
Visual			
Rhythmic visual stimuli	Newborn	Right	Crowell et al., 1973
Face recognition	7–9 years	Left field	Marcel and Rajan, 1975
	6–13 years	Left field	Witelson, 1973
	9–10 years	None	Diamond and Carey, 1977
Somatosensory			
Dichhaptic recognition	All ages	Left	Witelson, 1977
Motor			
Stepping	< 3 months	Right	Peters and Petrie, 1979
Head turning	Neonates	Right	Turkewitz, 1977
Grasp duration	1–4 months	Right	Caplan and Kinesbourne, 1976
Finger tapping	3–5 years	Right	Ingram, 1975
Strength	3–5 years	Right	Ingram, 1975
Gesturing	3–5 years	Right	Ingram, 1975
Head orientation	Neonates	Right	Michel, 1981

Asymmetry in the Auditory System. Asymmetry in the auditory system has been demonstrated in infants only a few weeks old. Entus combined the dichotic-listening technique with a test known by the awesome name of the nonnutritive high-amplitude sucking paradigm. In the study the infant was given the opportunity to suck on a nipple and then to learn that if it increased its sucking rate it would receive an auditory stimulus through one or the other side of a pair of earphones. Entus presented phonemes such as "ma" and "ba," or the note A (440 Hz) played on different instruments, such as the piano or viola. Entus found that the infants changed their sucking rate in such a way that they received more phonemes through the right earphone than the left, and more musical notes through the left earphone than the right. This evidence suggested that there was a lateralized prefer-ence—left for phonemes, right for notes—as early as 22 days. In support of this conclusion a variety of evoked-potential and electroencephalographic studies suggest that very young infants have similarly lateralized preferences for phonemes and tones. In addition, many studies using the standard dichotic listening technique have found an adultlike asymmetry in children three years of age and older.

Asymmetry in the Visual System. There have been many attempts to use the tachistoscopic method of visual presentation to demonstrate perceptual asymmetries in the visual system of children. In a thorough review, Witelson concluded that not one tachistoscopic study of left hemisphere specialization in children is free of methodological difficulty or provides unequivocal results. Tachistoscopic studies of right hemisphere specialization have been more convincing and have indicated right hemisphere effects in children as young as six years of age. From their use of a strobe-light test Crowell et al. even suggest a right hemisphere effect in newborns. Using findings that repetitive strobe-light flashes produce bilateral photic driving in adults—that is, particular EEG waves occurring in both hemispheres at the same frequency as the flash—he tested newborn babies for the same phenomenon. Newborns showed photic driving only in the right hemisphere (or in some cases not at all); Crowell interpreted this result as evidence of right hemisphere specialization for the perception of rhythmic visual stimuli.

Asymmetry in Motor Control The study of the development of hand preference is intriguing in view of the relation between hand preference and cerebral control of language. Thus, the emergence of hand preference (presumably for the right hand) is commonly inferred to be indicative of left hemisphere specialization. Although this inference is somewhat tenuous at best, it is nevertheless worthy of consideration. After hundreds of studies on this issue, considerable disagreement remains about results and their interpretation alike. The major problem is deciding how to measure hand preference. If frequency of reaching is taken as the measure, there appears to be a *left* hand preference at about four to five months, followed by a switch to a *right* hand preference at about six to nine months, which increases from then until eight to nine years. Measures of grasp duration, however, favor the right hand as early as one month of age. In general, although hand preference is evident in most tests by one year, the data at early ages are far from clear.

Observations favoring left hemisphere specialization for motor control by age three or earlier include increased right-hand gesturing during speech (as seen also in adults) and reduced speed for finger tapping with the right hand, but not the left, when in competition with talking—a finding similar to those of analogous experiments with adults.

A study by Ingram is intriguing: she found both left- and right-hand effects in the same children, according to the task tested. At age three the right hand was stronger, the right fingers tapped faster, and the right hand showed increased gesturing during speech. Thus, the right hand showed an adult response pattern. The left hand copied hand postures of the deaf alphabet and finger spacing of a hand position significantly better. The left-hand tasks may be interpreted as measuring spatial control of hand and finger movements, thus indicating that the right hemisphere is specialized for certain aspects of spatial motor control as early as age three. Curiously, this result is not obtained with adults.

Does Asymmetry Develop? According to many studies of the development of asymmetry, the differences become greater with age. Can this be taken as evidence that lateralization of function continues to develop? Apparently not, for the methodological and theoretical problems of such an inference have often been pointed out. Lateralization scores are usually used to indicate relative differences of function of the two hemispheres, not degree of difference or specialization. Therefore, to use difference scores across different ages to indicate development of lateralization would be inappropriate. The emergence of such differences may indicate the development of cognitive ability, not of its lateralization.

What Determines the Development of Asymmetry? According to an old doctrine called *Müller's law of specific nerve energy* an area of the brain performs its given function because it receives fibers from a given sensory system. For example, we see with the visual cortex because that region receives fibers from the eye. This doctrine's explanatory usefulness is open to dispute. And if the law is not an entirely adequate explanation of why we see with a particular area of the cortex (we could, for example, hear with color and see with sounds), what is the explanation for why we speak with one hemisphere? What is its special property that it can assume that function? What property allows the other hemisphere to support nonlanguage abilities? One explanation is that the anatomy of particular areas is well developed, making it easier for one hemisphere to adopt a given function than for the other. Thus, language becomes a left hemisphere function because the left temporal cortex is genetically programmed to be well developed and more easily subsumes language than the right; likewise, because the right hemisphere is well developed in other areas, it adopts other functions. We believe this the most likely explanation, although other theories have been proposed favoring either greater activity of the reticular activating system on one side than on the other, or environmental factors. Our explanation is at least consistent with the principles obtained from the cat's visual system. Lateralization is innate, but requires functional validation, as we shall see below.

Environmental Influences on Asymmetry. Although the evidence so far recounted suggests an inborn predisposition toward lateralization of cerebral function, there is convincing evidence that environmental factors play a significant role. Recall that although the cat's visual system appears functionally and anatomically mature when the eyes open, visual deprivation, especially of just one eye, seriously affects the system. Similarly, it is reasonable to suppose that environmental stimulation could enhance or retard the develop-

ment of other cerebral functions such as language. Two lines of evidence support this proposition: (1) the absence of normal cerebral lateralization in illiterate or deaf adults, and (2) anomalous hemispheric development following social isolation and experiential deprivation.

Asymmetry in Illiterate and Deaf People. Studies by Cameron et al. and by Wechsler have reported that aphasia is equally probable following either left or right hemisphere damage in illiterate persons. This is a provocative finding, for it implies that experience with language—particularly complex language skills such as reading and writing—somehow influences cerebral asymmetry.

An analogous finding is that literate, congenitally deaf persons have abnormal patterns of cerebral organization, as indicated by two different lines of work. First, according to Neville, two different laboratories have independently reported that congenitally deaf persons fail to show the usual right visual field superiority in tasks of linguistic processing. This failure could be interpreted as evidence that if experience with auditory language is absent, lateralization of some aspect or aspects of nonauditory language functions is abolished. Second, Neville reported that, during perception of line drawings, visual evoked potentials were significantly larger on the *right* in children with normal hearing, and significantly larger on the *left* in deaf children who used American Sign Language to communicate. Curiously, there was no asymmetry at all in children who could not sign but merely used pantomime to communicate. From the signers' left hemisphere effect for line drawings Neville inferred that the deaf signers acquired their sign language much as normal children acquire verbal language: with their left hemispheres. However, since sign language has a visuospatial component, certain visuospatial functions may have developed in the left hemisphere, producing an unexpected left hemisphere effect. The lack of asymmetry in nonsigners could mean that the absence of language experience somehow abolished certain aspects of cerebral asymmetry or, alternatively, that the expression of cerebral asymmetry depends on language experience. If the nonsigners learn Ameslan, and do so before puberty (the reasons are discussed below), they might develop an asymmetrical evoked-potential pattern similar to those of children who already sign.

Although congenital deafness may alter certain aspects of cerebral organization, Kimura, in reviewing 11 cases of signing disorders following brain damage, finds the similarity with speakers is remarkable. Her results are summarized in Table 24–3. Note that of the nine right-handed signers with left hemisphere lesions all had a signing disorder. In two left-handers, one had a disorder with a left hemisphere lesion and one had a disorder with a right hemisphere lesion. These values are just those that would be expected in a population of vocal communicators. Sign comprehension and writing comprehension were affected in much the same way as was signing, but reading was undisturbed. Kimura postulates that reading was spared because it is not syllabically based

(see the discussion below on patients with hemidecortications) but achieved by visual-to-visual matching. The instructive feature of Kimura's review is that it shows that the development of a language based on signs has the same anatomical basis as do regular vocal languages. This strongly supports the idea that language has a preferential base and that this base is anatomically determined.

Genie: The Effect of Social Isolation and Experiential Deprivation on Language. It is well known that deprivation retards development. An important question is whether deprivation retards or prevents the development of cerebral lateralization and, further, whether a child so deprived can "catch up," wholly or partly. Genie is a child whose isolation resulted from a deliberate attempt to keep her from normal social and experiential stimuli.

Genie was found when she was 13 years, 9 months, at which time she was an unsocialized, primitive human being, emotionally disturbed, unlearned, and without language. She had been taken into protective custody by the police, and, on November 4, 1970, was admitted into the Children's Hospital of Los Angeles for evaluation with a tentative diagnosis of severe malnutrition. She remained in the Rehabilitation Center of the hospital until August 13, 1971. At that time she entered a foster home where she has been living ever since as a member of the family.

When admitted to the hospital, Genie was painfully thin, had a distended abdomen, and appeared to be six or seven years younger than her age. She was 54.5 inches tall and weighed 62.25 pounds. She was unable to stand erect, could not chew solid or even semi-solid foods, had great difficulty in swallowing, was incontinent of feces and urine, and was mute.

The tragic and bizarre story which was uncovered revealed that for most of her life Genie suffered physical and social restriction,

TABLE 24–3

Manual signing disorders
in left- and right-handed patients

	Disorder with left hemisphere lesion	Disorder with right hemisphere lesion
Right-handers	9	0
Left-handers	1	1

Adapted from Kimura, 1981.

nutritional neglect, and extreme experiential deprivation. There is evidence that from about the age of 20 months until shortly before admission to the hospital Genie had been isolated in a small closed room, tied into a potty chair where she remained most or all hours of the day, sometimes overnight. A cloth harness, constructed to keep her from handling her feces was her only apparel of wear. When not strapped into the chair she was kept in a covered infant crib, also confined from the waist down. The door to the room was kept closed, and the windows were curtained. She was hurriedly fed (only cereal and baby food) and minimally cared for by her mother, who was almost blind during most of the years of Genie's isolation. There was no radio or TV in the house and the father's intolerance of noise of any kind kept any acoustic stimuli, which she received behind the closed door, to a minimum. (The first child born to this family died from pneumonia when three months old after being put in the garage because of noisy crying.) Genie was physically punished by the father if she made any sounds. According to the mother, the father and older brother never spoke to Genie although they barked like dogs at her. The mother was forbidden to spend more than a few minutes with Genie during feeding. (Fromkin et al., 1974, pp. 84–85)

At Genie's birth (by Caesarean section) she was 7 pounds, 7.5 ounces and according to the pediatrician's records was within normal weight limits at 11 months. There is no suggestion of retardation, her only serious physical anomaly being a dislocated hip.

It is unknown whether Genie ever began to speak words prior to her isolation, but when she was discovered she did not speak at all. Her only sound was a "throaty whimper." Even when angry, although she would scratch at her face, blow her nose violently into her clothes, and urinate, she would not vocalize, possibly because she had been whipped by her father when she did. Genie's inability to talk may

have been due to similar emotional factors or may have had a physiological basis. Comprehensive tests of language comprehension were first administered about 11 months after Genie's discovery. By this time Genie was able to understand and produce individual words and names, although her comprehension was far beyond her ability to use words. One source of her problems in using words for talking was probably a physical difficulty in learning the necessary neuromuscular controls over her vocal organs. After all, while other children were learning this control she was learning to repress all sounds. As a result, Genie's speech is in a monotone and very low volume, although it has shown marked improvement with time.

In spite of her physical problems with speech Genie is clearly learning language. Hers is similar to development in normal children in that her speech is governed by rules: her basic sentence elements are in a fixed order, and syntactic and semantic relations are expressed systematically. Her speech does, however, differ from that of normal children. For example, although her vocabulary is much larger than that of children with equivalent syntactic abilities, she clearly has more difficulty than normal children in learning rules of grammar. She uses no question words, no demonstratives, no particles, and no rejoinders. She produces negative sentences by the addition of the negative element to the beginning of the sentence rather than reorganizing the sentence as children at her stage in language development would do (e.g., "No can go").

Genie's cognitive development was quite rapid. In May 1973 her Stanford-Binet mental age was five to eight. Because this value far exceeds her linguistic abilities, Genie's right hemisphere functions may be far superior to her left hemisphere functions.

Results of her dichotic listening are provocatively unusual for a right-handed person: although both ears show normal hearing, there is a strong left-ear, hence right hemisphere, effect for both verbal and nonveral (environmental) sounds. In fact, the right ear is nearly totally suppressed, a phenomenon also characteristic of split-brain patients for the *left* ear. In short, the dichotic-listening results imply that Genie's right hemisphere is processing both verbal and nonverbal acoustic stimuli, as would be the case in people with a left hemispherectomy in childhood. The possibility that Genie is using her right hemisphere for language suggests that her capacity for language acquisition is limited, as it is in left hemispherectomy patients (see below). This conclusion is supported by her retarded development of syntactic skills despite possession of a large vocabulary.

To date, Genie has not been assessed for neuropsychological functions such as are measured by visuospatial or praxic tests. In view of the Leipmann-Kimura theory that the left hemisphere controls movement, it would be interesting to determine whether Genie has difficulty in performing sequential motor movements.

Genie's dichotic results suggest a curious puzzle: Why has deprivation of auditory and verbal experience caused a shift in speech lateralization? (Speculations of this type are risky at best, since there is no "average brain," and all inferences about brain function are based on group averages. Thus, any hypothesis about an individual must be treated as pure conjecture and heavily spiced with skepticism. After all, it is possible that Genie's speech would have developed in the right hemisphere even if she were raised normally.) Given this caution, we will consider different hypotheses to explain why Genie's right hemisphere has speech along with nonspeech functions.

At least three explanations for Genie's abnormal lateralization are plausible. The first hypothesis is that disuse of the left hemisphere (functional validation) may simply have resulted in degeneration. Thus, it would be interesting to have a CT scan of Genie's brain to see if there are any gross morphological changes. The second hypothesis is that in the absence of auditory stimulation the left hemisphere is now actively inhibited by the right hemisphere or by some other structure. This possibility is congruent with the studies done on monocular deprivation in cats. Recall that after monocular deprivation in kittens, the experienced eye actively inhibited input from the deprived eye. This inhibition could only be released by inhibiting the active cells pharmacologically. By analogy, Genie's left hemisphere could have been actively inhibited from assuming its function when the chance arose. Since Genie was not deprived of visuospatial experience, the right hemisphere would not have been inhibited from assuming its normal functions. The third hypothesis is that Genie's left hemisphere is now performing some other functions. In the absence of a thorough neuropsychological assessment, it is difficult to theorize just what the new functions might be. One possibility is that the left hemisphere was able to assume its preferred role in motor control, and in the absence of competition from speech functions the left hemisphere has an even greater control of motor functions than normal. This idea actually suggests increased cerebral lateralization for at least one function in Genie, but it remains to be tested. It is unfortunate that tests of praxic functions were not administered repeatedly throughout the period of language development.

BRAIN INJURY AND DEVELOPMENT

Although it was known in 1861 that damage to the left frontal cortex could abolish speech, by 1868 Cotard had observed that children who had received left frontal lesions developed normal adult language functions. This was the origin of the idea that brain injury has milder and short-lived effects if it is sustained in childhood. In the 1930s Kennard put the idea to scientific study. She compared the effects of unilateral motor cortex lesions on infant and adult monkeys. The impairments in the infant monkeys were milder than those of the adults. The generalization that sparing of function follows infant lesions became known as the **Kennard principle.** For a time the idea received wide acceptance and a good deal of experimental support but then, gradually, particularly in recent years, it became evident that earlier may not always be better, and then it became apparent that earlier may actually be worse. Of course, exactly which effect is obtained depends on the behavior under examination, the extent of brain damage, and the actual age of injury. With respect to cognitive function in humans, it is clear that speech survives early brain damage, but some elements of syntax and some nonlanguage functions may not survive, and general intellectual ability may in fact decline. In this section we shall examine some of the evidence that supports these conclusions. The discussion will deal mainly with language, not only because it has received the most study but also because functions lying outside the primary speech zones show less evidence of sparing of function even after early injury. Left temporal damage still produces specific impairments in memory, and left frontal lesions are still associated with enduring defects on tests such as the Wisconsin card-sorting test. Apparently the brain places an emphasis on preserving speech and will save it whenever possible.

Effect of Brain Damage on Language

It is now well known that language deficits resulting from cerebral injury in childhood are usually short-lived, and that recovery is nearly complete. Furthermore, transient language disorders following right hemisphere damage are commoner in children than in adults, the incidence running at about 8 percent and 2 percent respectively (see Table 24–4). The Basser study, which gave a value of 35 percent with aphasia, is thought to be inaccurate, since

TABLE 24–4

Summary of studies of aphasia resulting from unilateral lesions

	Age range of subjects	Number of cases	Percent with right hemi-sphere lesions
Childhood lesions			
Guttman, 1942	2–14	15	7
Alajouanine and Lhermitte, 1965	6–15	32	0
McCarthy, 1963	After language acquisition	114	4
Basser, 1962	Before 5	20	35
Hécaen, 1976	3½–15	17	11
Total	2–15	198	8
Adult lesions			
Russell and Espir, 1961	—	205	3
Hécaen, 1976	—	232	0.43
Total	—	437	1.6

Adapted from Krashen (1973) and Hécaen (1976).

many of the subjects may have had bilateral lesions.

Alajouanine and Lhermitte studied 32 cases of childhood aphasia, finding writing deficits in all and reading deficits in about half of the children, in addition to difficulty in speaking. Six months after the injury they observed total recovery of spontaneous language in about one-third, although significant improvement was noted in all the others. When reexamined at one year or more postinjury, 24 of the 32 children had normal or almost normal language, although 14 still had some degree of dysgraphia; 22 of the children were eventually able to return to school.

Similarly, Hécaen followed postinjury recovery of aphasia and related symptoms in 15 children with left hemisphere unilateral lesions, as summarized in Table 24–5. Besides disorders of speech, nearly all the children had disorders of writing and calculation as well. Of these 15 children, five showed complete recovery within six weeks to two years. Most of the remaining children showed considerable improvement, the only remaining deficit often being a mild difficulty in writing, a finding similar to that of Alajouanine and Lhermitte.

Woods and Teuber have studied about 50 patients with prenatal or early postnatal brain damage to either the left or the right hemisphere. Using normal siblings as controls they came to the following conclusions. (1) Language survives after early left-side injury. (2) Much of this survival seems attributable to occupancy of a potential language zone in the right hemisphere. (3) This shift of language location is not without a price, because some kinds of visuospatial orientation are impaired. (4) Early lesions of the right hemisphere produce deficits similar to those produced by similar lesions in adulthood. In other words, if a child sustains a lesion of the left hemisphere that produces right hemiplegia, language functions are remarkably more intact than after a comparable lesion in an adult, presumably because some, or all, of the language abilities have moved to the right hemisphere. However, language *crowds* into the right hemisphere at the expense of visuospatial functions. On the other hand, a lesion of the right hemisphere, which produces left hemiplegia, results in deficits on visuospatial tasks; apparently they do not crowd into the left hemisphere. These results are summarized in Figure 24–1. In this regard it is interesting to note that we are un-

TABLE 24–5

Frequency of different symptoms in 15 cases caused by left hemisphere lesions in childhood

	Number of cases	Percent	Evolution of symptoms
Mutism	9	60	From 5 days to 30 months
Articulatory disorders	12	80	Persistent in 4 cases
Auditory verbal comprehension disorders	6	40	Persistent in 1 case
Naming disorders	7	46	Persistent in 3 cases
Paraphasia	1	7	Disappearance
Reading disorders	9	60	Persistent in 3 cases
Writing disorders	13	86	Persistent in 7 cases
Facial apraxia	2		Transient
Acalculia	11		(Not reported)

Adapted from Hécaen, 1976.

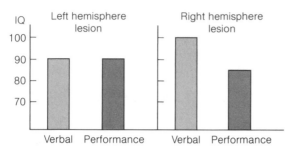

FIGURE 24–1. IQs on subtests of the Wechsler Intelligence Test for adults who while infants had suffered a lesion of the left or the right hemisphere, as determined by the occurrence of hemiparesis. Note that both verbal and performance scores are depressed by left hemisphere lesions, whereas only performance scores are depressed by right hemisphere lesions. The results suggest that if language moves to the right hemisphere, that hemisphere's functions are sacrificed to accommodate this shift. The results also suggest that right hemisphere functions do not shift sufficiently to interfere with language. (After Teuber, 1975.)

aware of any reports of visual neglect following early lesions to the right hemisphere, and further we must caution that the failure to observe sparing of function following right hemisphere damage may be due in part to the choice of behavioral tests.

If we accept the evidence that early brain damage produces sparing of language and that sparing may occur because the control of language is transferred to the opposite hemisphere, it is possible to address a set of three different questions. These concern the actual language functions that are transferred, the type of brain damage that causes them to be transferred, and the age range during which transfer can take place. The first two questions have been addressed experimentally by Rasmussen and Milner, but the third is as yet incompletely answered.

Using the carotial sodium Amytal and dichotic-listening tests Rasmussen and Milner localized language in a large number of patients who had received left hemisphere injury early in life but had returned to the hospital later in life because of complications. They found that the patients divided into three groups, as shown in Table 24–6: in one group speech was in the left hemisphere, in the second speech was represented bilaterally, and in the third speech was in the right hemisphere. The patients who had speech in the left hemisphere were found to have damage that did not invade the anterior speech zone (Broca's area) or the posterior speech zone (Wernicke's area). Examples of brain damage that did not produce a shift in language lateralization are shown in Figure 24–2 A. Both exemplar lesions are large yet the dichotic-listening test showed a right-ear advantage, and in the sodium Amytal tests the patients were mute on both naming (giving the names of objects, e.g., what is—experimenter holds up object) and repetition (e.g., name the days of the week in order) tasks after left hemisphere injection. The shading in the first portion of Figure 24–2 A shows the locations of the anterior and posterior speech zones. An example of a lesion in a patient that produced a complete shift of language to the right hemisphere is illustrated in Figure 24–2 B. This patient showed a left-ear advantage on the dichotic-listening test and was mute for

TABLE 24–6

Changes in hemispheric speech representation following early brain damage

| | | Percent with speech representation | | |
		Left	Bilateral	Right
No early damage	Right	96	0	4
	Left or mixed	70	15	15
Early damage	Right	81	7	12
	Left or mixed	28	19	53

Adapted from Rasmussen and Milner, 1975, pp. 248–249.

naming and repetition after right hemisphere sodium Amytal injection. Note that the lesion invaded both the anterior and posterior speech zones. That the lesion did invade both speech zones was typical for patients who developed right hemisphere speech after early left hemisphere lesions. Examples of the lesions in patients who had bilateral speech are shown in Figure 24–2 C and 24–2 D. The patient in Figure 24–2 C had a large left frontal lobe lesion at six years of age that included the anterior language zone. At 18 years of age the patient was right-handed and had a right-ear advantage for digits and a left-ear advantage for melodies. On the sodium Amytal tests, a left injection produced a disturbance in series repetition (counting, reciting the days of the week forward or backward, or oral spelling) but naming was less disturbed. A right hemisphere injection produced a disturbance in both series repetition and naming. Since it is assumed that the right-ear advantage for digits is an indication of left hemisphere speech and that the absence of series repetition after left hemisphere sodium Amytal injection is an indication of intact speech in the left posterior speech zone, it can be concluded that the lesion did not cause a complete shift of speech from the posterior left speech zone. Since naming was disturbed after a right hemisphere injection of sodium Amytal it is assumed that left hemisphere speech functions of the anterior zone had shifted to the right hemisphere. The patient in Figure 24–2 D had a large posterior lesion that was incurred at 2.5 years of age. Testing at 16 years of age showed that she was left-handed and had a left-ear advantage for both digits and melodies. Sodium Amytal tests showed that naming was disturbed by both left and right injections, whereas series repetition was done well after the left but not the right injection. In this case it is thought that the large posterior lesion incurred early in life had caused speech functions of the posterior zone

A   No shift in language

B   Complete shift of language

C   Shift of anterior speech functions

D   Shift of posterior speech functions

FIGURE 24–2. Relations between early brain damage and hemisphere changes in language organization. A. Anterior and posterior lesions after which language remained in the left hemisphere. The shaded portion of the first figure shows location of language zones. B. An anterior-posterior lesion that causes all language to move to the right hemisphere. C. An anterior lesion that causes the anterior speech zone to shift to the right hemisphere. D. A posterior lesion that caused the posterior speech zone to shift to the right hemisphere. (After Rasmussen and Milner, 1977.)

to shift to the right, while the anterior speech zone still retained some speech function.

The Invariance and Maturational Hypotheses

Explanations of recovery of language from early brain damage take two forms. The *invariance hypothesis* argues that the left hemisphere is specialized for language at birth and that the right hemisphere must acquire language abilities after the left hemisphere is damaged. The *maturational hypothesis* argues that both hemispheres are initially involved in language but gradually the left hemisphere becomes more specialized for language control. Lenneberg refined the maturational hypothesis by proposing that lateralization of function develops rapidly between the ages of two or three to five, and then proceeds more slowly until puberty, by which time it is complete. Lenneberg reasoned that if cerebral damage occurred in the potentially dominant hemisphere, recovery would be complete and rapid, because language would simply develop in the undamaged hemisphere. Furthermore, damage to either hemisphere would produce a transient language disturbance because language was still under the control of both hemispheres. Between the ages of three and 10 cerebral damage may produce aphasia but recovery occurs over time because the intact cerebral hemisphere is still able to take over. Damage after 10 would produce language disorders resembling those observed in adults, because the intact hemisphere becomes increasingly specialized and less able to adapt. By about age 14 the ability to reorganize is lost, and prognosis for recovery is poor. Lenneberg defined the time span from about age two to 14 as the critical period for the development of language and, more broadly, of cerebral lateralization. Krashen has subsequently revised Lenneberg's upper age limit

of 14 down to five years. Support for the maturational hypothesis comes, obviously, from the fact that children recover from aphasia, but also from the purported finding that **crossed aphasia** (i.e., aphasia from right hemisphere lesions) is commoner in children than adults.

The results that we have described to this point, particularly those of Rasmussen and Milner, support the invariance hypothesis. Their findings show that language has a strong affinity for the left hemisphere and will not abandon it unless an entire center is destroyed, and even then it might shift only partly to the other hemisphere. This affinity is thought to be based on the special innate anatomical organization of the left hemisphere—remember that the left planum temporale is larger than the right one. In the examination of their series of patients with early left hemisphere lesions, Rasmussen and Milner also noted that childhood injuries to the left hemisphere occurring after five years of age rarely changed speech patterns. They argued that recovery that occurs after about six years of age occurs not through transfer to the other hemisphere but by intrahemispheric reorganization, possibly with intact surrounding zones acquiring some control over speech. Further evidence for the invariance hypothesis comes from the study of Woods and Teuber. As is illustrated in Figure 24–1, left, but not right, hemisphere lesions cause a decline in both verbal and performance IQ scores, a result that argues against the idea that the right hemisphere has equal potential for language. Finally, the evidence that crossed aphasia is commoner in children than adults derives mainly from Basser's study, and Woods and Teuber have convincingly argued that these data are severely contaminated with bilateral effects.

Given that the invariance hypothesis is correct, there is evidence to suggest that functional validation must still occur; that is, practice with language is necessary to establish left preeminence. Woods has reported that if left hemisphere lesions occur before the first birthday both verbal and performance IQ are severely depressed by a right hemisphere lesion. If the right hemisphere lesion occurred after the first birthday, verbal scores were unimpaired but performance scores were still not normal. It seems likely that the results of the lesions before one year of age might be due to a disruption of verbal functions that had been insufficiently validated, or perhaps disrupted by the invasion of performance functions. We must note, however, that this suggestion is speculative, that IQ is at best an imprecise measure of language, and that a more systematic study of these patients using linguistic tests is warranted.

Effects of Hemidecortication

If a person has life-threatening seizures resulting from severe infantile cerebral injury, the neocortex of an entire hemisphere may be surgically removed to control the seizures. Although most such surgery is performed during the patient's early adolescence, it is sometimes done in the first year of life, before speech has developed. These latter cases are particularly germane to the question of how cerebral lateralization develops. If the hemispheres are functionally different at birth, then left and right hemispherectomies would be expected to produce differential effects on cognitive abilities. If they are not, then no cognitive differences would result from left or right hemidecortications.

Can One Hemisphere Take Over the Functions of the Other? The general results of recent studies of linguistic and visuospatial abilities in patients with unilateral hemidecortications support the conclusion that both hemispheres are functionally specialized, al-

though both hemispheres appear capable of assuming some functions usually performed by the missing hemisphere. Table 24–7 summarizes these data. Notice that the left hemidecortication produces no severe aphasia or obvious language deficits. Yet the right hemisphere cannot completely compensate for the left hemisphere, for the patients have deficits in using complex language. Note that right hemidecortication produces no severe deficits in visuospatial abilities. Yet the left hemisphere cannot completely compensate for the right hemisphere, since the patients have deficits in performing complex visuospatial tasks.

In an analysis of language abilities, Dennis and Whitaker found that unlike right hemisphere removals, left hemisphere removals produced deficits in understanding auditory language when the meaning was conveyed by complex syntactic structure, particularly if the sentence contained an error (e.g., "The tall guard wasn't shot by the armed robber"), and produced difficulty in determining sentence implication, integrating semantic and syntactic information to replace missing pronouns, and forming judgments of word interrelations in sentences. In an analysis of word comprehension, Dennis has found that both hemispheres understand the meaning of words and both hemispheres can spontaneously produce lists of names of things. When searching for words using different cues, the left hemisphere has an advantage over the right hemisphere. Both hemispheres can name an object from its picture or from its description but the left hemisphere can identify it on the basis of "rhymes with" whereas the right hemisphere is deficient in using this type of cue. In an analysis of reading skills, Dennis and her co-workers found that both hemispheres had almost equal ability in higher-order reading comprehension; however, the left hemisphere was superior to the right in reading and spelling unfa-

TABLE 24–7

Summary of effects of hemidecortication on verbal
and visuospatial abilities

Intelligence	Left hemidecorticate	Right hemidecorticate
	Low normal	Low normal
Language tests		
Simple	Normal	Normal
Complex (e.g. syntax)	Poor	Normal
Visuospatial tests		
Simple	Normal	Normal
Complex	Normal	Poor

Based on data from Kohn and Dennis (1974) and Dennis and Whitaker (1976).

miliar words, and in using sentence structure to achieve fluent reading. The left hemisphere also read prose passages with greater decoding accuracy, more fluency, and fewer errors that violated the sematic and syntactic structure of the sentence. The superiority of the left hemisphere seems to be its ability to manipulate and exploit language rules. The right hemisphere is not without its strengths in language. Performance was better with the right hemisphere in a task that required learning an association between nonsense words and symbols. In summarizing the studies on language Dennis suggests that if written language is thought of as a combination of meaning structure (morphology), sound structure (phonology), and picture structure (logography), then the isolated left hemisphere will show superior performance with morphology and phonology and inferior performance with logographic cues, whereas the isolated right hemisphere will show superior performance with logographic cues and inferior performance with morphological and phonological cues.

An almost analogous pattern of results is observed on tests of visuospatial function. Kohn and Dennis found that although patients with right hemisphere removals performed normally on simple tests of visuospatial function such as drawing, they were significantly impaired on complex tests such as maze problems or map-reading tests.

To summarize, each hemisphere can assume some of the opposite hemisphere's functions if the opposite hemisphere is removed during development, but neither hemisphere is totally capable of mediating all of the missing opposite's functions. Thus, although the developing brain gives evidence of considerable plasticity, there is convincing evidence against equipotentiality: both appear to have a processing capacity that likely has an innate structural basis. Furthermore, there seems to be a price for assuming new responsibilities. With few exceptions patients undergoing hemidecortication are of below-average, or at best only average, intelligence, and they are frequently less than normally proficient at tests of the intact hemisphere's function.

A Note of Dissent. Although the experiments of Dennis and her coworkers seem internally consistent and consonant with other lines of research on the organization of language (see Chapters 21 and 28), Bishop has questioned the methodological adequacy of the demonstrations. She points out that in the 1975 study of Kohn and Dennis two of five left decorticate patients understood reversible passive sentences, and one may have been too young to perform the task. Furthermore, Bishop argues that if subjects with comparable IQs are tested on the Kohn and Dennis task and then used as a control group, neither left nor right hemidecorticates differ from the control group. Likewise, she argues that the performance of the three subjects in the 1976 Dennis and Whitaker study also have performance scores that fall within the range of control values. In presenting these methodological criticisms, Bishop does not dispute the left-for-language hypothesis, but rather suggests that the evidence that supports it is weak. Bishop's criticisms are telling and point out the difficulties that are involved in drawing conclusions from studies on small numbers of subjects and in obtaining appropriate control groups to compare with people who have brain damage. At this writing, Dennis and coworkers have not had time to respond to Bishop's criticisms, and so we must point out only that there is a note of dissent concerning this research. At the same time we must also note that Zaidel (see Chapter 28) comes to similar conclusions about the superiority of the left hemisphere for language in hemidecorticate and split-brain patients, and so we must conclude that the left-for-language hypothesis maintains a relatively strong position, despite methodological questions about some of the studies that are presented in its support.

A THEORY OF COGNITIVE DEVELOPMENT

Three general theoretical positions can be postulated to account for the ontogeny of cerebral specialization. We have called these (1) the equipotential theory, (2) the left-for-language theory, and (3) the parallel-development theory. (We feel these terms are preferable and more explicit than the terms "maturational" and "invariance" used above.)

According to the *equipotential* theory either hemisphere can be specialized for either language or nonlanguage functions, and the occurrence of specialization is entirely a matter of chance. According to the *left-for-language* theory the left hemisphere is special and is organized genetically to develop language skills; the right hemisphere is postulated to be a dumping ground for whatever is left over. According to the *parallel-development* theory, both hemispheres, by virtue of their construction, play special roles, one hemisphere being destined to specialize in language and the other in nonlanguage functions. Although there are fairly good arguments for each theory, in our view a parallel-development theory that initially permits some flexibility or equipotentiality most usefully encompasses most of the available data. The cognitive functions of each hemisphere can be conceived hierarchically. Simple or lower-level functions are represented at the base of the hierarchy, corresponding to functions in primary, sensory, motor, language, or visuospatial areas. More complex or higher-level functions are represented further up the hierarchy, the most complex being at the top: these functions are the most lateralized. At birth the two hemispheres functionally overlap because each is processing low-level behaviors. By five years of age the newly developing higher-order cognitive processes have very little overlap, and each hemisphere thus becomes increasingly specialized. By puberty each hemisphere has developed its own unique functions (Figure 24–3).

Note that the cerebral hemispheres are not becoming more lateralized in development; rather, as Witelson has pointed out, the developing cognitive functions are built on the

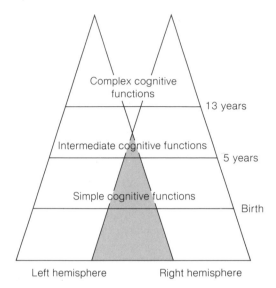

FIGURE 24–3. A model of the development of cognitive function in the left and right hemispheres of normal people. At the bottom of the pyramids cognitive functions are relatively simple (e.g., for language simple functions could include babbling and the use of simple nouns), and the functions of the two hemispheres overlap considerably. At the top of the pyramids, representing very complex functions, the functions of the two hemispheres do not overlap at all (e.g., for language complex functions could include the use of adult language structure). It is important to note that the hemispheres are not themselves becoming more lateralized with respect to a given function; rather, they are developing new functions that are more specialized. Since both hemispheres show functional overlap in the early years of life, each can adopt the functions of the other if brain damage has occurred at an early age.

lower functions, which are innately located in one hemisphere or the other.

All models of cerebral development provoke the question of how functions become restricted to one hemisphere, rather than becoming bilateral. In a series of papers, Moscovitch has emphasized the possibility that one hemisphere actively inhibits the other (recall our earlier discussion of the effects of monocular deprivation in cats), thus preventing the contralateral hemisphere from developing similar functions. This active inhibition presumably develops at about age five, as the corpus callosum becomes functional. Moscovitch proposes that this inhibitory process not only prevents the subsequent development of language processes in the right hemisphere, and vice versa, but also inhibits expression of the language processes already in the right hemisphere. Support for this idea comes from the observation that the right hemisphere of commissurotomy patients appears to have greater language abilities than expected from the study of normal patients, presumably because the right hemisphere is no longer subject to inhibition by the left. Furthermore, Netley reports that people born with no corpus callosum demonstrate little or no functional asymmetry as inferred from dichotic listening, suggesting that the absence of interhemispheric connection results in attenuated hemisphere differentiation. This phenomenon follows directly from the Moscovitch proposal.

EXPERIMENTAL APPROACHES TO EARLY RECOVERY

It is becoming increasingly clear that the mechanisms mediating recovery of function from injury sustained in infancy are behaviorally and anatomically quite different from the mechanisms that mediate recovery after lesions inflicted in adults. The best illustration of the role of age comes from a series of studies on the function of the dorsolateral and orbitofrontal areas of the prefrontal cortex.

The dorsolateral cortex receives projections from the parvocellular subdivision of the dorsomedial nucleus of the thalamus. In fact, the distribution of this projection defines this cortical zone. Many studies of the function of this area show that if it is damaged in adult monkeys, rats, or other animals, they show profound impairments of spatial delayed responses or spatial delayed alternations. The features of these tasks are that the animal must make a choice between two spatially located objects, and each trial is separated by a delay. For example, a monkey must remember that a peanut is located in one of two cups, but each trial is separated by a short delay during which it cannot see the cup. Generally, lesioned animals do not perform above chance on this task, and the deficit is not attributable to interference with performance by sensory or motor difficulties, surgical shock, or lack of opportunity to learn. That is, even though they seemingly "know" what to do they make errors. On a host of other tasks, such as visual discriminations, these monkeys show no deficits. In addition to showing this behavioral deficit, histological analysis shows that the projecting fibers from the dorsomedial nucleus die after lesioning, and the cell bodies of these fibers degenerate.

Akert et al. and subsequently others have removed the dorsolateral cortex of monkeys within the first two months of life and studied the monkeys on spatial reversals over the next year of life. During this time the monkeys show no impairment when compared with age-matched control animals. Nevertheless, degeneration of cells in the thalamus are found. These early studies seemed to suggest that other brain structures, most likely the basal ganglia, could assume this function. However, this simple interpretation was complicated by Goldman's 1971 finding that if the monkeys were tested for as long as two years, they gradually developed the adult deficit or, as it has been phrased, "they grew into the deficit." These results are instructive, first because they show that a subcortical structure can control the behavior in a seemingly normal way for a period of time, and second,

because they show that the function is "given up" with maturation.

More recently, Goldman and Galkin studied the behavior and anatomy of monkeys that had been removed from the womb before term, subjected to surgery, and then replaced. These animals show no deficits as infants or when mature and also show no cellular degeneration in the dorsomedial thalamus. Kolb and Nonneman have obtained identical results with the rat, which does not require preterm surgery because it is more immature at birth than the monkey. The studies of Goldman and Galkin and of Kolb and Nonneman imply that if cortical damage occurs sufficiently early in life, the brain is able to reorganize in some way to achieve complete compensation. One type of evidence for reorganization is that the monkeys have gyri and sulci not observed in normal monkeys. Other evidence is that cells of the dorsomedial nucleus remain intact, permitting the hypothesis that the new connections that they make most likely sustain behaviors of delayed alternation. Goldman and Galkin have suggested a number of types of reorganization that might account for the survival of these cells (Figure 24–4). (1) *Transient collaterals.* The fibers that enter the dorsolateral cortex from the dorsomedial thalamus may initially have collaterals going elsewhere, which under normal conditions degenerate, but which in instances of dorsolateral cortex damage survive. (2) *Oversupply.* There is an oversupply of neurons in the dorsomedial nucleus, but normally only those that innervate the dorsolateral cortex survive. (3) *Collateral sprouting.* The immature neurons do not die, because in early life they can sprout collaterals to new cortical areas and so replace their severed axons. (4) *Lesion-induced neurogenesis.* Although the original neurons are killed by the lesion, new cell bodies form and replace them. (5) *Autonomy of undifferentiated neurons.* Although normal neurons die if their target is destroyed, undifferentiated neurons can survive to make new connections. (6) *Rerouting.* If axons from the thalamus have not yet entered the neocortex, they are able to seek out and innervate alternate targets.

Many of the studies on animals with prefrontal cortex damage have assessed behavior using one test, or at most only a few tests. Kolb and Whishaw have adapted the neuropsychological procedures developed for humans and applied them to investigations in the rat. They tested rats that had received neonatal or adult frontal cortex damage on a "test battery" that evaluated many different aspects of the animals' learned and unlearned behavior. They found that learned behaviors (e.g., spatial reversals) were spared by the neonatal lesions but species-typical behaviors (e.g., nest building, food hoarding) were abolished. They interpreted the results to mean that what rats are preprogrammed to do cannot survive

Transient collaterals

Oversupply

Collateral sprouting

Lesion-induced neurogenesis

Autonomy of undifferentiated neurons

Rerouting

FIGURE 24–4. Diagram of possible alternative explanations of the preservation of neurons in the dorsomedial nucleus of the thalamus after surgical resection of the dorsolateral frontal cortex in the monkey prior to birth. Black circles indicate degenerated neurons; open circles, preserved neurons. (From P. S. Goldman and T. W. Galkin, Prenatal removal of frontal association cortex in the fetal rhesus monkey: Anatomical and functional consequences in postnatal life. *Brain Research,* 152:451–485, 1978. Reprinted with permission.)

lesions at any age, whereas things that are heavily dependent on learning are somehow spared by the early lesions. A second interesting aspect of their results was the finding that the brains of the neonatal-lesioned rats were reduced in size by 25 percent whereas the brains of adult-operated rats were shrunk by less than 12 percent. This size reduction, which in humans would be the equivalent of about 200 grams, was not due to a larger lesion size but was produced by shrinkage of the entire neocortex. Besides providing a possible explanation of the small brain size reported in a subset of retarded children, the results seem applicable to humans in another way. After frontal cortex damage in infancy, humans seem to show the same sparing of learned behaviors despite the loss of what could be called human-typical behaviors. The case history of the patient J.P. best illustrates this point.

At the age of 20, J.P. was referred for psychiatric examination because of his repeated difficulties with law enforcement agencies. A pneumoencephalogram plus follow-up exploratory surgery showed that J.P. had what seemed to be a congenital absence of both frontal lobes. J.P.'s behavior had always been peculiar. In his preschool years he was noted for his wandering, which carried him miles from home, and for his Chesterfielding or valet-like manners. He had school difficulties from the beginning. On one occasion his first-grade teacher had just written a letter to his parents complimenting them on having such a well-mannered child, when she looked up and found him exposing himself and masturbating before the class. He got by in school because of his abilities in language, but he failed the third and fourth grades and did not finish high school even after being sent to a variety of special schools. Throughout his life he was known for his wanderings and his love of taking cars and driving them hundreds of miles from home using the navigational criteria of "I steer by the compass and never make turns." In later life he was tested by Ralph Reitan, Brenda Milner, and others. His IQ was strictly average, but he failed all tests of frontal lobe function including the Category test and the Wisconsin card-sorting test. Halstead, after testing J.P., thought he resembled a Univac machine, so stereotyped were his responses. Everyone who met J.P. was struck by how dissociated he seemed from the world. He had no friends in life and had made no sexual contacts or other social attachments. He once took a girl out to dinner, but ran off with her purse when she went to the washroom. In school he was hated by all the boys. He was once described as a "stranger in the world without knowing it." Ackerly summarized his impressions of him in the following way: "What seemed to command our attention and sympathy was his 'aloneness'—detachment not from the immediate physical environment of things and people, but from anything beyond that—anything that gave meaning to life, love, friendship, comradeship. He is indeed a veritable stranger in this world with no other world to flee to for comfort." Throughout his life he was never able to hold a job for more than a few weeks. Ackerly seems to have pinpointed the dichotomy of his existence by describing him not as a case of mental deficiency but as a case of social deficiency.

The studies on frontal lobe function show that certain behaviors can be lost and others spared by early brain damage, and they also provide a number of novel hypotheses for why behaviors may survive early lesions. There are, however, at least three other types of effect that early brain damage can have that require mention. In some cases complete sparing of a behavior occurs, in others a behavior is completely lost, and in still others impairments may be more subtle and generalized. We will give an example and explanation of each type of case.

1. Complete sparing. It is well known that lateral hypothalamic lesions in adult animals produce immediate and short-term arrest of eating and drinking, chronic reductions in body weight, and changes in sensory responsiveness and arousal. Almli and coworkers have found that if large lesions are made in the lateral hypothalamus at different ages, the ensuing deficit depends very closely on the age at which the lesion was incurred. Lesions from birth on produce a decline in body weight; lesions from about seven days on produce consummatory deficits; finally, lesions from about 22 days of age on produce sensory disturbances and attenuated arousal. The explanation for this remarkable finding may be that drinking and feeding are supported by a number of different neural systems that traverse the lateral hypothalamic area. These may include fibers from the neocortex that are involved in producing appropriate motor movements of the mouth and tongue, and dopamine-containing fibers from the midbrain to caudate that are thought to facilitate eating. Because these fibers pass through the hypothalamus between day 1 and 22, the earlier lesions spare them and the later lesions section them. Presumably after the early lesions they simply grow around the lesion site. Since many behavioral deficits in adults may be due to disconnection, absence of deficits in infants that have received similar lesions may be attributable to events such as those described by Almli.

2. Complete loss. Although there is striking recovery from infant injury, as demonstrated in the experiments we have just described, equally careful studies have failed to obtain either recovery or compensation after infant lesions. Lawrence and Hopkins cut the corticospinal tract in infant monkeys and studied the monkeys as they matured. This tract controls speed, agility, and strength of distal movements, and more specifically it produces relatively independent finger movements in adult monkeys. When the monkeys operated on in infancy matured, they showed deficits identical to those of monkeys operated on as adults. Their speed, agility, and strength were reduced, and they were unable to make relatively independent finger movements, such as those requiring the opposition of thumb and forefinger to grasp small objects located in holes in wood boards. An important aspect of Lawrence and Hopkins' study showed that if any corticospinal fibers remained, some recovery occurred, but if all were gone, no recovery took place. Thus, if damage is complete, recovery is absent.

3. Generalized impairments. Many types of infant brain damage produce rather subtle but generalized impairments in behavior. This effect is not well understood but may occur because nonspecific brain systems are damaged. An example of such a nonspecific system is the noradrenaline projection from the brainstem to the forebrain. The projections of this system are very diffuse, going to all cortical regions. Noradrenaline is secreted by the terminals into extracellular space rather than onto specific terminal zones on the innervated neurons. Kasamatsu has suggested that noradrenaline acts to maintain neuronal plasticity, that is, to assist neurons to change anatomically and functionally so that they adapt to new internal and external influences. In an experimental demonstration of the putative role of noradrenaline, Kasamatsu and his coworkers occluded one eye of kittens until most cells in the visual cortex responded to stimulation of the open eye rather than to both eyes as is typical for the normal condition. If noradrenaline function was blocked, cells did not shift their responses to only the open eye. In cats in which the shift had occurred, noradrenaline infusions permitted the previously occluded eye to regain control of many cortical cells. It follows that if noradrenaline systems were damaged in infancy, there would be a generalized inability to adapt to environmental modification. O'Shea and his coworkers have supported this suggestion by demonstrating that the improvement in learning ability that is produced by raising rats in an enriched environment is completely absent if the rats are depleted of noradrenaline before enrichment. In addition, Sutherland and his coworkers have shown that the savings that occur if frontal cortex lesions are made in infancy are blocked by noradrenaline depletion. Speculatively, Kasamatsu's hypothesis may be applicable to other types of effects. In humans, the right hemisphere does not learn to speak if the left hemisphere is damaged in adulthood. Possibly the infant condition, in which the right hemisphere can learn to speak, could be restored to the adult brain if noradrenaline activity in the right hemisphere could be potentiated.

Summary. The process of brain maturation is long, lasting at least into early adulthood, but in the first five years of life the brain has a special ability to compensate for injury. Of all behaviors in humans, language appears the most resiliant to early brain injury. However, even in the case of language, recovery may be incomplete if function is moved from the left to the right hemisphere. The left hemisphere seems to have a special ability to deal with language rules. If brain damage occurs very early in life, before the first year is complete, some aspects of behavior may be disrupted rather than spared, apparently because too many demands are made on remaining neural systems. Experimental models of sparing of function provide a variety of explanations about how the immature brain compensates for damage.

REFERENCES

Ackerly, S. S. A case of paranatal bilateral frontal lobe defect observed for thirty years. In J. M. Warren and K. Akert, eds., *The Frontal Granular Cortex and Behavior,* New York: McGraw-Hill, 1964.

Akert, K., O. S. Orth, H. Harlow, and K. A. Schultz. Learned behavior of rhesus monkeys following neonatal bilateral prefrontal lobotomy. *Science* 132:1944–1945, 1960.

Alajouanine, T., and F. Lhermitte. Acquired aphasia in children. *Brain* 88:653–662, 1965.

Almli, R. C., D. L. Hill, N. T. McMullen, and R. S. Fisher. Newborn rats: Lateral hypothalamic damage and consummatory-sensorimotor ontogeny. *Physiology and Behavior* 22:767–773, 1979.

Basser, L. Hemiplegia of early onset and the faculty of speech with special reference to the effects of hemispherectomy. *Brain* 85:427–460, 1962.

Bishop, D. V. M. Linguistic impairment after hemidecortication for infantile hemiplegia? A reappraisal. *Quarterly Journal of Experimental Psychology, 35A*:199–207, 1963.

Blakemore, C., and D. E. Mitchell. Environmental modification of the visual cortex and the neural basis of learning and memory. *Nature* 241:467–468, 1973.

Bryden, M. P. *Laterality: Functional Asymmetry in the Intact Brain.* New York: Academic, 1982.

Cameron, R. F., R. D. Currier, and A. F. Haerer. Aphasia and literacy. *British Journal of Disorders of Communication* 6:161–163, 1971.

Caplan, P. J., and M. Kinesbourne. Baby drops the rattle: Asymmetry of duration of grasp by infants. *Child Development* 47:532–534, 1967.

Caviness, V. S., Jr., and R. L. Sidman. Time of origin of corresponding cell classes in the cerebral cortex of normal and reeler mutant mice: An autoradiographic analysis. *Journal of Comparative Neurology* 148:141–152, 1973.

Crowell, D. H., R. H. Jones, L. E. Kapuniai, and J. K. Nakagawa. Unilateral cortical activity in newborn humans: An early index of cerebral dominance? *Science* 180:205–208, 1973.

Curtiss, S. *Genie: A Psycholinguistic Study of a Modern-Day "Wild Child."* New York: Academic, 1978.

Dennis, M. Capacity and strategy for syntactic comprehension after left or right hemidecortication. *Brain and Language* 10:287–317, 1980.

Dennis, M. Language acquisition in a single hemisphere: Semantic organization. In D. Caplan, ed., *Biological Studies of Mental Processes*. Cambridge: MIT Press, 1980.

Dennis, M., M. Lovett, and C. A. Wiegel-Crump. Written language acquisition after left or right hemidecortication in infancy. *Brain and Language* 12:54–91, 1981.

Dennis, M., and H. A. Whitaker. Language acquisition following hemidecortication: Linguistic superiority of the left over the right hemisphere. *Brain and Language* 3:404–433, 1976.

Diamond, R., and S. Carey. Developmental changes in the representation of faces. *Journal of Experimental Child Psychology,* 23:1–22, 1977.

Entus, A. K. Hemispheric asymmetry in processing of dichotically presented speech and nonspeech stimuli by infants. In S. J. Segalowitz and F. A. Gruber, eds.. *Language Development and Neurological Theory*. New York: Academic, 1977.

Flechsig, P. *Anatomie des menschlichen Gehirns und Rückenmarks*. Leipzig: Georg Thieme, 1920.

Freud, S. *The Standard Edition of the Complete Psychological Works of Sigmund Freud*. J. Strachey, tr. and ed., in collaboration with A. Freud. London: Hogarth, 1954.

Fromkin, V. A., S. Krashen, S. Curtiss, D. Rigler, and M. Rigler. The development of language in Genie: A case of language acquisition beyond the "critical period." *Brain and Language* 1:81–107, 1974.

Goldman, P. S. Functional development of the prefrontal cortex in early life and the problem of neuronal plasticity. *Experimental Neurology* 32:366–387, 1971.

Goldman, P. S., and T. W. Galkin. Prenatal removal of frontal association cortex in the fetal rhesus monkey: Anatomical and functional consequences in postnatal life. *Brain Research* 152:451–485, 1978.

Guttman, E. Aphasia in children. *Brain* 65:205–219, 1942.

Harlow, H. F. *Learning to Love*. San Francisco: The Albion Publishing Co., 1971.

Hécaen, H. Acquired aphasia in children and the ontogenesis of hemispheric functional specialization. *Brain and Language* 3:114–134, 1976.

Hirsch, H. V. B., and D. N. Spinelli. Modification of the distribution of receptive field orientation in cats by selective visual exposure during development. *Experimental Brain Research* 13:509–527, 1971.

Hubel, D. H., and T. N. Wiesel. Receptive fields of cells in striate cortex of very young, visually inexperienced kittens. *Journal of Neurophysiology* 26:994–1002, 1963.

Ingram, D. Motor asymmetries in young children. *Neuropsychologia* 13:95–102, 1975.

Kasamatsu, T. Enhancement of neuronal plasticity by activating the norepinephrine system in the brain: A remedy for amlyopia. *Human Neurobiology* 1:49–54, 1982.

Kimura, D. Speech lateralization in young children as determined by an auditory test. *Journal of Comparative and Physiological Psychology* 56:899–902, 1963.

Kimura, D. Neural mechanisms in manual signing. *Sign Language Studies* 33:291–312, 1981.

Kimura, D., R. Battison, and B. Lubert. Impairment of nonlinguistic hand movements in a deaf aphasic. *Brain and Language* 3:566–571, 1976.

Knox, C. and D. Kimura. Cerebral processing of non-verbal sounds in boys and girls. *Neuropsychologia* 8:227–237, 1970.

Kohn, B., and M. Dennis. Selective impairments of visuo-spatial abilities in infantile hemiplegics after right hemidecortication. *Neuropsychologia* 12:505–512, 1974.

Kolb, B., and A. J. Nonneman. Sparing of function in rats with early prefrontal cortex lesions. *Brain Research* 151:135–148, 1978.

Kolb, B., and I. Q. Whishaw. Neonatal frontal lesions in the rat: Sparing of learned but not species typical behavior in the presence of reduced brain weight and cortical thickness. *Journal of Comparative and Physiological Psychology* 95:863–879, 1981.

Krashen, S. D. Lateralization, language learning and the critical period: Some new evidence. *Language Learning* 23:63–74, 1973.

Kratz, K. E., P. D. Spear, and D. C. Smith. Postcritical-period reversal of effects of monocular deprivation on striate cortex cells in the cat. *Journal of Neurophysiology* 39:501–511, 1976.

Lawrence, D. G., and D. A. Hopkins. The development of motor control in the rhesus monkey: Evidence concerning the role of corticomotorneuronal connections. *Brain* 99:235–254, 1976.

Lenneberg, E. *Biological Foundations of Language.* New York: Wiley, 1967.

Lomas, J., and A. Kertesz. Patterns of spontaneous recovery in aphasic groups: A study of adult stroke patients. *Brain and Language* 5:388–401, 1978.

Marcel, T. and P. Rajan. Lateral specialization for recognition of words and faces in good and poor readers. *Neuropsychologia* 13:489–497, 1975.

McCarthy, G., 1963. Quoted in Krashen, 1973.

Michel, G. F. Right handedness: A consequence of infant supine head-orientation preference? *Science* 212:685–687, 1981.

Milner, B. Psychological aspects of focal epilepsy and its neurological management. *Advances in Neurology* 8:299–321, 1975.

Molfese, D. L., and V. J. Molfese. Cortical responses of preterm infants to phonetic and nonphonetic speech stimuli. *Developmental Psychology* 16:574–581, 1980.

Moscovitch, M. The development of lateralization of language functions and its relation to cognitive and linguistic development: A review and some theoretical speculations. In S. J. Segalowitz and F. A. Gruber, eds., *Language Development and Neurological Theory.* New York: Academic, 1977.

Netley, C. Dichotic listening of callosal agenesis and Turner's syndrome patients. In S. J. Segalowitz and F. A. Gruber, eds., *Language Development and Neurological Theory*. New York: Academic, 1977.

Neville, H. Electroencephalographic testing of cerebral specialization in normal and congenitally deaf children: A preliminary report In S. J. Segalowitz and F. A. Gruber, eds., *Language Development and Neurological Theory*. New York: Academic, 1977.

O'Shea, L., M. Saari, B. A. Pappas, R. Ings, and K. Stauge. Neonatal 6-hydroxydopamine attenuates the neural and behavioral effects of enriched rearing in the rat. *Society for Neuroscience: Abstracts* 9, 558, 1983.

Peters, M., and B. F. Petrie. Functional asymmetries in the stepping reflex of human neonates. *Canadian Journal of Psychology* 33:198–200, 1979.

Piaget, J. *Biology and Knowledge*. Chicago: The University of Chicago Press, 1971.

Ramón y Cajal, S. *Recollections of My Life. Memoirs of the American Philosophical Society,* vol. 8, 1937.

Rasmussen, T., and B. Milner. Clinical and surgical studies of the cerebral speech areas in man. In K. J. Zulch, O. Creutzfeldt, and G. C. Galbraith, eds., *Cerebral Localization*. Berlin and New York: Springer-Verlag, 1975.

Rasmussen, T., and B. Milner. The role of early left-brain injury in determining lateralization of cerebral speech functions. *Annals of the New York Academy of Sciences* 299:355–369, 1977.

Russell, R., and M. Espir. *Traumatic Aphasia*. Oxford: Oxford University Press, 1961.

Schneider, G. E. Early lesions of superior colliculus: Factors affecting the formation of abnormal retinal projections. *Brain Behavior and Evolution* 8:73–109, 1973.

Segalowitz, S. J., and F. A. Gruber, eds. *Language Development and Neurological Theory*. New York: Academic, 1977.

Sidman, R. L. Development of interneuronal connections in brains of mutant mice. In F. P. Carlson, ed., *Physiological and Biochemical Aspects of Nervous Integration*. Englewood Cliffs, N.J.: Prentice-Hall, 1968.

Singh, J. A. L., and R. M. Zingg. *Wolf Children and Feral Man*. New York: Harper, 1940.

Skeels, H. M. Adult status of children with contrasting early life experiences. *Monographs of the Society for Research in Child Development* 31:1–65, 1966.

Sutherland, R. J., B. Kolb, I. Q. Whishaw, and J. B. Becker. Cortical noradrenaline depletion eliminates sparing of spatial learning after neonatal frontal cortex damage in the rat. *Neuroscience Letters* 32:125–130, 1982.

Teuber, H.-L. Recovery of function after brain injury in man. In *Outcomes of Severe Damage to the Nervous System,* Ciba Foundation Symposium 34. Amsterdam: Elsevier-North Holland, 1975.

Turkowitz, G. The development of lateral differentiation in the human infant. In S. J. Dimond and D. A. Blizard, eds., *Evolution and Lateralization of the Brain. Annals of the New York Academy of Science* 299:213–221, 1977.

Wechsler, A. F. Crossed aphasia in an illiterate dextral. *Brain and Language* 3:164–172, 1976.

Witelson, S. F. Early hemisphere specialization and interhemispheric plasticity: An empirical and theoretical review. In S. J. Segalowitz and F. A. Gruber, eds., *Language Development and Neurological Theory*. New York: Academic, 1977.

Woods, B. T. and H.-L. Teuber. Early onset of complementary specialization of cerebral hemispheres in man. *Transactions of the American Neurological Association* 98:113–117, 1973.

25

RECOVERY OF FUNCTION

On the afternoon of June 16, 1783, Dr. Samuel Johnson, the famed English lexicographer, sat for his portrait in the studio of Miss Frances Reynolds, the sadly untalented sister of Sir Joshua Reynolds. Despite his 73 years and marked obesity, Johnson afterwards walked the considerable distance from the studio to his home. He went to sleep at his usual hour in the evening and awoke according to his account around 3 a.m. on June 17. To his surprise and horror, he found that he could not speak. He immediately tested his mental faculties by successfully composing a prayer in Latin verse. Next he tried to loosen his powers of speech by drinking some wine, violating his recently acquired habits of temperance. The wine only put him back to sleep. Upon reawakening after sunrise, Johnson still could not speak. He found, however, that he could understand others and that he could write. His penmanship and composition were somewhat defective. . . . Johnson proceeded to summon his physicians, Drs. Brocklesby and Heberden, who came and examined him. They prescribed blisters on each side of the throat up to the ear, one on the head, and one on the back, along with salts of hartshorn (ammonium carbonate). Heberden, who was one of London's leading doctors,

predicted a speedy recovery. His confidence proved quite justified: the therapeutic regimen was so efficacious that Johnson's speech began returning within a day or two. Recovery proceeded smoothly over the next month, and even the mild disorders in writing lessened. Johnson finally was left with a slight but stable dysarthria until he succumbed to other causes later in the next year. (Rosner, 1974, p. 1)

The case of Dr. Johnson has been described and discussed a number of times by different neuroscientists because he was a famous and interesting person and because his transitory illness is not fully explained and invites speculation. (The reader may try a diagnosis and then compare the result with that published by Critchley.) Obviously, his aphasia provides an example of almost complete loss of a rather specific function (he could still write) and seemingly rapid and almost complete recovery. The story also contains a testimony to the knowledge and insight of his doctors because their prediction with regard to outcome was correct. There are, however, many questions the critical reader may wish to ask. How much weight should self-testimony be accorded? Did he in fact have a stroke or any other brain disorder? We can believe that he might discover, when alone in the middle of the night, that he could not speak because he was known to have the habit of talking to himself. But, since he was an eccentric, we might also believe that the stroke was faked for one or another purpose. Given that his disorder was real, what was it and where was it? Some neurologists have thought that the lesion was very small or was only a transitory blood clot. Others, such as Critchley, have speculated that because he could not speak but could think, compose Latin verse, and write might be evidence that he had bilateral speech. This latter idea may be negated in view of Murray's hypothesis that Johnson had Tourette's syndrome, which is thought to involve a dysfunction of the right hemisphere. Even given that Johnson had had a stroke and that all the testimony concerning it was correct, it might still be asked whether his is a representative case of recovery.

Luria described a different case in his book *The Man with a Shattered World*. The book describes the condition of a former soldier, Lyova Saletsky, who received a fractured skull and accompanying brain damage from a bullet wound in the battle of Smolensk. The damage was centered in the posterior left hemisphere intersections of the occipital, temporal, and parietal cortex. Luria first saw Saletsky three months after the injury and then at three-week intervals for the next 26 years. During this time Saletsky painfully and slowly "relearned" the art of reading and writing. (It may have been a matter of relearning to use his remaining skill rather than relearning the skill per se.) In doing so he compiled a diary, in which he gives a moving account of his initial deficits, recovery, and residual problems. The following is an example of what Saletsky had to say about his condition.

I remember nothing, absolutely nothing! Just separate bits of information that I sense have to do with one field or another. But that's all! I have no real knowledge of any subject. My past has just been wiped out!

Before my injury I understood everything people said and had no trouble learning any of the sciences. Afterwards I forgot everything I learned about science. All my education was gone.

I know that I went to elementary school, graduated with honors from the middle school, completed three years of courses at the Tula Polytechnic Institute, did advanced work in chemistry, and before the war, finished all these requirements ahead of time. I remember that I was on the western front, was wounded in the head in 1943 when we tried to break through the Germans' defense in Smolensk, and that I've never been able to put my life together again. But I can't remember what I did or studied, the sciences I learned, subjects I took. I've forgotten everything. Although I studied German for six years, I can't remember a word of it, can't even recognize a single letter. I also remember that I studied English for three straight years at the Institute. But I don't know a word of that either now. I've forgotten these languages so completely I might just as well never have learned them. Words like *trigonometry, solid geometry, chemistry, algebra*, etc., come to mind, but I have no idea what they mean.

All I remember from my years in the secondary school are some words (like signboards, names of subjects): *physics, chemistry, astronomy, trigonometry, German, English, agriculture, music*, ect., which don't mean anything to me now. I just sense that somehow they're familiar.

When I hear words like *verb, pronoun, adverb*, they also seem familiar, though I can't understand them. Naturally, I knew these words before I was wounded, even though I can't understand them now. For example, I'll hear a word like *stop!* I know this word has to do with grammar—that it's a verb. But that's all I know. A minute later, I'm likely even to forget the word *verb*—it just disappears. I still can't remember or understand grammar or geometry because my memory's gone, part of my brain removed.

Sometimes I'll pick up a textbook on geometry, physics, or grammar but get disgusted and toss it aside, since I can't make any sense out of textbooks, even those from the middle school. What's more, my head aches so badly from trying to understand them, that one look is enough to make me nervous and irritable. An unbearable kind of fatigue and loathing for it all comes over me. (Luria, 1972, pp. 140–142)

To these two celebrated examples we could add many more, who like Johnson showed dramatic spontaneous recovery, or who like Saletsky showed amazing strength and perseverance in compensating for their disability. But unlike Johnson, many people show little or no recovery, as Kertesz has described to be the case for global aphasia caused by cerebrovascular accidents. Many other people show much less resiliance than Saletsky. Here are two examples of patients we have known. H.P. was an extremely intelligent teacher who after a left hemisphere stroke, which occurred in middle-age, suffered from what might best be described as Broca's aphasia. Despite showing almost daily signs of excellent recovery and frequent excellent good humor and insight he committed suicide within months of his stroke. Knowing H.P. we cannot help feeling that this was his reasoned solution to an infirmity that he could not accept. Nevertheless, feelings of depression are common after brain damage, and his act may have been pathological rather than reasoned and free. D.S. was an equally intelligent middle-aged man who worked in the theater industry but whose real pleasure was his hobby of carpentry. After a right hemisphere stroke he no longer showed an interest in theater, cinema, or even watching TV and he no longer displayed any interest or skill in carpentry. His family did not under-

stand this change and was unable to give him any support. He remains in a passive and dependent condition and gives no indication of trying to improve his lot. Finally, there are cases in which recovery simply does not occur, as is illustrated by the Quinlan's story of their daughter, Karen Ann Quinlan.

Twenty-one years after her birth, Karen Ann Quinlan was returned to the same hospital, St. Clare's, in a deep coma from which she never roused. After attending a birthday party the night of 14 April, 1975 and consuming a few gin and tonics, she slipped into unconsciousness. No one ever determined exactly why. She had been on a crash diet to slim down to a size 7 bikini and had not eaten all day. It would later be found that she also had taken a mild "therapeutic" amount of a tranquilizer, and aspirin. Whatever the cause, Karen Ann fell quickly into a coma and for a period of time—no one ever knew exactly how long—she stopped breathing. The resulting oxygen starvation caused the cognitive area of her brain to die. In the hospital, Karen Ann was fed by tubes inserted in her nostrils and her breathing was supported by a respirator. Her weight dropped from 120 pounds to 90, 80, and finally to 70. Her body gradually contracted to the fetal position and became rigid. By the end of July, Karen Ann's family, on the advice of their physicians, Morse and Javed, gave their permission to remove the respirator that was assumed to be keeping their daughter alive. However, the attorney for the hospital, Theodore Einhorn, informed the Quinlans that as Karen Ann was over 21 they were not her legal guardians and that they would have to be appointed by a judge as legal guardians before their request would be followed. The subsequent legal cases, in which the family was represented by Paul Armstrong, a Legal Aid Society attorney, attracted international interest. The central issue of the case was whether Joseph Quinlan could be named her legal guardian for the purpose of authorizing the discontinuance of all extraordinary means of sustaining her life, since no recovery was expected and since medical science could not help her. The case was lost in the initial trial but was eventually won before the Supreme Court of New Jersey. This was a landmark decision because it was the first right-to-die ruling ever made in legal history. Karen Ann was subsequently removed from the respirator and moved to a nursing home. However, she continued to breathe on her own and remains unchanged at the nursing home today.

These examples show that we can be both optimistic and pessimistic about the prospects for recovery from brain damage. What we know today tells us that recovery depends on the type, location, and extent of brain damage and also on the attitude of the person and the attitude and support of physicians, therapists, and family. Our knowledge of each of these variables as they apply to any one person is uncertain. This is best demonstrated with the results illustrated in Figure 25–1. The figure summarizes the consequences of a closed head injury to 1285 patients that was of sufficient severity to produce six hours of coma, during which no eye opening occurred, no recognizable words were uttered, and no commands were followed. What is interesting is the enormous variation in the prospects for recovery. Over 40 percent of the patients die, but among those who survive the majority make a reasonably good recovery. It is important to note, however, that among those in the good recovery group less than 50 percent can return to work and many of these may not regain complete job competency. As Finger and Stein point out, many people have an expectation that recovery will not occur and they consequently do not encourage rehabilitation. Others may be overly optimistic. In the following section we describe the processes of recovery, the cellular processes that take place after brain damage, present evidence about how each may result in behavioral change, and present information about the prospects for recovery of function. Finally, we present results from some new experimental approaches that are directed toward restoring function.

EXAMPLES OF THE PROCESS OF FUNCTIONAL RECOVERY

Recovery is seldom a sudden restitution of function, but rather is usually a slow change that follows a relatively predictable sequence. Examination of the stages of the sequence and their associated behaviors reveals an apparent reemergence of lower-level functions in succession. More normal behavior is manifest only in the last stage of the sequence. In Hughlings-Jackson's terms the lesion or trauma produces a complete deevolution of the behavior followed by reevolution. (As Teitelbaum and his coworkers have pointed out tellingly, recovery often parallels the sequential develop

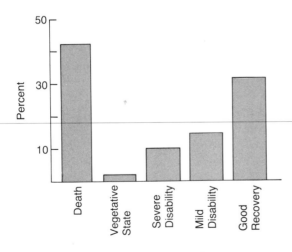

FIGURE 25–1. Recovery prospects from a closed head injury that produces six hours of coma. (After Levin, Benton, and Grossman, 1982.)

ment of the behavior in infants.) Several examples of such events are worth considering.

Recovery from Spinal Cord Section

Kuhn has given a detailed description of the effects of complete spinal cord transection in humans. He notes considerable variability in the extent to which spinal reflexes recover after cord section. Some people show virtually no recovery, and their muscles atrophy; others recover sufficiently that their legs will support their weight, and they show no muscle atrophy. For those who show pronounced recovery of spinal reflexes, Kuhn describes four major stages or steps in the process of recovery.

1. *Spinal shock.* Spinal shock is a state of profound depression of all reflexes below the level of section. Shock varies in severity from person to person and in duration, lasting from one to six weeks. Some reflexes, such as penile erection in males, may not be depressed at all. As stated above, for some few individuals there is no evidence of recovery beyond this stage.

2. *Minimal reflex activity.* In this stage slight flexion or extension of the foot, some toe twitches, and extension of the large toe occur. Anal and bladder reflexes for waste secretion may also be present.

3. *Flexor activity.* The first major reflexes to return are flexor reflexes, consisting of such movements as dorsiflexion of the big toe and fanning of the toe, dorsiflexion of the foot, and flexion of the leg and thigh. Stimuli found most effective in eliciting limb flexion were tactile, particularly effective were unpleasant stimuli, and the zones with the lowest thresholds were the foot area and the genital area.

4. *Extensor activity.* Extensor movements generally become apparent as early as six months after injury and continue to develop for years. They consist of extension and stiff-

ening of one or both legs; in some patients there is only a slight tightening of limbs, whereas in others the limbs assume pillarlike rigidity. In some people in the latter group this activity is sufficient to permit prolonged standing in warm water without support.

The most effective stimuli for eliciting extension were proprioceptive, such as stretching the flexors of the thigh muscles at the hip (as occurs during shifting from a sitting to a lying position) or squeezing the thigh muscles. Tactile stimulation became effective in eliciting extensor responses somewhat later, and the lowest thresholds were on the thigh or the back of the knee and spread distally to include the foot surface. It can be seen from this description that recovery from spinal cord section can be quite extensive. However, these people can make no voluntary movements and receive no sensation from below the area of the lesion.

Recovery from Hypothalamic Lesions

In 1951, Anand and Brobeck observed that lesions of the lateral hypothalamus of rats and cats produced **aphagia** (inability to eat or chew), which ultimately led to death. Teitelbaum and Stellar reported three years later that if the animals are artificially fed for a period of time, they recover the ability to eat. Analyzing this recovery process, Teitelbaum and Epstein found that feeding behavior recovered in an orderly sequence: first the animals ate only small amounts of wet food and maintained themselves on this diet, later they began to eat dry food, and eventually maintained themselves on dry food and water. Many workers have observed this sequence of recovery in many species of animals that have received hypothalamic and other types of brain lesions that affect feeding. Interestingly, this sequence of recovery bears close resemblance to the development of eating in young animals. Teitelbaum and others have thus argued that the process of recovery is analogous to the process of *encephalization:* ontogenetic development of behavior in the individual as successively higher levels of function mature.

In addition to their deficits in feeding, lateral hypothalamic lesioned animals display another behavioral abnormality that has been called *sensory neglect.* This phenomenon was first described by Marshall, Turner, and Teitelbaum, using a variety of simple but ingenious tests. Using Von Frey hairs, cotton swabs, and pins for testing tactile responsiveness, pieces of chocolate, Mennen shaving lotion, and ammonia for testing olfactory responsiveness, and various visual stimuli, they found that on the first day following the lesion the rats would only respond to stimuli if they were presented to the tip of the nose. Gradually, with recovery time, the area of the body to which the animal would orient increased, spreading from the tip of the nose to the front paws, to the rear paws, and finally to the back. There was a very close relation between the recovery of feeding and the recovery of sensory responsiveness to the snout and between the recovery of responsiveness to the body and the recovery of locomotion (see below).

The same technique of analyzing sequential behavioral changes has been extended to behaviors other than feeding. Numerous studies with many species of animals had suggested that large lesions of the posterior portions of the hypothalamus produce **somnolence** that leads eventually to death. In 1969, McGinty found that with care rats with such lesions would recover from the somnolence and eventually sleep less than normal rats. Analyzing the processes of recovery Robinson and Whishaw argued that the somnolence was due more to a loss of voluntary movement than to disruption of a sleep center. Sleep abated as movement recovered, and the residual impairment was an inability to initiate and maintain voluntary movement. More recently, Golani,

Wolgin, and Teitelbaum have supported this suggestion. To analyze the details of the recovery of movement, they used a version of the Eshkol-Wachman system of movement notation—originally developed for ballet choreography and analysis.

Figure 25–2 gives examples of sequential recovery of movement. Golani and his coworkers found that exploratory movements in the rat recover along several relatively independent dimensions that appear successively. During recovery the animal develops antigravity support, which allows it to stand and support its weight. The animal develops longitudinal movements that allow it to extend forward. The animal develops scans of the head in a forward and lateral direction, which progressively increases in amplitude over days until the animal can turn completely around as well as walk forward. Interestingly, each time the animal initiates walking it does so with the sequence of movements illustrated during recovery. These authors argue that the isolation of relatively independent dimensions of movement during recovery suggests the existence of corresponding neural systems. The development of movement in infant rats follows a similar sequence to that seen in recovery and also many of these components can be observed in the features of movements that are displayed each time a normal animal begins to move.

In the two examples given above the first effect of the lesion is manifest as an almost complete absence of eating or of certain kinds of movements. Both abilities recover, but do so in stages that appear to parallel behavioral development in infant animals. This parallelism suggests that recovery represents a sequential emergence of higher levels of function. Finally, if hypothalamic damage is not excessive, the animals recover a level of function that approximates normal. Many studies on animals with lesions indicate that if the initial

FIGURE 25–2. Recovery of (A) posture, (B) forward scanning, and (C) turning in a rat that had been given large posterior lateral hypothalamic lesions. Broken-line and solid-line drawings indicate the extreme positions that the rat assumes during each phase. Recovery occurs over time, in the sequence indicated by the Roman numerals. In each sequence recovery begins with the head and proceeds caudally. (After I. Golani, D. L. Wolgin, and P. Teitelbaum, A proposed natural geometry of recovery from akinesia in the lateral hypothalamic rat. *Brain Research,* 164:237–267, 1979. Reprinted with permission.)

lesions are small, the animals begin to recover at more advanced stages, but they nevertheless follow the same sequence. If the lesions are particularly large, recovery may be arrested short of completion.

Because it has been possible to develop clear descriptions of behavioral changes that follow lateral hypothalamic lesions, this preparation has become a favorite model for the study of recovery of function. A major recent thrust of research on recovery has been to investigate the biochemical changes that underlie recovery. Stricker and Zigmond have made a detailed study of the role that dopamine plays in this syndrome. The hypothalamic lesions do cut dopamine-containing fibers that are projecting to the basal ganglia, and the concomitant decrease in dopamine seems closely correlated with many of the symptoms of the lesions. Further evidence for this comes from studies in which dopamine is selectively depleted with the neurotoxin 6-hydroxydopamine. Following depletion, many of the symptoms peculiar to the lateral hypothalamic syndrome are induced. Some of the recovery that follows the lesions also seems to be attributable to recovery in dopamine systems. The changes that are postulated to underlie this recovery are illustrated in Figure 25–3 and include (1) increased firing in the remaining dopamine cells, (2) sprouting of the remaining dopamine cells so that they can fill in for cells that have been destroyed, (3) an increase in the number of dopamine receptors, permitting a more potent action of the remaining dopamine, (4) a decrease in the activity of cells that are normally antagonistic to dopamine, and (5) an increased release of dopamine from the remaining terminals. The range of changes that occur after the lesions is quite surprising, but they are also a testimony to the remarkable capacity of the brain to restore homeostasis, that is, its normal biochemical balance. Of course, dopamine decreases are not the only changes that follow hypothalamic lesions, but the research on dopamine changes provides a good model for studying changes in other neurochemical systems.

Recovery from Motor Cortex Damage

Twitchell has given a very detailed description of recovery from hemiplegia produced by thrombosis, embolism, or stroke of the middle cerebral artery. The recovery sequence closely parallels the development of reaching and the grasp response described by Twitchell in infants. Immediately following arterial occlusion there was onset of hemiplegia marked by complete flaccidity of the muscles and loss of all reflexes and voluntary movements. Recovery

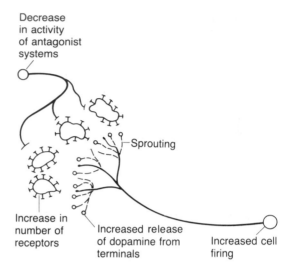

FIGURE 25–3. Hypothetical changes in dopamine and allied systems that might underlie behavior recovery that takes place after the system has been damaged.

occurred over a period of days or weeks and followed a relatively orderly sequence in each patient. Some patients recovered relatively normal use of their limbs; for others, recovery was arrested at one or another stage. Complete recovery of use of the arms, when it occurred, appeared between 23 and 40 days after the lesion. Recovery occurred in the following sequence: (1) return of tendon and stretch reflexes, (2) development of rigidity, (3) grasping that was facilitated by, or occurred as part of, proprioception (that is, as part of postural reflexes of turning, righting, etc.), (4) development of voluntary grasping (this involved recovery of movement in the sequence of shoulder, elbow, wrist, and hand, first in the flexor musculature, then in the extensor musculature), (5) facilitation of grasping by tactual stimulation of the hand, and, finally, (6) grasping that occurred predominantly under voluntary control. Voluntary grasping continued to improve until independent movements of the fingers were well developed. About 30 percent of patients reached the last stage of recovery; the others showed arrested recovery at one of the preceding stages.

In these patients, loss of function was initially profound, and in many cases it resulted in complete suppression of all reflexes, including spinal reflexes, so that the muscles were left completely flaccid. The sequential recovery can be thought of as involving first the return of spinal-tendon and stretch reflexes, then rigidity and proprioceptive facilitation from the midbrain, then tactile facilitation from the forebrain, and finally the return of voluntary control. The actual degree of recovery was no doubt determined by the extent of cortical damage. Some patients who never went through the latter stages probably had the most severe cortical damage.

Recovery from Aphasia

Kertesz has recently reviewed the prospects of recovery from aphasia with examples of his own case histories. An example of recovery from each of his different patient subgroups is shown in Figure 25–4. All of the patients received the Western Aphasia Battery, which assesses spontaneous speech content, fluency, comprehension, repetition, etc., from which an aphasia quotient was derived. Kertesz makes the following generalizations from this work. (1) Posttraumatic (head injury) patients showed the most rapid, and often almost complete, recovery, whereas recovery in stroke patients was less pronounced and in some groups may be almost absent. (2) Initial deficits in anomic patients were the least severe and initial deficits in global aphasics were the most severe, with intermediate severity occurring for other groups. The actual rate of recovery, given initial impairments, was often quite

similar in all groups. (3) There was a tendency, when recovery occurred, that the patient progressed to one of the other stages, but recovery usually stopped with anomic aphasia. (4) Most recovery occurred in the first three months (not illustrated in Figure 25–4), with some recovery occurring in the next six months and less recovery occurring in the following six months. Thereafter little or no recovery occurred. (5) There was some evidence that younger patients showed better recovery, and the effects of intelligence, occupation, and sex in these patients were slight if present. (6) The language components that were the most resistant to brain damage were naming, oral imitation, comprehension of nouns, and yes-no responses, functions that may be partly mediated by the right hemisphere. Kertesz's analysis of

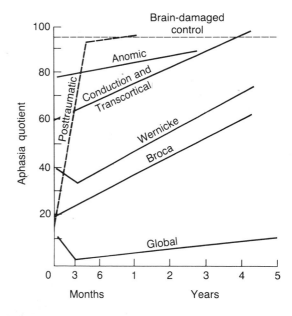

FIGURE 25–4. Initial deficits and recovery in stroke patients with different language disorders (solid lines) and a posttrauma patient (dotted line). Each line is a representative patient. (After Kertesz, 1979.)

aphasia is not based on the linguistic properties of language, but unquestionably such analysis is necessary. It may also be worthwhile to introduce a word of caution with respect to the sequences of recovery. Basso, Capitani, and Zanobio note that patients who are fluent (Wernicke's) do not turn into nonfluent (Broca's) aphasics. This is understandable because the lesion locations for each type are thought to be distinct.

Recovery from Amnesia

There are many reports of the loss of memory and its subsequent recovery following brain lesions or concussions. There is some difference in opinion on the sequence of events during recovery. Barbizet reports a case that illustrates one point of view, or possibly one type of syndrome of recovery. A 40-year-old man suffered a head trauma and was in a coma for seven weeks. Five months after the trauma he was completely amnesic for the two preceding years and had gross memory disturbances for events back to early childhood. Eight months after trauma the period of complete amnesia had shrunk to one year, and the period of partial amnesia extended back to the age of four. Sixteen months after trauma his amnesia was limited to the two-week period before trauma. Thus, his recovery represented a progressive shrinkage of the amnesia, from past to present.

Whitty and Zangwill report a somewhat different pattern of recovery following less severe head injury. They report that as a rule retrograde amnesias are very short, usually of a few seconds' duration. If they are longer, the shrinkage of amnesia may not be strictly chronological. Sometimes more recent events are recalled first and then serve as a magnet for piecing together a continuous memory.

Despite the difference of opinion (a not uncommon event in areas of memory research,

and one that may be attributable to differences in type of damage, location, etc.), both of the above reports present a period of complete amnesia, a period of recovery either of time or events, and a period of residual deficit. The nature of the deficit and the processes of recovery seem reminiscent of those we have just described for other types of deficits; that is, a sequential recovery from diaschisis with some residual deficit. The parallel between the recovery of memory and the recovery from aphagia, paralysis, etc., suggests that recovery from all types of brain trauma involves some common processes.

Descriptions of recovery as a sequential development have obvious practical and theoretical utility. From a practical perspective good sequential descriptions allow any patient to be monitored for rate and degree of recovery. If recovery is arrested before completion, residual abilities can be understood within the context of the recovery stage reached. Theoretically, stages of recovery provide insights into the brain's organization and provide background information for enhancing recovery or for overcoming residual deficits.

Summary

Recovery follows some kinds of brain damage. It may involve recovery in the remaining portions of an incompletely damaged neural system or recovery from the suppression of function within a system. An interesting feature of recovery is that it can be gradual and orderly and proceed in what appears to be stages. In some ways these stages seem to parallel the well-known rostral-caudal and proximal-distal ontological development of the body and of behavior. The recapitulation of development as seen in recovery from spinal shock or motor cortex damage in humans or feeding and walking in the rat is remarkable but can also be used as a diagnostic indication of how recovery is proceeding. It is not clear that cognitive functions show the same orderly sequence of recovery, but speech sometimes recovers in a sequence of global to anomic aphasia and memory sometimes returns in a past-present sequence. More knowledge about how cognitive functions recover may depend on progress in analyzing their normal structure.

CELLULAR EVENTS ASSOCIATED WITH BRAIN DAMAGE

Brain damage produces a number of short, intermediate, and long-term changes in brain tissue in addition to the actual loss of tissue caused by the initial insult. Precisely what changes occur will depend on the type of brain damage, and so, for simplicity, the following descriptions derive from the changes that follow brain lesions. Terms associated with these processes are defined in Table 25–1.

Changes at the Site of Damage

A lesion made either by a puncture wound or ablation leaves a vacuole or cavity of variable size. Due to degeneration of surrounding tissue, accumulation of fluid, and shrinkage of surrounding tissue the cavity may expand in size for about a week and then begin to constrict. With time it may completely disappear and thus may not be visible on CAT scans. The shrinkage of the cavity may cause distortions of surrounding tissue such that the ventricles expand to compensate for the loss in tissue volume. Ventricular expansion may be visible on CAT scans and provide a clue that damage has been incurred. Within about an hour after damage dead tissue surrounds the cavity, and surrounding this area of **necrosis** is an area of tissue consisting of injured, dead, and normal

cells. Within 24 hours phagocytes (astrocytes and microglia) infiltrate the area to remove debris. By three to seven days new capillaries proliferate in the area. These processes may continue for several months until the debris is removed and only the glial cells remain. Inspection of stained tissue may show many small, dark glial cells filling the area, a process called **gliosis,** and among these the astrocytes form a scar in the area. The scar may hamper or block any functional regeneration of remaining neural cells.

Changes Distal to the Site of Damage

Damage in one area not only kills local cells but may cut the fibers of cells located at a distance and also produce changes in cells that previously innervated the region or were innervated by it. These changes may involve the breakdown or death of the tissue, a process called *degeneration*. There are a number of kinds of degeneration, which seem to involve different processes. The location of and the terms for some of these processes are illustrated in Figure 24–5.

When a nerve is severed, the portion distal to the cut always degenerates. This fact was first noted by Waller in the early 1850s and is so certain that its occurrence is thought to constitute the only law of neuroanatomy. Such degeneration is called **Wallerian** or **anterograde degeneration.** The process of Wallerian degeneration in the central nervous system is different in part from what occurs in the peripheral nervous system. Centrally, the axons degenerate, as does the myelin that wraps around them, and there is little or no regeneration. The damage can be visualized in the following way. Normal myelin can be stained dark blue by certain stains (e.g., the Weigert method). In the absence of myelin, portions of the brain where the axons had been take up no

TABLE 25–1

Compensatory mechanisms that may follow brain damage

Term	Definition
Behavioral compensation	Use of a new or different behavioral strategy to compensate for a behavior lost due to brain damage, e.g., notetaking to compensate for loss of memory.
Collateral sprouting	The growth of collaterals of axons to replace lost axons or to innervate targets that have lost other afferents.
Denervation supersensitivity	The proliferation of receptors on a nerve or muscle when innervation is interrupted that results in an increase in response when residual afferents are stimulated or when chemical agonists are applied.
Disinhibition	Removal of inhibitory actions of a system usually by destroying it or blocking its action pharmacologically.
Nerve growth factor	A protein that may be secreted by glial cells that promotes growth in damaged neurons and facilitates regeneration and reinnervation by cut axons.
Regeneration	Process by which damaged neurons, axons, or terminals regrow and establish their previous connections.
Rerouting	Process by which axons or their collaterals seek out new targets when their normal destination has been removed.
Silent synapses	A hypothetical synapse that is thought to be present but whose function is not behaviorally evident until the function of some other part of the system is disrupted.
Sparing	A concept that refers to a process that allows certain behaviors or aspects of behavior to survive brain damage.
Sprouting	Growth of nerve fibers to innervate new targets, particularly if they have been vacated by other terminals.
Substitution	The idea that an unoccupied or underused area of the brain will assume functions of a damaged area (not in vogue today).
Transient collaterals	Collaterals that at some time during development innervated targets that they subsequently abandon as development proceeds.
Vicariation	A version of substitution theory that suggests that the functions of damaged areas can be assumed by adjacent areas. The term is unlikely to catch on.

stain and so leave a negative image of the route that had been taken by the axon. In the peripheral nervous system the process is different in that some regeneration occurs. The Schwann cells that form the myelin do not all die, and they subsequently multiply and form a bridge that regenerating fibers can cross to reinnervate their target. Reinnervation may not occur in the central nervous system because the oligodendrites that form its myelin do not proliferate and also because scarring may block regrowth. The end feet of cut axons also change, becoming dense and small. This reaction occurs within a day or two and the material may be visible for months if certain stains (e.g., Fink-Heimer) are used. The degenera-

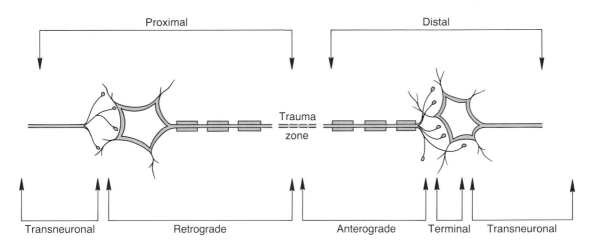

FIGURE 25–5. The spatial terminology for cell and fiber degeneration. (After Beresford, 1965.)

tion of the end feet is called **terminal degeneration** and, as is noted elsewhere, it is employed as a useful sign of the destination of different neural systems.

The proximal portions of the axon and the cell body may not always degenerate, but if they do, the process is called **retrograde degeneration.** In the cell body the Nissl substance disappears, the nucleus is displaced to the periphery of the cell, and the cell may swell to double its normal size. For some neurons (e.g., motor neurons) retrograde degeneration is reversible, whereas in others (e.g., thalamic neurons) it is not. In the former case the cells return to normal size, but in the latter they shrink and are removed by phagocytosis. Retrograde degeneration can be detected because the absence of Nissl substance makes the cell colorless, a process called *chromatolysis,* and this can be detected by the negative image the cells leave because they have lost their affinity for Nissl stains.

Cells that innervate or are innervated by a degenerating neuron may also die, a process called *transneuronal degeneration.* This process was first observed in the visual system. When the optic nerve is cut, cells of the lateral geniculate body completely degenerate. It is thought that the cells degenerate either because they require an optimal level of stimulation from the optic nerve to survive or because some necessary trophic substance is supplied by its end feet. (A similar type of process appears to occur in muscles because when their nerves are cut, they shrink and waste away.) Transneuronal degeneration may occur across more than one synapse; for example, cells in the visual cortex may also begin to die after the lateral geniculate body degenerates. Transneuronal degeneration may also occur in the opposite direction, in the cells of innervation. The former process is referred to as anterograde and the latter as retrograde transneuronal degeneration. Transneuronal degeneration may also be associated with accumulating deposits of calcium, a process called *calcification.* For example, in response to neocortex damage calcification may occur in degenerating thalamic neurons (also a site of retrograde degeneration) and in the basal ganglia (a possible site of secondary transneuronal degeneration). These deposits can be so pronounced that they are easily seen in histological material or with CAT scans. The reasons for calcification and the way that it occurs are not known, but its presence in CAT scans can be taken as an indication of certain kinds of cortical or subcortical damage.

The occurrence of these different degenerative processes provides evidence relevant to a number of issues that the reader might wish to consider. First, the fact that degenerative changes occur in so many places and in so many ways makes it impossible to state that even the most refined lesion can be localized. For example, a small ablation in the frontal cortex may be easily visualized and may appear to be localized, but retrograde degeneration and calcification will occur in the thalamus, secondary transneuronal degeneration and calcification will appear in the basal ganglia, and Wallerian and terminal degeneration will appear throughout the neocortex, brainstem and spinal cord, etc. Clearly, brain damage cannot be strictly localized. Second, it is important to note that degeneration has been a key not only to understanding brain damage but also to understanding how the different parts of the brain are connected with one another. Schoenfeld and Hamilton have argued that a thorough analysis of these changes should be a part of the proper assessment of all types of brain damage. Third, many of these degenerative changes are known to continue for years, but as yet we have no idea how they are associated with changes in behavior. Fourth, degeneration may be different if brain damage occurs in infancy (see Chapter 24).

PHYSIOLOGICAL EVENTS ASSOCIATED WITH BRAIN DAMAGE

One of the earliest theories of recovery of function was formulated by Munk in 1881. He suggested that regions of the brain that were not otherwise occupied could assume functions previously mediated by the injured area. The area substituting for the damaged one would ordinarily not have become involved in mediating the function in question. However, there is little evidence that any portions of the brain are standing by unused until required. Subsequent proposals variously suggested that recovery occurs through regrowth, compensation by surrounding areas, removal of inhibition from surrounding areas, etc. Munk's and some subsequent proposals failed to recognize that the initial deficits may not have been entirely due to focal damage.

Von Monakow recognized another factor. In 1911 he formulated the concept that he called **diaschisis** (from the Greek, meaning to split in two or to split apart): after a brain injury not only is neural tissue and its function lost, but several neural areas related to the damaged area are also depressed and their function is consequently absent for a period of time. In von Monakow's words:

> What characterizes all kinds of shock is a temporary cessation of function which affects a wide expanse of physiologically built up functions, and a restitution which goes on in well defined phases, sometimes shorter, sometimes longer, sometimes even retrospectively in the shape of fragments of functions in retrograde amnesias. The diaschisis proper has its point of attack beyond the limits of anatomically disturbed tissue in those parts of the grey substance which are connected with the focus by fibers. (von Monakow, 1911, p. 241)

The term diaschisis has been described by some as peculiar at best and horrible at worst, because what neural changes are to be encompassed within its meaning have never been precisely specified. Von Monakow meant that some aspects of recovery could be attributed to reemergence of function of the depressed zones rather than to plasticity, rewiring, sprouting of remaining fibers, or other neural changes that might be occurring at the same time. In the absence of any proper neural correlate for diaschisis some people have equated the term with shock. Certainly, shock is easier to pronounce and spell than diaschisis, although it implies an overall suspension of function rather than a splitting of function. Rather than debate the merits of the terms, we shall accept both here and describe some examples of neural and other changes that contribute to some of the immediate deficits that follow brain damage.

1. **Shock.** Marshall Hall in 1841 recognized that damage to the spinal cord resulted in a temporary loss of spinal reflexes, a phenomenon that became known as spinal shock. Sherrington in the early 1900s demonstrated that the shock was caused by depriving the spinal cord of its connections from the brain. Cutting the cord or transecting it with the local anesthetic procaine produced shock, but recutting it after reflexes had recovered did not reinstate shock. The duration of shock seems related to the amount of input that the spinal cord receives, as can be inferred from two sets of data. Shock lasts for days in humans, a number of hours in cats, and is almost absent in frogs, suggesting a relation between the number of descending fibers and shock duration. Shock also has a shorter duration if only some of the input to the spinal cord is interrupted or if it is interrupted in a number of stages. The details of how removal of input produces shock are not fully understood. It is hypothesized that spinal cells have an optimal resting excitation that is maintained in part by the release of neural transmitter substances from descending fibers. When this tonic influence is lost, the cells are depressed and return to normal resting excitability only gradually. Support for this idea comes from

work by Grillner in cats. He found that pharmacological agents that stimulated spinal cord noradrenaline receptors could arrest spinal shock. The understanding of spinal shock has played an important role in the therapy of people who have received spinal injury. Before World War I it was believed that reflexes were permanently abolished. In 1917 Head and Riddoch showed that if infections were controlled, patients could be maintained indefinitely and that reflexes began to return within two to three weeks. By analogy, the principle of spinal shock can be generalized to other parts of the brain with the assumption that cells everywhere will show temporary depression when their input is removed. Indeed, as noted above, some die when deafferentated.

2. **Edema.** Edema (from the Greek for swelling), or swelling of tissue following trauma, occurs in the area surrounding the lesion but may, through pressure and other mechanisms, affect distant areas. In general, interstitial (between cell) tissue is like a collapsed balloon with respect to fluid, and in the brain it contains less fluid than other tissue. Due to either increased capillary pressure, changes in constituency of capillary fluid, or increased porosity of the capillaries, fluid flows into or accumulates in the interstitial space, causing it to balloon. The ensuing pressure likely depresses neuronal function. Edema, as well as many other posttraumatic symptoms, can be lessened by cortisone. (It has been suggested that excessive use of cortisone so effectively suppresses symptoms that patients may walk directly to the morgue. Clearly, it is difficult to balance the ameliorative effects of symptom suppression against the ameliorative actions of the body's own restorative functions.) Some posttraumatic deficits may be caused by edema. The drop in IQ that occurs after cortical surgery for the treatment of epilepsy, as reported by Milner, is shown in Figure 25–6. Immediately after surgery, IQ, irrespective of

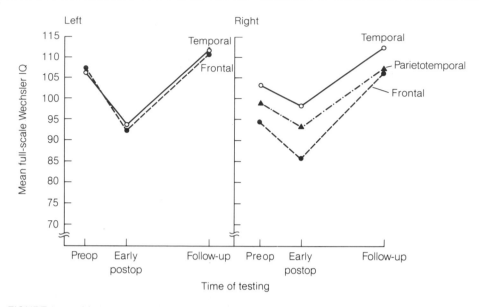

FIGURE 25–6. Mean preoperative, early postoperative, and long-term follow-up Wechsler IQ rating for 51 patients (38 male, 13 female) classed according to side and site of the cortical excisions carried out to relieve epilepsy. Number of cases: left temporal, 19; left frontal, 6; right temporal, 13; right frontal, 6; right parietotemporal, 7. (From B. Milner, Psychological aspects of focal epilepsy and its neurosurgical management. In D. P. Purpura, J. K. Penry, and R. D. Walker, eds., *Advances in Neurology*, vol. 8. New York: Raven Press. Copyright © 1975. Reprinted with permission.)

the lesion location (temporal, frontal, parietal), drops and then returns to preoperative levels within a year. The initial drop may be due in part to edema, because it is lessened by treatment with cortisone.

3. Blood Flow. The amount or rate of blood flow through the arteries of the brain can be used as a measure of its metabolic activity. It is thought that blood flow is controlled by CO_2 that is released by tissue metabolic activity; accordingly, if activity is high, then CO_2 release will be high, which will in turn increase blood flow. Blood flow can be measured by placing special detectors on the skull, which measure the flow of a radioactive inert gas that has been injected into the carotid artery. The more blood that flows, the higher the radioactivity count. Using this technique with brain-damaged patients, Skinhøj was able to show an immediate reduction in blood flow after injury

had occurred, and Meyer and his coworkers were able to detect a reduction in blood flow for as long as a month after injury, even in the intact hemisphere. It is thought that when tissue is damaged, its metabolic activity drops, causing a decrease in the release of CO_2 and a concomitant reduction in blood flow. Presumably, distant neural areas show decreased activity because they lose contacts with the damaged area and reflect this by decreased metabolic activity, decreased CO_2 release, and reduced blood flow. Clearly, these events conspire to reduce overall brain activity, which will in turn be reflected in a lowering of behavioral function.

4. Neurotransmitter Release. The levels of many brain neurotransmitters are known to change after brain damage, but these neurotransmitters have not been exhaustively examined nor have their changes been correlated with behavioral changes. Here we will give only one example of the types of correlations that are being attempted. In an animal model of human stroke, Robinson and his coworkers have cut the middle cerebral artery on one side of the rat brain and measured brain catecholamines (noradrenaline and dopamine) in various locations. They found reduced levels of these transmitters in many brain areas five days later, with recovery, and even overcompensation, occurring three weeks later. Robinson, influenced by the catecholamine hypothesis of mental illness, proposes that both the physical and the behavioral apathy that follows strokes may be caused in part by the decline in catecholamine levels. Obviously, this is an intuitively appealing hypothesis. We may note, however, that this hypothesis depends on the correctness of this explanation of mental illness and that it also does not exclude other possible behavioral-transmitter relations. Hassler and his coworkers are now reporting many complex changes in the concentrations of transmitters and other chemicals after brain damage.

5. Glucose Uptake. The Sokoloff technique of deoxyglucose labeling has been used by Pappius to evaluate changes in the brain after trauma. The technique involves injecting [^{14}C]-labeled deoxyglucose into the circulatory system. The deoxyglucose has many of the same biochemical properties of glucose, and it is mistaken for glucose by energy-requiring active brain cells and so crosses the blood-brain barrier to enter brain cells as an energy source. Unlike glucose, its metabolism is relatively incomplete, and because it is unable to pass back out of the cells, it accumulates in them for a period of time. If the brain is removed and cut about an hour after injection and placed on a film negative, the film will receive the most intense exposure from the [^{14}C] in areas that had high glucose utilization. Pappius, realizing that brain metabolism and function are closely coupled, damaged the

neocortex of rats and then measured glucose uptake over a number of days. In the neocortex ipsilateral to the lesion glucose utilization fell by over 60 percent three days after the injury and did not return to normal until five days after it. Metabolism also fell by nearly 25 percent in the undamaged hemisphere. When rats were treated with steroids before, or just after, brain damage, the decline in metabolic activity was only about 20 percent in the damaged hemisphere and about 10 percent in the undamaged hemisphere. Pappius was able to show that the decline in metabolic activity was not due entirely to edema and so must be caused by some as yet unknown process. These results provide another explanation for the behavioral depression that follows brain damage.

6. Changes in Electrical Activity. Changes in the electrical activity of neurons may, of course, reflect any or all of the physiological events mentioned above. Nevertheless, electrical activity does change following brain damage, and it can be used as an index of posttraumatic function. Glassman has observed transient suppression of sensory-evoked potentials and reduction in fast EEG activity near areas of damage in the cat neocortex, and such changes also occur in humans. It is also well known that brainstem damage produces many changes in forebrain EEG activity, at least in part because the damage cuts ascending fibers of systems that are responsible for producing forebrain EEG activity. In an illustrative study Kolb and Whishaw made lesions in a large number of brainstem locations and observed that forebrain EEG activity that depends on noncholinergic systems could be transiently abolished by certain types of brain damage. In many cases recovery in these noncholinergic systems was very gradual, lasting for two or more weeks. In a study of single-cell activity Barnes, Joynt, and Schottelius observed that motor neurons in the spinal cord became transiently hyperpolarized (more difficult to fire) after the spinal cord was transiently disconnected with a cold block. Although this explains loss of reflex activity, it does not explain whether hyperpolarization is due to withdrawal of excitation from the brain orto the imposition of inhibition from residual circuitry.

Summary. These examples of brain changes following trauma illustrate that there is not one physiological event that can be unequivocally related to the depression of function that follows brain damage. Rather, there seems to be a series of parallel changes, which together account for alterations in behavior. It is likely that immediate declines in postinjury function have an adaptive function—that of partially immobilizing the person so that restorative processes can proceed. As intuitively sensible as this proposal seems to be, however, at least one rather provocative study suggests that it should not be uncritically accepted. Feeney, Gonzales, and Law trained rats to walk on a narrow beam and then subjected them to unilateral neocortex damage. After damage, they measured the number of times the rats failed to correctly place their contralateral paws when walking on the beam. Relatively normal walking was usually restored by about 30 days postinjury. If the rats were treated with amphetamine (a catecholamine stimulant that produces locomotion in rats), they recovered within about seven days. If they were treated with haloperidol (a dopaminergic antagonist that blocks locomotion) or restrained, recovery was profoundly slowed. These results, which have substantial indirect support in the literature, are interpreted by Feeney and coworkers as a demonstration that rehabilitation should involve almost immediate drug and behavioral therapy, rather than restraint. In conclusion, we again point out that we have not identified any single mechanism as accounting for what could be called diaschisis. But the reader may wish to refer to a lively exchange between West and his coworkers and Markowitsch and Pritzel concerning attempts to obtain a definition of diaschisis at the cellular level.

POSSIBLE MECHANISMS RESPONSIBLE FOR RECOVERY

So far we have considered mechanisms thought to produce shock and recovery from shock, but a substantial portion of overall recovery is thought to involve reorganization of remaining undamaged tissue, or else reorganization of tissue around the area of the lesion. Flourens first propounded the latter idea, but Lashley brought it to prominence in the first half of this century.

Lashley believed that recovery of function was not only expected but was relatively easy to explain since the brain worked on the principles of mass action (the entire cortex participates in each function) and equipotentiality (each area of the cortex is equally able to assume control of any given behavior). Although Lashley's original position was extreme, he moderated it, applying the notions of mass action and equipotentiality only to functional areas. The following experiment illustrates the type of evidence that Lashley brought forth in support of his position. He electrically stimulated the area of the precentral gyrus of rhesus monkeys on four separate occasions over a period of 18 days. On each test he obtained relatively constant responses from each site stimulated, and on different tests he found that arm and leg areas, etc., remained relatively fixed. However, within any one area stimulation of the same point on different tests resulted in widely different movements, and at different times the same movement was obtained from separate and shifting areas. These results suggested to Lashley that "within the segmental areas the various parts of the cortex may be equipotential for the production of all of the movements within that area" (Lashley, 1929, p. 154).

Subsequent work has given Lashley's conclusion little support, because use of more refined techniques to perform the same experiments did not confirm his results. Doty and his coworkers repeatedly stimulated the motor cortex of dogs and found that the movements obtained from a given site are amazingly constant over long periods of time. Craggs and Rushton implanted an array of electrodes into the cortex of a baboon and found remarkable stability of response with repeated stimulation. In Lashley's experiments the surgical procedures were repeated on each test, whereas in Doty's and in Craggs and Rushton's the animals were chronically implanted so that after initial surgery the electrodes were fixed and no further surgical trauma occurred. It seems likely that Lashley's results can be attributed in part to trauma (tissue edema, etc.), and in part to slight differences in the placement of his electrodes. Certainly it is now accepted that Doty's findings on what is called the *stability of points* negate the belief that recovery occurs because of equipotentiality alone.

Strictly speaking, equipotentiality means that every subarea of a region is involved in mediating a given function. Although as shown above there is little evidence to support such a strict view, there is evidence that under certain circumstances equipotentiality, if more flexibly defined, is realized. In this view an area may play no role in the control of a particular behavior until a lesion occurs, at which point reorganization takes place, giving other areas, particularly adjacent ones, some part of the damaged area's function. The experiments of Glees and Cole support just such a hypothesis. They identified the thumb area of the monkey neocortex with electrical stimulation, removed the area, and then remapped the surrounding tissue after a period of recovery. During recovery the animals began to use the thumb, and when the cortex was remapped, the areas surrounding the lesion were found to produce thumb movements.

A modified equipotentiality interpretation may explain the recovery in the following case reported by Bucy, Keplinger, and Siqueira. They studied a man with a pyramidal tract sectioned in the lower brainstem as a treatment for involuntary movements. During the first 24 hours after surgery he had complete flaccid hemiplegia, followed by slight return of voluntary movement in his extremities. By the 10th day he was able to stand alone and walk with assistance. By the 24th day he could walk with a walker, and by the 29th day he could walk unaided. Within seven months maximum recovery seemed to have been reached, and he could move his feet, hands, fingers, and toes with only slight impairment. At autopsy, two and a half years later, about 17 percent of his pyramidal tract fibers were found to be intact. The recovery in his ability to move his toes and fingers seems attributable to that remaining 17 percent, doing the job previously done by the entire tract. This suggests that the system displays substantial equipotentiality. Lawrence and Kuyper's experiments with pyramidal tract lesions in rhesus monkeys might be interpreted as supporting this conclusion. They found that a few remaining pyramidal tract fibers could support relatively independent finger movements, apparently irrespective of the location of the fibers. If all the fibers were removed, there was no recovery of finger movement.

If it is accepted that functional areas have the ability to compensate for damage, how does this occur? Several neural mechanisms have been suggested as important in mediating such recovery, including (1) regeneration, (2) sprouting, (3) denervation supersensitivity, and (4) disinhibition or release of potential compensatory zones from inhibition. Associated with these mechanisms are several possible ways of facilitating the processes of recovery. In attempts to account for recovery a number of terms have become popular; some of the commonest of these are defined in Table 25–2.

Regeneration

Regeneration is a process by which neurons damaged by trauma regrow connections to the area they previously innervated. Regeneration is a well-known and common occurrence in the peripheral nervous system, where both sensory and motor neurons send forth new fibers to reinnervate their previous targets (Figure 25–7). It is believed that Schwann cells, the cells that provide myelin on peripheral fibers, multiply and provide a tube or tunnel that guides the regenerating fibers to their appropriate destination.

The stimulus to search for and promote regeneration in the mammalian brain comes in large part from studies on amphibians. They display almost complete regeneration of nervous system elements after brain damage. Studies by Sperry and others have shown that regenerating axons can circumvent scarring and form topographically correct connections that reestablish normal behavior. Given that this occurs in amphibians, it is thought that the same regeneration could be promoted in the mammalian brain if only the mechanisms of regeneration in the amphibian brain were understood.

There have been a number of attempts to devise ways of facilitating regeneration. One is the use of a substance called *nerve-growth factor*

TABLE 25–2

Degenerative events following brain damage	
Term	Definition
Anterograde degeneration	Also called orthograde or Wallerian degeneration. The certain degeneration of an axon after it has been cut from the cell body.
Astrocyte activity	Astrocytes invade areas of damage to remove debris and through attachments made by their many processes seal or scar the area.
Calcification	Accumulation of large deposits of calcium at some locations where neural degeneration takes place. Deposits can be seen on brain scans.
Chromatolyses	Literally, color dissolution. After injury, fatigue, or exhaustion, cell Nissl substance breaks down. Loss of Nissl and affinity for stain makes the cell colorless to microscopic examination.
Gliosis	Replacement of cell bodies by glial cells in areas undergoing degeneration.
Necrosis	Localized death of individual cells or groups of cells.
Phagocytosis	Removal of dead cells by mitochondria and astrocytes.
Retrograde degeneration	The death of the remaining axon, cell body, and dendrites after the axon is cut. The process may be reversible before it is complete.
Terminal degeneration	The shrinkage and degeneration of terminals after the axon is cut from the cell body.
Transneuronal degeneration	The death of neurons that innervate or are innervated by a damaged or destroyed neuron.

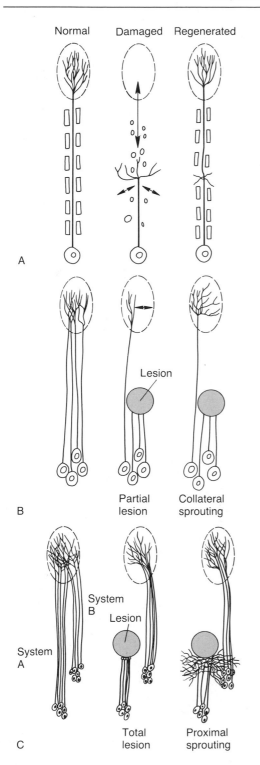

Normal   Damaged   Regenerated

A

Lesion

Partial   Collateral
lesion   sprouting

B

System
B
Lesion

System
A

System
B

Total   Proximal
lesion   sprouting

C

(NGF), a high-molecular-weight protein that is either produced or taken up from glia by nerve terminals and then transported to the cell body to play some role in maintaining normal growth or the health of a cell. There have been a number of attempts to determine whether injection of NGF into lesioned areas promotes functional regeneration, but as yet there has been no conclusive evidence that it does so.

Two approaches have been formulated for developing ways of helping regeneration fibers to bridge areas of scarring. One is to build artificial tubes or bridges across the area of scarring; the second is to place relatively undifferentiated neural tissue in the lesion to provide a medium through which regenerating fibers can grow. Kromer, Björklund, and Stenevi have reported some success with this technique. They sectioned the cholinergic pathway, which innervates the septum from the hippocampus, transplanted embryonic brain tissue into the gap, and found that regenerating cholinergic fibers grew through the bridge to reinnervate the hippocampus in what appeared to be a normal fashion. A particularly interesting feature of these results is that the embryonic tissue, in addition to providing a bridge, stimulates the damaged system to regenerate. These experiments appear to provide one of the most promising avenues for developing ways of stimulating functional regeneration.

FIGURE 25–7. Three models of axonal sprouting by which lesioned central axons might reestablish functional connections. A. True regeneration of severed axons involving regrowth of the axon back to its target site. Present in the peripheral nervous system and in invertebrates and in central nervous system of rats under favorable conditions. B. Collateral sprouting in intact neurons. Known to occur and be functional in the brain catecholamine and serotonin fibers. C. Reinnervation of systems that have been disconnected, as yet a hypothetical explanation of recovery. (After Björklund, 1979).

Sprouting

Some early studies on the effect of sectioning some of the afferent fibers to muscles suggested that the remaining fibers sprouted branches that occupied the sites left vacant by the lesioned axons. Convincing evidence now shows that similar sprouting takes place in the brain after lesions (Figure 25–7 B). Lynch and his coworkers and others have examined the rate at which sprouting occurs and have addressed the question of whether the newly formed connections are functional. Using the rat's hippocampus as their model they cut one of the inputs to the granule cells of the hippocampus. They then addressed the question of function by recording evoked potential from the denervated area. In addition, they examined the anatomical basis of regrowth by staining the hippocampus with chemicals that highlight the synaptic terminals of interest so that synaptic distribution could be assessed with the electron microscope. Their results show the following. (1) Remaining fibers send sprouts to reinnervate vacated portions of the granule cells. (2) Other fiber systems from adjacent portions of the cell sprout and reinnervate the unoccupied area. (3) Even fibers not connected with the cells grow and occupy a deserted space. The process of sprouting appears to be quite rapid and may be complete in seven to 10 days. Evoked potentials indicate that the new connections are electrophysiologically functional. Whether they are behaviorally functional is open to inquiry.

Another form of sprouting is shown in Figure 25–7 C. In this case the path of one of two interconnecting systems has been severed and so the remaining system has sent connections to interdigitate with the proximal portions of the severed axons. It is not known if such hypothetical connections are functional.

Denervation Supersensitivity

The idea of denervation supersensitivity arose from the work of Cannon and Rosenblueth in 1949. They found that when the afferent fibers to a muscle were cut, the muscle became hyperresponsive to the application of its neurotransmitter. Hypersensitivity is presumed to occur because receptors proliferate on the muscle cell in areas where they were not previously located. As a result a given amount of drug produces a greater effect because there are more receptors available to be stimulated. Similar receptor proliferation is thought to occur in the brain.

Denervation supersensitivity appears to be a particularly pronounced occurrence after certain biochemical lesions of the nervous system. For example, it has been found that when the dopamine terminals of the brain are destroyed with a neurotoxin, animals previously unaffected by injections of L–dopa (which, recall, is converted into dopamine in the brain) become profoundly activated by the drug. It is suggested that this effect occurs because the removal of dopamine synapses produces a proliferation of dopamine receptors, which then give an enormous response to stimulation from what ordinarily might be considered a small amount of dopamine.

A question remains about denervation supersensitivity: Is it a mechanism with some adaptive or compensatory value? There is a certain appeal in the idea that supersensitivity may compensate for reductions in neurotransmitter supply (caused by lesions, poisons, or aging), but as yet there is no evidence to suggest that this happens.

Disinhibition of Potential Compensatory Zones

In 1971, Wall and Egger mapped the thalamic and neocortical regions in which stimulation of a rat's forelimb or hindlimb resulted in an evoked potential. After then cutting the pathway from the lower spinal cord to the brain to sever the connections with the hindlimb, they again stimulated the forelimb or hindlimb. As expected, there was no response in the hindlimb regions, but the forelimb region was normal. After three days, however, there was a remarkable change. The region that had previously exhibited evoked potentials on stimulation of the hindlimb now showed these potentials on stimulation of the forelimb. The response looked normal, as if it had always been wired up to the forelimb. Why?

Most available evidence indicates that sprouting could not account for the effect and that there must be preexisting *silent synapses.* Evoked potentials elicited over pathways formed by sprouting generally take between seven and 10 days to occur. It seems likely, therefore, that fibers from the forelimb were always connected to the hindlimb area but were kept under some form of inhibition and thus were not functional. Once fibers from the hindlimb area were severed the competing input was lost and the area became functionally a forelimb area. These findings seem to suggest that an area that could *potentially* become involved in response is larger than mapping studies usually suggest. The results also suggest that the areas may not become involved in a response unless competing or inhibitory systems are abolished; that is, unless *disinhibition* occurs. A good example of the applicability of this idea has been previously mentioned. If one eye of a kitten is occluded, the cells that it should normally drive are taken over by the non-occluded eye. In fact, the animal appears completely blind to stimulation of the previously occluded eye. However, Kratz et al. have found that if the good eye is removed, the previously blind eye becomes functional to a rather surprising extent. The blindness of the previously occluded eye seems to be due to inhibition from the good eye. Duffy et al. found that drugs that block inhibiting synapses (bicuculline) were also able to restore vision to the blind eye. In fact, in a rather ingenious experiment Sherman and Guillery et al. destroyed a small part of one retina and occluded the other eye. When the occluder was removed, the animal was blind in all parts of the occluded eye except that part corresponding to the damaged portion of the retina of the nonoccluded eye. Apparently areas of the cortex that would normally receive input from the damaged part of the retina require input to inhibit the function of the corresponding area of the other eye.

These findings suggest that in various parts of the brain there is considerable overlap in innervation, but that specificity is maintained through inhibition. Removal of inhibition allows some takeover by the previously inhibited area. How general is this effect? The answer is not known, but Geschwind has raised the question of whether the recovery of language is mediated by such a mechanism. He suggests that language may be learned in both hemispheres, but that its use in the subordinate hemisphere is inhibited in some way. Damage in the dominant hemisphere disinhibits the subordinate hemisphere, and recovery can be attributed to this release. Although there is not much firm evidence to support this suggestion, it illustrates an imaginative use of the concept of disinhibition.

CHRONIC EFFECTS OF BRAIN DAMAGE IN ADULTS

The use of such words as "plasticity" and the emphasis placed on recovery of function in a great deal of basic research give the impression that the brain has an unlimited potential for recovery and reorganization after injury. Although there is a paucity of information on long-term recovery, on the basis of the available evidence the following generalizations can be made. (1) Recovery is likely in complex behaviors that are comprised of many components through processes that are referred to as *behavioral compensation*. (2) Recovery is most pronounced with incomplete lesions, such as those common after trauma from concussions or penetrating head wounds. (3) Recovery is unlikely for specific functions controlled by localized brain areas if all of the area is removed. Even in making these generalizations, we must emphasize that the available evidence indicates that there are always residual and permanent deficits after brain damage, and that extensive recovery is the exception, not the rule.

Behavioral Compensation

The ability to be employed and self-supporting is unquestionably dependent on many behavioral abilities and configurations of those abilities. Brain damage may affect some of those behaviors more than others, but there are numerous possibilities for compensation. Studies by Dresser and his coworkers show that when gainful employment is used as a measure of recovery, as was done for veterans injured in the Korean War, recovery was pronounced. Approximately 80 percent were employed. This measure gives the highest rate of recovery of any we have found in the literature and strongly suggests that some factor such as behavioral compensation is operating. This is not to minimize in any way the seriousness of the problem that 20 percent were not employed. Nor does it speak to the quality of employment. Oddy and Humphrey suggest that work is not a sensitive index of recovery. Forty-eight of their 54 closed head injury patients were back at work within two years, but

many were restricted in their work activity and believed that they had not regained their full working capacity. Other aspects of their social life also suffered, as they had not resumed all leisure time activities and social contacts. Interestingly, of all aspects of social relations, those with siblings suffered most. Oddy and Humphrey emphasize that therapy should not be directed only toward return to work but also toward leisure activities and social relations.

One way of examining what the chronic effects of brain damage are and how individuals cope is to study self-reports of people who have been brain damaged. Generally, very little attention is given to these reports, but they provide a valuable insight into questions of recovery. Fredrick Linge, a clinical psychologist we know, has described the changes that he has undergone after suffering brain damage in an automobile accident. He was in a coma for the first week after the accident and was not expected to achieve significant recovery. Nevertheless, he was able to return to a relatively demanding clinical practice about a year after his accident. But he was changed by the brain damage and had to make changes in his life style and work routine to cope. He describes his adjustments in the following way:

> In learning to live with my brain damage, I have found through trial and error that certain things help greatly and others hinder my coping. In order to learn and retain information best, I try to eliminate as many distractions as possible and concentrate all my mental energy on the task at hand. A structured, routine, well-organized and serene atmosphere at home and as far as possible at work, is vital to me. In the past I enjoyed a rather chaotic life style, but I now find that I want "a place for everything and everything in its place." When remembering is difficult, order and habit make the minutiae of daily living much easier.

In learning to live what is essentially a new life style he recognizes changes that seemed for the worst but also some that seemed for the better. On the one hand he states:

> I cannot cope with anger as well as I was able to do before my accident. Rage, related to my losses, does not lie just under the surface waiting to explode as it did earlier in my recovery. Yet, like any other person living in the real world, situations arise which make me justifiably angry. Before my accident, it took a lot to make me angry, and I am still, today, slow to anger. The difference is that now, once I become angry, I find it impossible to "put the brakes on" and I attribute this directly to my brain damage. It is extremely frightening to me to find myself in this state, and I still have not worked out a truly satisfactory solution, except insofar as I try to avoid anger-provoking situations or try to deal with them before they become too provoking.

On the other hand, he states:

> My one-track mind seems to help me to take each day as it comes without excessive worry and to enjoy the simple things of life in a way that I never did before. As well, I seem to be a more effective therapist, since I stick to the basic issues at hand and have more empathy with others than I did previously. (Linge, 1980, pp. 6–7)

The self-report by Linge shows that studies on recovery cannot be limited to measures such as reemployment or even renewed social contacts. These measures may, in many cases, indicate that recovery is complete, but they do not detail how the individual has changed, and has changed other aspects of the world, in order to cope. It is noteworthy that Linge was a professional psychologist who lived in a social milieu in which people were willing to help him reestablish himself. Many people who do not have, or who have not established, a similar position will have a much more difficult time "recovering." This is not an important point for understanding the chronic effects of brain damage. Linge makes our point well by stating that not only must the brain-damaged person change the external environment, the person must change the internal environment as well. We can go still further and state that studies on recovery of function are incomplete if they do not examine both these aspects of the brain-damaged person.

Recovery from Traumatic Lesions

As noted above, Kertesz has reported that after traumatic injuries greater recovery from aphasia is possible than after cerebrovascular accidents (Figure 25–4). This is probably because strokes damage large areas of the brain, both cortically and subcortically, and in doing so remove entire functional areas, whereas damage from traumatic injuries may be more diffuse and spare some parts of many areas. For example, a small residual part of a system may mediate substantial recovery, as was the case for the patient described above who recovered nearly normal motor abilities with 17 percent of the pyramidal tract. Studies on war veterans have also shown that there are good prospects for recovery from penetrating head injuries.

In Teuber's analysis the deficits of war veterans on tests given one week after injury were compared with those given 20 years later. These patients are excellent for study because they received standard tests after induction into the Army and were relatively young at the time of injury, the immediate aftermath of the injury is documented, and the kind and extent of recovery can be documented through prolonged follow-up by veterans' services. A summary of the results is given in Figure 25–8. They reveal that 4 percent shows some recovery from motor defects, 36 percent showed some recovery from somatosensory defects, 43 percent showed some recovery from visual defects, and 24 percent showed some recovery from initial dysphasia. These findings are probably quite reliable if we can general-

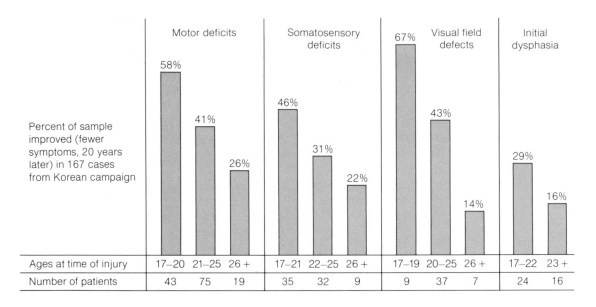

	Motor deficits			Somatosensory deficits			Visual field defects			Initial dysphasia	
Ages at time of injury	17–20	21–25	26 +	17–21	22–25	26 +	17–19	20–25	26 +	17–22	23 +
Number of patients	43	75	19	35	32	9	9	37	7	24	16

FIGURE 25–8. Estimated improvement from initial examination (within no more than one week of injury) and follow-up examination (20 years later) for some body regions (extremities, sides of face) for which symptoms were recorded (reflex changes, paralysis, weakness) for the motor system; noted sensory losses for the somatosensory system; estimated improvement in the visual field (diminution in number of quadrants known to be affected) and in symptoms interpreted as dysphasia. Note the advantage of groups of lower age at the time of wounding. (After Teuber, 1975.)

ize from the visual- field tests; according to Teuber, the Harms procedure of determining field defects allows for an extremely accurate assessment and is highly reliable in the hands of different testers at different times. Two comments can be made about Teuber's analysis. First, it must be noted that more than half of the patient population showed no recovery at all, and the failure of more than 75 percent of patients to show recovery from dysphasia is not encouraging. The latter figure is supported by Luria's report that 66 percent of his dysphasic patients show no recovery. Second, the analysis is not quantitative and there is no estimate of the degree of recovery. A study on a larger population of war veterans, those from Viet Nam, has been made by Mohr and his coworkers. In general, their results are consistent with those of Teuber

in that a great deal of recovery of function is to be expected from penetrating brain injury. In fact, Mohr reports more extensive recovery from aphasia (34 percent) than does Teuber and reports that the recovery continued for years after injury. An addendum to these studies may be made. Zihl and Cramon report that practice in localizing lights led to an increase in visual field in partially blind patients, an increase that would not have occurred without practice. It is not known what effect specific therapy may have had on the patients reported in the veteran studies.

Recovery from Surgical Lesions

Throughout this book we have emphasized that localized brain damage can produce specific impairments. The studies on patients with atrophic lesions have been used to provide a data base from which tests are obtained and the tests are then used for diagnostic purposes. Quite clearly, if recovery is at all pronounced, the diagnostic utility of the tests will be lessened; that is, a given test would not be useful if it did not reveal brain damage after a certain recovery period had passed. With this idea in mind it seems pertinent to ask: How reliable are the tests with respect to recovery time from surgery? Fortunately, an answer to the question can be obtained because the tests have been given to patients within days of surgery and up to as long as 20 years after surgery. Unfortunately, the effects of recovery seem so frequently to have been absent that the breakdown of data at different test-retest intervals is not reported. Table 25–3 summarizes the results from some studies in which tests were given a few days before surgery, within 20 days after surgery, and one to 20 years after surgery. The results show that after dorsolateral frontal lesions there is no recovery in card sorting, after right

temporal lesions there is no recovery in recall of the Rey figure, and after cerebral lesions there is no recovery in finger position sense or arm movement copying. The finding of no recovery is also reported in some other studies. Jones-Gottman and Milner tested patient groups within two weeks of surgery and one or more years later on tests of spontaneous drawing. The subjects were told to invent as many unnamable drawings as they could within five minutes. Although all patient groups showed some reduction in performance relative to control groups, patients with right frontal lesions were the most impaired, and there were no differences in performance in patients tested shortly after surgery and those tested more than a year after it. There also seems to be little or no recovery in memory after bilateral hippocampal removal. In a 14-year follow up, Milner, Corkin, and Teuber report that the amnesic patient H.M. had a presurgical IQ of 104, at two-year follow up of 112, and at nine-year follow up of 118. Yet despite this improvement in intelligence score, his anterograde amnesia remained essentially unchanged.

TABLE 25–3

Presurgical, postsurgical, and follow-up performance on neuropsychological tests by patients with cortical lesions						
Test	Lesion	Preop	Postop	Followup	Control	Reference
Card-sorting categories	Frontal	3.3	1.4	1.3	4.6	Milner, 1963
Card-sorting errors	Frontal	54.9	73.2	78.2	37.7	Milner, 1963
Rey-figure copy score	Right temporal	31.2	30.6	29.8	34.9	Taylor, 1969
Rey-figure recall score	Right temporal	15.4	15.3	13.8	24.2	Taylor, 1969
Finger position sense	Central					
Incidence of deficit (%)						
Ipsilateral		24	14	6	—	Taylor, 1969
Contralateral		36	43	65	—	
Arm movement copying	Left parietal		73	75.8	90.2	Kolb and Milner, 1981

In the case of H.M. the improvement in IQ was probably due to a lessening of epileptic seizures. In some studies on patients with atrophic lesions a degree of recovery has been noted on some tests. Milner in 1975 reported that patients with left temporal lesions have preoperative verbal memory scores of 12, early postoperative scores of 4.4, and five to 20 year follow-up scores of 8. This improvement is significant. There are a number of possible explanations for why recovery should have occurred on this test. First, the score is a composite of logical memory (recall of stories) and paired-associate learning. It is not clear which component of the test recovered. Blakemore and Falconer studied paired-associate learning in 86 temporal lobectomy patients for up to 10 years after surgery. They found the deficit lasted for two to three years but thereafter there was progressive recovery, provided the patients were young. Hence recovery could have been due to improvement in one facet of the task. Second, Jones has shown that if left temporal lobe patients are taught to use imagery (i.e., for the associate word pair "bouquet-elephant" they imagine an elephant with a bouquet of flowers in its trunk), they show substantial improvement in memory. Hence, recovery may have been due to the development of alternate memory strategies. Third, temporal cortex must have rather special properties to allow rapid memory storage. This property probably also makes it especially prone to epilepsy. It is possible, this postulate accepted, that if any of the area remains, it retains a special capacity for plasticity that is not evident in other brain areas. Considered together, although recovery occurs on this test, it is not clear that recovery is due to recovery of verbal memory per se. In summary, we feel that the results from some of the studies reported here are very important to the question of recovery of function. The implications of the results are that if the test is specific for certain brain areas and if the lesions remove the entire area, recovery will not occur. What makes this position particularly persuasive for us is that the surgical patients had tumors or epilepsy at the site of the lesions, which could have encouraged the function to move elsewhere. Yet there is little or no evidence in the test results to suggest that any such transfer took place.

VARIABLES AFFECTING RECOVERY

There are many variables other than just lesion size that affect the rate of recovery from brain damage. These are not discussed fully in many papers because measurements are so difficult to make, patient groups are often small to begin with, which precludes fractionation, or simply because a particular researcher may not think that they are important. These variables include age, sex, handedness, intelligence, and personality. Each of these variables will not be discussed here in full, but overall it is thought that if one is to incur brain damage, recovery will be best if one is a young, intelligent, optimistic, left-handed female. Youth is one of the easier variables to measure. Teuber and co-workers have found that on a number of tests, recovery by soldiers from natural lesions in the 17 to 20 age group is greater than in the 21 to 25 age group, which in turn is greater than for the age group 26 and over (Figure 25–8). Perhaps 40 is the upper limit, for Milner reports that patients over 40 who have removals near the posterior temporal speech zone in the left hemisphere show less recovery than younger patients. It is noteworthy that age does not always appear as a significant factor in studies of recovery, as noted by Kertesz. It should also be remembered that age is a contributing factor to many kinds of brain damage; that is, strokes and other kinds of brain abnormality are common in older people and these are also just the people who may be showing declines in motor and cognitive function due to the normal processes of aging. Thus, recovery may tend to be obscured by aging.

A number of experimental models have been developed to examine the effects of age on recovery of function. Gall, McWilliams, and Lynch have damaged one of the afferents to the granule cells of the hippocampus and then examined sprouting by the remaining hippocampal afferents. They found that in infant rats sprouting was extensive and invaded the entire dendritic field of the granule cells, in 21-day-old rats sprouting was attenuated, but in adult rats sprouting was virtually absent. If one assumes, therefore, that something like sprouting underlies some aspects of recovery of function, then this provides a convincing model for a neural basis for enhanced recovery in younger individuals. Contrasted to this approach, it should be noted that other researchers find that function can often be disrupted more profoundly in animals that receive injury in infancy than occurs if injury is incurred in adulthood. Some of this evidence was reviewed in Chapter 24. Some anatomical evidence to support such effects can also be mentioned. Figure 25–9 shows the brain weight of rats that received small parietal cortex lesions in adulthood, at five days of age, and at one day of age. Note that the infant lesions produce a greater reduction in brain weight than the adult lesions and also that the weight reduction was quite profound for the one-day group. This difference was not due to lesion size or to differences in tissue removed. In fact, when the brains were weighed at intervals after the one-day lesions, it was found that the difference only emerged when the rats were juvenile. The one-day rats also showed many behavioral abnormalities when adult. They were retarded in acquiring various tasks that adults could perform quite well, and they were prone to attacks of epilepsy. It seems to us that future research

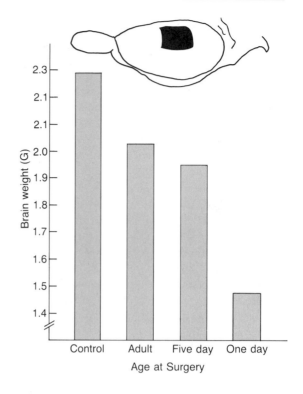

FIGURE 25–9. Brain weights of control rats and rats that received parietal lesions (see insert) as adults or at five days and one-day of age. (After Whishaw and Kolb, 1984.)

will have to carefully examine just what kind of changes can promote recovery of function as contrasted with those that might actually have a negative impact on recovery. At present, it seems sufficient to note that whatever changes do take place, the experimental evidence seems quite convincing that they are more likely to take place at younger, as contrasted with older, ages.

Handedness and sex, both for much the same reason, may influence the outcome of brain damage. Recall that a number of theories argue there is less lateralization, or some other organizational differences, in the female than in the male brain. Likewise, familial left-handers are thought to be less lateralized in function than right-handers. For both groups it is thought that damage in a particular location can be ameliorated to some extent by the remaining functional portions of the system that are located in the undamaged hemisphere. There is an inherent logical weakness in this view. It is this: if part of a functional area is located elsewhere and remains undamaged, then the lesions are really not complete and behavioral comparisons of recovery will be confounded. A similar sort of confounding may well be applicable to considerations of the factor of intelligence. Although the ultimate recovery of a very intelligent individual may be excellent in relation to the recovery of others, their actual residual deficit may be equal simply because they would normally function at a higher level. The question of personality is still more difficult to evaluate. It is widely thought that optimistic, extroverted, or easygoing people have a better prognosis. Yet personality is notoriously difficult to measure, and brain damage may change personality.

Just as the study of animals has provided animal models of how age influences brain changes after damage, similar studies provide evidence that sex effects can be examined in experimental animal paradigms. Loy and Milner have examined axonal sprouting of noradrenaline fibers into the hippocampus after damage was inflicted on certain hippocampal afferents. They found that sprouting was more vigorous in younger animals than in older animals and that at both ages sprouting was more extensive in female animals. The reason for the sex difference is not obvious, but there are two possible explanations. It is possible that female sex hormones promote sprouting in female rats or alternatively that male sex hormones create a biochemical climate that inhibits sprouting in male animals. As a way of balancing the advantage that this experiment

appears to accord to female rats, Yu reports just the opposite sex-related effect in a different experimental paradigm. Yu cut the hypoglossal nerve in male and female rats and then measured the rate at which it grew back to innervate the tongue. The regeneration rate was faster in the male rats, and furthermore, the administration of testosterone to either sex accelerated regeneration. These seemingly contradictory findings should not seem surprising, since sex-related brain research is still in its formative stages, but the results do illustrate the importance of considering sex a relevant variable in the study of recovery of function.

Summary

Adults who receive brain damage show better recovery if the damage is caused by head injury than if it is caused by cerebrovascular accident. This is because trauma frequently spares more tissue than strokes. The more extensive damage appears to be, the poorer are the prospects for recovery. When the measure of recovery is a complex skill, comprised of many components, recovery may be extensive because there are many strategies available for obtaining the same end. When a very specific skill is tested, no recovery occurs if the entire neural area sustaining that skill is destroyed.

THERAPEUTIC APPROACHES TO BRAIN DAMAGE

The idea and the techniques of transplanting neural tissue in mammals go back to the first decade of this century. Yet until a few years ago the idea that neural transplantation had any practical possibilities was viewed as rather remote. This view is now radically changed. First, the brain appears sheltered from the normal rejection processes that hamper transplant success in the rest of the body. As a result, successful grafts can be made not only within the body but between individuals and across species. The following are the prerequisites for successful grafts. First, Surger and Olsen have found that fetal grafts survive best. Tissue taken from prenatal rats survives well, tissue from rats a few days or weeks old survives poorly, and tissue from adult rats fails to survive at all. Second, the grafts need to receive a blood supply quickly. To accomplish this many experiments are done in which grafts are made in the anterior chamber of the eye or near the vessel-rich pia of the ventricles. Stenevi and his coworkers found that when neonatal noradrenergic neurons were transplanted to this site, about 500 of a total of 1500 neurons were present six months later. The transplants seem to show a high degree of normal differentiation and organization. They also make connections with the host tissue. An example from the hippocampus will demonstrate this point. The circuitry of the hippocampus is well known from anatomical and electrophysiological studies. One of its inputs is from the anteriorly located septum. Cholinergic cells in this region make highly specific connections with certain portions of the dendrites of hippocampal neurons. If this pathway is cut, the cholinergic terminals will disappear from the hippocampus. If a transplant of septal cells is placed in the location of the cut, its fibers will grow into the hippocampus and in one to three months will reoccupy the dendritic zones previously occupied by septal cells. The accuracy of the terminal occupation on the cells can be confirmed histochemically. An AChe (acetylcholinesterase) stain produces a large black band coloring a specific area of the dendrites of hippocampal cells. After the transplant has taken, the AChe-stained zone reappears in its appropriate location. A particularly positive feature of the grafts is that when placed almost anywhere, they send axons to make appropri-

ate connections. As a result the graft works when placed in the zone of damage, in the ventricle, or at other sites convenient for the technological manipulations of the experimenter. The embryonic cells seem to have a homing instinct as well as a passport no longer available to adult cells and so travel through the nervous system at will. A word of caution! The transplants may not only go to their appropriate locations but may be promiscuous and make other contacts. This aspect of their behavior has not been adequately controlled.

The newly formed connections made by grafts are behaviorally functional. Dunnett, trained rats to alternate their responses to two arms of a T-maze for a reward. This is easy and presumably fun for the normal rat, but not for rats with transected septal axons. They persistently run to the same side in the maze. After brain grafts with septal cells, correct alternation performance is gradually restored to almost 89 percent of normal levels as the graft makes its new connections.

The application of the technology of brain grafts is obvious. After brain damage, degenerating tissue is simply replaced. An almost immediate application is to Parkinson's and Alzheimer's disease, both of which seem to be caused by the loss of a specific group of cells. Recall that in the case of Parkinson's disease cells of the substantia nigra degenerate and consequently the brain is depleted of the transmitter substance dopamine, which the cells supply to their terminals. The loss of dopamine produces the constellation of symptoms that constitute the disease. Figure 25–10 gives a box diagram of the presumed role of dopamine as a behavioral modulator in the normal brain. The figure shows the parkinsonian (or the rat analogue) condition. A putative remedy for the disease is to place a brain graft of embryonic cells into the brain as is shown in the figure. Does it work? Perlow and coworkers destroyed the dopamine system on one side of the

A Intact

B Dopamine lesion

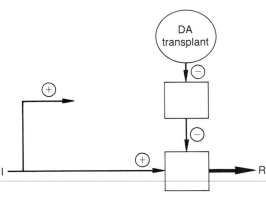

C Dopamine transplant

brain of rats and replaced it with a graft of fetal dopamine cells. The dopamine cell transplant reduced parkinsonian symptoms (abnormal turning induced by apomorphine) by about 50 percent. Björklund and coworkers have obtained the same therapeutic effects with grafts into rats with bilateral dopamine system damage. The application of this technology to humans is obvious and is already in the experimental stage. Even the supply of dopamine cells is not an obstacle to progress since cells seem transplantable across species and since dopamine cells from other parts of the body, such as the adrenal cortex, seem effective. Much the same approach can be used with Alzheimer's disease, which is now thought to result from a loss of cholinergic cells that project to the neocortex, in much the same way that cholinergic septal cells project to the hippocampus, and which are important for the maintenance of memory. Still, it is worth noting that the experimental research has been done with rats. Their brains are very small and grafts need but send fibers a few millimeters to form functional connections. As yet there is no evidence that grafts will be as successful in the large human brain.

FIGURE 25–10. Proposed mode of action of the DA-producing brain grafts in the promotion of behavioral recovery. A. The behavioral response (R) evoked by an activating sensory input (I) is modulated through an inhibitory control mechanism of which the dopamine (DA) pool forms an important part. B. The response can no longer occur in the absence of dopamine. C. The sensory response pathway is reopened by the dopamine transplant.

REFERENCES

Anand, B. K., and J. R. Brobeck. Hypothalamic control of food intake. *Yale Journal of Biology and Medicine* 24:123–140, 1951.

Barbizet, J. *Human Memory and Its Pathology*. San Francisco: Freeman, 1970.

Barnes, C. D., R. T. Joynt, and B. A. Schottelius. Motor neuron resting potentials in spinal shock. *American Journal of Physiology* 203:1113–1116, 1962.

Basso, A., E. Capitani, and E. Zanobio. Pattern of recovery of oral and written expression and comprehension in aphasic patients. *Behavioral Brain Research* 6:115–128, 1982.

Beresford, W. A. A discussion of retrograde changes in nerve fibers. *Progress in Brain Research* 14:33–57, 1965.

Björklund, A., M. Segal, and U. Stenevi. Functional reinnervation of rat hippocampus by locus coeruleus implants. *Brain Research* 170:409–426, 1979.

Björklund, A., and U. Stenevi. Regeneration of monoaminergic and cholinergic neurons in the mammalian central nervous system. *Physiological Reviews* 59:62–100, 1979.

Björklund, A., U. Stenevi, S. B. Dunnett, and S. D. Iversen. Function reactivation of the deafferented neostriatum by nigrae transplants. *Nature* 289:1–3, 1981.

Blakemore, C. B., and M. A. Falconer. Long-term effects of anterior temporal lobectomy on certain cognitive functions. *Journal of Neurology, Neurosurgery and Psychiatry* 30:364–367, 1967.

Bucy, P. C., J. E. Keplinger, and E. B. Siqueira. Destruction of the "pyramidal tract" in man. *Journal of Neurosurgery* 21:385–398, 1964.

Cannon, W. B., and A. Rosenblueth. *The Supersensitivity of Denervated Structures*. New York: Macmillan, 1949.

Craggs, M. D., and D. N. Rushton. The stability of the electrical stimulation map of the motor cortex of the anesthetized baboon. *Brain* 99:575–600, 1976.

Critchley, M. Dr. Samuel Johnson's aphasia. *Medical History* 6:27–44, 1962.

Doty, R. W. Conditioned reflexes formed and evoked by brain stimulation. In D. E. Sheer, ed., *Electrical Stimulation of the Brain*. Austin: University of Texas Press, 1961.

Dresser, A. C., A. M. Meirowsky, G. H. Weiss, M. L. McNeel, A. G. Simon, and W. F. Caveness. Gainful employment following head injury. *Archives of Neurology* 29:111–116, 1973.

Duffy, F. H., S. R. Snodgrass, J. L. Burchfield, and J. L. Conway. Bicuculline reversal of deprivation amblyopia in the cat. *Nature* 260:256–257, 1976.

Dunnett, S. B., W. C. Low, S. D. Iversen, U. Stenevi, and A. Björklund. Septal transplants restore maze learning in rats with fornix-fimbria lesions. *Brain Research* 251:335–348, 1982.

Eshkol, N., and A. Wachmann. *Movement Notation*. London: Weidenfeld and Nicolson, 1958.

Feeney, D. M., A. Gonzales, and W. A. Law. Amphetamine, haloperidol, and experience interact to affect rate of recovery after motor cortex injury. *Science* 217:855–857, 1982.

Finger, S., and D. G. Stein. *Brain Damage and Recovery*. New York: Academic, 1982.

Flourens, P. Investigations of the properties and the functions of the various parts which compose the cerebral mass. In G. von Bonin, ed., *The Cerebral Cortex*. Springfield, Ill.: Charles C Thomas, 1960.

Gall, C., R. McWilliams, and G. Lynch. Accelerated rates of synaptogenesis by "sprouting" afferents in the immature hippocampal formation. *Journal of Comparative Neurology* 193:1047–1061, 1980.

Geschwind, N. Late changes in the nervous system: An overview. In D. G. Stein, J. J. Rosen, and N. Butters, eds., *Plasticity and Recovery of Function in the Central Nervous System.* New York: Academic, 1974.

Glassman, R. B. Recovery following sensorimotor cortical damage: Evoked potentials, brain stimulation and motor control. *Experimental Neurology* 33:16–29, 1971.

Glees, P., and J. Cole. Recovery of skilled motor function after small repeated lesions of motor cortex in macaque. *Journal of Neurophysiology* 13:137–148, 1950.

Golani, I., D. L. Wolgin, and P. Teitelbaum. A proposed natural geometry of recovery from akinesia in the lateral hypothalamic rat. *Brain Research* 164:237–267, 1979.

Grillner, S. Locomotion in the spinal cat. In R. B. Stein, K. G. Pearson, R. S. Smith, and J. B. Redford, eds., *Control of Posture and Locomotion.* New York: Plenum, 1973.

Guillery, R. W. Binocular competition in the control of geniculate cell growth. *Journal of Comparative Neurology* 144:117–130, 1972.

Hall, M. *On the Diseases and Derangements of the Nervous System.* London: Baillière, 1841.

Hassler, R., P. Haug, C. Nitsch, J. S. Kim, and K. Paik. Effect of motor and premotor cortex ablation on concentrations of amino acids, monoamines, and acetylcholine and on the ultrastructure in rat striatum. A confirmation of glutamate as the specific cortico-striatal transmitter. *Journal of Neurochemistry* 38:1087–1098, 1982.

Head, H., and G. Riddoch. The automatic bladder, excessive sweating and some other reflex conditions in gross injuries of the spinal cord. *Brain* 15:188–263, 1917.

Hughlings-Jackson, J. *Selected Writings of John Hughlings-Jackson,* J. Taylor, ed. London: Hodder, 1932.

Jones, M. K. Imagery as a mnemonic aid after left temporal lobectomy: Contrast between material-specific and generalized memory disorders. *Neuropsychologia* 12:21–30, 1974.

Jones-Gottman, M., and B. Milner. Design fluency: The invention of nonsense drawings after focal cortical lesions. *Neuropsychologia* 15:653–674, 1977.

Kertesz, A. *Aphasia and Associated Disorders.* New York: Grune & Stratton, 1979.

Kolb, B., and B. Milner. Performance of complex arm and facial movements after focal brain lesions. *Neuropsychologia* 19:491–503, 1981.

Kolb, B., and I. Q. Whishaw. Effects of brain lesions and atropine on hippocampal and neocortical electroencephalograms in the rat. *Experimental Neurology* 56:1–22,

Kratz, K. E., P. D. Spear, and C. D. Smith. Postcritical-period reversal of effects of monocular deprivation on striate cortex cells in the cat. *Journal of Neurophysiology* 39:501–511, 1976.

Kromer, L. F., A. Björklund, and U. Stenevi. Innervation of embryonic hippocampal implants by regenerating axons of cholinergic neurons in the adult rat. *Brain Research* 210:153–171, 1980.

Kuhn, R. A. Functional capacity of the isolated human spinal cord. *Brain* 73:1–51, 1950.

Lashley, K. S. *Brain Mechanisms and Intelligence.* Chicago: The University of Chicago Press, 1929.

Lashley, K. S. Temporal variation in the function of the gyrus precentralis in primates. *American Journal of Physiology* 65:585–602, 1923.

Lawrence, D. G., and H. G. J. M. Kuypers. The functional organization of the motor system in the monkey: I. The effects of bilateral pyramidal lesions. *Brain* 81:1–14, 1968.

Levin, H. S., A. L. Benton, and R. G. Grossman. *Neurobehavioral Consequences of Closed Head Injury.* New York: Oxford, 1982.

Linge, F. What does it feel like to be brain-damaged? *Canada's Mental Health* 28:4–7, 1980.

Loy, R., and T. A. Milner. Sexual dimorphism in extent of axonal sprouting in rat hippocampus. *Science* 208:1282–1284, 1980.

Luria, A. R. *The Man with a Shattered World.* Lynn Solotoroff, New York: Basic Books, Jonathan Cape, Ltd., 1972.

Lynch, G., G. Rose, C. Gall, and C. W. Cotman. In M. Statini, ed., *Golgi Centennial Symposium Proceedings.* New York: Raven Press, 1975.

Lynch, G. S., S. Deadwyler, and C. W. Cotman. Post lesion axonal growth produces permanent functional connections. *Science* 180:1364–1366, 1973.

Markowitsch, H. J., and M. Pritzel. Von Monakow's diaschisis concept: Comments on West et al. (1976). *Behavioral Biology* 22:411–412, 1978.

Marshall, J. F., B. H. Turner, and P. Teitelbaum. Sensory neglect produced by lateral hypothalamic damage. *Science* 174:523–525, 1971.

McGinty, D. J. Somnolence, recovery and hypersomnia following ventromedial diencephalic lesions in the rat. *Electroencephalography and Clinical Neurophysiology* 26:70–79, 1969.

Meyer, J. S., M. Shinohara, T. Kauda, Y. Fukuuchi, A. D. Ericsson, and N. N. Kole. Diaschisis resulting from acute unilateral cerebral infarction. *Archives of Neurology* 23:241–247, 1970.

Milner, B. Effects of different brain lesions on card sorting. *Archives of Neurology* 9:90–100, 1963.

Milner, B. Psychological aspects of focal epilepsy and its neurosurgical management. *Advances in Neurology* 8:299–321, 1975.

Milner, B., S. Corkin, and H.-L. Teuber. Further analysis of the hippocampal amnesic syndrome: 14-year follow-up study of H.M. *Neuropsychologia* 6:215–234, 1968.

Mohr, J. P., G. H. Weiss, W. F. Caveness, J. D. Dillon, J. P. Kistler, A. M. Meirowsky, and B. L. Rish. Language and motor disorders after penetrating head injury in Viet Nam. *Neurology* 30:1273–1279, 1980.

Monakow, C. V. von. *Lokalization der Hirnfunktionen. Journal für Psychologie und Neurologie,* 17:185–200, 1911. Reprinted in G. von Bonin, *The Cerebral Cortex.* Springfield, Ill.: Charles C Thomas, 1960.

Munk, H. *Über die Funktionen der Grosshirnrinde. Gesammelte Mitteilungen aus den Jahren.* 1877–1880. Berlin: August Hershwald, 1881.

Murray, T. J. Dr. Samuel Johnson's Abnormal movements. In A. J. Friedhoff and T. N. Chase, eds., *Advances in Neurology,* vol. 35. New York: Raven Press, 1982.

Oddy, M., and M. Humphrey. Social recovery during the year following severe head injury. *Journal of Neurology, Neurosurgery, and Psychiatry* 43:798–802, 1980.

Pappius, H. M. Dexamethasone and local cerebral glucose utilization in freeze-traumatized rat brain. *Annals of Neurology* 12:157–162, 1982.

Pappius, H. M. Local cerebral glucose utilization in thermally traumatized rat brain. *Annals of Neurology* 9:484–491, 1981

Perlow, M. J., W. J. Freed, B. J. Hoffer, A. Sager, L. Olson, and R. J. Wyatt. Brain grafts reduce motor abnormalities produced by destruction of nigrostriatal dopamine system. *Science* 204:643–647, 1979.

Quinlan, J., and J. Quinlan. *Karen Ann: The Quinlans Tell Their Story.* Toronto: Doubleday, 1977.

Robinson, R. G., F. E. Bloom, and E. L. F. Battenberg. A fluorescent histochemical study of changes in noradrenergic neurons following experimental cerebral infarction in the rat. *Brain Research* 132:259–272, 1977.

Robinson, T. E., and I. Q. Whishaw. Effects of posterior hypothalamic lesions on voluntary behavior and hippocampal electroencephalograms in the rat. *Journal of Comparative and Physiological Psychology* 86:768–786, 1974.

Rosner, B. B. Recovery of function and localization of function in historical perspective. In D. G. Stein, J. J. Rosen, and N. Butters, eds., *Plasticity and Recovery of Function in the Central Nervous System.* New York: Academic, 1974.

Schoenfeld, T. A., and L. W. Hamilton. Secondary brain changes following lesions: A new paradigm for lesion experimentation. *Physiology and Behavior* 18:951–967, 1977.

Seiger, A., and L. Olson. Quantification of fiber growth in transplanted monoamine neurons. *Cell Tissue Research* 179:285–316, 1977.

Sherman, S. M., R. W. Guillery, J. H. Gaas, and K. J. Sanderson. Behavioral electrophysiological and morphological studies of binocular competition in development of geniculocortical pathways of cats. *Journal of Comparative Neurology* 158:1–18, 1974.

Sherrington, C. S. *The Integrative Action of the Nervous System,* 2nd ed. New Haven: Yale University Press, 1947.

Skinhøj, E. Bilateral depression of CSF in unilateral cerebral diseases. *Acta Neurologica Scandinavica,* suppl. 14, 41:161–163, 1965.

Sokoloff, L. The deoxyglucose method: Theory and practice. *European Neurology* 20:137–145, 1981.

Sperry, R. W. Mechanisms of neural maturation. In S. S. Stevens, ed., *Handbook of Experimental Psychology.* New York: Wiley, 1965.

Stenevi, U., A. Björklund, and N.-A. Svendgaard. Transplantation of central and peripheral monoamine neurons to the adult rat brain: Techniques and conditions for survival. *Brain Research* 114:1–20, 1976.

Stricker, E. M., and M. J. Zigmond. Recovery of function after damage to central catecholamine-containing neurons: A neurochemical model for the lateral hypothalamic syndrome. In J. M. Sprague and A. N. Epstein, eds., *Progress in Psychobiology and Physiological Psychology,* vol. 6. New York: Academic, 1976.

Taylor, L. B. Localization of cerebral lesions by psychological testing. *Clinical Neurosurgery* 16:269–287, 1969.

Taylor, L. B. Psychological assessment of neurosurgical patients. In T. Rasmussen and R. Marino, eds., *Functional Neurosurgery.* New York: Raven Press, 1979.

Teitelbaum, P., and A. N. Epstein. The lateral hypothalamic syndrome: Recovery of feeding and drinking after lateral hypothalamic lesions. *Psychological Review* 69:74–90, 1962.

Teitelbaum, P., and E. Stellar. Recovery from the failure to eat produced by hypothalamic lesions. *Science* 120:893–895, 1954.

Teuber, H.-L. Recovery of function after brain injury in man. In *Outcome of Severe Damage to the Nervous System,* Ciba Foundation Symposium 34. Amsterdam: Elsevier North-Holland, 1975.

Twitchell, T. E. The automatic grasping response of infants. *Neuropsychologia* 3:247–259, 1965.

Twitchell, T. E. The restoration of motor function following hemiplegia in man. *Brain* 74:443–480, 1951.

Wall, P. D., and M. D. Egger. Formation of new connections in adult rat brains after partial deafferentation. *Nature* 232:542–545, 1971.

Waller, A. V. Experiments on the section of the glossopharyngial and hypoglossal nerves of the frog, and observations of the alterations produced thereby in the structure of their primitive fibers. *Philosophical Transactions* 140:423–429, 1850.

West, J. R. The concept of diaschisis: A reply to Markowitsch and Pritzel. *Behavioral Biology* 22:413–416, 1978.

West, J. R., S. A. Deadwyler, C. W. Cotman, and G. S. Lynch. An experimental test of diaschisis. *Behavioral Biology* 18:419–425, 1976.

Whishaw, I. Q., and B. Kolb. Behavioral and anatomical studies of rats with complete or partial decortication in infancy. In C. R. Almli and S. Finger, eds., *The Behavioral Biology of Early Brain Damage.* New York: Academic, 1984.

Whitty, C. W. M., and O. L. Zangwill. Traumatic amnesia. In C. W. M. Whitty and O. L. Zangwill, eds., *Amnesia.* London: Butterworths, 1966.

Yu, W. H. A. Sex differences in the regeneration of the hypoglossal nerve in rats. *Brain Research* 238:404–406, 1982.

Zihl, J., and D. von Cramon. Restitution of visual field in patients with damage to the geniculostriate visual pathway. *Human Neurobiology* 8:5–8, 1982.

PART SEVEN

APPLIED HUMAN NEUROPSYCHOLOGY

This last part of the book describes the application of the fundamental principles of human neuropsychology to both neuropsychological assessment and the understanding of a variety of socioeducational problems. Chapters 26 and 27 describe the principles and applications of neuropsychological assessment. In no other area is the application of neuropsychological testing used more than in the field of education: Chapter 28 describes the application of neuropsychology in the study of learning disabilities. There has been a gradual movement to apply neuropsychological testing procedures to psychiatric populations, and so Chapter 29 describes some of the concepts that are emerging from this research. Finally, for the use of those who are interested in the details of testing and scoring, we have included norms that we have compiled from studies that have used the tests described in this book.

The true potential of neuropsychology lies not only in its contribution to the understanding of brain function but also—and this will be its real test—in the applicability of the basic knowledge to human problems. There are moral and ethical responsibilities to apply the basic knowledge wisely, with the utmost care and caution. Neuroscientists in other areas will be watching with a very critical eye. Perhaps the major difficulty in successful application of neuropsychological principles is the problem of individual differences. Up to this point in the book we have emphasized the consistent relation between brain function and behavior. In practice, however, brain-behavior relations vary considerably from person to person. Such variability can be attributed to a number of factors. For example, individuals in the general population vary widely in their ability at any particular skill, and this variance influences the effects of brain injury or dysfunction. An architect with injury to the right hemisphere may suffer deficits in visuospatial analysis that make it impossible for him or her to return to work as an architect— even though he or she is still better at visuospatial ability than the average person! Further, personality variables influence a person's response to brain injury and affect the degree of recovery following it. In other disciplines in applied neurology, variation, although it must also be contended with, is less of a burden because those disciplines deal largely with physical signs and symptoms that are much less variant than the differences in cognitive processes measured by neuropsychologists. It is for this reason that neuropsychological principles must be applied carefully and conservatively to avoid serious errors harmful both to individual patients and (less importantly) to the reputation of a field with so much potential. Thus, those who would be called neuropsychologists *must* have a solid grounding in the fundamentals of neuroscience, and in neuropsychology in particular. Throughout this book we have emphasized the importance of a basic understanding of how the nervous system operates, to its minute particulars, whether it be a neuron or a synapse. Failure to learn basic lessons before applying neuropsychological principles will only ensure, at best, mediocrity or, worse, incompetence. At the same time, competent neuropsychologists must not be *overly* cautious, because if the competent fail to apply the basic knowledge, the incompetent will surely fill the field.

26

NEUROPSYCHOLOGICAL ASSESSMENT

After World War II many neuropsychological laboratories were established in Europe and North America. These have been principally responsible for the development of neuropsychological assessment as a tool in clinical neurology. We make no attempt to thoroughly review all the tests used in neurological assessment (we recommend Lezak's book for further discussion of the range of available tests). Rather, we review: (1) the rationale and goals of neuropsychological assessment, (2) the types of disorders for which it is most useful, (3) the characteristics of useful neuropsychological tests, (4) currently used formal test batteries, and (5) examples of an informal composite battery.

RATIONALE OF ASSESSMENT

Throughout Chapters 7 to 23 we have seen that circumscribed lesions in different cortical regions may produce discrete behavioral changes. In Chapters 16, 17, and 18 we argued that it would thus seem reasonable to assume that one could work backward from this knowledge to localize unknown brain damage. That is, given a particular behavioral change, one should be able to predict the site or sites of the disturbance most likely causing the behavioral change. There are, however, several problems in working backward in such a manner. First, research patients are often chosen for specific reasons. For example, whereas patients with rapidly expanding tumors would not be chosen for research, because the results are so difficult to interpret, neurosurgical patients, on the other hand, are ideal research subjects because the extent of damage is known. This difference in etiology of the neurological disorder might therefore be expected to make assessment difficult if the tests are based on data collected from patients with totally different etiologies.

The second problem is related to the size of the lesion and the sensitivity of the tests. If a large region of the brain is dysfunctioning, then the assessment test need not be particularly sensitive to demonstrate the dysfunction. On the other hand, if the lesion is small, the behavioral effect may be rather specific (as we have seen). For example, a lesion in the right somatosensory representation of the face may produce very subtle sensory changes, and unless specific tests of nonverbal fluency are used (see Chapter 18), the cognitive changes may go unnoticed, even with dozens of tests.

The third problem, a related one, is assessment time. Since neuropsychological tests must be sensitive to changes in a vast number of behaviors and skills, many different tests must be administered for a diagnosis to be made. Thus, existing one-shot tests of organic impairment, organicity, or brain dysfunction are invalid when used alone. Although it is true that many people with brain damage do poorly on some of these tests, it is also true that many people with known brain damage do well on them. And even among those people who are impaired at them, there is no localization of the neurological problem. In addition, there is the continual problem of false positives. Individuals may be impaired at *particular* tests for many reasons, only one of which may be brain damage or dysfunction. An adequate assessment requires time, often six or more hours, which clearly requires more than one sitting with the subject.

The fourth problem is that various factors may interact with the brain pathology to make interpretation of test results difficult. Tests are seldom developed for subjects who are 80 years old or who are culturally disadvantaged. Test scores therefore cannot be interpreted with strict cutoff criteria—that is, performance below a particular level cannot always be taken as indicating brain damage. Further, intelligence alters the investigators' expectations of performance on different tests: someone with an IQ of 130 may be relatively impaired on a test

of verbal memory but, compared to someone with an IQ of 90, may appear normal. Thus, unlike standard psychometric assessment, neuropsychological assessment must be flexible. This clearly makes interpretation difficult and requires extensive training in fundamental neuropsychology and neurology as well as in neuropsychological assessment.

A final problem is that current neuropsychological assessment procedures cannot easily discriminate between people with extensive brain damage and people with gross cerebral *dysfunction* such as occurs in schizophrenia. Although schizophrenic individuals would not appear to have focalized lesions, they do certainly appear to have grossly dysfunctioning brains.

Goals of Neuropsychological Assessment

The goal of assessment in general clinical psychology is the diagnosis of the disorder for the purpose of effecting behavioral change. For example, intelligence and achievement tests may be given to schoolchildren as a means of trying to identify particular problem areas, as an aid in teaching. Similarly, personality tests are used with an eye toward defining and curing a behavioral disorder.

The goals in clinical neuropsychology are different in some respects. First, the assessment aims to diagnose the presence of cortical damage or dysfunction and to localize it where possible. Second, assessment is used to facilitate patient care as well as rehabilitation. A related goal is to identify unusual brain organization that may occur in left-handers or in people with childhood brain injury. This information is particularly valuable to the surgeon, who would not wish to inadvertently remove primary speech zones during surgery. In such disorders as focal epilepsy the primary evidence corroborating abnormal EEG may be behavioral, because radiological procedures often fail to demonstrate the abnormal brain tissue giving rise to the seizures. In addition, because some recovery of function may be expected following brain injury, this recovery must be documented not only with rehabilitation in mind but also to determine the effectiveness of any medical treatment, particularly for neoplasms or vascular abnormalities. Further, the patient and the family must understand the patient's possible residual deficits so that realistic life goals and rehabilitation programs can be planned.

Application of Neuropsychological Assessment to Specific Disorders

Neuropsychological assessment is most useful on people with cerebral vascular disorders, acute traumatic lesions, neoplasms, and epilepsy; it is of limited value on people with infections of the brain, progressive brain disease such as multiple sclerosis, or dementias, all of which are not localized. Once a person behaves as if demented, test results have little validity.

The importance of comprehensive neuropsychological assessments in people with cerebral vascular disorders or traumatic lesions cannot be overemphasized: in such people a partial assessment is often worse than none at all. For example, standardized intelligence tests may produce results that misleadingly suggest dementia, because IQ tests emphasize verbal skills and ignore other skills necessary for day-to-day living. On the other hand, just the opposite may also be true: people with normal or near normal IQs may fail to perform normally on other tests of specific mental functions critically important in normal daily activities. An inadequate assessment may fail to diagnose these deficits, leading to invalid conclusions about an individual's neuropsychological functioning.

In the case of cerebral tumors, neuropsychological studies may provide baselines for assessing initial and later effects of surgery, irradiation, or chemotherapy. In the absence of radiological evidence such studies may also promote proper clinical neurological assessment by providing evidence of brain dysfunction resulting from disease processes.

Neuropsychological assessment has a most important diagnostic role in the preoperative localization of lesions in focal epilepsy. It is not uncommon for focal epileptics to demonstrate no positive signs in radiological or other neurological tests while demonstrating clearly localized behavioral deficits. Further, particularly in the case of temporal lobe epilepsy, where there may be risk to memory, neuropsychological assessment may be invaluable in identifying hippocampal damage in the hemisphere contralateral to the major focus.

Finally, neuropsychological assessment is beginning to be used to evaluate undesirable side effects of various pharmacological treatments, particularly in the treatment of movement disorders such as Parkinson's disease. Because the effects of various pharmacological treatments for both psychiatric and neurological disorders are as yet poorly understood, side effects of high or chronic doses of various drugs are common. Neuropsychological assessment can provide an objective measure of unwanted deficits in cognitive functioning.

Although neuropsychological assessment has many roles and goals in the diagnosis and treatment of neurological disease, we must emphasize a serious concern. Hebb once wrote, "a half-baked psychologist is worse than none at all." It is also true that "a half-baked neuropsychologist is worse than none at all." Neuropsychological assessment is complex and requires extensive training to properly evaluate the results. Experience in interpreting personality or intelligence tests is not sufficient background to begin neuro-psychological assessment.

Intelligence Testing in Neuropsychological Assessment

Most neuropsychological assessments begin with either the Wechsler Adult Intelligence Scale (WAIS) or its recent revision, the WAIS-R. These two versions are necessary for repeated testing, and they correlate highly with each other. The Wechsler scales have proved invaluable in providing a base level of cognitive functioning. McFie has also found them to be extremely useful diagnostic tools in themselves. These scales present a distinct advantage: they provide separate scores for verbal and for performance sub-tests, as well as an overall IQ.

The verbal scale consists of six subtests. (1) Information: questions such as "Where is Egypt?" "Who wrote *Hamlet*?" (2) Compre-hension: questions requiring some reflection before answering, e.g., "Why are child-labor laws needed?" (3) Arithmetic: e.g., "How many hours will it take a man to walk 24 miles at the rate of three miles an hour?" (4) Similar-ities: the subject is asked in what way two items are alike, e.g., an orange and a banana, an egg and a seed. (5) Digit span: tests the num-ber of digits that can be repeated in correct sequence, forward and backward. (6) Vocab-ulary: asks for the meaning of words ranging from easy (e.g., winter) to difficult (e.g., travesty).

The performance scale consists of five sub-tests: (1) Digit symbol: nine symbols (e.g., + are paired with digits 1–9 in a key above the response sheet. The task is to pencil in as many of the symbols corresponding to each of 90 digits as possible in 90 seconds. This requires rapid eye movement and short-term visual store. (2) Picture completion: the subject indi-cates what is missing in each of a series of pic-

tures. (3) Block design: red and white blocks must be used to form a design presented on a card. (4) Picture arrangement: several cards with cartoonlike drawings are presented in mixed-up order, and the subject is required to order them so that they tell a coherent story. (5) Object assembly: pieces of simple jigsaw puzzles are given to the subject who must assemble them as quickly as possible.

Although the distinction between the verbal and performance subtests is serendipitous, the subtests have proved extremely useful as a rough measure of left and right hemisphere function, respectively. The IQs obtained on the verbal and performance sections both have a mean of 100 and a standard deviation of 15. A difference of more than 10 points between the verbal and performance scores is usually taken to be a clinically significant difference, al-though statistically this interpretation is some-what liberal. A number of studies have shown that well-defined left hemisphere lesions pro-duce a relatively low verbal IQ, whereas well-defined right hemisphere lesions produce a re-latively low performance IQ. Diffuse damage, on the other hand, tends to produce a low performance IQ, leading to the erroneous be-lief that the verbal-performance IQ difference is not diagnostically useful. Although a re-duced performance IQ is not definitive, it is rare to obtain a relatively low verbal IQ, and its appearance should not be ignored.

TEST BATTERIES

It is evident that to be thorough a useful neuropsychological assessment requires a ser-ies of different tests. Hence neuropsychologi-cal batteries have been developed that are given routinely as a group. Basically, there are two types of test batteries: those that constitute a formal battery of commercially available tests, and those that are informal composite batteries assembled for use with particular populations. The choice of one type over another depends largely on the nature of the clinical question being addressed and on the nature of the population being assessed. On the whole, the ready-made batteries are not as good as the less formal composite batteries, although they have the important advantage of being much easier to obtain. We shall consider three well-known formal batteries (Halstead-Reitan, Luria's Neuropsychological Investigation, and the Luria-Nebraska Neuropsychological Battery) and provide an example of a composite test battery. First, however, we shall consider the characteristics of useful batteries.

Characteristics of Useful Neuropsychological Batteries

At least five important criteria characterize useful neuropsychological tests.

1. *Thoroughness.* To be useful a group of tests must test a wide variety of functions. They must identify the hemisphere containing speech; measure general intelligence and memory; measure sensory, perceptual, and motor functions; assess language functions; and, finally, examine frontal lobe function.

Laterality of speech is most easily determined by a verbal dichotic-listening test, and general intelligence is most frequently measured by one of the Wechsler scales. Memory testing requires consideration of both verbal and nonverbal aspects as well as short-term and long-term memory. The Wechsler memory scale, widely used as a general test of memory, is primarily verbal and must be supplemented with visual tests.

Visual and auditory sensory functions are usually thoroughly examined by neurologists, but somatosensory function is not—largely because it is tedious and time consuming to

do so. If there is any evidence of a lesion to the central regions, somatosensory tests are invaluable. Motor functions such as reflexes, balance, gait, and the like are usually thoroughly examined by neurologists, but praxic functions frequently are not, again because of time limitations. Tests of apraxia are, however, easy to administer and score and should be included if practical.

Language functions can be assessed by tests of the subject's speech and also by the many tests of aphasia, reading, writing, and arithmetic abilities. Tests of language functions should not be limited to a simple conversation, for subtle defects may often be overlooked.

Finally, a thorough assessment protocol will include tests of left and right frontal lobe function.

2. *Ease and cost.* Tests should be easy to administer and score. Much of the testing often must be done by psychometrists, and the results interpreted by the neuropsychologist. Thus, it is essential that tests be given in a standard format and scored objectively so that the neuropsychologist can be assured of consistent results from tests being administered by more than one psychometrist. The tests should also be inexpensive. Cost constraints are not a good reason to administer a partial assessment protocol.

3. *Time.* Tests should not take excessively long to administer. Because subjects are often weak and easily tired, it is desirable to complete testing as quickly as possible without compromising thoroughness.

4. *Adaptability.* Often subjects are not very mobile, possibly being restricted to wheelchairs or even bedridden. It is therefore essential that the tests be portable and adaptable to varying constraints determined by the health of the subject.

5. *Flexibility.* Research is continually improving tests and devising newer, better ones.

It is important that tests be substituted or improved in the light of new data. Test batteries that employ complex formulas or cut-off scores are thus less desirable because they necessarily lose their flexibility.

Halstead-Reitan Battery

The most widely known battery is the Halstead-Reitan battery, presumably because it is the most readily available. Essentially it is based on a series of tests originally devised by Halstead in the late 1940s. It began as a battery of seven tests selected for their power to discriminate between patients with frontal lobe lesions and other patient groups or normal controls. The current version of the battery consists of about 10 basic tests, eight of which are listed below and several others of which are given mention.

1. *Wechsler intelligence scale.* Either the WAIS, WAIS-R, or the Wechsler-Bellevue intelligence scale, Form I, is administered.

2. *Category test.* A category test is primarily a test of abstracting ability. A variety of stimulus figures varying in size, shape, number, intensity, color, and location are projected on a screen for the subject's viewing. These figures can be grouped by abstract principles, and it is the subject's task to determine the principle. This test is sensitive to left or right frontal lobe damage.

3. *Critical flicker fusion test.* The rate at which flashing lights appear steady or fused into a constant light is assessed by using a light-flashing stroboscope. This test is often not included in the battery.

4. *Tactual-performance test.* The Seguin-Goddard form board test described in our discussion of parietal lobe tests in Chapter 16 is a tactual-performance test. Blindfolded subjects are asked to place blocks of wood of various shapes (square, star, half-moon, etc.) into holes of similar shape in the form board; later they are asked, without having seen the board, to draw it from memory. Although Halstead and Reitan believed this was a frontal lobe test, many authors, including ourselves, have found that frontal lobe patients are not impaired at this task whereas right parietal patients are. Indeed, it is difficult to understand why this test would have been considered a test of frontal lobe pathology.

5. *Rhythm test.* The rhythm test, a subtest of the Seashore test of musical talent, requires the subject to discriminate between like and unlike pairs of musical beats. Subjects with right temporal lobe removals are impaired at this task.

6. *Speech-sounds perception test.* The speech-sounds perception test is an auditory acuity test in which the subject listens to a tape recording of 60 spoken nonsense words, all of which have an "ee" vowel sound in the middle with different beginning and ending consonant sounds. The subject selects the word heard from a series of alternatives. This is a test of left hemisphere function, presumably taxing mainly either the left posterior temporal-parietal cortex around Wernicke's area or possibly the left face area.

7. *Finger-oscillation test.* On the finger-oscillation test the subject's finger-tapping speed is measured on a key resembling a Morse code key. Halstead found a slight slowing of tapping speed in patients with cortical lesions, and Reitan has claimed this test to be one of the most sensitive in the battery. This conclusion is not universally accepted and we have found the test to be unreliable in lateralizing pathology, especially if the lesion is in the temporal or occipital cortex.

8. *Time-sense test.* A time-sense test measures the subject's visual-motor reaction time and ability to estimate elapsed time. The task is to watch a clock hand rotate around a clock

face and then to estimate sweep time from memory. The memory component of this test has not proved useful and is not generally used.

9. *Auxiliary tests*. Other tests included in the original battery but not always administered include the trail-making test, aphasia screening test, and Minnesota Multiphasic Personality Inventory (MMPI). The trail-making test requires subjects to draw lines to connect either consecutive numbers or letters scattered randomly on a page and in a second part to alternate between the two sequences (i.e., A-1-B-2-C-3 . . .); the aphasia screening test is an altered version of the Wepman aphasia test; and the MMPI is a widely used self-report questionnaire alleged to diagnose psychiatric abnormalities.

To ascertain the presence of brain damage, a summary value is obtained, known as the *Halstead Impairment Index*. This index is determined by counting the number of tests on which the results fall in the range characteristic of the performance of brain-damaged subjects.

Although the Halstead-Reitan battery is widely used and has been an important pioneer effort in neuropsychological assessment, it is subject to a number of serious criticisms. The tests are not theoretically based, but rather are largely derived from 27 tests that Halstead originally chose in hopes of finding tests to identify subjects with frontal lesions. Thus, the 10 tests that are used are really clinically based and are difficult to interpret theoretically. Furthermore, the norms for the tests are not well-founded, being based on a small sample. Memory functions are poorly and naively assessed, even though more probably is known about memory and its assessment than about any other cerebral function. In addition, the tests are not sensitive enough, because many subjects with small focalized lesions would have no significant abnormalities on the battery. The test is sensitive to the effects of aging on behavior and cannot reliably discriminate between subjects 45 years of age or older and brain-damaged subjects. An additional problem is that the battery, and particularly the category test, is not really portable and is thus difficult to administer to bedridden subjects. The most serious problem, however, is that the battery, although containing a large number of tests, does not meet our criteria of thoroughness (as discussed above). There is no measure of somatosensory function, praxic function, or gnostic function. Furthermore, there is evidence that the tests used are highly correlated, and therefore redundant, and that some of the individual tests (e.g., the trail-making test) may actually be better predictors of brain damage than the impairment index. A final problem, by no means unique to the Halstead-Reitan battery, is its inability to distinguish between psychotic and brain-damaged subjects. For example, Watson et al. found that Reitan-trained examiners were unable to differentiate, at better than a chance level, patients with known brain damage from patients diagnosed as schizophrenic. This inability is a chronic problem of all neuropsychological batteries, no doubt reflecting the gross frontal and temporal lobe dysfunction in schizophrenia discussed in previous chapters.

Because of the limitations of the original Halstead-Reitan battery, there have been numerous attempts to modify it for specific populations (see Lezak for examples). Many clinicians have added their own tests, especially tests of memory, to supplement the basic battery. What is needed, however, is a thorough revision of the battery with updated and extended norms and validation studies on subjects with verified lesions, incorporating many of the improvements that have been made by different groups.

Luria's Neuropsychological Investigation

Luria's test battery is not widely known in the Western world, having been first published in English as a battery by Christensen in 1975. Based on about 35 years of research by Luria and his colleagues in the Soviet Union, it is probably the most thorough battery available, as the summary of the tests in Table 26–1 shows. Because the nonpsychometric nature of Luria's battery makes it difficult to describe all of the tests briefly, we have presented an example of one test and its interpretation in Tables 26–2 and 26–3.

The principal advantages of Luria's battery are the following. (1) It is based on theoretical principles of neuropsychological functioning, making the interpretation a logical conclusion of the theory. (2) It is thorough, inexpensive, easy to administer, flexible, and brief, taking only about one hour to administer. (3) It measures the actual behavior of the subject rather than inferred cognitive processes, thus making interpretation more straightforward. There are, however, also disadvantages of the Luria procedure. (1) The scoring is subjective and is based on clinical experience. It is unlikely that a novice to neuropsychology or neurology could easily master the interpretation without extensive training. On the other hand, experienced neuropsychologists or neurologists ought to find the battery easy to learn. (2) Because the manual that accompanies the battery offers no validation studies, it must be taken on faith that the tests really measure what Luria claims they do. This criticism is the most serious, because most Western neuropsychologists are likely to continue to use psychometric assessment tools reporting validation studies.

The Luria-Nebraska Neuropsychological Battery

This recently devised test battery is an attempt to standardize the Luria test procedures, but it

TABLE 26–1

Summary of Luria's neuropsychological investigation

1. Determination of cerebral dominance
2. Investigation of motor functions
   a. Motor functions of the hands
   b. Oral praxis
   c. Speech regulation of the motor act
3. Investigation of acousticomotor organization
   a. Perception and reproduction of pitch relations
   b. Perception and reproduction of rhythmic structures
4. Investigation of the higher cutaneous and kinesthetic functions
   a. Cutaneous sensation
   b. Muscle and joint sensation
   c. Stereognosis
5. Investigation of the higher visual functions
   a. Visual perception of objects and pictures
   b. Spatial orientation
   c. Intellectual operations in space
6. Investigation of impressive speech
   a. Phonemic hearing
   b. Word comprehension
   c. Understanding of simple sentences
   d. Understanding of logical grammatical structures
7. Investigation of the higher visual functions
   a. Articulation of speech sounds
   b. Reflected (repetitive) speech
   c. The nominative function of speech
   d. Narrative speech
8. Investigation of writing and reading
   a. Phonetic analysis and synthesis of words
   b. Writing
   c. Reading
9. Investigation of arithmetical skill
   a. Comprehension of number structure
   b. Arithmetical operations
10. Investigation of memory processes
    a. The learning process
    b. Retention and retrieval
    c. Logical memorizing
11. Investigation of intellectual processes
    a. Understanding of thematic pictures and texts
    b. Concept formation
    c. Discursive intellectual activity

Adapted from Christensen, 1975.

TABLE 26–2

Example of Luria's assessment tests.
Test 1, Investigation of higher visual functions

Procedure	Materials

1. Investigation of objects and pictures
  a. The patient is asked to examine carefully objects or clearly drawn pictures of objects (with no time limit) and to name them.
    If speech is disturbed, nonverbal communication can be used.
  b. The patient is asked to examine and name complicated or indistinct pictures of objects.
  c. The patient is asked to examine and name pictures of objects that are scribbled over or superimposed one on another (Poppelreuter's test).
  d. The patient is asked to identify a figure in a complex design (Gottschaldt).
  e. The patient is asked to complete a structure from which a portion is missing by choosing from a series of offered insets the one that matches the particular structure (example from Raven's test). No time limit is imposed.
	Objects and pictures

The presentation of these tests may be varied. The figure may be presented for only a short period of time, or the pictures may be presented in the wrong position.

In simplified forms the patient is asked to trace the outline of the figure with his finger, or he may be given leading questions, or the examiner may point to any one of the essential signs.

From Christensen, 1975, p. 69.

should not be considered as a substitute for Luria's Neuropsychological Investigation. Golden and his colleagues have selected items from Christensen's manual on the basis of whether they discriminated between normal subjects and neurologically impaired subjects to produce a standardized administration and scoring procedure for the Christensen tests. A score is thus obtained for most of the measures summarized in Table 26–1. Although the idea of standardizing the test items is sound, in so doing a very different test battery than that used by Luria has been produced. "It is not the items, per se, but the manner in which Luria made use of them as a means of testing hypotheses concerning various abilities, deficits or functions which is his method and his unique contribution to neuropsychological assessment. Consequently, the incorporation of items drawn from Luria's work into a standardized test should not be interpreted to mean that the test is an operationalization or standardization of Luria's method" (Spiers, 1981, p. 339).

Golden and his colleagues have been very energetic over the past few years and have published an impressive number of papers on their battery. Nevertheless, the battery has not been widely accepted by neuropsychologists. "A considerable gap separates the evaluations of this battery made by Golden and his colleagues from those by neuropsychologists who are not affiliated with them. Golden and his group, without exception, offer data supporting their claims that this battery is a diagnostically efficient instrument. Other neuropsychologists have concluded that the battery is unreliable" (Lezak, 1983, p. 570).

TABLE 26-3

Interpretative guideline for Luria's test of objects and pictures

Behavior	Lesion
1. Perception of objects and pictures	
Objects and pictures	
The patient perceives only one sign—the most conspicuous or prominent—but fails to correlate it with the other signs or to integrate the necessary group of signs; he draws premature conclusions regarding the meaning of the pictures, guessing at it from a single fragment that he has perceived. E.g., he may identify the pair of spectacles . . . as "a bicycle" because he cannot synthesize two circles and a series of lines into the required image. In less marked cases these difficulties are only brought to light during the examination of the most complex visual structures. The patient hardly ever expresses confident opinions regarding the meaning of pictures; he is constantly in doubt or he complains of his poor eyesight.	Lesions in the occipitoparietal divisions of the cortex. *Optic agnosia*
The patient can perceive a picture and evaluate it properly, but he can only perceive one picture or one element at a time.	*Simultaneous agnosia*
The patient loses sight of the whole picture if he examines its details. His examination of the objects is accompanied by ataxia of gaze.	
The patient looks at the picture passively; he does not change the direction of his gaze and he does not seem to attempt to "seek out" the identifying signs; usually he reaches a confident conclusion about what the picture represents; he shows no doubt and there is no attempt at correction.	Lesion of the frontal lobes
The patient evaluates the picture in the position it is shown to him; he does not turn it over and he makes no attempt to invert it mentally. Complex visual stimuli give him the impression of chaos. . . . He may also persevere in the same perception, i.e., the different pictures begin to be interpreted in the same way.	
The patient neglects the left side.	Lesion of the right hemisphere

From Christensen, 1975, pp. 72–73.

Our reading of the literature leads us to concur with Lezak. The usefulness and validity of this battery is far from proved. Neuropsychologists would be better advised to use Christensen's version of Luria's procedures or one of the composite batteries described below than to use the Luria-Nebraska.

Informal Composite Batteries

In the course of studying the consequences of brain injury psychologists have devised many tests with which to demonstrate double dissociation of different cortical regions. Many of these tests are inappropriate for clinical application, but some are particularly well suited for use in the diagnosis of brain injury. By using tests of this sort it is possible to assemble informal test batteries that can be easily changed with additions or subtractions to suit the assessment problems of individual subjects. Examples of this form of informal composite battery are described by Benton et al., Newcombe, Smith, and Lezak. Because of our affiliation with the Montreal Neurological Institute, we have chosen to use the tests derived from over 30 years of research on neurosurgical patients by Brenda Milner, Laughlin Taylor, and their colleagues. In addition, we have borrowed tests from others, particularly Doreen Kimura and H.-L. Teuber and his associates. We describe these tests briefly here and provide a more extensive description, including normative data, in Chapter 30.

The tests in this battery are based primarily on research with patients with surgical excisions for indolent tumors or epilepsy. Although not all of the tests were developed in Montreal, all have been extensively researched on neurosurgical patients before and after surgery, as well as later in follow up, sometimes pursued over periods of 20 years after surgery.

Table 26–4 summarizes the tests in the battery, most of which have been discussed in other contexts earlier in the book (see Chapters 16–18); each test will therefore be discussed only briefly. First, general intelligence and speech lateralization are assessed using standard techniques, namely Wechsler scales and dichotic digits or words. Visuoperceptual abilities are assessed by a series of pictures making up the McGill picture-anomalies test: looking at a series of pictures, each containing something strange or unusual, the subject must point to the oddity in the picture. The Mooney faces test requires the subject, examining an incomplete sketch of a face, to perceive the face, and then indicate the sex and age of the person. Finally, the Rey complex figure is copied as accurately as possible. The Mooney faces and the Rey figure are particularly sensitive to right parietal lobe damage, whereas the McGill picture anomalies is most sensitive to right temporal lobe damage.

Memory is assessed by a number of tests. The widely used Wechsler memory scale complements the Wechsler intelligence scales and includes subtests of general information

TABLE 26–4

An example of an informal composite battery[a]

1. Determination of speech lateralization
   a. Handedness questionnaire
   b. Dichotic digits or words

2. General intelligence: WAIS or WAIS-R

3. Visuoperceptual
   a. McGill picture anomalies
   b. Mooney faces
   c. Rey complex figures—copy

4. Memory
   a. Wechsler memory scale
   b. Rey complex figures—delayed recall
   c. Delayed recall of stories, paired associates, and drawings
   d. Corsi block span

5. Spatial
   a. Right-left differentiation
   b. Semmes body-placing test

6. Somatosensory
   a. Passive movement
   b. Point localization
   c. Two-point discrimination
   d. Simultaneous extinction

7. Language
   a. Object naming
   b. Chapman-Cook speed of reading
   c. Spelling
   d. Phonetic discrimination
   e. Token test

8. Hippocampal function
   a. Corsi recurring blocks
   b. Hebb recurring digits

9. Frontal lobe
   a. Wisconsin card-sorting test
   b. Chicago word fluency test

10. Motor function
    a. Dynamometer
    b. Kimura box test
    c. Complex arm and facial movement copying

[a]Based largely on research done at the Montreal Neurological Institute.

drawings, and paired associates, these items (names of heads of state) and orientation (date, etc.), recall of simple logical stories, forward and backward recall of strings of digits, a paired-associates list, and simple drawings. In addition to immediate recall of the stories, must be recalled after a delay of about 30 minutes. Finally, there is a delayed recall of a complex figure previously copied. The verbal-memory tests are sensitive to left temporal lobe damage, the nonverbal tests to right temporal lobe damage.

Among the spatial tests are a right-left differentiation test and the Semmes body-placing test. Somatosensory tests include tests of sensitivity of the hands, face, and feet to light touch and passive movement. Language functions are assessed by standard tests of naming, reading, spelling, and language comprehension, the only unusual test being that of phonetic discrimination, described in the frontal lobe chapter. Tests of hippocampal, frontal lobe, and motor function have all been discussed previously, in Chapters 16 through 18.

The principal advantage of using the Montreal tests is that the hundreds of research cases on which they are based have surgically induced lesions that were carefully photographed and sketched by the surgeons so that test performance could be accurately correlated with lesion location and extent. Since the patients were tested both preoperatively and postoperatively, as well as in follow up, those tests that were not reliable indicators of localized brain injury have been eliminated. Furthermore, although the original research patients were usually epileptic, subsequent studies have shown the tests to be even more sensitive to other disorders such as strokes and tumors, and they can be used to discriminate between individuals with different types of disorders, as described in the following chapters.

REFERENCES

Benton, A. L., D. deS. Hamsher, N. R. Varney, and O. Spreen. *Contributions to Neuropsychological Assessment: A Clinical Manual.* New York: Oxford University Press, 1983.

Christensen, A.-L. *Luria's Neuropsychological Investigation.* New York: Spectrum Publications, 1975.

Golden, C. J. A standardized version of Luria's neuropsychological tests. In S. Filskov and T. J. Boll, eds., *Handbook of Clinical Neuropsychology.* New York: Wiley-Interscience, 1981.

Kimura, D., and J. McGlone. *Neuropsychology Test Procedures.* Manual used at the University Hospital, London, Ontario, Canada, 1983.

Lezak, M. D. *Neuropsychological Assessment,* 2nd ed. New York: Oxford University Press, 1983.

McFie, J. *Assessment of Organic Intellectual Impairment.* New York: Wiley, 1975.

Newcombe, F. *Missile Wounds of the Brain.* London: Oxford University Press, 1969.

Reitan, R. M., and L. A. Davison. *Clinical Neuropsychology: Current Status and Application.* New York: Wiley, 1974.

Smith, A. Principles underlying human brain functions in neuropsychological sequelae of different neuropathological processes. In S. B. Filskov and T. J. Boll, eds., *Handbook of Clinical Neuropsychology.* New York: Wiley-Interscience, 1981.

Spiers, P. A. Have they come to praise Luria or to bury him: The Luria-Nebraska controversy. *Journal of Consulting and Clinical Psychology,* 49:331–341, 1981.

Taylor, L. B. Psychological assessment of neurosurgical patients. In T. Rasmussen and R. Marino, eds., *Functional Neurosurgery*. New York: Raven Press, 1979.

Watson, C. G., R. W. Thomas, D. Anderson, and J. Felling. Differentiation of organics from schizophrenics by use of the Reitan–Halstead organic test battery. *Journal of Consulting and Clinical Psychology* 32:679–684, 1968.

27

APPLICATIONS OF
NEUROPSYCHOLOGICAL ASSESSMENT

Having surveyed the basic principles of neuropsychological theory and assessment, we now provide examples of the application of the tests and theory to clinical problems by presenting case histories to illustrate the use of neuropsychological tests in neuropsychological assessment. In this chapter we describe the test results and case histories of 12 patients: four neurosurgical cases, four neurological cases, and four miscellaneous cases. These cases will provide a feel for the clinical application of neuropsychological tests and will provide an introduction to the next two chapters, in which we consider the use of these tests to study disorders that do not have known neurological correlates: learning disabilities and mental disorders.

NEUROSURGICAL CASES

To illustrate the application of neuropsychological tests to neurosurgical cases we have borrowed four cases from Laughlin Taylor at the Montreal Neurological Hospital. We also refer the reader to Chapter 14, where we contrasted two other such patients.

Case 1

This 33-year-old man had a history of seizures beginning four years before his admission to the hospital. His neurological examination on admission was negative, but he was having increasingly frequent seizures, which were characterized by head and eyes turning to the right: a pattern that suggests supplementary motor cortex involvement. Radiological and EEG studies suggested a left frontal lobe lesion, a suggestion that was confirmed at operation when a poorly differentiated astrocytoma was removed, as illustrated in Figure 27–1. This man was given the composite Montreal battery similar to the one summarized in Table 26–4, and the significant results are summarized in Figure 27–1. The only difficulty the patient experienced preoperatively was in doing the Wisconsin card-sorting test, where numerous perservative errors were made and only one category was correctly sorted. Two weeks after surgery all the intelligence ratings, memory quotient, and delayed verbal recall scores decreased, but these scores remained in essentially the same ratio to one another. Other tests were essentially unchanged, the only sig-

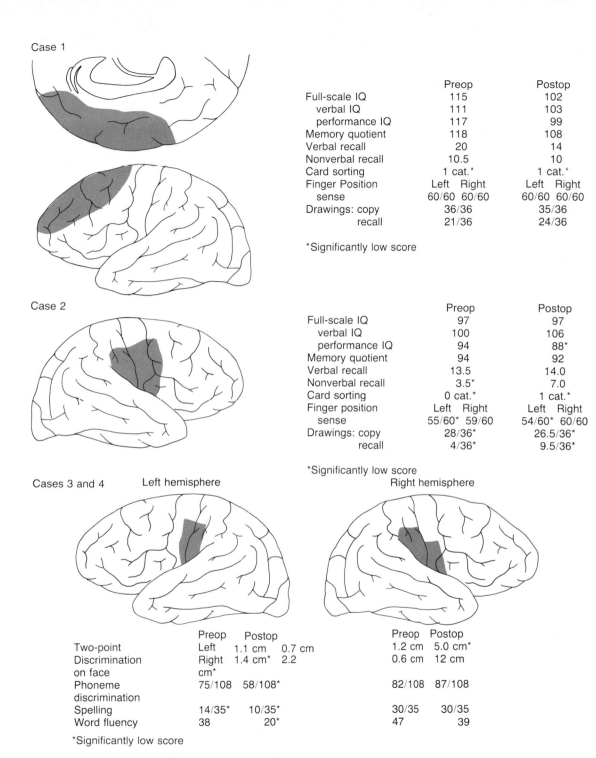

Case 1

	Preop	Postop
Full-scale IQ	115	102
verbal IQ	111	103
performance IQ	117	99
Memory quotient	118	108
Verbal recall	20	14
Nonverbal recall	10.5	10
Card sorting	1 cat.*	1 cat.*
Finger Position sense	Left Right 60/60 60/60	Left Right 60/60 60/60
Drawings: copy	36/36	35/36
recall	21/36	24/36

*Significantly low score

Case 2

	Preop	Postop
Full-scale IQ	97	97
verbal IQ	100	106
performance IQ	94	88*
Memory quotient	94	92
Verbal recall	13.5	14.0
Nonverbal recall	3.5*	7.0
Card sorting	0 cat.*	1 cat.*
Finger position sense	Left Right 55/60* 59/60	Left Right 54/60* 60/60
Drawings: copy	28/36*	26.5/36*
recall	4/36*	9.5/36*

*Significantly low score

Cases 3 and 4   Left hemisphere   Right hemisphere

	Preop	Postop		Preop	Postop
Two-point Discrimination on face	Left 1.1 cm Right 1.4 cm*	0.7 cm 2.2 cm*		1.2 cm 0.6 cm	5.0 cm* 12 cm
Phoneme discrimination	75/108	58/108*		82/108	87/108
Spelling	14/35*	10/35*		30/35	30/35
Word fluency	38	20*		47	39

*Significantly low score

FIGURE 27–1. Psychological test results before and after operation for four cases. (After Taylor 1969, 1979.)

nificantly low score again being on the sorting test. If this patient were like other patients with similar lesions, it is likely that on follow up a year after surgery his intelligence ratings and memory scores would have returned to the preoperative level, although his card sorting would be unlikely to show any improvement. Furthermore, he would almost certainly have had a chronic deficit in copying sequences of movements of the face, although he was not given this test.

Case 2

This 26-year-old man had a history of eight years of seizures dating back to an episode of meningitis in which he was thought to have an intracerebral abcess. Subsequently he developed seizures beginning in the left side of his face and hand, and he was referred as a candidate for surgery since his seizures were uncontrolled by medication. Before surgery, the patient scored within normal limits on tests of intelligence and general memory, although he did have difficulty with delayed recall of verbal material. He had slight defects of finger position sense on the left hand, which together with some weakness in the left arm and leg pointed to damage in the right central area. In addition, he had difficulty in copying and recalling the Rey complex figure and was unable to sort cards in the Wisconsin test, results suggesting that his lesion might extend into frontal and temporal areas as well.

The right face area and a region extending into the right frontal lobe were removed at surgery. After this removal there remained some residual epileptiform abnormality in both the frontal lobe and the superior temporal gyrus. Postoperative testing showed improvement both in verbal IQ and in long-term verbal memory, but the patient had persisting difficulties on the card-sorting test, with finger

position sense on the left hand, and on the copy and recall of the Rey figure. There was also a decline in performance IQ. The difficulty with finger position is to be expected with the removal in this man, but the continuing difficulties with card sorting and the Rey figure imply that dysfunctioning areas remain in his right hemisphere, as reflected by the residual spiking in the frontal and temporal regions.

Cases 3 and 4

These two cases are presented together to emphasize the contrasting effects of their left and right hemisphere removals, respectively. Both of patients had longstanding epilepsy of unknown origins. The left hemisphere patient, a 13-year-old boy, had a total removal of the precentral and postcentral face area, whereas the right hemisphere patient, a 23-year-old man, had a similar removal on the left and additional removal of some parietal cortex, as illustrated in Figure 27–1.

Preoperatively, both patients had average intelligence and memory ratings, which were unaffected by the surgery. The left hemisphere patient performed normally on all preoperative tests, however. Following surgery, the left hemisphere patient continued to have a sensory loss on the right side of his face and impaired spelling, but in addition he now had difficulty with phoneme discrimination and word fluency. These symptoms are typical of patients with left face area lesions, as described in Chapter 18. In contrast, the patient with a similar removal of the right face area had a large sensory loss on the left side of his face, but showed no other significant deficits. Curiously, when we tested these patients at the copying of sequences of facial movements, they showed no impairment whatsoever, although there was a slight contralateral weakness in moving the face. This result suggests that the sensory and motor control of the face are organized rather differently.

Summary of Neurosurgical Cases

These four cases, in conjunction with those in Chapter 14, provide us with several lessons. First, neuropsychological tests can measure specific functions of the brain; they are not measures of general brain damage. Second, neuropsychological tests can discriminate and doubly dissociate quite small areas of damage in neurosurgical cases. This implies that these tests would be extremely sensitive to more global pathology such as strokes or tumors, and indeed they are. In addition, however, the sensitivity of the tests suggests that they may be useful in identifying poorly developed functions in other populations such as learning-disabled children. We return to this point in the next chapter. Third, the test results indicate that neuropsychological tests can reflect the absence of brain tissue or the presence of damaged or disturbed tissue. Fourth, it should be apparent that intelligence tests by themselves are not reliable measures of brain damage. Although the temporal lobe patients described in Chapter 14 did exhibit large decreases in IQ, similar drops were not seen in the four cases described here, even though three of them did have other cognitive deficits. Finally, it is obvious that a broad range of tests must be used, including careful measurement of somatosensory functions, if an accurate picture of cerebral functioning is to be obtained.

NEUROLOGICAL CASES

Few neuropsychologists have the good fortune to study or assess neurosurgical patients. More commonly, patients are referred by neurologists or other physicians after a stroke or some other naturally occurring disease. Assessment in these cases is far more difficult, but as we shall see in the following examples, composite test batteries can still be very useful in describing the functional state of the remaining brain.

Case 5

This 28-year-old right-handed woman had undergone emergency surgery following the bursting of a aneurysm in the right temporal lobe. Surgical reports indicated that portions of the right temporal and parietal cortex were damaged, and she had a left quadrantic hemianopsia, indicating that the lesion extended posteriorly into the visual cortex. She was referred to us two years after the accident, at which time she was in good health and attending a university, but she was having social problems as well as difficulty with mathematics. The results of her neurological assessment are summarized in Table 27–1, where it can be seen that she experienced several deficits consistent with right posterior damage. Her performance IQ was 10 points lower than her verbal IQ, she had difficulty obtaining closure on the Mooney faces test, and her recall of visual material was well below the level expected for a woman of her age and intelligence. In contrast, she performed within expected limits on tests of left hemisphere and frontal lobe function.

Case 6

A 22-year-old woman was referred to us by a clinical psychologist to assess the possibility of "organic" dysfunction. She had on several occasions engaged in bizarre behaviors such as undressing in public and urinating on other people and on one occasion had attacked her roommate. Following these episodes she was confused and amnesic for her behavior during the "attack" as well as for the period just prior to the outburst. Her neuropsychological test results indicated that her left temporal lobe was abnormal, because her verbal memory as well as reading and object-naming were impaired (see Table 27–1). Our diagnosis of temporal lobe epilepsy with a left-side focus was partially confirmed by a neurologist when EEG studies showed left hemisphere abnormality. As frequently occurs in epilepsy, a CT scan failed to reveal any unusual features, and there is nothing in the woman's history to account for the epilepsy. The seizures are completely controlled with Dilantin, but her neuropsychological deficits remain.

Case 7

This 60-year-old woman suffered a stroke that, from her CT scan, appeared to be localized in the face area and Broca's area on the left. She was referred to us a year after the stroke because of her poor progress with the speech pathologist in regaining her speech. In view of her marked dysphasia we first administered a token test, only to find that although this woman appeared to understand many of the things spoken to her, she was severely dysphasic, obtaining a very poor score on the token test. In view of this result, we gave her only a modified battery, designed to answer the referral question of what could be expected if she were to continue speech therapy. Her test results, which are summarized in Table 27–1, showed that she was of average intelligence when measured with a nonverbal test, and she performed normally on all nonverbal tests of memory and perception administered. In contrast, she had real difficulty in copying movements, even though she had no hemiparesis. Indeed, she was totally unable to copy sequences of facial movements, although she could manage individual facial movements, with some

difficulty. These results led us to conclude that this woman was aphasic and had a facial apraxia, leading us to be pessimistic about her chances for further recovery of speech functions.

Case 8

This is the case of a 37-year-old man who had been in a traffic accident some 15 years earlier. He was in a coma for six weeks and suffered secondary injury from brain infection. At the time of his accident, he was a student in a graduate program in journalism, having previously obtained a B.A. with honors in English literature. When we first met him, he had severe motor problems, needing canes to walk, and was both apraxic and ataxic. He had great difficulty in pronouncing words, especially when hurried or stressed, but careful language testing on the token test revealed no aphasic symptoms; his language problems were entirely anarthric. Since the time of his accident this man had lived at home with his parents and had not learned the social skills necessary to cope with his handicap. In short, he was being treated as though he was retarded and was being completely looked after by his family. Indeed, the patient himself believed he was retarded and he was very reluctant to attempt rehabilitation programs. At the urging of his family we gave him a thorough assessment to evaluate his potential. His results were surprising, even to us. As summarized in Table 27–1, his IQ was superior (WAIS verbal IQ of 127), and although he had deficits on some tests, especially those involving motor skills, his performance on most tests was average or above average. Despite his obvious motor handicaps, this man clearly was not retarded. Armed with our test results we were able to show him and his family that he could look after himself and should seek occupational therapy through a government agency for the handicapped.

TABLE 27–1

Examples of neuropsychological assessments of neurological patients

Test	Normal control	Case 5 Right temporal aneurysm	Case 6 Left temporal epilepsy	Case 7 Left hemi- sphere stroke	Case 8 Traffic accident
1. Speech lateralization dichotic words:					
left ear	25	18	2*	F	16
right ear	46	50	15	F	25
handedness	R	R	R	R	R
2. General intelligence					
full-scale IQ	107	113	104	F	115
verbal IQ	109	117	95*	F	127
performance IQ	105	107*	111	108	96*
3. Visuoperceptual					
Mooney faces (abbreviated)	18/19	12/19*	16/19	16/19	17/19
Rey complex figures—copy	32/36	24/36*	31/36	30/36	34/36
4. Memory					
Wechsler memory quotient	107	115	87*	F	100*
Rey complex figures—recall	22/36	11/36*	18/36*	17/36	13/36*
delayed recall of stories and paired associates	13	17	7*	—	23
delayed recall of drawings	12	6*	10	9	2*
5. Spatial					
right-left differentiation	52/60	48/60	43/60	51/60	35/60*
Semmes body placing	32/35	30/35	30/35	—	35/35
6. Language					
reading	12	12	7*	F	20
object-naming	23/36	20/26	14/26*	F	—
7. Frontal lobe					
Wisconsin card-sorting test	6.0 cat.	5.8 cat.	4.0 cat.	3.0 cat.	2.4 cat.*
Chicago word fluency	62	50	38	F	52
Motor function					
complex arm	92%	94%	89%	72%	82%
face	88%	90%	89%	20%	30%

*Abnormally poor score.
F = could not be assessed because of dysphasia.

Summary of Neurological Cases

Most neurological referrals are not intended to diagnose brain damage; as this has already been done by the neurologist; modern radiological technology can identify most brain pathology, with the exception of some epilepsies. CT scans and similar devices do not describe the particular behavioral symtoms that an individual may experience, however, and this is where careful neuropsychological assessment can be very helpful both in understanding the disorder and in planning rehabilitation. Again, we must emphasize that a thorough battery of tests is necessary for these functions, to identify both the weaknesses and the strengths of each individual.

EXAMPLES OF OTHER DISORDERS

Neuropsychologists are often asked to assess people without known neurological disease. In many of these cases there is a need to identify the cognitive deficits and strengths that different people have in order to plan rehabilitative programs or to identify the correct institutional placements. It is foolish for the psychologist to try to identify brain pathology in these people since it is almost certainly not focal and cannot be verified by other means. Nevertheless, the study of individuals with certain disorders may provide insight into the nature of the causes of the disease, a point we return to in the next two chapters.

Case 9

This 31-year-old man was diagnosed independently by two psychiatrists as being schizophrenic. When assessed by us, he had been on a small dose of chlorpromazine for two days and appeared rather lucid, having no delusions or hallucinations during the testing. His test results, however, showed serious neuropsychological abnormalities, especially in tests of frontal and temporal lobe function (see Table 27–2). We have found a similar pattern of abnormality in other diagnosed schizophrenics; we shall return to this in Chapter 29.

Case 10

Although Gilles de la Tourette's syndrome is relatively rare, diagnosis of this disease has become commoner in recent years, possibly because the symptoms are becoming better known. We have seen about 60 such cases from all across North America in the past few years and present a representative case. This was a nine-year-old boy who was displaying frequent facial and body tics, as well as some involuntary vocalizations. Although he was reported to have had a difficult birth, his developmental milestones were normal and there was no evidence of neurological disease. He was, however, having difficulty in school and his tics were making his social adjustment difficult. His intelligence rating was strictly average, although his performance IQ was eight points lower than his verbal IQ. His long- and short-term verbal memory were within normal limits but his visual memory was very poor; his copy and recall of the Rey figure were typical of a child four years younger. Perhaps surprisingly, however, this boy did not perform poorly on other tests, particularly those normally performed poorly by children with learning disabilities. We have found that this boy's pattern of test results is typical of both children and adults diagnosed as having Gilles de la Tourette's syndrome, although the cause of the tics and the cognitive deficits remains unknown. In view of the very poor visual memory skills in these people it is important for them to plan occupations not requiring heavy demands on visual memory.

Case 11

This 10-year-old boy was referred to us by a local school psychologist because of his slow progress and difficult peer relations. He had no history of neurological disease and had experienced normal developmental milestones. His intelligence rating was average, although his performance score showed an advantage of 17 points. His digit span was especially poor, as he was unable to recall more than five digits even with repeated testing. His memory rating

TABLE 27–2

Examples of neuropsychological assessments of nonneurological patients

Test	Case 9 Schizo-phrenic	Case 10 Gilles de la Tourette	Case 11 Learning disabled	Case 12 Dementia
1. General intelligence				
Full-scale IQ	98	100	94	86
Verbal IQ	100	103	87*	89
Performance IQ	95	95	104	87
2. Visuoperceptual				
Mooney faces	15/19	20/26	26/26	11/26*
Rey figure—copy	35/36	18/26*	15/36*	0*
3. Memory				
Wechsler memory quotient	90*	81*	92	66*
Rey figure—recall	1/36*	6/36*	7/36*	0*
Delayed recall of stories and paired associates	8*	18	19	0*
Delayed recall of drawings	9	6*	8	0*
4. Spatial				
Right-left differentiation	44/60	42/60	27/60*	30/60*
Semmes body placing	16/35*	29/35	22/35*	25/35*
5. Frontal lobe				
Wisconsin card-sorting test	2.5 cat.*	6.0 cat.	5.0 cat.	0 cat.*
Chicago word fluency	30*	22[a]	30[a]	4*

*Abnormally poor score.
[a]Within acceptable range for this age.

was also within the average range, although he had difficulty with the immediate recall of short stories, a result consistent with his poor immediate recall of digits. Further, he had difficulty with both the copy and the recall of the Rey figure, scoring well below the expected range for his age. Like most learning-disabled children, this boy also had real difficulty in differentiating left from right, scoring at a chance level. Performance on most other tests was, however, within normal limits, a pattern we find to be typical of children with learning difficulties.

Case 12

This 40-year-old man had been admitted to a nursing home, apparently suffering from some type of presenile dementia. His neurological exam was negative, but when we first saw him, he was incontinent and generally unresponsive. This latter symptom made testing very difficult, although with urging he did complete most tests given to him. Intelligence testing revealed a low-average IQ, a result that contrasted with his apparent dementia. Memory testing revealed significant dysfunction, however, as he was completely unable to recall even very simple drawings. He was unable to copy the Rey figure and performed very poorly on every other test given to him, a result consistent with his dementia. In this case neuropsychological testing only confirmed the obvious, and led us to be rather pessimistic regarding the man's future.

Summary

We have chosen a variety of cases in this last section to illustrate the range in test patterns that can be expected from individuals without obvious neurological disorders. The use of tests with these individuals must be very judicious and is best directed toward the planning of remedial programs. Nevertheless, neuropsychological testing of these cases may offer some insight into the nature of the disorders, as we shall see in the next chapter.

The technology of neuropsychology can be applied to virtually any problem in which psychologists use traditional assessment techniques. This range includes general counseling, vocational guidance, assessment of juvenile delinquents for the courts, assessment related to legal matters such as suits arising from injuries in traffic accidents, and placement of retarded people in occupational-training programs. Neuropsychology does not offer a panacea for any of these problems, but it can add an important tool to the arsenal used in general psychological assessment.

A Word of Caution

We have emphasized the usefulness of neuropsychological information for a variety of applied settings, but we would be remiss if we failed to caution against overuse or abuse of this information. As useful as neuropsychological data can be for general counseling, we are not proposing that neuropsychological technology be applied to every person who sees a neurologist, psychologist, psychiatrist, counselor, etc. First, it would be a waste of resources, since the vast majority of clinical problems presented to mental health and counseling services are related to problems in coping with everyday life and are largely unrelated to neurological functioning, at least at our current state of knowledge.

Second, there is a real risk of labeling people as brain damaged or organic because of failure to perform normally on particular tests. There are numerous reasons for poor performance on psychological tests, only one of which is actual brain damage. In the absence of physical symptoms or a sudden change in behavior it would be an error to assume the cause of poor performance to be brain damage. Furthermore, there is a tendency to assume that identifying a person as brain damaged solves the clinical problem, and to stop there. This is of course a false assumption, since the goal of the clinician is treatment as well as assessment. Labeling a person as brain damaged does little in the way of treatment and may actually deter treatment if the label is interpreted as meaning that nothing can be done. Indeed, we have found that the decision to administer and to use neuropsychological information requires a healthy dose of common sense in addition to technical savvy.

REFERENCES

Taylor, L. B. Localisation of cerebral lesions by psychological testing. *Clinical Neurosurgery* 16:269–287, 1969.

Taylor, L. B. Psychological assessment of neurosurgical patients. In T. Rasmussen and R. Marino, eds., *Functional Neurosurgery*. New York: Raven Press, 1979

28
LEARNING DISABILITIES

Once upon a time, the animals decided they must do something heroic to meet the problems of a "new world." So they organized a school. They adopted an activity curriculum consisting of running, climbing, swimming, and flying. To make it easier to administer the curriculum, all the animals took all the subjects. The duck was excellent in swimming, in fact better than his instructor. But he made only passing grades in flying and was very poor in running. Since he was slow in running, he had to drop swimming and stay after school to practice running. This was kept up until his web feet were badly worn and he was only average in swimming. But average was quite acceptable, so nobody worried about that—except the duck. The rabbit started at the top of his class in running, but had a nervous breakdown because of so much makeup work in swimming. The squirrel was excellent in climbing, but he developed frustrations in flying class because his teacher made him start from the ground up instead of from the treetop down. He developed "charlie horses" from overexertion and he got a C in climbing and a D in running. The eagle was a problem child and was severely disciplined. In climbing classes he beat all the others to the top of the tree, but insisted on using his own way to get there. At the end of the year an abnormal eel that could swim exceedingly well, and also run, climb, and fly a little, had the highest marks and was class valedictorian. The prairie dog stayed out of school and fought the tax levy because the administration would not add digging and burrowing to the curriculum. They apprenticed their child to a badger and later joined the groundhogs and gophers to start a free school. (Author unknown, but told by Sam Rabinovich.)

This fable expresses one view of the challenge for neuropsychology in education. Are learning problems a manifestation of disabilities or individual variation? Large numbers of children enter schools in which they are required to master a core curriculum. Some of them are completely unable to meet any demands of the school system they enter, some learn but only with great difficulty, some have to repeat one or more grades, some graduate but fail to master certain subject areas, and some even graduate without mastering basic knowledge in any area. For those who fail, the educational experience often leaves emotional and attitudinal scars that are carried throughout life. Of course, the difficulties that individuals encounter in school can have any of a number of causes. A child may be disturbed by an unhappy home life, be bored by school, dislike school, dislike a teacher, have no aptitude for school, have low "intelligence," or have a physical handicap, including brain damage. Some school systems may be equipped to assess these kinds of problems and deal with them objectively. Most have no resources for either assessment or remediation. Whether or not a school system is equipped to deal with the learning problems of an individual, neuropsychology now receives enough publicity that the question of whether a child has a brain or cognitive problem that precludes effective learning will probably arise.

Although neuropsychological assessment can often produce a useful answer to this question, there are general issues that require consideration. If someone has a problem in school, is it because they are not sufficiently intelligent? If they have a problem in a school subject, could it not be that they have a unique brain with propensities for some subjects but not for others? Let us consider these issues.

Traditionally, many people have held the view that intelligence is an entity that is normally distributed throughout the population: some people are very intelligent, most are average, and some are retarded. Gould has traced the history of this idea, and he as well as others has criticized the view that there is an entity "intelligence" that can be measured with tests. Nevertheless, the application of this view in education quite naturally leads to the conclusion that school performance should be normally distributed; that is, some children should do well and others should fail. Fulfillment of this expectation produces no strong desire to label certain children as learning disabled or to search for new strategies of instruction for those whose progress is not excellent. Neuropsychology provides a quite different perspective if one wishes to consider it. Ideas of localization and lateralization of function provide the theoretical background for the idea that there will be a lot of variation in the abilities of different individuals. A person may be a good musician but a poor artist, a good writer but a poor mathematician, a good historian but a poor scientist, etc. A person may also do poorly in every academic sphere but still have talents to be a success in life. If the idea of individual abilities based on individual differences in brain function is accepted, focus is removed from the emphasis on general intelligence and directed toward special skills. When the neuropsychological approach is adopted, it generally contains the following assumptions. (1) A disability may exist in only one or a few spheres of endeavor. (2) A specific disability or skill can be detected using a neuropsychological testing procedure. (3) If one method or strategy of instruction is unsuccessful, another might be more successful. (4) It should be possible to predict a strategy for remediation of a learning disability from the neuropsychological test results. Although none of these assumptions has yet received anything like adequate scientific support, at least one reason that neuropsychology is becoming a popular approach is that the assumptions do hold out more hope for helping learning-disabled children than does the view that they are simply not intelligent enough to succeed. Even if neuropsychology offers no help in remediation, however, it may still be useful for purposes of counseling. The case of Ms. P. illustrates this point. For Ms. P. it was not a cure for her problems, or a substitute for other types of therapy, but it did provide her with information about her problems that she had been unable to obtain elsewhere.

Ms. P., a 19-year-old woman, was referred to us by a friend of hers. She was working as a nurse's aide and had found her work so enjoyable that she was considering entering a nursing program. However, she had not completed high school and generally had a poor academic record. She came to us for guidance as to whether or not she could handle the nursing program. In discussing her academic record we learned that Ms. P. had particular difficulty with language skills, and her reading was so poor that she was unable to pass the written exam for a driver's license. In view of Ms. P's real interest in further education in nursing we decided to administer a complete neuropsychological battery to see if the requisite cognitive abilities were present. The results showed an overall IQ on the WAIS of 85, but there was a 32-point spread between her verbal IQ of 74 and her performance IQ of 106—a difference so large as to suggest that her left hemisphere was functioning very poorly at best. Her performance on specific tests of left hemisphere function confirmed this hypothesis, because her verbal memory, verbal fluency, spelling, reading, and arithmetic skills were extremely poor. On the other hand, her spatial skills were good, as were her nonverbal memory and her performance on tests such as the Wisconsin card-sorting and Semmes body-placing tests. In short, her language skills were those of a six-year-old although she had attended school for 11 years. This verbal ability contrasted with her other abilities, which were normal for a person of her age.

In view of the test results we explained to Ms. P. our belief that it was unlikely that she could handle a nursing program because of her deficient language skills. We believed also that she was unlikely to develop these skills, especially since—as we inadvertently discovered—none of her five brothers and sisters could read either! We explained to Ms. P. that she was by no means retarded, but that just as some people had no musical ability whatsoever, she had no verbal ability. (Further, we were able to arrange an aural administration of the driver's test, which she passed.) Finally, we explained Ms. P.'s problem to her husband, a well-educated man with a master's degree. In the short time they had been married he had become totally frustrated with her inability to balance the back account, read recipes, etc., and was beginning to believe his wife was either "crazy or retarded." What the marital outcome will be we do not know, but at least Mr. P. now has an understanding of his wife's problem, and they are able to work out domestic routines to circumvent her handicap.

DEFINING A LEARNING DISABILITY

The appellation learning disability is an umbrella term that is used to refer to a wide variety of school-related problems. The key feature of the term, and one that accounts for its popularity, is the implication that the disability is much like a physical handicap, and were it absent, the individual would be completely normal. A number of formal definitions of learning disabilities have been proposed. They usually include assumptions to the effect that the individual has adequate intelligence, opportunity to learn, adequate instruction, and an adequate home environment, yet still does not succeed. These definitional features are illustrated by the definition of dyslexia devised by the World Federation of Neurology: "A disorder manifested by difficulty in learning to read despite conventional instruction, adequate intelligence, and sociocultural opportunity. It is dependent upon fundamental cognitive disabilities which are frequently of constitutional origin." Virtually every phase of this and similar definitions has been disputed. For example, why should it be called a disorder? What is meant by conventional instruction? What is meant by adequate intelligence, etc.? To appreciate the difficulties with definitions, some of the history of ideas about learning disabilities is helpful.

Much of the early history of learning disabilities, as well as most current literature, had as its central concern one disability: dyslexia, an inability to read properly. The history of dyslexia has been recounted by Critchley, who points out that ideas about dyslexia emerged within an "aphasiological context," so that it was thought of as being due to brain damage that occurred in language areas at an early age. In the study of adult-acquired reading disorders, Kussmaul in 1877 is thought to have been the first person to specifically isolate "word blindness," or an inability to read that was caused by brain damage and that persisted in the presence of intact sight and speech. In 1892 Dejerine placed the responsible lesion in the posterior portions of the left hemisphere. The word dyslexia was coined by Berlin in 1887. When James Hinshelwood (1895), a Glasgow eye surgeon, and Pringle Morgan (1896), a Seaford general practitioner, first observed students who were incapable of learning to read, they assumed that their reading failed to develop because their prerequisite brain areas were absent or abnormal. It seemed logical to conclude that developmental dyslexia (congenital dyslexia) was similar in form to acquired dyslexia (dyslexia due to brain damage after reading had been achieved). Largely

due to the work of Samuel T. Orton in the 1920s and 1930s this view was gradually replaced with the belief that it was delayed function, not anatomical absence, that caused the disorder. Orton, the director of a medical clinic in Iowa, noted that dyslexia was correlated with left-handedness and tendencies toward letter and word reversals or inversions when learning to read or write. Orton thought that the nondominant hemisphere, which he postulated had a reversed image of things, was excessively dominant or not sufficiently controlled. He also suggested that if the instructor was clever or persevered, education could establish normal dominance and thus normal reading. When sociologists and educational psychologists became interested in learning disabilities, they thought environmental explanations, rather than neurological explanations, could account for dyslexia. This was perhaps motivated by the belief, or hope, that environmental causes could be reversed more easily than neurological ones. Recent developments in neuropsychology are now reviving the popularity of hypotheses that brain abnormalities are causal in many learning disabilities.

The idea that there is a specific reading deficit, which is not due to inadequate intelligence, had its origin in the initial observations of dyslexics: many individuals understood well what was said to them, although they could not read, and some excelled in other subjects, such as mathematics, or excelled in other endeavors. A more formal examination of this postulate has been made by Rutter and Yule. They made the assumption that if reading ability were distributed as a normal curve, they would expect to find 2.28 percent of the school-age population to be retarded in both reading and intelligence. An examination of a large population of children from a number of different studies showed specific reading retardation in 3.5 percent of Isle of Wight 10 year olds, 4.5 percent of Isle of Wight 14 year olds, and over 6 percent of

London 10 year olds. The number in excess of 2.28 percent were individuals who were retarded in reading but not in intelligence. On the basis of these data Rutter and Yule argue that there is a "hump" at the lower end of the reading distribution produced by a population of poor readers who do have adequate intelligence but are impaired at reading. They called this group *specifically reading retarded* as compared to *reading-backward*. Rutter and Yule also called attention to some additional differences between those who are specifically reading retarded and those who are backward. Among the reading-backward the sex ratio was equal, but among the specifically reading retarded 76 percent were boys. In the backward group, 11 percent had a known brain disorder, but none of the specifically reading retarded group had such a condition. The backward group also had a higher incidence of motor, praxic, speech, and other developmental abnormalities. When the developmental progress of the two groups was compared in reading and arithmetic, the specifically reading retarded group made less progress in reading and spelling than the backward group, but they made more progress in arithmetic. Rutter and Yule go to some length to point out that specific reading retardation is not the same as dyslexia as that term is traditionally defined; nevertheless, they were successful in demonstrating that a learning disability that does not involve general retardation exists.

The term learning disability had its origins in a talk given in 1963 by Samuel A. Kirk. Kirk argued for better descriptions of children's school problems, but he excluded children with sensory handicaps and mental retardation from the children he called learning disabled. His definition and address were influential because members of his audience got together and formed the "Association for Children with Learning Disabilities," and this society in turn popularized the label. Gaddes has pointed out

that it is unfortunate that many subsequent definitions have stressed the exclusion of other disabilities, because this has led to the erroneous belief that learning disabilities can only be present in children with at least average intelligence. He correctly points out that low intelligence and a learning disability may both have the same cause.

The idea that neurological abnormalities are a primary causal factor in learning disorders has received growing attention in recent years, but few areas in neuroscience have occasioned such discord. It seems that there is a desire to accept the brain hypothesis but at the same time lessen its implications. This has resulted in a proliferation of terms that ostensibly attempt to dissociate the learning disabled from the retarded and brain damaged. In a light vein, Fry published a "Do-It-Yourself Terminology Generator," shown in Table 28–1, to emphasize the proliferation of terms in the field and the inaccuracies in description. From this list about 2000 terms can be fabricated that have been or could be used to describe the syndromes observed.

TABLE 28–1

"Do-It-Yourself Terminology Generator" [a]

Secondary	Nervous	Deficit
Minimal	Brain	Dysfunction
Mild	Cerebral	Damage
Minor	Neurological	Disorder
Chronic	Neurologic	Desynchronization
Diffuse	CNS	Handicap
Specific	Language	Disability
Primary	Reading	Retardation
Developmental	Perceptual	Deficiency
Disorganized	Impulsive	Impairment
Organic	Visual-motor	Pathology
Clumsy	Behavior	Syndrome
Functional	Psychoneurologic	Complex

[a]Directions: Select any word from first column, add any word from second and third columns. If you don't like the result, try again. It will mean about the same thing. (From Fry, 1968. Reprinted with permission of Edward Fry and the International Reading Association.)

The Incidence of Learning Disabilities

Disagreements over the definition of learning disabilities make it difficult to estimate their incidence. Gaddes tried to determine the proportion of children with learning disabilities as reported in various prevalence studies from both North America and Europe. He found that most estimates of the need for special training for learning disabilities range from between 10 and 15 percent of the school-age population, although only about 2 percent actually receive special education. A problem in collecting prevalence estimates is that a learning disability is an emerging problem. When children enter the first grade, few are as yet learning disabled. One popular method of defining a learning disability is to use a two-year cutoff criterion; that is, if an individual is two years behind as determined by a standard test, then that individual is learning disabled. When this criterion is used, then less than 1 percent of six year olds are disabled, 2 percent of seven year olds are disabled, and so on until at age 19, 25 percent would be disabled. This emerging incidence occurs because the learning disabled are falling behind at a rate that is proportional to their degree of impairment. Even these kinds of calculations may be difficult to apply in certain regions. For example, the Wide Range Achievement Test (WRAT) is frequently used to determine grade equivalent performance. When Snart, Dennis, and Brailsford gave the test to children in Stettler, an Alberta town with a population of about 5000, they found that the average child performed two years ahead of the expected grade norms. That is, a child two years behind in that school system would actually be classified as normal by WRAT criteria. Another way of collecting estimates could be to ask teachers how many children in their classes are receiving special help and, therefore, could be learning disabled. Unfortunately, many schools cannot provide such information because they have no resources for special education and so do not use that kind of classification. Myklebust suggests that reading (or any other academic skill) can be assessed by deriving a learning quotient based on the child's performance, age, grade, etc. Regardless of what measure is used, it may well be necessary to derive norms for performance in any area before fully objective definitions of what constitutes a learning disability for that area can be obtained.

Types of Learning Disabilities

We would like to provide the reader with a simple classification of learning disabilities along with some estimate of their incidence. All we can say, however, is that the classification and incidence reflect rather well the emphasis placed on appropriate conduct and certain academic specialties in school systems. Good behavior, reading, arithmetic, and spelling are areas of emphasis in all schools, and learning-disability classification reflects this emphasis. Although art, music, and physical education are taught in most schools, referrals for failure in these areas are extremely uncommon. Were art, and not reading, the core subject in the early years of school, we suspect that current catalogues of types of disabilities would be quite different. These comments are not made entirely tongue in cheek. If one purpose of neuropsychological assessment is to evaluate cognitive function, a restricted emphasis will unquestionably lead to a restricted view about what constitutes normal cognitive function.

There are a number of classifications of learning disabilities, but those in neuropsychology emphasize disorders of reading. In summarizing syndromes presented to a clinic specializing in learning disabilities over a two-year period, Denckla reports that of 484 children aged six to 16, 76 percent were classified as primarily dyslexic, with or without some associated problems, and 18 percent were classified as hyperactive. Thus, reading and behavior problems were the commonest reasons for referral. The Diagnostic and Statistical Manual of Mental Disorders (DSM III) provides a number of classifications of disorders arising in childhood. Excluding mental retardation and mental disorders, the DSM III describes disorders in reading, arithmetic, and motor activity along with some mixed classifications. The U.S. Department of Health, Education and Welfare identifies 10 characteristics as most often cited by various authors as being associated with a learning disability: (1) hyperactivity; (2) perceptual-motor impairments; (3) emotional lability; (4) general coordination deficits; (5) disorders of attention (short attention span, distractibility, perseveration); (6) impulsivity; (7) disorders of memory and thinking; (8) specific learning disabilities, including especially those of reading (dyslexia), arithmetic, writing, and spelling; (9) disorders of speech and hearing; and (10) equivocal neurological signs and irregular EEG. It must be noted that not all learning-disabled children exhibit all the symptoms. Critchley points out that for every learning-disabled child with coordination problems, there is a child with better than normal coordination. This variability underscores the points that not all learning disabilities are the same and that there are presumably multiple causes. Some authors categorize the learning disabilities into four symptom complexes, which are not mutually exclusive: (1) dyslexia-dysgraphia, (2) motor-perceptual, (3) language delay, and (4) hyperactivity. For the purposes of this chapter we shall concentrate our attention on dyslexia, since it provides a good model for the study of learning disabilities in general and is usually a central school problem of learning-disabled individuals.

CAUSES OF LEARNING DISABILITIES

Five major factors are most frequently cited as possible causes of learning disabilities: (1) structural damage, (2) brain dysfunction, (3) abnormal cerebral lateralization, (4) maturational lag, and (5) environmental deprivation. Although no data unequivocally and totally support any one of these theories, there is reason to believe that all these factors may contribute to disabilities.

Structural Damage

Since the symptoms of brain damage in adulthood resemble childhood learning disabilities (e.g., dyslexia), the cause of learning disabilities may be structural damage, perhaps resulting from birth trauma, encephalitis, anoxia, etc.; in general, causes similar to those that produce cerebral palsy (Table 12–2). Although no doubt a cause for a small minority of children, structural damage is not likely to be the cause in most children, since many neurological symptoms associated with brain damage in adults are not typically observed in children. For example, childred with developmental dyslexia do not have hemianopsias or scotomas, which are symptoms that would certainly occur in a large percentage of dyslexic adults. Further, to date EEG studies have not demonstrated structural damage: abnormal EEGs similar to those correlated with known brain damage are not consistently correlated with learning disabilities.

Since clear evidence of brain damage is absent in many children who have learning disorders, Gaddes suggests that they be classified as a group separate from those with brain damage and those with minimal brain damage. He suggests the brain damage classification be reserved for those who have what are called "hard signs": brain tumor, bleeding, penetrat ing injury, hemiplegia, etc. He suggests that children with minimal brain damage are those who have what are called "soft neurological signs": developmental delay, language retardation, motor clumsiness, perceptual deficits, right-left problems, hyperactivity, poor body image, poor hand-eye coordination, etc. Children with learning disabilities would be those with none of these signs, but with a specific difficulty in one or more school subjects. Some people may find these distinctions problematical. For educators there is little advantage to the distinction since any group may have a learning disability that requires their special attention. Children with learning disabilities may also have some of the "soft signs" such as left-right confusion but still show no evidence of structural damage. Nevertheless, the classification is worth mentioning because it does direct attention to a conventional view: that is, many learning disabilities do not seem to be accompanied by obvious structural damage.

The idea that structural damage is involved in learning disabilities cannot be dismissed until anatomical studies have been made, at autopsy, on the brains of learning-disabled individuals. At present only a few studies have been reported. Drake examined the brain of a 12-year-old boy who died of cerebral hemorrhage. In school he had been impaired in arithmetic, writing, and reading, but he had normal intelligence. Autopsy showed that there were atypical gyral patterns in the parietal lobes, an atrophied corpus callosum, and neurons in the underlying white matter that should have migrated to the cortex. Galaburda and Kemper have examined the brain of a 20-year-old male who had previously had a reading disability despite average intelligence. Visual inspection of the brain showed it to be normal, but microscopic examination showed several left hemisphere abnormalities. Polymicrogyria (numerous small convolutions) and other architectural abnormalities were found in the left parietal cortex. The right hemisphere was normal. Galaburda and Eidelberg have subsequently reported subcortical abnormalities, in the medial geniculate nucleus and the lateral posterior nucleus of the thalamus, of the same individual. They suggest that the bilateral subcortical abnormalities may have been related to the left parietal abnormalities. But even if they were not, outflow from the intact right hemisphere would have been abnormal since the thalamic structures with which it must interrelate were abnormal. This, they suggest, would explain why the intact right hemisphere of this individual had not developed the ability to mediate normal reading. Although these studies are intriguing, they do not make a convincing case of themselves. First, the number of subjects is small. Second, both individuals had been epileptic and had displayed other problems at one time, so that neither was a case of a "pure" learning disability. Still, this line of research should provide valuable information in the future. The Orton Dyslexia Society has designated the Galaburda-Geschwind laboratories as a "brain bank" for anatomical research on dyslexia.

Brain Dysfunction

It is not necessary to have direct brain damage to have neurological deficits. As we noted earlier, for example, there is little doubt that schizophrenia results from abnormal brain function, but brain lesions do not produce schizophrenia. Rather, some abnormal physiological or biochemical process is most likely responsible. A similar logic has been applied to the study of learning disabilities: such disabilities may result, not from direct damage, but from malfunction of some portion of the cerebral cortex. Tentative support for this view comes from electrophysiological recording studies associating specific high-frequency EEG abnormalities with various types of learning disabilities. These studies are controversial, however. In a review Hughes concludes that EEG and AEP studies of children with learning disabilities are encouraging enough to justify further investigation of these techniques as diagnostic tools, but to date no firm conclusions have been reached.

One view of the brain dysfunction hypothesis holds that the dysfunction results from defective "arousal mechanisms." Since the neocortex is normally activated by subcortical structures, it is argued that if the subcortical input were missing or abnormal, then a particular cortical region would dysfunction. This conclusion has been inferred from two principal sources. First, Douglas and her colleagues have found that learning-disabled children have difficulty on continuous-performance tests requiring them to react to particular stimuli while ignoring others. Similarly, reaction-time studies show the children to have slower mean reaction times to signals. On tests of visual searching—in which the child is asked to search among several alternatives to find a picture identical to a standard picture—the learning-disabled children choose impulsively and quickly, making many more errors than normal children, who perform more slowly. Douglas concludes that the deficits on these types of tasks result from some form of inadequate cerebral activation. It could be predicted that learning disabilities, or some types, at least, should improve with drugs that increase cerebral activation. This is indeed the case: both amphetamine and caffeine, cerebral stimulants, improve performance on the Douglas et al. tests and are frequently used effectively in the treatment of hyperactive children.

An alternative dysfunction theory proposes that brain malfunction results from abnormal metabolism, due either to diet or to abnormal metabolic processes. Recent work has shown that if diet is modified—especially if foods containing sugar are reduced—learning dis-

abilities are significantly mitigated. This finding supports the idea that inadequate diet may contribute to learning disabilities by causing abnormal brain function. One difficulty in treating learning disabilities with proper nutrition is that people's needs for various minerals, vitamins, etc., vary widely. It may be that some children require certain nutrients in amounts far exceeding the usual. For example, vitamin D resistant rickets is a disorder requiring amounts of vitamin D that would be lethal to most people. Although it is conceivable that extremely large amounts of some vitamin or mineral are required in children with learning disorders, the missing factor would be extremely difficult to identify. A recent study is intriguing in this respect. Analyzing specimens of hair from normal and learning-disabled children, Pihl and Parkes found significant differences between the groups in the levels of sodium, cadmium, cobalt, lead, manganese, chromium, and lithium. When levels of these elements were measured in the hair, it was possible to accurately pick 98 percent of all the children diagnosed as learning disabled from a second sample of children. Although Pihl and Parkes could not identify the cause of the abnormal levels of trace elements, their success in diagnosing additional children leads us to seriously consider biochemical factors as causal factors in learning disabilities.

Abnormal Cerebral Lateralization

Around 1900 there were several reports of children with normal intelligence who appeared unable to learn to read, exhibiting so-called developmental dyslexia. In 1925, Orton began to study such children, and he proposed that some anomaly in cerebral dominance was responsible for the difficulties; he termed such dyslexia *strephosymbolia* (from the Greek, meaning twisted symbols). Orton's concept (and term) was largely ignored until its revival in the 1960s, with the growing interest in human neuropsychology. Today a variety of theories rest on the premise that learning disabilities result from reduced or abnormal cerebral lateralization. This premise is based on the assumption that, since language is lateralized in the left hemisphere of most adults, such lateralization must be advantageous, and its absence would be deleterious to the acquisition of language skills. Normal lateralization could be absent for a number of reasons. For example, we noted earlier that some inhibitory process may normally act to prevent left hemisphere functions from developing in the right hemisphere, and vice versa. If this inhibitory process were inactive, the brain would be less asymmetrical. Inhibition could be absent because of a number of factors, retarded myelinization of the corpus callosum being one.

Orton's explanation of learning disabilities would seem to be easy to evaluate experimentally. For example, if children were divided into two groups (normal and learning disabled) and then tested for dichotic and visual field asymmetries, the disabled group should not show asymmetries. In the past 20 years dozens of studies have examined dichotic and visual field asymmetries in this way, but the data are far from unequivocal. Satz concludes:

> One might ask what light the preceding review of laterality studies sheds, if any, on the problem of cerebral dominance and reading disability. The answer should be—not much. The reason for this somewhat discouraging view lies in the numerous methodological and conceptual problems that continue to plague research efforts in this area. (Satz, 1976, p. 288)

Proposing a somewhat different theory of abnormal cerebral lateralization, Witelson argues that there may be an association between developmental dyslexia and two neurological abnormalities: a lack of right hemi-

sphere specialization for spatial processing, and a dysfunction in left hemisphere processing of linguistic functions. That is, being located in both hemispheres, spatial functions result in an interference with the left hemisphere's processing of linguistic functions. The person approaches linguistic functions in a visual-holistic manner rather than a phonetic-analytic manner, which would be expected to produce deficits in language but superiority in spatial skills.

Because of current popular interest in hemispheric asymmetry, the belief that impaired cerebral lateralization is the source of problems in learning-disabled children has become attractive. Kinsbourne and Hiscock have been outspoken critics of this theory. Their principle criticism centers on the assumption that reduced lateralization of language should be detrimental to language development and school performance. As discussed in Chapter 15, anomalous language lateralization in left-handers is not consistently correlated with cognitive deficit, nor is left-handedness consistently correlated with learning disability. We concur with Kinsbourne and Hiscock's criticisms.

Maturational Lag

The maturational-lag hypothesis postulates that cognitive functions involved in language, reading, and other complex behaviors are organized hierarchically, and that the levels in the hierarchy develop sequentially during ontogeny. Should one level of the hierarchy be slow to develop, the entire hierarchy is retarded in development, since higher functions depend on the integrity of lower ones. The delayed maturation of cortical functions could result from a variety of factors: two examples are delayed myelinization of a particular region, and slow development of the connections of association regions, which delays the hookup of sensory and motor regions with associative cortex. Although some studies suggest that various functions in learning-disabled children are slow in maturing, the type of study needed here is a careful longitudinal analysis of children tested on a large number of perceptual, motor, and cognitive skills for a period of 10 to 15 years. When learning-disabled children have been reexamined in adulthood, they have been found to still have their characteristic impairments. For example, Frauenheim studied 40 adults who were diagnosed as dyslexic in childhood and found that on test performance and on self-report evaluations they were essentially unchanged from the time of diagnosis. This result does not support the maturational-lag hypothesis.

Environmental Deprivation

The work of Rosensweig, Krech, Bennett, Diamond, and their colleagues has shown that environmental factors can alter the neocortical development of rats. Rats raised in enriched environments have a thicker cortex with increased numbers of dendritic spines compared with rats raised in impoverished environments. This work implies, then, that the environment in which children are raised may affect behavior indirectly by altering brain development. The notion has considerable appeal and has led to the development of programs such as Operation Headstart. To date there is no unequivocal experimental evidence that environmental factors, short of impoverishment such as that suffered by Genie (Chapter 24), can produce learning disabilities. However, Money has argued in a "feisty" review that institutional confinement, neglect, and child abuse can cause retarded intellectual development and even retardation in physical growth. Accordingly, he states that environmental deprivation should rank high on the list of causes of learning disabilities and should be actively investigated.

Do Learning Disabilities Have a Genetic Basis?

Any consideration of the possibility that learning disorders have a genetic basis must recognize some of the obstacles to the demonstration. First, as discussed above, learning disabilities may have many environmental causes, which must be excluded from genetic causes. Since it is not clear in individual cases what a putative cause might be, such exclusions are typically difficult to make. Second, learning disabilities take many forms. At present, criteria for categorizing types of learning disabilities are poorly developed. Third, the incidence of learning disabilities is related to the quality of schooling. Average length of schooling and the demands made by schools on students have undergone rapid change in the past two generations. Thus, it is difficult to compare the reading abilities of many children with those of their parents. Fourth, learning-disabled individuals are typically of average intelligence, as are their parents, and as we shall see, people of strictly average intelligence (that is, full-scale IQs around 100) generally find school difficult. Fifth, the ability to read is itself probably inherited, making it difficult to sort out the contribution made by inherited reading skill as compared with a supposed inherited causal factor underlying a disability. Despite the difficulties in doing this kind of research, the possibility of genetic causes has been repeatedly raised. As early as 1905, Thomas noted the familial nature of "word blindness," and since then many authors have made reference to the high incidence of learning disabilities within certain families. Two other types of evidence also support the genetic hypothesis. For dyslexia the ratio of about four males to one female is commonly reported (see Critchley for a summary of studies between 1927 and 1968). If only environmental factors were responsible, a more equal sex ratio would be expected. Twin studies also find a higher incidence of dyslexia in identical as compared with fraternal twins. Despite the familial nature of learning disabilities, however, attempts by Defries and Decker and others have not been successful in relating this incidence to any genetic model. Therefore, it is simply not certain that disabilities are inherited, although considerable evidence seems to support the inheritance hypothesis.

DYSLEXIA

Reading is a complex business that requires a number of abilities to perform. These include letter identification skill, phonological skill (converting letters into sounds using certain rules), grapheme skills (the visual gestalt of a word is used to access a previously learned sound), sequencing skills in which a number of sounds are analyzed and combined in sequence, and short-term memory skills to retain pieces of information as they are sequentially extracted from written material. Acquired information is also important. Knowledge of words in the form of a **lexicon** (a dictionary-like store), containing their meanings, knowledge of the way in which they can be combined, and information about the ideas with which they can be associated are importantly related to reading. Thus, reading is a multiprocess and multistage behavior. As such it is possible, in theory if not in fact, for it to be disrupted in many different ways.

It is generally accepted that reading can be accomplished in one of two ways. Consider the following example, which illustrates the two ways. Imagine that you are reading a novel about a man named Fzylx from Worcester. Let us assume that you have never encountered either the man's name or his hometown before. When you read the names, you would presumably attempt to pronounce the various letters to arrive at a satisfactory pronunciation of the words. Suppose that the next day you overhear two people discussing a novel about a man named Felix from Wooster. At first, you might be struck by the similarity between the plot of your book and theirs, until you realize that they are actually talking about Fzylx from Worcester! What has happened? When you read Fzylx and Worcester, you encountered two common problems in reading English. First, you had to read a name that is not English and so you have no rules by which to read it. You may feel comfortable with your pronunciation, since it allows you to read it, but you are likely to be wrong. Second, you encounter an irregular word; that is, a word that is not pronounced the way it is spelled. The only way to pronounce this type of word correctly is to memorize the word. This type of reading is called **grapheme** reading (sometimes called lexical reading). It can be used for regular words as well, but it must be used for irregular words or words that are not found in English. Incidentally, it is also the way Arabic numerals must be read (e.g., 4) and the way international symbolic road and direction signs must be read. The other way to read is to do what you tried to do with Fzylx and Worcester. You simply convert a letter or group of letters into sounds (phonemes) that will provide the clue to the meaning of the words. Stated differently, the sounds that you get by analyzing letter groups will lead you to the correct pronunciation and you will be able to access your memory, or lexicon, for the meaning and connotation of the word. This is known as **phonological** reading.

Bradley and Bryant have suggested that the phonological procedure is used by beginning readers, but that as reading skill is attained the graphemic procedure becomes more important. They suggest that the transition occurs between six and 10 years of age. Thus, normal reading initially involves phonological skills and then later becomes dependent on grapheme skills. This may be why many people find it hard to find typographical errors when they proofread. Rather than reading phonologically, they read graphemically and, with practice at graphemic reading, only part of the word need be read before attention is shifted to the next word. If the spelling error is not within the portion of the word "read," it will not be noticed. As we shall see below, it has been suggested that whereas phonological reading must be a function of the left hemisphere, grapheme reading may be a function of the right hemisphere.

Given that there are two reading processes, two or three different kinds of impairments, which could occur at different ages, should be observed. A child who is incompetent in the phonological procedure will have difficulty in the early stages of reading. A child who is competent in the phonological procedure but who is incompetent in the grapheme procedure will have difficulty later on. Frith has demonstrated just such types of age-related disabilities among poor readers. It may also follow that a child who is impaired at the first type will be hampered in making the transition to the second type as well. We should note here that by no means would these types of impairments exhaust the class of poor-reader types. People with a poor short-term auditory memory may not correctly derive the sense of written material that they read because they forget the meaning of phrases as they proceed. This type of disability may be particularly obvious at still older ages, once reading material becomes more complex. People with poor long-term memory may not understand the sense of words despite good decoding skills simply because they do not have much information about the meaning of the words. This type of individuals would be like English-speaking people who are reading Italian. They would be able to read the words because they know phonetic rules, but they would not understand what they read because they would not know what the words meant. In fact, people who are demented are often just like this. They can read but they understand nothing.

There are three approaches to the analysis of the problems of the dyslexic individual. One is to identify the reading problem without regard to its underlying causes. Such an approach may also give some information about underlying causes, but this is by no means certain. A second approach is to describe and analyze the dyslexic in a variety of different ways, cataloging various symptoms, in order to come to conclusions about underlying causes. A third way is to use neuropsychological assessment procedures, derived from research on adult brain-damaged patients, to evaluate brain and cognitive function in the disabled reader and relate that information to the reading disorder. All three approaches have generated interesting insights into the dyslexic individual, although it would be correct to say that the amount and complexity of the information they have generated is astonishing. As a testament to the cornucopia of theories and findings it might be enlightening to catalogue some theories of dyslexia and then to discuss a selected few later on.

Malatesha and Dougan have reviewed studies that provide various subclassifications of dyslexia. They found that seven studies describe two subtypes, 21 studies describe three subtypes, and three studies describe four subtypes. To add to this complexity, most subtypes in most of the different studies are derived in quite different ways, using different assessment techniques and different classification criteria. Some studies emphasize visual and auditory processing differences, some emphasize hemisphere specialization, some emphasize memory differences, some emphasize deficits in certain aspects of reading, whereas others are based on postulated types of brain damage or dysfunction, etc. It appears to us that the problem of classification and subclassification will remain complex. As we shall describe below, there is a great deal of variation in test performance even in individuals who are reported to have the same type of learning disability. It would seem, therefore, that assessment providing a number of different evaluation criteria combined with counseling directed toward the special problems of each individual will remain the most effective approach to both research and remediation.

Language Analysis

Based on the analysis of reading, writing, and spelling patterns, Boder has proposed that there are three subtypes of dyslexia: dysphonetic, dyseidetic, and dysphonetic-dyseidetic. As we shall discuss, these groups correspond quite closely to those described above that include individuals having a disability in phonological processing, grapheme processing, or a combined deficit of both types of processing.

1. *Dysphonetic.* The dysphonetic subgroup is the largest (>60 percent). These types of reading-disabled individuals are thought to have a disability in developing phonic- and word-analysis skill; that is, they are unable to decode written words or to write them using phonic or sound principles. They recognize the words on the basis of visual patterns and confuse words with similar visual patterns (e.g.,

diesel and dress) or meanings (e.g., planet and moon).

2. *Dyseidetic.* Dyseidetic individuals have deficits in recognizing words by their visual configurations, but they are able to use phonic skills to read them or render a relatively correct spelling. They have difficulty in developing a sight vocabulary. Their misreadings involve phonic renditions (talc for talk) as do their misspellings (laf for laugh).

3. *Dysphonetic-Dyseidetic.* This group consists of individuals who combine both types of deficits and are unable to develop either a sight or a phonic vocabulary. They are essentially alexic.

The three groups are discriminated by using a diagnostic screening test that assesses their ability to discriminate known and unknown words. The Boder classification is similar to a number of other classifications, particularly that of Johnson and Myklebust, who also divide dyslexics into subgroups with primary impairments in visual procession (recognizing words by sight) and auditory procession (recognizing words by sound). The approach is also similar to that divised by Coltheart and others, which is described in Chapter 21 and illustrated in Figures 21–6 and 21–7. Although the latter models were initially designed to analyze acquired dyslexia, they can be applied equally well to developmental dyslexia.

The reading tests described to this point depend on the fact that some education in reading has taken place. Bradley and Bryant have developed an interesting approach that is initially reading-independent. They have tested children's ability in sound categorization before they started to read. The tests involve giving the child three or four words and asking it to pick out the word that does not share a phoneme in common with the others. For example, in the series "hill, pig, and pin," hill would be the correct choice; in the series "cot, pot, and hat," hat would be the correct choice, and in the series "pin, bun, and gun," pin would be the correct choice. They found that when the same children were older and had started to learn to read, those who were initially poor at sound categorization were those who became backward in reading and spelling. They argue that the initial insensitivity to rhyme and alliteration is causal to subsequent reading impairment, because if the children who were initially impaired were given special training on rhyme and alliteration, their reading was far less impaired after training in reading began. According to Bradley and Bryant, at least one cause of reading deficiency would be a basic deficiency in phonological awareness.

It is possible that children who are at risk for learning disabilities could be detected still earlier. Frith has suggested that articulation of babies' babbling may give clues about those who are at risk. Tees and his coworkers have reported that young infants can detect differences between all known speech sounds, but as they acquire language their detection abilities become restricted to only those sounds used in their own language, which they are exposed to daily. It is possible, according to Tees, that the acquisition of language-related discrimination may be retarded or poorly developed in those who are at risk for learning disabilities. Should these possibilities prove correct, remediation in the use of phonic skills, such as that suggested by Bradley and Bryant, could be begun as early as the first year of life.

Analysis of Correlated Deficits

On the surface it might be hoped that reading deficits would display themselves in a straightforward manner. This seems not to be the case, because it has long been known that dyslexic individuals have a wide variety of different symptoms that occur in clusters and that vary considerably between individuals. We cannot discuss each of the many peculiar symptoms here, but for the reader's information they are listed in Table 28–2 along with some relevant references. Note, we do not pretend that this list is complete. We suggest that these symptoms should not be thought of as necessarily uninformative, unrelated, or irrelevant. On the basis of the simplest postulate, they might all be produced by a common underlying deficit. We need only turn to the description of the symptoms of Parkinson's disease, which although many and complex are produced by the absence of only a few brain cells containing the neurotransmitter dopamine, for reassurance that complex symptoms do not invariably indicate complex underlying causes. Dyslexia may be associated with many kinds of symptoms because language has a superordinate role in the control of behavior, because there is an intimate relation between the control of language and the control of movement, and because development of dyslexia itself may produce secondary symptoms. Just the same, attempts have been made to see if the various symptoms are causally related to dyslexia. Rutter suggests that clumsiness and incoordination; difficulties in the perception of spatial relations; directional confusion; right–left confusion; disordered temporal orientation; difficulties in naming colors and recognizing the meaning of pictures; inadequate, inconsistent, or mixed cerebral dominance; bizarre spelling; and a family history of reading difficulties do seem related to dyslexia, but it is not clear that the relation is causal. On the other hand, he concludes that low intelligence and mixed-handedness are definitely not important as causal factors. Vellutino has specifically asked which of the capacities of visual perception and visual memory, intersensory integration, temporal order and recall, and verbal processing are of central importance to reading. On the basis of a review of the available research and

TABLE 28–2

Deficits associated with dyslexia

Deficit	Reference	Deficit	Reference
Asymmetry	Gordon, 1980; Orton, 1925, 1937; Silver and Hagen, 1982		Perfetti and Hogaboam, 1975; Spring, 1976
Attention	Douglas, 1976	Orientation (left-right, etc.)	Benton, 1959; Myklebust and Johnson, 1962
Auditory and visual	Myklebust and Johnson, 1962; Wepman, 1960, 1961	Rhythmic movements	Bradley and Bryant, 1983; Klicpera, Wolff, and Drake, 1981
Cerebellar-vestibular	Ayres, 1978; Frank and Levinson, 1976; Levinson, 1980	Serial ordering	Bakker, 1972; Corkin, 1974
		Spatial frequency	Lovegrove, Heddle, and Slaghuis, 1980
Development	Critchely, 1964; Satz, Rarden, and Ross, 1971; Satz and Sparrow, 1970	Spatial-general	Witelson, 1974
		Speech-motor sequencing	Frith, 1981
Dichotic listening	Bryden, 1970; Zurif and Carlson, 1970	Temporal sequencing	Johnson and Mykelbust, 1967
Dyschrometria (time-telling)	Myklebust and Johnson, 1962	Topographic (map-reading)	Myklebust and Johnson, 1962
EEG	Ahn et al., 1980; Duffy et al., 1980; Maccario et al., 1982	Verbal	Jorm, 1979; Vellutino, 1977
		Visuomotor (letter reversals, etc.)	Orton, 1925, 1937
Eye movements	Pavlidis, 1981; Pirozzolo and Rayner, 1977; Zangwill and Blakemore, 1972	Visual processing	Lyle and Goyen, 1975
		WAIS (verbal-performance	Reed, 1967; Huelsman, 1970
Intersensory integration	Birch, 1962; Birch and Belmont, 1965	WAIS (subtests)	Graham and Kamano, 1968; Hunter and Johnson, 1971; Rugel, 1974; Lyle and Goyen, 1969
Memory	Myklebust and Johnson, 1962; Lyle, 1968		
Motor	Orton, 1937; McFie, 1952		
Naming or fluency	Denckla, 1972; Denckla and Rudel, 1976; Eakin and Douglas, 1971;		

logical arguments, he finds that only a deficit in verbal processing is causally related to dyslexia. He suggests that many of the other deficits occur because tests require verbal processing for their solution. When the verbal component of the test is removed, there is improvement or even normalcy. There have also been suggestions that eye movement deficits are causal to dyslexia. Pirozzolo and Hansch have reviewed this literature and argue that it is unlikely that eye movement problems cause dyslexia, but they do admit that for some dyslexics eye movement abnormalities may be part of the underlying pathology that complicates dyslexia. In sum, the concensus about correlated deficits is that they are not causal to dyslexia. Some may themselves be symptoms of the underlying pathology, some may compound the disability, and some may produce other kinds of learning disabilities, but dyslexia seems to be due to some abnormality in language-related brain systems. Vellutino concludes that the normal reader should be seen as a verbal gymnast who can use a variety of devices for reading, whereas the impaired reader does not have this armamentarium.

NEUROPSYCHOLOGICAL EVALUATION

Neuropsychological assessment should offer insight into the abilities of individual learning-disabled children because it assesses performance on a wide range of tests sensitive to all areas of brain function. Usually children are not dyslexic or dyscalculic alone but have a number of associated symptoms. Teachers and parents are usually unaware of the associated deficits, and once the deficits are explained, it is often easier for both to understand the nature of the handicaps. The tests should also be able to distinguish between children who have central reading impairments and those who have problems caused by emotional or environmental causes. Consideration of individual test results should also give some suggestions for strategies for special instruction. Details about the application of various neuropsychological assessment procedures can be obtained from reviews such as those by Denckla, Gaddes, and Rourke. Perhaps the most obvious question that should be asked about such application is whether tests derived from studies on adult brain-damaged populations are applicable to children. Our own studies on dyslexic children suggest that they are applicable, provided that some care in interpretation is taken.

There have been many studies on the IQ test results of learning-disabled children. Rugel has summarized the results from studies that included a total of 1521 reading-disabled children and 554 control children. We have produced a graphic representation of these results in Figure 28–1. The dyslexic group displays low subscale

scores on four tests: arithmetic, coding, information, and digit span. This profile, typical in many studies, is referred to as the "ACID" profile. Dyslexic children typically have a mean full-scale IQ that averages about seven points lower than that of control children, but their mean IQ is roughly 100. Whishaw and Kolb have found that children over eight show the ACID profile, whereas those younger than eight may often not show a deficit in the information or arithmetic subscales. This suggests that these deficits in older children and adults are secondary to the underlying impairment that produces dyslexia. Performance on both tests will depend on acquisition of school-related skills, so that it seems reasonable that if school performance is deficient, deficits will emerge as the children fall behind. Deficits in coding and digit span may be more directly related to the underlying impairment that produces dyslexia. We should point out that some studies do not find emerging deficits on these tests; the different results may be related to the dyslexia population studied or the age groups included in the study. Lyle and Goyen did not find emerging deficits in information and arithmetic, but the impairments that they did find were not pronounced and the groups included in the study were quite young. We feel that the age-related trends are important if the Wechsler Intelligence Scale for Children (WISC) test pattern is used for diagnosis. First, it explains commonly observed IQ decreases that are found when children are tested before eight years of age and again when they are older. Second, it suggests that the values of the WISC patterns are less useful for the diagnosis of very young children.

Although the IQ of dyslexic children is average, typically very few high scores are found. In a group of 30 children and adults we found only two individuals with full-scale IQs as high as 114. This makes it difficult to find adequate control groups with which to compare dyslexic children. Whishaw and

FIGURE 28–1. Intelligence test profiles of developmental dyslexic and control subjects. (FS means full-scale IQ.) (After Rugel, 1974.)

Kolb used two control groups, one consisting of children who were referred for testing because they had poor grades and the other consisting of children who were selected from classes because their school performance was strictly average; that is, they had no failing grades and no grades that were above average. The poor-grades group had a mean IQ of 110 and the average-grade group had a mean IQ of 120. This result may be idiosyncratic to the study area, but it does have implications for counseling. In most Canadian school systems an average IQ of about 110

seems prerequisite for high school graduation and an average IQ of about 115 seems prerequisite for university entrance. Thus, in addition to their specific disability, the dyslexic groups will be at a disadvantage to their classmates with respect to potential for school success, a point that should be considered when advising parents and schools with respect to remedial instruction and future prospects.

Many researchers have commented that there are large verbal-performance IQ differences in dyslexic individuals, and it has

Age 6 6 6 7 7 7 7 7 8 8 9 10 10 10 10 10 10 11 11 11 11 11 11 12 12 12 13 13 14 15 16 16 17 19 20 22 26 29 38
Sex M M F M M M F M M M M M M M M F M F M M F M M M M F F M F M M F M M F M M

Handed R L L R R R R L L R R R L R L R R L R L L R R R R R R L L R R R R L R L R
Dominant ear R L R L R R L L L R R R L L R L L R R R R R L L L R L L L R R L L R R L L L R

IQ
Verbal   10 4 3 1   10   9 3   7   19   11 9 7 6   11   13
Performance   38 2   2 11 5 12 7 1 7 12 19   6   9 5 5 5 9   19   34   9 14

Information
Comprehension
Arithmetic
Similarities
Digit span
Vocabulary

Digit symbol
Picture completion
Block design
Picture arrangement
Object assembly

Memory quotient

FIGURE 28–2. Scatter in WISC performance and age, sex, and handedness for developmental dyslexic subjects. Large dots show scores one standard deviation below the population norm; small dots, scores three-quarters of a standard deviation below the population norm. Note the scatter on subtest scores. (After Whishaw and Kolb, 1984.)

been suggested that two different types of dyslexics can be identified on the basis of these scores. In addition, Denckla has pointed to the "scatter" of the IQ subscores. Figure 28–2 illustrates both of these features in a population of 30 dyslexics ranging in age from six to 38. The figure also gives information about handedness, dominant ear on a dichotic-listening test, and Wechsler memory quotient. Although verbal-performance differences and scatter of subtest results are a feature of this group, Whishaw and Kolb were unsuccessful in organizing these results into meaningful subgroups. Nevertheless, for the experienced counselor the pattern displayed by any individual may be meaningful.

In comparing the dyslexic group to the control groups on other tests of our composite test battery, it was found that the tests did discriminate between the two groups, but their effectiveness was dependent in part on the individual's age. This age-dependent effect was particularly clear in three different tests. In the test of left-right differentiation (Figure 28–3) neither control nor dyslexic children were able to score above chance if they were younger than eight years old. After the age of eight the control children performed well whereas the dyslexic groups continued to perform at chance. A different kind of emerging difference was found on tests of word fluency, in which differences did not occur at younger than eight years but became increasingly large in older age groups (Figure 28–4). This result seems to suggest that control children show increasingly improved fluency performance whereas the dyslexic group remains almost static. A third pattern was obtained on the Semmes body-placing task (Figure 28–5). Here, significant group differences only emerged in adults, and then they seemed to depend on the fact that adult control subjects displayed vir-

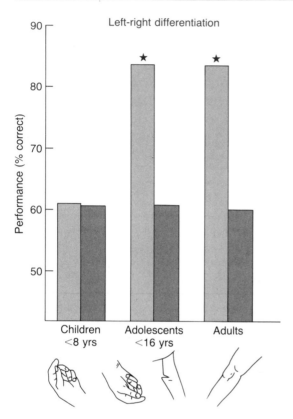

FIGURE 28–3. Performance on the left-right discrimination test by control (open bars) and dyslexic (shaded bars) subjects. Stars signify significant group differences. (After Whishaw and Kolb, 1984.)

tually perfect performance on the tests. The results of these various tests suggest to us that although the tests can be applied to children with some success, a great deal of caution in interpretation is required for the younger children, and retesting at different ages is worthwhile.

The overall performance of dyslexic subjects on tests of our composite test-battery is illustrated in Figure 28–6. This summary shows performance on tests sensitive to left and right hemisphere function and to the function of different lobes. The measures represent standard deviations below performance of the control group. It is noteworthy that some deficits appear on all tests but the Wisconsin card-sorting test and the Mooney faces test: tests thought to be sensitive to frontal lobe and right parietal function respectively. The largest overall deficits occurred on tests of left-right discrimination, paired-associate learning, verbal IQ, memory quotient, word fluency, and performance IQ. The common feature of these tests is that they are sensitive to function of the parietal lobes, particularly the left parietal lobe.

THE NEURAL BASIS OF DYSLEXIA

There are a number of hypotheses about what neural abnormalities cause dyslexia. One view, articulated most emphatically by Jorm, is that dyslexia is caused by a genetically based dysfunction of the left inferior parietal lobule. This argument is based on the assumption that the major problem encountered by dyslexics is that of accessing the meaning of written words via phonological recoding. Jorm's hypothesis is not inconsistent with some longstanding views of dyslexia, but support for it as an exclusive hypothesis would require that other kinds of damage in the left hemisphere could not produce dyslexia and also that dyslexia could not be caused by damage to the right hemisphere. Of course, unequivocal answers about what other areas of the brain might contribute to dyslexia cannot be given, but other possibilities cannot be excluded. It is worth noting here that the traditional view of language function is that it resides almost exclusively in the left hemisphere. Therefore, it is usual to assign language disabilities to abnormalities in the left hemisphere and to assign residual language capacities that survive brain damage to the remaining portions of the left hemisphere. There is, however, some evidence that the right hemisphere does have significant language abilities and that language capacities surviving left hemisphere damage may be the product of the right hemisphere. If both of these possibilities are realities, then they open other avenues for understanding dyslexia. First, if the right hemisphere does have language abilities, damage to it could cause a reading impairment resulting in a form of dyslexia. Second, if the right hemisphere has language abilities, the reading that survives left hemisphere damage may be the product of the right hemisphere and not the product of residual parts of the left hemisphere. Since these options provide some interesting possibilities for understanding some of the symptoms of dyslexia, we shall briefly review some evidence supporting the hypothesis for right hemisphere language.

Coltheart, in reviewing evidence for right hemisphere language, suggests that if the right hemisphere is questioned in a subtle way, evidence that it has language abilities is found. If it is simply asked to read or speak, it displays no language abilities at all. He and his colleagues have examined the reading abilities of patients who had received extensive damage to both the posterior and anterior speech zones of the left hemisphere. These patients display a fascinating reading syndrome called **deep dyslexia.** When asked to read words, they make semantic errors (e.g., play for act, close for shut), visual errors (e.g., queue for quiz, duel for deuce), and derivational errors (e.g., wisdom for wise, born for birth), and they are completely unable to derive phonology from print or to effectively read low-imagery words or

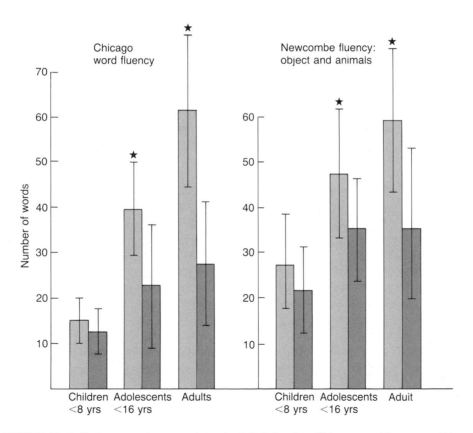

FIGURE 28–4. Performance (mean and standard deviations) on Chicago word fluency and Newcombe objects and animals fluency tests by control (open bars) and dyslexic (shaded bars) subjects. Stars signify significant group differences. (After Whishaw and Kolb, 1984.)

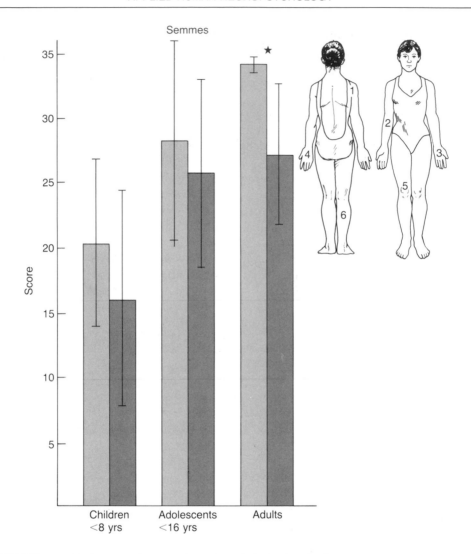

FIGURE 28–5. Performance (mean and standard deviations) on the Semmes body-placing test by control (open bars) and dyslexic (shaded bars) subjects. Star signifies significant group differences. (After Whishaw and Kolb, 1984.)

function words. As an example of a disability with function words, a patient could read *fly* when it appeared in the sentence, "The *fly* buzzed in my ear," but could not read it when it appeared in the sentence, "The bird will *fly* away." Coltheart suggests that these errors in reading are not produced by residual portions of the left hemisphere because all the symptoms appear together as a group in all the patients irrespective of the location of the left hemisphere brain damage. He suggests then that the patients are reading with their right hemisphere and the errors that they make reveal something about the way the right hemisphere deals with language. The errors suggest that the right hemisphere reads using grapheme procedures, hence the visual errors; its comprehension is limited to concrete words, hence the derivational errors; and its analytical capacities are largely associational, hence the categorically correct semantic errors.

Support for Coltheart's view comes from at least one other study on focal brain damaged patients, but one in which the patients had damage that was largely restricted to Broca's area. Langmore and Canter suggest that the spelling errors of the Broca's area patients are

attributable to the grapheme spelling strategy of the right hemisphere.

One other line of research also suggests that the right hemisphere has a certain form of language ability. Zaidel has made an extensive study of patients with corpus callosum sections. These patients have two intact hemispheres but the language abilities of each hemisphere can be examined separately by presenting words or other stimuli to each hemisphere selectively. Zaidel's experiments are comprehensive and cannot be reported here in detail, but they demonstrate that the right hemisphere

FIGURE 28–6. Summary of performance of developmental dyslexic and control groups. Left, theoretical relation between tests and hemisphere; middle, theoretical relation between tests and lobes; right, deficit (standard deviations) in dyslexic group as contrasted with a control group. (After Whishaw and Kolb, 1984.)

is largely mute, has no short-term verbal memory, and cannot read phrases, but that it can read simple concrete words using grapheme cues. The left hemisphere, in contrast, can perform grapheme-to-phonetic conversions, perform grammatical analysis, read phrases, and has short-term verbal memory, but it seems least specialized for semantic analysis. Zaidel suggests that these findings are applicable for understanding the underlying problems of learning-disabled children. Specifically, analysis of the disabilities of dyslexic children should reveal groups who function either with the right hemisphere or the left hemisphere, resembling the callosal-sectioned patients with respect to some of their reading disabilities.

If we accept the evidence from these three lines of research, it seems logical to conclude that both hemispheres in normal individuals may be involved in reading. The left hemisphere does phonological and grammatical analysis whereas the right hemisphere is involved in grapheme analysis and the extraction of certain kinds of semantic information. Interestingly, Pirozzolo and Rayner, using a tachistoscopic study, have even suggested that the visual system segregates these two types of information as reading progresses. They suggest that during normal reading foveal vision (from the center of the retina) is used by the left hemisphere for phonetic decoding, while peripheral vision is used by the right hemisphere for grapheme decoding. The dual-process notion also suggests to us that damage to either the right or the left hemisphere could produce dyslexia but that its characteristics after each type of damage might be different. It is possible, however, that things could be even more complex than this because any hypothetical damage is thought to occur early in life, which permits the brain to make various adjustments as maturation proceeds. Also, dyslexic individuals have a variety of associated symptoms, which often differ between one

individual and another. In the following sections we shall speculate on three neural models that might be relevant to explanations of dyslexia. All three models include the assumption that verbal language will be preserved irrespective of the type of damage to either cortex because speech acquisition takes place very early in life. Reading may not receive a similar priority for sparing, since its acquisition occurs relatively late in life.

In Chapter 24 we described the language abilities of people who had received surgical removal of the left or right hemisphere when they were very young. The studies of Dennis and her coworkers show that although either hemisphere can learn to speak, there are language deficits that suggest there are constraints on the skills that each hemisphere is able to acquire. Stated simply, the isolated left hemisphere shows superior performance in dealing with the meaning of words and their sound structure whereas the right hemisphere shows superior performance when dealing with the visual structure of words. If one takes an extreme position and assumes that dyslexic individuals have unilateral impairments as severe as the hemispherectomized people studied by Dennis, it can be postulated that there are two types of dyslexics. One group would have language completely lateralized on the left, and this group would be impaired at grapheme reading. They would be able to read regular words and show no impairments in the early stages of reading, but they would show impaired sight reading when older and would not be able to read or spell irregular words. They would also be impaired in decoding numbers and other symbols that cannot be translated into phonetic form. The second group would have language completely lateralized to the right. They would be impaired at phonological reading and would have trouble converting letters into sounds using phonetic rules. They would be impaired in initial attempts to acquire phonetic reading but would eventually be able to recognize words and symbols, such as numbers, by sight. Interestingly, these two groups would correspond to Boder's dyseidetic and dysphonetic types of dyslexics.

Of course, this extreme hypothesis does not correspond to what is known about dyslexia. Dyslexic individuals do have two intact hemispheres, but if they have subtle damage to either the left or the right hemisphere something like the impairments given in this description might be true. It is likely, however, that their speech organization is more complex. In Chapter 24 we described the organization of language in people who received cortical damage prior to five years of age. Recall that Rasmussen and Milner found that these people could be divided into three groups: in the first, speech was in the right hemisphere, in the second, speech was in the left hemisphere, and in the third, speech was represented bilaterally. The last group could be further subdivided depending on which of the two speech zones was shifted to the opposite hemisphere. Using this model it could be postulated that there are more than two kinds of dyslexia. Two types, a left or a right hemisphere type, might be similar to those described above. Other types would include individuals in whom the left posterior zone was shifted to the right, who would be poor at phonetic reading (assuming the phonetic analysis is a function of the posterior cortex), and individuals in whom the anterior zone had shifted to the right, who would be poor at phonetic spelling (assuming that language production is a function of the anterior cortex).

There is still a third possibility, one that might be the most plausible, although it also does not exclude either model described above. These might be individuals in whom speech is "normally" lateralized but who have weaknesses in, rather than the complete loss of, one or another speech zone. For these individuals

the brain areas involved in reading would be those that are used by normal readers, but there would be a range of abnormalities from subtle to severe depending on the extent of the anatomical abnormality. Their deficits would not be absolute, but they would be proportional to the demands made on reading abilities.

We can represent these various possibilities in the form of a table (Table 28–3). For the purposes of example, we have assumed that phonetic reading is performed by the left posterior hemisphere and phonetic spelling is done by the left anterior hemisphere, whereas grapheme reading is done by the right posterior hemisphere and grapheme spelling is done by the right anterior hemisphere. Using this example, it can be seen that there are a variety of deficits that can occur depending on the site of any anatomical abnormality. Some other symptoms of dyslexia might also be generated using this model. If one assumes, for example, that handedness is specified in most people by the function of the left posterior cortex, then it can be seen that for some types of dyslexia there might be alterations in handedness. In fact, depending on what kind of function one might like to attribute to any particular brain region, hypotheses for most types of learning disabilities, including their associated symptoms, could be derived from this type of model. We emphasize, however, that we do not present this model as dogma, but simply as an example of how the characteristics of various learning disabilities might be understood.

ADULT OUTCOME OF LEARNING DISABILITIES

There are a variety of views about the outcome of children with learning disabilities. The most optimistic outcome study is reported by Critchley, in which 20 dyslexic boys attended a

TABLE 28-3

Model of reading and spelling abilities associated with
different types of neural organization

Neural structure present	Reading-spelling performance
Left hemisphere only	Phonetic reading and spelling
Right hemisphere only	Grapheme reading and spelling
Broca left; Wernicke right	Phonetic spelling–grapheme reading
Wernicke left; Broca right	Phonetic reading–grapheme spelling
Weak left or right Broca	Poor phonetic or grapheme spelling
Weak left or right Wernicke	Poor phonetic or grapheme reading

private school and received special instruction according to the Orton-Gillingham-Stillman method. The eventual occupations held by these individuals were two medical doctors, one college professor, one lawyer, two research scientists, six owners or managers of businesses, one school principal, three teachers, one actor, one factory foreman, and one skilled laborer. There are some reports in the popular press of similar, though perhaps not so absolute, success of various private schools for learning-disabled individuals. The majority of these studies do not report such optimistic outcomes and the most thorough of them gives frankly pessimistic results about academic outcome. Spreen has examined the progress of 203 learning-disabled individuals over a 10-year period. The sample included a group who was diagnosed as learning disabled with no neurological impairments, a group diagnosed as minimal brain damaged, and a group that had definite brain damage. The learning-disabled group were compared with

52 control individuals. The following conclusions derive from the assessments, personal interviews, parental interviews, and other observations made on these groups.

1. Typically the control group fared better than the learning-disabled group, who fared better than the minimal brain damaged group, who fared better than the brain-damaged group in all areas of assessment. Spreen argues that this has important implications since educators may not think that the presence or absence of neurological impairments is relevant to the outcome of school programs. It was also found that all three handicapped groups were inferior to the control group in all areas of study including art and physical education. They also had a poorer attitude toward school.

2. Individuals in all but the control group suffered through a miserable and usually short school career and then suffered a miserable social life full of disappointments and failures. They also had a relatively poor chance for advanced training and skilled employment. They did not, however, have a higher incidence of juvenile delinquency or psychiatric problems.

3. Interviews with subjects and their parents gave similar factual information about their situation. Parents, however, tended to report more serious effects on the well-being, happiness, and social interaction of their children than were reported by the children. The children also had less clear memories of their childhood than the control children. As the subjects aged they developed firmer plans for their future and made better occupational adjustments, but they also gave increasingly poorer impressions of their school experiences. The eventual social adjustments in females were poorer than they were in males.

In all, although learning-disabled individuals eventually managed to make personal adjustments and find jobs, their dislike of and dissatisfaction with school remained. The major evidence from this and other follow-up studies also suggests that the effects of remedial educational programs were not particularly significant, except perhaps for those individuals with very high IQ scores. Reports of extravagant success seem to derive largely from private schools that select only high-IQ students from relatively affluent homes.

We should perhaps end this section by asking whether there is a challenge for neuropsychology in the area of learning disabilities or whether all available avenues of remediation have been fairly tried. We think that there is a challenge. First, we think that the impairments of each individual child have to be adequately assessed in order to assess the cognitive deficits that are likely to be particular to each child. Second, once specific problem areas of individual children have been identified, specialized teaching programs can be devised to circumvent the neuropsychological handicaps. Third, we feel there may be little point in trying to teach children those things that it seems clear they are not going to learn. It may be that education should be more explicitly directed to the acquisition of skills that may be subsequently used to gain employment. Fourth, we feel that counseling should be an important part of the educational process both for the learning-disabled individual and for parents. Counseling should be directed not only toward helping them overcome their own negative attitudes toward the educational system but also toward helping them come to understand their own unique handicaps, including some strategies that they can use to circumvent some of their handicaps. Fifth, we feel that there should be continued research into altered education strategies that are consistent with neuropsychological findings. Erickson, Chase, and Faloon have demonstrated that digit span in a subject of average intelligence could be increased from seven to nine with 230 hours of training. Could similar training of learning-disabled children, who have poor short-term verbal memory, improve this memory to permit them to deal more effectively with certain aspects of school course work that they are attempting to acquire?

HYPERACTIVITY

The hyperactive child syndrome is distinguished from other types of learning disabilities because its major feature is that the child is a behavioral problem in school and all aspects of school performance are usually disrupted. Hyperactive children may have specific learning disabilities in addition to hyperactivity, and these may contribute to hyperactivity. A number of diagnostic labels have been given to hyperactive children, and accordingly they have been classed as minimal brain dysfunction, hyperkinetic child, hyperkinetic impulsive disorder, etc. DSM III gives the following characteristics of the disorder:

1. Excessive general hyperactivity or motor restlessness for the child's age. In preschool and early school years, there may be incessant haphazard, impulsive running, climbing, or crawling. During middle childhood or adolescence, marked inability to sit still, up and down activity, and fidgeting are characteristic. The activity differs from the norms for the age both in quality and quantity.

2. Difficulty in sustaining attention, such as inability to complete tasks initiated or a disorganized approach to tasks. The child frequently "forgets" demands made or tasks assigned and shows poor attention in unstructured situations or when demands are made for independent, unsupervised performance.

3. Impulsive behavior.

4. Duration of at least one year.

It is thought that in infancy hyperactive children are characterized by poor and irregular sleep, colic, and feeding problems. It is thought they are not cuddly and do not like to be held still for long. Later they are described as skipping walking in favor of running, and as being driven to handle and play with everything. By the time they reach kindergarten they are demanding, do not listen, and do not play well with other children. Other people, outside the home, may begin to reject the child because of its behavior. By the time the child enters school, its activity, low tolerance for frustration, poor concentration, and poor self-esteem lead to a referral for assessment. By adolescence the individual is a school failure, and 25 to 50 percent may begin to encounter problems with the law. Their behavior remains restless, they withdraw from school, and they fail in developing social relations and in maintaining steady employment.

The hyperactive child syndrome is extremely common and is described by Weiss and Hechtman as the commonest behavioral disturbance among children. Estimates of its incidence vary because of problems with definition and differences in tolerance shown by different societies. The ratio of boys to girls is described as being as high as 5:1 to 9:1. In the Isle of Wight study made by Rutter an incidence of one in 1000 was reported, but in North America, where the tolerance for hyperactive behavior seems lower, estimates of incidence as high as six in 100 have been reported. It does seem that parents' and teachers' estimates of what comprises normal behavior may be unrealistic, for Weiss and Hechtman note that in surveys of parents and teachers as many as 50 percent of children are reported as hyperactive. Interestingly, Gaddes has commented that as yet no measures of activity have been made from hyperactive children to quantify objectively their "activity."

The cause of hyperactivity is simply not known. Suggested causes have been brain damage, encephalitis, genetics, dopamine decreases, food allergies, high lead concentrations, and various home and school environments. It is unlikely that there is a single cause, and hence comprehensive, multidisciplinary assessment is recommended.

Recommended therapy includes counseling for the child and parent and careful structuring of the home and school environments. Beginning in the 1960s and continuing to the present, treatment with amphetaminelike stimulant drugs such as Ritalin has been popular. The effectiveness of Ritalin or other drug treatment as a long-term solution is doubted. When Ritalin is effective, it may be because, as a stimulant, it allows the individual to concentrate on the tasks at hand. The drug may also have a general sedating effect on children.

The prognosis for hyperactive children has been reported by Weiss and Hechtman as being relatively poor. Their life style continues to be impulsive and often marked by geographical moves, accidents, problems with the law, etc. In later life their major problems may be with poor self-esteem and social skills, but they are not regarded as hyperactive by their employers, and they do not become mentally disturbed or adult criminals.

REFERENCES

Ahn, H., L. Princhep, E. R. John, H. Baird, M. Trepeten, and H. Kaye. Developmental equations reflect brain dysfunctions. *Science* 210:1259–1262, 1980.

Ayres, A. J. Learning disabilities and the vestibular system. *Journal of Learning Disabilities* 11:11–29, 1978.

Bakker, D. J. *Temporal Order in Disturbed Reading: Developmental and Neuropsychological Aspects in Normal and Reading-Retarded Children.* Rotterdam: Rotterdam University Press, 1972.

Benton, A. *Right-left discrimination and finger localization.* New York: Hoeber-Harper, 1959.

Birch, H. G. Dyslexia and maturation of visual function. In J. Money, ed., *Reading Disability: Progress and Research Needs in Dyslexia.* Baltimore: John Hopkins Press, 1962.

Birch, H. G., and L. Belmont. Auditory-visual integration, intelligence, and reading ability in school children. *Perceptual and Motor Skills* 20:295–305, 1965.

Boder, E. Developmental dyslexia: A diagnostic screening procedure based on three characteristic patterns of reading and spelling. *Learning Disorders* 4:298–342, 1971.

Bradley, L., and P. E. Bryant. Categorizing sounds and learning to read—A causal connection. *Nature* 301:419–421, 1983.

Bruck, M. The suitability of early French immersion programs for the language disabled child. *Canadian Journal of Education* 34:50–73, 1978.

Bryden, M. P. Laterality effects in dichotic listening: Relations with handedness and reading disability in children. *Neuropsychologia* 8:443–450, 1970.

Coltheart, M. Deep dyslexia: A right hemisphere hypothesis. In M. Coltheart, K. E. Patterson, and J. Marshall, eds., *Deep Dyslexia.* London: Routledge, 1980.

Corkin, S. Serial ordering deficits in inferior readers. *Neuropsychologia* 12:347–354, 1974.

Critchley, M. *Developmental Dyslexia.* Springfield, Ill.: Charles C Thomas, 1964.

Defries, J. C., and S. N. Decker. Genetic aspects of reading disability: A family study. In R. N. Malatesha and P. G. Aaron, eds., *Reading Disorders: Varieties and Treatments.* New York: Academic, 1982.

Denckla, M. B. Color-naming defects in dyslexic boys. *Cortex* 8:164–176, 1972.

Denckla, M. B. Critical review of "electroencephalographic and neurophysiological studies in dyslexia." In A. L. Benton and D. Pearl, eds., *Dyslexia: An Appraisal of Current Knowledge.* New York: Oxford University Press, 1978.

Denckla, M. B., and R. Rudel. Naming of object-drawings by dyslexia and other learning disabled children. *Brain and Language* 13:1–15, 1976.

Dennis, M. Capacity and strategy for syntatic comprehension after left or right hemidecortication. *Brain and Language* 10:287–317, 1980.

Douglas, V. I. Perceptual and cognitive factors as determinants of learning disabilities: A review chapter with special emphasis on attentional factors. In R. M. Knights and D. J. Bakker, eds., *The Neuropsychology of Learning Disorders.* Baltimore: University Park Press, 1976.

Drake, W. Clinical and pathological findings in a child with a developmental learning disability. *Journal of Learning Disabilities* 1:468–475, 1968.

Duffy, F. H., M. B. Denckla, P. H. Bartels, and G. Sandini. Dyslexia: Regional differences in brain electrical activity by topographic mapping. *Annals of Neurology* 7:412–420, 1980.

Eakin, S., and V. I. Douglas. "Automatization" and oral reading problems in children. *Journal of Learning Disabilities* 4:31–38, 1971.

Erickson, K. A., W. G. Chase, and S. Faloon. Acquisition of a memory skill. *Science* 208:1181–1182, 1980.

Frank, J., and H. H. Levinson. Dysmetric dyslexia and dyspraxia. *Academic Therapy* 11:133–143, 1976.

Frauenheim, J. G. Academic achievement characteristics of adult males who were diagnosed as dyslexic in childhood. *Journal of Learning Disabilities* 11:476–483, 1978.

Frith, U. Experimental approaches to developmental dyslexia. *Psychological Research* 43:97–109, 1981.

Fry, E. A do-it-yourself terminology generator. *Journal of Reading* 11:428–430, 1968.

Gaddes, W. H. *Learning Disabilities and Brain Function.* New York: Springer-Verlag, 1980.

Gaddes, W. H. Prevalence estimates and the need for definition of learning disabilities. In R. M. Knights and D. J. Bakker, eds., *The Neuropsychology of Learning Disorders.* Baltimore: University Park Press, 1976.

Galaburda, A. M., and D. Eidelberg. Symmetry and asymmetry in the human posterior thalamus. II. Thalamic lesions in a case of development dyslexia. *Archives of Neurology* 39:333–336, 1982.

Galaburda, A. M., and T. L. Kemper. Cytoarchitectonic abnormalities in developmental dyslexia. A case study. *Annals of Neurology* 6:94–100, 1979.

Gordon, H. W. Cognitive asymmetry in dyslexic families. *Neuropsychologia* 18:645–656, 1980.

Gould, S. J. *The Mismeasurement of Man.* New York: Norton, 1981.

Graham, E. E., and D. Kamano. Reading failure as a factor in the WAIS subtest patterns of youthful offenders. *Journal of Clinical Psychology* 14:302–305, 1958.

Huelsman, C. B. The WISC syndrome for disabled readers. *Perceptual and Motor Skills* 30:535–550, 1970.

Hughes, J. R. Electroencephalographic and neurophysiological studies in dyslexia. In A. L. Benton and D. Pearl, eds., *Dyslexia: An Appraisal of Current Knowledge.* New York: Oxford University Press, 1978.

Hunter, E. J., and L. C. Johnson. Developmental and psychological differences between readers and nonreaders. *Journal of Learning Disabilities* 4:572–577, 1971.

Johnson, D. J., and H. R. Myklebust. *Learning Disabilities.* New York: Grune & Stratton, 1967.

Jorm, A. F. The cognitive and neurological basis of developmental dyslexia: A theoretical framework and review. *Cognition* 7:19–33, 1979.

Kinsbourne, M., and M. Hiscock. Does cerebral dominance develop? In S. J. Segalowitz and F. A. Gruber, eds., *Language Development and Neurological Theory.* New York: Academic, 1977.

Klicpera, C., P. H. Wolff, and C. Drake. Bimanual co-ordination in adolescent boys with reading retardation. *Developmental Medicine and Child Neurology* 23:617–625, 1981.

Langmore, S. E., and G. J. Canter. Written spelling deficit of Broca's aphasics. *Brain and Language* 18:293–314, 1983.

Levinson, H. N. *Dyslexia.* New York: Springer-Verlag, 1980.

Lovegrove, W. J., M. Heddle, and W. Slaghuis. Reading disability: Spatial frequency specific deficits in visual information store. *Neuropsychologia* 18:111–115, 1980.

Lyle, J. G. Performance of retarded readers on the memory-for-designs test. *Perceptual and Motor Skills* 26:851–854, 1968.

Lyle, J. G., and J. D. Goyen. Performance of retarded readers on the WISC and educational tests. *Journal of Abnormal Psychology* 74:105–112, 1969.

Lyle, J. G., and J. D. Goyen. Effect of speed of exposure and difficulty of discrimination on visual recognition of retarded readers. *Journal of Abnormal Psychology* 84:673–676, 1975.

Maccario, M., S. J. Hefferen, S. J. Keblusek, and K. A. Lipinski. Developmental dysphasia and electroencephalographic abnormalities. *Developmental Medicine and Child Neurology* 24:141–155, 1982.

Malatesha, R. N., and D. R. Dougan. Clinical subtypes of developmental dyslexia: Resolution to an irresolute problem. In R. N. Malatesha and P. G. Aaron, eds., *Reading Disorders*. New York: Academic, 1982.

McFie, J. Cerebral dominance in cases of reading disability. *Journal of Neurology and Psychiatry* 15:194–199, 1952.

Money, J. Child abuse: Growth failure, IQ deficit, and learning disability. *Journal of Learning Disabilities* 15:579–582, 1982.

Myklebust, H. R., and D. Johnson. Dyslexia in children. *Exceptional Children* 29:14–25, 1962.

Orton, S. T. *Reading, Writing and Speech Problems in Children*. New York: Norton, 1937.

Orton, S. T. Word-blindness in school children. *Archives of Neurology and Psychiatry* 14:581–615, 1925.

Pavlidis, G. Th. Do eye movements hold the key to dyslexia? *Neuropsychologia* 19:57–64, 1981.

Perfetti, C. A., and T. Hogaboam. The relationship between single word decoding and reading comprehension skill. *Journal of Educational Psychology* 67:461–469, 1975.

Pihl, R. O., and M. Parkes. Hair element content in learning disabled children. *Science* 198:204–206, 1977.

Pirozzolo, F. J., and E. C. Hansch. The neurobiology of developmental reading disorders. In R. N. Malatesha and P. G. Aaron, eds., *Reading Disorders: Varieties and Treatments*. New York: Academic, 1982.

Pirozzolo, F. J., and K. Rayner. Hemispheric specialization in reading and word recognition. *Brain and Language* 4:248–261, 1977.

Reed, J. C. Reading achievement as related to differences between WISC verbal and performance I.Q.'s. *Child Development* 38:835–840, 1967.

Rosensweig, M. R., D. Krech, E. L. Bennett, and M. C. Diamond. Effects of environmental complexity and training on brain chemistry and anatomy: A replication and extension. *Journal of Comparative and Physiological Psychology* 55:427–429, 1962.

Rourke, B. P. Neuropsychological assessment of children with learning disabilities. In S. B. Filskov and T. J. Boll, eds., *Handbook of Clinical Neuropsychology*. New York: Wiley, 1981.

Rugel, R. P. WISC subtest scores of disabled readers: A review with respect to Bannatyne's categorization. *Journal of Learning Disability* 17:48–55, 1974.

Rutter, M., and W. Yule. The concept of specific reading retardation. *Journal of Child Psychology and Psychiatry* 16:181–197, 1975.

Satz, P. Cerebral dominance and reading disability: An old problem revisited. In R. M. Knights and D. J. Bakker, eds., *The Neuropsychology of Learning Disorders*. Baltimore: University Park Press, 1976.

Satz, P., and S. S. Sparrow. Specific developmental dyslexia: A theoretical formulation. In D. Bakker and P. Satz, eds., *Specific Reading Disability: Advances in Theory and Method*. Rotterdam: Rotterdam University Press, 1970.

Satz, P., D. Rarden, and J. Ross. An evaluation of a theory of specific developmental dyslexia. *Child Development* 42:1009–1021, 1971.

Silver, A. A., and R. A. Hagen. A unifying concept for the neuropsychological organization of children with reading disability. *Developmental and Behavioral Pediatrics* 3:127–132, 1982.

Snart, F., S. Dennis, and A. Brailsford. Concerns regarding the wide range achievement test. *Canadian Psychology* 24:99–104, 1983.

Spreen, O. Neuropsychology of learning disorders: Post-conference review. In R. M. Knights and D. J. Bakker, eds., *The Neuropsychology of Learning Disorders*. Baltimore: University Park Press, 1976.

Spring, C. Encoding speed and memory span in dyslexic children. *The Journal of Special Education* 10:35–40, 1976.

Tees, R. C., and J. Werker. The development of speech perception: Evidence of functional decline in neonatal ability. Paper given at Winter Conference on Brain Research, Keystone, Colorado, January, 1981.

U.S. Department of Health, Education and Welfare. Minimal brain dysfunction in children. *National Institute of Neurological Diseases Monograph* 3:1–18, 1966.

Vellutino, F. R. Alternative conceptualizations of dyslexia: Evidence in support of a verbal-deficit hypothesis. *Howard Educational Review* 47:334–353, 1977.

Vellutino, F. R. Toward an understanding of dyslexia: Psychological factors in specific reading disability. In A. L. Benton and D. Pearl, eds., *Dyslexia: An Appraisal of Current Knowledge*. New York: Oxford University Press, 1978.

Weiss, G., and L. Hechtman. The hyperactive child syndrome. *Science* 205:1348–1354, 1979.

Wepman, J. M. Auditory discrimination, speech and reading. *The Reading Teacher* 9:325–333, 1960.

Wepman, J. M. The interrelationships of hearing, speech and reading. *The Reading Teacher* 14:245–247, 1961.

Whishaw, I. Q., and B. Kolb. Neuropsychological assessment of children and adults with developmental dyslexia. In R. N. Malatesha and H. A. Whitaker, eds., *Dyslexia: A Global Issue*. The Hague: Martinus Nijhoff, 1984.

Witelson, S. F. Early hemisphere specialization and interhemispheric plasticity, an empirical and theoretical review. In S. J. Segalowitz and F. A. Gruber, eds., *Language Development and Neurological Theory*. New York: Academic, 1977.

Witelson, S. F. Hemispheric specialization for linguistic and nonlinguistic tactual perception using a dichotomous stimulation technique. *Cortex* 11:3–17, 1974.

Zaidel, E. The split and half brains as models of congenital language disability. In C. L. Ludlow and M. E. Doran-Quine, eds., *The Neuropsychological Basis of Language Disorders in Children*. National Institute of Neurological and Communicative Disorders and Stroke, 22. Bethesda, Md., 1978.

Zangwill, O. L., and C. Blakemore. Dyslexia: Reversal of eye-movements during reading. *Neuropsychologia* 10:371–373, 1972.

Zurif, E. B., and G. Carlson. Dyslexia in relation to cerebral dominance and temporal analysis. *Neuropsychologia* 81:351–361, 1970.

29

PSYCHIATRIC AND MOTOR DISORDERS

Advances in neuropsychological assessment have led to an increase in the use of neuropsychological tests in psychiatric settings. Psychiatric diagnosis is always difficult at best, and neuropsychological evaluations may provide objective information to aid in classifying patients for treatment as well as in evaluating prognosis. It may also help understanding of the problems that patients have. There is, however, a lot of misunderstanding about the nature and potential of neuropsychological tests. Perhaps because of the attempts to use one-shot tests of "organicity" as in the Bender-Gestalt or MMPI, clinical psychologists are frequently asked to help determine whether patients' behavioral disturbances are "functional" or "organic" in nature. In other words, the psychologist is being asked for an opinion on whether the abnormal behavior in a patient can be ascribed to brain dysfunction or to some other "mental" disorder. This question is clearly inappropriate. As we have seen, especially in Chapters 14 through 25, the question to ask is not whether or not someone's brain is functioning normally. Normal brain function is

hardly a "yes" or "no" issue. Clinically, it may be more reasonable to ask (1) whether a patient is experiencing neuropsychological deficits that could account for the observed behavioral symptoms, and (2) whether the test profile is suggestive of a particular diagnosis. Of course, the second question assumes that different disorders are associated with particular patterns of test results. This is the major topic of this chapter. We shall ask whether some of the commoner "psychiatric" and "motor" disorders are associated with consistent neuropsychological profiles and whether these profiles appear robust enough to help in diagnosis. Because the literature is so large we have been selective in our discussion and have tried to select those studies that are comprehensive or particularly incisive.

SCHIZOPHRENIA

Speculation concerning a biological cause of schizophrenia has led to repeated attempts to identify structural abnormalities in the brains of schizophrenics (Chapter 22). Although the results have often proved equivocal, it does appear as though there is some abnormality in the mesocortical dopaminergic system. Further, there is good evidence that neither the frontal nor the temporal lobes are functioning normally in schizophrenia. In view of this, we should expect to find significant impairment in the performance of neuropsychological tests by schizophrenics, and we do.

Heaton and Crowley reviewed 132 studies published between 1960 and 1978 that considered the accuracy of neuropsychological tests in discriminating patients with various psychiatric diagnoses from patients with known brain damage. Overall, Heaton and Crowley conclude that, with the exception of chronic schizophrenia, the majority (75 percent) of psychiatric patients could be correctly classified. Hence there appears to be a general consensus that schizophrenics do poorly on neuropsychological tests. The crucial question, however, is *how* they do poorly.

Over the past decade a view has emerged suggesting that schizophrenics may do especially poorly on tests of left hemisphere function. Flor-Henry has emphasized left temporal lobe dysfunction as a characteristic of schizophrenic patients, although he does not exclude the possibility of poor performance on frontal lobe tests as well. Similarly, other researchers such as Piran, Bigler, and Cohen have been struck with an apparent shift in handedness and eye dominance to the left in schizophrenics, again suggesting left hemisphere pathology. It does seem puzzling, however, that neuropsychological impairments would be restricted just to tests sensitive to left hemisphere function since the biological evidence would lead one to anticipate a bilateral impairment. More recent evidence suggests that this may indeed be the case. There is good evidence that if schizophrenics are tested on a broad range of tests known to be sensitive to both left and right hemisphere function, they perform poorly on tests believed to measure both left and right frontal or temporal lobe function. For example, we studied the performance of schizophrenic patients on a composite battery similar to the one summarized in Chapter 26 but included additional tests of frontal lobe function, including the copying of complex facial movements (Figure 18–2) and the Gotman-Milner design fluency test (Figure 18–7). The results showed that schizophrenics were significantly impaired, relative to age-matched controls, on every test sensitive to frontal and temporal lobe function but performed with normal limits on tests sensitive to parietal lobe function (see Table 30–10).

Overall, it appears that schizophrenics do perform poorly on neuropsychological measures and that they may have a reliable pattern of test results, in which they perform poorly on tests of long-term verbal and nonverbal memory, as well as on tests sensitive to left or right frontal lobe function. Performance on tests of visual discrimination, spatial orientation, and short-term verbal and nonverbal memory appears to be less affected, and in most schizophrenics these tests appear to be performed normally. We must caution, however, that people who have been chronically institutionalized as schizophrenics may not perform normally on *any* tests, rendering the assessment of them futile at best. (For a detailed account of the effects of antipsychotic medication on test performance see Heaton and Crowley.)

AFFECTIVE DISORDERS

In our discussion of biological correlates of affective disorders in Chapter 22 we considered possible neurochemical abnormalities in affective disorders but, unlike for the data for schizophrenia, we were unable to provide much more than circumstantial evidence in support of any proposed abnormality. There is a similar dearth of information about the neuropsychological test performance of people with affective disorders. Heaton and his colleagues summarize only six studies on affective patients, and all of these used only one or two measures. Flor-Henry and others have suggested that affective patients do especially poorly on tests sensitive to right hemisphere function, but their neuropsychological evidence is not yet compelling. We must conclude that to date there does not appear to be a reliable pattern of neuropsychological test results for people with different affective disorders.

TOURETTE'S SYNDROME

Although Tourette's syndrome is less common than schizophrenia or affective disorders, it has attracted a lot of interest, in large part because of the interesting symptoms and because of the activity of the Tourette Syndrome Association. Scattered reports of specific biological disturbances associated with Tourette's syndrome have appeared in the literature, but pathological studies are virtually nonexistent, and even the clinical boundaries of the syndrome are in dispute (see Chapter 12 for a detailed discussion of common symptoms). Most of the inferences about the biological nature of Tourette's syndrome have been derived from the studies of the therapeutic effects of drugs such as haloperidol, the current drug of choice in this disease. Neuropsychological studies thus have much to offer both in the diagnosis of Tourette's syndrome and in the study of the neurological basis of the disorder.

The extensive volume on Tourette's syndrome, which was edited by Friedhoff and Chase, contains virtually all of the neuro-

psychological studies on Tourette's patients (see Table 29–1). Whereas standard neuropsychological test batteries (e.g., the Halstead-Reitan battery) do not identify consistent abnormalities in Tourette's patients, there nevertheless may be a distinctive and reliable pattern of test results. Sutherland and his colleagues gave a composite test battery to a large sample of children and adults with Tourette's syndrome and found a consistent pattern of results. The patients were especially bad at drawing and remembering complex geometric figures, although they also performed poorly on the Chicago word fluency test and recall of the Wechsler logical stories (see Table 29–1). The poor performance of these patients on the Rey figure was particularly striking since even patients with superior verbal IQs, such as the adult Tourette patient illustrated in Figure 29–1, performed very poorly, even when compared with control children or schizophrenic patients. These results, as well as similar findings by Shapiro, suggest that Tourette's patients may have a right frontotemporal dysfunction, but owing to the limited number of studies published to date, this conclusion must be considered tentative.

TABLE 29–1

Representative neuropsychological studies of psychiatric and motor disorders

Disease	Basic reference
Schizophrenia	Flor-Henry and Yeudall, 1979
	Kolb and Whishaw, 1983
Affective disorders	Flor-Henry and Yeudall, 1979
Tourette's syndrome	Shapiro et al., 1974
	Sutherland et al., 1982
Parkinson's disease	Pirozzolo et al., 1982
	Bowen et al., 1972
Huntington's disease	Fedio et al., 1979
	Wexler, 1979

Rey complex Figure

Copy   Recall

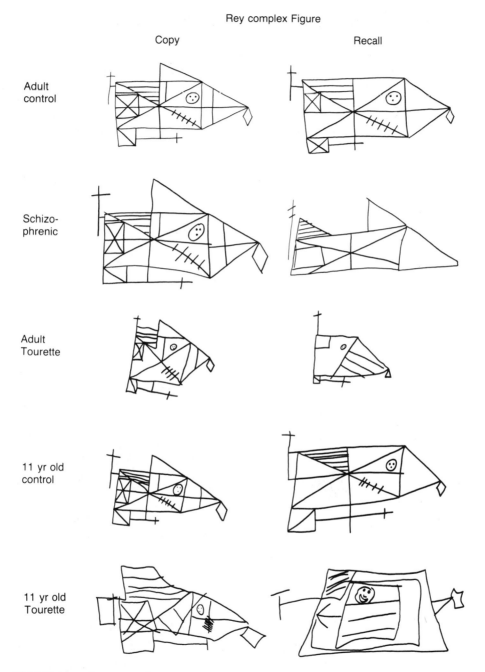

Adult
control

Schizo-
phrenic

Adult
Tourette

11 yr old
control

11 yr old
Tourette

FIGURE 29–1. Representative performance by a normal adult control, a schizophrenic, an adult Tourette, a normal child, and a Tourette child on the Rey complex figure, copying and recall. The Tourette patients are impaired at both the copy and the recall; the schizophrenic patient is impaired only at the recall. (After Sutherland et al., 1982.)

PARKINSON'S DISEASE

The pathology of Parkinson's disease is probably the best studied of all the pathologies of degenerative diseases (see Chapter 12), but the extent of neocortical abnormality remains controversial. Parkinson patients who are clearly demented at death have been known for some time to show structural cortical changes similar to those of Alzheimer's disease (see Chapter 6), but it has more recently been suggested that Alzheimer-like neocortical abnormalities may be a characteristic of all Parkinson patients. For example, Hakim and Mathieson found that of 34 Parkinson patients' brains they examined, only one did not have clear evidence of Alzheimer-like abnormalities. Further, of the 34 patients, only 19 were claimed to have shown any clinical evidence of dementia, although no psychological tests were done on their sample.

Neuropsychological investigations in other populations have confirmed the possibility of a general cognitive deterioration in Parkinson patients. For example, in their extensive study Pirozzolo et al. found Parkinson patients to be significantly impaired relative to age-matched controls on several subtests of the WAIS (information, digit span, digit symbol, and block design) and on measures of verbal memory (logical stories, paired associates) and visual-spatial ability. Similar results have been reported by others, and in addition, Parkinson patients are impaired at the Wisconsin card-sorting test and on Semmes et al.'s tests of personal and extrapersonal spatial orientation (Figure 18–5). In contrast, however, there is no evidence of aphasia, agnosia, or apraxia in Parkinson patients. In sum, Parkinson patients appear to do poorly at a broad range of neuropsychological tests and do not present any obvious pattern of test results that could distinguish them from people with other central degenerative diseases such as Alzheimer's disease.

HUNTINGTON'S DISEASE

Huntington's disease is another degenerative disorder (Chapter 12) that has recently become of particular interest to neuropsychologists, primarily because it may be possible to identify cognitive markers for the disease before the motor symptoms first appear. This is especially important for genetic counseling since there is currently no way to diagnose the disease until the degenerative motor symptoms appear. Neuropsychological studies have thus tended to compare known Huntington's patients to control subjects as well as to people who could be considered "at risk" for Huntington's since they had at least one parent with the disease. Extensive studies by Fedio et al. and by Wexler have shown that it may in fact be possible to identify those "at risk" people who will develop Huntington's disease. These authors have found that patients known to have Huntington's disease are impaired at a broad range of memory (e.g., Wechsler memory scale, recall of the Rey figure), perceptual (e.g., copy of the Rey figure, tachistoscopic and dichaptic recognition), and various frontal lobe tests (e.g., Chicago word fluency, stylus maze). People in the "at risk" groups appeared to perform poorly only at the frontal lobe tests, suggesting that these tests might be useful as predictors of the disease. This will be seen in the coming years as the subjects from these studies do, or do not, begin to display other symptoms.

CONCLUSIONS

Neuropsychological tests are likely to be used increasingly in the assessment of people with both "motor" and "psychiatric" disorders. There is evidence that people with some diseases may show distinctive patterns of test results (e.g., schizophrenia, Tourette's, Huntington's) whereas those with other diseases may not (e.g., Parkinson's). Skillful use of neuropsychological test results for people with the disorders discussed here, as well as for people with other less well studied diseases, may prove invaluable in the future both in differential diagnosis and patient management. We must emphasize, however, that these tests are not properly used merely as measures of "organicity." When carefully chosen and used, the results of neuropsychological tests present a reliable measure of the cognitive capacities of people; we have a reasonable degree of confidence that the profiles of neuropsychological deficits in different diseases reflect the anatomically and physiologically unique neurological dysfunction underlying these different disorders.

REFERENCES

Bowen, F. P., M. M. Hoehn, and M. D. Yahr. Parkinsonism: Alterations in spatial orientation as determined by a route walking test. *Neuropsychologia* 10:335–361, 1972.

Fedio, P., C. S. Cox, A. Neophytides, G. Canal-Frederick, and T. N. Chase. Neuropsychological profile of Huntington's disease: Patients and those at risk. *Advances in Neurology* 23:239–256, 1979.

Flor-Henry, P. Lateralized temporal-limbic dysfunction and psychopathology. *Annals of the New York Academy of Science* 280:777–795, 1976.

Flor-Henry, P., and L. T. Yeudall. Neuropsychological investigation of schizophrenia and manic-depressive psychosis. In J. Gruzelier and P. Flor-Henry, eds., *Hemisphere Asymmetries of Function in Psychopathology*. Amsterdam: Elsevier North-Holland, 1979.

Friedhoff, A. J., and T. N. Chase, eds. *Gilles de la Tourette Syndrome. Advances in Neurology*, vol. 35. New York: Raven Press, 1982.

Gruzelier, J., and P. Flor-Henry, eds. *Hemisphere Asymmetries of Function in Psychopathology*. Amsterdam: Elsevier North-Holland, 1979.

Hakim, A. M., and G. Mathieson. Dementia in Parkinson disease: A neuropathologic study. *Neurology* 29:1209–1214, 1979.

Heaton, R. K., L. E. Badde, and K. L. Johnson. Neuropsychological test results associated with psychiatric disorders in adults. *Psychological Bulletin* 85:141–162, 1978.

Heaton, R. K., and T. J. Crowley. Effects of psychiatric disorders and their somatic treatments on neuropsychological test results. In S. B. Gilskov and G. J. Boll, eds., *Handbook of Clinical Neuropsychology*. New York: Wiley, 1981.

Incagnoli, T., and R. Kane. Neuropsychological functioning in Tourette syndrome. *Advances in Neurology* 35:305–310, 1982.

Joschko, M., and B. Rourke. Neuropsychological dimensions of Tourette syndrome: Test-retest stability and implications for intervention. *Advances in Neurology* 35:297–304, 1982.

Kolb, B., and I. Q. Whishaw. Performance of schizophrenic patients on tests sensitive to left or right frontal, temporal, or parietal function in neurological patients. *Journal of Nervous and Mental Disease* 171:435–443, 1983.

Piran, N., E. D. Bigler, and D. Cohen. Motoric laterality and eye dominance suggest unique pattern of cerebral organization in schizophrenia. *Archives of General Psychiatry* 39:1010, 1982.

Pirozzolo, F. J., E. C. Hansch, J. A. Mortimer, D. D. Webster, and M. A. Kuskowski. Dementia in Parkinson disease: A neuropsychological analysis. *Brain and Cognition* 1:71–83, 1982.

Shapiro, E., E. K. Shapiro, and J. Clarkin. Clinical psychological testing in Tourette's syndrome. *Journal of Personality Assessment* 38:464–478, 1974.

Sutherland, R. J., B. Kolb, W. M. Schoel, I. Q. Whishaw, and D. Davies. Neuropsychological assessment of children and adults with Tourette syndrome: A comparison with learning disabilities and schizophrenia. *Advances in Neurology* 35:311–322, 1982.

Wexler, N. S. Perceptual-motor, cognitive, and emotional characteristics of person at risk for Huntington's disease. *Advances in Neurology* 23:257–272, 1979.

30

NEUROPSYCHOLOGICAL TEST
PROCEDURES AND NORMS

A major disadvantage of using an informal composition test battery in neuropsychological assessment is that the tests are seldom given as a group to a single population of normal controls. Thus, the testing conditions for control and patient populations may be rather different, especially if taking one test affects performance on others. Further, the neurological patients must often be compared across studies and their data are seldom compiled. Finally, there is seldom any information regarding the test performance of people other than neurological patients, making it difficult to evaluate neurological patients with other disorders such as schizophrenia or alcoholism in addition to their neurological complaint.

In this final chapter we provide such information for a group of tests that we have found to be very useful clinically over the past 10 years (see Table 26–4). These tests are largely drawn from tests devised and validated by others, especially at the Montreal Neurological Institute, and should not be construed to form a formal battery. Rather, they should be seen as a collection of tests that may be especially applicable to some types of patient populations or certain research questions. Cutoff scores can-

not be used with these tests; rather it is the idiosyncratic pattern of test results for each case that must be considered in the light of the basic information in earlier chapters of this text. Many of the tests can be constructed from the descriptions or references provided. Some are available commercially from DK Consultants (Department of Psychology, University Hospital, London, Canada) and related tests, which accompany Benton et al.'s manual, are available from Oxford University Press, New York.

In this chapter we briefly review the tests and then summarize norms for normal controls of different ages, summarize published data from neurological patients, and provide our original data from patients diagnosed as schizophrenic, alcoholic, learning disabled, or Gilles de la Tourette's. In addition, we summarize the performance of a sample of left-handed university students.

THE TESTS

General Intelligence
We normally administer the Wechsler scale appropriate for the age of the patient. In the

event that a Wechsler scale has been administered recently by another psychologist, the Peabody picture vocabulary test can be given as a quick validation of the Wechsler score; in our experience the Peabody score is usually about five points higher than the verbal IQ on the WAIS. As we mentioned earlier, intelligence ratings serve primarily as a valuable reference for the validity and interpretation of other test data, especially memory scores, and do not in themselves offer a great deal of help in localizing brain injuries.

Speech Lateralization

The best noninvasive test of speech lateralization is dichotic listening. The original Kimura tapes (available from DK Consultants) are as good as any for this purpose, although for very bright subjects there may be a ceiling effect. It must be remembered that dichotic listening is not a foolproof measure of speech lateralization; it is merely a means of inferring the likely locus of speech, and scores may be influenced by many methodological factors (see Chapter 14).

Visuoperceptual Tests

Three useful tests of visual perceptual skills are the copy of the Rey figure, the Mooney closure test (for a similar test see Kimura and McGlone), and a test of drawing (see Table 30–1). The complex figure test was devised by Rey to investigate both perceptual organization and visual memory in brain-damaged subjects (see Figure 10–2). The Rey figure has been extensively used and studied and has been found to be a very sensitive measure both of perceptual-motor skill and of visual memory. Osterrieth standardized Rey's procedure, Visser prepared a manual for it, and a summary of the scoring

criteria are found in Lezak. A recent study by Binder is informative, as he showed how stroke patients tend to lose the overall configuration of the design: right hemisphere patients tend to leave out units of the test whereas left hemisphere patients tend to fragment the test, rather than drawing it as a unit. Taylor finds that frontal lobe patients, especially right frontal lobe patients, tend to be sloppy in their production of the copy, although the test is neither distorted nor fragmented. Thus, although the copy of the Rey figure is often perceived to be a test of right posterior function, it is more complex, and interpretation of the score must consider both the actual score and the configuration of the design. Table 30–2 provides means and standard deviations for copy and recall of the Rey figure for a randomly selected sample of school-aged subjects collected from the Lethbridge public and separate school systems.

The Mooney faces test (see Figure 10–2) has also been extensively researched and found to be selectively sensitive to right posterior lesions. In our experience normal subjects are almost never impaired at this test, nor are many pathological groups such as schizophrenics, and so the presence of a deficit on this test must be taken seriously.

Like many psychologists, we use a drawing test because it allows subjects to relax with a more familiar task and because it is sensitive to many kinds of disorders. We use a draw-a-bicycle task since bicycles are well known to everyone and because they are very complex. The orientation of the bicycle (left or right) is taken by some to be clinically significant, but we have not found it so. One difficulty with using drawing tests is that there are seldom any objective criteria for their scoring. We have devised a scoring protocol for bicycles and have normed this test on hundreds of subjects (see Tables 30–3 and 30–4). In addition to our scoring criteria, we look for relative inatten-

TABLE 30–1

Summary of published means for neurological patients

| Test | Patient group | | | | | | |
| | Frontal | | Temporal | | Parietal | | |
	Left	Right	Left	Right	Left	Right	
Visuoperceptual							
Mooney faces	38/44	39/44	38/44	35/44		31/44*	Milner, 1980
Rey copy			33/36	30/36			Taylor, 1969
Memory							
Delayed verbal recall	18.1	15	9.6*	16.5	15	17	Milner, 1967
Digit span	6.1	6.3	5.5*	6.5	5.6*	6.8	Newcombe, 1969
Recurring figures			21/40	9/40	23/40	24/40	Milner, 1967
Rey recall			22/36	14/36*			Taylor, 1969
Spatial							
Semmes figures	24.35	30/35*	32/35	32/35	27/35*	33/35	Teuber, 1964
Right-left	75%	83%	72%	78%	50%	76%	See text
Language							
Newcombe fluency I	27	30	22*	28	23*	27	Newcombe, 1969
Newcombe fluency II	16	18	15	19	16	17	Newcombe, 1969
Newcombe fluency III	13	15	11*	14	13	14	Newcombe, 1969
Chapman-Cook			11*	17			Milner, 1967
Reading							
Frontal lobe							
Wisconsin card:							
Categories[a]	3.3*	3.3*	5.3	5.3	4.5	4.5	Milner, 1964
Perseverative errors	40*	40*	9	9	22	22	Milner, 1964
Chicago fluency	35*	57	58	58	44*		Milner, 1964, 1967

* Differs significantly from control.

[a] Data from left and right hemisphere lesions are not separated in the published reports.

tion to one side of the page or drawing and at the size of the drawing, as it is claimed that left hemisphere lesions decrease drawing size whereas right hemisphere lesions increase the size.

Memory

Milner's extensive studies linking certain memory functions with the temporal lobes have provided several tests useful for assessing memory functions. Although the Wechsler memory scale is not a sensitive test of memory, it is a useful starting point. After completing the standard Wechsler memory scale we administer a delayed recall of the drawings, stories, and paired associates with a delay of about 20 minutes. Although it is unusual for patients to have difficulty with the simple Wechsler drawings, poor recall must be considered significant. Milner has found the delayed recall of the stories and paired associates to be especially sensitive to left temporal lobe damage, as summarized in Table 30–1, where "delayed verbal recall" refers to the sum of the two stories and a single attempt at recall of the paired associates.

TABLE 30–2

Rey figure copy and recall scores (mean and standard deviation)
for school subjects aged 6 to 18

Age	Sex	(n)	Rey copy		Rey recall	
			Mean	S.D.	Mean	S.D.
6	♀	(111)	16.96	7.86	10.79	5.80
	♂	(81)	16.25	8.16	10.18	5.81
	Total	(192)	16.66	7.97	10.53	5.80
7	♀	(184)	21.03	7.76	13.18	5.86
	♂	(169)	21.57	7.59	13.99	6.69
	Total	(353)	21.29	7.67	13.57	6.28
8	♀	(155)	23.74	7.97	16.36	6.45
	♂	(192)	23.57	8.04	16.32	7.03
	Total	(347)	23.64	8.00	16.34	6.77
9	♀	(154)	26.61	6.87	18.29	6.27
	♂	(175)	26.33	7.01	19.07	6.06
	Total	(329)	26.46	6.94	18.71	6.16
10	♀	(146)	27.95	7.13	19.83	6.53
	♂	(155)	26.50	7.95	19.64	6.89
	Total	(301)	27.20	7.58	19.73	6.71
11	♀	(126)	29.29	6.75	22.88	6.33
	♂	(154)	28.06	7.73	22.35	6.92
	Total	(280)	28.61	7.31	22.59	6.65
12	♀	(119)	30.54	7.29	23.25	6.16
	♂	(106)	29.84	5.95	23.15	6.65
	Total	(225)	30.21	6.69	23.20	6.38
13	♀	(106)	32.80	4.15	24.47	6.38
	♂	(131)	32.50	4.52	24.69	6.25
	Total	(237)	32.63	4.35	24.59	6.29
14	♀	(89)	33.46	3.20	26.28	5.56
	♂	(91)	33.60	3.19	26.21	5.27
	Total	(180)	33.53	3.18	26.24	5.40
15	♀	(48)	33.62	3.10	26.39	6.63
	♂	(68)	33.60	2.92	25.73	6.18
	Total	(116)	33.60	2.98	26.00	6.35
16	♀	(30)	34.63	1.13	26.43	5.64
	♂	(40)	34.49	1.65	27.29	5.33
	Total	(70)	34.55	1.45	26.92	5.44
17	♀	(38)	34.86	1.51	25.63	6.34
	♂	(39)	34.73	2.12	27.31	5.56
	Total	(77)	34.79	1.83	26.49	5.97
18	♀	(19)	34.37	3.58	26.05	5.93
	♂	(14)	33.79	3.66	27.46	3.15
	Total	(33)	34.12	3.57	26.65	4.93

TABLE 30–3

Scoring procedure for draw-a-bicycle test [a]		
Part	Representation	Score
Wheels	2 circles	2 (1 for each wheel)
	2 tires	1
	Spokes	2 (any spokes; 1 for each wheel)
Frame	Front wheel	1
	Back wheel	1
	Middle "V"	1
	Seat	1
	Handlebars	1
Drive	Rear wheel sprocket	1
	Front sprocket	1
	Chain	1
	2 pedals	1
	2 pedal supports	1
Function	Can coast	1
	Can be driven	1
	Parts in the right place	1
	Parts in proportion	1
	Well drawn	1
		20

[a] In our sample 49.6 percent of females and 46.6 percent of males pointed the bicycle to the left.

Long-term recall of visual material is assessed using both a delayed (30 min) recall of the Rey figure and the Kimura recurring figures test, which is available from DK Consultants. In the former test, the subjects are asked to reproduce as exactly as they can the complex geometric figure that they drew earlier. Patients with right temporal lobe lesions are especially poor at this, although frontal lobe patients may embellish their drawings and should be encouraged to draw only what they actually recall. The same scoring criteria are used for the recall as for the copy. In the recurring figures test, subjects are shown a series of nonsense drawings (see Figure 20–9), which they are to remember. They are then shown a much larger series and asked to pick out the ones they saw previously. Again, right temporal lobe patients are especially poor at this test.

In addition to measures of long-term memory it is useful to assess short-term verbal and nonverbal memory. Digit span is the commonest way to assess verbal short-term memory, and the Corsi block span test is a very useful analogue for nonverbal short-term memory. In the latter test the visual span is determined using the block board illustrated in Figure 20–7. The subject's task is to copy the sequence demonstrated by the examiner, as described in Chapter 20 for the span + 1 test. Although there are no published data for this test, Milner and her associates find that right parietal lobe patients have reduced block spans, just as left parietal lobe patients have reduced digit spans. We have not yet completed a normative study on this test, but as a general rule of thumb one can expect the block span to be one fewer than the digit span.

TABLE 30–4

Draw-a-bicycle test
(Means and standard deviations)

Age	Sex	(n)	Mean	S.D.	Age	Sex	(n)	Mean	S.D.
2–4	♀	(16)	3.0	1.7	13	♀	(115)	9.8	2.8
	♂	(15)	3.7	2.5		♂	(119)	12.8	3.6
	Total	(31)	3.2	2.1		Total	(234)	11.3	3.6
5	♀	(22)	4.6	2.4	14	♀	(129)	10.8	3.3
	♂	(15)	6.2	3.8		♂	(120)	12.6	3.5
	Total	(37)	5.3	2.9		Total	(249)	11.6	3.5
6	♀	(20)	6.5	2.3	15	♀	(197)	10.6	2.8
	♂	(19)	6.4	2.7		♂	(188)	13.6	3.4
	Total	(39)	6.5	2.5		Total	(385)	12.0	3.4
7	♀	(24)	6.1	2.1	16	♀	(182)	10.7	3.9
	♂	(29)	8.0	2.8		♂	(207)	13.5	3.6
	Total	(53)	7.1	2.7		Total	(389)	12.2	3.6
8	♀	(22)	7.5	2.0	17	♀	(174)	10.9	3.0
	♂	(16)	9.3	2.4		♂	(187)	13.5	3.8
	Total	(38)	8.3	2.3		Total	(361)	12.2	3.7
9	♀	(24)	8.2	1.9	18	♀	(119)	12.1	3.4
	♂	(16)	10.1	2.9		♂	(98)	14.2	3.9
	Total	(40)	9.0	2.3		Total	(217)	13.1	3.8
10	♀	(27)	9.6	2.3	19	♀	(46)	12.6	3.7
	♂	(27)	11.4	4.0		♂	(35)	14.2	4.0
	Total	(54)	10.5	3.3		Total	(81)	13.3	3.9
11	♀	(17)	9.1	1.7	20–29	♀	(116)	11.4	3.9
	♂	(25)	11.8	3.8		♂	(133)	14.1	4.0
	Total	(42)	10.8	3.3		Total	(249)	12.8	4.1
12	♀	(47)	10.6	3.4	30–50	♀	(43)	11.1	3.9
	♂	(60)	12.0	3.4		♂	(16)	11.1	3.9
	Total	(107)	11.4	3.5		Total	(59)	11.0	3.9

Spatial Orientation

Two tests of spatial orientation were drawn from the extensive studies of Semmes and her colleagues. In the right-left differentiation test the subject is shown a series of pictures of body parts (hands, arms, eyes, ears, legs) and clothing (lapels, shoes) and asked to determine if each is of the left or right. Most people find this test difficult, scoring only about 80 percent correct. Patients with left parietal lesions respond strictly at chance, however. Although data for neurological patients are not published for this test, we have computed scores for those patients studied by Kolb and Milner and have summarized them in Table 30–1. Other excellent tests of right-left discrimination are found in Benton's manual.

In the body-placing test (see Figure 18–4) the subject is shown five drawings similar to those in Figure 18–4 and the task is to point to the location of each of the numbers on the subject's own body. Patients with frontal lobe lesions are poor at this task, largely because they point inaccurately. Patients with left parietal lobe lesions confuse left and right in the test, a deficit that also leads to impaired performance (see Table 30–1). This test can be constructed by using the model in Figure 18–4 and placing numbers on the following locations: (1) front view: right cheek, right palm, left shoulder; rear view: left shoulder, left hand; (2) front view: left forehead, right forearm, right shin; rear view: left shoulder, right elbow, left hand; (3) front view: left shoulder, right wrist, left thumb, right knee; rear view: right shoulder, left forearm, middle finger; (4) front view: left ear, right thumb, left forearm, right knee; rear view: left ear, left shoulder, left middle finger, right calf; (5) front view: left eye, right wrist, right little finger, left ring finger, right shin; rear view: left thumb, left middle finger, right first finger, right knee.

Somatosensory Testing

Three tests are especially useful for identifying somatosensory defects: two-point discrimination, point localization, and position sense. Detailed procedures for these tests can be found in Corkin et al. Briefly, in the two-point discrimination test the subject's ability to tell if the palm has been touched with one or two probes is determined. The point localization test determines how close two touches need

to be for the subject to perceive them to be in exactly the same place. This test can be administered either to the palm, the foot, or the face. Finally, the position sense test is a measure of the sensitivity of the digits to induced movement up or down.

Lesions that invade the core somatosensory cortex of the precentral gyrus severely disturb somatosensation on the contralateral hand, as summarized in Table 30–5. Although these tests may be tedious to administer, patients with central lesions may only show a deficit on careful somatosensory testing, as illustrated by Case 4 described in Chapter 26.

Language

We normally use three language tests: the token test, the Newcombe fluency test, and the Chapman-Cook speed of reading test. As we have mentioned earlier, the token test is an aphasia screening test that we give only to those subjects in whom language comprehension difficulties are suspected. De Renzi and Vignolo present clear instructions and norms for this test, which can be purchased from

TABLE 30–5

Summary of Corkin et al. somatosensory data			
	2-Point	Point Localization	Position sense
A. Control data			
Right hand	7.6 ± 2.0 mm	3.28 ± 2.62 mm	58/60+
Left hand	8.0 ± 1.9 mm	3.04 ± 2.48 mm	58/60+
B. Patient data[a]			
Parietal [b]:			
Ipsilateral hand	0%	26%	6%
Contralateral hand	78%	81%	78%
Frontal or temporal:			
Ipsilateral hand	3%	0%	0%
Contralateral hand	0%	5%	5%

[a]Numbers indicate the percentage of patients whose score deviated from the control value by more than 2.54 × control standard deviation.
[b]Only those parietal lobe patients whose lesions had invaded the precentral gyrus are included.

University Park Press, 233 East Redwood St., Baltimore, Maryland 21202.

The Newcombe fluency tests require the patient to produce orally the names of as many objects (Test I), animals (Test II), or animal-color-animal-color alternations (Test III) as possible in one minute each. Although a simple test for most people, left hemisphere patients consistently score below the level of control or right hemisphere patients, the greatest deficit appearing in patients with left posterior temporal or parietal lobe lesions. Finally, we often administer a reading test such as the Wide Range Achievement Test (WRAT) or the Chapman-Cook speed of reading test. Both of these tests are available from most suppliers of psychometric instruments.

Frontal Lobe Tests

The frontal lobes are the most difficult regions to assess using psychological tests because it is difficult to find tests appropriate for routine clinical use that dissociate the left and right frontal lobes. The best test of frontal lobe function available is the Wisconsin card-sorting test, which can be purchased from Psychological Assessment Resources, Inc., P.O. Box 98, Odessa, Florida 33556 (see Figure 18–4). A modified, shorter version has been published by Nelson. According to Milner, patients with left dorsolateral frontal lesions (around area 9) are the most impaired at this task although patients with right dorsolateral lesions are also impaired. Damage to the orbitofrontal cortex may be without effect. Another useful test is the Chicago word fluency test (Table 30–6), which, in contrast to the card-sorting test, is most sensitive to orbitofrontal damage and less affected by dorsolateral lesions. Again, both left and right hemisphere lesions impair performance on this test, although somewhat more so on the left.

Miscellaneous Tests

Depending on the referral question, we routinely add other tests to our assessment, especially the Kimura manual sequence box, the copying of arm and facial movements, a handedness questionnaire, and a measure of hand strength. All these tests are described in detail in Kimura and McGlone, and any test materials necessary can be purchased from DK Consultants.

SUBJECT POPULATIONS

Perhaps the most frustrating impediment to the use of a composite collection of tests taken from research reports is that data for normal control subjects are often not provided, the main comparison being the relative performance of two or more groups of neurological patients. We have therefore undertaken to establish norms for normal control subjects on the tests that we use routinely. Further, since many neurological referrals are confounded by psychiatric diagnoses as well, we have compiled data on people with diagnoses of chronic alcoholism and schizophrenia and availed ourselves of the opportunity to study people with Tourette's syndrome. Finally, since we have used our tests to assess the cognitive development of children making slow progress in school, we have collected data from a sample of schoolage children.

Normal Subjects

We administered the entire collection of tests to 107 adult control subjects, which we have broken down by age and sex in Table 30–7. We recruited "average" people by contacting various local community organizations and self-help groups to solicit volunteers. Children were obtained from local school systems

TABLE 30–6

Chicago word fluency norms [a]

Age (yrs.)	Total			Female			Male		
	n	$\overline{x}$	S.D.	n	$\overline{x}$	S.D.	n	$\overline{x}$	S.D.
6	80	9.28	4.47	40	9.85	4.58	40	8.70	4.33
7	133	15.87	8.22	72	17.22	8.20	61	14.26	8.00
8	197	21.52	9.29	85	23.72	10.34	112	19.85	8.05
9	208	25.93	10.18	90	28.41	9.93	118	24.03	10.01
10	189	29.98	11.92	86	33.16	11.83	103	27.32	11.39
11	146	37.08	11.98	75	39.03	10.57	71	35.01	13.07
12	140	40.58	13.00	84	44.52	12.98	56	34.61	10.61
13	167	45.07	14.10	76	51.37	13.65	91	39.81	12.26
14	175	48.46	14.72	85	52.64	14.30	90	44.52	14.08
15	120	47.35	15.22	51	51.57	13.28	69	44.23	15.88
16	69	48.28	13.69	28	53.43	10.54	41	44.76	14.56
17	79	49.65	17.51	37	53.65	17.63	42	46.12	16.83
18	30	61.47	15.29	18	64.22	14.98	12	57.33	15.42

[a]The test requires the subject to write as many words as possible beginning with the letter "s" in five minutes and as many four-letter words as possible beginning with the letter "c" in four minutes. Results are totals for both sets of responses.

TABLE 30–7

Summary of control data[a]

	Age group				
	5–9	10–15	16–30	31–44	45–60
n	6	14	67	26	14
Intelligence					
Verbal IQ	116 ± 9.6	118 ± 13.4	116 ± 10.0	114 ± 9.4	120 ± 10.6
Performance IQ	123 ± 10.1	118 ± 12.4	116 ± 9.9	114 ± 12.7	121 ± 13.2
Full-scale IQ	122 ± 5.1	120 ± 13.2	117 ± 8.5	115 ± 10.5	123 ± 11.4
Visuoperceptual					
Mooney faces	22.6 ± 1.2	22.7 ± 2.2	22.4 ± 2.0	23.2 ± 2.2	19.9 ± 5.1
Rey copy	16.4 ± 9.8	32.6 ± 3.5	35.1 ± 1.5	33.2 ± 6.1	34.5 ± 2.1
Memory					
MQ	95 ± 6.7	112 ± 13.8	108 ± 12.0	114 ± 15.1	123 ± 16.1
Delayed stories	20.3 ± 6.9	13.8 ± 5.4	12.8 ± 6.9	14.7 ± 4.7	13.5 ± 4.1
Delayed associates	8.0 ± 1.7	9.5 ± 1.2	7.7 ± 3.5	8.4 ± 3.2	7.4 ± 3.4
Digit span	12.2 ± 3.5	11.6 ± 2.5	11.0 ± 2.6	10.8 ± 2.8	9.3 ± 2.5
Recurring figures	—	—	24.7 ± 7.8	21.7 ± 10.9	21.6 ± 7.1
Rey recall	11.6 ± 7.1	22.9 ± 6.8	22.7 ± 7.0	19.5 ± 6.7	18.3 ± 6.7
Spatial					
Semmes figures	20.5 ± 6.5	30.2 ± 6.1	31.1 ± 2.8	33.7 ± 1.7	34.2 ± 1.2
Right-left	60 ± 1.1	80 ± 10.5	84 ± 5.7	84 ± 6.2	79 ± 6.3
Language					
Newcombe I	29.0 ± 10.9	27.3 ± 14.0	28.9 ± 7.7	25.4 ± 7.1	27.8 ± 5.2
II	9.2 ± 2.7	13.2 ± 3.8	22.5 ± 4.4	20.9 ± 3.8	19.5 ± 3.6
III	—	—	17.0 ± 6.9	16.2 ± 3.6	16.2 ± 3.3
Frontal lobe					
Wisconsin card	2.6 ± 2.1*	4.9 ± 2.2*	5.8 ± 4.7	5.3 ± 1.6	6.0 ± 0.0
Chicago fluency	16.3 ± 4.9	39.7 ± 12.8	64.0 ± 15.9	66.6 ± 17.6	58.7 ± 25.6

[a]Numbers represent means and standard deviations.   *Only one deck of cards was used.

by searching for "average" students or by testing entire classrooms of students. The left-handed subjects were entirely composed of a freshman university population since we were interested in seeing if this admittedly select group would be impaired relative to right-handers at any of the tests. They were not! The designation of familial and nonfamilial left-hander was made by asking the students if they had any close relatives (parents, grandparents, aunts, uncles, or siblings) who were also left-handed.

Schizophrenic Subjects

Two psychiatrists independently diagnosed these subjects as schizophrenic using the DSM-III criteria. None of the patients had any history of prior neurological illness or substance abuse, and none had clinically obvious neuroleptic side effects at the time of testing. All of the patients had been on a neuroleptic for at least 24 hours before testing began. They had a mean age of 29 years, a mean of 12 years of education, and an average of 3.6 prior admissions with the same diagnosis at discharge.

Alcoholic Subjects

The alcoholic subjects were recruited from a local Alcoholics Anonymous group and a government alcohol treatment center. They were all self-proclaimed alcoholics and reported an abusive drinking history of from five to 20 years and had suffered physical (hospitalization) and/or psychosocial consequences (marital breakdown, loss of employment, conflict with the law, etc.) as a result of their excessive drinking. They were between 19 and 55 years of age and had eight to 14 years of education. All of the alcoholic subjects had been abstinent for more than four months.

Learning Disabled

These children were referred by the local school systems as having severe difficulties in school, especially in reading, in spite of intelligence ratings within the average range. Children with obvious emotional problems were not included in the sample.

Gilles de la Tourette

Although Tourette's syndrome is a relatively rare disorder, we had an opportunity to study a large group of these patients. We include them in our patient population here because they provide an example of how neuropsychological tests may provide insight into the nature of disorders of unknown etiology and because they have a unique pattern of test results. These subjects were obtained from a local health unit, the Canadian Tourette Society, and the American Tourette Syndrome Association. Some of these subjects were receiving no medication at the time of testing; the others were receiving pimozide, haloperidol, clonidine, or Cogentin.

TEST SCORES

We will not extensively discuss the test results, as most of these data have been discussed in the previous two chapters. Rather, we have summarized the data into tables, which can be used by others for comparison purposes.

Normal Controls

Test results for normal controls are divided arbitrarily into three age groups: 16 to 29 years, 30 to 44 years, and 45 to 60 years (see Table 30–7). A further analysis was made to determine if there might be differences related to gender, and these data are summarized in Table 30–8, along with the scores for

TABLE 30–8

Summary of data by handedness and gender[a]

	Group				
	Right	Left familial	Left non-familial	Male	Female
Age	29.2	19.3–1.86	20.8–4.3	29.7	29
n	107	34	22	30	77
Intelligence					
Verbal IQ	116 ± 10	120 ± 9.7	116 ± 9.1	116 ± 11.2	116 ± 9.5
Performance IQ	116 ± 11	116 ± 11.9	119 ± 9.2	112 ± 9.5	117 ± 11.1
Full-scale IQ	117 ± 9	120 ± 10	119 ± 8.8	115 ± 10	117 ± 9
Visuoperceptual					
Mooney faces	22 ± 3	21.5 ± 1.1	21.9 ± 1.3	21.9 ± 4.1	22.3 ± 2.4
Rey copy	34.5 ± 3.4	35.3 ± 1.4	35.2 ± 1.2	34.9 ± 1.4	34.4 ± 3.9
Memory					
MQ	112 ± 15	113 ± 15.3	109 ± 11.9	107 ± 12.8	114 ± 14.8
Delayed stories	19.4 ± 0.5	18.8 ± 6.5	14.9 ± 6.4	12.1 ± 5.6	14 ± 6.2
Delayed associates	17.3 ± 2.8	9.4 ± 1.8	9.2 ± 1.7	7.2 ± 3.5	8.1 ± 3.4
Digit span	10.7 ± 2.7	12.1 ± 2.6	11.2 ± 2.2	10.3 ± 3.0	10.9 ± 2.5
Recurring figures	23 ± 7.9	—	—	19.3 ± 7.3	24.2 ± 8.7
Rey recall	21.7 ± 7	25.1 ± 6.2	26 ± 6.3	19.9 ± 5.9	21.7 ± 7.4
Spatial					
Semmes figures	33 ± 2.1	32.6 ± 3.1	32.8 ± 2.6	33.5 ± 2.5	33.4 ± 2.4
Right-left	84 ± 6	83 ± 6.9	87 ± 2.3	84 ± 5.1	83 ± 6.3
Language					
Newcombe I	28 ± 7.4	28 ± 6.3	24.4 ± 7.4	26.5 ± 7.2	28.4 ± 7.4
II	22 ± 4.3	22.5 ± 6.9	20 ± 4.6	22 ± 5.3	21.5 ± 3.9
III	16.7 ± 5.6	16.2 ± 3.8	16 ± 2.3	16.5 ± 4	16.8 ± 6.1
Frontal lobe					
Wisconsin card	5.6 ± 1	4.8 ± 1.2*	4.4 ± 0.9*	5.6 ± 1.1	5.7 ± 1.1
Chicago fluency	64 ± 18	69 ± 18.9	60.0 ± 13.3	60 ± 2.0	65 ± 16.6

[a]Numbers represent means and standard deviations.
*Only one deck of cards was used.

left-handers. There was very little difference in the performance of people as they aged, although visual memory scores did appear to deteriorate somewhat. There were no obvious gender differences or differences related to handedness.

In order to determine the relation between the different tests, all the adult control subjects were pooled and each test was correlated with every other test. Correlations coefficients exceeding .3 ($p < .01$) were considered significant and are summarized in Table 30–9. Perhaps the most interesting correlations are those between intelligence and memory scores and between intelligence and Chicago fluency scores. In view of these correlations it is obviously difficult to consider using cutoff scores for patient groups since the cutoff must slide with IQ. Finally, age correlates positively with Wechsler memory quotient (MQ). This result implies that the age correction on the MQ is too liberal, a factor that should be considered in assessing memory in older patients.

TABLE 30–9

Summary of all cross correlations

Test	Verb. IQ	Perf. IQ	Full IQ	Wechsler MQ	Stories	Paired assoc.	Delayed stories	Delayed assoc.	Wechsler figs.	Delayed figs.	Rey recall	Kimura figs.	Digit span	Left-right	Newcombe I	= II	= III	Rey copy	Mooney	Block span	Card sorting	Chicago	Semmes
Verbal IQ																							
Performance IQ	*																						
Full-scale IQ	*	*																					
Wechsler MQ	*	*	*																				
Stories	*		*	*																			
Paired associates	*	*	*	*	*																		
Delayed stories				*	*	*																	
Delayed assoc.																							
Wechsler figs.																							
Delayed figs.				*																			
Rey recall										*													
Kimura figs.		*								*													
Digit span	*		*	*																			
Left-right																							
Newcombe I																							
II															*								
III																*							
Rey copy											*												
Mooney closure																							
Block span																							
Card sorting																							
Chicago fluency	*		*	*	*														*				*
Semmes placing																							

*Indicates correlations over +.3 (p < .01).

The test scores for children have been summarized in Table 30–7 by dividing the children into two age groups. Comparison of the adults' and children's scores reveals that children find many of the tests more difficult than adults, a difference that is no doubt related to the level of cognitive development in children. A different set of simpler logical stories was used for the young children, since in our experience they had difficulty in understanding Wechsler stories.

Patient Groups

Each of the patient groups displays a different pattern of test results (see Table 30–10).

Schizophrenic patients are impaired at every test of frontal and temporal lobe function but perform normally on tests believed to measure parietal lobe function. Those diagnosed as having Tourette's syndrome had an unusual pattern of test results suggestive of right orbito-frontal dysfunction, although there is no known neurological correlate of this. Learning-disabled children perform especially poorly at tests sensitive to left parietal and temporal lobe function, although some children have a severe disability at drawing the Rey figure as well. Finally, alcoholics are surprisingly normal at most of our tests, a significant impairment appearing only at long-term recall of the Rey figure.

TABLE 30–10

Summary of data by patient group

	Tourette's		Schizophrenic	Alcoholic	Learning disabled	
Age	10–14 yrs	15+ yrs	28.5 yrs	40 yrs	5–9 yrs	10–15 yrs
n	14	12	30	23	17	31
Intelligence						
Verbal IQ	108	113	105*	114	102	101
Performance IQ	101	105	95*	112	102	100
Full-scale IQ	106	110	98*	114	102	102
Visuoperceptual						
Mooney faces	22.6	23	20	21	19.5	22
Rey copy	28	31	32.5	32.9	18*	29.1
Memory						
MQ	102	100	89*	110	85	98
Delayed stories	13	11.8	6.7*	14.1	14.6	12.6
Delayed P.A.L.	9.1	8.8	8.4*	9.3	7.6	9.2
Digit span	11.8	12.4	11.0	10.3	7.7	8.8
Recurring figures	—	—	—	—	—	—
Rey recall	17.2*	20.1*	10.8*	16.75*	7.8*	18.1*
Spatial						
Semmes figures	30	32	30	33.3	18.7	27
Right-left	75	80	77	80	63*	69*
Language						
Newcombe I	27	34	25	25	15	24
II	17	22	20	20	13	17
III	13	16	14	15	6	13
Frontal lobe						
Wisconsin card	4.5	5	2.9*	3.9	3.7	5.1
Chicago fluency	34*	46*	36*	55.5	19	32

*Differs significantly from control scores.

CONCLUDING COMMENTS

The tests that we have described in this chapter represent only a small fraction of the tests used in neuropsychological assessment, but they have been used extensively for neurological patients (see Taylor), for those undergoing psychiatric surgery (see Corkin et al.) and stereotaxic surgery for Parkinson's disease, and for the assessment of children with learning disorders. We have found them to be useful and reliable measures both for routine clinical assessments and as a starting point for various research projects. There are, of course, many aspects of cerebral function that these tests do not measure, and other specific tests may be necessary for particular assessment questions and patient populations. Nevertheless, the data we have summarized in this chapter should be useful complements to the manuals by Benton et al. and Kimura and McGlone and to the excellent assessment text by Lezak. We caution, however, that none of these sources can be used validly without a thorough understanding of the basic material of this text.

The usefulness of any scientific endeavor is eventually measured by its technological applicability to the betterment of humankind. We believe that in the decades to come neuropsychology will indeed be applied to a plethora of human problems. It is up to those in the field to apply it wisely.

REFERENCES

Benton, A. L. Psychological testing. In A. B. Baker and L. H. Baker, eds., *Clinical Neurology,* vol. 1. Philadelphia: Harper & Row, 1982.

Benton, A. L., K. deS. Hamsher, N. R. Varney, and O. Spreen. *Contributions to Neuropsychological Assessment.* New York: Oxford University Press, 1983.

Binder, L. M. Constructional strategies on complex figure drawings after unilateral brain damage. *Journal of Clinical Neuropsychology* 4:51–58, 1982.

Corkin, S., B. Milner, and T. Rasmussen. Somatosensory thresholds: Contrasting effects of postcentral-gyrus and posterior parietal-lobe excisions. *Archives of Neurology* 23:41–58, 1970.

Corkin, S., H.-L. Teuber, and T. E. Twitchell. A study of cingulatomy in man: A summary. In W. H. Sweet, ed., *Neurosurgical Treatment in Psychiatry, Pain and Epilepsy.* Baltimore: University Park Press, 1977.

Kimura, D., and J. McGlone. *Neuropsychology Test Procedures.* University of Western Ontario, London, Ontario, 1983.

Kolb, B., and B. Milner. Performance of complex arm and facial movements after focal brain lesions. *Neuropsychologia* 4:491–503, 1981.

Kolb, B., and I. Q. Whishaw. Performance of schizophrenic patients on tests sensitive to left or right frontal, temporal, or parietal function in neurological patients. *Journal of Nervous and Mental Disease,* 171:435–443, 1983.

Lezak, M. D. *Neuropsychological Assessment,* 2nd ed. New York: Oxford University Press, 1983.

Milner, B. Brain mechanisms suggested by studies of temporal lobes. In F. L. Darley, ed., *Brain Mechanisms Underlying Speech and Language.* New York: Grune & Stratton, 1967.

Milner, B. Complementary functional specializations of the human cerebral hemispheres. In R. Levi-Montalcini, ed., *Nerve Cells, Transmitters and Behavior.* Vatican City: Pont. Acad. Scientiarum, 1980.

Milner, B. Some effects of frontal lobectomy in man. In J. M. Warren and K. Akert, eds., *Frontal Granular Cortex and Behavior.* New York: McGraw-Hill, 1964.

Newcombe, F. *Missile Wounds of the Brain.* London: Oxford University Press, 1969.

Renzi, E. de., and L. A. Vignolo. The token test: A sensitive test to detect disturbances in aphasics. *Brain* 85:665–678, 1962.

Semmes, J., S. Weinstein, L. Ghent, and H.-L. Teuber. Correlates of impaired orientation in personal and extrapersonal space. *Brain* 86:747–772, 1963.

Sutherland, R. J., B. Kolb, W. M. Schoel, I. Q. Whishaw, and D. Davies. Neuropsychological assessment of children and adults with Tourette syndrome: A comparison with learning disabilities and schizophrenia. In A. J. Friedhoff and T. N. Chase, eds., *Gilles de la Tourette Syndrome.* New York: Raven Press, 1982.

Taylor, L. B. Localisation of cerebral lesions by psychological testing. *Clinical Neurosurgery* 16:269–287, 1969.

Taylor, L. B. Psychological assessment of neurosurgical patients. In T. Rasmussen and R. Marino, eds., *Functional Neurosurgery.* New York: Raven Press, 1979.

Teuber, H.-L. The riddle of frontal lobe function in man. In J. M. Warren and K. Akert, eds., *Frontal Granular Cortex and Behavior.* New York: McGraw-Hill, 1964.

Visser, R. S. H. *Manual of the Complex Figure Test*. Amsterdam: Swets and Zeitlinger, 1973.

Whishaw, I. Q., and B. Kolb. Neuropsychological assessment of children and adults with developmental dyslexia. In R. N. Malatesha and H. A. Whitaker, eds., *Dyslexia: A Global Issue*. Boston: Martinus Nijhoff, 1984.

GLOSSARY

Ablation. Intentional destruction or removal of portions of the brain or spinal cord; brain lesion.

Absence attack. Temporary loss of consciousness in some forms of epilepsy.

Acalculia. Inability to perform mathematical operations.

Accessory cells. Cells that, originating from germinal cells (spongioblasts), contribute to the support, nourishment, conduction, and repair of neurons; occasionally the origins of tumors. The accessory cells are the astrocytes; oligodendrocytes; and ependymal, microglial, and Schwann cells.

Achromatopsia. Inability to distinguish different hues despite normally pigmented cells in the retina. Sometimes called cortical color blindness.

Acopia. Inability to copy a geometric design.

Acquired dyslexia. When an individual who can read suffers brain damage and can no longer read, the dyslexia is referred to as acquired, to distinguish it from developmental dyslexia, which is a failure to learn to read.

Action potential. The brief electrical impulse by which information is conducted along an axon. It results from brief changes in the membrane's permeability to potassium and sodium ions.

Afferent. Conducting toward the central nervous system or toward its higher centers.

Afferent paresis. Loss of kinesthetic feedback resulting from lesions to the postcentral gyrus (areas 1, 2, 3), producing clumsy movements.

Agnosia. Partial or complete inability—unexplainable by a defect in elementary sensation or by a reduced level of alertness—to recognize sensory stimuli.

Agraphia. Decline or loss of the ability to write.

Akathisia. A condition of motor restlessness, ranging from a feeling of inner disquiet to an inability to sit or lie quietly.

Akinesia. Absence or poverty of movement.

Akinetic seizures. Seizures producing temporary paralysis of muscles. Characterized by a sudden collapse without warning. Commonest in children.

Alexia. Inability to read.

Allesthesia. The sensation of touch experienced at a point remote from the place touched.

Alpha rhythm. A regular (approximately 10 Hz) wave pattern in the EEG, found in most subjects when they are relaxed with eyes closed.

Amativeness. Inclination to love. Localized by the phrenologists in the nape of the neck.

Amblyopia. Dimness of vision without obvious impairment of the eye itself.

Ammon's horn. Part of the hippocampus.

Amnesia. Partial or total loss of memory.

Amusia. Inability to produce (motor) or to comprehend (sensory) musical sounds.

Amygdala. A set of nuclei in the base of the temporal lobe; part of the limbic system.

Anarthria. Incoordination of the musculature of the mouth, resulting in speechlessness.

Anastomosis. The connection between parallel blood vessels such that they can communicate their blood flows.

Aneurysm. Vascular dilations resulting from localized defects in vascular elasticity; a sac is formed by the dilation of the walls of an artery or of a vein and is filled with blood.

Angiography. Radiographic imaging of blood vessels filled with a contrast medium.

Angioma. Collections of abnormal blood vessels, including capillary, venous, and arteriovenous malformations, resulting in abnormal blood flow.

Angular gyrus. Gyrus in the parietal lobe corresponding roughly to Brodmann's area 39. Important in language functions.

Anomia. Difficulty in finding words, especially those naming objects.

Anopia. Loss of vision.

Anosmia. Absence of the sense of smell.

Anosodiaphoria. Indifference to illness.

Anosognosia. Loss of ability to recognize or to acknowledge bodily defect; usually associated with right parietal lesions.

Anterior commissure. Fiber tract that joins the temporal lobes.

Anterograde amnesia. Inability to remember events subsequent to some disturbance of the brain such as head injury, electroconvulsive shock, or certain degenerative diseases.

Anterograde degeneration. When a nerve cell is damaged, it completely or partly degenerates. Degeneration of the parts of the cell that lie distal to the trauma, with the cell body used as reference, is called anterograde degeneration. For example, when an axon is cut, anterograde degeneration occurs in the section from the cut to the synaptic terminals.

Aphagia. Inability to eat or chew.

Aphasia. Defect or loss of power of expression by speech, writing, or signs or of comprehending spoken or written language due to injury or disease of the brain.

Apraxia. Inability to carry out purposeful movements in the absence of paralysis or paresis.

Arachnoid. A thin sheet of delicate collagenous connective tissue that follows the contours of the brain.

Archicortex. Portion of cerebral cortex that develops in association with olfactory cortex and is phylogenetically older than the neopallium and lacks its layered structure. Also called archipallium, allocortex, and olfactory cortex. Corresponds to the dentate gyrus and hippocampal gyrus in mature mammals.

Arcuate fasciculus. A long bundle of fibers joining Wernicke's and Broca's areas.

Argyll Robertson pupil. Constriction of the pupil to accommodation, but not to light.

Used to diagnose damage to the midbrain relays of the third nerve (oculomotor).

Asomatognosia. Loss of knowledge or sensory awareness of one's own body and bodily condition. May occur on one or both sides of the body. Most commonly results from damage to the right parietal lobe.

Association cortex. All cortex that is not specialized motor or sensory cortex. (The term survives from an earlier belief that inputs from the different senses meet and become associated.)

Astereognosis. Inability, with no defect of elementary tactile sensation, to recognize familiar objects by touch.

Astrocytes. A type of glial cell. *See also* accessory cells.

Astrocytoma. A slow-growing brain tumor resulting from the growth of astrocytes.

Asymbolia. Inability to employ a conventional sign to stand for another object or event.

Ataxia. Failure of muscular coordination; any of various irregularities of muscular action.

ATP. Adenosine triphosphate, a molecule important to cellular energy metabolism. The conversion of ATP to ADP (adenine diphosphate) liberates energy. ATP can also be converted to cyclic AMP, which serves as an intermediate messenger in the production of postsynaptic potentials by some neurotransmitters, and in the mediation of the effects of polypeptide hormones.

Auditory agnosia. Impaired capacity to identify nonverbal acoustic stimuli.

Automatic behaviors. Stereotyped units of behavior linked in a fixed sequence, e.g., grooming and chewing. Also called reflexive, consummatory, and respondent behaviors.

Autoradiography. Radiolabeled substances when injected are incorporated into cells and transported along their processes. If the tissue is exposed to a photographic film it "takes its own picture" and reveals the route taken by the radiolabeled substance.

Autotopagnosia. Inability to localize and name the parts of one's own body; e.g., finger agnosia (*see* agnosia).

Average evoked potential (AEP). The computerized average of a number of evoked potentials from sensory input.

Axon. A thin neuronal process that transmits action potentials away from the cell body to other neurons (or to muscles or glands).

Axon hillock. The site of origin of a nerve impulse.

Basal ganglia. A group of large nuclei in the forebrain, including the caudate nucleus, putamen, globus pallidus, claustrum, and amygdala.

Bell-Magendie law. The law, named after its cofounders, states that the dorsal roots of the spinal cord are sensory and the ventral roots of the spinal cord are motor.

Beta rhythm. Irregular EEG activity of 13–30 Hz generally associated with alert state.

Bilateral. Occurring on or applying to both sides of the body.

Binocular deprivation. Removal of visual stimulation from both eyes by raising an animal in the dark, bandaging the eyes, etc.

Bitemporal hemianopsia. Loss of vision in both temporal fields due to damage to the medial region of the optic chiasm.

Brain abcess. A localized collection of pus in the brain formed from tissues that have disintegrated as a result of infection.

Brain scan. *See* radioisotope scan.

Brainstem. Defined in this book to include the hypothalamus, midbrain, and hindbrain.

Some authorities also include the thalamus and basal ganglia.

Broca's aphasia. An expressive or nonfluent aphasia; chiefly a defect of speech; results from a lesion to Broca's area.

Broca's area. A region of the left frontal lobe (frontal operculum) believed to be involved in the production of language. Damage results in Broca's aphasia.

Brodmann's map. A map of the cerebral cortex devised by Brodmann; it is based on cytoarchitectonic structure and labels anatomical areas by number. (Conforms remarkably closely to functional areas based on lesion and recording studies.)

Calcification. The accumulation of calcium in various brain regions after brain damage.

Caudate nucleus. A nucleus of the basal ganglia.

Cell assembly. A hypothetical collection of neurons that become functionally connected; proposed by Hebb to be the basis of ideation, perception, and memory.

Central sulcus. A fissure running from the dorsal border of the hemisphere near its midpoint, obliquely downward and forward until it nearly meets the lateral fissure, dividing the frontal and parietal lobes. Also called fissure of Rolando.

Cerebellum. A major structure of the hindbrain specialized for motor coordination.

Cerebral arteriosclerosis. Condition marked by loss of elasticity and by thickening and hardening of the arteries. Eventually results in dementia.

Cerebral compression. A contraction of the brain substance due to an injury that has caused hemorrhage and the development of a hematoma.

Cerebral contusion. A vascular injury resulting in bruising and edema and hemorrhage of capillaries.

Cerebral cortex. The layer of gray matter on the surface of the cerebral hemispheres composed of neurons and their synaptic connections that form 4 to 6 sublayers.

Cerebral laceration. A contusion severe enough to physically breach the brain substance.

Cerebral vascular accident. *See* stroke.

Cerebrospinal fluid (CSF). A clear, colorless solution of sodium chloride and other salts that fills the ventricles inside the brain and circulates around the brain beneath the arachnoid layer in the subarachnoid space.

Chromatolysis. The loss of protein in a damaged cell results in loss of its ability to absorb stain; hence literally the breakdown of its ability to be colored.

Chromosome. Strands of DNA combined with protein in the nucleus of each cell that contain the genetic code determining the structure and function of the individual.

Cingulate cortex. A strip of limbic cortex lying just above the corpus callosum along the medial walls of the cerebral hemispheres.

Class-common behaviors. Those behaviors and behavioral capacities common to all members of a phylogenetic class.

Color agnosia. Inability to associate particular colors with objects or objects with colors.

Color anomia. Inability to name colors; generally associated with other aphasic symptoms. Also called color aphasia.

Commissure. A bundle of fibers connecting corresponding points on the two sides of the central nervous system.

Commissurotomy. Surgical disconnection of the two hemispheres by cutting the corpus callosum.

Concussion. A condition of widespread paralysis of the functions of the brain that occurs immediately after a blow on the head.

Conduction aphasia. A type of fluent aphasia in which, despite alleged normal comprehension of spoken language, words are repeated incorrectly.

Constructional apraxia. The inability to perform well-rehearsed and familiar sequences of movements involved in making or preparing something. The deficit is not attributable to an inability to move or to perform the individual acts required for the task.

Contralateral. Residing in the side of the body opposite the reference point.

Contralateral neglect. Neglect of part of the body and/or space contralateral to the lesion.

Contrast x-ray. Radiographic procedure using the injection of radio-opaque dye or air into the ventricles, or of dye into the arteries, for purposes of diagnosis.

Corollary discharge. Transmission by one area of the brain to another, informing the latter area of the former's actions. Commonly used more specifically for a signal from the motor system to the sensory systems that a particular movement is being produced.

Corpus callosum. Fiber system connecting the homotopic areas of the two hemispheres. Split-brain patients are those whose corpus callosum has been severed.

Cortex. An external layer. In this text, synonymous with neocortex.

Cranial nerves. A set of 12 pairs of nerves conveying sensory and motor signals to and from the head.

Crossed aphasia. The aphasia that results from damage to the right hemisphere.

CT scan. Computerized tomography. An x-ray procedure in which a computer draws a map from the measured densities of the brain; superior to a conventional x-ray since it provides a three-dimensional representation of the brain. Also called by the trade name EMI-Scan.

Cytoarchitectonic map. A map of the cortex based on the organization, structure, and distribution of the cells.

Decerebrate rigidity. Excessive tone in all muscles, producing extension of the limbs and dorsoflexion of the head because antigravity musculature overpowers other muscles; caused by brainstem or cerebellar lesions.

Declarative memory. The type of memory that is illustrated by the ability of an individual to recount the details of events, including time, place, and circumstances, as compared with the ability to perform some act or behavior. Quite literally it refers to the ability to recount what one knows. The ability is lost in many types of amnesia.

Decortication. Removal of the cortex of the brain.

Decussation. Crossing of pathways from one side of the brain to the other.

Deep dyslexia. A reading impairment that follows large lesions to the hemisphere dominant for speech. It is characterized by a peculiar constellation of errors that suggests the reading is being performed by the non-dominant hemisphere.

Delusions. Beliefs opposed to reality but firmly held despite evidence of their falsity; characteristic of some types of psychotic disorders.

Dendrites. Treelike processes at the receiving end of the neuron.

Denervation supersensitivity. A condition of increased susceptibility to drugs, resulting from proliferation of receptors after denervation (removal of terminations) of an area.

Deoxyribonucleic acid. *See* DNA.

Depolarization. Inward transfer of positive ions erasing a difference of potential between the inside and the outside of the neuron.

Dermatome. The area of skin supplied with afferent nerve fibers by a single spinal dorsal root.

Desynchronization. A change in EEG activity from a high-amplitude slow pattern to low-amplitude fast pattern.

Developmental dyslexia. The inability to learn adequate reading skills even when opportunity and appropriate instruction are given.

Diaschisis. A special kind of shock following brain damage in which areas connected to the damaged area show a transitory arrest of function.

Dichaptic. A procedure for simultaneously presenting two different objects to each hand to determine which hand is most effective at identifying the object.

Dichotic listening. A procedure of simultaneously presenting a different auditory input to each ear through stereophonic earphones.

Diencephalon. A region of the brain that includes the hypothalamus, thalamus, and epithalamus.

Diplopia. Perception of two images of a single object; double vision.

Disconnection. Severing, by damage or by surgery, of the fibers that connect two areas of the brain such that the two areas can no longer communicate; also, the condition that results.

Disinhibition. Removal of inhibition from a system.

Dissolution. According to an unproved theory, the condition whereby disease or damage in the highest levels of the brain would produce not loss of function but rather a repertory of simpler behaviors as seen in animals who have not evolved that particular brain structure.

Distal. Being away from or distant to some point.

DNA. Deoxyribonucleic acid, a long, complex macromolecule consisting of two interconnected helical strands. Strands of DNA, along with their associated proteins, constitute the chromosomes, which contain the genetic information of the animal.

Dorsal root. The fibers that carry sensory information enter the dorsal (posterior in humans) portion of the spinal cord; those that enter each segment of the cord are collected together in a nerve, called a dorsal root.

Dorsal root ganglion. The cell bodies of the sensory fibers are located adjacent to the portion of the spinal cord into which their axons enter. The protuberance produced by their aggregation is called the dorsal root ganglion.

Dorsomedial thalamus. A thalamic nucleus providing a major afferent input to the prefrontal cortex; degenerates in Korsakoff's disease, leading to a severe amnesic syndrome.

Double dissociation. An experimental technique whereby two areas of neocortex are functionally dissociated by two behavioral tests, each test being affected by a lesion to one zone and not the other.

Dura mater. A tough, double layer of collagenous fiber enclosing the brain in a kind of loose sack.

Dysarthria. Difficulty in speech production caused by incoordination of the speech apparatus.

Dyscalculia. Difficulty in performing arithmetical operations.

Dyseidetic. Individuals who have difficulty recognizing words by their visual configurations.

Dyskinesia. Any disturbance of movement.

Dyslexia. A difficulty in reading.

Dysphasia. Impairment of speech caused by damage to the central nervous system.

Dysphonetic. Individuals who are unable to decode words or recognize them using phonic or sound principles.

Efferent. Conducting away from higher centers in the central nervous system and toward a muscle or gland.

Electroconvulsive shock therapy (ECT or ECS). The application of a massive electric shock across the brain, as a treatment for affective disorders.

Electroencephalogram (EEG). Electrical potentials recorded by placing electrodes on the scalp or in the brain.

Electromyography (EMG). Recording of electrical activity of the muscles as well as the electrical response of the peripheral nerves.

Embolism. The sudden blocking of an artery or a vein by a blood clot, bubble of air, deposit of oil or fat, or small mass of cells deposited by the blood current.

Encephalitis. Inflammation of the central nervous system as a result of infection.

Encephalization. The process by which higher structures such as the cerebral cortex have taken over the functions of the lower centers; may imply either a phylogenetic or an ontogenetic shift of function.

Encephalization quotient (EQ). The ratio of the actual brain size to the expected brain size for a typical mammal of that body size.

Encephalomalacia. Softening of the brain, resulting from vascular disorders caused by inadequate blood flow.

Encephalopathy. Chemical, physical, allergic, or toxic inflammation of the central nervous system.

Encorticalization. The process by which the cerebral cortex has taken over the functions of the lower centers; may imply either a phylogenetic or an ontogenetic shift of function.

Endoplasmic reticulum (ER). An extensive internal membrane system in the cytoplasm. Ribosomes attach to part of ER to form the rough ER.

Ependymal cells. Glial cells forming the lining of the ventricles; some produce cerebrospinal fluid.

Epilepsy. A condition characterized by recurrent seizures of various types associated with a disturbance of consciousness.

Epithalamus. A collection of nuclei forming the phylogenetically most primitive region of the thalamus; includes the habenulae, pineal body, and stria medullaris.

Equipotentiality hypothesis. The hypothesis that each part of a given area of brain is able to encode or produce the behavior normally controlled by the entire area.

Ergotamine. A drug used in the treatment of migraine and tension headaches that acts by constricting cerebral arteries.

Evoked potential (EP). A short train of large, slow waves recorded from the scalp, reflecting dendritic activity.

Extinction. A term used in learning theory that refers to the fact that the probability that a behavior will occur decreases if reinforcement is withheld.

Fasciculation. A small local contraction of muscles, visible through the skin, representing a spontaneous discharge of a number of fibers innervated by a single motor nerve filament.

Festination. Tendency to engage in behavior at faster and faster speeds; usually refers to walking, but can include other behaviors such as talking and thinking.

Fissure. A cleft, produced by folds of the neocortex, that extends to the ventricles.

Fluent aphasia. Refers to a speech disorder in which a person articulates words in a languagelike fashion but what is said actually makes little sense. Also called Wernicke's aphasia; it usually results from damage to the left posterior cortex.

Focal seizures. Seizures that begin locally and then spread; e.g., from one finger to the whole body.

Forebrain. Term used in this book for the cerebral hemispheres, basal ganglia, thalamus, amygdala, hippocampus, and septum.

Frontal lobes. All the neocortex forward of the central sulcus.

Frontal operculum. The upper region of the inferior frontal gyrus.

Functional maps. Maps of the cortex constructed by stimulating areas of the brain electrically and noting elicited behavior, or by recording electrical activity during certain behaviors. Such maps relate specific behaviors to brain areas.

Functional validation. According to theory, the need of a neural system for sensory stimulation if it is to become fully functional.

Generalized seizures. Bilaterally symmetrical seizures without a local onset.

Geniculostriate system. A system consisting of projections from the retina of the eye to the lateral geniculate nucleus of the thalamus, then to areas 17, 18, 19, and then to 20, 21; involved in perception of form, color, and pattern.

Gerstmann syndrome. A collection of symptoms due to left parietal lesion, alleged to include finger agnosia, right-left confusion, acalculia, and agraphia. A source of some controversy.

Glial cells. Supportive cells of the central nervous system.

Glioblastoma. A highly malignant, rapidly growing brain tumor; commonest in adults over 35 years of age; results from the sudden growth of spongioblasts.

Glioma. Any brain tumor that arises from glial cells.

Gliosis. Glial cells migrate to and proliferate in areas of neural tissue where damage has occurred. Their presence serves as a sign of tissue damage.

Globus pallidus. Literally, means pale globe or sphere. Part of the basal ganglia that receives projections from the caudate nucleus and sends projections to the ventral lateral nucleus of the thalamus.

Gnosis. Knowledge.

Golgi apparatus. A complex of parallel membranes in the cytoplasm that wraps the product of a secretory cell or a protein manufactured by a nerve cell.

Graded potential. An electrical potential in a neuron or receptor cell that changes with the intensity of the stimulus. Also known as a generator potential.

Grand mal. Seizure characterized by loss of consciousness and stereotyped, generalized convulsions.

Grapheme. Term referring to the pictorial qualities of a written word that permits it to be understood without being sounded out; a group of letters that conveys a meaning.

Graphesthesia. The ability to identify numbers or letters traced on the skin with a blunt object.

Gray matter. Any brain area composed predominantly of cell bodies.

Gyrus. A convolution of the cortex of the cerebral hemispheres.

Habituation. Gradual quantitative decrease of a response after repeated exposure to a stimulus.

Hallucinations. Perceptions for which there are no appropriate external stimuli; characteristic of some types of psychotic disorders.

Hematoma. A local swelling or tumor filled with effused blood.

Hemiparesis. Muscular weakness affecting one side of the body.

Hemiplegia. Paralysis of one side of the body.

Hemispherectomy. Removal of a cerebral hemisphere.

Hindbrain. A region of the brain that consists primarily of the cerebellum, medulla, pons, and fourth ventricle.

Hippocampus. Primitive cortical structure lying in the anterior medial region of the temporal lobe.

Homeostasis. The maintenance of a chemically and physically constant internal environment.

Homonymous hemianopsia. Total loss of vision due to complete cuts of the optic tract, lateral geniculate body, or area 17.

6-Hydroxydopamine. A chemical that is selectively taken up by axons and terminals of noradrenergic or dopaminergic neurons and acts as a poison, damaging or killing them.

Hypermetamorphosis. A tendency to attend and react to every visual stimulus, leading to mental distraction and confusion.

Hyperpolarization. The process by which a nerve membrane becomes more resistant to the passage of sodium ions and consequently more difficult to excite with adequate stimulation. During hyperpolarization the electrical charge on the inside of the membrane relative to the outside becomes more negative.

Hypothalamus. Collection of nuclei located below the thalamus; involved in nearly all behavior including movement, feeding, sexual activity, sleeping, emotional expression, temperature regulation, and endocrine regulation.

Idiopathic seizures. Seizure disorders that appear to arise spontaneously and in the absence of other diseases of the central nervous system.

Illusions. False or misinterpreted sensory impressions of real sensory images.

Infarct. An area of dead or dying tissue resulting from an obstruction of the blood vessels normally supplying the region.

Infection. Invasion of the body by disease-producing microorganisms and the reaction of the tissues to their presence.

Inferior colliculus. The nucleus of the tectum of the midbrain that receives auditory projections and is involved in whole body orientation to auditory stimuli.

Interneuron. Any neuron lying between a sensory neuron and a motor neuron.

Ipsilateral. Located on the same side of the body as the point of reference.

Isolation syndrome. *See* transcortical aphasia.

Kennard principle. Early brain damage produces less severe behavioral effects than brain damage incurred later in life. The term was coined after Kennard reported this phenomenon in a series of papers based on the study of neonatally brain damaged monkeys.

Kindling. Production of epilepsy by repeated stimulation; e.g., by an electrode in the brain.

Klüver-Bucy syndrome. A group of symptoms resulting from bilateral damage to the temporal lobes. Characterized especially by hypersexuality, excessive oral behavior, and visual agnosia.

Korsakoff's syndrome. An amnesic syndrome resulting from degeneration of the dorsomedial thalamic nucleus; produced by chronic alcoholism.

Korsakoff-Wernicke disease. A metabolic disorder of the central nervous system due to a lack of vitamin B_1 (thiamin); often associated with chronic alcoholism.

Lateral fissure. A deep cleft on the basal surface of the brain that extends laterally, posteriorly, and upward, thus separating the temporal and parietal lobes. Also called Sylvian fissure.

Laterality. Side of the brain that controls a given function; hence studies of laterality are devoted to determining which side of the brain controls various functions.

Lesion. Any damage to the nervous system.

Lexicon. A dictionary, or memory store, in the brain that contains words and their meanings.

Limbic system. An elaboration of the structures of the limbic lobe to form a hypothetical functional system originally believed to be important in controlling affective behavior. The neural systems that line the inside wall of the neocortex.

Lipofuscin granules. Dark-pigmented substance that accumulates in brain cells as they age.

Localization of function. Hypothetically, the control of each kind of behavior by a different specific brain area.

Lysomes. One of the small bodies containing digestive enzymes seen with the electron microscope in many types of cells.

Macular sparing. A condition in which the central region of the visual field is not lost even though temporal and/or nasal fields are.

Mass action hypothesis. The hypothesis that the entire neocortex participates in every behavior.

Massa intermedia. Mass of gray matter that connects the left and right thalami across the midline.

Medulla oblongata. The portion of the hindbrain immediately rostral to the spinal cord.

Medulloblastoma. Highly malignant brain tumor found almost exclusively in the cerebella of children; results from the growth of germinal cells, which infiltrate the cerebellum.

Meninges. The three layers of protective tissue—the dura mater, arachnoid, and pia mater—that encase the brain and spinal cord.

Meningioma. An encapsulated brain tumor growing from the meninges.

Meningitis. Inflammation of the meninges.

Mesencephalon. Middle brain; term for the middle one of the three primary embryonic vesicles, which subsequently comprises the tectum and tegmentum.

Metastatic tumor. A tumor that occurs through the transfer of tumor cells from elsewhere in the body.

Microfilaments. Small tubelike processes in cells, the function of which is uncertain, but they may be involved in controlling the shape, movement, or fluidity of the cytoplasm or substances within the cell.

Microtubules. Fiberlike substances in the soma and processes of nerve cells that are involved in transporting substances from the soma to the distal elements of the cell or from distal portions of the cell to the soma.

Midbrain. The short segment between the forebrain and hindbrain including the tectum and tegmentum.

Migraine. A type of headache characterized by an aching, throbbing pain, frequently unilateral. It may be preceded by a visual aura presumed to result from ischemia of the occipital cortex induced by vasoconstriction of cerebral arteries.

Mitochondria. A complex organelle within the cell that through a number of processes produces most of the cell's energy.

Monocular blindness. Blindness in one eye caused by destruction of its retina or optic nerve.

Monocular deprivation. Deprivation of visual experience to one eye by closure, bandaging, etc.

Motoneurone. Sherrington's term for the unit formed by motor neurons and the muscle fiber to which their axon terminations are connected.

Motor neuron. A neuron that has its cell body in the spinal cord and that projects to muscles.

Motor program. A hypothetical neural circuit so arranged that it produces a certain type of movement, for example, walking.

Mycotic infection. Invasion of the nervous system by a fungus.

Myelin. The lipid substance forming an insulating sheath around certain nerve fibers; formed by oligodendroglia in the central nervous system and by Schwann cells in the peripheral nervous system.

Myelinization. Formation of myelin on axons. Used by some people as an index of maturation.

Myoclonic spasms. Massive seizures consisting of sudden flexions or extensions of the body and often beginning with a cry.

Narcolepsy. Condition in which a person is overcome by uncontrollable, recurrent, brief episodes of sleep.

Nasal hemianopsia. Loss of vision of one nasal field due to damage to the lateral region of the optic chiasm.

Natural selection. A proposition in the theory of evolution that animals with certain adaptive characteristics will survive in certain environments and pass on their genet-ic characteristics to their offspring, while less fortunate animals, lacking those characteristics, die off.

Necrosis. Cell death or death of tissue, usually as individual cells, groups of cells, or in small, localized areas.

Neocortex. Newest layer of the brain, forming the outer layer or "new bark"; has four to six layers of cells. In this text, synonymous with cortex.

Nerve growth factor (NGF). A protein that plays some role in maintaining the growth of a cell.

Nerve impulse. Movement or propagation of an action potential along the length of an axon; begins at a point close to the cell body and travels away from it.

Neuroblast. Any embryonic cell that develops into a neuron.

Neurofibril. Any of numerous fibrils making up part of the internal structure of a neuron; may be active in transporting precursor chemicals for the synthesis of neurotransmitters.

Neuroleptic drug. A drug that has antipsychotic action affecting principally psychomotor activity and is generally without hypnotic effects.

Neurologist. A physician specializing in the treatment of disorders of the nervous system.

Neuron. The basic unit of the nervous system; the nerve cell; its function is to transmit and store information; includes the cell body (soma), many processes called dendrites, and an axon.

Neuropsychology. The study of the relation between brain function and behavior.

Neurotoxin. Any substance that is poisonous or destructive to nerve tissue; e.g., 6-hydroxydopamine, placed in the ventricles of the brain, will selectively destroy the noradrenaline and dopamine systems.

Neurotransmitter. A chemical released from a synapse in response to an action potential and acting on postsynaptic receptors to change the resting potential of the receiving cell; chemically transmits information from one neuron to another.

Neurotropic viruses. Those viruses having a strong affinity for cells of the central nervous system, as opposed to pantropic viruses, which attack any body tissue.

NMR. Nuclear magnetic resonance. An imaging procedure in which a computer draws a map from the measured changes in the magnetic resonance of atoms in the brain.

Node of Ranvier. A space separating the Schwann cells that form the covering or myelin on a nerve axon; because the nerve impulse jumps from one node to the next its propagation is accelerated.

Nonfluent aphasia. An inability or impairment of speech that follows brain damage, particularly to the frontal part of the hemisphere dominant for speech, and which is characterized by difficulty in articulating words.

Noradrenergic neurons. Neurons that contain noradrenaline in their synapses or use noradrenaline as their neurotransmitter.

Nucleolus. An organelle within the nucleus of a cell that produces ribosomes.

Nucleus. A spherical structure in the soma of cells; contains DNA; also, a group of cells forming a cluster that can be identified histologically.

Nystagmus. Constant, tiny eye movements that occur involuntarily and have a variety of causes.

Occipital horns. Most posterior projections of the lateral ventricles that protrude into the occipital lobe.

Occipital lobes. A general area of the cortex lying in the back part of the head.

Olfaction. The sense of smell or the act of smelling.

Oligodendrocytes. Specialized support or glial cells in the brain that form a covering or myelin on nerve cells to speed the nerve impulse. Also called oligodendroglia.

Optic ataxia. A deficit in the visual control of reaching and other movements as well as a deficit in eye movements.

Optic chiasm. The point at which the optic nerve from one eye partially crosses to join the other, forming a junction at the base of the brain.

Orbital frontal cortex. Cortex that lies adjacent to the cavity containing the eye but that, anatomically defined, receives projections from the dorsomedial nucleus of the thalamus.

Organic brain syndrome. A general term for behavioral disorders that result from brain malfunction attributable to known or unknown causes.

Paleocortex. That portion of the cerebral cortex forming the pyriform cortex and parahippocampal gyrus. Also called the paleopallium.

Pantropic viruses. Those viruses that attack any body tissue. *See also* neurotropic viruses.

Papilledema. Swelling of the optic disk; caused by increased pressure from cerebrospinal fluid. Used as a diagnostic indicator of tumors or other swellings in the brain.

Paragraphia. The writing of incorrect words or perseveration in writing the same word.

Paralimbic cortex. A term for areas of three-layered cortex that is adjacent to the classically defined limbic cortex and has a direct connection with limbic cortex, e.g., cingulate cortex.

Paraphasia. The production of unintended syllables, words, or phrases during speaking.

Parasite. An organism living on or within another living organism (the host) at the expense of the host.

Paresis. A general term for loss of physical and mental ability due to brain disease, particularly from syphilitic infection; a term for slight or incomplete paralysis.

Parietal lobes. A general region of the brain lying beneath the parietal bone.

Parkinson's disease. A disease of the motor system that is correlated with a loss of dopamine in the brain and is characterized by tremors, rigidity, and reduction in voluntary movement.

Perception. A cognition resulting from the activity of cells in the various sensory regions of the neocortex beyond the primary sensory cortex.

Peripheral nerves. Those nerves that lie outside the spinal cord and the brain.

Perseveration. Tendency to repeatedly emit the same verbal or motor response to varied stimuli.

PET. Positron emission tomography. An imaging technique in which a subject is given a radioactively labeled compound such as glucose, which is metabolized by the brain, and the radioactivity is later recorded by a special detector.

Petit mal. Seizure characterized by a loss of awareness during which there is no motor activity except blinking and/or turning of the head, rolling of the eyes, etc.; of brief duration (10 seconds typically).

Phagocytes. Cells that engulf microorganisms, other cells, and foreign particles.

Phoneme. A unit of sound that forms a word or part of a word.

Phonological. Refers to sound, as in theories of reading that emphasize the role of sound in decoding the meaning of words.

Phrenology. The study of the relation between the skull's surface features and mental faculties. Long discredited.

Pia mater. A moderately tough connective tissue that clings to the surface of the brain.

Pineal body. An unsymmetrical structure in the epithalamus, thought by Descartes to be the seat of the soul, but now thought to be involved in circadian rhythms.

Planum temporale. The cortical area just posterior to the auditory cortex'; Heschl's gyrus' within the Sylvian fissure.

Plasticity. According to theory, the ability of the brain to change in various ways to compensate for loss of function due to damage.

Pneumoencephalography. An x-ray technique in which the cerebrospinal fluid is replaced by air introduced by a lumbar puncture.

Polyribosomes. Structures formed by the combination of mRNA and ribosomes that serve as the actual sites for protein synthesis.

Pons. A portion of the hindbrain; composed mostly of motor fiber tracts going to such areas as the cerebellum and spinal tract.

Postsynaptic membrane. The membrane lying adjacent to a synaptic connection across the synaptic space from the terminal.

Praxis. An action, movement, or series of movements.

Precentral gyrus. The gyrus lying in front of the central sulcus.

Preferred cognitive mode. Use of one type of thought process in preference to another, e.g., visuospatial instead of verbal; sometimes attributed to the assumed superior function of one hemisphere over the other.

Prefrontal cortex. Cortex lying in front of primary and secondary motor cortex; thus, tertiary or association cortex in the frontal lobe.

Presynaptic membrane. The terminal membrane adjacent to the subsynaptic space.

Primary projection area. An area of the brain that first receives a connection from another system.

Primary sensory area. An area of the cortex that first receives projections from a sensory system.

Primary zones. Areas of the cortex that first receive projections from sensory systems or that project most directly to muscles.

Procedural memory. Memory for certain ways of doing things or for certain movements. This memory system is thought to be independent from memory used to "tell about" the ability.

Projection maps. Maps of the cortex made by tracing axons from the sensory systems into the brain and by tracing axons from the neocortex to the motor systems of the brainstem and spinal cord.

Prosencephalon. Front brain; term for the most anterior part of the embryonic brain, which subsequently evolves into the telencephalon and diencephalon.

Prosody. The variation in stress, pitch, and rhythm of speech by which different shades of meaning are conveyed.

Prosopagnosia. Inability, not explained by defective visual acuity or reduced consciousness or alertness, to recognize familiar faces. Very rare in pure form, and thought to be secondary to right parietal lesions.

Proximal. Being close to something.

Pseudodepression. A condition of personality following frontal lobe lesion in which apathy, indifference, and loss of initiative are apparent symptoms but are not accompanied by a sense of depression in the patient.

Pseudopsychopathic. Describing a condition of personality following frontal lobe lesion in which immature behavior, lack of tact and restraint, and other behaviors symptomatic of psychopathology are apparent but are not accompanied by the equivalent mental or emotional components of psychopathology.

Psychoactive drug. Any chemical substance that alters mood or behavior by altering the functions of the brain.

Psychometrics. The science of measuring human abilities.

Psychosis. A major mental disorder of organic or emotional origin in which the individual's ability to think, respond emotionally, remember, communicate, interpret reality, and behave appropriately is sufficiently impaired so that the ordinary demands of life cannot be met. The term is applicable to conditions having a wide range of severity and duration (e.g., schizophrenia, depression).

Psychosurgery. Surgical intervention to sever fibers connecting one part of the brain with another or to remove or destroy brain tissue with the intent of modifying or altering disturbances of behavior, thought content, or mood for which no organic pathological cause can be demonstrated by established tests and techniques (e.g., lobotomy).

Ptosis. Drooping of the upper eyelid from paralysis of the third nerve (oculomotor).

Pulvinar. Thalamic nucleus that receives projections from the visual cortex and superior colliculus and sends connections to secondary and tertiary temporal and parietal cortex.

Putamen. A nucleus of the basal ganglia complex.

Putative transmitters. Chemicals strongly suspected of being neurotransmitters but not conclusively proved to be so.

Pyramidal cells. Cells that have a pyramidal-shaped cell body. They usually send information from one region of the cortex to some other brain area.

Pyramidalis area. Area 4.

Quadrantic hemianopsia. Blindness in one quadrant of the visual field due to some damage to the optic tract, lateral geniculate body, or area 17.

Radioisotope scan. Scanning of the cranial surface with a Geiger counter after an intraveneous injection of a radioisotope has been given, to detect tumors, vascular disturbances, atrophy, etc.

Reading backward. Individuals who are unable to read irrespective of the cause.

Reafference. Confirmation by one part of the nervous system of the activity in another. *See also* corollary discharge.

Receptive field. The area from which a stimulus can activate a sensory receptor.

Reciprocal inhibition. Activation of one muscle group with inhibition of its antagonists.

Red nucleus. A nucleus in the anterior portion of the tegmentum that is the source of a major motor projection.

Regeneration. A process by which neurons damaged by trauma regrow connections to the area that they previously innervated.

Resting potential. Normal voltage across a nerve cell membrane; varies between 60 and 90 millivolts in the cells of different animals.

Reticular formation. A mixture of nerve cells and fibers in the lower and ventral portion of the brainstem, extending from the spinal cord to the thalamus and giving rise to important ascending and descending systems.

Reticular matter. An area of the nervous system composed of intermixed cell bodies and axons; has a mottled gray and white or netlike appearance.

Retrograde amnesia. Inability to remember events that occurred prior to the onset of amnesia.

Retrograde degeneration. Degeneration of a nerve cell that occurs between the site of damage and the cell body and includes the cell body and all of its remaining processes.

Rhinencephalon. Alternative term for the limbic system, means smell brain.

Rhombencephalon. The hindmost posterior embryonic part of the brain, which divides into the metencephalon and myelencephalon.

Ribonucleic acid. *See* RNA.

Righting reflex. A reflex whereby an animal placed in an inverted posture returns to upright; survives low decerebration, hence a reflex.

RNA. Ribonucleic acid, a complex macromolecule composed of a sequence of nucleotide bases attached to a sugar-phosphate backbone. Messenger RNA (mRNA) delivers genetic information from a portion of a chromosome to a ribosome (ribosomal or rRNA), where the appropriate molecules of transfer RNA (tRNA) assemble the appropriate amino acids to produce the polypeptide coded for by the active portion of the chromosome.

Roentgenography. Photography using x-rays.

Saccule. One of two vestibular receptors of the middle ear; stimulated when the head is oriented normally; maintains head and body in an upright position.

Saltatory conduction. Propagation of a nerve impulse on a myelinated axon; charac terized by its leaping from one node of Ranvier to another.

Schizophrenia. A type of psychosis characterized by disordered cognitive functioning and poor social adjustment (literally splitting of thought and emotive processes); probably due to brain malfunction.

Schwann cells. Glial cells that form myelin in the peripheral nervous system.

Scotoma. Small blind spot in the visual field caused by small lesions or epileptic focus or migraines of the occipital lobe.

Secondary projection area. An area of the cortex that receives projections from or sends projections to a primary projection area.

Sensation. The result of activity of receptors and their associated afferent pathways to the corresponding primary sensory neocortical areas.

Sensory aphasia. *See* Wernicke's aphasia.

Septum. A nucleus in the limbic system that when lesioned in rats produces sham rage and abolishes the theta EEG waveform.

Sexual selection. A process of evolution in which the processes involved in determining who mates with whom also determines the characteristics of the offspring that will be produced.

Simultaneous extinction. Second stage of recovery from contralateral neglect; characterized by response to stimuli on the neglected side as if there were a simultaneous stimulation on the contralateral side.

Soma. Cell body.

Somatosensory zone. Any region of the brain responsible for analyzing sensations of fine touch and pressure and possibly of pain and temperature.

Somnolence. Sleepiness; excessive drowsiness.

Sparing. The saving (sparing) of some brain functions from disruption after the occurrence of a lesion early in life (usually before that function has developed).

Spatial summation. Tendency of two adjacent events to summate; hence two adjacent postsynaptic potentials add or subtract.

Specifically reading retarded. Individuals who have adequate intelligence to read but cannot read.

Spinal cord. The part of the nervous system enclosed in the vertebral column.

Spinal reflex. Response obtained when only the spinal cord is functioning.

Splenium. A bandlike structure, but term is used to refer to the posterior rounded end of the corpus callosum.

Spongioblasts. Immature cells that develop into glial cells.

Sprouting. The phenomenon following partial damage whereby remaining portions of a neuron or other neurons sprout terminations to connect to the previously innervated area.

Stellate cell. Nerve cells that are characterized by having a star-shaped cell body. They serve largely as association cells whose processes remain within the region of the brain in which the cell body is.

Stereognosis. The recognition of objects through the sense of touch.

Stimulation. The act of applying a stimulus or an irritant to something; the occurrence of such a stimulus or an irritant.

Stimulus. An irritant or event that causes a change in action of some brain area.

Storage granules. Vesicles in the terminal that are presumed to store neurotransmitters.

Stretch reflex. The contraction of a muscle to resist stretching; mediated through a muscle spindle, a special sensory receptor system in the muscle.

Stroke. The sudden appearance of neurological symptoms as a result of severe interruption of blood flow.

Substantia nigra. A nucleus area in the midbrain containing the cell bodies of axons containing dopamine. In freshly prepared human tissue the region appears black, hence the name (Latin, meaning black substance).

Sulcus. A small cleft produced by folding of the cortex.

Superior colliculus. Nucleus of the tectum in the midbrain that receives visual projections and is involved in whole body reflexes to visual stimuli.

Supplementary motor cortex. A relatively small region of the cortex that lies outside the primary motor cortex but that when stimulated will also produce movements.

Surface dyslexia. An inability to read words on the basis of their pictographic or grapheme representations while retaining the ability to read using phonological or sounding-out procedures.

Sylvian fissure. *See* lateral fissure.

Synapse. The junction between an axonal terminal and another cell.

Synaptic knob. Another term for end foot; also called synapsis, synapse, bouton termineau, terminal knob.

Synaptic vesicles. Small vesicles visible in electron-microscope pictures of terminals; believed to contain neurotransmitter.

Tachistoscope. A mechanical apparatus consisting of a projector, viewer, and screen by which visual stimuli can be presented to selective portions of the visual field.

Tactile; tactual. Pertaining to the sense of touch.

Tectopulvinar system. Portion of the visual system that functions to locate visual stimuli. Includes superior colliculus, posterior thalamus, and areas 20 and 21.

Tectum. The area of the midbrain above the cerebral aqueduct (the roof); consists of the superior and inferior colliculi, which mediate whole body response to visual and auditory stimuli, respectively.

Tegmentum. The area of the midbrain below the cerebral aqueduct (the floor); contains sensory and motor tracts and a number of nuclei.

Telencephalon. Term for the endbrain; includes the cortex, basal ganglia, limbic system, and olfactory bulbs.

Temporal lobes. Lobes found laterally on the head, below the lateral sulci adjacent to the temporal bones.

Temporal summation. Tendency of two events related in time to summate; hence two temporally related postsynaptic potentials add or subtract.

Terminal degeneration. Degeneration of the terminals of neurons. It can be detected by selective tissue staining.

Tertiary projection area. An area of the cortex that receives projections from or sends projections to a secondary projection area. Also known as association cortex.

Thalamus. A group of nuclei of the diencephalon.

Thermoregulation. The ability to regulate body temperature.

Theta rhythm. A brain rhythm with a frequency of 4 to 7 Hz.

Threshold. The point at which a stimulus produces a response.

Thrombosis. A plug or clot in a blood vessel, formed by the coagulation of blood.

Topographic maps. Maps of the neocortex showing various features, projections, cell distributions, etc.

Tract. A large collection of axons coursing together within the central nervous system.

Transcortical aphasia. Aphasia in which people can repeat and understand words and name objects but cannot speak spontaneously, or can repeat words but cannot comprehend them.

Transient ischemia. A short-lived condition of inadequate supply of blood to a brain area.

Transneuronal degeneration. The degeneration of cells that synapse with or are synapsed onto by a damaged cell, e.g., section of optic tracts results in the degeneration of lateral geniculate body cells.

Tumor. A mass of new tissue that persists and grows independently; a neoplasm; it surrounds tissue and has no physiologic use.

Uncinate fasciculus. A fiber tract connecting temporal and frontal cortex; a hooked or curved tract.

Unilateral visual neglect. Neglect of all sensory events of one or more modalities of stimulation when the stimulation is restricted to one half of the world as defined by the central axis of the body.

Unit activity. The electrical potential of a single cell.

Ventral root. The tract of fibers leaving the spinal cord, hence motor, on the ventral portion of the spinal cord of animals or on the anterior portion of humans.

Ventricles. The cavities of the brain that contain cerebrospinal fluid.

Ventriculography. An x-ray technique whereby, to highlight the contours of the ventricles, an opaque medium is introduced into the ventricle through a cannula inserted through the skull.

Vestibular system. A sensory system with receptors in the middle ear that respond to body position and movement.

Virus. An encapsulated aggregate of nucleic acid causing infection and nonspecific lesions.

Visual agnosia. Inability to combine visual impressions into complete patterns— therefore an inability to recognize objects; inability to perceive objects and to draw or copy them.

Voluntary movement. Any movement that takes an animal from one place to another; can be elicited by lower-level sensory input and/or executed through lower and postural support and reflex systems. Also called appetitive, instrumental, purposive, and operant movement.

Wallerian degeneration. Degeneration of that portion of a neuron that lies distal to the site of damage when the cell body is used as the point of reference. *See* anterograde degeneration.

Wernicke's aphasia. Inability to comprehend speech or to produce meaningful speech; follows lesions to posterior cortex.

Wernicke's area. The posterior portion of the superior temporal gyrus, roughly equivalent to area 22.

White matter. Those areas of the nervous system rich in axons covered with glial cells.

INDEX OF NAMES

INDEX OF TOPICS